久保帯人

...you ...ing the very first volume of Bleach. I worked really hard writing it. Please treat it kindly.
Sincerely,
Tite Kubo

BLEACH is author Tite Kubo's second title. Kubo made his debut with *ZOMBIE POWDER*, a four-volume series for *WEEKLY SHONEN JUMP*. To date, *BLEACH* has been translated into numerous languages and has also inspired an animated TV series that began airing in Japan in 2004. Beginning its serialization in 2001, *BLEACH* is still a mainstay in the pages of *WEEKLY SHONEN JUMP*. In 2005, *BLEACH* was awarded the prestigious Shogakukan Manga Award in the *shonen* (boys) category.

BLEACH
3-in-1 Edition

SHONEN JUMP Manga Omnibus Edition Volume 1
A compilation of the graphic novel volumes 1–3

STORY AND ART BY
TITE KUBO

English Adaptation/Lance Caselman
Translation/Joe Yamazaki
Touch-up Art & Lettering/Andy Ristaino (volumes 1-2), Dave Lanphear (volume 3)
Design - Manga Edition/Sean Lee
Design - Omnibus Edition /Fawn Lau
Editor - Manga Edition/Kit Fox
Editor - Omnibus Edition /Alexis Kirsch

Printed in the U.S.A.

Published by VIZ Media, LLC
P.O. Box 77010
San Francisco, CA 94107

10 9 8 7 6 5 4
Omnibus edition first printing, June 2011
Fourth printing, July 2012

www.viz.com

THE WORLD'S
MOST POPULAR MANGA
www.shonenjump.com

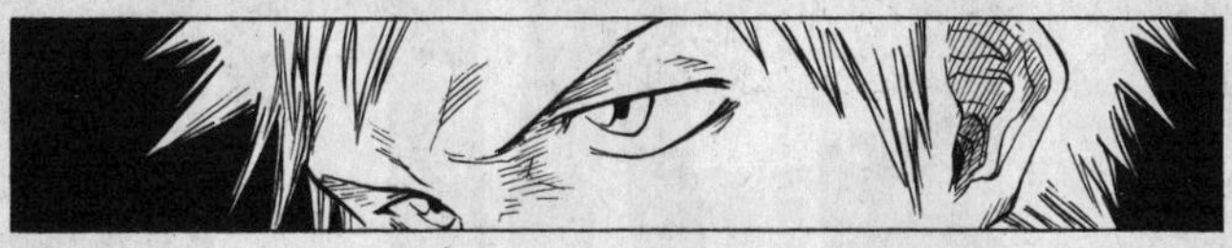

We fear that which we cannot see

BLEACH1

DEATH & STRAWBERRY

Shonen Jump Manga

BLEACH 1

DEATH & STRAWBERRY

Contents

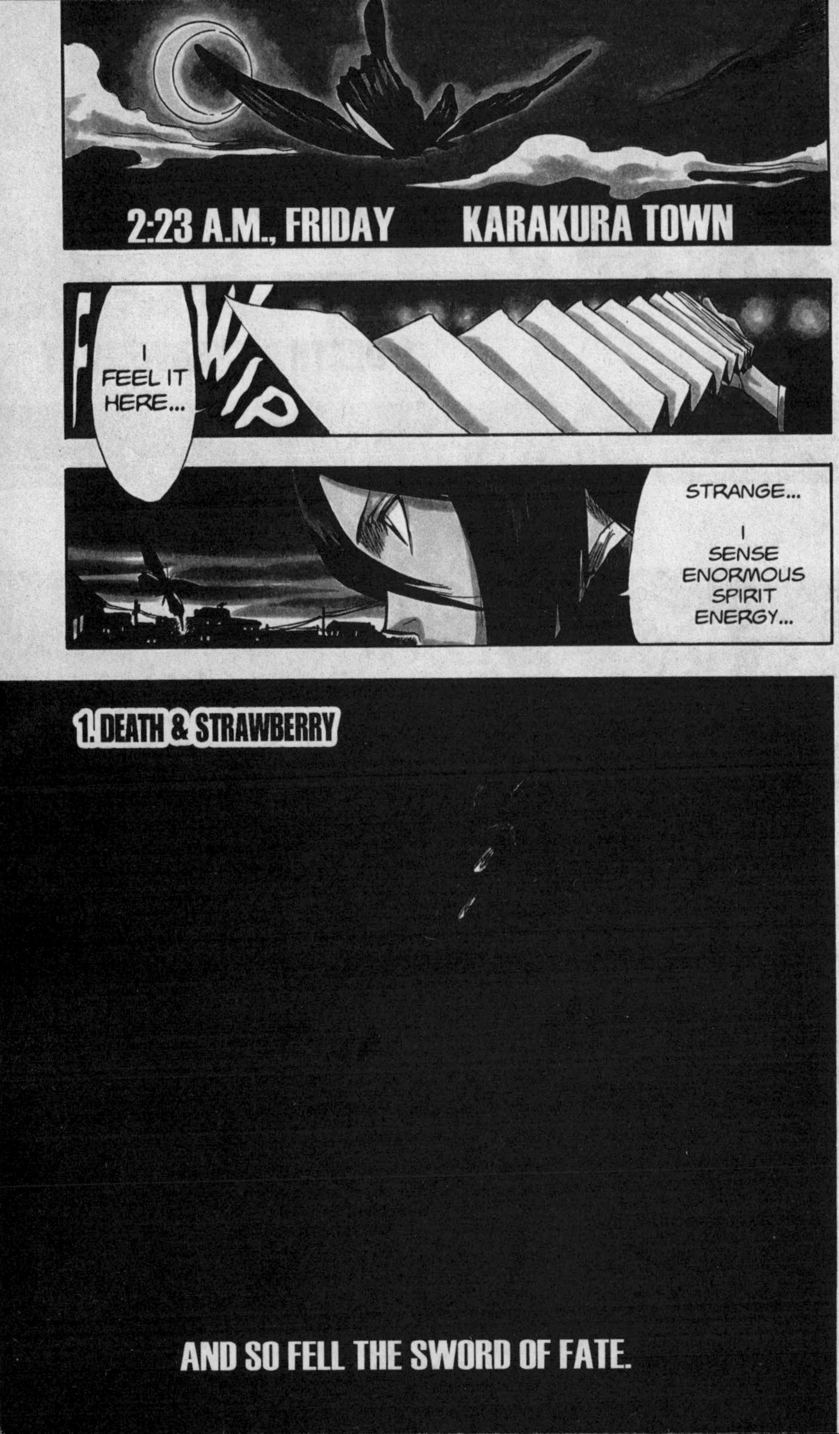

2:23 A.M., FRIDAY   KARAKURA TOWN

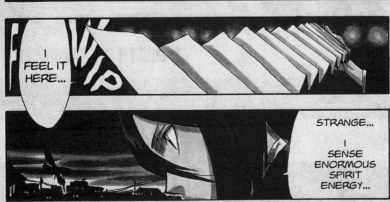

FWIP

I FEEL IT HERE...

STRANGE...

I SENSE ENORMOUS SPIRIT ENERGY...

1. DEATH & STRAWBERRY

AND SO FELL THE SWORD OF FATE.

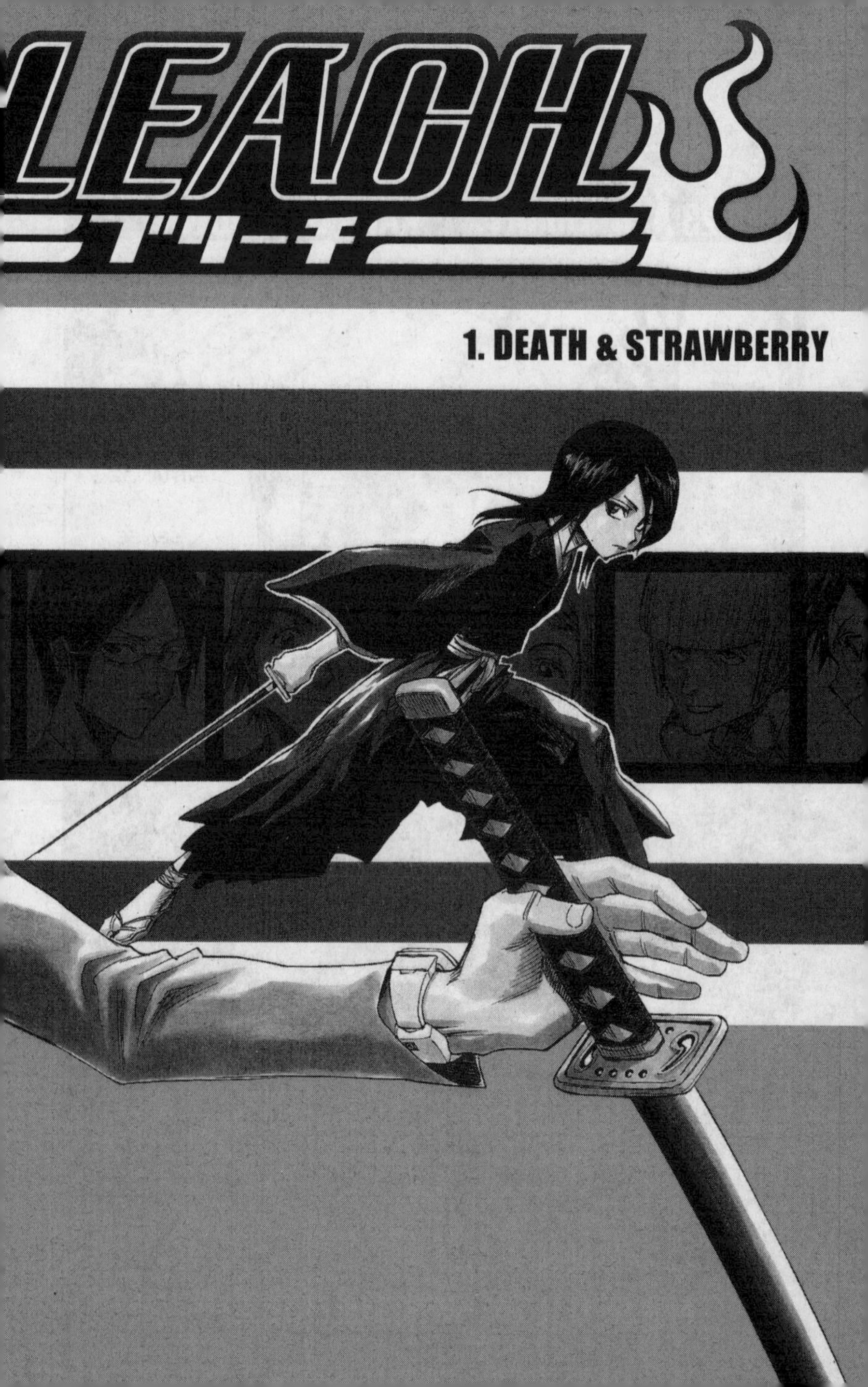
ブリーチ
1. DEATH & STRAWBERRY

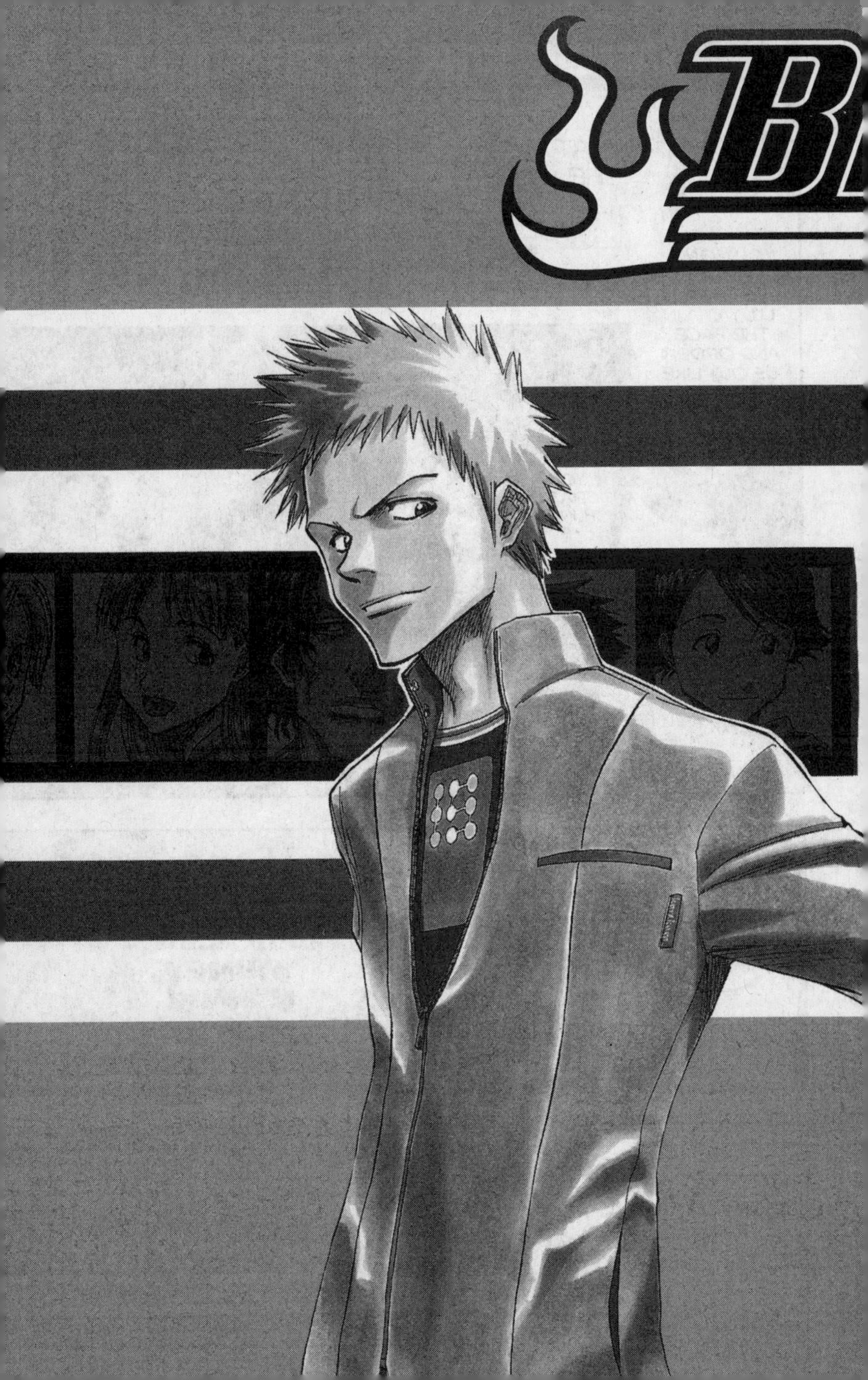

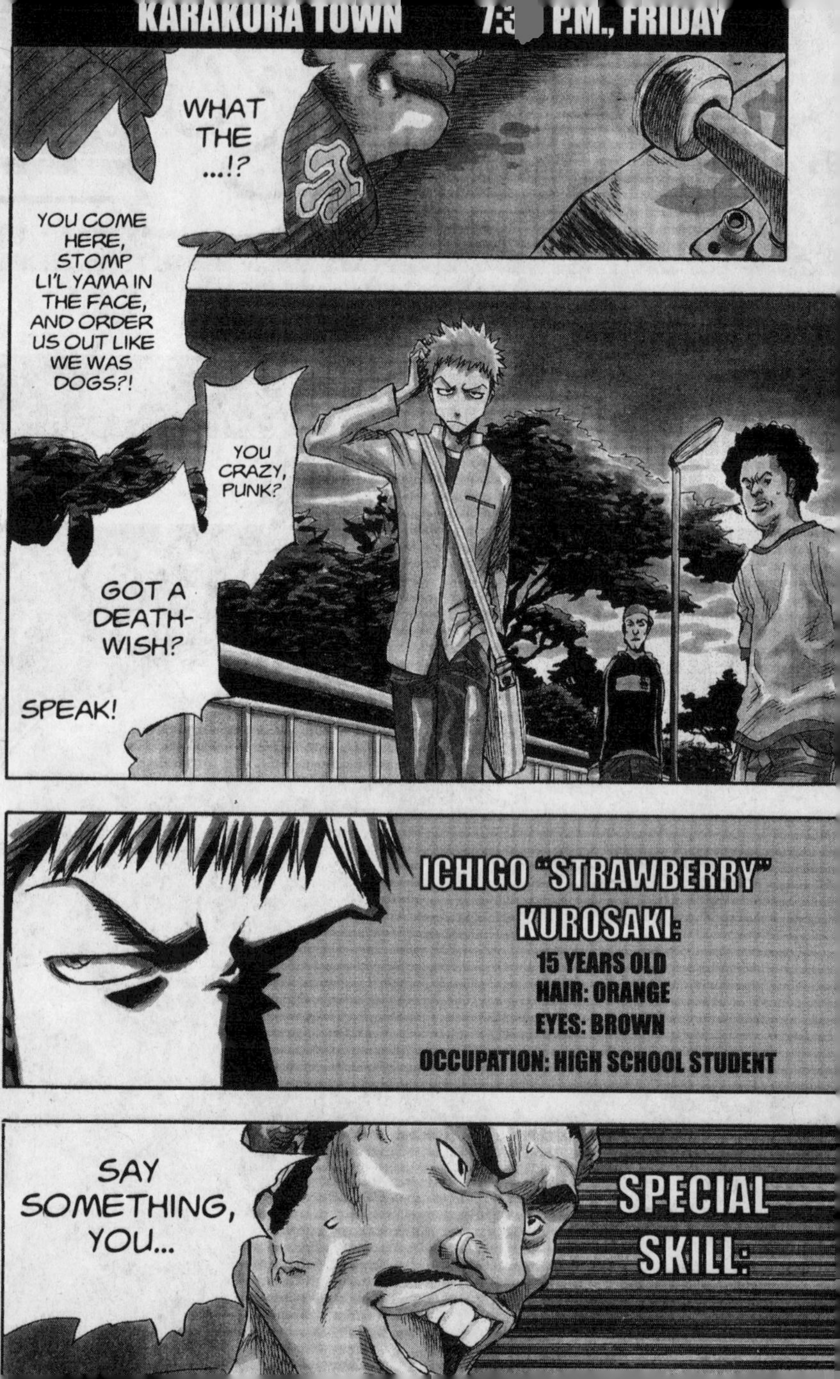
KARAKURA TOWN 7:3[redacted] P.M., FRIDAY
WHAT THE ...!?
YOU COME HERE, STOMP LI'L YAMA IN THE FACE, AND ORDER US OUT LIKE WE WAS DOGS?!
YOU CRAZY, PUNK?
GOT A DEATH-WISH?
SPEAK!
ICHIGO "STRAWBERRY" KUROSAKI:
15 YEARS OLD
HAIR: ORANGE
EYES: BROWN
OCCUPATION: HIGH SCHOOL STUDENT
SPECIAL SKILL:
SAY SOMETHING, YOU...

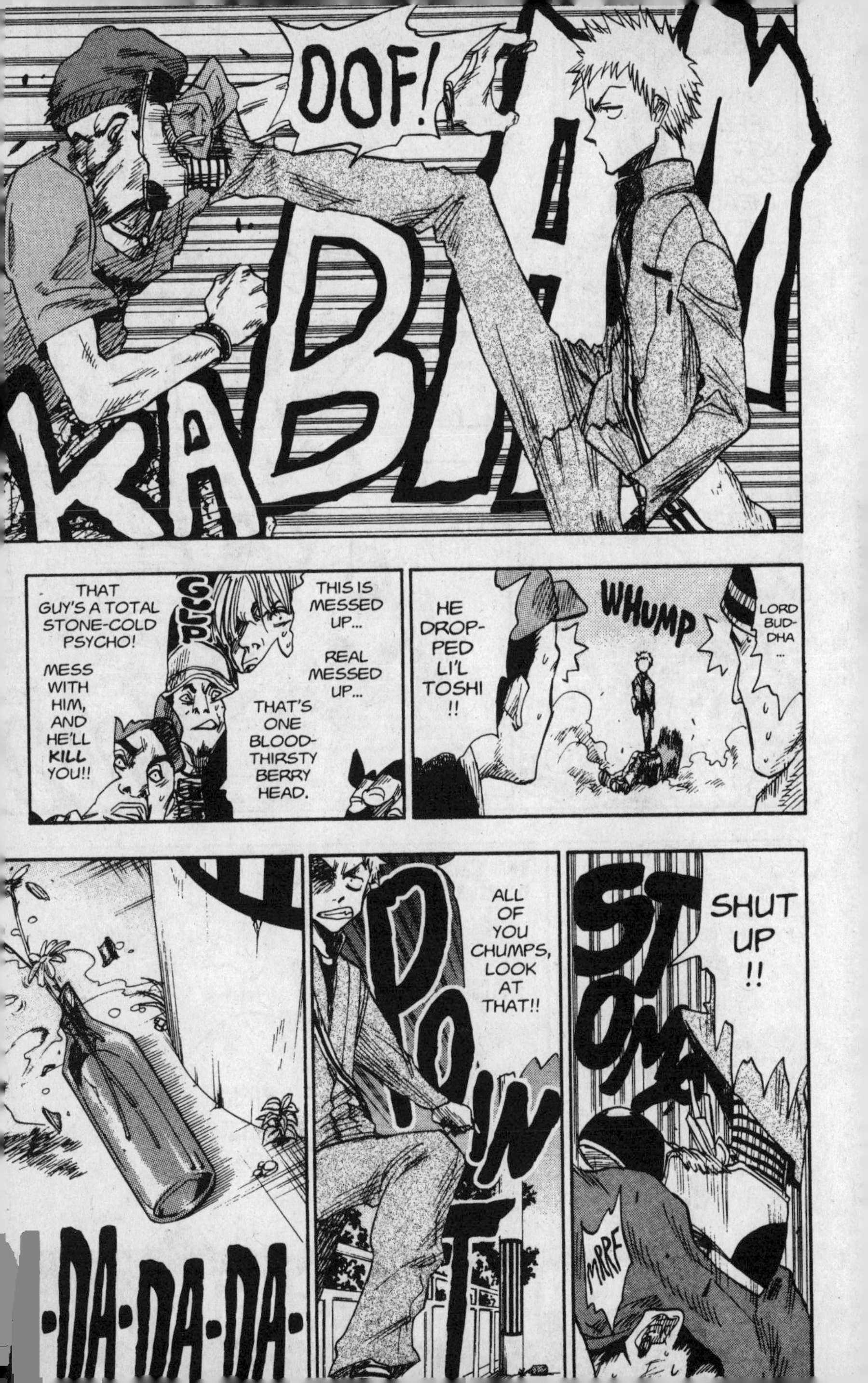

OOF!
LORD BUDDHA ...
WHUMP
HE DROPPED LI'L TOSHI !!
THIS IS MESSED UP... REAL MESSED UP...
GULP
THAT'S ONE BLOODTHIRSTY BERRY HEAD.
THAT GUY'S A TOTAL STONE-COLD PSYCHO!
MESS WITH HIM, AND HE'LL **KILL** YOU!!
SHUT UP !!
MRRF
ALL OF YOU CHUMPS, LOOK AT THAT!!
-DA-DA-DA-DA-

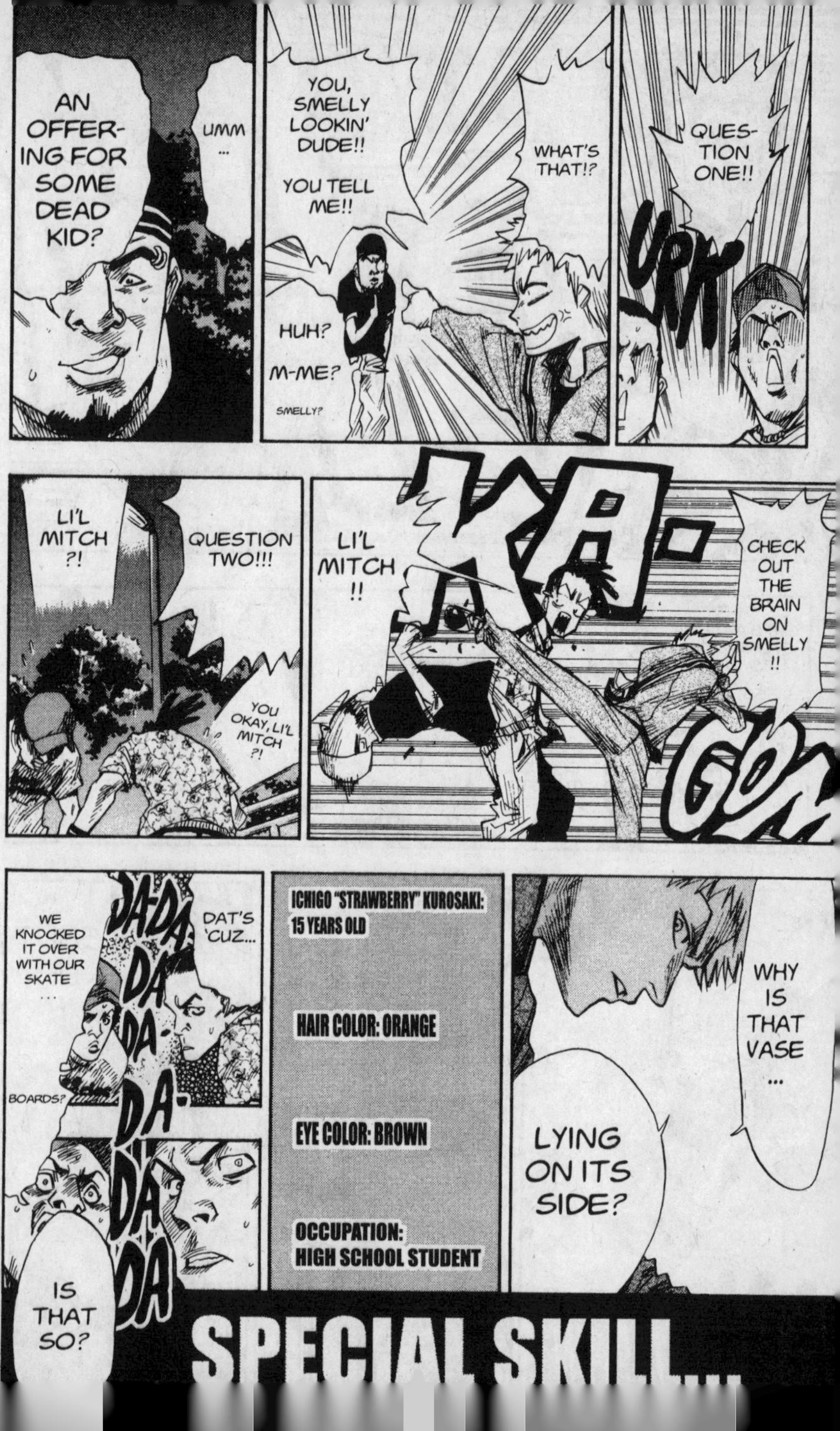
QUES-TION ONE!!
UPP
WHAT'S THAT!?
YOU, SMELLY LOOKIN' DUDE!!
YOU TELL ME!!
HUH?
M-ME?
SMELLY?
UMM ...
AN OFFERING FOR SOME DEAD KID?
CHECK OUT THE BRAIN ON SMELLY !!
KA-
GON
LI'L MITCH !!
QUESTION TWO!!!
LI'L MITCH ?!
YOU OKAY, LI'L MITCH ?!
WHY IS THAT VASE ...
LYING ON ITS SIDE?
ICHIGO "STRAWBERRY" KUROSAKI: 15 YEARS OLD
HAIR COLOR: ORANGE
EYE COLOR: BROWN
OCCUPATION: HIGH SCHOOL STUDENT
DAT'S 'CUZ...
WE KNOCKED IT OVER WITH OUR SKATE ...
BOARDS?
DA-DA-DA-DA-DA-DA-DA-DA
IS THAT SO?
SPECIAL SKILL...

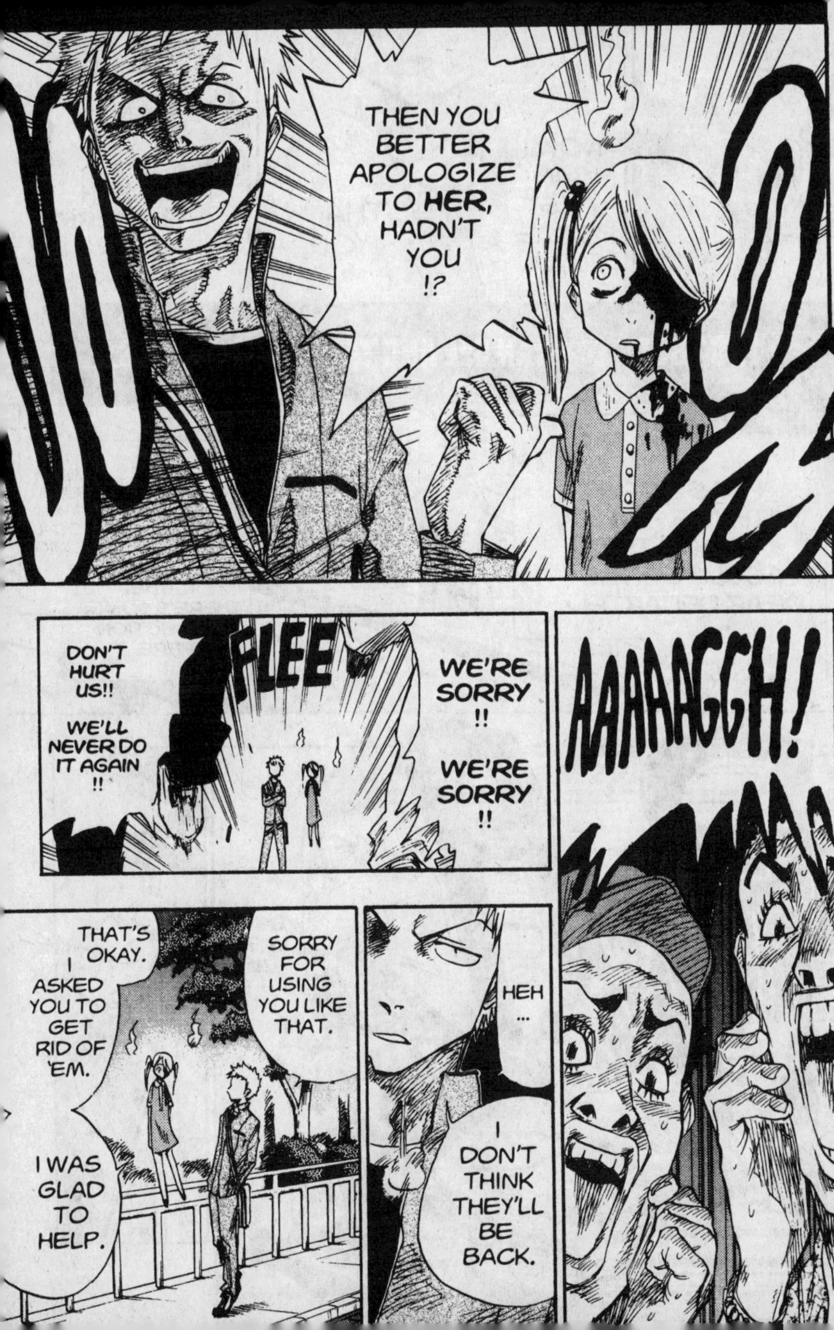

THEN YOU BETTER APOLOGIZE TO HER, HADN'T YOU !?
AAAAAGGH!
WE'RE SORRY !!
WE'RE SORRY !!
FLEE
DON'T HURT US!!
WE'LL NEVER DO IT AGAIN !!
HEH ...
I DON'T THINK THEY'LL BE BACK.
SORRY FOR USING YOU LIKE THAT.
THAT'S OKAY.
I ASKED YOU TO GET RID OF 'EM.
I WAS GLAD TO HELP.

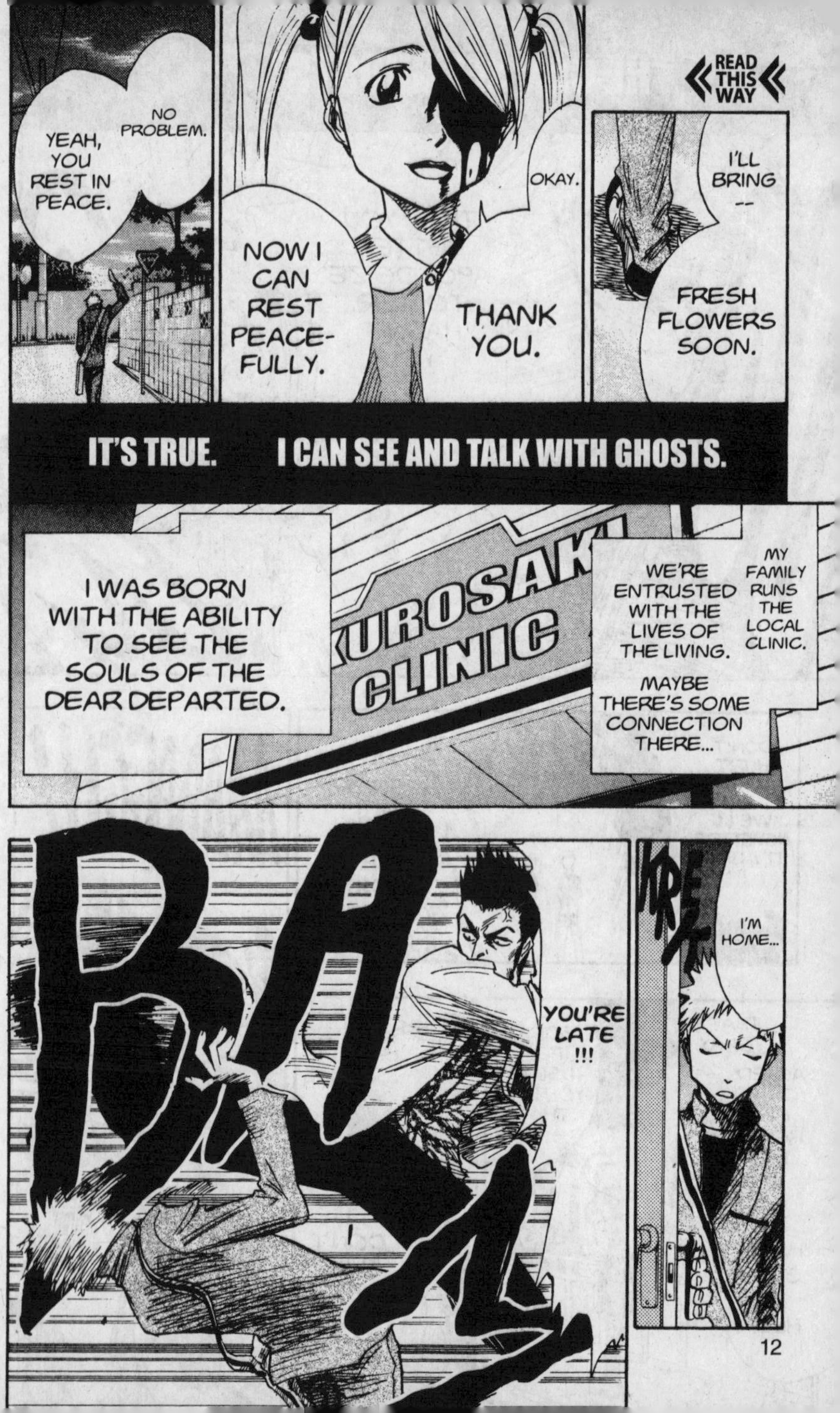
READ THIS WAY
I'LL BRING -- FRESH FLOWERS SOON.
OKAY.
THANK YOU.
NOW I CAN REST PEACEFULLY.
NO PROBLEM.
YEAH, YOU REST IN PEACE.
IT'S TRUE. I CAN SEE AND TALK WITH GHOSTS.
MY FAMILY RUNS THE LOCAL CLINIC.
WE'RE ENTRUSTED WITH THE LIVES OF THE LIVING.
MAYBE THERE'S SOME CONNECTION THERE...
CLINIC
I WAS BORN WITH THE ABILITY TO SEE THE SOULS OF THE DEAR DEPARTED.
I'M HOME...
YOU'RE LATE!!!
BA

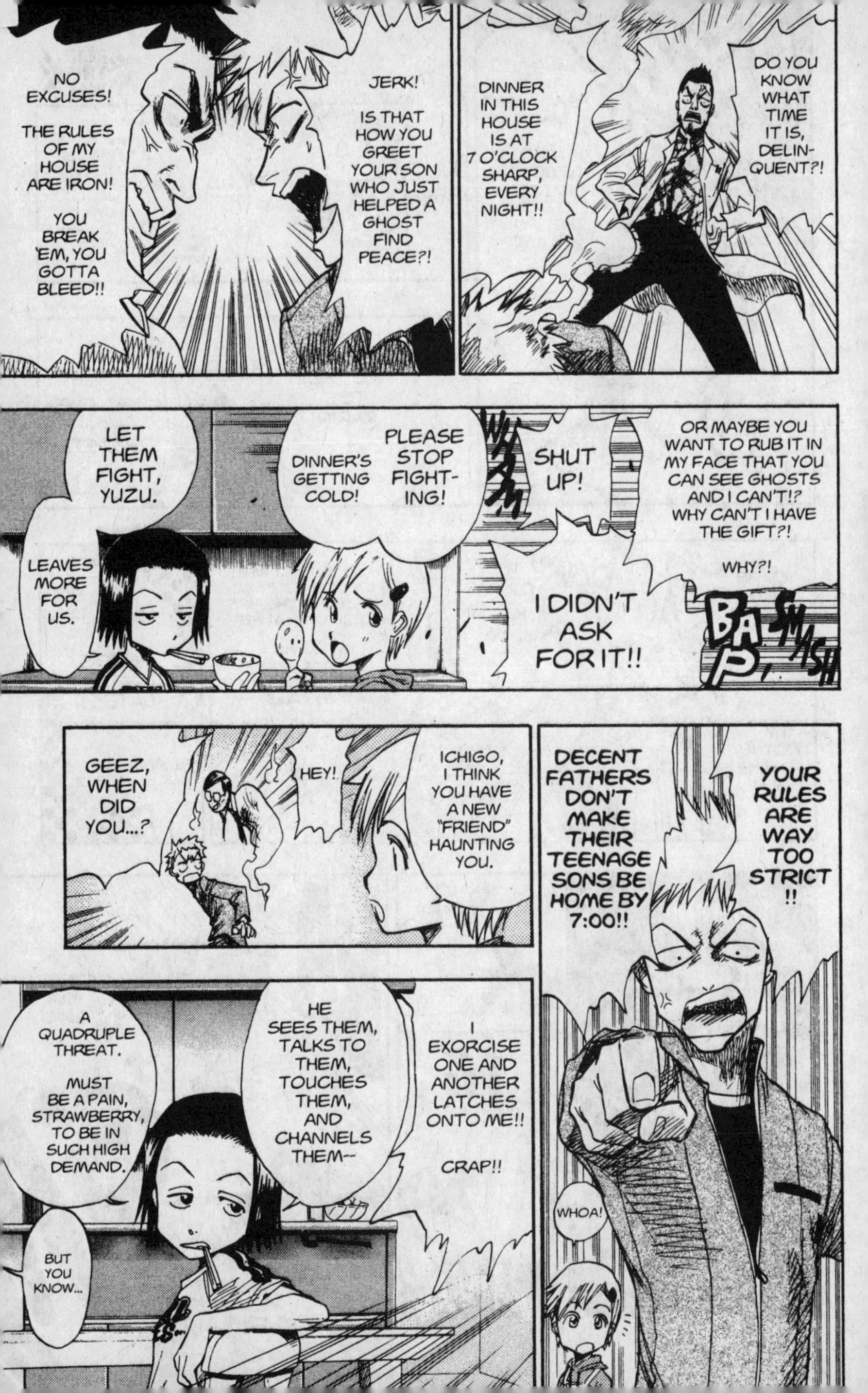
DO YOU KNOW WHAT TIME IT IS, DELINQUENT?!
DINNER IN THIS HOUSE IS AT 7 O'CLOCK SHARP, EVERY NIGHT!!
JERK!
IS THAT HOW YOU GREET YOUR SON WHO JUST HELPED A GHOST FIND PEACE?!
NO EXCUSES!
THE RULES OF MY HOUSE ARE IRON!
YOU BREAK 'EM, YOU GOTTA BLEED!!
OR MAYBE YOU WANT TO RUB IT IN MY FACE THAT YOU CAN SEE GHOSTS AND I CAN'T!? WHY CAN'T I HAVE THE GIFT?!
WHY?!
BAP, SMASH
SHUT UP!
WHAM
I DIDN'T ASK FOR IT!!
PLEASE STOP FIGHTING!
DINNER'S GETTING COLD!
LET THEM FIGHT, YUZU.
LEAVES MORE FOR US.
YOUR RULES ARE WAY TOO STRICT!!
DECENT FATHERS DON'T MAKE THEIR TEENAGE SONS BE HOME BY 7:00!!
WHOA!
ICHIGO, I THINK YOU HAVE A NEW "FRIEND" HAUNTING YOU.
HEY!
GEEZ, WHEN DID YOU...?
I EXORCISE ONE AND ANOTHER LATCHES ONTO ME!!
CRAP!!
HE SEES THEM, TALKS TO THEM, TOUCHES THEM, AND CHANNELS THEM--
A QUADRUPLE THREAT.
MUST BE A PAIN, STRAWBERRY, TO BE IN SUCH HIGH DEMAND.
BUT YOU KNOW...

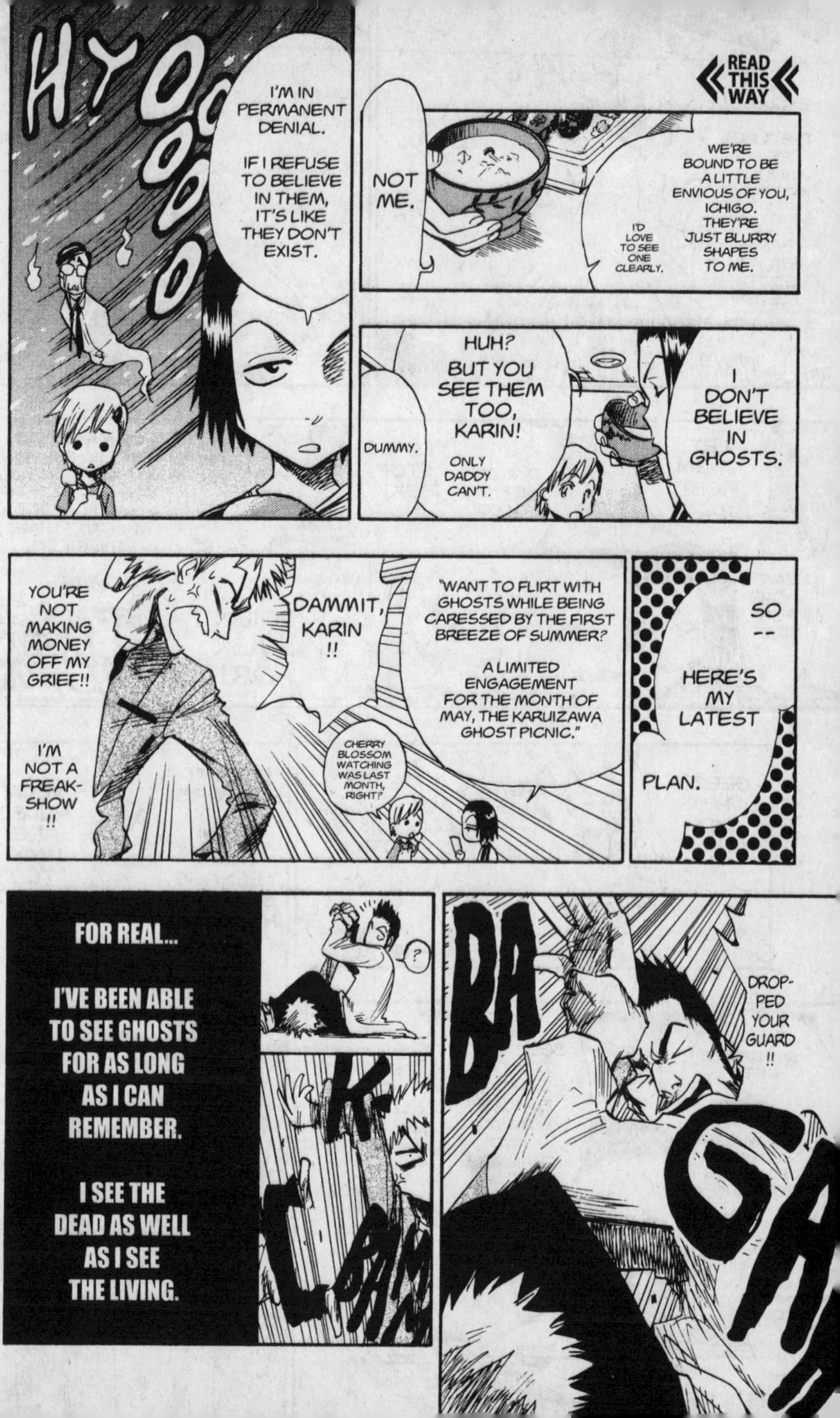
READ THIS WAY
WE'RE BOUND TO BE A LITTLE ENVIOUS OF YOU, ICHIGO. THEY'RE JUST BLURRY SHAPES TO ME.
I'D LOVE TO SEE ONE CLEARLY.
NOT ME.
I DON'T BELIEVE IN GHOSTS.
HUH? BUT YOU SEE THEM TOO, KARIN!
ONLY DADDY CAN'T.
DUMMY.
I'M IN PERMANENT DENIAL.
IF I REFUSE TO BELIEVE IN THEM, IT'S LIKE THEY DON'T EXIST.
HYOOOOOOO
SO -- HERE'S MY LATEST PLAN.
"WANT TO FLIRT WITH GHOSTS WHILE BEING CARESSED BY THE FIRST BREEZE OF SUMMER?
A LIMITED ENGAGEMENT FOR THE MONTH OF MAY, THE KARUIZAWA GHOST PICNIC."
CHERRY BLOSSOM WATCHING WAS LAST MONTH, RIGHT?
DAMMIT, KARIN!!
YOU'RE NOT MAKING MONEY OFF MY GRIEF!!
I'M NOT A FREAK-SHOW!!
BA
DROP-PED YOUR GUARD!!
GA
?
K
BAM
FOR REAL...
I'VE BEEN ABLE TO SEE GHOSTS FOR AS LONG AS I CAN REMEMBER.
I SEE THE DEAD AS WELL AS I SEE THE LIVING.

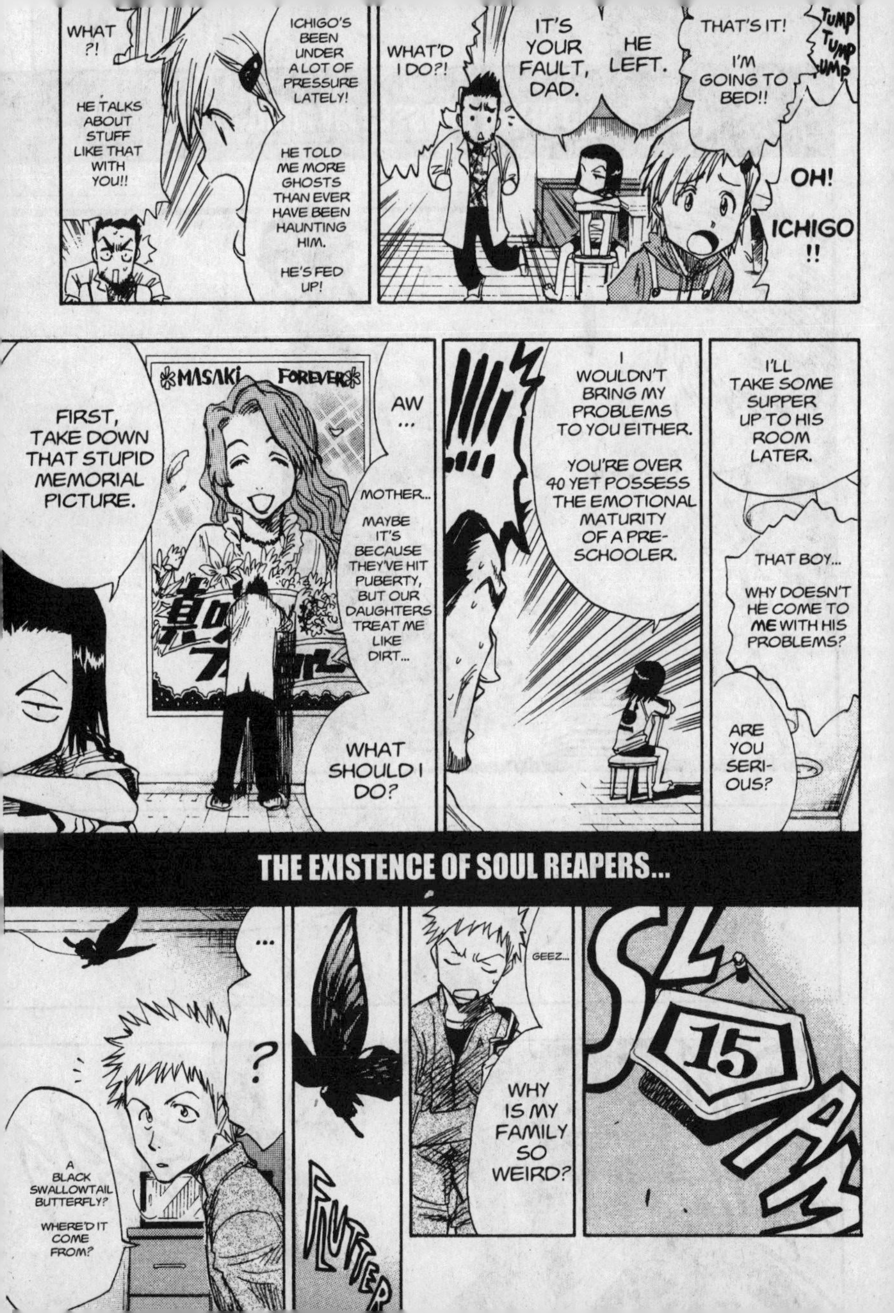
TUMP TUMP TUMP
THAT'S IT! I'M GOING TO BED!!
HE LEFT.
IT'S YOUR FAULT, DAD.
OH! ICHIGO!!
WHAT'D I DO?!
ICHIGO'S BEEN UNDER A LOT OF PRESSURE LATELY!
HE TOLD ME MORE GHOSTS THAN EVER HAVE BEEN HAUNTING HIM.
HE'S FED UP!
WHAT?!
HE TALKS ABOUT STUFF LIKE THAT WITH YOU!!
I'LL TAKE SOME SUPPER UP TO HIS ROOM LATER.
THAT BOY...
WHY DOESN'T HE COME TO ME WITH HIS PROBLEMS?
ARE YOU SERIOUS?
I WOULDN'T BRING MY PROBLEMS TO YOU EITHER.
YOU'RE OVER 40 YET POSSESS THE EMOTIONAL MATURITY OF A PRE-SCHOOLER.
MASAKI FOREVER
AW ...
MOTHER... MAYBE IT'S BECAUSE THEY'VE HIT PUBERTY, BUT OUR DAUGHTERS TREAT ME LIKE DIRT...
FIRST, TAKE DOWN THAT STUPID MEMORIAL PICTURE.
WHAT SHOULD I DO?
THE EXISTENCE OF SOUL REAPERS...
SLAM
15
GEEZ...
WHY IS MY FAMILY SO WEIRD?
FLUTTER
...
?
A BLACK SWALLOWTAIL BUTTERFLY?
WHERE'D IT COME FROM?

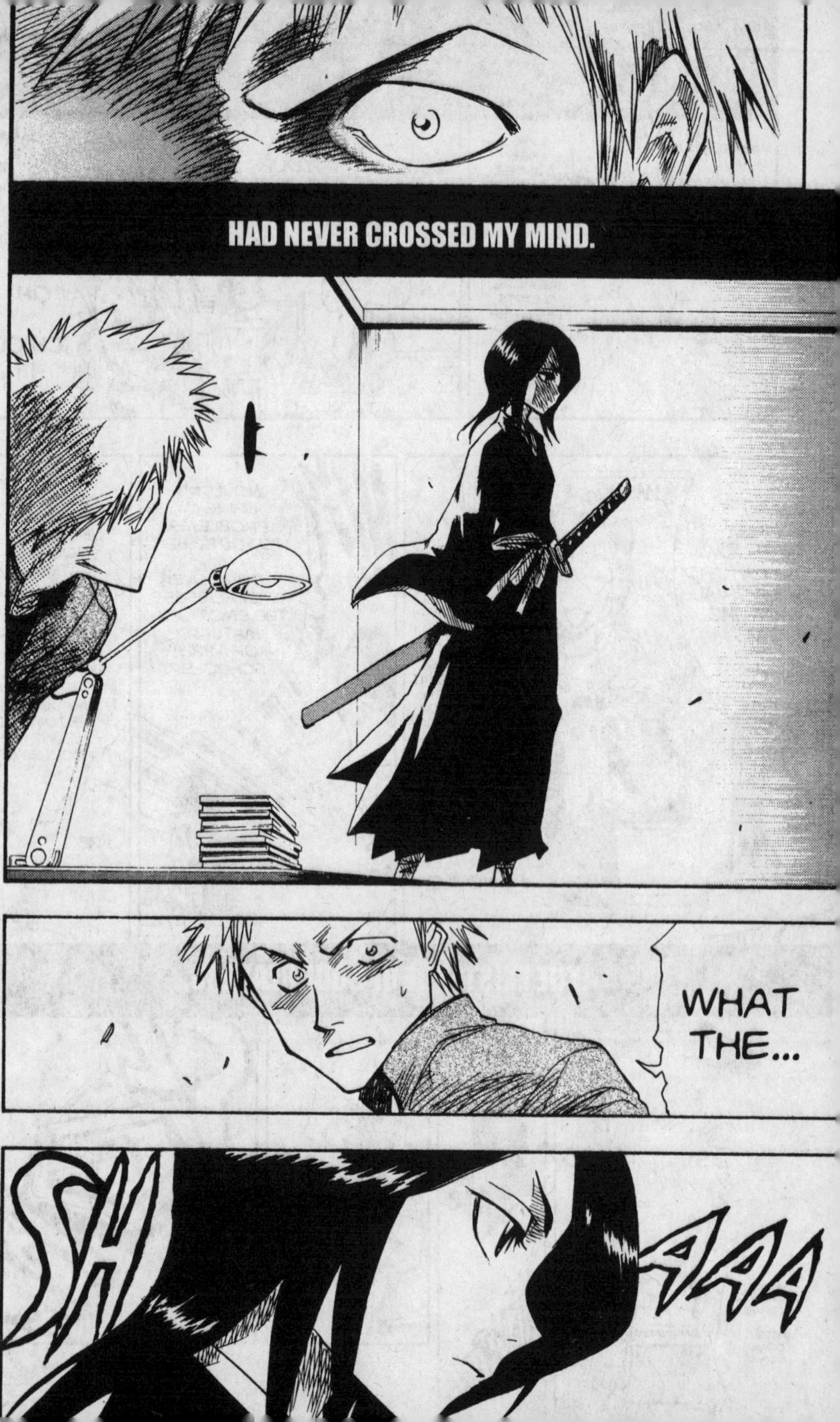
HAD NEVER CROSSED MY MIND.
WHAT THE...
SHAAA

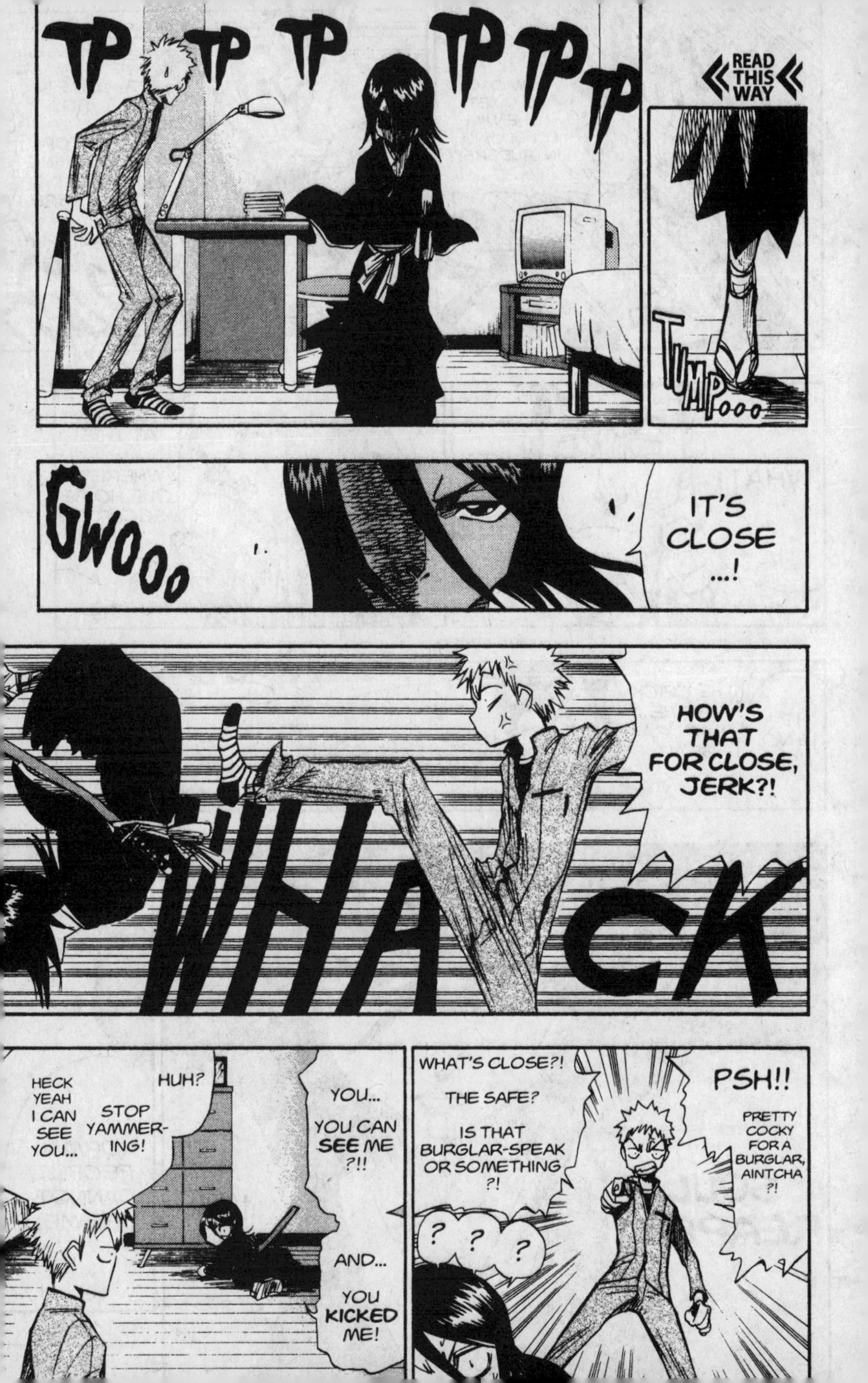
READ THIS WAY
TUMPooo
TP TP TP TP TP TP TP
IT'S CLOSE ...!
GWOOO
HOW'S THAT FOR CLOSE, JERK?!
WHACK
PSH!!
PRETTY COCKY FOR A BURGLAR, AINTCHA ?!
WHAT'S CLOSE?!
THE SAFE?
IS THAT BURGLAR-SPEAK OR SOMETHING ?!
? ? ?
YOU...
YOU CAN SEE ME ?!!
AND...
YOU KICKED ME!
HUH?
STOP YAMMER-ING!
HECK YEAH I CAN SEE YOU...

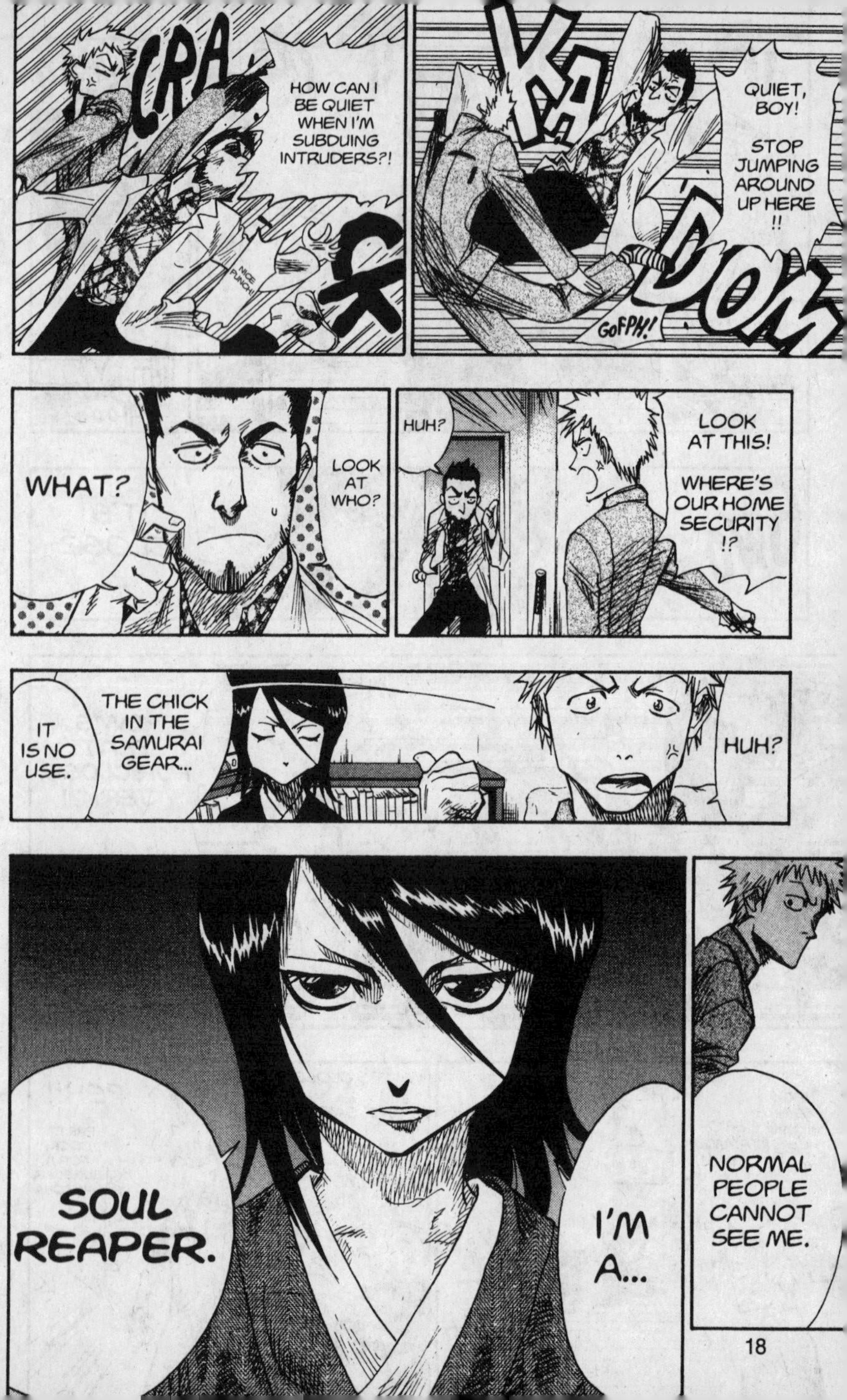
QUIET, BOY!
STOP JUMPING AROUND UP HERE !!
KA
DOM
GoFPH!
CRA
HOW CAN I BE QUIET WHEN I'M SUBDUING INTRUDERS?!
NICE PUNCH!
CK
LOOK AT THIS!
WHERE'S OUR HOME SECURITY !?
HUH?
LOOK AT WHO?
WHAT?
HUH?
THE CHICK IN THE SAMURAI GEAR...
IT IS NO USE.
NORMAL PEOPLE CANNOT SEE ME.
I'M A...
SOUL REAPER.

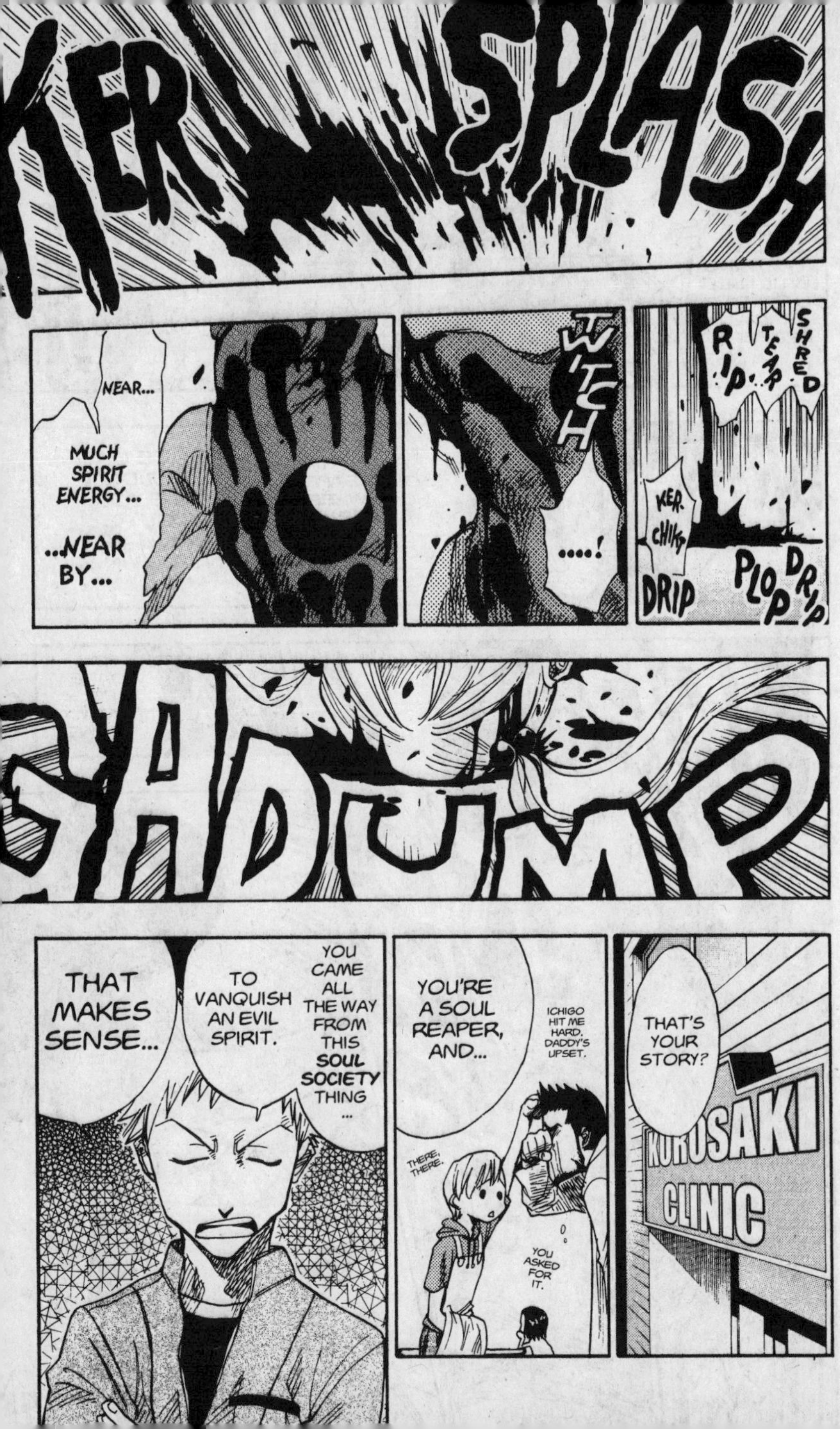
KERSPLASH
RIP
TEAR
SHRED
KER-CHIKS
DRIP
PLOP
DRIP
TWITCH
....!
NEAR...
MUCH SPIRIT ENERGY...
...NEAR BY...
GADUMP
THAT'S YOUR STORY?
KUROSAKI CLINIC
YOU'RE A SOUL REAPER, AND...
ICHIGO HIT ME HARD. DADDY'S UPSET.
THERE, THERE.
YOU ASKED FOR IT.
YOU CAME ALL THE WAY FROM THIS SOUL SOCIETY THING...
TO VANQUISH AN EVIL SPIRIT.
THAT MAKES SENSE...

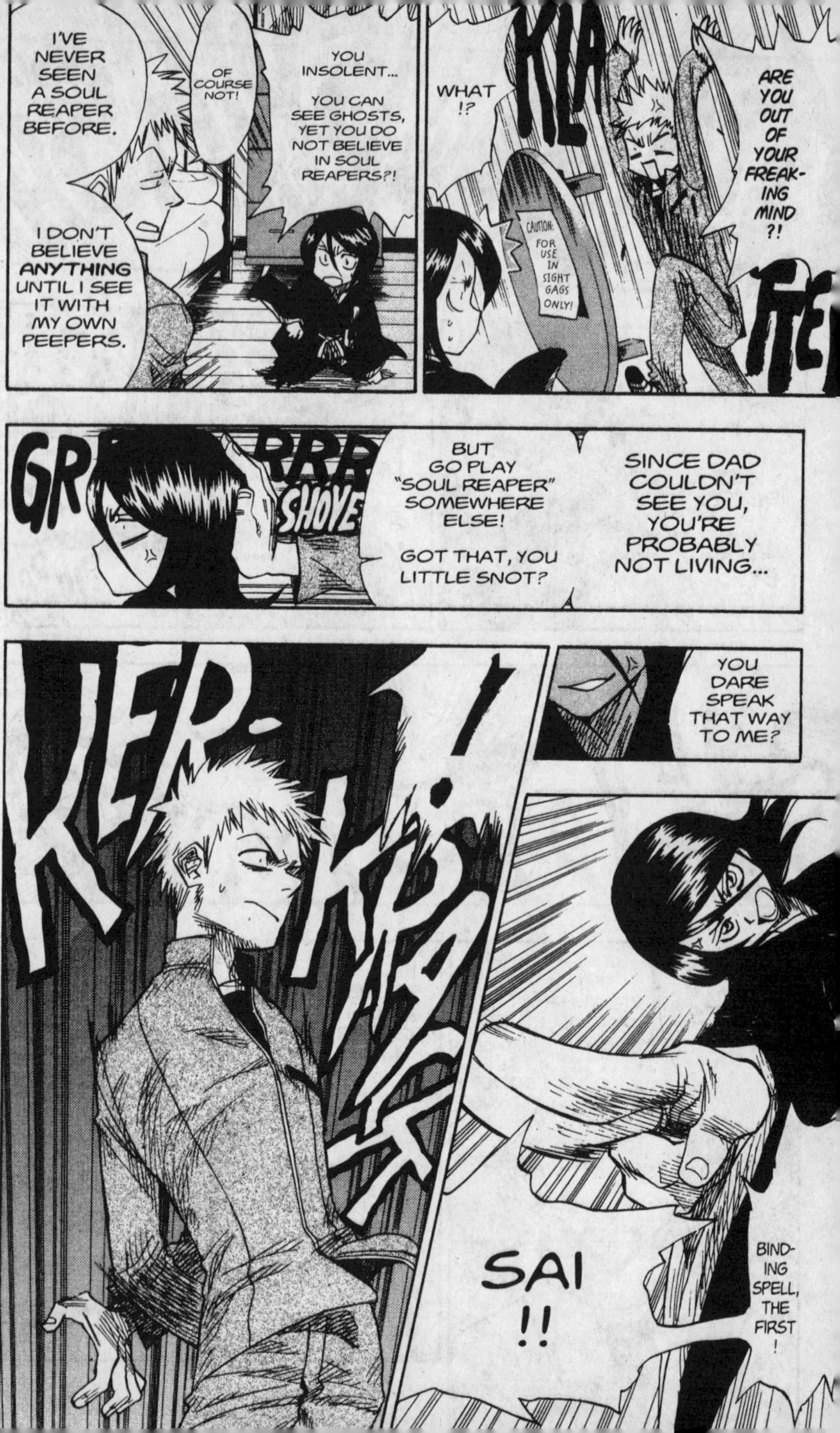
ARE YOU OUT OF YOUR FREAKING MIND?!
KLA
WHAT !?
CAUTION: FOR USE IN SIGHT GAGS ONLY!
YOU INSOLENT...
YOU CAN SEE GHOSTS, YET YOU DO NOT BELIEVE IN SOUL REAPERS?!
OF COURSE NOT!
I'VE NEVER SEEN A SOUL REAPER BEFORE.
I DON'T BELIEVE **ANYTHING** UNTIL I SEE IT WITH MY OWN PEEPERS.
SINCE DAD COULDN'T SEE YOU, YOU'RE PROBABLY NOT LIVING...
BUT GO PLAY "SOUL REAPER" SOMEWHERE ELSE!
GOT THAT, YOU LITTLE SNOT?
SHOVE
GRRRR
YOU DARE SPEAK THAT WAY TO ME?
BINDING SPELL, THE FIRST!
SAI !!
KLER-

READ THIS WAY

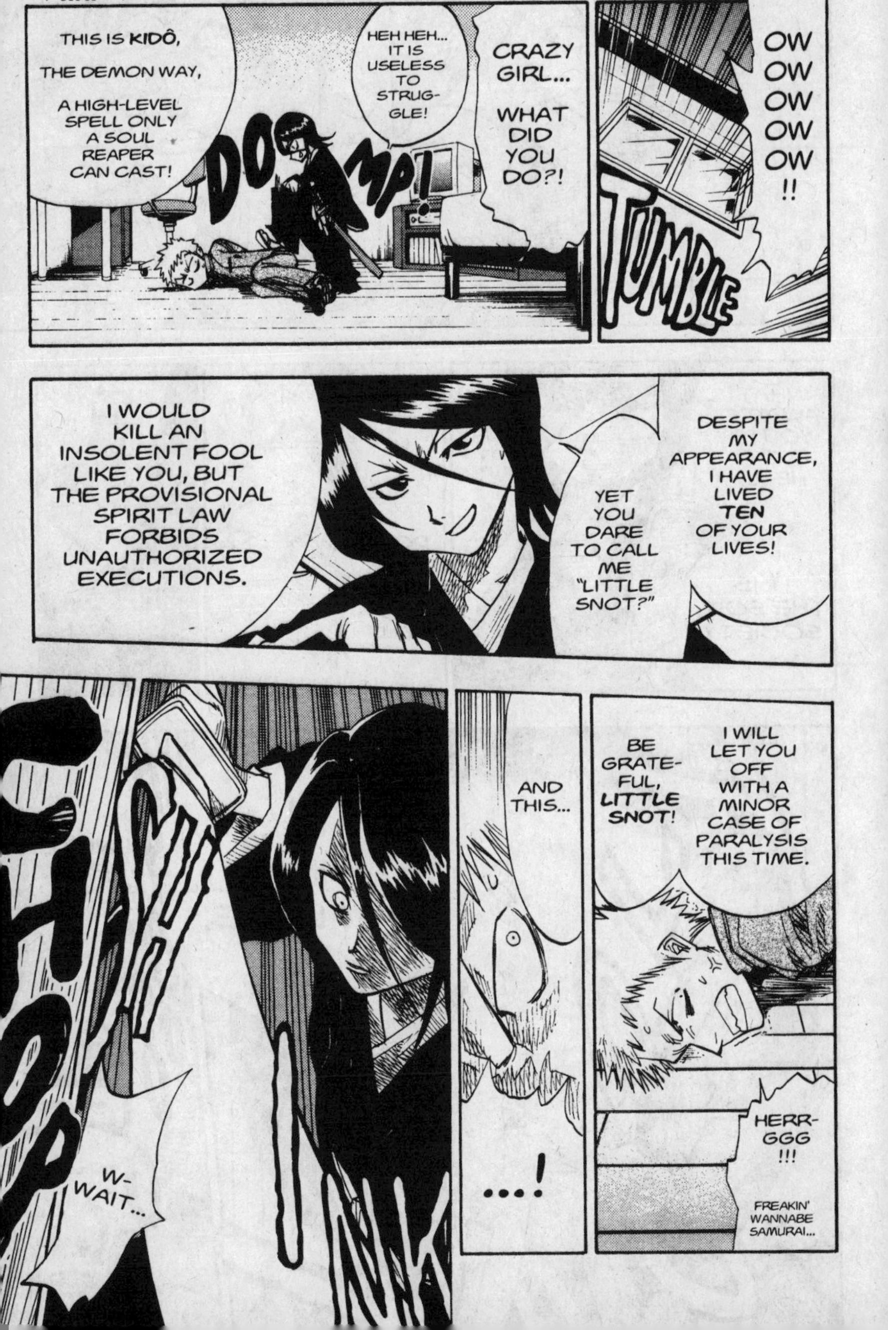

OW OW OW OW OW!!
TUMBLE
CRAZY GIRL... WHAT DID YOU DO?!
HEH HEH... IT IS USELESS TO STRUG-GLE!
THIS IS KIDÔ, THE DEMON WAY, A HIGH-LEVEL SPELL ONLY A SOUL REAPER CAN CAST!
DOOMP!
DESPITE MY APPEARANCE, I HAVE LIVED TEN OF YOUR LIVES!
YET YOU DARE TO CALL ME "LITTLE SNOT?"
I WOULD KILL AN INSOLENT FOOL LIKE YOU, BUT THE PROVISIONAL SPIRIT LAW FORBIDS UNAUTHORIZED EXECUTIONS.
I WILL LET YOU OFF WITH A MINOR CASE OF PARALYSIS THIS TIME.
BE GRATE-FUL, LITTLE SNOT!
HERR-GGG!!!
FREAKIN' WANNABE SAMURAI...
AND THIS...
...!
W-WAIT...

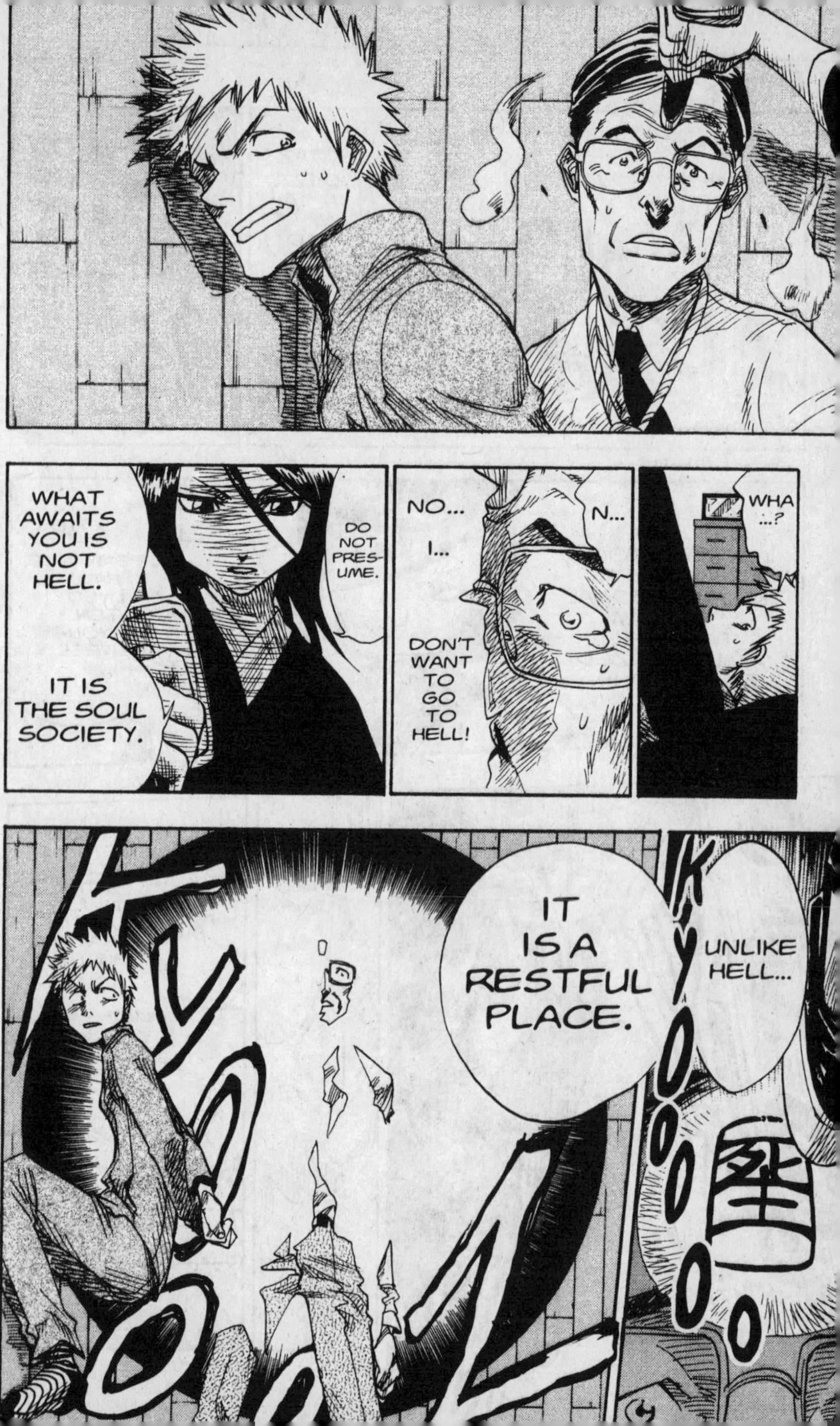
WHA ...?
N...
NO...
I...
DON'T WANT TO GO TO HELL!
DO NOT PRESUME.
WHAT AWAITS YOU IS NOT HELL.
IT IS THE SOUL SOCIETY.
UNLIKE HELL...
IT IS A RESTFUL PLACE.

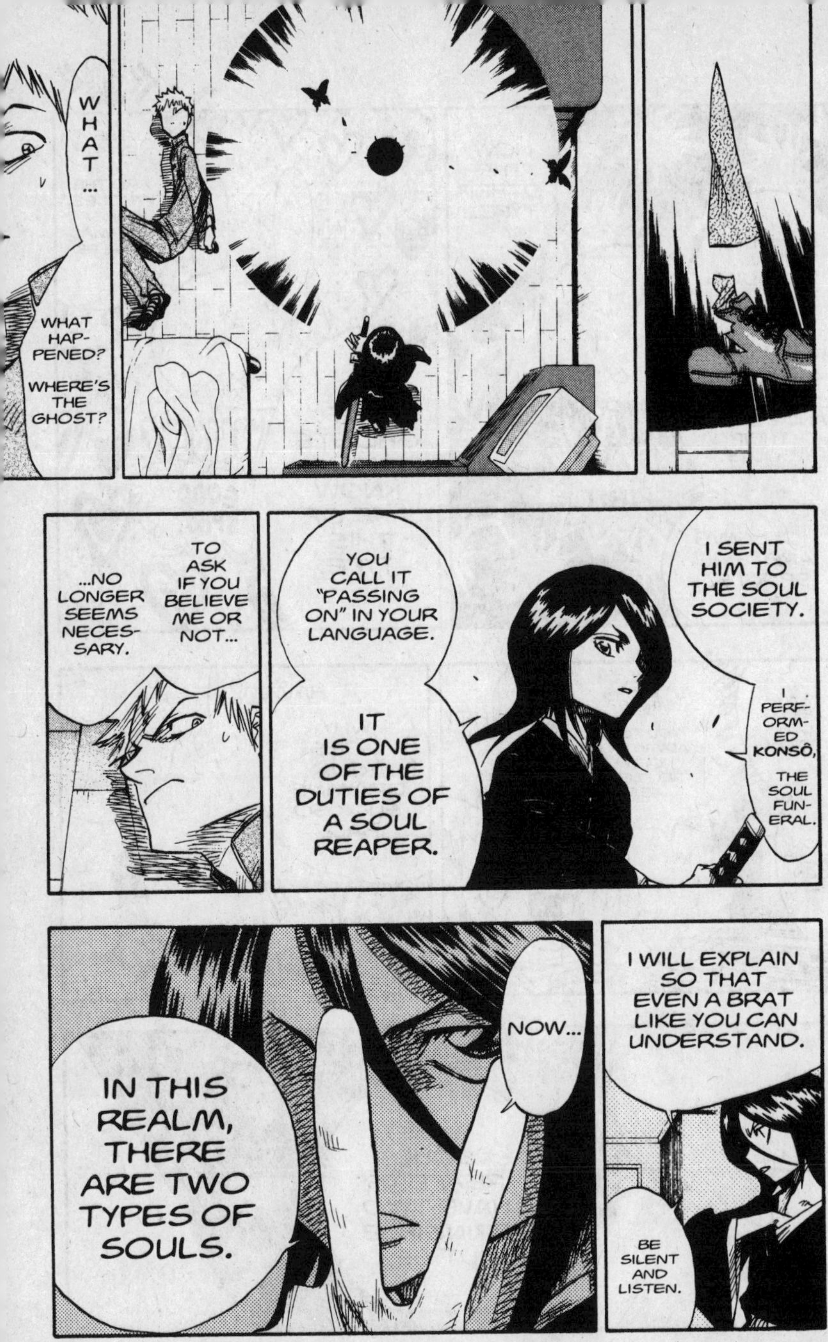
WHAT...
WHAT HAPPENED?
WHERE'S THE GHOST?
I SENT HIM TO THE SOUL SOCIETY.
I PERFORMED KONSÔ, THE SOUL FUNERAL.
YOU CALL IT "PASSING ON" IN YOUR LANGUAGE.
IT IS ONE OF THE DUTIES OF A SOUL REAPER.
TO ASK IF YOU BELIEVE ME OR NOT...
...NO LONGER SEEMS NECESSARY.
I WILL EXPLAIN SO THAT EVEN A BRAT LIKE YOU CAN UNDERSTAND.
BE SILENT AND LISTEN.
NOW...
IN THIS REALM, THERE ARE TWO TYPES OF SOULS.

READ THIS WAY

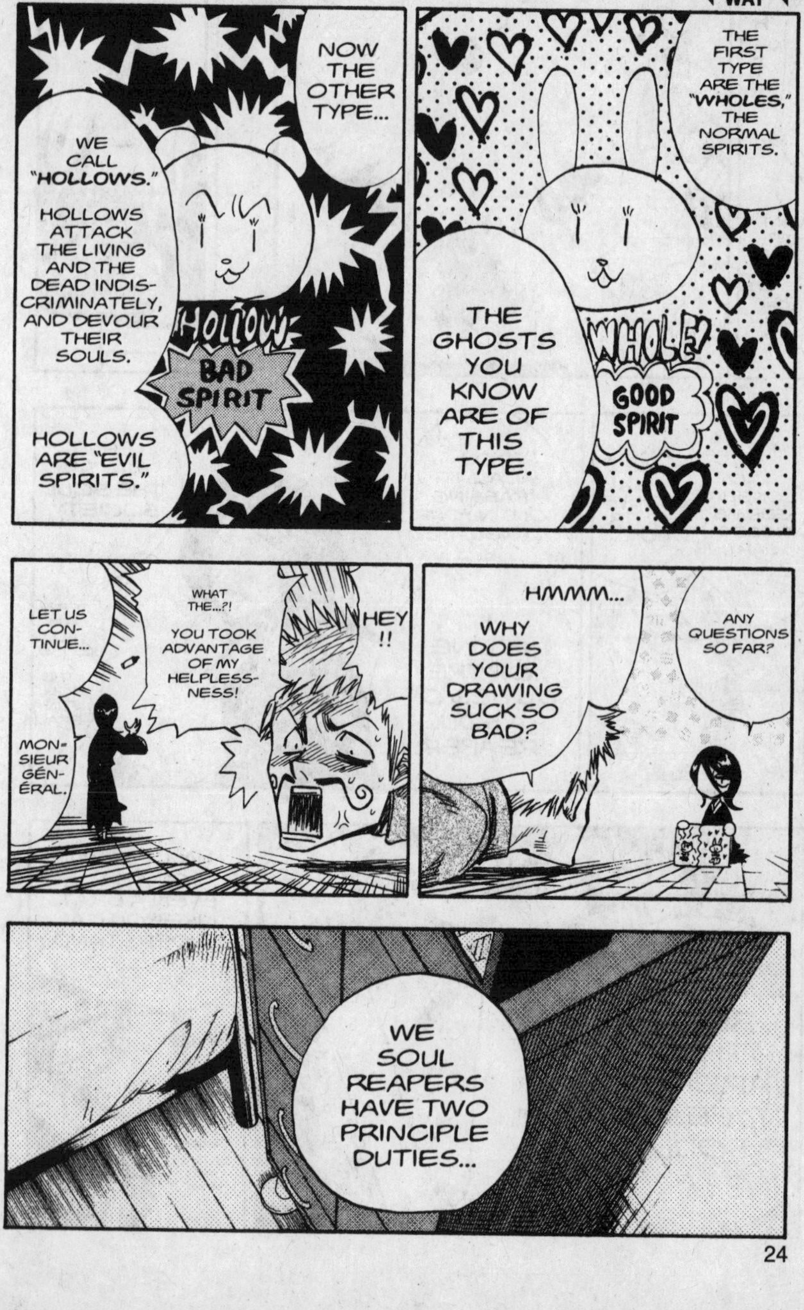
THE FIRST TYPE ARE THE "WHOLES," THE NORMAL SPIRITS.
THE GHOSTS YOU KNOW ARE OF THIS TYPE.
WHOLE!
GOOD SPIRIT
NOW THE OTHER TYPE...
WE CALL "HOLLOWS."
HOLLOWS ATTACK THE LIVING AND THE DEAD INDISCRIMINATELY, AND DEVOUR THEIR SOULS.
HOLLOW
BAD SPIRIT
HOLLOWS ARE "EVIL SPIRITS."
ANY QUESTIONS SO FAR?
HMMM...
WHY DOES YOUR DRAWING SUCK SO BAD?
HEY!!
WHAT THE...?!
YOU TOOK ADVANTAGE OF MY HELPLESSNESS!
LET US CONTINUE...
MONSIEUR GÉNÉRAL.
WE SOUL REAPERS HAVE TWO PRINCIPLE DUTIES...

READ THIS WAY

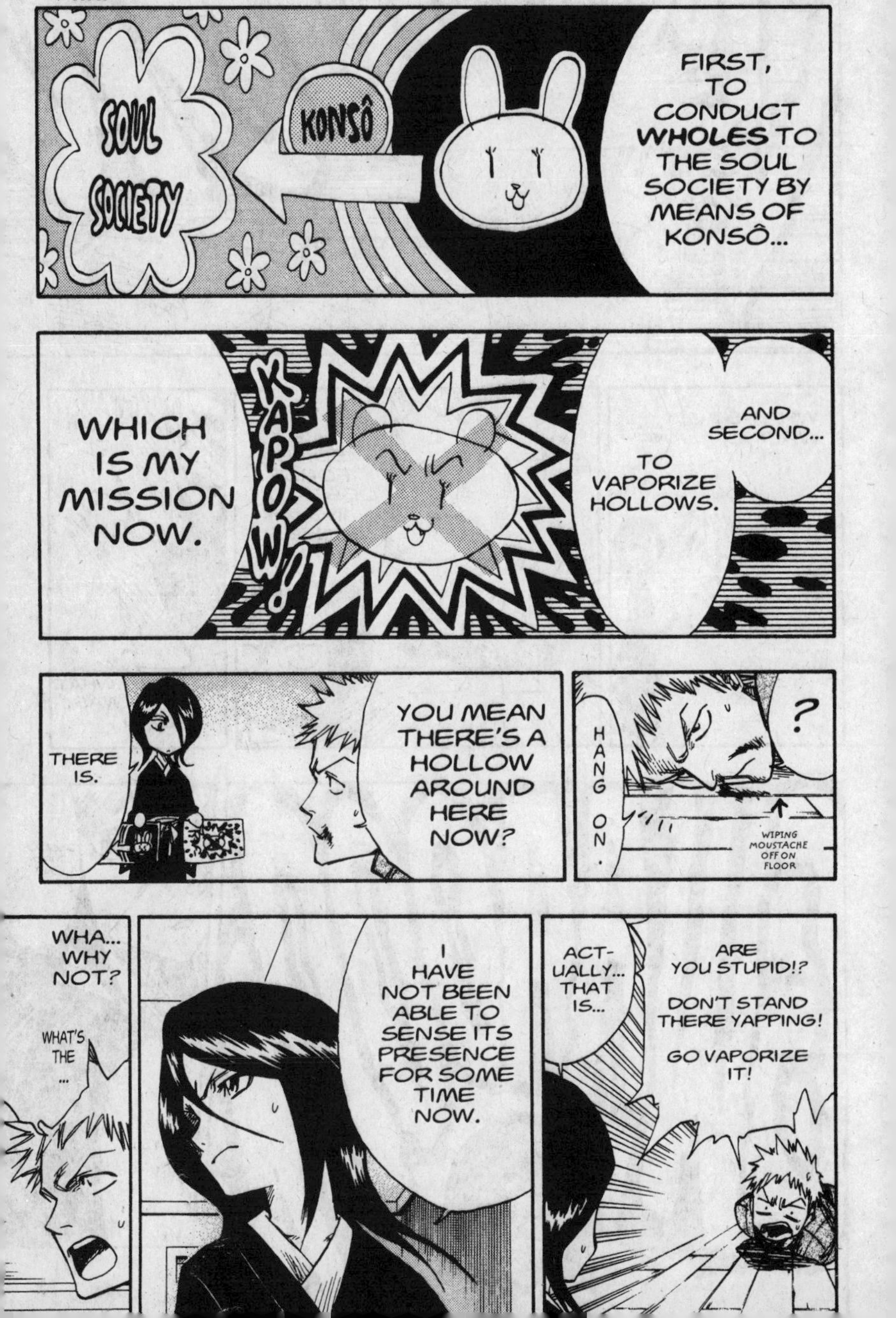
FIRST, TO CONDUCT WHOLES TO THE SOUL SOCIETY BY MEANS OF KONSÔ...
KONSÔ
SOUL SOCIETY
AND SECOND...
TO VAPORIZE HOLLOWS.
KAPOW!
WHICH IS MY MISSION NOW.
?
HANG ON.
WIPING MOUSTACHE OFF ON FLOOR
YOU MEAN THERE'S A HOLLOW AROUND HERE NOW?
THERE IS.
ARE YOU STUPID!? DON'T STAND THERE YAPPING! GO VAPORIZE IT!
ACTUALLY... THAT IS...
I HAVE NOT BEEN ABLE TO SENSE ITS PRESENCE FOR SOME TIME NOW.
WHA... WHY NOT?
WHAT'S THE ...

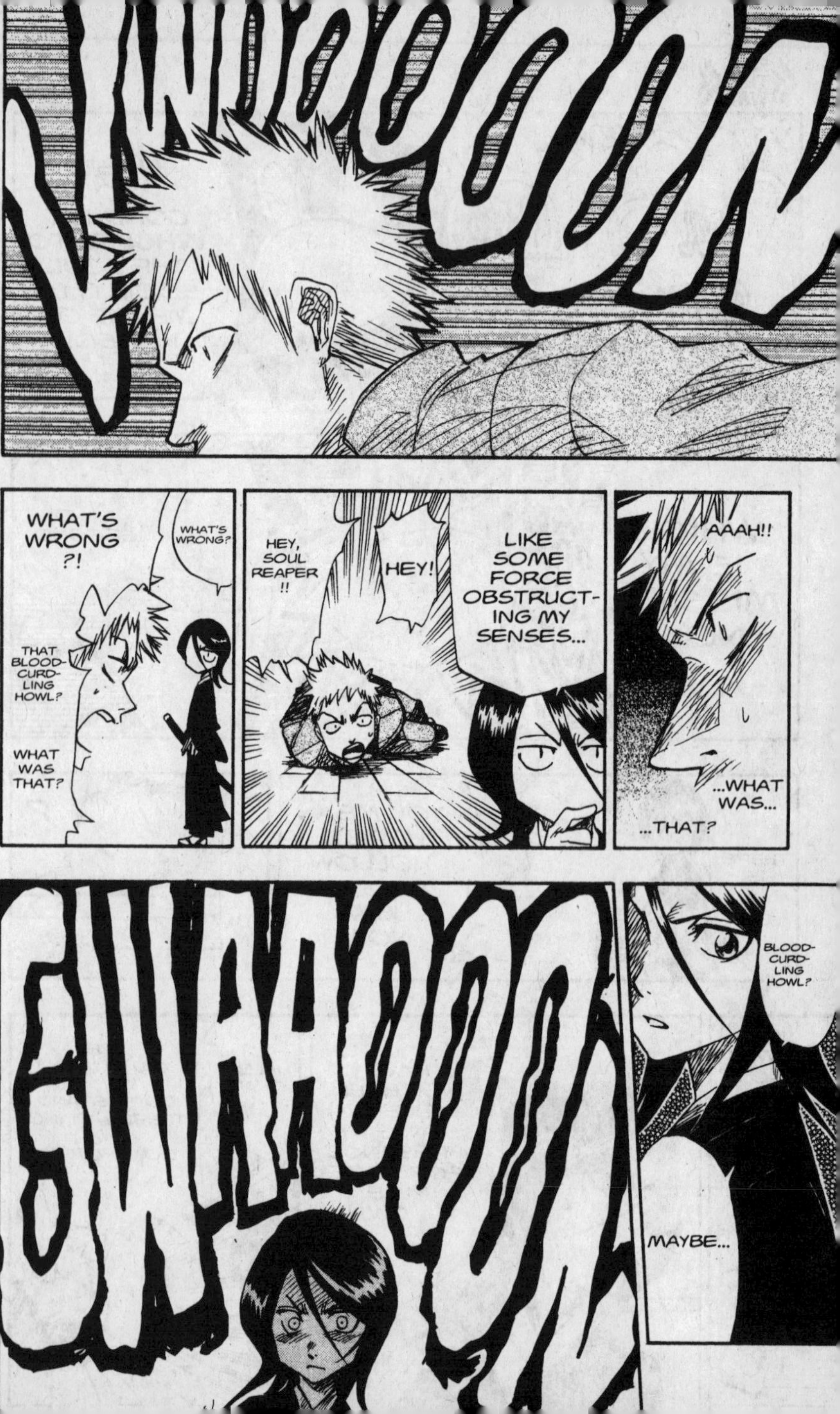
AAAH!!
...WHAT WAS...
...THAT?
LIKE SOME FORCE OBSTRUCTING MY SENSES...
HEY!
HEY, SOUL REAPER!!
WHAT'S WRONG?
WHAT'S WRONG ?!
THAT BLOOD-CURDLING HOWL?
WHAT WAS THAT?
BLOOD-CURDLING HOWL?
MAYBE...

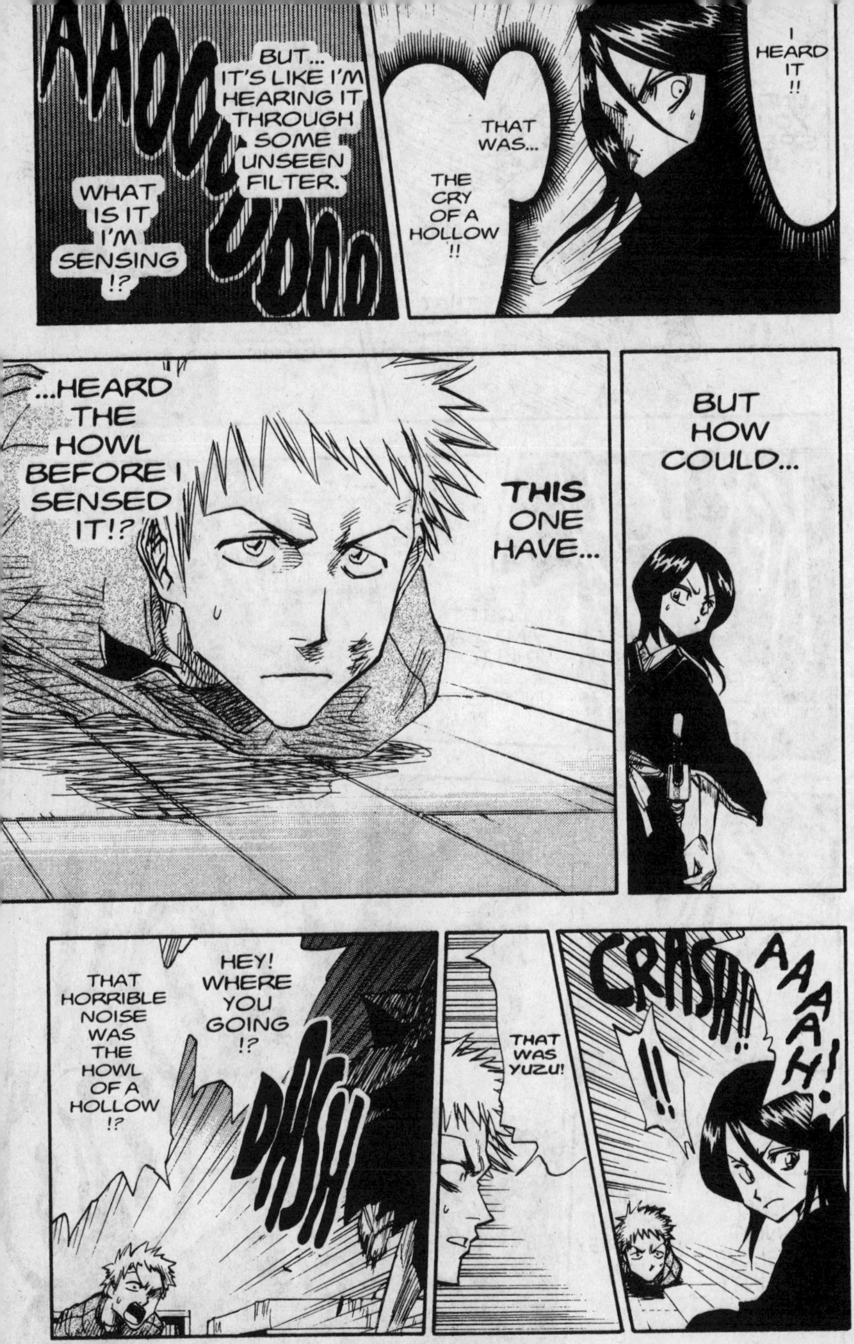
I HEARD IT !!
THAT WAS...
THE CRY OF A HOLLOW !!
AAOOOUOOO
BUT... IT'S LIKE I'M HEARING IT THROUGH SOME UNSEEN FILTER.
WHAT IS IT I'M SENSING !?
BUT HOW COULD...
THIS ONE HAVE...
...HEARD THE HOWL BEFORE I SENSED IT!?
CRASH!!
AAAAH!
!!
THAT WAS YUZU!
HEY! WHERE YOU GOING !?
DASH
THAT HORRIBLE NOISE WAS THE HOWL OF A HOLLOW !?

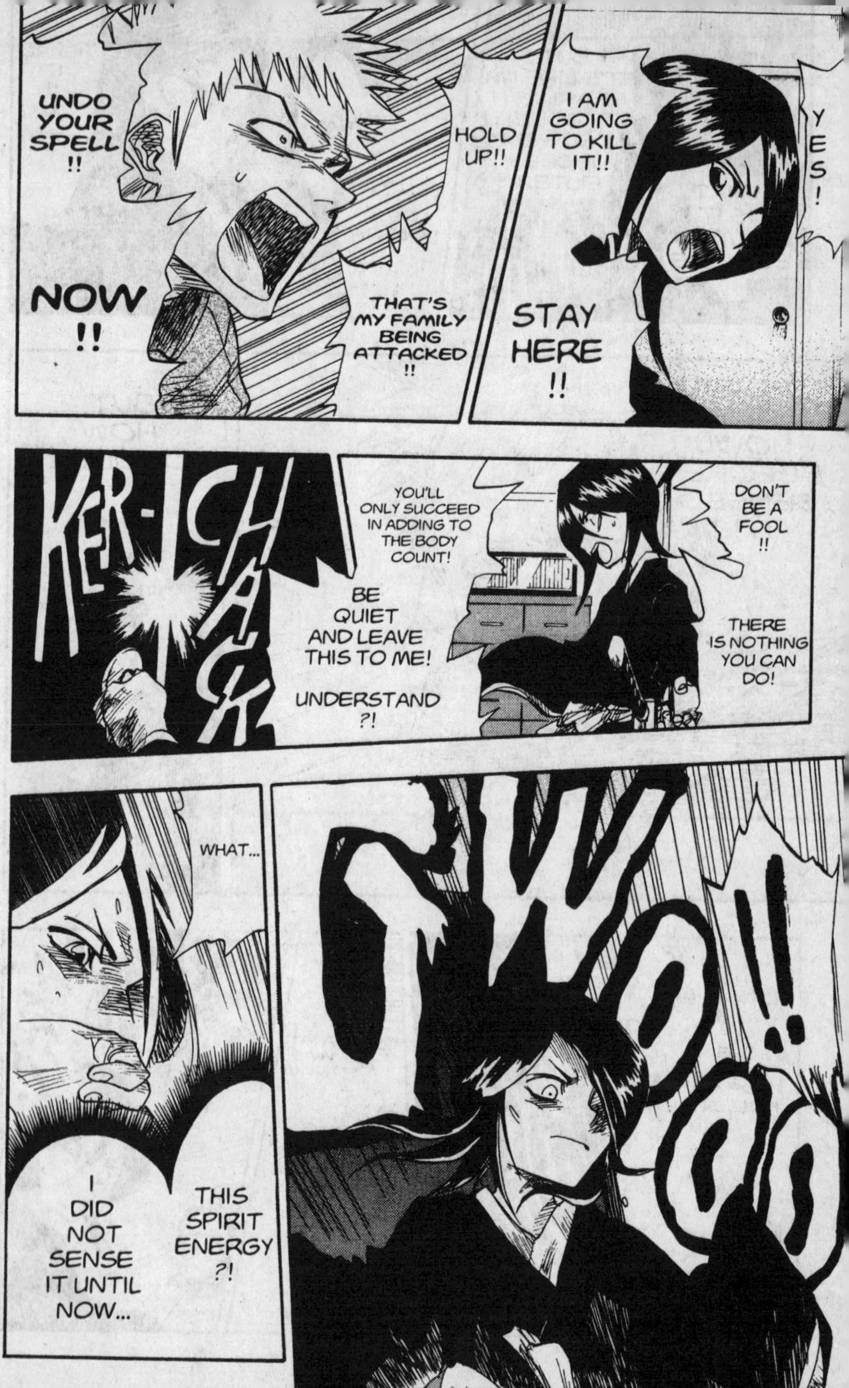
YES!
I AM GOING TO KILL IT!!
STAY HERE!!
HOLD UP!!
UNDO YOUR SPELL!!
THAT'S MY FAMILY BEING ATTACKED!!
NOW!!
DON'T BE A FOOL!!
YOU'LL ONLY SUCCEED IN ADDING TO THE BODY COUNT!
THERE IS NOTHING YOU CAN DO!
BE QUIET AND LEAVE THIS TO ME!
UNDERSTAND?!
KER-ICHACK
WOOOO!!
WHAT...
THIS SPIRIT ENERGY?!
I DID NOT SENSE IT UNTIL NOW...

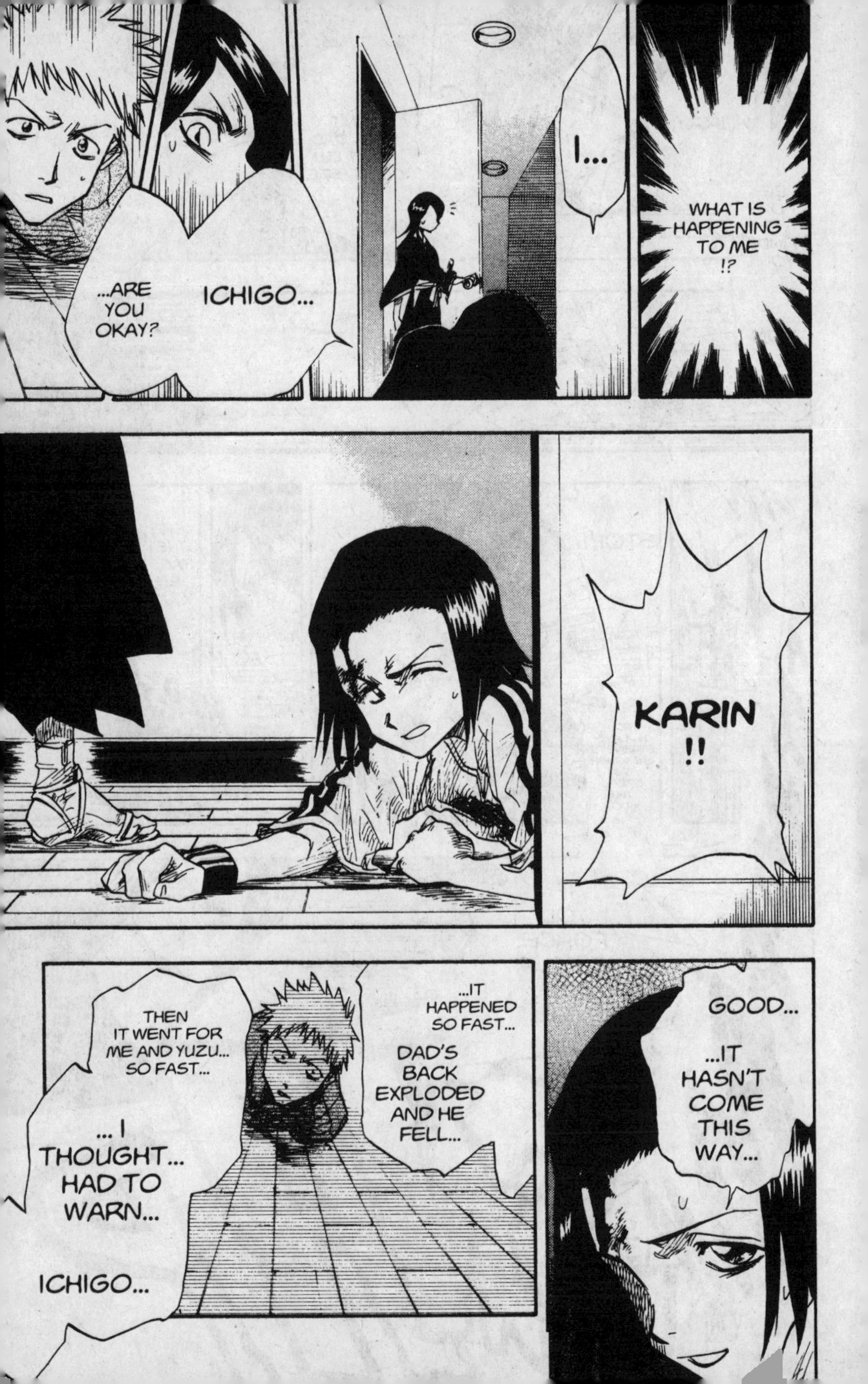
WHAT IS HAPPENING TO ME !?
I...
ICHIGO...
...ARE YOU OKAY?
KARIN !!
GOOD...
...IT HASN'T COME THIS WAY...
...IT HAPPENED SO FAST...
DAD'S BACK EXPLODED AND HE FELL...
THEN IT WENT FOR ME AND YUZU... SO FAST...
... I THOUGHT... HAD TO WARN...
ICHIGO...

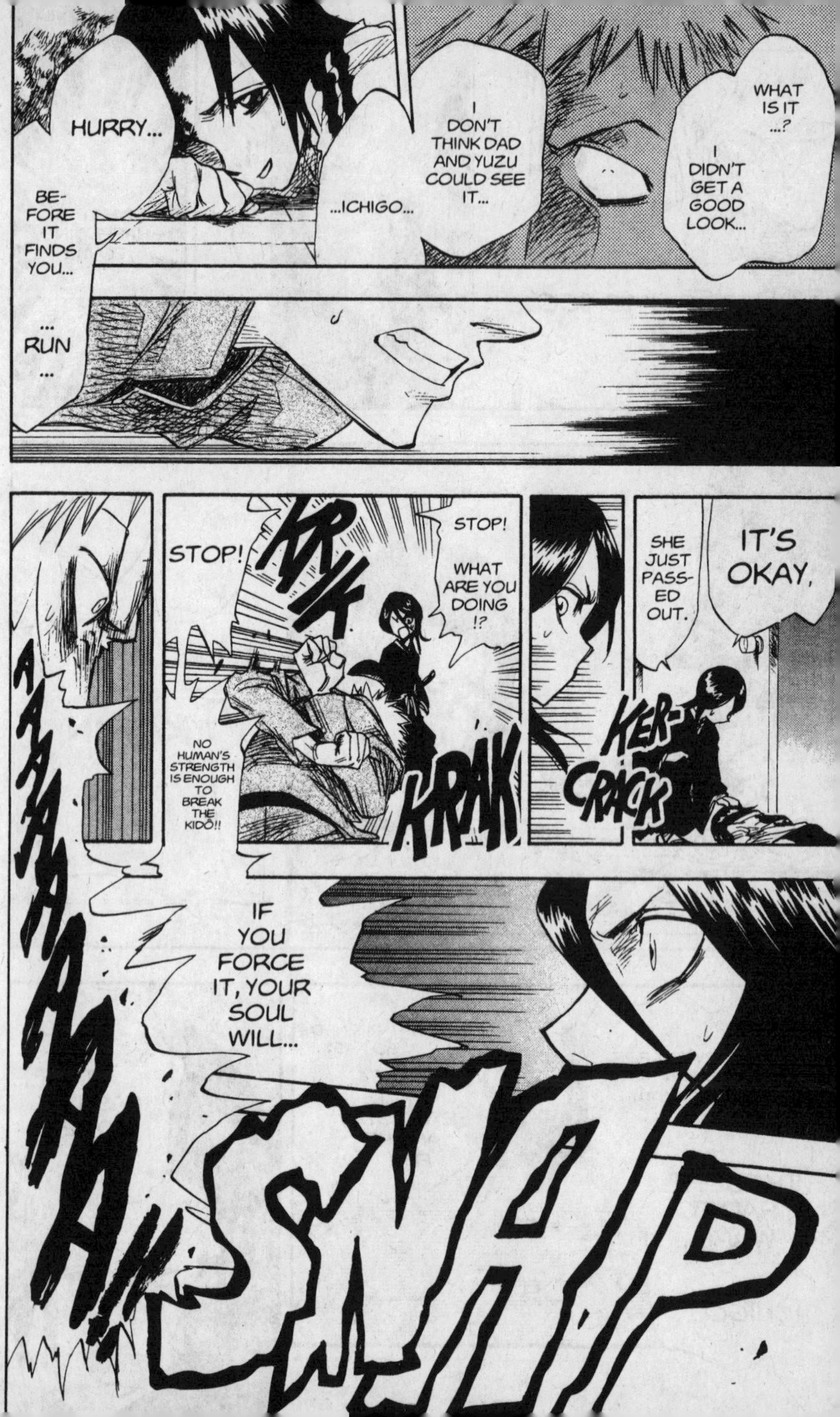
WHAT IS IT ...?
I DIDN'T GET A GOOD LOOK...
I DON'T THINK DAD AND YUZU COULD SEE IT...
...ICHIGO...
HURRY...
BEFORE IT FINDS YOU...
...RUN...
IT'S OKAY,
SHE JUST PASSED OUT.
KER-CRACK
STOP!
WHAT ARE YOU DOING!?
KRIK
KRAK
STOP!
NO HUMAN'S STRENGTH IS ENOUGH TO BREAK THE KIDÔ!!
AAAAAAAAAH!!
IF YOU FORCE IT, YOUR SOUL WILL...
SNAP

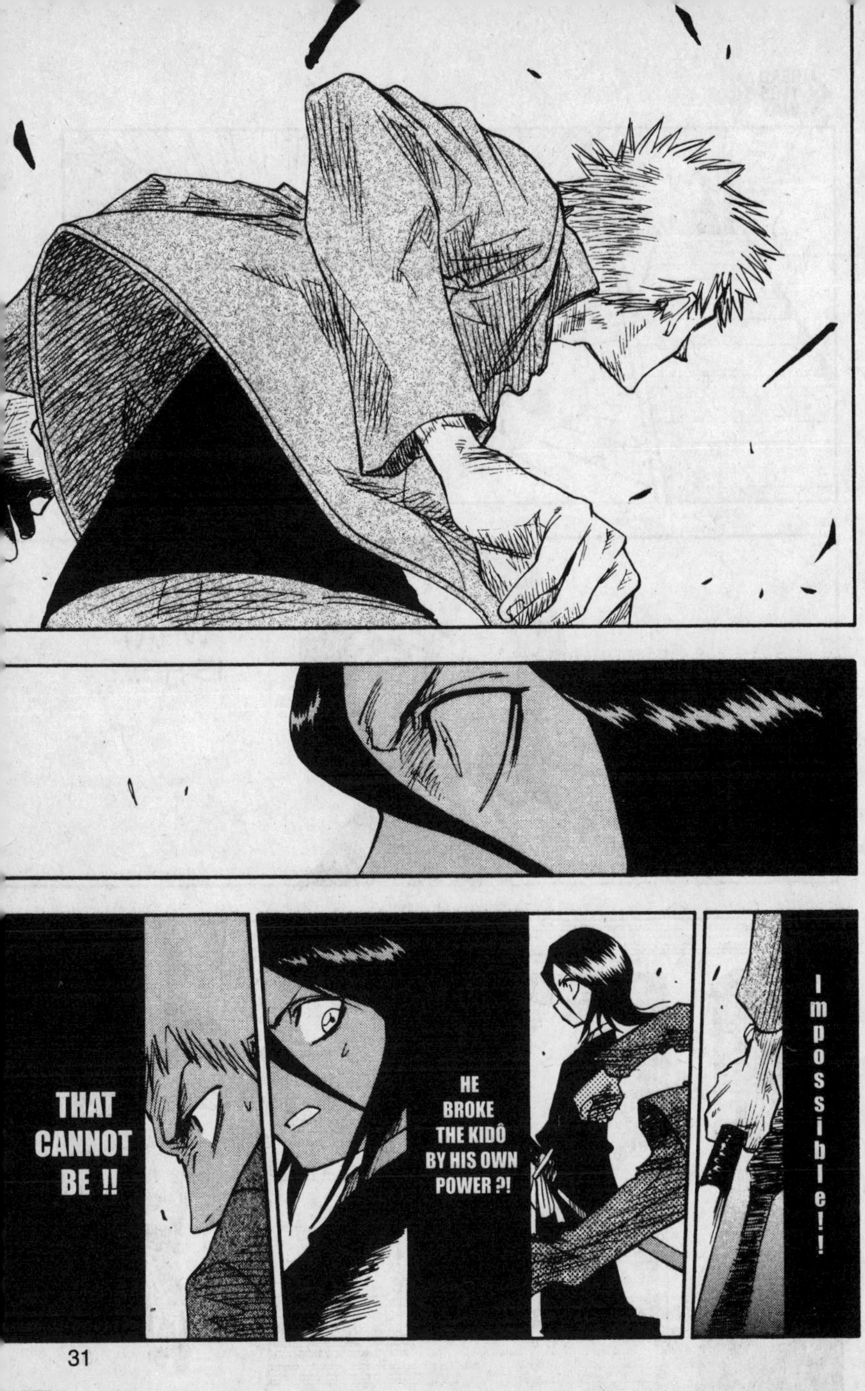
Impossible!!
HE BROKE THE KIDÔ BY HIS OWN POWER ?!
THAT CANNOT BE !!

READ THIS WAY

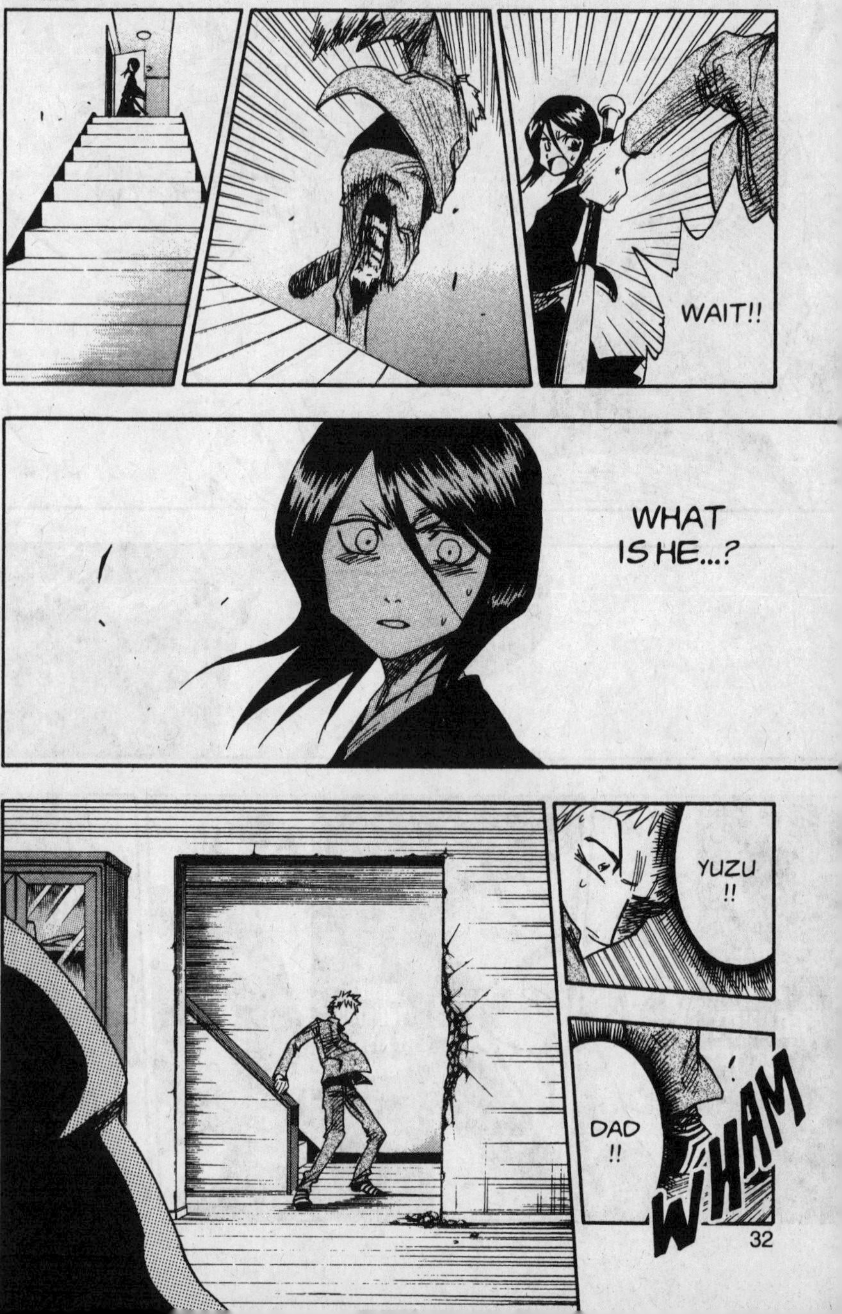
WAIT!!
WHAT IS HE...?
YUZU !!
DAD !!
WHAM

READ THIS WAY

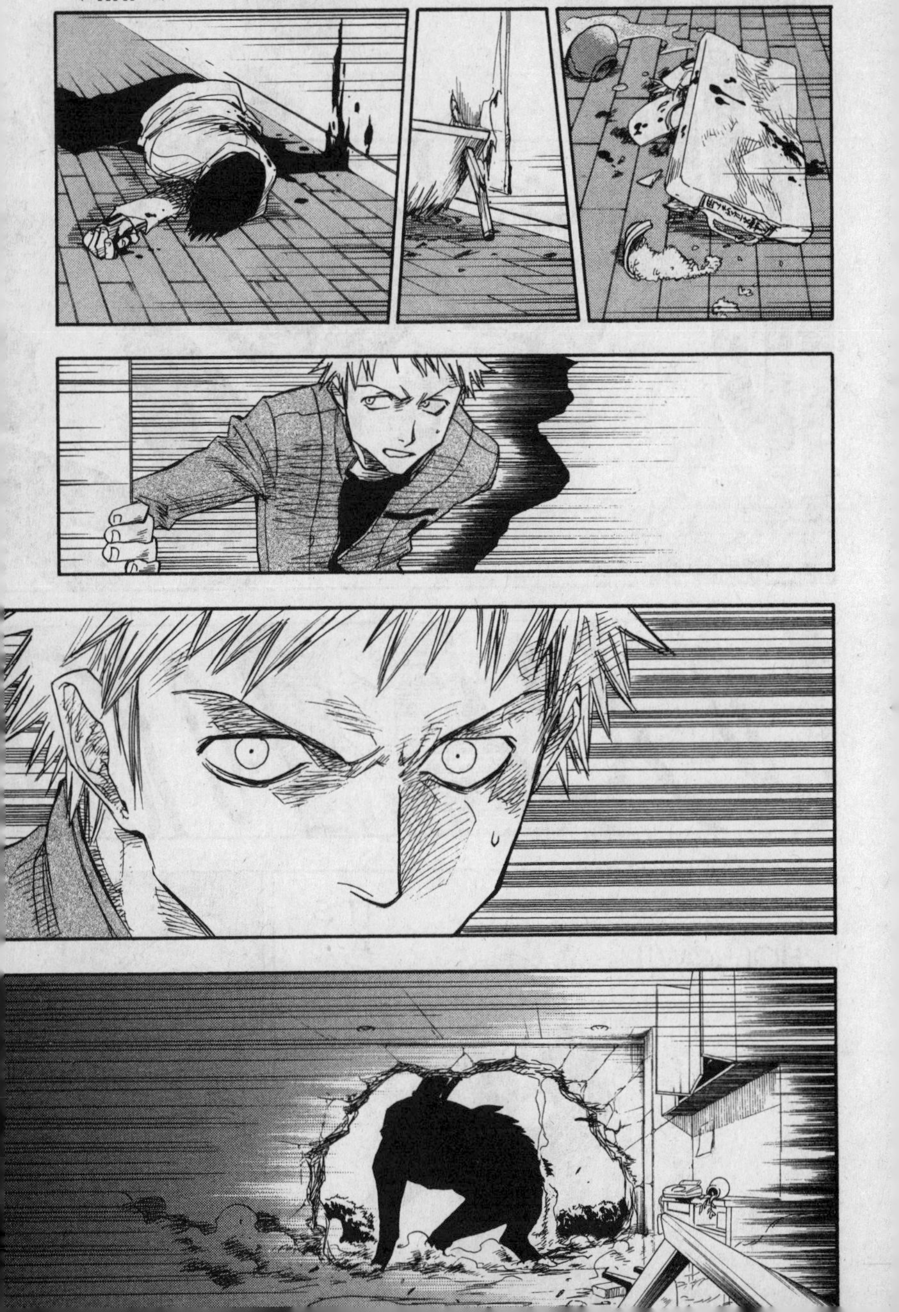

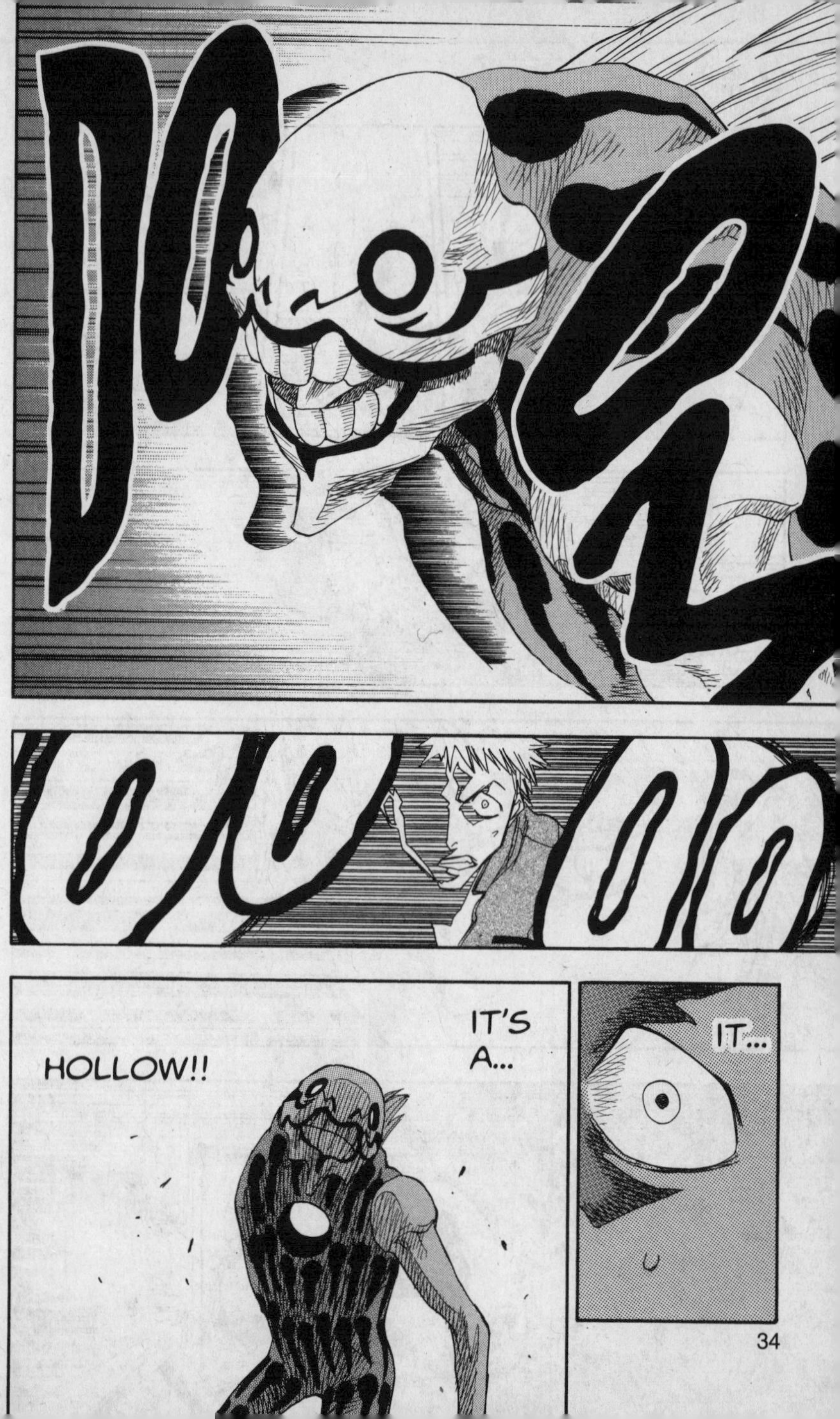
IT...
IT'S A...
HOLLOW!!

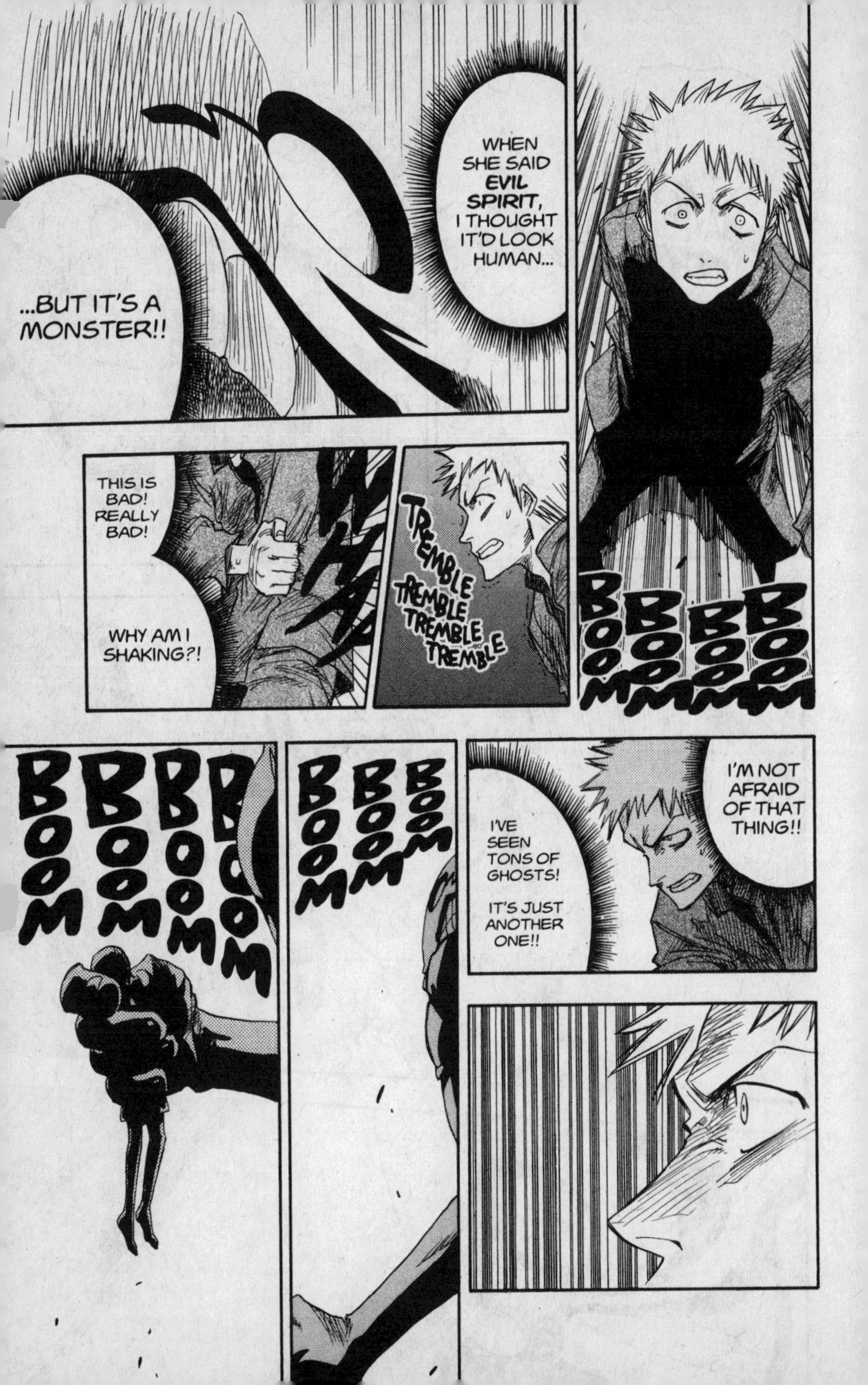
BOOM BOOM BOOM BOOM BOOM
WHEN SHE SAID EVIL SPIRIT, I THOUGHT IT'D LOOK HUMAN...
...BUT IT'S A MONSTER!!
TREMBLE TREMBLE TREMBLE TREMBLE
THIS IS BAD! REALLY BAD!
WHY AM I SHAKING?!
I'M NOT AFRAID OF THAT THING!!
I'VE SEEN TONS OF GHOSTS!
IT'S JUST ANOTHER ONE!!
BOOOM BOOOM BOOOM
BOOOM BOOOM BOOOOM BOOOOMM

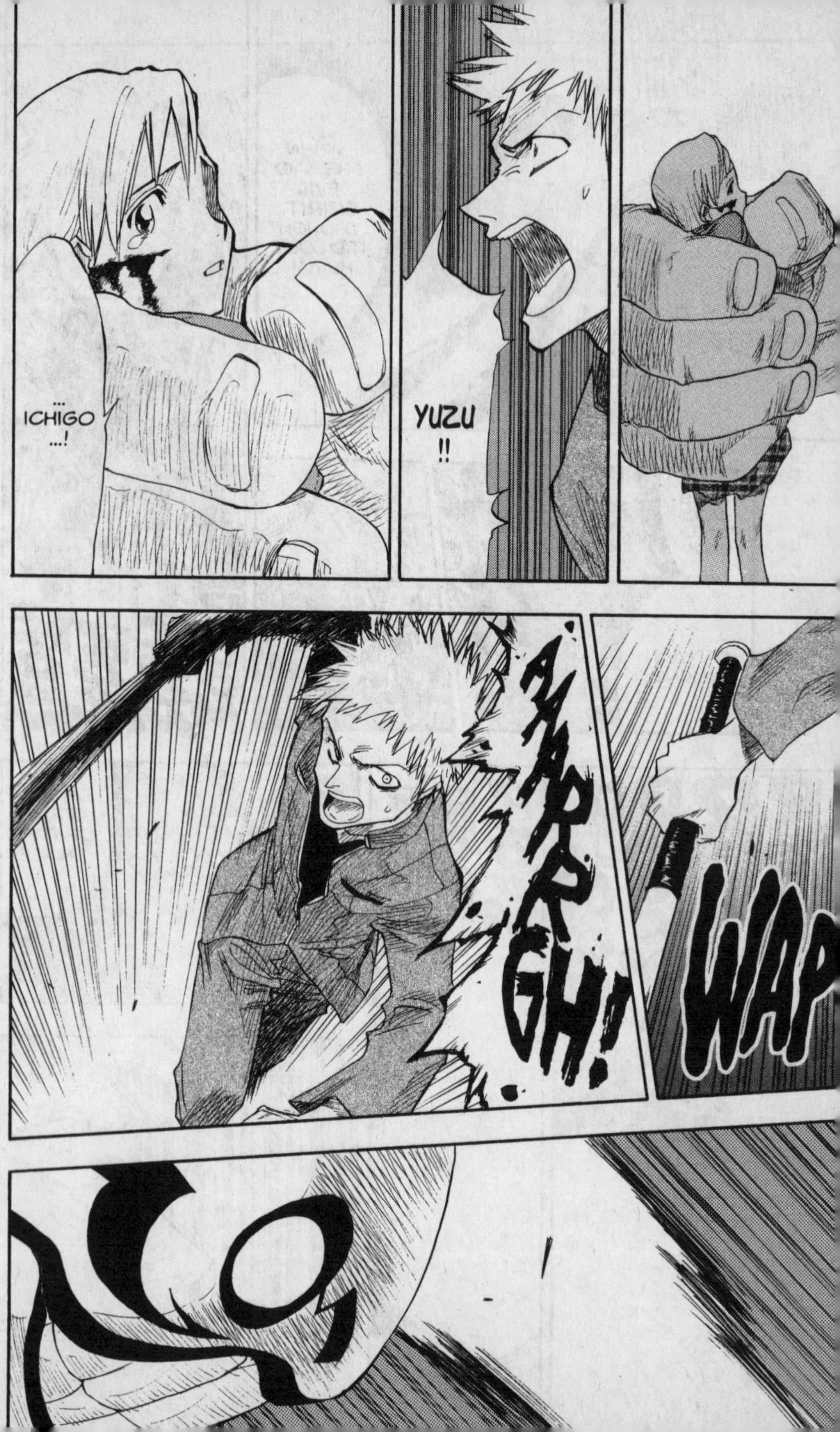
YUZU
!!
...
ICHIGO
...!
WAP
AAARRGH!

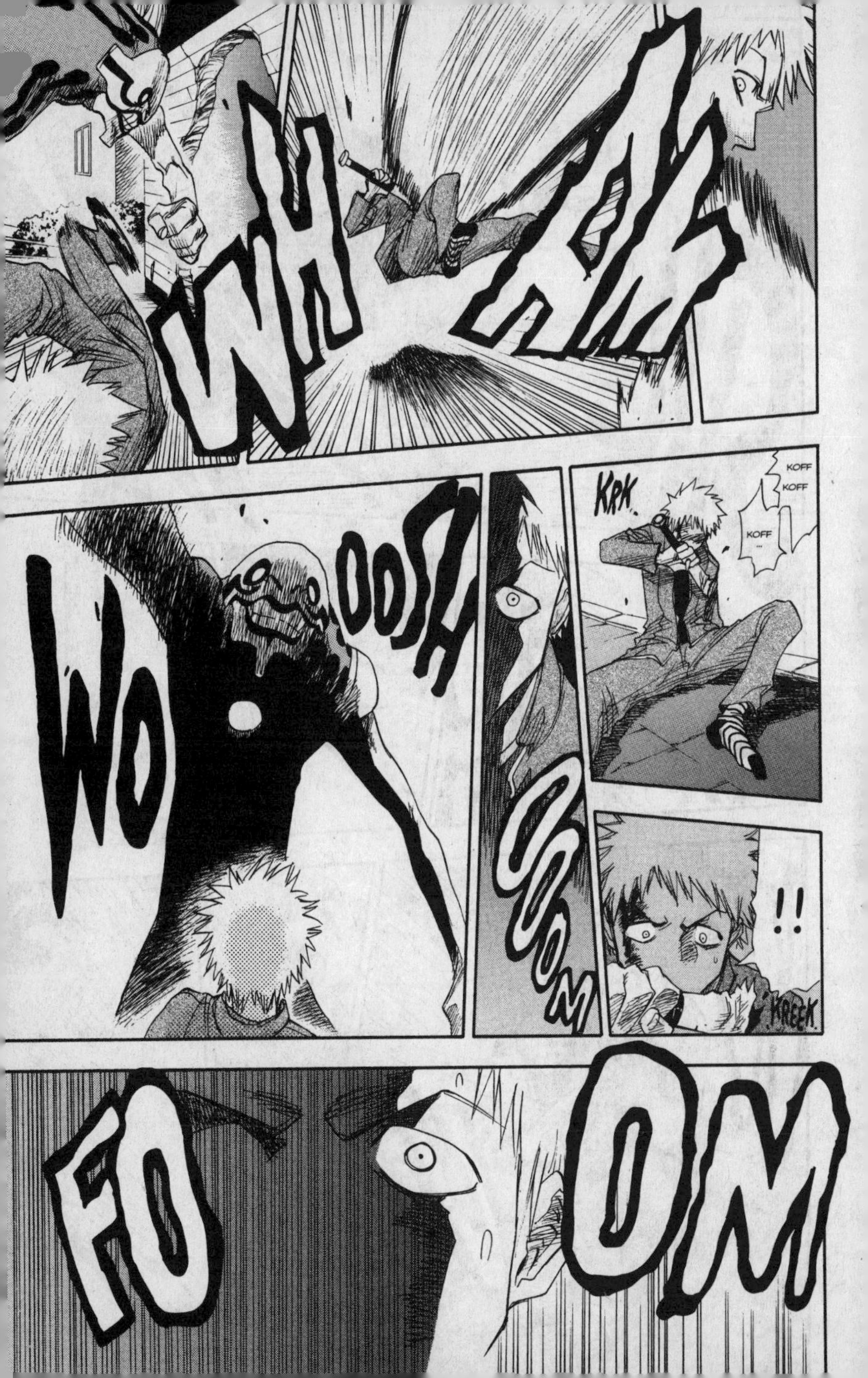
WHAM
KRK
KOFF
KOFF
KOFF
...
!!
KREEK
OOOOOM
WOOOSH
FOOM

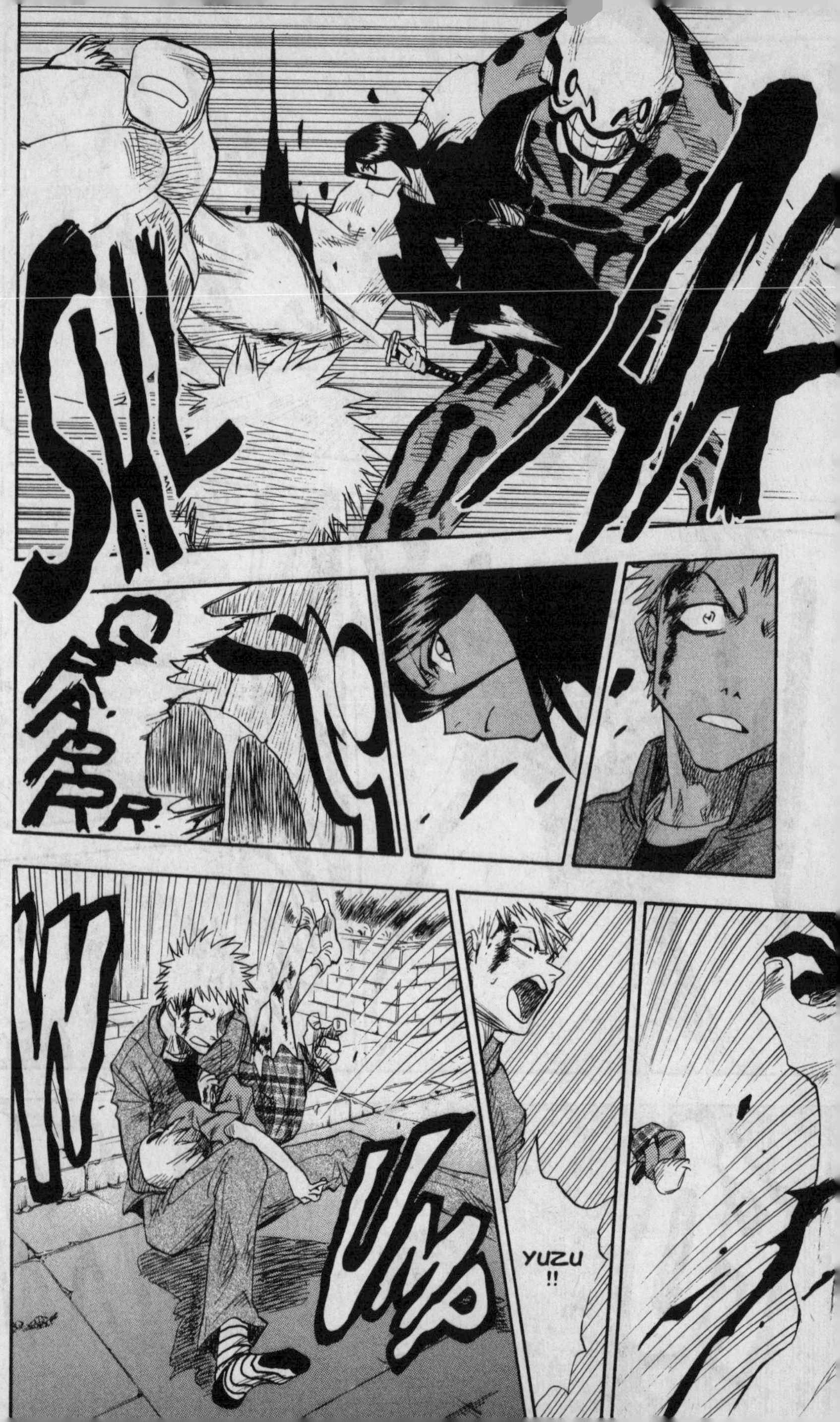
GRAPRR
YUZU !!

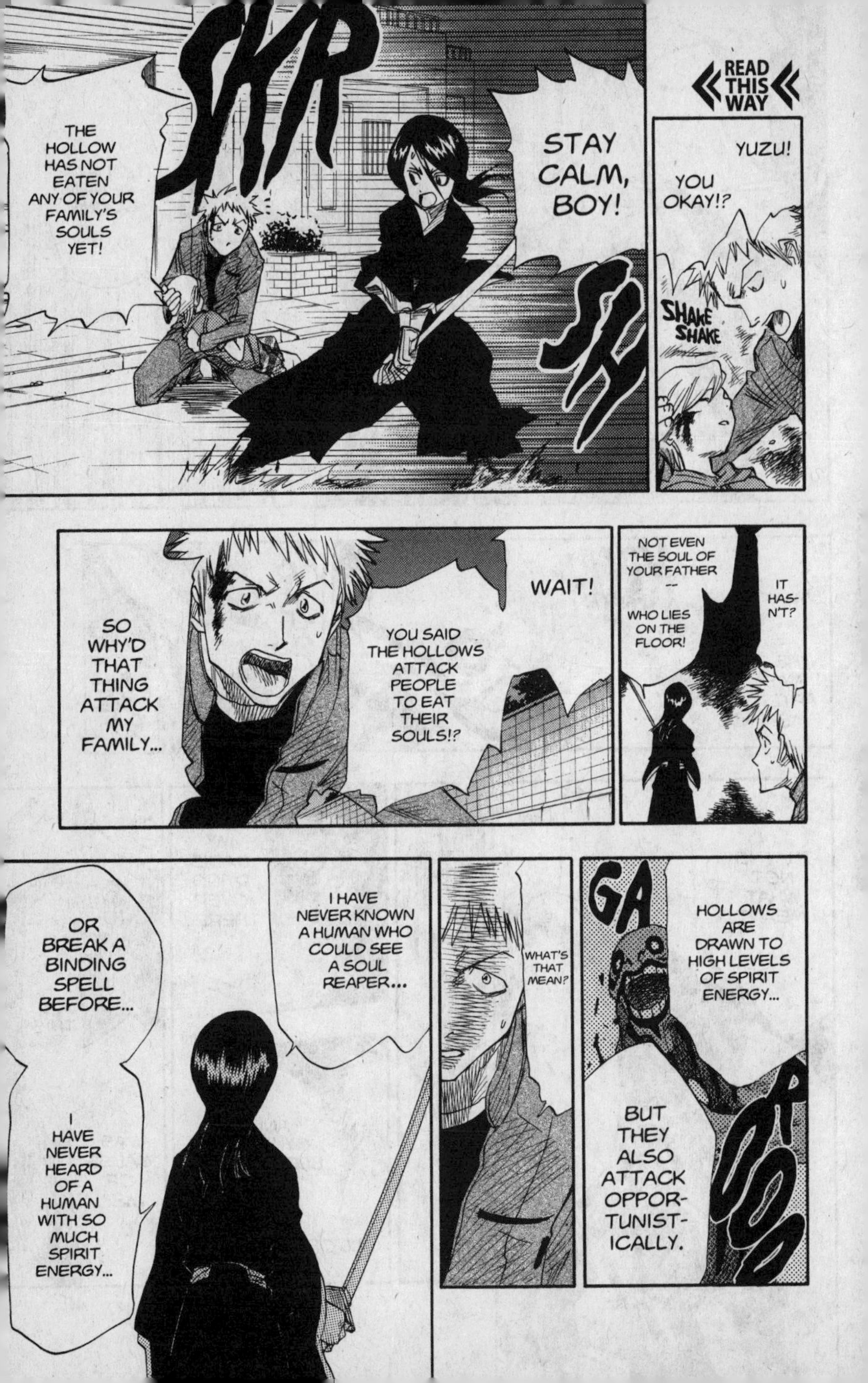
READ THIS WAY
YUZU!
YOU OKAY!?
SHAKE SHAKE
STAY CALM, BOY!
THE HOLLOW HAS NOT EATEN ANY OF YOUR FAMILY'S SOULS YET!
IT HAS-N'T?
NOT EVEN THE SOUL OF YOUR FATHER -- WHO LIES ON THE FLOOR!
WAIT!
YOU SAID THE HOLLOWS ATTACK PEOPLE TO EAT THEIR SOULS!?
SO WHY'D THAT THING ATTACK MY FAMILY...
GA
HOLLOWS ARE DRAWN TO HIGH LEVELS OF SPIRIT ENERGY...
BUT THEY ALSO ATTACK OPPOR-TUNIST-ICALLY.
WHAT'S THAT MEAN?
I HAVE NEVER KNOWN A HUMAN WHO COULD SEE A SOUL REAPER...
OR BREAK A BINDING SPELL BEFORE...
I HAVE NEVER HEARD OF A HUMAN WITH SO MUCH SPIRIT ENERGY...

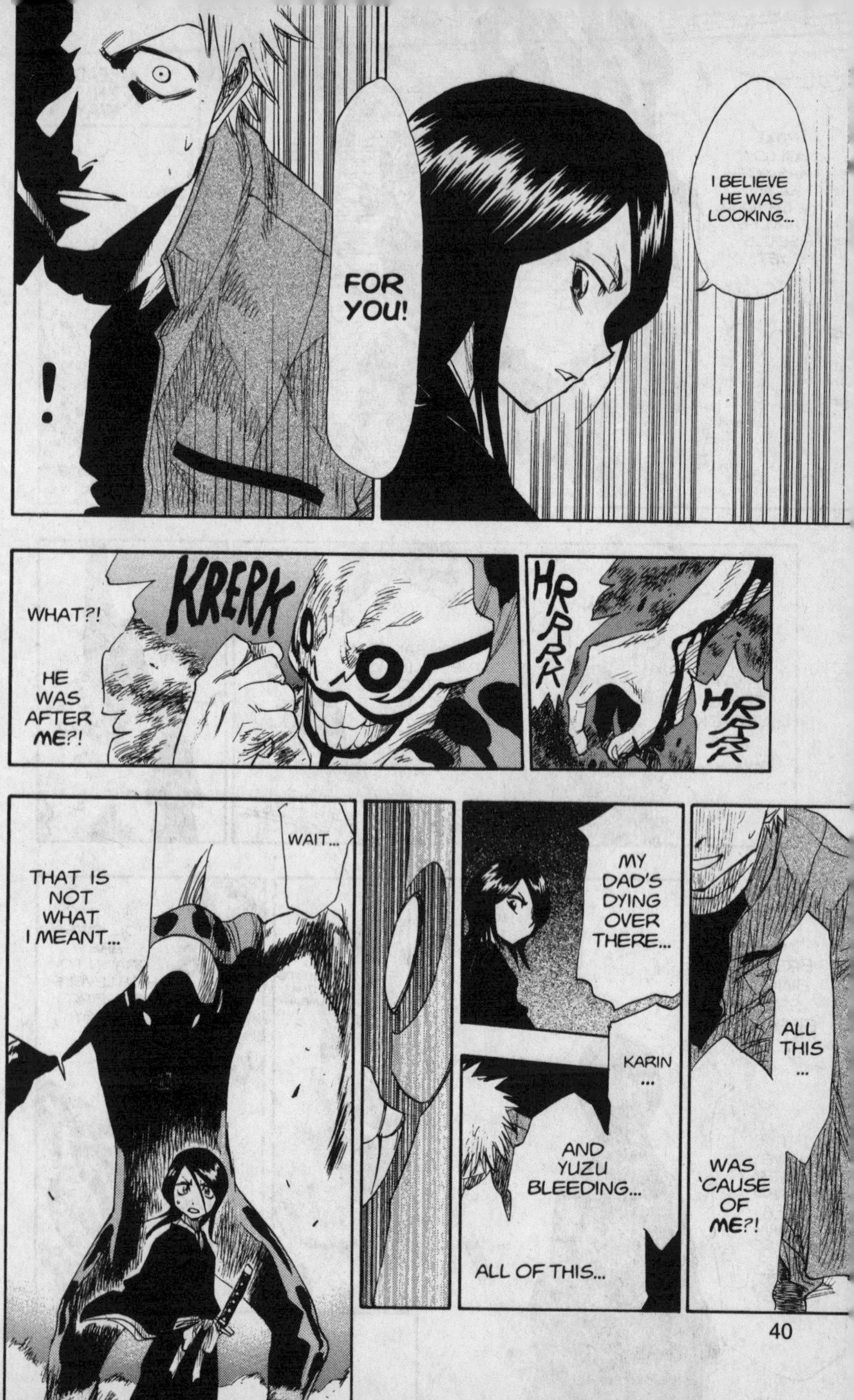
I BELIEVE HE WAS LOOKING...
FOR YOU!
!
HRRRK
HRRRK
KRERK
WHAT?!
HE WAS AFTER ME?!
ALL THIS...
WAS 'CAUSE OF ME?!
MY DAD'S DYING OVER THERE...
KARIN...
AND YUZU BLEEDING...
ALL OF THIS...
WAIT...
THAT IS NOT WHAT I MEANT...

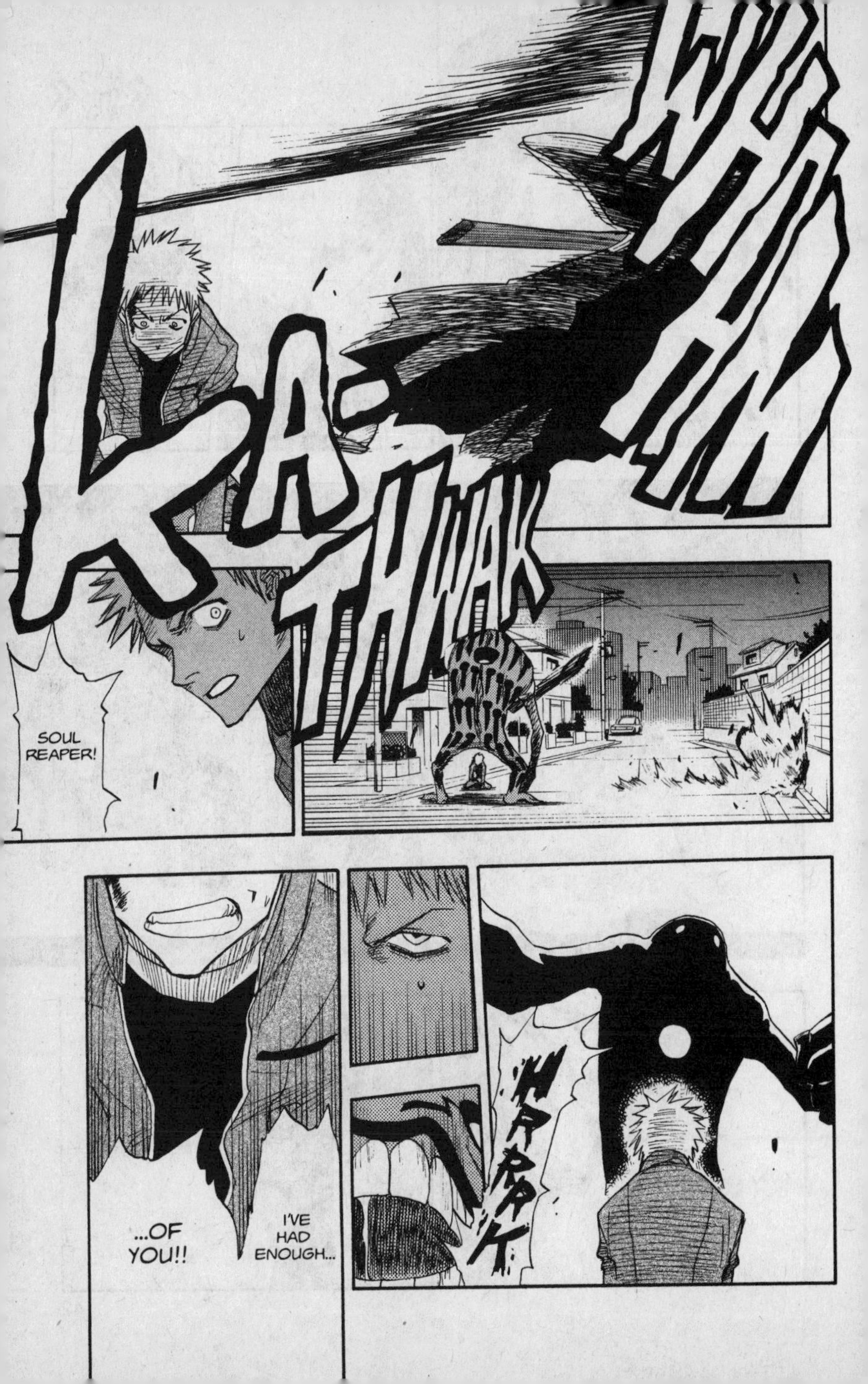
KA-THWAK
SOUL REAPER!
HRRRK
I'VE HAD ENOUGH...
...OF YOU!!

READ THIS WAY

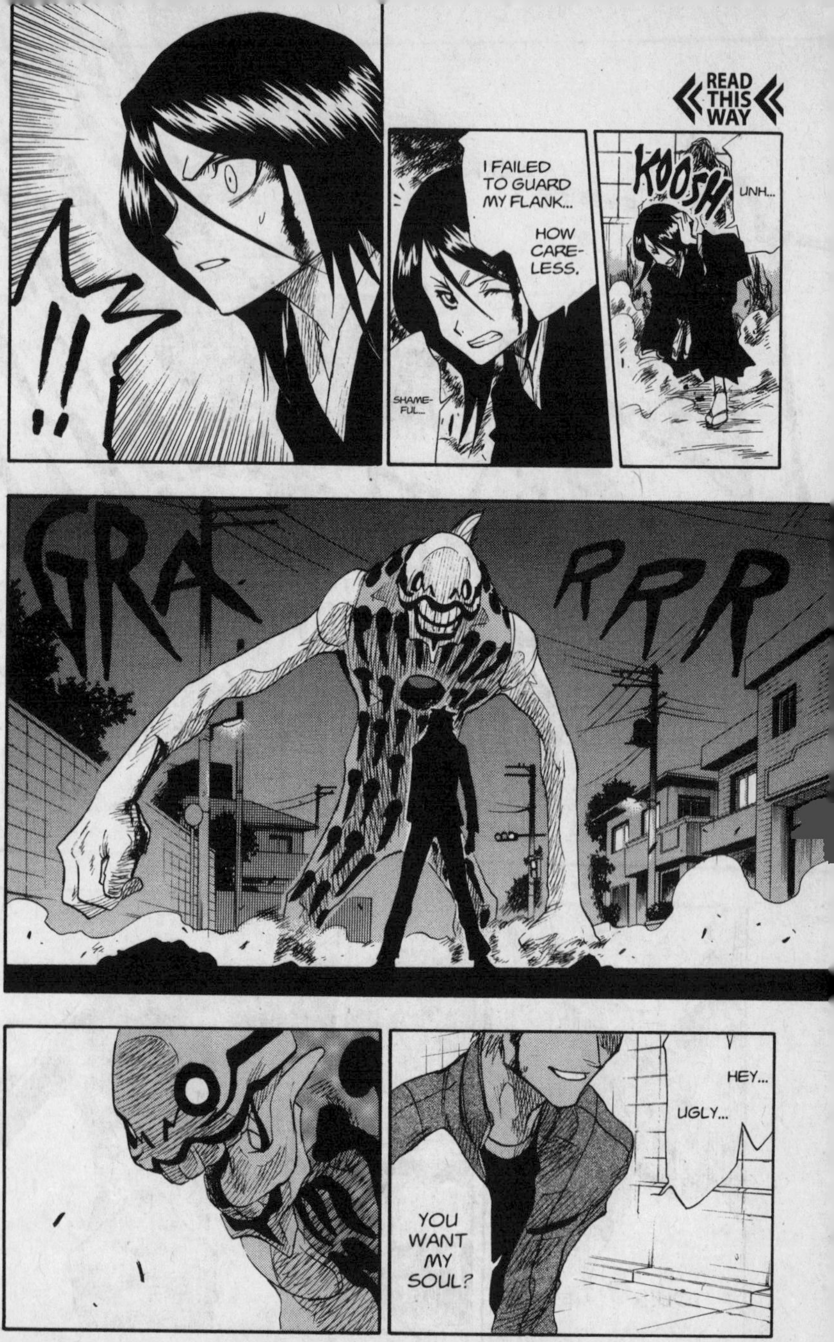
KOOSH
UNH...
I FAILED TO GUARD MY FLANK...
HOW CARE-LESS.
SHAME-FUL...
!!
GRA
RRR
HEY...
UGLY...
YOU WANT MY SOUL?

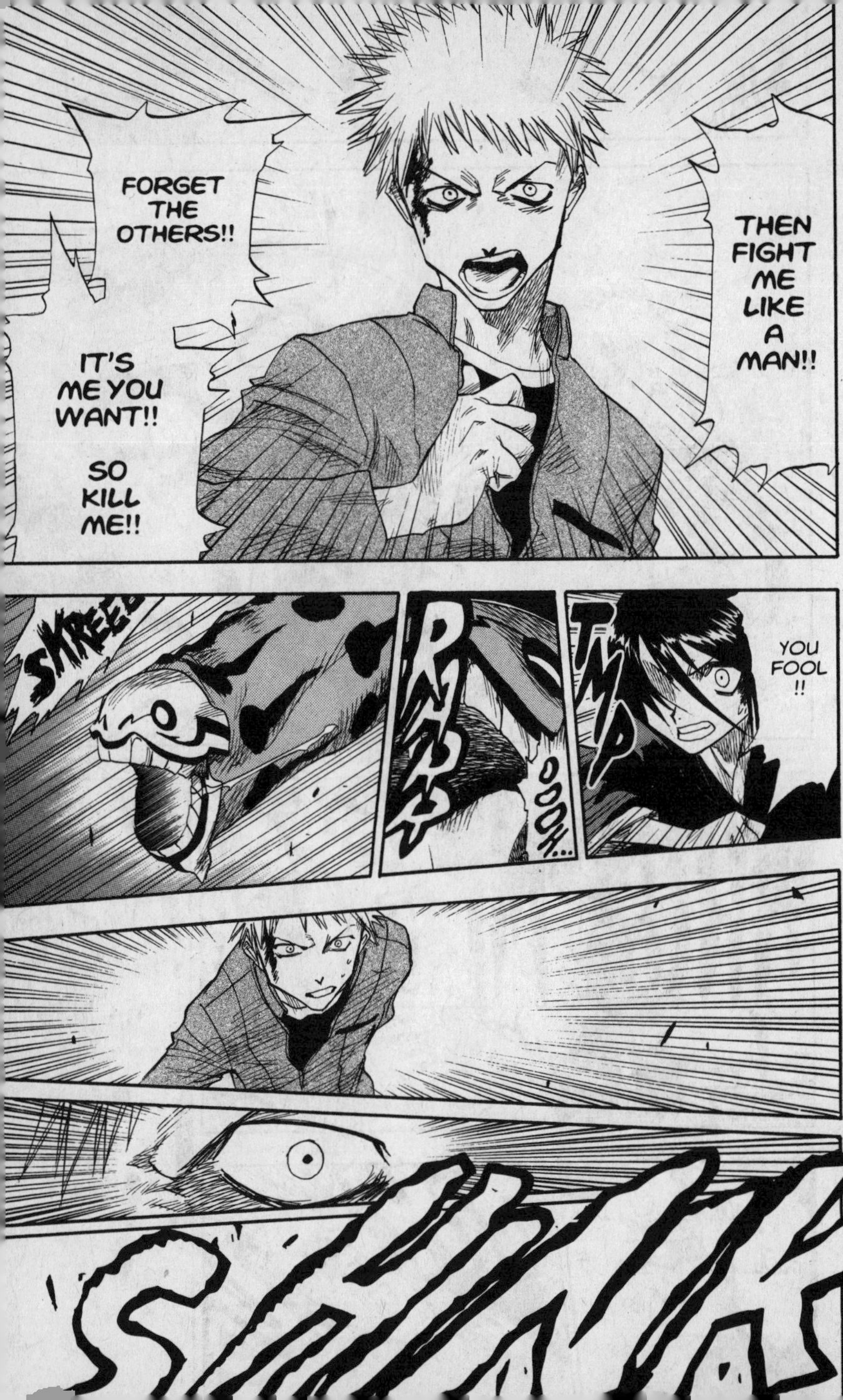
THEN FIGHT ME LIKE A MAN!!
FORGET THE OTHERS!!
IT'S ME YOU WANT!!
SO KILL ME!!
TMP
YOU FOOL!!
OOOH...
SKREEE

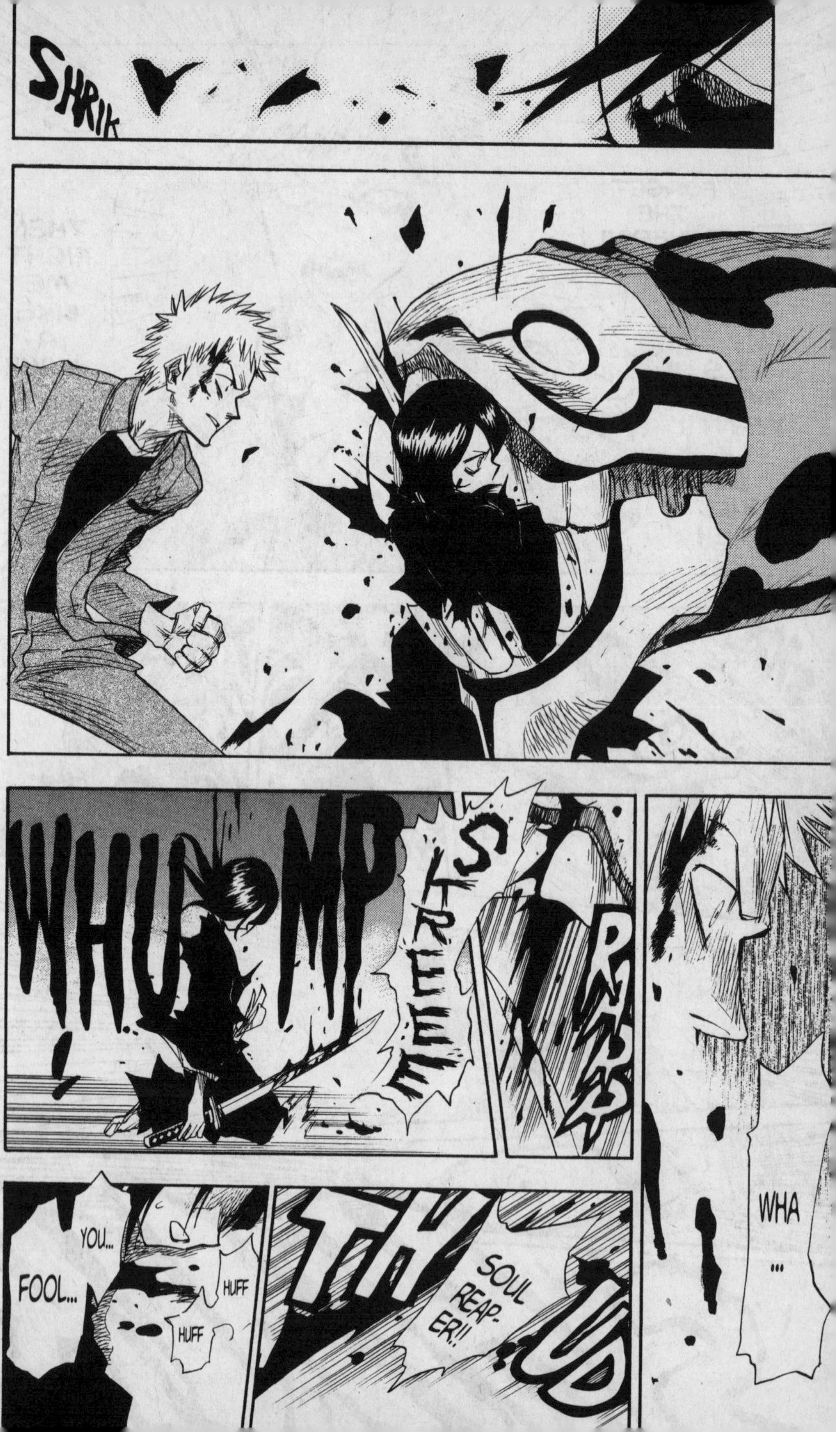
SHRIK
WHA ...
SKREEEE
WHUMP
THUD
SOUL REAP-ER!!
YOU...
FOOL...
HUFF
HUFF

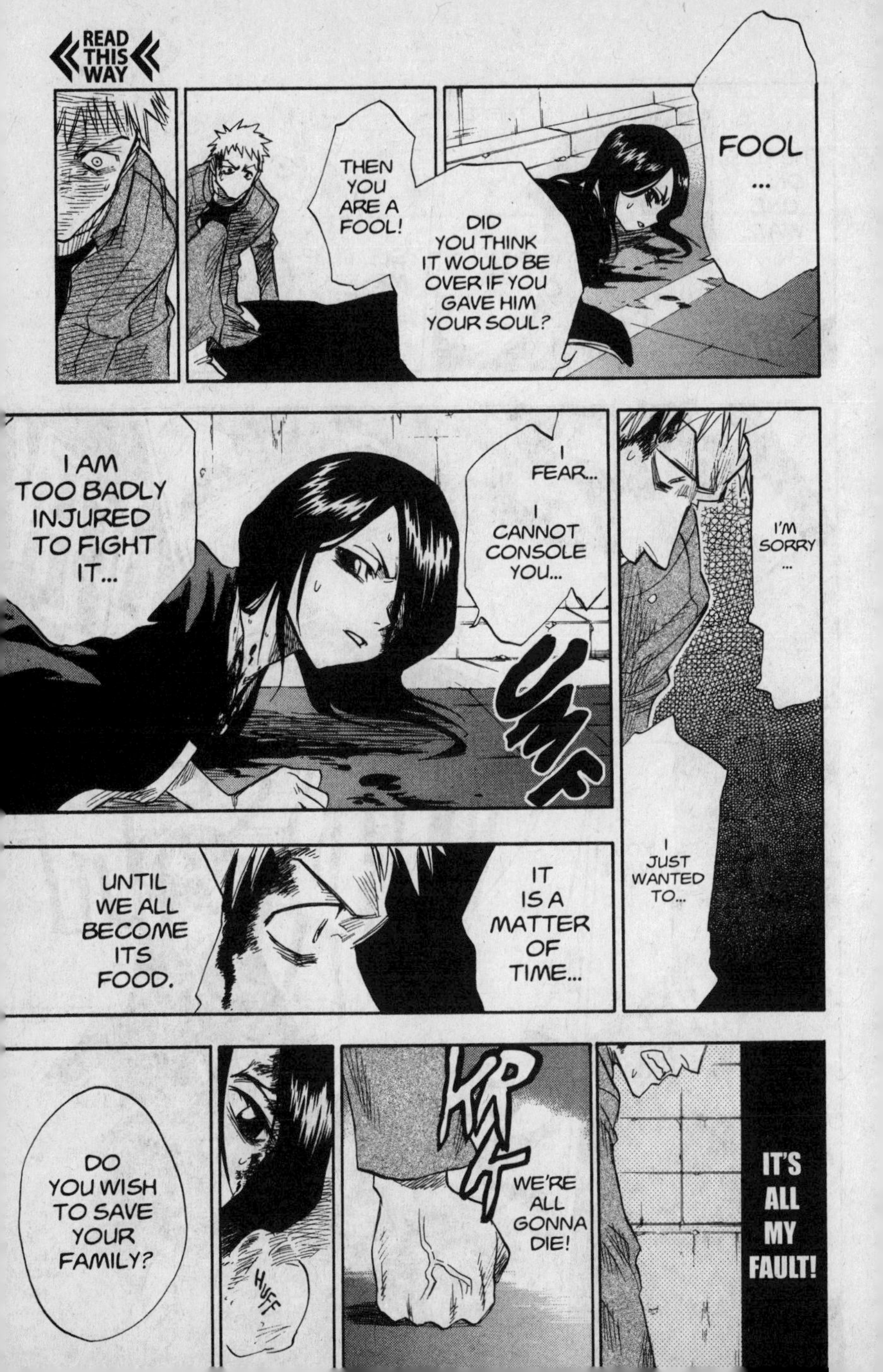
READ THIS WAY
FOOL ...
DID YOU THINK IT WOULD BE OVER IF YOU GAVE HIM YOUR SOUL?
THEN YOU ARE A FOOL!
I'M SORRY ...
I JUST WANTED TO...
I FEAR... I CANNOT CONSOLE YOU...
UMF
I AM TOO BADLY INJURED TO FIGHT IT...
IT IS A MATTER OF TIME...
UNTIL WE ALL BECOME ITS FOOD.
IT'S ALL MY FAULT!
KRK
WE'RE ALL GONNA DIE!
HUFF
DO YOU WISH TO SAVE YOUR FAMILY?

READ THIS WAY

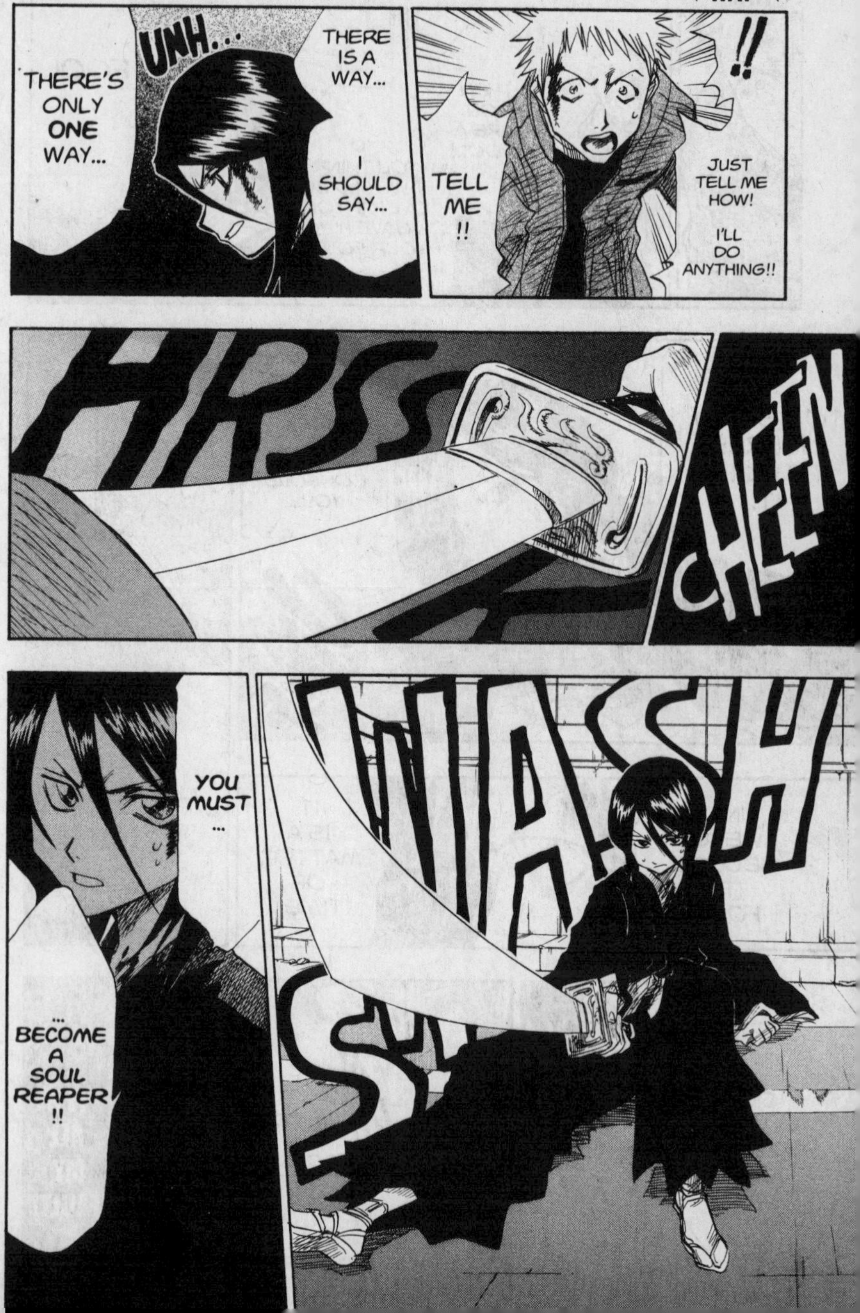
!!
JUST TELL ME HOW!
I'LL DO ANYTHING!!
TELL ME !!
UNH...
THERE IS A WAY...
I SHOULD SAY...
THERE'S ONLY ONE WAY...
CHEEN
HRSS
SWASH
YOU MUST ...
... BECOME A SOUL REAPER !!

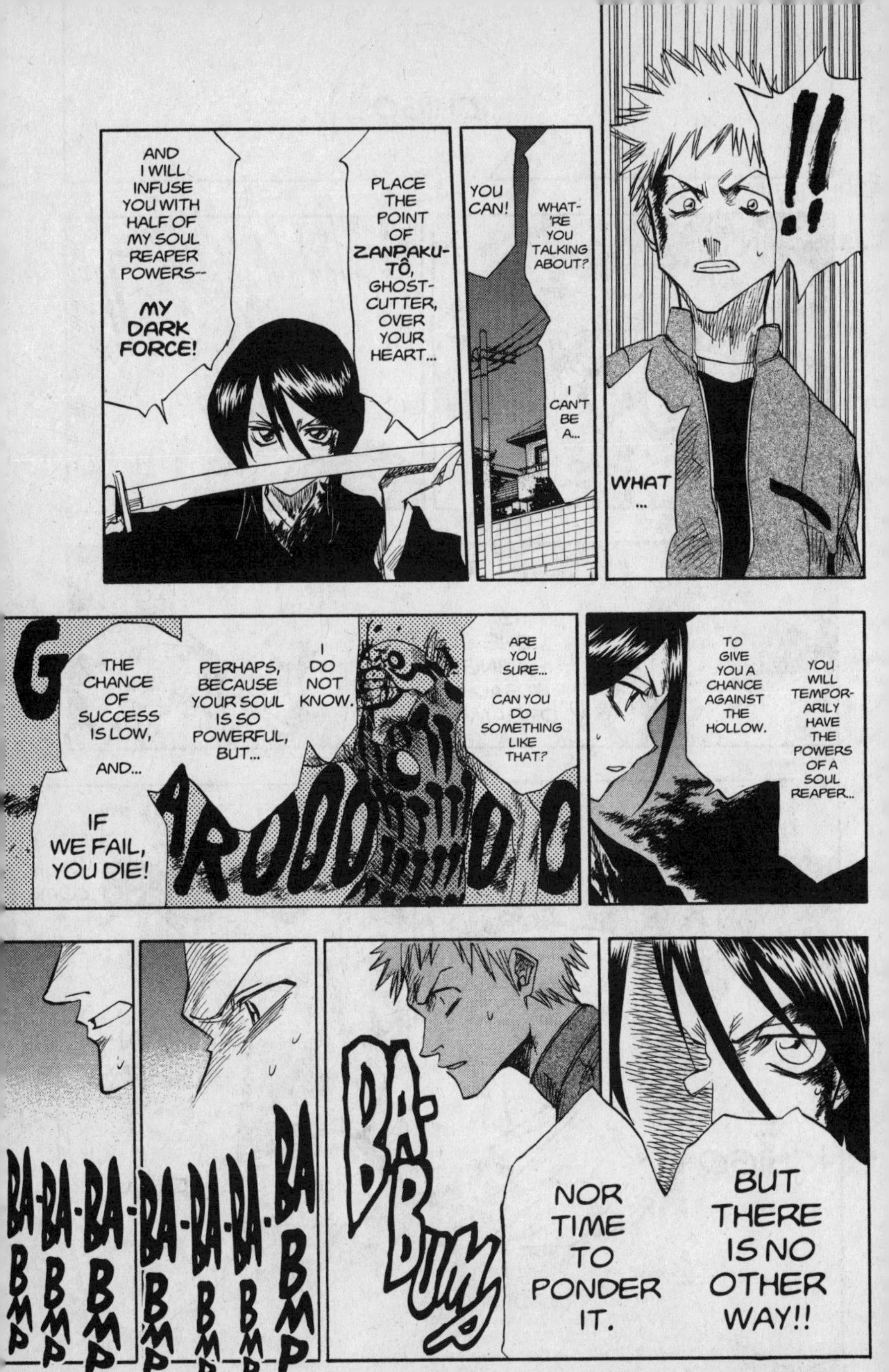

!!
WHAT...
WHAT-'RE YOU TALKING ABOUT?
YOU CAN!
I CAN'T BE A...
PLACE THE POINT OF ZANPAKU-TÔ, GHOST-CUTTER, OVER YOUR HEART...
AND I WILL INFUSE YOU WITH HALF OF MY SOUL REAPER POWERS--
MY DARK FORCE!
YOU WILL TEMPORARILY HAVE THE POWERS OF A SOUL REAPER...
TO GIVE YOU A CHANCE AGAINST THE HOLLOW.
ARE YOU SURE...
CAN YOU DO SOMETHING LIKE THAT?
I DO NOT KNOW.
GAROOO.......OO
PERHAPS, BECAUSE YOUR SOUL IS SO POWERFUL, BUT...
THE CHANCE OF SUCCESS IS LOW,
AND...
IF WE FAIL, YOU DIE!
BUT THERE IS NO OTHER WAY!!
NOR TIME TO PONDER IT.
BA-BUMP
BA-BUMP-BA-BUMP-BA-BUMP-BA-BUMP-
BA-BUMP-BA-BUMP-BA-BUMP-

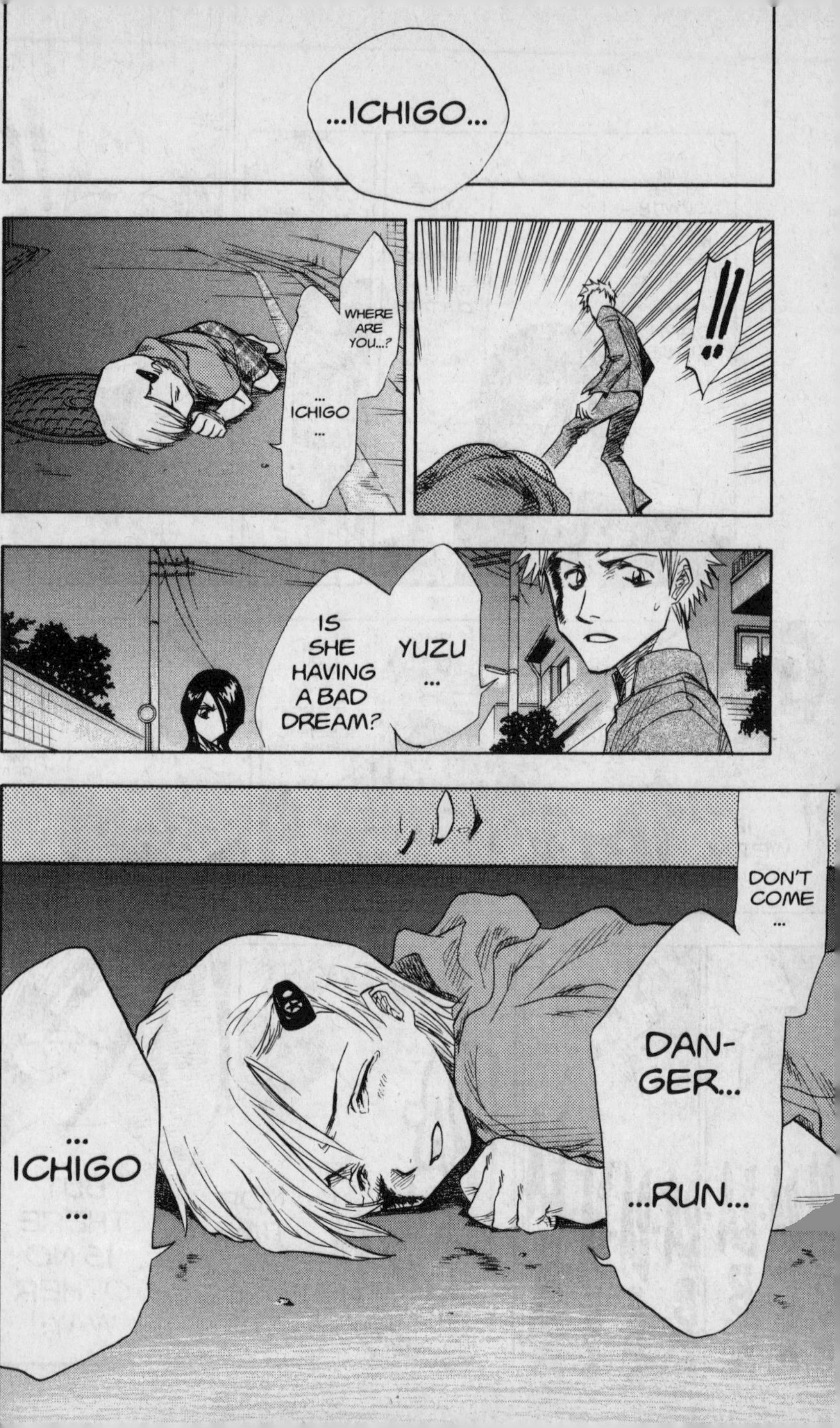
...ICHIGO...
!!
WHERE ARE YOU...?
...ICHIGO...
YUZU...
IS SHE HAVING A BAD DREAM?
DON'T COME...
DAN-GER...
...RUN...
...ICHIGO...

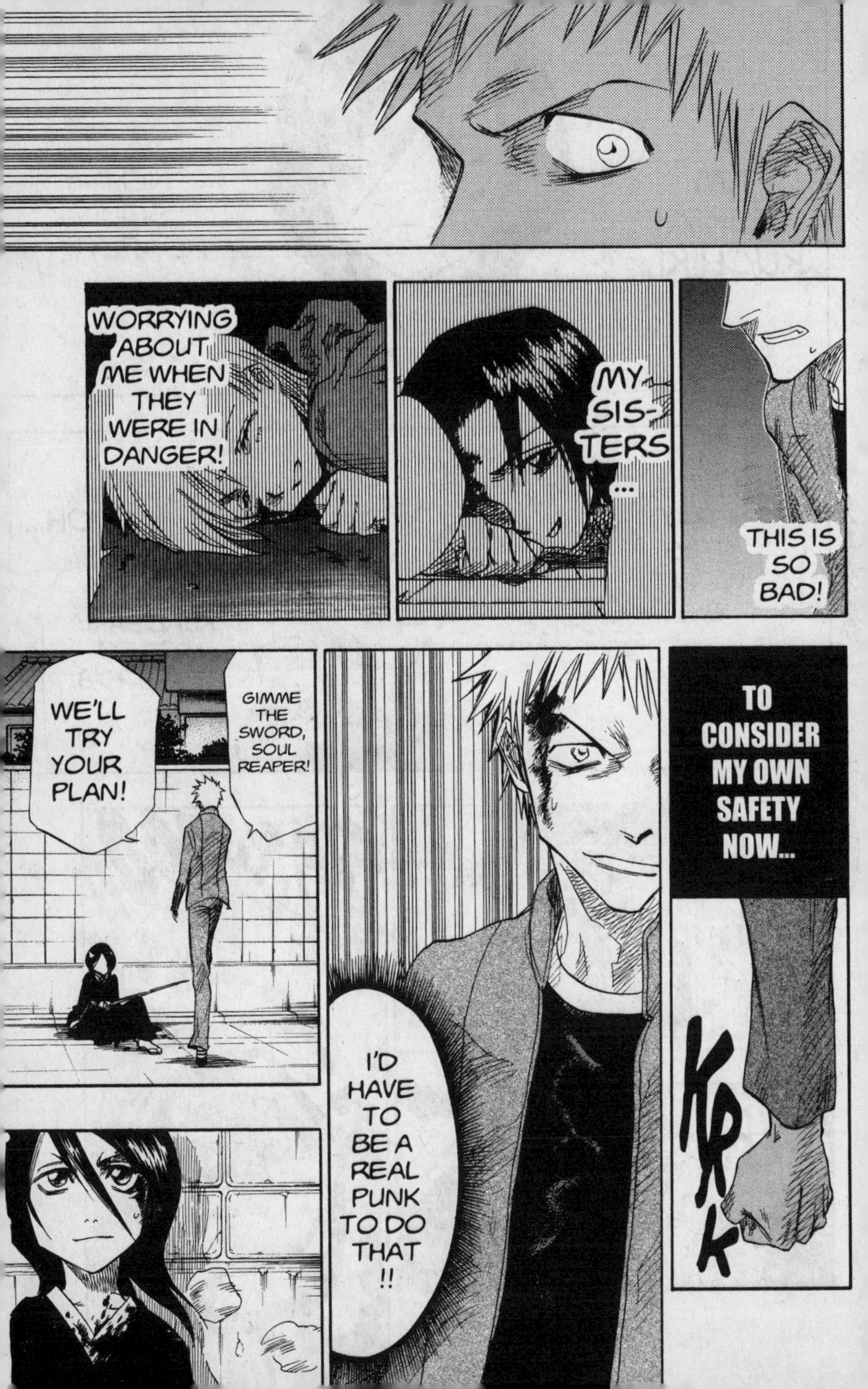
THIS IS SO BAD!
MY SIS-TERS...
WORRYING ABOUT ME WHEN THEY WERE IN DANGER!
TO CONSIDER MY OWN SAFETY NOW...
KRK
I'D HAVE TO BE A REAL PUNK TO DO THAT!!
GIMME THE SWORD, SOUL REAPER!
WE'LL TRY YOUR PLAN!

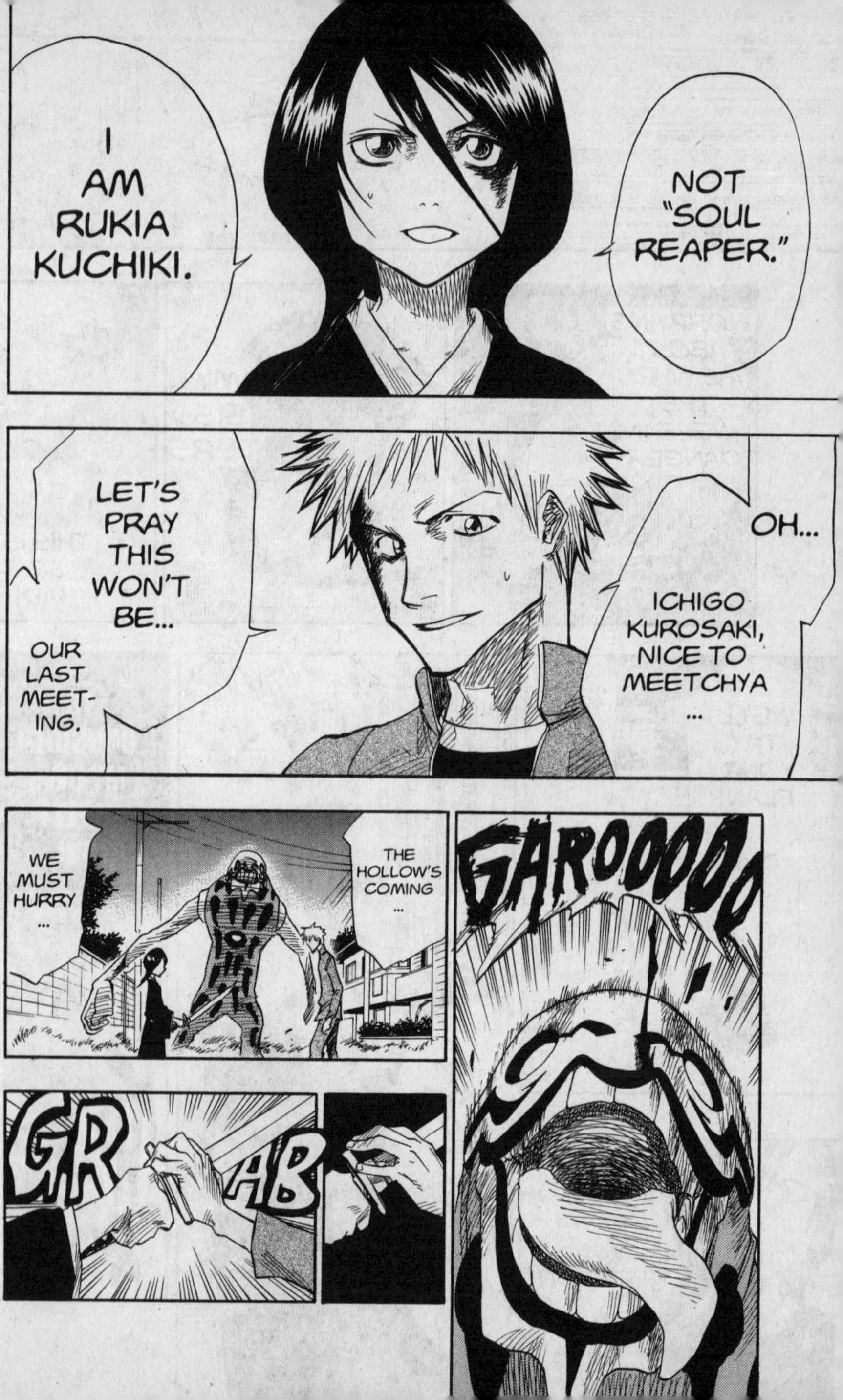
NOT "SOUL REAPER."
I AM RUKIA KUCHIKI.
OH... ICHIGO KUROSAKI, NICE TO MEETCHYA...
LET'S PRAY THIS WON'T BE... OUR LAST MEET-ING.
GAROOOOO
THE HOLLOW'S COMING...
WE MUST HURRY...
GRAB

READ THIS WAY

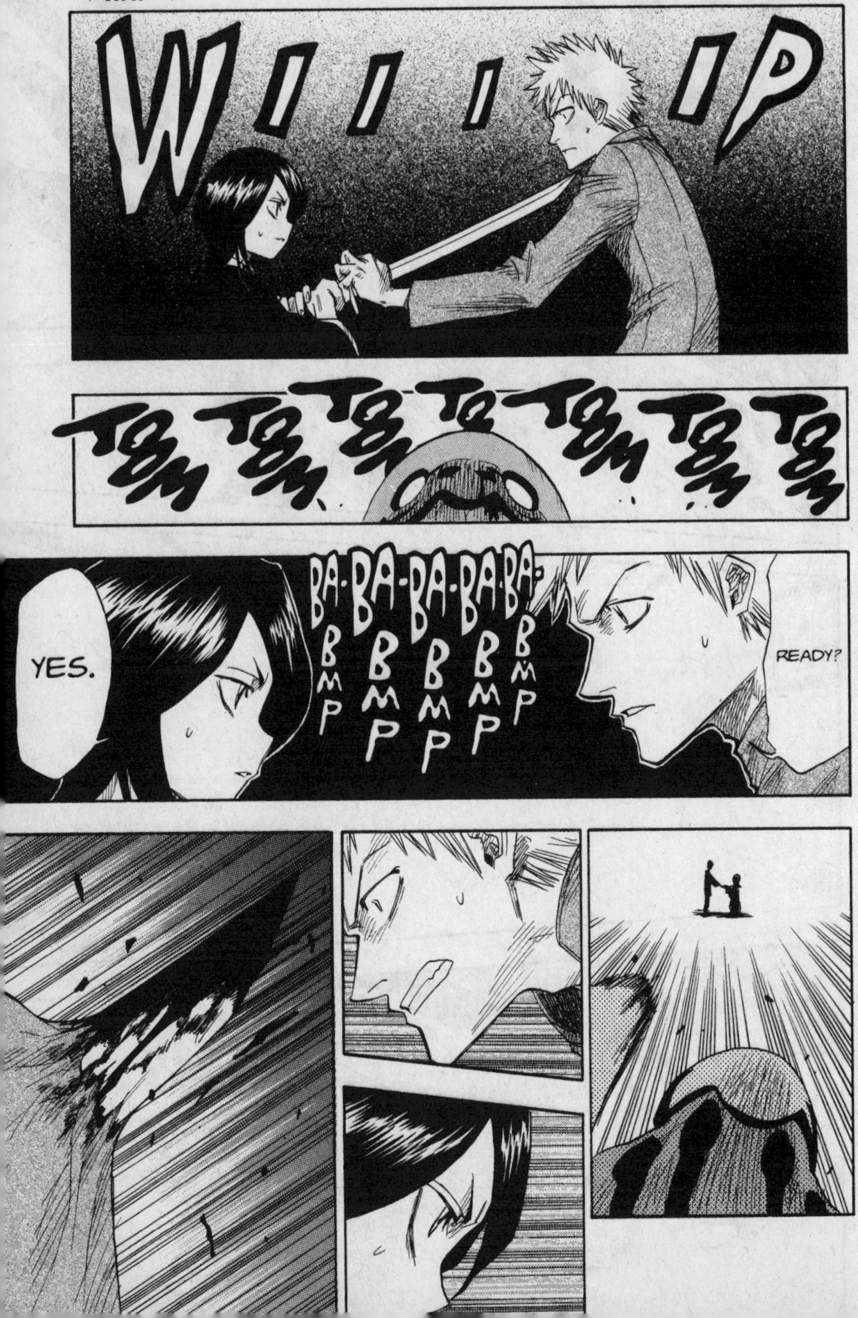
WIIIIIP
TOM TOM TO TO TOM TOM TOM
READY?
BA-BA-BA-BA-BA-
BMP BMP BMP BMP BMP
YES.

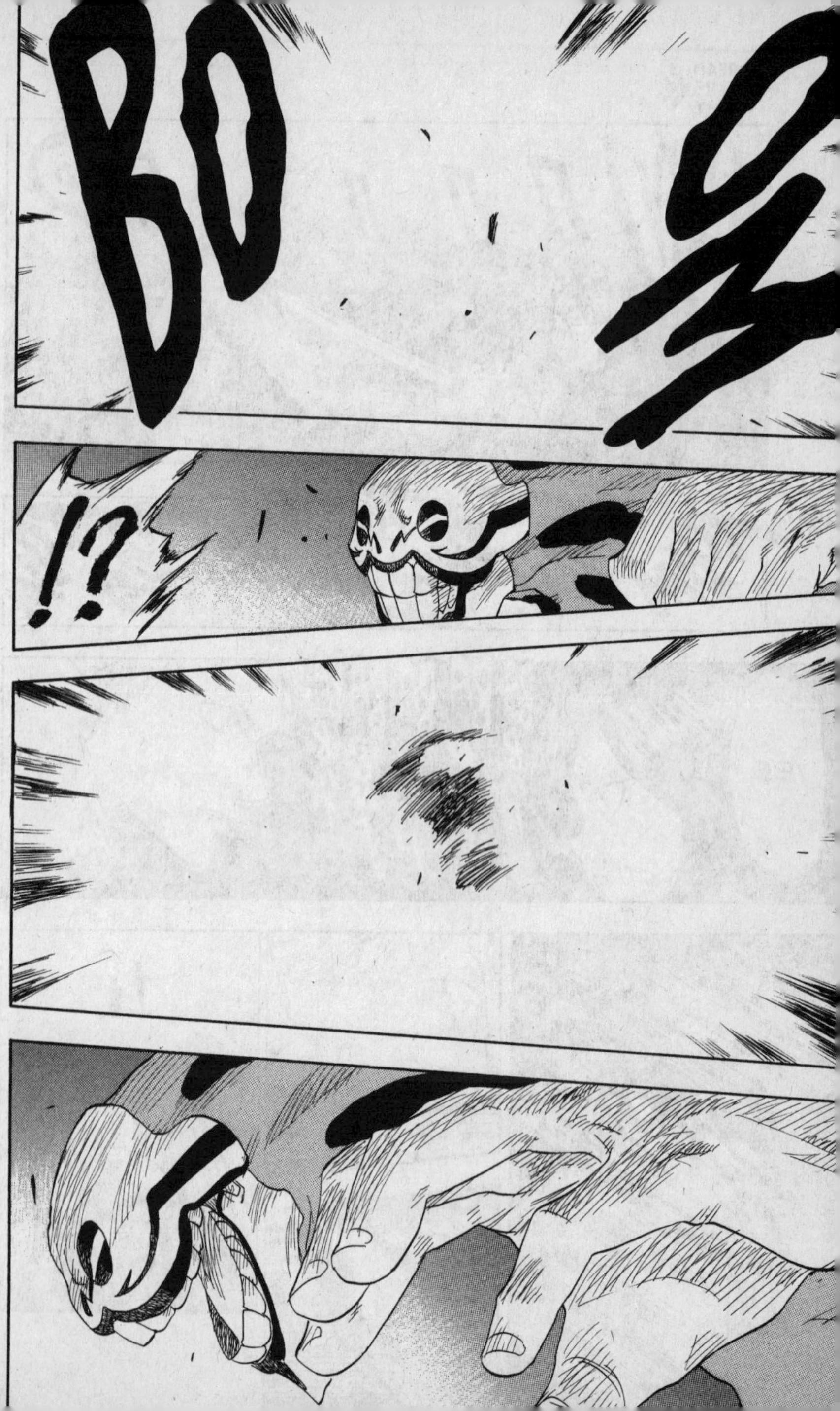
BOOM
!?

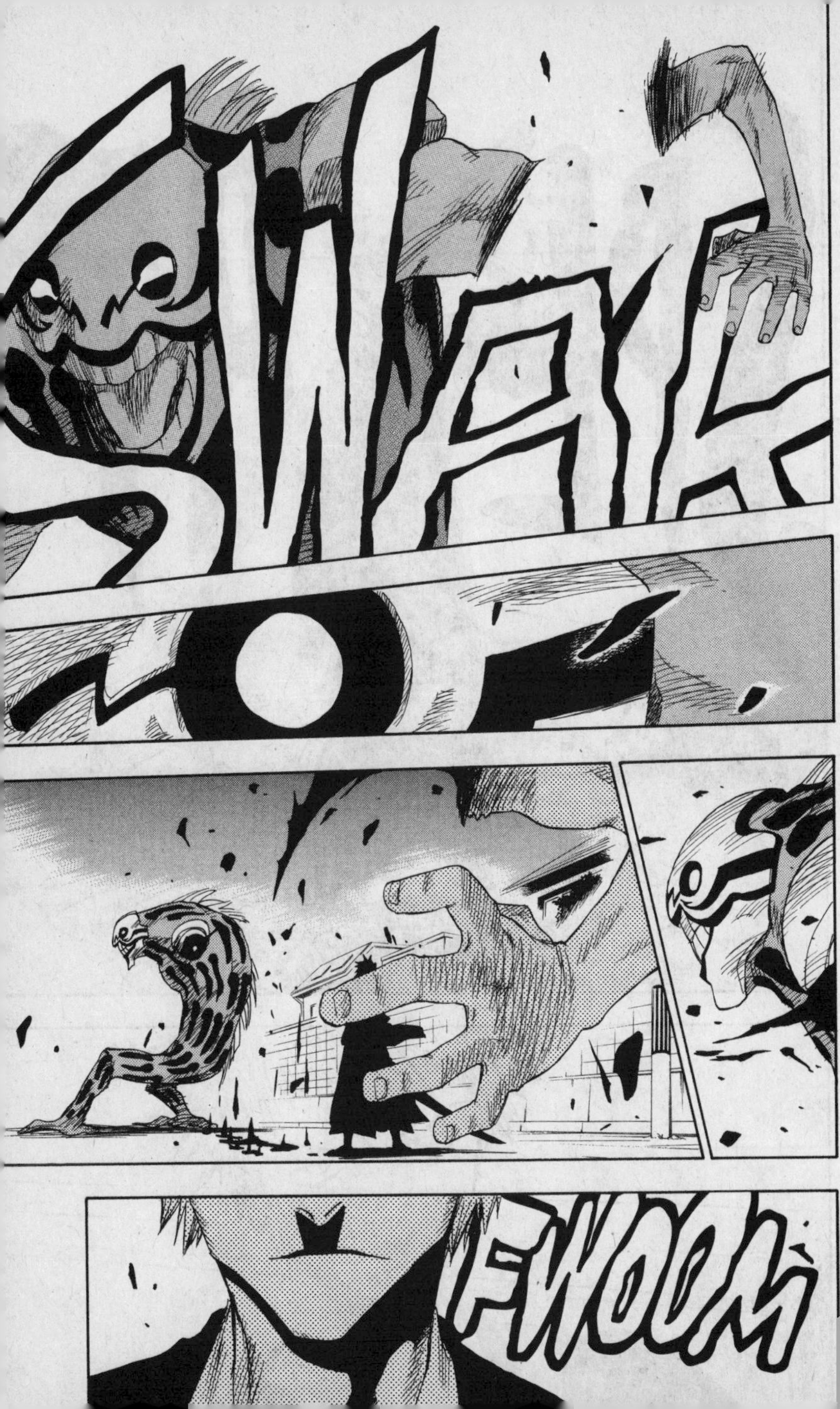
SWAK
FWOOM

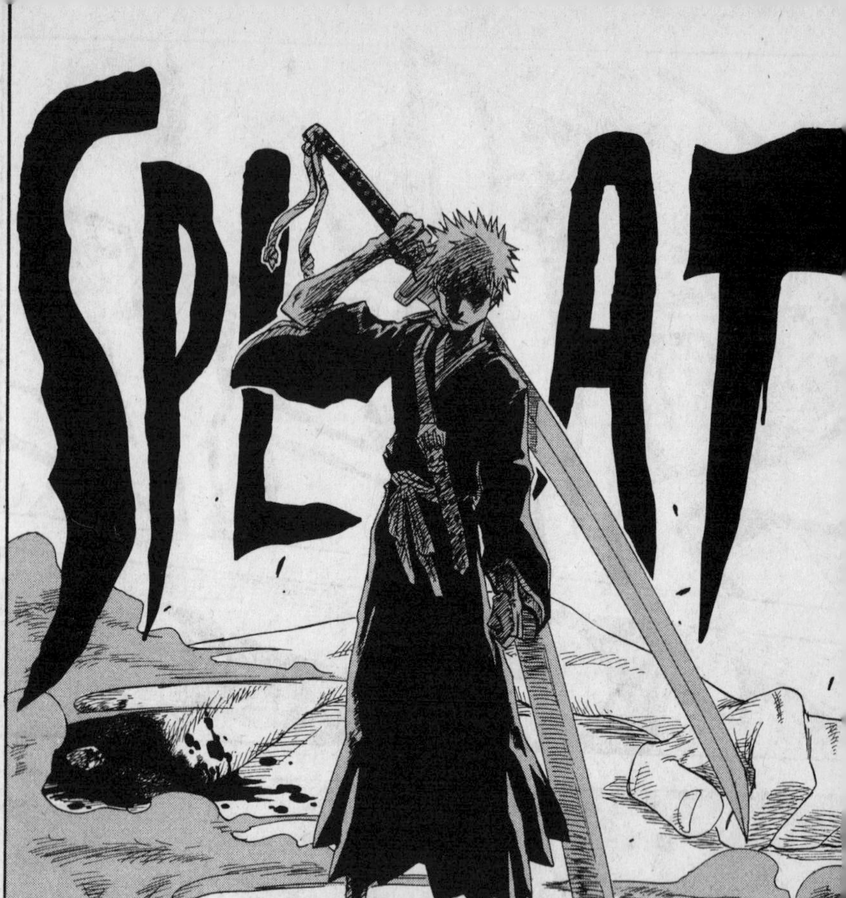
SPLAT
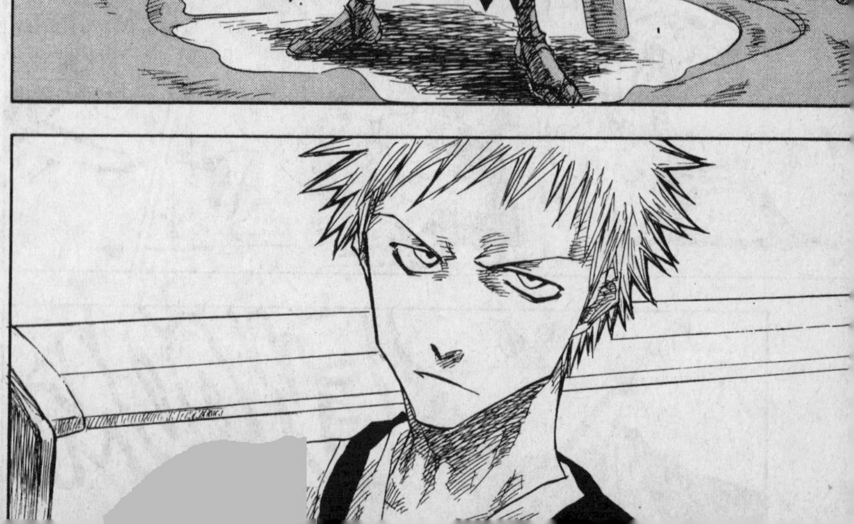

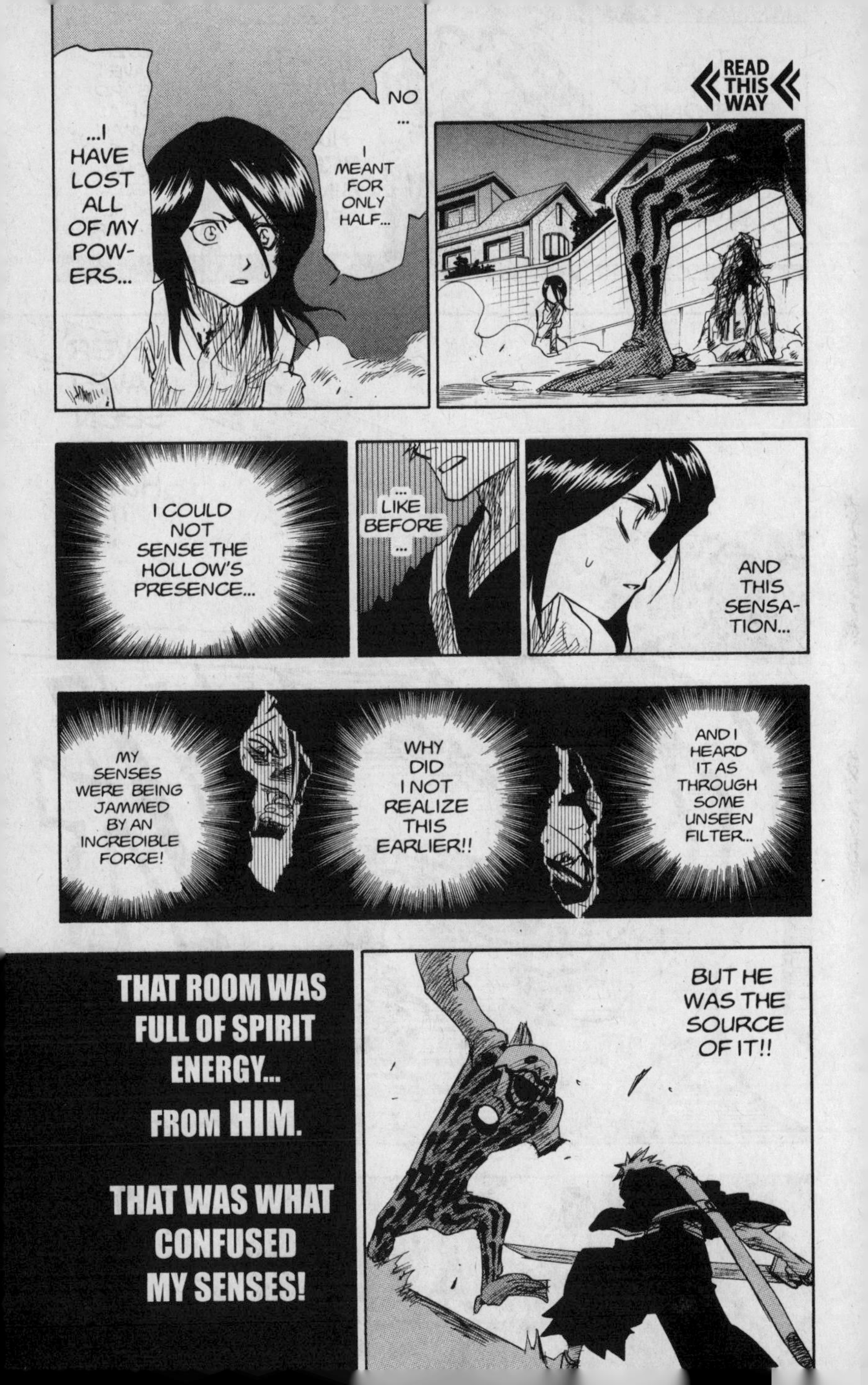
READ THIS WAY
NO ...
I MEANT FOR ONLY HALF...
...I HAVE LOST ALL OF MY POWERS...
AND THIS SENSATION...
... LIKE BEFORE ...
I COULD NOT SENSE THE HOLLOW'S PRESENCE...
AND I HEARD IT AS THROUGH SOME UNSEEN FILTER...
WHY DID I NOT REALIZE THIS EARLIER!!
MY SENSES WERE BEING JAMMED BY AN INCREDIBLE FORCE!
BUT HE WAS THE SOURCE OF IT!!
THAT ROOM WAS FULL OF SPIRIT ENERGY... FROM HIM.
THAT WAS WHAT CONFUSED MY SENSES!

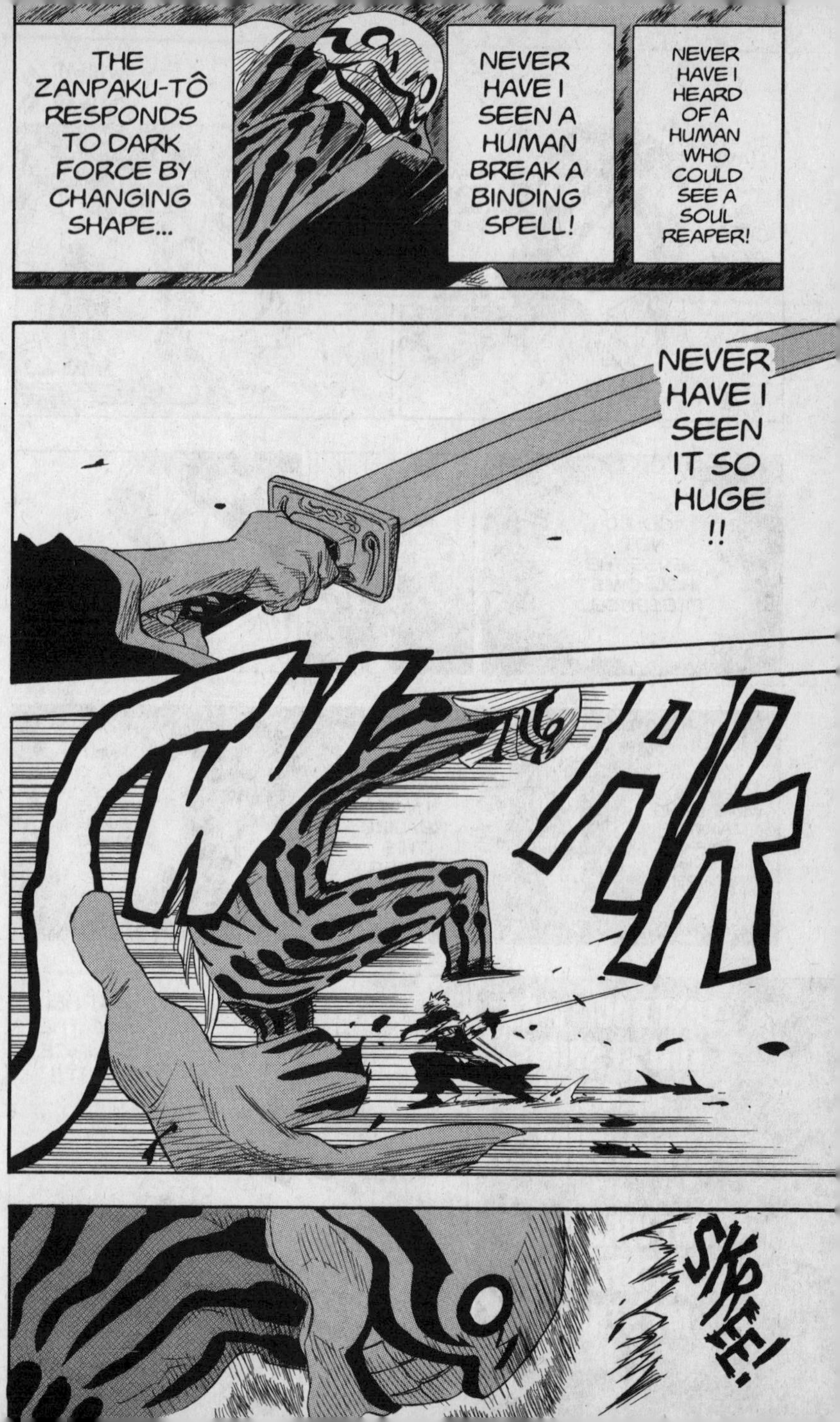
NEVER HAVE I HEARD OF A HUMAN WHO COULD SEE A SOUL REAPER!
NEVER HAVE I SEEN A HUMAN BREAK A BINDING SPELL!
THE ZANPAKU-TÔ RESPONDS TO DARK FORCE BY CHANGING SHAPE...
NEVER HAVE I SEEN IT SO HUGE !!
CHLIK
SKREE!

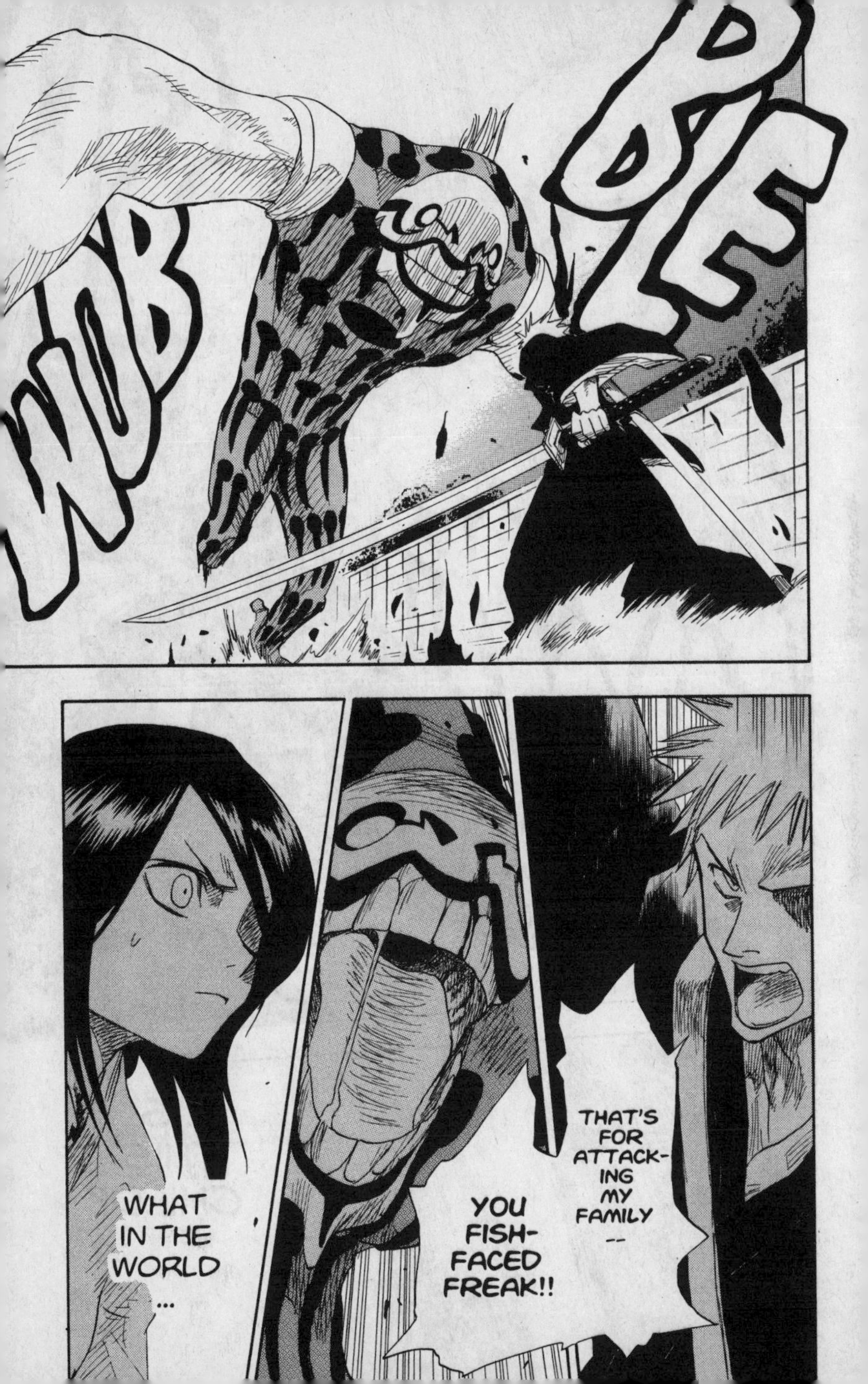
THAT'S FOR ATTACKING MY FAMILY --
YOU FISH-FACED FREAK!!
WHAT IN THE WORLD ...

SK
SK
SK

SWA

...IS
THIS
CHILD?

READ THIS WAY

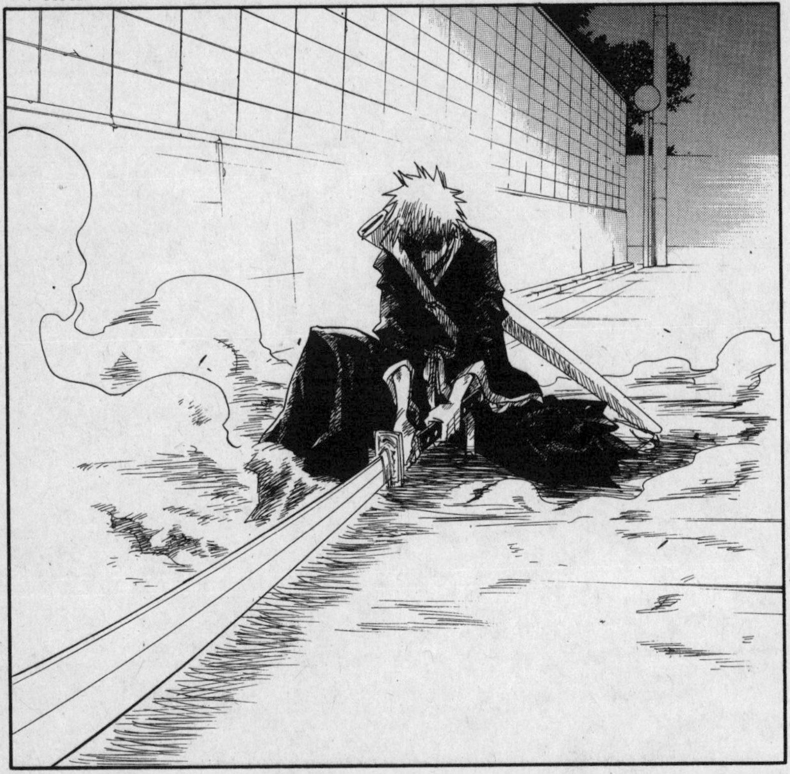

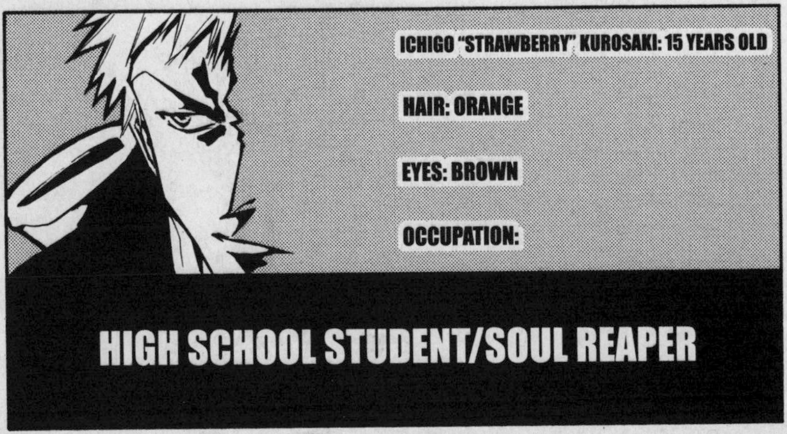
ICHIGO "STRAWBERRY" KUROSAKI: 15 YEARS OLD
HAIR: ORANGE
EYES: BROWN
OCCUPATION:
HIGH SCHOOL STUDENT/SOUL REAPER

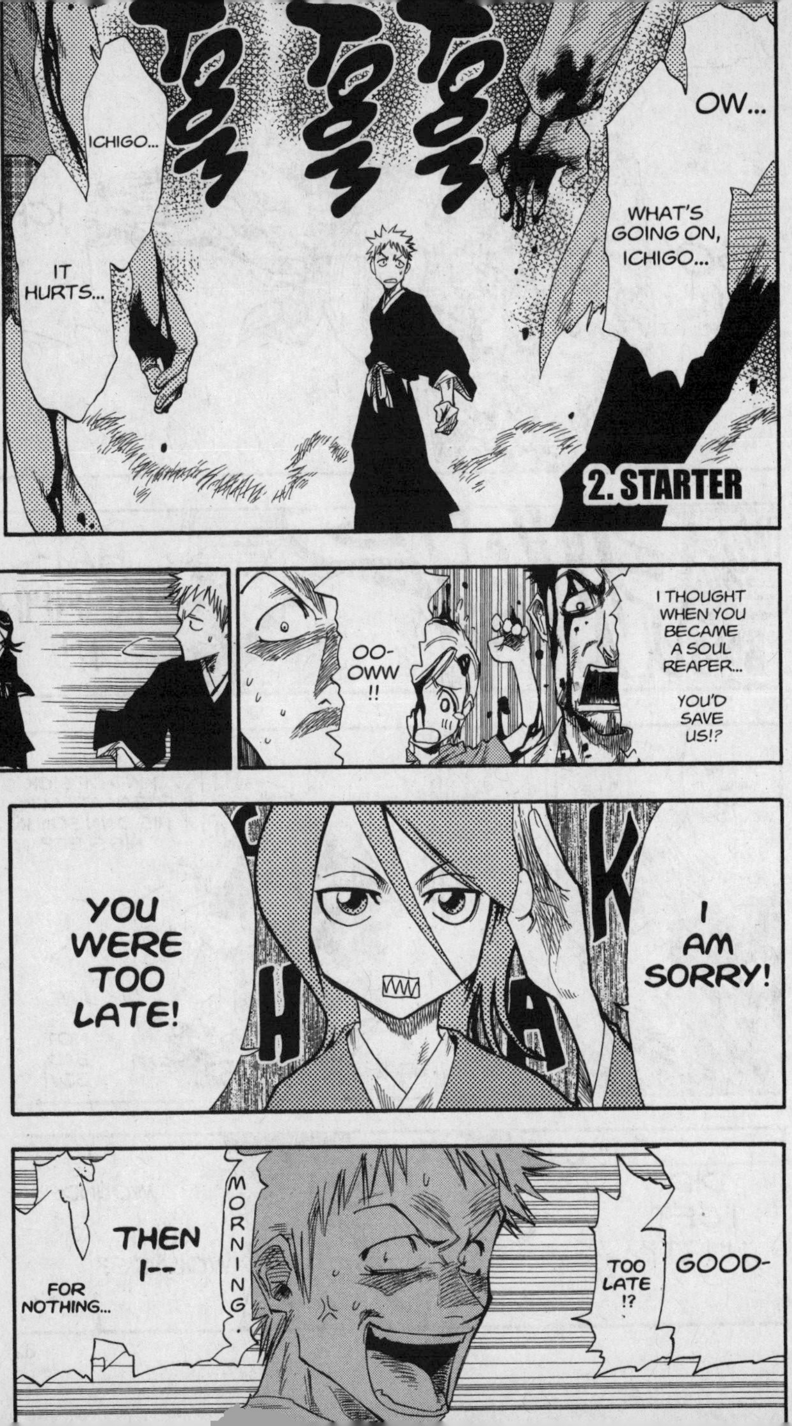
OW...
WHAT'S GOING ON, ICHIGO...
ICHIGO...
IT HURTS...
2. STARTER
I THOUGHT WHEN YOU BECAME A SOUL REAPER...
YOU'D SAVE US!?
OO-OWW !!
I AM SORRY!
YOU WERE TOO LATE!
GOOD-
TOO LATE !?
MORNING.
THEN I--
FOR NOTHING...

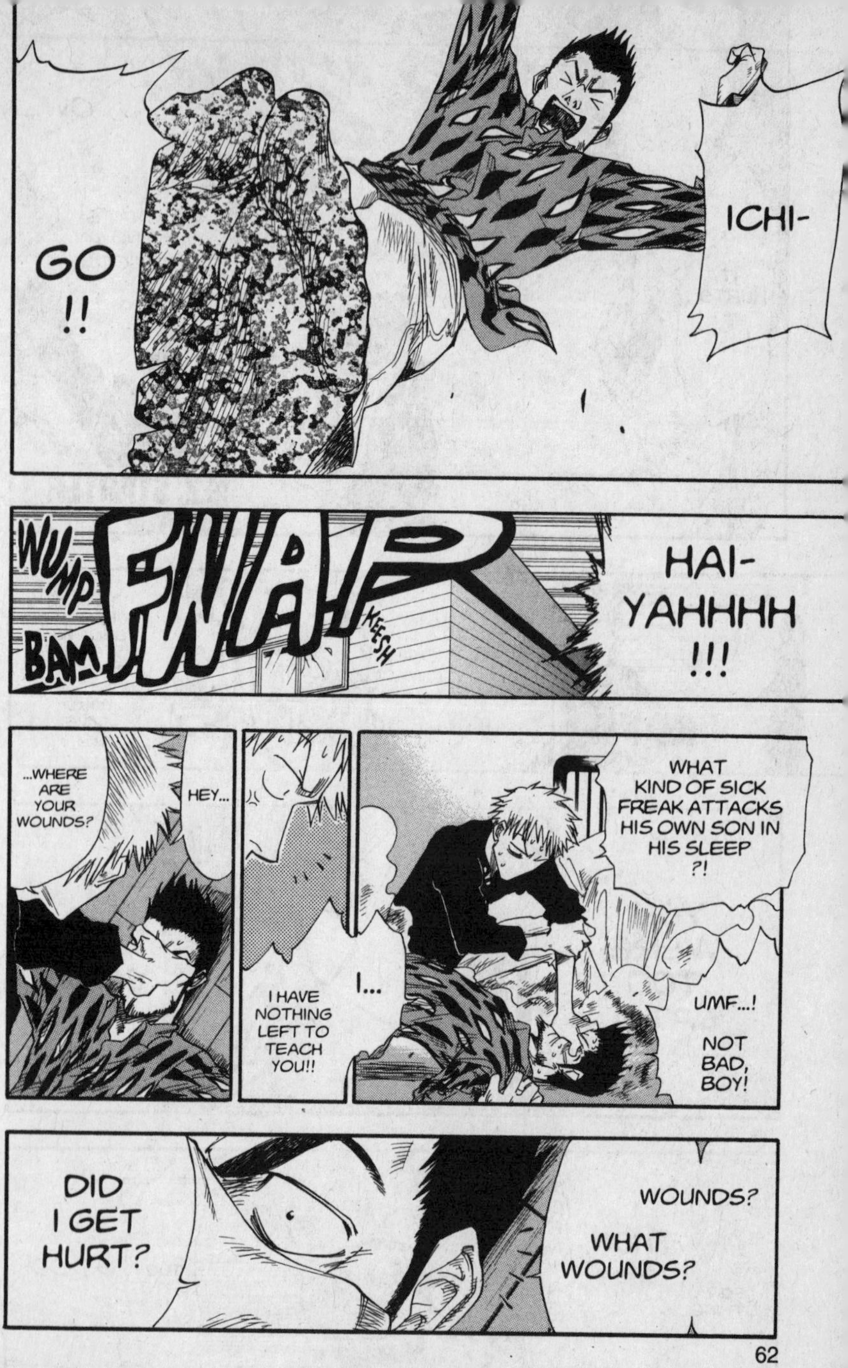
ICHI-
GO !!
HAI-YAHHHH !!!
FWAP
KEESH
WUMP
BAM
WHAT KIND OF SICK FREAK ATTACKS HIS OWN SON IN HIS SLEEP ?!
UMF...!
NOT BAD, BOY!
I...
I HAVE NOTHING LEFT TO TEACH YOU!!
HEY...
...WHERE ARE YOUR WOUNDS?
WOUNDS?
WHAT WOUNDS?
DID I GET HURT?

BLEACH ブリーチ

2. STARTER

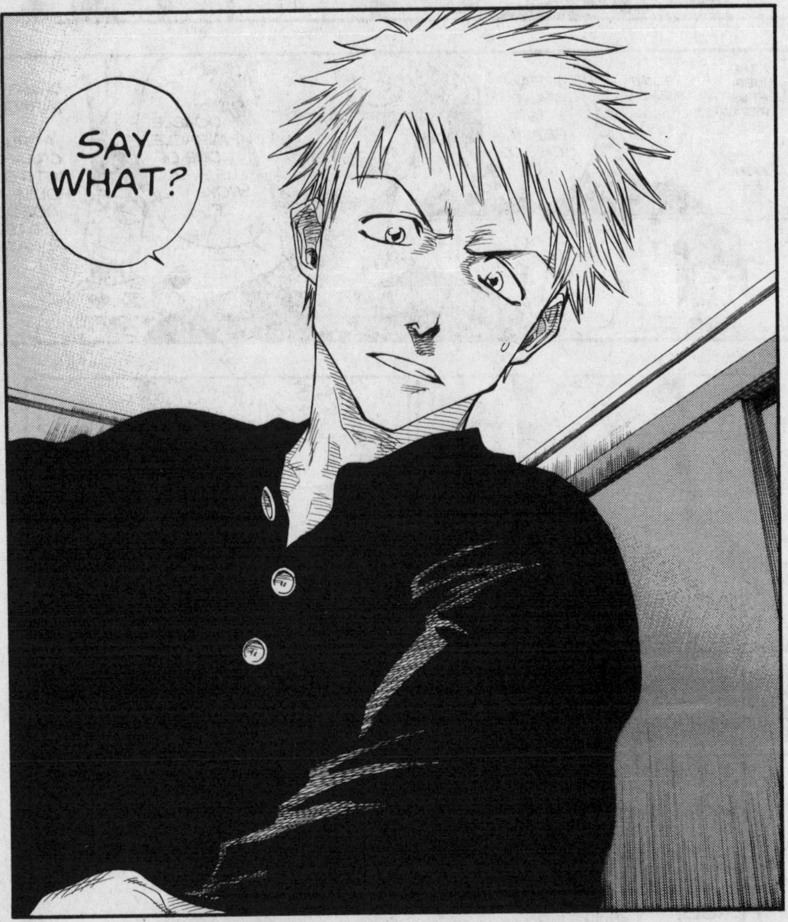
SAY WHAT?

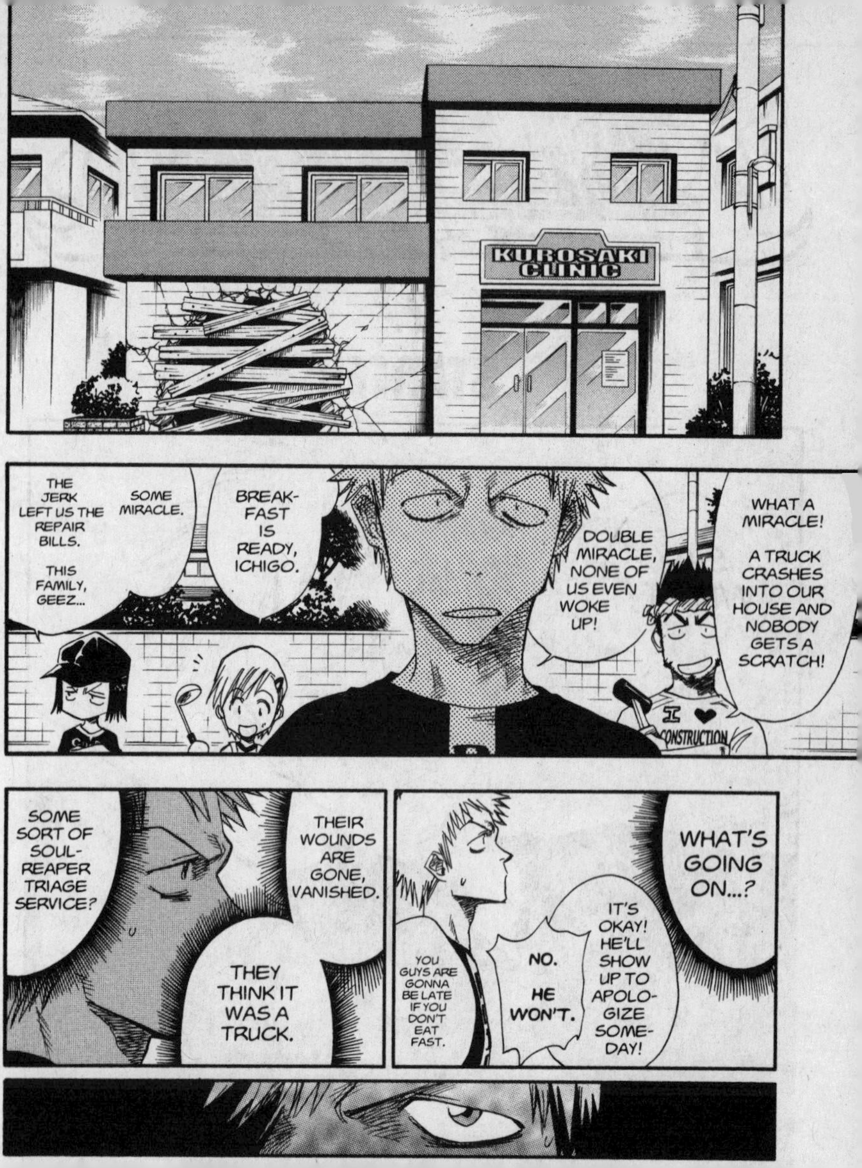
KUROSAKI CLINIC
WHAT A MIRACLE! A TRUCK CRASHES INTO OUR HOUSE AND NOBODY GETS A SCRATCH!
DOUBLE MIRACLE, NONE OF US EVEN WOKE UP!
I ♥ CONSTRUCTION
BREAK-FAST IS READY, ICHIGO.
SOME MIRACLE.
THE JERK LEFT US THE REPAIR BILLS. THIS FAMILY, GEEZ...
WHAT'S GOING ON...?
IT'S OKAY! HE'LL SHOW UP TO APOLO-GIZE SOME-DAY!
NO. HE WON'T.
YOU GUYS ARE GONNA BE LATE IF YOU DON'T EAT FAST.
THEIR WOUNDS ARE GONE, VANISHED.
SOME SORT OF SOUL-REAPER TRIAGE SERVICE?
THEY THINK IT WAS A TRUCK.

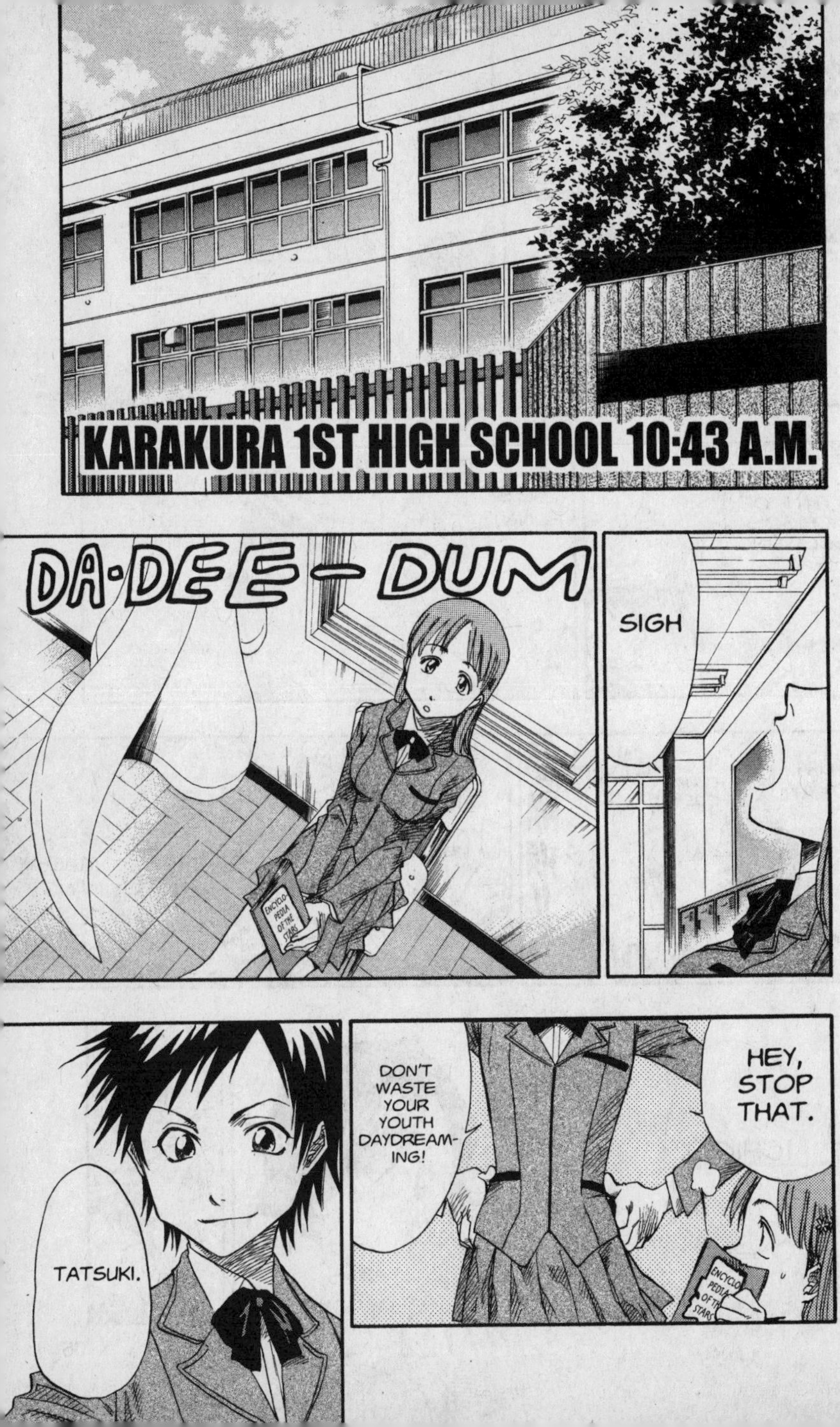
KARAKURA 1ST HIGH SCHOOL 10:43 A.M.
SIGH
DA-DEE-DUM
ENCYCLOPEDIA OF THE STARS
HEY, STOP THAT.
DON'T WASTE YOUR YOUTH DAYDREAMING!
ENCYCLOPEDIA OF THE STARS
TATSUKI.

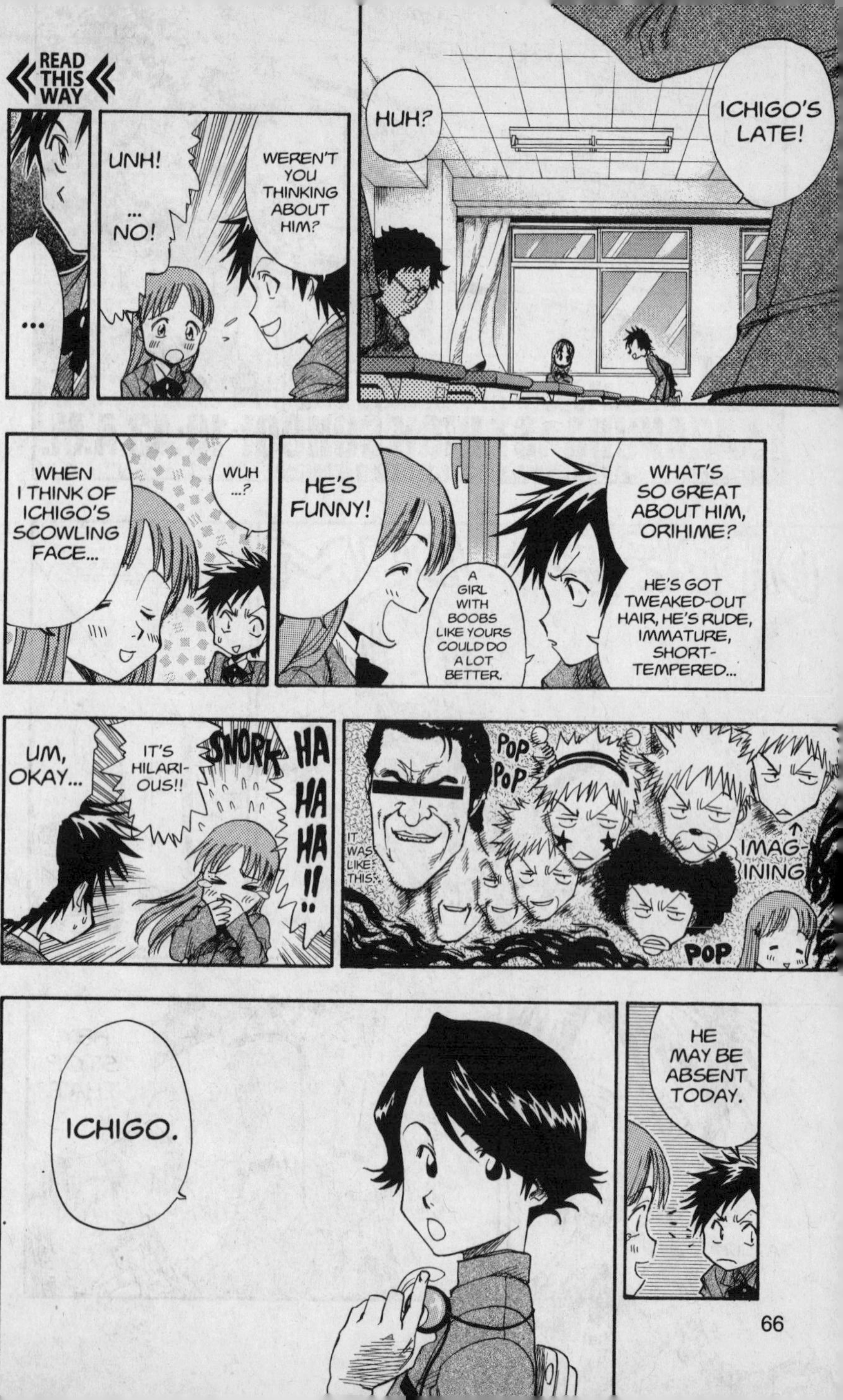
READ THIS WAY
ICHIGO'S LATE!
HUH?
WEREN'T YOU THINKING ABOUT HIM?
UNH!
... NO!
...
WHAT'S SO GREAT ABOUT HIM, ORIHIME?
HE'S GOT TWEAKED-OUT HAIR, HE'S RUDE, IMMATURE, SHORT-TEMPERED...
A GIRL WITH BOOBS LIKE YOURS COULD DO A LOT BETTER.
HE'S FUNNY!
WUH ...?
WHEN I THINK OF ICHIGO'S SCOWLING FACE...
POP POP
IMAG-INING
IT WAS LIKE THIS.
POP
HA HA HA!!
SNORK
IT'S HILARI-OUS!!
UM, OKAY...
HE MAY BE ABSENT TODAY.
ICHIGO.

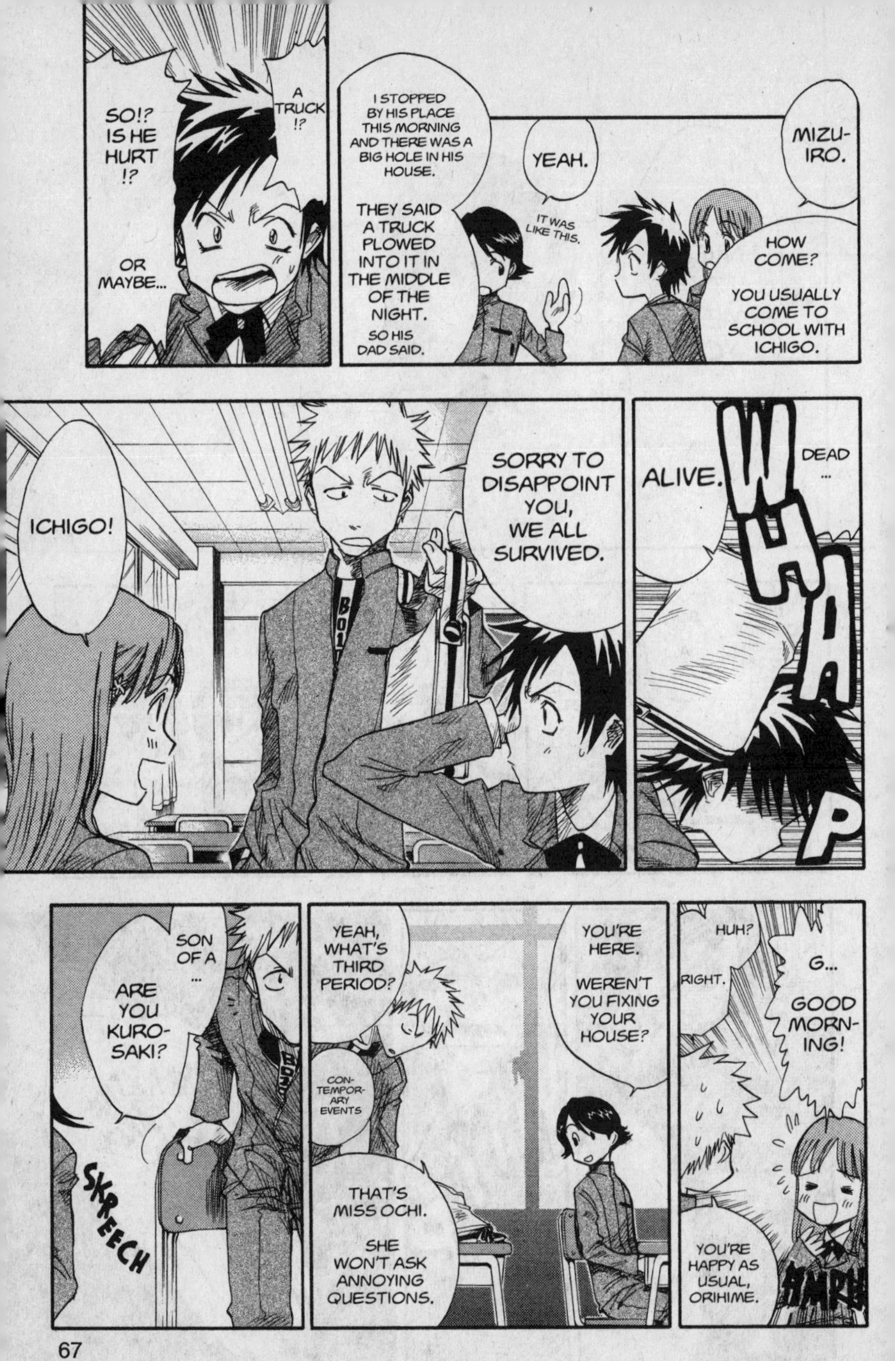
MIZU-IRO.
HOW COME?
YOU USUALLY COME TO SCHOOL WITH ICHIGO.
YEAH.
IT WAS LIKE THIS.
I STOPPED BY HIS PLACE THIS MORNING AND THERE WAS A BIG HOLE IN HIS HOUSE.
THEY SAID A TRUCK PLOWED INTO IT IN THE MIDDLE OF THE NIGHT.
SO HIS DAD SAID.
A TRUCK !?
SO!? IS HE HURT !?
OR MAYBE...
DEAD ...
WHAP
ALIVE.
SORRY TO DISAPPOINT YOU, WE ALL SURVIVED.
ICHIGO!
G...
GOOD MORN-ING!
HUH?
RIGHT.
YOU'RE HAPPY AS USUAL, ORIHIME.
YOU'RE HERE.
WEREN'T YOU FIXING YOUR HOUSE?
YEAH, WHAT'S THIRD PERIOD?
CON-TEMPOR-ARY EVENTS
THAT'S MISS OCHI.
SHE WON'T ASK ANNOYING QUESTIONS.
SON OF A ...
ARE YOU KURO-SAKI?
SKREECH

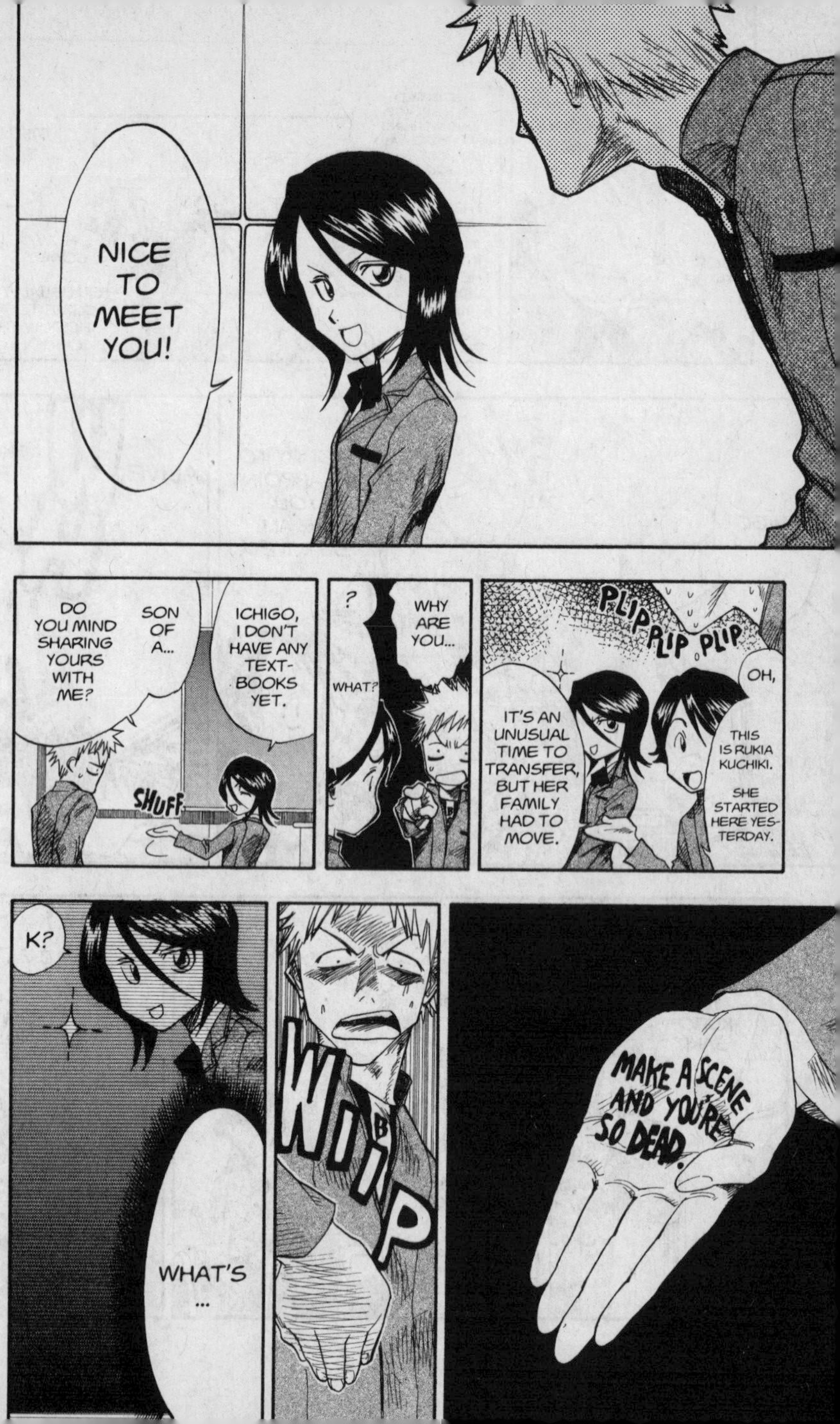
NICE TO MEET YOU!
PLIP PLIP PLIP
OH,
THIS IS RUKIA KUCHIKI.
SHE STARTED HERE YESTERDAY.
IT'S AN UNUSUAL TIME TO TRANSFER, BUT HER FAMILY HAD TO MOVE.
WHY ARE YOU...
?
WHAT?
ICHIGO, I DON'T HAVE ANY TEXTBOOKS YET.
SON OF A...
DO YOU MIND SHARING YOURS WITH ME?
SHUFF
MAKE A SCENE AND YOU'RE SO DEAD.
WHIP
K?
WHAT'S ...

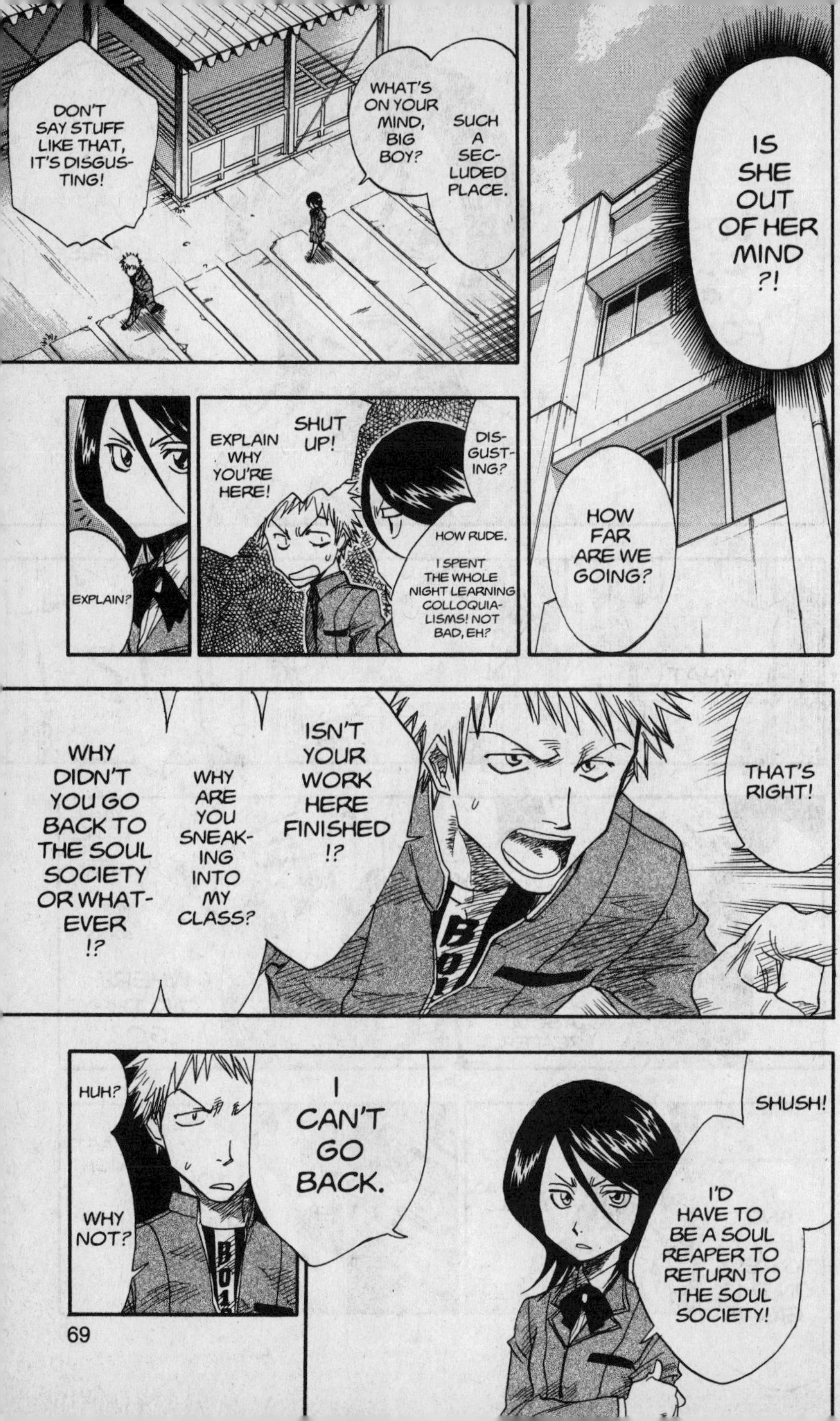
IS SHE OUT OF HER MIND ?!
HOW FAR ARE WE GOING?
WHAT'S ON YOUR MIND, BIG BOY?
SUCH A SEC-LUDED PLACE.
DON'T SAY STUFF LIKE THAT, IT'S DISGUS-TING!
DIS-GUST-ING?
HOW RUDE.
I SPENT THE WHOLE NIGHT LEARNING COLLOQUIA-LISMS! NOT BAD, EH?
SHUT UP!
EXPLAIN WHY YOU'RE HERE!
EXPLAIN?
THAT'S RIGHT!
ISN'T YOUR WORK HERE FINISHED !?
WHY ARE YOU SNEAK-ING INTO MY CLASS?
WHY DIDN'T YOU GO BACK TO THE SOUL SOCIETY OR WHAT-EVER !?
I CAN'T GO BACK.
HUH?
WHY NOT?
SHUSH!
I'D HAVE TO BE A SOUL REAPER TO RETURN TO THE SOUL SOCIETY!

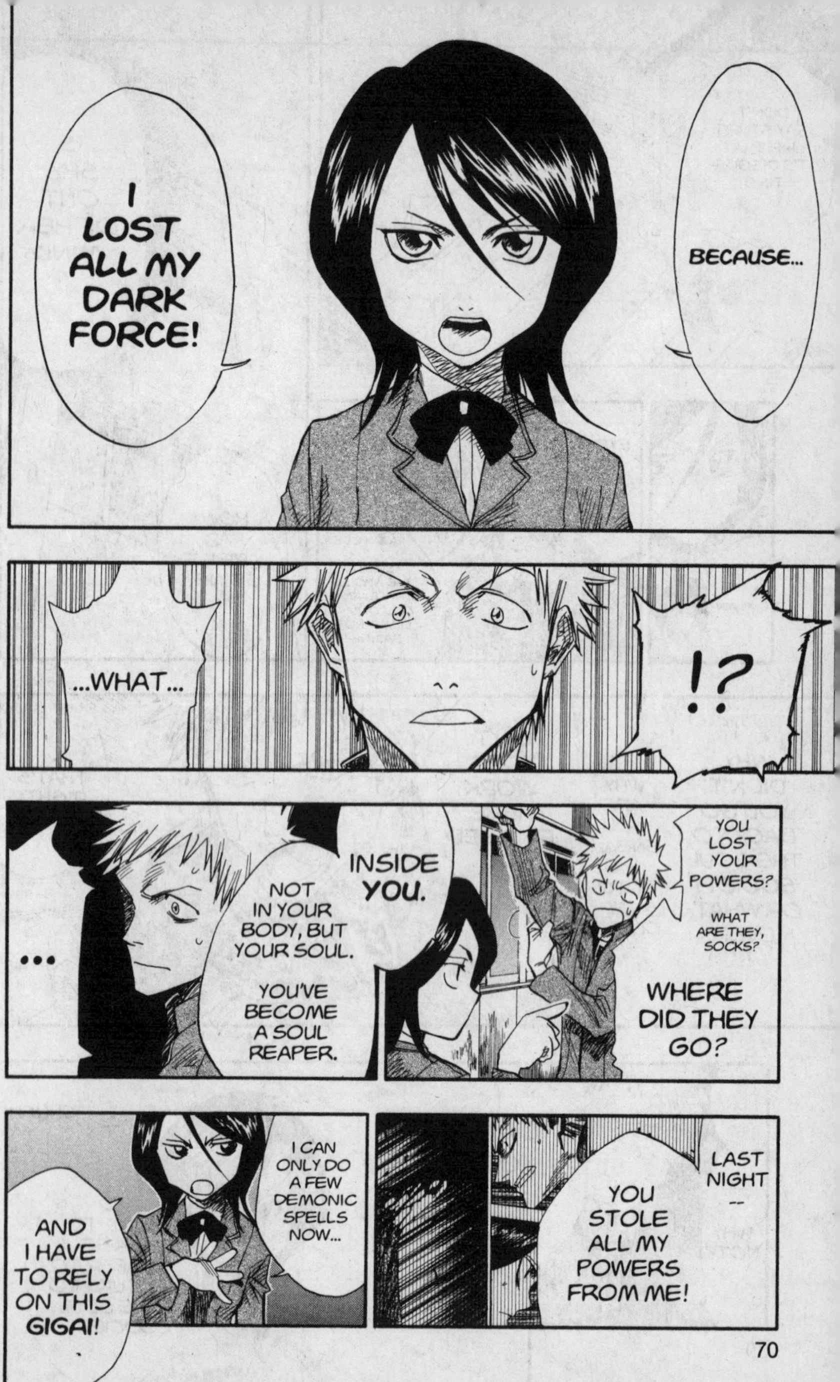
BECAUSE...
I LOST ALL MY DARK FORCE!
!?
...WHAT...
YOU LOST YOUR POWERS?
WHAT ARE THEY, SOCKS?
WHERE DID THEY GO?
INSIDE YOU.
NOT IN YOUR BODY, BUT YOUR SOUL.
YOU'VE BECOME A SOUL REAPER.
...
LAST NIGHT --
YOU STOLE ALL MY POWERS FROM ME!
I CAN ONLY DO A FEW DEMONIC SPELLS NOW...
AND I HAVE TO RELY ON THIS GIGAI!

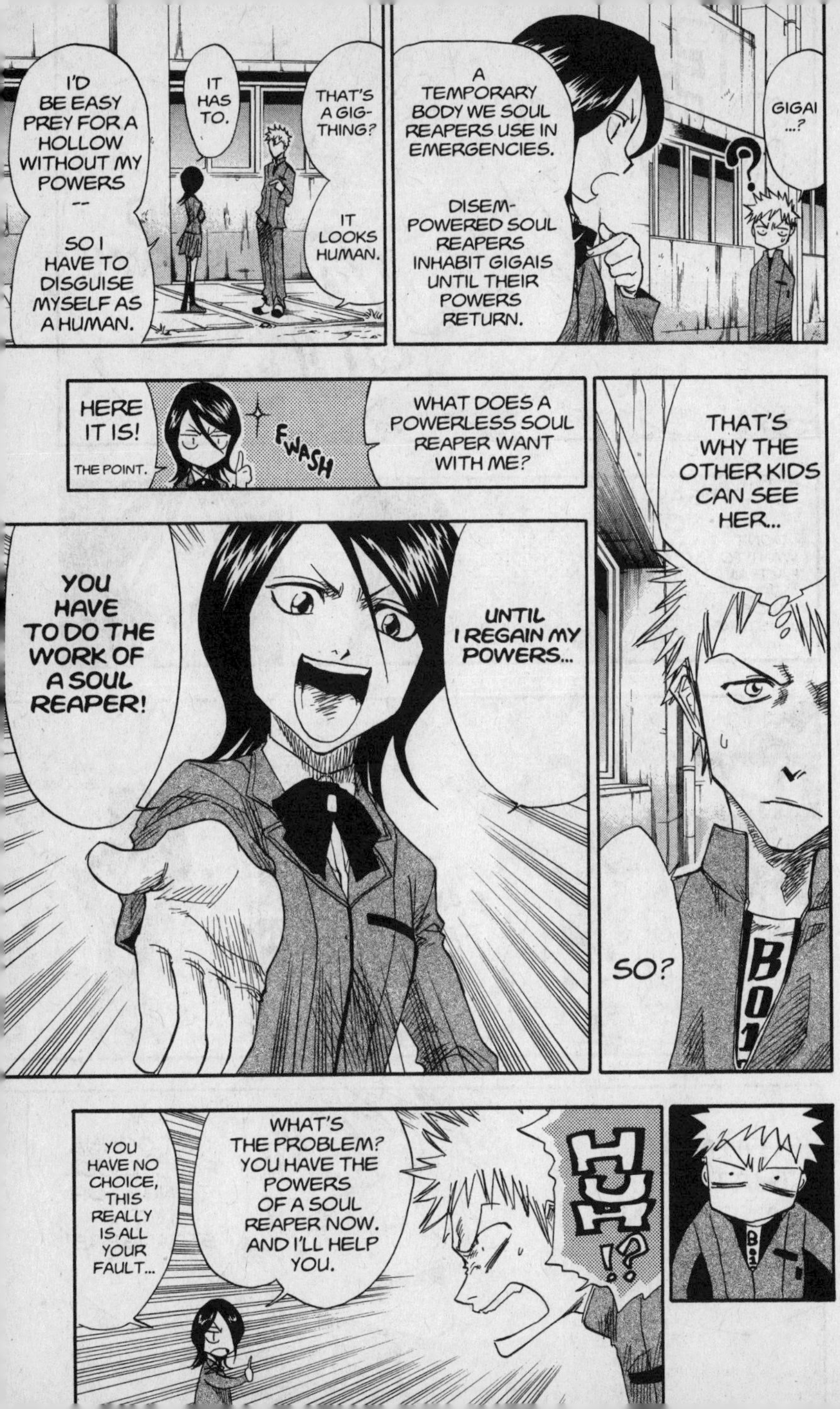
GIGAI ...?
A TEMPORARY BODY WE SOUL REAPERS USE IN EMERGENCIES.
DISEMPOWERED SOUL REAPERS INHABIT GIGAIS UNTIL THEIR POWERS RETURN.
THAT'S A GIG-THING?
IT LOOKS HUMAN.
IT HAS TO.
I'D BE EASY PREY FOR A HOLLOW WITHOUT MY POWERS --
SO I HAVE TO DISGUISE MYSELF AS A HUMAN.
THAT'S WHY THE OTHER KIDS CAN SEE HER...
SO?
WHAT DOES A POWERLESS SOUL REAPER WANT WITH ME?
FWASH
HERE IT IS!
THE POINT.
UNTIL I REGAIN MY POWERS...
YOU HAVE TO DO THE WORK OF A SOUL REAPER!
HUH!?
WHAT'S THE PROBLEM? YOU HAVE THE POWERS OF A SOUL REAPER NOW. AND I'LL HELP YOU.
YOU HAVE NO CHOICE, THIS REALLY IS ALL YOUR FAULT...

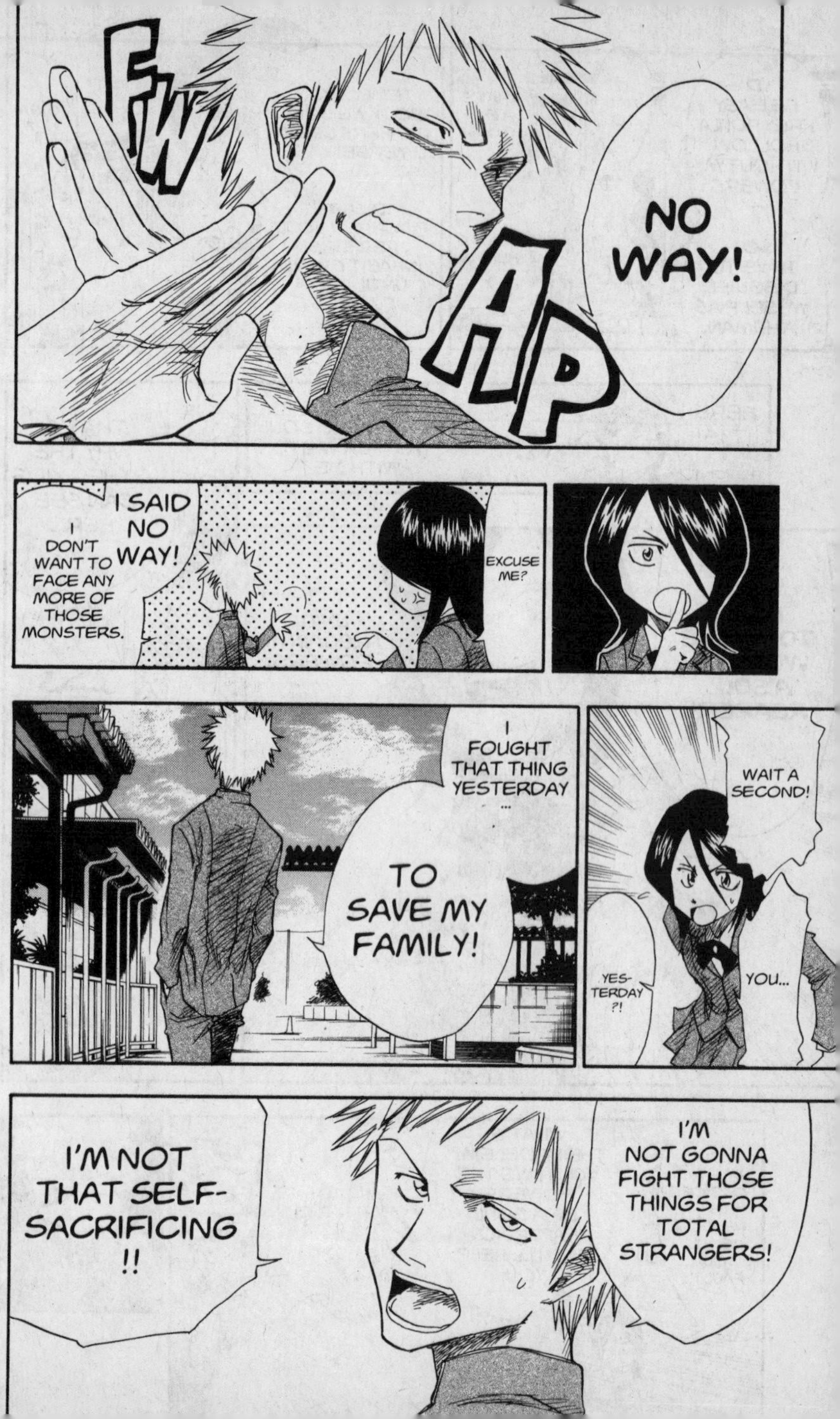
FWAP
NO WAY!
EXCUSE ME?
I SAID NO WAY!
I DON'T WANT TO FACE ANY MORE OF THOSE MONSTERS.
WAIT A SECOND!
YOU...
YES-TERDAY?!
I FOUGHT THAT THING YESTERDAY...
TO SAVE MY FAMILY!
I'M NOT GONNA FIGHT THOSE THINGS FOR TOTAL STRANGERS!
I'M NOT THAT SELF-SACRIFICING!!

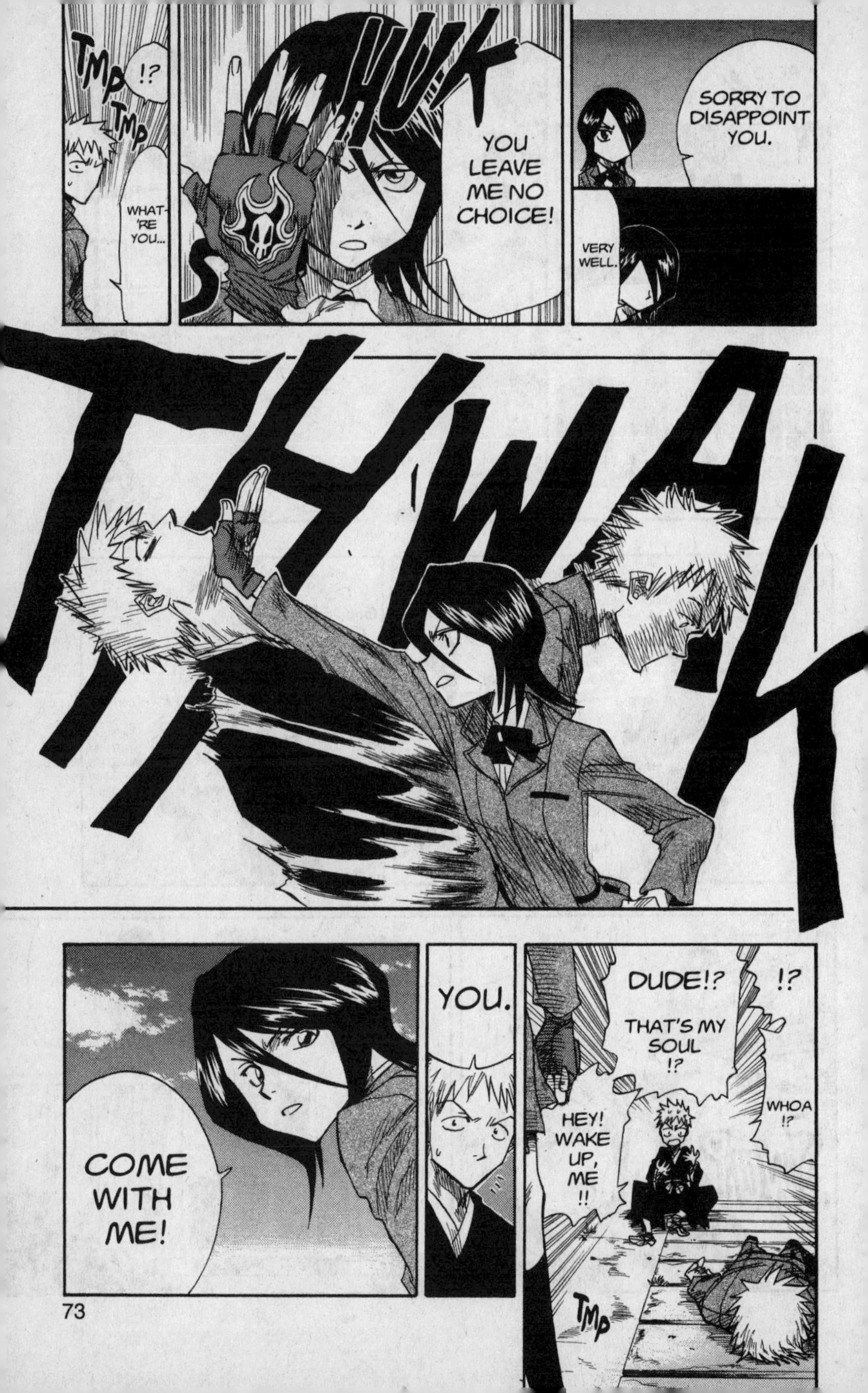
SORRY TO DISAPPOINT YOU.
VERY WELL.
HUK
YOU LEAVE ME NO CHOICE!
!?
TMP TMP
WHAT-'RE YOU...
THWAK
!?
DUDE!?
THAT'S MY SOUL !?
WHOA !?
HEY! WAKE UP, ME !!
TMP
YOU.
COME WITH ME!

READ THIS WAY

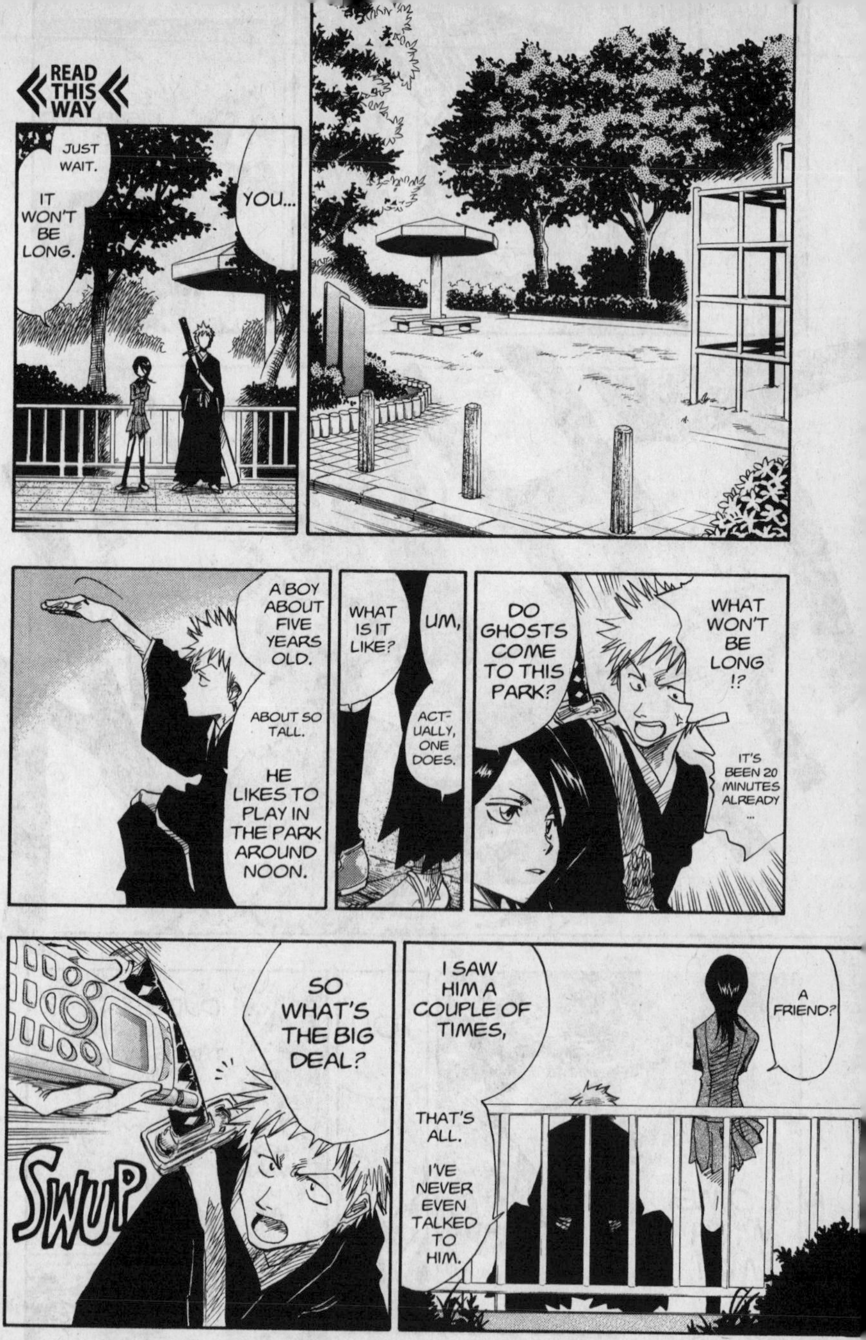
YOU...
JUST WAIT.
IT WON'T BE LONG.
WHAT WON'T BE LONG!?
IT'S BEEN 20 MINUTES ALREADY...
DO GHOSTS COME TO THIS PARK?
UM,
ACT-UALLY, ONE DOES.
WHAT IS IT LIKE?
A BOY ABOUT FIVE YEARS OLD.
ABOUT SO TALL.
HE LIKES TO PLAY IN THE PARK AROUND NOON.
A FRIEND?
I SAW HIM A COUPLE OF TIMES,
THAT'S ALL.
I'VE NEVER EVEN TALKED TO HIM.
SO WHAT'S THE BIG DEAL?
SWUP

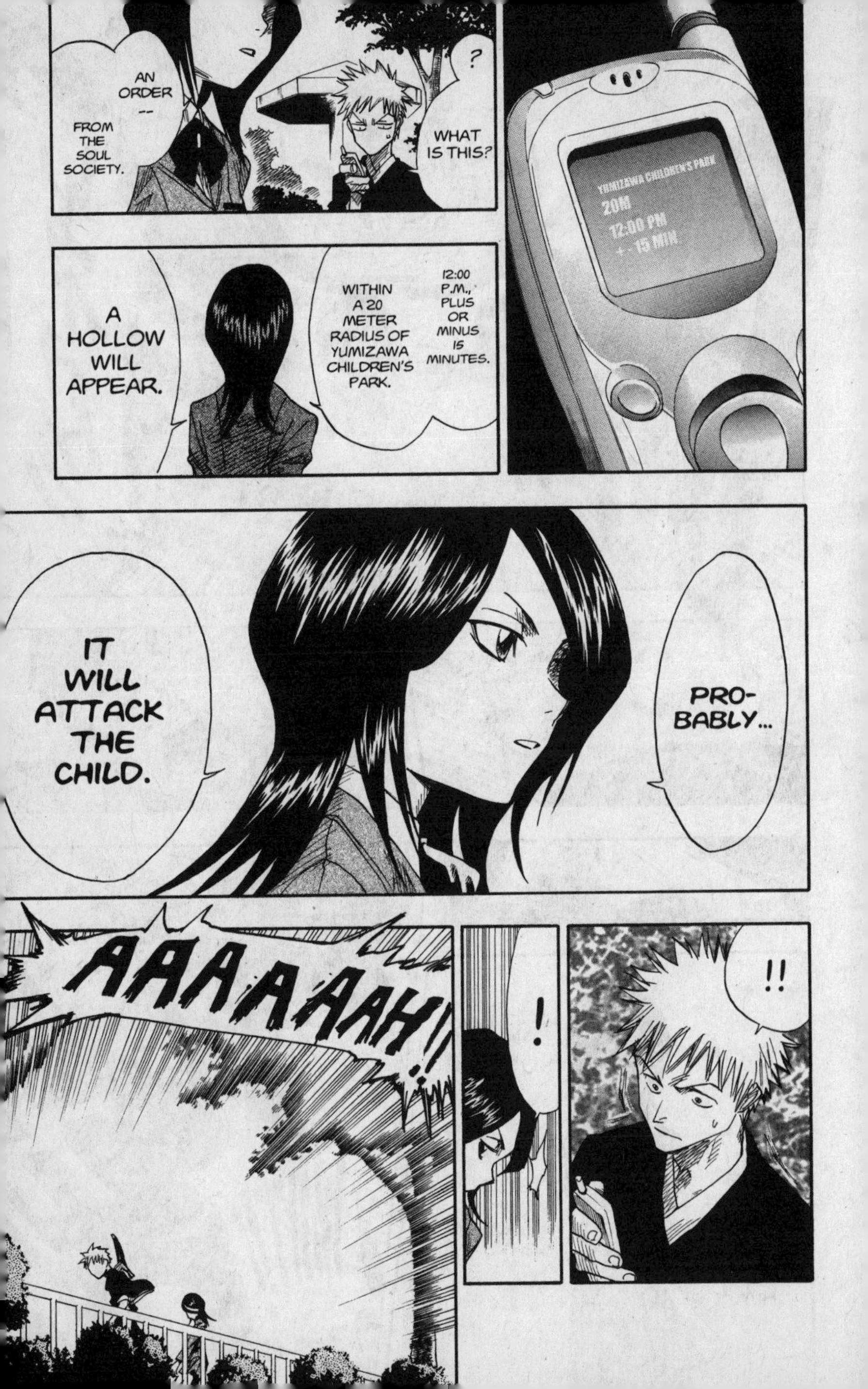
YUMIZAWA CHILDREN'S PARK
20M
12:00 PM
+- 15 MIN
?
WHAT IS THIS?
AN ORDER -- FROM THE SOUL SOCIETY.
12:00 P.M., PLUS OR MINUS 15 MINUTES.
WITHIN A 20 METER RADIUS OF YUMIZAWA CHILDREN'S PARK.
A HOLLOW WILL APPEAR.
PRO-BABLY...
IT WILL ATTACK THE CHILD.
!!
!
AAAAAAAH!!

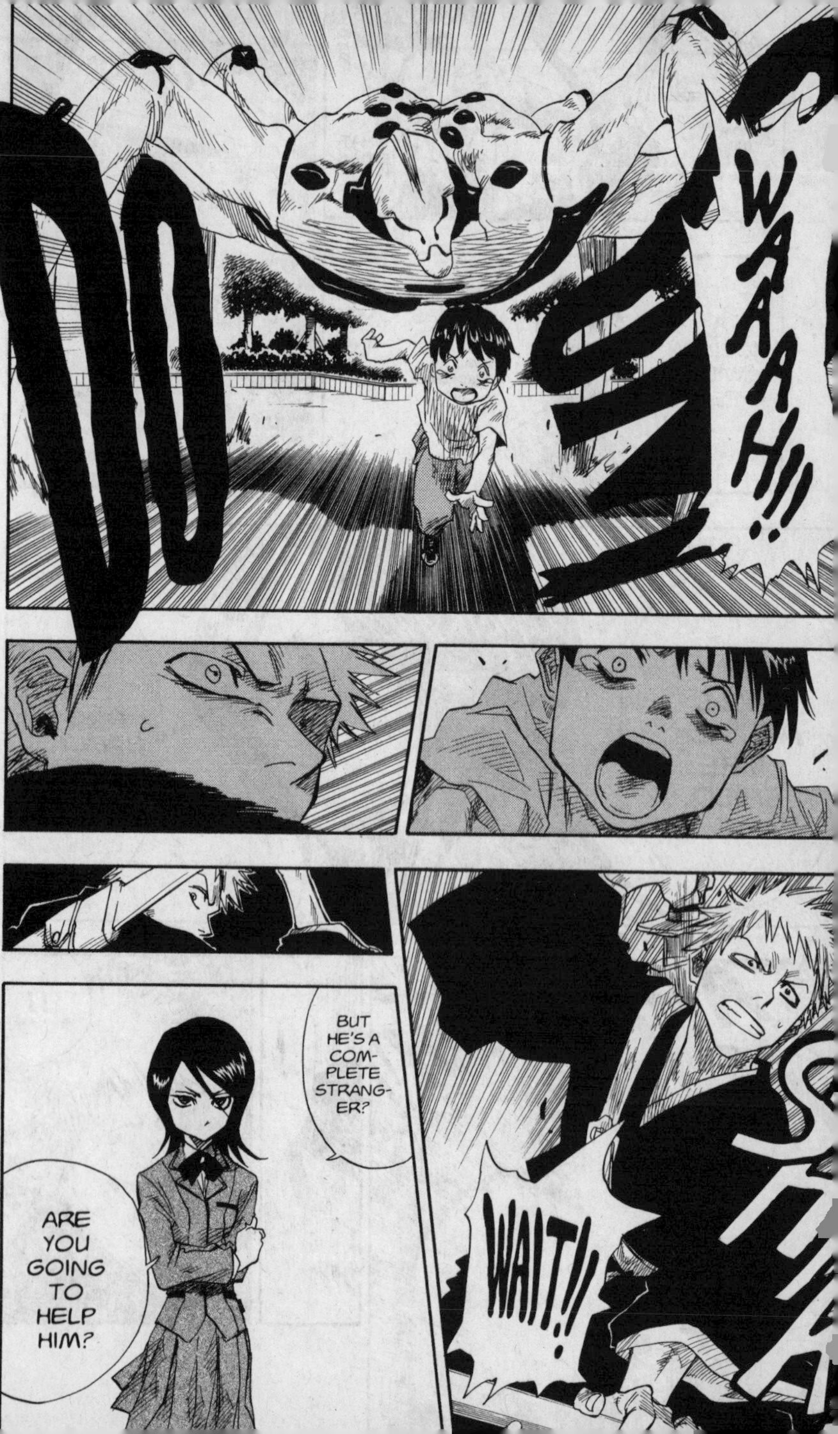
WAAAH!!!
DO
WAIT!!
BUT HE'S A COMPLETE STRANGER?
ARE YOU GOING TO HELP HIM?

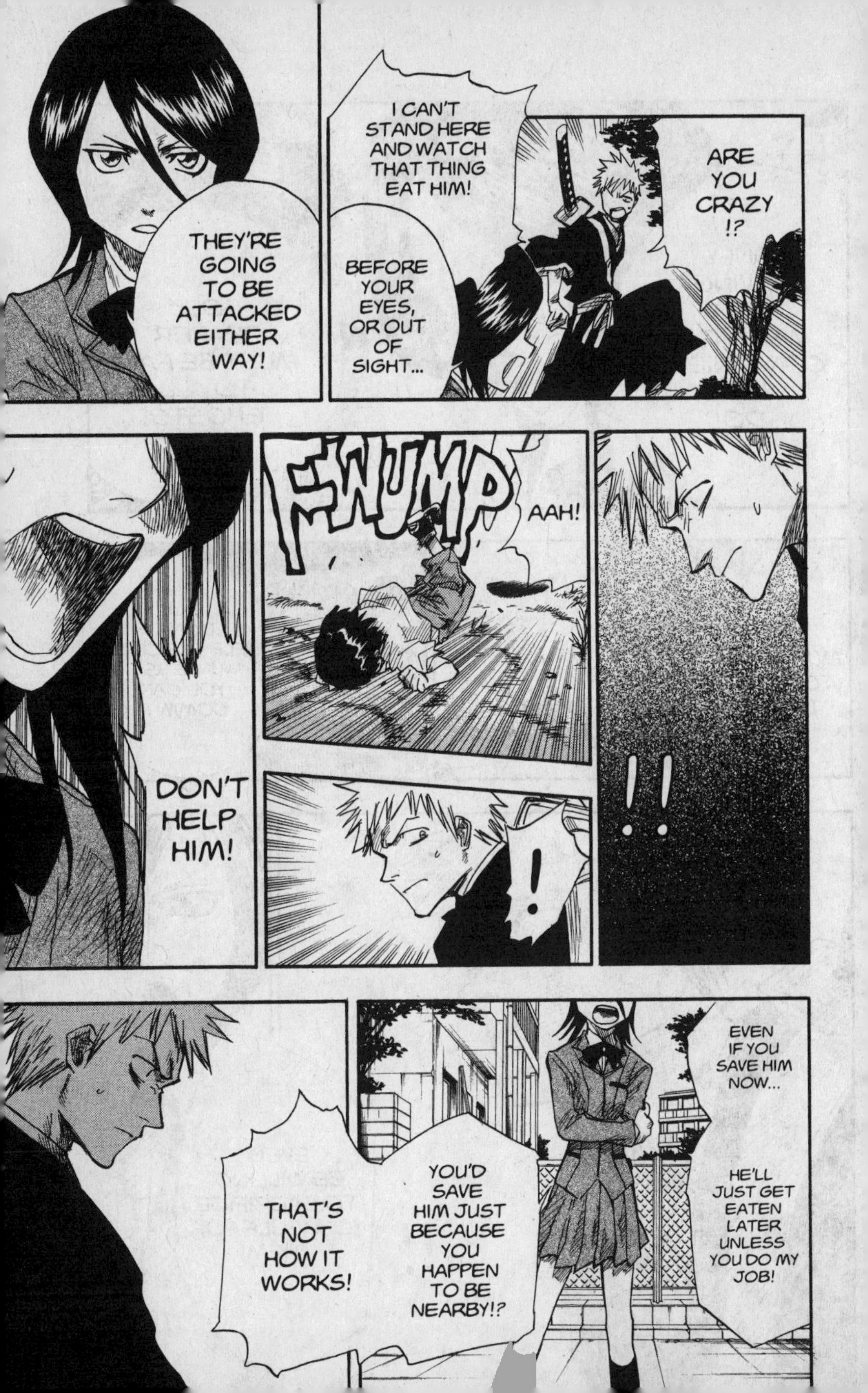
ARE YOU CRAZY !?
I CAN'T STAND HERE AND WATCH THAT THING EAT HIM!
BEFORE YOUR EYES, OR OUT OF SIGHT...
THEY'RE GOING TO BE ATTACKED EITHER WAY!
!!
FWUMP
AAH!
!
DON'T HELP HIM!
EVEN IF YOU SAVE HIM NOW...
HE'LL JUST GET EATEN LATER UNLESS YOU DO MY JOB!
YOU'D SAVE HIM JUST BECAUSE YOU HAPPEN TO BE NEARBY!?
THAT'S NOT HOW IT WORKS!

READ THIS WAY

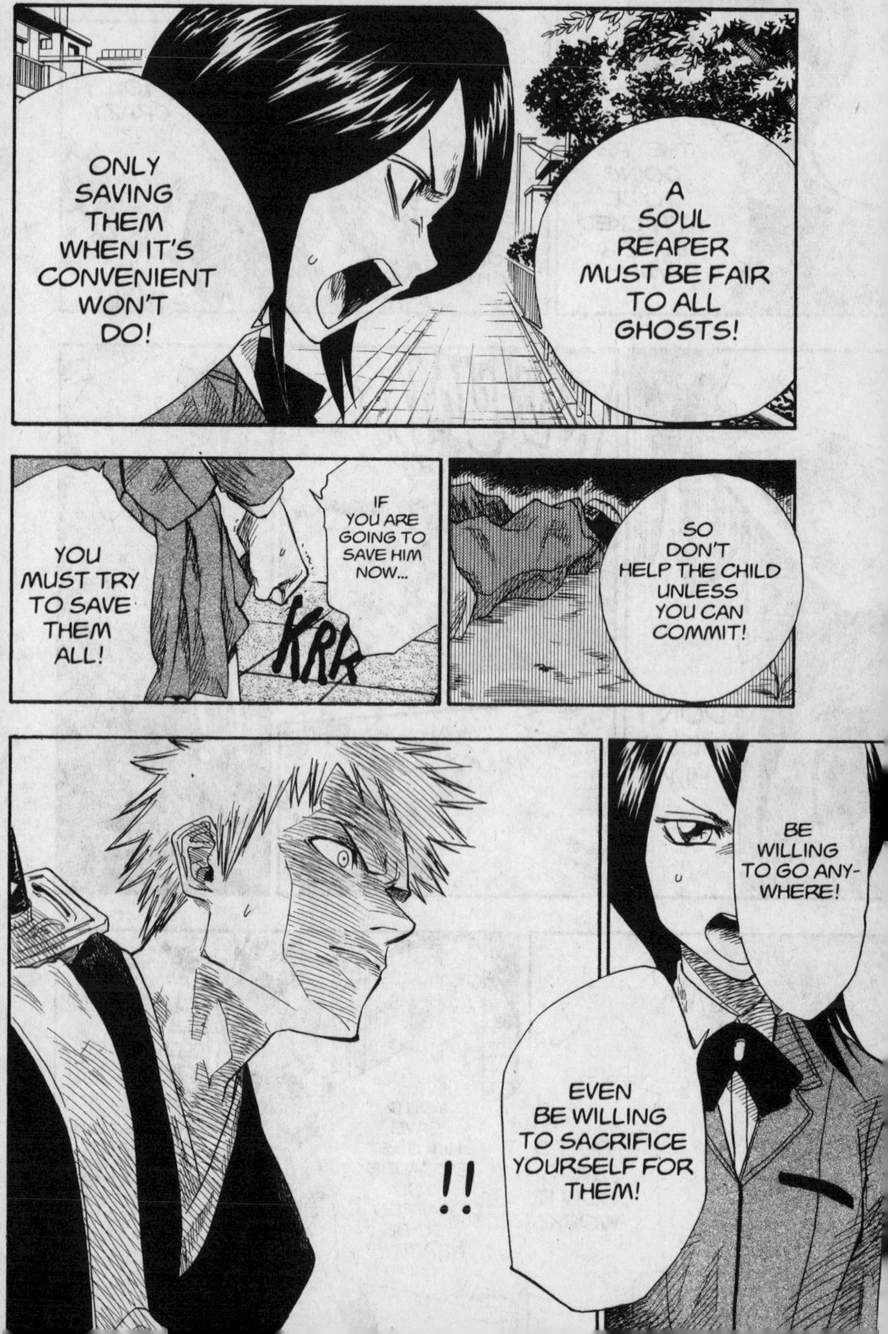
A SOUL REAPER MUST BE FAIR TO ALL GHOSTS!
ONLY SAVING THEM WHEN IT'S CONVENIENT WON'T DO!
SO DON'T HELP THE CHILD UNLESS YOU CAN COMMIT!
IF YOU ARE GOING TO SAVE HIM NOW...
KRK
YOU MUST TRY TO SAVE THEM ALL!
BE WILLING TO GO ANY-WHERE!
EVEN BE WILLING TO SACRIFICE YOURSELF FOR THEM!
!!

READ THIS WAY

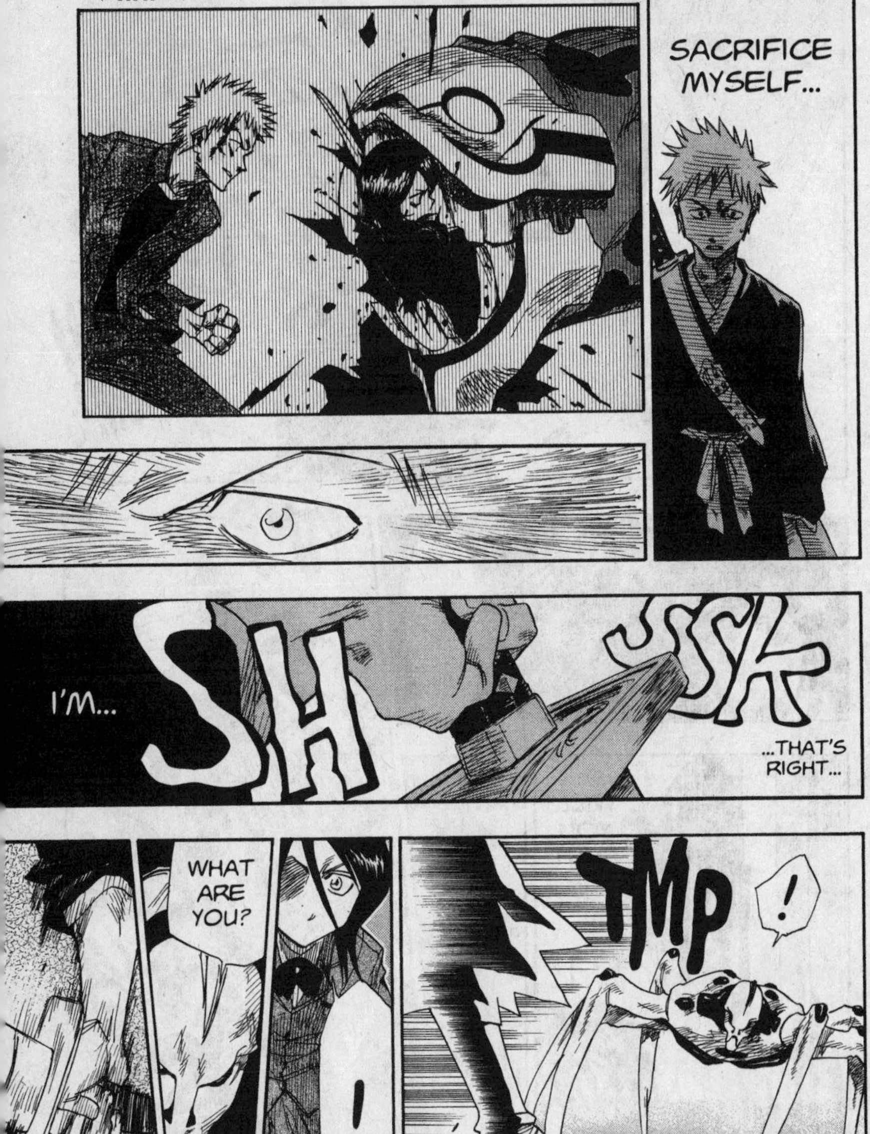

SACRIFICE MYSELF...
...THAT'S RIGHT...
SHSSK
I'M...
!
TMP
WHAT ARE YOU?
!

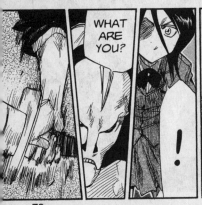

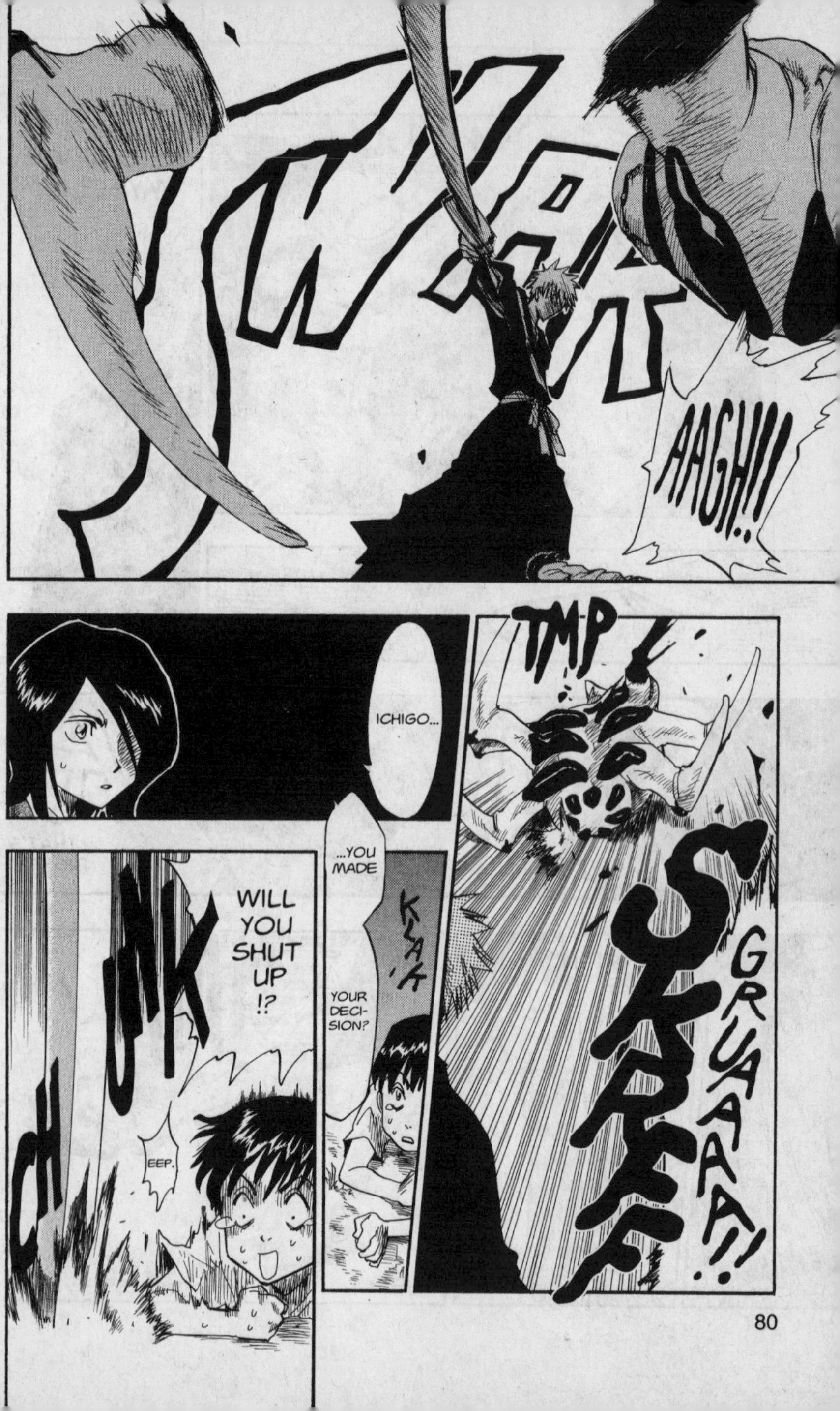
WHAK
AAGH!!..
TMP
GRUAAAA!!
ICHIGO...
...YOU MADE YOUR DECISION?
KLAK
WILL YOU SHUT UP!?
CHUNK
EEP.

READ THIS WAY

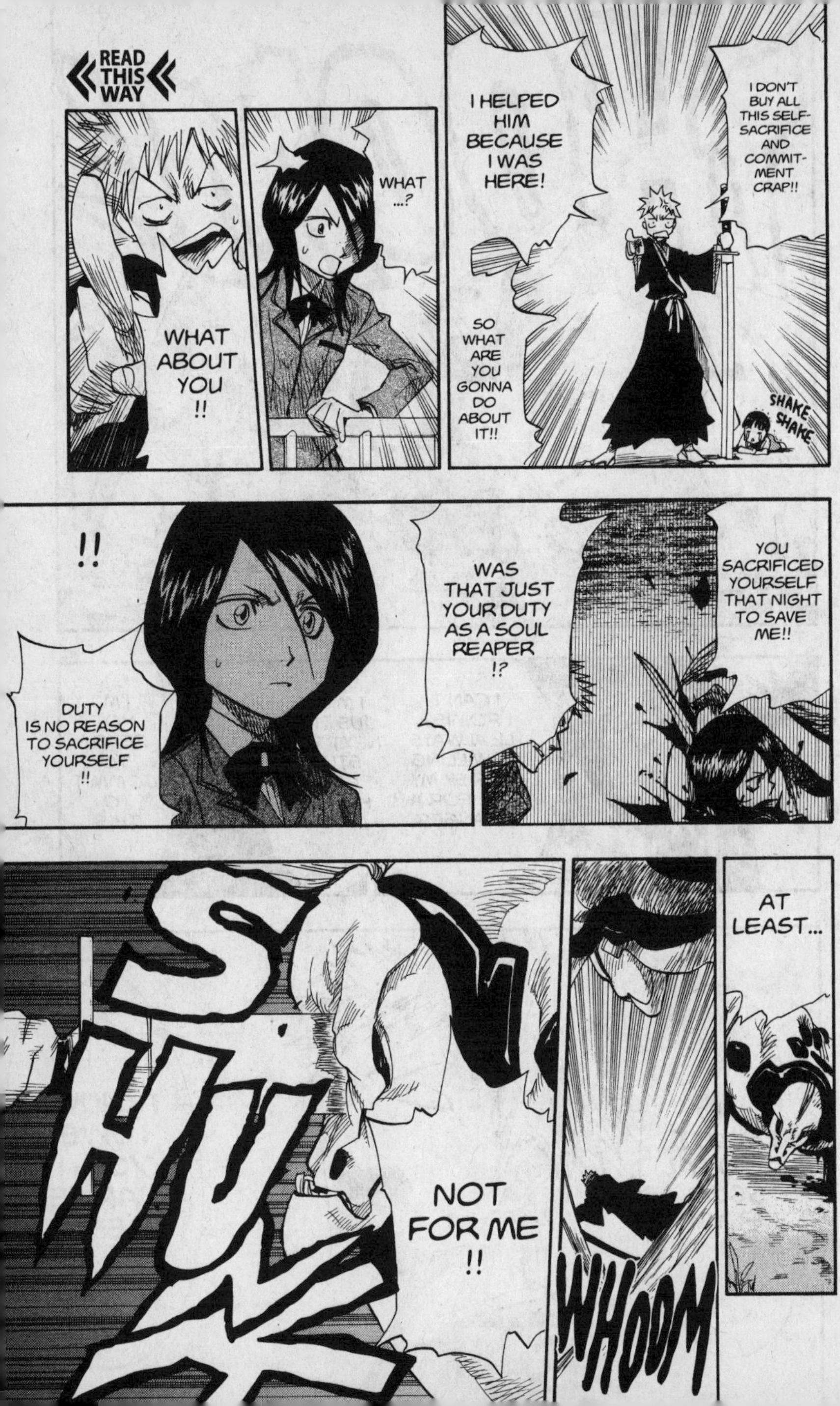
I DON'T BUY ALL THIS SELF-SACRIFICE AND COMMITMENT CRAP!!
I HELPED HIM BECAUSE I WAS HERE!
SO WHAT ARE YOU GONNA DO ABOUT IT!!
SHAKE SHAKE
WHAT ...?
WHAT ABOUT YOU !!
YOU SACRIFICED YOURSELF THAT NIGHT TO SAVE ME!!
WAS THAT JUST YOUR DUTY AS A SOUL REAPER !?
!!
DUTY IS NO REASON TO SACRIFICE YOURSELF !!
AT LEAST...
WHOOM
NOT FOR ME !!

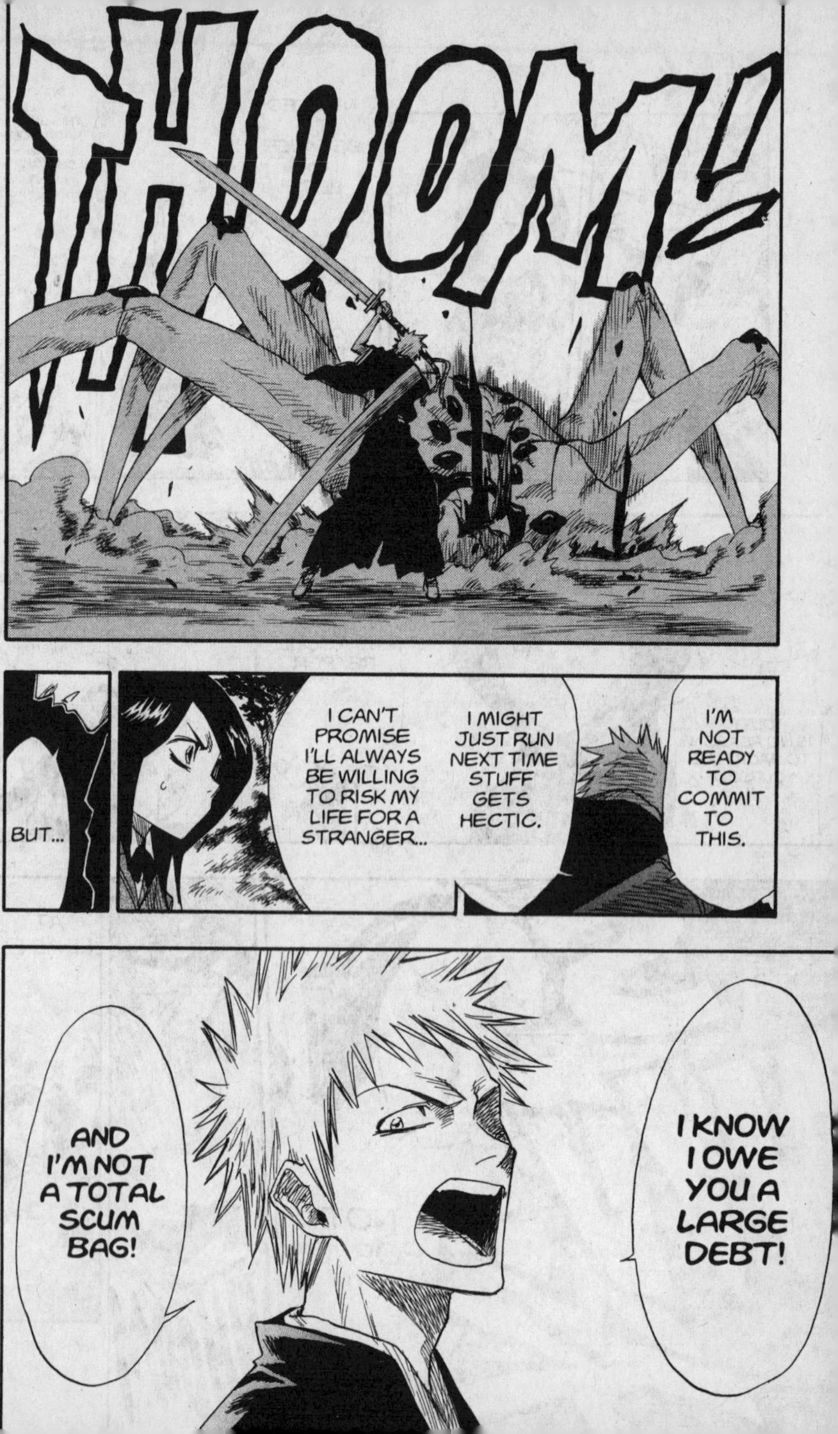
THOOM!
I'M NOT READY TO COMMIT TO THIS.
I MIGHT JUST RUN NEXT TIME STUFF GETS HECTIC.
I CAN'T PROMISE I'LL ALWAYS BE WILLING TO RISK MY LIFE FOR A STRANGER...
BUT...
I KNOW I OWE YOU A LARGE DEBT!
AND I'M NOT A TOTAL SCUM BAG!

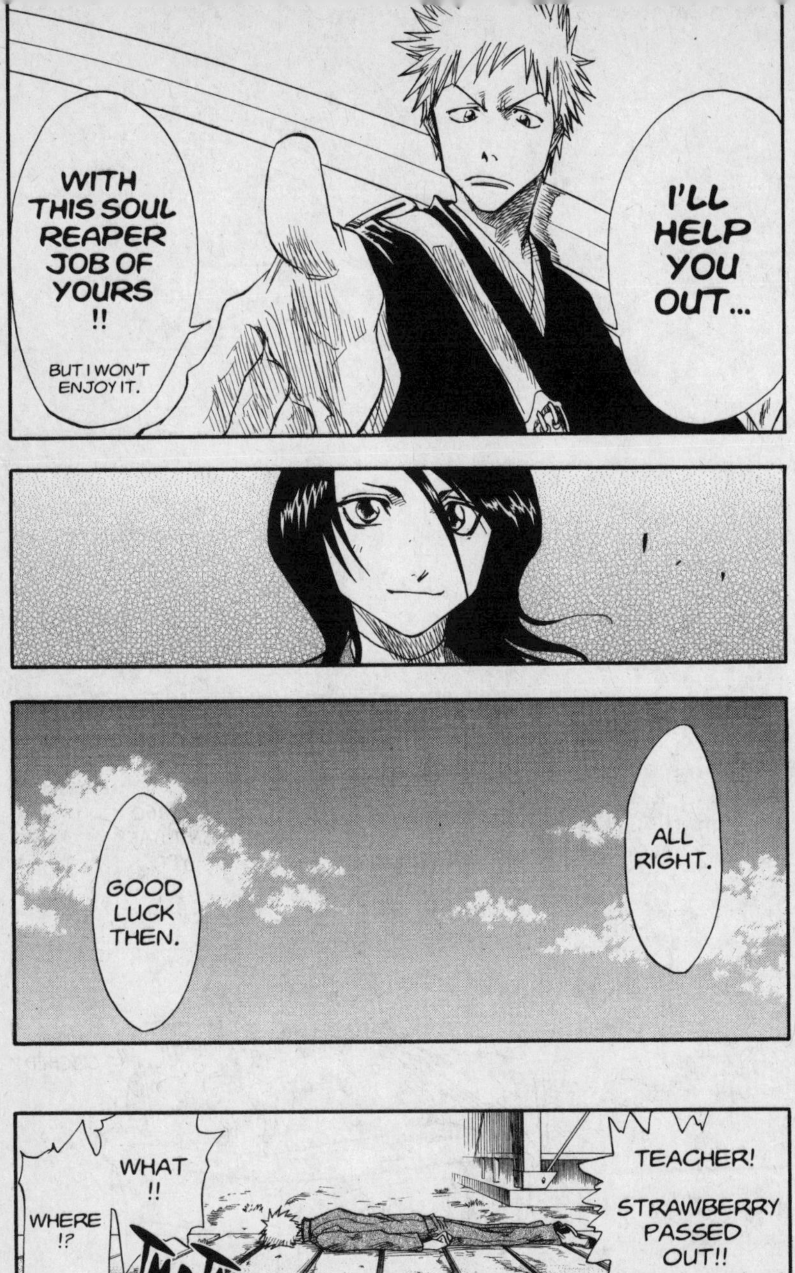
I'LL HELP YOU OUT...
WITH THIS SOUL REAPER JOB OF YOURS !!
BUT I WON'T ENJOY IT.
ALL RIGHT.
GOOD LUCK THEN.
TEACHER!
STRAWBERRY PASSED OUT!!
TMP TMP
WHAT !!
WHERE !?

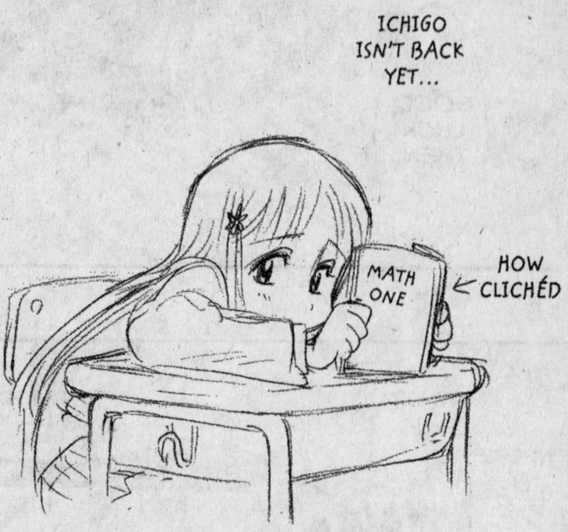
ICHIGO ISN'T BACK YET...
MATH ONE
HOW CLICHÉD

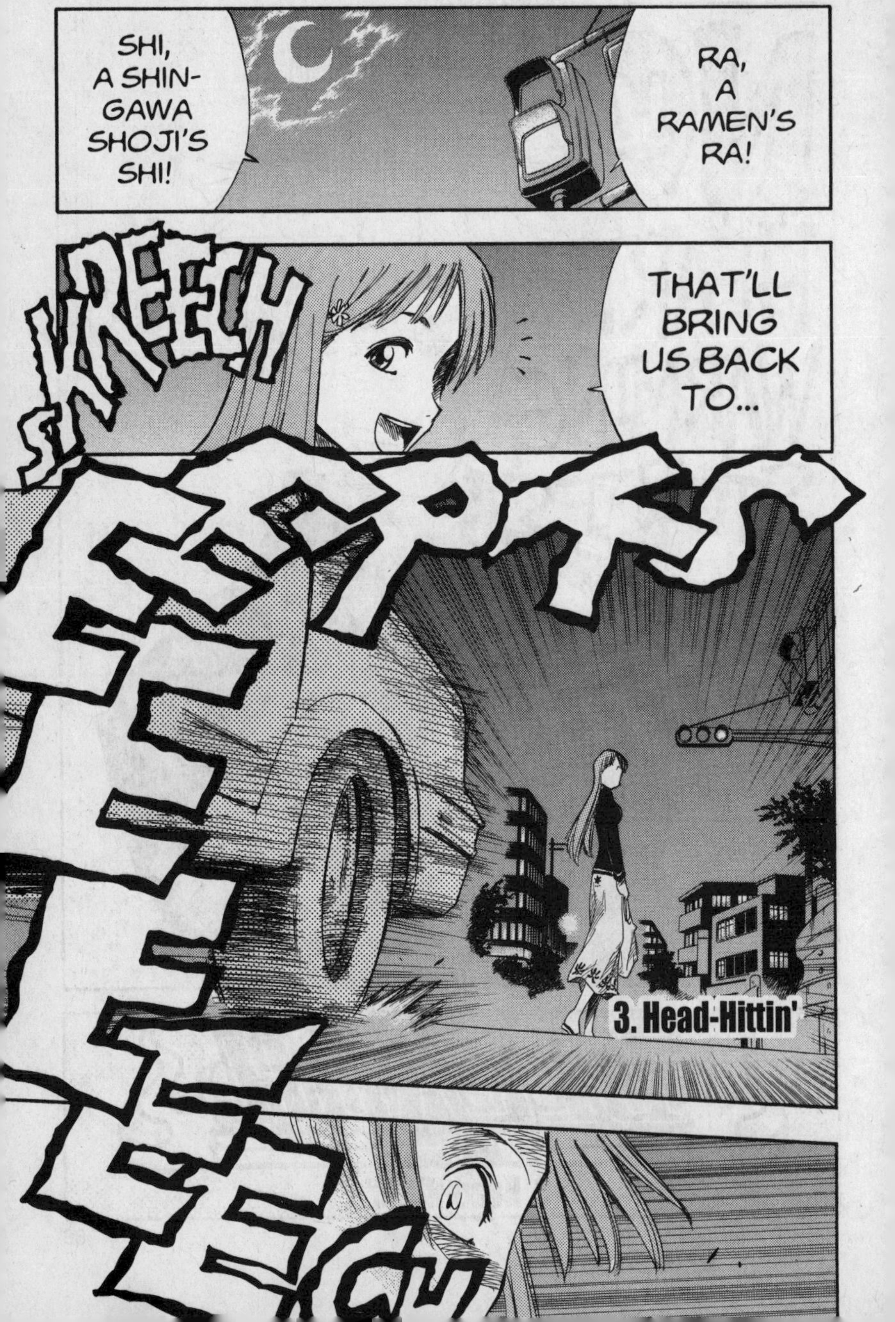
RA, A RAMEN'S RA!
SHI, A SHIN-GAWA SHOJI'S SHI!
THAT'LL BRING US BACK TO...
SKREECH
SKREECH
3. Head-Hittin'

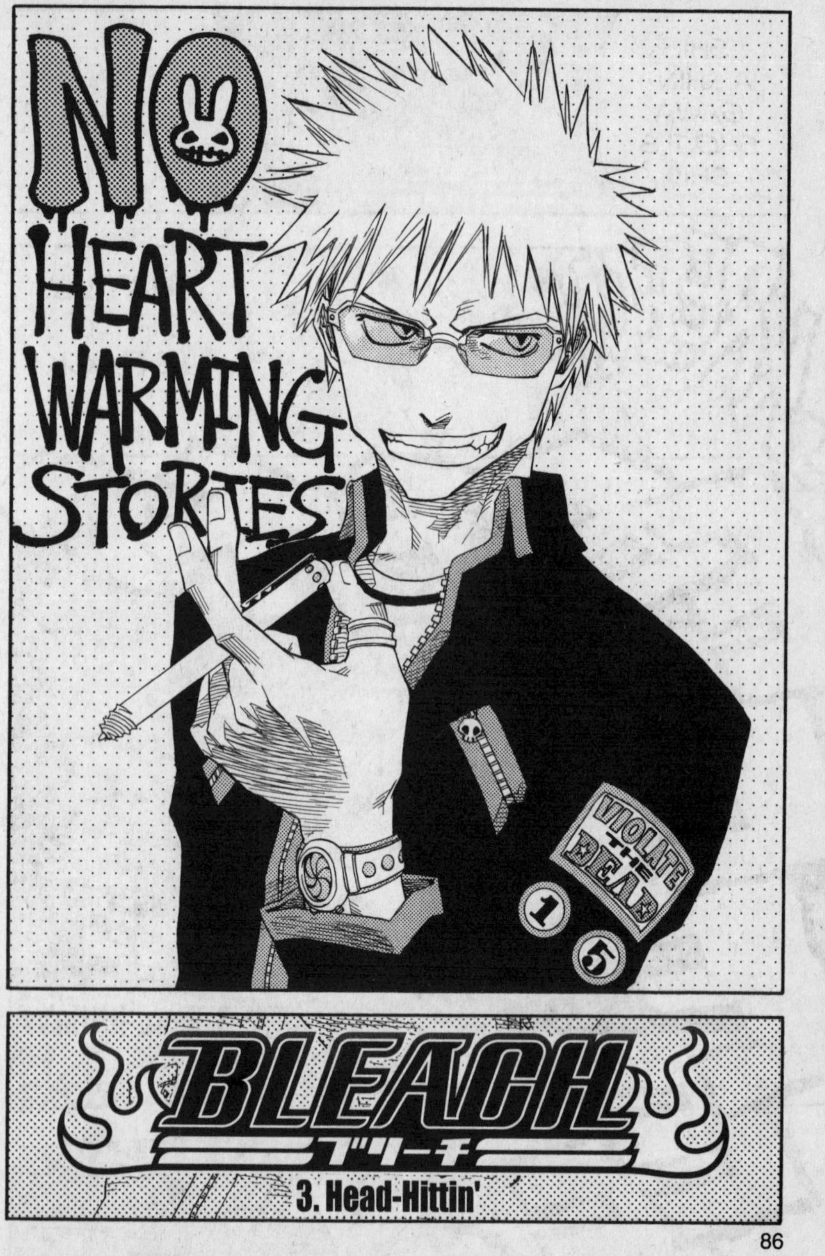
NO HEART WARMING STORIES
VIOLATE THE DEAD
1
5

BLEACH

ブリーチ

3. Head-Hittin'

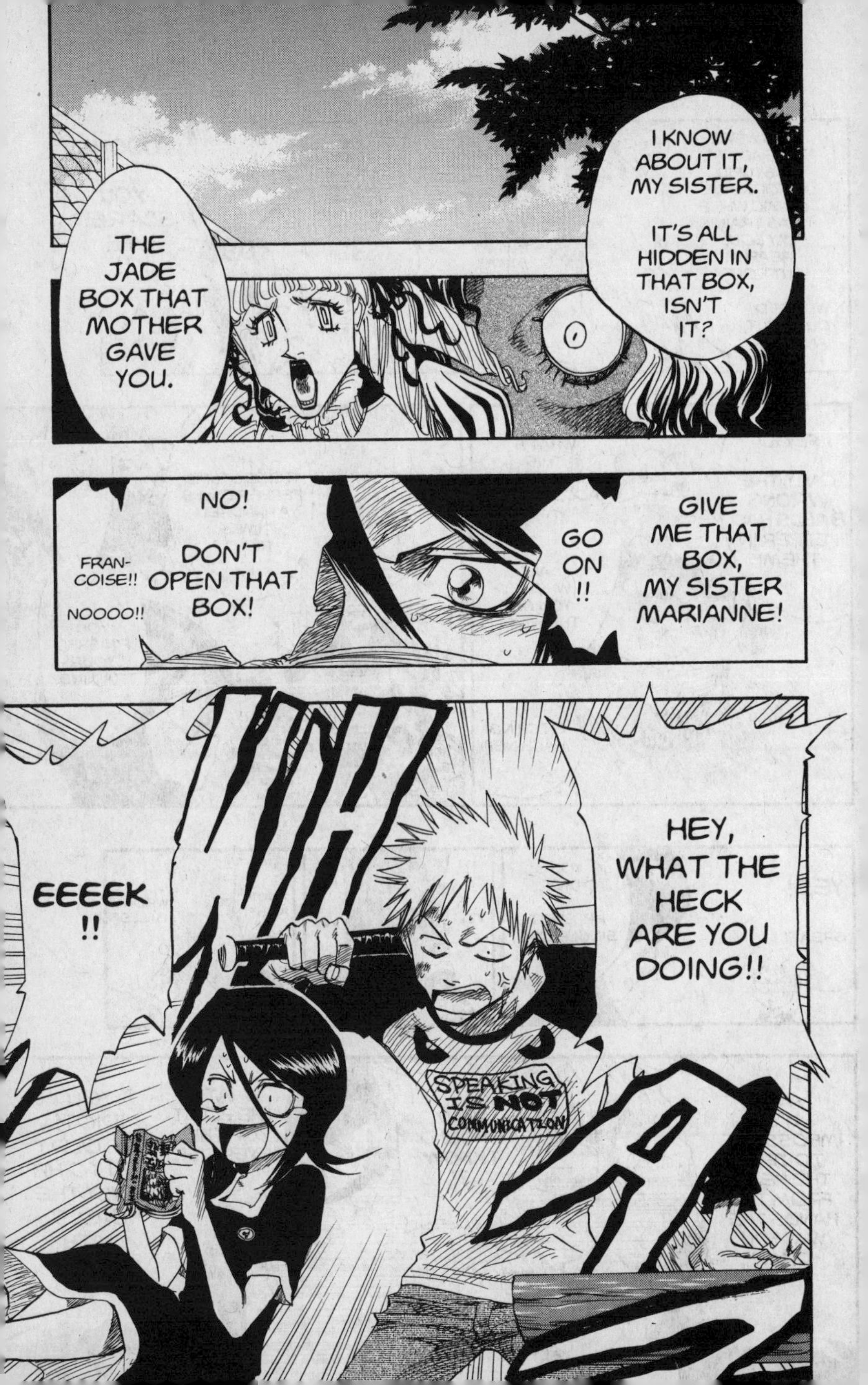
I KNOW ABOUT IT, MY SISTER.
IT'S ALL HIDDEN IN THAT BOX, ISN'T IT?
THE JADE BOX THAT MOTHER GAVE YOU.
GIVE ME THAT BOX, MY SISTER MARIANNE!
GO ON !!
NO!
DON'T OPEN THAT BOX!
FRAN-COISE!!
NOOOO!!
HEY, WHAT THE HECK ARE YOU DOING!!
EEEEK !!
SPEAKING IS NOT COMMUNICATION

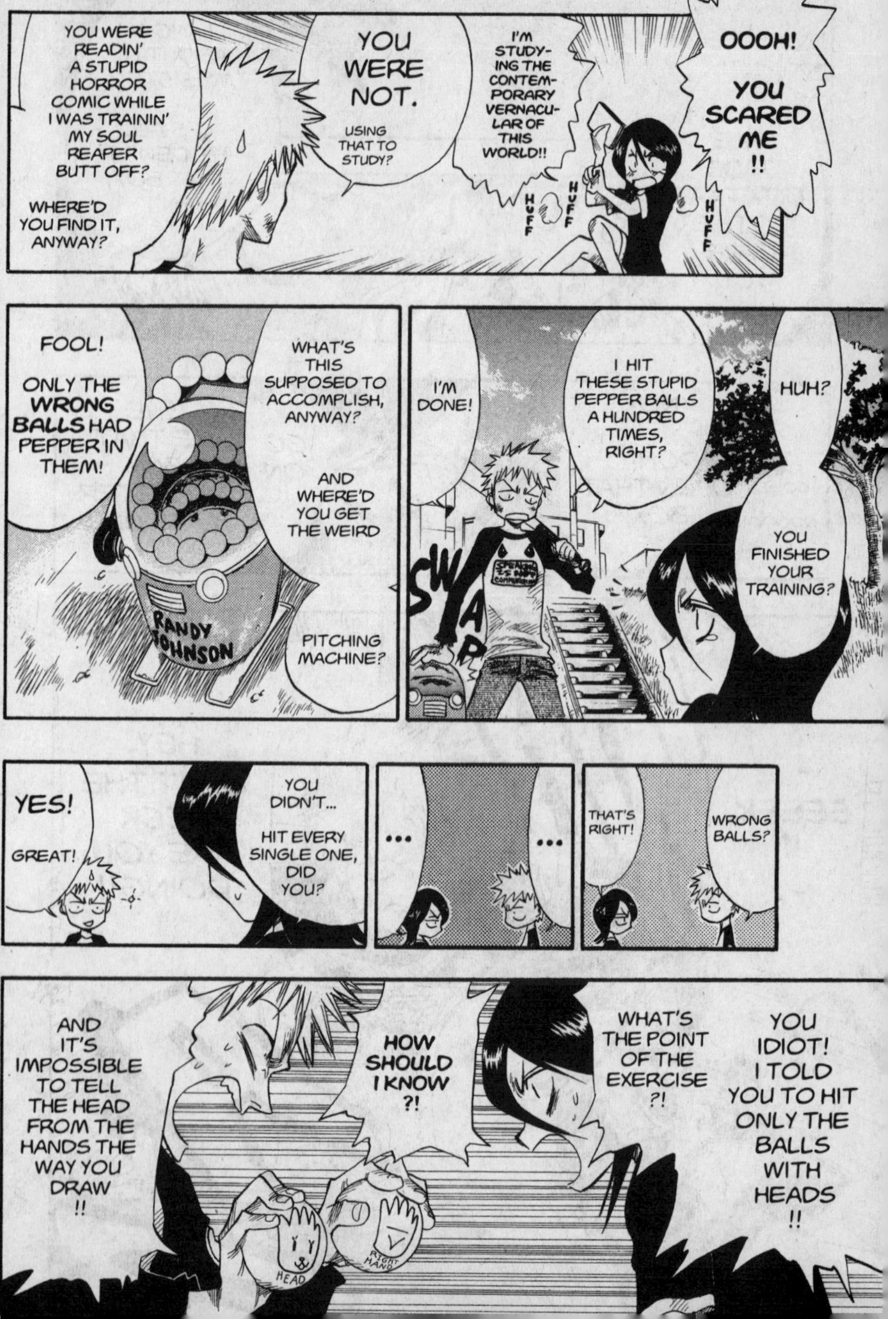
OOOH! YOU SCARED ME!!
HUFF HUFF HUFF
I'M STUDYING THE CONTEMPORARY VERNACULAR OF THIS WORLD!!
YOU WERE NOT.
USING THAT TO STUDY?
YOU WERE READIN' A STUPID HORROR COMIC WHILE I WAS TRAININ' MY SOUL REAPER BUTT OFF?
WHERE'D YOU FIND IT, ANYWAY?
HUH?
YOU FINISHED YOUR TRAINING?
I HIT THESE STUPID PEPPER BALLS A HUNDRED TIMES, RIGHT?
I'M DONE!
SWAP
WHAT'S THIS SUPPOSED TO ACCOMPLISH, ANYWAY?
AND WHERE'D YOU GET THE WEIRD
PITCHING MACHINE?
FOOL! ONLY THE WRONG BALLS HAD PEPPER IN THEM!
RANDY JOHNSON
WRONG BALLS?
THAT'S RIGHT!
...
...
YOU DIDN'T... HIT EVERY SINGLE ONE, DID YOU?
YES!
GREAT!
YOU IDIOT! I TOLD YOU TO HIT ONLY THE BALLS WITH HEADS!!
WHAT'S THE POINT OF THE EXERCISE?!
HOW SHOULD I KNOW?!
AND IT'S IMPOSSIBLE TO TELL THE HEAD FROM THE HANDS THE WAY YOU DRAW!!
RIGHT HAND
HEAD

READ THIS WAY

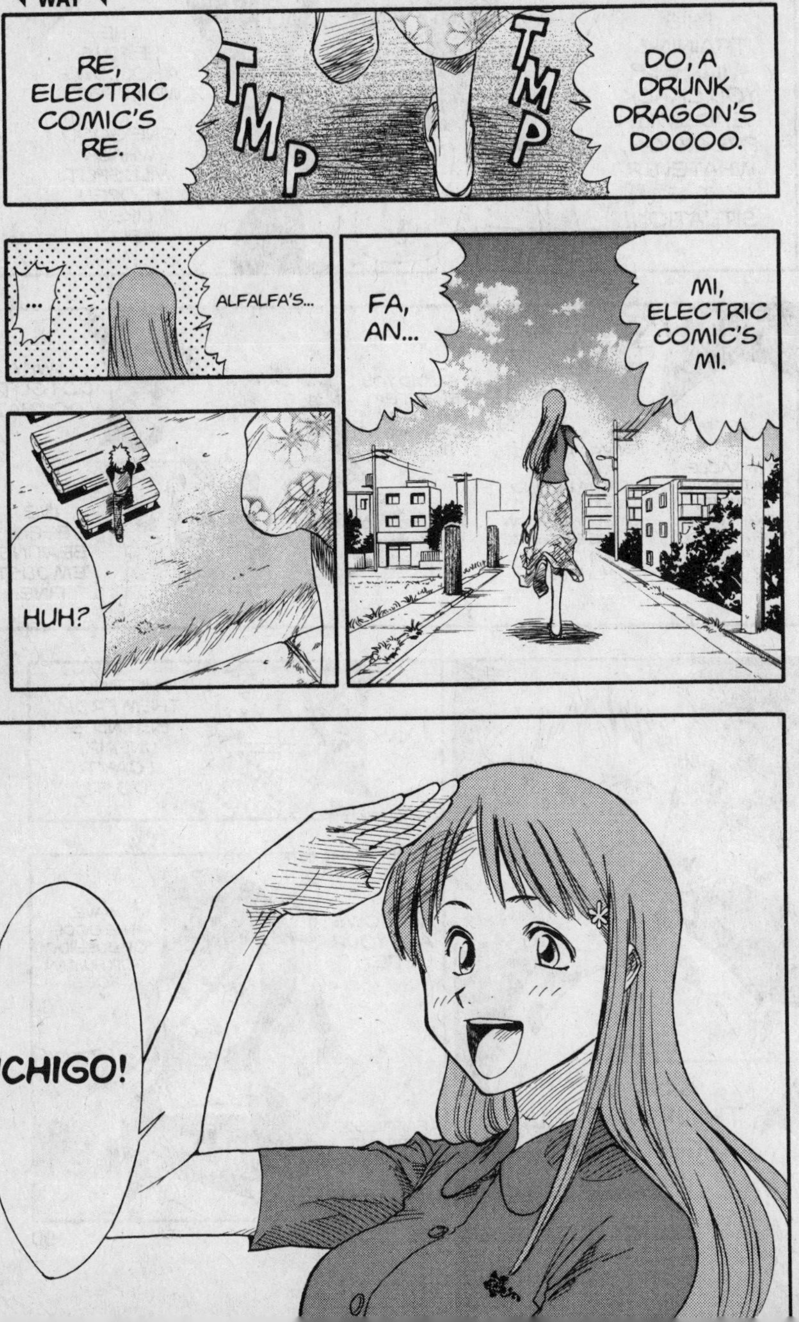
DO, A DRUNK DRAGON'S DOOOO.
TMP
TMP
RE, ELECTRIC COMIC'S RE.
MI, ELECTRIC COMIC'S MI.
FA, AN...
ALFALFA'S...
...
HUH?
ICHIGO!

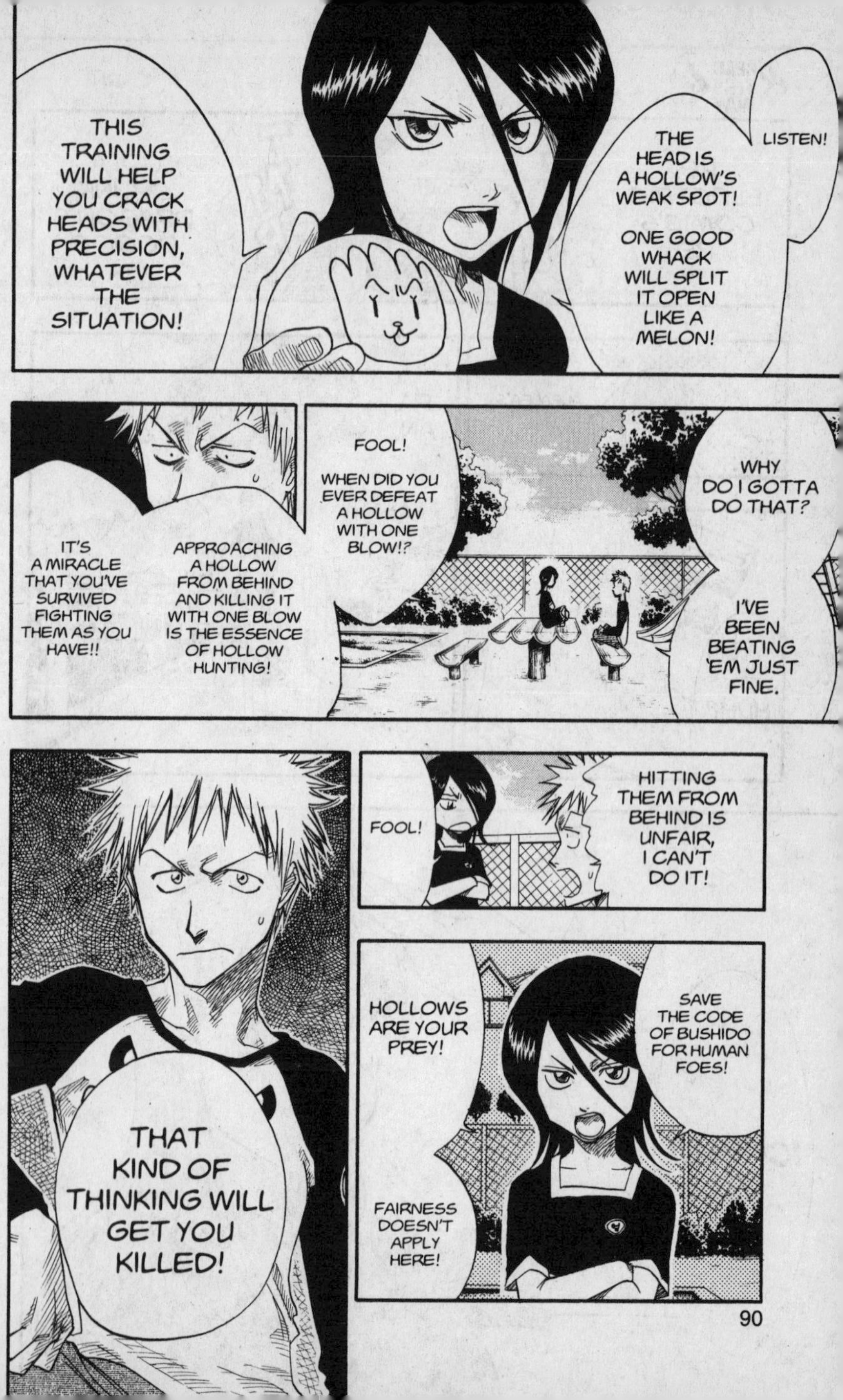

LISTEN!
THE HEAD IS A HOLLOW'S WEAK SPOT!
ONE GOOD WHACK WILL SPLIT IT OPEN LIKE A MELON!
THIS TRAINING WILL HELP YOU CRACK HEADS WITH PRECISION, WHATEVER THE SITUATION!
WHY DO I GOTTA DO THAT?
I'VE BEEN BEATING 'EM JUST FINE.
FOOL!
WHEN DID YOU EVER DEFEAT A HOLLOW WITH ONE BLOW!?
APPROACHING A HOLLOW FROM BEHIND AND KILLING IT WITH ONE BLOW IS THE ESSENCE OF HOLLOW HUNTING!
IT'S A MIRACLE THAT YOU'VE SURVIVED FIGHTING THEM AS YOU HAVE!!
HITTING THEM FROM BEHIND IS UNFAIR, I CAN'T DO IT!
FOOL!
SAVE THE CODE OF BUSHIDO FOR HUMAN FOES!
HOLLOWS ARE YOUR PREY!
FAIRNESS DOESN'T APPLY HERE!
THAT KIND OF THINKING WILL GET YOU KILLED!

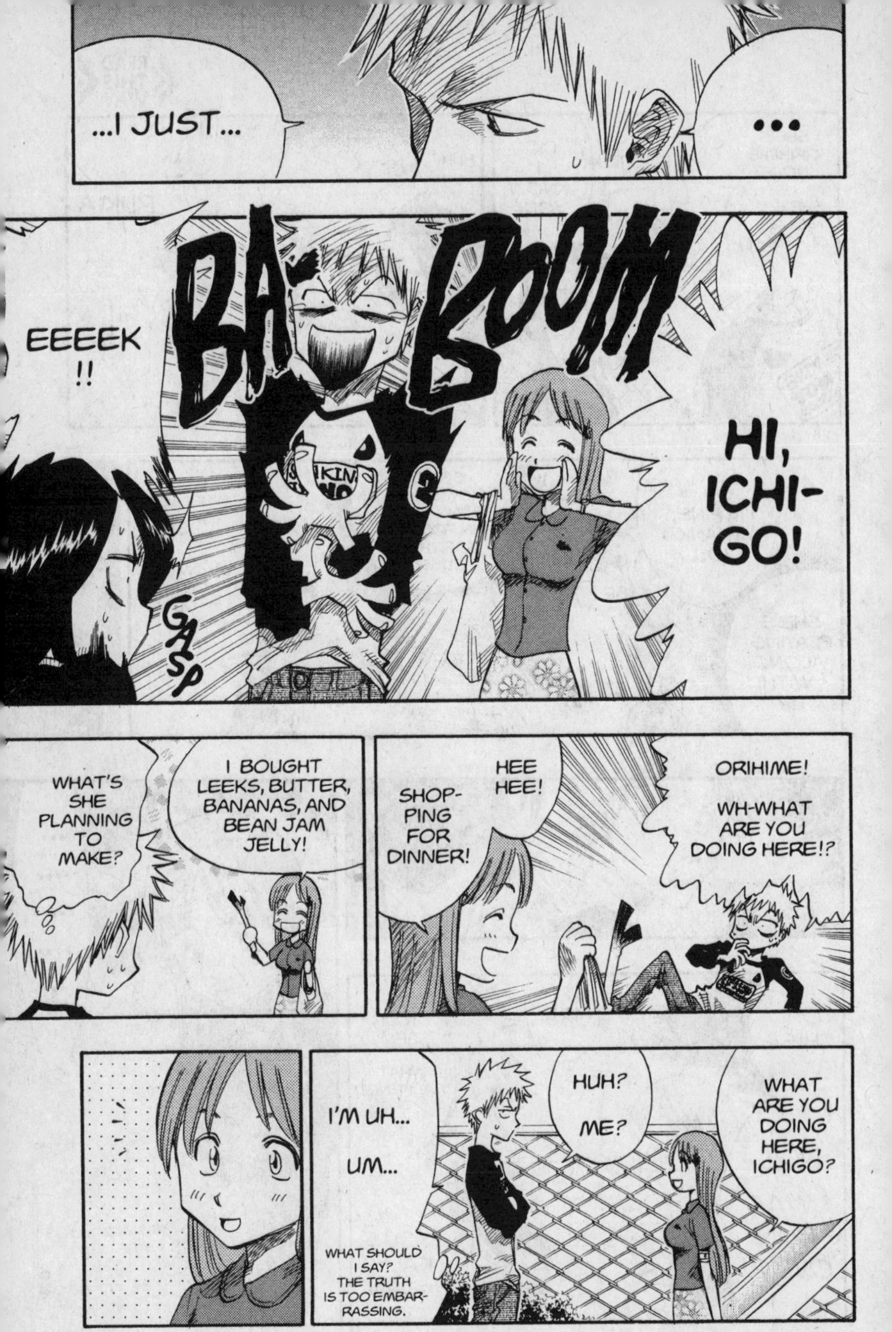
...
...I JUST...
BA-BOOM
HI, ICHI-GO!
EEEEK!!
GASP
ORIHIME!
WH-WHAT ARE YOU DOING HERE!?
HEE HEE!
SHOP-PING FOR DINNER!
I BOUGHT LEEKS, BUTTER, BANANAS, AND BEAN JAM JELLY!
WHAT'S SHE PLANNING TO MAKE?
WHAT ARE YOU DOING HERE, ICHIGO?
HUH?
ME?
I'M UH...
UM...
WHAT SHOULD I SAY? THE TRUTH IS TOO EMBAR-RASSING.

READ THIS WAY

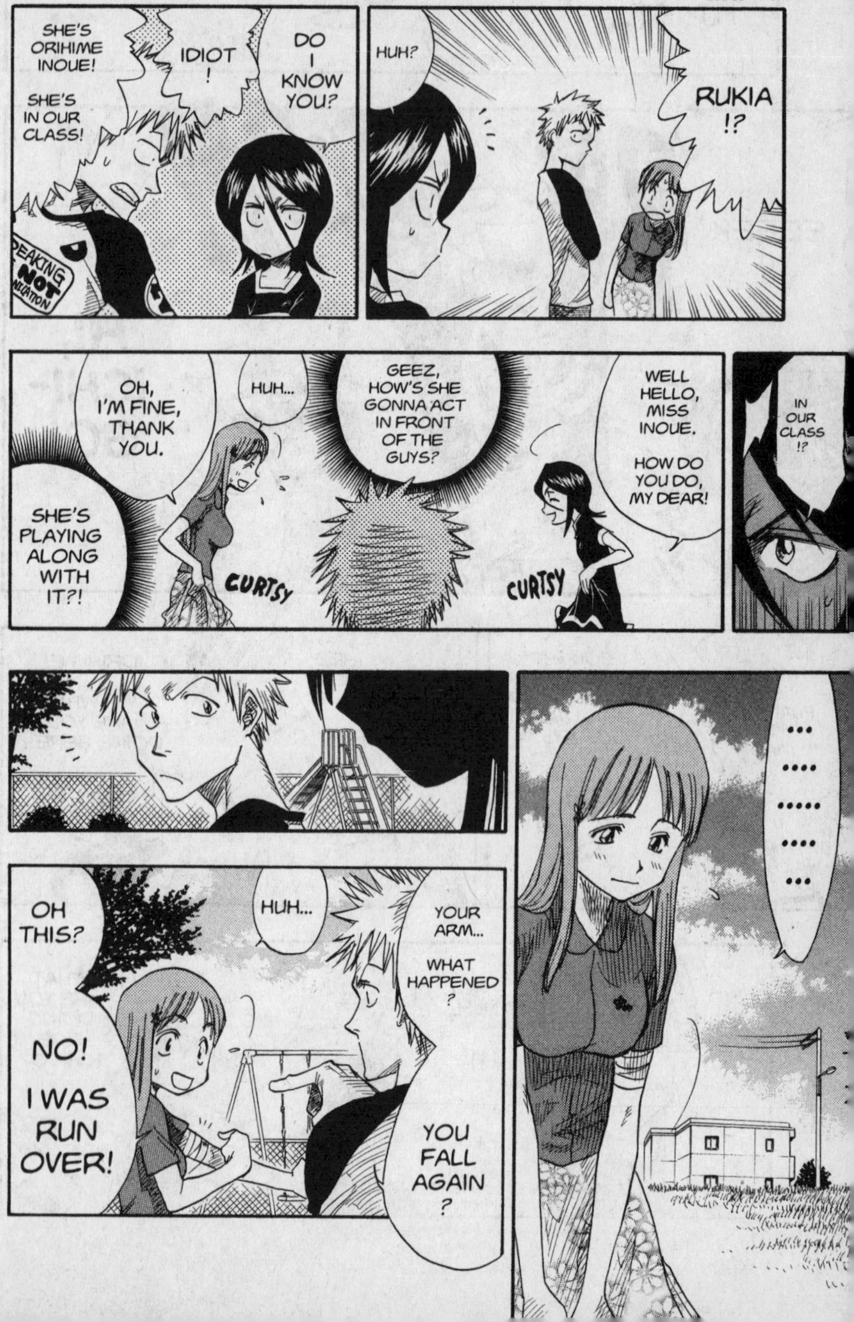
RUKIA !?
HUH?
DO I KNOW YOU?
IDIOT!
SHE'S ORIHIME INOUE!
SHE'S IN OUR CLASS!
IN OUR CLASS !?
WELL HELLO, MISS INOUE.
HOW DO YOU DO, MY DEAR!
CURTSY
GEEZ, HOW'S SHE GONNA ACT IN FRONT OF THE GUYS?
HUH...
OH, I'M FINE, THANK YOU.
CURTSY
SHE'S PLAYING ALONG WITH IT?!
... .
YOUR ARM...
WHAT HAPPENED ?
HUH...
OH THIS?
YOU FALL AGAIN ?
NO!
I WAS RUN OVER!

READ THIS WAY

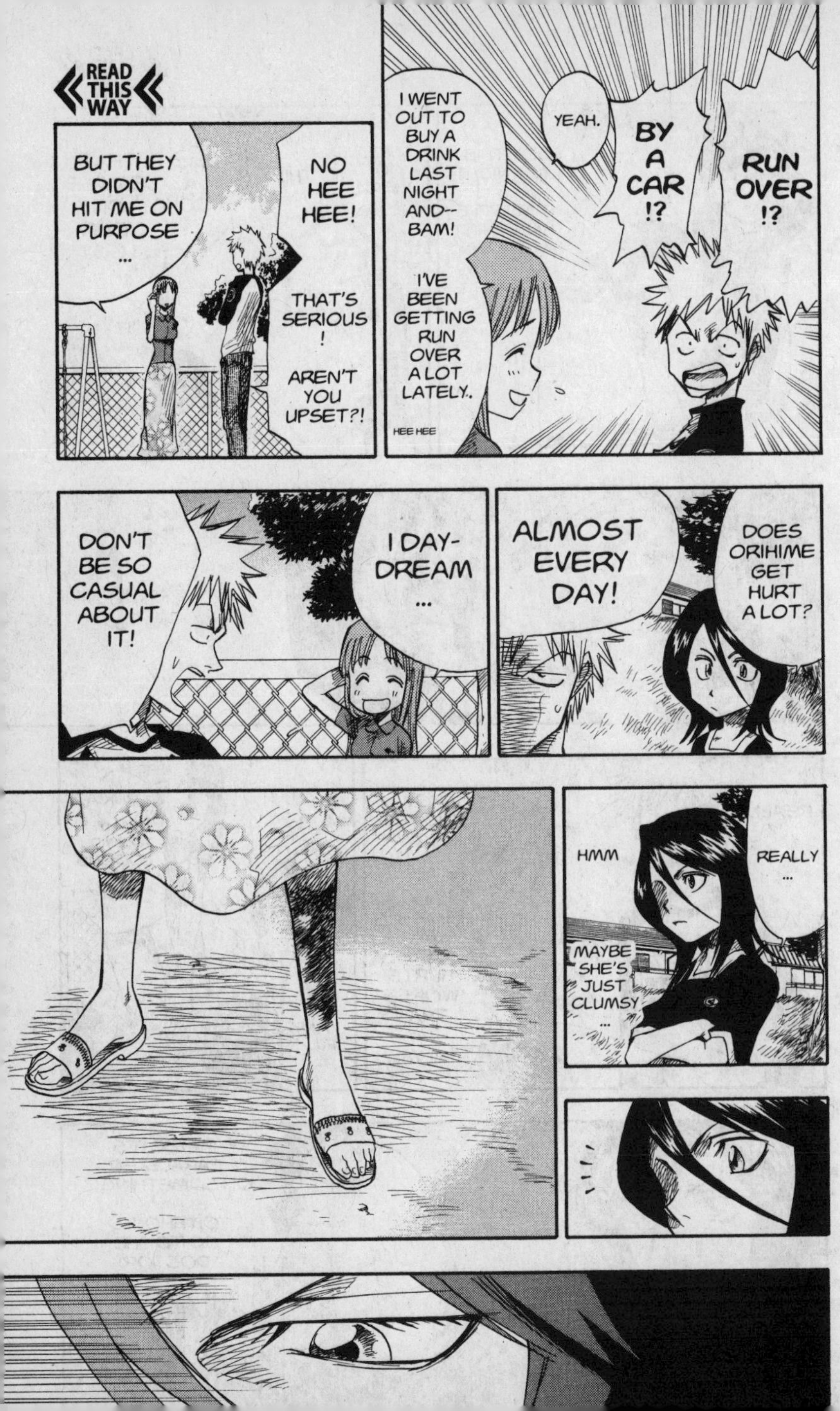
RUN OVER !?
BY A CAR !?
YEAH.
I WENT OUT TO BUY A DRINK LAST NIGHT AND-- BAM!
I'VE BEEN GETTING RUN OVER A LOT LATELY..
HEE HEE
NO HEE HEE!
THAT'S SERIOUS! AREN'T YOU UPSET?!
BUT THEY DIDN'T HIT ME ON PURPOSE ...
DOES ORIHIME GET HURT A LOT?
ALMOST EVERY DAY!
I DAY-DREAM ...
DON'T BE SO CASUAL ABOUT IT!
REALLY ...
HMM
MAYBE SHE'S JUST CLUMSY ...

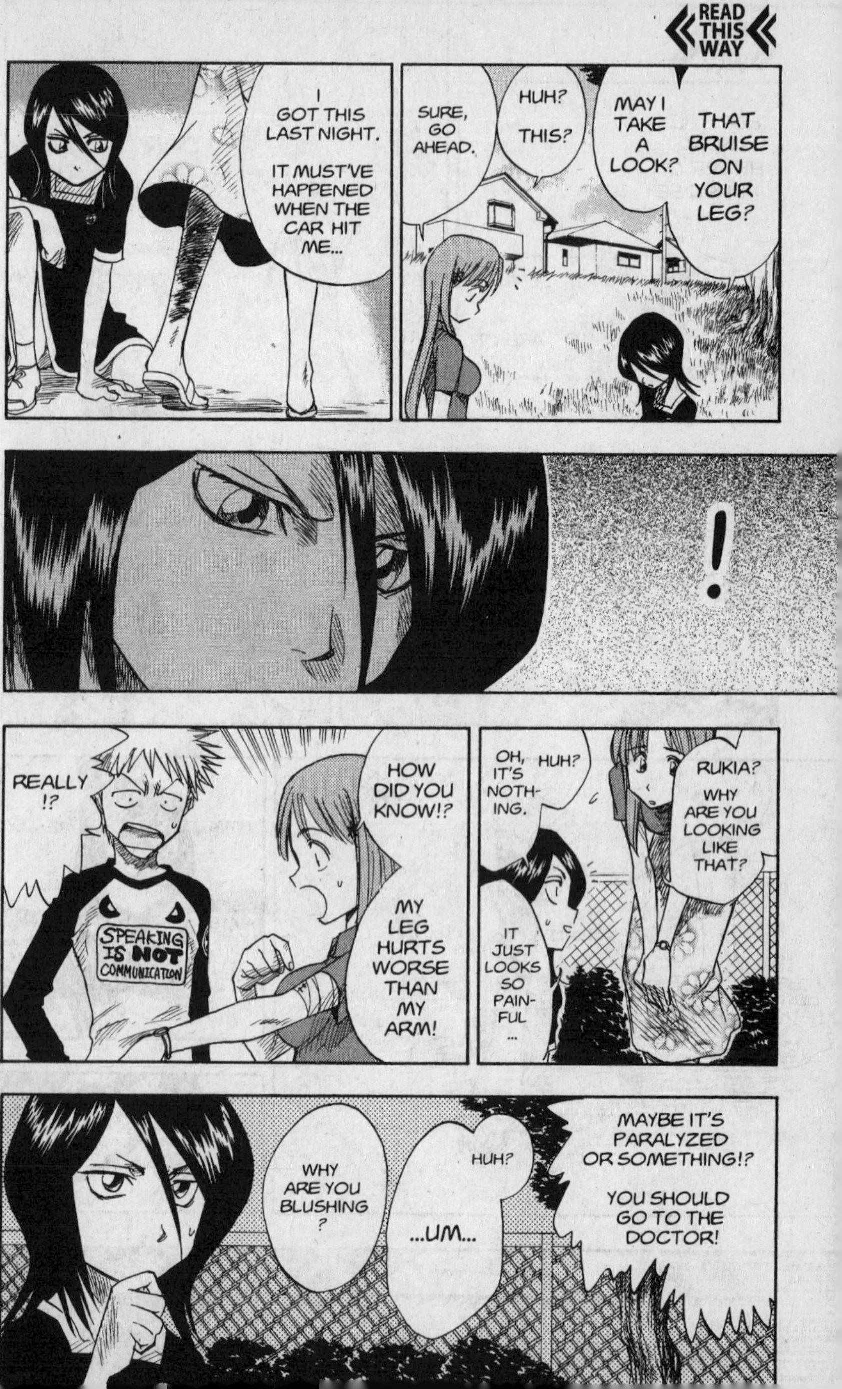
READ THIS WAY
THAT BRUISE ON YOUR LEG?
MAY I TAKE A LOOK?
HUH? THIS?
SURE, GO AHEAD.
I GOT THIS LAST NIGHT. IT MUST'VE HAPPENED WHEN THE CAR HIT ME...
!
RUKIA? WHY ARE YOU LOOKING LIKE THAT?
HUH?
OH, IT'S NOTHING.
IT JUST LOOKS SO PAINFUL...
HOW DID YOU KNOW!? MY LEG HURTS WORSE THAN MY ARM!
REALLY!?
SPEAKING IS NOT COMMUNICATION
MAYBE IT'S PARALYZED OR SOMETHING!? YOU SHOULD GO TO THE DOCTOR!
HUH?
...UM...
WHY ARE YOU BLUSHING?

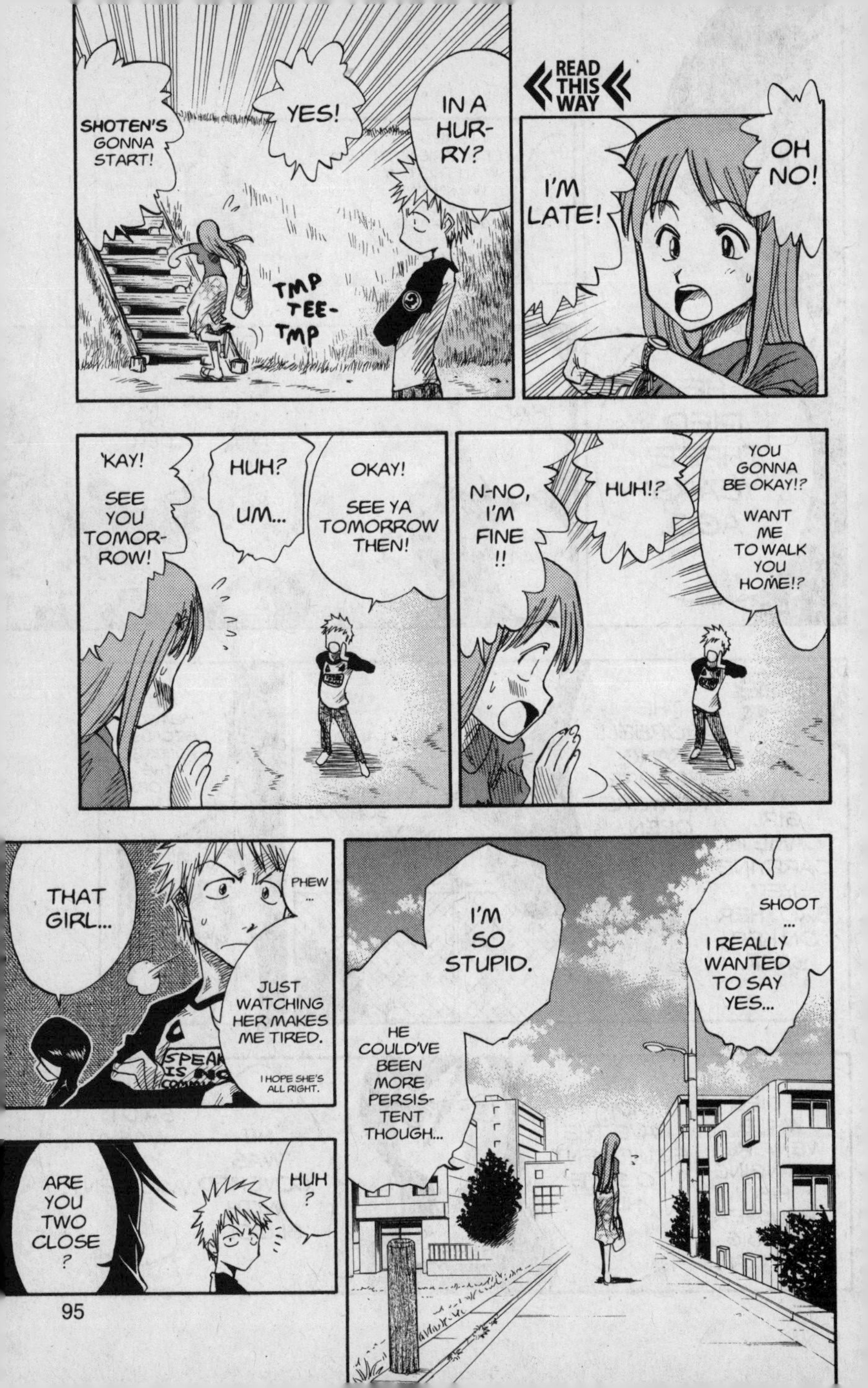
READ THIS WAY
OH NO!
I'M LATE!
IN A HUR-RY?
YES!
SHOTEN'S GONNA START!
TMP TEE-TMP
YOU GONNA BE OKAY!? WANT ME TO WALK YOU HOME!?
HUH!?
N-NO, I'M FINE!!
OKAY! SEE YA TOMORROW THEN!
HUH? UM...
'KAY! SEE YOU TOMOR-ROW!
SHOOT... I REALLY WANTED TO SAY YES...
I'M SO STUPID.
HE COULD'VE BEEN MORE PERSIS-TENT THOUGH...
PHEW...
JUST WATCHING HER MAKES ME TIRED.
I HOPE SHE'S ALL RIGHT.
THAT GIRL...
HUH?
ARE YOU TWO CLOSE?

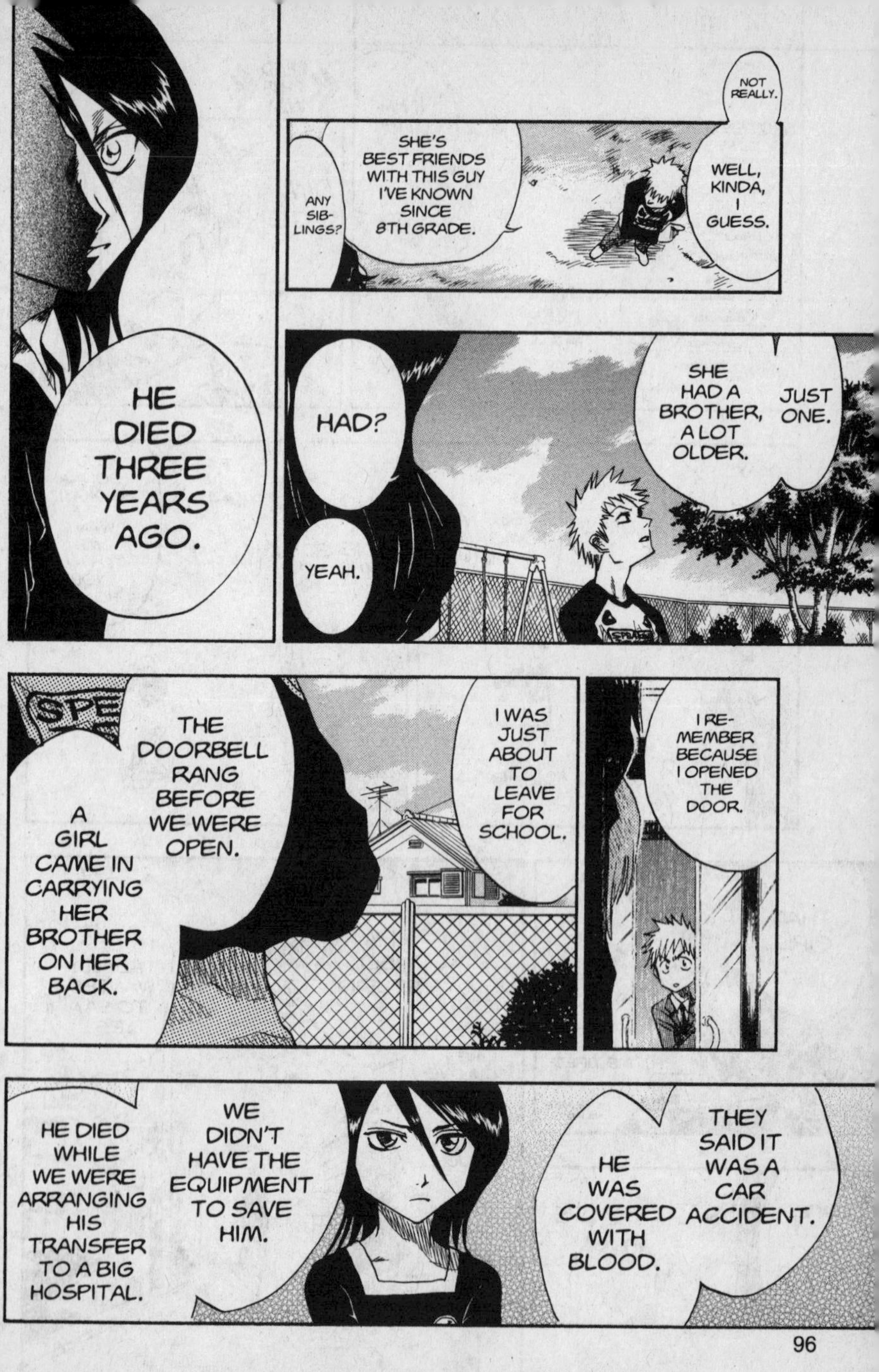
NOT REALLY.
WELL, KINDA, I GUESS.
SHE'S BEST FRIENDS WITH THIS GUY I'VE KNOWN SINCE 8TH GRADE.
ANY SIB-LINGS?
JUST ONE.
SHE HAD A BROTHER, A LOT OLDER.
HAD?
YEAH.
HE DIED THREE YEARS AGO.
I RE-MEMBER BECAUSE I OPENED THE DOOR.
I WAS JUST ABOUT TO LEAVE FOR SCHOOL.
THE DOORBELL RANG BEFORE WE WERE OPEN.
A GIRL CAME IN CARRYING HER BROTHER ON HER BACK.
THEY SAID IT WAS A CAR ACCIDENT.
HE WAS COVERED WITH BLOOD.
WE DIDN'T HAVE THE EQUIPMENT TO SAVE HIM.
HE DIED WHILE WE WERE ARRANGING HIS TRANSFER TO A BIG HOSPITAL.

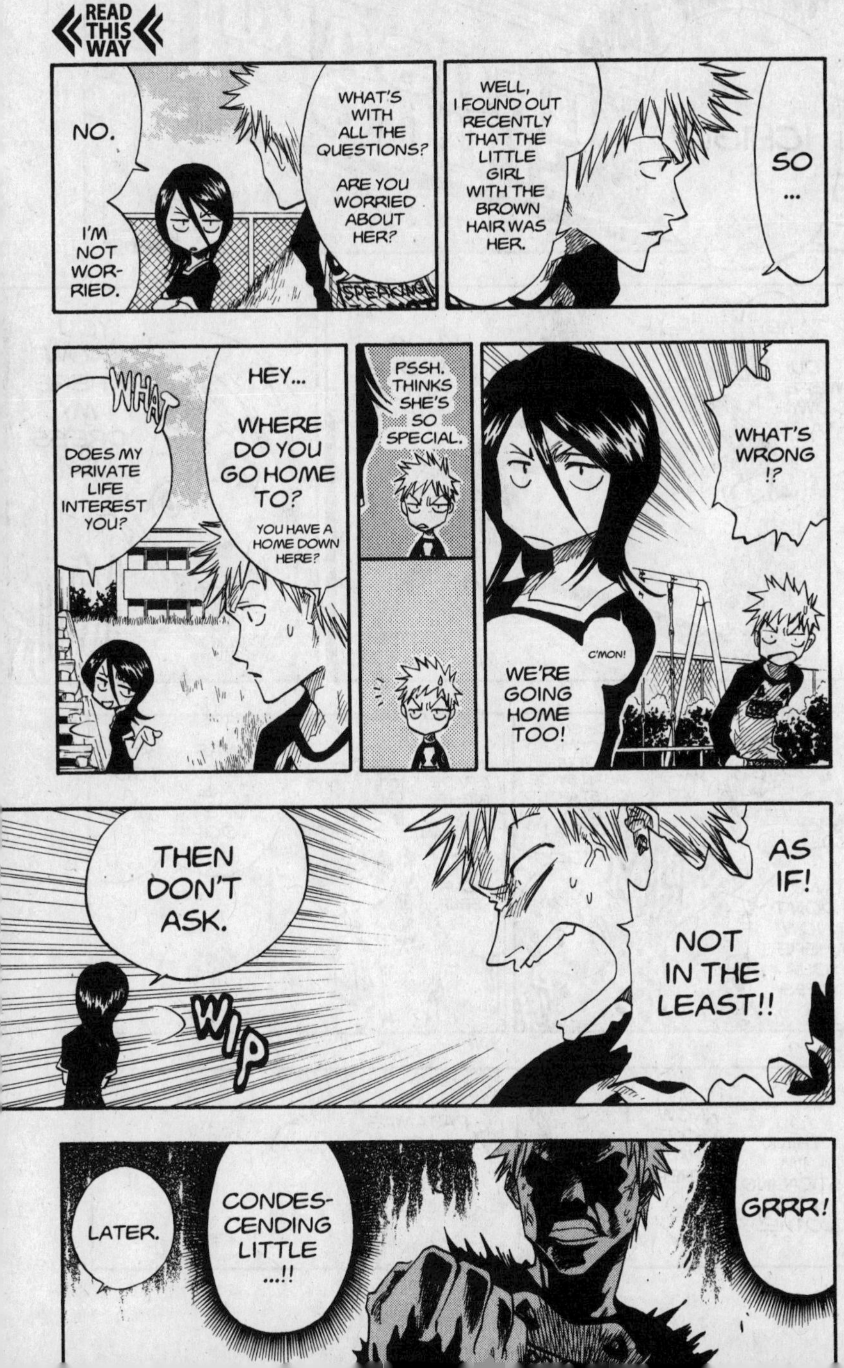
READ THIS WAY
SO ...
WELL, I FOUND OUT RECENTLY THAT THE LITTLE GIRL WITH THE BROWN HAIR WAS HER.
WHAT'S WITH ALL THE QUESTIONS?
ARE YOU WORRIED ABOUT HER?
SPEAKING
NO.
I'M NOT WORRIED.
WHAT'S WRONG !?
C'MON!
WE'RE GOING HOME TOO!
PSSH. THINKS SHE'S SO SPECIAL.
HEY...
WHERE DO YOU GO HOME TO?
YOU HAVE A HOME DOWN HERE?
WHAT DOES MY PRIVATE LIFE INTEREST YOU?
AS IF!
NOT IN THE LEAST!!
THEN DON'T ASK.
WIP
GRRR!
CONDESCENDING LITTLE ...!!
LATER.

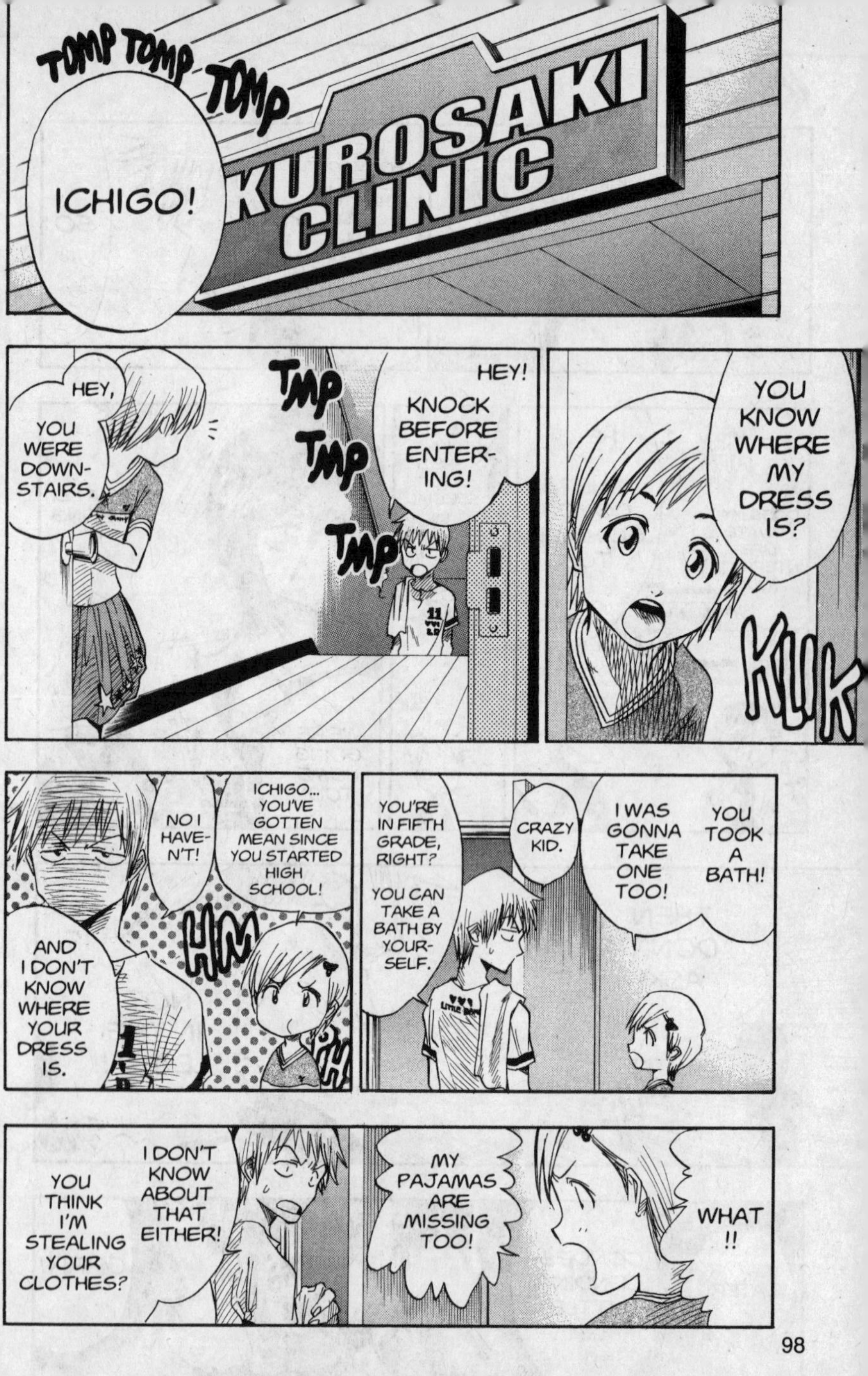
TOMP TOMP TOMP TOMP
ICHIGO!
KUROSAKI CLINIC
YOU KNOW WHERE MY DRESS IS?
KLIK
HEY! KNOCK BEFORE ENTERING!
TMP TMP TMP
HEY, YOU WERE DOWNSTAIRS.
YOU TOOK A BATH!
I WAS GONNA TAKE ONE TOO!
CRAZY KID.
YOU'RE IN FIFTH GRADE, RIGHT? YOU CAN TAKE A BATH BY YOURSELF.
ICHIGO... YOU'VE GOTTEN MEAN SINCE YOU STARTED HIGH SCHOOL!
NO I HAVEN'T!
HM
AND I DON'T KNOW WHERE YOUR DRESS IS.
WHAT!!
MY PAJAMAS ARE MISSING TOO!
I DON'T KNOW ABOUT THAT EITHER!
YOU THINK I'M STEALING YOUR CLOTHES?

READ THIS WAY

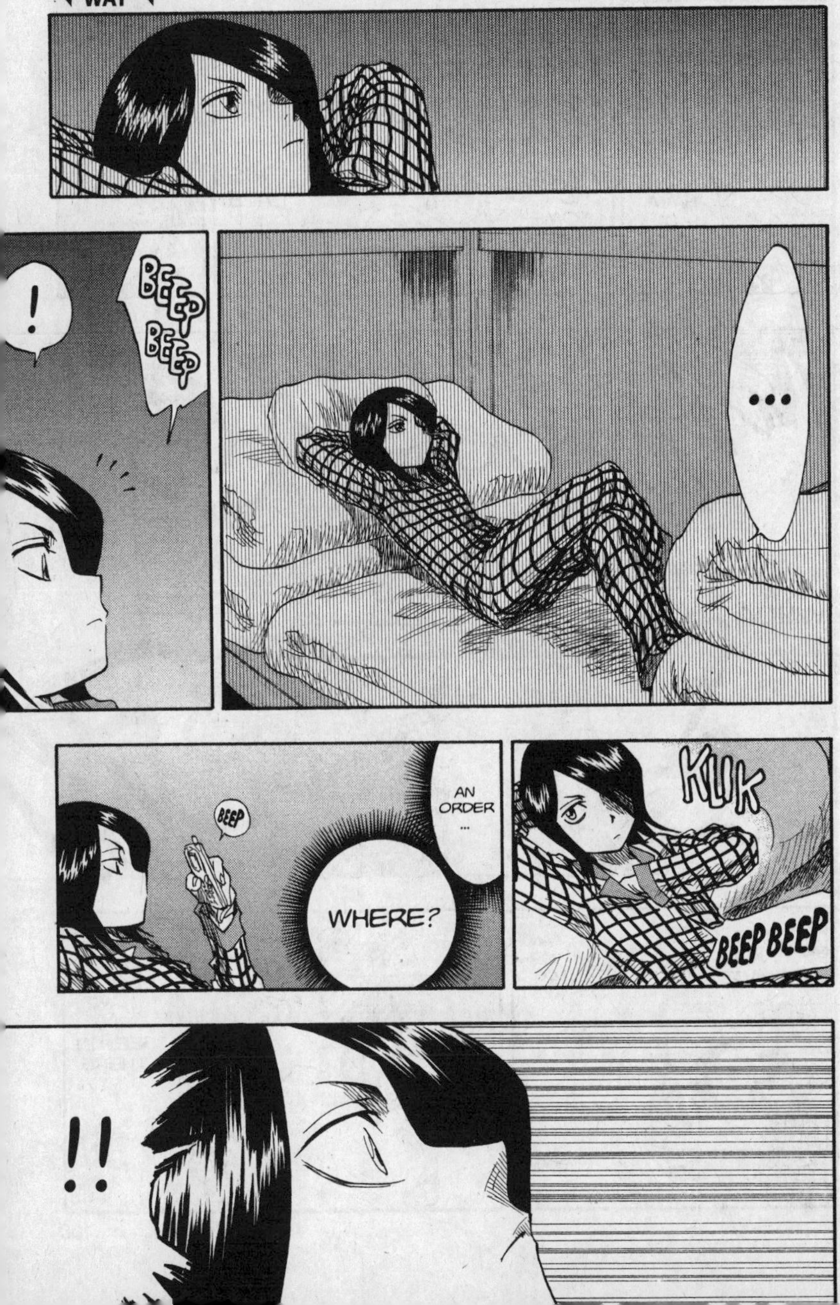
...
BEEP BEEP
!
KLIK
BEEP BEEP
AN ORDER ...
BEEP
WHERE?
!!

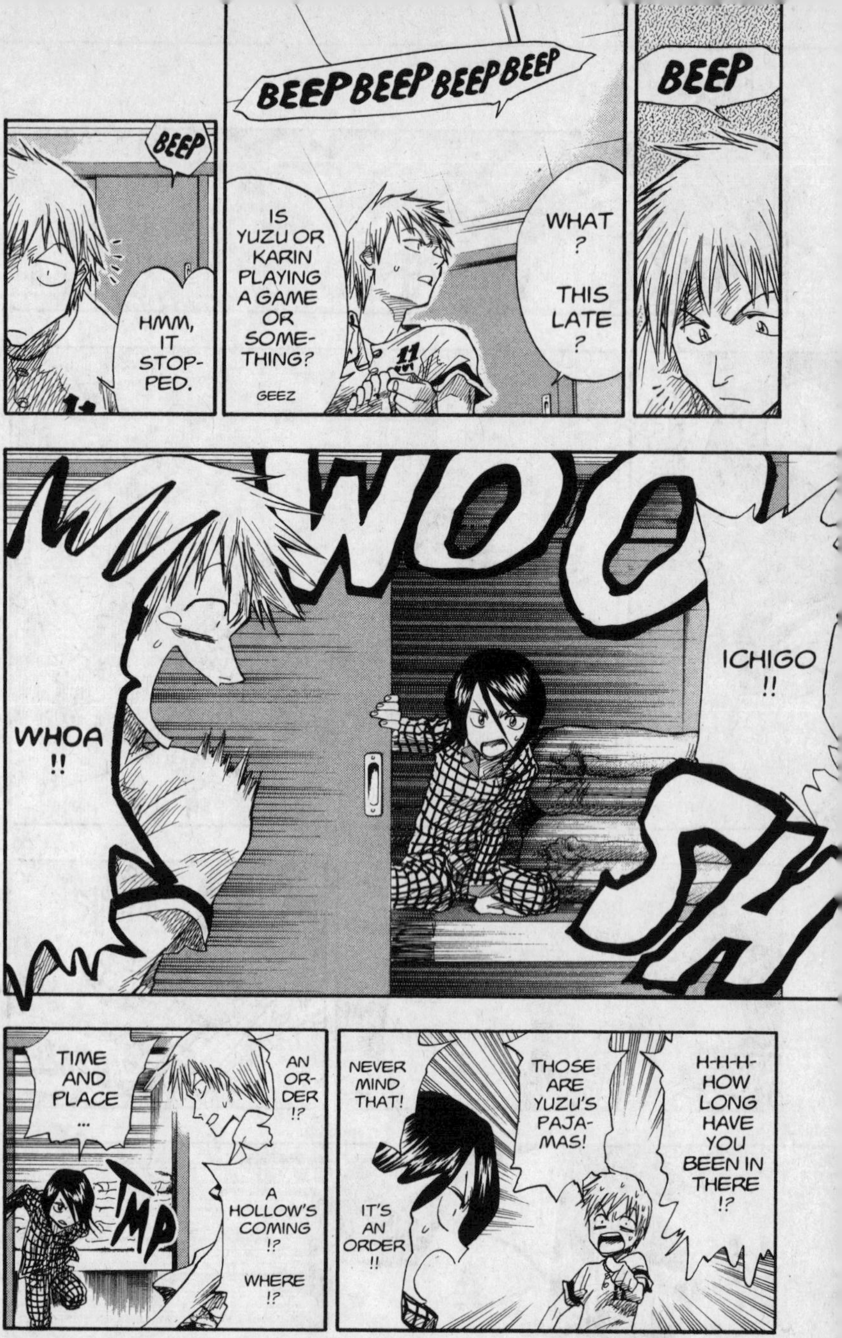
BEEP
BEEP BEEP BEEP BEEP
WHAT? THIS LATE?
IS YUZU OR KARIN PLAYING A GAME OR SOMETHING?
GEEZ
BEEP
HMM, IT STOPPED.
WOOSH
ICHIGO!!
WHOA!!
H-H-H-HOW LONG HAVE YOU BEEN IN THERE!?
THOSE ARE YUZU'S PAJAMAS!
NEVER MIND THAT!
IT'S AN ORDER!!
AN ORDER!?
A HOLLOW'S COMING!?
WHERE!?
TIME AND PLACE...
TMP

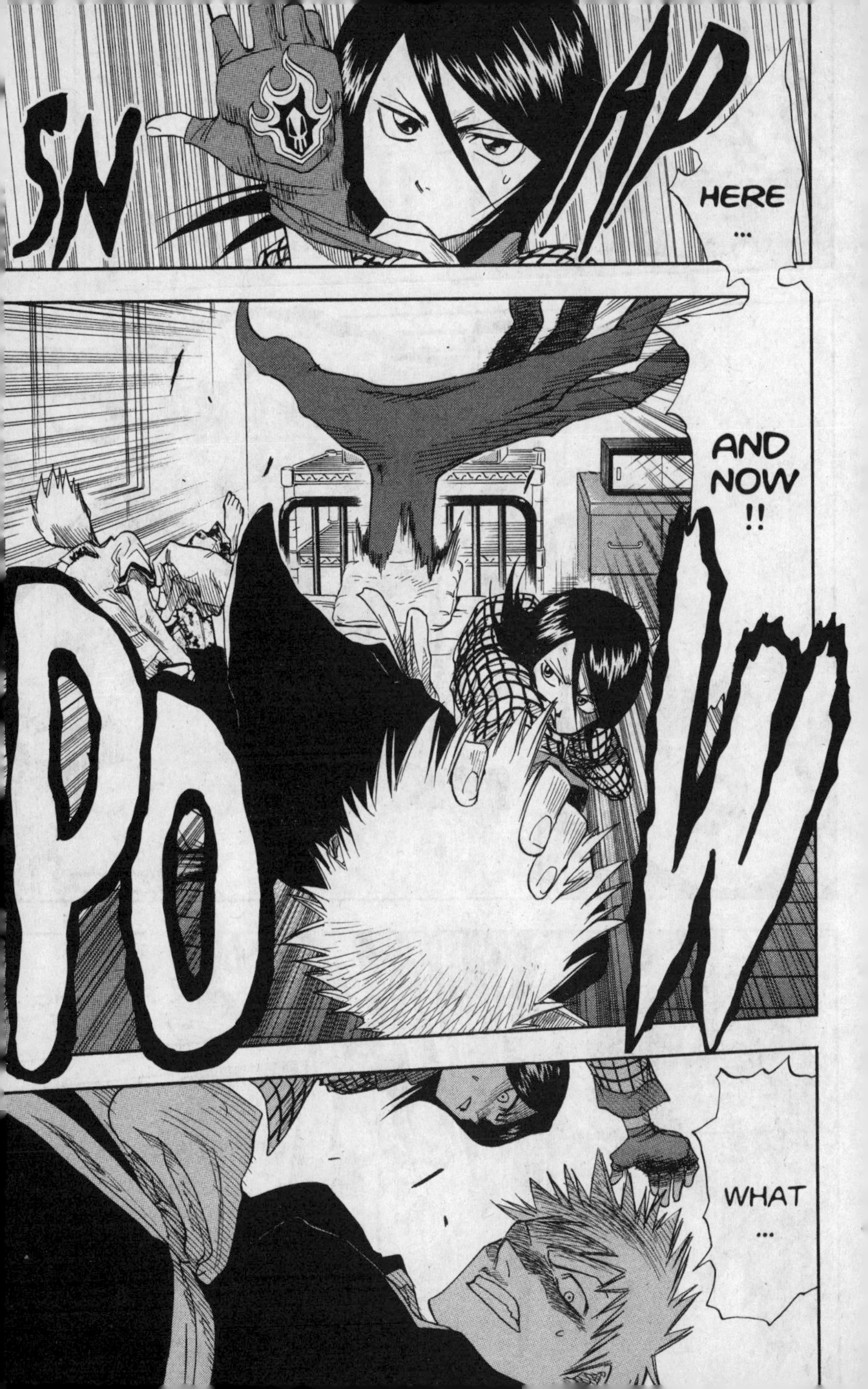
SNAP
HERE ...
AND NOW !!
POW
WHAT ...

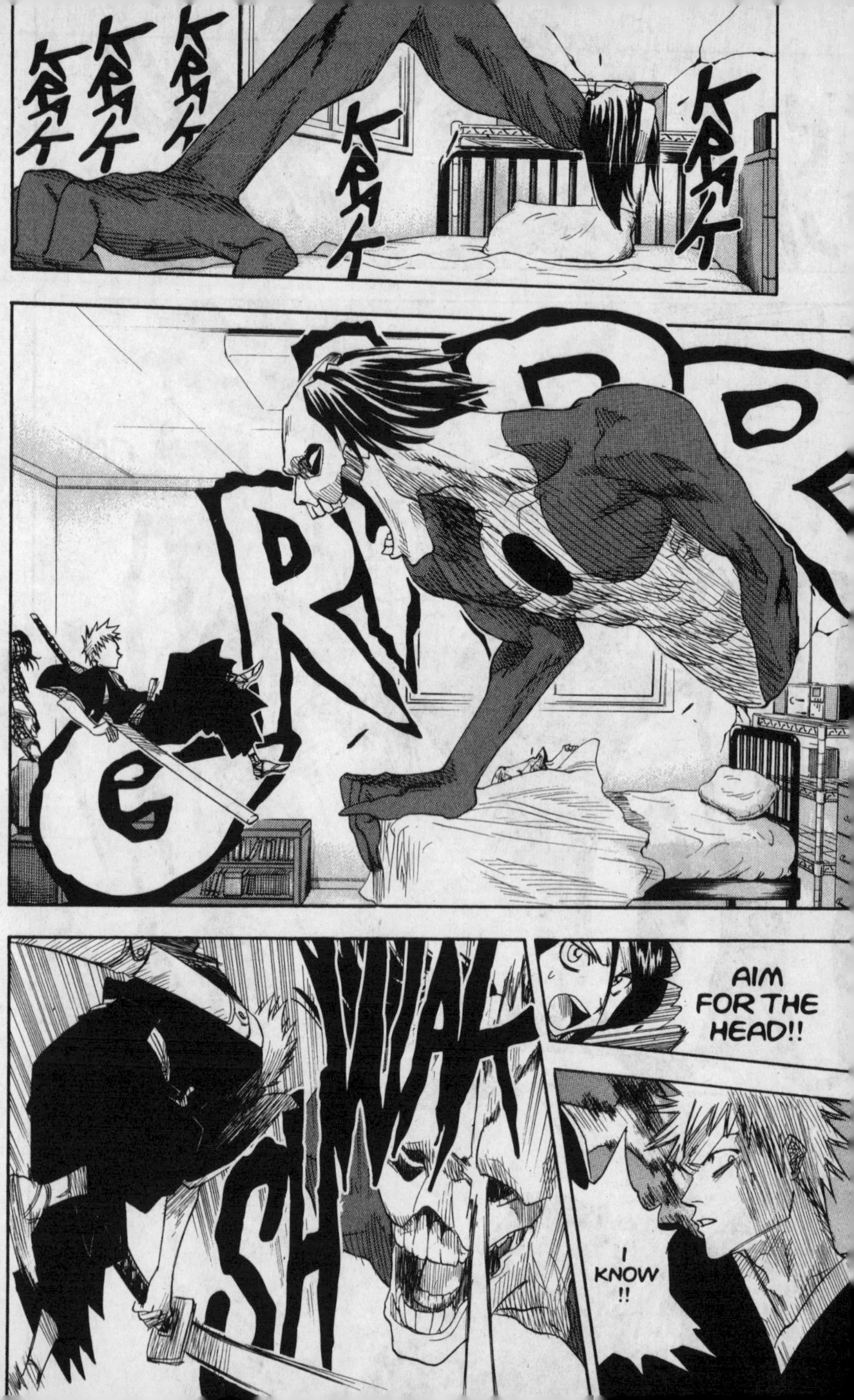

KRAK
KRAK
KRAK
KRAK
KRAK
AIM FOR THE HEAD!!
I KNOW!!

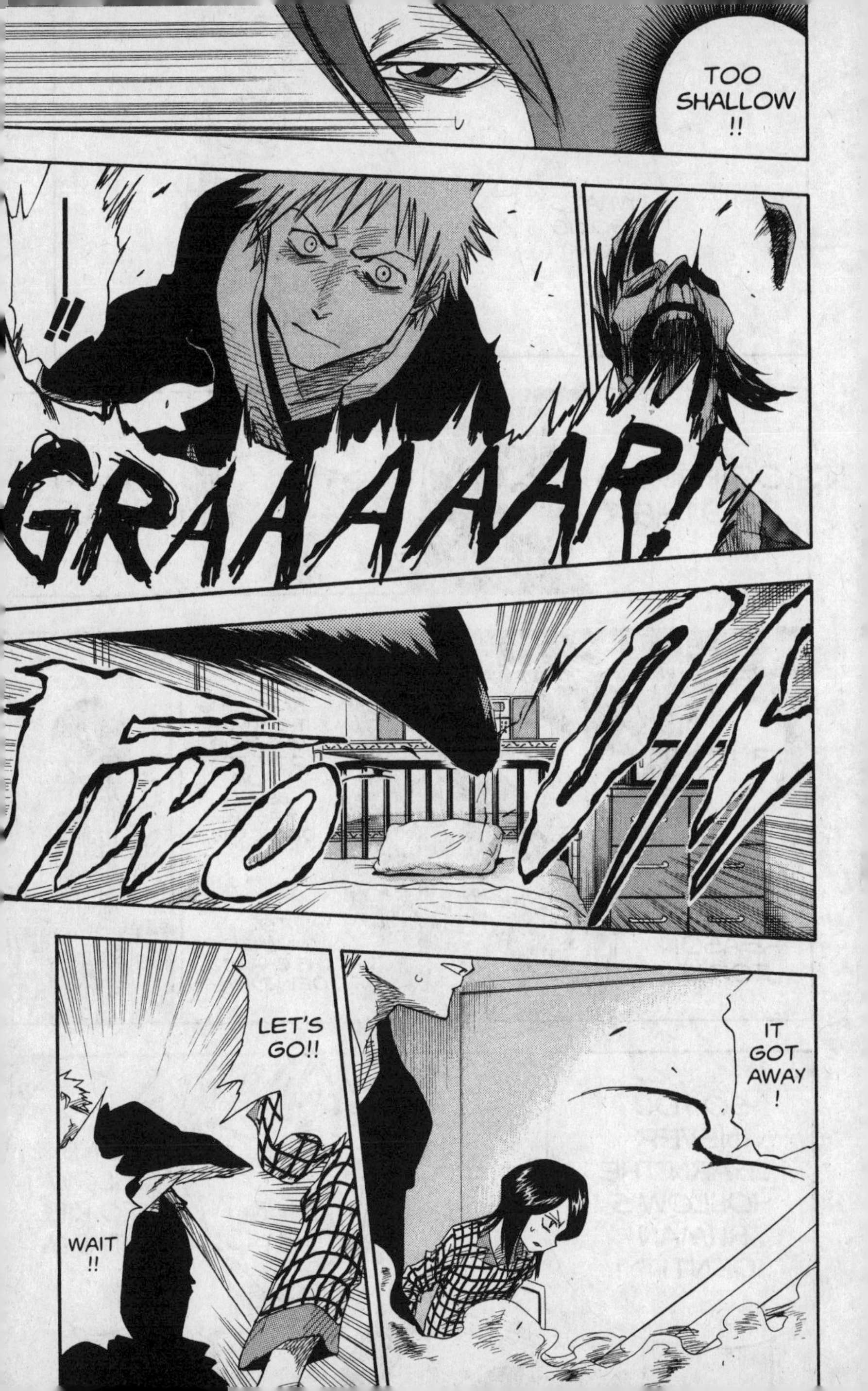
TOO SHALLOW !!
!!
GRAAAAR!
WOOM
IT GOT AWAY!
LET'S GO!!
WAIT !!

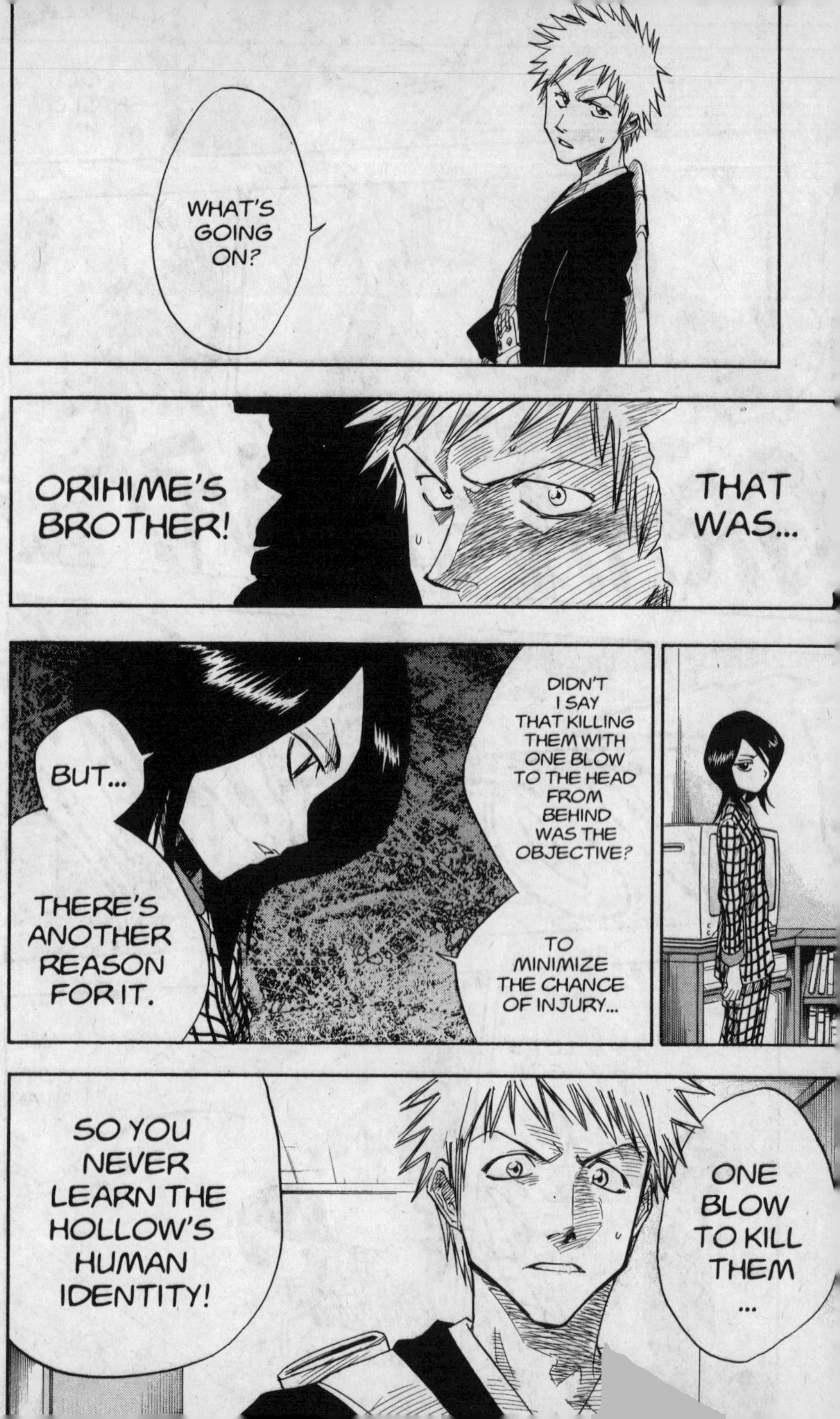
WHAT'S GOING ON?
THAT WAS...
ORIHIME'S BROTHER!
DIDN'T I SAY THAT KILLING THEM WITH ONE BLOW TO THE HEAD FROM BEHIND WAS THE OBJECTIVE?
TO MINIMIZE THE CHANCE OF INJURY...
BUT...
THERE'S ANOTHER REASON FOR IT.
ONE BLOW TO KILL THEM ...
SO YOU NEVER LEARN THE HOLLOW'S HUMAN IDENTITY!

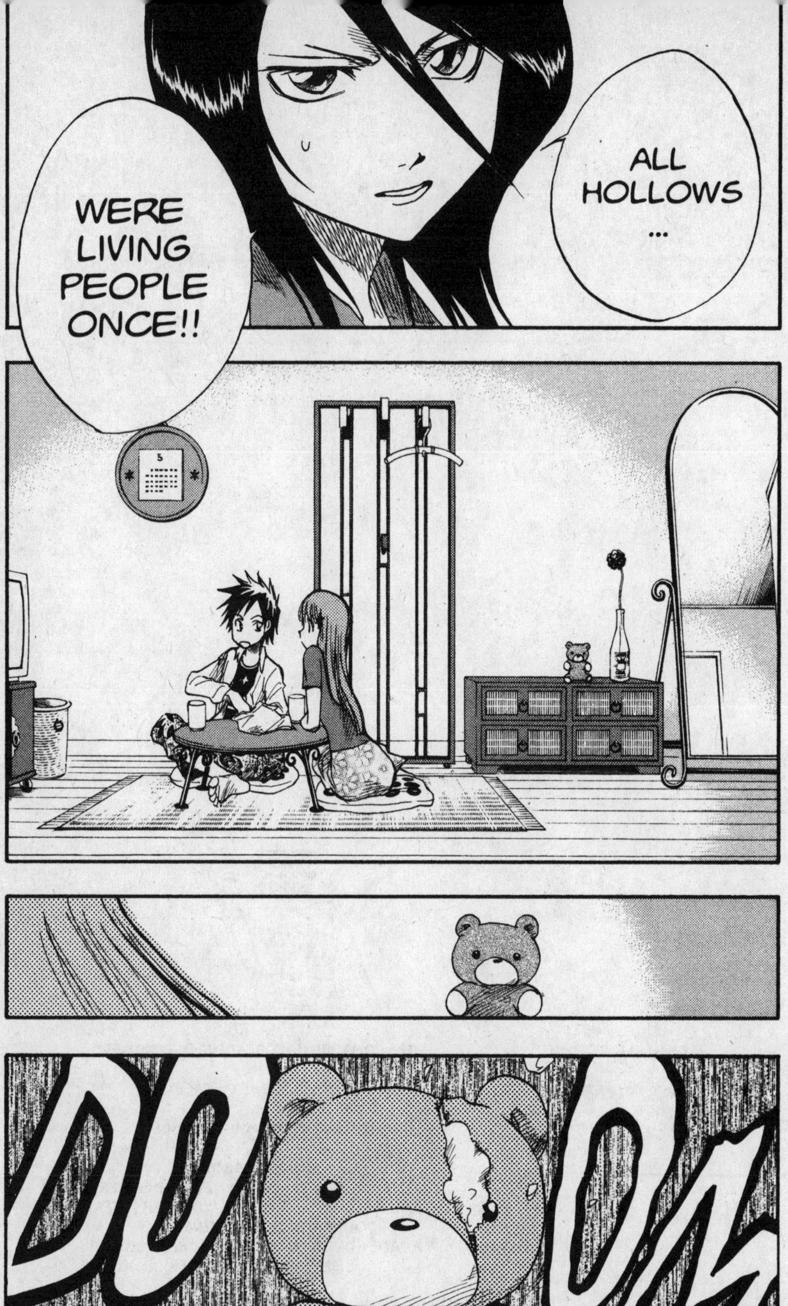
ALL HOLLOWS ...
WERE LIVING PEOPLE ONCE!!
DOOM

SMALL ITEMS SERIES 1

THE COMIC RUKIA IS READING IN EPISODE 3.

"THE JADE HERMITAGE"

WRITTEN BY: MARIE HATSUE

A STORY ABOUT
SOFT-MASOCHIST MARIANNE (OLDER SISTER)
AND HARD-GAY FRANCOISE (YOUNGER SISTER)
DOING ALL SORTS OF THINGS OVER
A JADE BOX GIVEN TO THEM BY THEIR MOTHER
(52-YEAR-OLD-WRESTLER).

SUPER SCARY STUFF

4. WHY DO YOU EAT IT?

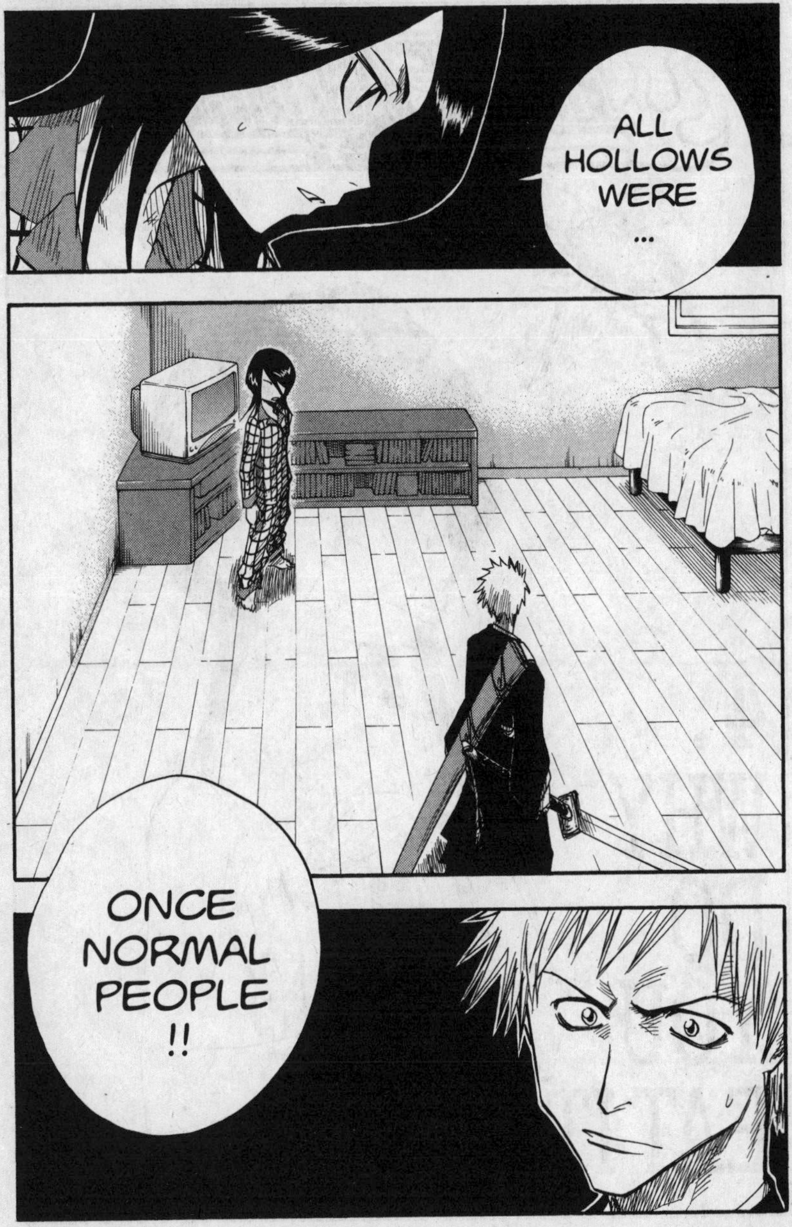
ALL HOLLOWS WERE ...
ONCE NORMAL PEOPLE !!

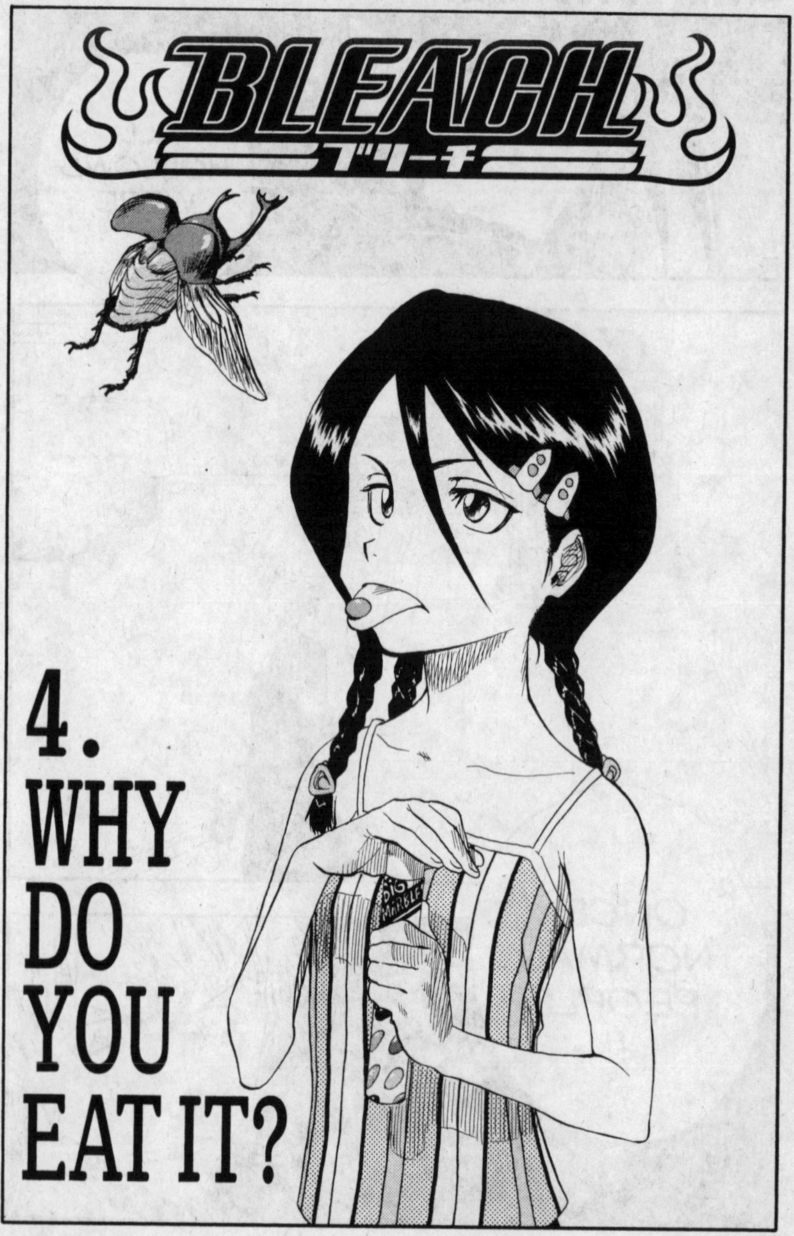
BLEACH
ブリーチ
4. WHY DO YOU EAT IT?
BIG MARBLE

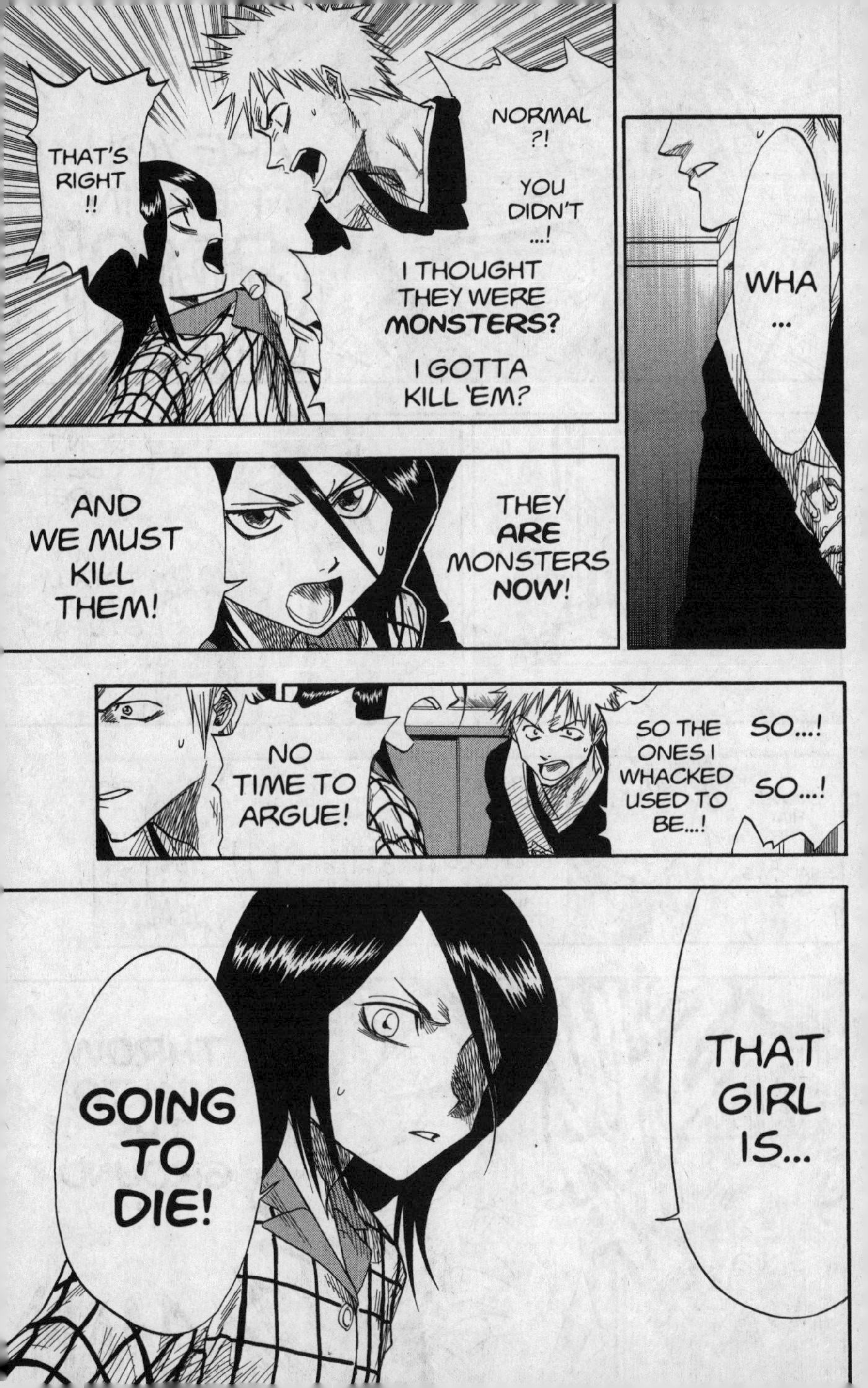
WHA ...
NORMAL ?!
YOU DIDN'T ...!
I THOUGHT THEY WERE MONSTERS?
I GOTTA KILL 'EM?
THAT'S RIGHT !!
THEY ARE MONSTERS NOW!
AND WE MUST KILL THEM!
SO...!
SO...!
SO THE ONES I WHACKED USED TO BE...!
NO TIME TO ARGUE!
THAT GIRL IS...
GOING TO DIE!

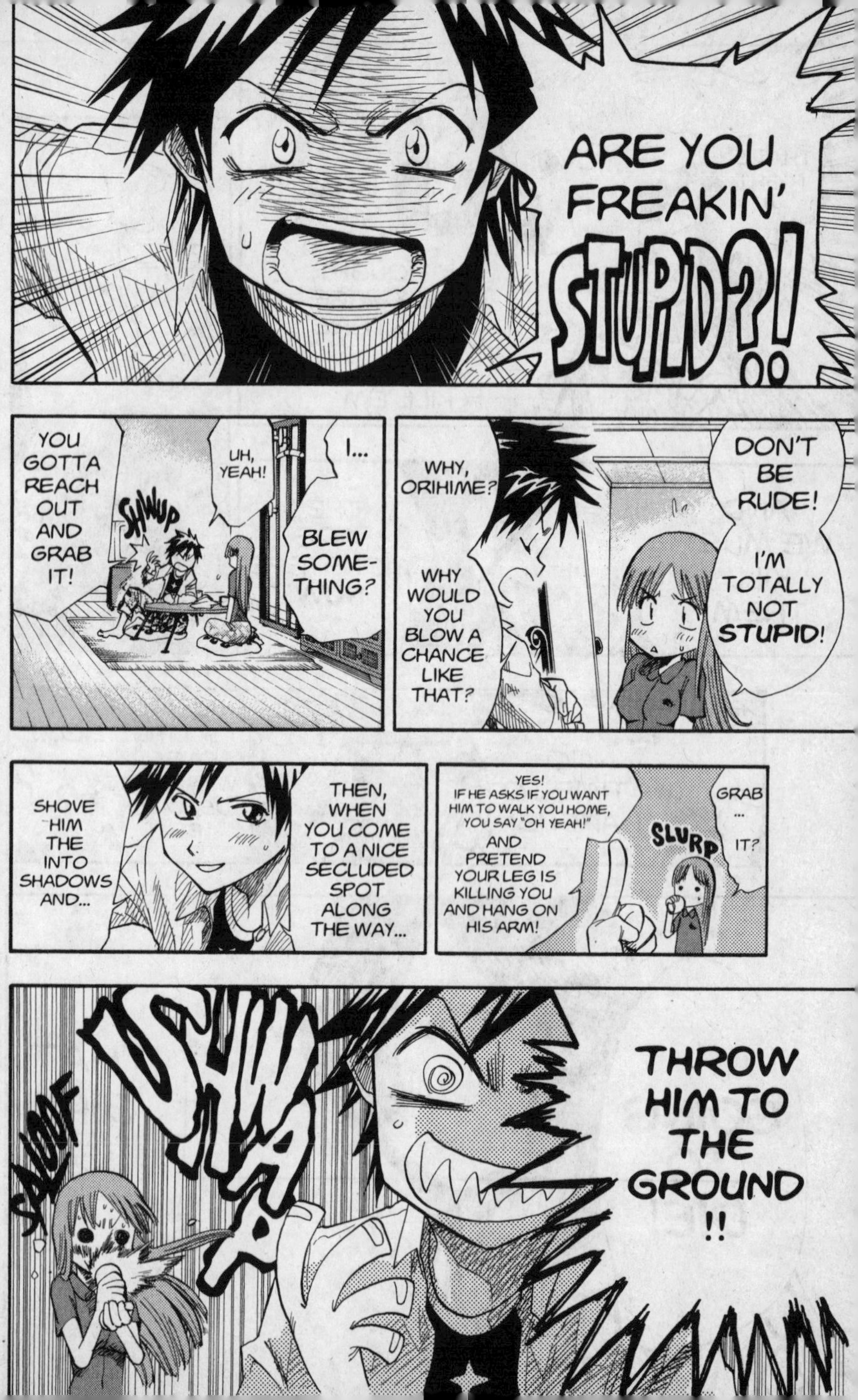
ARE YOU FREAKIN' STUPID?!
DON'T BE RUDE!
I'M TOTALLY NOT STUPID!
WHY, ORIHIME?
WHY WOULD YOU BLOW A CHANCE LIKE THAT?
I...
BLEW SOMETHING?
UH, YEAH!
YOU GOTTA REACH OUT AND GRAB IT!
SHWUP
GRAB ... IT?
YES! IF HE ASKS IF YOU WANT HIM TO WALK YOU HOME, YOU SAY "OH YEAH!"
SLURP
AND PRETEND YOUR LEG IS KILLING YOU AND HANG ON HIS ARM!
THEN, WHEN YOU COME TO A NICE SECLUDED SPOT ALONG THE WAY...
SHOVE HIM THE INTO SHADOWS AND...
THROW HIM TO THE GROUND!!
SPLOOF

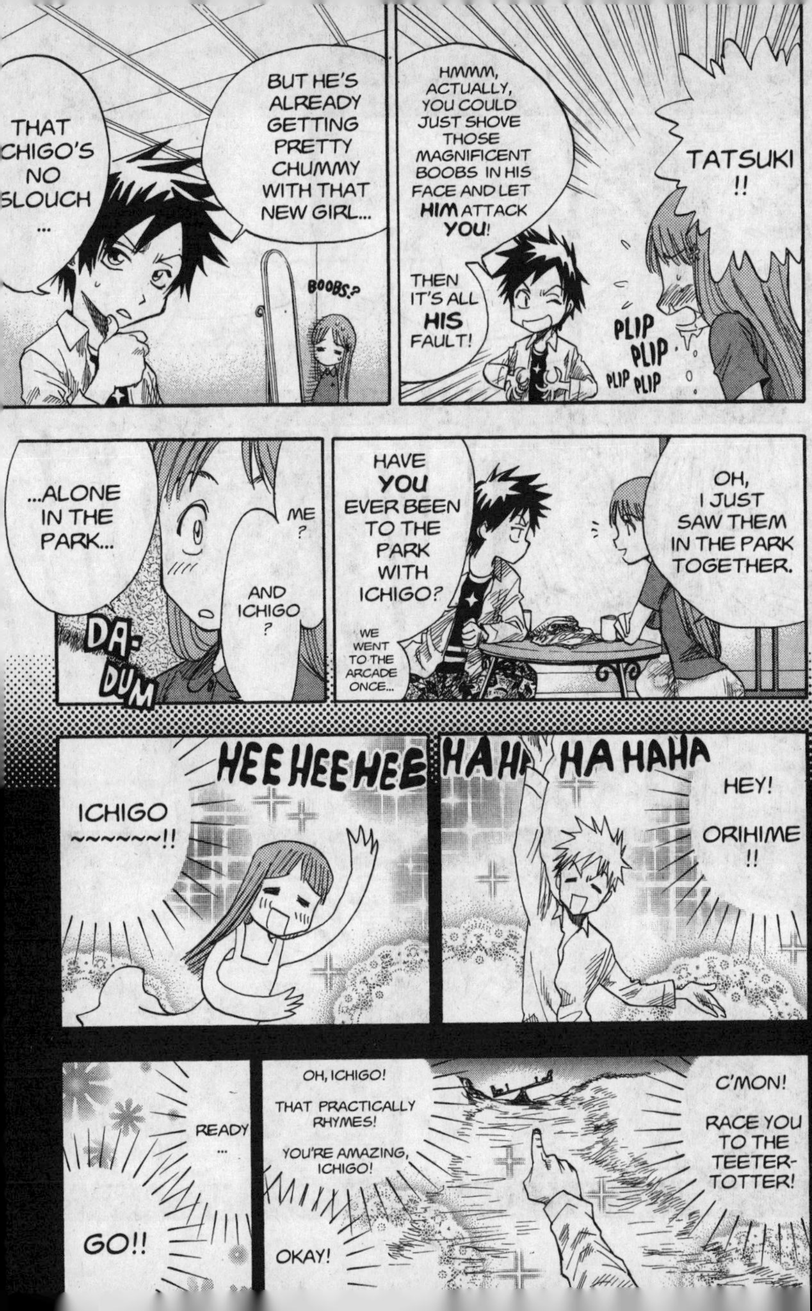
TATSUKI !!
HMMM, ACTUALLY, YOU COULD JUST SHOVE THOSE MAGNIFICENT BOOBS IN HIS FACE AND LET HIM ATTACK YOU!
THEN IT'S ALL HIS FAULT!
PLIP PLIP PLIP PLIP
BUT HE'S ALREADY GETTING PRETTY CHUMMY WITH THAT NEW GIRL...
THAT ICHIGO'S NO SLOUCH ...
BOOBS?
OH, I JUST SAW THEM IN THE PARK TOGETHER.
HAVE YOU EVER BEEN TO THE PARK WITH ICHIGO?
WE WENT TO THE ARCADE ONCE...
ME?
AND ICHIGO?
...ALONE IN THE PARK...
DA-DUM
HA HAHA
HAHA
HEY!
ORIHIME !!
HEE HEE HEE
ICHIGO ~~~~~~!!
C'MON!
RACE YOU TO THE TEETER-TOTTER!
OH, ICHIGO!
THAT PRACTICALLY RHYMES!
YOU'RE AMAZING, ICHIGO!
OKAY!
READY ...
GO!!

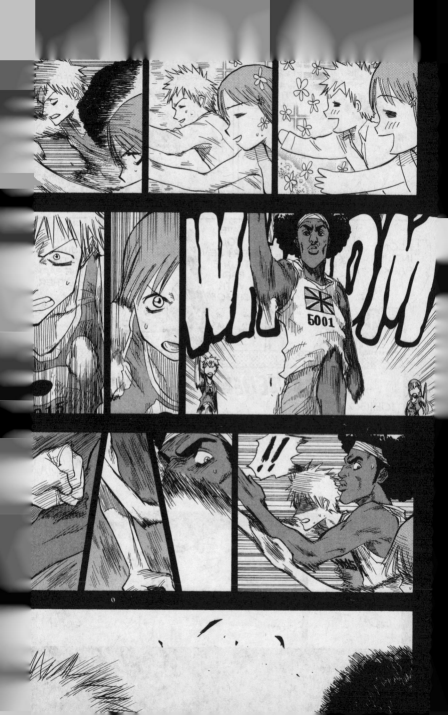

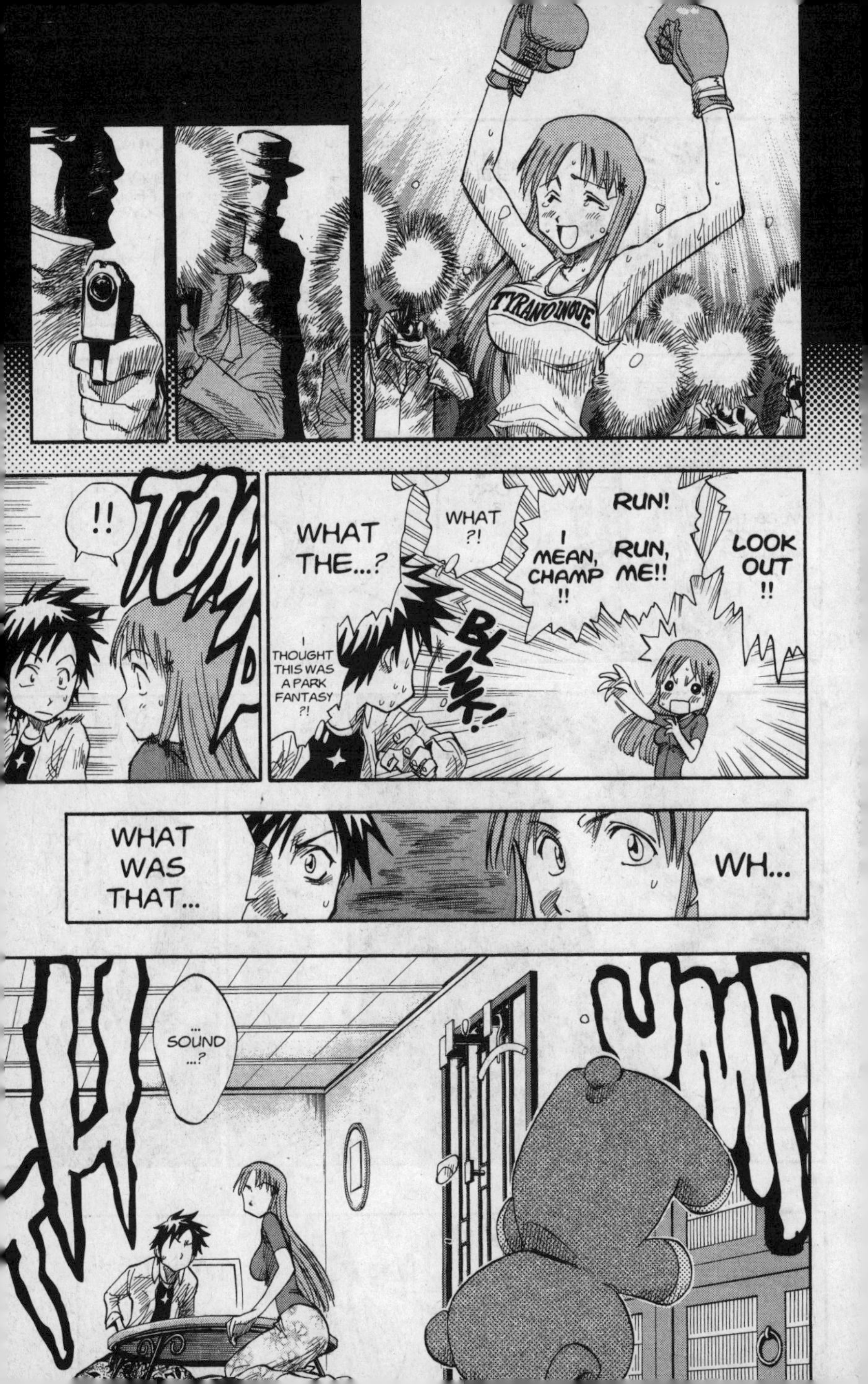
TYRANO INOUE
LOOK OUT !!
RUN!
RUN, ME!!
I MEAN, CHAMP !!
WHAT ?!
WHAT THE...?
I THOUGHT THIS WAS A PARK FANTASY ?!
BLINK!
!!
WH...
WHAT WAS THAT...
... SOUND ...?

READ THIS WAY

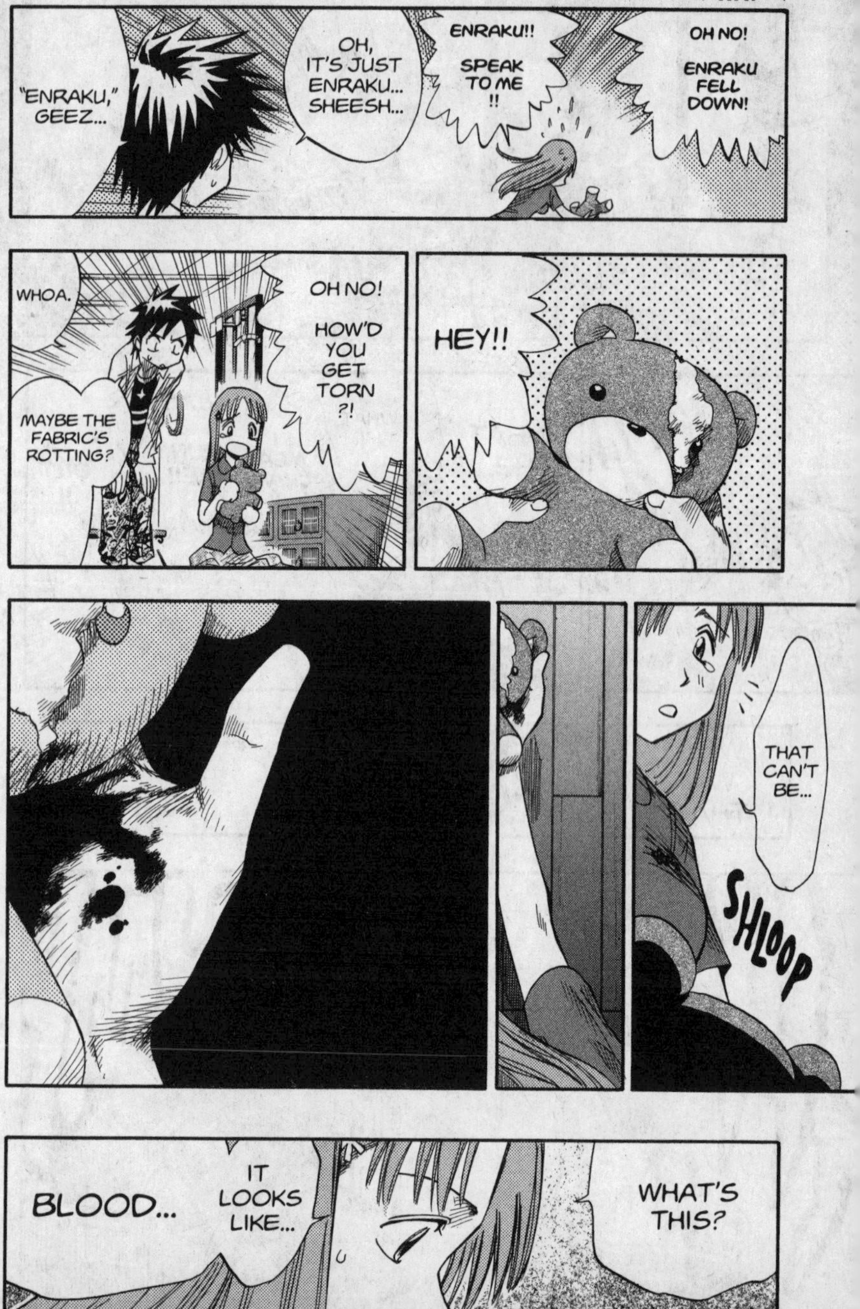
OH NO!
ENRAKU FELL DOWN!
ENRAKU!!
SPEAK TO ME !!
OH, IT'S JUST ENRAKU... SHEESH...
"ENRAKU," GEEZ...
HEY!!
OH NO!
HOW'D YOU GET TORN ?!
WHOA.
MAYBE THE FABRIC'S ROTTING?
THAT CAN'T BE...
SHLOOP
WHAT'S THIS?
IT LOOKS LIKE...
BLOOD...

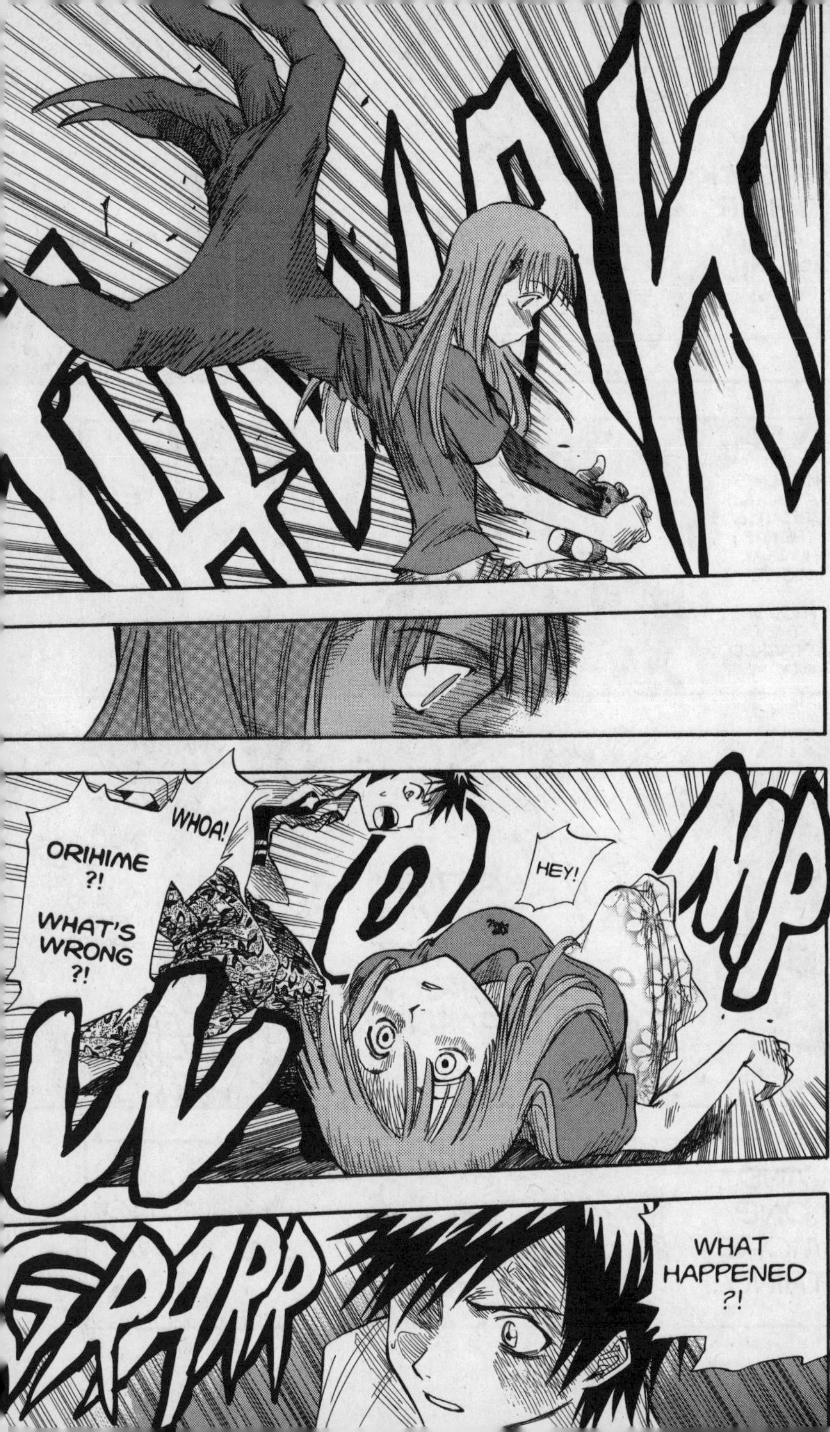
HEY!
WHOA!
ORIHIME ?!
WHAT'S WRONG ?!
WHAT HAPPENED ?!

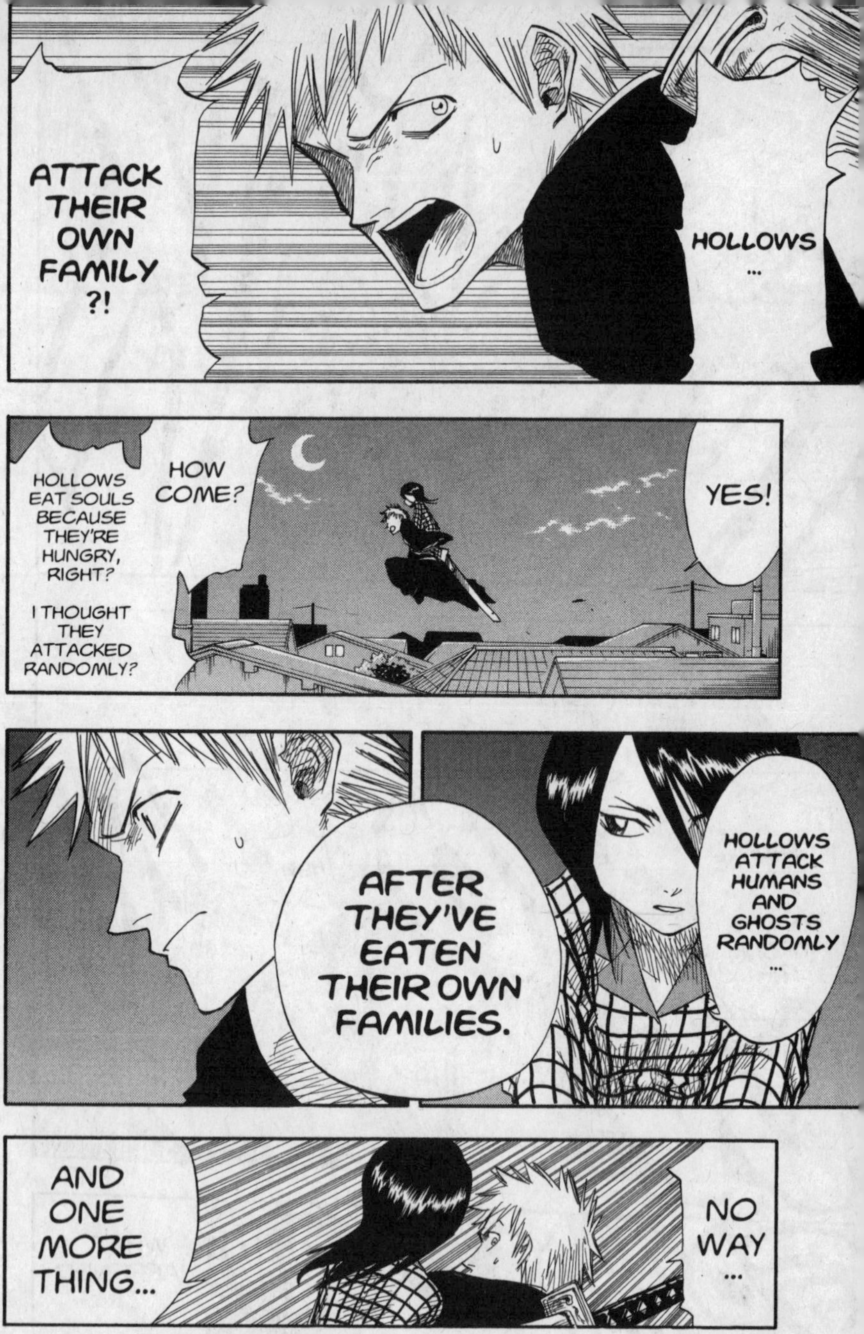
HOLLOWS ...
ATTACK THEIR OWN FAMILY ?!
YES!
HOW COME?
HOLLOWS EAT SOULS BECAUSE THEY'RE HUNGRY, RIGHT?
I THOUGHT THEY ATTACKED RANDOMLY?
HOLLOWS ATTACK HUMANS AND GHOSTS RANDOMLY ...
AFTER THEY'VE EATEN THEIR OWN FAMILIES.
NO WAY ...
AND ONE MORE THING...

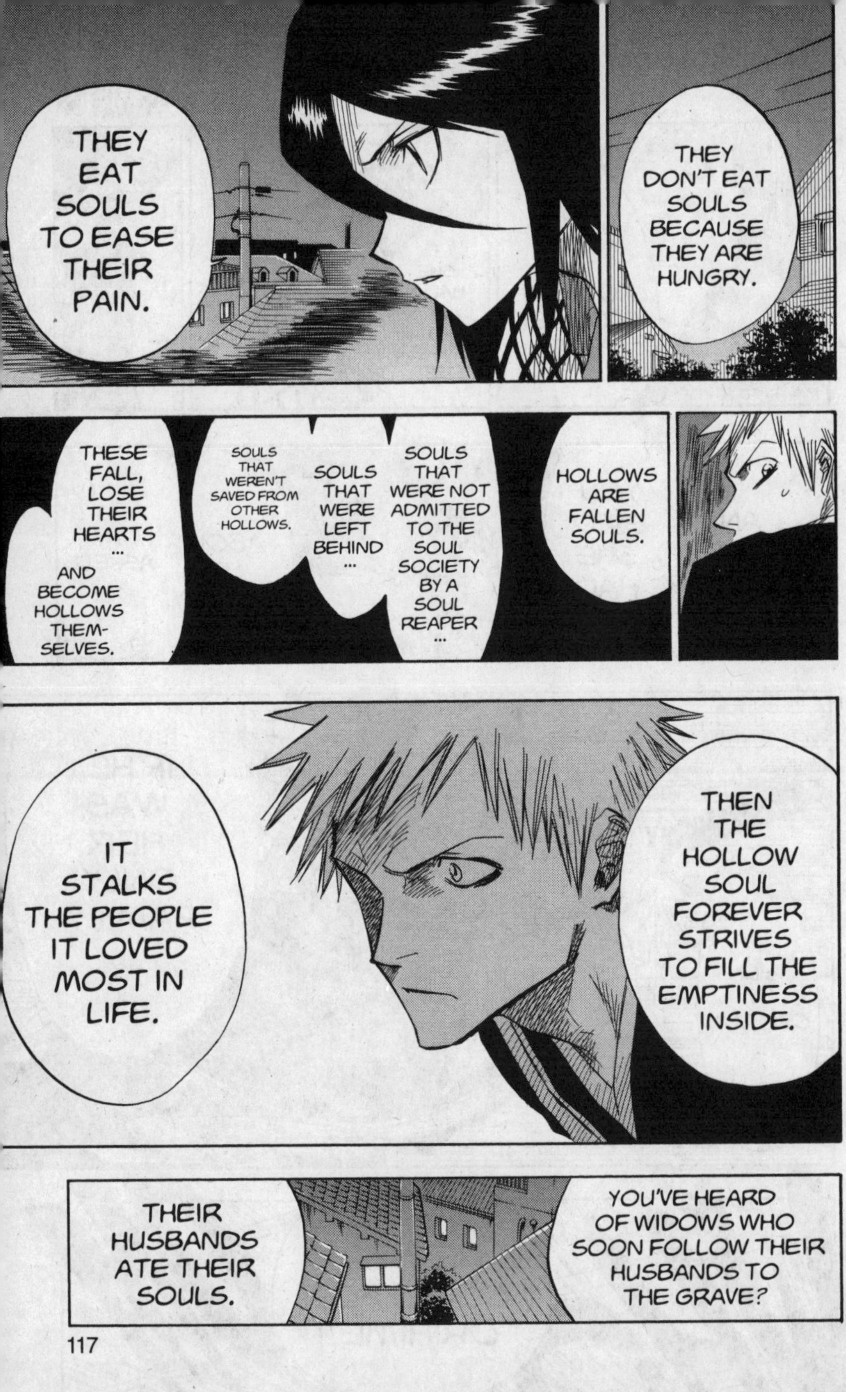
THEY DON'T EAT SOULS BECAUSE THEY ARE HUNGRY.
THEY EAT SOULS TO EASE THEIR PAIN.
HOLLOWS ARE FALLEN SOULS.
SOULS THAT WERE NOT ADMITTED TO THE SOUL SOCIETY BY A SOUL REAPER ...
SOULS THAT WERE LEFT BEHIND ...
SOULS THAT WEREN'T SAVED FROM OTHER HOLLOWS.
THESE FALL, LOSE THEIR HEARTS ...
AND BECOME HOLLOWS THEM-SELVES.
THEN THE HOLLOW SOUL FOREVER STRIVES TO FILL THE EMPTINESS INSIDE.
IT STALKS THE PEOPLE IT LOVED MOST IN LIFE.
YOU'VE HEARD OF WIDOWS WHO SOON FOLLOW THEIR HUSBANDS TO THE GRAVE?
THEIR HUSBANDS ATE THEIR SOULS.

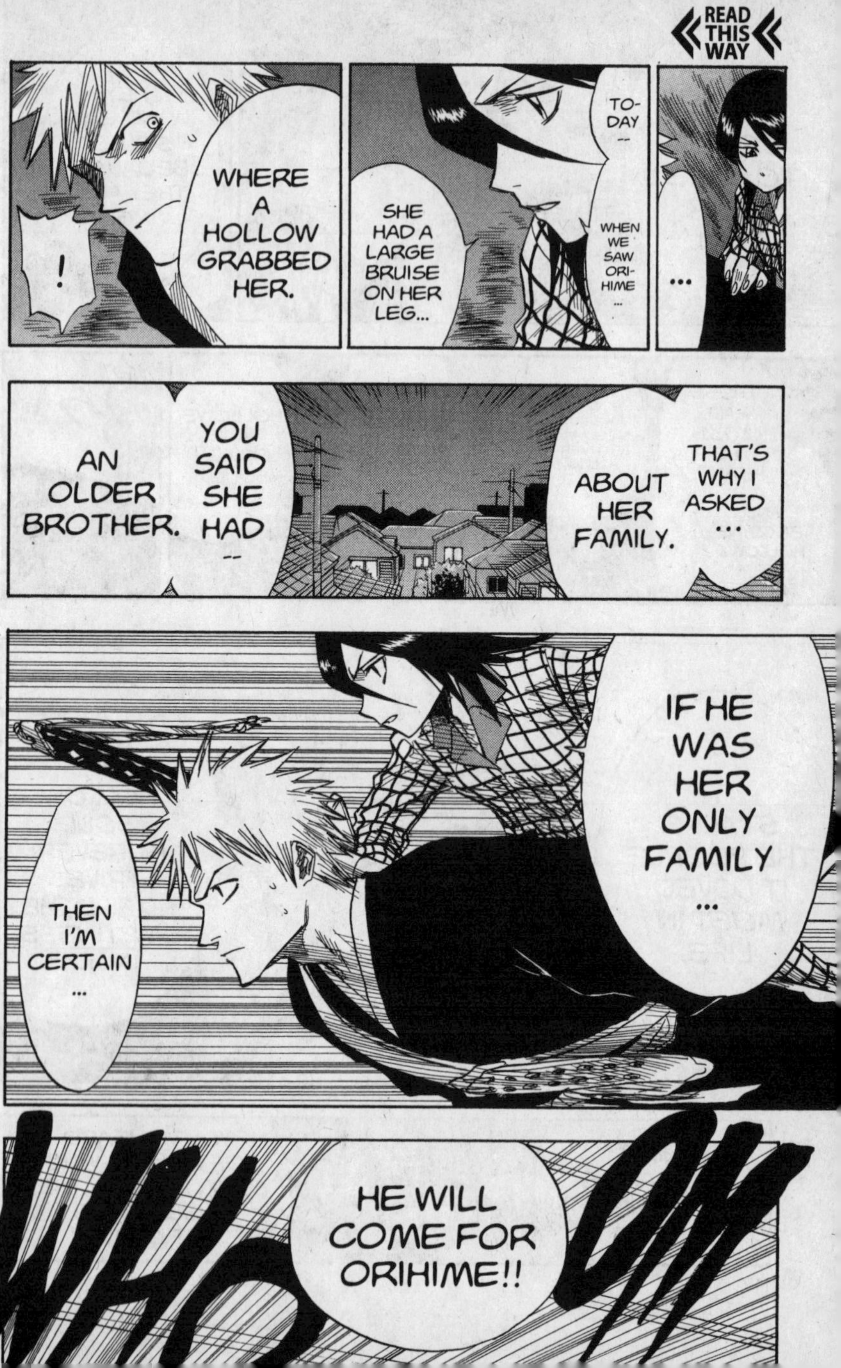
READ THIS WAY
...
TO-DAY -- WHEN WE SAW ORI-HIME ...
SHE HAD A LARGE BRUISE ON HER LEG...
WHERE A HOLLOW GRABBED HER.
!
THAT'S WHY I ASKED ...
ABOUT HER FAMILY.
YOU SAID SHE HAD --
AN OLDER BROTHER.
IF HE WAS HER ONLY FAMILY ...
THEN I'M CERTAIN ...
WHOOM
HE WILL COME FOR ORIHIME!!

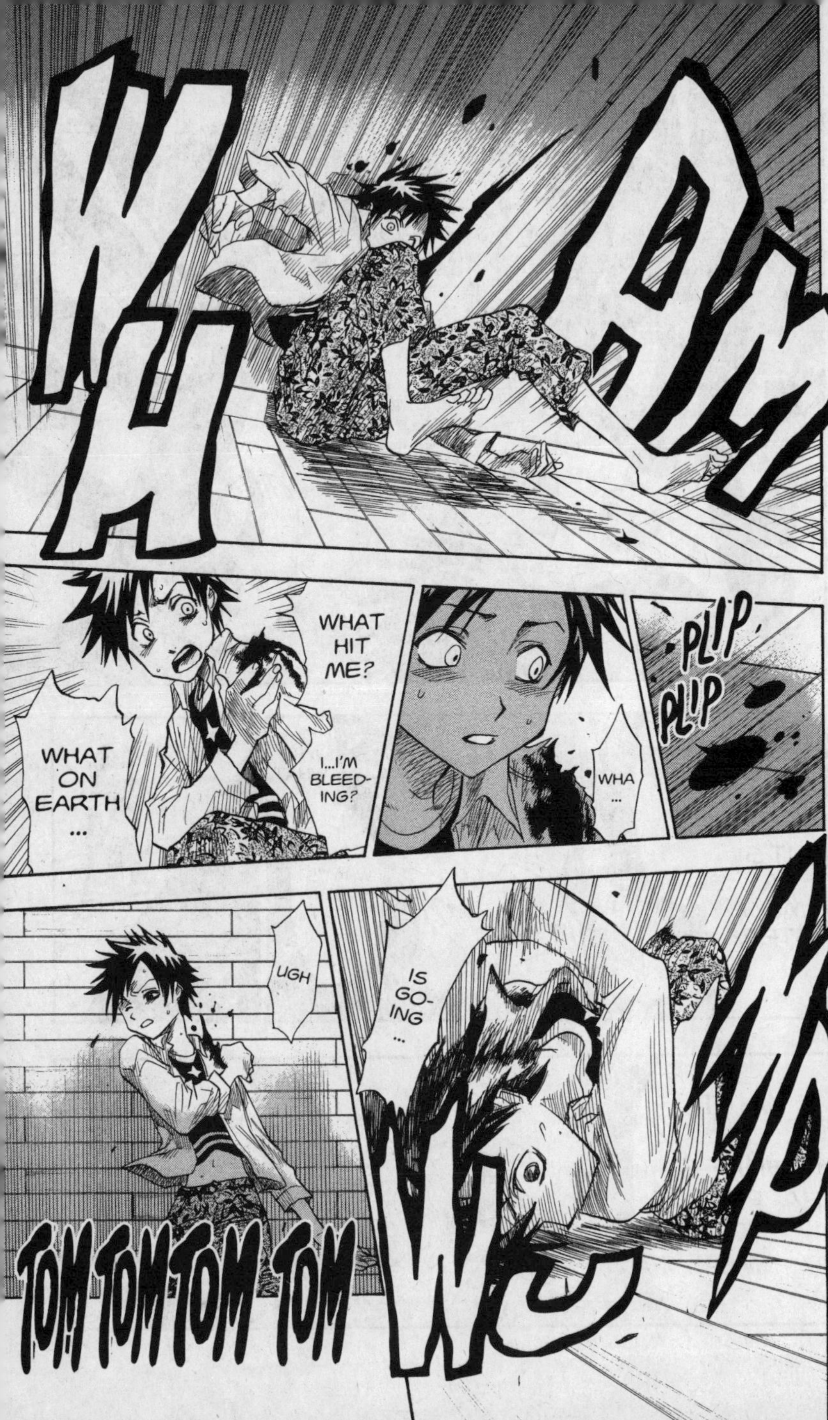
WHAM
PLIP PLIP
WHA...
WHAT HIT ME?
I...I'M BLEEDING?
WHAT ON EARTH...
IS GOING...
UGH
TOM TOM TOM TOM

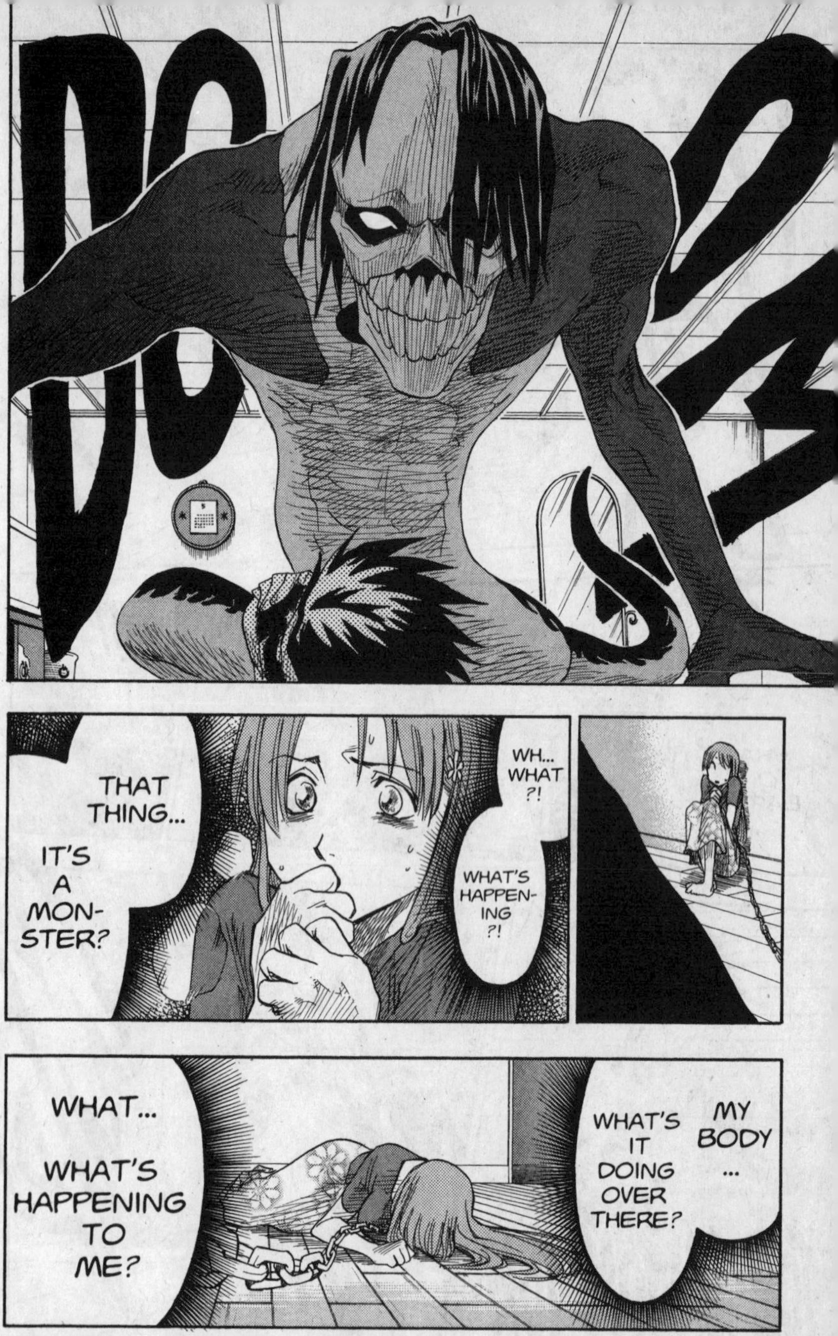
WH... WHAT ?!
WHAT'S HAPPENING ?!
THAT THING...
IT'S A MONSTER?
MY BODY ...
WHAT'S IT DOING OVER THERE?
WHAT...
WHAT'S HAPPENING TO ME?

READ THIS WAY

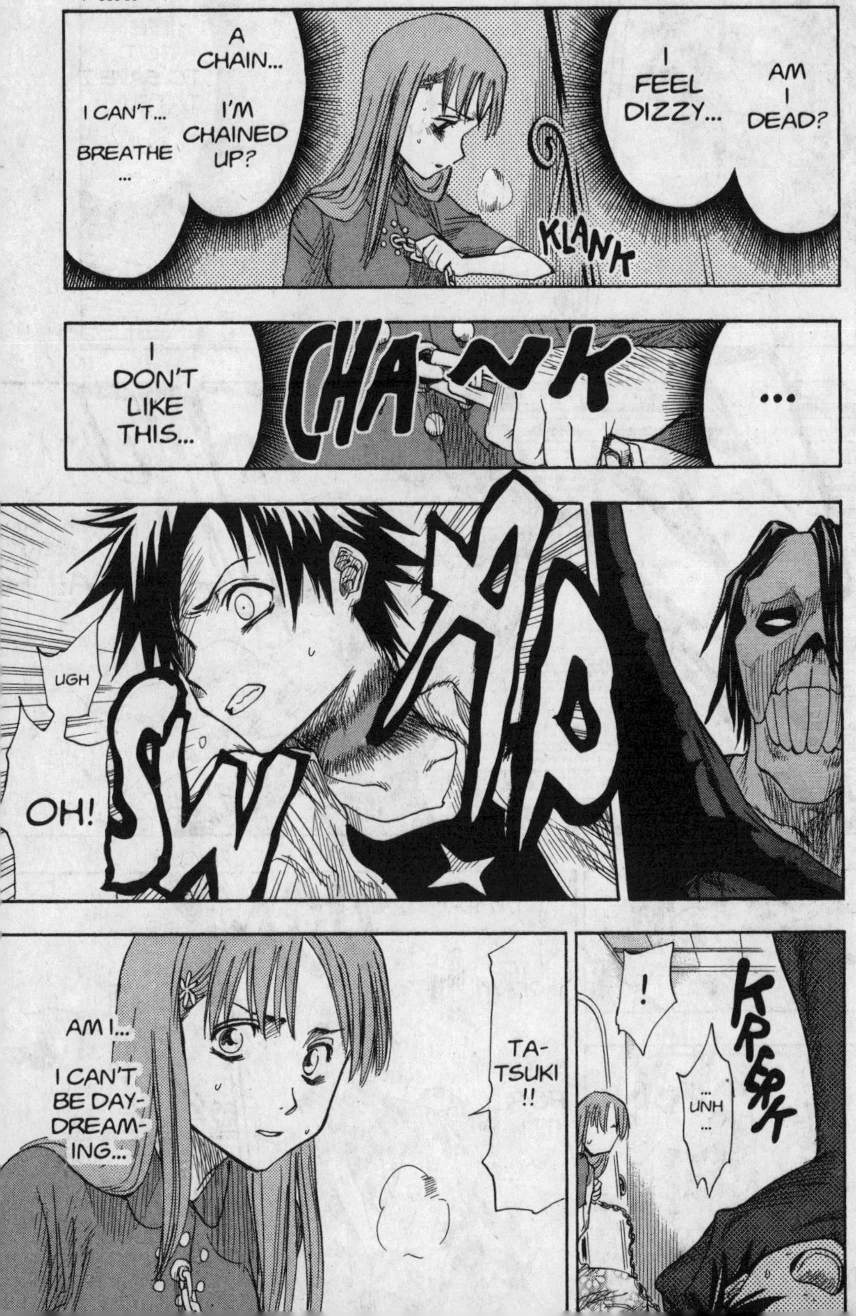
AM I DEAD?
I FEEL DIZZY...
KLANK
A CHAIN...
I'M CHAINED UP?
I CAN'T... BREATHE...
...
CHANK
I DON'T LIKE THIS...
SWOOP
UGH
OH!
KRERK
!
...UNH...
TA-TSUKI!!
AM I...
I CAN'T BE DAY-DREAMING...

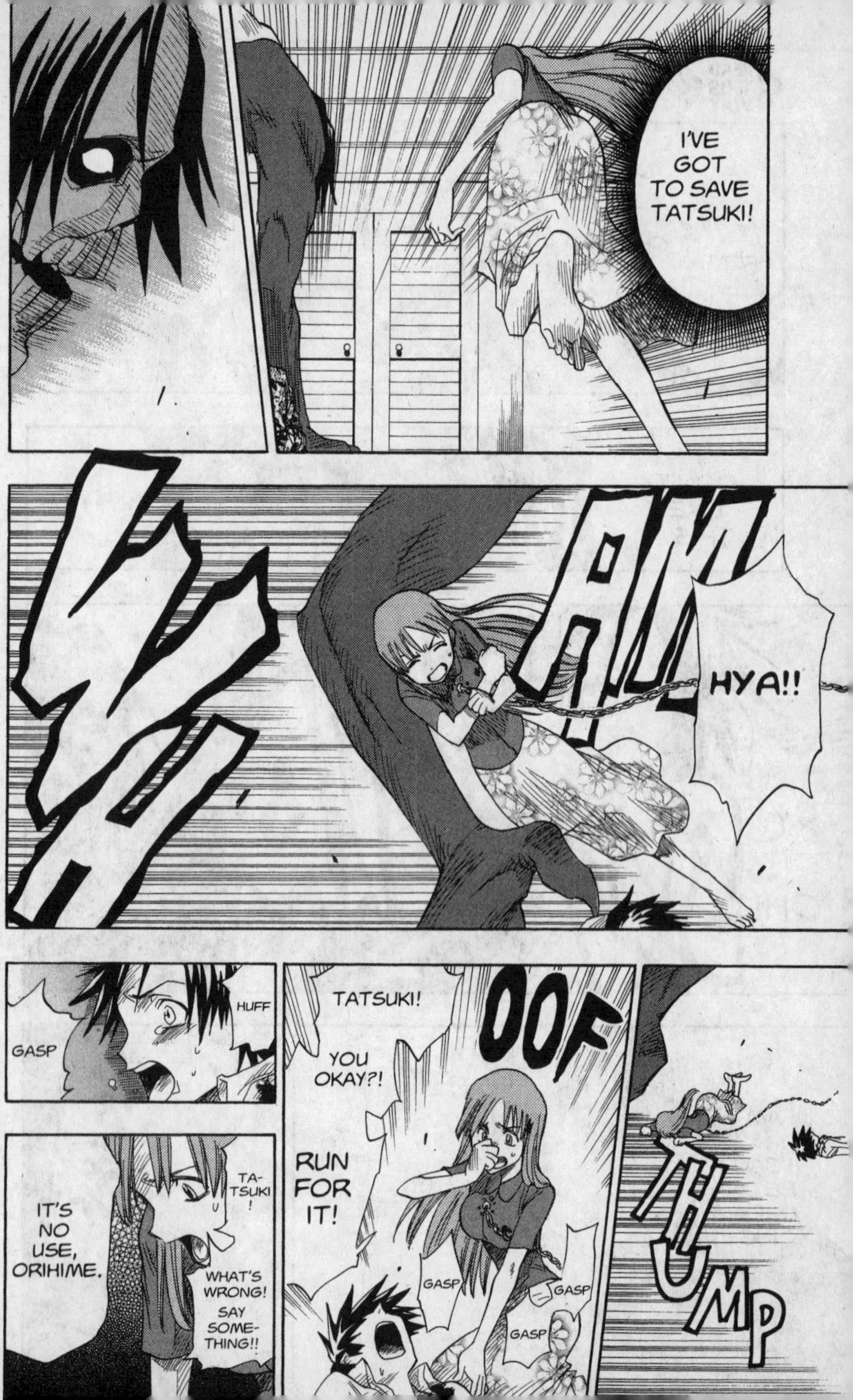
I'VE GOT TO SAVE TATSUKI!
HYA!!
OOF
THUMP
TATSUKI!
YOU OKAY?!
RUN FOR IT!
GASP
GASP
GASP
HUFF
GASP
TA-TSUKI!
WHAT'S WRONG! SAY SOME-THING!!
IT'S NO USE, ORIHIME.

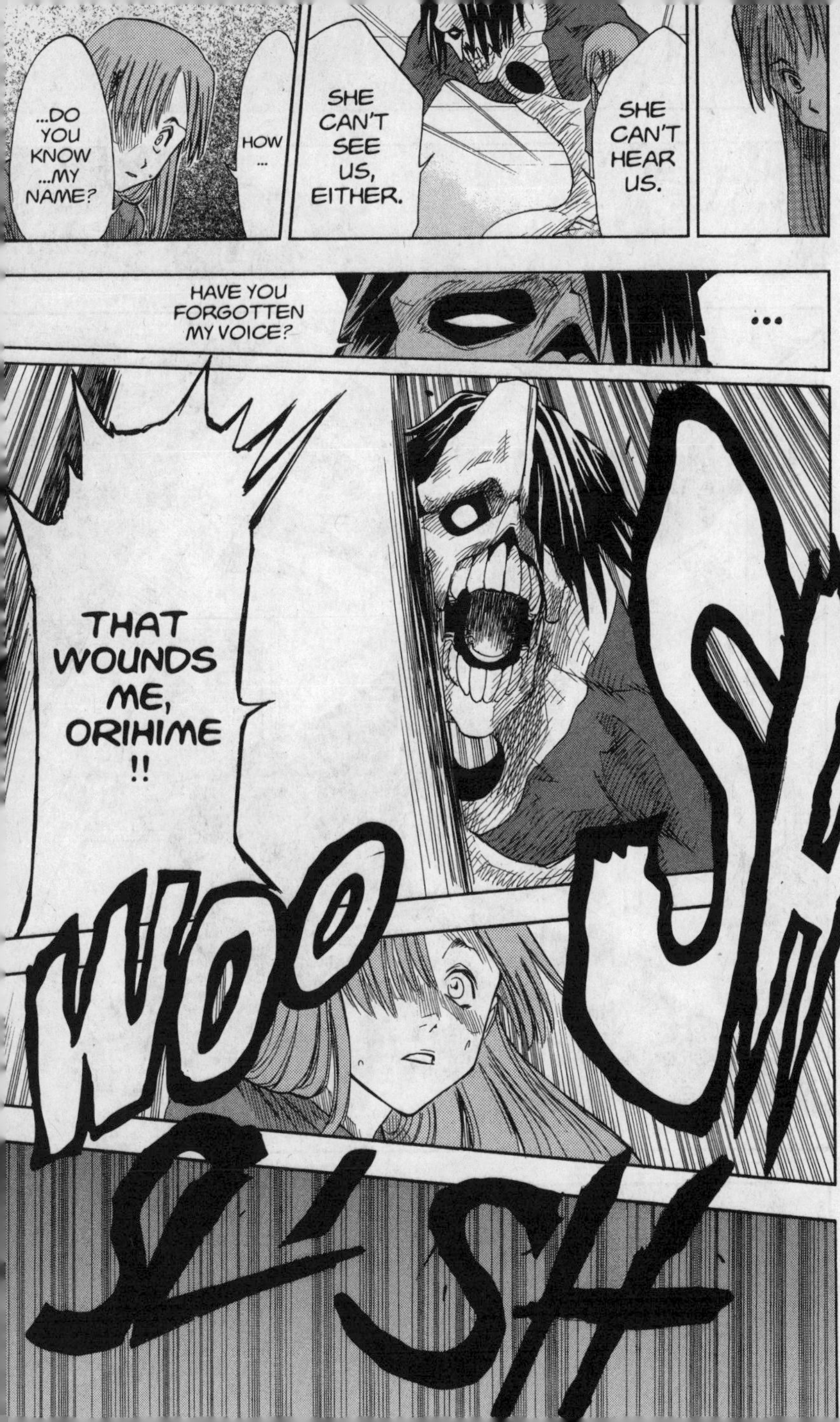
SHE CAN'T HEAR US.
SHE CAN'T SEE US, EITHER.
HOW ...
...DO YOU KNOW ...MY NAME?
...
HAVE YOU FORGOTTEN MY VOICE?
THAT WOUNDS ME, ORIHIME !!
WOOSH

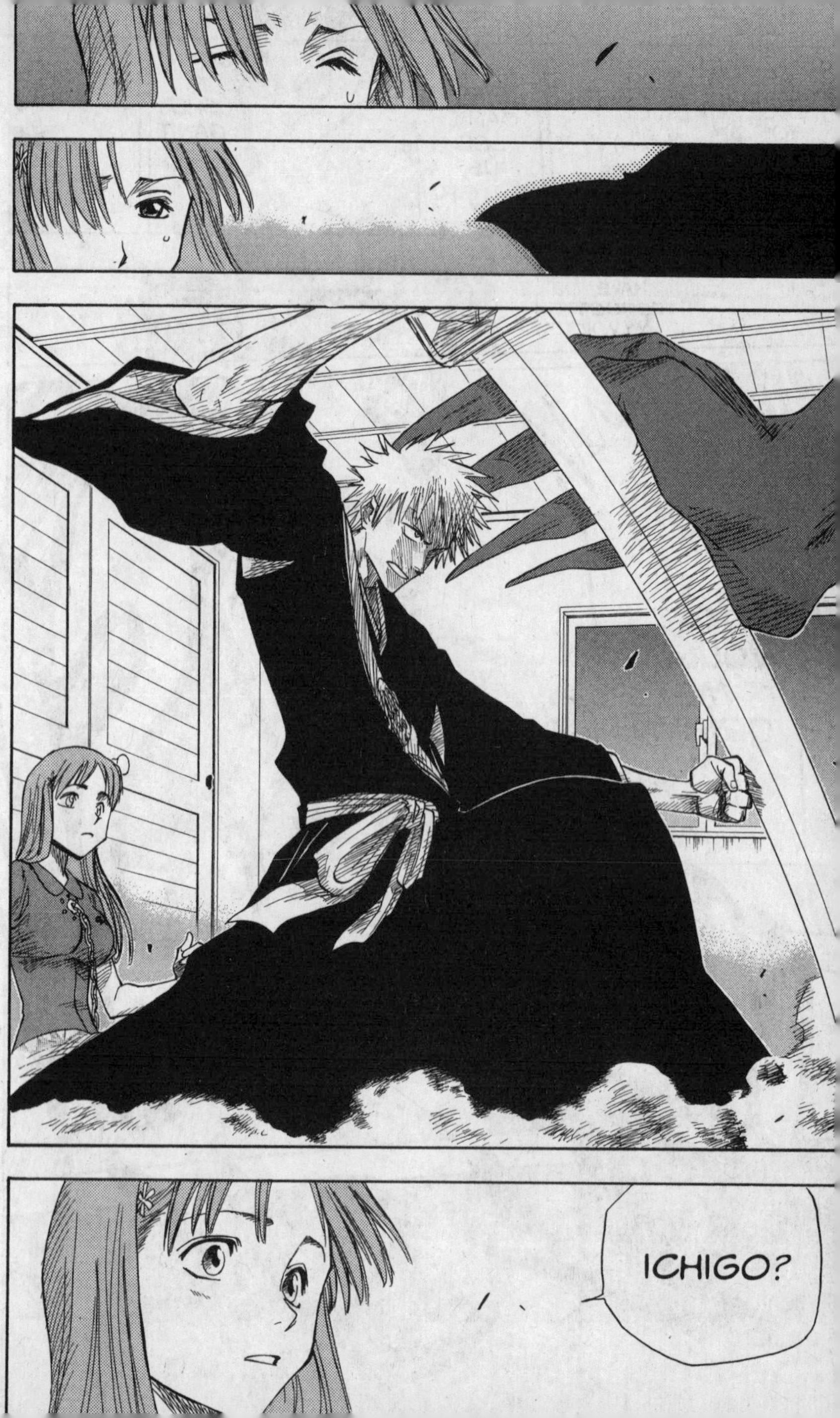
ICHIGO?

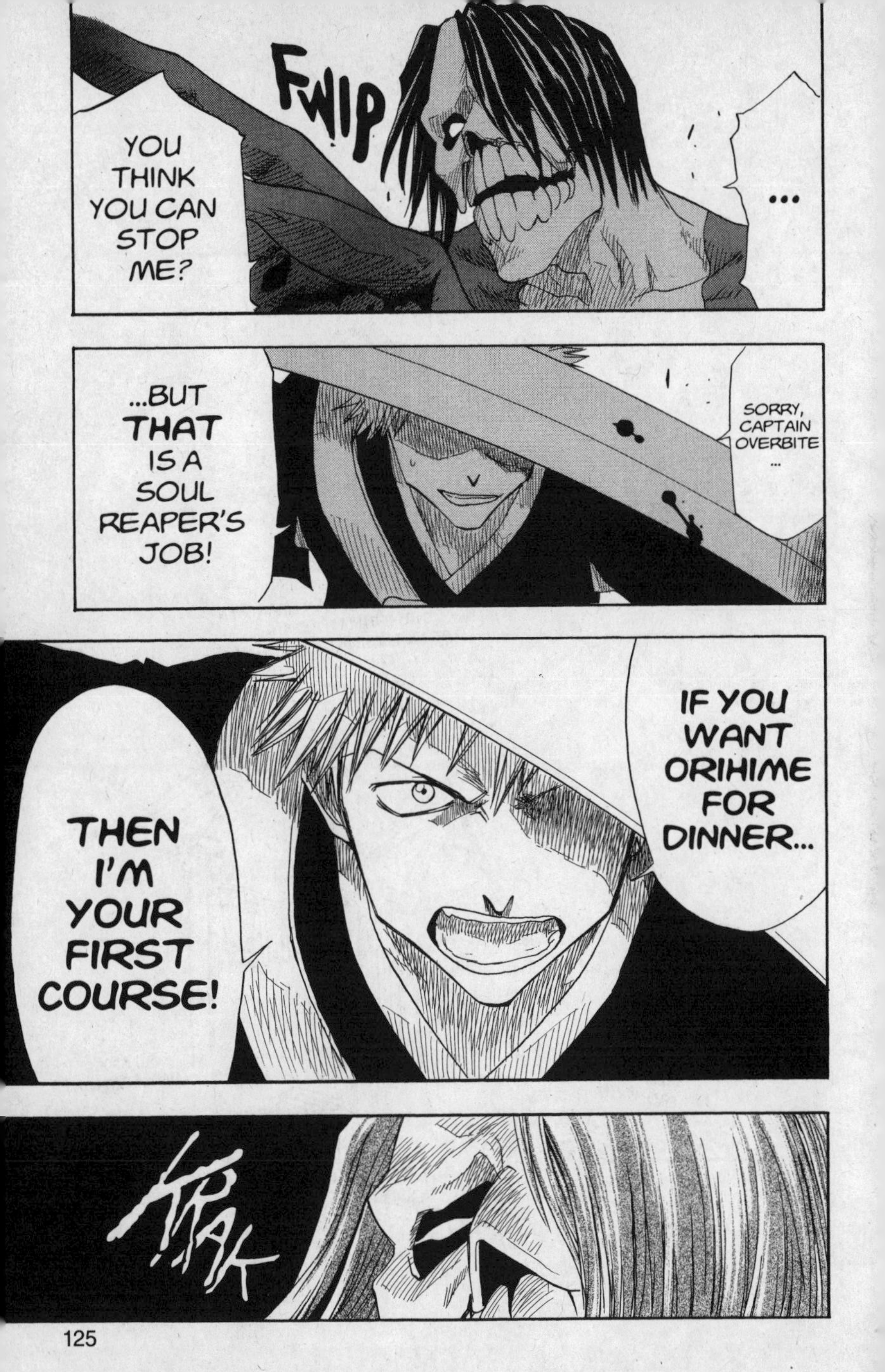
FWIP
...
YOU THINK YOU CAN STOP ME?
SORRY, CAPTAIN OVERBITE...
...BUT **THAT** IS A SOUL REAPER'S JOB!
IF YOU WANT ORIHIME FOR DINNER...
THEN I'M YOUR FIRST COURSE!
KRAK

ORIHIME'S HOUSE IS AN APARTMENT.
THIS IS THE STREET SIDE.
APT. 202 IS THE INOUE RESIDENCE

INOUE
EMPTY UNIT
MORITA (ON VACATION)
IWAO (SEPARATED FROM WIFE)

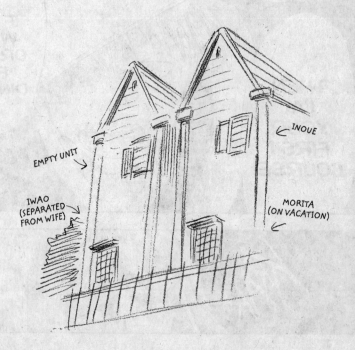

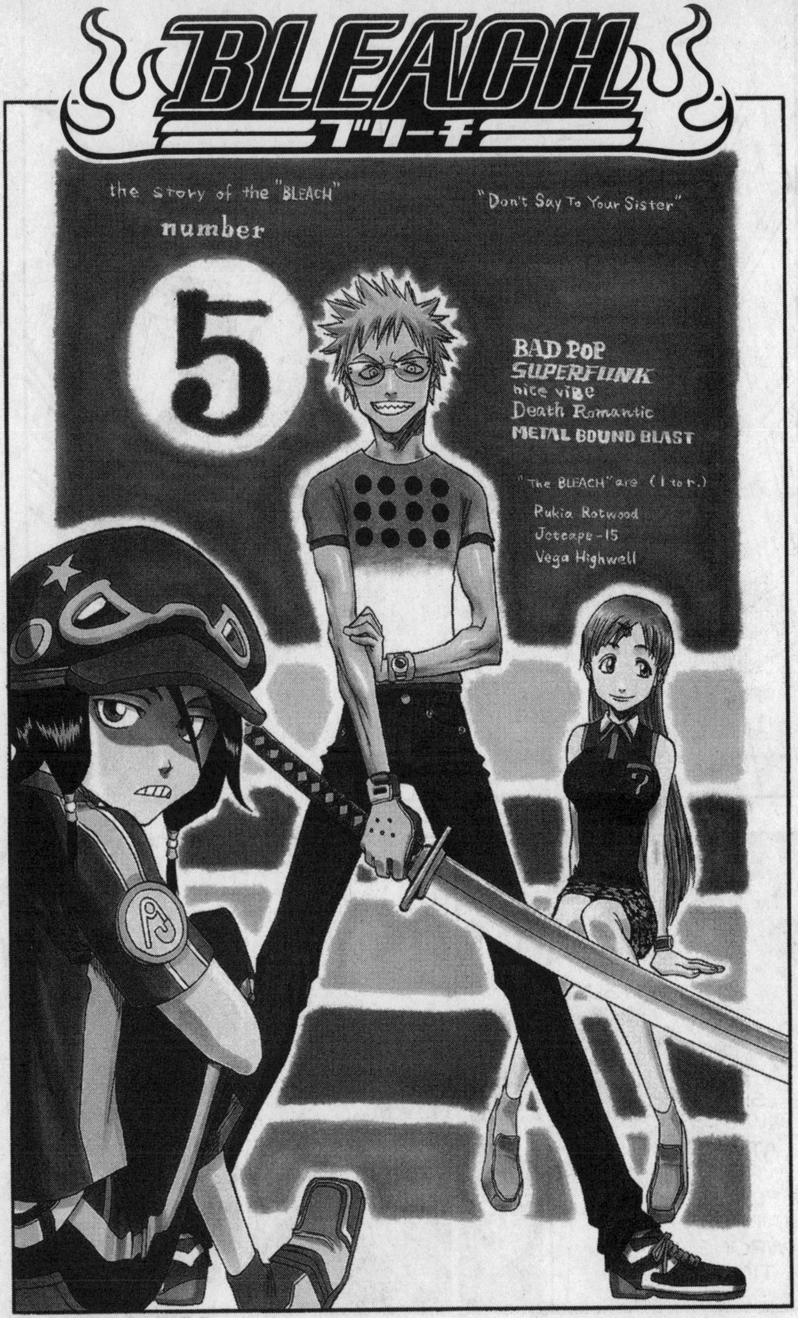

5. BINDA BLINDA

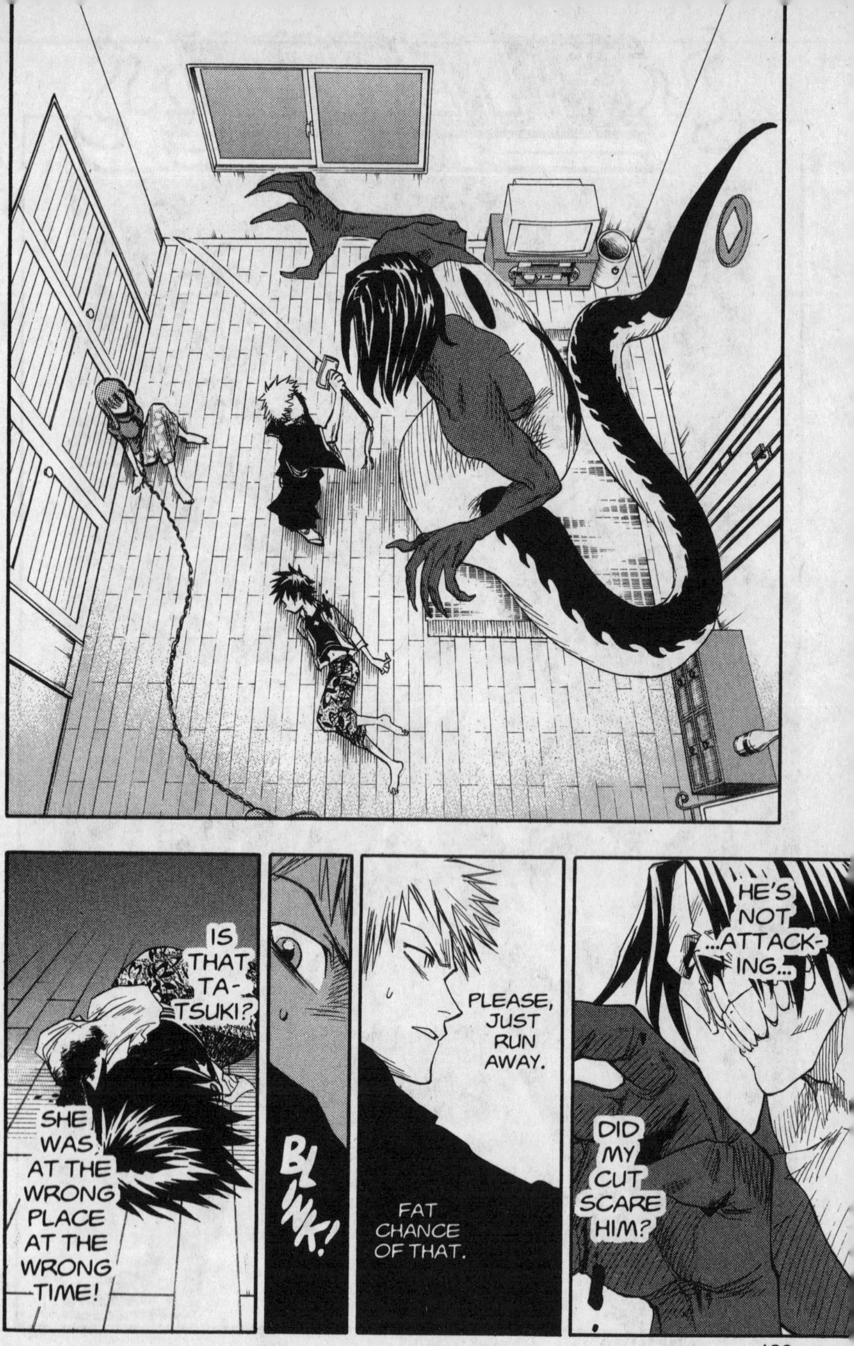
HE'S NOT ...ATTACKING...
DID MY CUT SCARE HIM?
PLEASE, JUST RUN AWAY.
FAT CHANCE OF THAT.
BLINK!
IS THAT TATSUKI?
SHE WAS AT THE WRONG PLACE AT THE WRONG TIME!

WHO
....?

THERE'S SOMEONE ELSE LYING OVER THERE...

....?

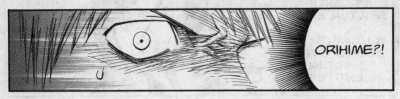

ORIHIME?!

I KNEW IT!

HEY!

BUT...

SHE'S STANDING BEHIND ME!

W
I
P

IT'S YOU, ICHIGO!!

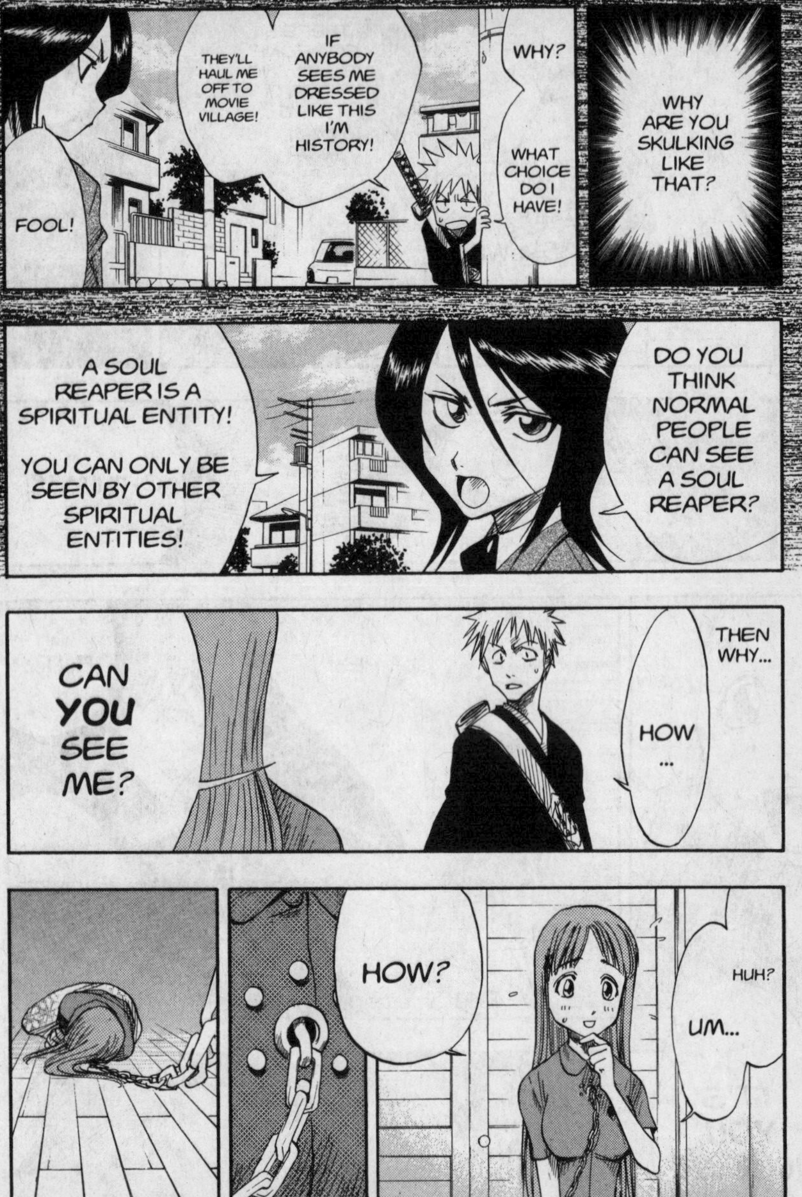
WHY ARE YOU SKULKING LIKE THAT?
WHY?
WHAT CHOICE DO I HAVE!
IF ANYBODY SEES ME DRESSED LIKE THIS I'M HISTORY!
THEY'LL HAUL ME OFF TO MOVIE VILLAGE!
FOOL!
DO YOU THINK NORMAL PEOPLE CAN SEE A SOUL REAPER?
A SOUL REAPER IS A SPIRITUAL ENTITY!
YOU CAN ONLY BE SEEN BY OTHER SPIRITUAL ENTITIES!
THEN WHY...
HOW ...
CAN YOU SEE ME?
HUH?
UM...
HOW?

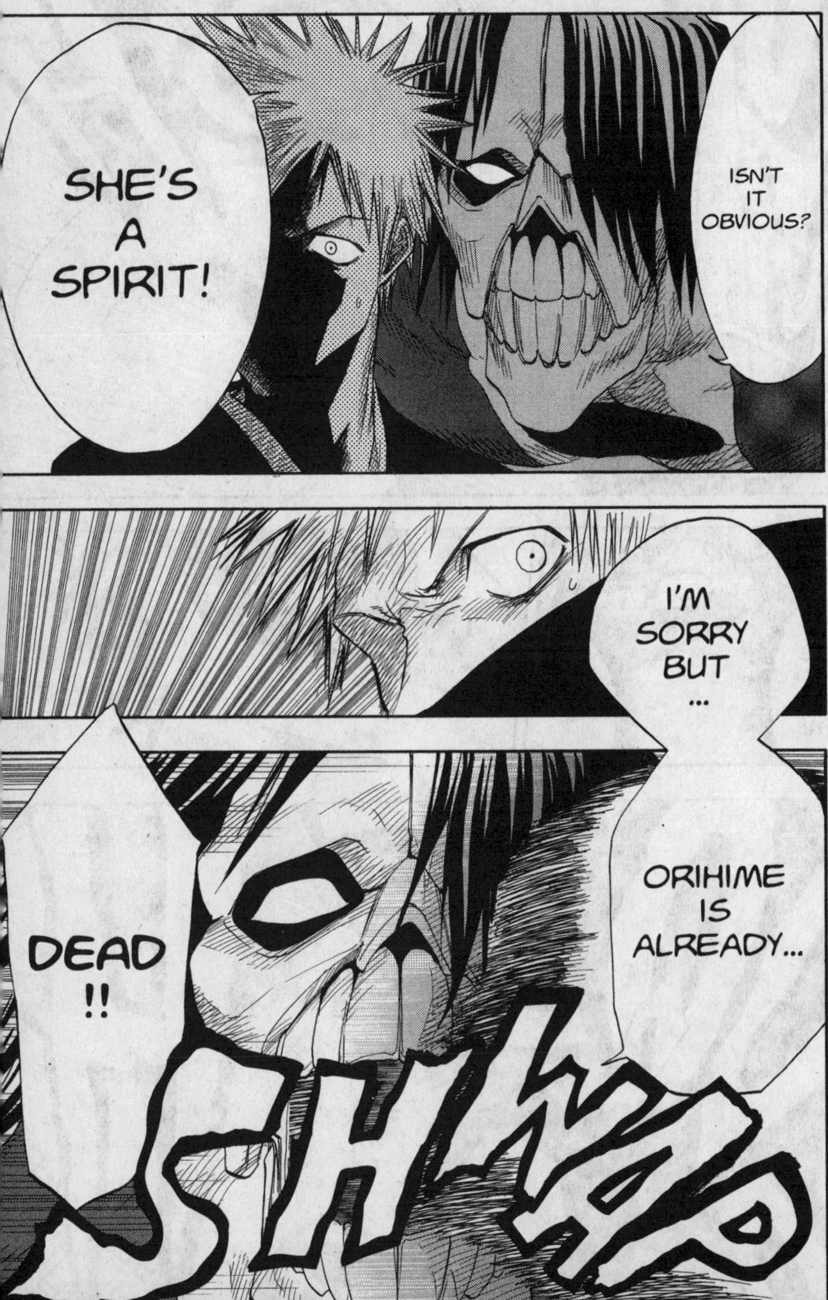
ISN'T IT OBVIOUS?
SHE'S A SPIRIT!
I'M SORRY BUT ...
ORIHIME IS ALREADY...
DEAD !!
SHHAP

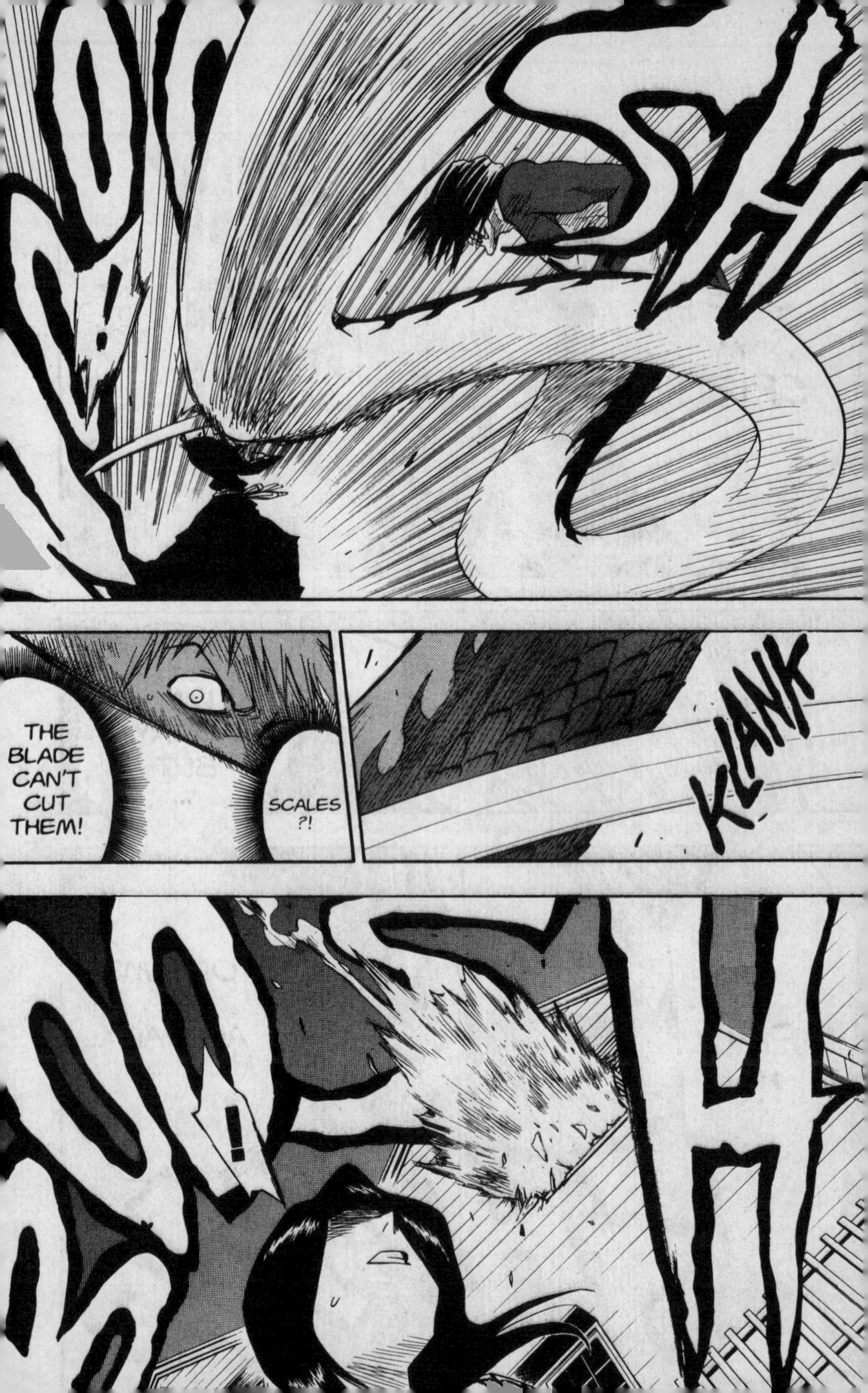
KLANK
SCALES ?!
THE BLADE CAN'T CUT THEM!

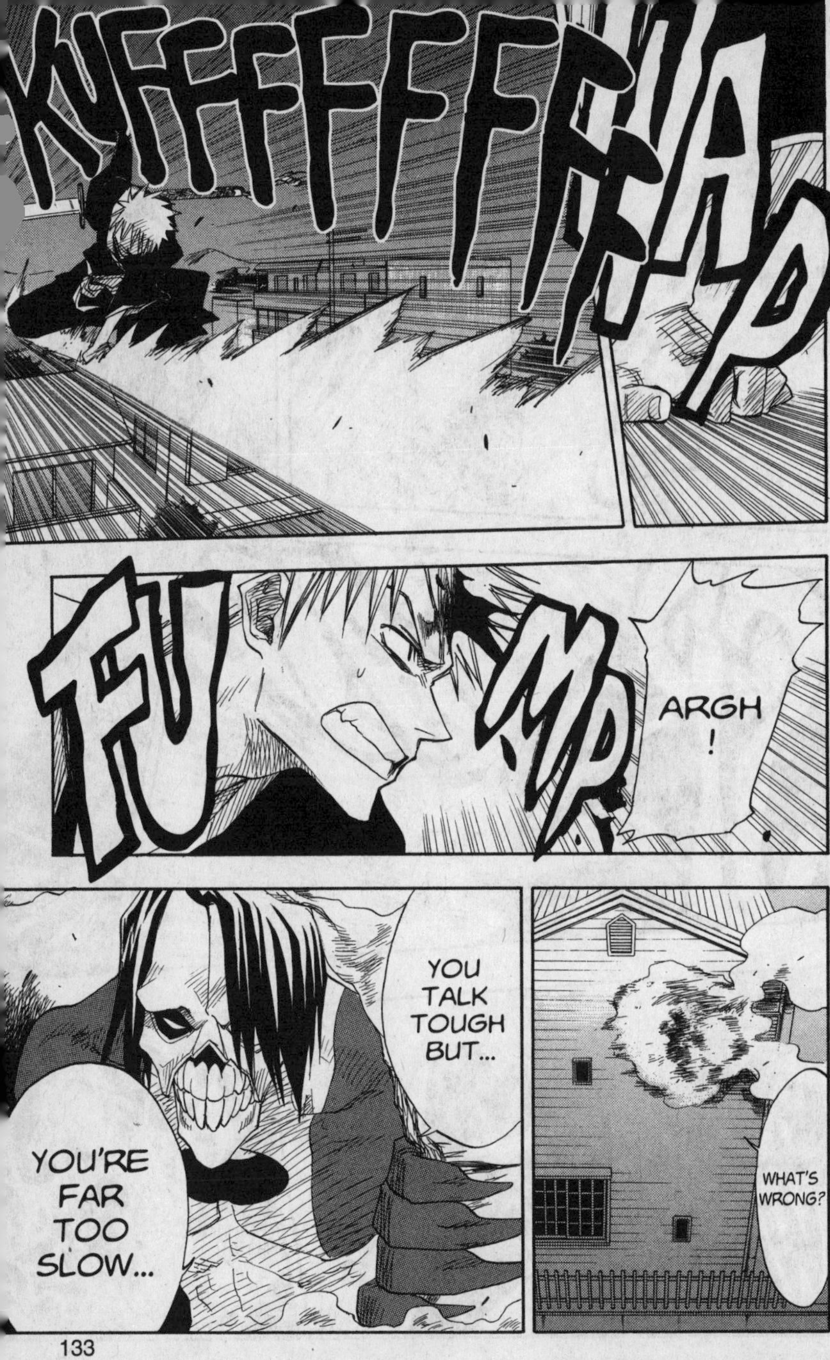
KYFFFFFFFFFWAP
ARGH!
FUMP
WHAT'S WRONG?
YOU TALK TOUGH BUT...
YOU'RE FAR TOO SLOW...

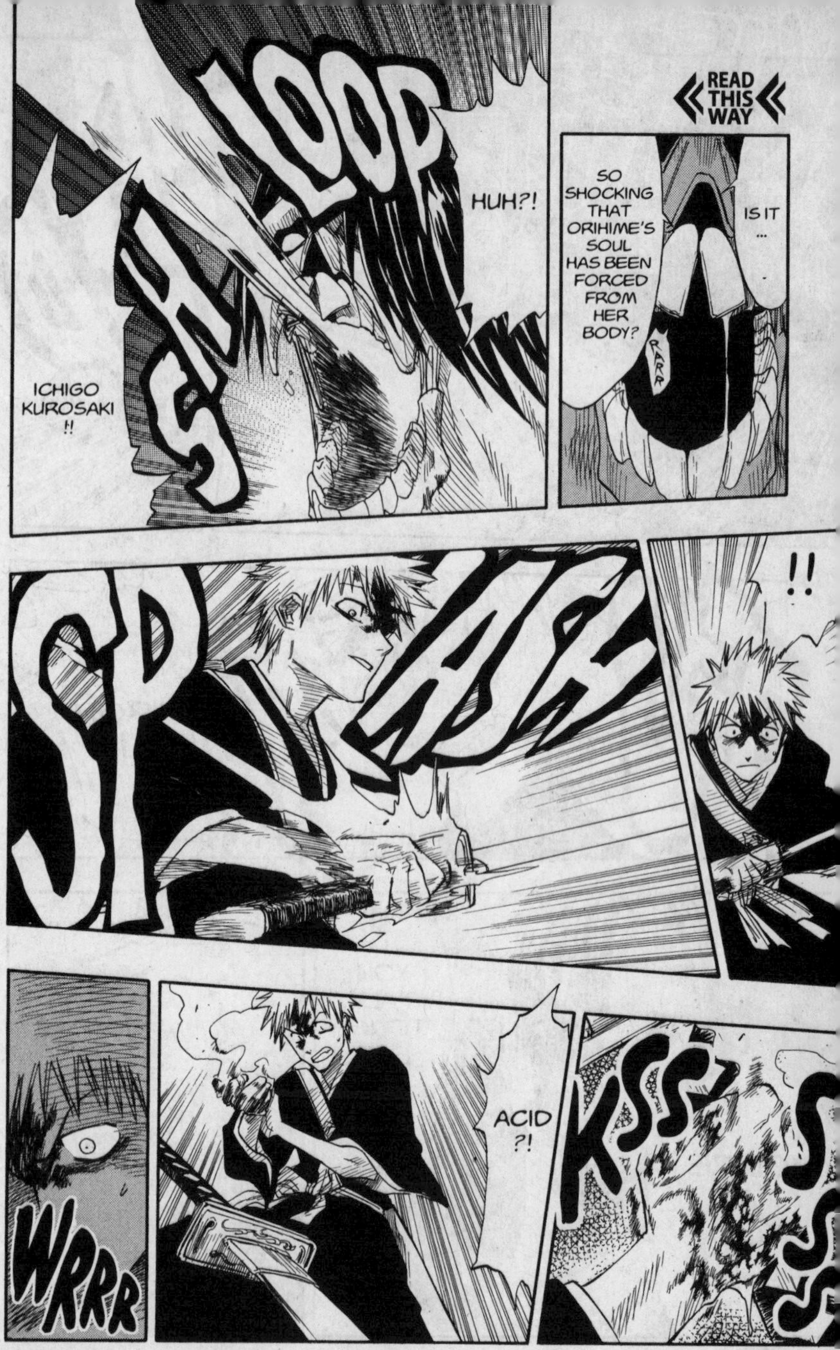
READ THIS WAY
IS IT ...
SO SHOCKING THAT ORIHIME'S SOUL HAS BEEN FORCED FROM HER BODY?
RARR
HUH?!
SHLOOP
ICHIGO KUROSAKI !!
!!
SP ASH
KSSS
ACID ?!
WRRR

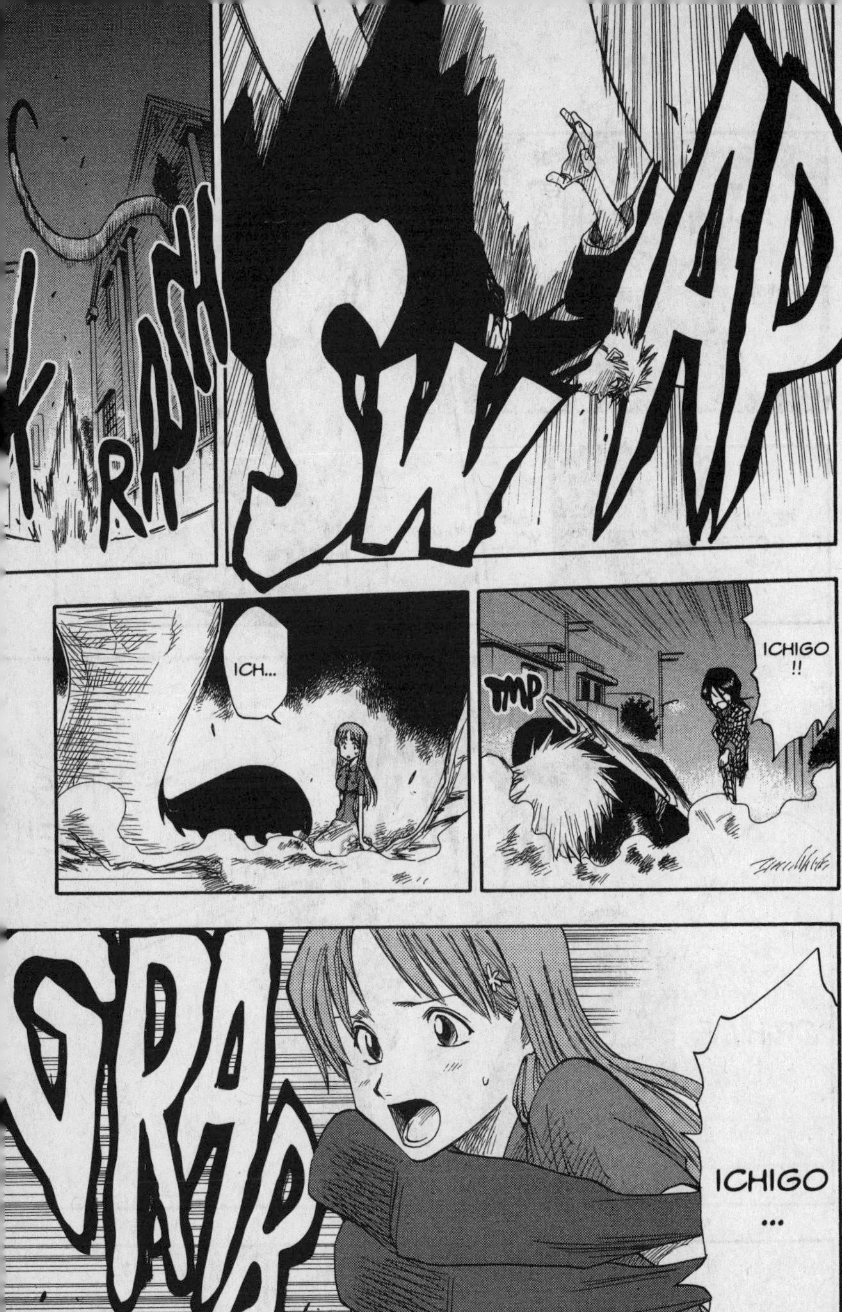
SWAP
KRASH
ICHIGO !!
TMP
ICH...
ICHIGO ...

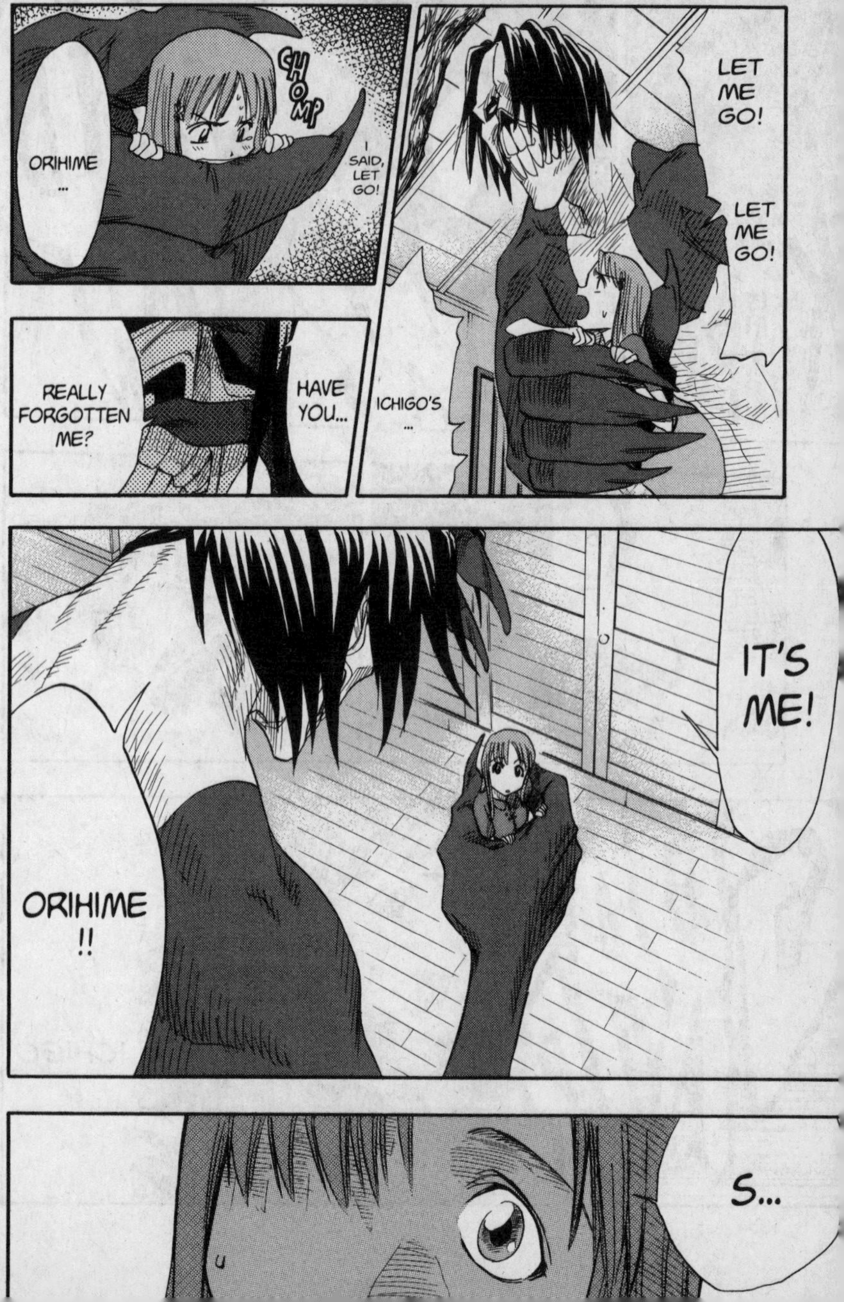
LET ME GO!
LET ME GO!
ICHIGO'S ...
CHOMP
I SAID, LET GO!
ORIHIME ...
HAVE YOU...
REALLY FORGOTTEN ME?
IT'S ME!
ORIHIME !!
S...

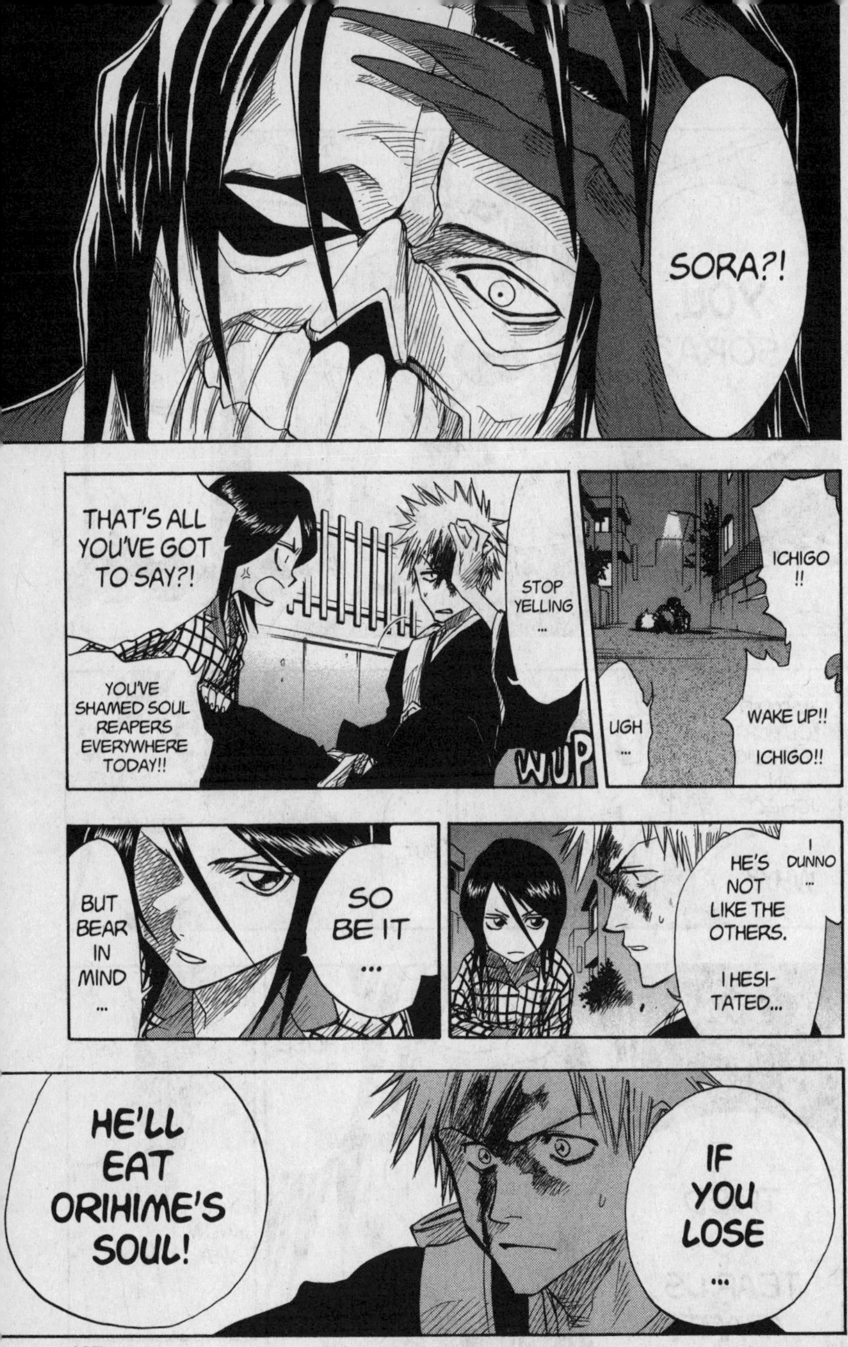
SORA?!
ICHIGO!!
WAKE UP!! ICHIGO!!
UGH...
STOP YELLING...
THAT'S ALL YOU'VE GOT TO SAY?!
WUP
YOU'VE SHAMED SOUL REAPERS EVERYWHERE TODAY!!
I DUNNO...
HE'S NOT LIKE THE OTHERS. I HESITATED...
SO BE IT...
BUT BEAR IN MIND...
IF YOU LOSE...
HE'LL EAT ORIHIME'S SOUL!

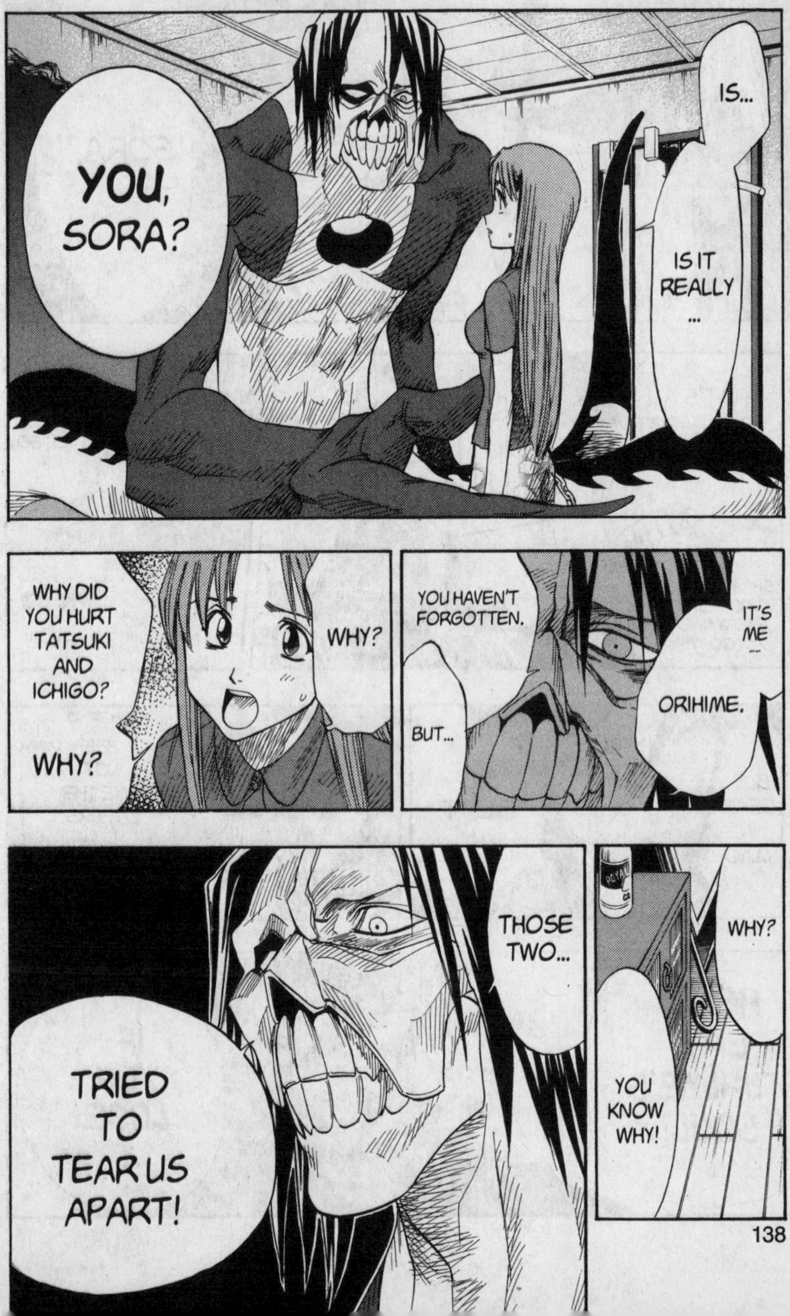
IS...
IS IT REALLY ...
YOU, SORA?
IT'S ME --
ORIHIME.
YOU HAVEN'T FORGOTTEN.
BUT...
WHY?
WHY DID YOU HURT TATSUKI AND ICHIGO?
WHY?
WHY?
YOU KNOW WHY!
THOSE TWO...
TRIED TO TEAR US APART!

READ THIS WAY

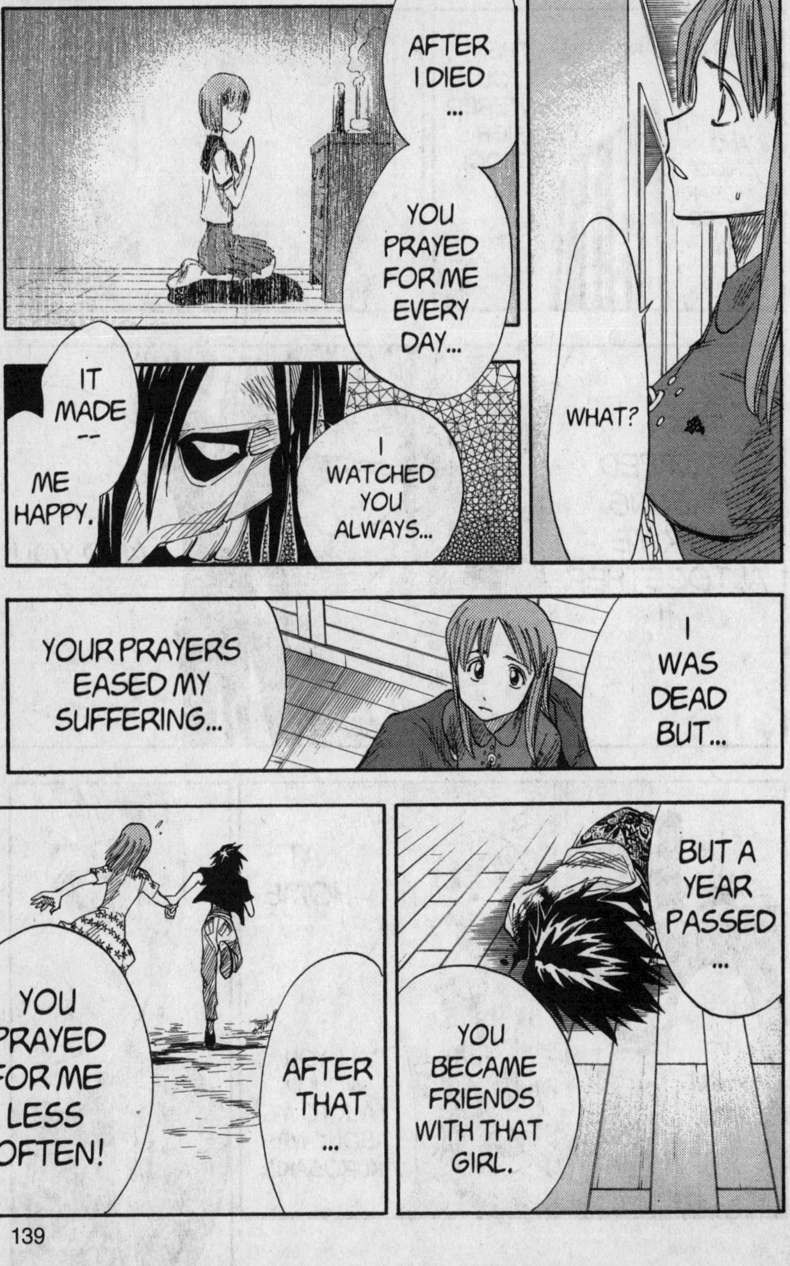
WHAT?
AFTER I DIED ...
YOU PRAYED FOR ME EVERY DAY...
I WATCHED YOU ALWAYS...
IT MADE -- ME HAPPY.
I WAS DEAD BUT...
YOUR PRAYERS EASED MY SUFFERING...
BUT A YEAR PASSED ...
YOU BECAME FRIENDS WITH THAT GIRL.
AFTER THAT ...
YOU PRAYED FOR ME LESS OFTEN!

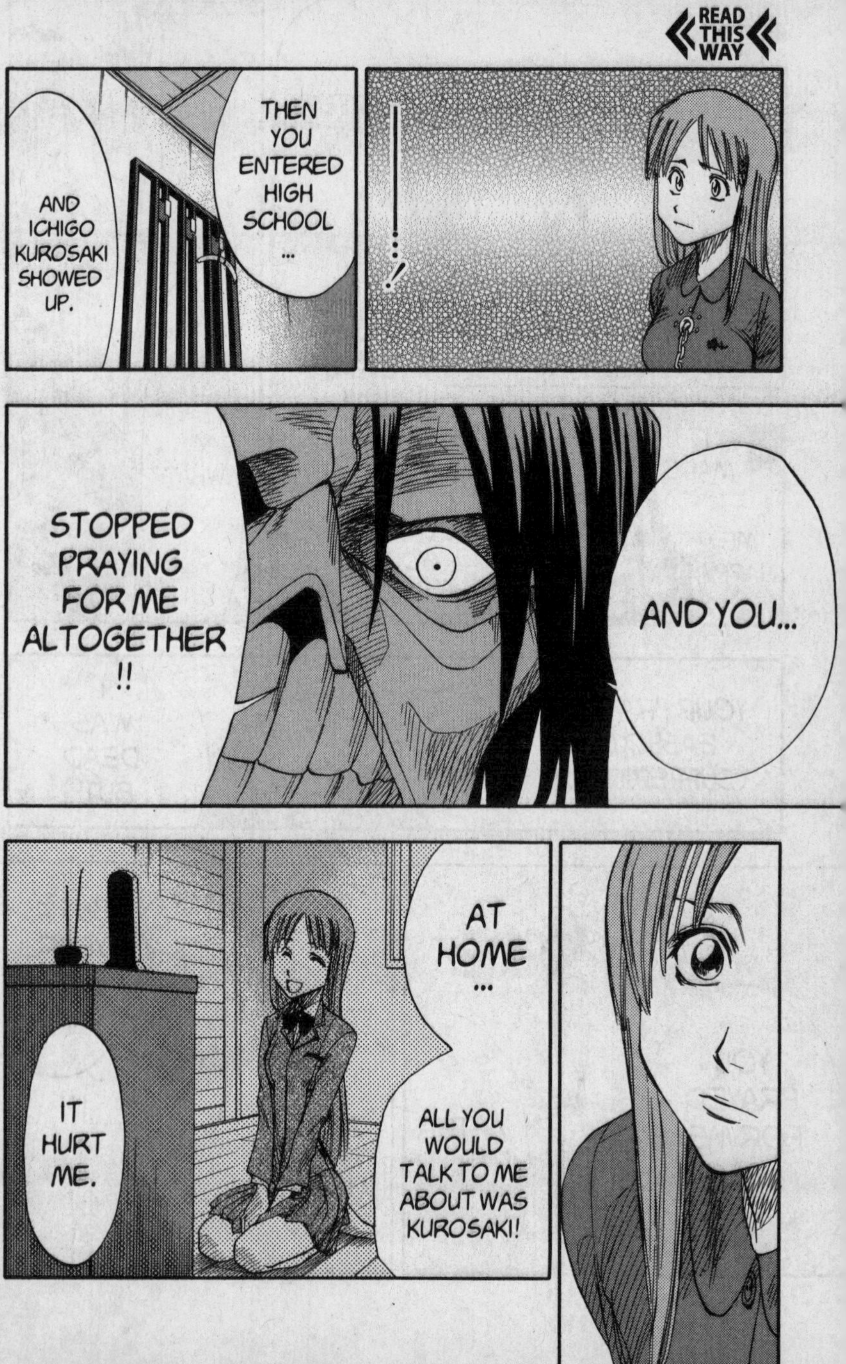
READ THIS WAY
......!
THEN YOU ENTERED HIGH SCHOOL ...
AND ICHIGO KUROSAKI SHOWED UP.
AND YOU...
STOPPED PRAYING FOR ME ALTOGETHER !!
AT HOME ...
ALL YOU WOULD TALK TO ME ABOUT WAS KUROSAKI!
IT HURT ME.

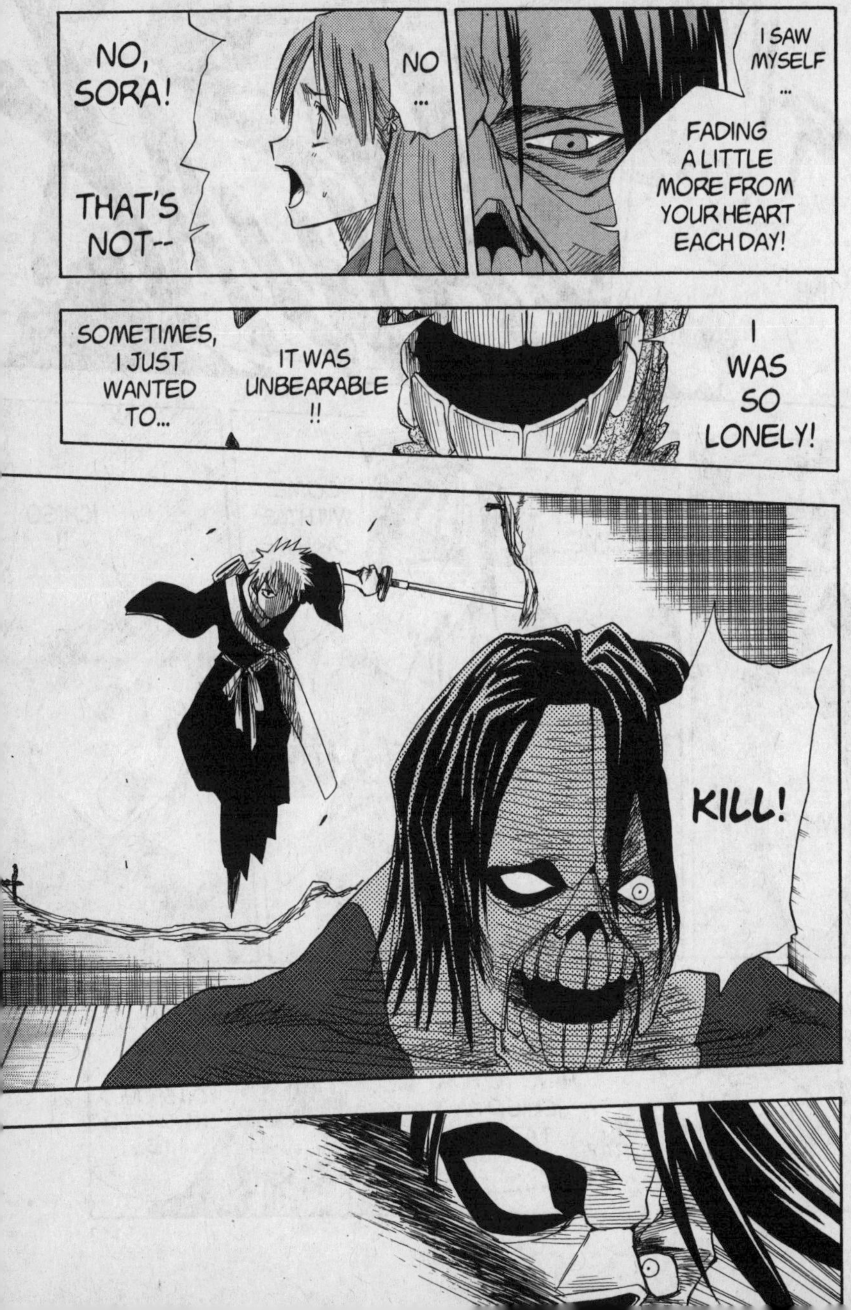
I SAW MYSELF ... FADING A LITTLE MORE FROM YOUR HEART EACH DAY!
NO ...
NO, SORA!
THAT'S NOT--
I WAS SO LONELY!
IT WAS UNBEARABLE !!
SOMETIMES, I JUST WANTED TO...
KILL!

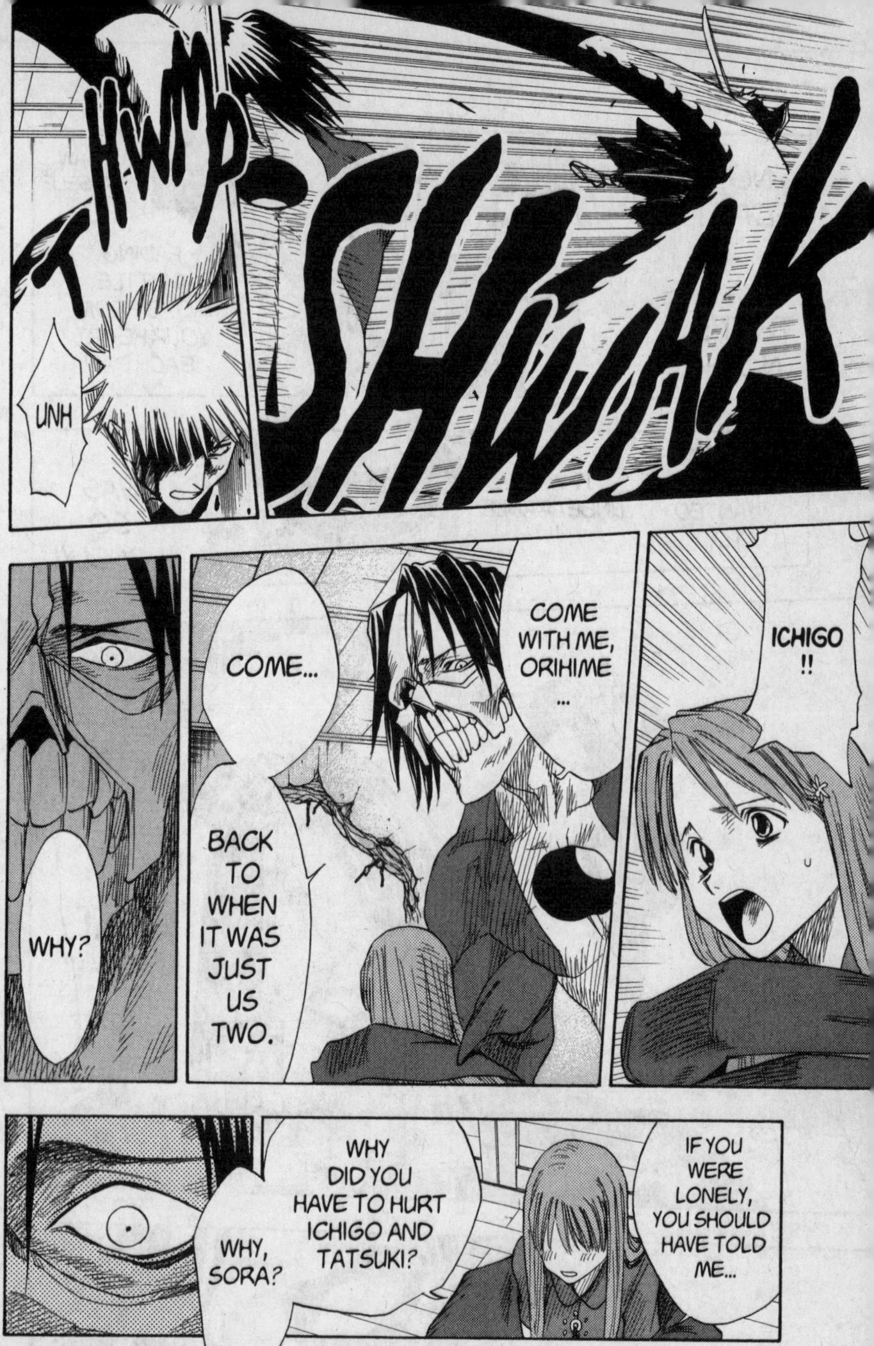
SHWAK
THWMP
UNH
ICHIGO !!
COME WITH ME, ORIHIME ...
COME...
BACK TO WHEN IT WAS JUST US TWO.
WHY?
IF YOU WERE LONELY, YOU SHOULD HAVE TOLD ME...
WHY DID YOU HAVE TO HURT ICHIGO AND TATSUKI?
WHY, SORA?

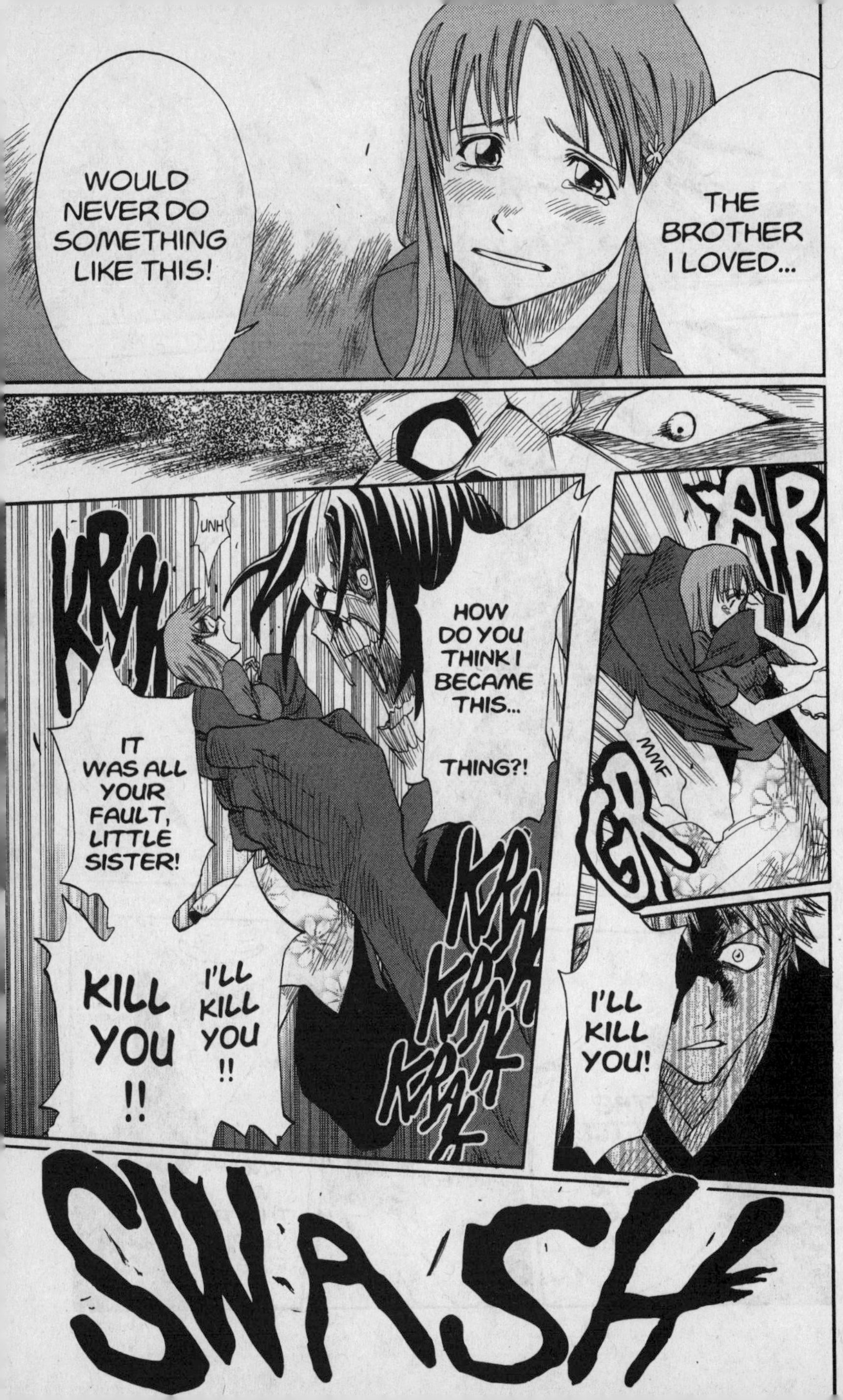
THE BROTHER I LOVED...
WOULD NEVER DO SOMETHING LIKE THIS!
GRAB
MMF
I'LL KILL YOU!
HOW DO YOU THINK I BECAME THIS...
THING?!
UNH
KRAK
IT WAS ALL YOUR FAULT, LITTLE SISTER!
KRAK KRAK KRAK
I'LL KILL YOU !!
KILL YOU !!
SWASH

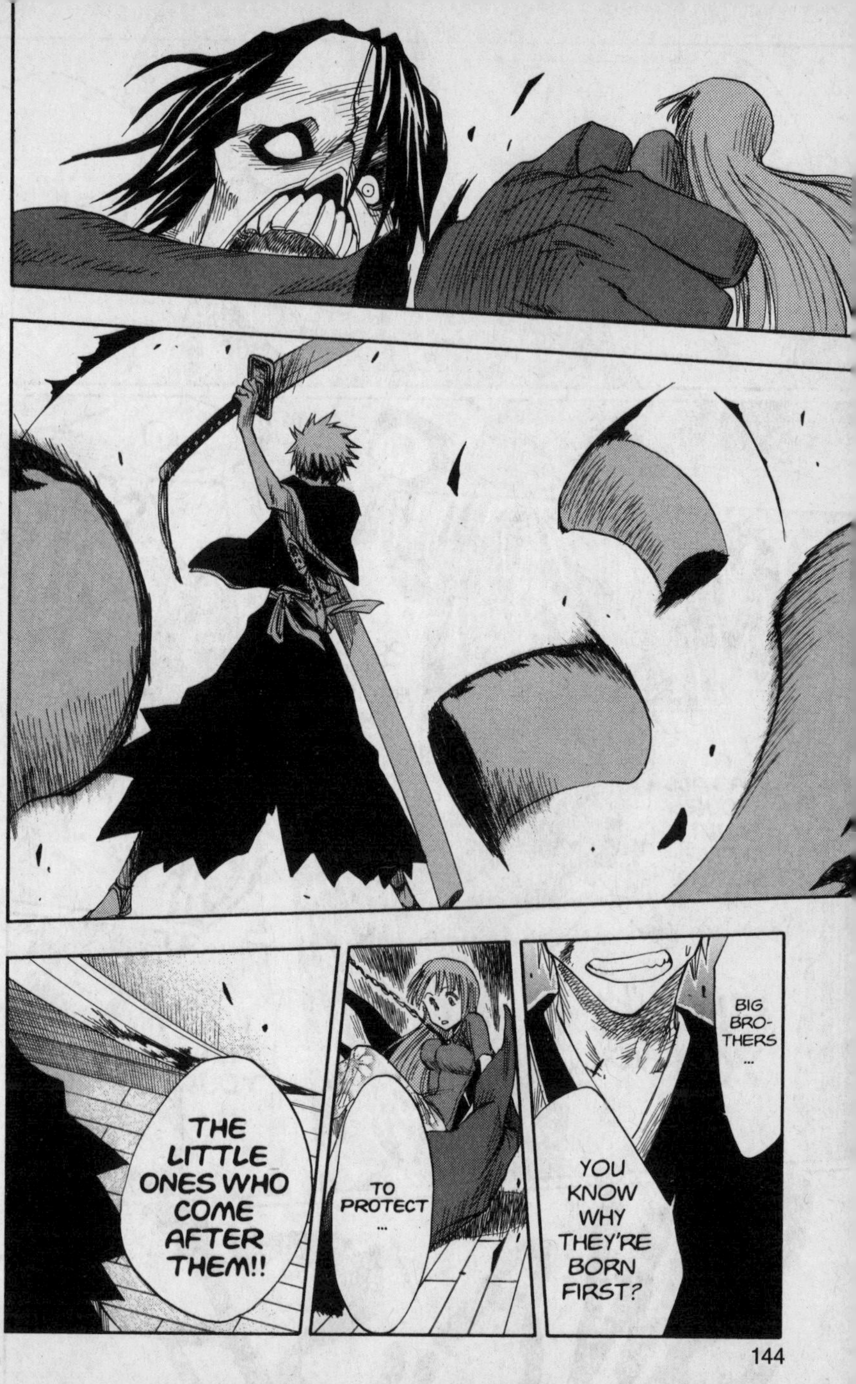
BIG BROTHERS...
YOU KNOW WHY THEY'RE BORN FIRST?
TO PROTECT...
THE LITTLE ONES WHO COME AFTER THEM!!

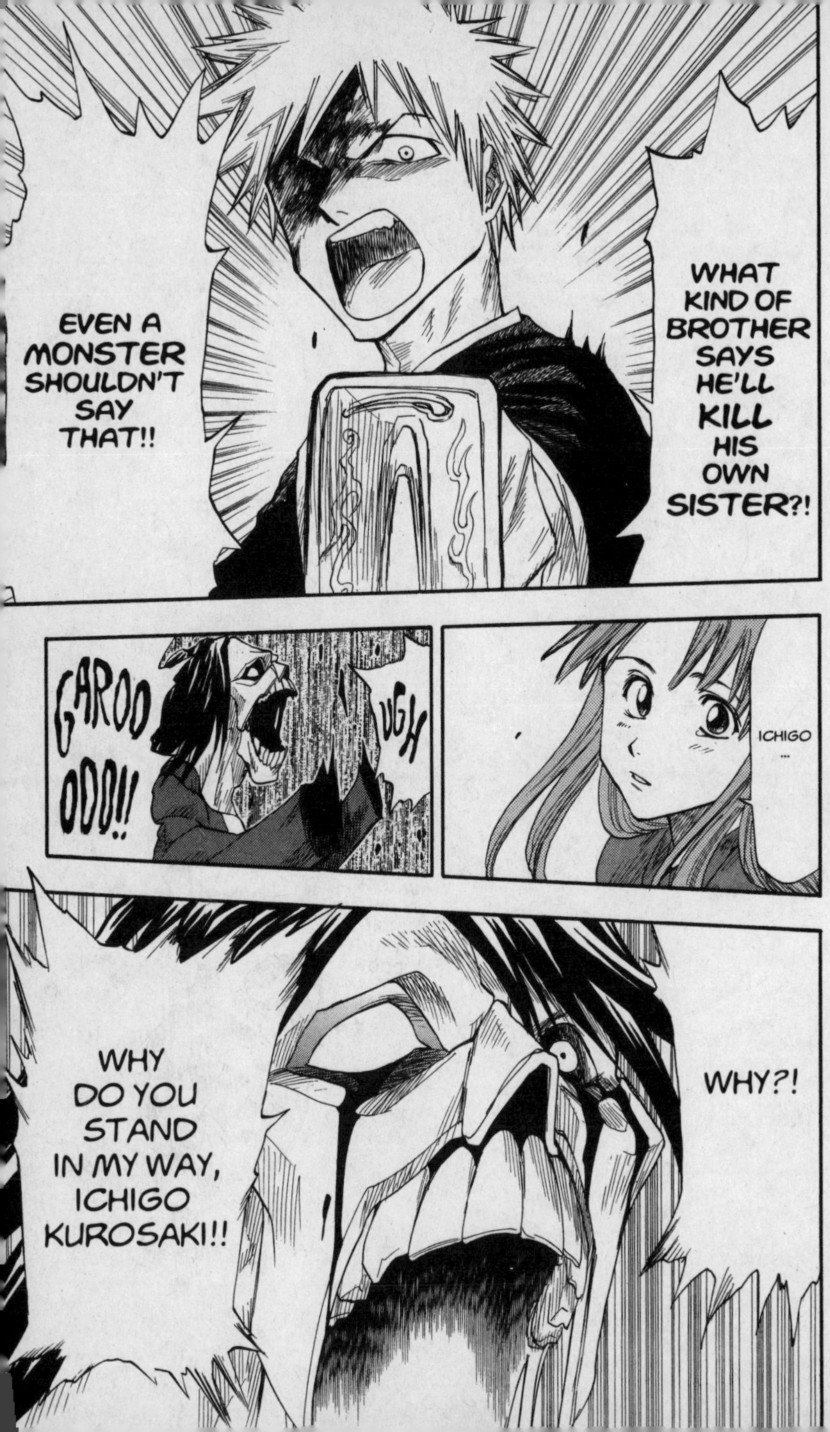
WHAT KIND OF BROTHER SAYS HE'LL KILL HIS OWN SISTER?!
EVEN A MONSTER SHOULDN'T SAY THAT!!
ICHIGO ...
UGH
GAROOODO!!
WHY?!
WHY DO YOU STAND IN MY WAY, ICHIGO KUROSAKI!!

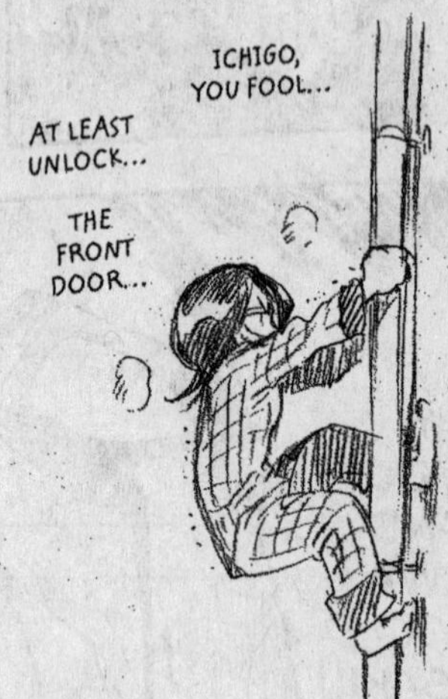
ICHIGO, YOU FOOL...
AT LEAST UNLOCK...
THE FRONT DOOR...

6. Microcrack.

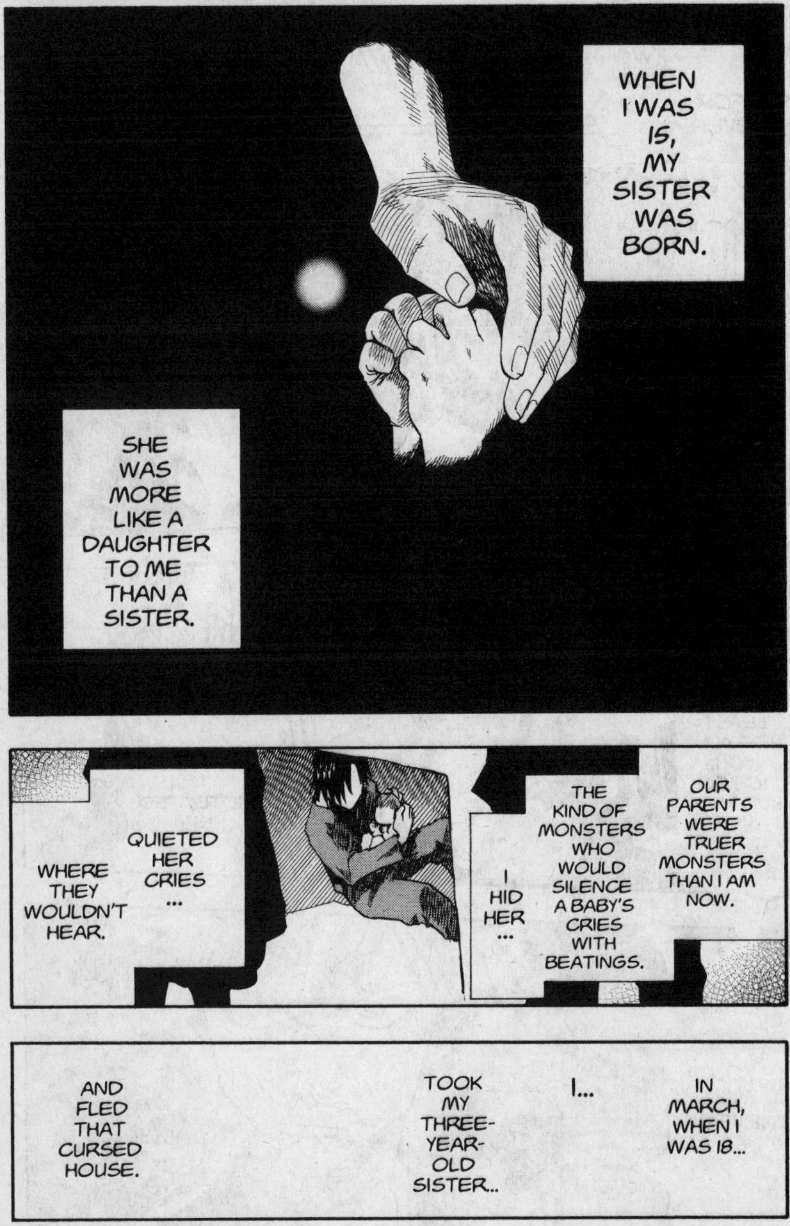
WHEN I WAS 15, MY SISTER WAS BORN.
SHE WAS MORE LIKE A DAUGHTER TO ME THAN A SISTER.
OUR PARENTS WERE TRUER MONSTERS THAN I AM NOW.
THE KIND OF MONSTERS WHO WOULD SILENCE A BABY'S CRIES WITH BEATINGS.
I HID HER...
QUIETED HER CRIES...
WHERE THEY WOULDN'T HEAR.
IN MARCH, WHEN I WAS 18...
I...
TOOK MY THREE-YEAR-OLD SISTER...
AND FLED THAT CURSED HOUSE.

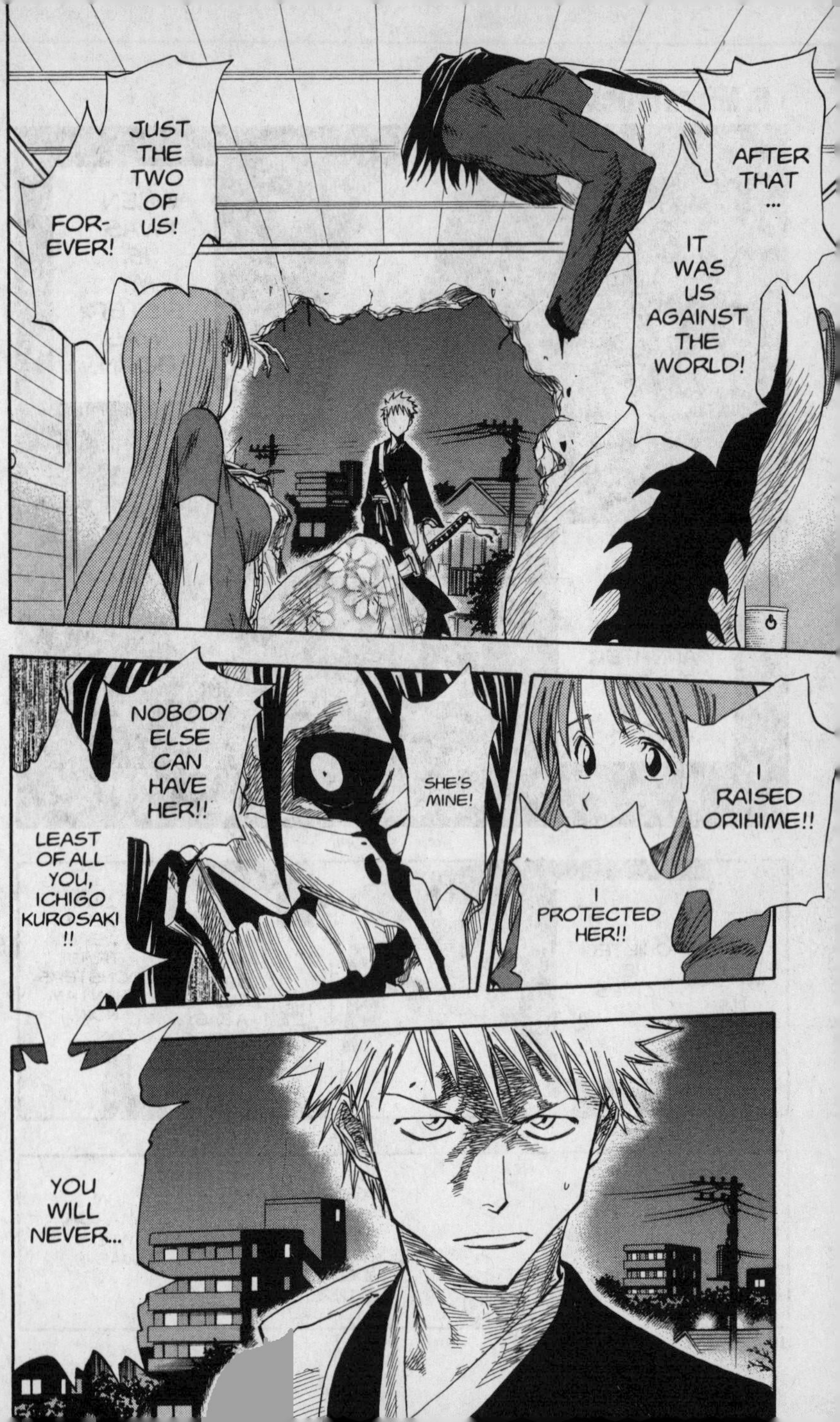
AFTER THAT...
IT WAS US AGAINST THE WORLD!
JUST THE TWO OF US!
FOR-EVER!
I RAISED ORIHIME!!
I PROTECTED HER!!
SHE'S MINE!
NOBODY ELSE CAN HAVE HER!!
LEAST OF ALL YOU, ICHIGO KUROSAKI!!
YOU WILL NEVER...

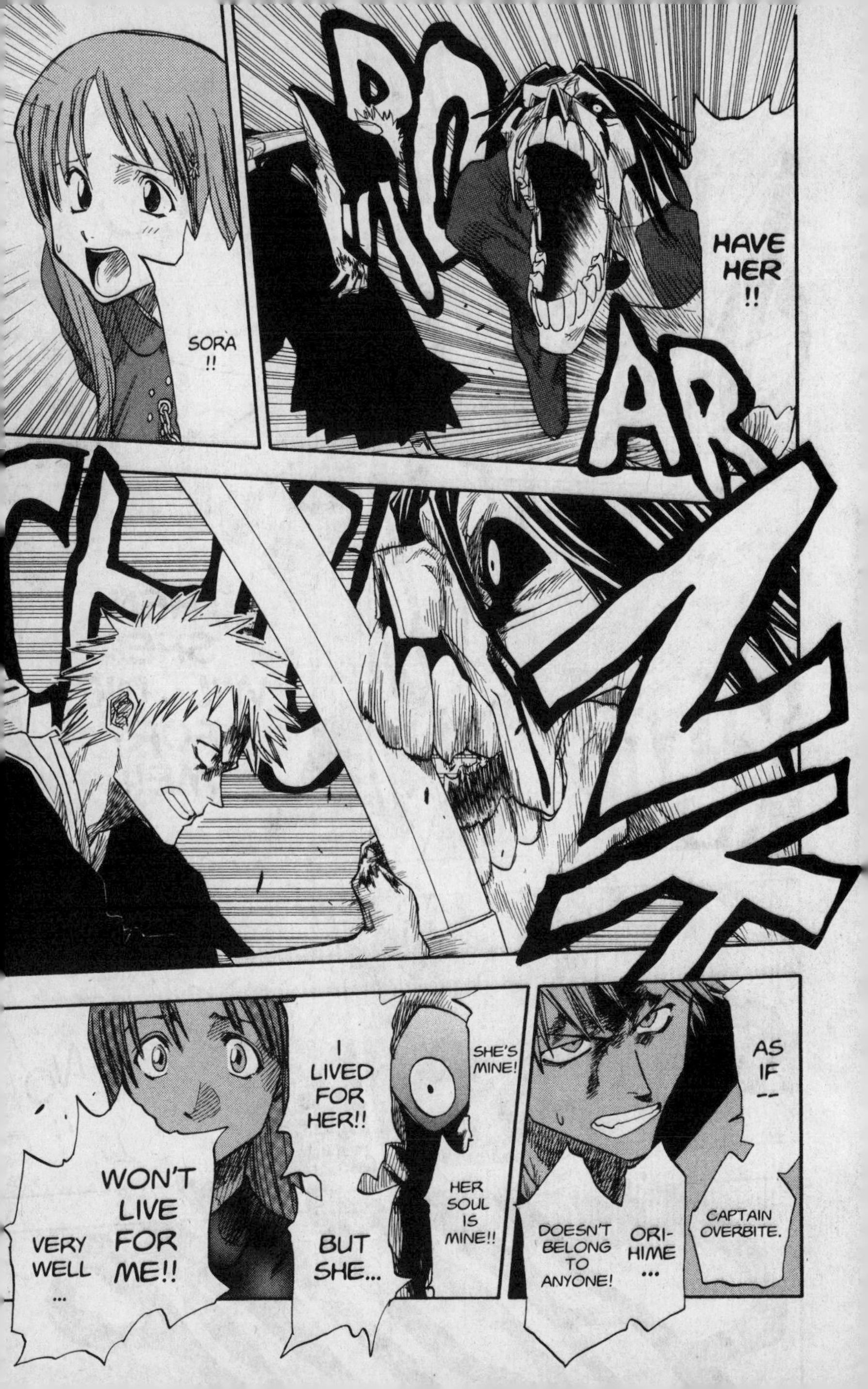
HAVE HER !!
ROAR
SORA !!
AS IF --
CAPTAIN OVERBITE.
ORI-HIME ...
DOESN'T BELONG TO ANYONE!
SHE'S MINE!
I LIVED FOR HER!!
HER SOUL IS MINE!!
BUT SHE...
WON'T LIVE FOR ME!!
VERY WELL ...

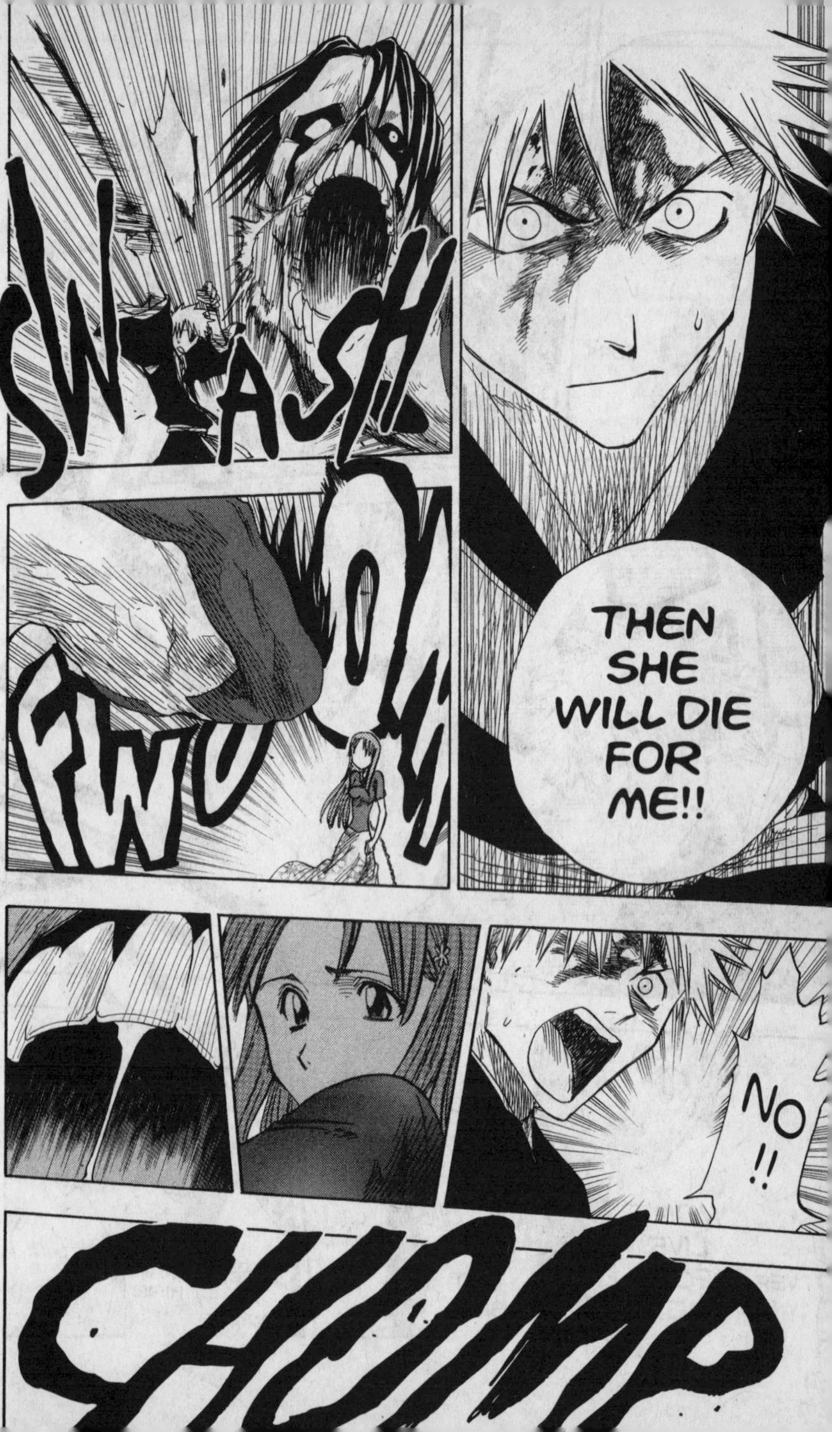
SWASH
THEN SHE WILL DIE FOR ME!!
FWOOM
NO!!
CHOMP

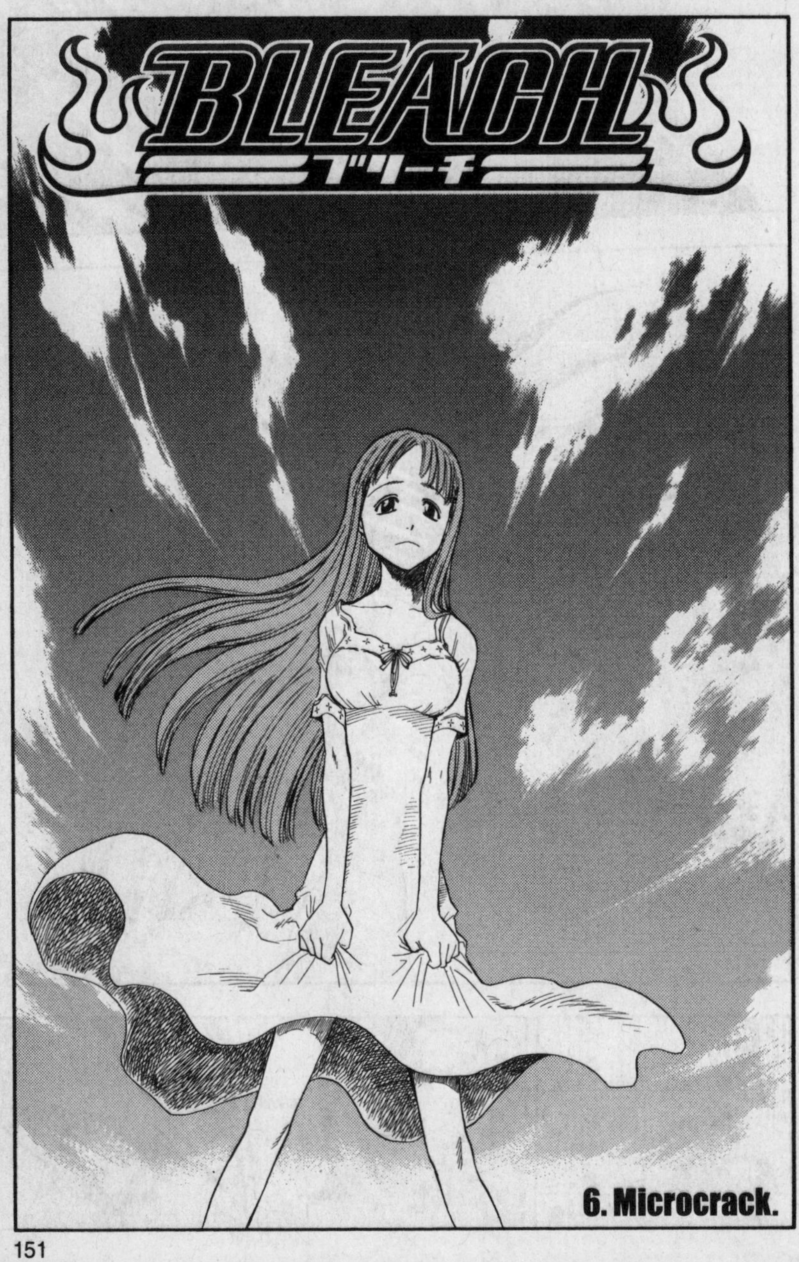
BLEACH
ブリーチ
6. Microcrack.

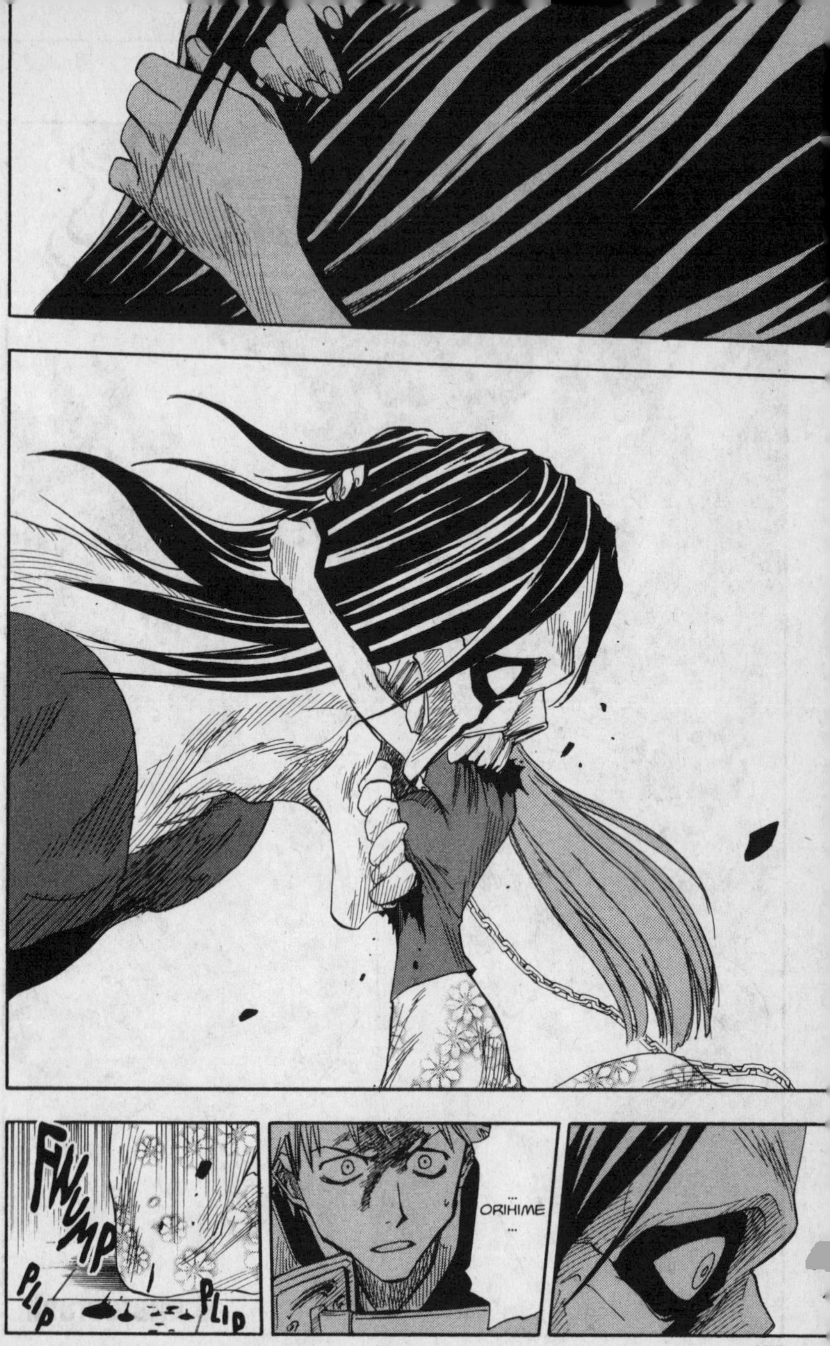
...
ORIHIME
...
FWUMP
PLIP
PLIP

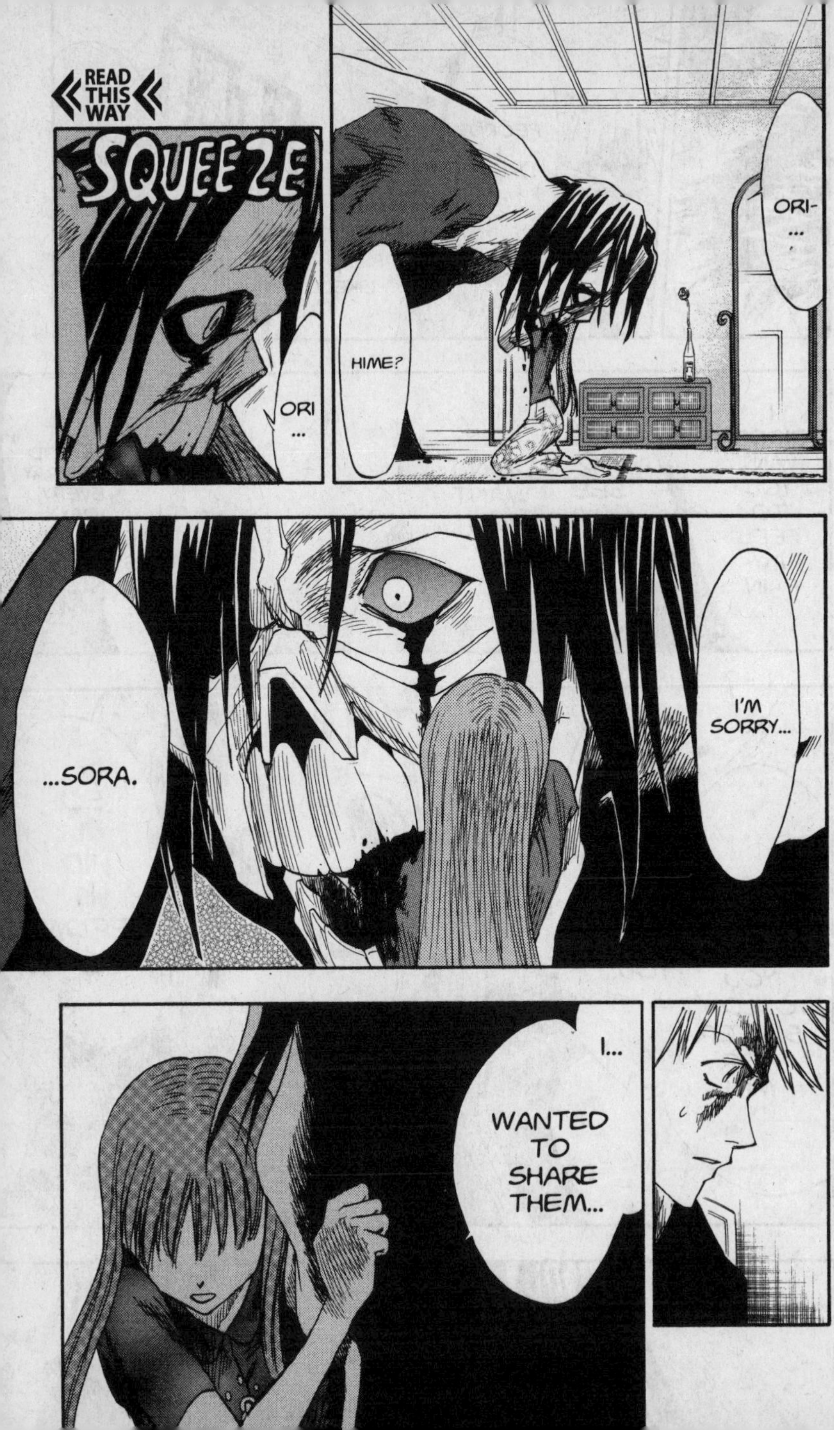
READ THIS WAY
ORI-...
HIME?
SQUEEZE
ORI ...
I'M SORRY...
...SORA.
I... WANTED TO SHARE THEM...

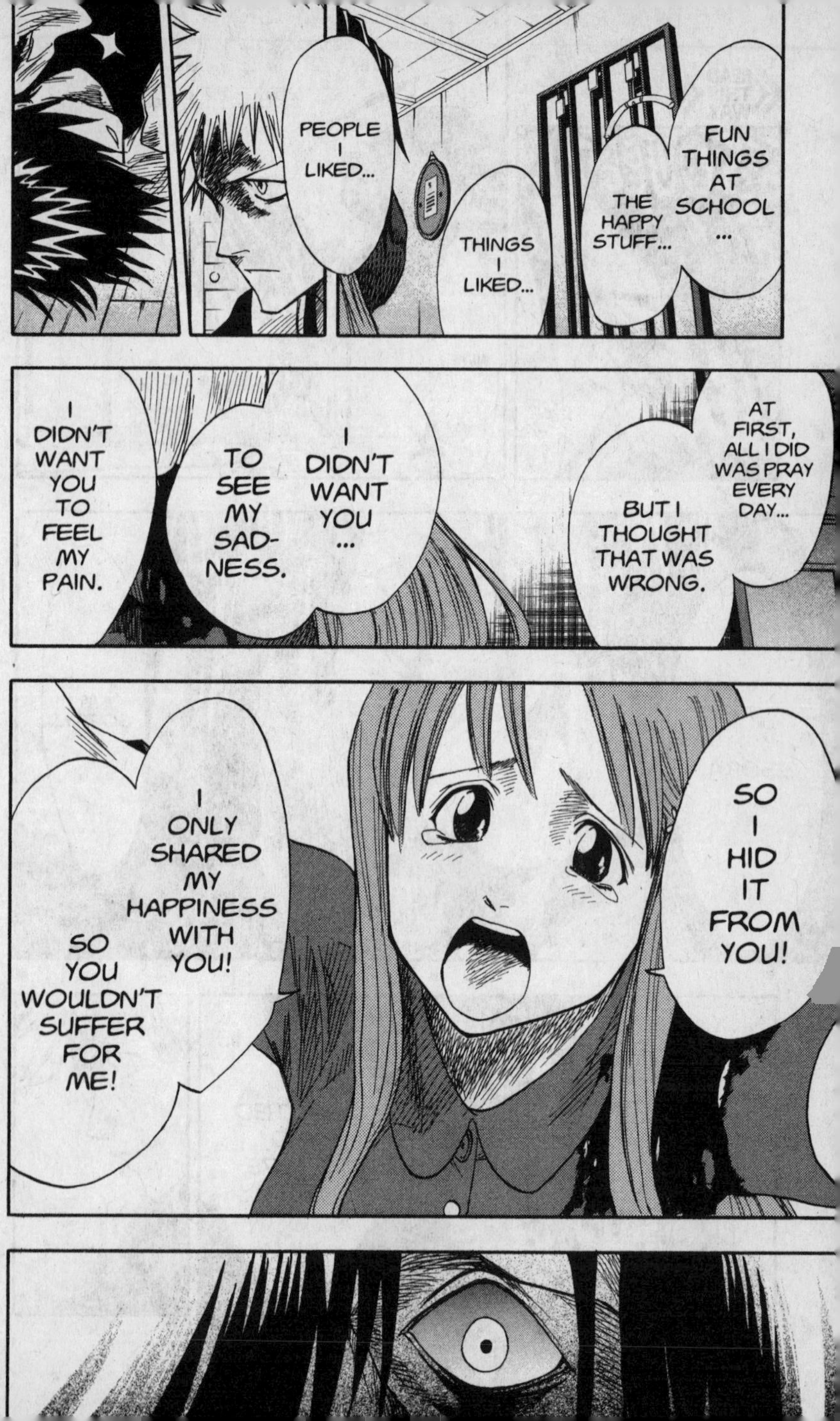
FUN THINGS AT SCHOOL ...
THE HAPPY STUFF...
THINGS I LIKED...
PEOPLE I LIKED...
AT FIRST, ALL I DID WAS PRAY EVERY DAY...
BUT I THOUGHT THAT WAS WRONG.
I DIDN'T WANT YOU ...
TO SEE MY SAD-NESS.
I DIDN'T WANT YOU TO FEEL MY PAIN.
SO I HID IT FROM YOU!
I ONLY SHARED MY HAPPINESS WITH YOU!
SO YOU WOULDN'T SUFFER FOR ME!

READ THIS WAY

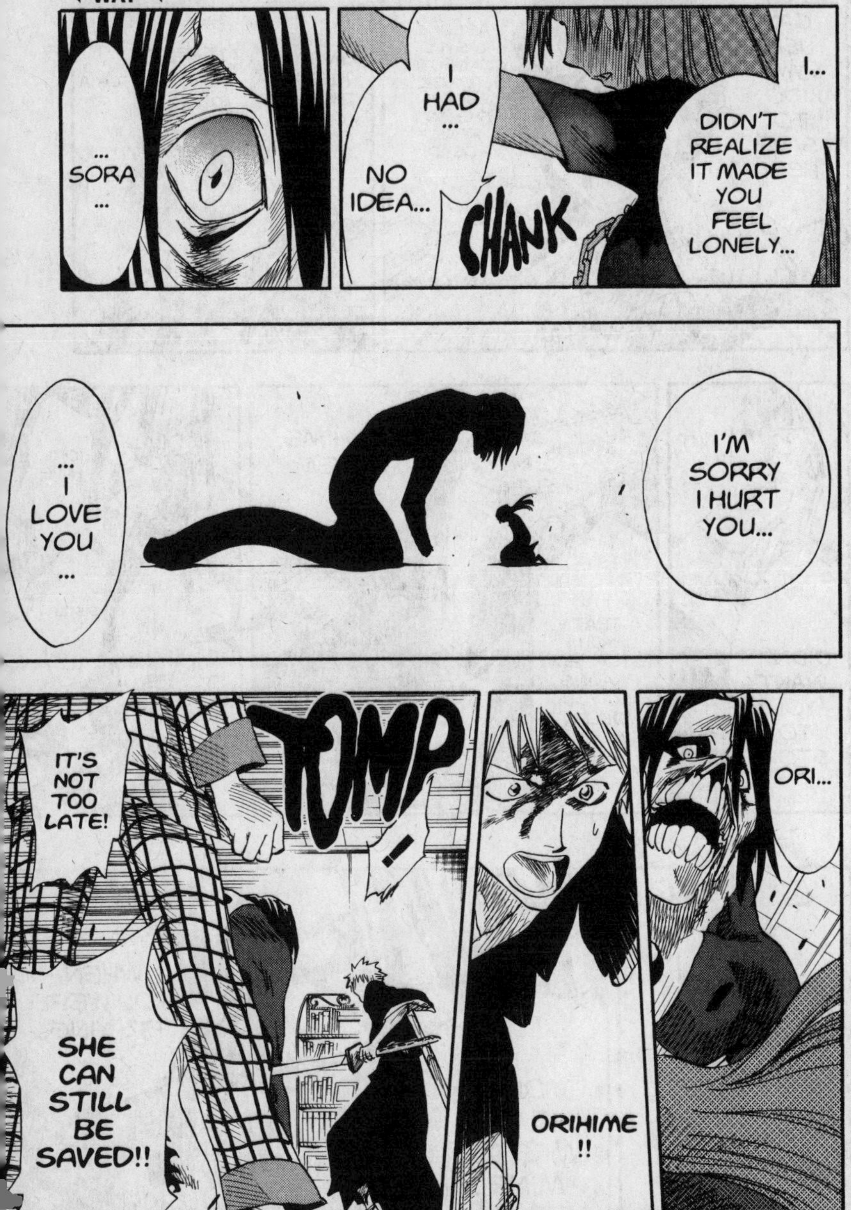
I...
DIDN'T REALIZE IT MADE YOU FEEL LONELY...
I HAD ... NO IDEA...
CHANK
... SORA ...
I'M SORRY I HURT YOU...
... I LOVE YOU ...
ORI...
ORIHIME !!
TOMP
IT'S NOT TOO LATE!
SHE CAN STILL BE SAVED!!

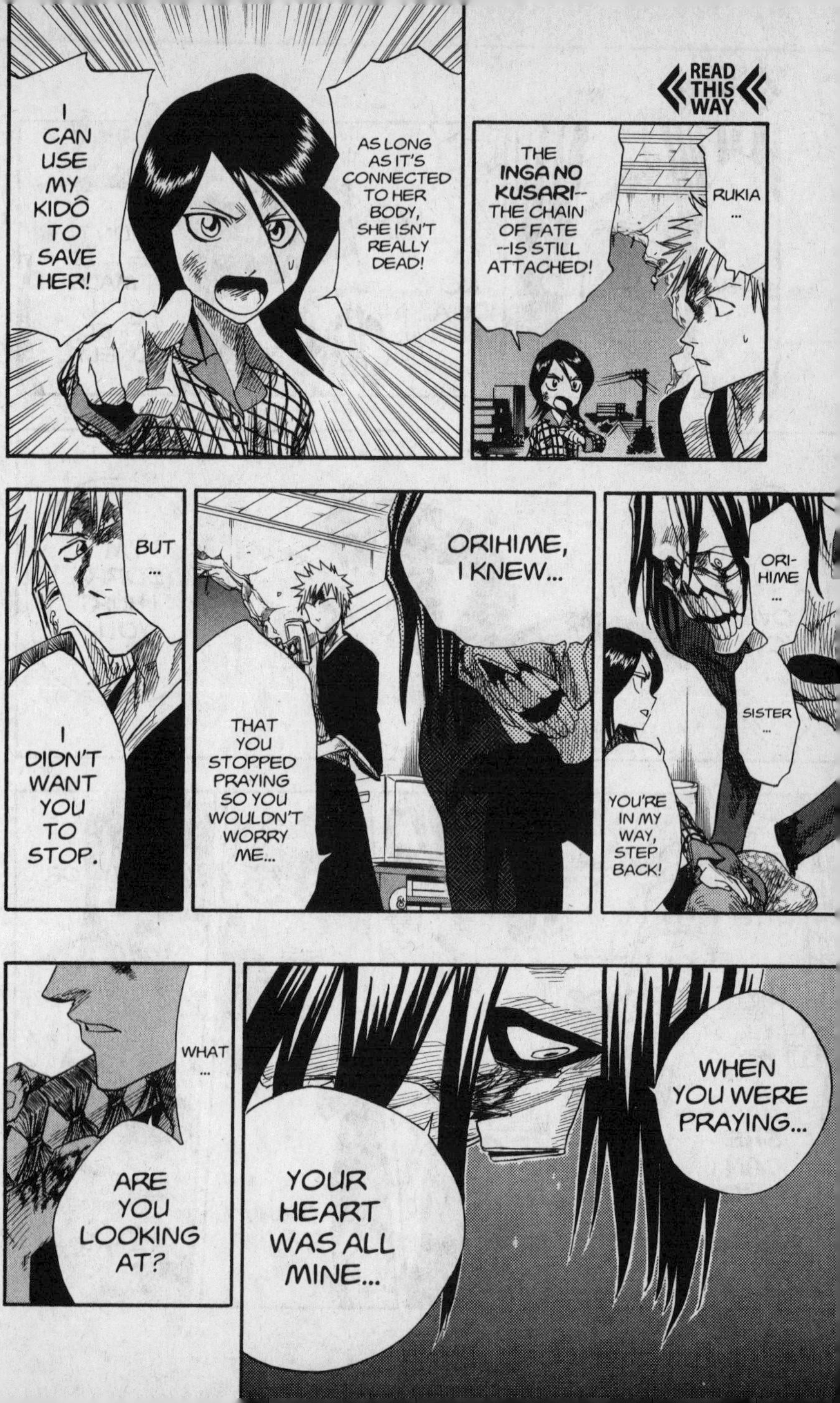
READ THIS WAY
RUKIA ...
THE INGA NO KUSARI-- THE CHAIN OF FATE --IS STILL ATTACHED!
AS LONG AS IT'S CONNECTED TO HER BODY, SHE ISN'T REALLY DEAD!
I CAN USE MY KIDÔ TO SAVE HER!
ORI-HIME ...
SISTER ...
YOU'RE IN MY WAY, STEP BACK!
ORIHIME, I KNEW...
THAT YOU STOPPED PRAYING SO YOU WOULDN'T WORRY ME...
BUT ...
I DIDN'T WANT YOU TO STOP.
WHEN YOU WERE PRAYING...
YOUR HEART WAS ALL MINE...
WHAT ...
ARE YOU LOOKING AT?

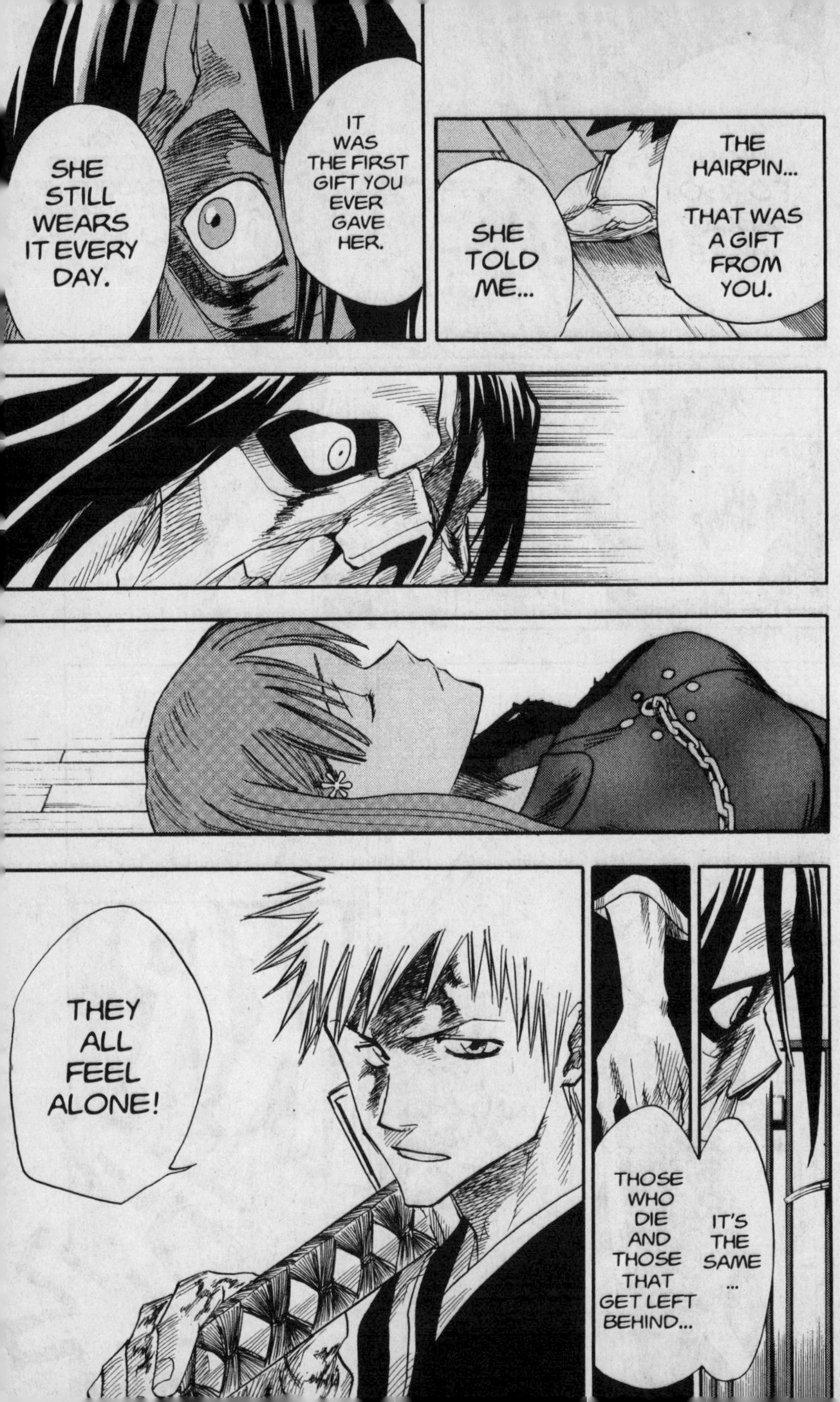
THE HAIRPIN... THAT WAS A GIFT FROM YOU.
SHE TOLD ME...
IT WAS THE FIRST GIFT YOU EVER GAVE HER.
SHE STILL WEARS IT EVERY DAY.
IT'S THE SAME...
THOSE WHO DIE AND THOSE THAT GET LEFT BEHIND...
THEY ALL FEEL ALONE!

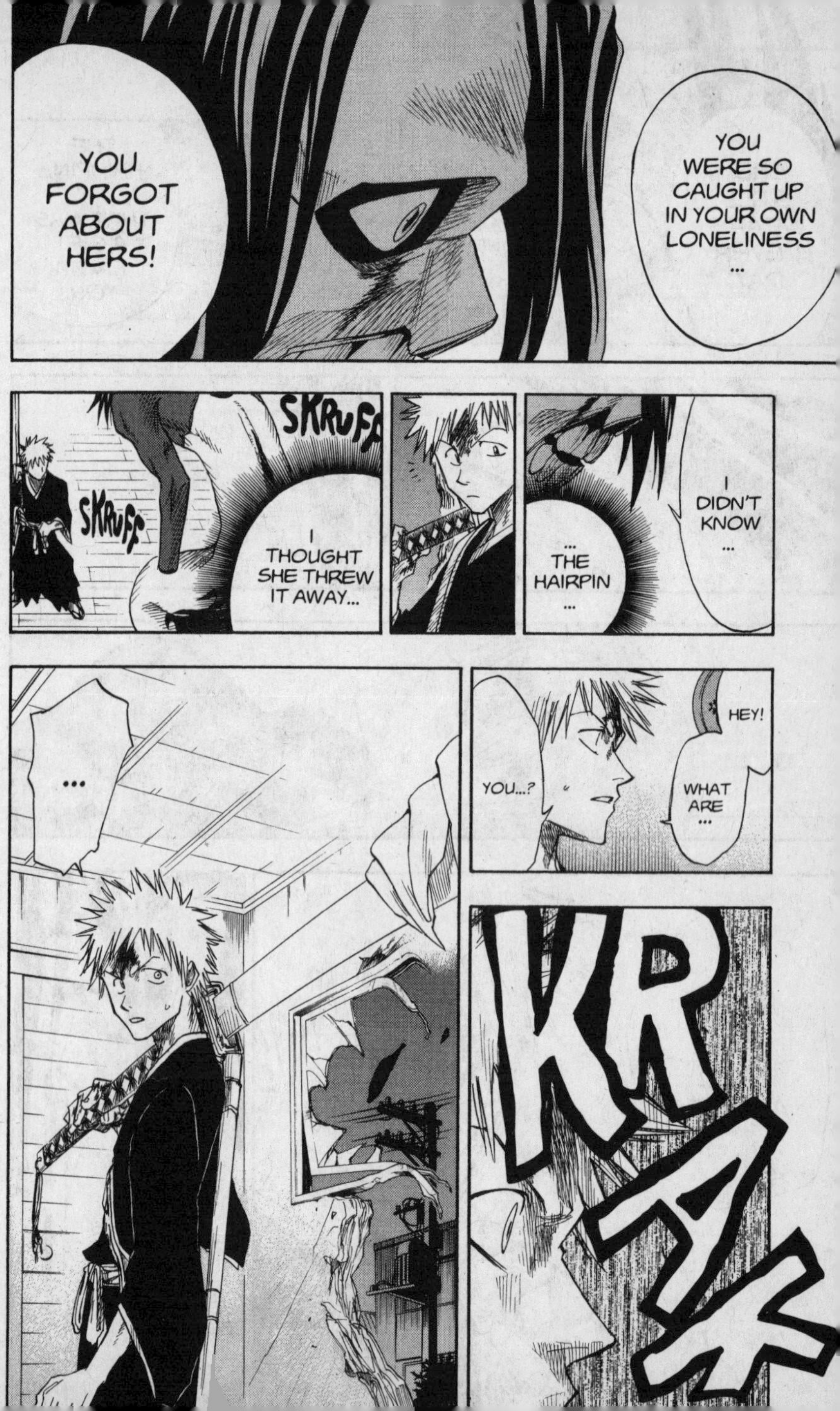
YOU WERE SO CAUGHT UP IN YOUR OWN LONELINESS ...
YOU FORGOT ABOUT HERS!
I DIDN'T KNOW ...
... THE HAIRPIN ...
SKRUFF
I THOUGHT SHE THREW IT AWAY...
SKRUFF
HEY!
WHAT ARE ...
YOU...?
KRAK
...

READ THIS WAY

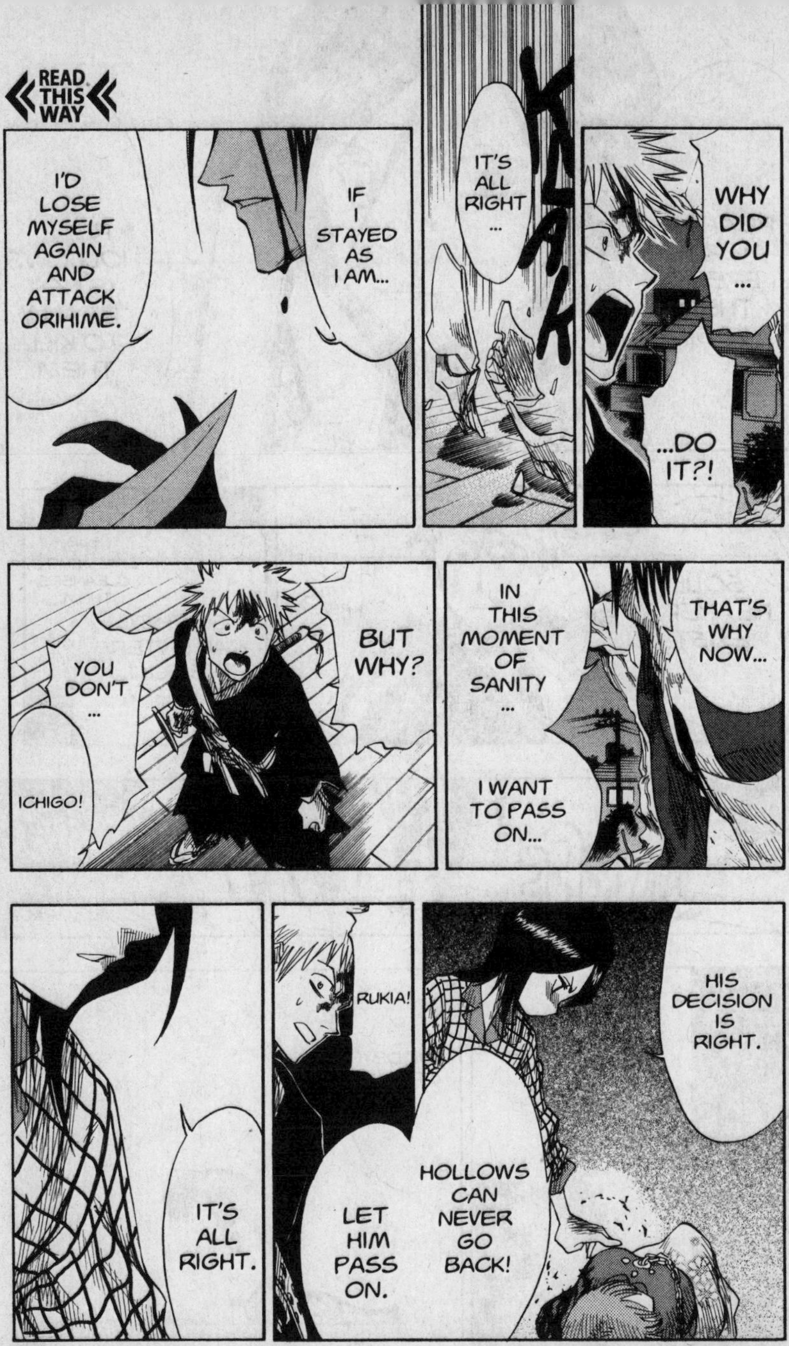
WHY DID YOU ...
...DO IT?!
KLAK
IT'S ALL RIGHT ...
IF I STAYED AS I AM...
I'D LOSE MYSELF AGAIN AND ATTACK ORIHIME.
THAT'S WHY NOW...
IN THIS MOMENT OF SANITY ...
I WANT TO PASS ON...
BUT WHY?
YOU DON'T ...
ICHIGO!
HIS DECISION IS RIGHT.
HOLLOWS CAN NEVER GO BACK!
LET HIM PASS ON.
RUKIA!
IT'S ALL RIGHT.

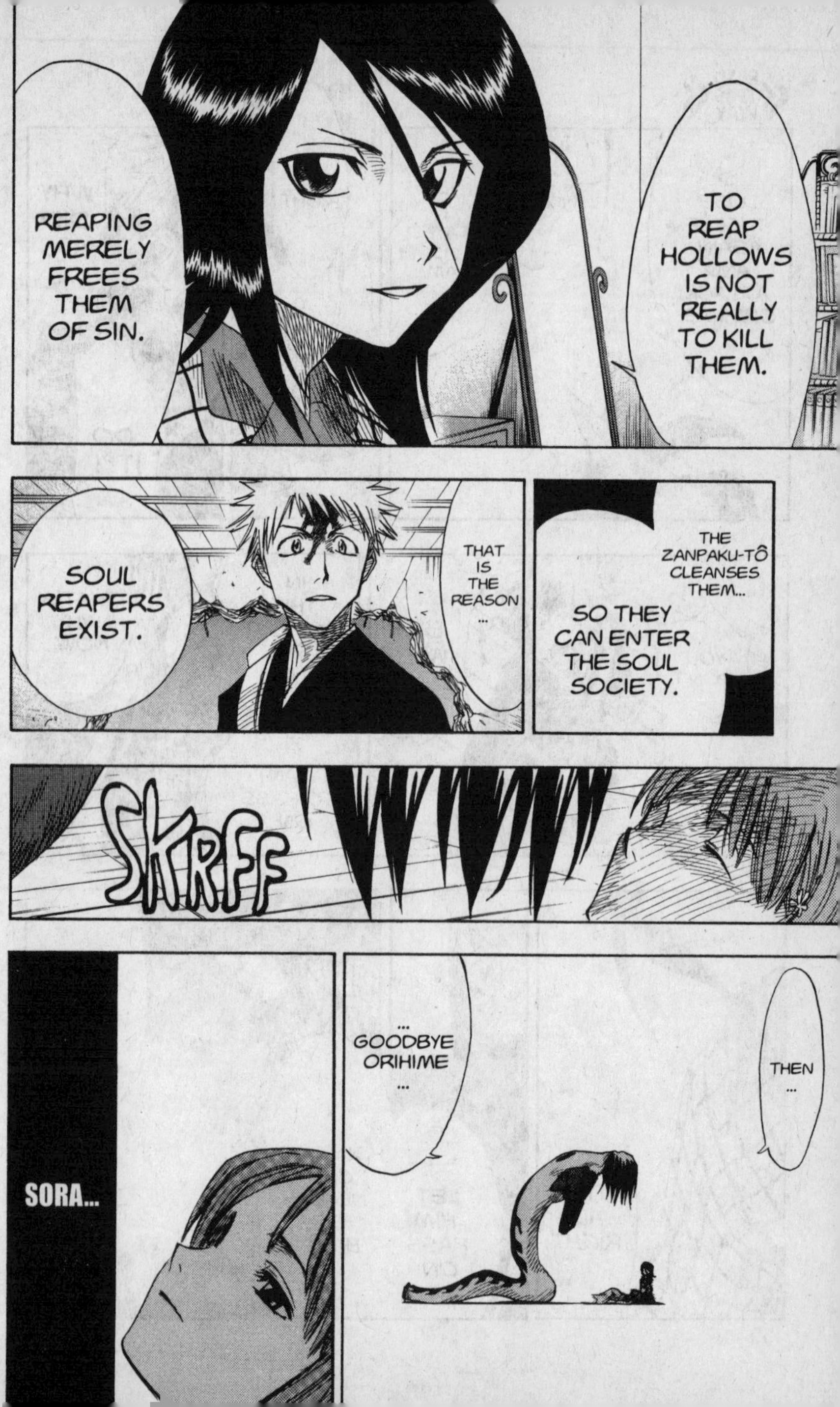
TO REAP HOLLOWS IS NOT REALLY TO KILL THEM.
REAPING MERELY FREES THEM OF SIN.
THE ZANPAKU-TÔ CLEANSES THEM...
SO THEY CAN ENTER THE SOUL SOCIETY.
THAT IS THE REASON ...
SOUL REAPERS EXIST.
SKRFF
THEN ...
... GOODBYE ORIHIME ...
SORA...

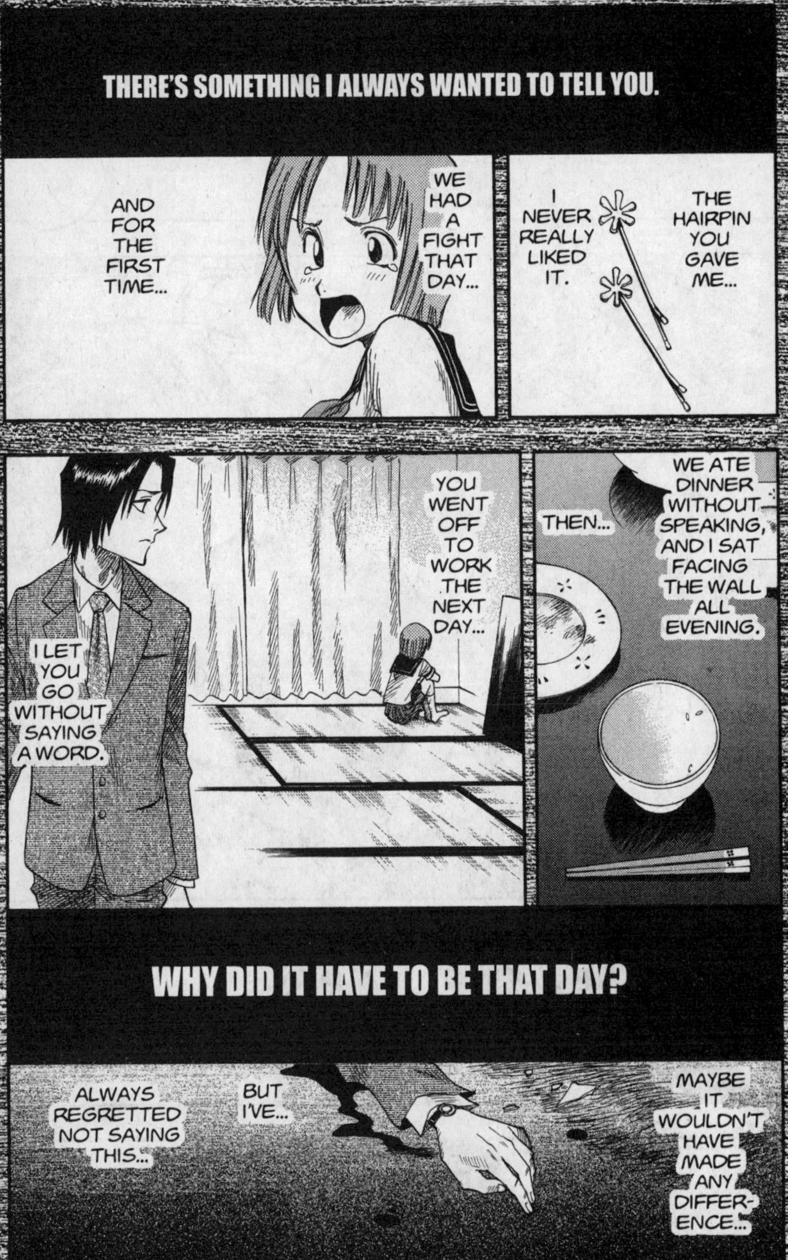
THERE'S SOMETHING I ALWAYS WANTED TO TELL YOU.
THE HAIRPIN YOU GAVE ME...
I NEVER REALLY LIKED IT.
WE HAD A FIGHT THAT DAY...
AND FOR THE FIRST TIME...
WE ATE DINNER WITHOUT SPEAKING, AND I SAT FACING THE WALL ALL EVENING.
THEN...
YOU WENT OFF TO WORK THE NEXT DAY...
I LET YOU GO WITHOUT SAYING A WORD.
WHY DID IT HAVE TO BE THAT DAY?
MAYBE IT WOULDN'T HAVE MADE ANY DIFFER-ENCE...
BUT I'VE...
ALWAYS REGRETTED NOT SAYING THIS...

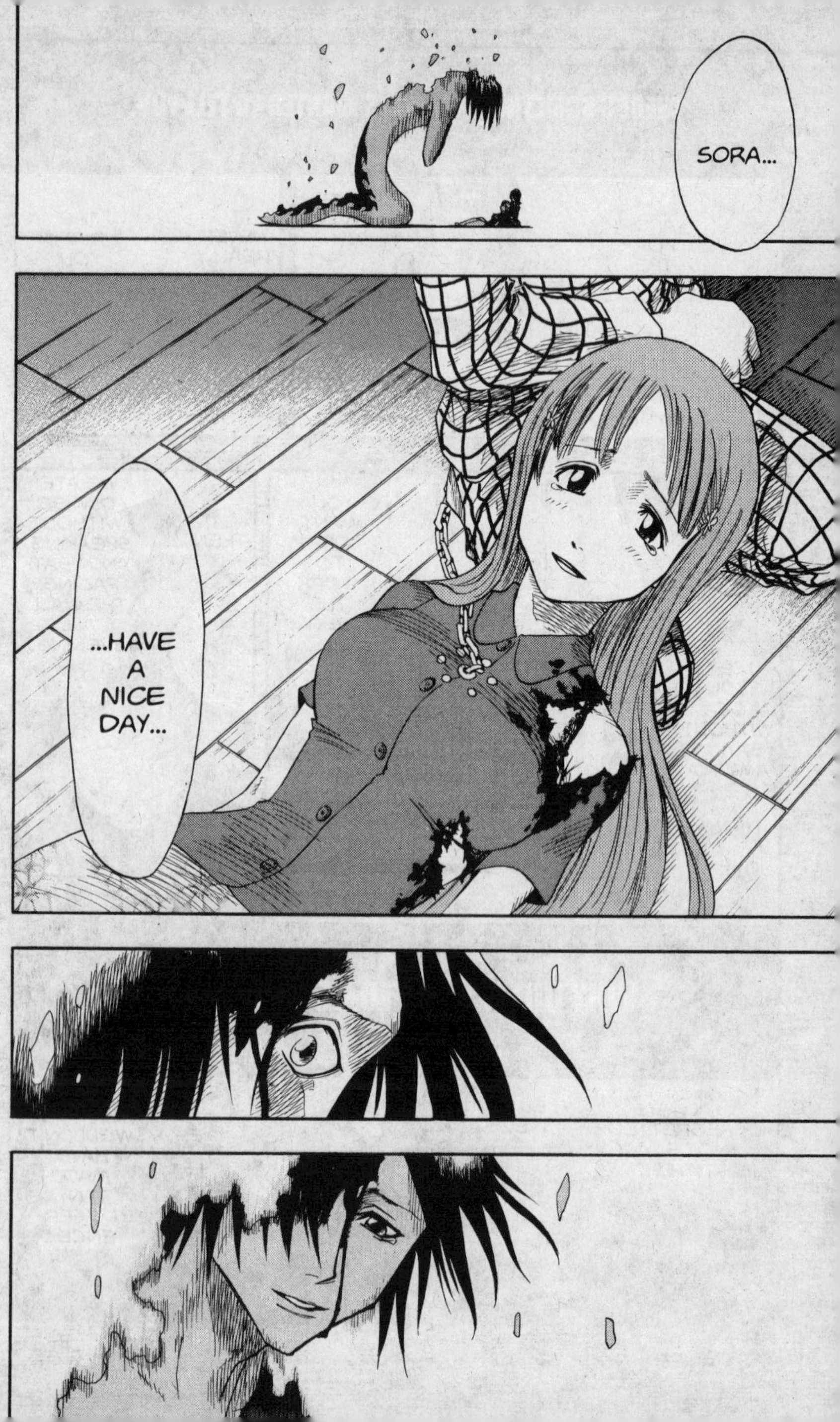
SORA...
...HAVE A NICE DAY...

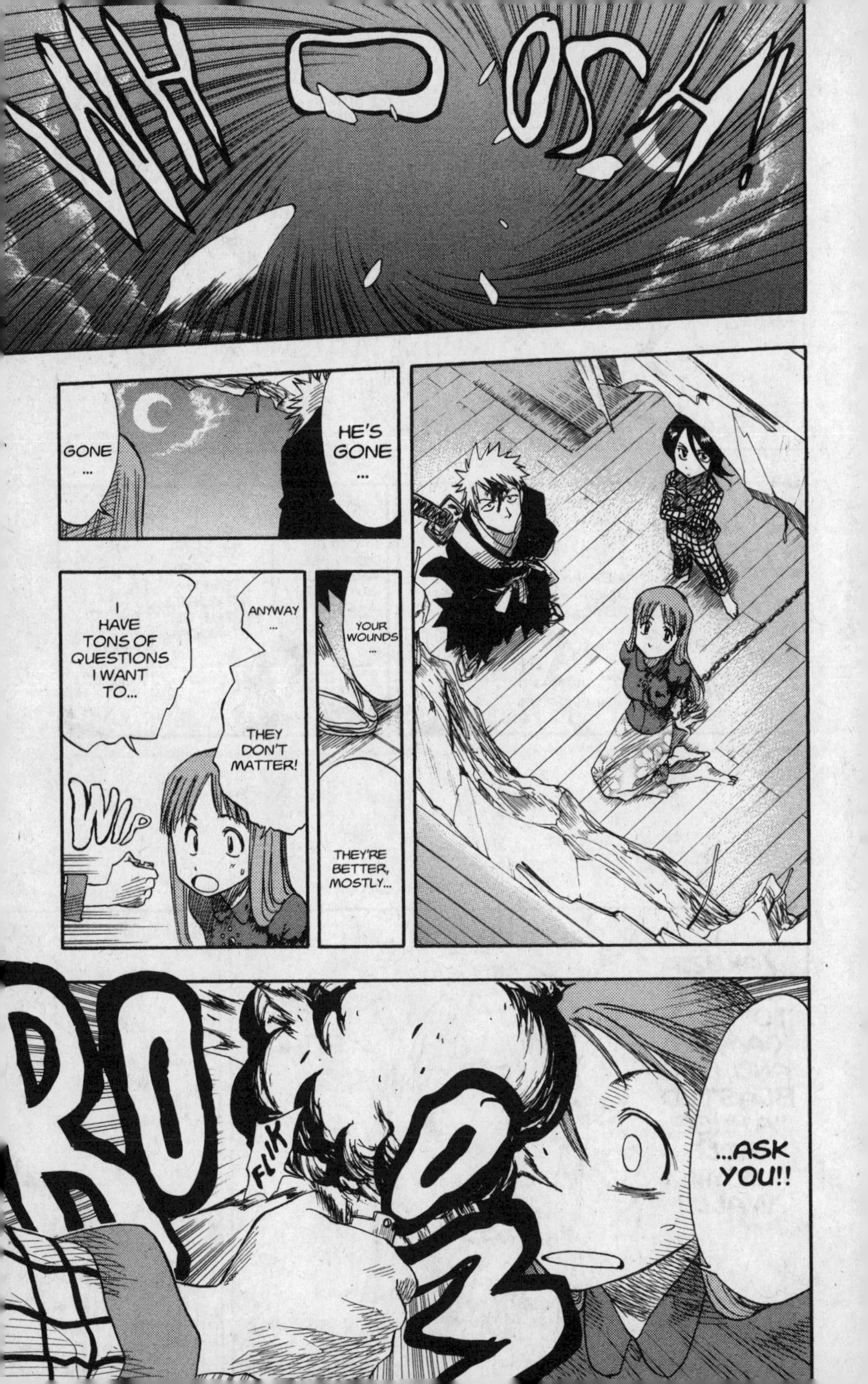
WHOOSH!
HE'S GONE...
GONE...
YOUR WOUNDS...
THEY'RE BETTER, MOSTLY...
ANYWAY...
THEY DON'T MATTER!
I HAVE TONS OF QUESTIONS I WANT TO...
WIP
...ASK YOU!!
FLIK

READ THIS WAY

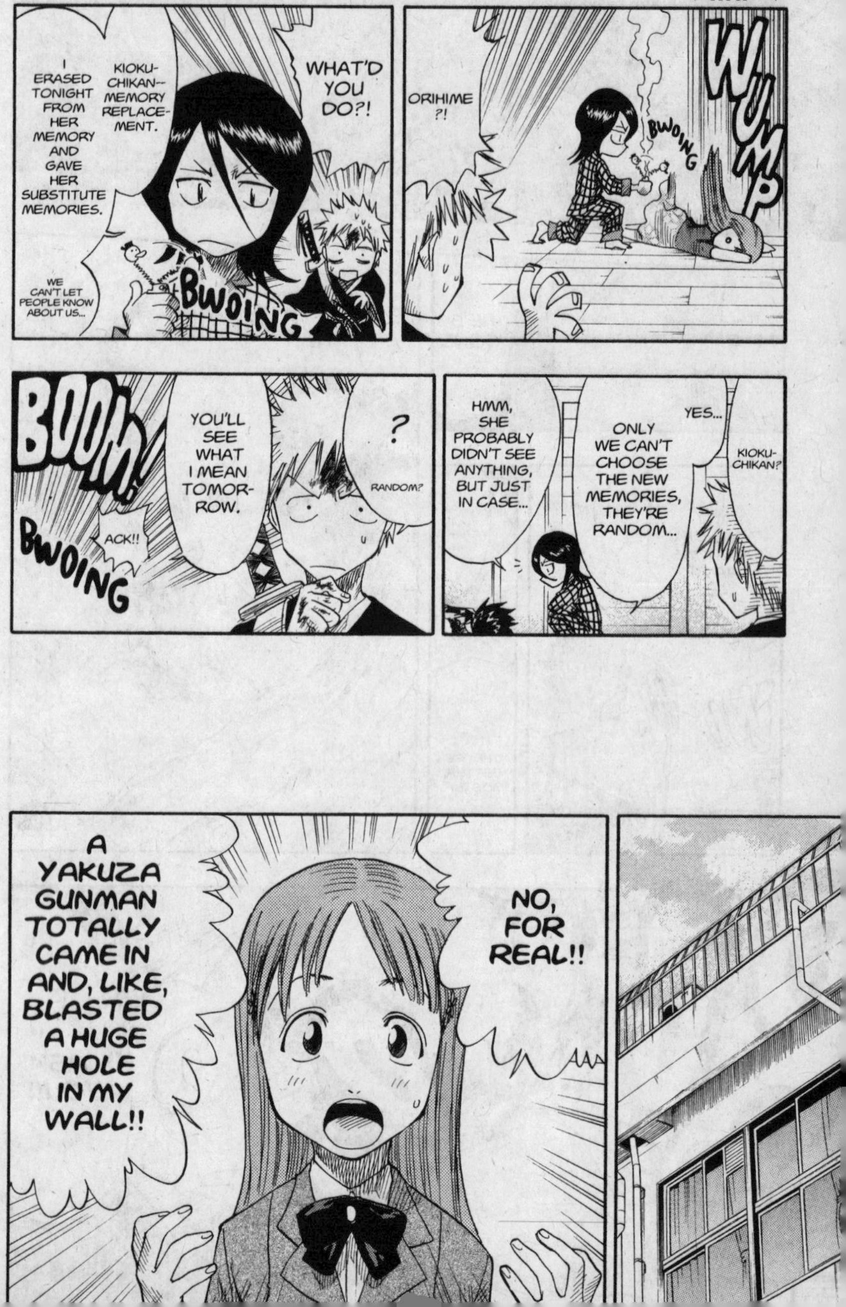
WUMP
BWOING
ORIHIME ?!
WHAT'D YOU DO?!
KIOKU-CHIKAN--MEMORY REPLACEMENT.
I ERASED TONIGHT FROM HER MEMORY AND GAVE HER SUBSTITUTE MEMORIES.
BWOING
WE CAN'T LET PEOPLE KNOW ABOUT US...
KIOKU-CHIKAN?
YES...
ONLY WE CAN'T CHOOSE THE NEW MEMORIES, THEY'RE RANDOM...
HMM, SHE PROBABLY DIDN'T SEE ANYTHING, BUT JUST IN CASE...
?
RANDOM?
YOU'LL SEE WHAT I MEAN TOMORROW.
BOOM!
ACK!!
BWOING
NO, FOR REAL!!
A YAKUZA GUNMAN TOTALLY CAME IN AND, LIKE, BLASTED A HUGE HOLE IN MY WALL!!

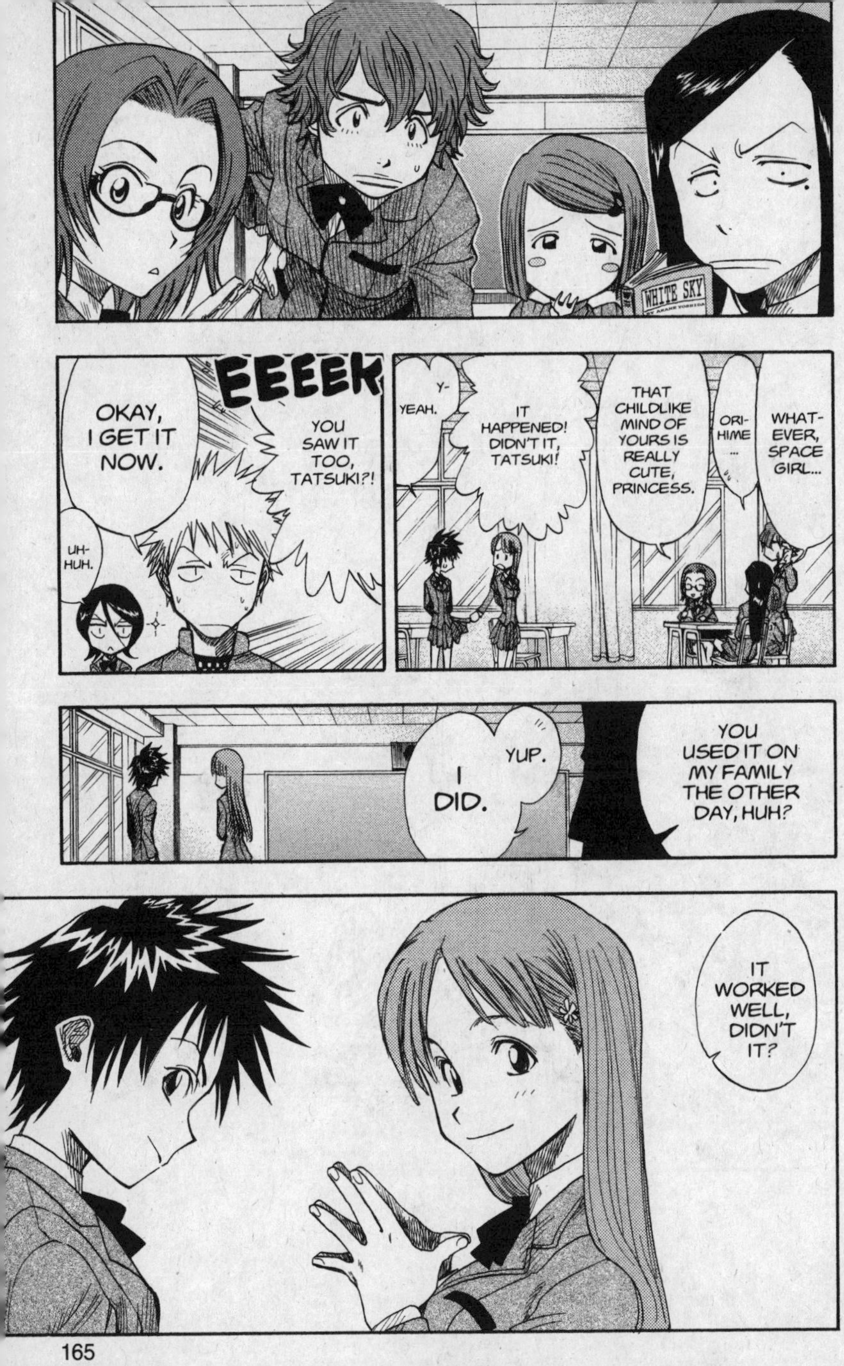
WHITE SKY
WHAT-EVER, SPACE GIRL...
ORI-HIME ...
THAT CHILDLIKE MIND OF YOURS IS REALLY CUTE, PRINCESS.
IT HAPPENED! DIDN'T IT, TATSUKI!
Y- YEAH.
EEEEK
YOU SAW IT TOO, TATSUKI?!
OKAY, I GET IT NOW.
UH-HUH.
YOU USED IT ON MY FAMILY THE OTHER DAY, HUH?
YUP.
I DID.
IT WORKED WELL, DIDN'T IT?

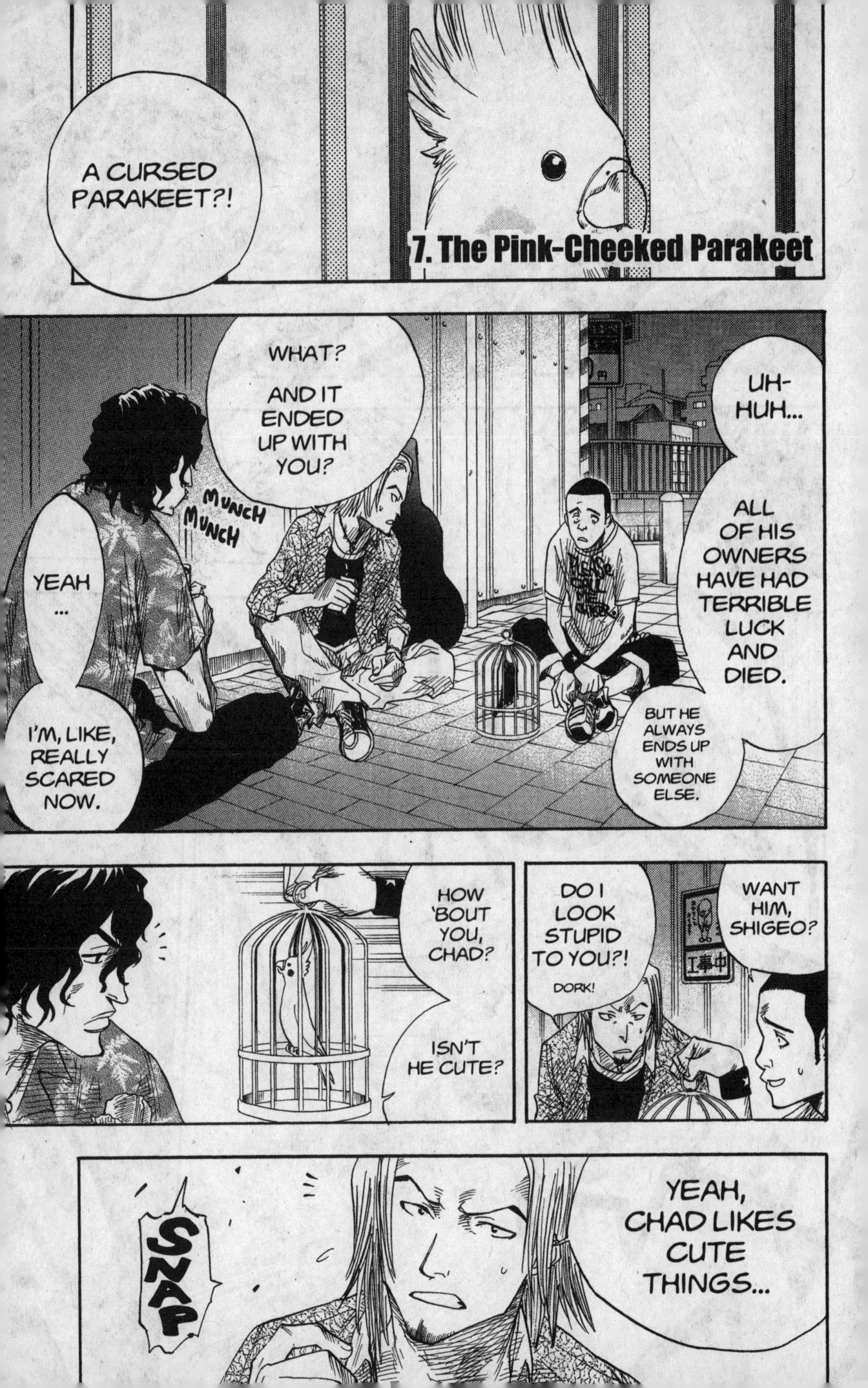
A CURSED PARAKEET?!
7. The Pink-Cheeked Parakeet
UH-HUH...
ALL OF HIS OWNERS HAVE HAD TERRIBLE LUCK AND DIED.
BUT HE ALWAYS ENDS UP WITH SOMEONE ELSE.
WHAT?
AND IT ENDED UP WITH YOU?
MUNCH MUNCH
YEAH ...
I'M, LIKE, REALLY SCARED NOW.
WANT HIM, SHIGEO?
工事中
DO I LOOK STUPID TO YOU?!
DORK!
HOW 'BOUT YOU, CHAD?
ISN'T HE CUTE?
YEAH, CHAD LIKES CUTE THINGS...
SNAP

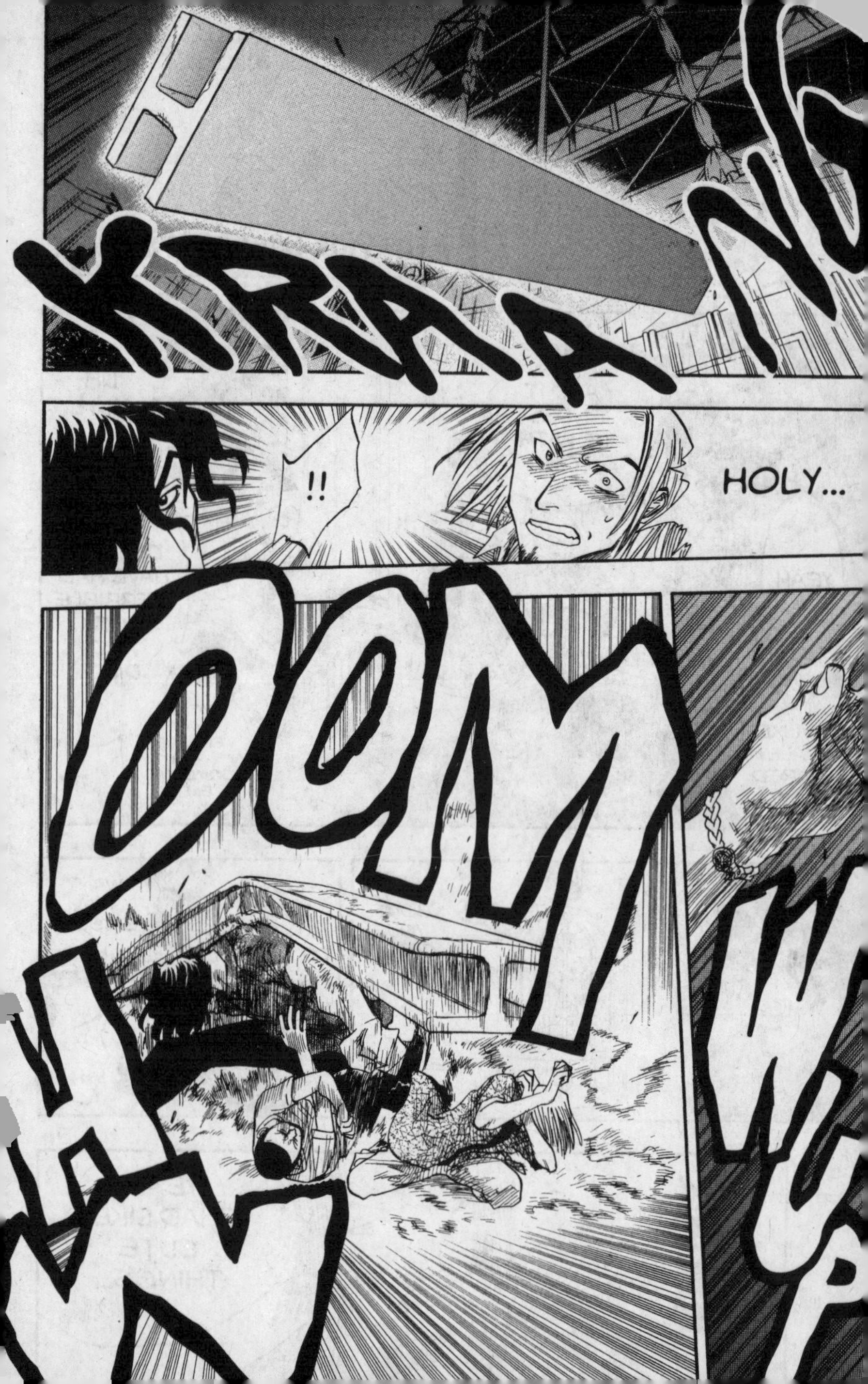
KRRAANG
HOLY...
!!
OOM

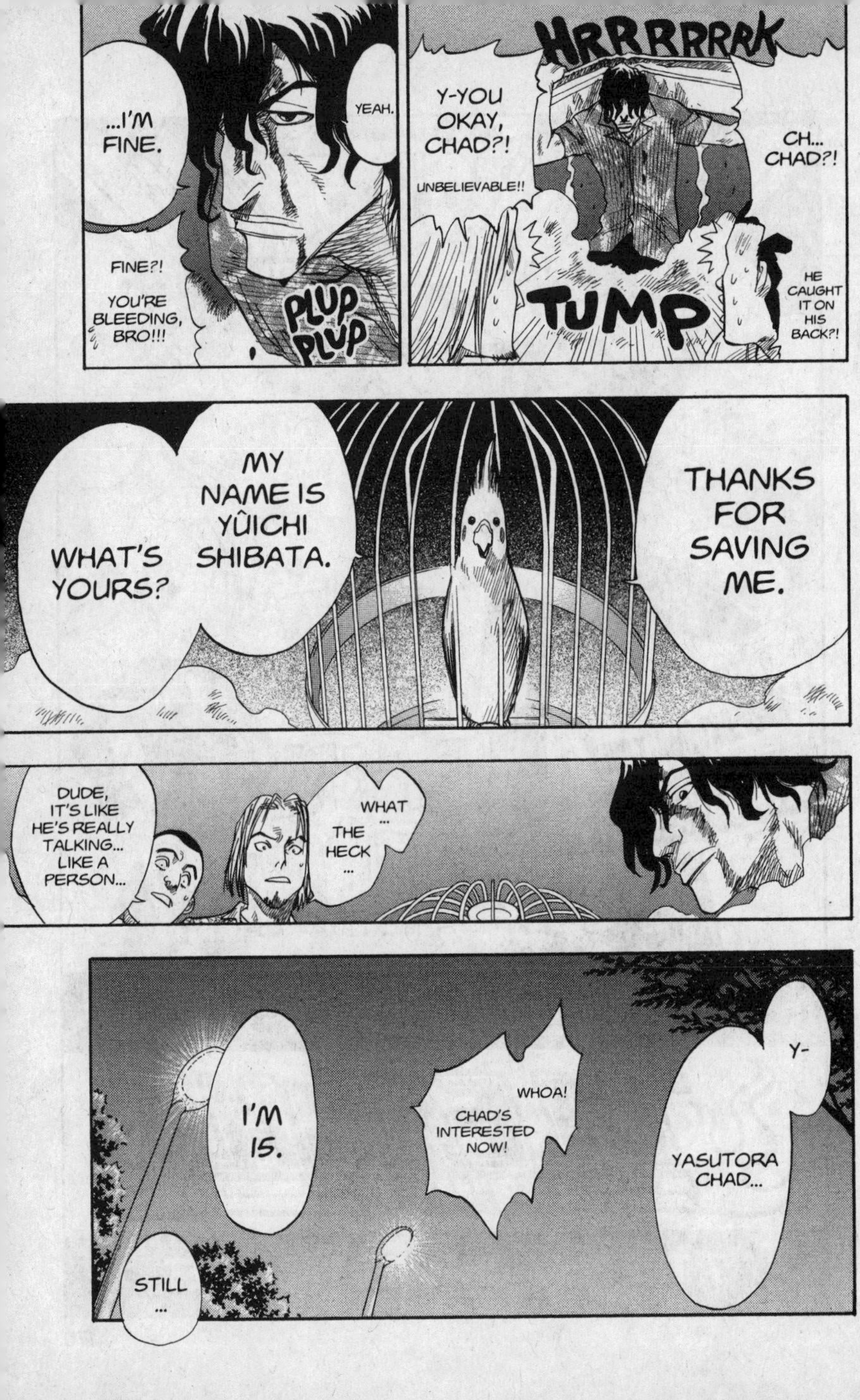
HRRRRRRK
CH... CHAD?!
Y-YOU OKAY, CHAD?!
UNBELIEVABLE!!
HE CAUGHT IT ON HIS BACK?!
TUMP
YEAH.
...I'M FINE.
PLUP PLUP
FINE?! YOU'RE BLEEDING, BRO!!!
THANKS FOR SAVING ME.
MY NAME IS YÛICHI SHIBATA.
WHAT'S YOURS?
WHAT... THE HECK...
DUDE, IT'S LIKE HE'S REALLY TALKING... LIKE A PERSON...
Y-
YASUTORA CHAD...
WHOA! CHAD'S INTERESTED NOW!
I'M IS.
STILL...

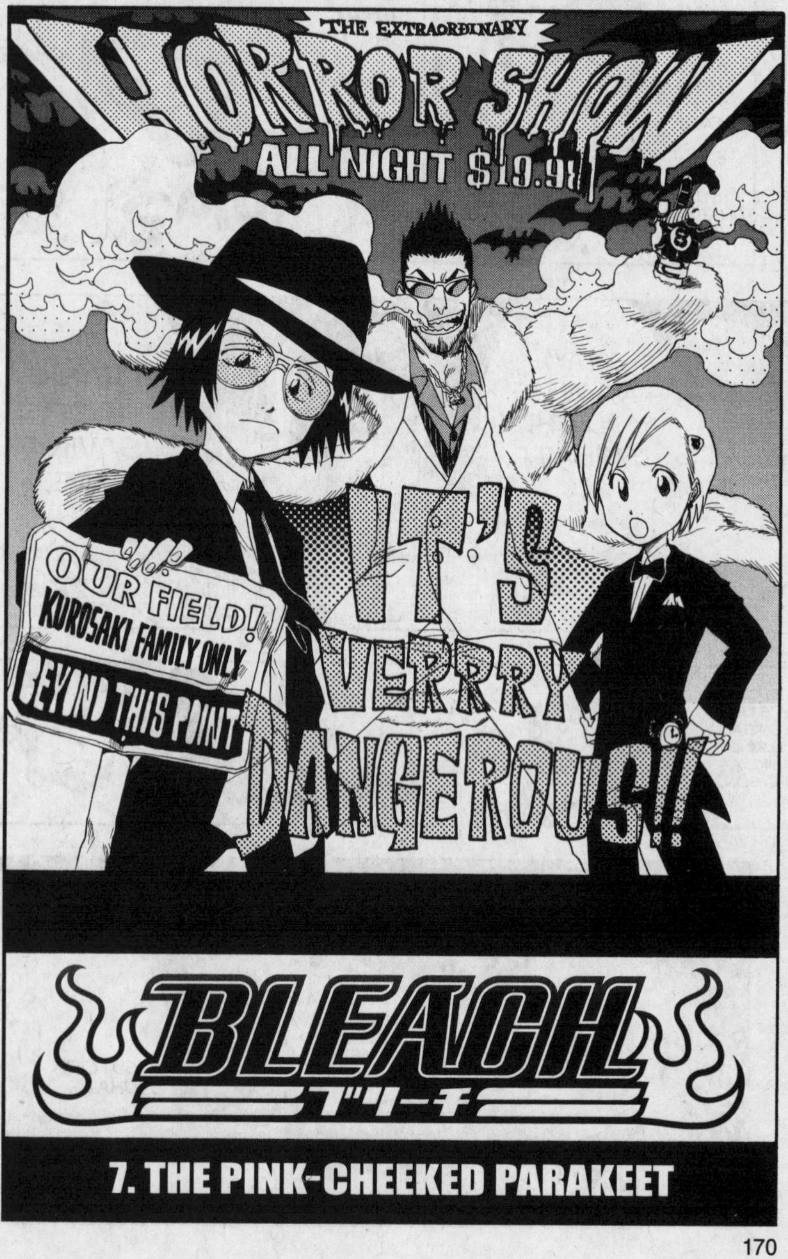
THE EXTRAORDINARY
HORROR SHOW
ALL NIGHT $19.98
OUR FIELD!
KUROSAKI FAMILY ONLY
BEYOND THIS POINT
IT'S VERRRY DANGEROUS!!
BLEACH
ブリーチ
7. THE PINK-CHEEKED PARAKEET

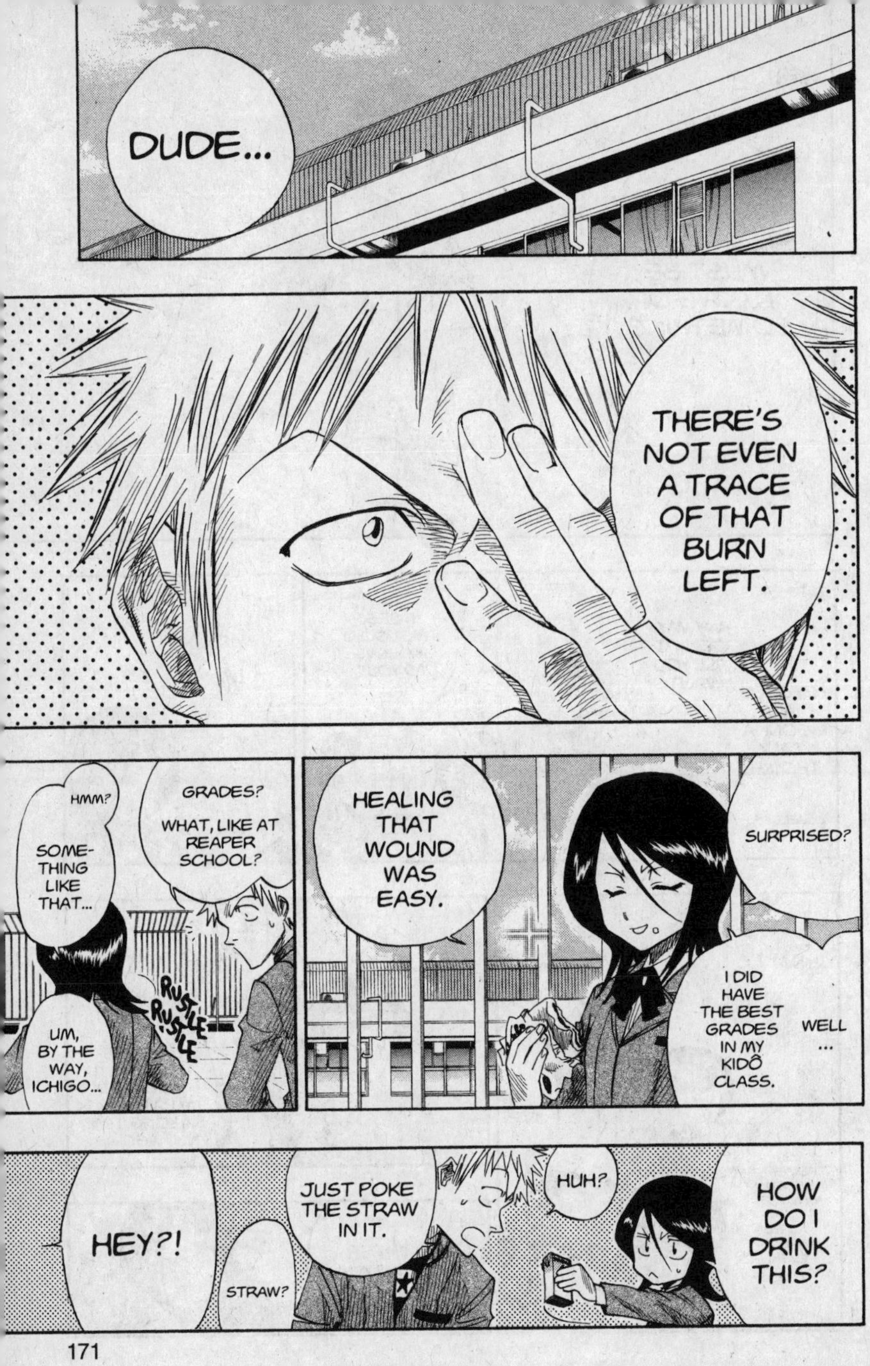
DUDE...
THERE'S NOT EVEN A TRACE OF THAT BURN LEFT.
SURPRISED?
HEALING THAT WOUND WAS EASY.
WELL...
I DID HAVE THE BEST GRADES IN MY KIDÔ CLASS.
GRADES? WHAT, LIKE AT REAPER SCHOOL?
HMM? SOME-THING LIKE THAT...
RUSTLE RUSTLE
UM, BY THE WAY, ICHIGO...
HOW DO I DRINK THIS?
HUH?
JUST POKE THE STRAW IN IT.
STRAW?
HEY?!

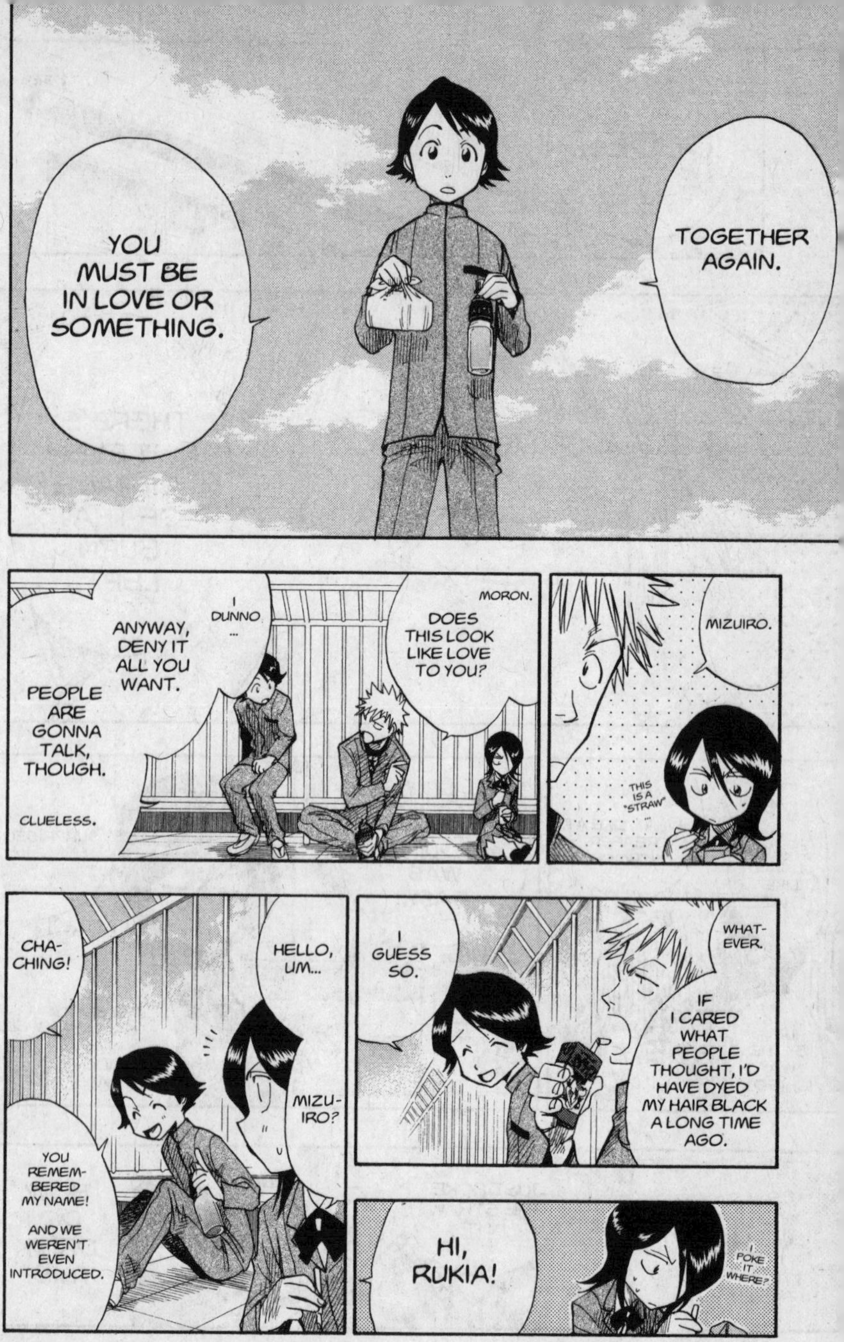
TOGETHER AGAIN.
YOU MUST BE IN LOVE OR SOMETHING.
MIZUIRO.
THIS IS A "STRAW"...
MORON.
DOES THIS LOOK LIKE LOVE TO YOU?
I DUNNO...
ANYWAY, DENY IT ALL YOU WANT.
PEOPLE ARE GONNA TALK, THOUGH.
CLUELESS.
WHAT-EVER.
IF I CARED WHAT PEOPLE THOUGHT, I'D HAVE DYED MY HAIR BLACK A LONG TIME AGO.
I GUESS SO.
I POKE IT WHERE?
HI, RUKIA!
HELLO, UM...
CHA-CHING!
MIZU-IRO?
YOU REMEM-BERED MY NAME!
AND WE WEREN'T EVEN INTRODUCED.

READ THIS WAY

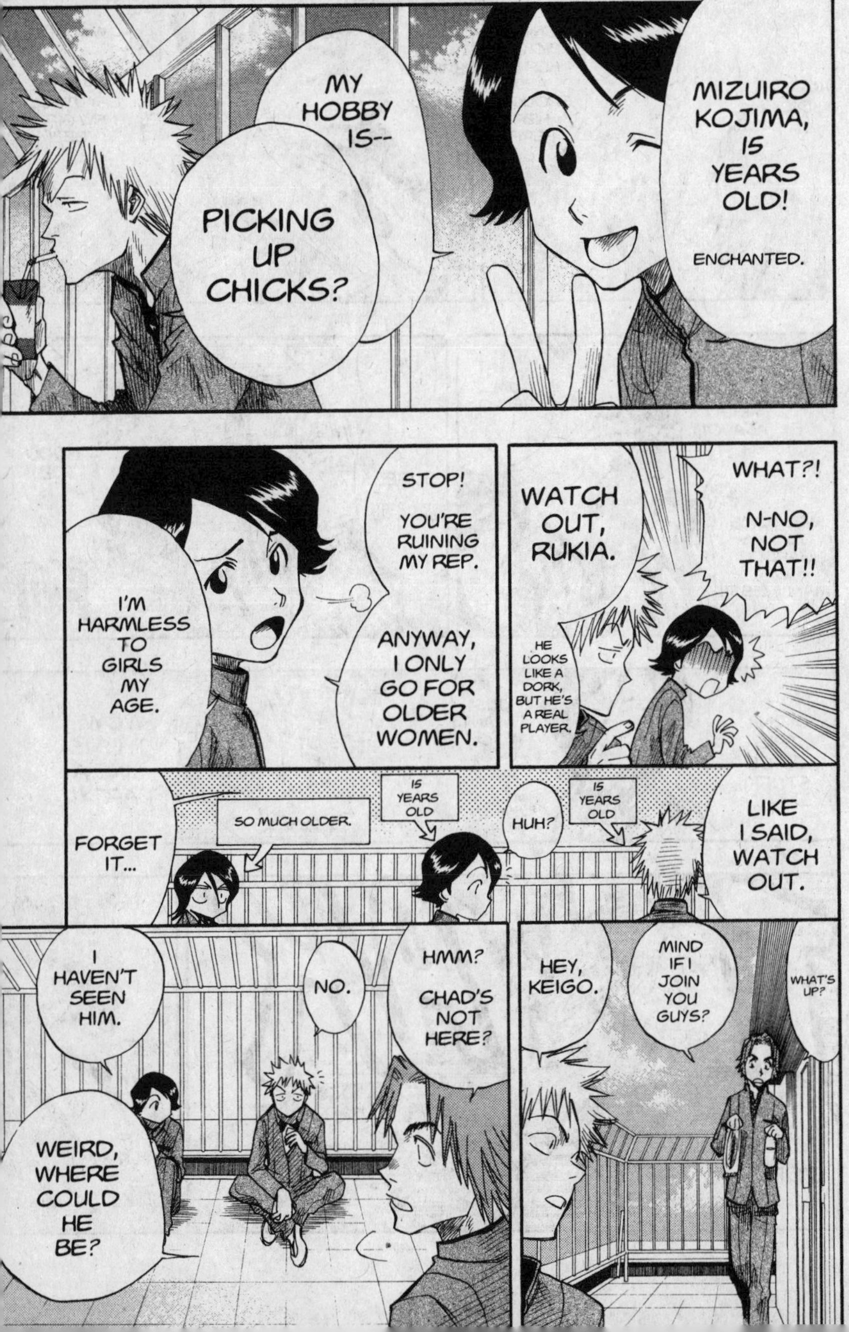
MIZUIRO KOJIMA, 15 YEARS OLD!
ENCHANTED.
MY HOBBY IS--
PICKING UP CHICKS?
WHAT?!
N-NO, NOT THAT!!
WATCH OUT, RUKIA.
HE LOOKS LIKE A DORK, BUT HE'S A REAL PLAYER.
STOP!
YOU'RE RUINING MY REP.
ANYWAY, I ONLY GO FOR OLDER WOMEN.
I'M HARMLESS TO GIRLS MY AGE.
LIKE I SAID, WATCH OUT.
15 YEARS OLD
HUH?
15 YEARS OLD
SO MUCH OLDER.
FORGET IT...
WHAT'S UP?
MIND IF I JOIN YOU GUYS?
HEY, KEIGO.
HMM?
CHAD'S NOT HERE?
NO.
I HAVEN'T SEEN HIM.
WEIRD, WHERE COULD HE BE?

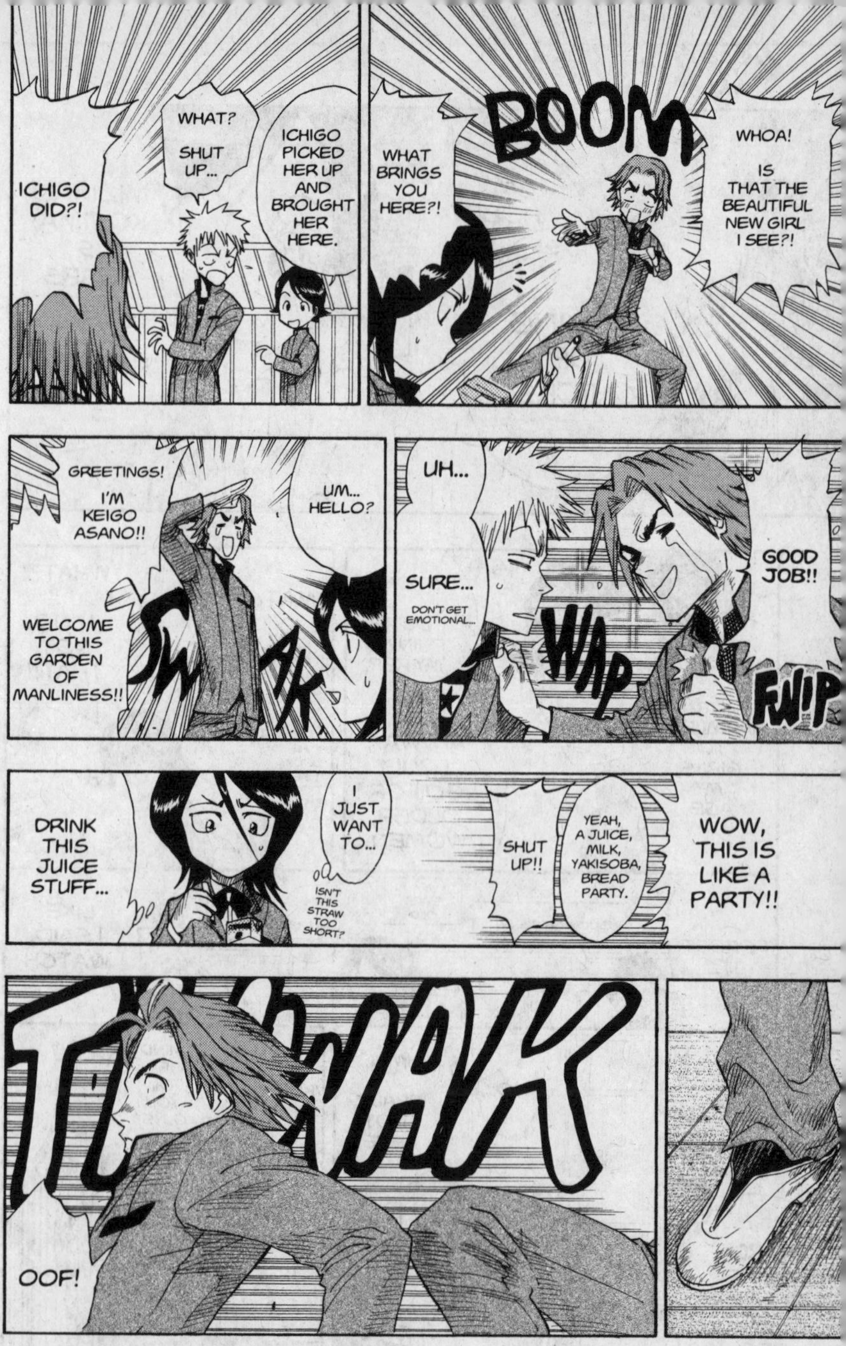
BOOM
WHOA! IS THAT THE BEAUTIFUL NEW GIRL I SEE?!
WHAT BRINGS YOU HERE?!
ICHIGO PICKED HER UP AND BROUGHT HER HERE.
WHAT? SHUT UP...
ICHIGO DID?!
GOOD JOB!!
FWIP
WAP
UH... SURE...
DON'T GET EMOTIONAL...
UM... HELLO?
GREETINGS! I'M KEIGO ASANO!!
WELCOME TO THIS GARDEN OF MANLINESS!!
WOW, THIS IS LIKE A PARTY!!
YEAH, A JUICE, MILK, YAKISOBA, BREAD PARTY.
SHUT UP!!
I JUST WANT TO...
ISN'T THIS STRAW TOO SHORT?
DRINK THIS JUICE STUFF...
OOF!

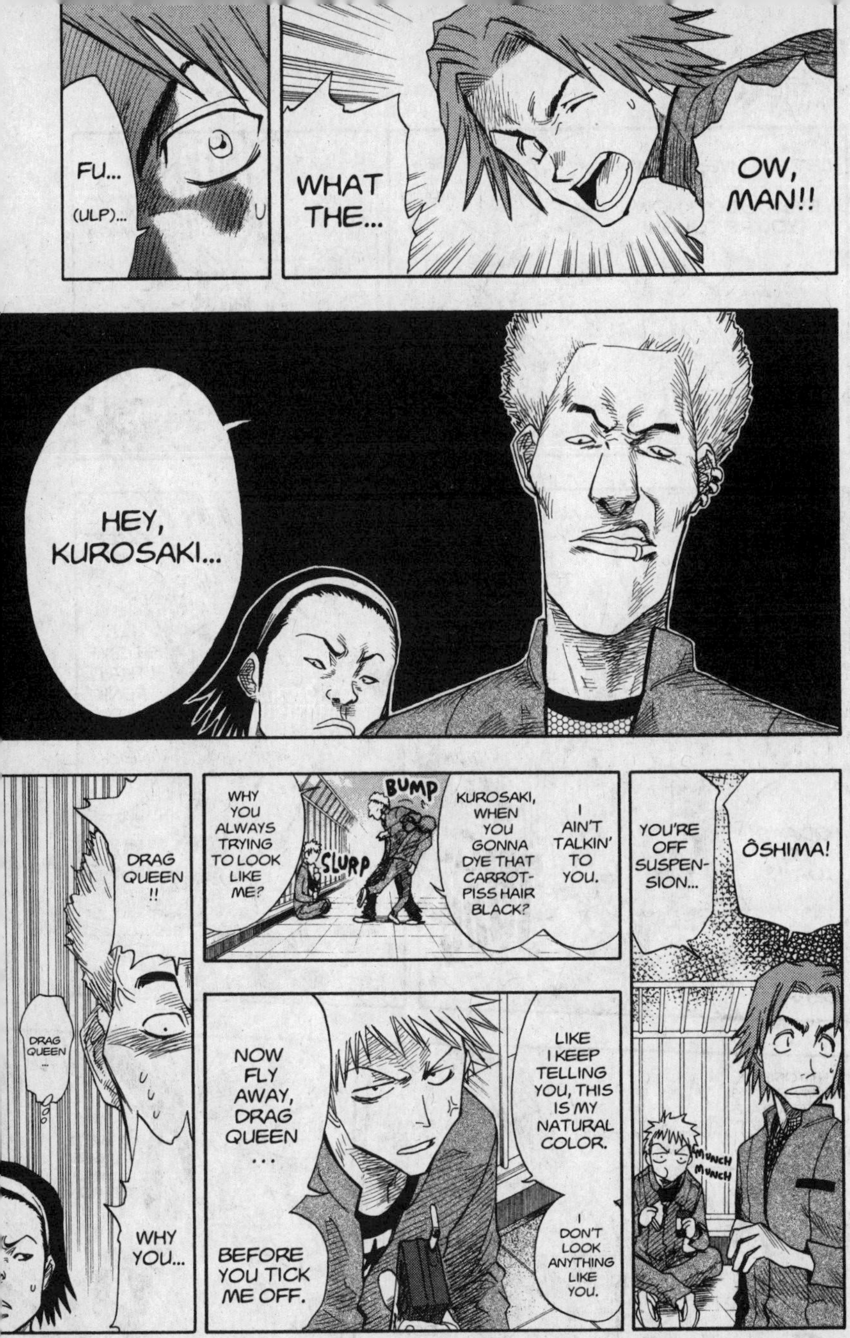
OW, MAN!!
WHAT THE...
FU...
(ULP)...
HEY, KUROSAKI...
ÔSHIMA!
YOU'RE OFF SUSPENSION...
MUNCH MUNCH
I AIN'T TALKIN' TO YOU.
KUROSAKI, WHEN YOU GONNA DYE THAT CARROT-PISS HAIR BLACK?
BUMP
SLURP
WHY YOU ALWAYS TRYING TO LOOK LIKE ME?
LIKE I KEEP TELLING YOU, THIS IS MY NATURAL COLOR.
I DON'T LOOK ANYTHING LIKE YOU.
NOW FLY AWAY, DRAG QUEEN . . .
BEFORE YOU TICK ME OFF.
DRAG QUEEN !!
DRAG QUEEN ...
WHY YOU...

READ THIS WAY

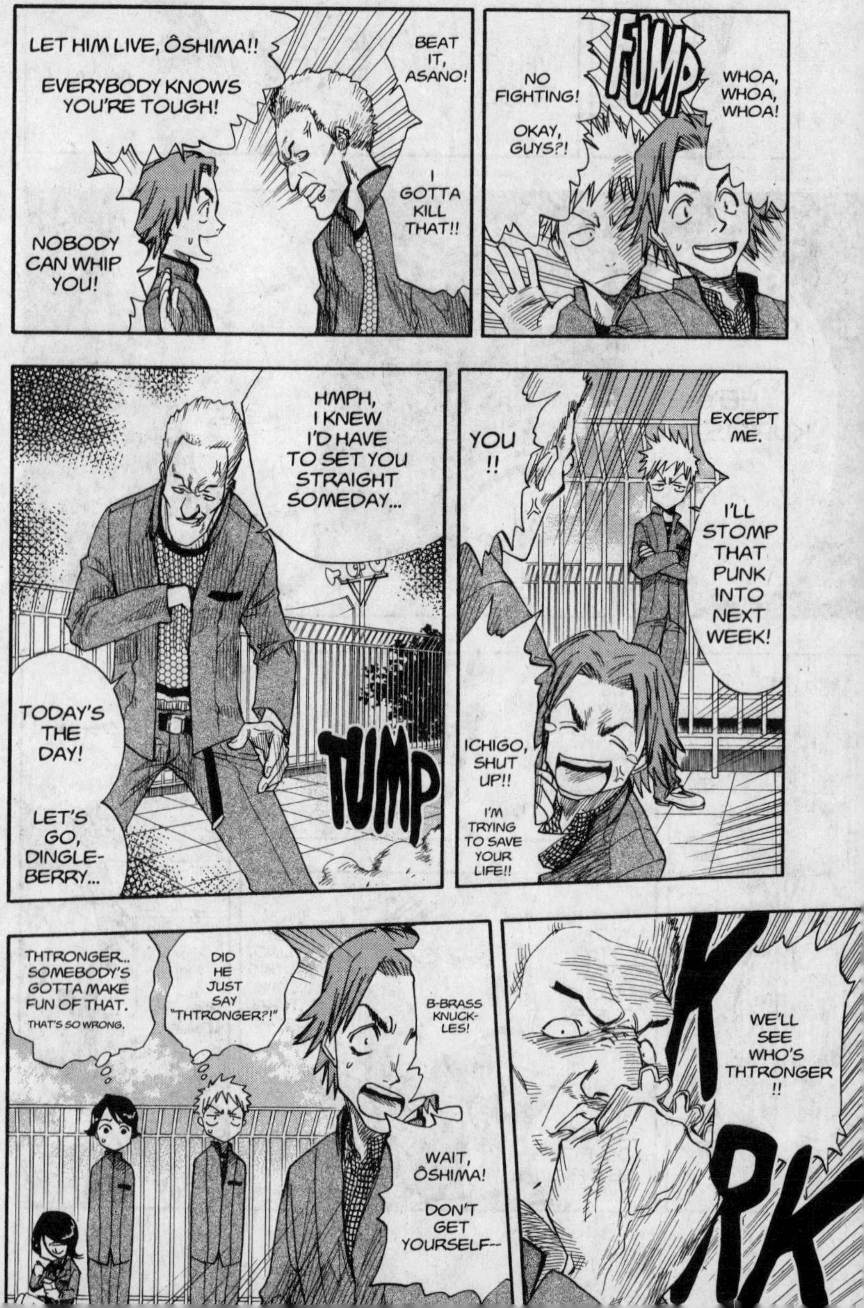
WHOA, WHOA, WHOA!
FUMP
NO FIGHTING!
OKAY, GUYS?!
BEAT IT, ASANO!
LET HIM LIVE, ÔSHIMA!!
EVERYBODY KNOWS YOU'RE TOUGH!
I GOTTA KILL THAT!!
NOBODY CAN WHIP YOU!
EXCEPT ME.
YOU!!
I'LL STOMP THAT PUNK INTO NEXT WEEK!
ICHIGO, SHUT UP!!
I'M TRYING TO SAVE YOUR LIFE!!
HMPH, I KNEW I'D HAVE TO SET YOU STRAIGHT SOMEDAY...
TODAY'S THE DAY!
TUMP
LET'S GO, DINGLE-BERRY...
K
WE'LL SEE WHO'S THTRONGER!!
RK
B-BRASS KNUCK-LES!
DID HE JUST SAY "THTRONGER?!"
THTRONGER.. SOMEBODY'S GOTTA MAKE FUN OF THAT.
THAT'S SO WRONG.
WAIT, ÔSHIMA!
DON'T GET YOURSELF--

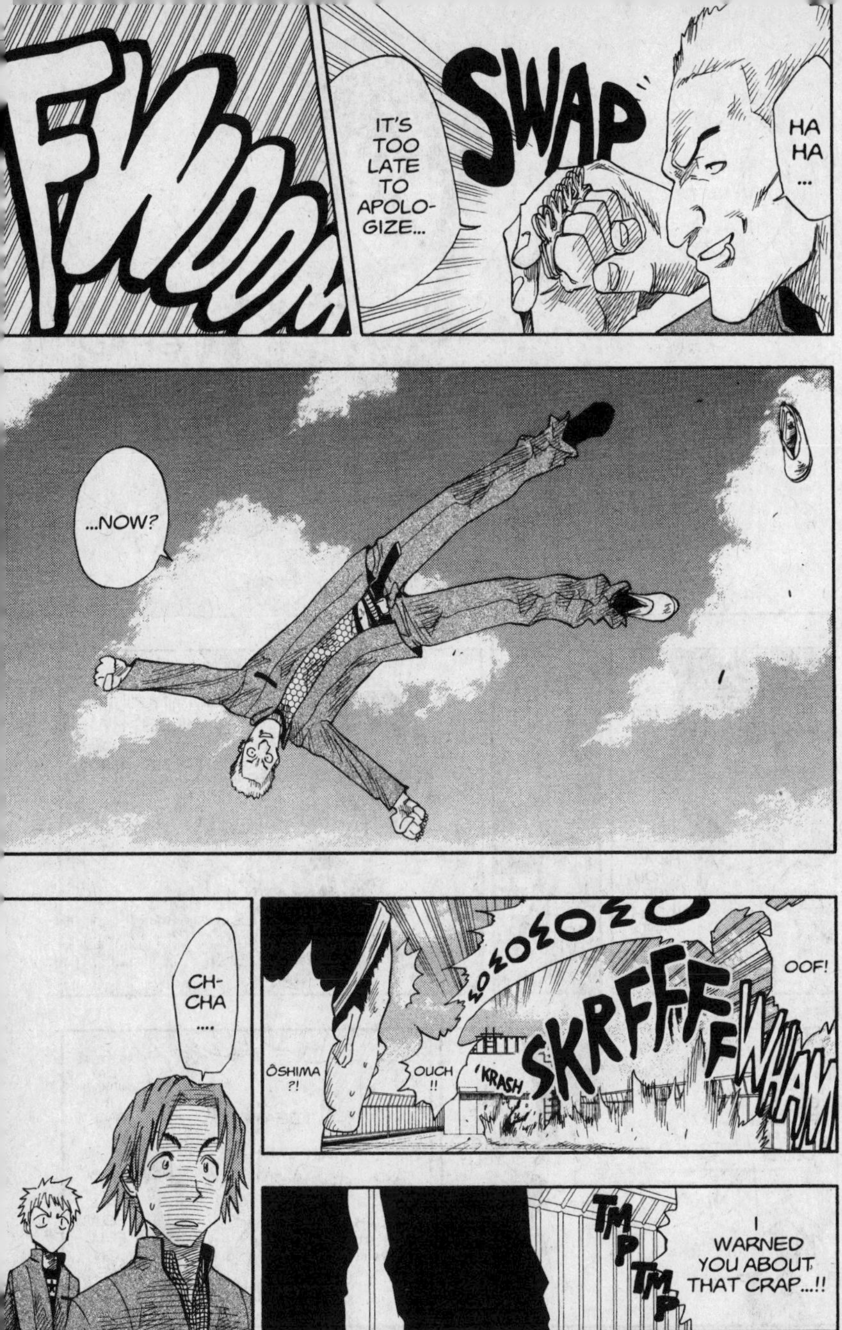
HA HA ...
SWAP
IT'S TOO LATE TO APOLOGIZE...
...NOW?
OOF!
WHAM
SKRFFFF
KRASH
OUCH !!
ÔSHIMA ?!
I WARNED YOU ABOUT THAT CRAP...!!
TMP TMP
CH- CHA ....

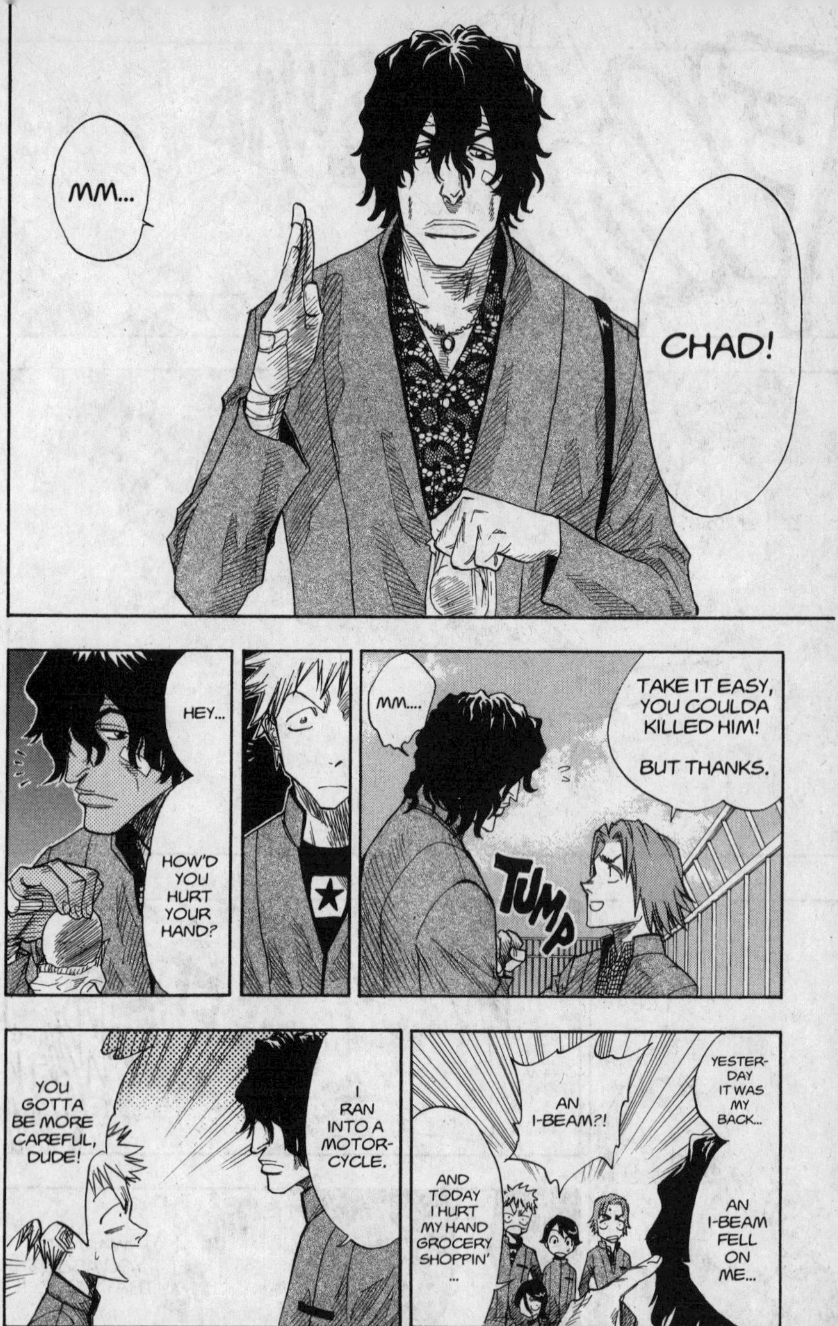
CHAD!
MM...
TAKE IT EASY, YOU COULDA KILLED HIM!
BUT THANKS.
TUMP
MM....
HEY...
HOW'D YOU HURT YOUR HAND?
YESTER-DAY IT WAS MY BACK...
AN I-BEAM FELL ON ME...
AN I-BEAM?!
AND TODAY I HURT MY HAND GROCERY SHOPPIN'...
I RAN INTO A MOTOR-CYCLE.
YOU GOTTA BE MORE CAREFUL, DUDE!

READ THIS WAY

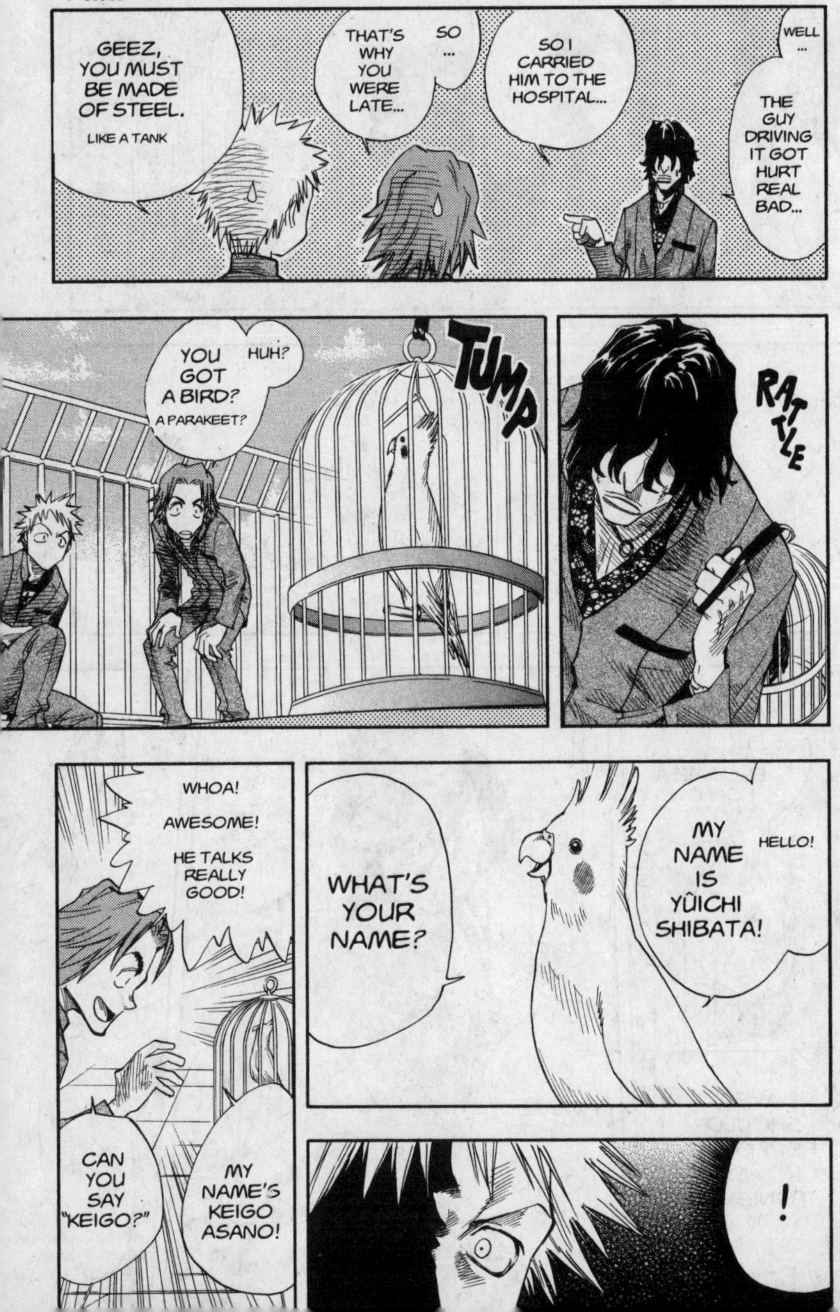
WELL ...
THE GUY DRIVING IT GOT HURT REAL BAD...
SO I CARRIED HIM TO THE HOSPITAL...
SO ...
THAT'S WHY YOU WERE LATE...
GEEZ, YOU MUST BE MADE OF STEEL.
LIKE A TANK
RATTLE
TUMP
HUH?
YOU GOT A BIRD?
A PARAKEET?
HELLO!
MY NAME IS YÛICHI SHIBATA!
WHAT'S YOUR NAME?
!
WHOA!
AWESOME!
HE TALKS REALLY GOOD!
MY NAME'S KEIGO ASANO!
CAN YOU SAY "KEIGO?"

READ THIS WAY

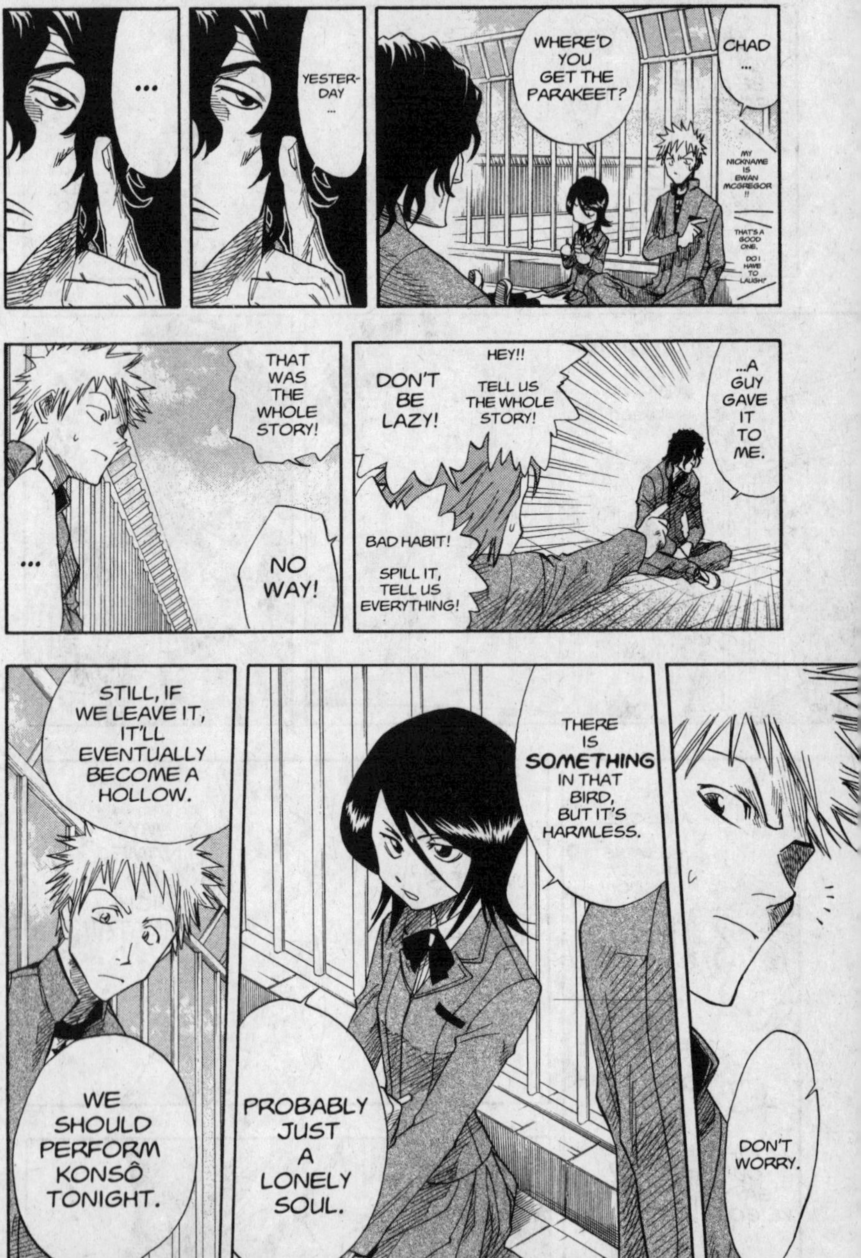
CHAD ...
WHERE'D YOU GET THE PARAKEET?
MY NICKNAME IS EWAN MCGREGOR !!
THAT'S A GOOD ONE. DO I HAVE TO LAUGH?
YESTER-DAY ...
...
...A GUY GAVE IT TO ME.
HEY!! TELL US THE WHOLE STORY!
DON'T BE LAZY!
BAD HABIT! SPILL IT, TELL US EVERYTHING!
THAT WAS THE WHOLE STORY!
NO WAY!
...
THERE IS **SOMETHING** IN THAT BIRD, BUT IT'S HARMLESS.
DON'T WORRY.
PROBABLY JUST A LONELY SOUL.
STILL, IF WE LEAVE IT, IT'LL EVENTUALLY BECOME A HOLLOW.
WE SHOULD PERFORM KONSÔ TONIGHT.

READ THIS WAY

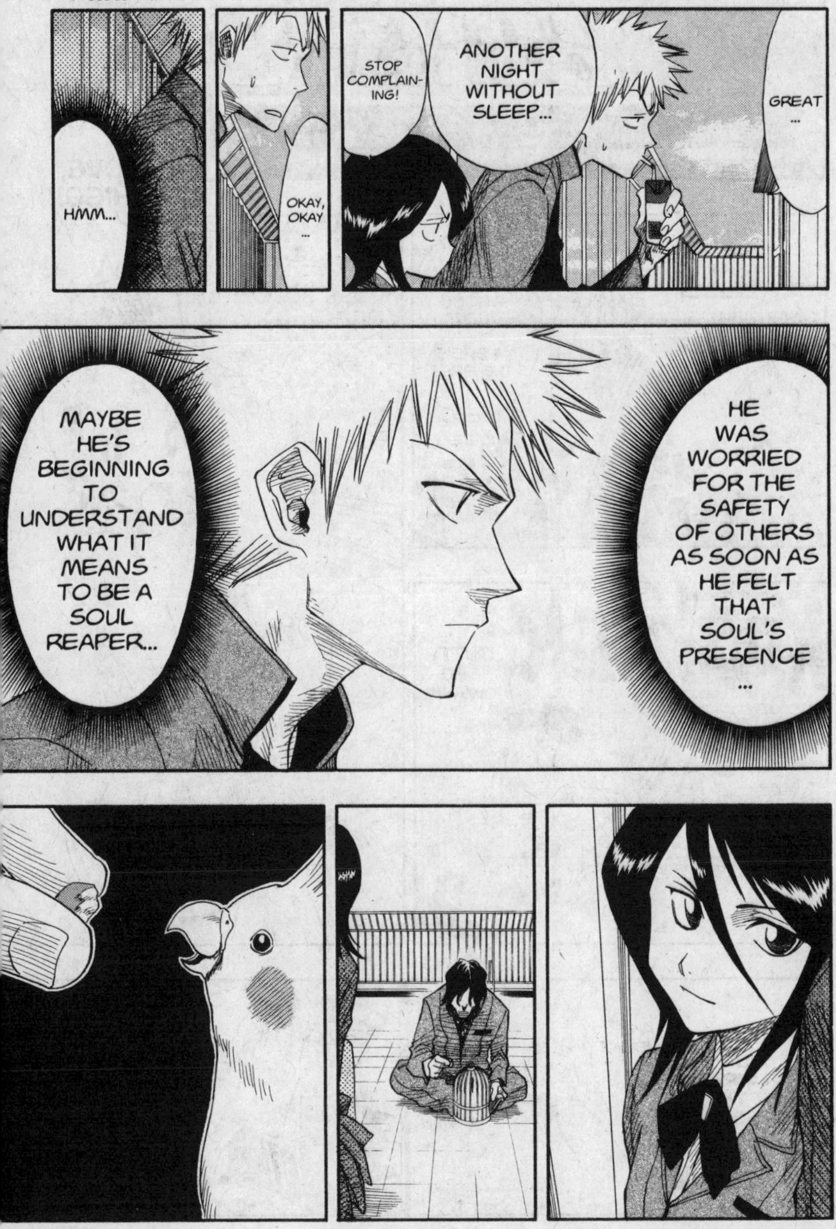
GREAT ...
ANOTHER NIGHT WITHOUT SLEEP...
STOP COMPLAINING!
OKAY, OKAY ...
HMM...
HE WAS WORRIED FOR THE SAFETY OF OTHERS AS SOON AS HE FELT THAT SOUL'S PRESENCE ...
MAYBE HE'S BEGINNING TO UNDERSTAND WHAT IT MEANS TO BE A SOUL REAPER...

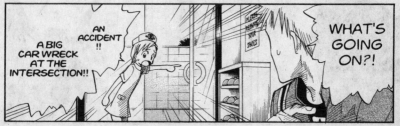

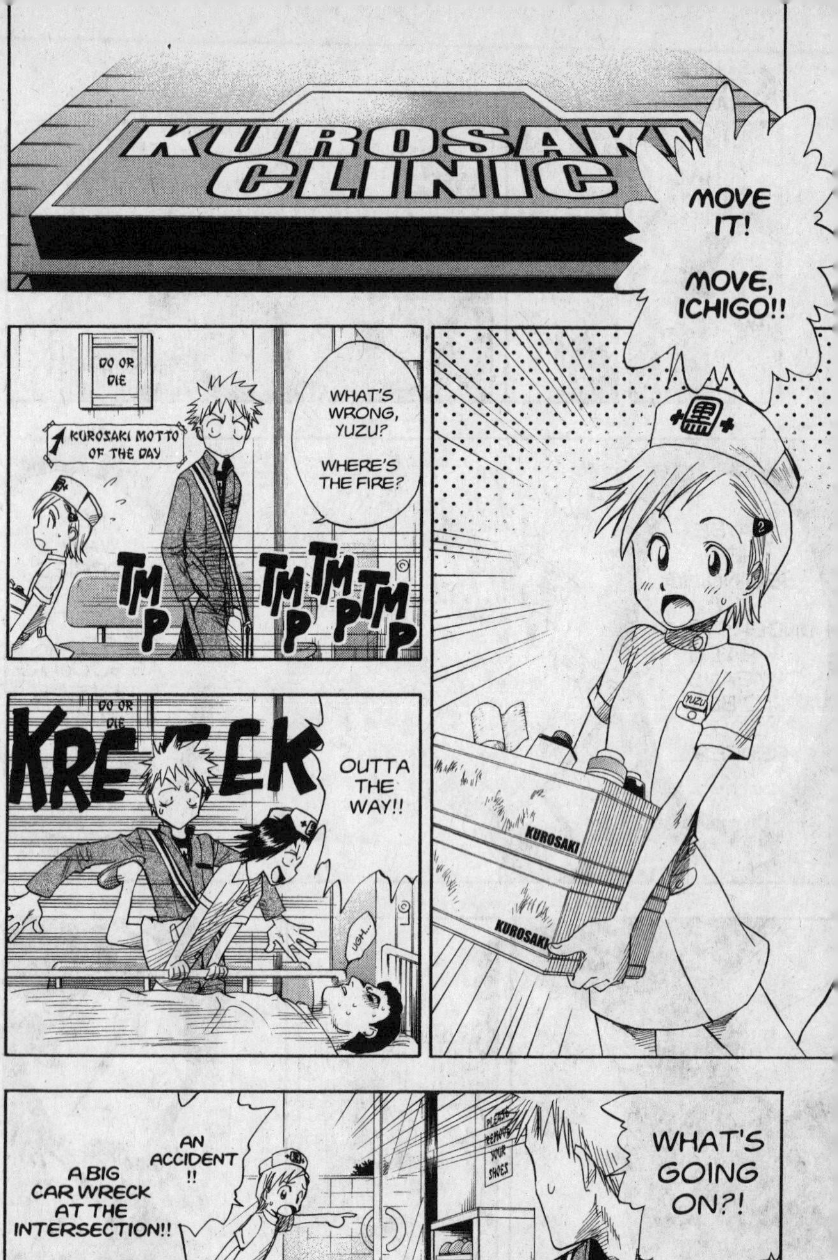
KUROSAKI CLINIC
MOVE IT!
MOVE, ICHIGO!!
YUZU
KUROSAKI
KUROSAKI
DO OR DIE
KUROSAKI MOTTO OF THE DAY
WHAT'S WRONG, YUZU?
WHERE'S THE FIRE?
TMP
TMP TMP TMP
DO OR DIE
KREEEK
OUTTA THE WAY!!
UGH...
PLEASE REMOVE YOUR SHOES
WHAT'S GOING ON?!
AN ACCIDENT!!
A BIG CAR WRECK AT THE INTERSECTION!!

READ THIS WAY

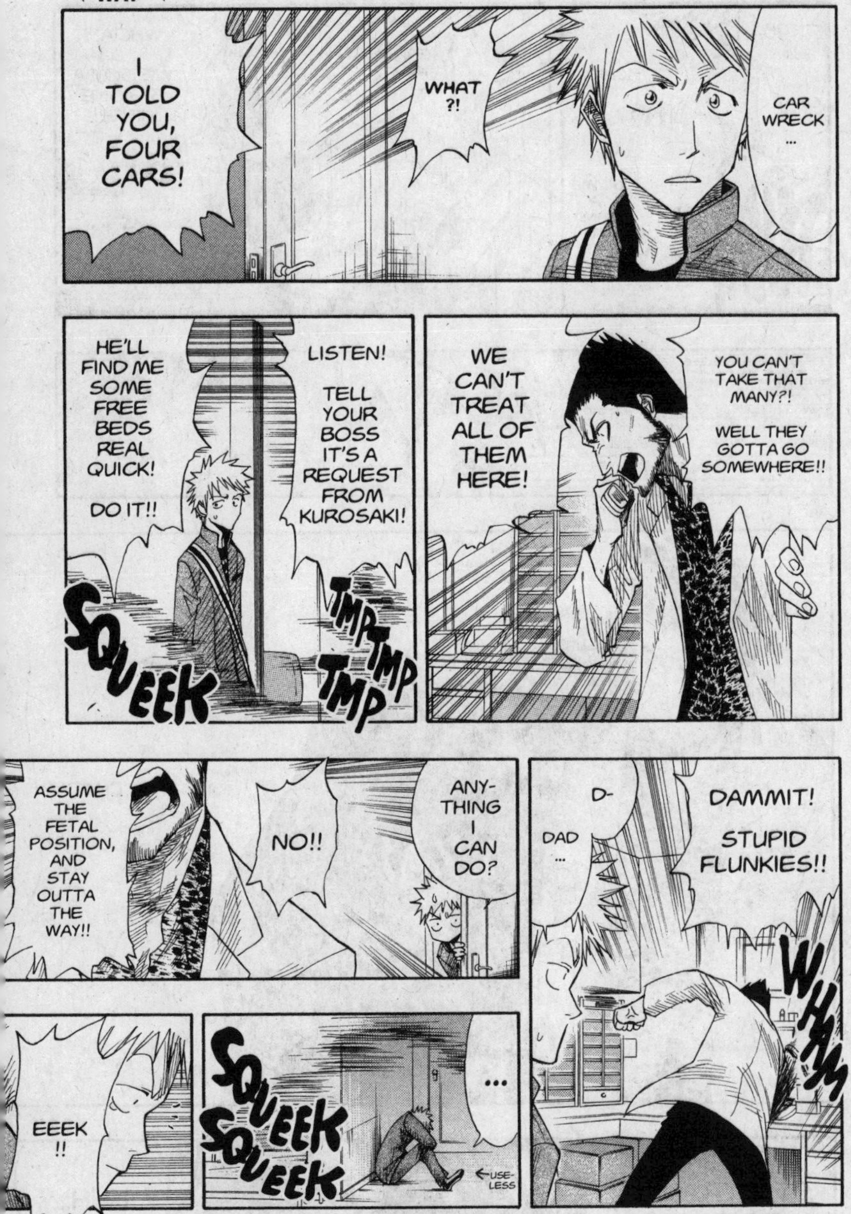
CAR WRECK ...
WHAT ?!
I TOLD YOU, FOUR CARS!
YOU CAN'T TAKE THAT MANY?!
WELL THEY GOTTA GO SOMEWHERE!!
WE CAN'T TREAT ALL OF THEM HERE!
LISTEN!
TELL YOUR BOSS IT'S A REQUEST FROM KUROSAKI!
HE'LL FIND ME SOME FREE BEDS REAL QUICK!
DO IT!!
TMPTMP TMP
SQUEEK
DAMMIT!
STUPID FLUNKIES!!
D-
DAD ...
WHAM
ANY-THING I CAN DO?
NO!!
ASSUME THE FETAL POSITION, AND STAY OUTTA THE WAY!!
...
SQUEEK SQUEEK
←USE-LESS
EEEK !!

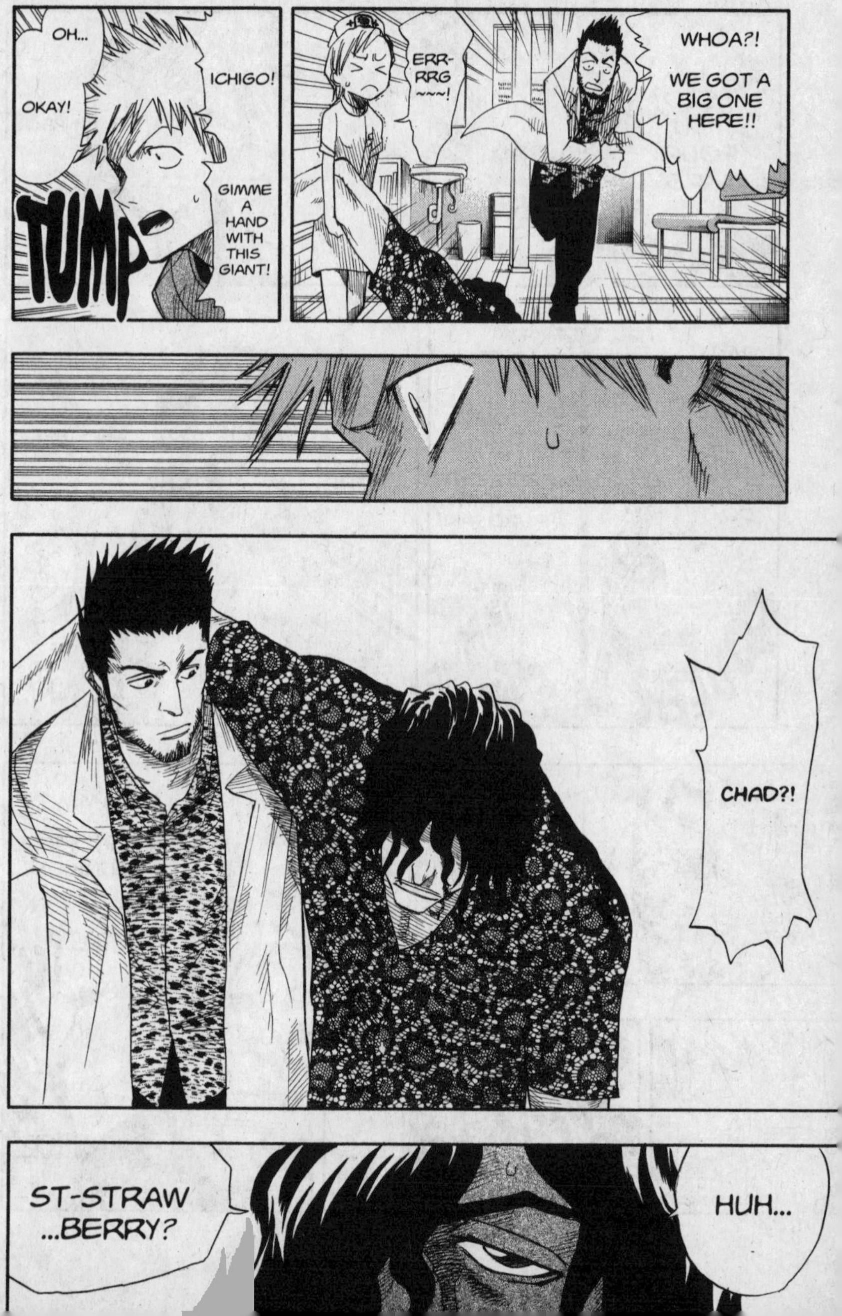
WHOA?!
WE GOT A BIG ONE HERE!!
ERR-RRG ~~~!
ICHIGO!
GIMME A HAND WITH THIS GIANT!
OH...
OKAY!
TUMP
CHAD?!
HUH...
ST-STRAW ...BERRY?

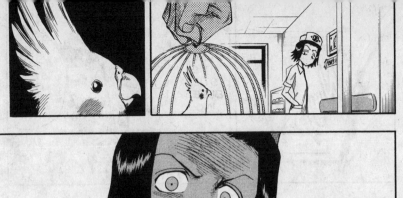

WHOA...

WHAT A HOR-RIBLE WOUND

THIS FEEL-ING!

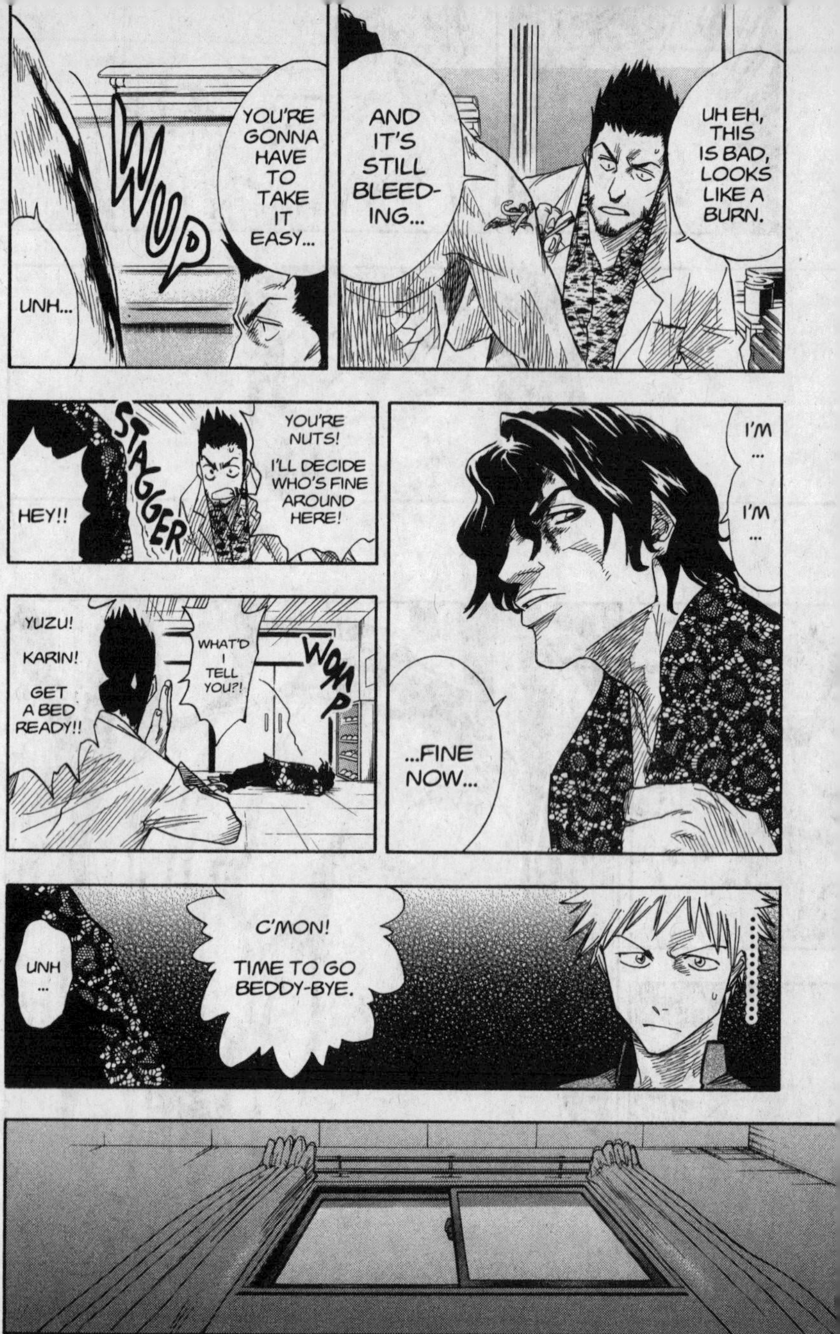
UH EH, THIS IS BAD, LOOKS LIKE A BURN.
AND IT'S STILL BLEEDING...
YOU'RE GONNA HAVE TO TAKE IT EASY...
WUP
UNH...
I'M ...
I'M ...
...FINE NOW...
YOU'RE NUTS!
I'LL DECIDE WHO'S FINE AROUND HERE!
STAGGER
HEY!!
WOMP
WHAT'D I TELL YOU?!
YUZU!
KARIN!
GET A BED READY!!
C'MON!
TIME TO GO BEDDY-BYE.
UNH ...

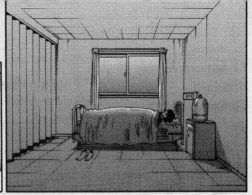

I FELT IT ALL THE WAY IN HERE.

OF COURSE.

I SENSED NO EVIL IN THE PARAKEET BUT...

HIS WOUND...

REEKS OF HOLLOW..!

DO YOU FEEL IT?

TO BE CONTINUED IN VOL. 2!

OVERALL ATTENDANCE SCORE 13	ICHIGO KUROSAKI	クロサキ・イチゴ
MALE STUDENT ATTENDANCE SCORE 6		

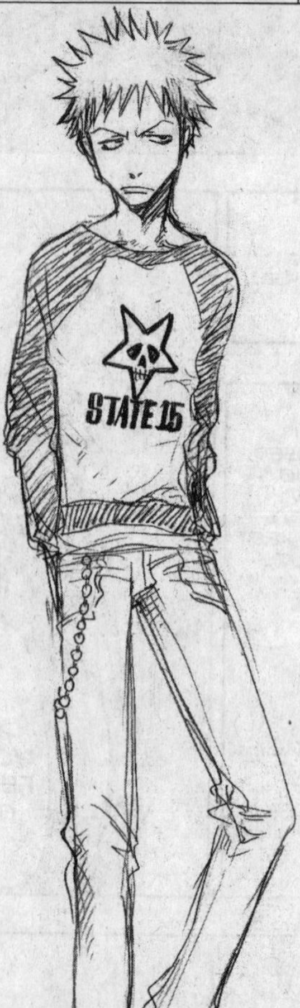
STATE 15

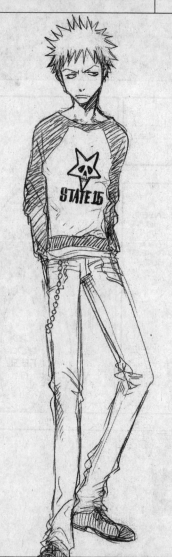

174 CM
61 KG
BLOOD TYPE AO.
D.O.B. JULY 15TH

- LIKES SLIM FIT SHIRTS AND PANTS
- LIKES CHOCOLATE AND KARASHI MENTAIKO
- FAVORITE CELEBRITIES ARE MIKE NESS AND AL PACINO
- PERSON HE RESPECTS MOST IS WILLIAM SHAKESPEARE
- HOW TO PRONOUNCE NAME, ICHIGO EMPHASIS ON THE "I." ACCENTED LIKE "ECHIGO."

THEME SONG

BAD RELIGION

"NEWS FROM THE FRONT"

RECORDED IN
"STRANGER THAN FICTION"

OVERALL ATTENDANCE SCORE 11	**RUKIA KUCHIKI**	クチキ・ルキア
FEMALE STUDENT ATTENDANCE SCORE 6		

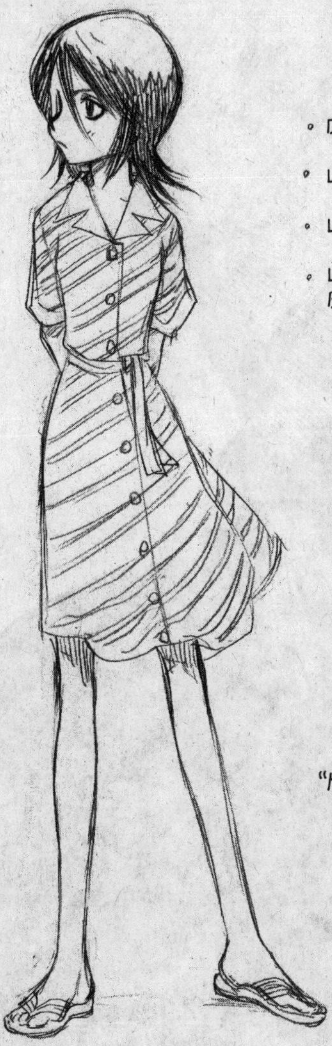

144 CM
33 KG
D.O.B. JANUARY 14TH

- DOESN'T LIKE TIGHT CLOTHES
- LIKES CLIMBING TO HIGH PLACES
- LIKES RABBIT-RELATED ITEMS
- LIKES CUCUMBER AND SHIRA-TAMA. BUT THE LIST COULD GET LONGER.

THEME SONG

ASHLEY MACISAAC

"WING-STOCK"

RECORDED IN
"HI HOW ARE YOU TODAY?"

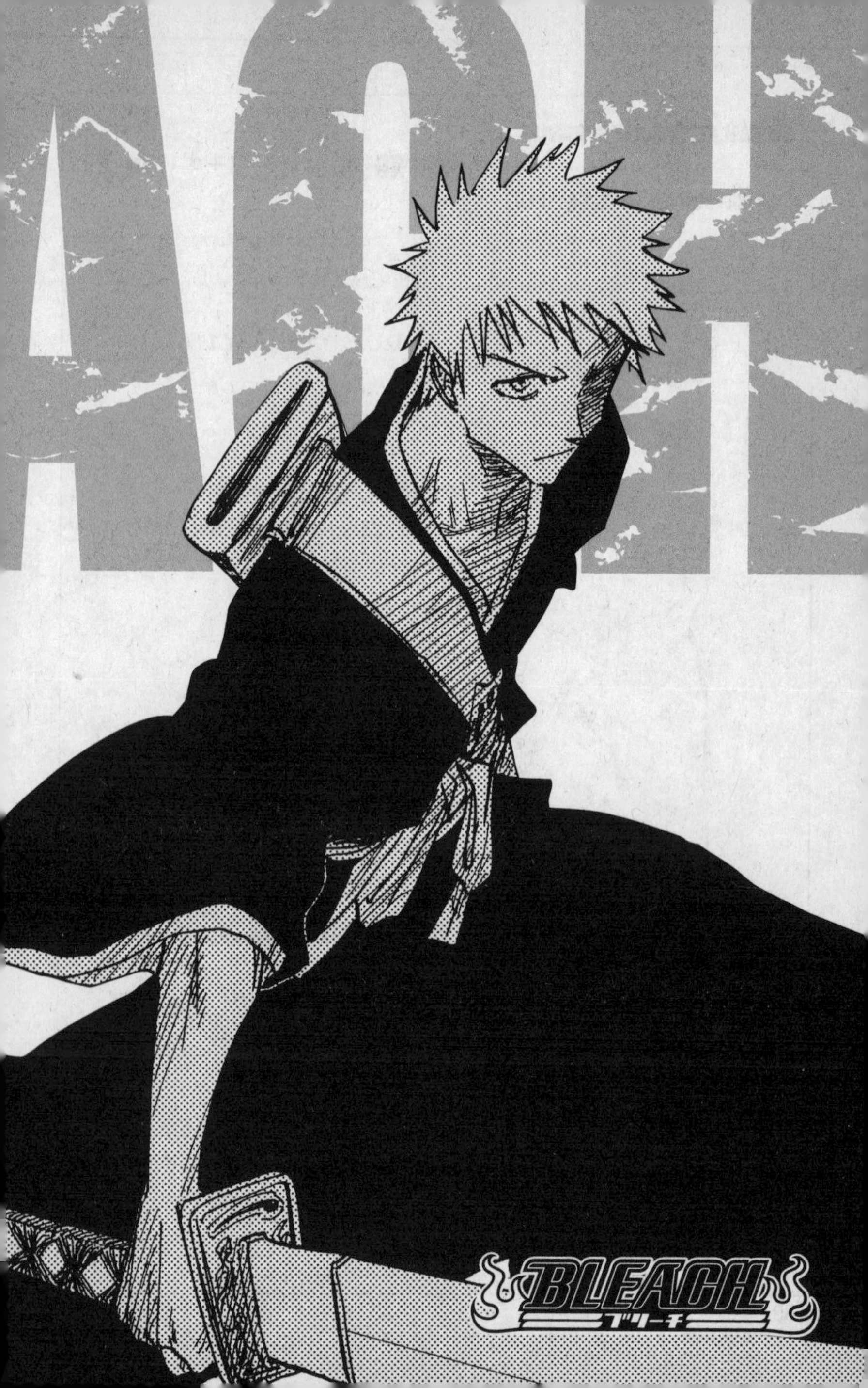
BLEACH
ブリーチ

- •A little girly
- •Fancy
- •Has a ribbon
- •Doesn't taste good
- •Twisting body

I'm gaining weight.
Not good. Very not good.
I don't know what to do. Any suggestions?
Let me know if there's a good diet out
there. Preferably something fast and easy...
without a lot of dietary restrictions...and
that will make me popular with the ladies.

-Tite Kubo

BLEACH

BLEACH
ブリーチ

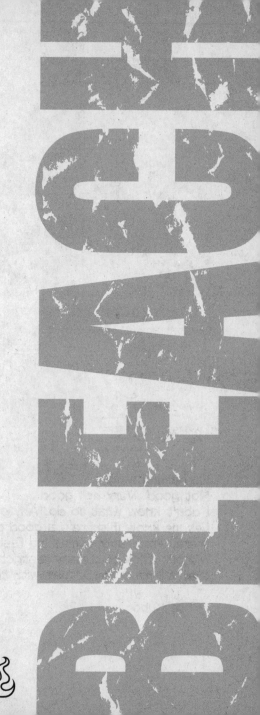

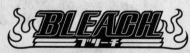

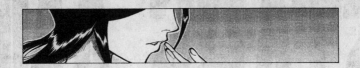

People have hope

Because they cannot see Death standing behind them

BLEACH2 GOODBYE PARAKEET, GOOD NIGHT MY SISTA

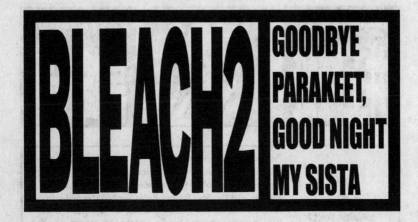

STARS AND

Rukia Kuchiki

Orihime Inoue

Ichigo Kurosaki

★ plot

Fifteen-year-old Ichigo "Strawberry" Kurosaki can see ghosts. Otherwise, he was a typical (?) high school student until the day a Hollow—a malevolent lost soul—came to eat him, and the Soul Reaper Rukia Kuchiki stepped into his life. To defeat the Hollow and save his family, Ichigo let Rukia transfer some of her Soul Reaper powers to him. But when Rukia was left powerless, she recruited Ichigo for her war against the murderous, soul-gobbling Hollows. Now, Ichigo's near-invincible classmate Chad has turned up at the family clinic with strange wounds—and a mysterious parakeet!?

BLEACH ALL

有沢竜貴

Tatsuki Arisawa

茶渡泰虎

Yasutora "Chad" Sado

Kisuke Urahara

浦原喜助

STORIES

BLEACH 2

GOODBYE PARAKEET, GOOD NIGHT MY SISTA

Contents

8. Chase Chad Around

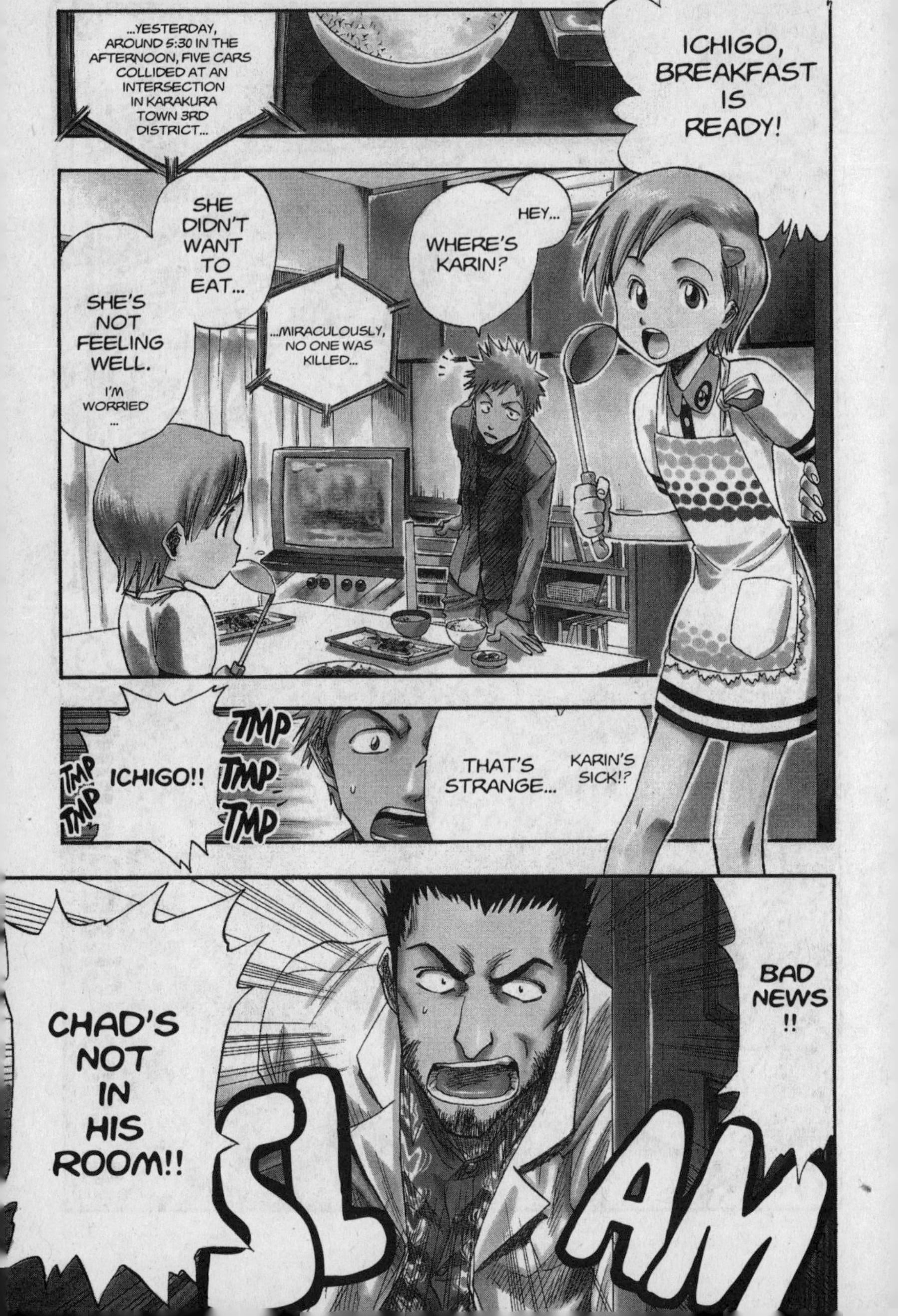
ICHIGO, BREAKFAST IS READY!
...YESTERDAY, AROUND 5:30 IN THE AFTERNOON, FIVE CARS COLLIDED AT AN INTERSECTION IN KARAKURA TOWN 3RD DISTRICT...
HEY...
WHERE'S KARIN?
...MIRACULOUSLY, NO ONE WAS KILLED...
SHE DIDN'T WANT TO EAT...
SHE'S NOT FEELING WELL.
I'M WORRIED ...
KARIN'S SICK!?
THAT'S STRANGE...
TMP TMP TMP
ICHIGO!!
TMP TMP
BAD NEWS !!
CHAD'S NOT IN HIS ROOM!!
SLAM

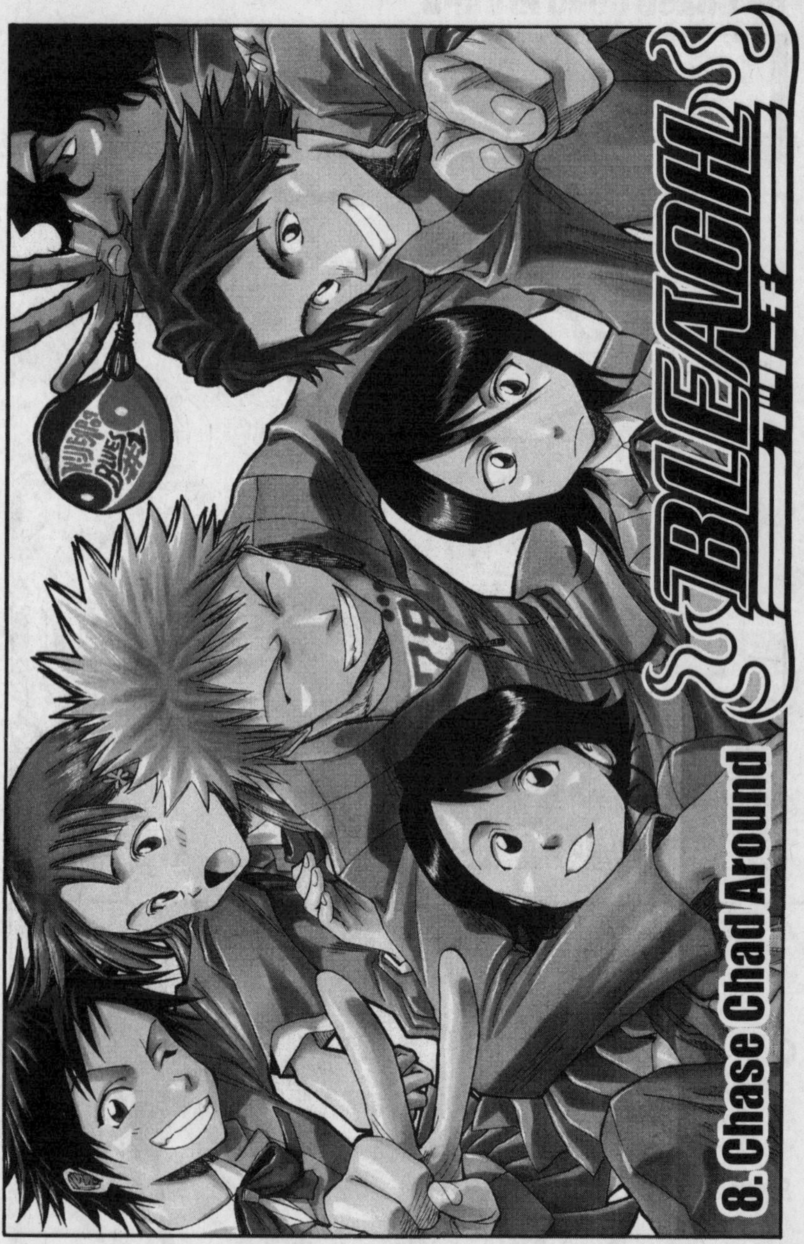
BLEACH
ブリーチ
8. Chase Chad Around

READ THIS WAY

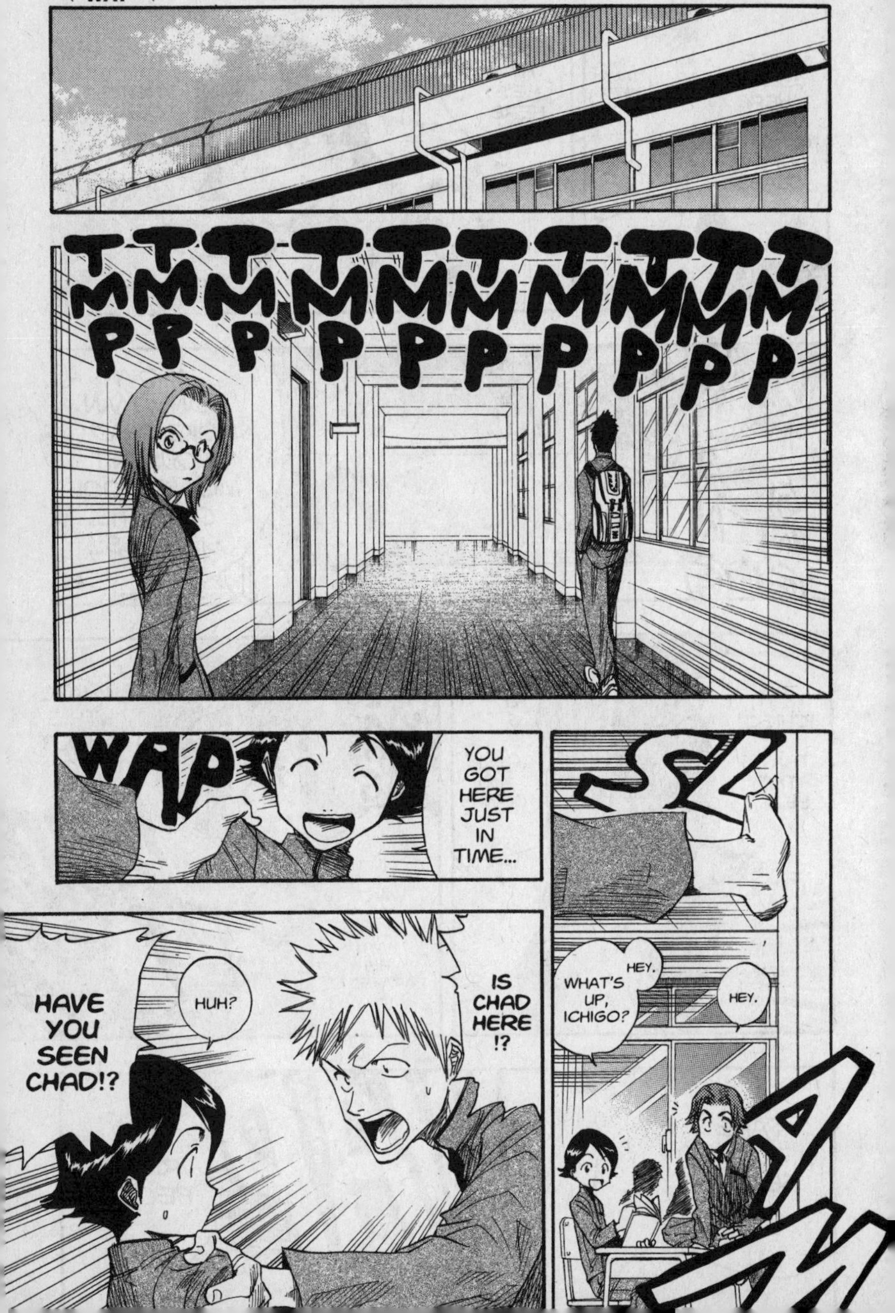
TMP TMP TMP TMP TMP TMP TMP TMP TMP TMP
SL
HEY. WHAT'S UP, ICHIGO?
HEY.
AM
YOU GOT HERE JUST IN TIME...
WAP
IS CHAD HERE!?
HUH?
HAVE YOU SEEN CHAD!?

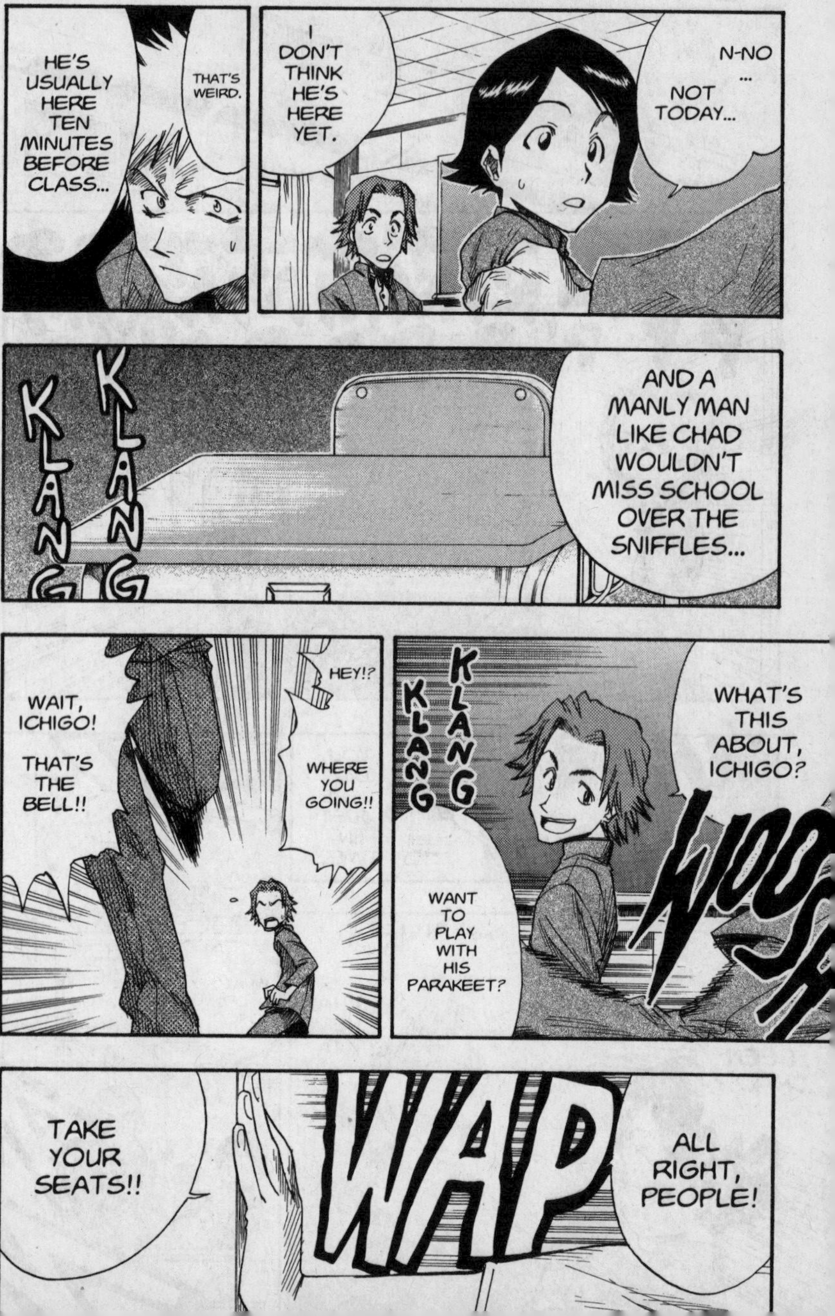
N-NO ... NOT TODAY...
I DON'T THINK HE'S HERE YET.
THAT'S WEIRD.
HE'S USUALLY HERE TEN MINUTES BEFORE CLASS...
AND A MANLY MAN LIKE CHAD WOULDN'T MISS SCHOOL OVER THE SNIFFLES...
KLANG
KLANG
KLANG
KLANG
WHAT'S THIS ABOUT, ICHIGO?
WANT TO PLAY WITH HIS PARAKEET?
WOOSH
HEY!?
WHERE YOU GOING!!
WAIT, ICHIGO!
THAT'S THE BELL!!
ALL RIGHT, PEOPLE!
WAP
TAKE YOUR SEATS!!

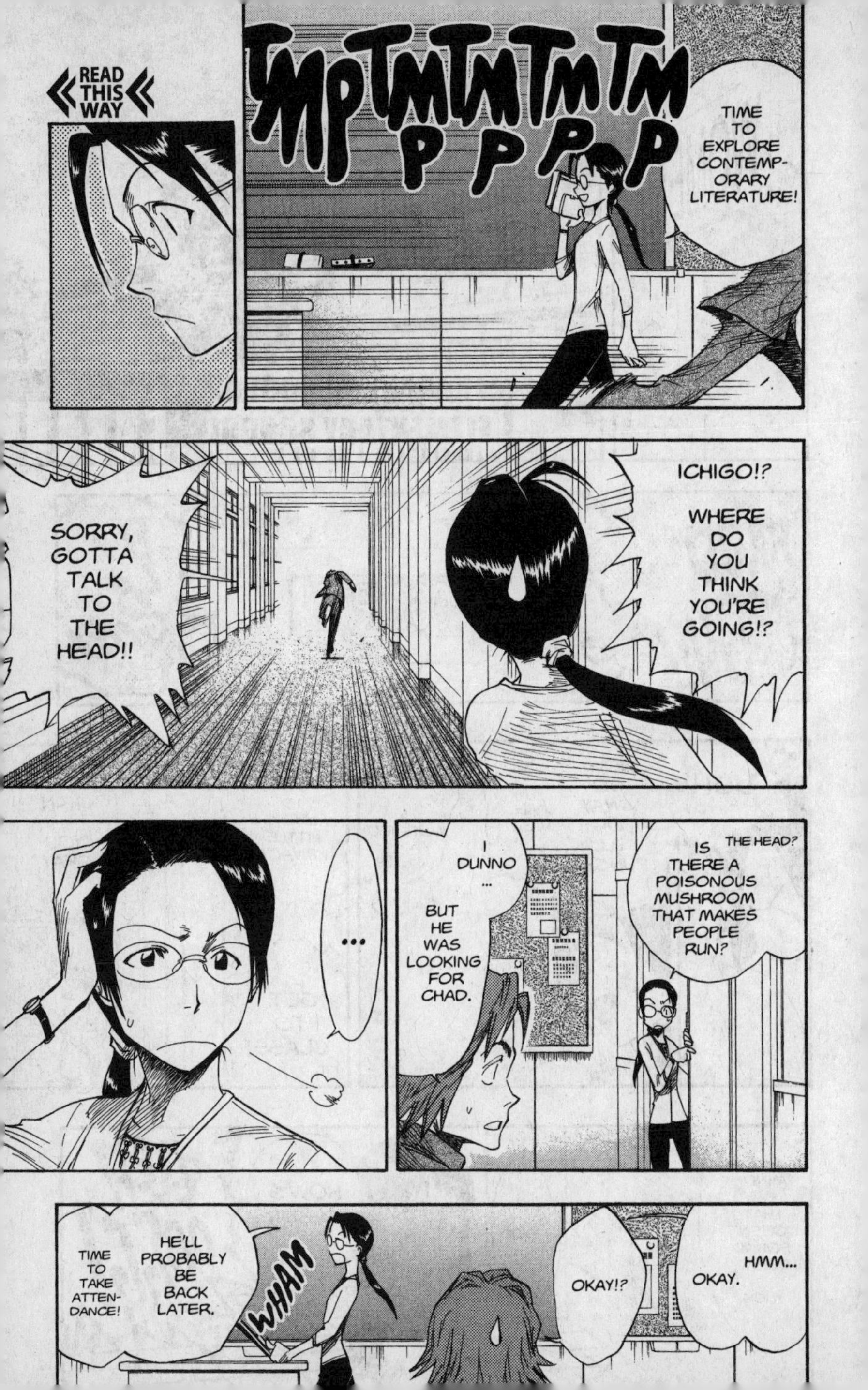
READ THIS WAY
TMPTMTMTMTM PPPP
TIME TO EXPLORE CONTEMPORARY LITERATURE!
ICHIGO!? WHERE DO YOU THINK YOU'RE GOING!?
SORRY, GOTTA TALK TO THE HEAD!!
THE HEAD?
IS THERE A POISONOUS MUSHROOM THAT MAKES PEOPLE RUN?
I DUNNO... BUT HE WAS LOOKING FOR CHAD.
...
HMM... OKAY.
OKAY!?
WHAM
HE'LL PROBABLY BE BACK LATER.
TIME TO TAKE ATTENDANCE!

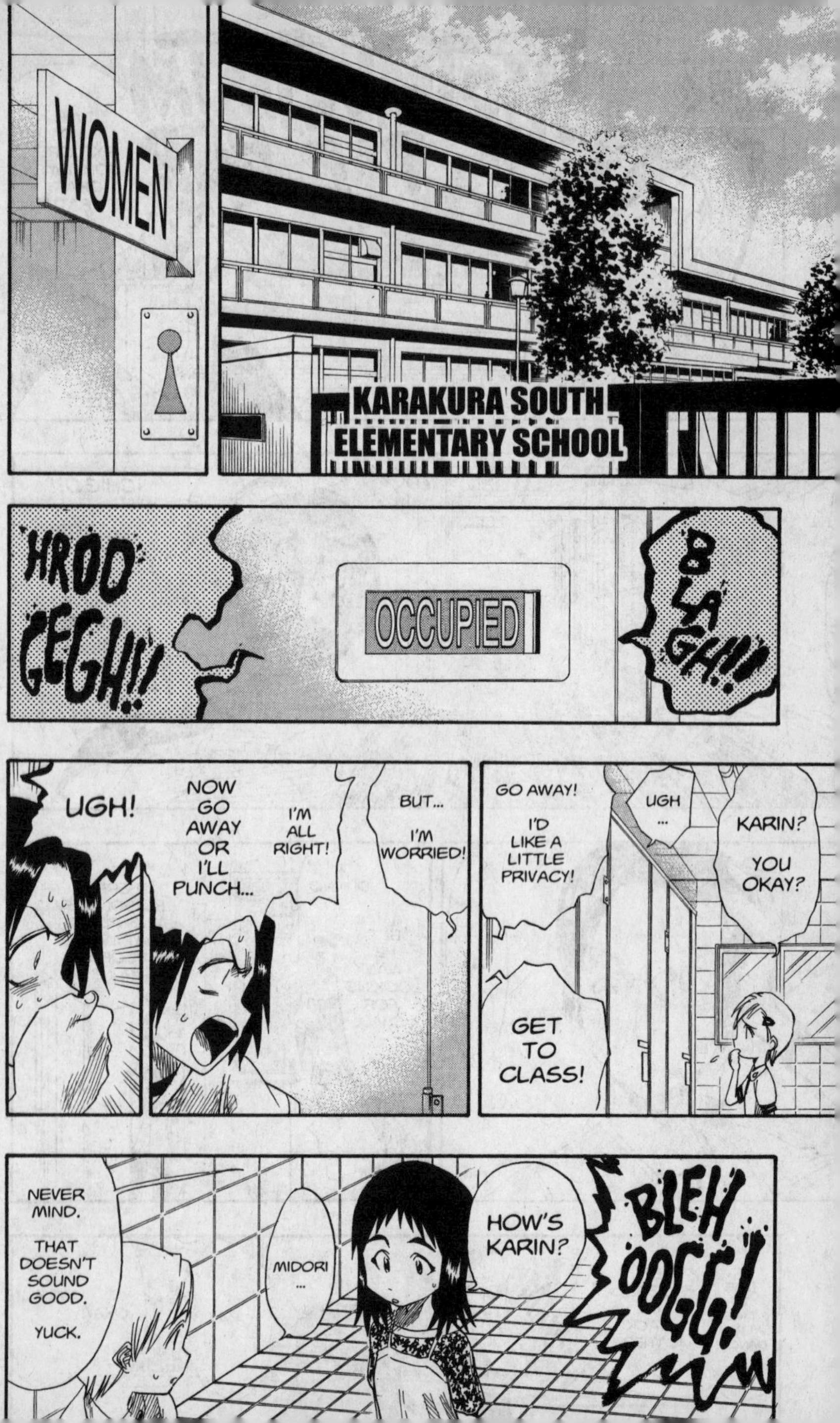
WOMEN
KARAKURA SOUTH ELEMENTARY SCHOOL
BLAGH!!!
OCCUPIED
HROOGEGH!!
KARIN? YOU OKAY?
UGH...
GO AWAY! I'D LIKE A LITTLE PRIVACY!
GET TO CLASS!
BUT... I'M WORRIED!
I'M ALL RIGHT!
NOW GO AWAY OR I'LL PUNCH...
UGH!
BLEH OOGG!
HOW'S KARIN?
MIDORI...
NEVER MIND. THAT DOESN'T SOUND GOOD. YUCK.

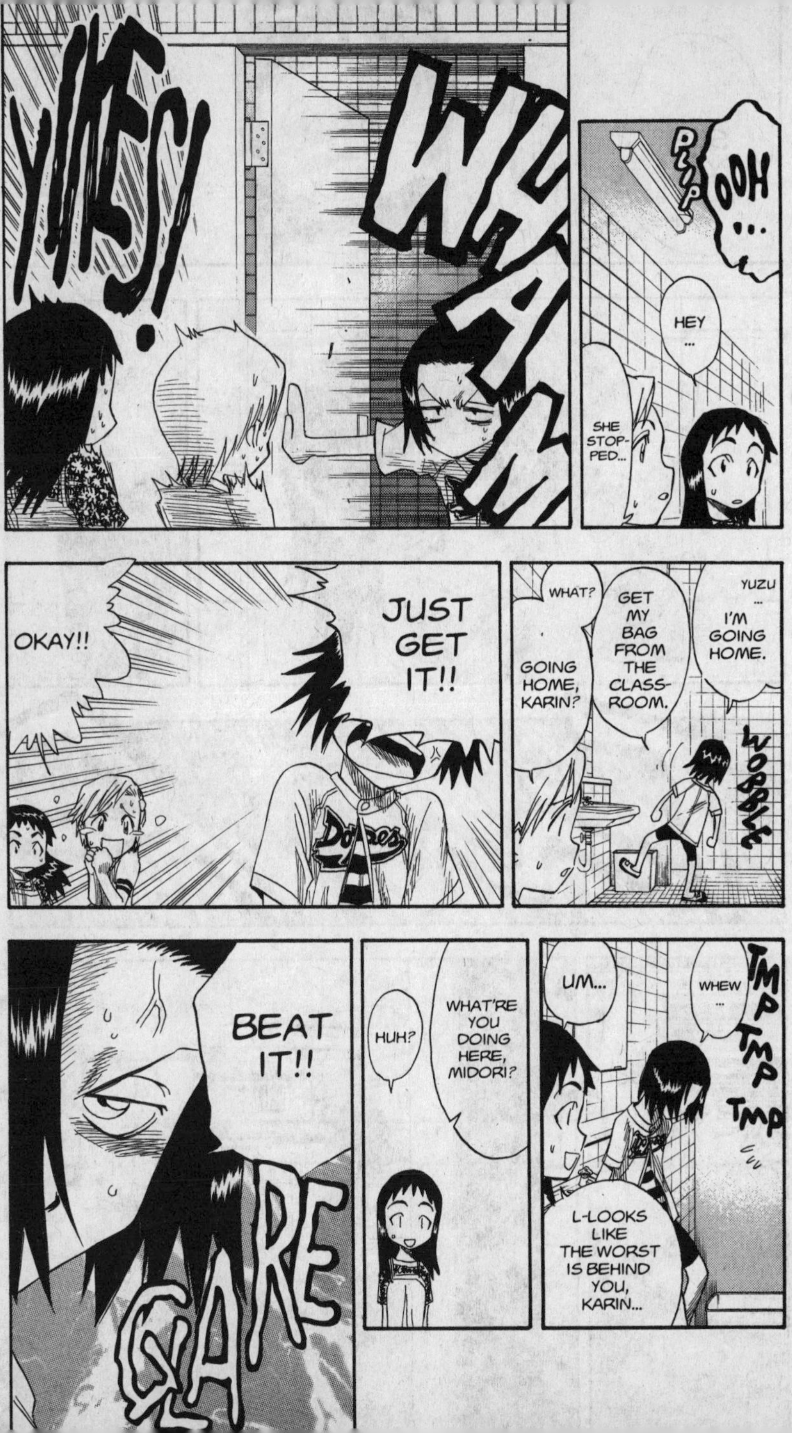
OOH ...
PLIP
HEY ...
SHE STOP-PED...
WHAM
YAAAS!
YUZU ... I'M GOING HOME.
GET MY BAG FROM THE CLASS-ROOM.
WHAT?
GOING HOME, KARIN?
WOBBLE
JUST GET IT!!
OKAY!!
WHEW ...
TMP TMP TMP TMP
UM...
L-LOOKS LIKE THE WORST IS BEHIND YOU, KARIN...
WHAT'RE YOU DOING HERE, MIDORI?
HUH?
BEAT IT!!
GAARE

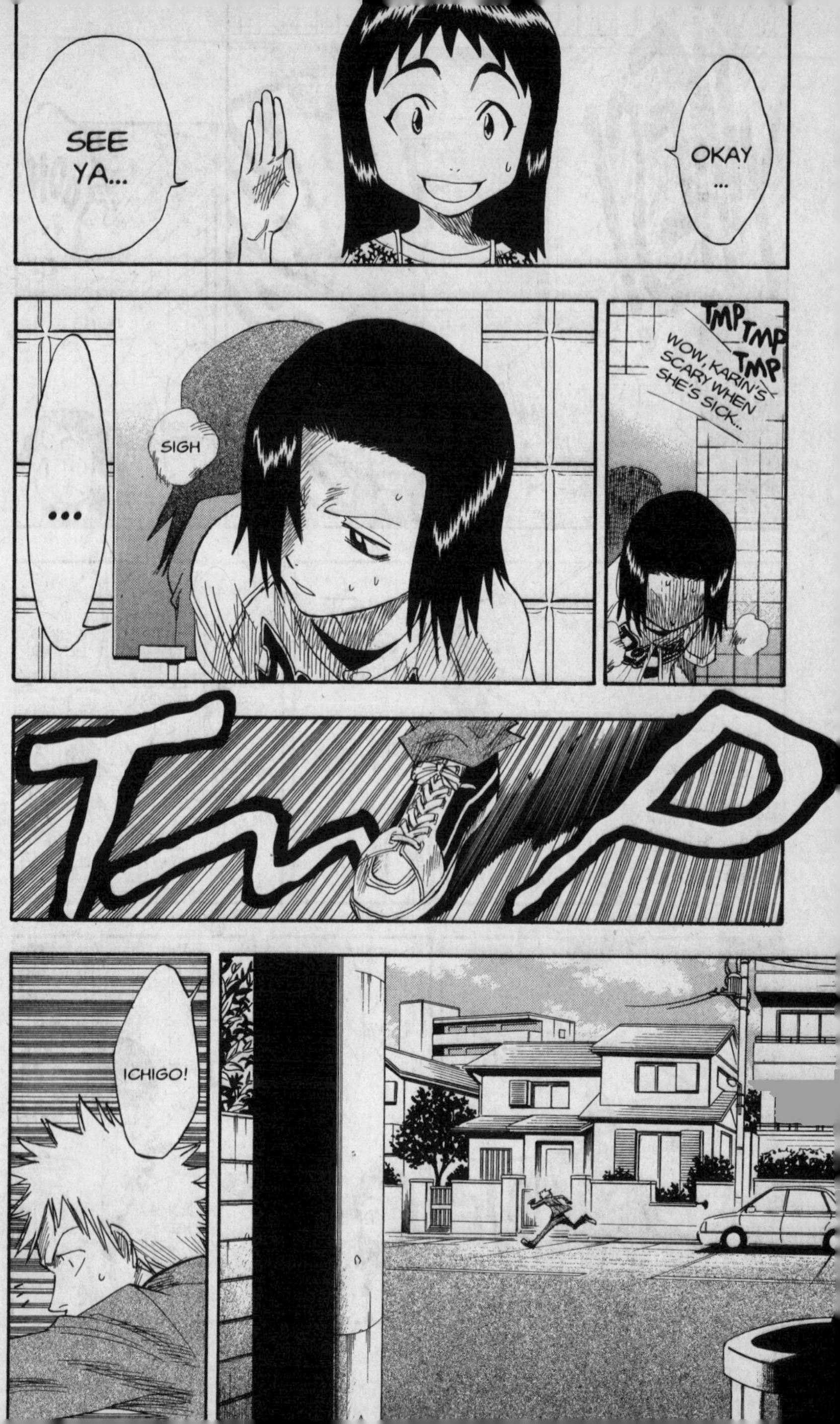
OKAY ...
SEE YA...
TMP TMP TMP
WOW, KARIN'S SCARY WHEN SHE'S SICK...
SIGH
...
TMP
ICHIGO!

READ THIS WAY

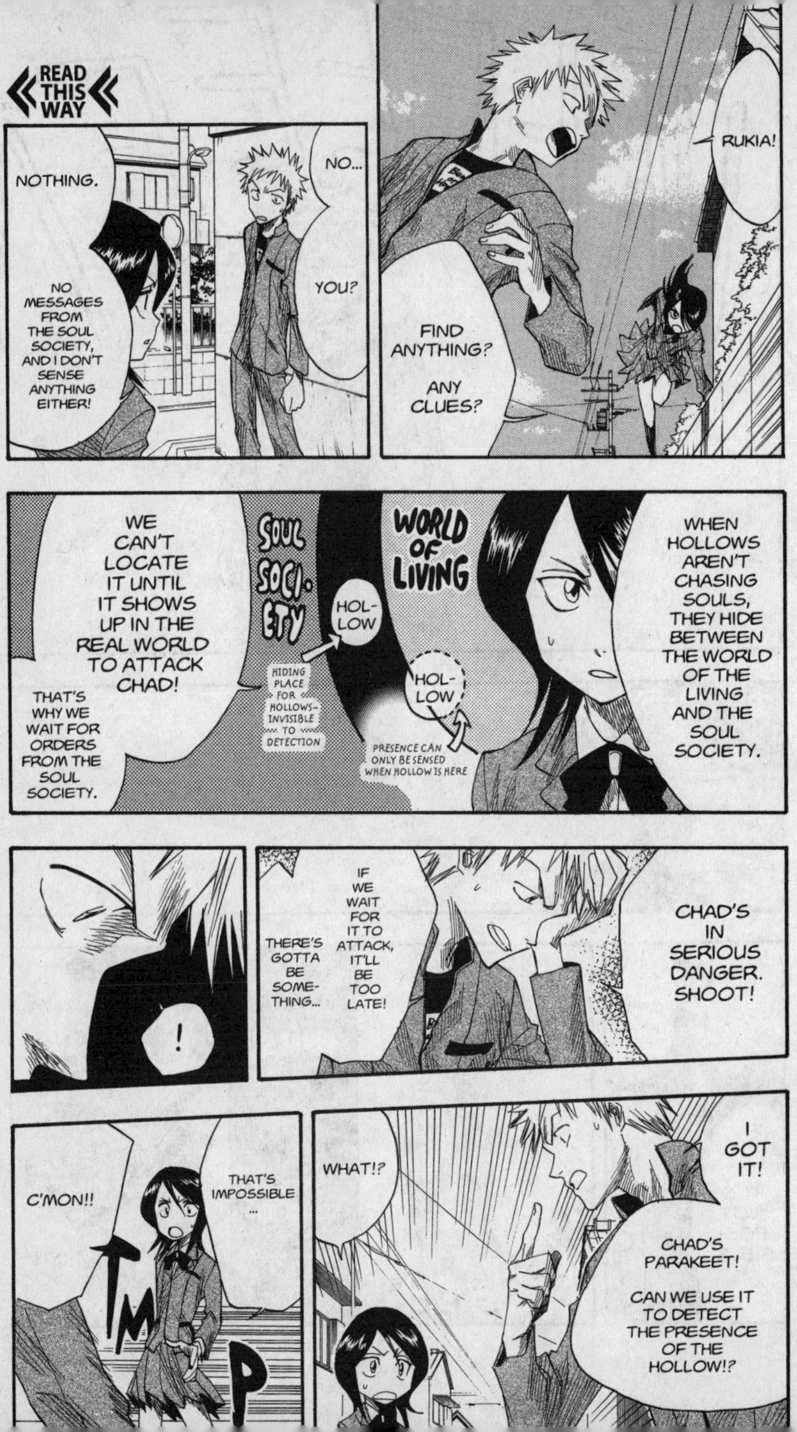

RUKIA!
FIND ANYTHING?
ANY CLUES?
NO...
YOU?
NOTHING.
NO MESSAGES FROM THE SOUL SOCIETY, AND I DON'T SENSE ANYTHING EITHER!
WHEN HOLLOWS AREN'T CHASING SOULS, THEY HIDE BETWEEN THE WORLD OF THE LIVING AND THE SOUL SOCIETY.
WORLD OF LIVING
HOL-LOW
PRESENCE CAN ONLY BE SENSED WHEN HOLLOW IS HERE
SOUL SOCI-ETY
HOL-LOW
HIDING PLACE FOR HOLLOWS- INVISIBLE TO DETECTION
WE CAN'T LOCATE IT UNTIL IT SHOWS UP IN THE REAL WORLD TO ATTACK CHAD!
THAT'S WHY WE WAIT FOR ORDERS FROM THE SOUL SOCIETY.
CHAD'S IN SERIOUS DANGER. SHOOT!
IF WE WAIT FOR IT TO ATTACK, IT'LL BE TOO LATE!
THERE'S GOTTA BE SOME-THING...
!
I GOT IT!
CHAD'S PARAKEET!
CAN WE USE IT TO DETECT THE PRESENCE OF THE HOLLOW!?
WHAT!?
THAT'S IMPOSSIBLE ...
C'MON!!
TMP

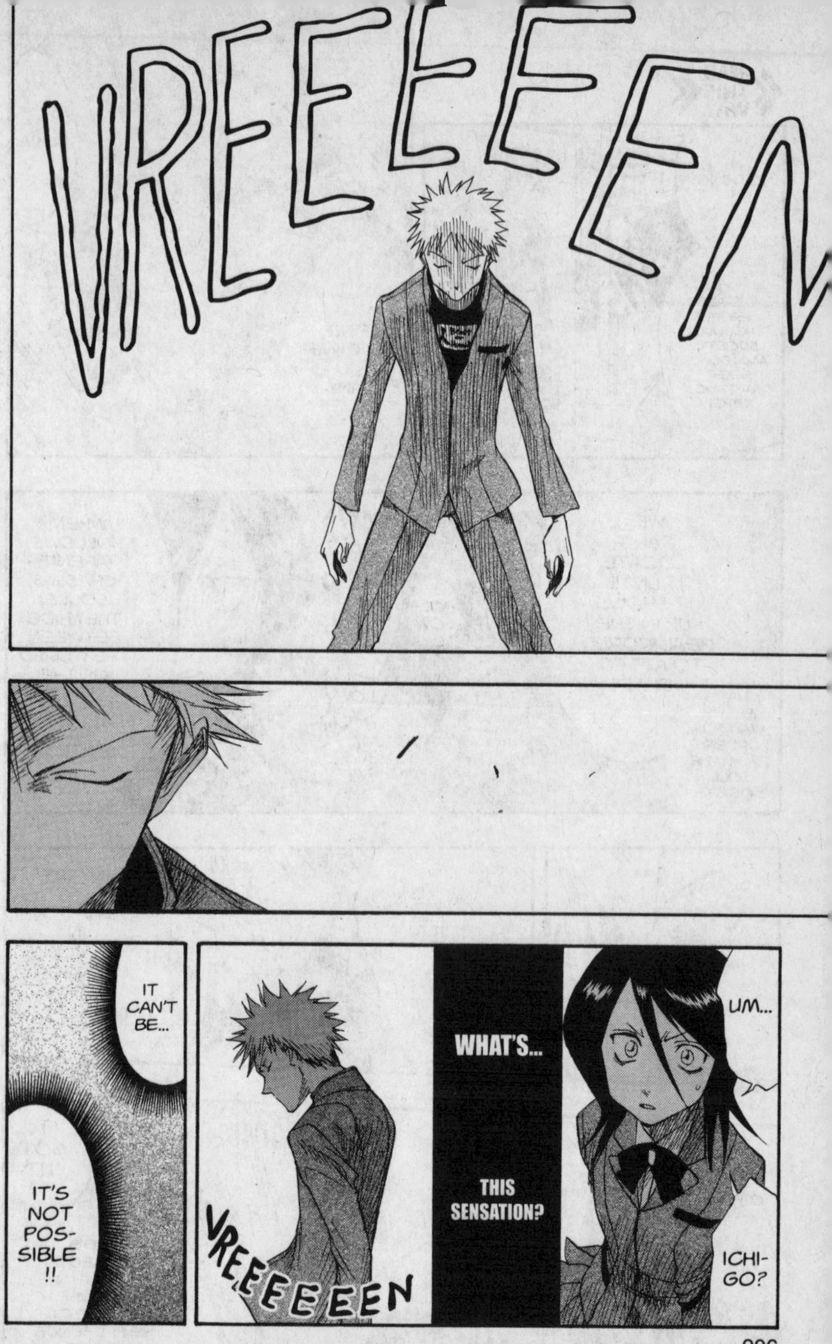
VREEEEEN
UM...
ICHI-GO?
WHAT'S...
THIS SENSATION?
VREEEEEEN
IT CAN'T BE...
IT'S NOT POS-SIBLE!!

READ THIS WAY

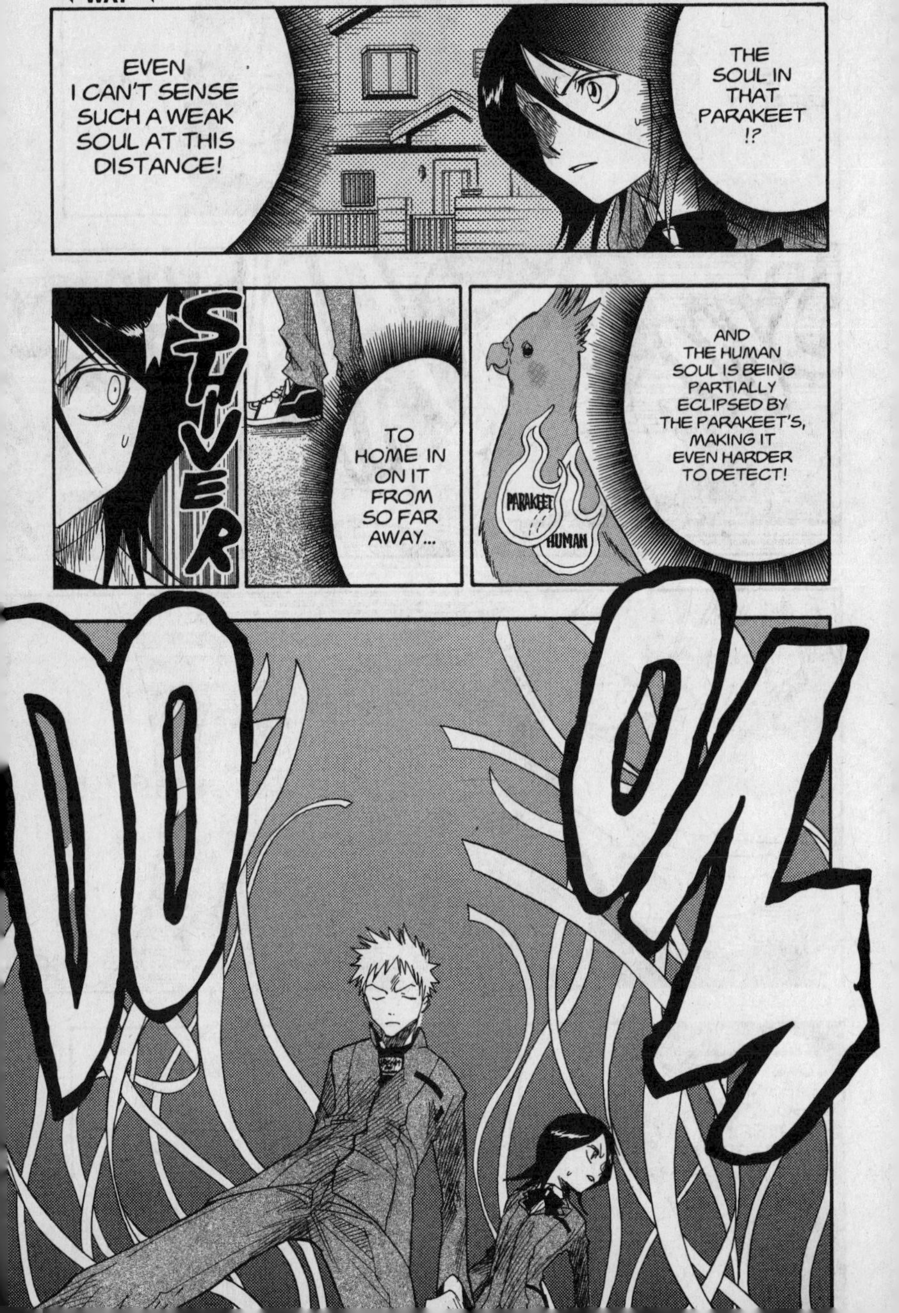

THE SOUL IN THAT PARAKEET !?
EVEN I CAN'T SENSE SUCH A WEAK SOUL AT THIS DISTANCE!
AND THE HUMAN SOUL IS BEING PARTIALLY ECLIPSED BY THE PARAKEET'S, MAKING IT EVEN HARDER TO DETECT!
PARAKEET
HUMAN
TO HOME IN ON IT FROM SO FAR AWAY...
SHIVER
DOOM

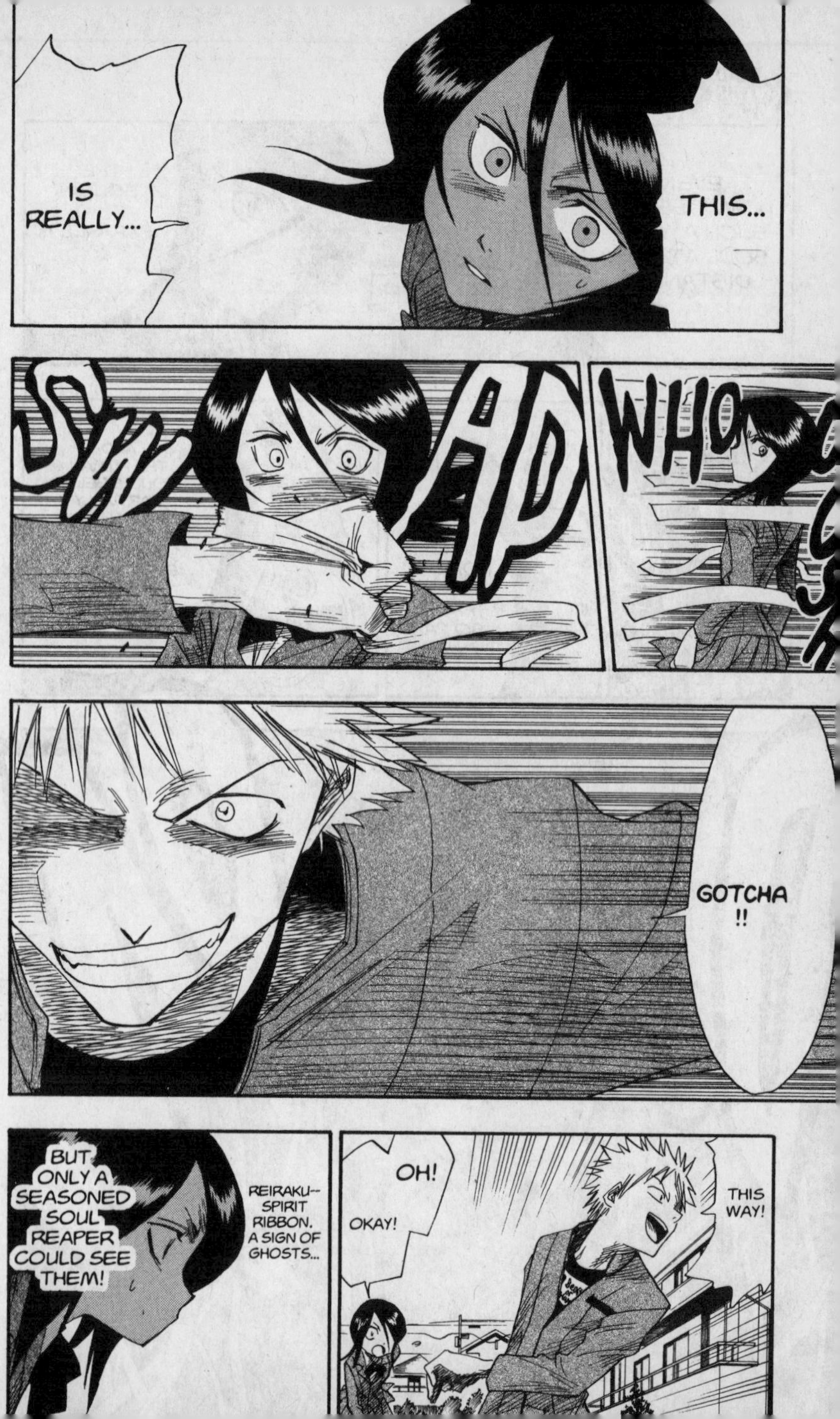
THIS...
IS REALLY...
GOTCHA !!
THIS WAY!
OH!
OKAY!
REIRAKU-- SPIRIT RIBBON. A SIGN OF GHOSTS...
BUT ONLY A SEASONED SOUL REAPER COULD SEE THEM!

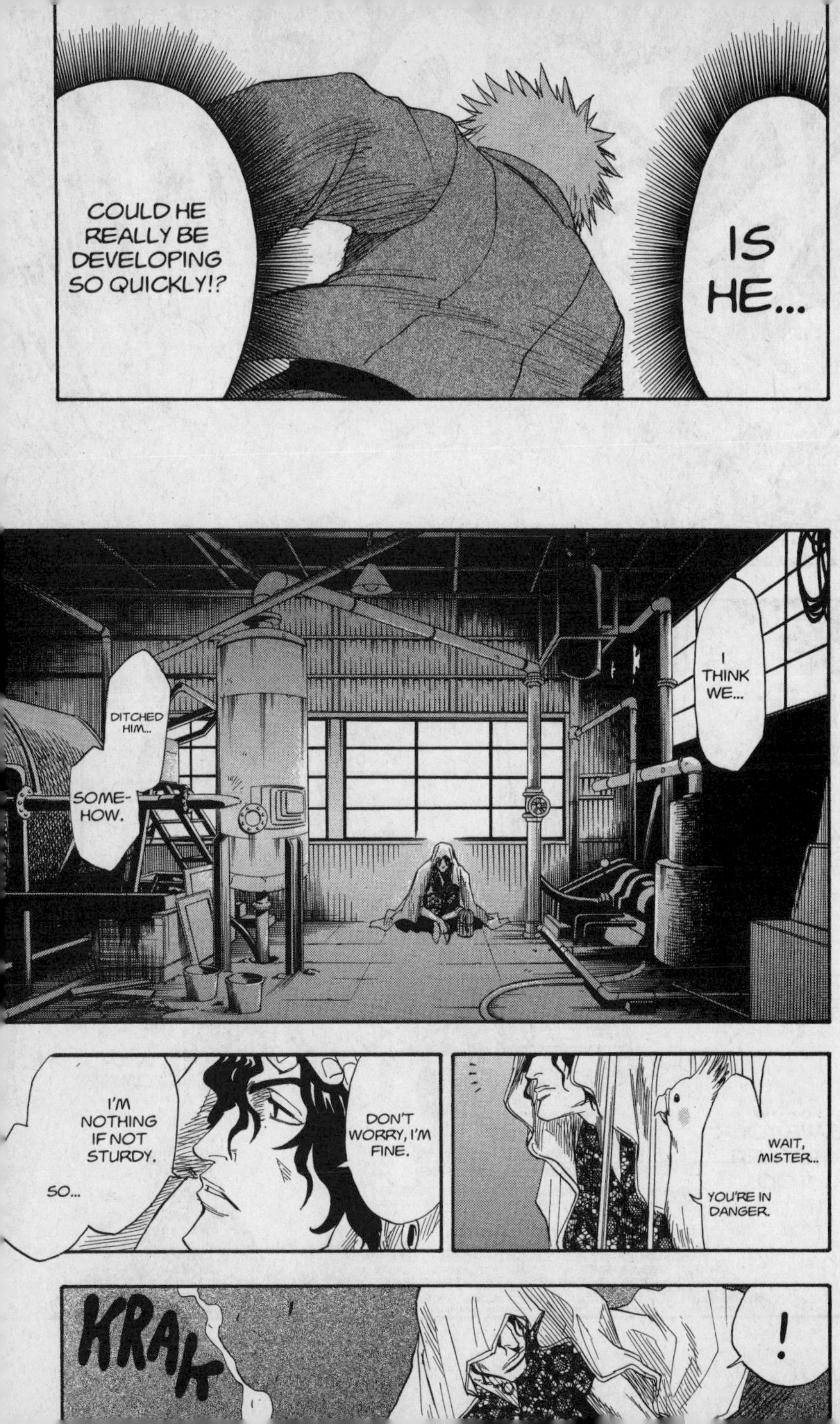
IS HE...
COULD HE REALLY BE DEVELOPING SO QUICKLY!?
I THINK WE...
DITCHED HIM...
SOME-HOW.
WAIT, MISTER..
YOU'RE IN DANGER.
DON'T WORRY, I'M FINE.
I'M NOTHING IF NOT STURDY.
SO...
!
KRAK

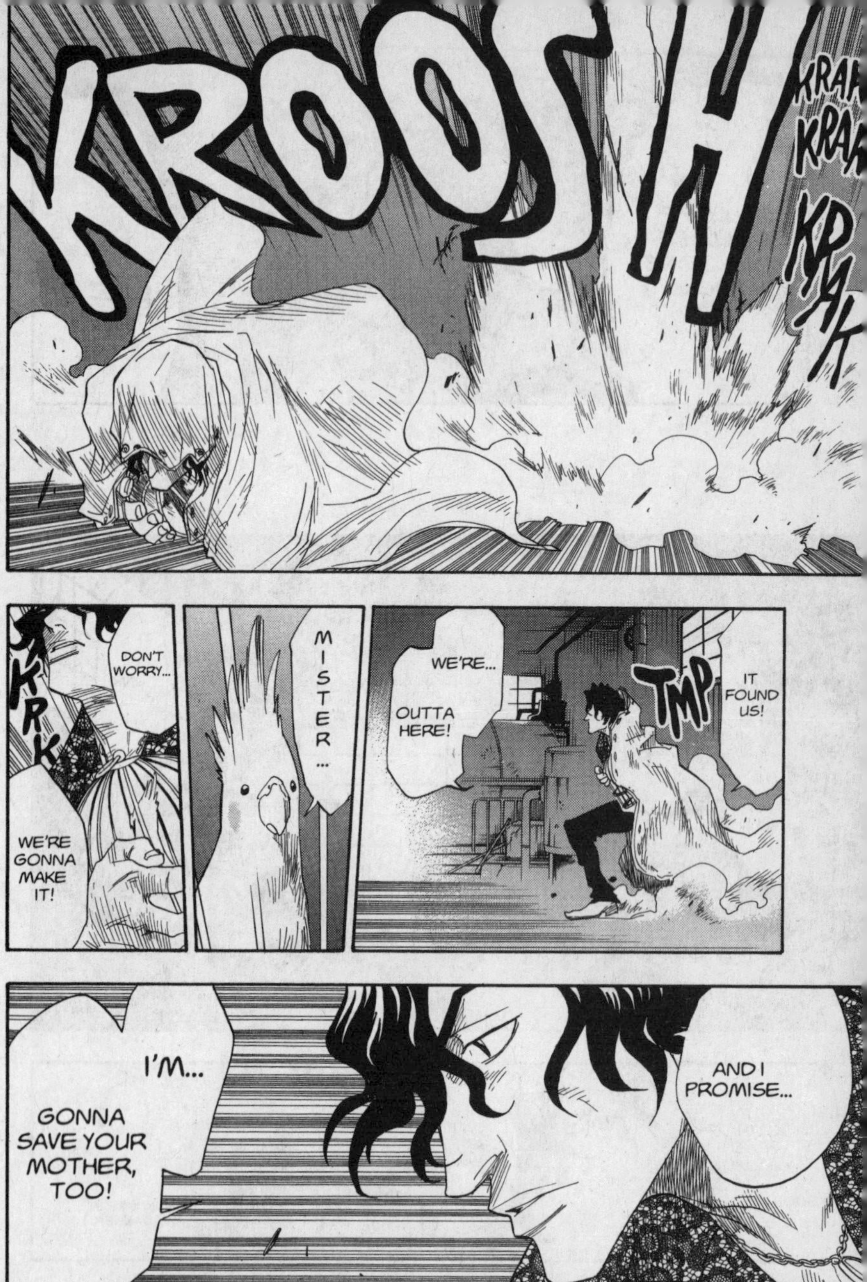
KROOSH
IT FOUND US!
TMP
WE'RE...
OUTTA HERE!
MISTER ...
DON'T WORRY...
KRK
WE'RE GONNA MAKE IT!
AND I PROMISE...
I'M...
GONNA SAVE YOUR MOTHER, TOO!

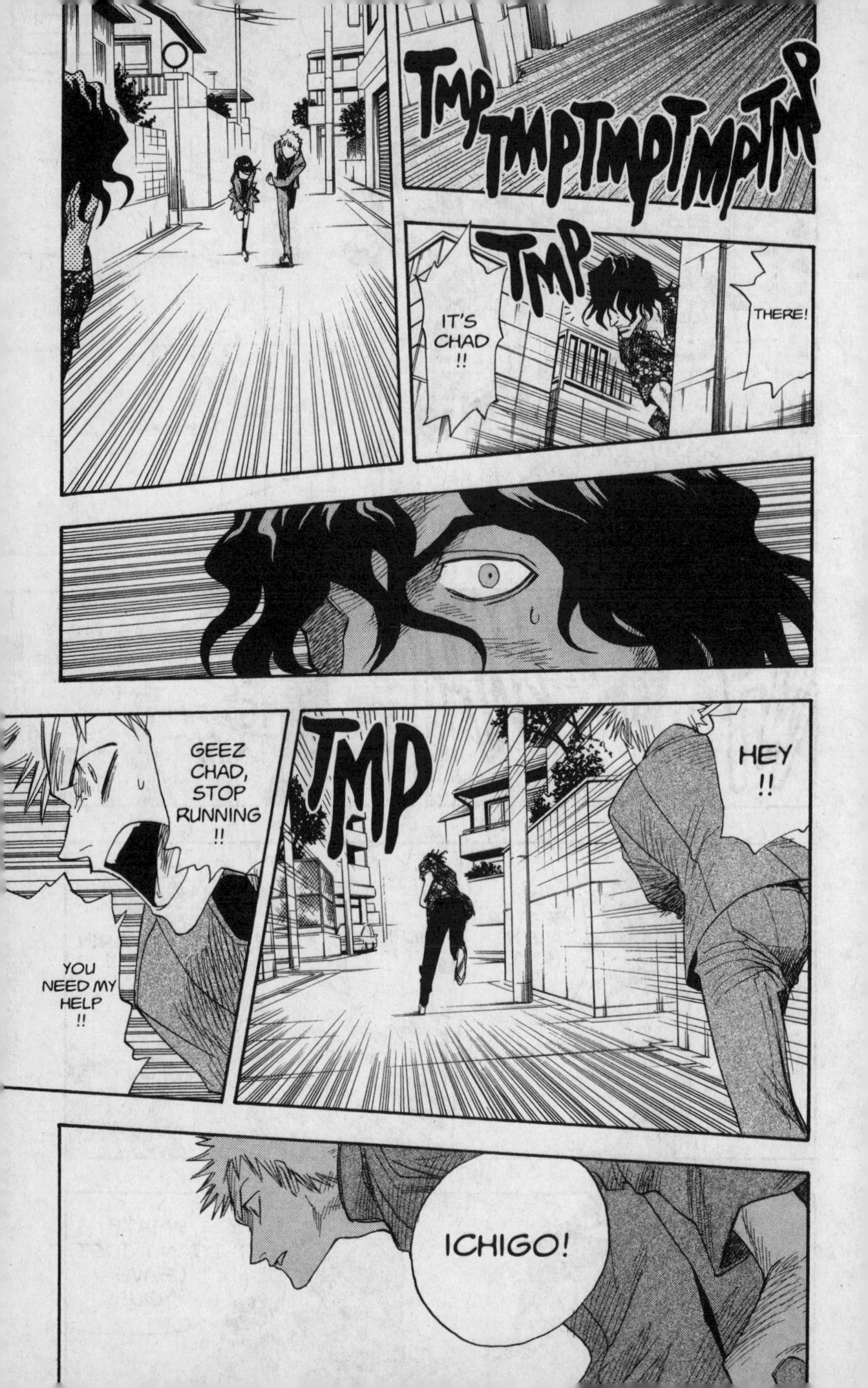
TMP TMPTMPTMPTMP
THERE!
TMP
IT'S CHAD !!
HEY !!
TMP
GEEZ CHAD, STOP RUNNING !!
YOU NEED MY HELP !!
ICHIGO!

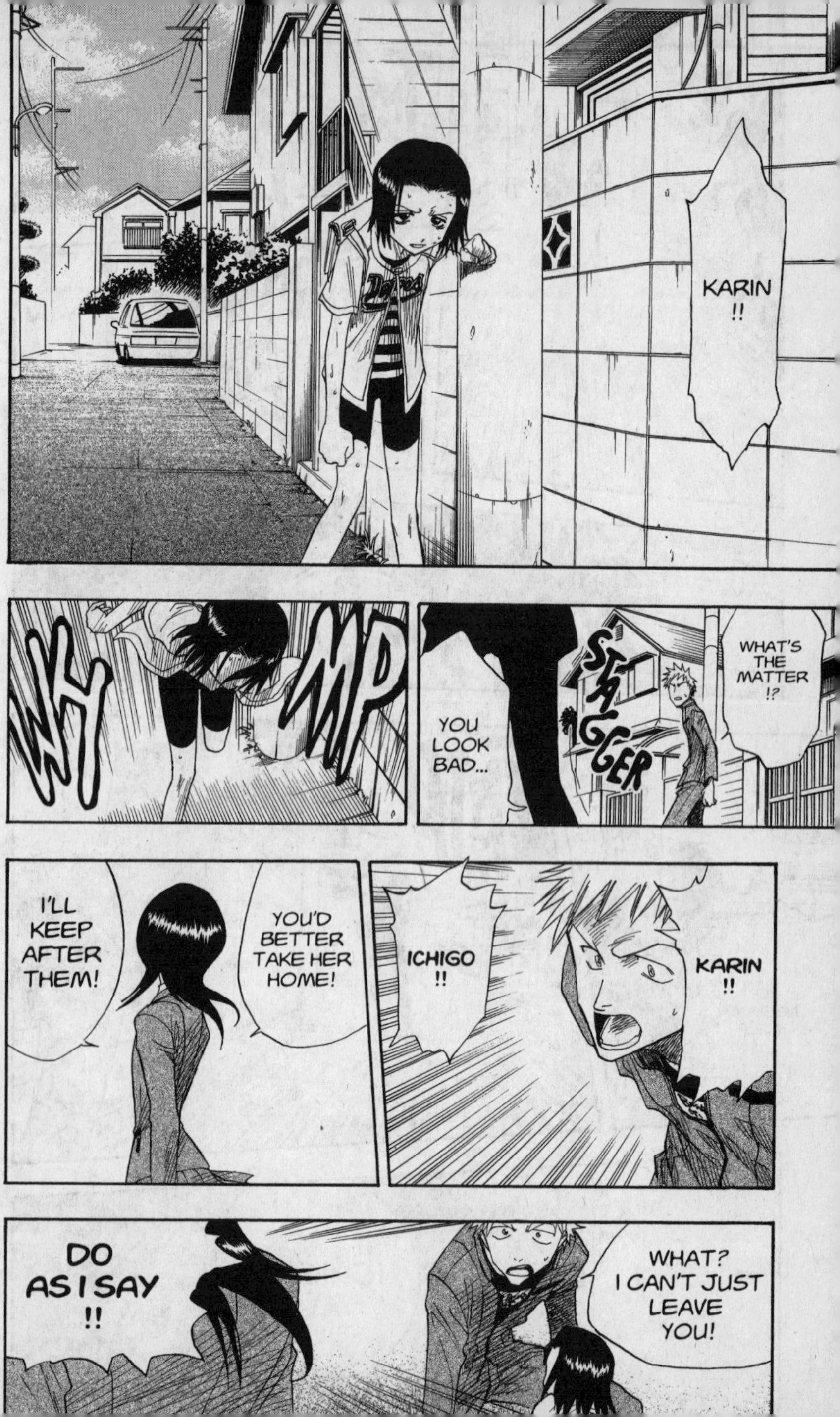
KARIN!!
WHAT'S THE MATTER!?
STAGGER
YOU LOOK BAD...
WH
MP
KARIN!!
ICHIGO!!
YOU'D BETTER TAKE HER HOME!
I'LL KEEP AFTER THEM!
WHAT? I CAN'T JUST LEAVE YOU!
DO AS I SAY!!

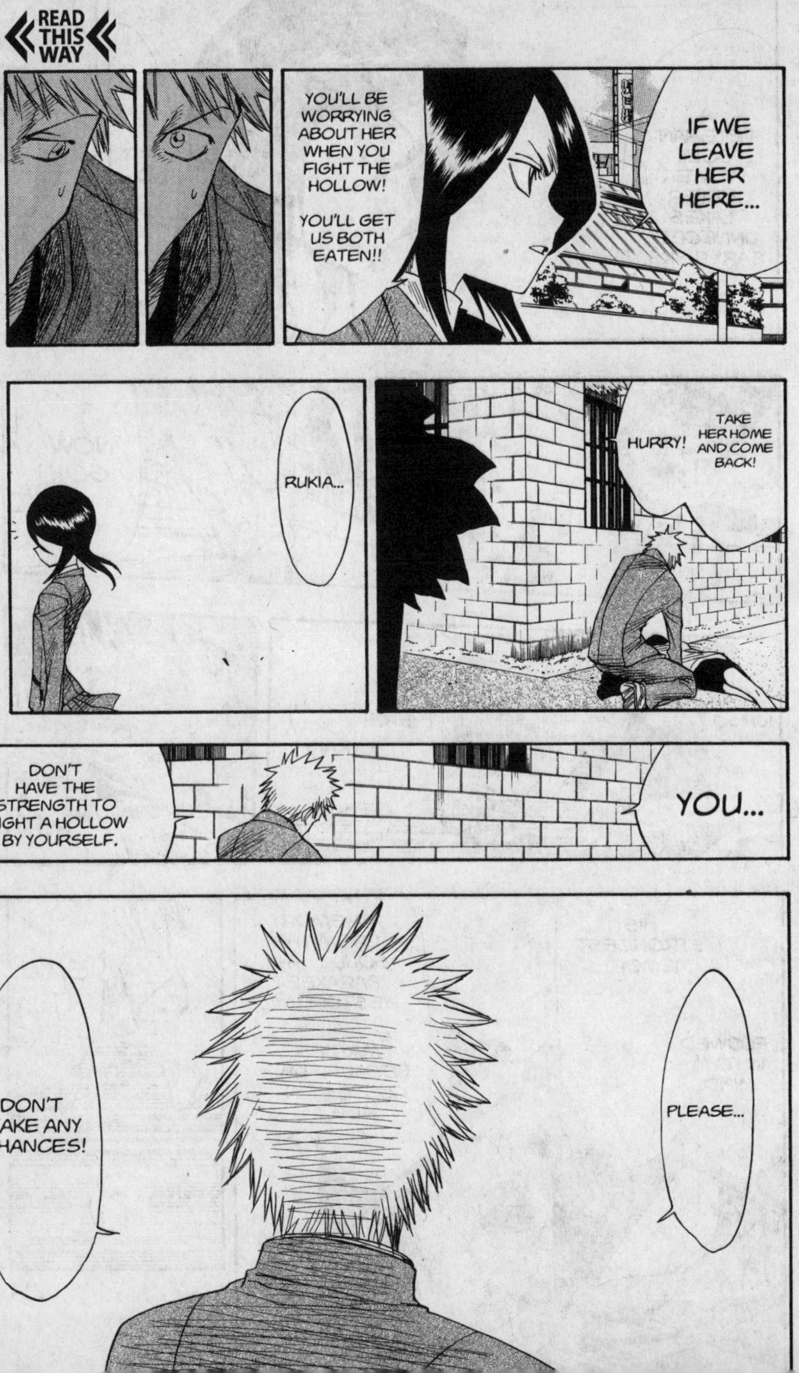
READ THIS WAY
IF WE LEAVE HER HERE...
YOU'LL BE WORRYING ABOUT HER WHEN YOU FIGHT THE HOLLOW!
YOU'LL GET US BOTH EATEN!!
HURRY!
TAKE HER HOME AND COME BACK!
RUKIA...
YOU...
DON'T HAVE THE STRENGTH TO FIGHT A HOLLOW BY YOURSELF.
PLEASE...
DON'T TAKE ANY CHANCES!

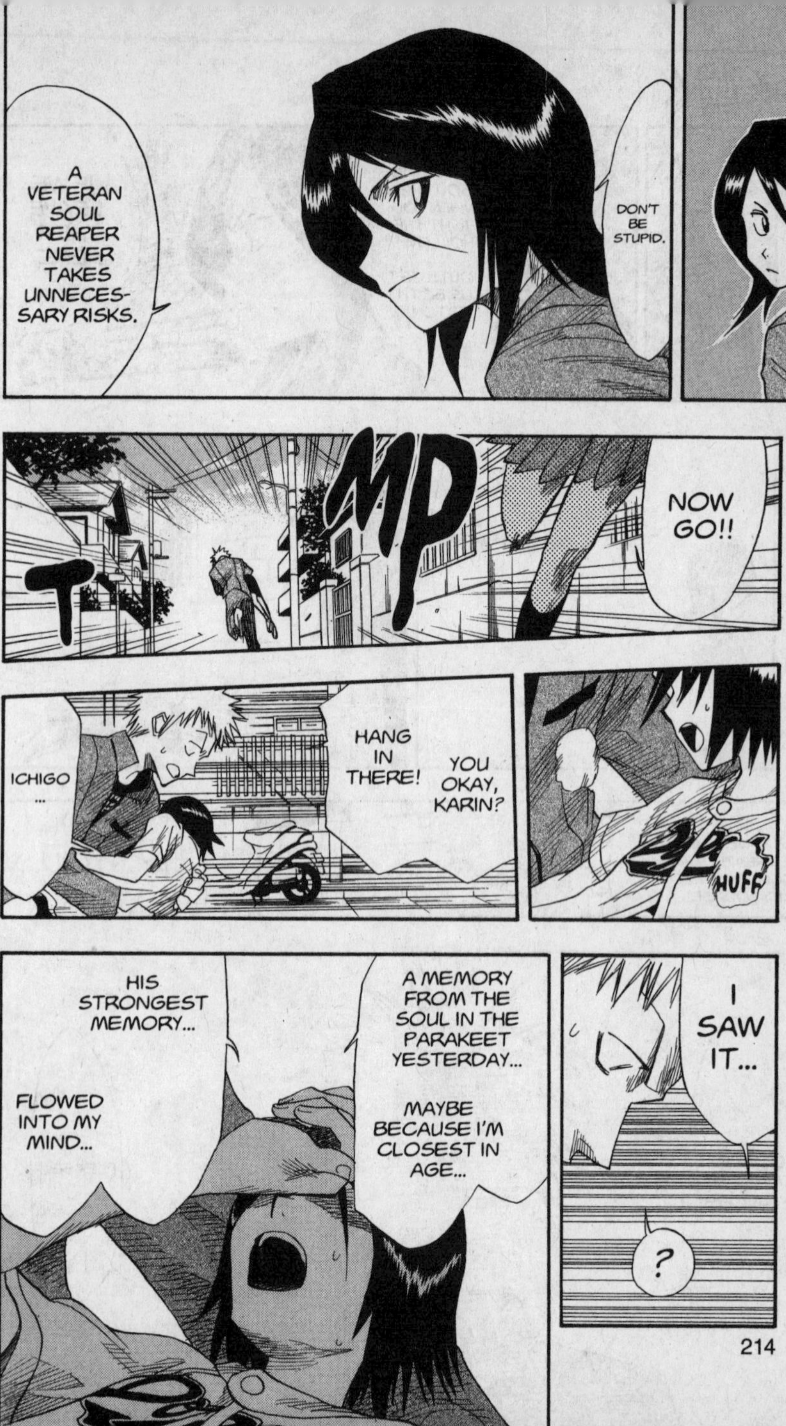
DON'T BE STUPID.
A VETERAN SOUL REAPER NEVER TAKES UNNECES-SARY RISKS.
NOW GO!!
MP
T
HUFF
YOU OKAY, KARIN?
HANG IN THERE!
ICHIGO ...
I SAW IT...
?
A MEMORY FROM THE SOUL IN THE PARAKEET YESTERDAY...
MAYBE BECAUSE I'M CLOSEST IN AGE...
HIS STRONGEST MEMORY...
FLOWED INTO MY MIND...

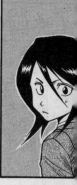

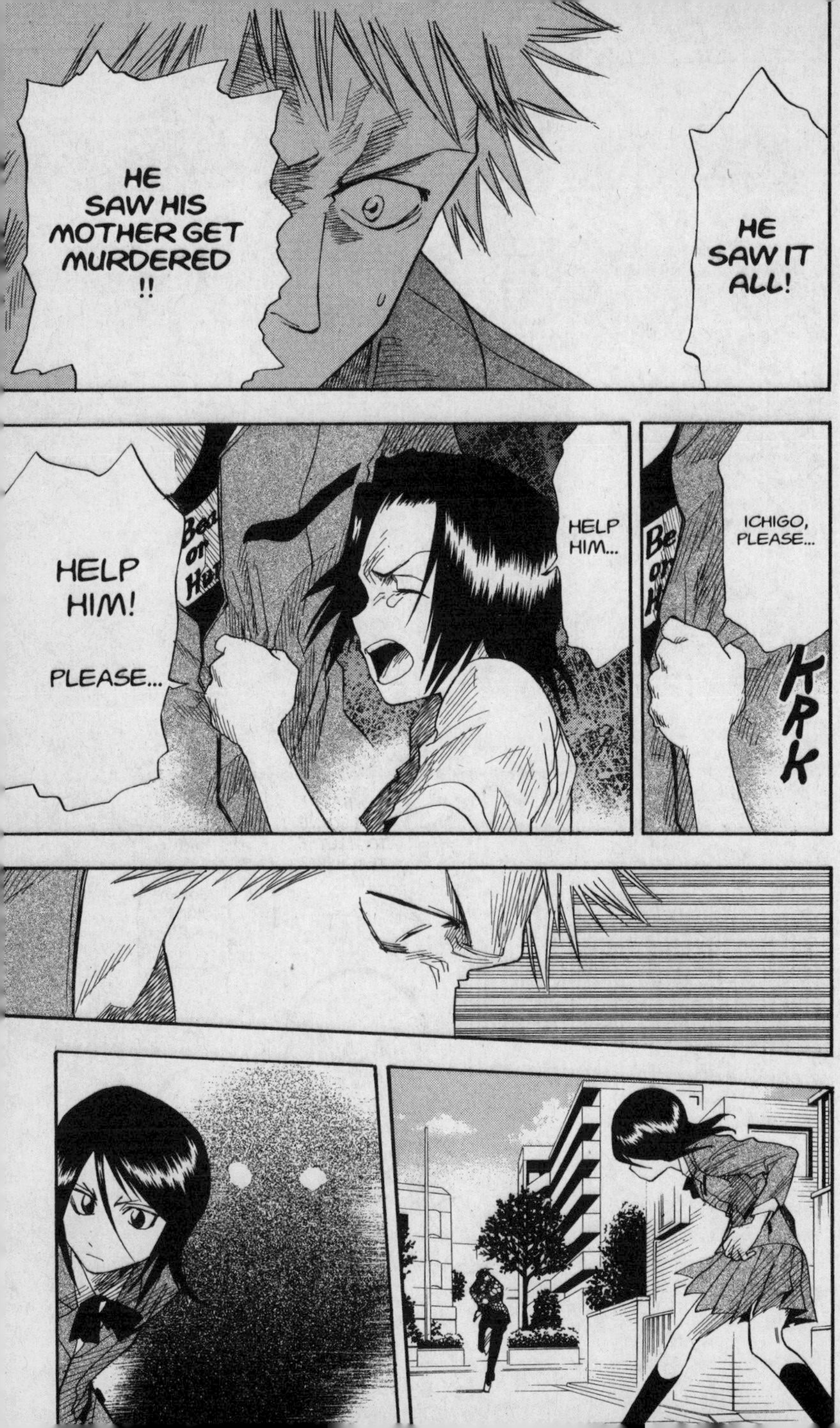
HE SAW IT ALL!
HE SAW HIS MOTHER GET MURDERED !!
ICHIGO, PLEASE...
KRK
HELP HIM...
HELP HIM!
PLEASE...

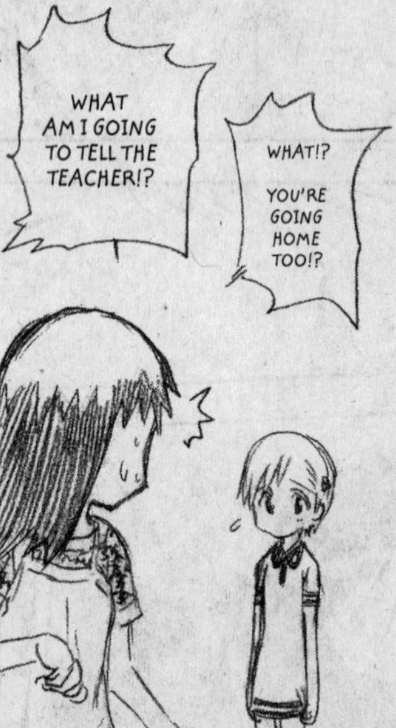
WHAT!? YOU'RE GOING HOME TOO!?
WHAT AM I GOING TO TELL THE TEACHER!?

9. Monster and a Transfer (Struck Down)

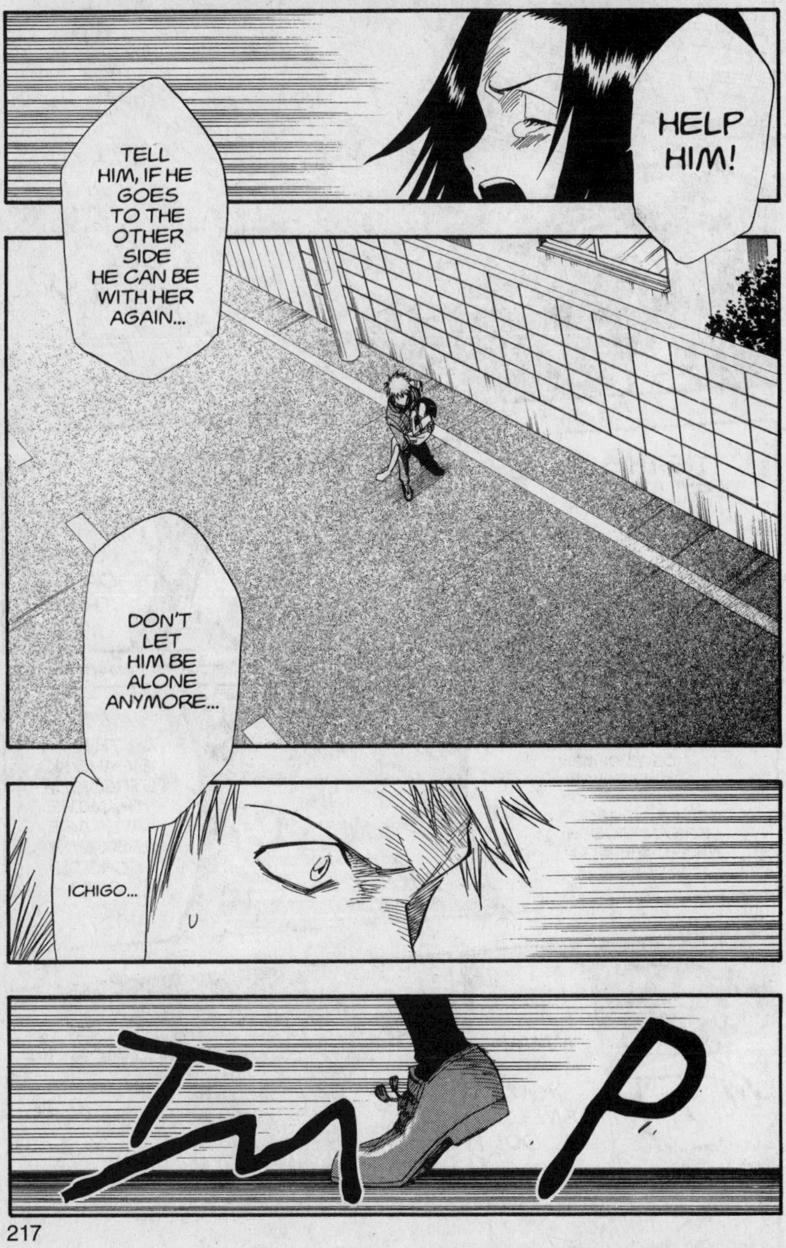

HELP HIM!
TELL HIM, IF HE GOES TO THE OTHER SIDE HE CAN BE WITH HER AGAIN...
DON'T LET HIM BE ALONE ANYMORE...
ICHIGO...
TMP

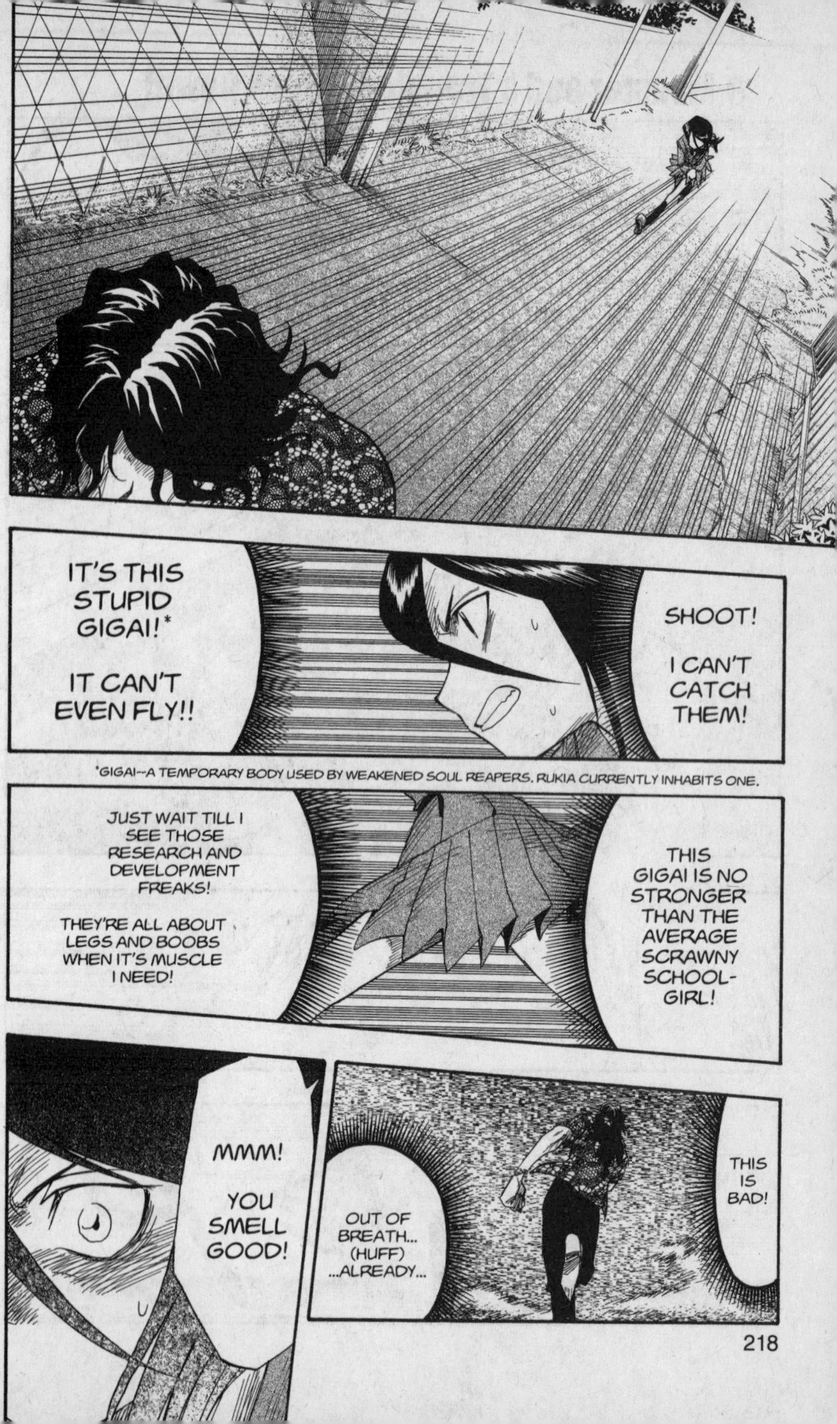
SHOOT!
I CAN'T CATCH THEM!
IT'S THIS STUPID GIGAI!*
IT CAN'T EVEN FLY!!
*GIGAI--A TEMPORARY BODY USED BY WEAKENED SOUL REAPERS. RUKIA CURRENTLY INHABITS ONE.
THIS GIGAI IS NO STRONGER THAN THE AVERAGE SCRAWNY SCHOOL-GIRL!
JUST WAIT TILL I SEE THOSE RESEARCH AND DEVELOPMENT FREAKS!
THEY'RE ALL ABOUT LEGS AND BOOBS WHEN IT'S MUSCLE I NEED!
THIS IS BAD!
OUT OF BREATH... (HUFF) ...ALREADY...
MMM!
YOU SMELL GOOD!

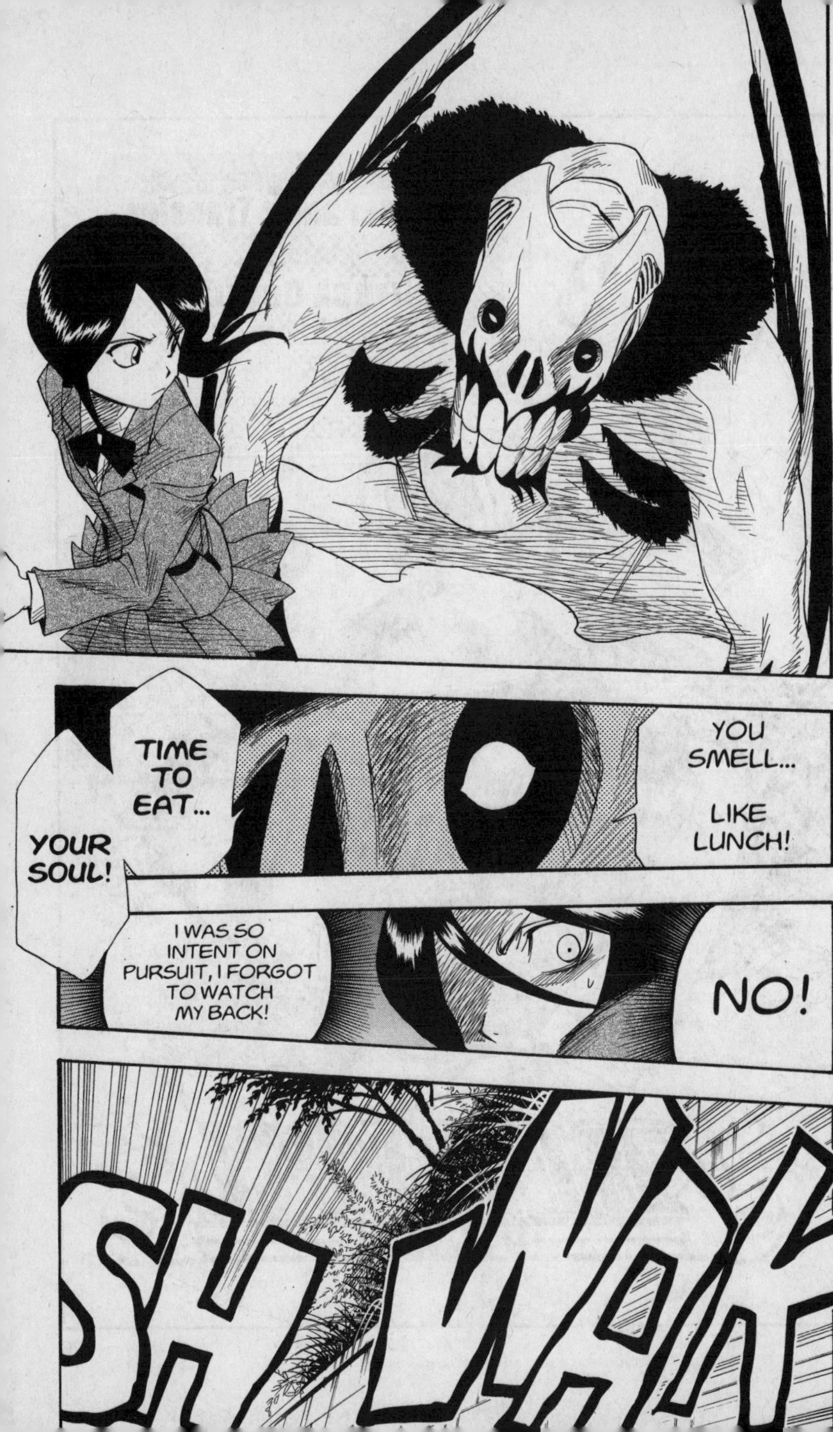
YOU SMELL...
LIKE LUNCH!
TIME TO EAT...
YOUR SOUL!
NO!
I WAS SO INTENT ON PURSUIT, I FORGOT TO WATCH MY BACK!
SHWAK

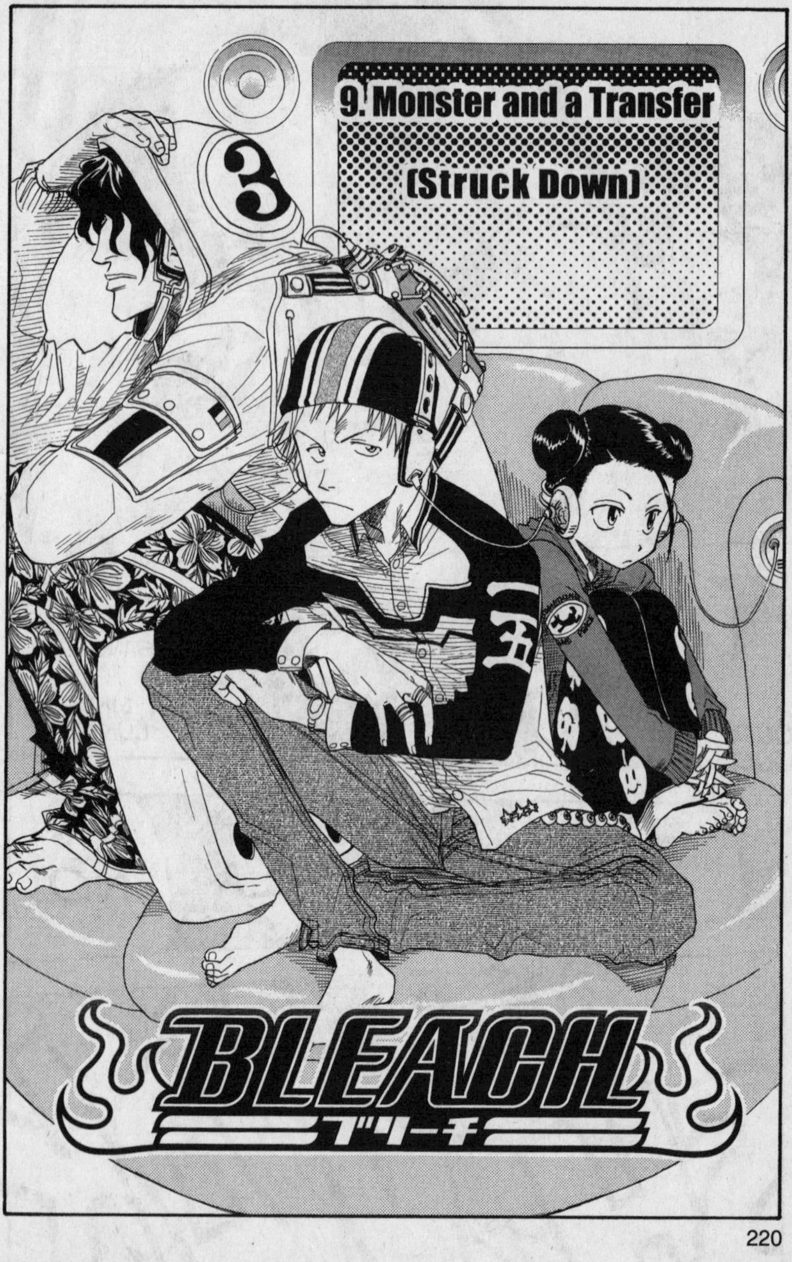
9. Monster and a Transfer
(Struck Down)
BLEACH
ブリーチ

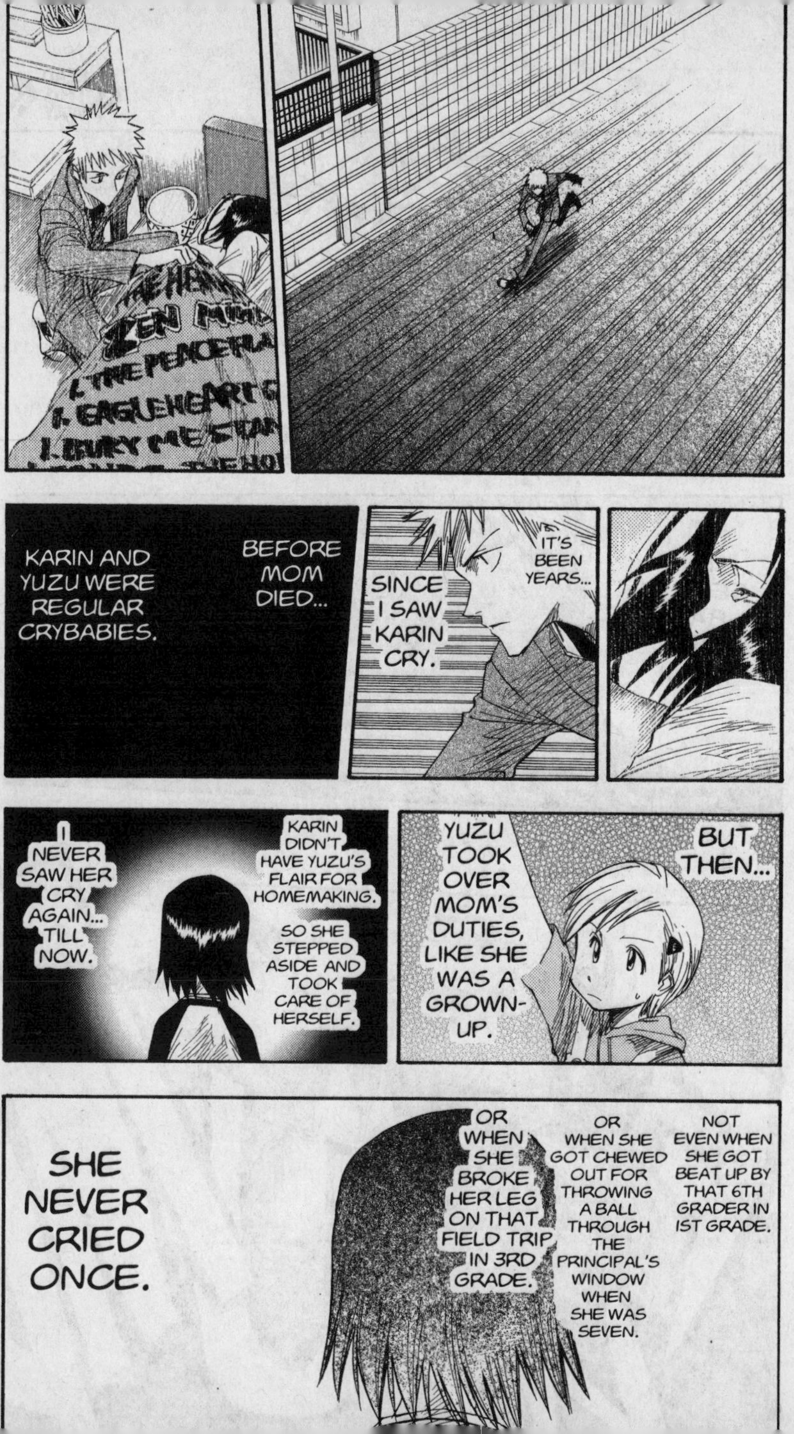
IT'S BEEN YEARS...
SINCE I SAW KARIN CRY.
BEFORE MOM DIED...
KARIN AND YUZU WERE REGULAR CRYBABIES.
BUT THEN...
YUZU TOOK OVER MOM'S DUTIES, LIKE SHE WAS A GROWN-UP.
KARIN DIDN'T HAVE YUZU'S FLAIR FOR HOMEMAKING.
SO SHE STEPPED ASIDE AND TOOK CARE OF HERSELF.
I NEVER SAW HER CRY AGAIN... TILL NOW.
NOT EVEN WHEN SHE GOT BEAT UP BY THAT 6TH GRADER IN 1ST GRADE.
OR WHEN SHE GOT CHEWED OUT FOR THROWING A BALL THROUGH THE PRINCIPAL'S WINDOW WHEN SHE WAS SEVEN.
OR WHEN SHE BROKE HER LEG ON THAT FIELD TRIP IN 3RD GRADE.
SHE NEVER CRIED ONCE.

READ THIS WAY

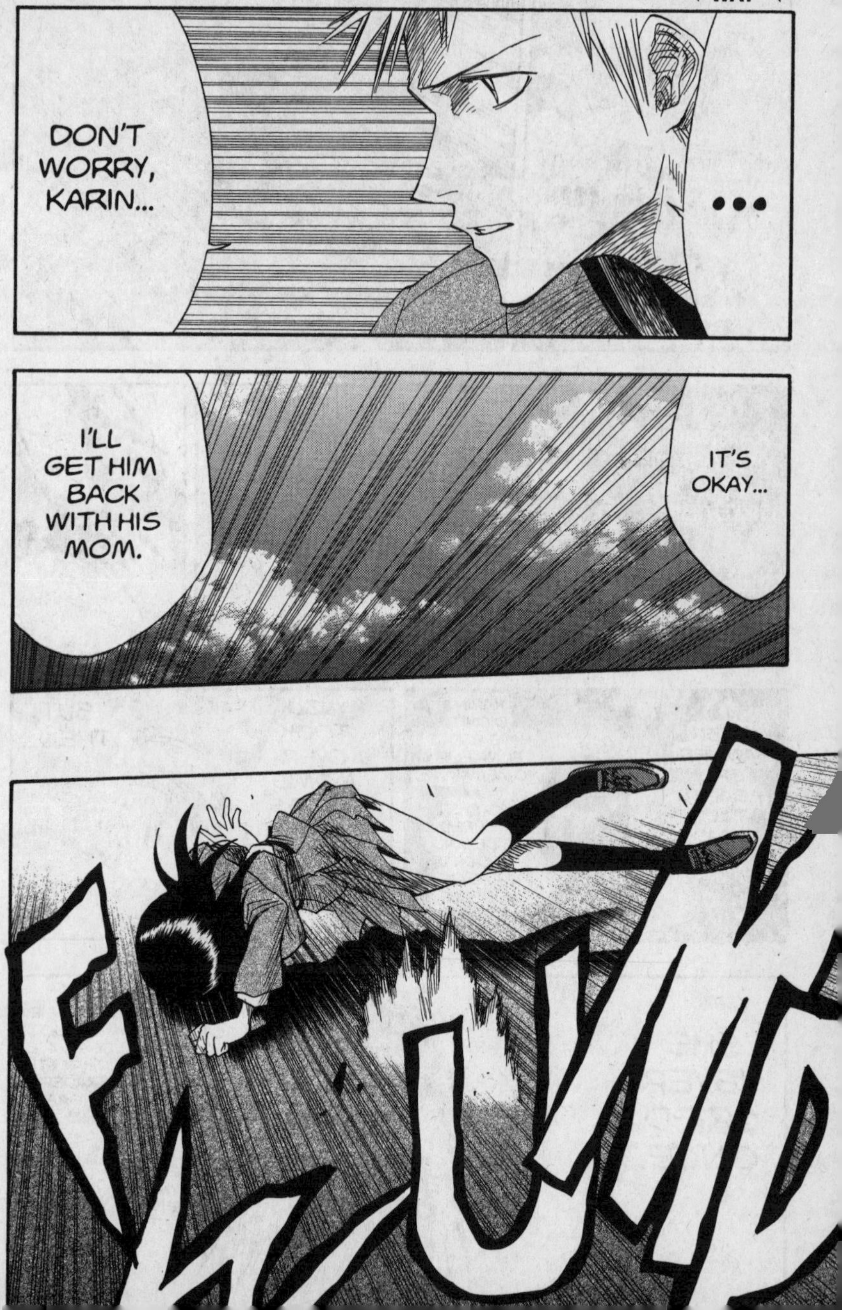
...
DON'T WORRY, KARIN...
IT'S OKAY...
I'LL GET HIM BACK WITH HIS MOM.

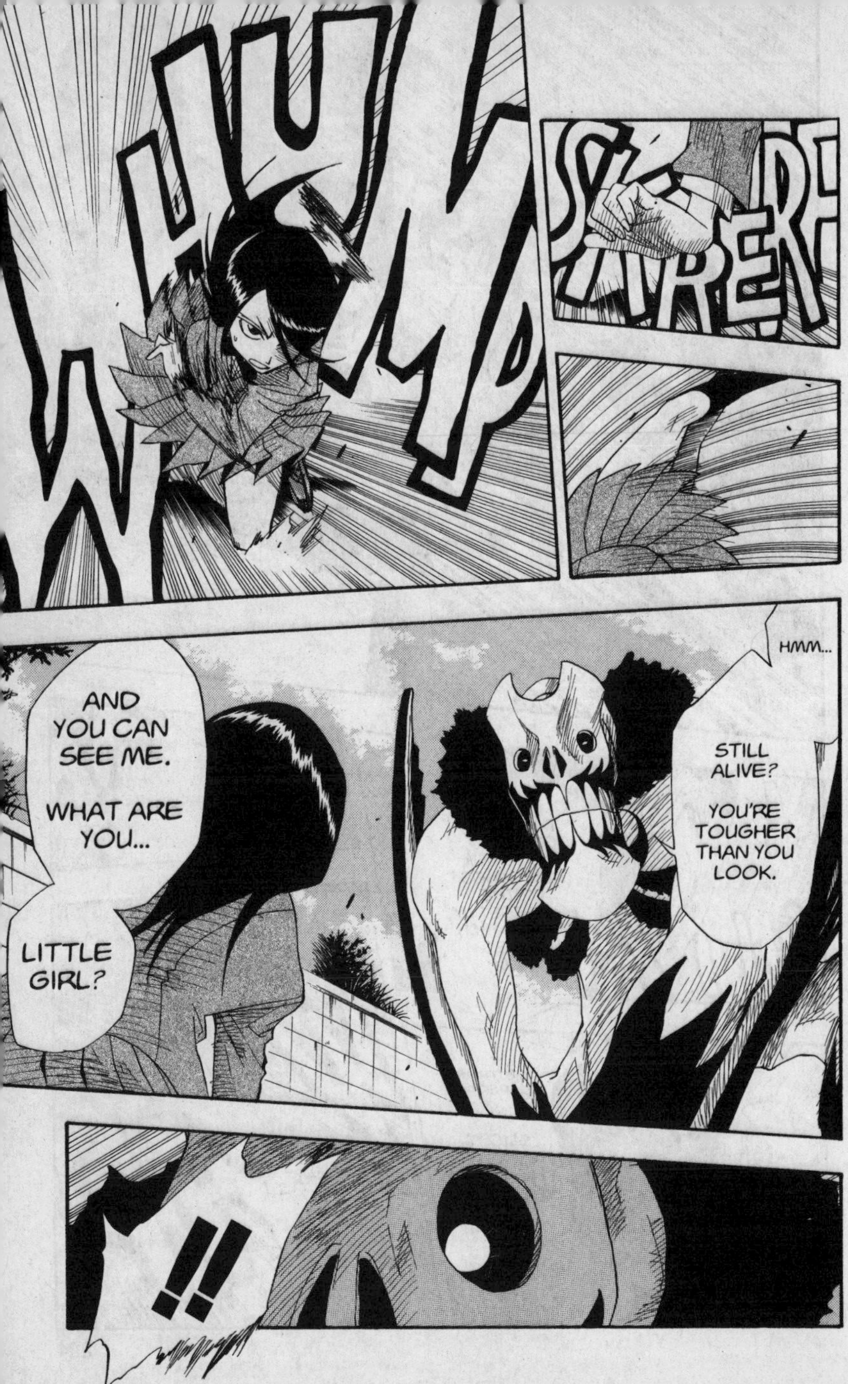
WHUMP
HMM...
STILL ALIVE?
YOU'RE TOUGHER THAN YOU LOOK.
AND YOU CAN SEE ME.
WHAT ARE YOU...
LITTLE GIRL?
!!

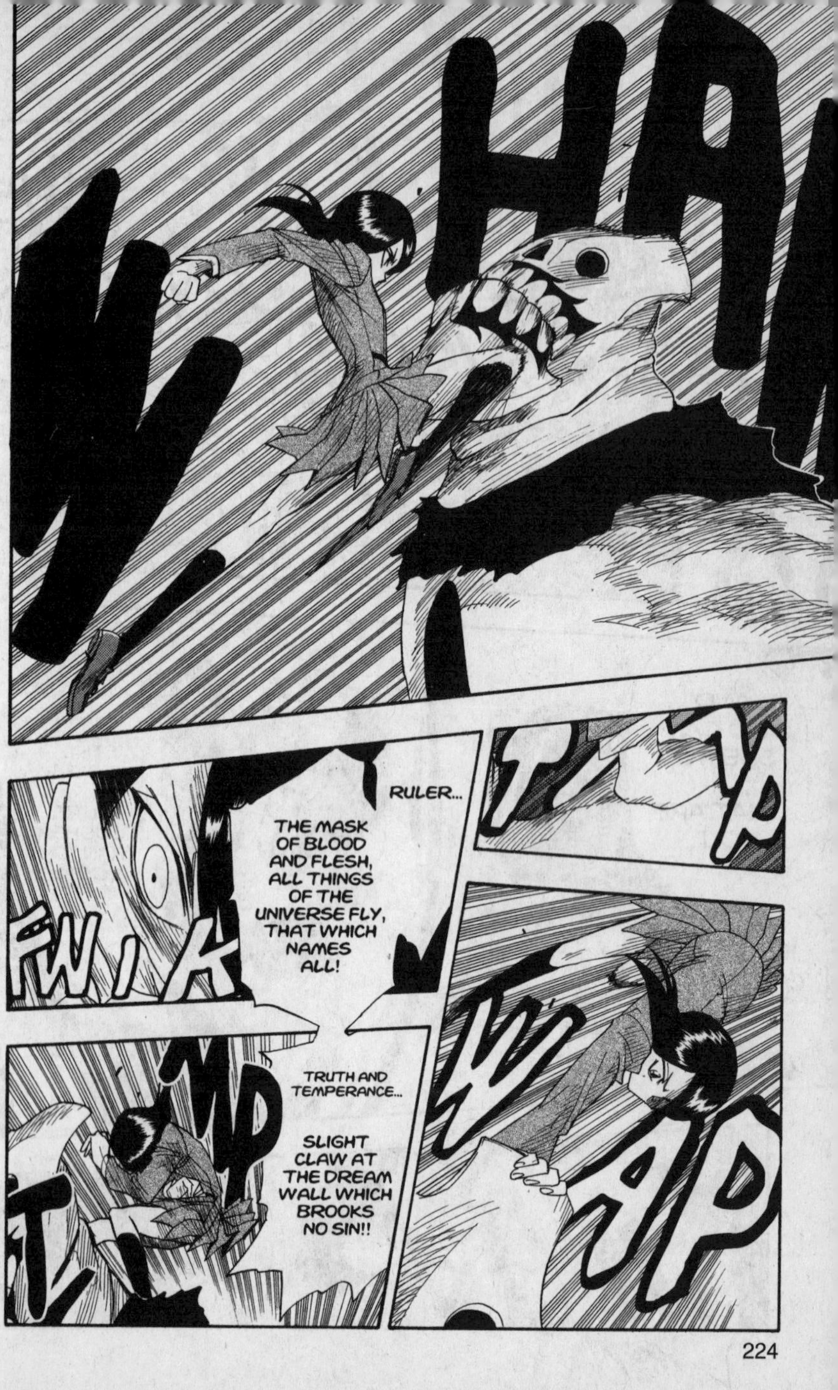
RULER...
THE MASK OF BLOOD AND FLESH, ALL THINGS OF THE UNIVERSE FLY, THAT WHICH NAMES ALL!
TRUTH AND TEMPERANCE...
SLIGHT CLAW AT THE DREAM WALL WHICH BROOKS NO SIN!!

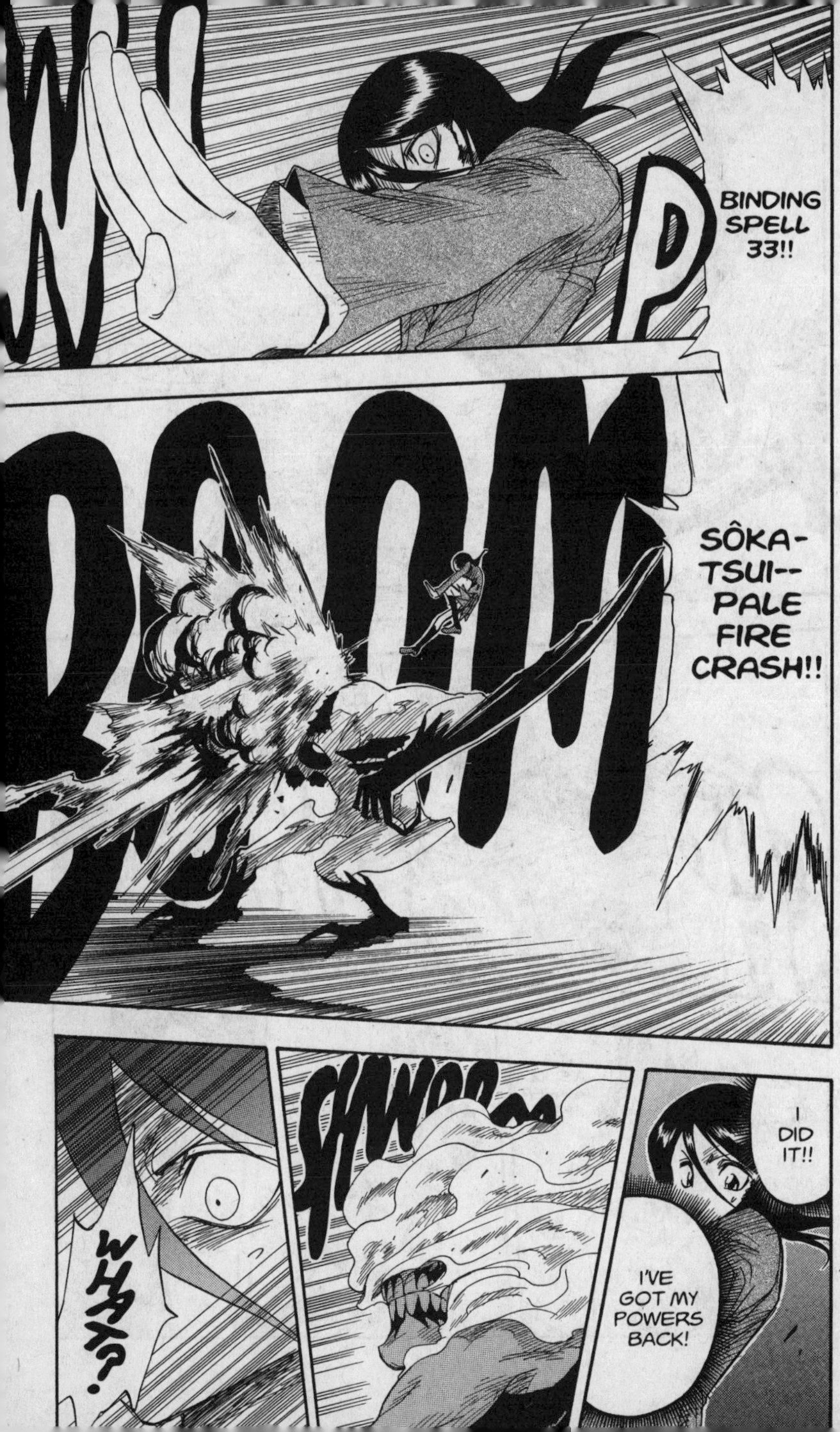
BINDING SPELL 33!!
SÔKA-TSUI--PALE FIRE CRASH!!
I DID IT!!
I'VE GOT MY POWERS BACK!
WHAT?!

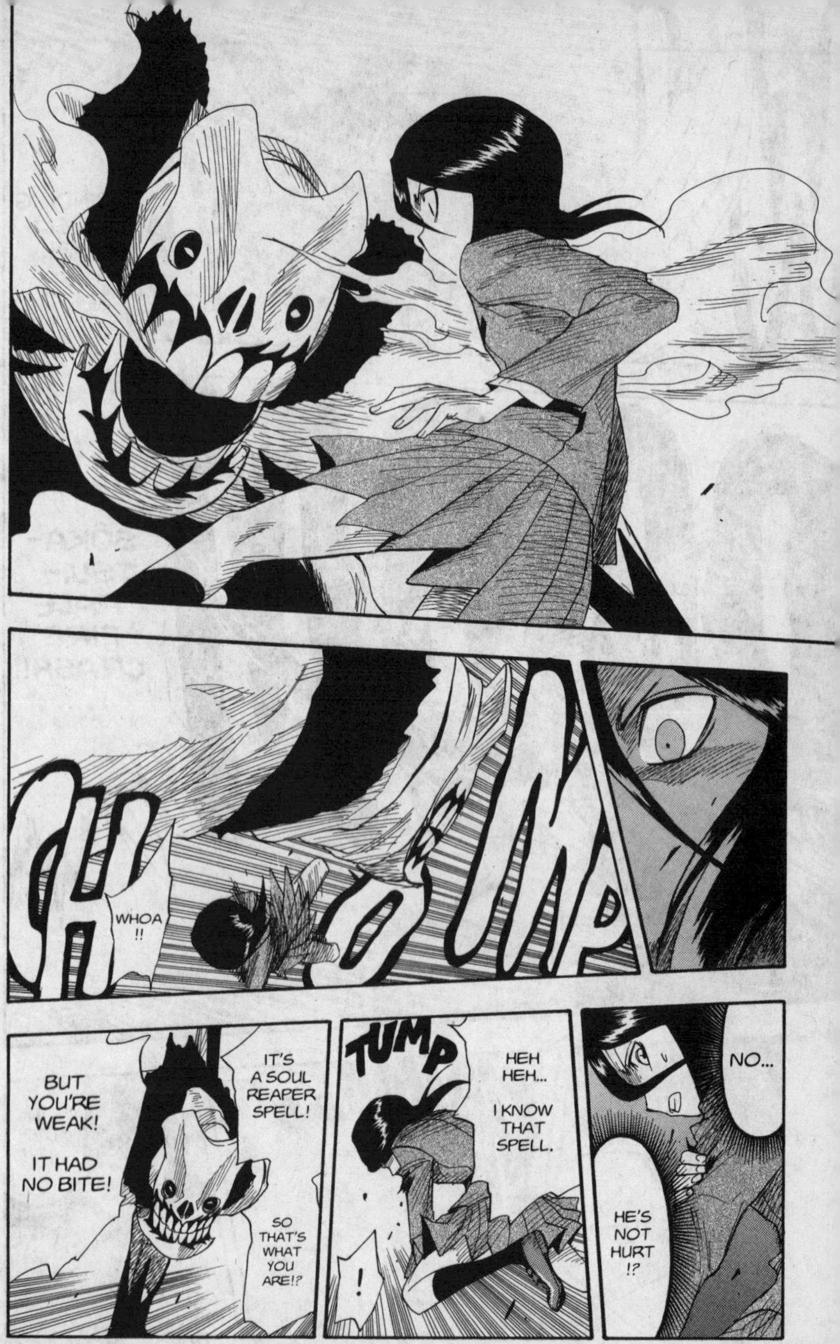
CHOMP
WHOA !!
NO...
HE'S NOT HURT !?
TUMP
HEH HEH...
I KNOW THAT SPELL.
!
IT'S A SOUL REAPER SPELL!
BUT YOU'RE WEAK!
IT HAD NO BITE!
SO THAT'S WHAT YOU ARE!?

READ THIS WAY

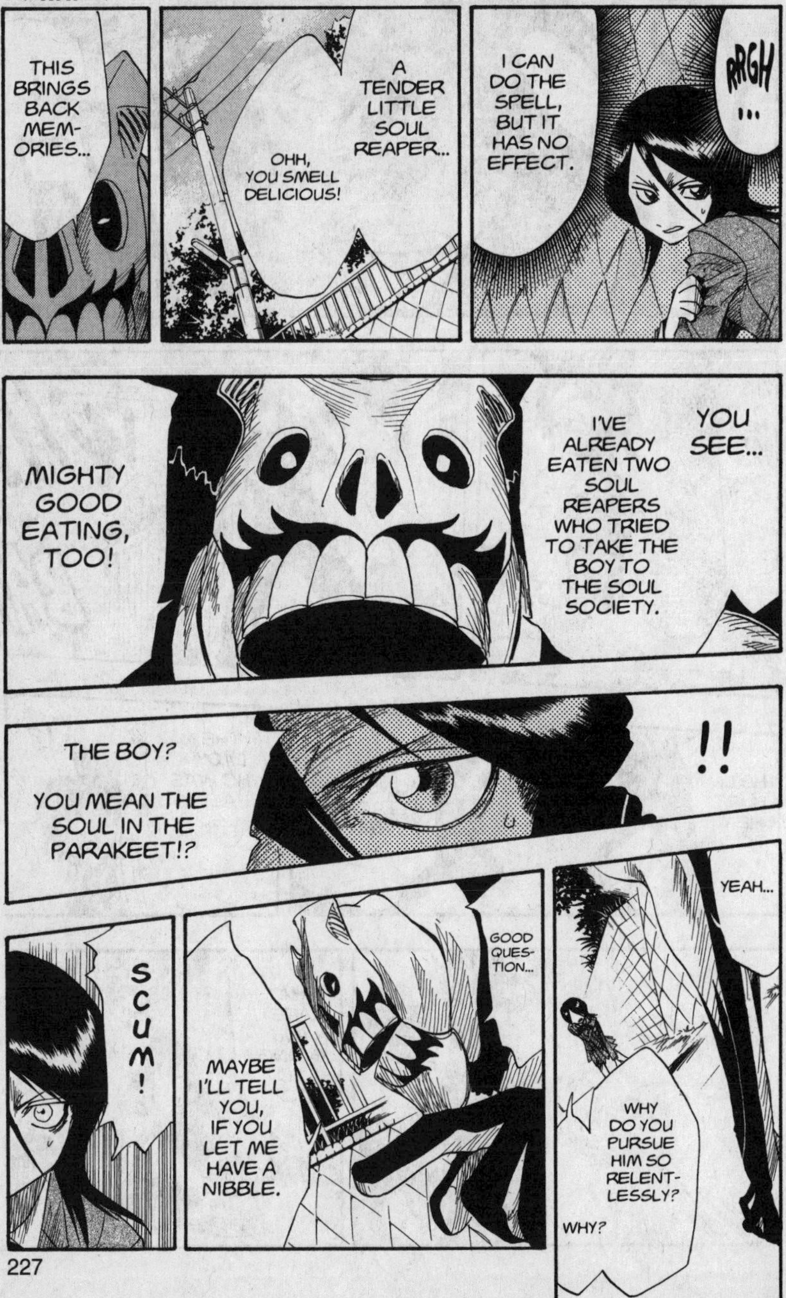
RRGH...
I CAN DO THE SPELL, BUT IT HAS NO EFFECT.
A TENDER LITTLE SOUL REAPER...
OHH, YOU SMELL DELICIOUS!
THIS BRINGS BACK MEMORIES...
YOU SEE...
I'VE ALREADY EATEN TWO SOUL REAPERS WHO TRIED TO TAKE THE BOY TO THE SOUL SOCIETY.
MIGHTY GOOD EATING, TOO!
!!
THE BOY?
YOU MEAN THE SOUL IN THE PARAKEET!?
YEAH...
WHY DO YOU PURSUE HIM SO RELENTLESSLY?
WHY?
GOOD QUESTION...
MAYBE I'LL TELL YOU, IF YOU LET ME HAVE A NIBBLE.
SCUM!

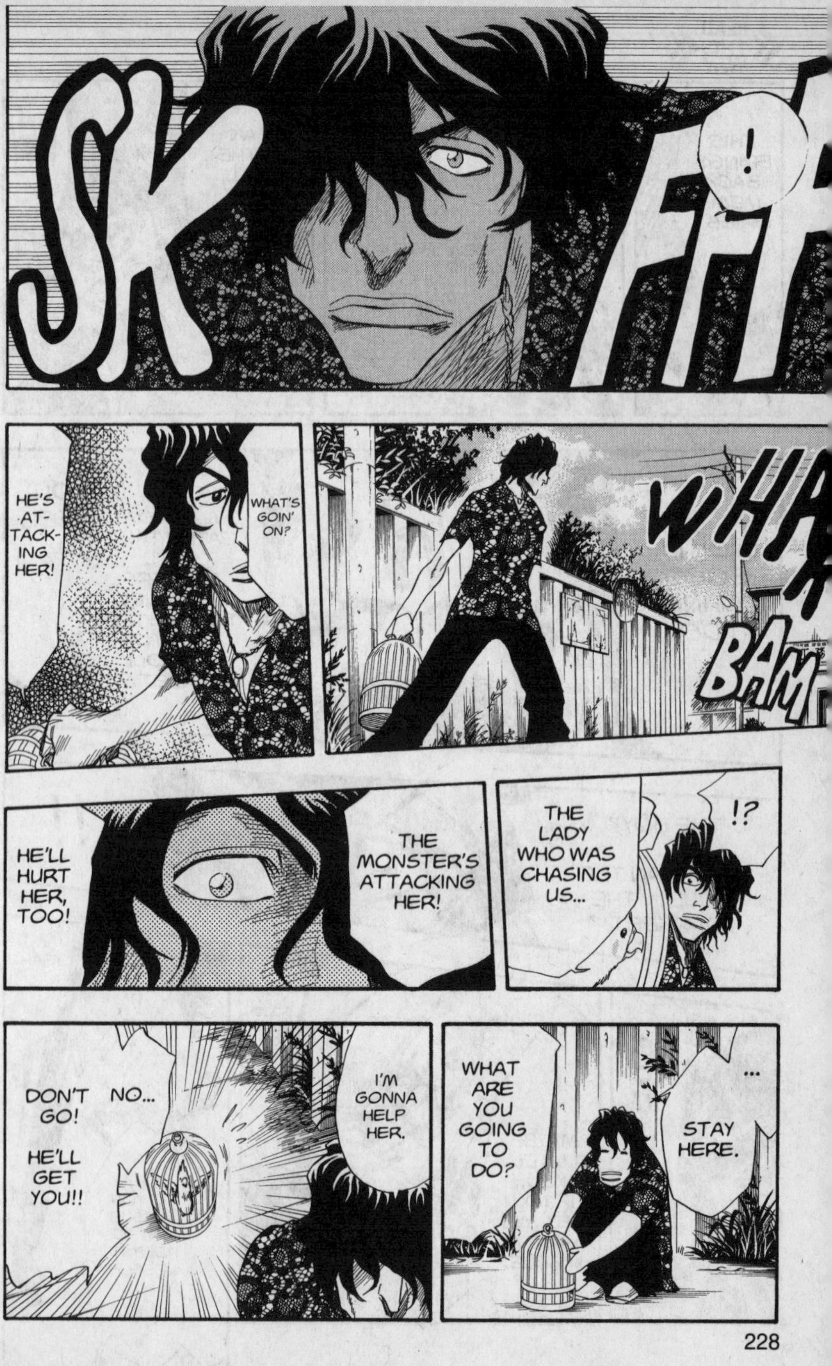
!
SK
FF
WHA
BAM
WHAT'S GOIN' ON?
HE'S AT-TACK-ING HER!
!?
THE LADY WHO WAS CHASING US...
THE MONSTER'S ATTACKING HER!
HE'LL HURT HER, TOO!
...
STAY HERE.
WHAT ARE YOU GOING TO DO?
I'M GONNA HELP HER.
NO...
DON'T GO!
HE'LL GET YOU!!

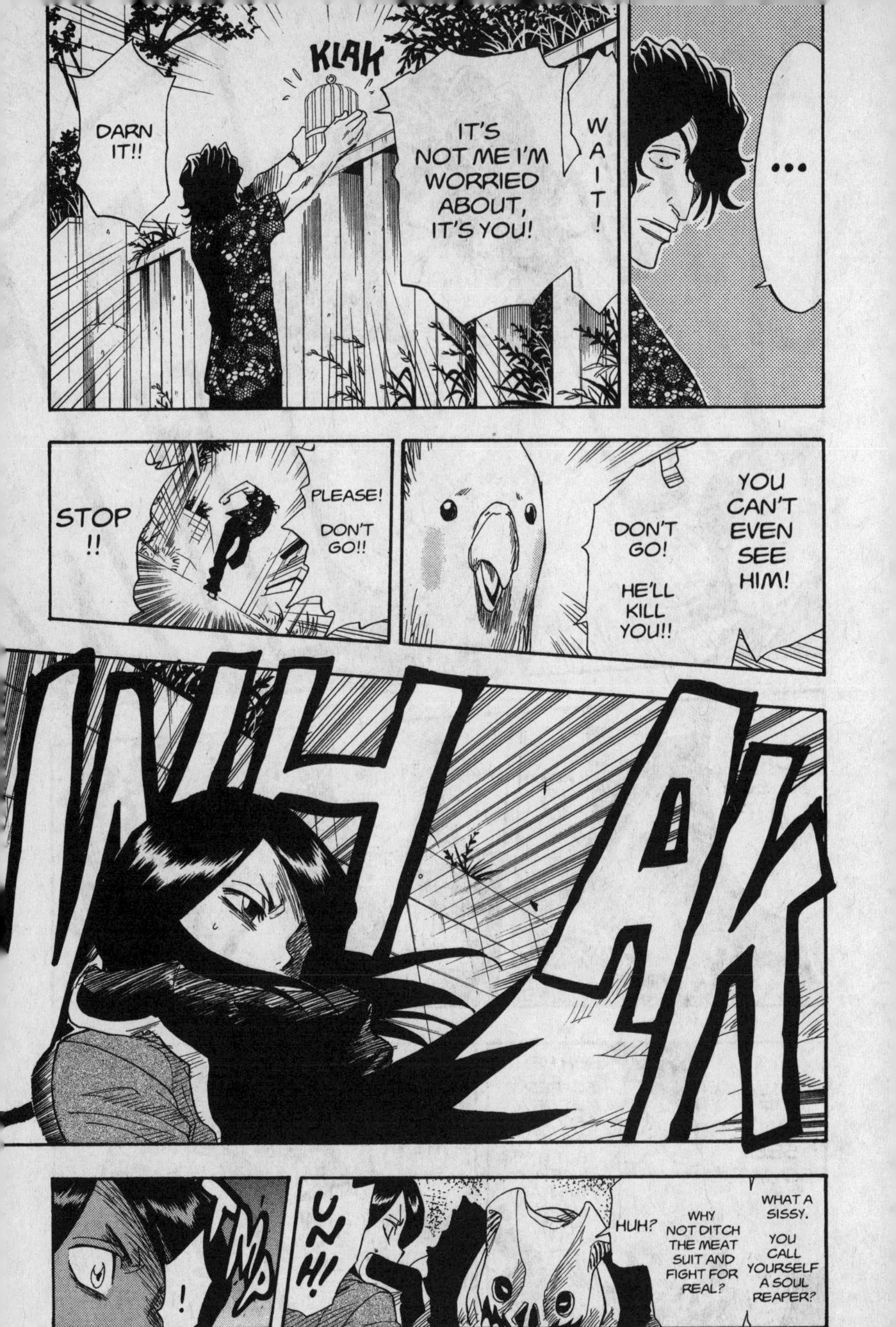
...
WAIT!
IT'S NOT ME I'M WORRIED ABOUT, IT'S YOU!
KLAK
DARN IT!!
YOU CAN'T EVEN SEE HIM!
DON'T GO!
HE'LL KILL YOU!!
PLEASE!
DON'T GO!!
STOP !!
WHAT A SISSY.
YOU CALL YOURSELF A SOUL REAPER?
WHY NOT DITCH THE MEAT SUIT AND FIGHT FOR REAL?
HUH?
UNH!
TMP
!

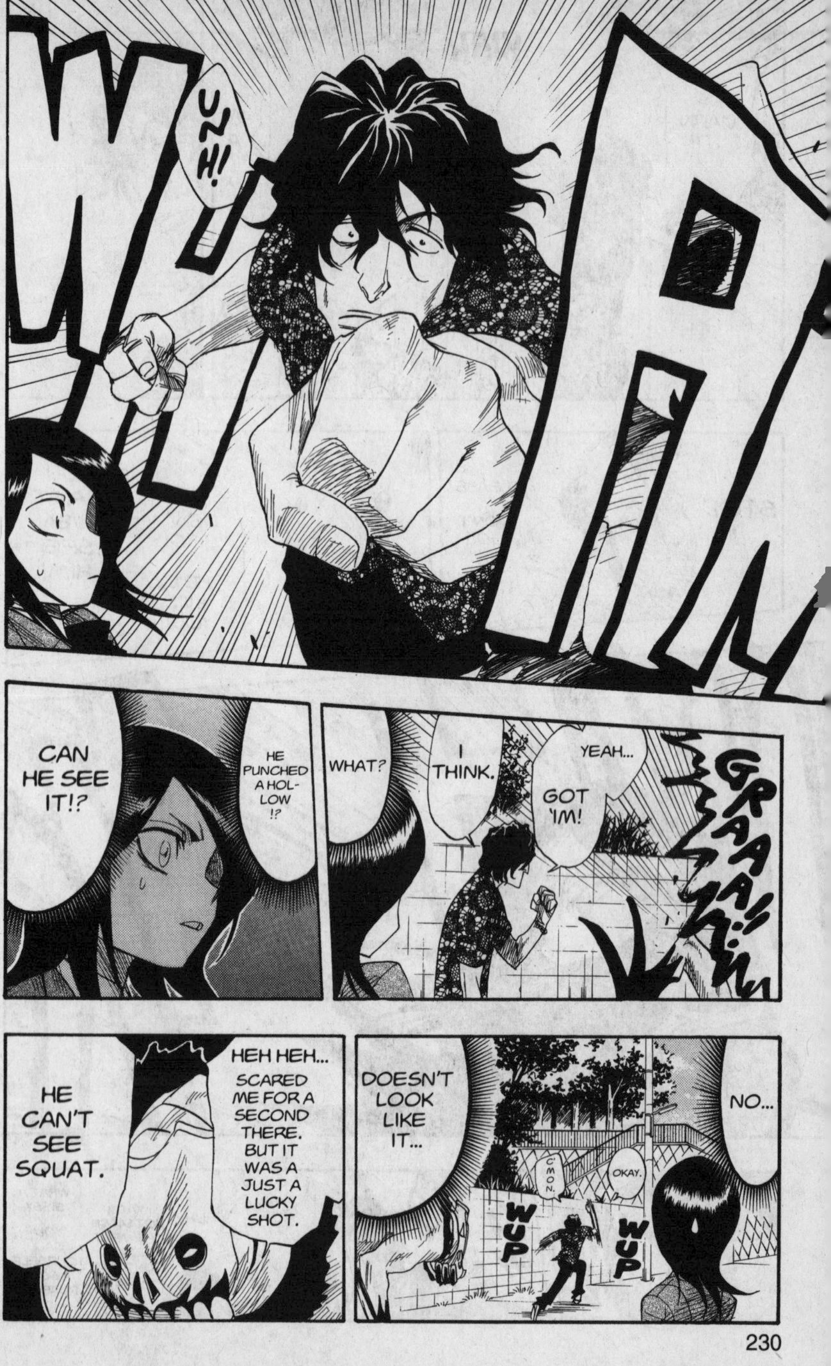
UNH!
GRAAAA!!
YEAH... GOT 'IM!
I THINK.
WHAT?
HE PUNCHED A HOL-LOW!?
CAN HE SEE IT!?
NO...
OKAY.
C'MON.
WUP
WUP
DOESN'T LOOK LIKE IT...
HEH HEH... SCARED ME FOR A SECOND THERE. BUT IT WAS A JUST A LUCKY SHOT.
HE CAN'T SEE SQUAT.

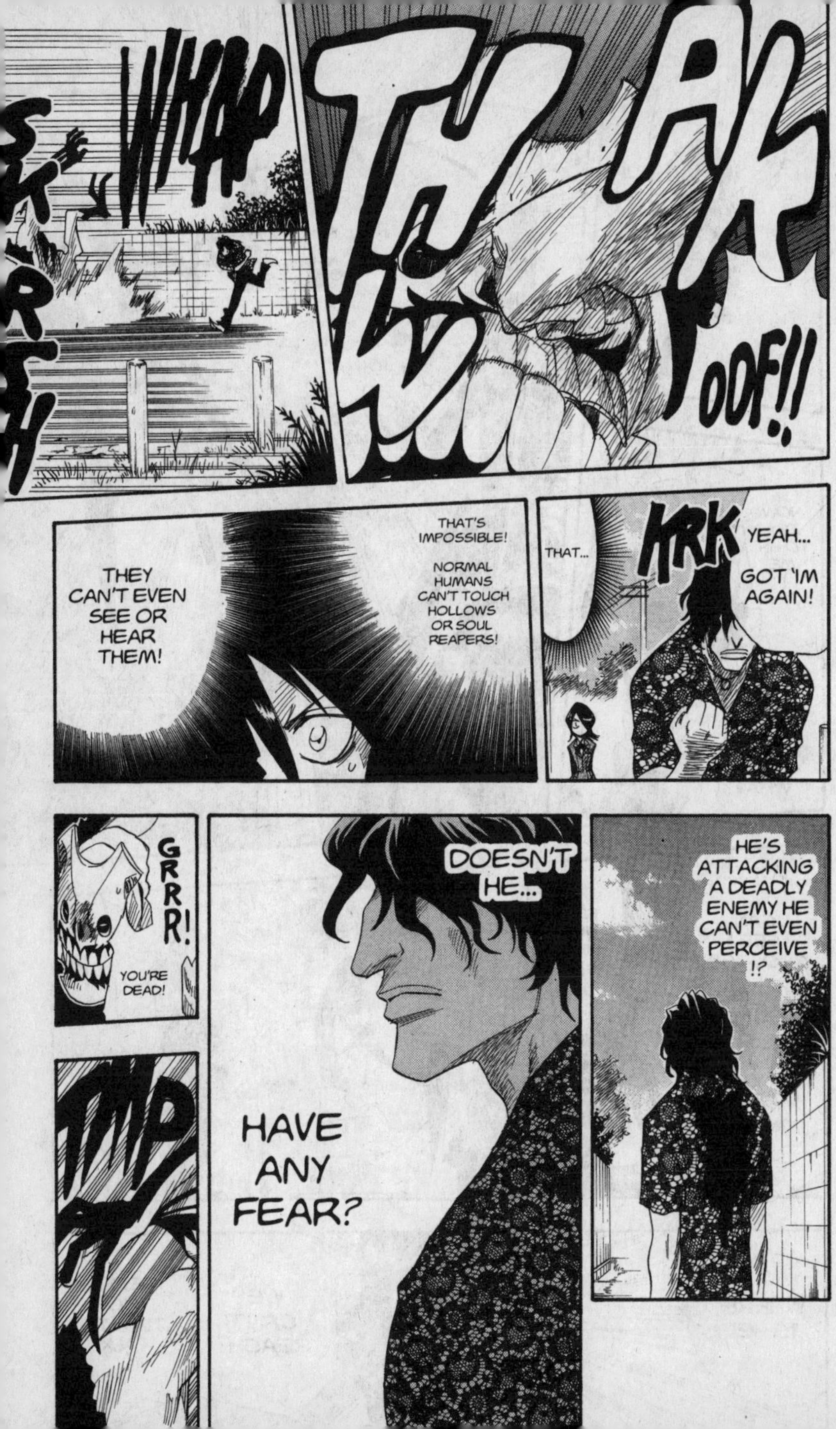
OOF!!
WHAP
THAT...
KRK
YEAH... GOT 'IM AGAIN!
THAT'S IMPOSSIBLE!
NORMAL HUMANS CAN'T TOUCH HOLLOWS OR SOUL REAPERS!
THEY CAN'T EVEN SEE OR HEAR THEM!
HE'S ATTACKING A DEADLY ENEMY HE CAN'T EVEN PERCEIVE!?
DOESN'T HE...
HAVE ANY FEAR?
GRRR!
YOU'RE DEAD!

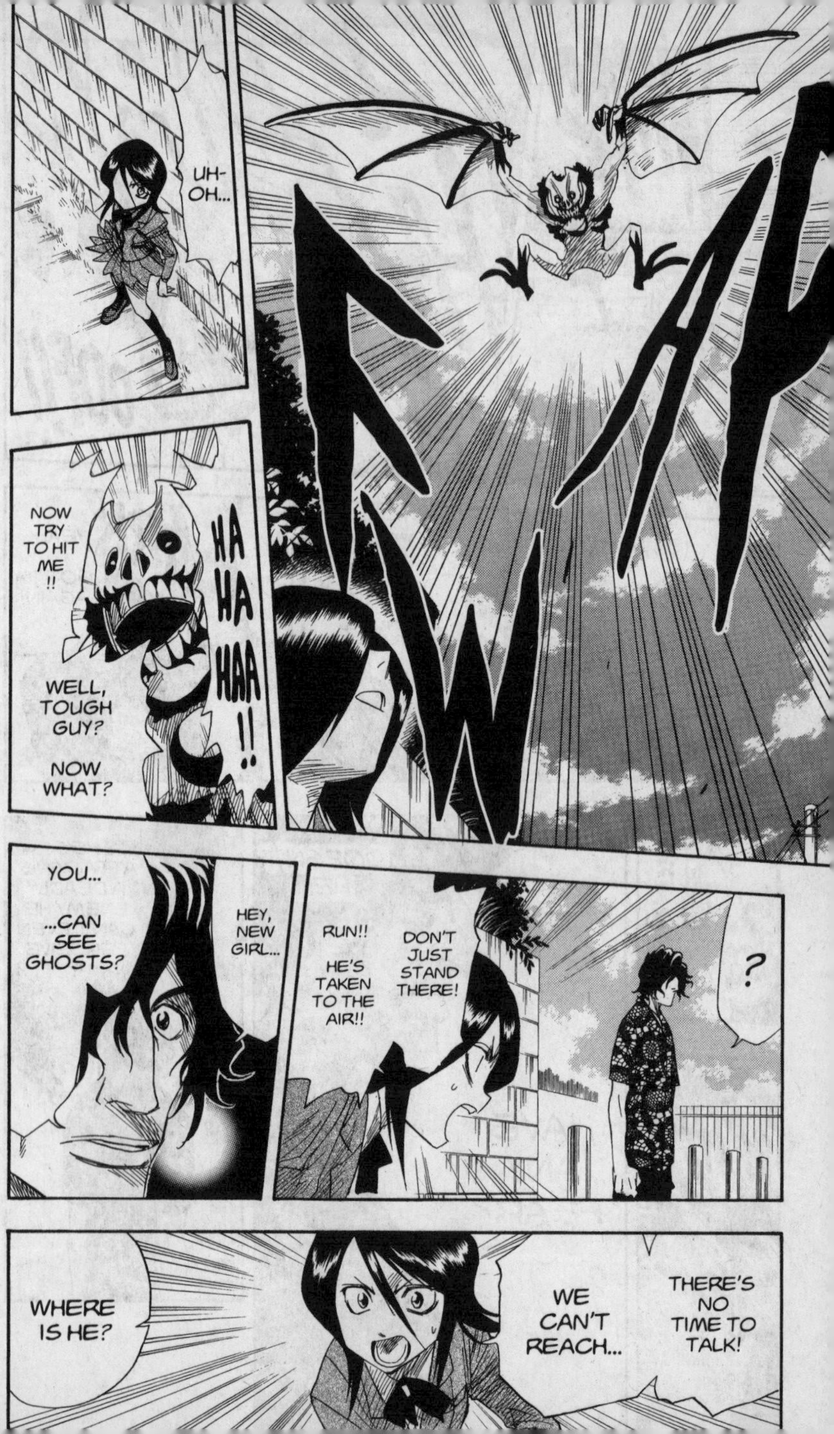
FWAP
UH-OH...
HA HA HAA!!
NOW TRY TO HIT ME!!
WELL, TOUGH GUY?
NOW WHAT?
?
DON'T JUST STAND THERE!
RUN!!
HE'S TAKEN TO THE AIR!!
HEY, NEW GIRL...
YOU...
...CAN SEE GHOSTS?
THERE'S NO TIME TO TALK!
WE CAN'T REACH...
WHERE IS HE?

READ THIS WAY

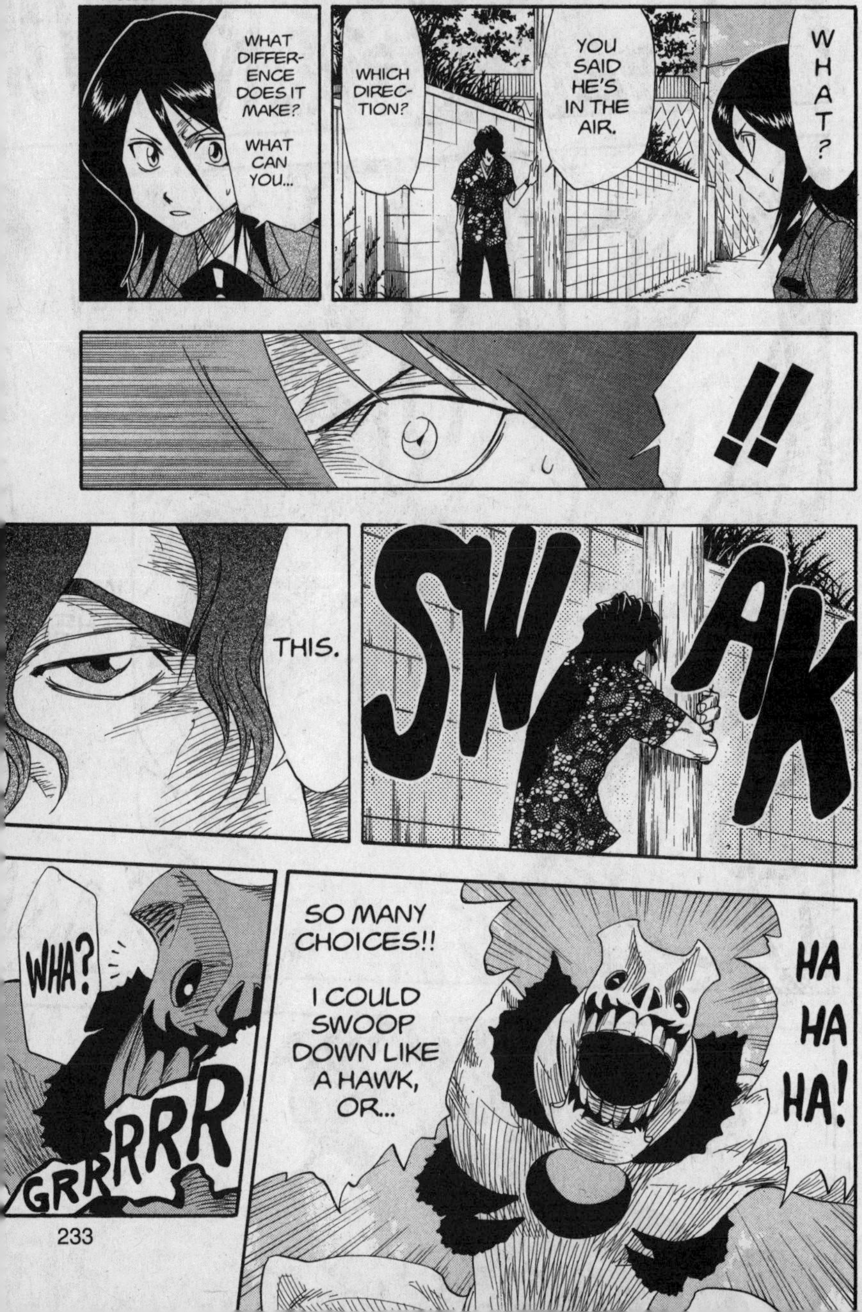

WHAT?
YOU SAID HE'S IN THE AIR.
WHICH DIRECTION?
WHAT DIFFERENCE DOES IT MAKE?
WHAT CAN YOU...
!!
SWAK
THIS.
HA HA HA!
SO MANY CHOICES!!
I COULD SWOOP DOWN LIKE A HAWK, OR...
WHA?
GRRRRR

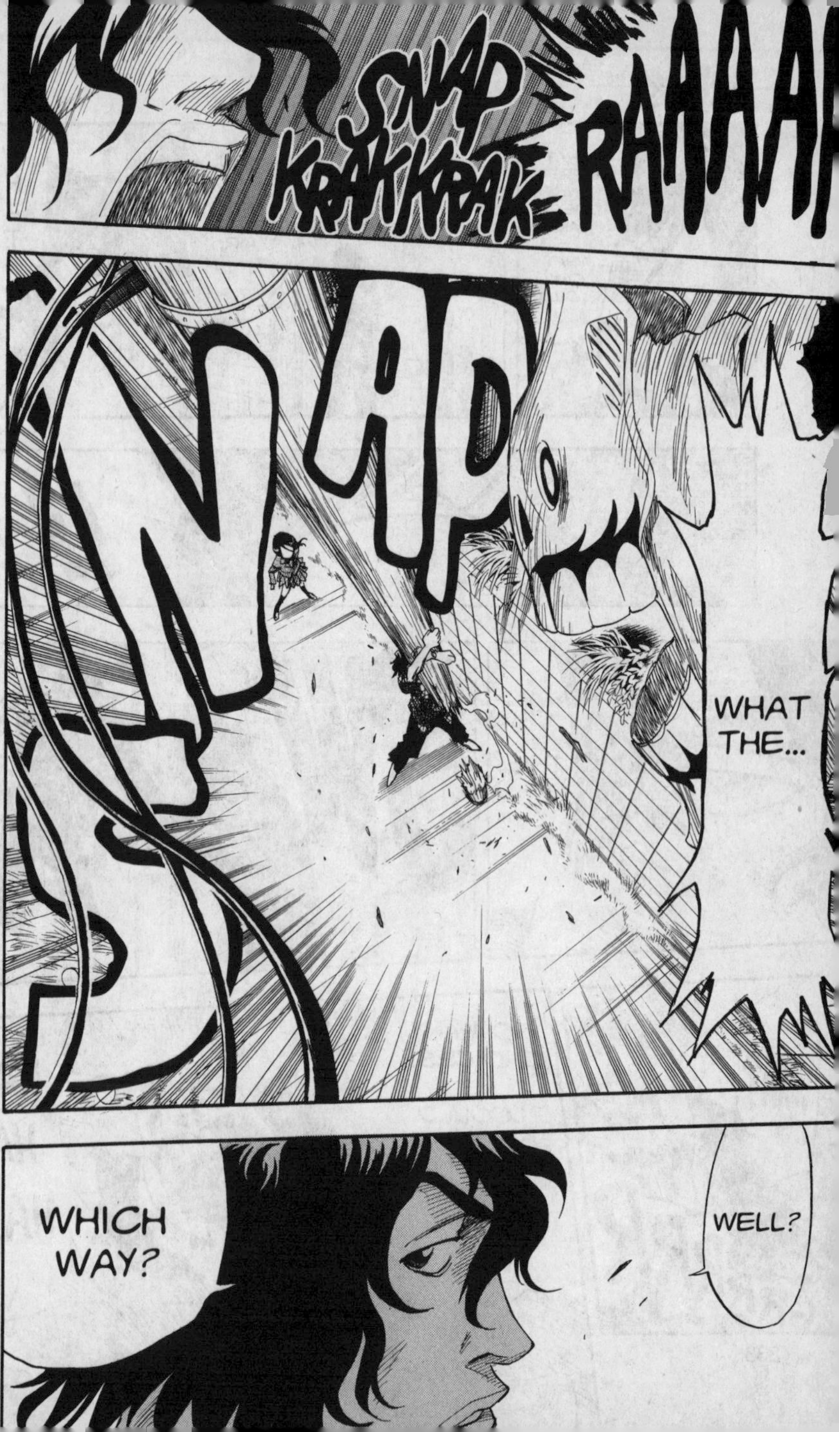
RAAAAA
SNAP KRAKKRAK
SNAP
WHAT THE...
WELL?
WHICH WAY?

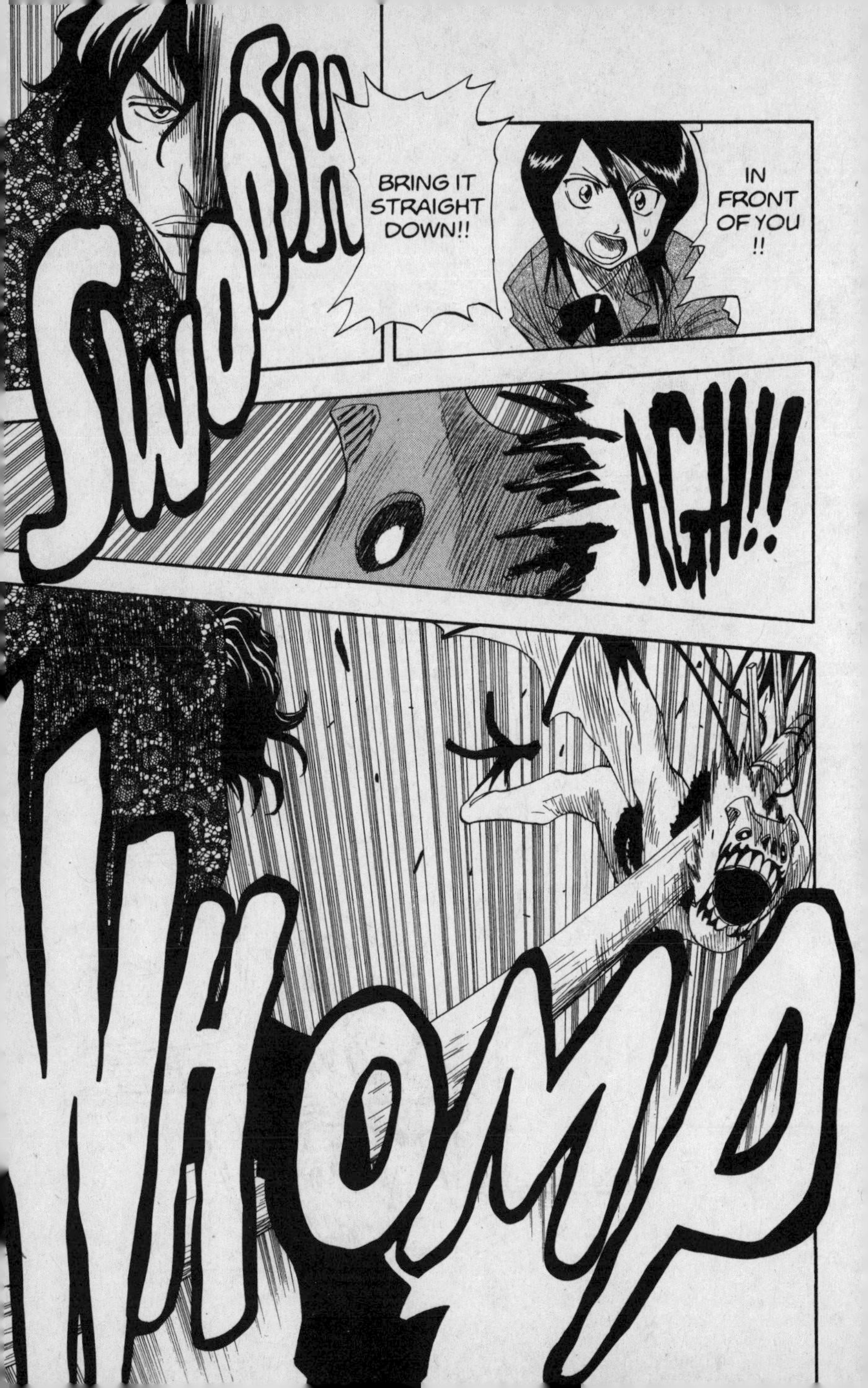
IN FRONT OF YOU !!
BRING IT STRAIGHT DOWN!!
SWOOSH
ACH!!
CHOMP

POWER OUTAGE

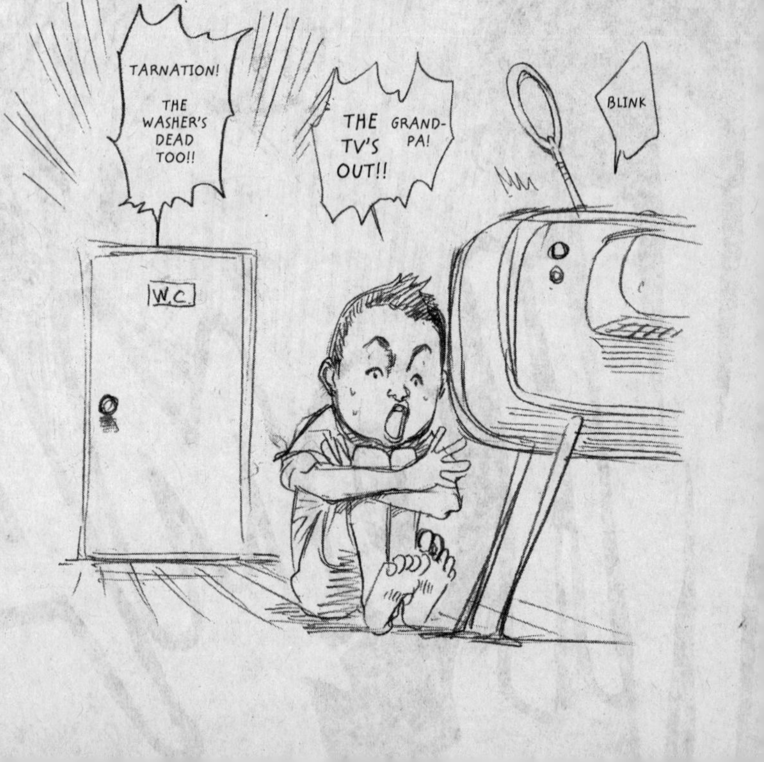
BLINK
GRAND-PA!
THE TV'S OUT!!
TARNATION!
THE WASHER'S DEAD TOO!!
W.C.

10. Monster and a Transfer, Part 2
[The Deathberry]

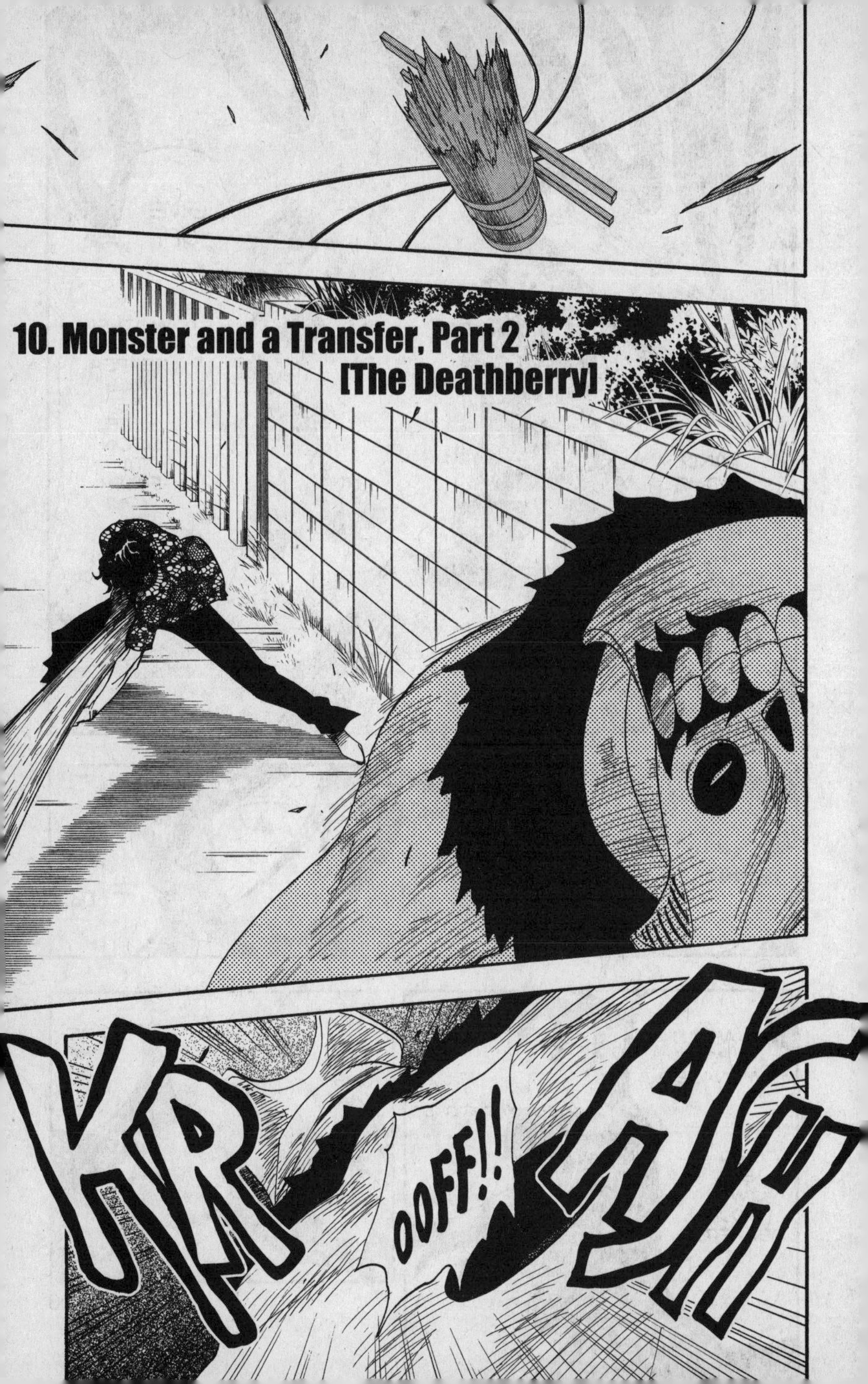
KRAA
OOFF!!

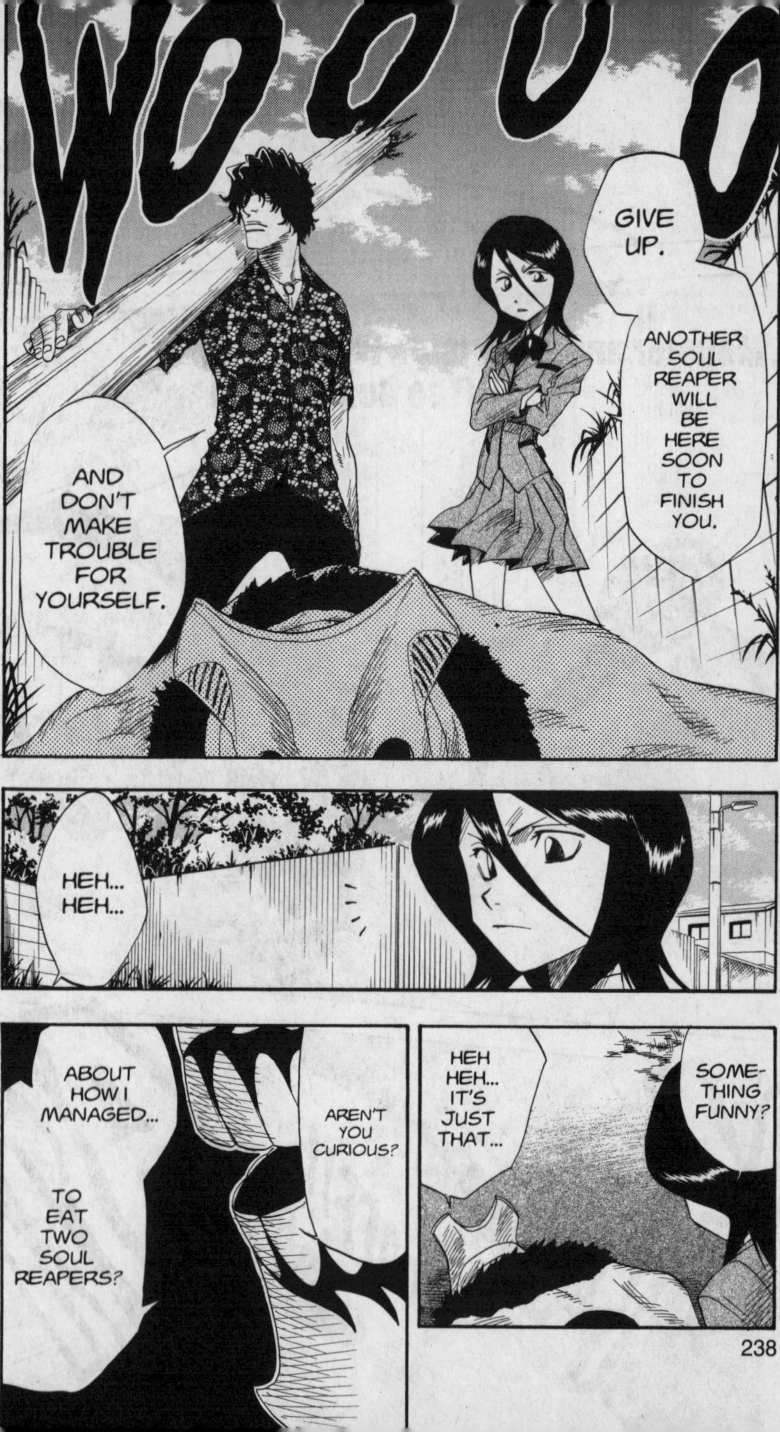
WOOOOO
GIVE UP.
ANOTHER SOUL REAPER WILL BE HERE SOON TO FINISH YOU.
AND DON'T MAKE TROUBLE FOR YOURSELF.
HEH... HEH...
SOME-THING FUNNY?
HEH HEH... IT'S JUST THAT...
AREN'T YOU CURIOUS?
ABOUT HOW I MANAGED...
TO EAT TWO SOUL REAPERS?

READ THIS WAY

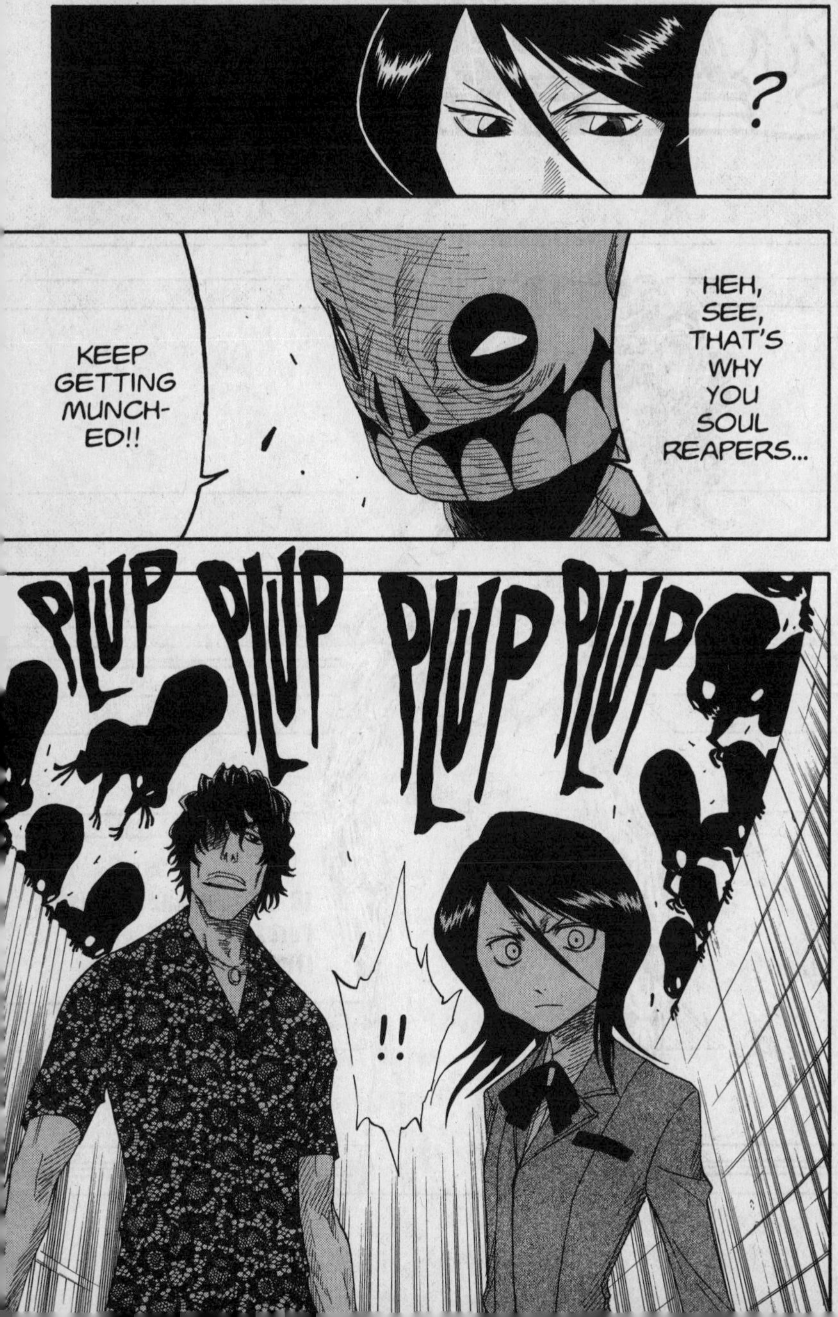
?
HEH, SEE, THAT'S WHY YOU SOUL REAPERS...
KEEP GETTING MUNCH-ED!!
PLUP PLUP PLUP PLUP
!!

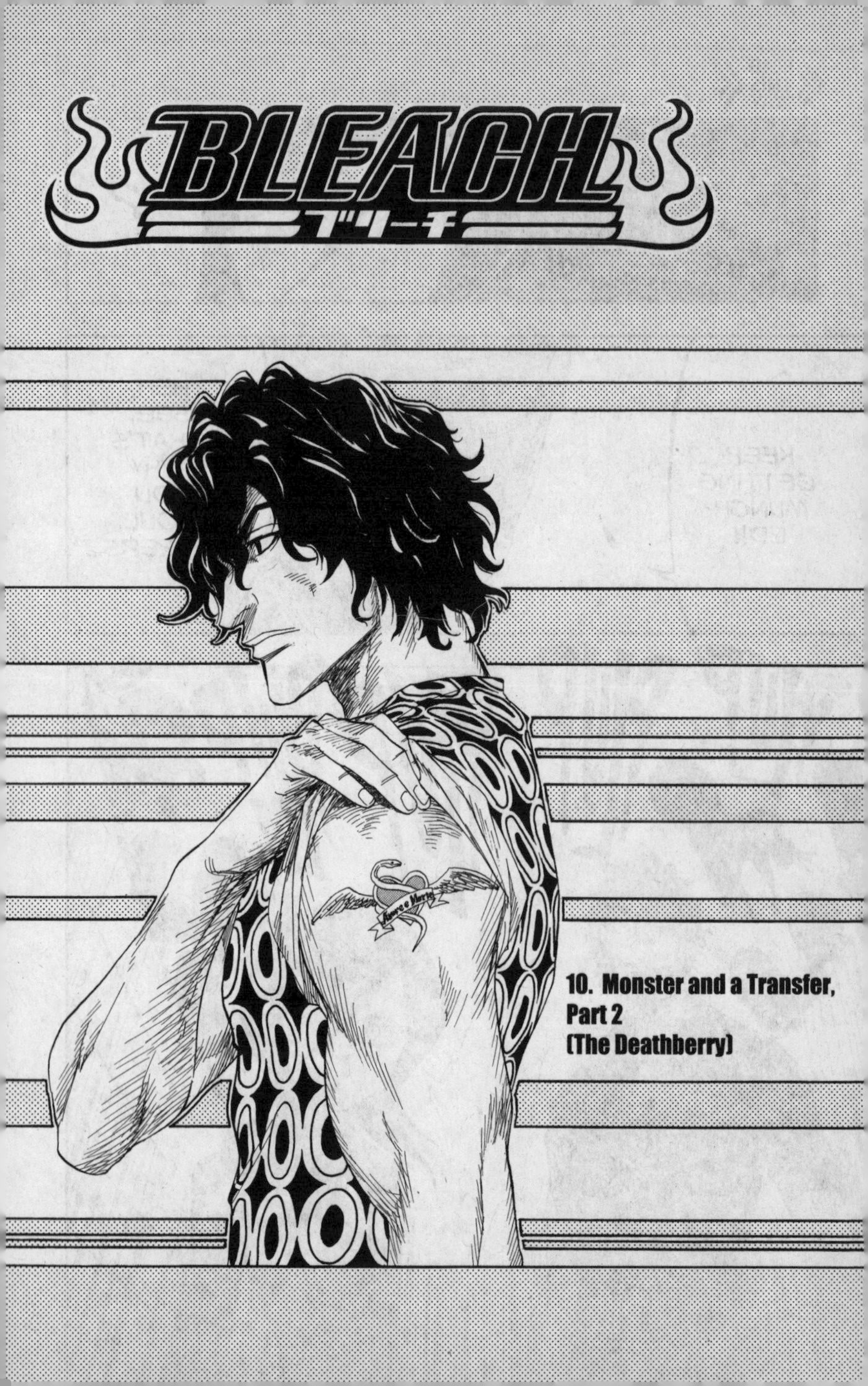
BLEACH
ブリーチ
10. Monster and a Transfer, Part 2
(The Deathberry)

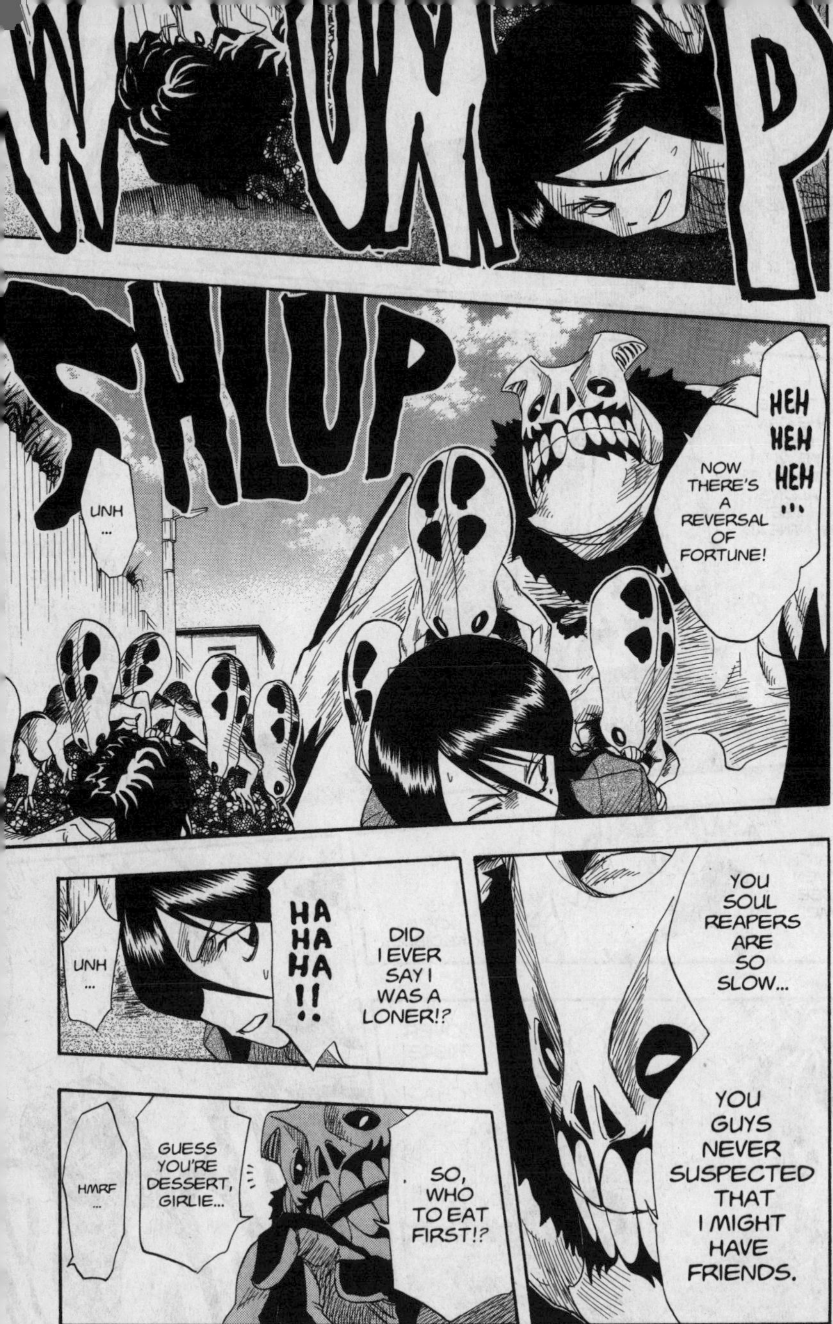
WHUMP
SHLUP
HEH HEH HEH...
NOW THERE'S A REVERSAL OF FORTUNE!
UNH...
YOU SOUL REAPERS ARE SO SLOW...
YOU GUYS NEVER SUSPECTED THAT I MIGHT HAVE FRIENDS.
DID I EVER SAY I WAS A LONER!?
HA HA HA!!
UNH...
SO, WHO TO EAT FIRST!?
GUESS YOU'RE DESSERT, GIRLIE...
HMRF...

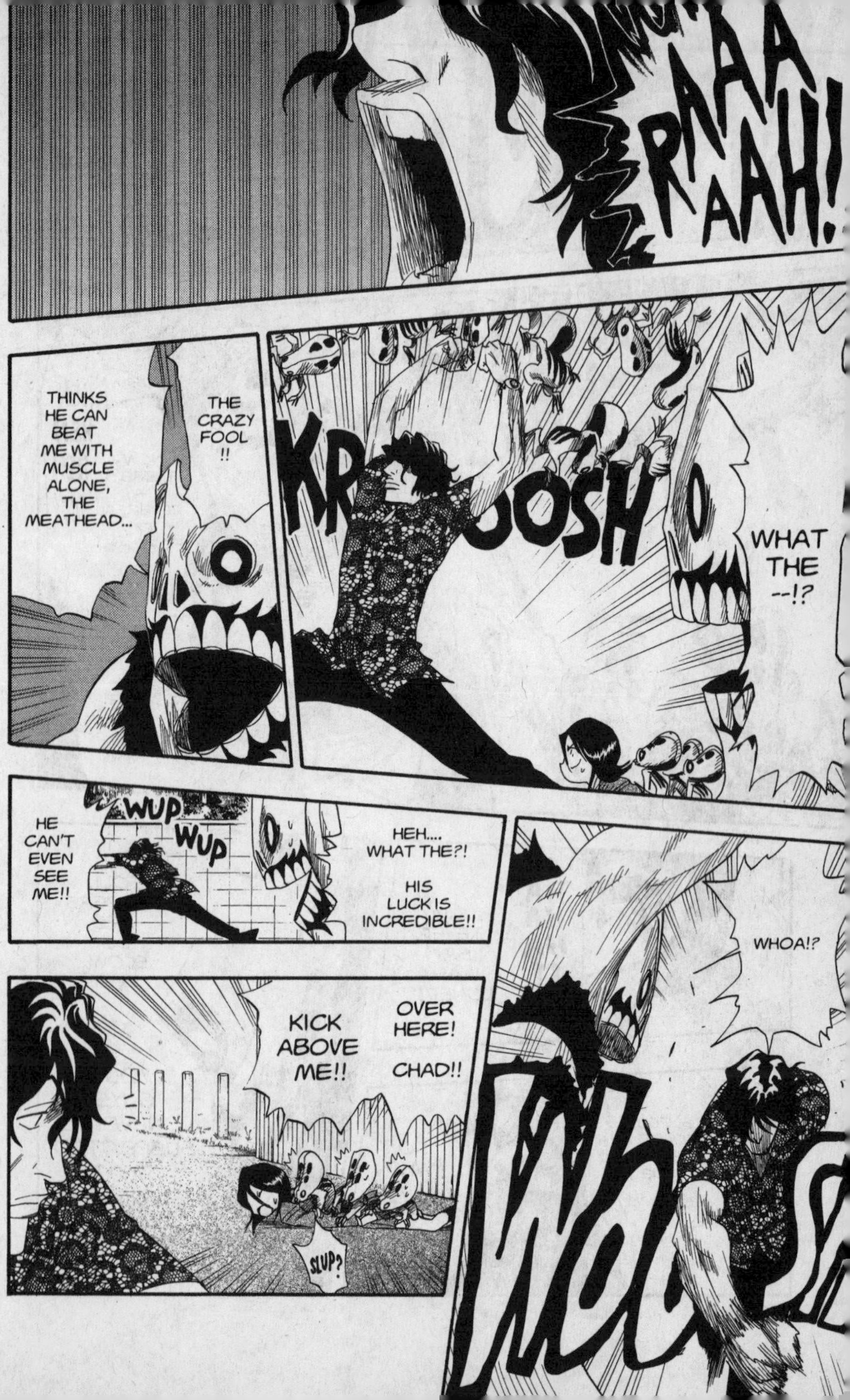
RAAAAAH!
KROOSH
WHAT THE --!?
THE CRAZY FOOL!!
THINKS HE CAN BEAT ME WITH MUSCLE ALONE, THE MEATHEAD...
WHOA!?
HEH.... WHAT THE?!
HIS LUCK IS INCREDIBLE!!
WUP
WUP
HE CAN'T EVEN SEE ME!!
OVER HERE!
CHAD!!
KICK ABOVE ME!!
SLUP?

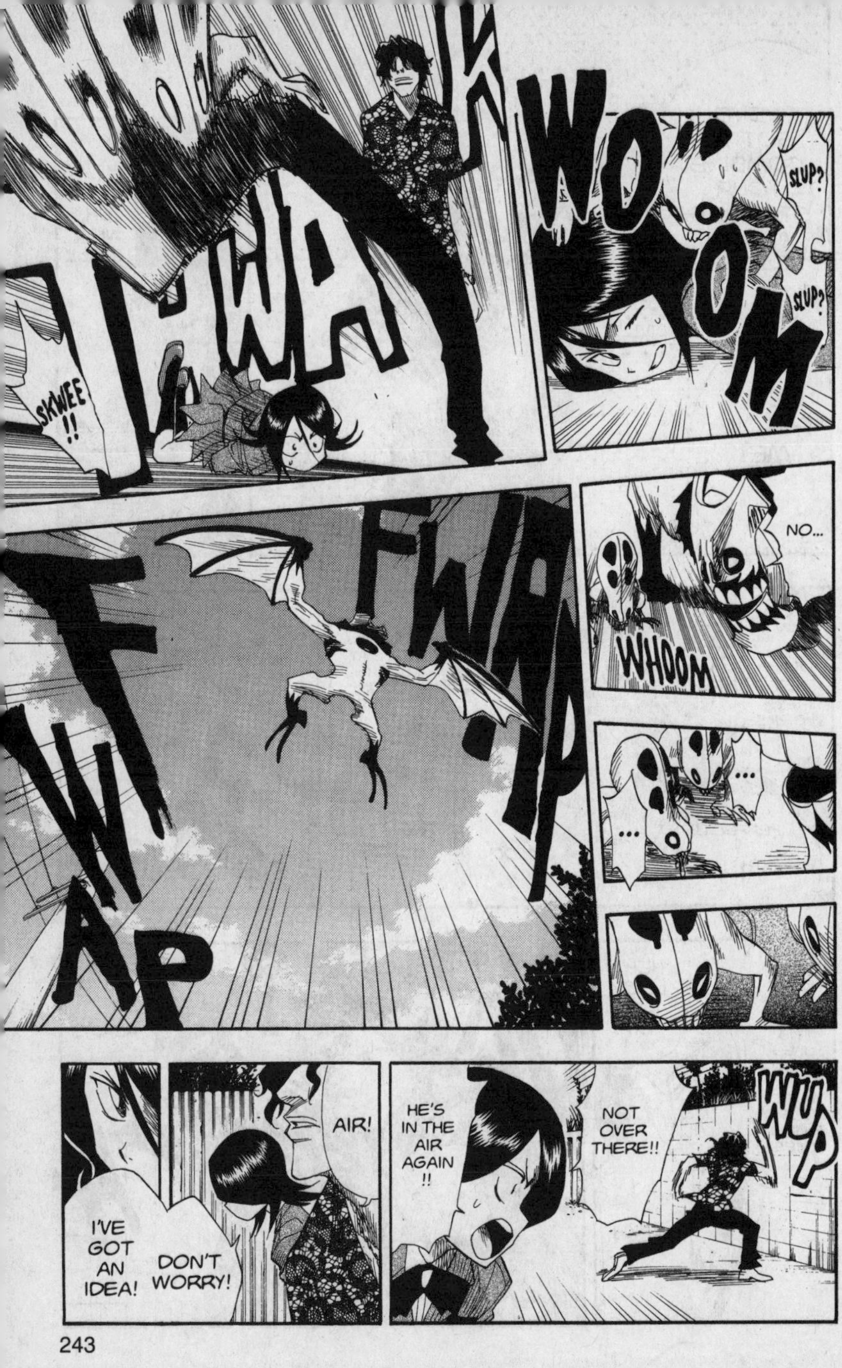
SLUP?
SLUP?
WOOOM
SKWEE !!
NO...
WHOOM
...
...
FWAP
FWAP
WUP
NOT OVER THERE!!
HE'S IN THE AIR AGAIN !!
AIR!
DON'T WORRY!
I'VE GOT AN IDEA!

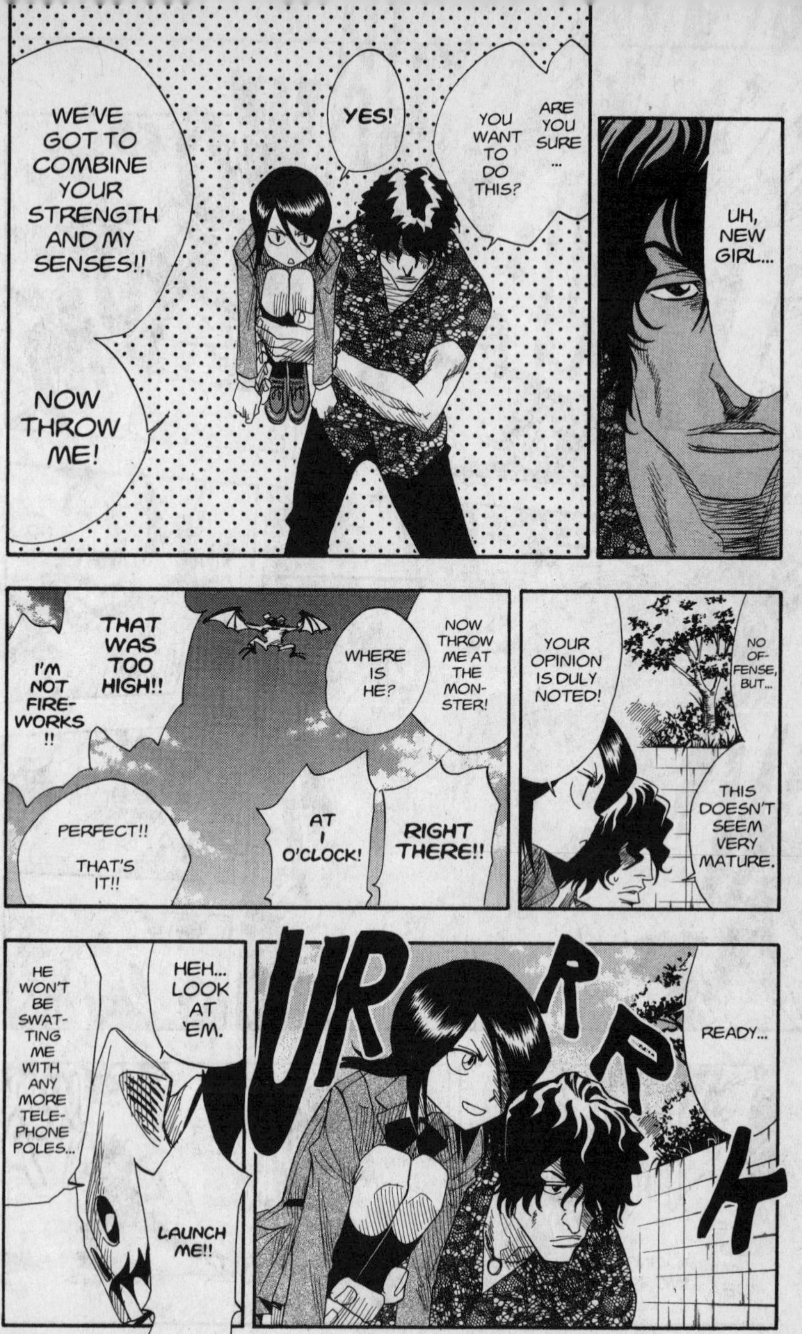
UH, NEW GIRL...
ARE YOU SURE...
YOU WANT TO DO THIS?
YES!
WE'VE GOT TO COMBINE YOUR STRENGTH AND MY SENSES!!
NOW THROW ME!
NO OFFENSE, BUT...
THIS DOESN'T SEEM VERY MATURE.
YOUR OPINION IS DULY NOTED!
NOW THROW ME AT THE MONSTER!
WHERE IS HE?
RIGHT THERE!!
AT 1 O'CLOCK!
THAT WAS TOO HIGH!!
I'M NOT FIREWORKS!!
PERFECT!!
THAT'S IT!!
READY...
URRRK
HEH... LOOK AT 'EM.
HE WON'T BE SWATTING ME WITH ANY MORE TELEPHONE POLES...
LAUNCH ME!!

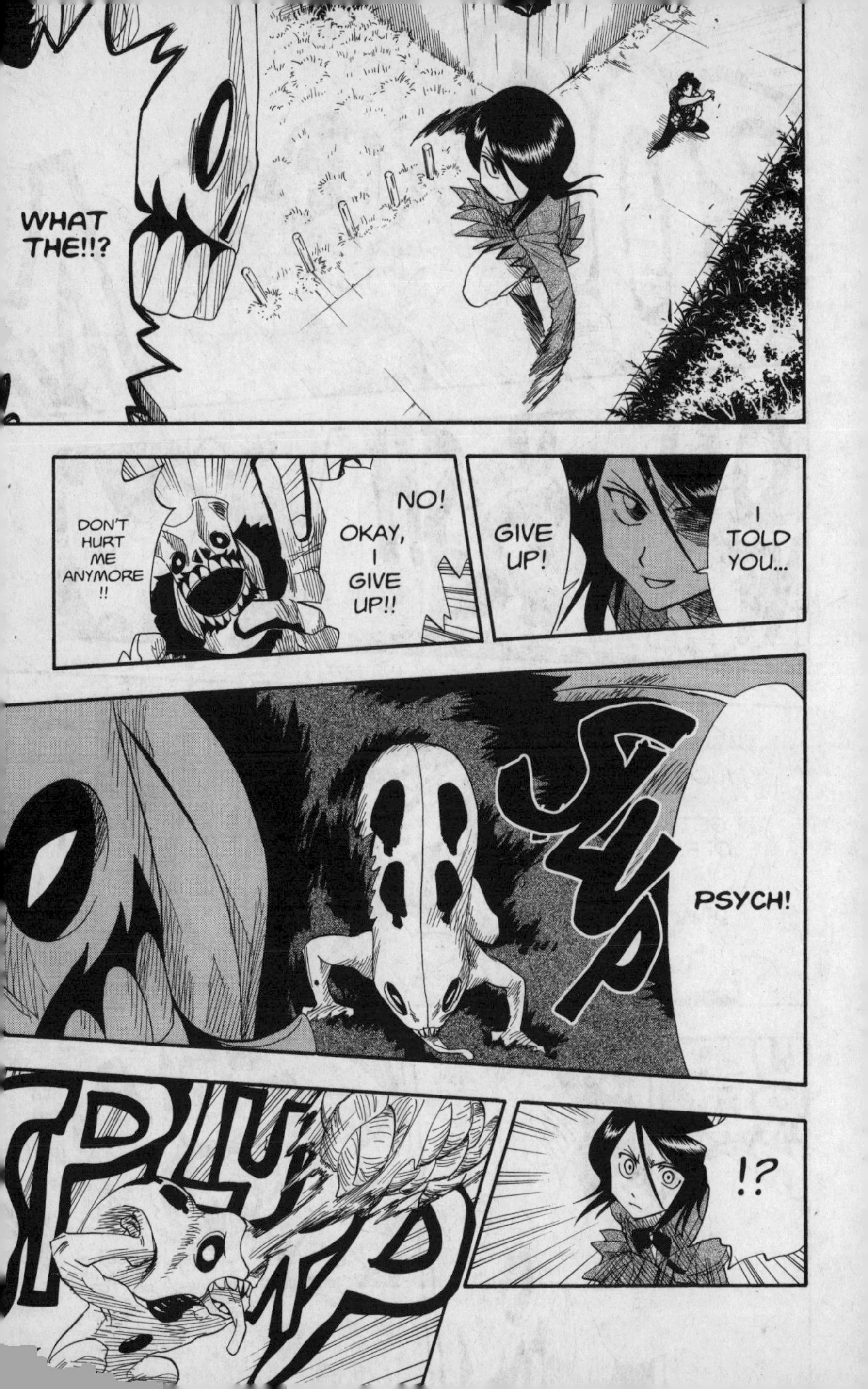
WHAT THE!!?
I TOLD YOU...
GIVE UP!
NO!
OKAY, I GIVE UP!!
DON'T HURT ME ANYMORE!!
PSYCH!
!?

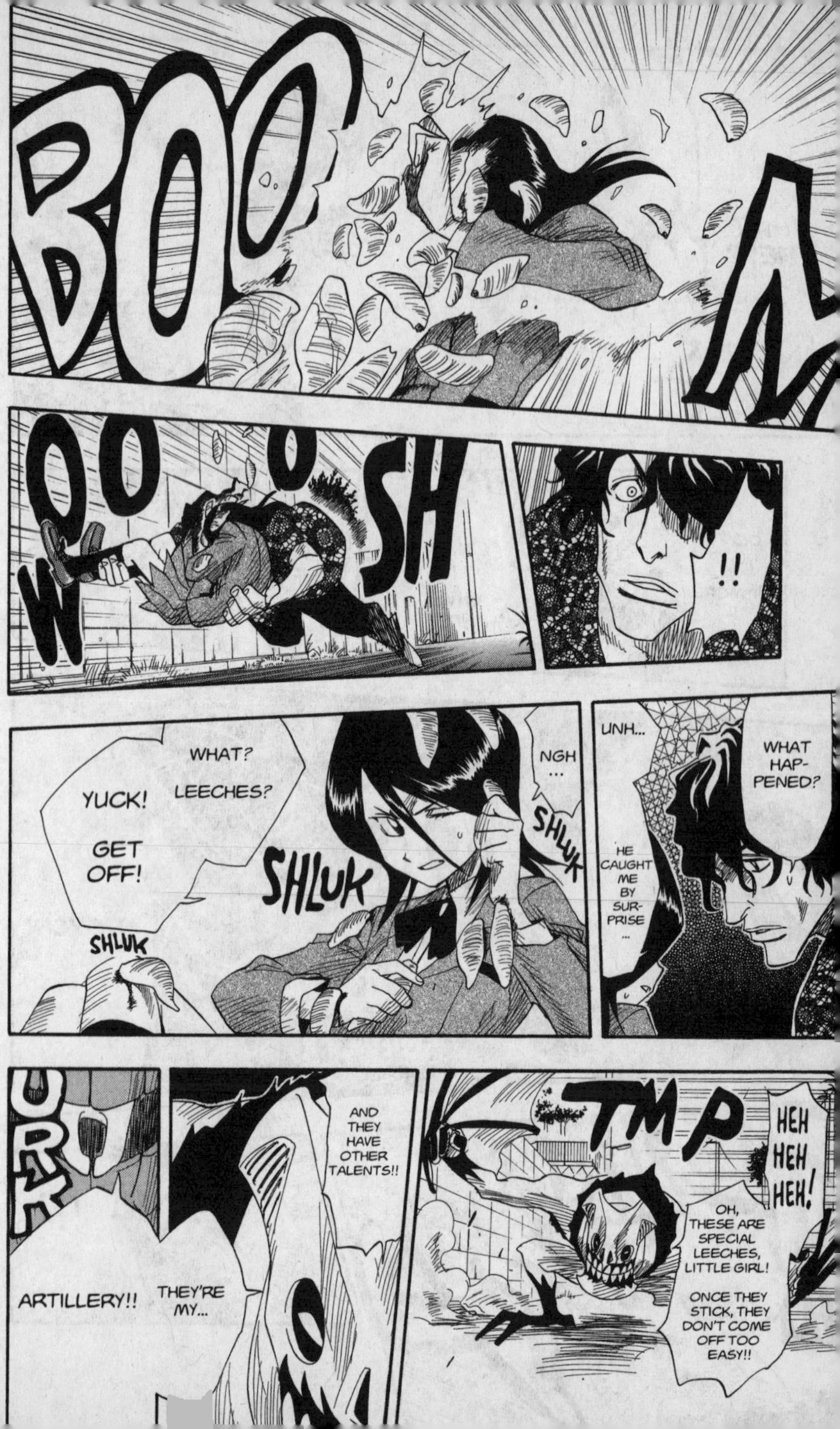
BOOOM
!!
WOOOSH
WHAT HAP-PENED?
UNH...
HE CAUGHT ME BY SUR-PRISE...
NGH...
SHLUK
WHAT? LEECHES?
YUCK! GET OFF!
SHLUK
SHLUK
TMP
HEH HEH HEH!
OH, THESE ARE SPECIAL LEECHES, LITTLE GIRL!
ONCE THEY STICK, THEY DON'T COME OFF TOO EASY!!
AND THEY HAVE OTHER TALENTS!!
THEY'RE MY...
URK
ARTILLERY!!

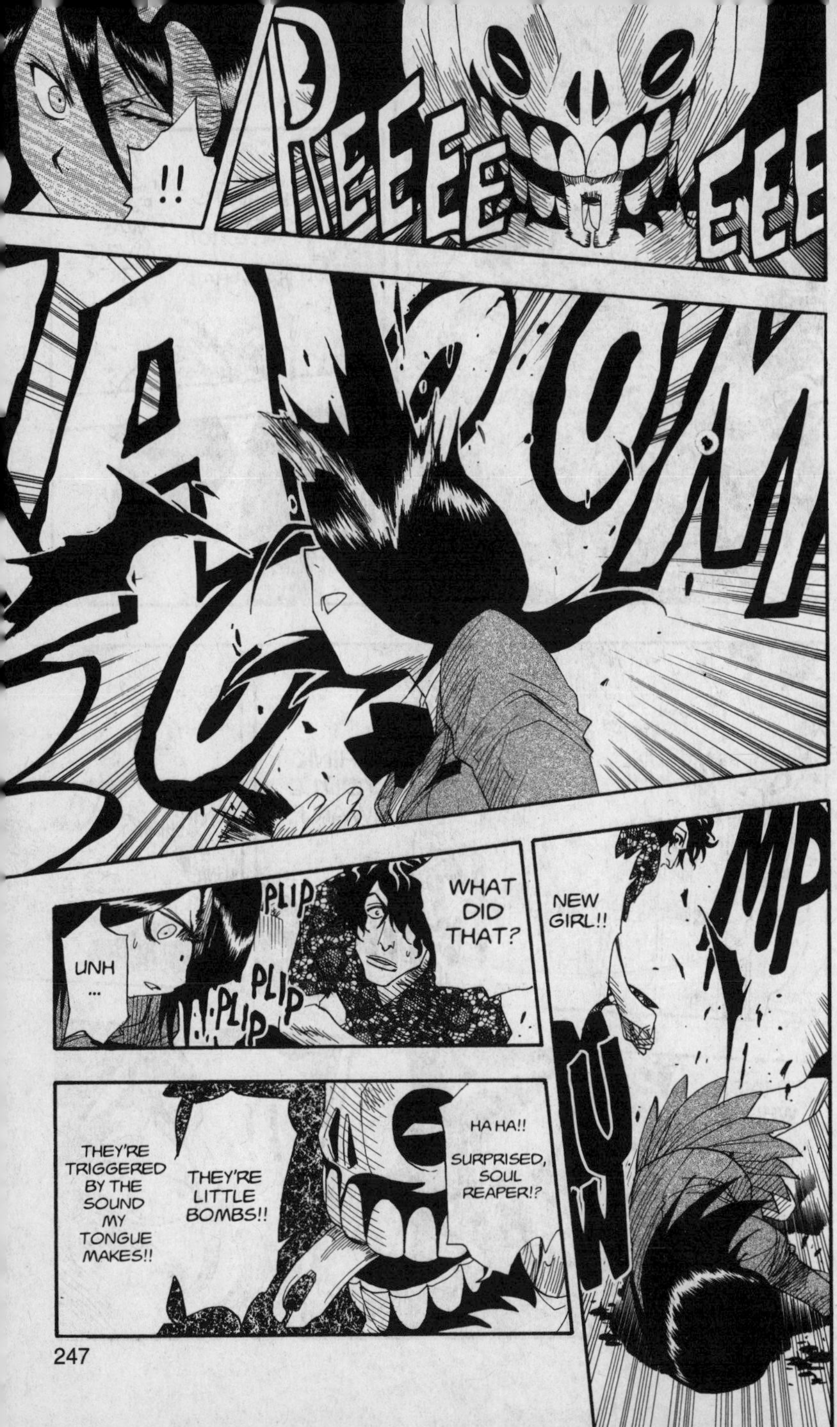
EEE
!!
NEW GIRL!!
MP
WHAT DID THAT?
PLIP
PLIP
PLIP
UNH ...
HA HA!!
SURPRISED, SOUL REAPER!?
THEY'RE LITTLE BOMBS!!
THEY'RE TRIGGERED BY THE SOUND MY TONGUE MAKES!!

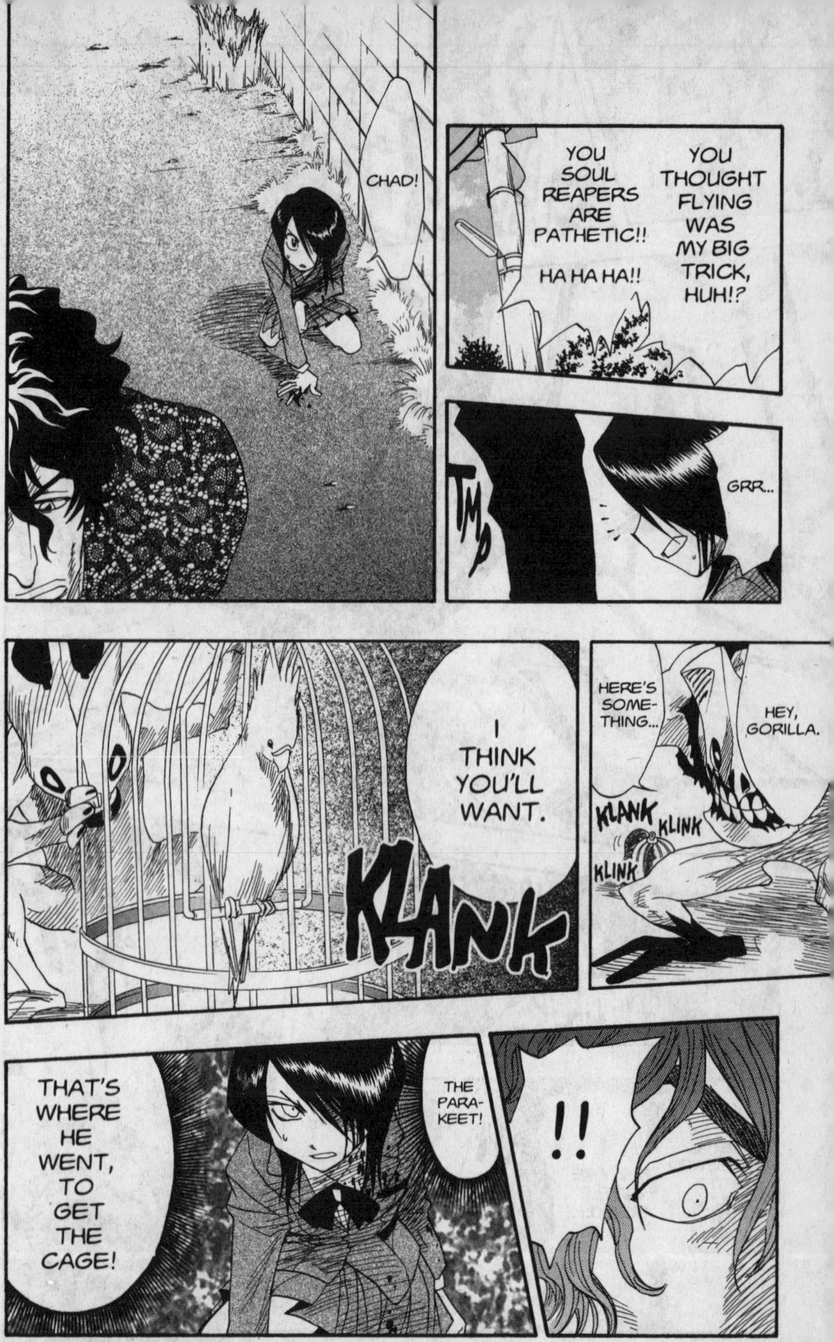
YOU THOUGHT FLYING WAS MY BIG TRICK, HUH!?
YOU SOUL REAPERS ARE PATHETIC!!
HA HA HA!!
GRR...
TMP
CHAD!
HEY, GORILLA.
HERE'S SOME-THING...
KLANK
KLINK
KLINK
I THINK YOU'LL WANT.
KLANK
!!
THE PARA-KEET!
THAT'S WHERE HE WENT, TO GET THE CAGE!

READ THIS WAY

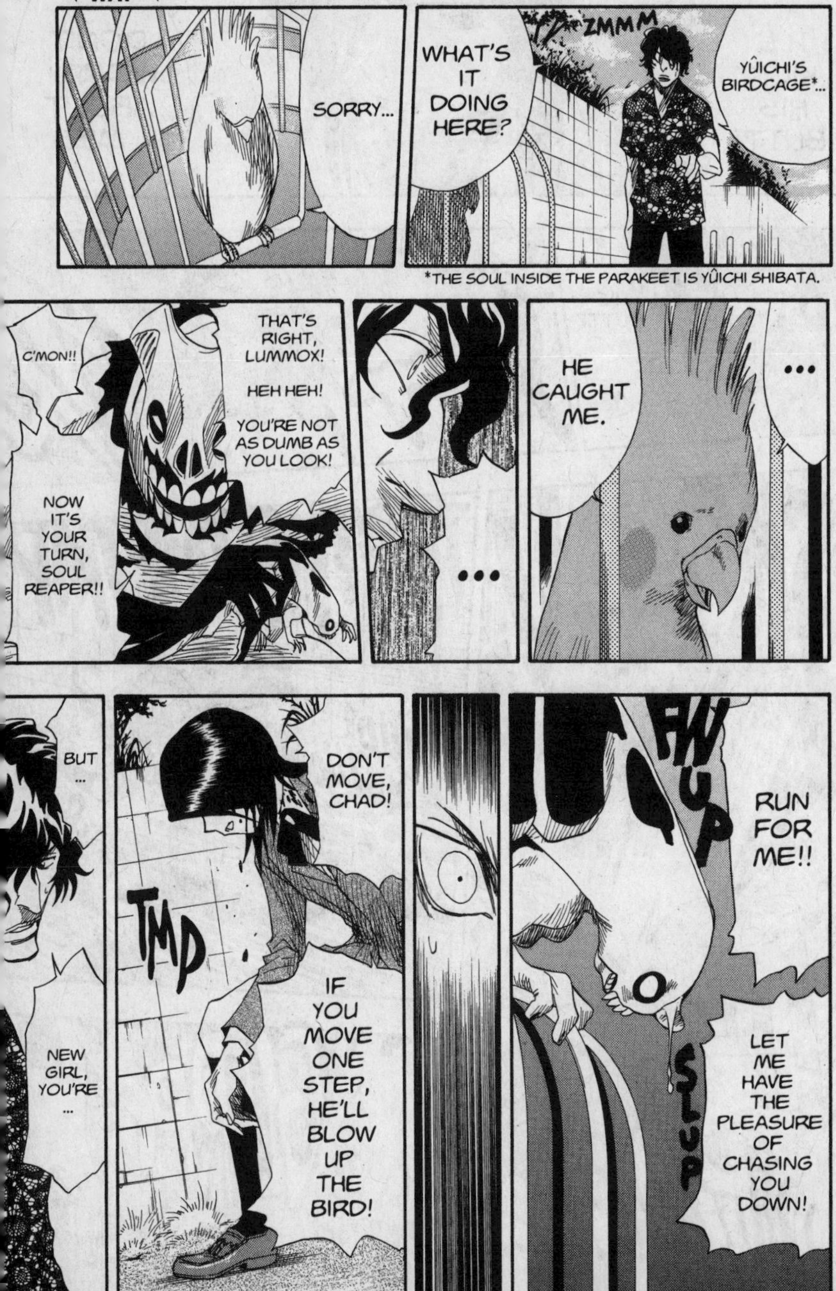
ZMMM
YÛICHI'S BIRDCAGE*...
WHAT'S IT DOING HERE?
SORRY...
*THE SOUL INSIDE THE PARAKEET IS YÛICHI SHIBATA.
...
HE CAUGHT ME.
...
THAT'S RIGHT, LUMMOX!
HEH HEH!
YOU'RE NOT AS DUMB AS YOU LOOK!
C'MON!!
NOW IT'S YOUR TURN, SOUL REAPER!!
FWUP
RUN FOR ME!!
SLUP
LET ME HAVE THE PLEASURE OF CHASING YOU DOWN!
DON'T MOVE, CHAD!
TMP
IF YOU MOVE ONE STEP, HE'LL BLOW UP THE BIRD!
BUT ...
NEW GIRL, YOU'RE ...

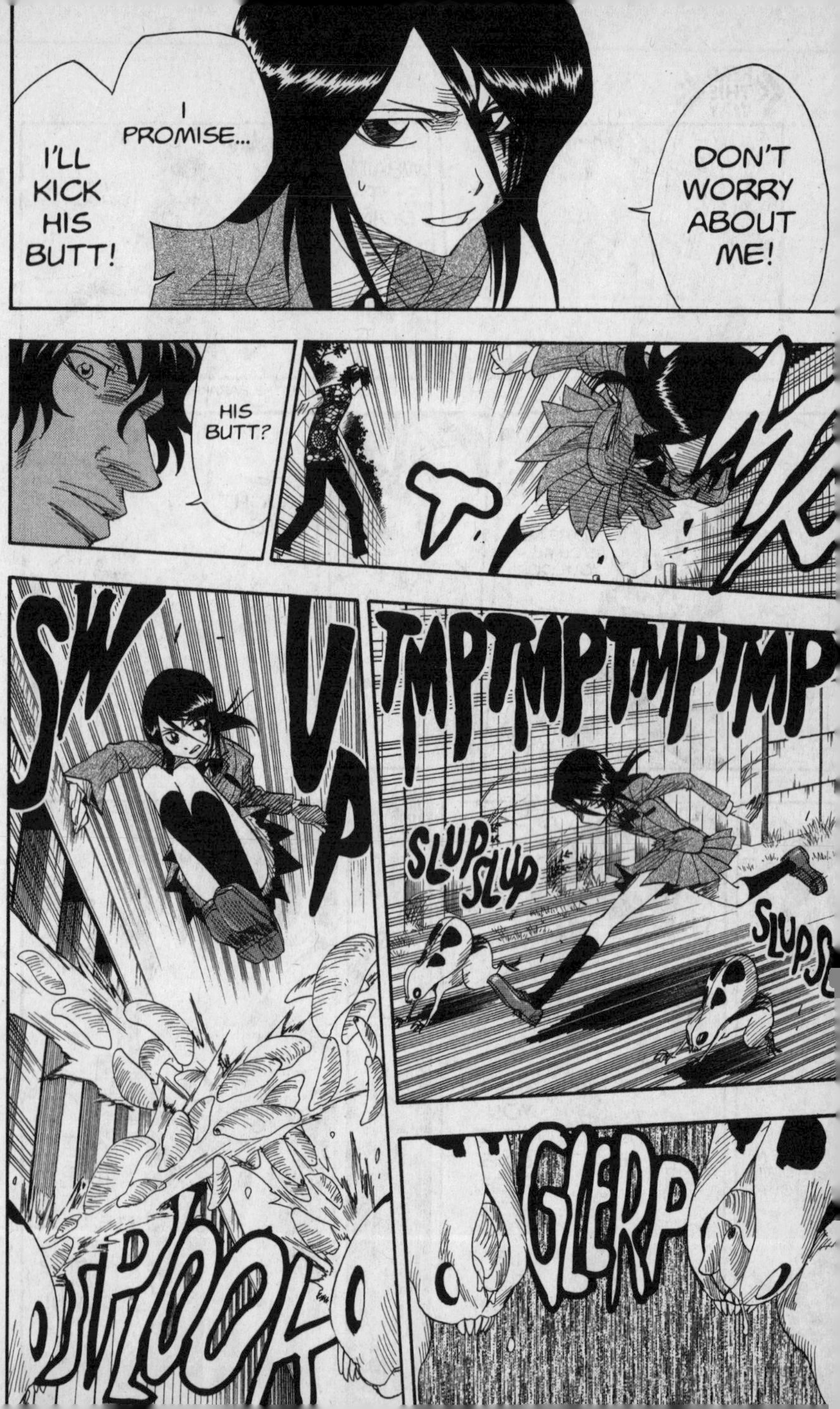
DON'T WORRY ABOUT ME!
I PROMISE... I'LL KICK HIS BUTT!
HIS BUTT?
TMPTMPTMPTMP
SLUP SLUP
GLERP
SWUP

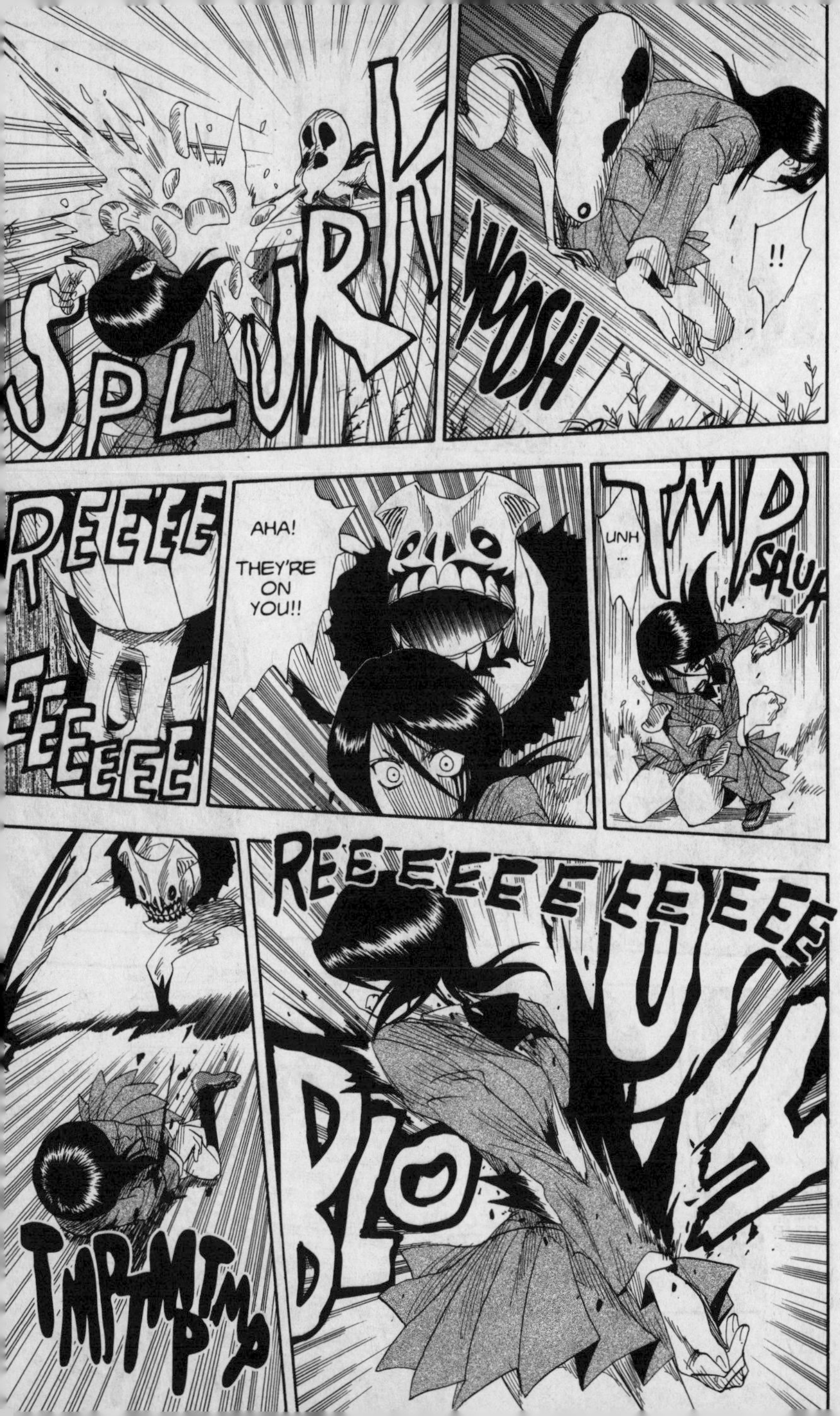
!!
WOOSH
SPLURK
TMP
SPLUK
UNH ...
AHA!
THEY'RE ON YOU!!
REEEEEEEEEEE
REEEEEEEEEEEE
TMPTMPTMP

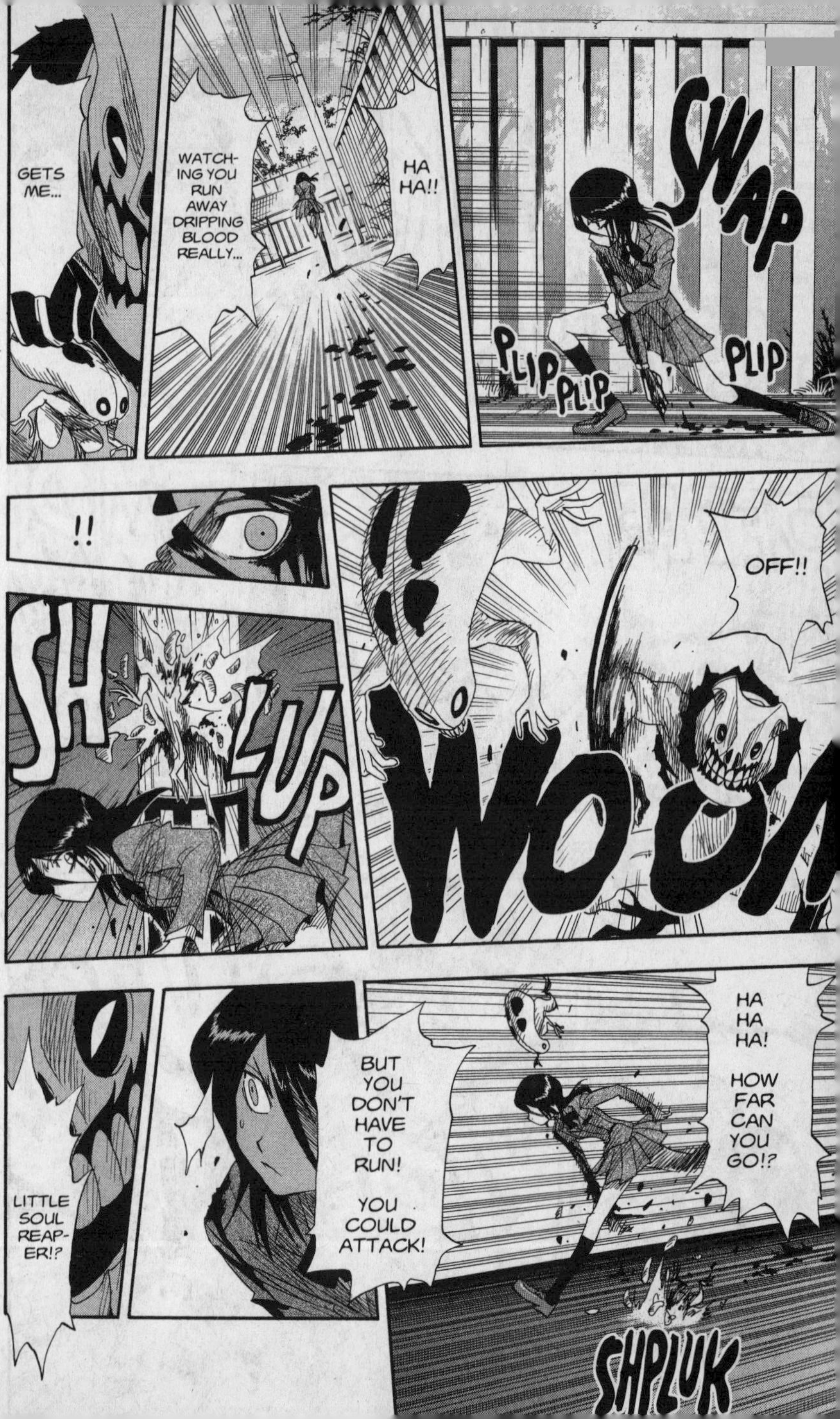
SWAP
PLIP
PLIP
PLIP
HA HA!!
WATCHING YOU RUN AWAY DRIPPING BLOOD REALLY...
GETS ME...
OFF!!
WOO
!!
SHLUP
HA HA HA!
HOW FAR CAN YOU GO!?
SHPLUK
BUT YOU DON'T HAVE TO RUN!
YOU COULD ATTACK!
LITTLE SOUL REAPER!?

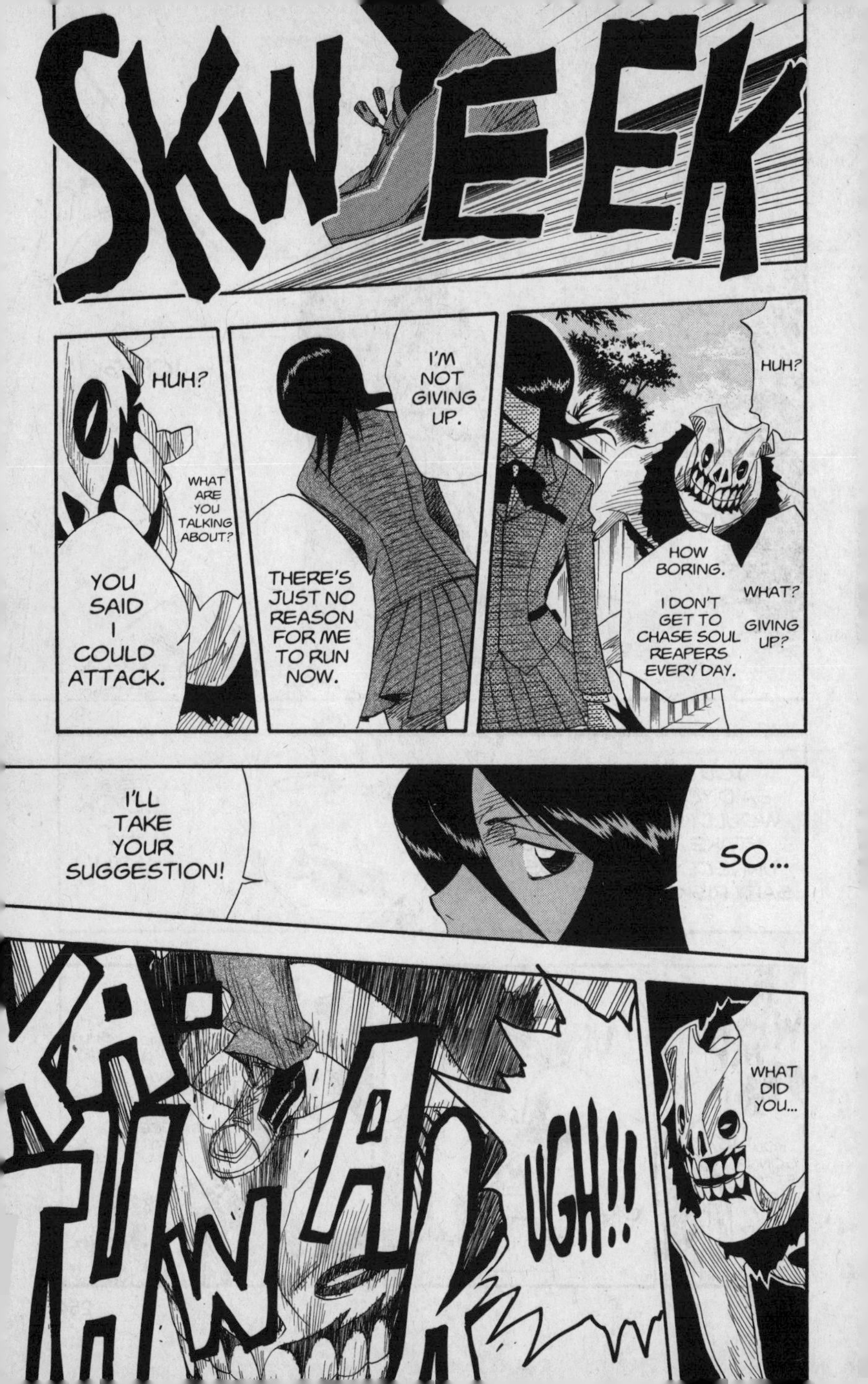
SKWEEEK
HUH?
HOW BORING.
I DON'T GET TO CHASE SOUL REAPERS EVERY DAY.
WHAT?
GIVING UP?
I'M NOT GIVING UP.
THERE'S JUST NO REASON FOR ME TO RUN NOW.
HUH?
WHAT ARE YOU TALKING ABOUT?
YOU SAID I COULD ATTACK.
SO...
I'LL TAKE YOUR SUGGESTION!
WHAT DID YOU...
UGH!!
THWAK

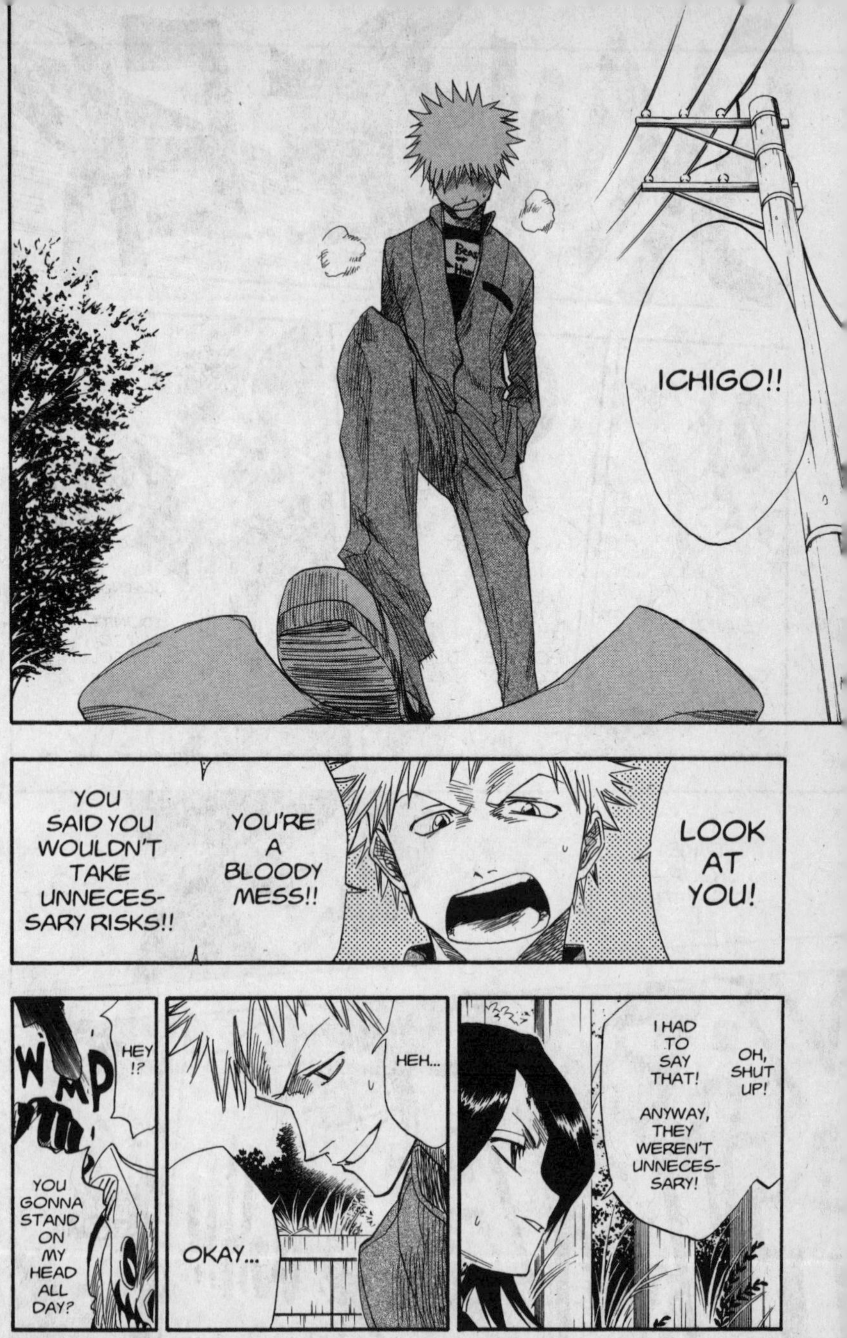
ICHIGO!!
LOOK AT YOU!
YOU'RE A BLOODY MESS!!
YOU SAID YOU WOULDN'T TAKE UNNECES-SARY RISKS!!
OH, SHUT UP!
I HAD TO SAY THAT!
ANYWAY, THEY WEREN'T UNNECES-SARY!
HEH...
OKAY...
WMP
HEY !?
YOU GONNA STAND ON MY HEAD ALL DAY?

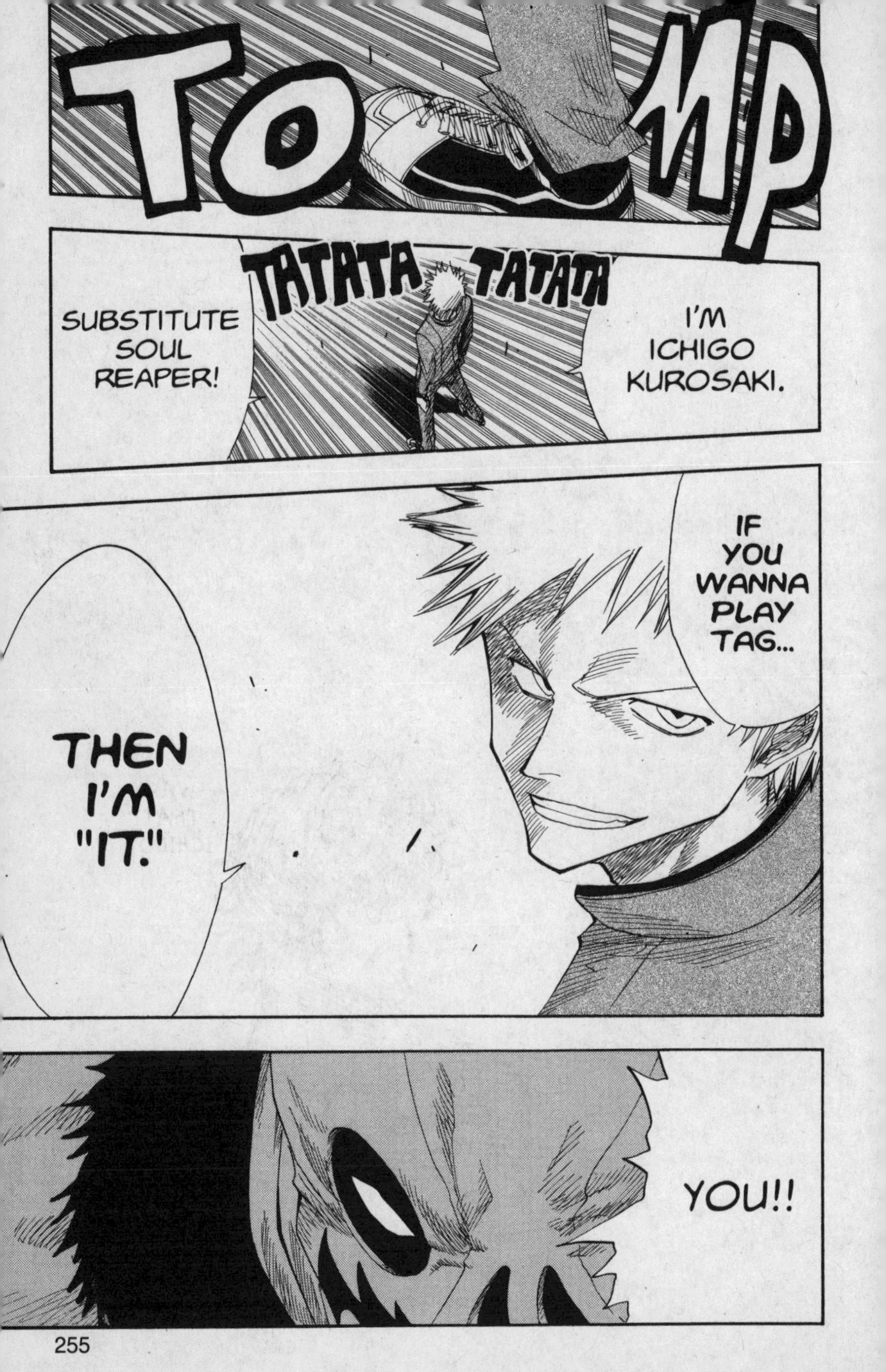
TOMP
TATATA TATATA
I'M ICHIGO KUROSAKI.
SUBSTITUTE SOUL REAPER!
IF YOU WANNA PLAY TAG...
THEN I'M "IT."
YOU!!

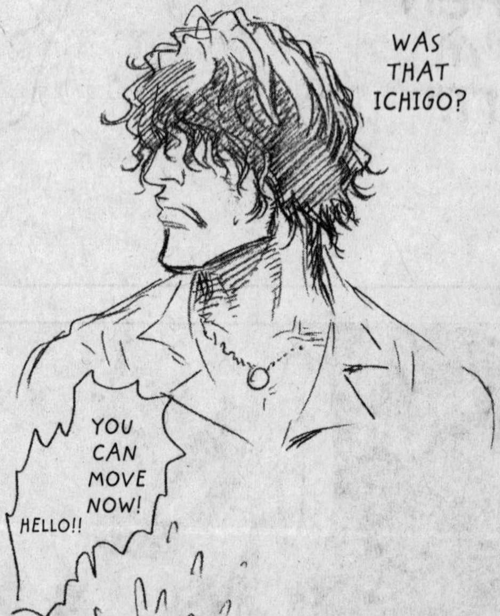
WAS THAT ICHIGO?
YOU CAN MOVE NOW!
HELLO!!

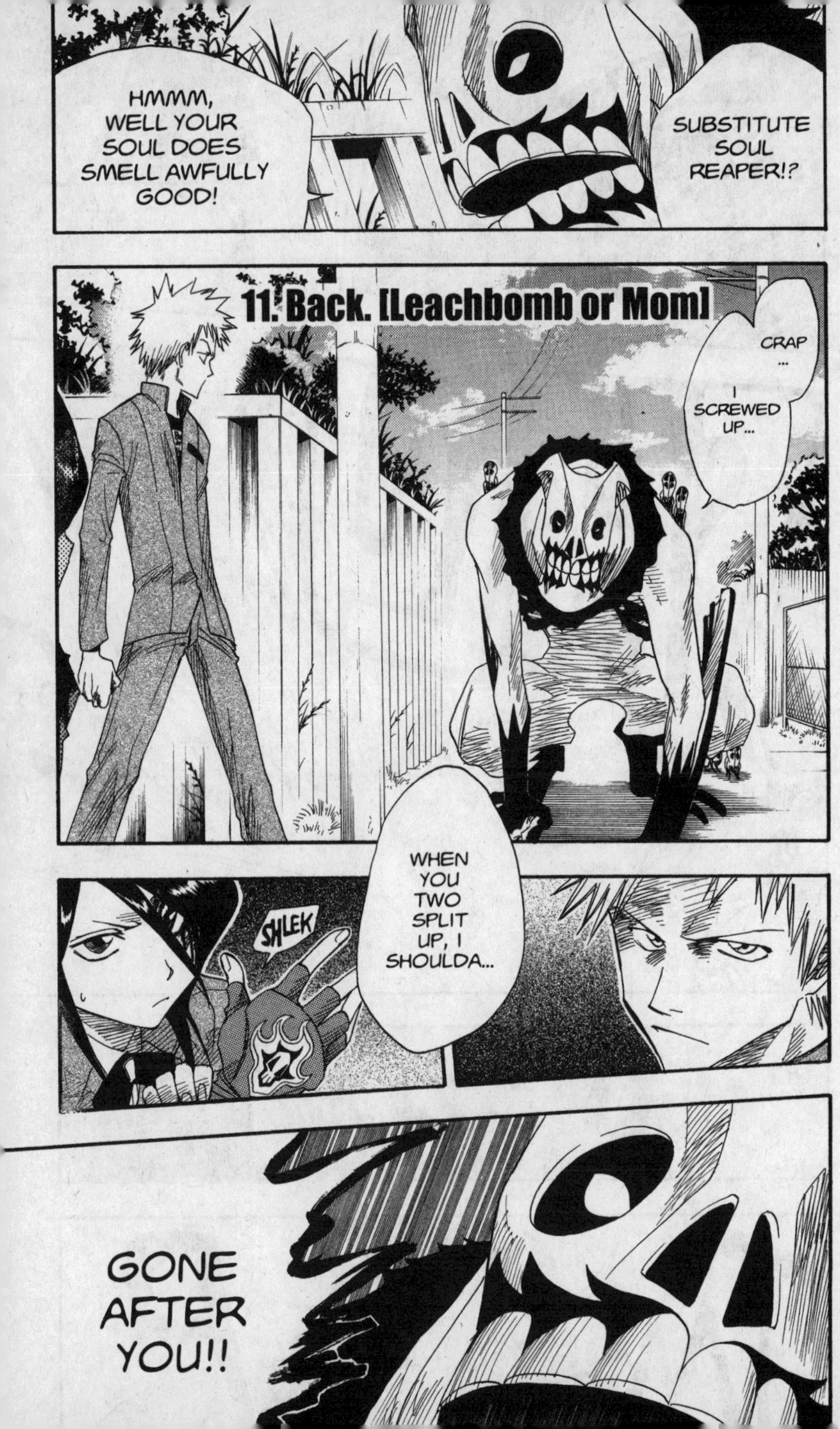
SUBSTITUTE SOUL REAPER!?
HMMM, WELL YOUR SOUL DOES SMELL AWFULLY GOOD!
11. Back. [Leachbomb or Mom]
CRAP ... I SCREWED UP...
WHEN YOU TWO SPLIT UP, I SHOULDA...
SHLEK
GONE AFTER YOU!!

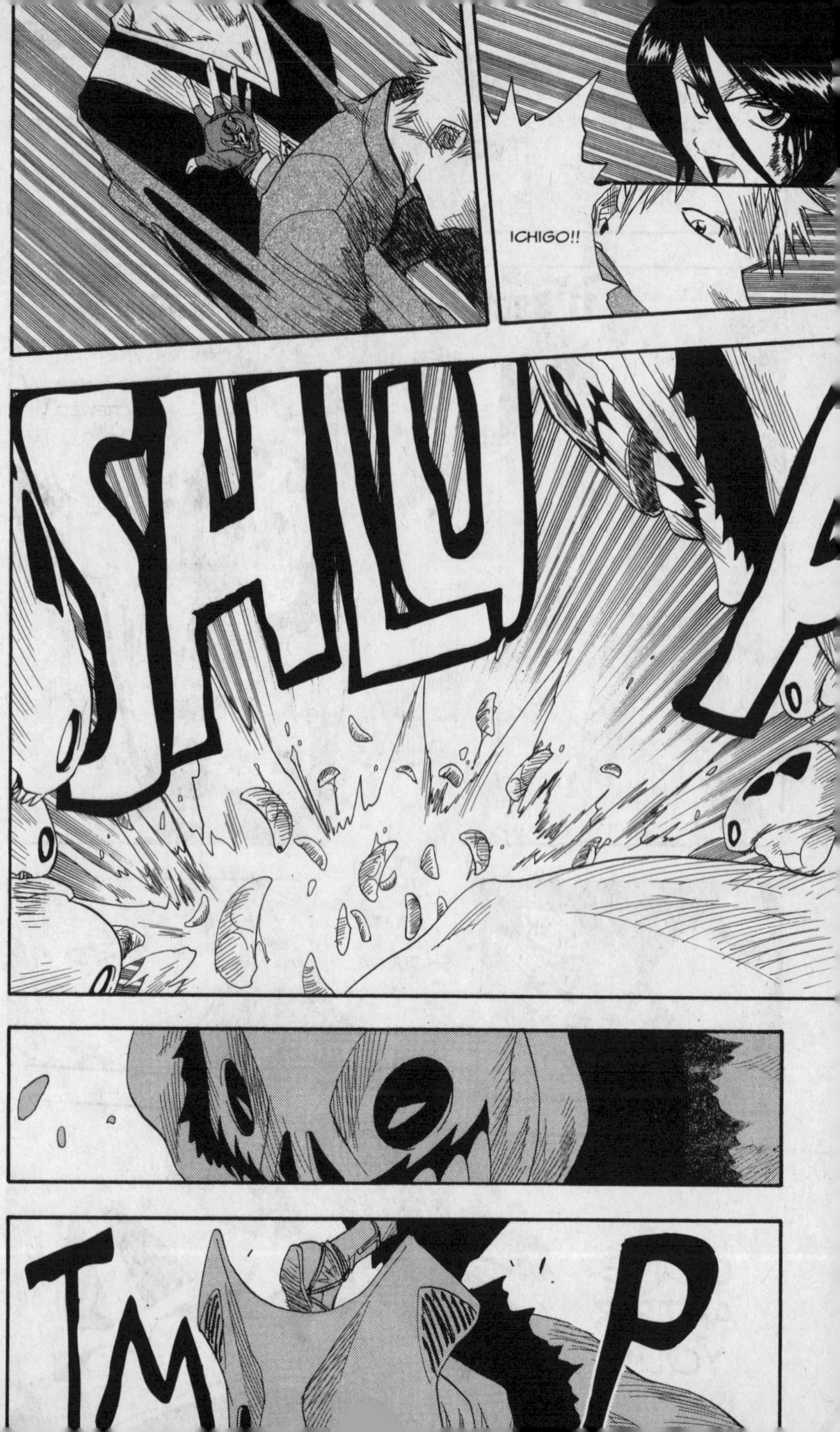
ICHIGO!!
SHUA
TMP

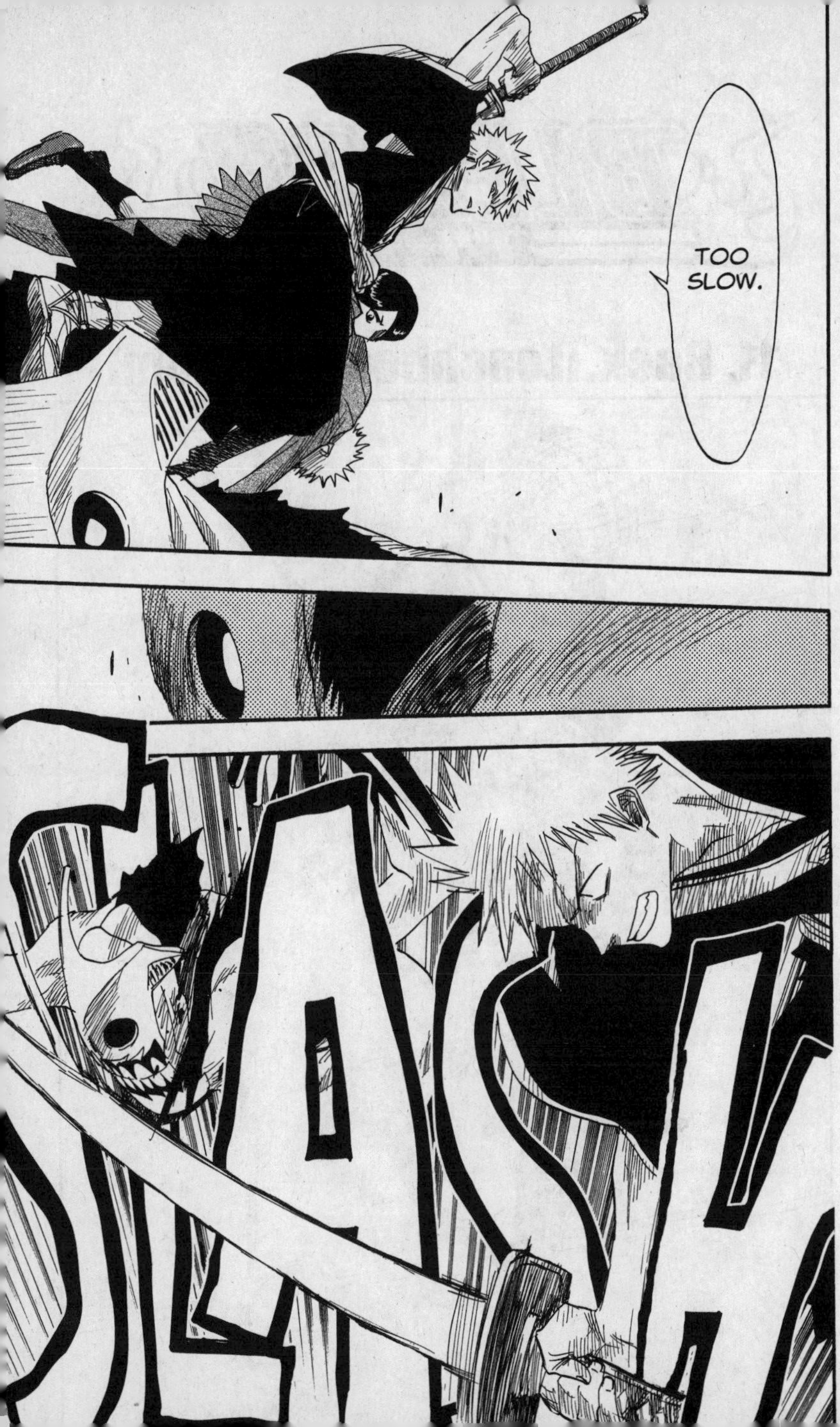
TOO SLOW.

BLEACH
ブリーチ

11. Back. [Leachbomb or Mom]

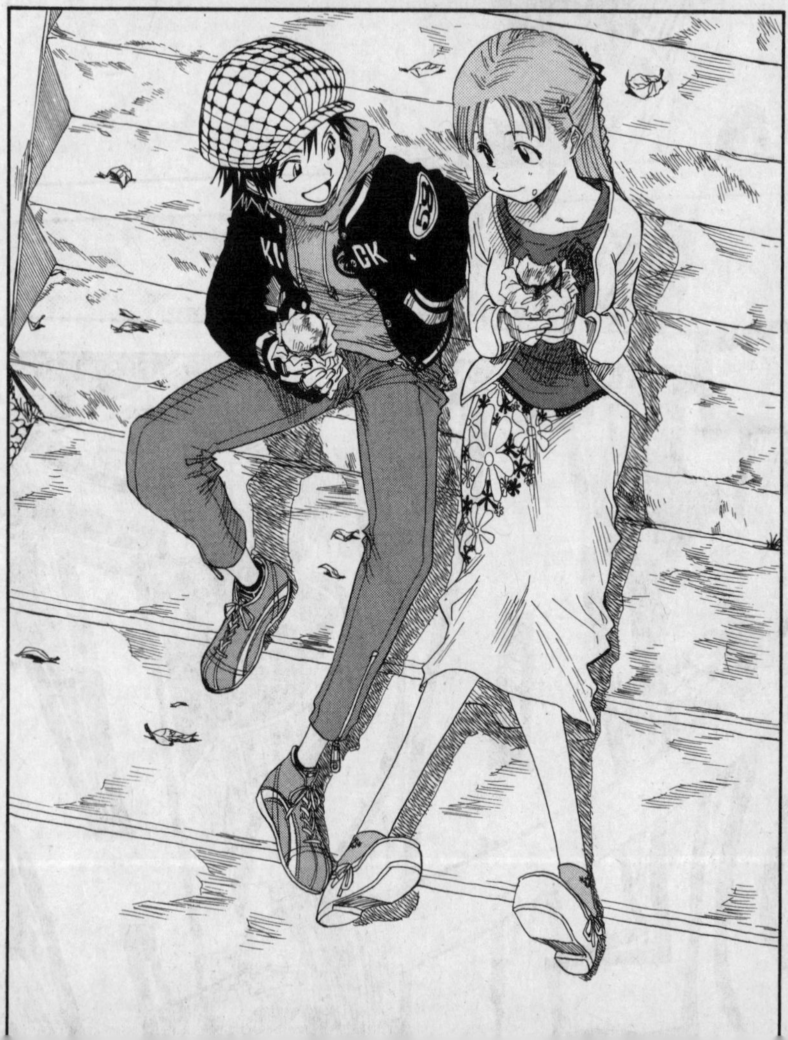

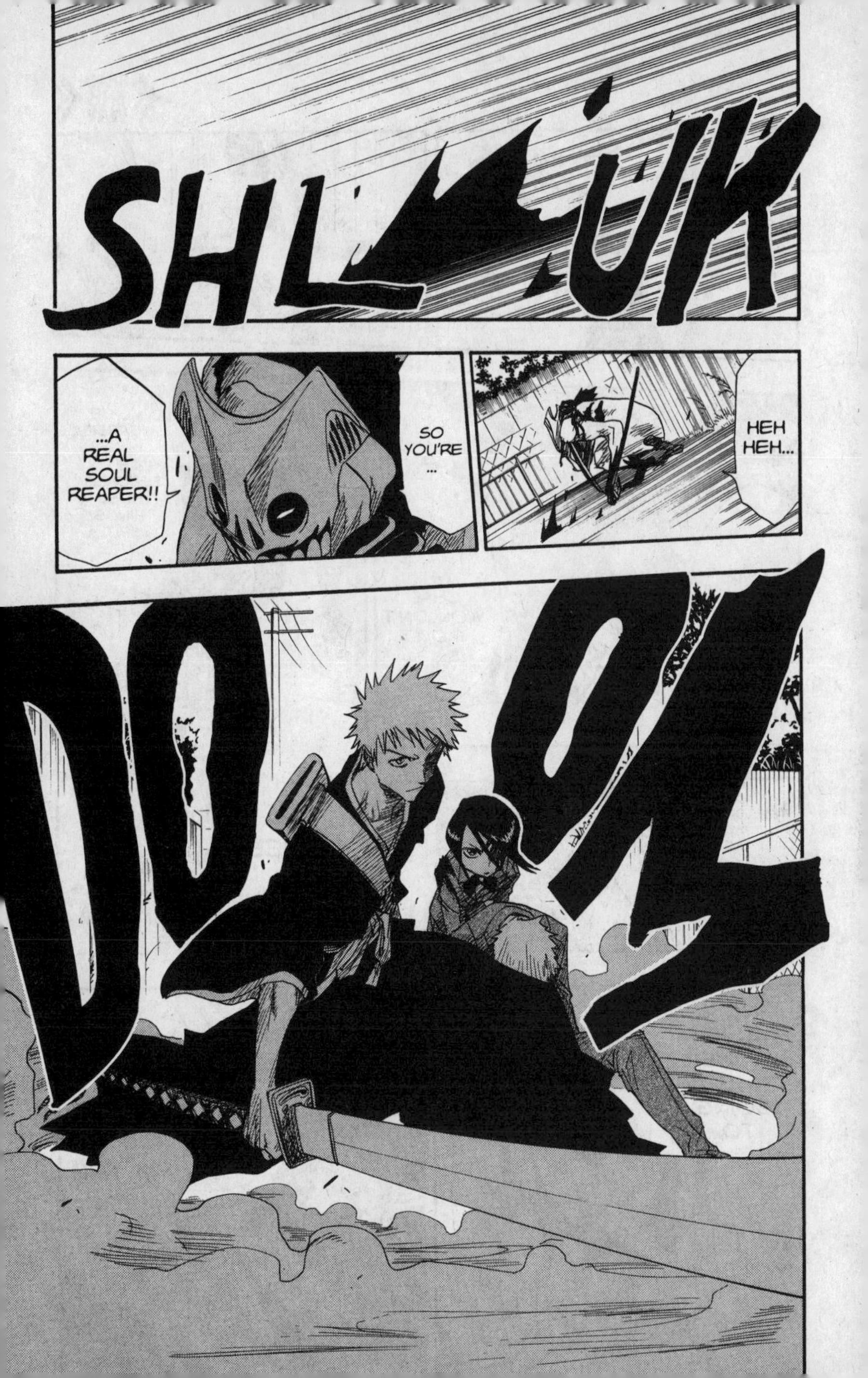
SHLUK
HEH HEH...
SO YOU'RE ...
...A REAL SOUL REAPER!!
DOOM

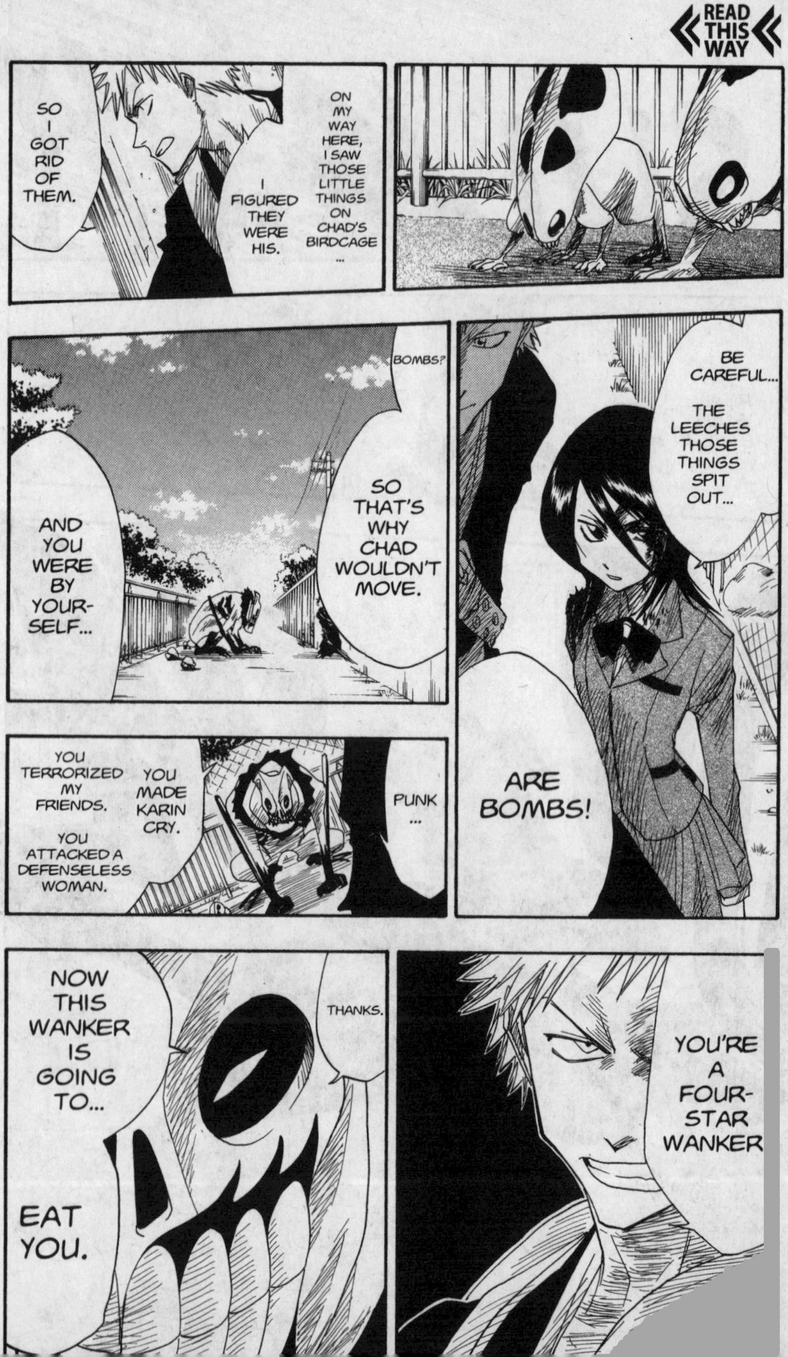
READ THIS WAY
ON MY WAY HERE, I SAW THOSE LITTLE THINGS ON CHAD'S BIRDCAGE...
I FIGURED THEY WERE HIS.
SO I GOT RID OF THEM.
BE CAREFUL... THE LEECHES THOSE THINGS SPIT OUT...
ARE BOMBS!
BOMBS?
SO THAT'S WHY CHAD WOULDN'T MOVE.
AND YOU WERE BY YOURSELF...
PUNK...
YOU MADE KARIN CRY.
YOU TERRORIZED MY FRIENDS.
YOU ATTACKED A DEFENSELESS WOMAN.
YOU'RE A FOUR-STAR WANKER
THANKS.
NOW THIS WANKER IS GOING TO...
EAT YOU.

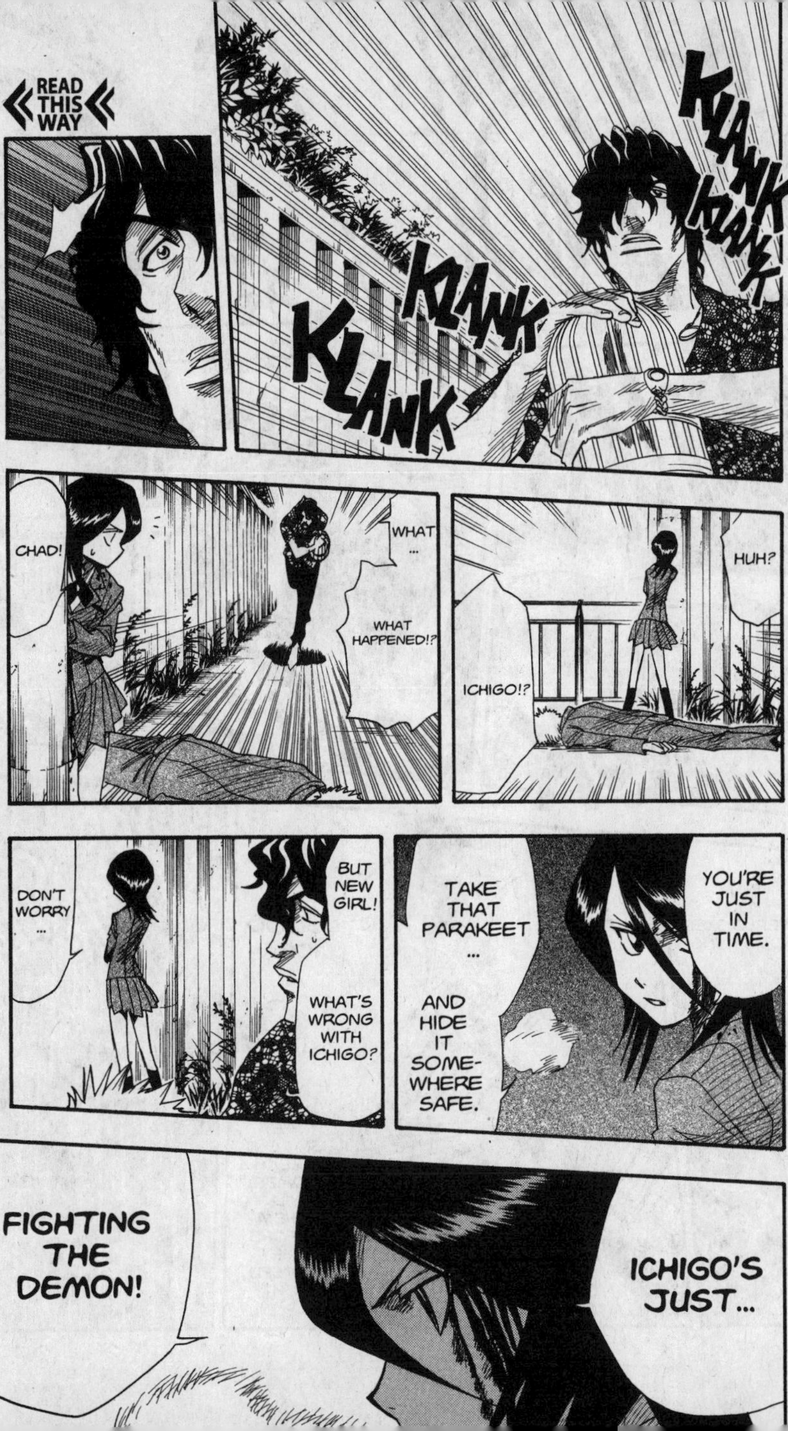
READ THIS WAY
KLANK KLANK
KLANK KLANK
HUH?
ICHIGO!?
WHAT ...
WHAT HAPPENED!?
CHAD!
YOU'RE JUST IN TIME.
TAKE THAT PARAKEET ...
AND HIDE IT SOMEWHERE SAFE.
BUT NEW GIRL!
WHAT'S WRONG WITH ICHIGO?
DON'T WORRY ...
ICHIGO'S JUST...
FIGHTING THE DEMON!

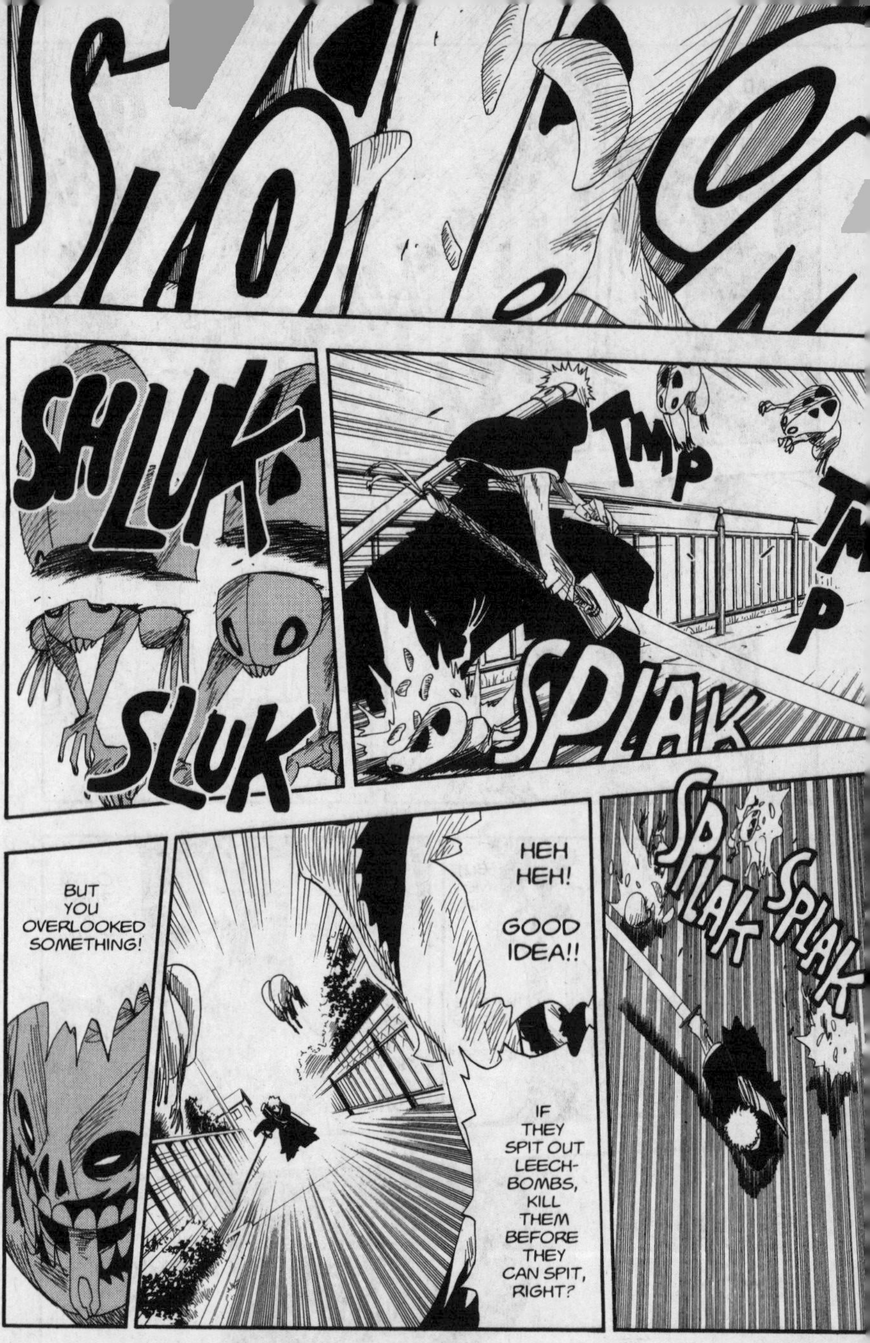
TMP
TMP
SPLAK
SHLUK
SLUK
SPLAK
SPLAK
HEH HEH!
GOOD IDEA!!
IF THEY SPIT OUT LEECH-BOMBS, KILL THEM BEFORE THEY CAN SPIT, RIGHT?
BUT YOU OVERLOOKED SOMETHING!

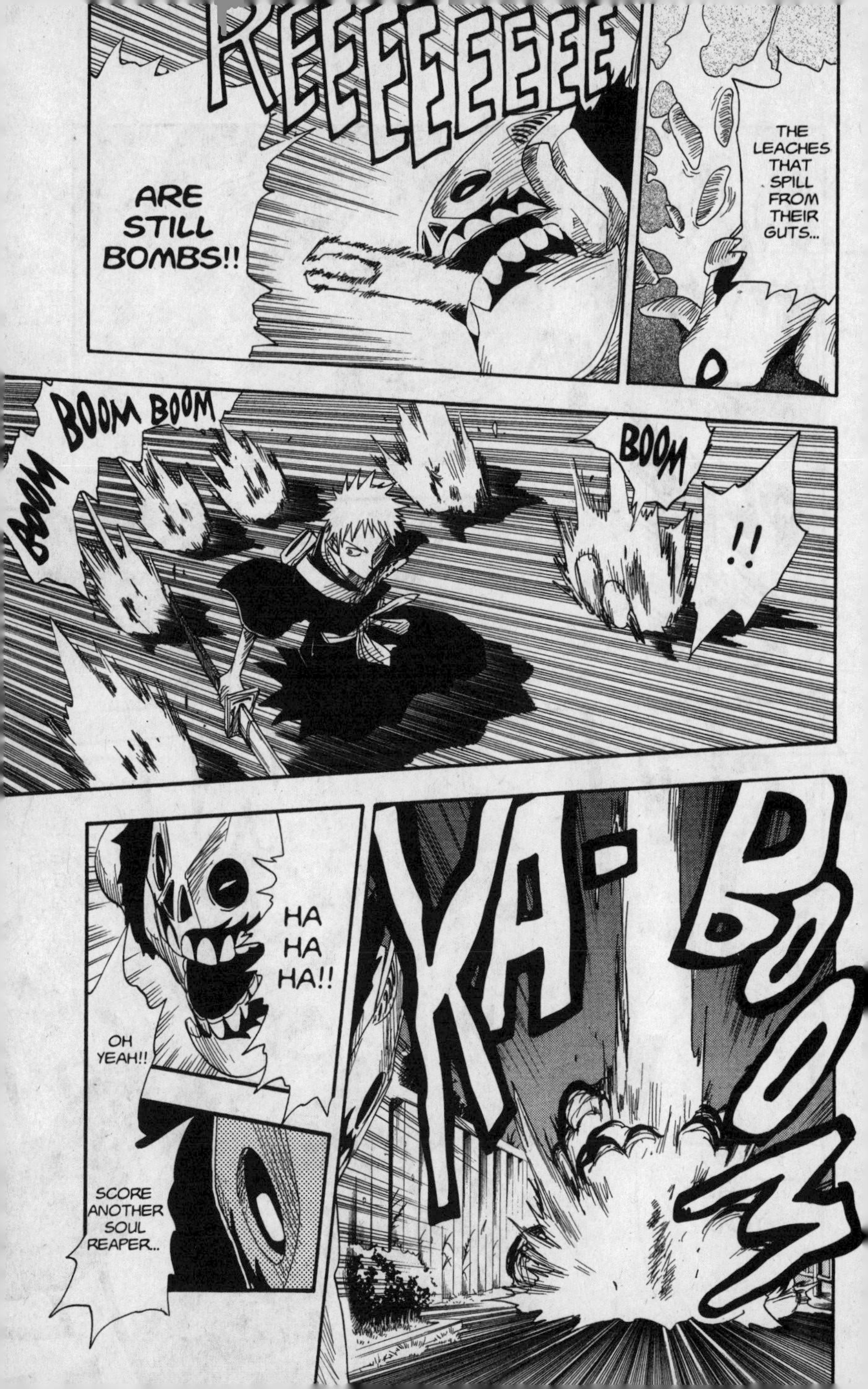
THE LEACHES THAT SPILL FROM THEIR GUTS...
REEEEEEEE
ARE STILL BOMBS!!
BOOM
!!
BOOM BOOM
BOOM
YA-BOOM
HA HA HA!!
OH YEAH!!
SCORE ANOTHER SOUL REAPER..

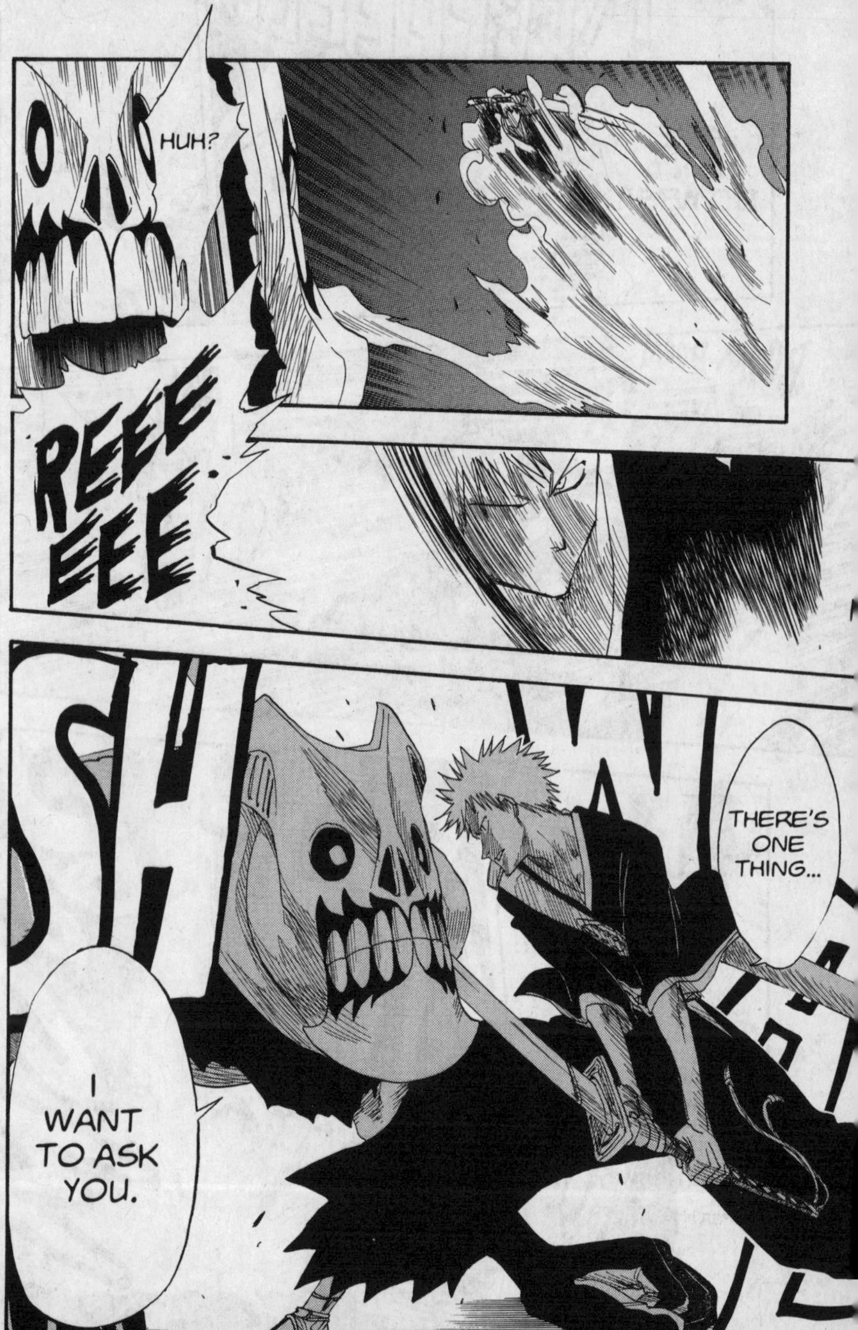
HUH?
REEEEEE
THERE'S ONE THING...
I WANT TO ASK YOU.

READ THIS WAY

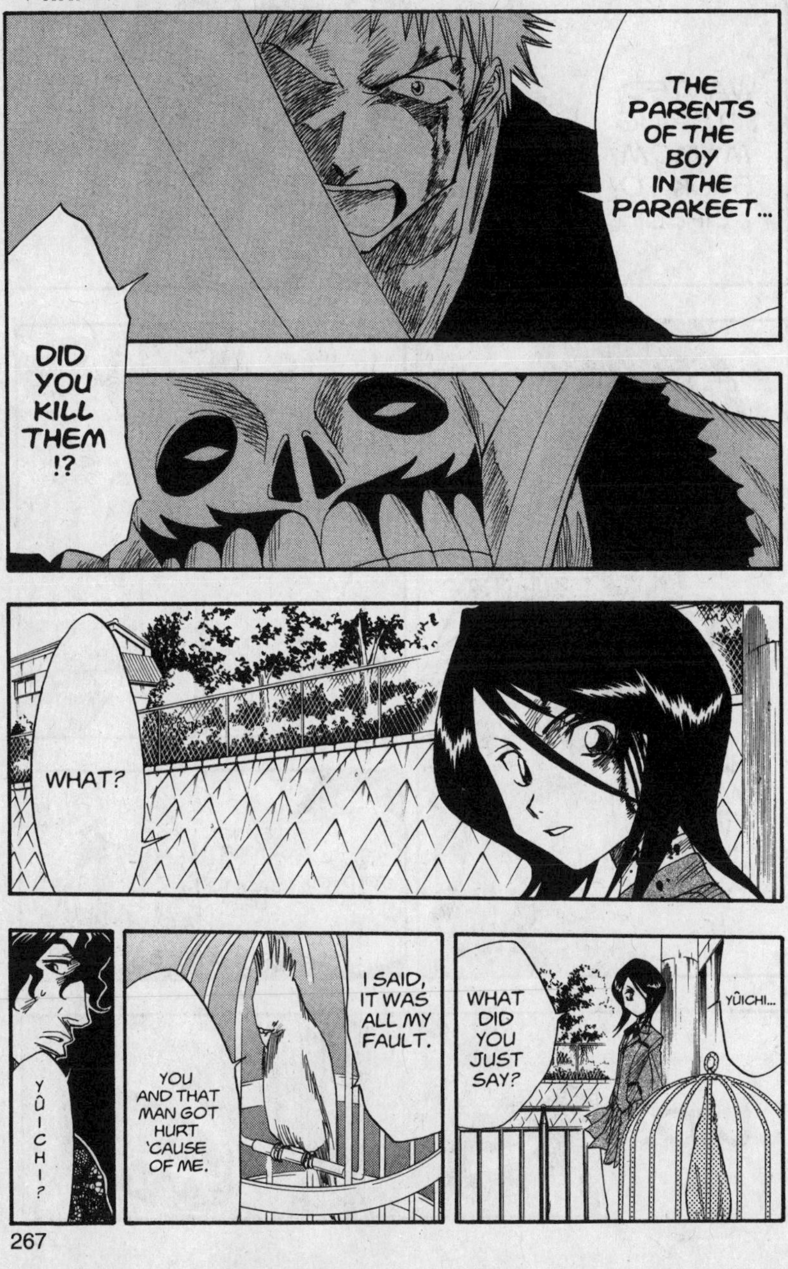

THE PARENTS OF THE BOY IN THE PARAKEET...
DID YOU KILL THEM !?
WHAT?
YÛICHI...
WHAT DID YOU JUST SAY?
I SAID, IT WAS ALL MY FAULT.
YOU AND THAT MAN GOT HURT 'CAUSE OF ME.
YÛICHI?

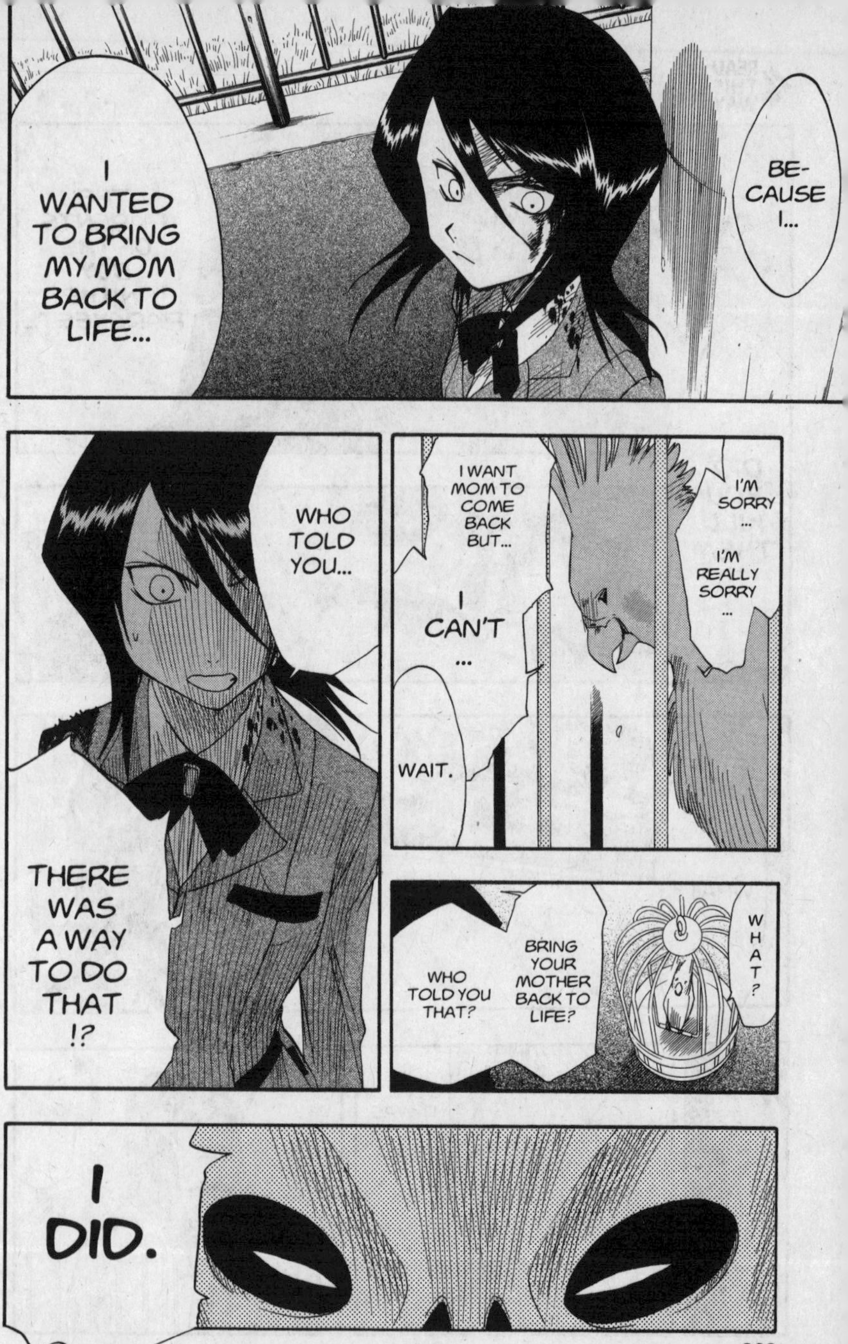
BE-CAUSE I...
I WANTED TO BRING MY MOM BACK TO LIFE...
I'M SORRY... I'M REALLY SORRY...
I WANT MOM TO COME BACK BUT...
I CAN'T...
WAIT.
WHAT?
BRING YOUR MOTHER BACK TO LIFE?
WHO TOLD YOU THAT?
WHO TOLD YOU...
THERE WAS A WAY TO DO THAT!?
I DID.

READ THIS WAY

!
I KILLED THE BRAT'S MOMMY!
ABOUT FIVE YEARS AGO...
BACK WHEN I WAS STILL ALIVE!
THEY CALLED ME A SERIAL KILLER.
I TRAVELED AROUND, HUNTING.
KILLED EIGHT PEOPLE.
THEY EVEN TALKED ABOUT ME ON TV!
I WAS FAMOUS, A REAL CELEBRITY!
THE KID'S MOTHER...
WAS MY FINAL SCORE!
SHE WAS SWEET.
I STABBED HER A DOZEN TIMES, AND SHE STILL RAN AWAY BLEEDING...
TRYING TO PROTECT THE KID.

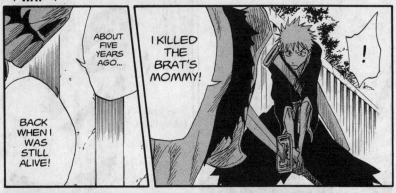

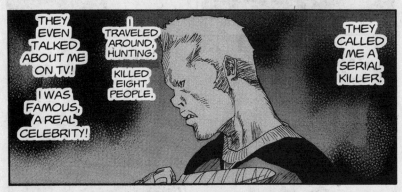

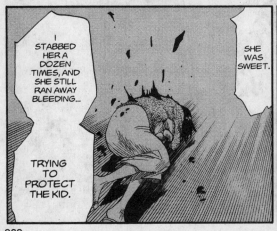

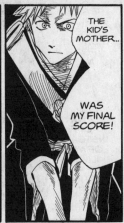

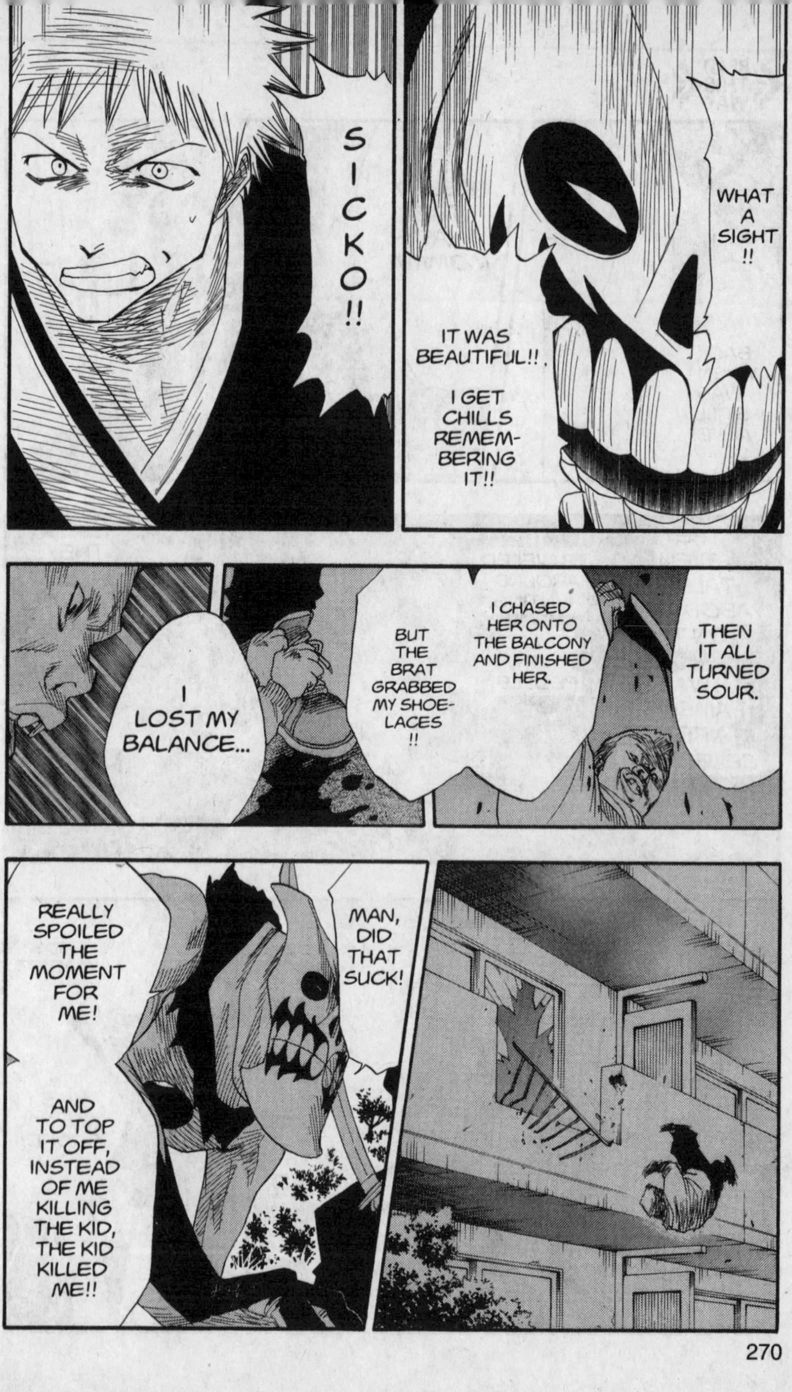
WHAT A SIGHT!!
IT WAS BEAUTIFUL!!
I GET CHILLS REMEM-BERING IT!!
SICKO!!
THEN IT ALL TURNED SOUR.
I CHASED HER ONTO THE BALCONY AND FINISHED HER.
BUT THE BRAT GRABBED MY SHOE-LACES!!
I LOST MY BALANCE...
MAN, DID THAT SUCK!
REALLY SPOILED THE MOMENT FOR ME!
AND TO TOP IT OFF, INSTEAD OF ME KILLING THE KID, THE KID KILLED ME!!

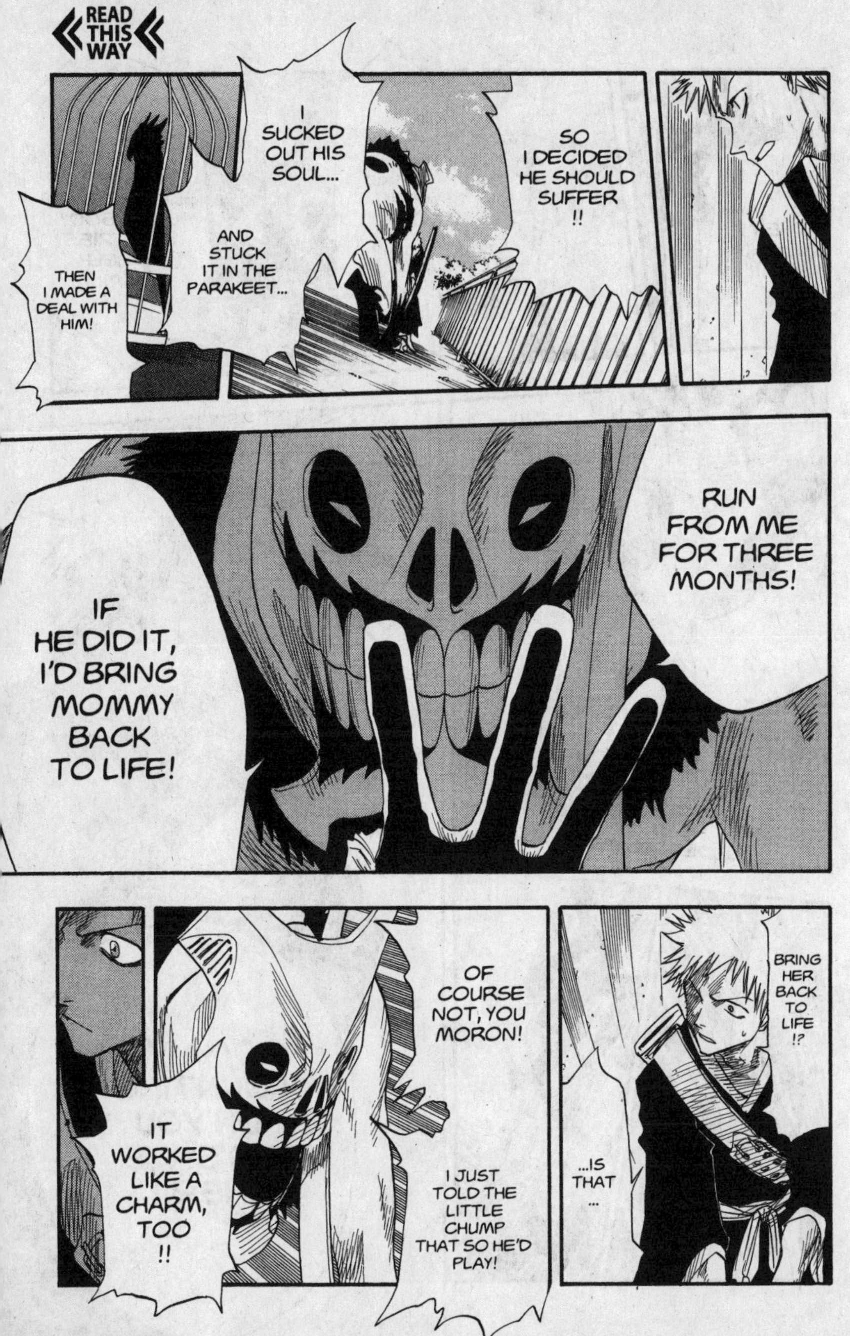
READ THIS WAY
SO I DECIDED HE SHOULD SUFFER !!
I SUCKED OUT HIS SOUL...
AND STUCK IT IN THE PARAKEET...
THEN I MADE A DEAL WITH HIM!
RUN FROM ME FOR THREE MONTHS!
IF HE DID IT, I'D BRING MOMMY BACK TO LIFE!
BRING HER BACK TO LIFE !?
...IS THAT ...
OF COURSE NOT, YOU MORON!
I JUST TOLD THE LITTLE CHUMP THAT SO HE'D PLAY!
IT WORKED LIKE A CHARM, TOO !!

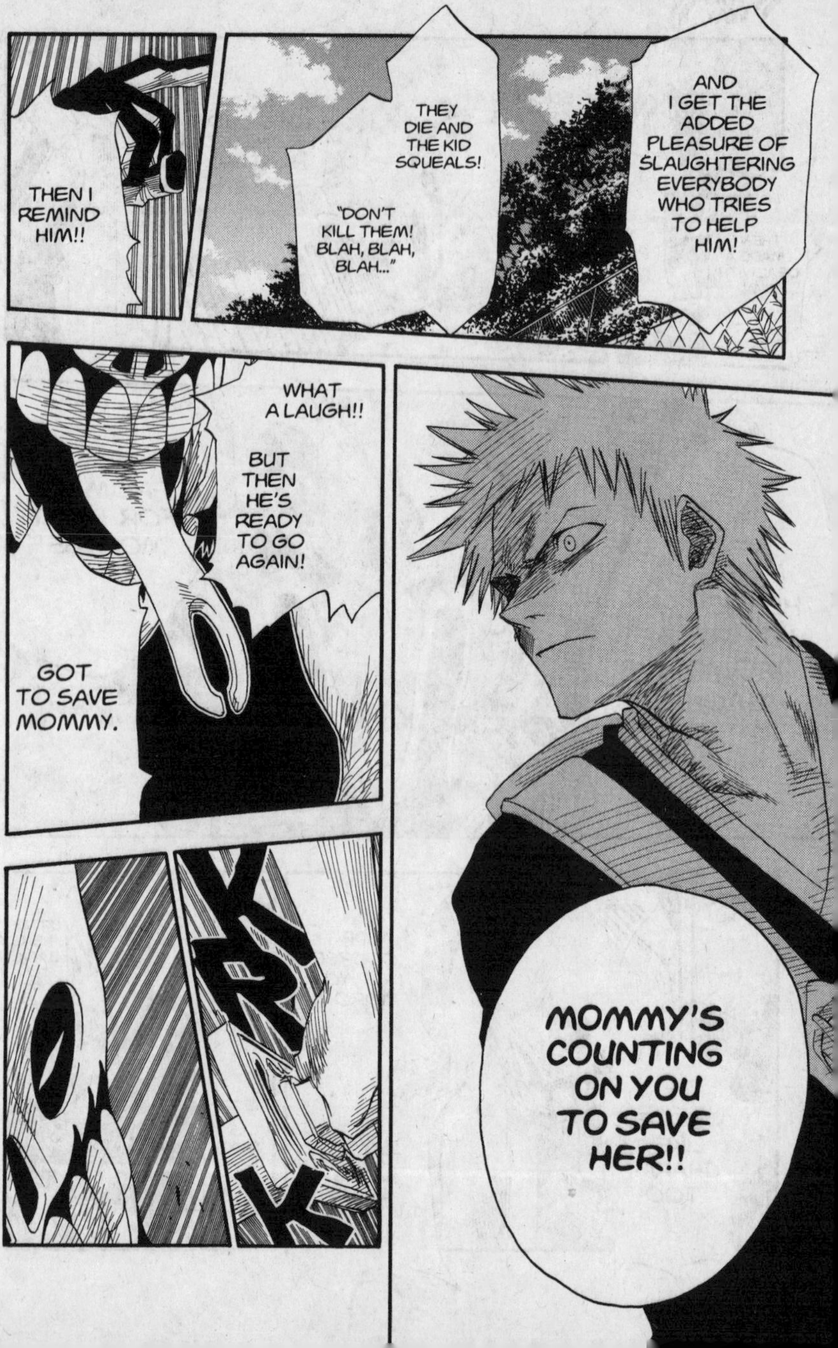
AND I GET THE ADDED PLEASURE OF SLAUGHTERING EVERYBODY WHO TRIES TO HELP HIM!
THEY DIE AND THE KID SQUEALS!
"DON'T KILL THEM! BLAH, BLAH, BLAH..."
THEN I REMIND HIM!!
MOMMY'S COUNTING ON YOU TO SAVE HER!!
WHAT A LAUGH!!
BUT THEN HE'S READY TO GO AGAIN!
GOT TO SAVE MOMMY.

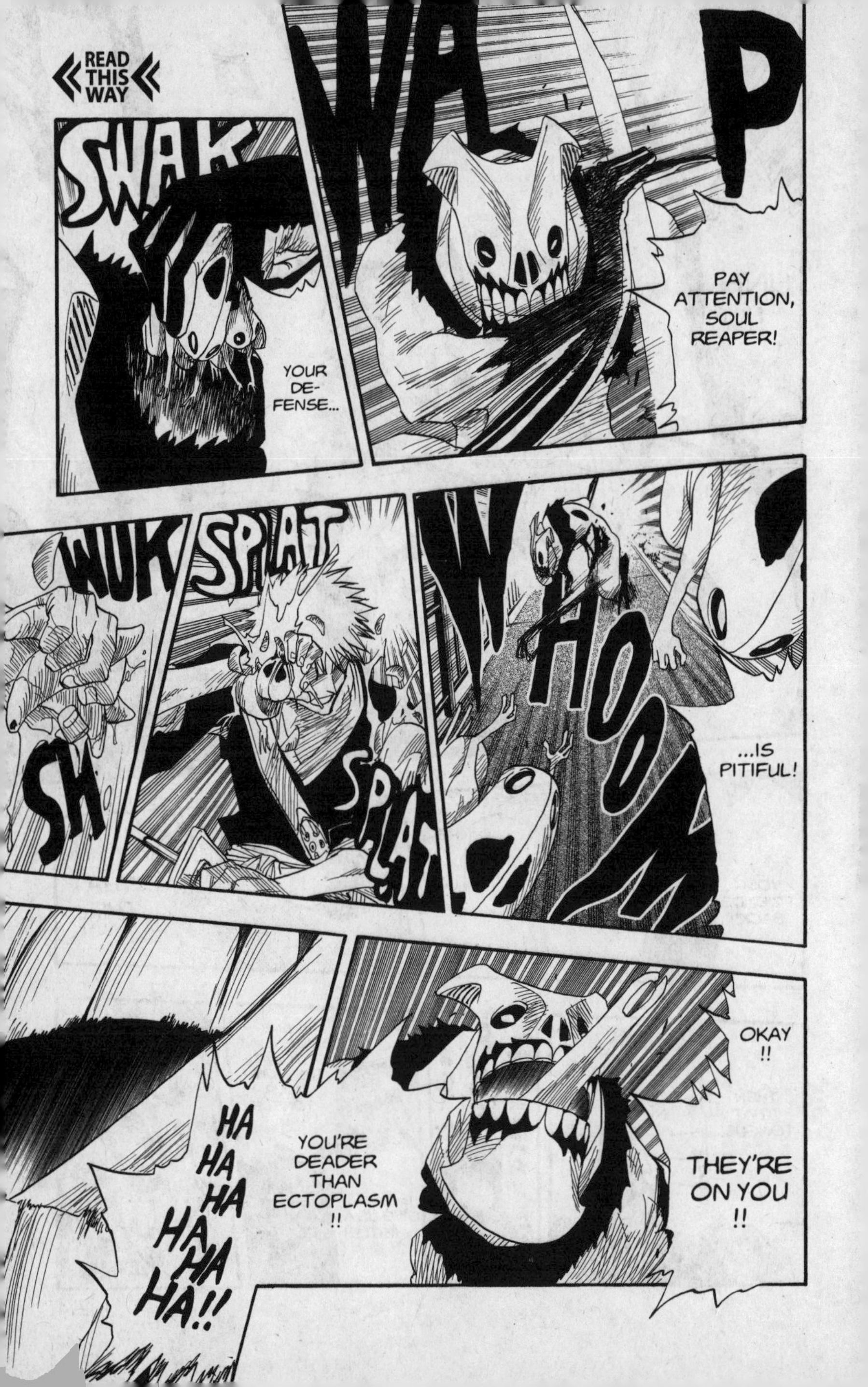
READ THIS WAY
WAP
PAY ATTENTION, SOUL REAPER!
SWAK
YOUR DE-FENSE...
WHOOM
...IS PITIFUL!
SPLAT
SPLAT
WUK
SH
OKAY !!
THEY'RE ON YOU !!
YOU'RE DEADER THAN ECTOPLASM !!
HA HA HA HA HA HA!!

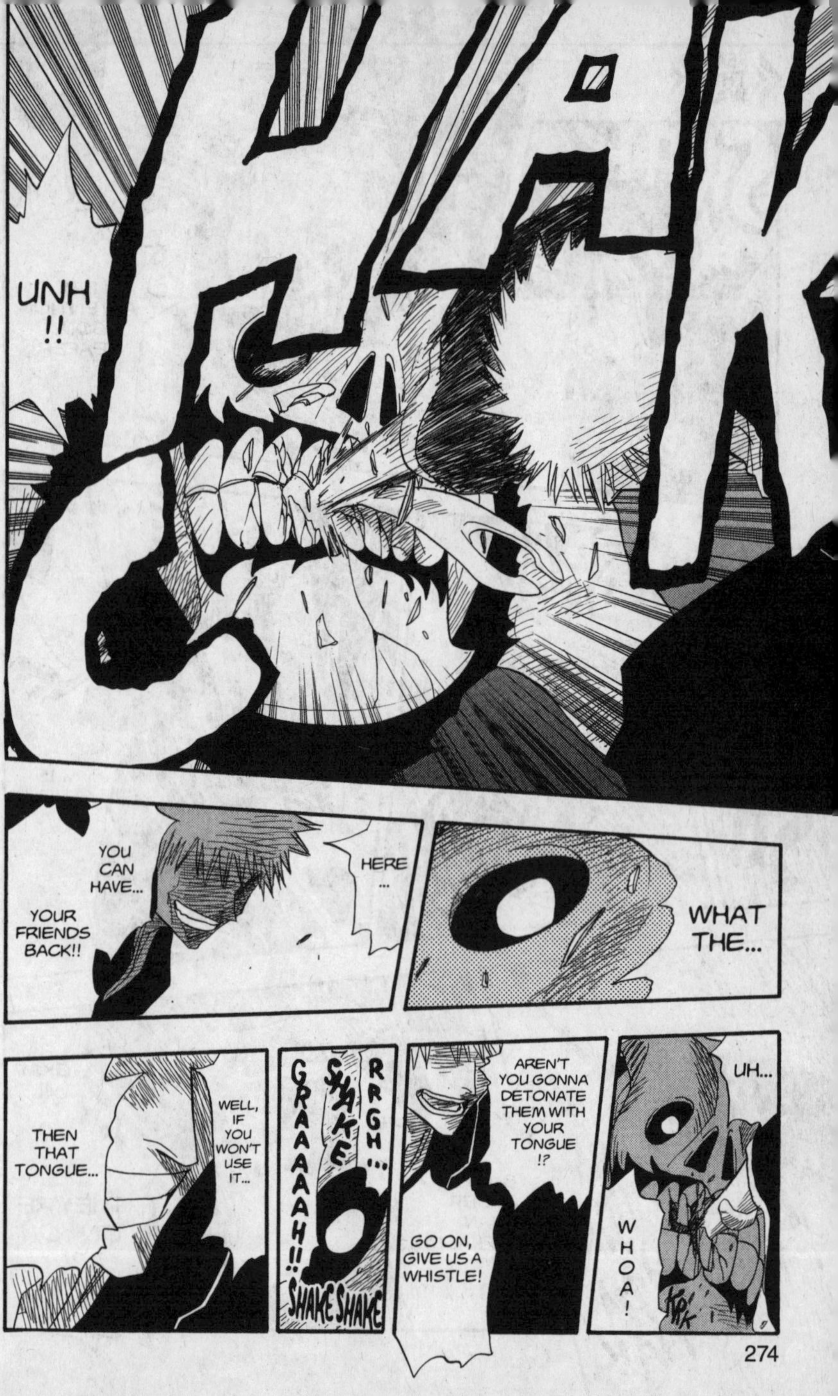

UNH !!
WHAT THE...
HERE...
YOU CAN HAVE...
YOUR FRIENDS BACK!!
UH...
WHOA!
AREN'T YOU GONNA DETONATE THEM WITH YOUR TONGUE !?
GO ON, GIVE US A WHISTLE!
RRGH...
SHAKE
GRAAAAAAAH!!
SHAKE SHAKE
WELL, IF YOU WON'T USE IT...
THEN THAT TONGUE...

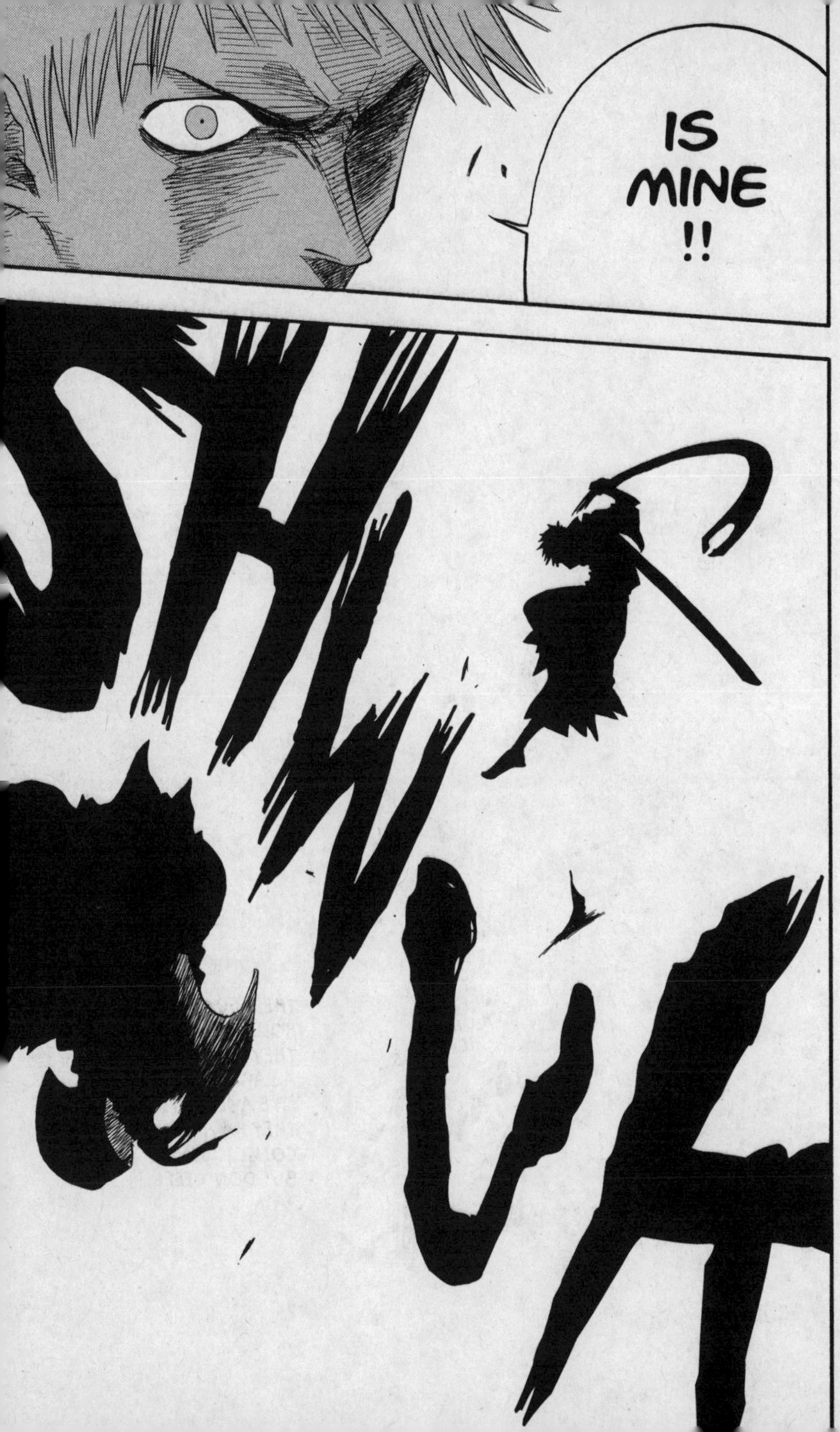
IS MINE !!
SHWUH

UH-OH.
THE TONGUE...

THESE GUYS AREN'T HOLLOWS. THEY'RE PARTS OF A LARGER ENTITY, LIKE A SECRETION. THEY HAVE SOME CONSCIOUSNESS BUT DON'T FEEL PAIN.

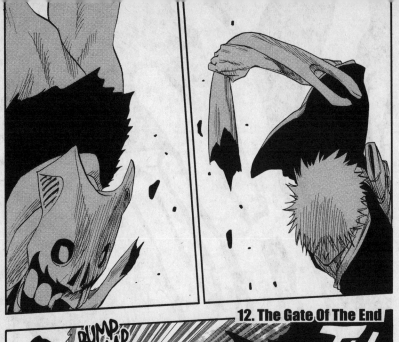

12. The Gate Of The End

GRRAH!!

BUMP BUMP SKRUFF

TUMP

UGH...

YOU RIPPED OUT MY TONGUE!!

YOU THON OF A...!!

URG...

PLOP

PLOP PLOP

KOFF...

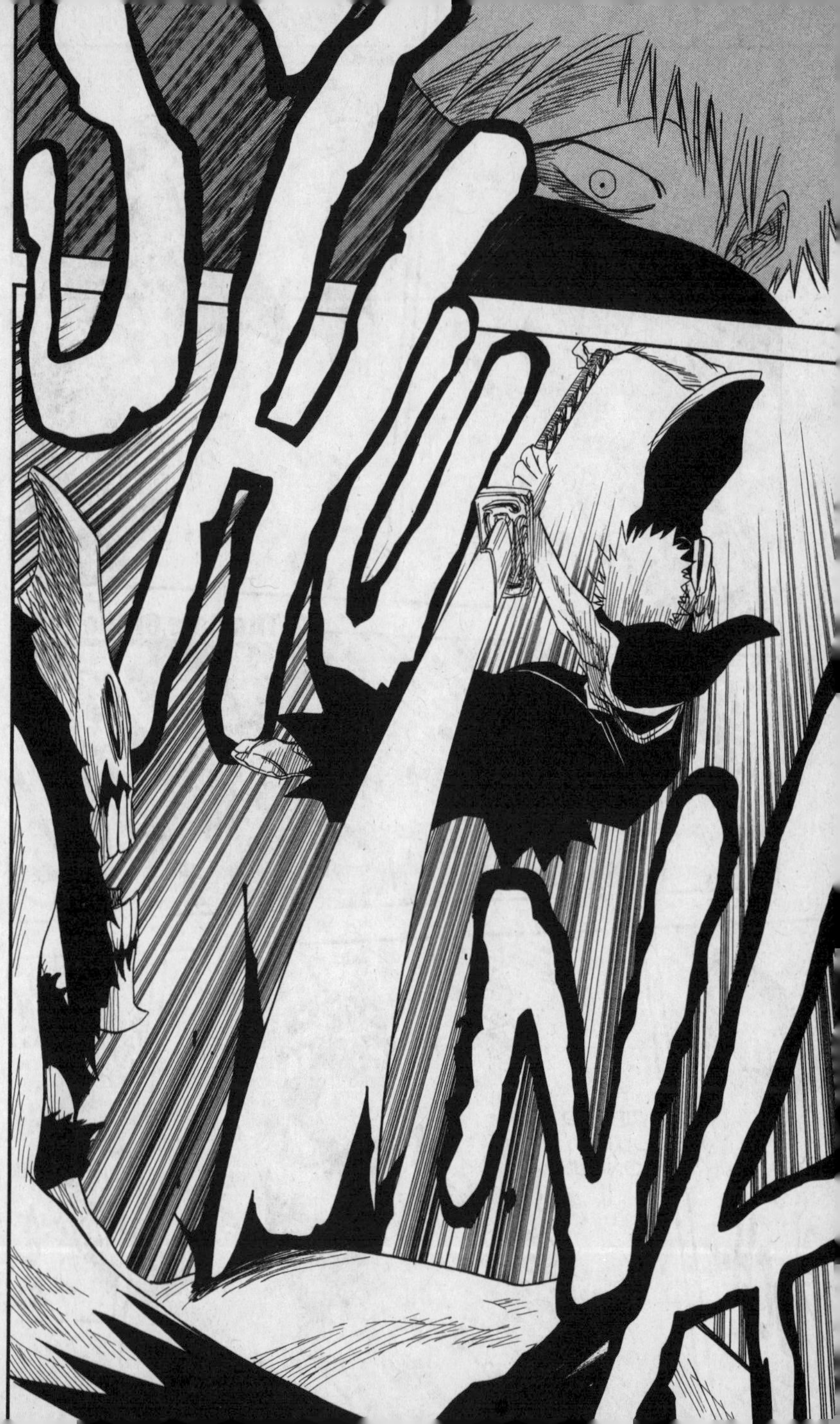

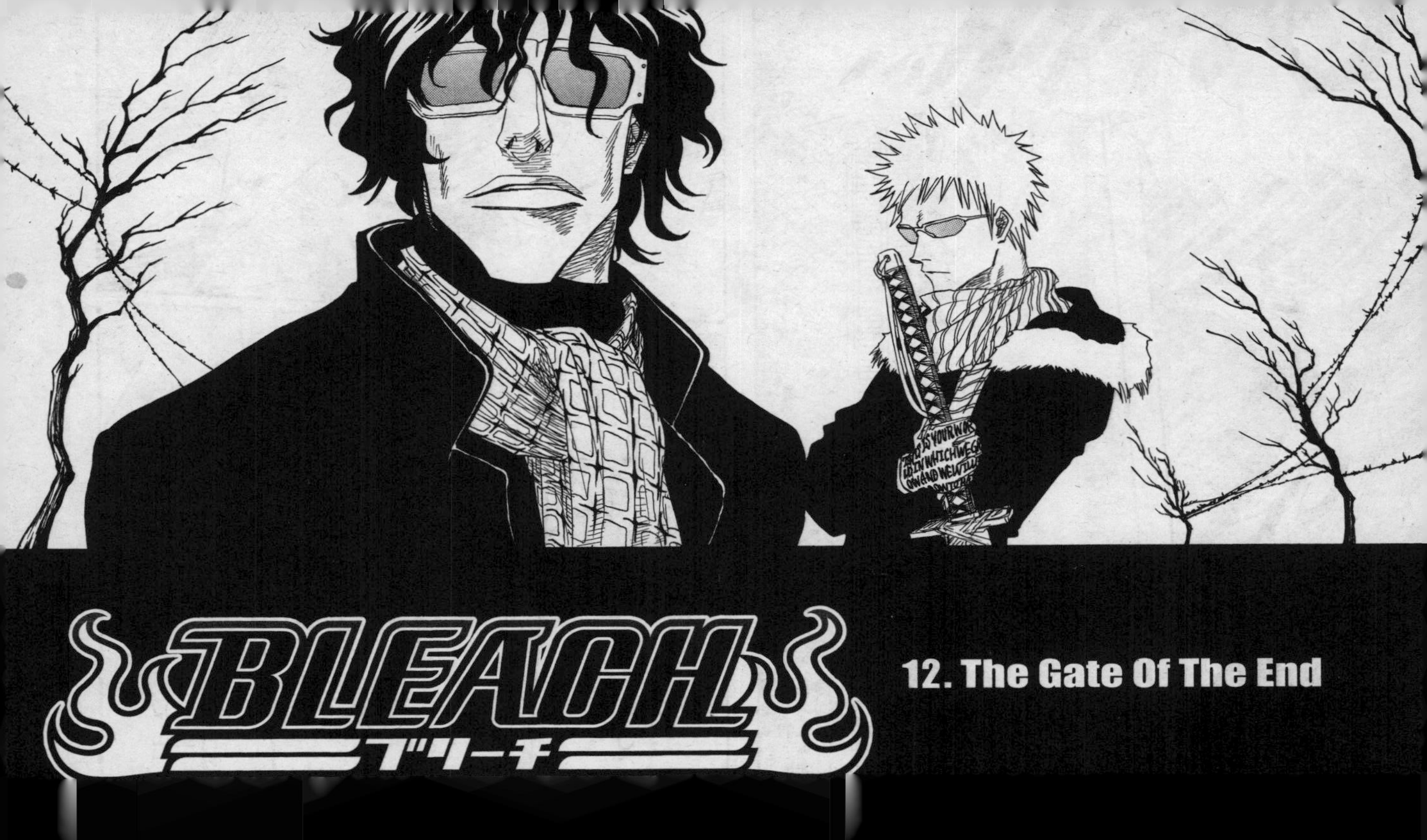

12. The Gate Of The End

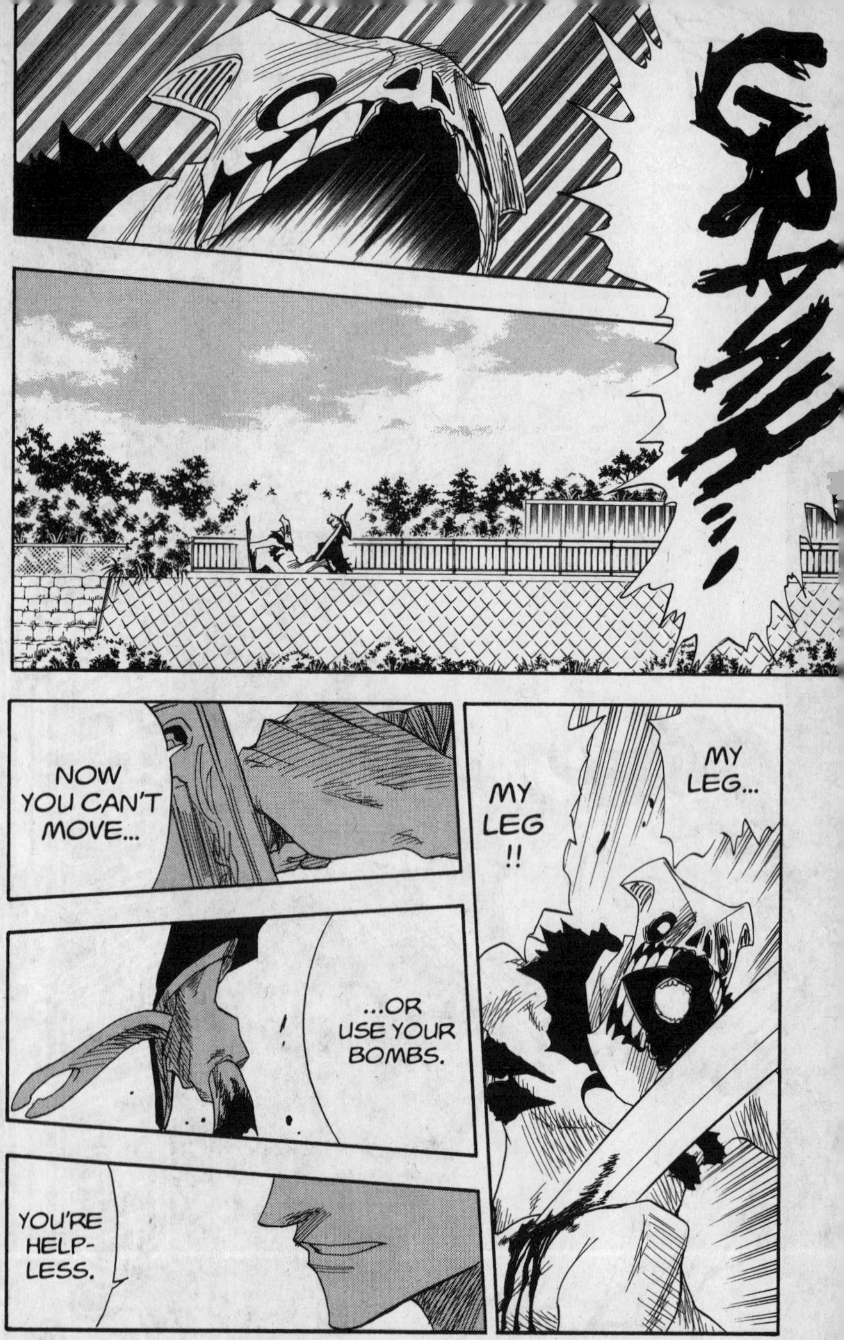
GRAAH...
MY LEG...
MY LEG!!
NOW YOU CAN'T MOVE...
...OR USE YOUR BOMBS.
YOU'RE HELPLESS.

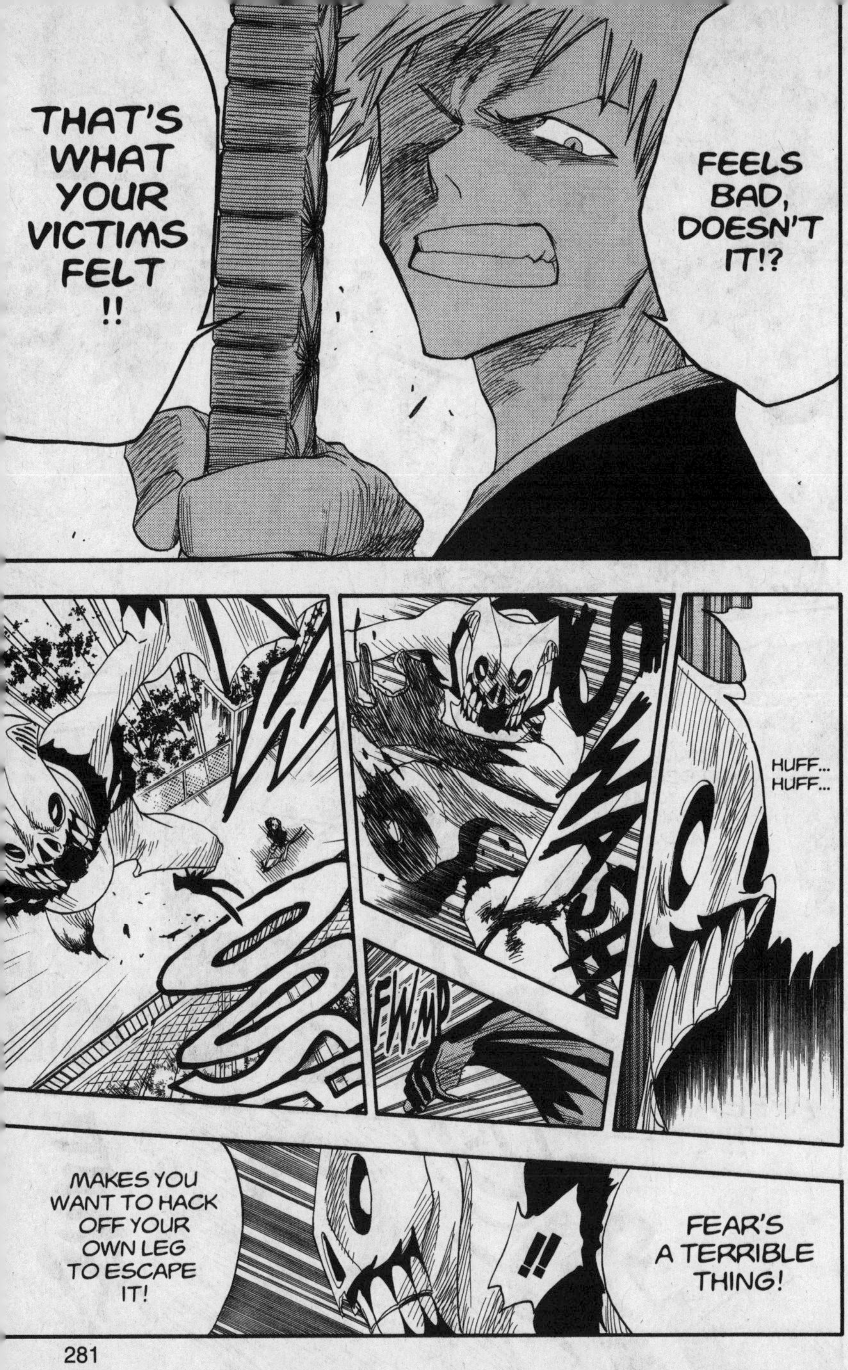
FEELS BAD, DOESN'T IT!?
THAT'S WHAT YOUR VICTIMS FELT!!
HUFF... HUFF...
SWASH
FWMP
FEAR'S A TERRIBLE THING!
!!
MAKES YOU WANT TO HACK OFF YOUR OWN LEG TO ESCAPE IT!

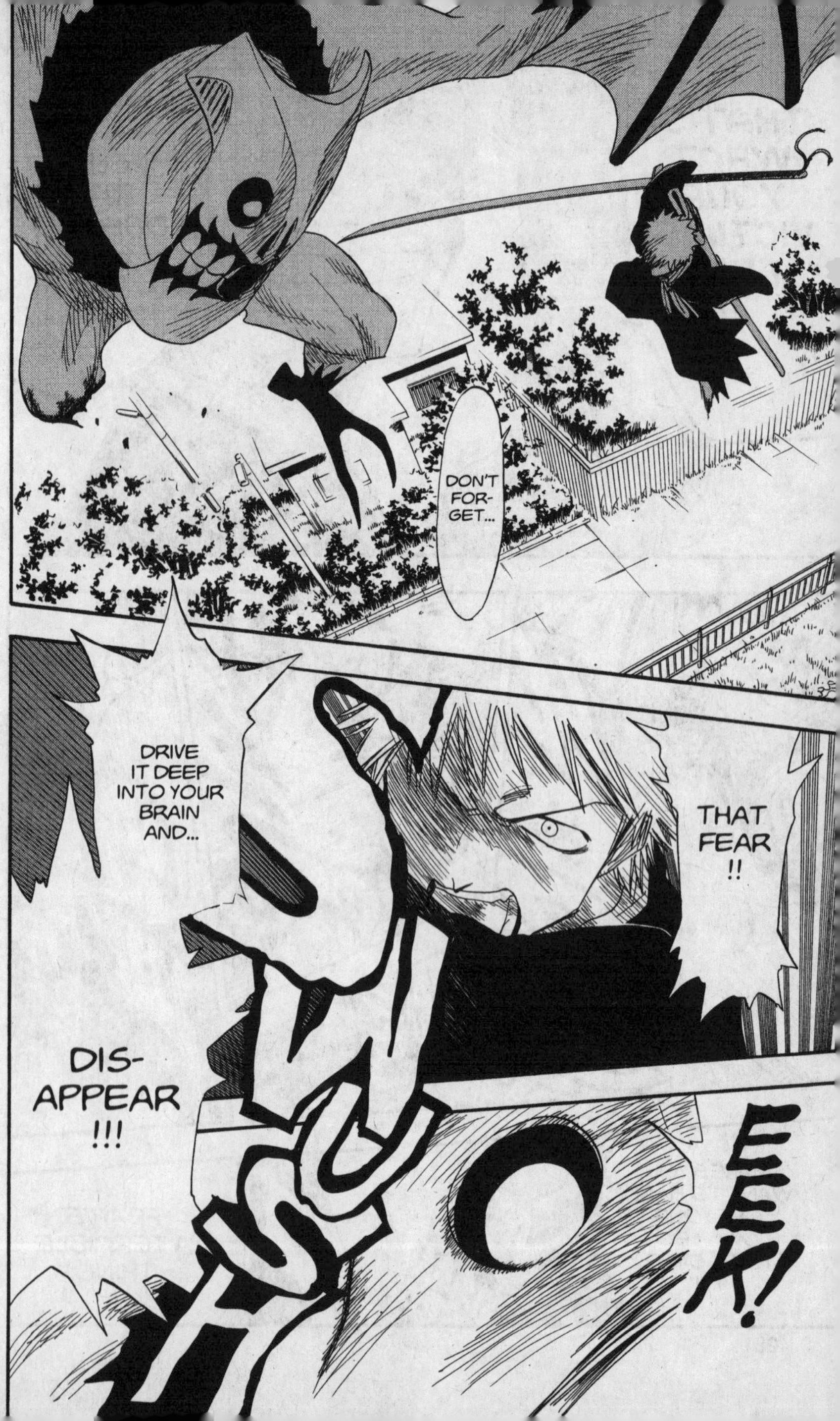
DON'T FORGET...
THAT FEAR!!
DRIVE IT DEEP INTO YOUR BRAIN AND...
EEEK!
DIS-APPEAR!!!

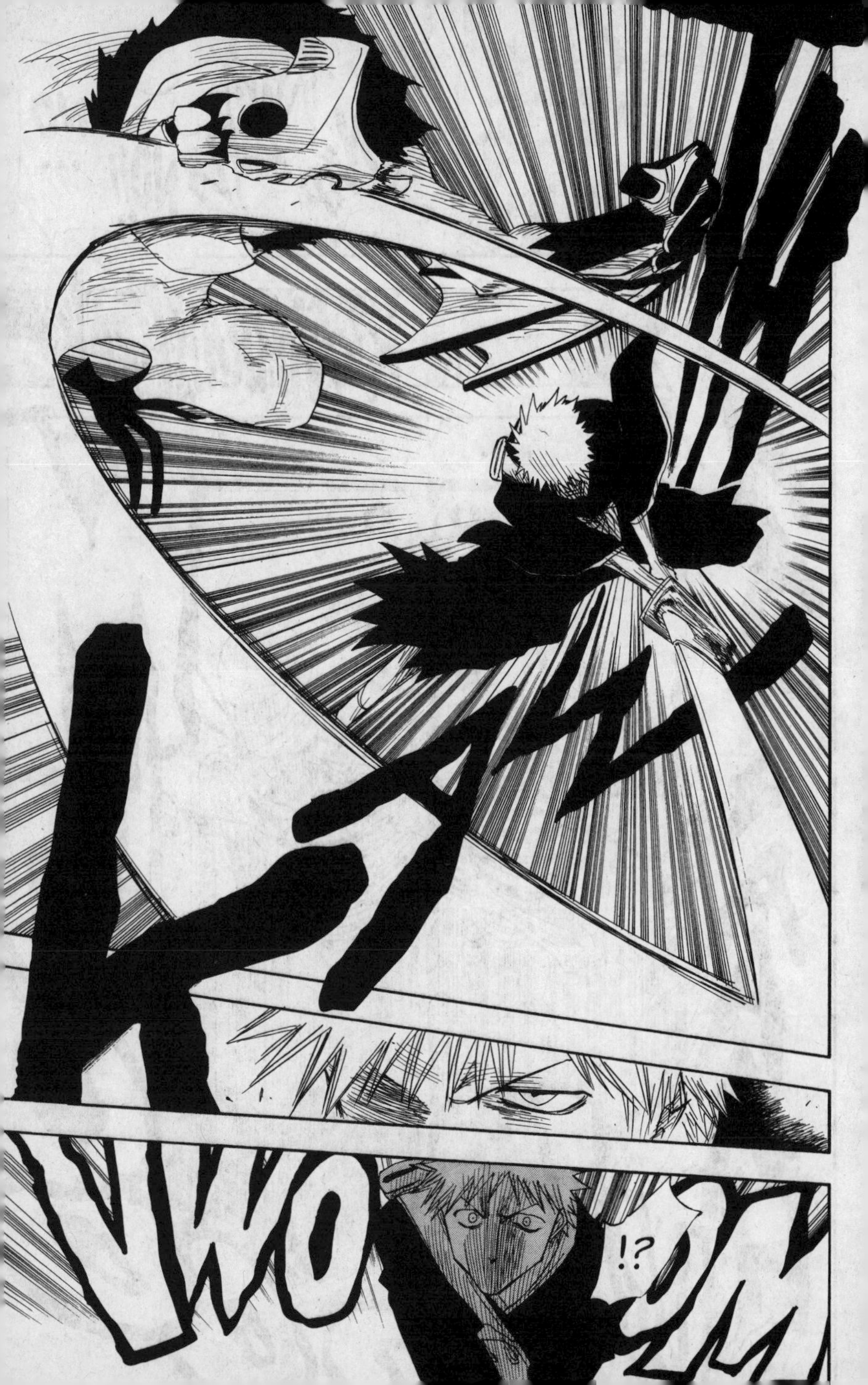
KZZZM
!?
VWOOM

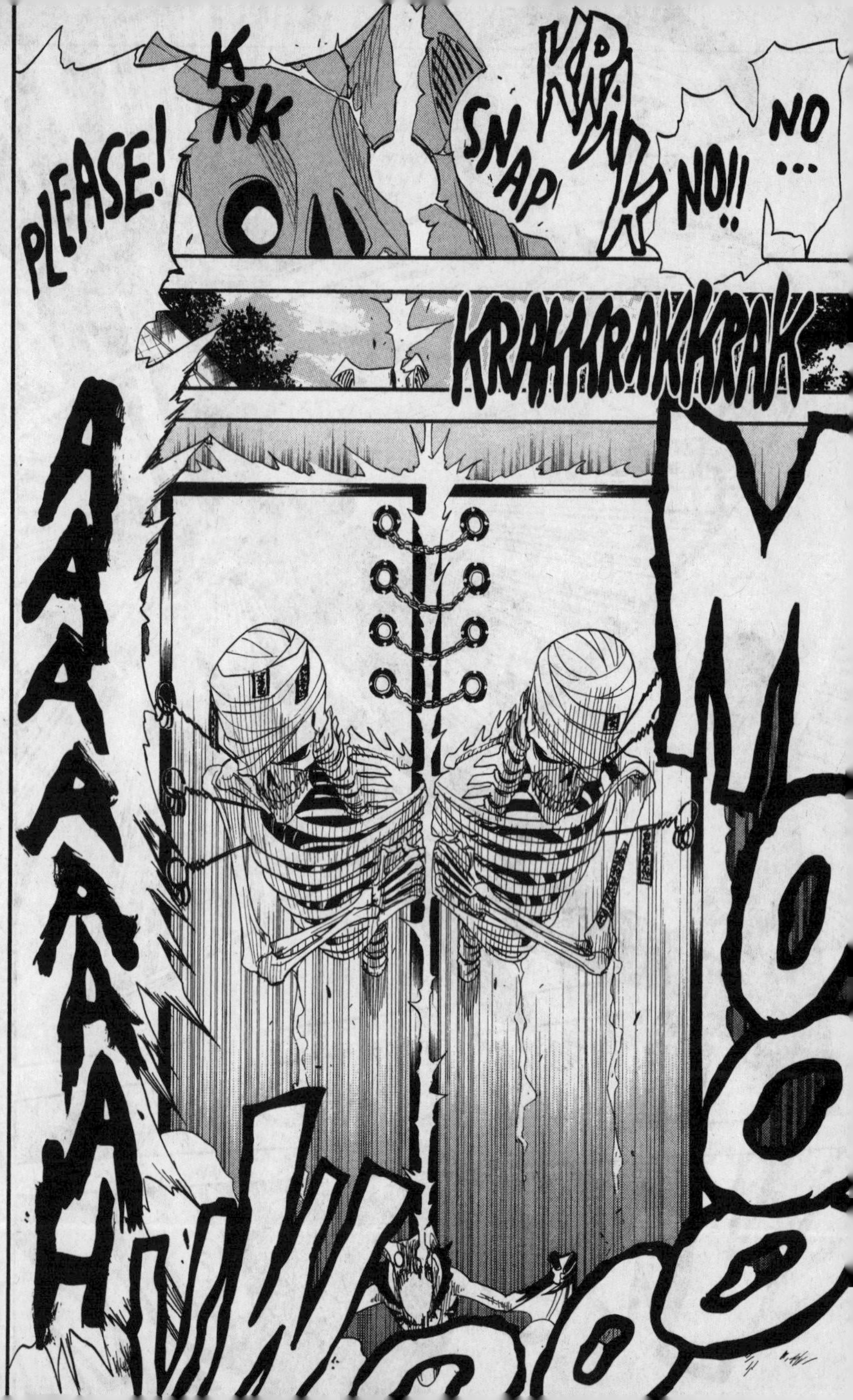
NO...
NO!!
KRAKK
SNAP
KRK
RK
PLEASE!
KRAKKRAKKRAK
VUOOOOO
AAAAAAAAAH!!

READ THIS WAY

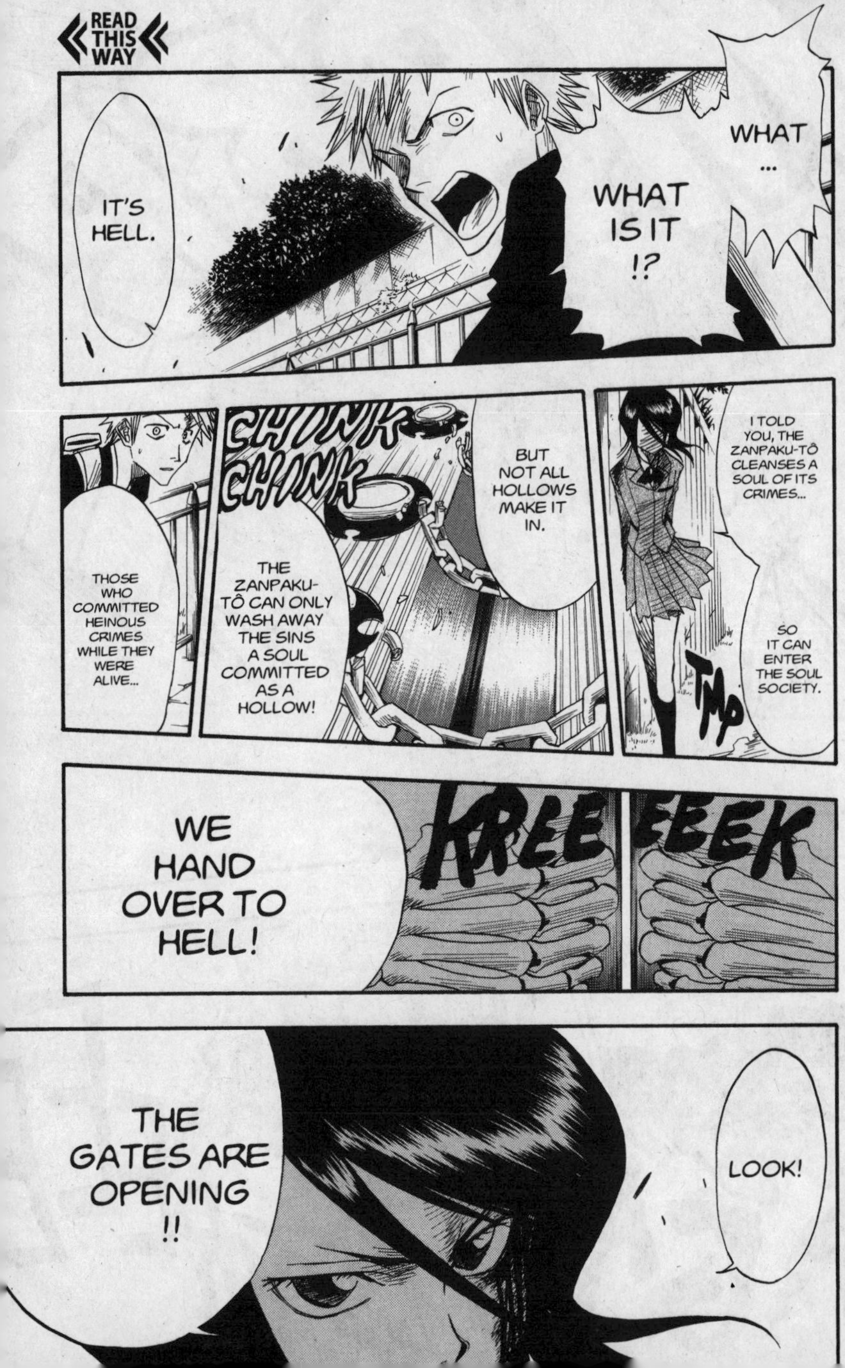
WHAT ...
WHAT IS IT !?
IT'S HELL.
I TOLD YOU, THE ZANPAKU-TÔ CLEANSES A SOUL OF ITS CRIMES...
SO IT CAN ENTER THE SOUL SOCIETY.
TMP
BUT NOT ALL HOLLOWS MAKE IT IN.
CHINK
CHINK
THE ZANPAKU-TÔ CAN ONLY WASH AWAY THE SINS A SOUL COMMITTED AS A HOLLOW!
THOSE WHO COMMITTED HEINOUS CRIMES WHILE THEY WERE ALIVE...
KREEEEEK
WE HAND OVER TO HELL!
LOOK!
THE GATES ARE OPENING !!

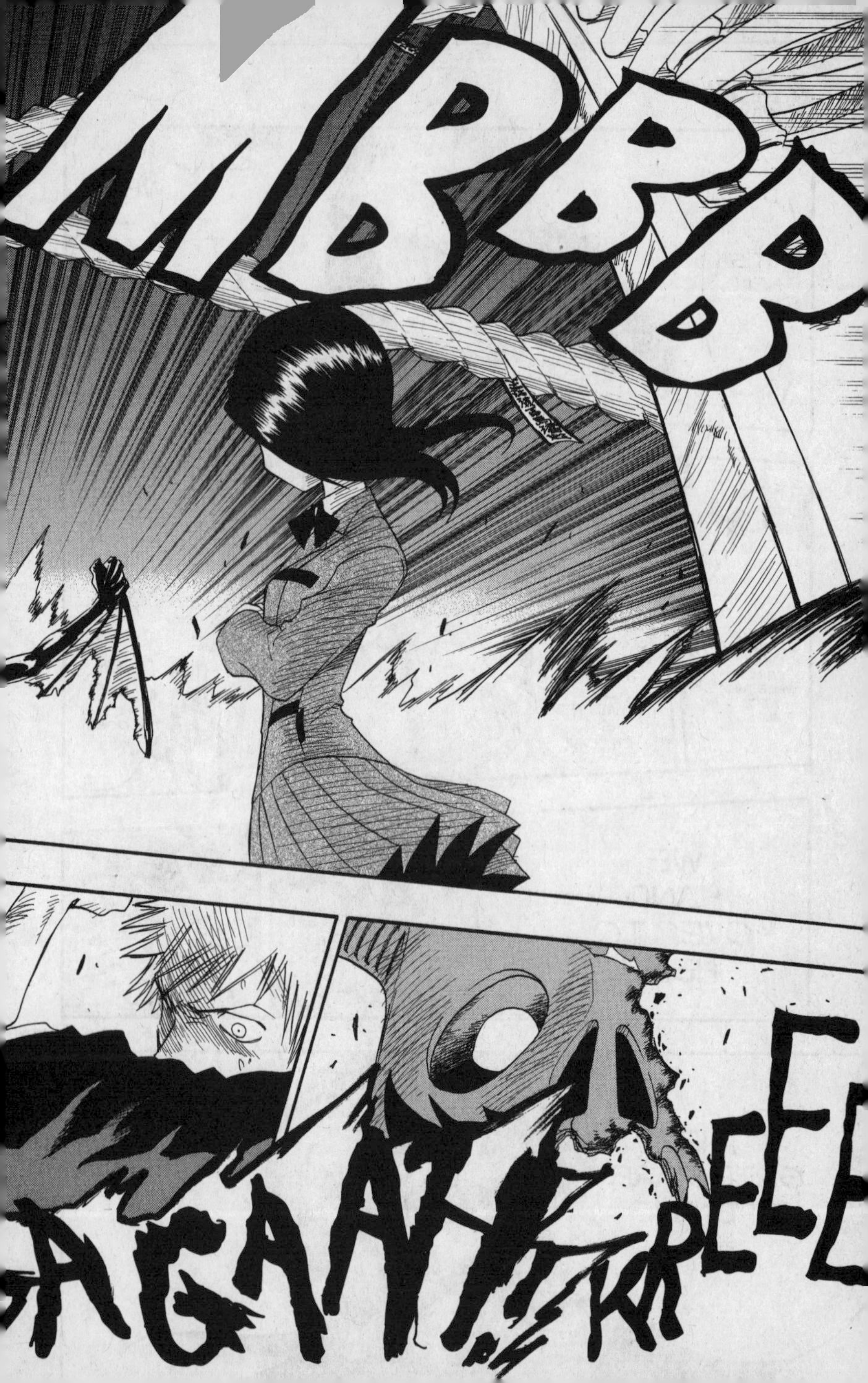

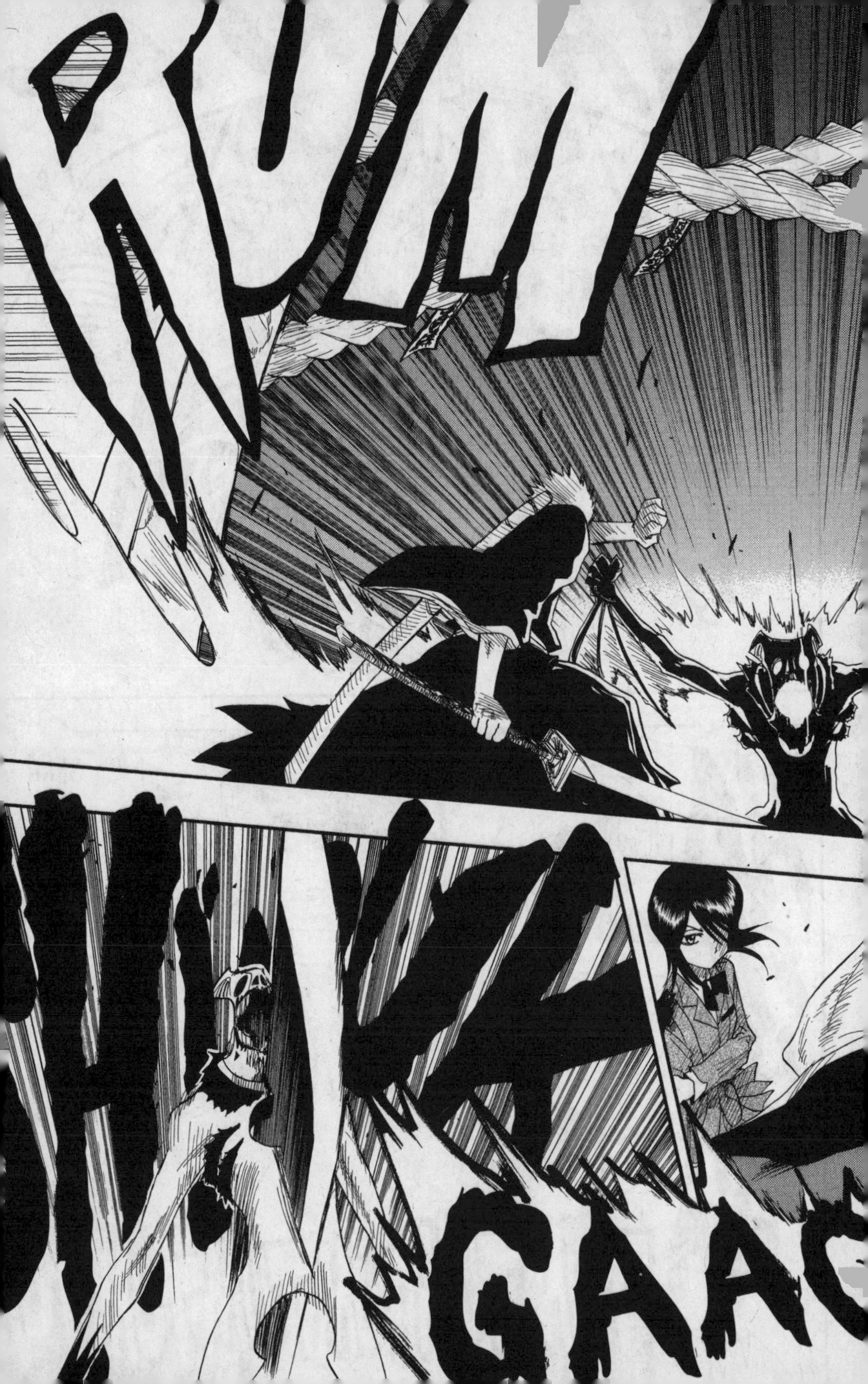

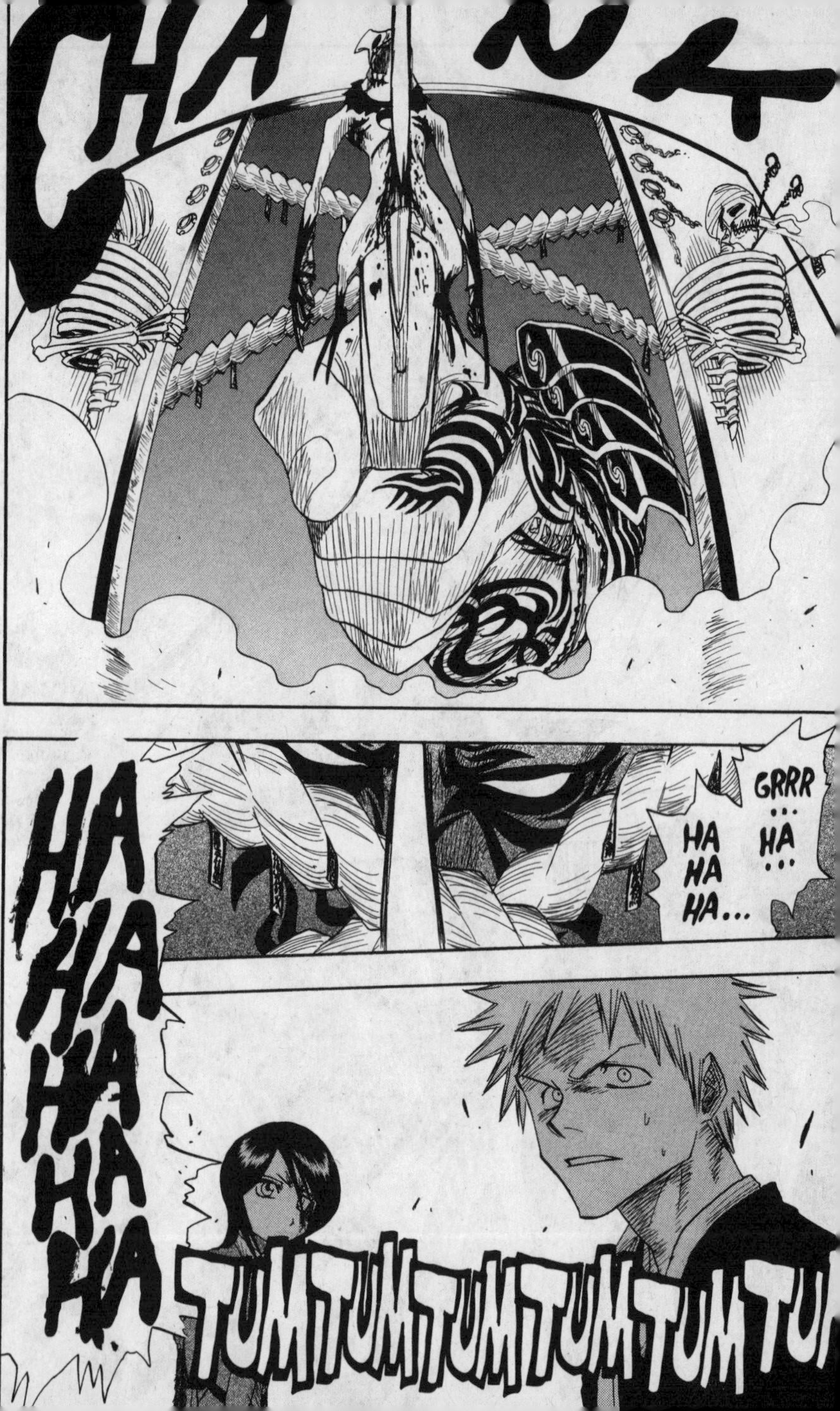
CHANK
GRRR... HA!...
HA HA HA...
HA HA HA HA HA HA HA HA
TUM TUM TUM TUM TUM TU

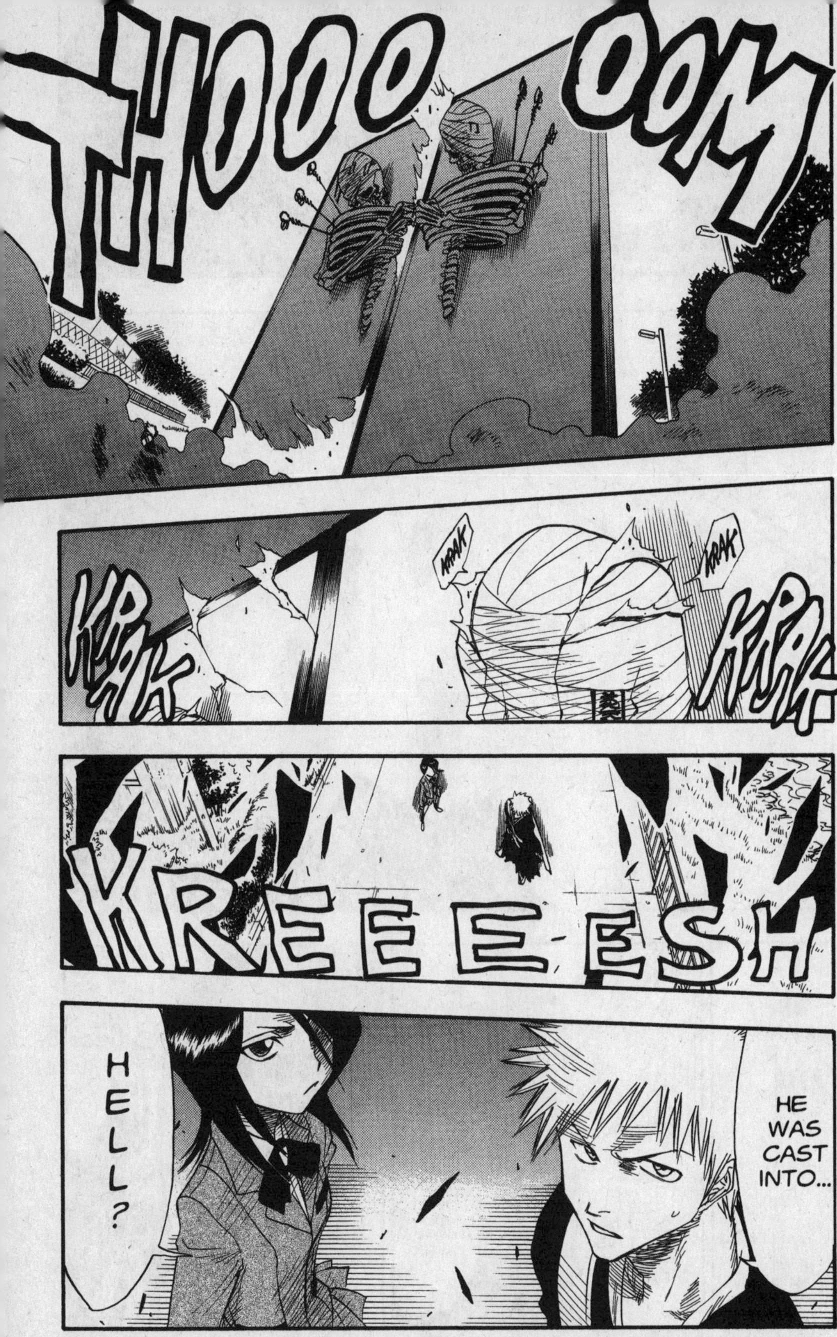
THOOOOOM
KRAK
KRAK
KRAK
KRAK
KREEESH
HE WAS CAST INTO...
HELL?

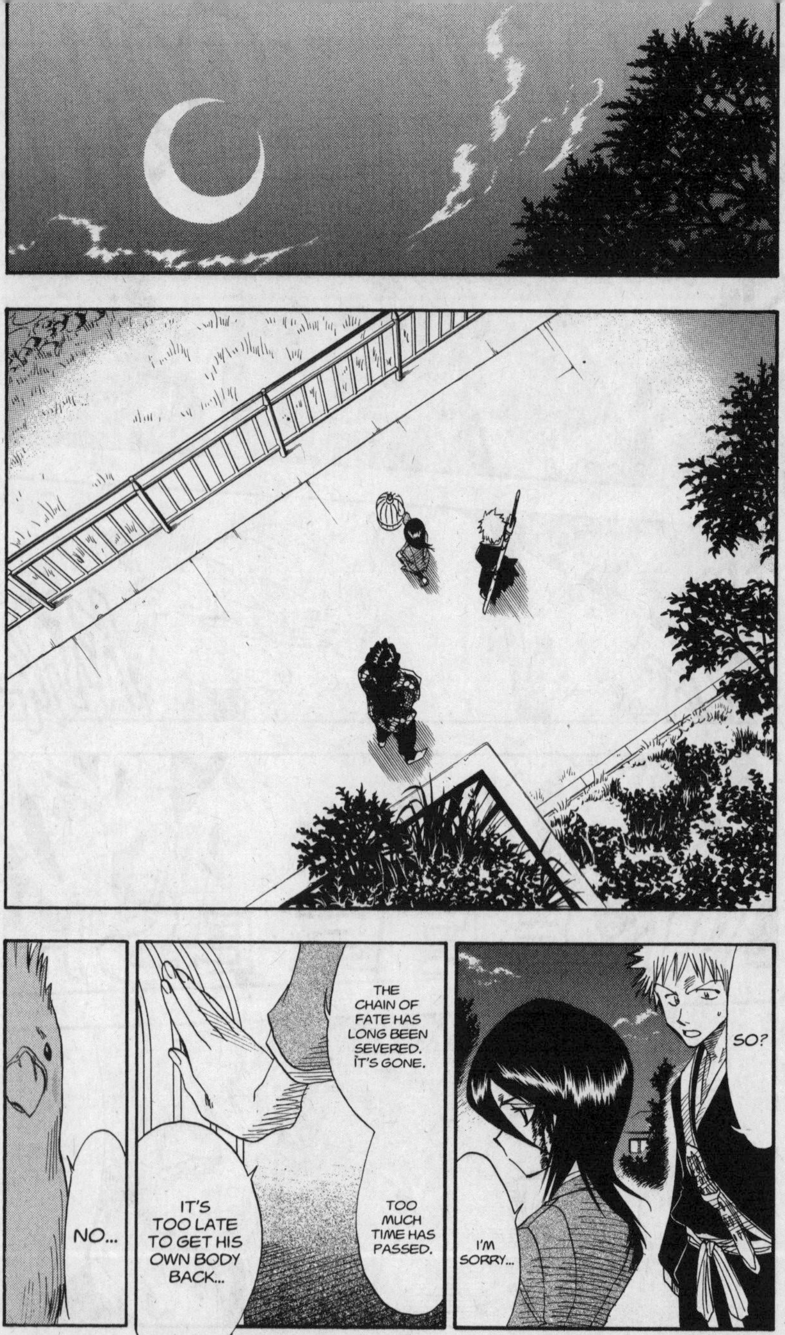
SO?
I'M SORRY...
THE CHAIN OF FATE HAS LONG BEEN SEVERED. IT'S GONE.
TOO MUCH TIME HAS PASSED.
IT'S TOO LATE TO GET HIS OWN BODY BACK...
NO...

READ THIS WAY

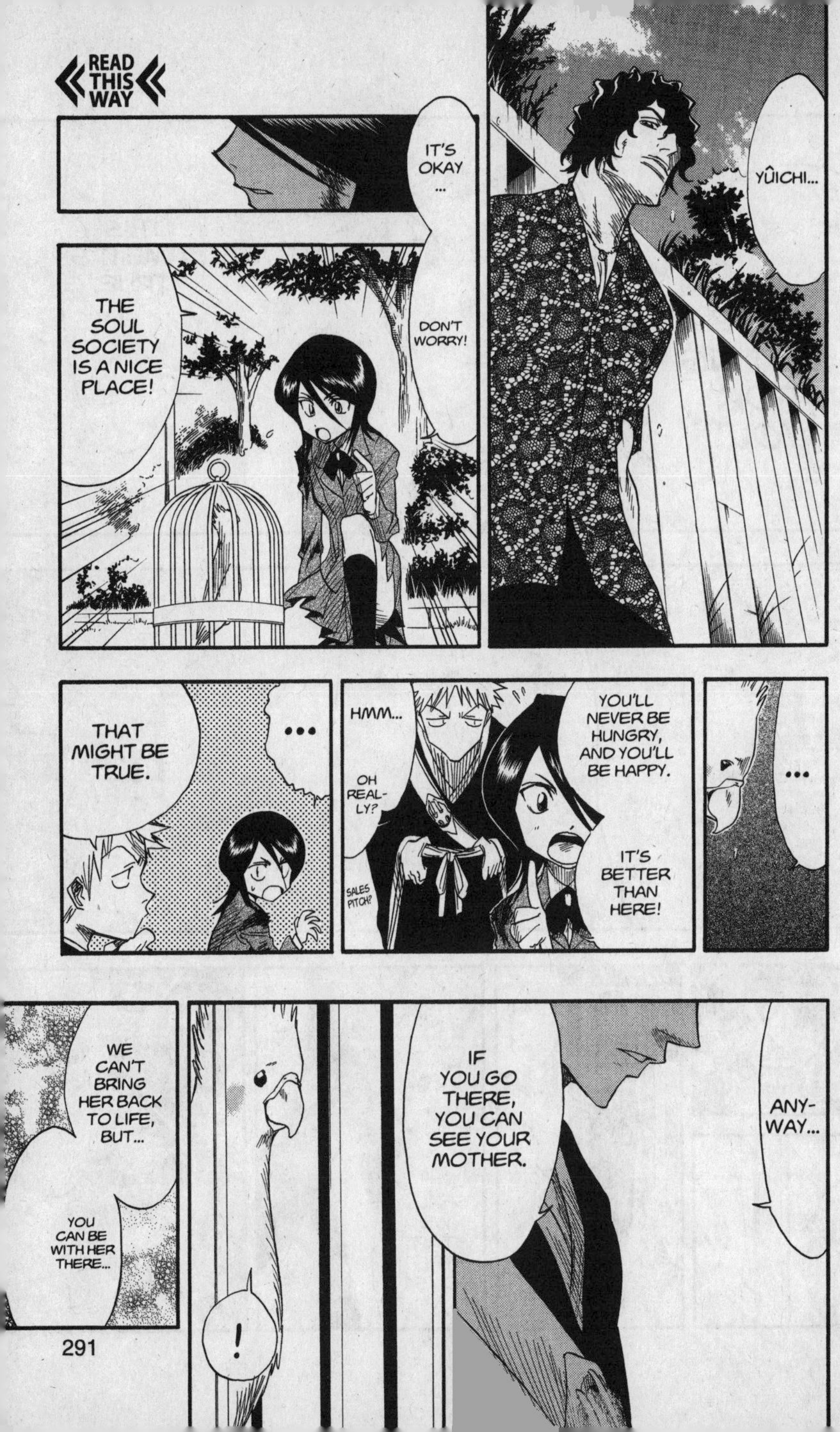
YÛICHI...
IT'S OKAY...
DON'T WORRY!
THE SOUL SOCIETY IS A NICE PLACE!
...
YOU'LL NEVER BE HUNGRY, AND YOU'LL BE HAPPY.
IT'S BETTER THAN HERE!
HMM...
OH REAL-LY?
SALES PITCH?
...
THAT MIGHT BE TRUE.
ANY-WAY...
IF YOU GO THERE, YOU CAN SEE YOUR MOTHER.
!
WE CAN'T BRING HER BACK TO LIFE, BUT...
YOU CAN BE WITH HER THERE...

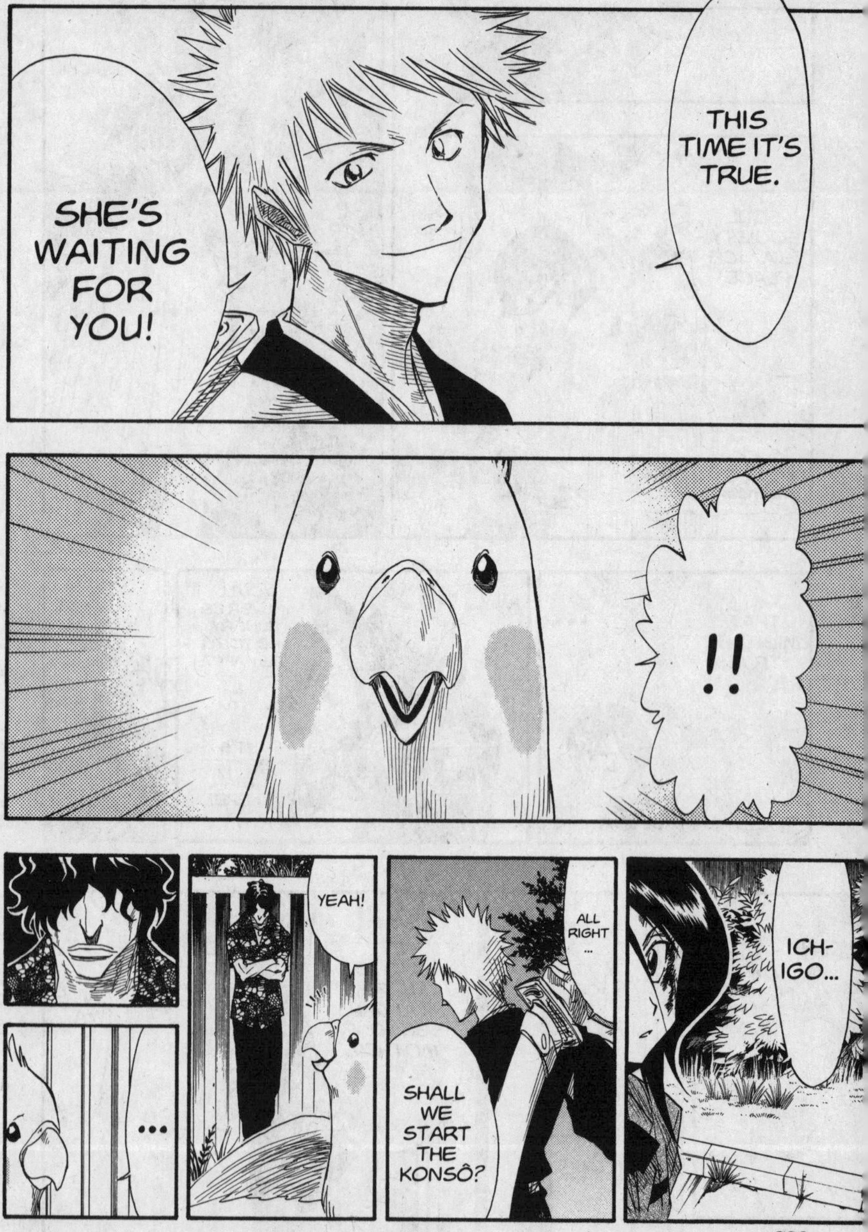
THIS TIME IT'S TRUE.
SHE'S WAITING FOR YOU!
!!
ICH-IGO...
ALL RIGHT ...
SHALL WE START THE KONSÔ?
YEAH!
...

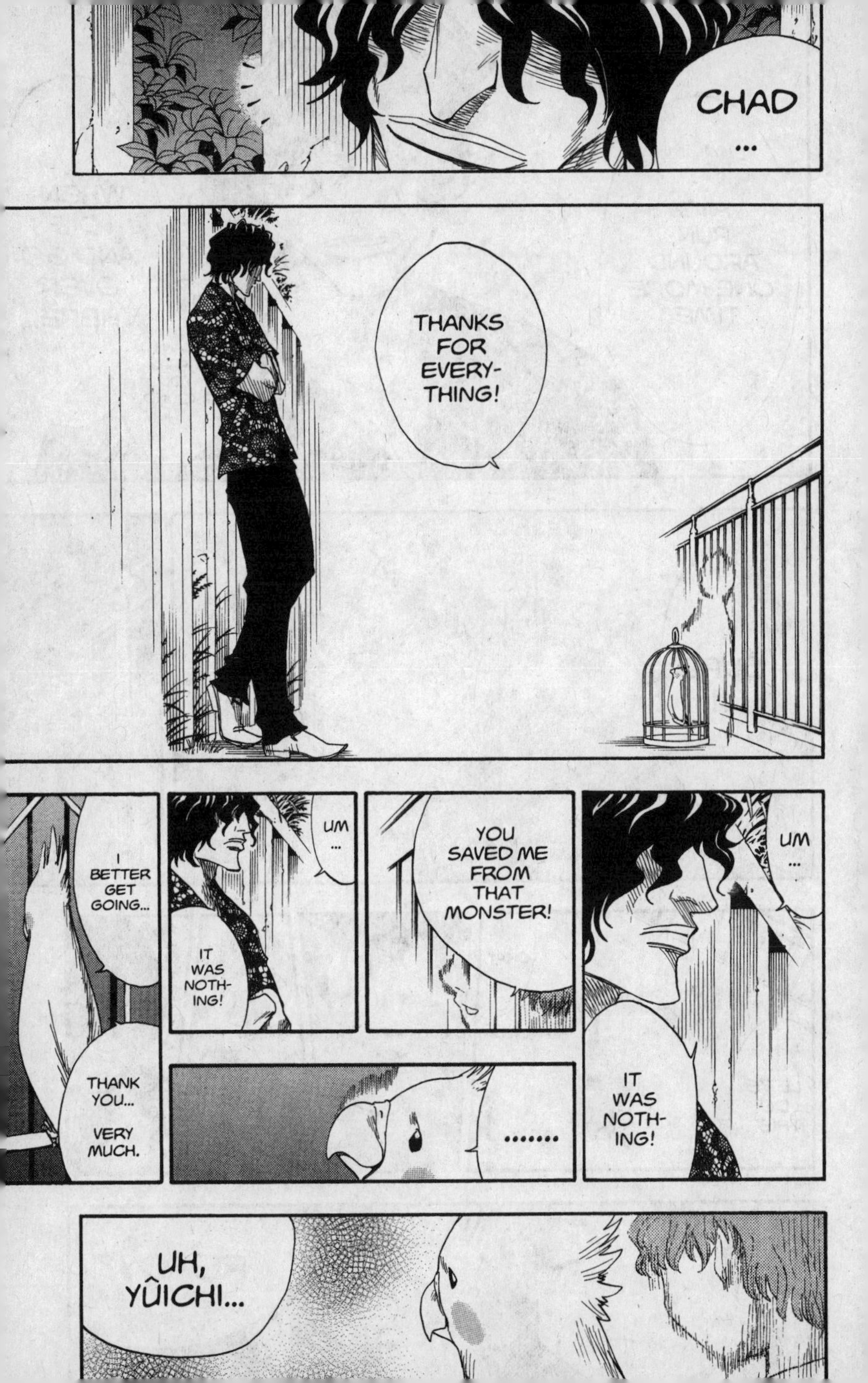
CHAD
...
THANKS FOR EVERY-THING!
UM
...
IT WAS NOTH-ING!
YOU SAVED ME FROM THAT MONSTER!
UM
...
IT WAS NOTH-ING!
....
I BETTER GET GOING...
THANK YOU...
VERY MUCH.
UH, YÛICHI...

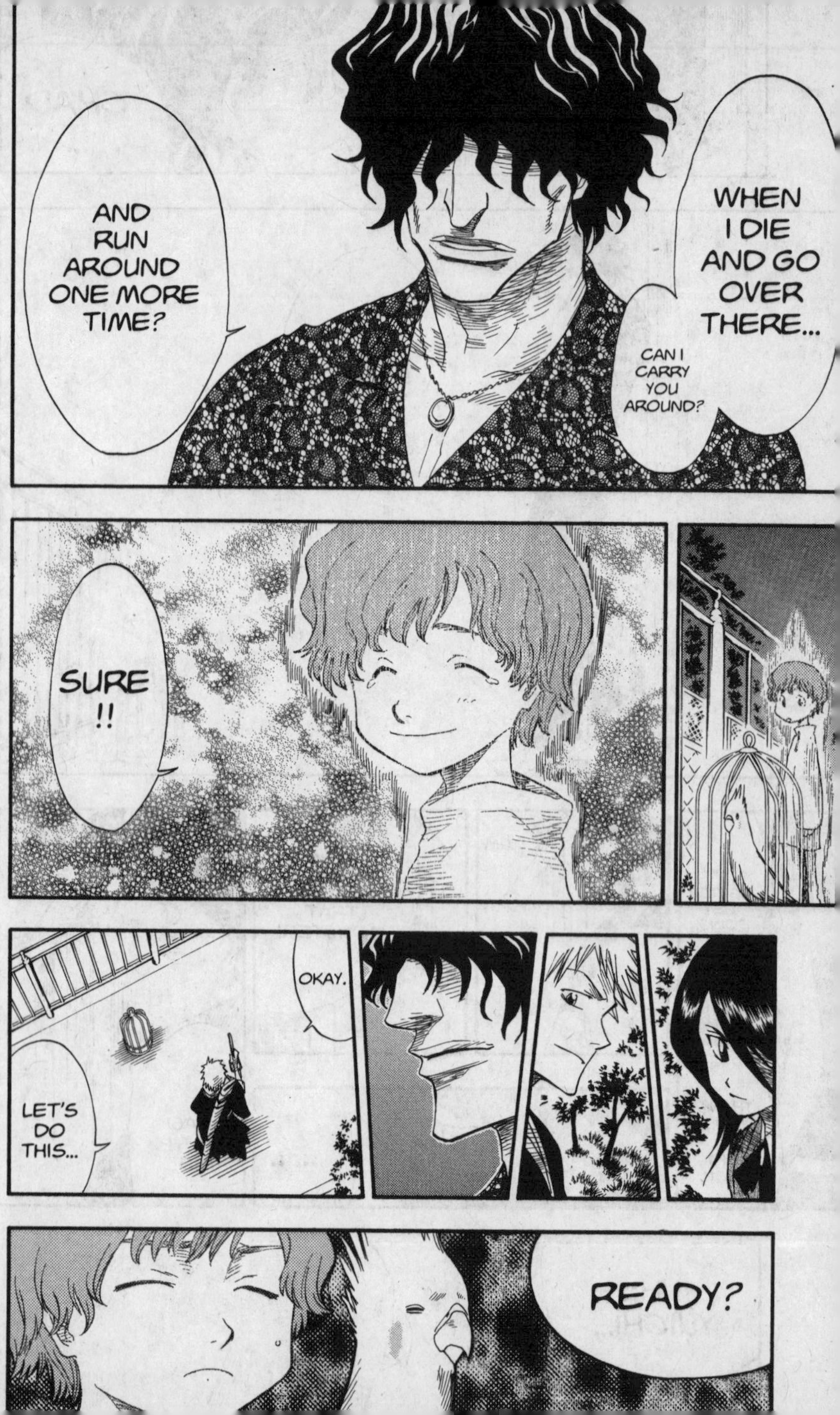
WHEN I DIE AND GO OVER THERE...
CAN I CARRY YOU AROUND?
AND RUN AROUND ONE MORE TIME?
SURE!!
OKAY.
LET'S DO THIS...
READY?

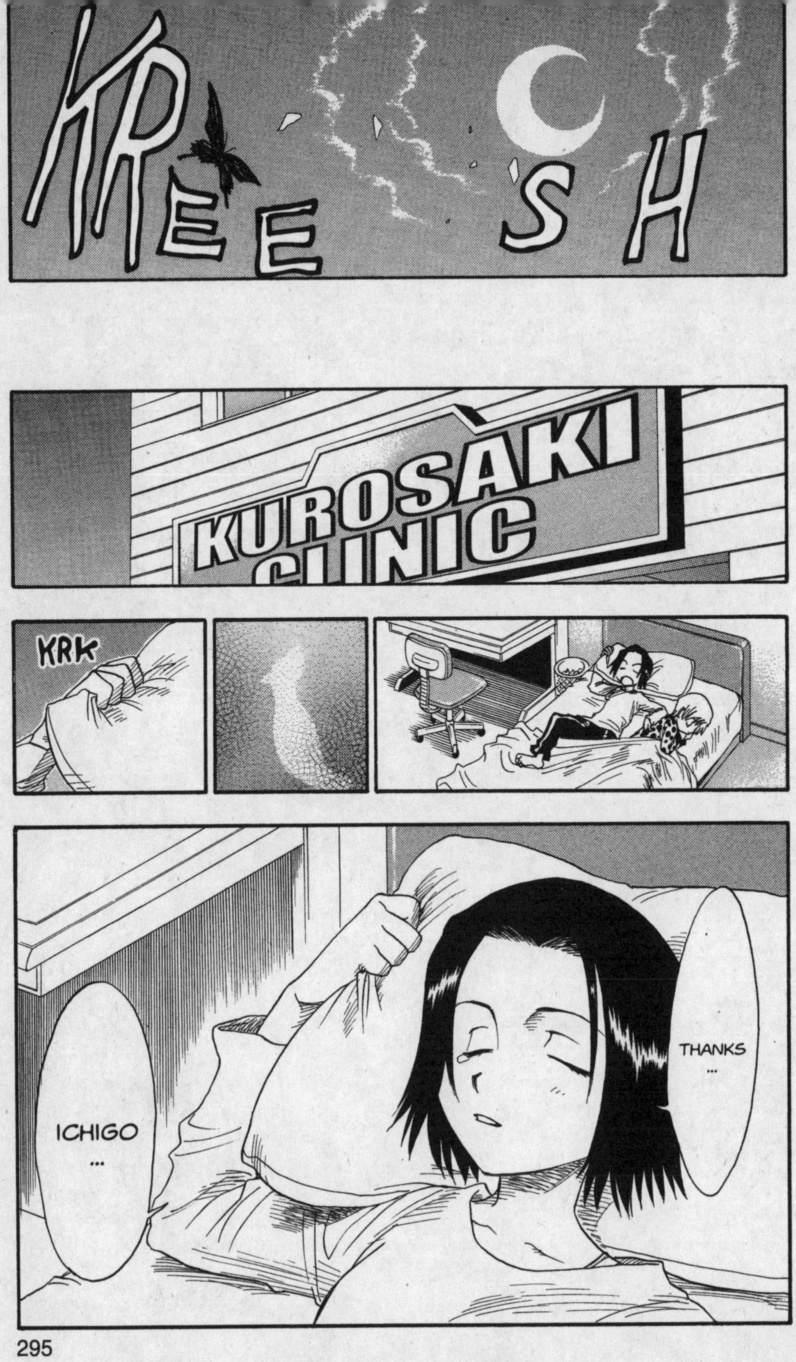
KREESH
KUROSAKI CLINIC
KRK
THANKS ...
ICHIGO ...

13. BAD STANDARD

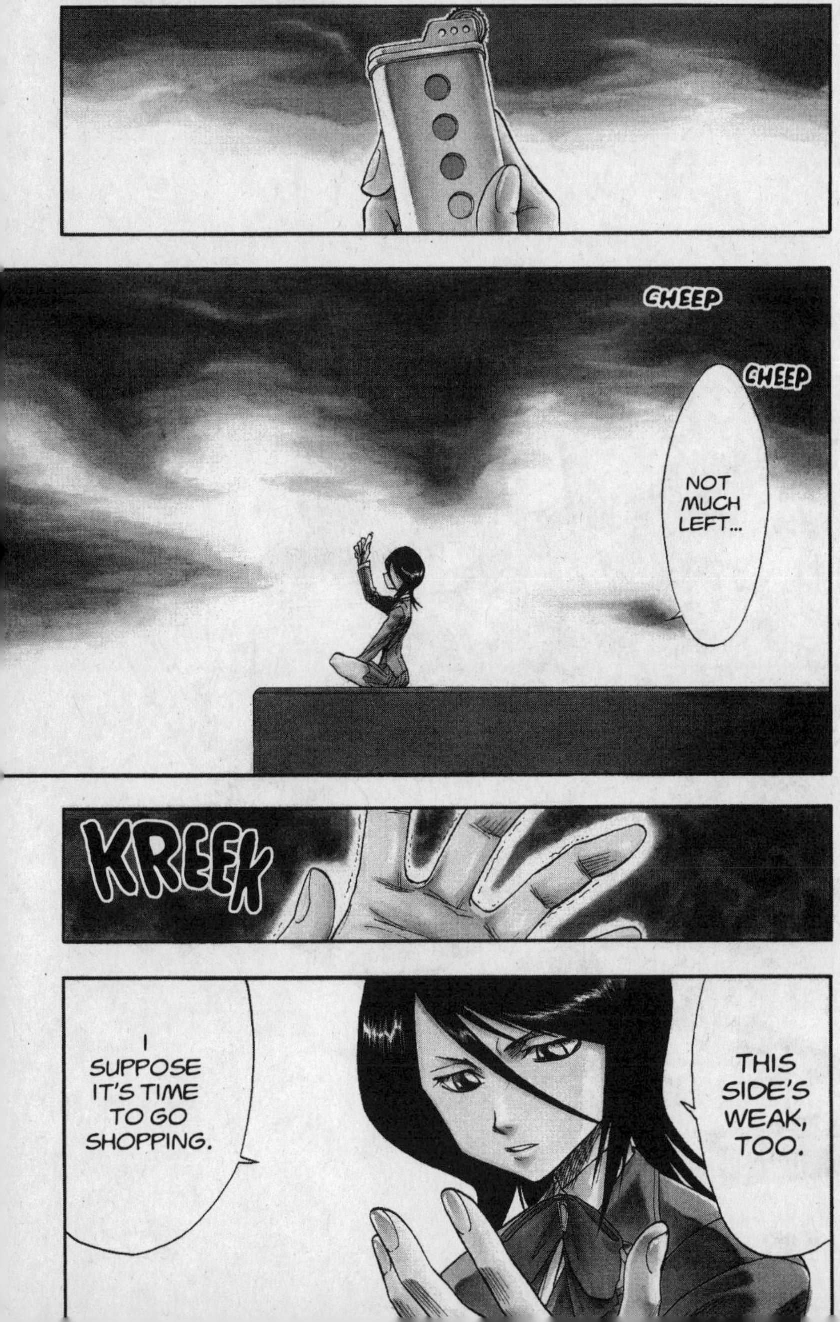
CHEEP
CHEEP
NOT MUCH LEFT...
KREEK
THIS SIDE'S WEAK, TOO.
I SUPPOSE IT'S TIME TO GO SHOPPING.

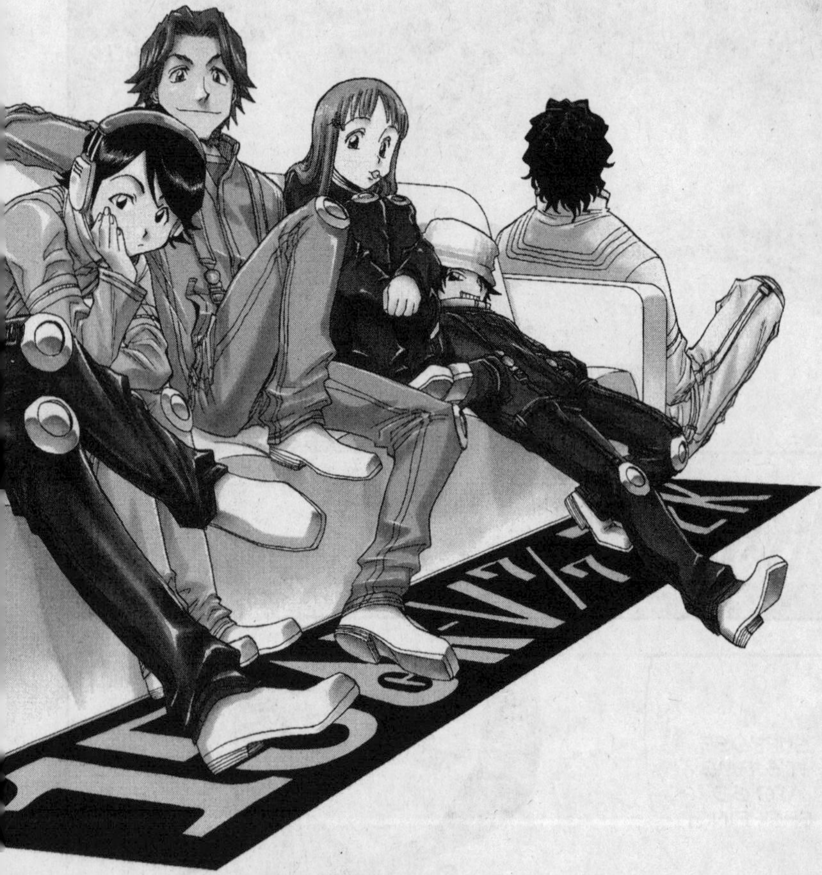

13. BAD STANDARD

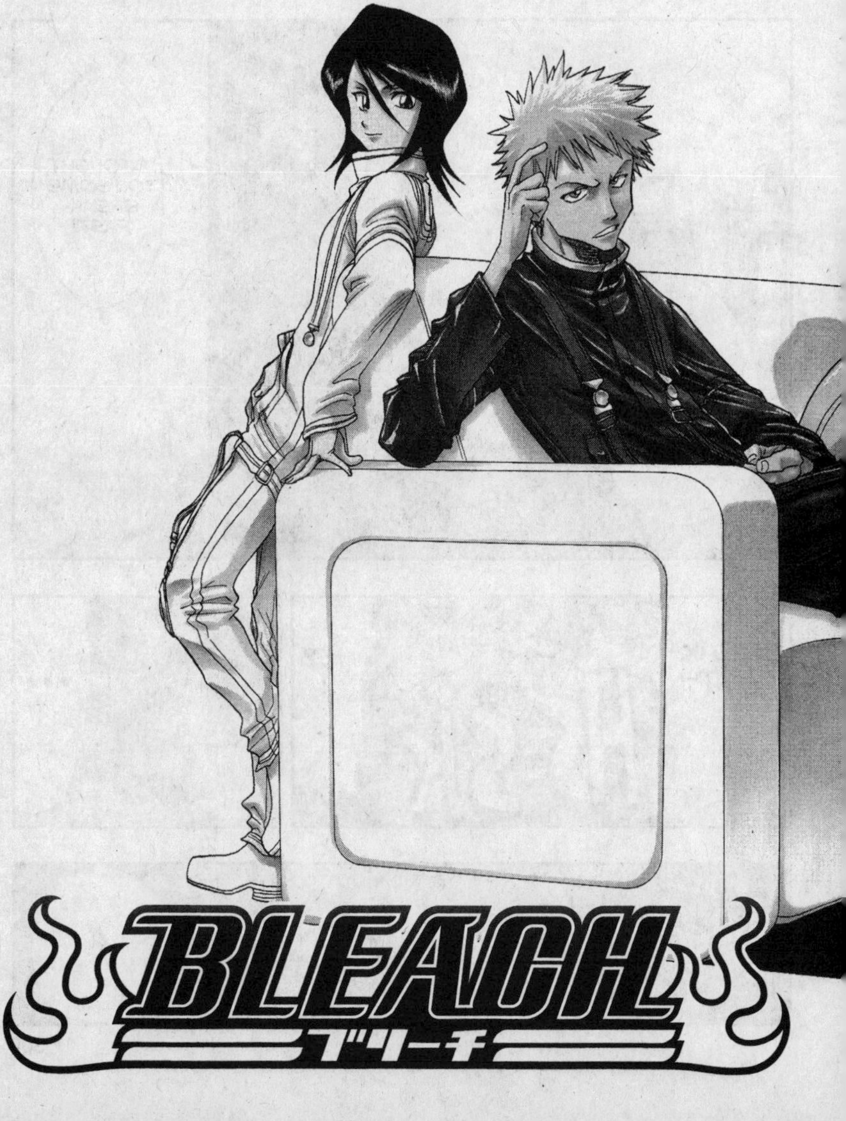
BLEACH
ブリーチ

READ THIS WAY

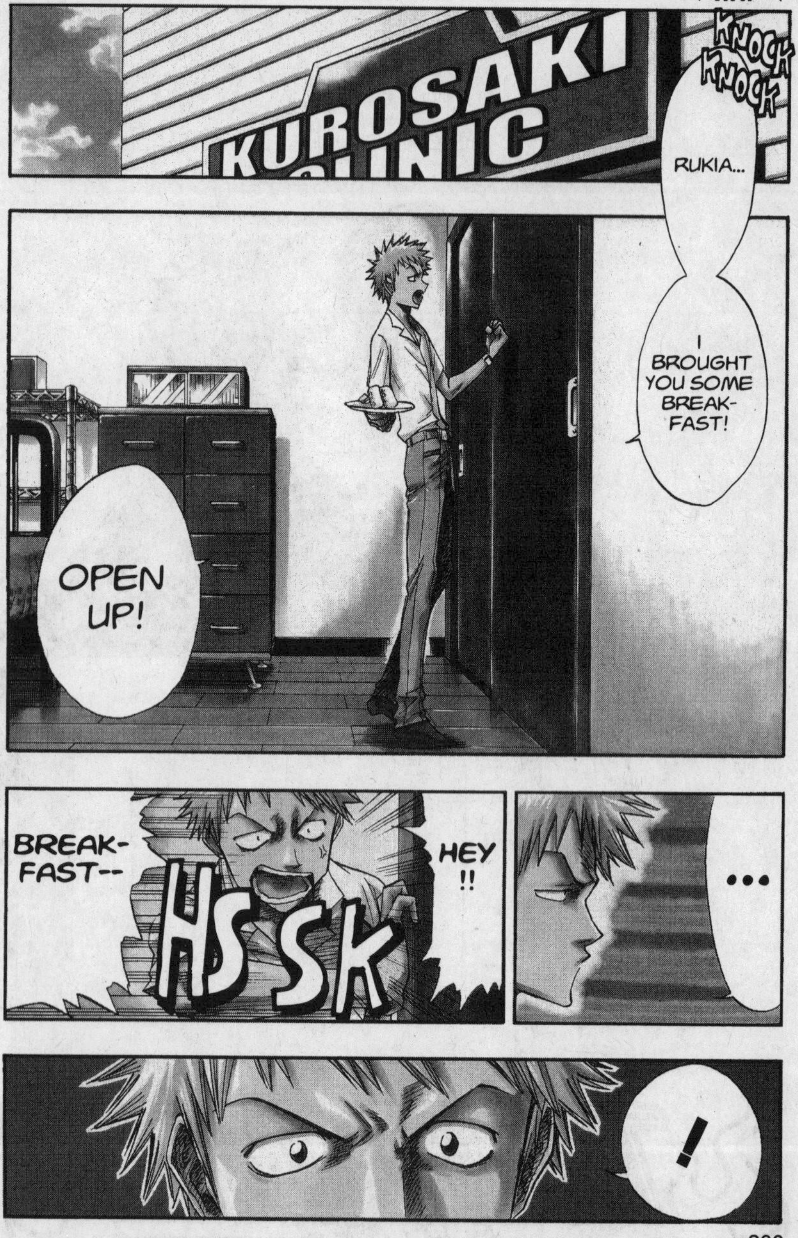
KUROSAKI CLINIC
KNOCK KNOCK
RUKIA...
I BROUGHT YOU SOME BREAK-FAST!
OPEN UP!
...
HEY !!
HSSK
BREAK-FAST--
!

READ THIS WAY

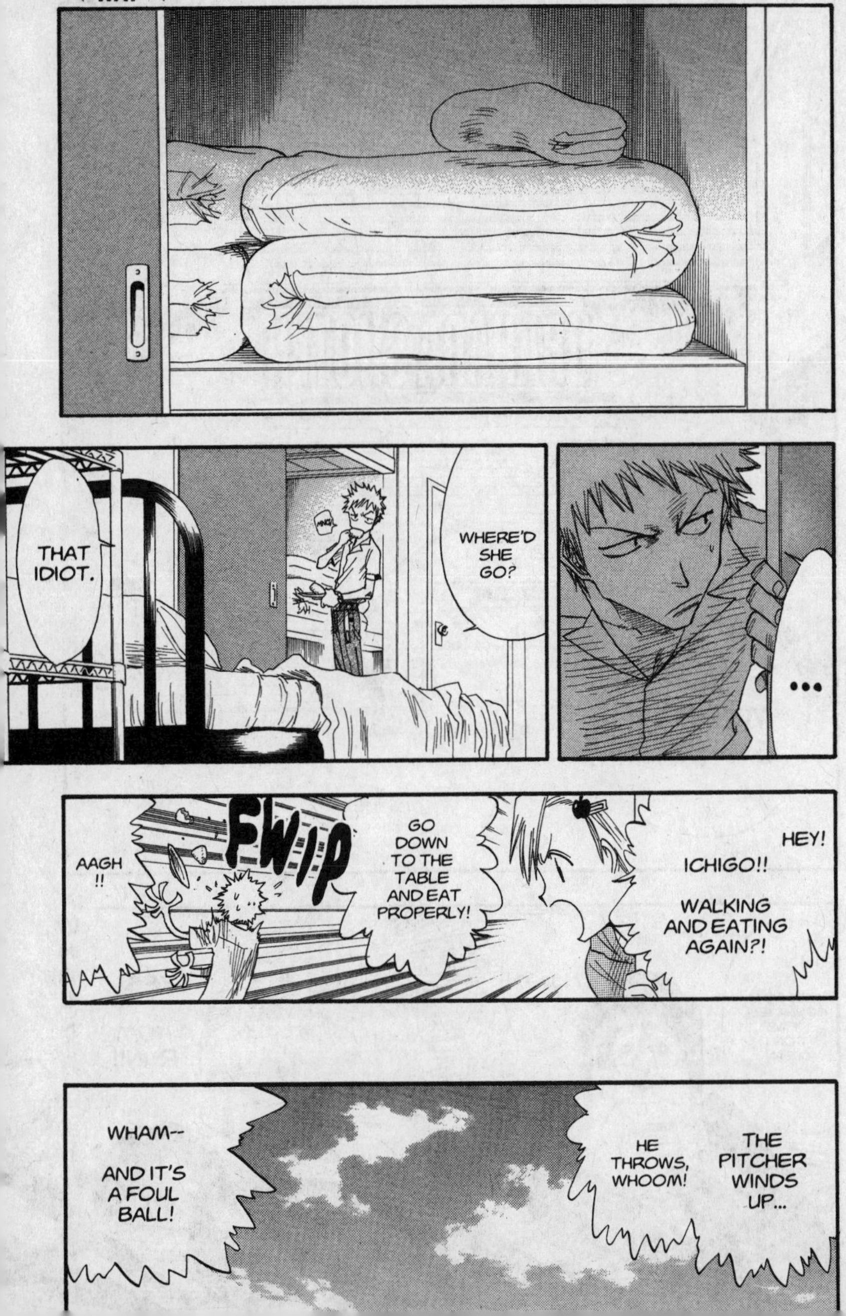
...
WHERE'D SHE GO?
THAT IDIOT.
HEY!
ICHIGO!!
WALKING AND EATING AGAIN?!
GO DOWN TO THE TABLE AND EAT PROPERLY!
FWIP
AAGH!!
THE PITCHER WINDS UP...
HE THROWS, WHOOM!
WHAM--
AND IT'S A FOUL BALL!

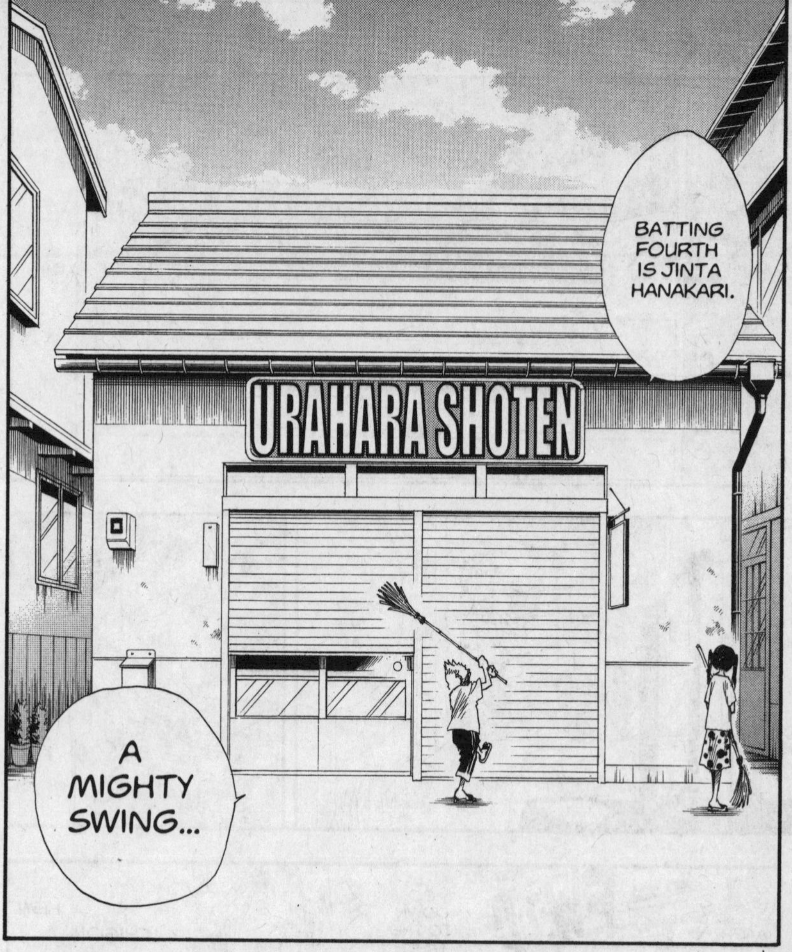
BATTING FOURTH IS JINTA HANAKARI.
URAHARA SHOTEN
A MIGHTY SWING...
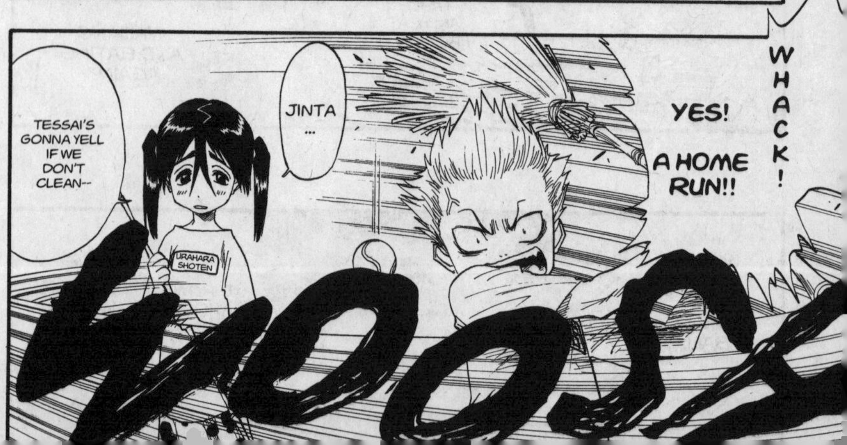
WHACK!
YES! A HOME RUN!!
JINTA ...
TESSAI'S GONNA YELL IF WE DON'T CLEAN--
URAHARA SHOTEN

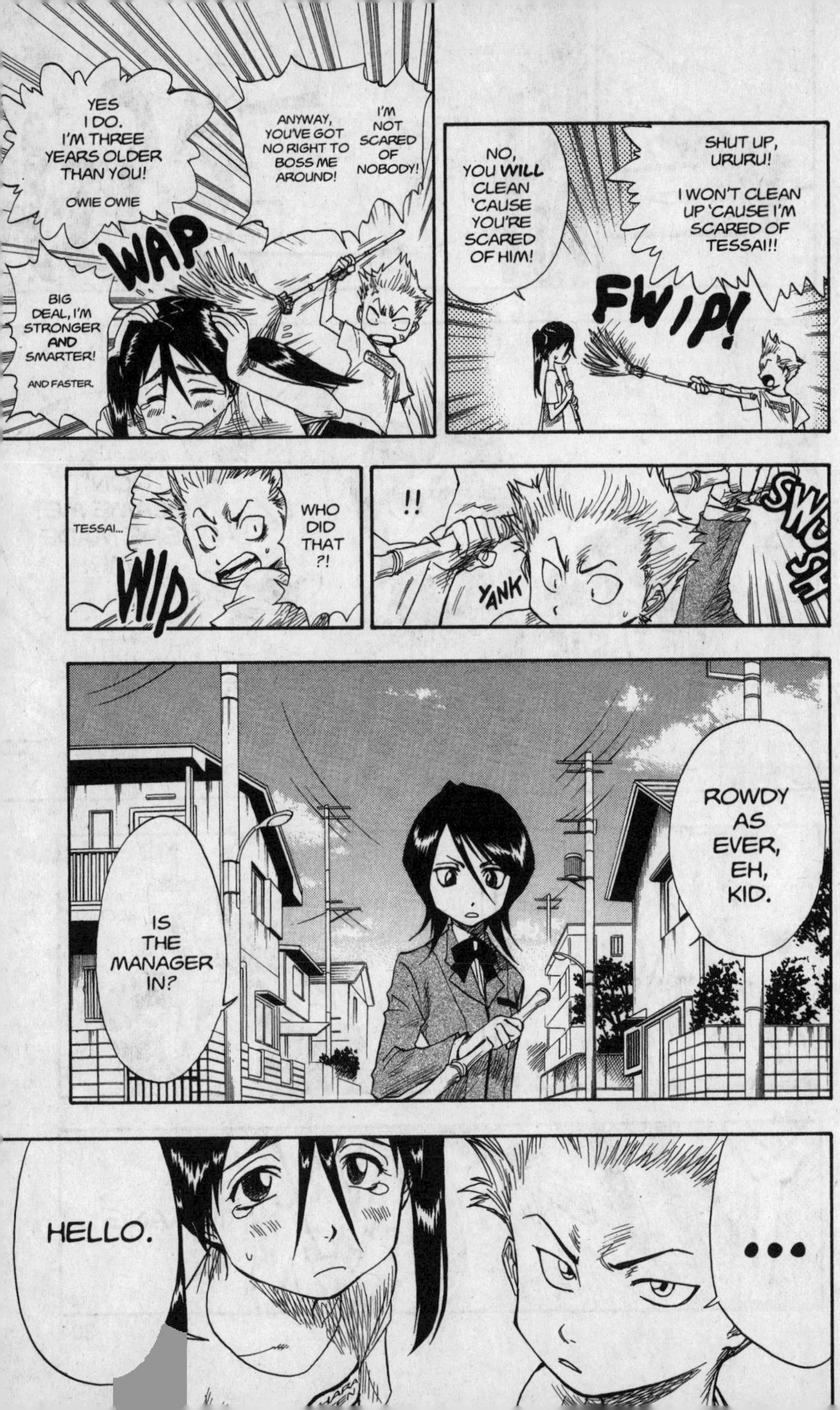
SHUT UP, URURU!
I WON'T CLEAN UP 'CAUSE I'M SCARED OF TESSAI!!
NO, YOU WILL CLEAN 'CAUSE YOU'RE SCARED OF HIM!
FWIP!
I'M NOT SCARED OF NOBODY!
ANYWAY, YOU'VE GOT NO RIGHT TO BOSS ME AROUND!
YES I DO. I'M THREE YEARS OLDER THAN YOU!
OWIE OWIE
WAP
BIG DEAL, I'M STRONGER AND SMARTER!
AND FASTER.
SWUSH
!!
YANK
WHO DID THAT ?!
TESSAI...
WIP
ROWDY AS EVER, EH, KID.
IS THE MANAGER IN?
...
HELLO.

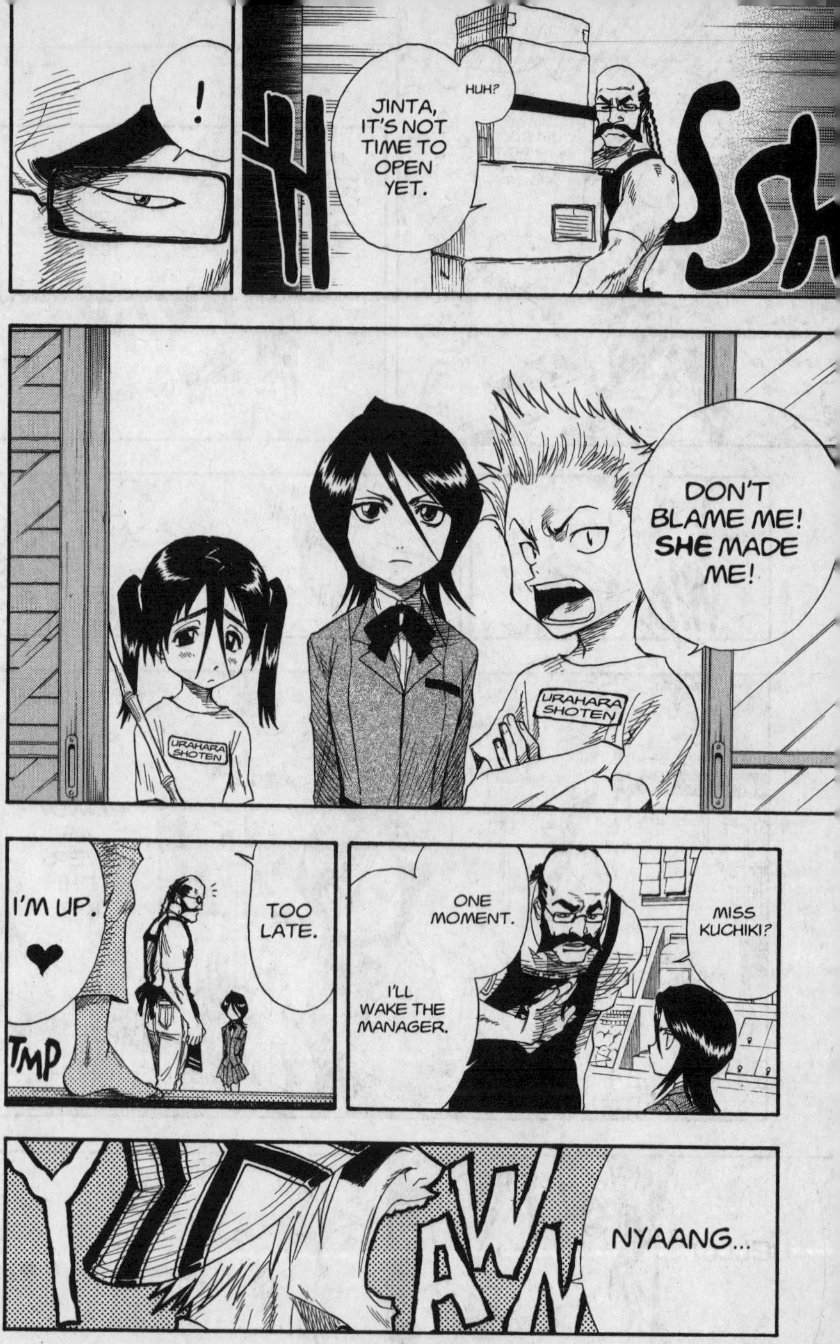

SSH
HUH?
JINTA, IT'S NOT TIME TO OPEN YET.
!
DON'T BLAME ME! SHE MADE ME!
MISS KUCHIKI?
ONE MOMENT.
I'LL WAKE THE MANAGER.
TOO LATE.
I'M UP. ♥
TMP
NYAANG...
YAWN

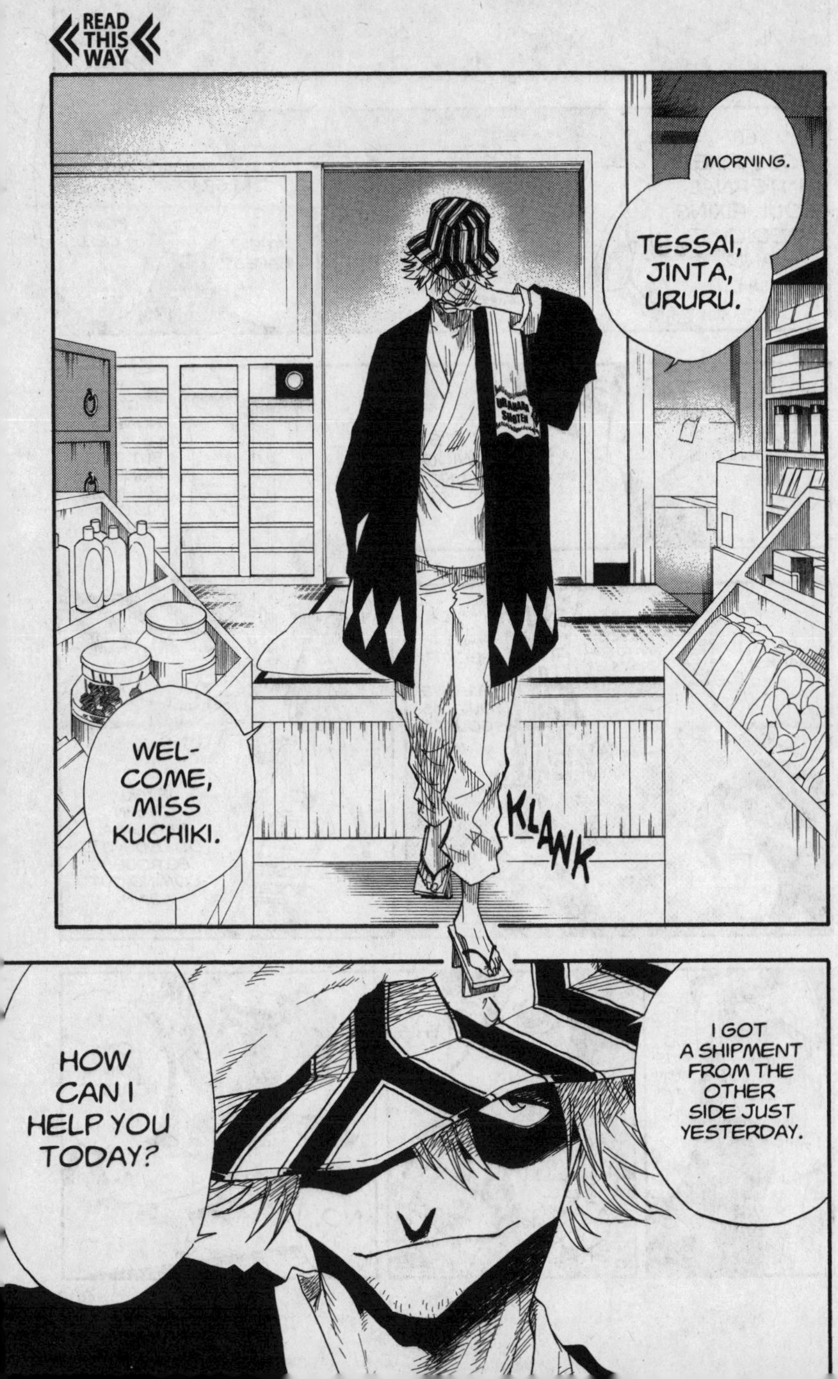
READ THIS WAY
MORNING.
TESSAI, JINTA, URURU.
WEL- COME, MISS KUCHIKI.
KLANK
URAHARA SHOTEN
I GOT A SHIPMENT FROM THE OTHER SIDE JUST YESTERDAY.
HOW CAN I HELP YOU TODAY?

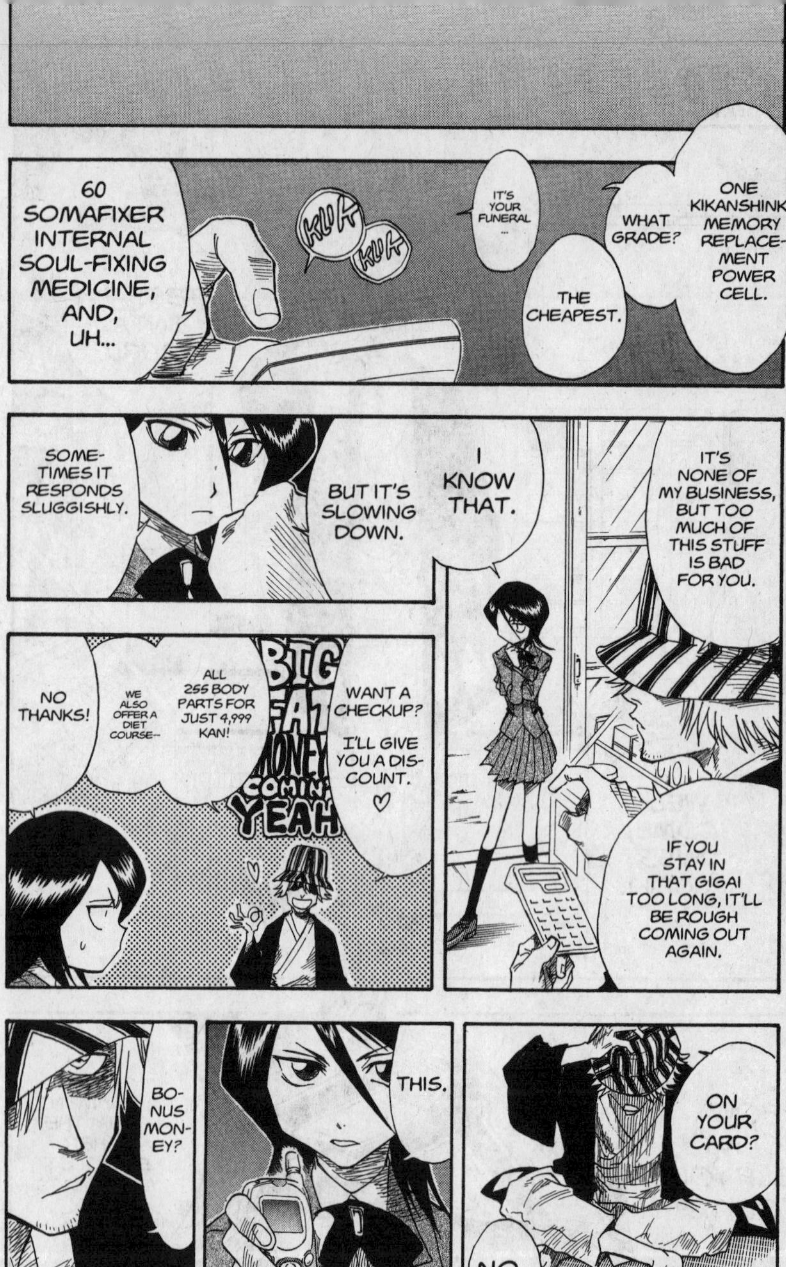
ONE KIKANSHINKI MEMORY REPLACEMENT POWER CELL.
WHAT GRADE?
THE CHEAPEST.
IT'S YOUR FUNERAL...
KLIK
KLIK
60 SOMAFIXER INTERNAL SOUL-FIXING MEDICINE, AND, UH...
IT'S NONE OF MY BUSINESS, BUT TOO MUCH OF THIS STUFF IS BAD FOR YOU.
I KNOW THAT.
IF YOU STAY IN THAT GIGAI TOO LONG, IT'LL BE ROUGH COMING OUT AGAIN.
BUT IT'S SLOWING DOWN.
SOMETIMES IT RESPONDS SLUGGISHLY.
WANT A CHECKUP?
I'LL GIVE YOU A DISCOUNT. ♡
BIG FAT MONEY COMIN' YEAH
ALL 255 BODY PARTS FOR JUST 4,999 KAN!
WE ALSO OFFER A DIET COURSE--
NO THANKS!
ON YOUR CARD?
NO.
THIS.
BONUS MONEY?

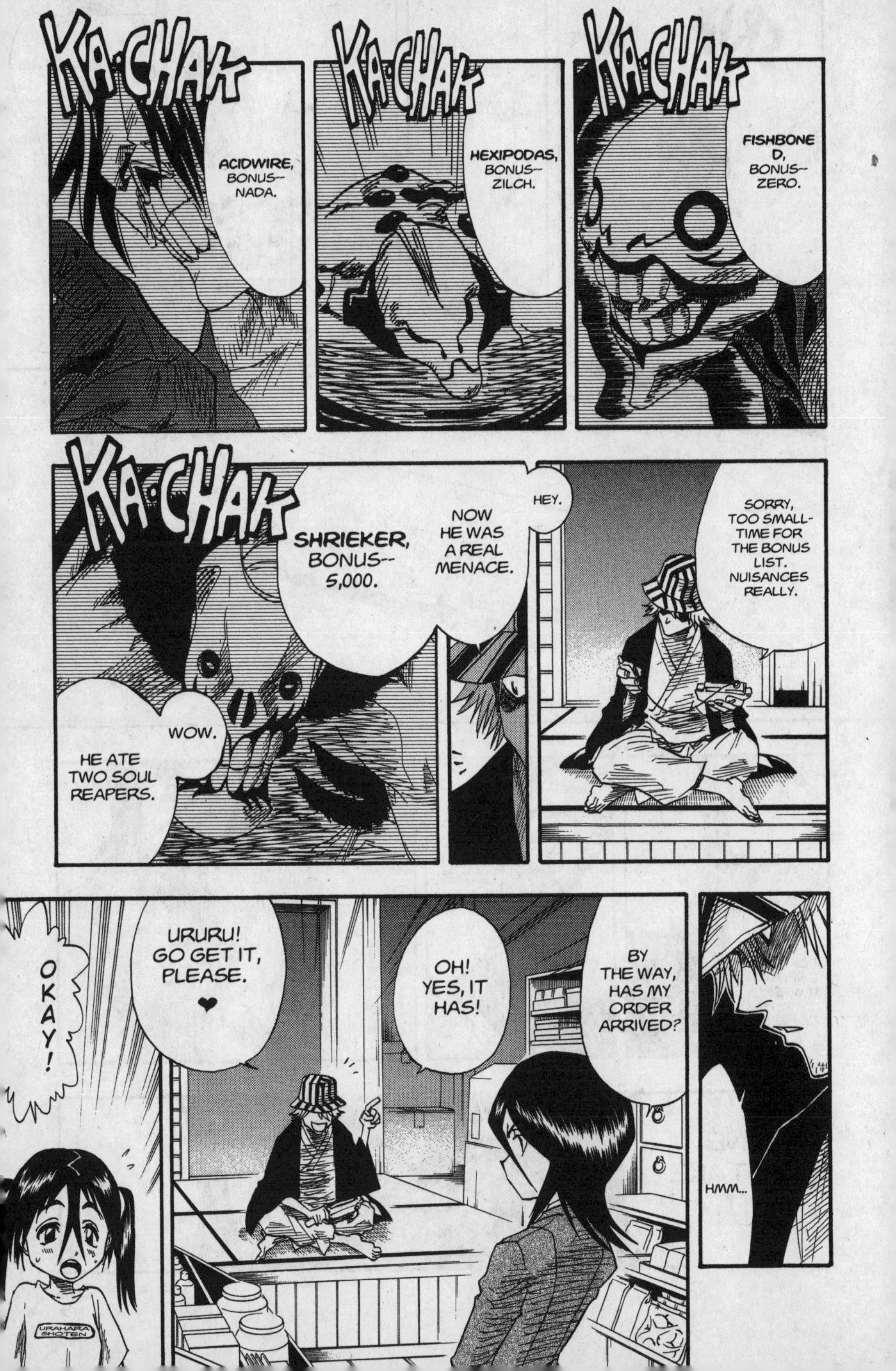
KA-CHAK
FISHBONE D, BONUS--ZERO.
KA-CHAK
HEXIPODAS, BONUS--ZILCH.
KA-CHAK
ACIDWIRE, BONUS--NADA.
SORRY, TOO SMALL-TIME FOR THE BONUS LIST. NUISANCES REALLY.
HEY.
KA-CHAK
SHRIEKER, BONUS--5,000.
NOW HE WAS A REAL MENACE.
WOW.
HE ATE TWO SOUL REAPERS.
HMM...
BY THE WAY, HAS MY ORDER ARRIVED?
OH! YES, IT HAS!
URURU! GO GET IT, PLEASE. ❤
OKAY!
URAHARA SHOTEN

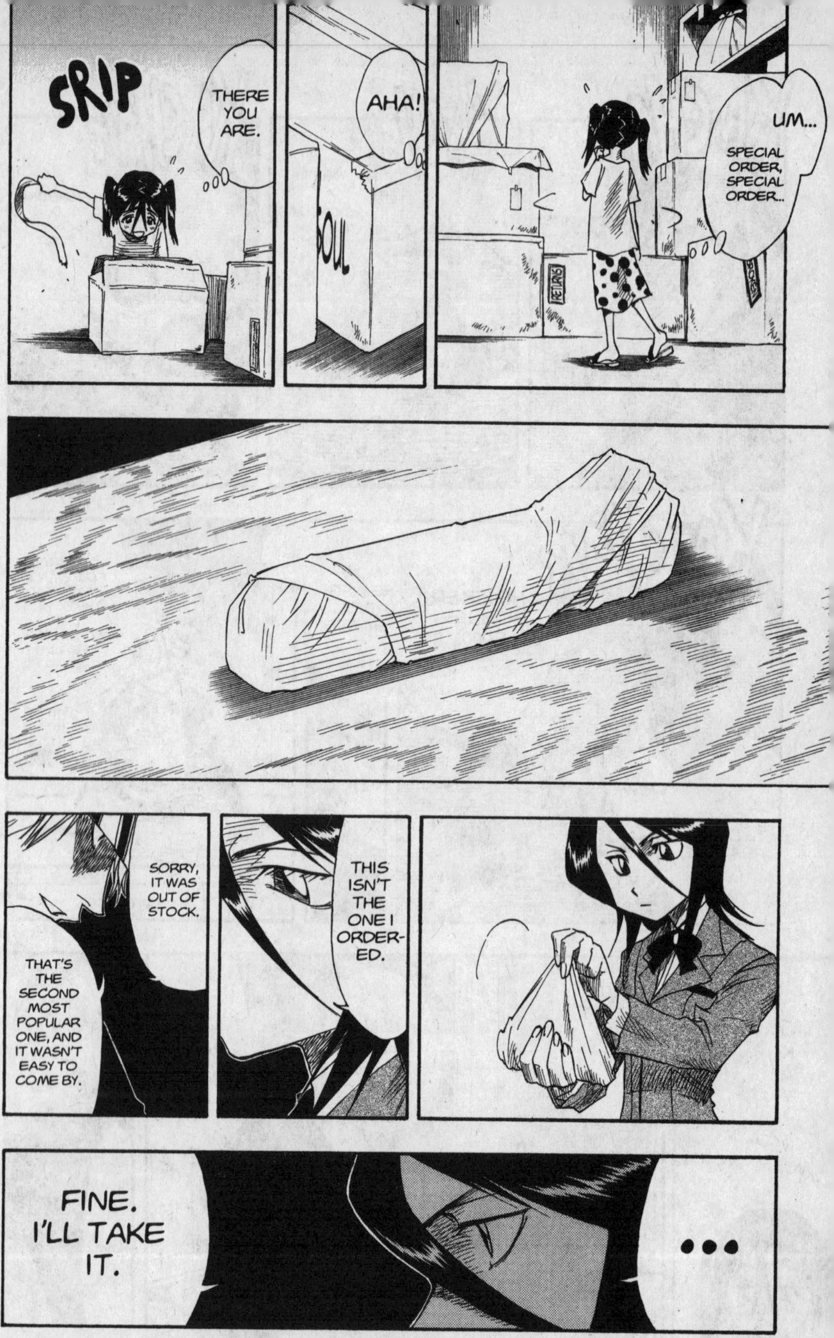
UM...
SPECIAL ORDER, SPECIAL ORDER...
RETURNS
AHA!
SOUL
THERE YOU ARE.
SRIP
THIS ISN'T THE ONE I ORDERED.
SORRY, IT WAS OUT OF STOCK.
THAT'S THE SECOND MOST POPULAR ONE, AND IT WASN'T EASY TO COME BY.
...
FINE. I'LL TAKE IT.

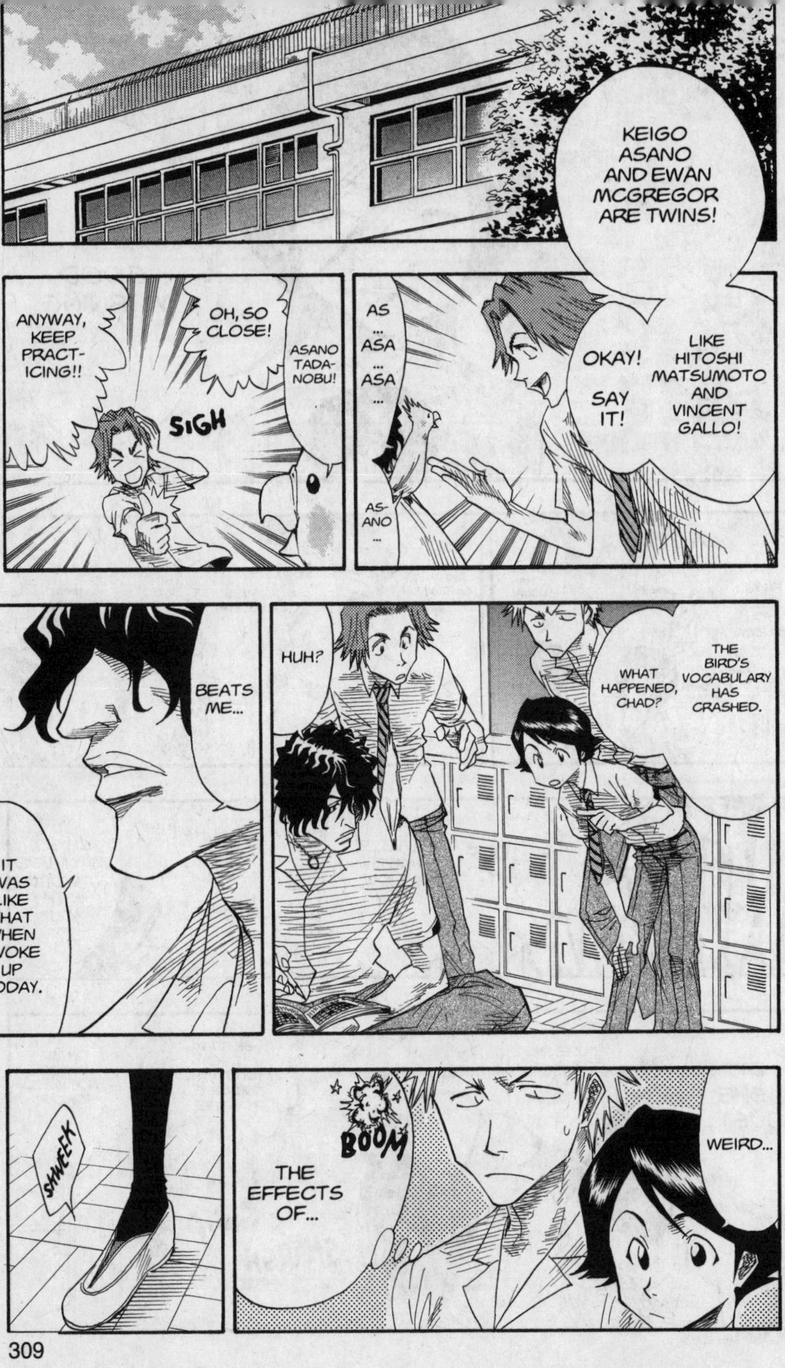
KEIGO ASANO AND EWAN MCGREGOR ARE TWINS!
LIKE HITOSHI MATSUMOTO AND VINCENT GALLO!
OKAY! SAY IT!
AS ... ASA ... ASA ...
AS-ANO ...
ASANO TADA-NOBU!
OH, SO CLOSE!
SIGH
ANYWAY, KEEP PRACT-ICING!!
THE BIRD'S VOCABULARY HAS CRASHED.
WHAT HAPPENED, CHAD?
HUH?
BEATS ME...
IT WAS LIKE THAT WHEN I WOKE UP TODAY.
WEIRD...
BOOM
THE EFFECTS OF...
SHWEEK

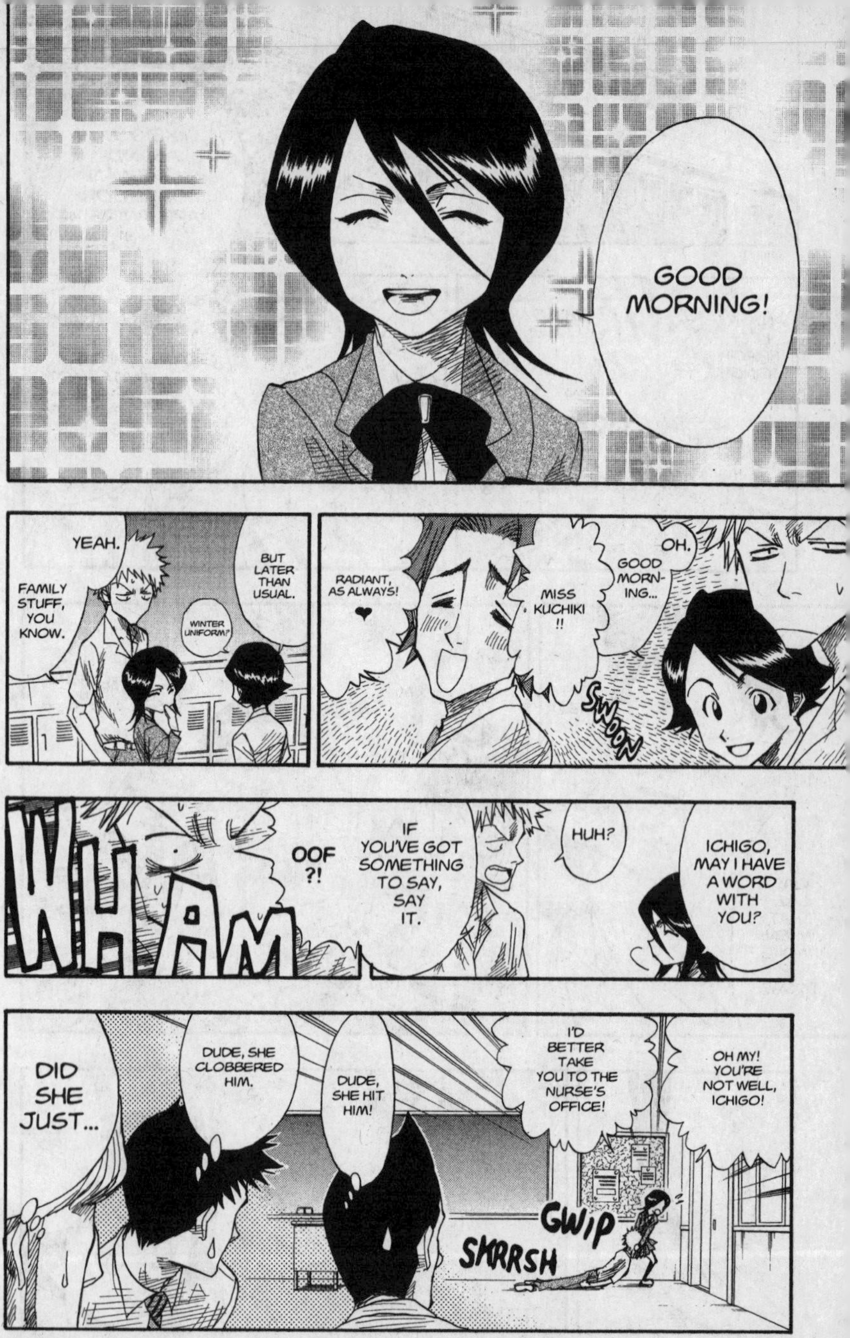
GOOD MORNING!
OH.
GOOD MORNING...
MISS KUCHIKI!!
RADIANT, AS ALWAYS! ❤
SWOON
BUT LATER THAN USUAL.
WINTER UNIFORM?
YEAH.
FAMILY STUFF, YOU KNOW.
ICHIGO, MAY I HAVE A WORD WITH YOU?
HUH?
IF YOU'VE GOT SOMETHING TO SAY, SAY IT.
OOF ?!
WHAM
OH MY! YOU'RE NOT WELL, ICHIGO!
I'D BETTER TAKE YOU TO THE NURSE'S OFFICE!
GWIP
SKRRSH
DUDE, SHE HIT HIM!
DUDE, SHE CLOBBERED HIM.
DID SHE JUST...

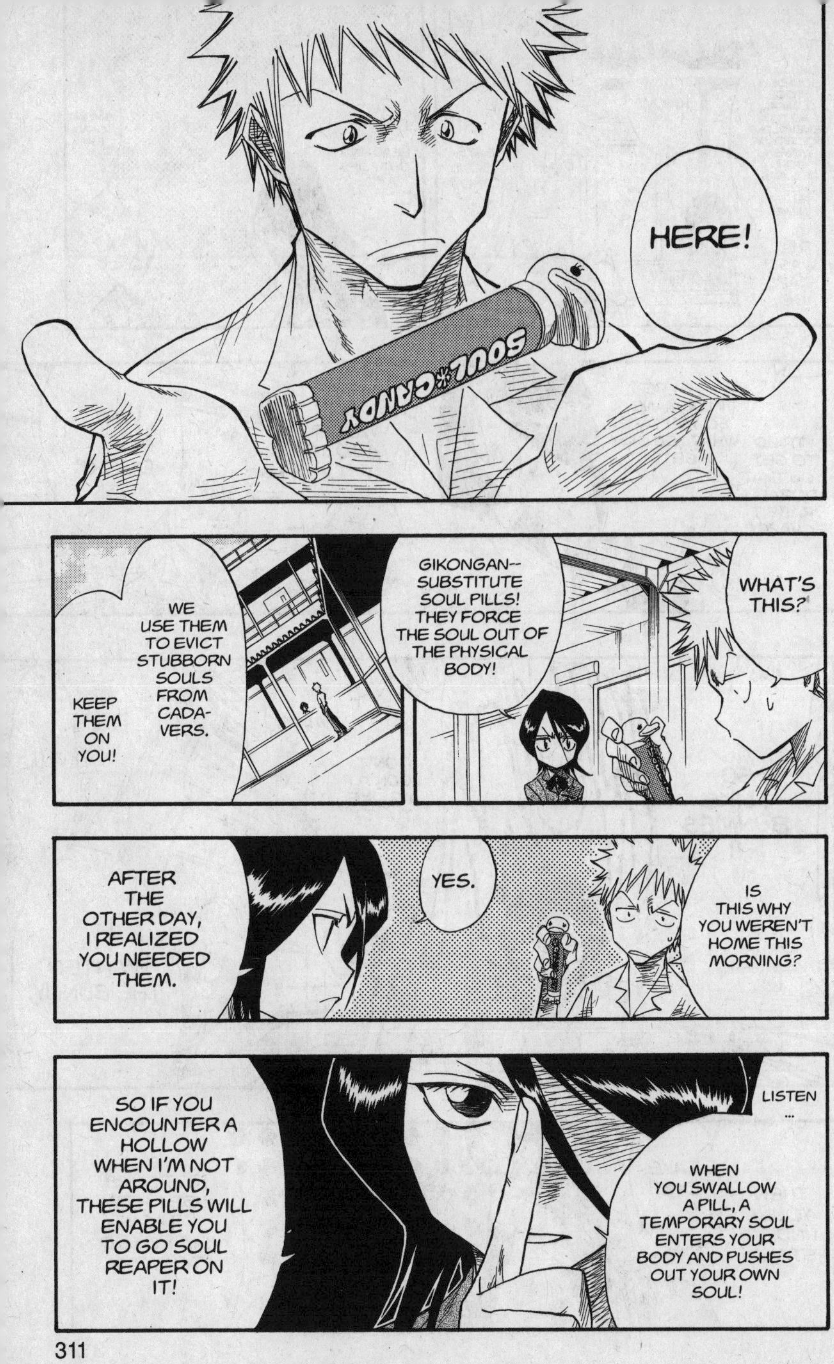
HERE!
SOUL*CANDY
WHAT'S THIS?
GIKONGAN--SUBSTITUTE SOUL PILLS! THEY FORCE THE SOUL OUT OF THE PHYSICAL BODY!
WE USE THEM TO EVICT STUBBORN SOULS FROM CADAVERS.
KEEP THEM ON YOU!
IS THIS WHY YOU WEREN'T HOME THIS MORNING?
YES.
AFTER THE OTHER DAY, I REALIZED YOU NEEDED THEM.
LISTEN...
WHEN YOU SWALLOW A PILL, A TEMPORARY SOUL ENTERS YOUR BODY AND PUSHES OUT YOUR OWN SOUL!
SO IF YOU ENCOUNTER A HOLLOW WHEN I'M NOT AROUND, THESE PILLS WILL ENABLE YOU TO GO SOUL REAPER ON IT!

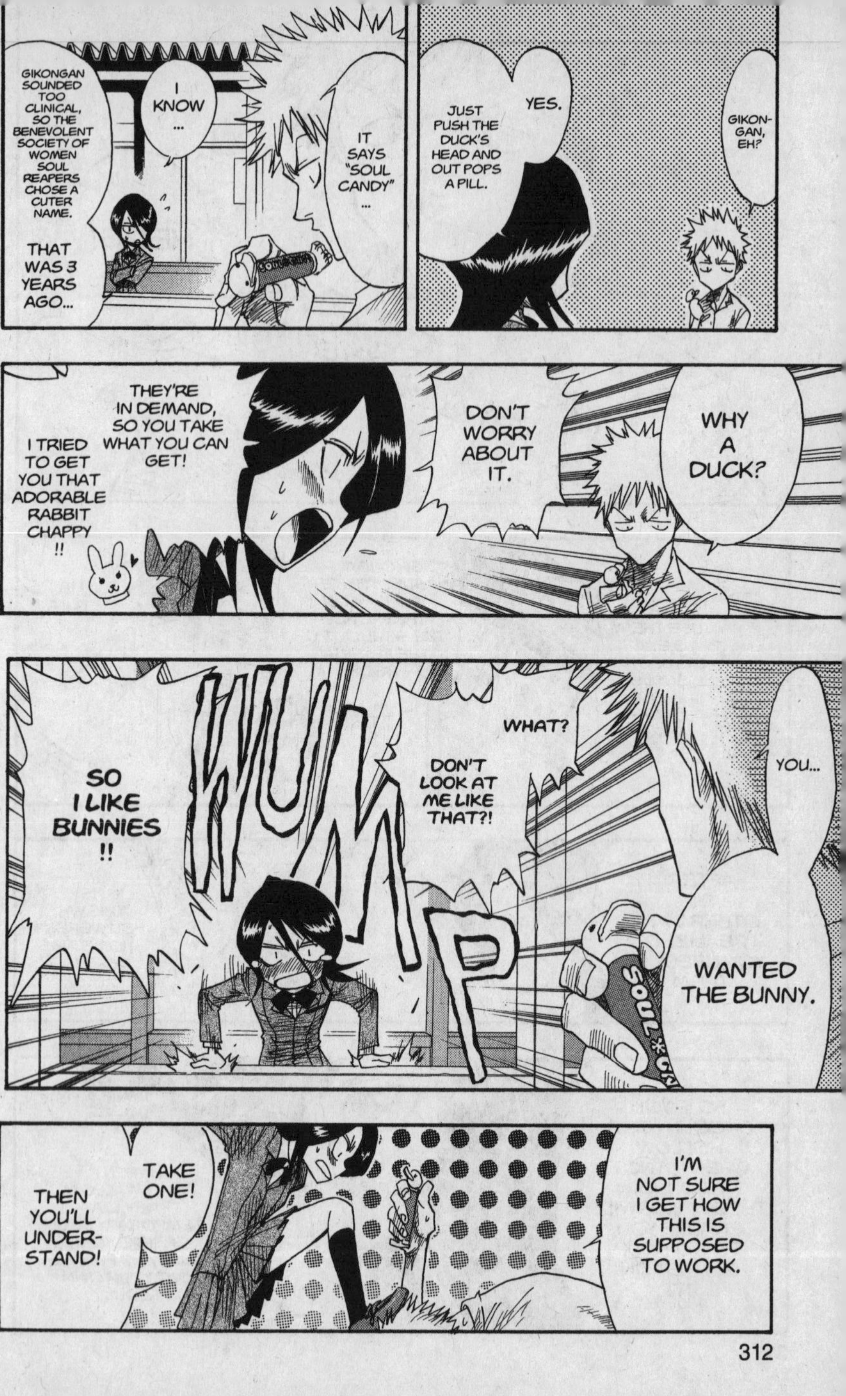

GIKON-GAN, EH?
YES.
JUST PUSH THE DUCK'S HEAD AND OUT POPS A PILL.
IT SAYS "SOUL CANDY"...
I KNOW...
GIKONGAN SOUNDED TOO CLINICAL, SO THE BENEVOLENT SOCIETY OF WOMEN SOUL REAPERS CHOSE A CUTER NAME.
THAT WAS 3 YEARS AGO...
WHY A DUCK?
DON'T WORRY ABOUT IT.
THEY'RE IN DEMAND, SO YOU TAKE WHAT YOU CAN GET!
I TRIED TO GET YOU THAT ADORABLE RABBIT CHAPPY!!
YOU...
WANTED THE BUNNY.
WHAT?
DON'T LOOK AT ME LIKE THAT?!
WUMP
SO I LIKE BUNNIES!!
I'M NOT SURE I GET HOW THIS IS SUPPOSED TO WORK.
TAKE ONE!
THEN YOU'LL UNDERSTAND!

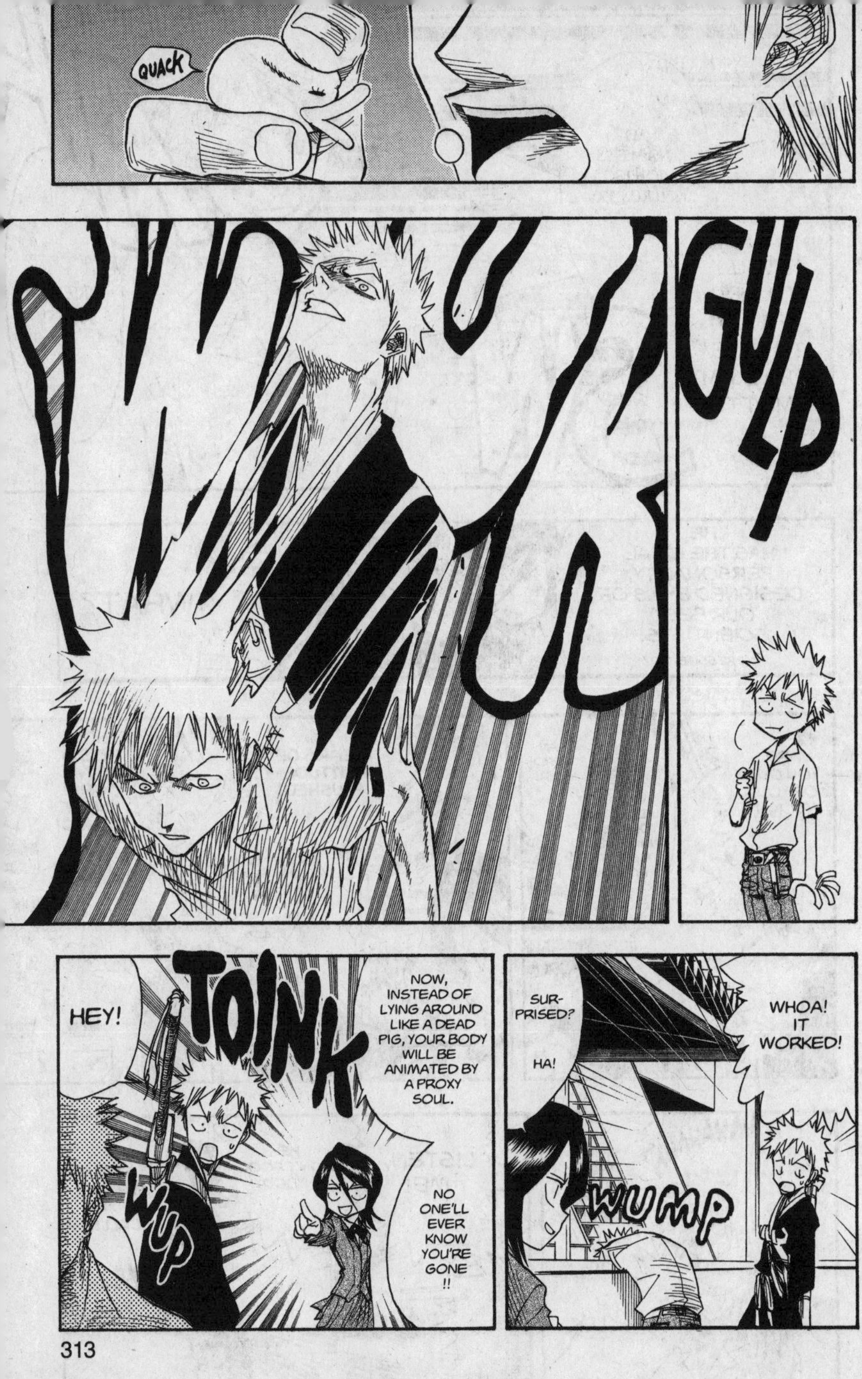
QUACK
GULP
WHOA! IT WORKED!
SUR-PRISED?
HA!
WUMP
NOW, INSTEAD OF LYING AROUND LIKE A DEAD PIG, YOUR BODY WILL BE ANIMATED BY A PROXY SOUL.
TOINK
HEY!
NO ONE'LL EVER KNOW YOU'RE GONE !!
WUP

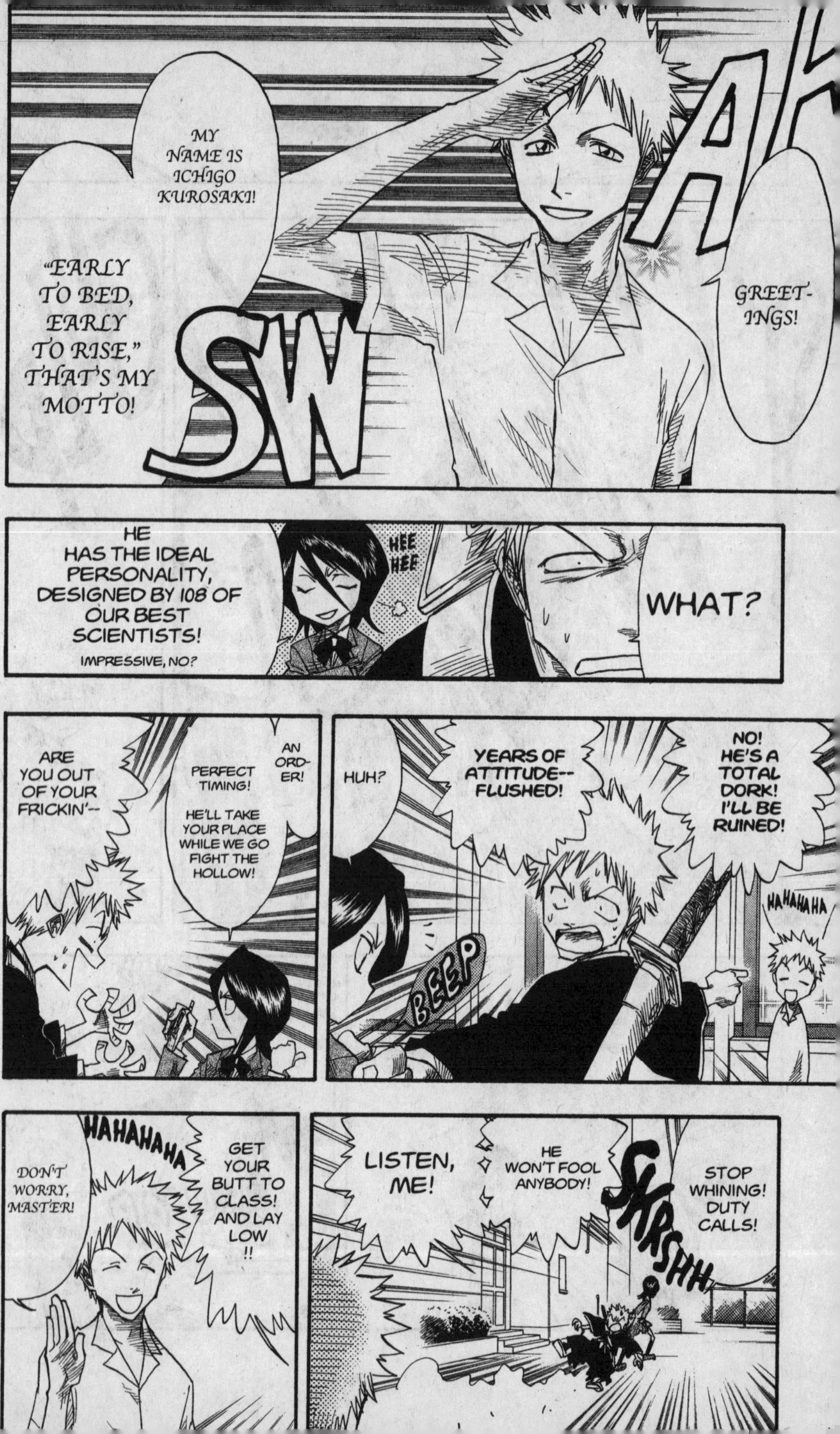
AH
GREET-INGS!
MY NAME IS ICHIGO KUROSAKI!
SW
"EARLY TO BED, EARLY TO RISE," THAT'S MY MOTTO!
WHAT?
HEE HEE
HE HAS THE IDEAL PERSONALITY, DESIGNED BY 108 OF OUR BEST SCIENTISTS!
IMPRESSIVE, NO?
NO! HE'S A TOTAL DORK! I'LL BE RUINED!
HAHAHAHA
YEARS OF ATTITUDE--FLUSHED!
HUH?
BEEP
AN ORDER!
PERFECT TIMING!
HE'LL TAKE YOUR PLACE WHILE WE GO FIGHT THE HOLLOW!
ARE YOU OUT OF YOUR FRICKIN'--
STOP WHINING! DUTY CALLS!
SKRSHH
HE WON'T FOOL ANYBODY!
LISTEN, ME!
GET YOUR BUTT TO CLASS! AND LAY LOW !!
HAHAHAHA
DON'T WORRY, MASTER!

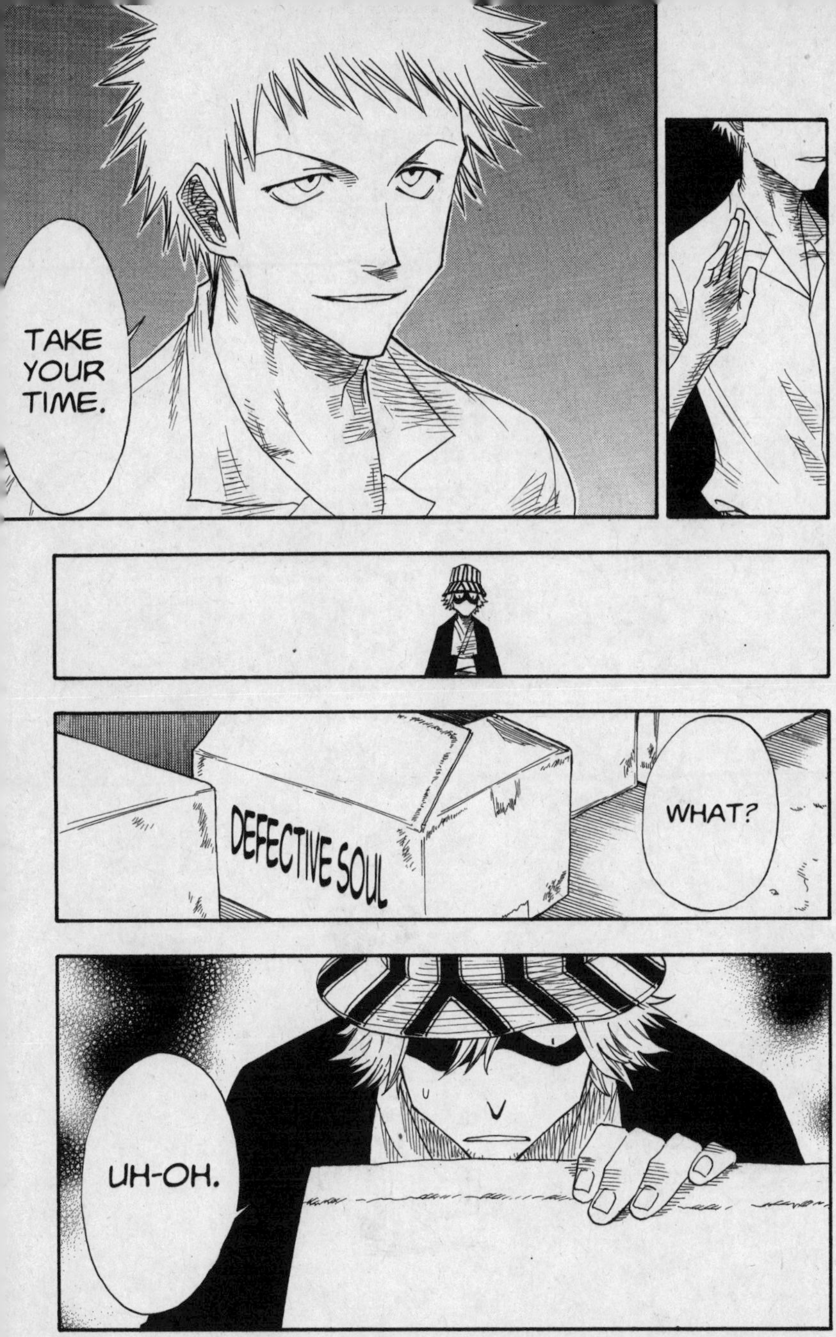
TAKE YOUR TIME.
WHAT?
DEFECTIVE SOUL
UH-OH.

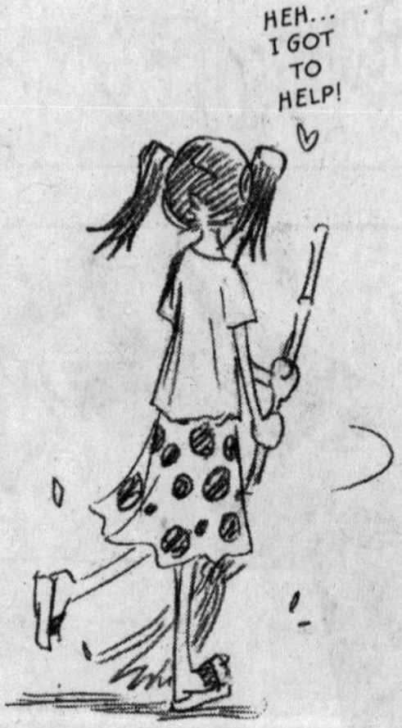
HEH... I GOT TO HELP!

14. School Daze!!!

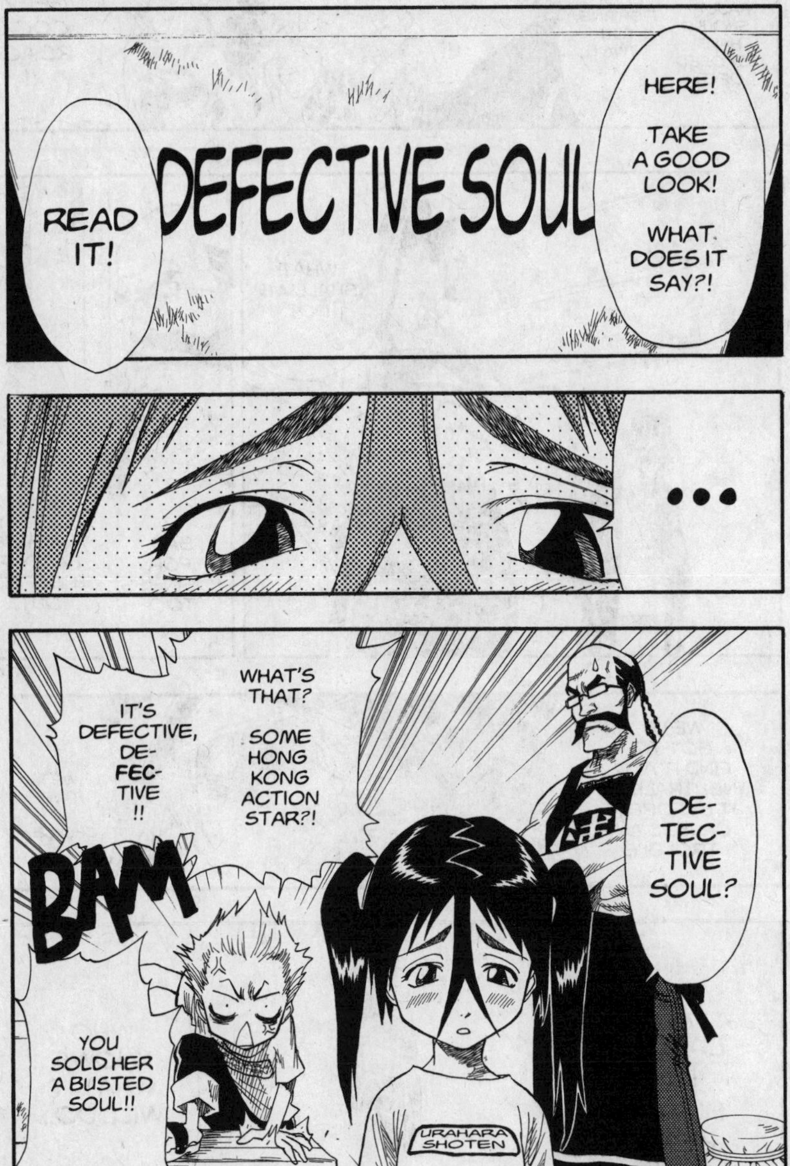
HERE! TAKE A GOOD LOOK! WHAT DOES IT SAY?!
DEFECTIVE SOUL
READ IT!
...
DE-TEC-TIVE SOUL?
WHAT'S THAT? SOME HONG KONG ACTION STAR?!
IT'S DEFECTIVE, DE-FEC-TIVE!!
BAM
YOU SOLD HER A BUSTED SOUL!!
URAHARA SHOTEN

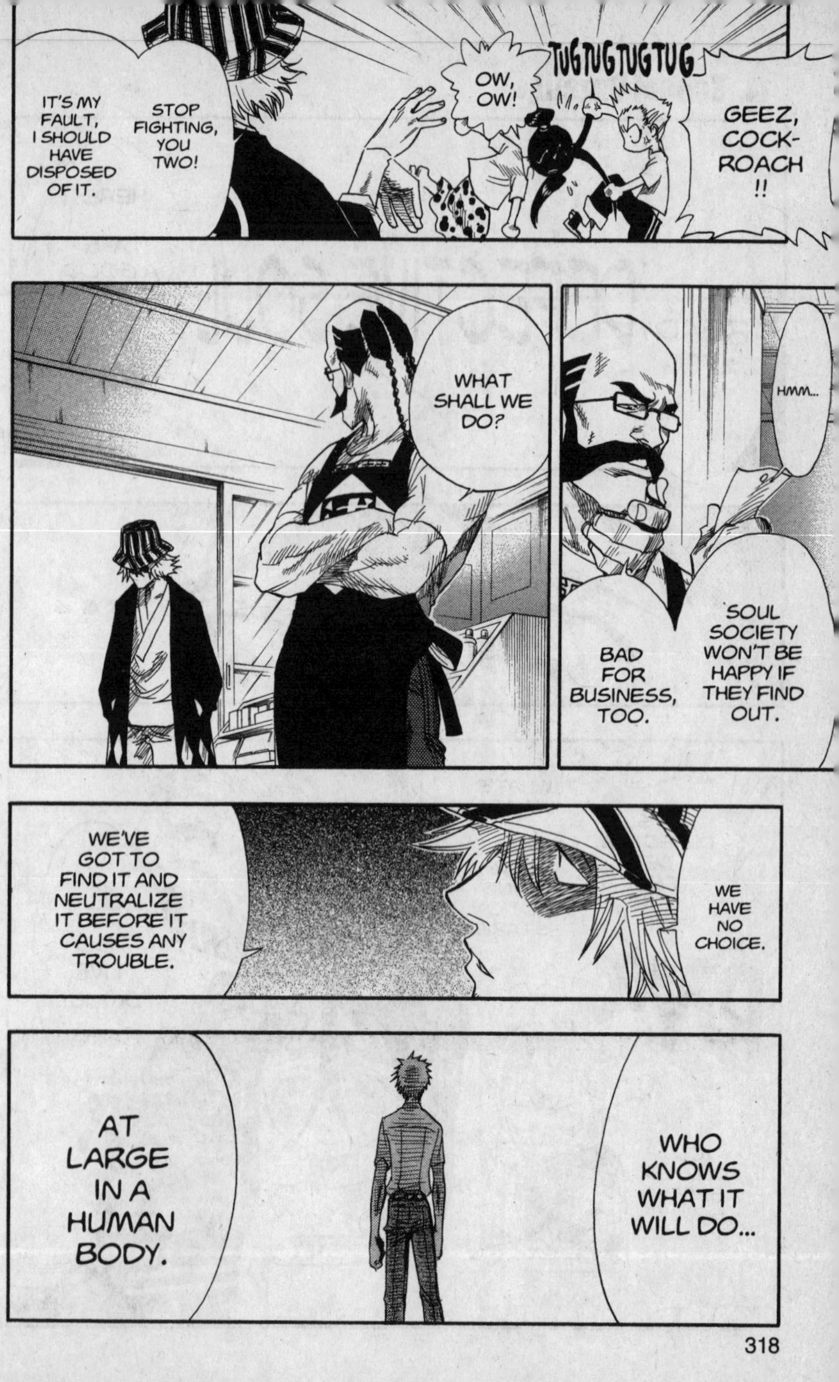
GEEZ, COCKROACH!!
TUGTUGTUGTUG
OW, OW!
STOP FIGHTING, YOU TWO!
IT'S MY FAULT, I SHOULD HAVE DISPOSED OF IT.
HMM...
SOUL SOCIETY WON'T BE HAPPY IF THEY FIND OUT.
BAD FOR BUSINESS, TOO.
WHAT SHALL WE DO?
WE HAVE NO CHOICE.
WE'VE GOT TO FIND IT AND NEUTRALIZE IT BEFORE IT CAUSES ANY TROUBLE.
WHO KNOWS WHAT IT WILL DO...
AT LARGE IN A HUMAN BODY.

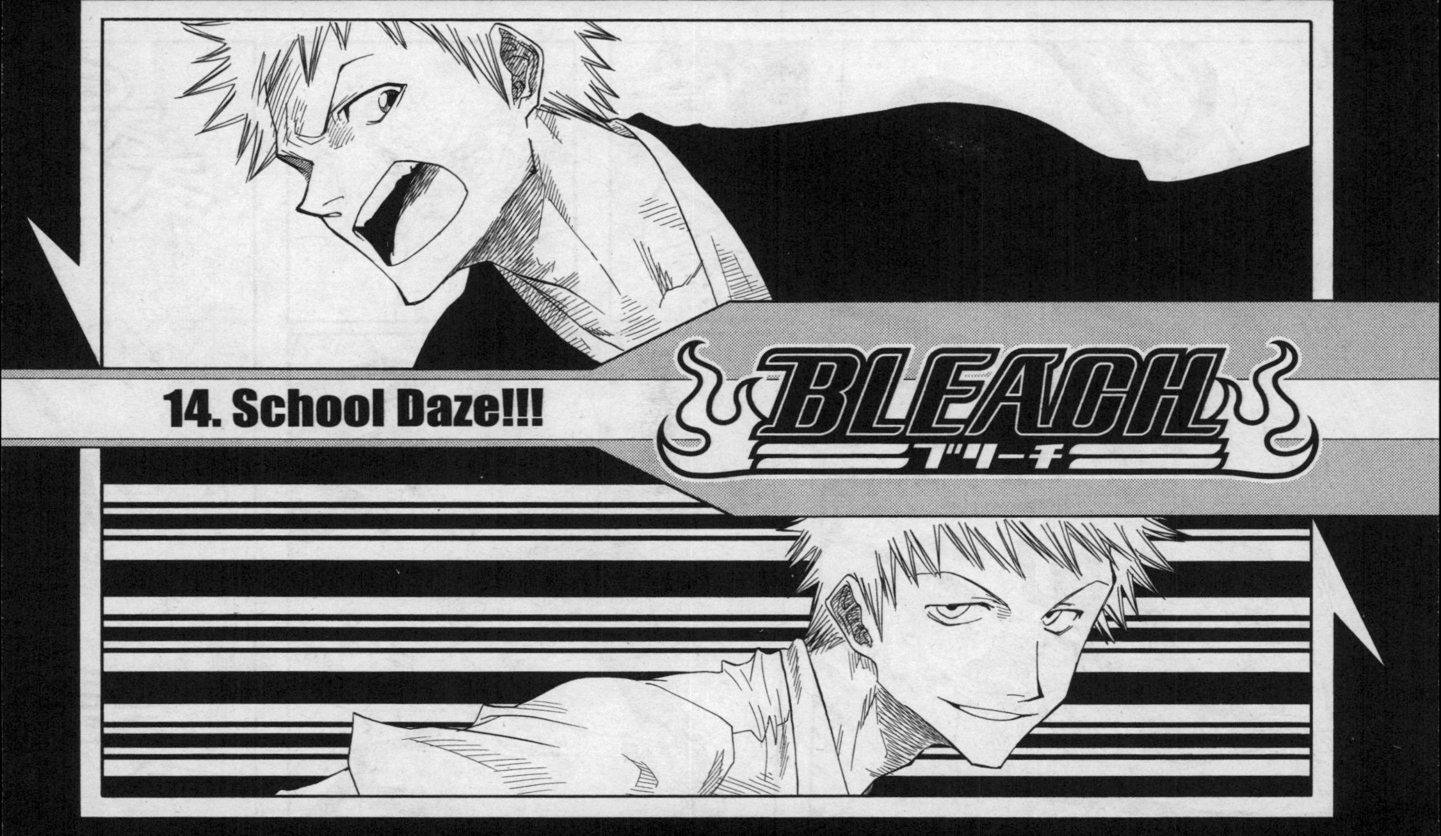
BLEACH
ブリーチ
14. School Daze!!!

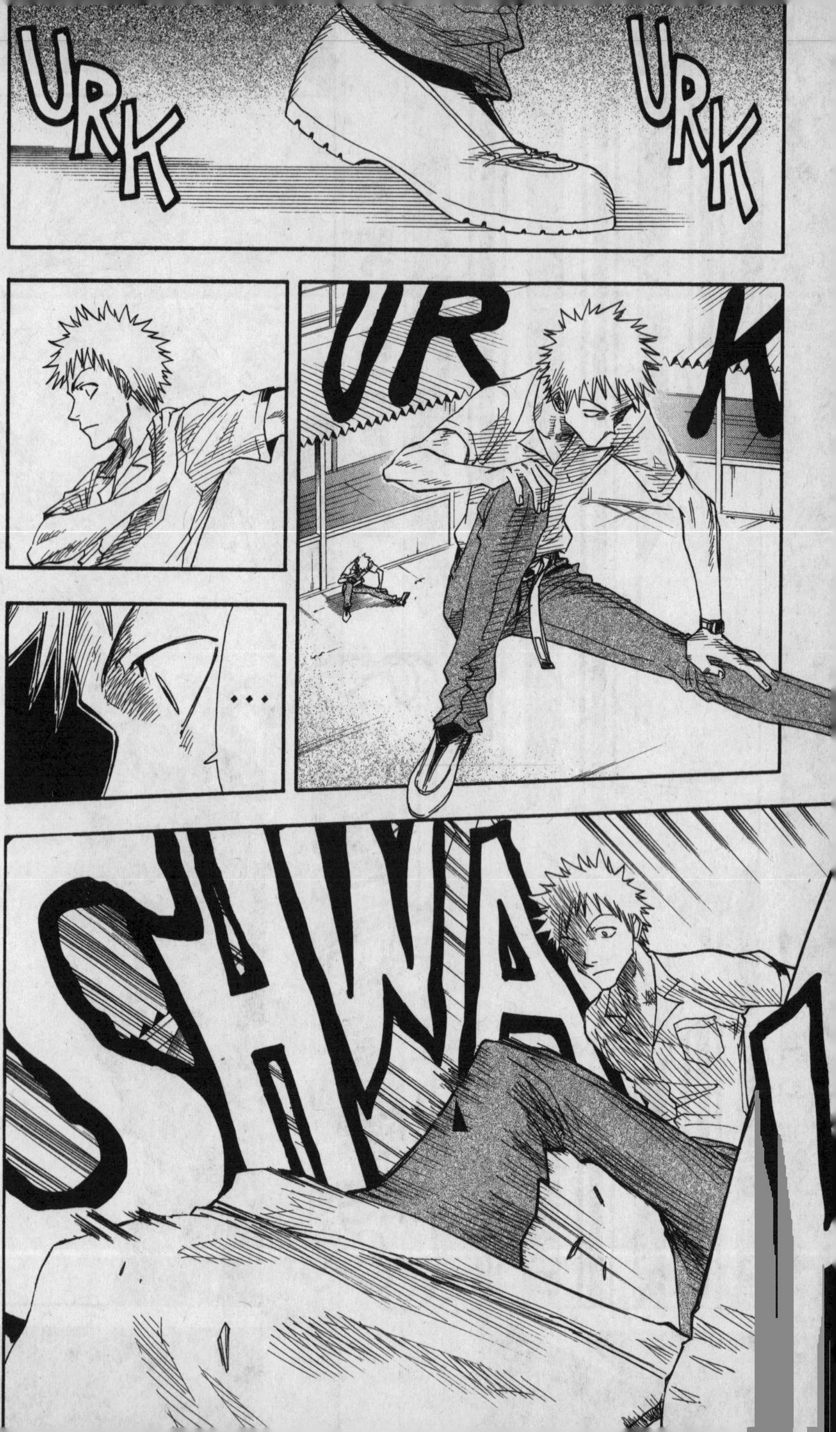
URK
URK
...
SHWA

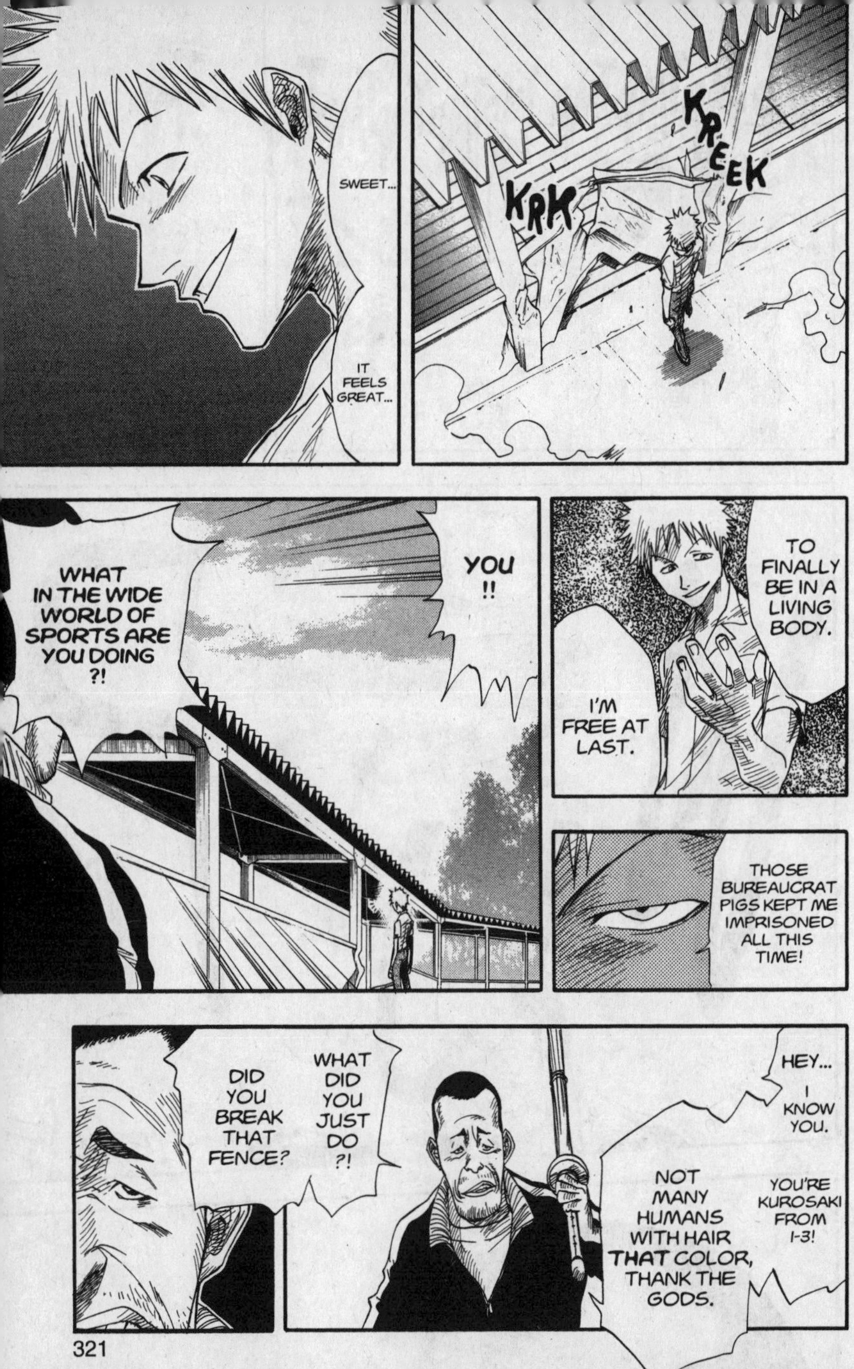
KREEK
KRK
SWEET...
IT FEELS GREAT...
TO FINALLY BE IN A LIVING BODY.
I'M FREE AT LAST.
THOSE BUREAUCRAT PIGS KEPT ME IMPRISONED ALL THIS TIME!
YOU !!
WHAT IN THE WIDE WORLD OF SPORTS ARE YOU DOING ?!
HEY...
I KNOW YOU.
YOU'RE KUROSAKI FROM 1-3!
NOT MANY HUMANS WITH HAIR THAT COLOR, THANK THE GODS.
WHAT DID YOU JUST DO ?!
DID YOU BREAK THAT FENCE?

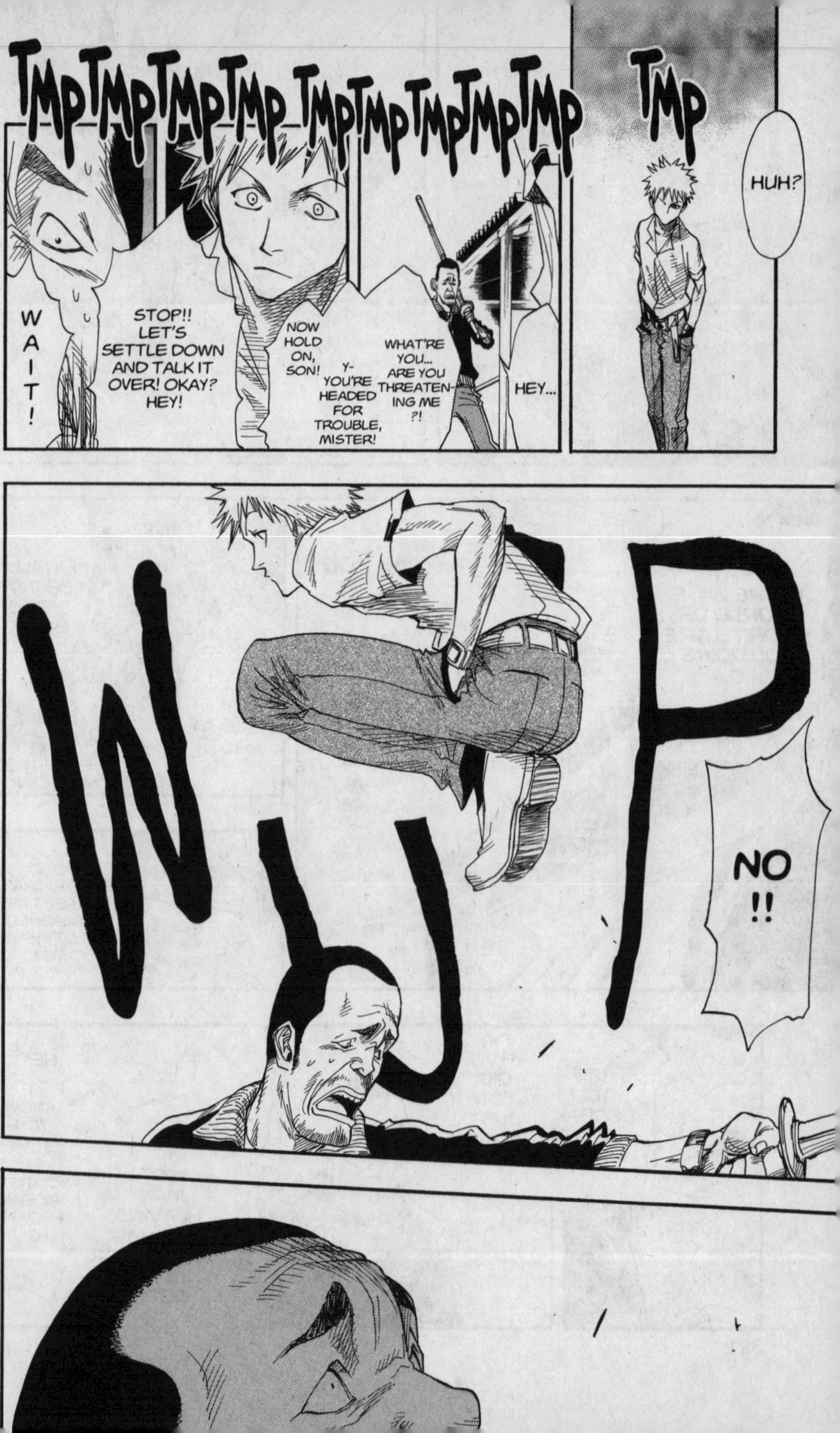
TMP
HUH?
TMP TMP TMP TMP TMP TMP TMP TMP TMP
HEY...
WHAT'RE YOU... ARE YOU THREATENING ME?!
Y- YOU'RE HEADED FOR TROUBLE, MISTER!
NOW HOLD ON, SON!
STOP!! LET'S SETTLE DOWN AND TALK IT OVER! OKAY? HEY!
WAIT!
NO!!
WUP

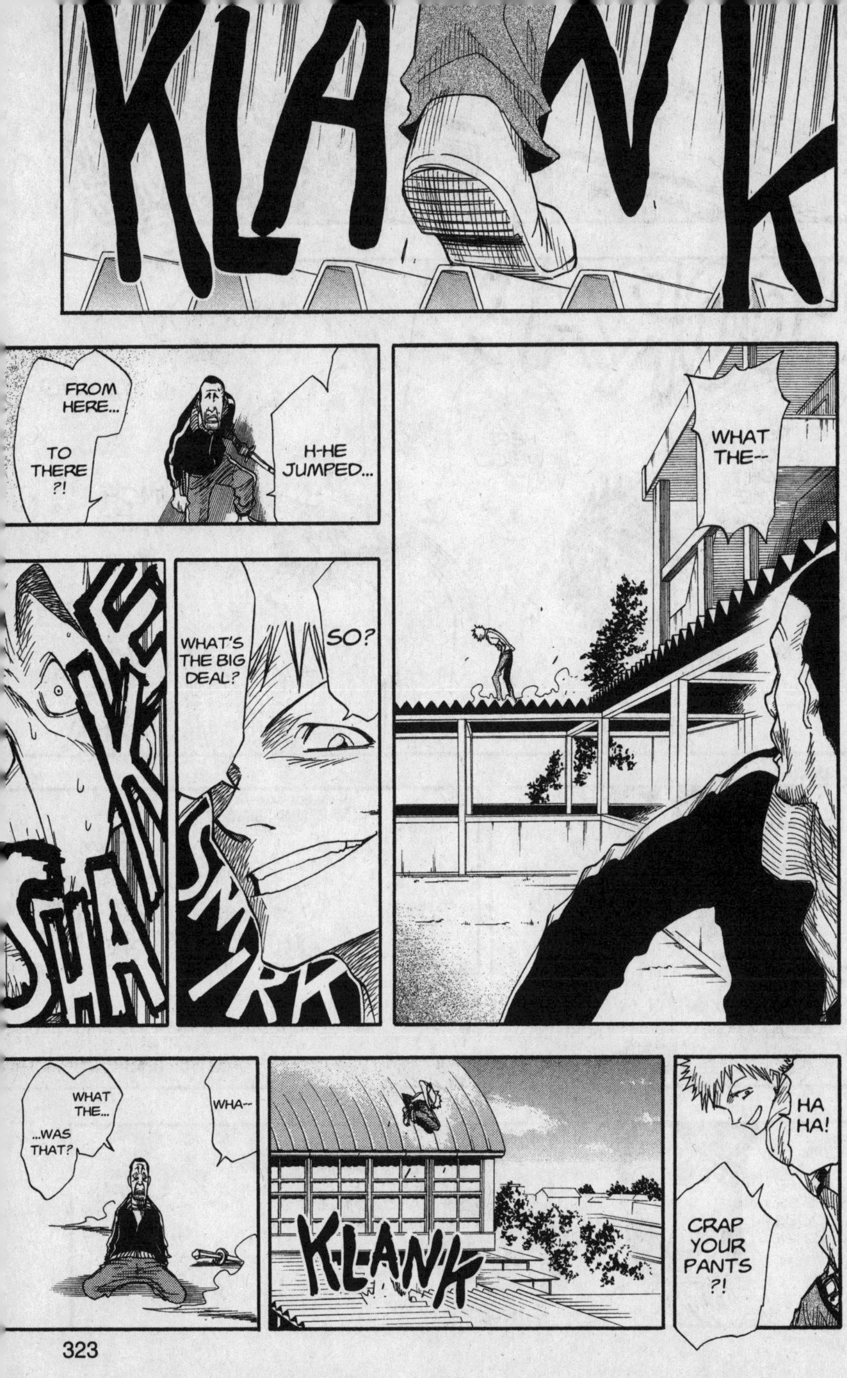
KLANK
WHAT THE--
H-HE JUMPED...
FROM HERE...
TO THERE ?!
SO?
WHAT'S THE BIG DEAL?
SMIRK
SHAK
HA HA!
CRAP YOUR PANTS ?!
KLANK
WHA--
WHAT THE...
...WAS THAT?

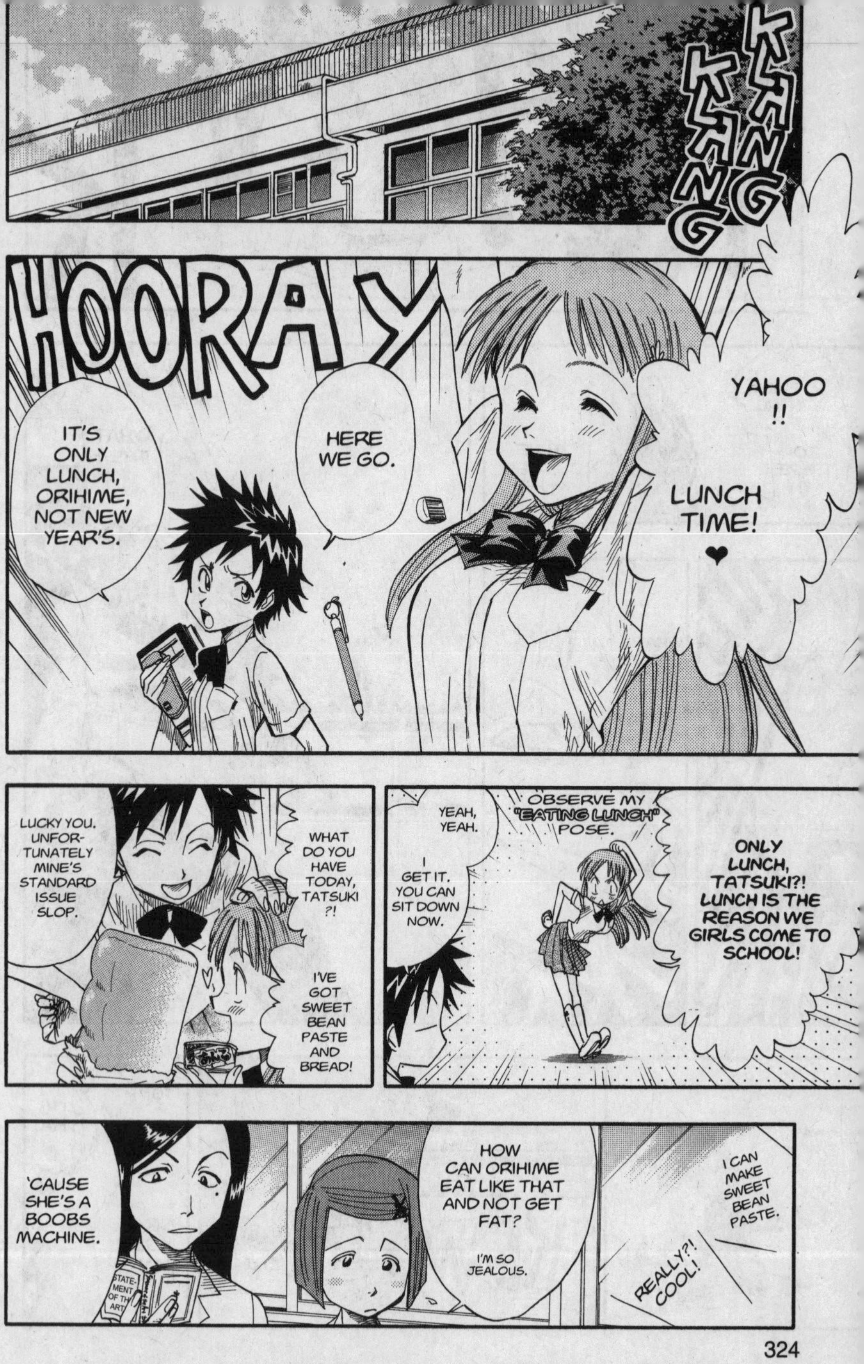

KLANG KLANG
HOORAY
YAHOO!!
LUNCH TIME! ❤
HERE WE GO.
IT'S ONLY LUNCH, ORIHIME, NOT NEW YEAR'S.
ONLY LUNCH, TATSUKI?! LUNCH IS THE REASON WE GIRLS COME TO SCHOOL!
OBSERVE MY "EATING LUNCH" POSE.
YEAH, YEAH.
I GET IT. YOU CAN SIT DOWN NOW.
WHAT DO YOU HAVE TODAY, TATSUKI?!
I'VE GOT SWEET BEAN PASTE AND BREAD!
LUCKY YOU. UNFORTUNATELY MINE'S STANDARD ISSUE SLOP.
I CAN MAKE SWEET BEAN PASTE.
REALLY?! COOL!
HOW CAN ORIHIME EAT LIKE THAT AND NOT GET FAT?
I'M SO JEALOUS.
'CAUSE SHE'S A BOOBS MACHINE.
STATEMENT OF TH ART

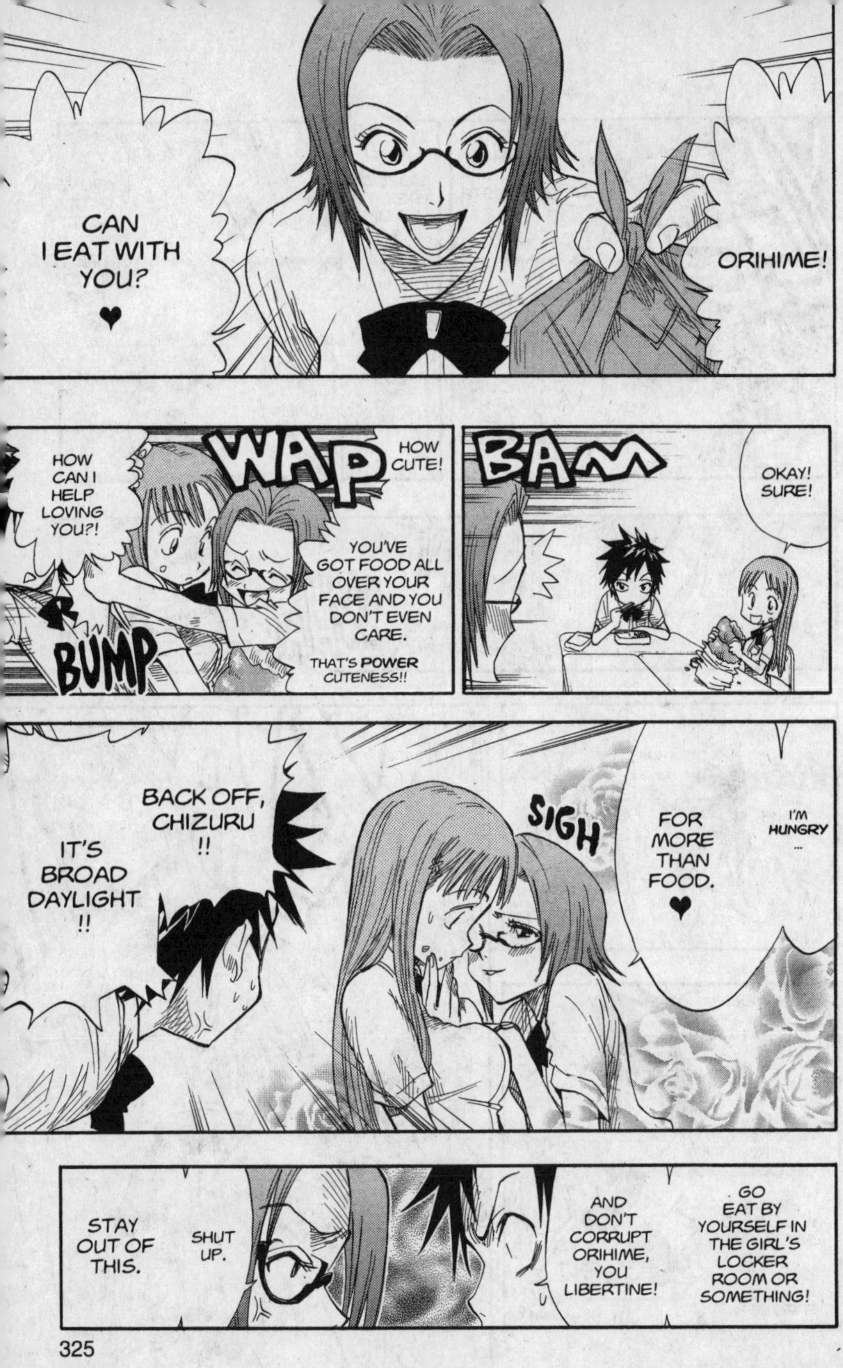
ORIHIME!
CAN I EAT WITH YOU? ♥
OKAY! SURE!
BAM
WAP
HOW CUTE!
YOU'VE GOT FOOD ALL OVER YOUR FACE AND YOU DON'T EVEN CARE.
THAT'S **POWER** CUTENESS!!
HOW CAN I HELP LOVING YOU?!
BUMP
I'M **HUNGRY** ...
FOR MORE THAN FOOD. ♥
SIGH
BACK OFF, CHIZURU !!
IT'S BROAD DAYLIGHT !!
GO EAT BY YOURSELF IN THE GIRL'S LOCKER ROOM OR SOMETHING!
AND DON'T CORRUPT ORIHIME, YOU LIBERTINE!
SHUT UP.
STAY OUT OF THIS.

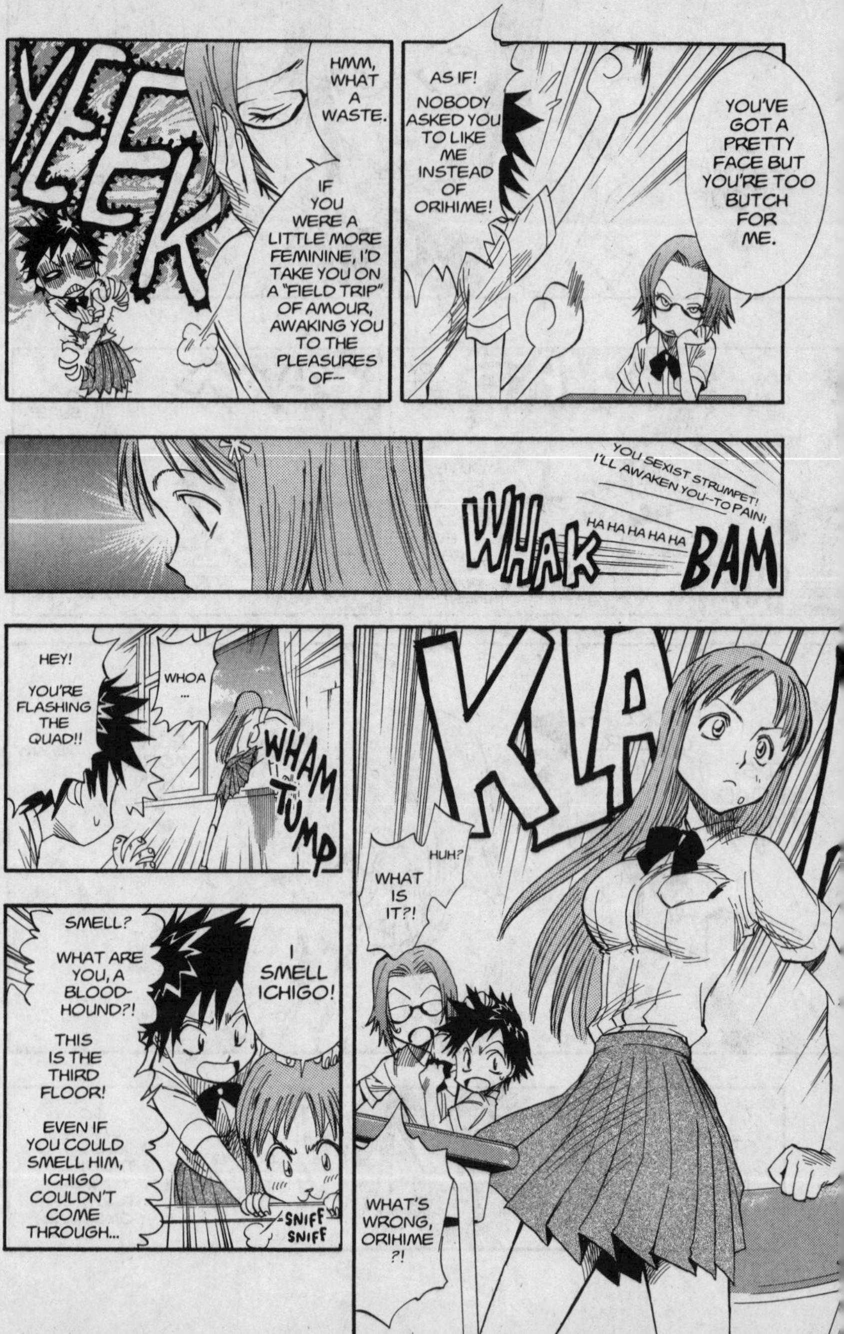
YOU'VE GOT A PRETTY FACE BUT YOU'RE TOO BUTCH FOR ME.
AS IF! NOBODY ASKED YOU TO LIKE ME INSTEAD OF ORIHIME!
HMM, WHAT A WASTE.
IF YOU WERE A LITTLE MORE FEMININE, I'D TAKE YOU ON A "FIELD TRIP" OF AMOUR, AWAKING YOU TO THE PLEASURES OF--
YEEK
YOU SEXIST STRUMPET! I'LL AWAKEN YOU--TO PAIN!
BAM
HA HA HA HA HA
WHAK
KLA
HUH?
WHAT IS IT?!
WHAT'S WRONG, ORIHIME?!
WHAM
TUMP
WHOA...
HEY! YOU'RE FLASHING THE QUAD!!
I SMELL ICHIGO!
SNIFF SNIFF
SMELL? WHAT ARE YOU, A BLOOD-HOUND?! THIS IS THE THIRD FLOOR! EVEN IF YOU COULD SMELL HIM, ICHIGO COULDN'T COME THROUGH...

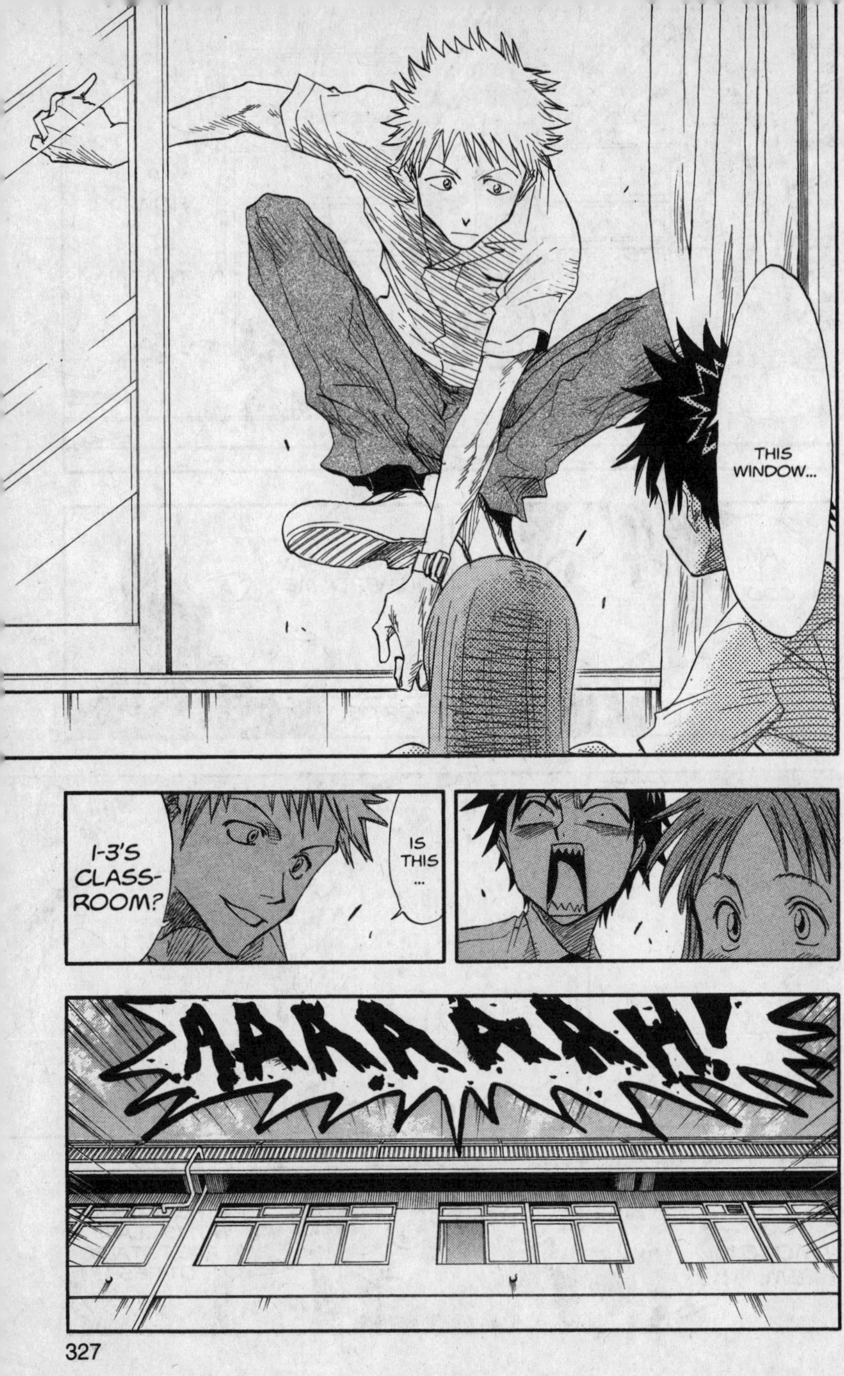
THIS WINDOW...
IS THIS ...
I-3'S CLASS-ROOM?
AARRRRH!

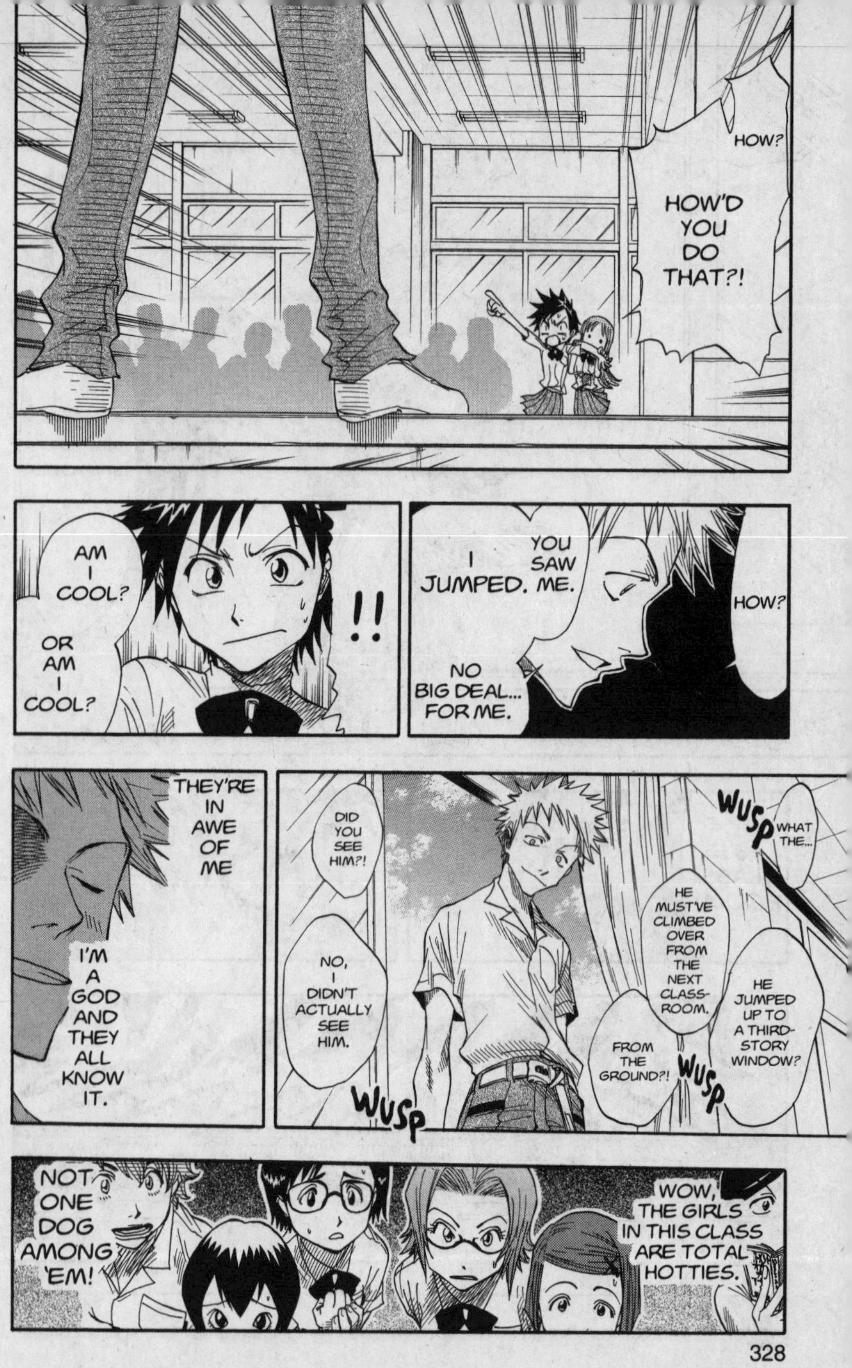
HOW?
HOW'D YOU DO THAT?!
HOW?
I JUMPED. YOU SAW ME.
NO BIG DEAL... FOR ME.
!!
AM I COOL?
OR AM I COOL?
WUSP
WHAT THE...
HE MUST'VE CLIMBED OVER FROM THE NEXT CLASS-ROOM.
HE JUMPED UP TO A THIRD-STORY WINDOW?
FROM THE GROUND?!
WUSP
DID YOU SEE HIM?!
NO, I DIDN'T ACTUALLY SEE HIM.
WUSP
THEY'RE IN AWE OF ME
I'M A GOD AND THEY ALL KNOW IT.
WOW, THE GIRLS IN THIS CLASS ARE TOTAL HOTTIES.
NOT ONE DOG AMONG 'EM!

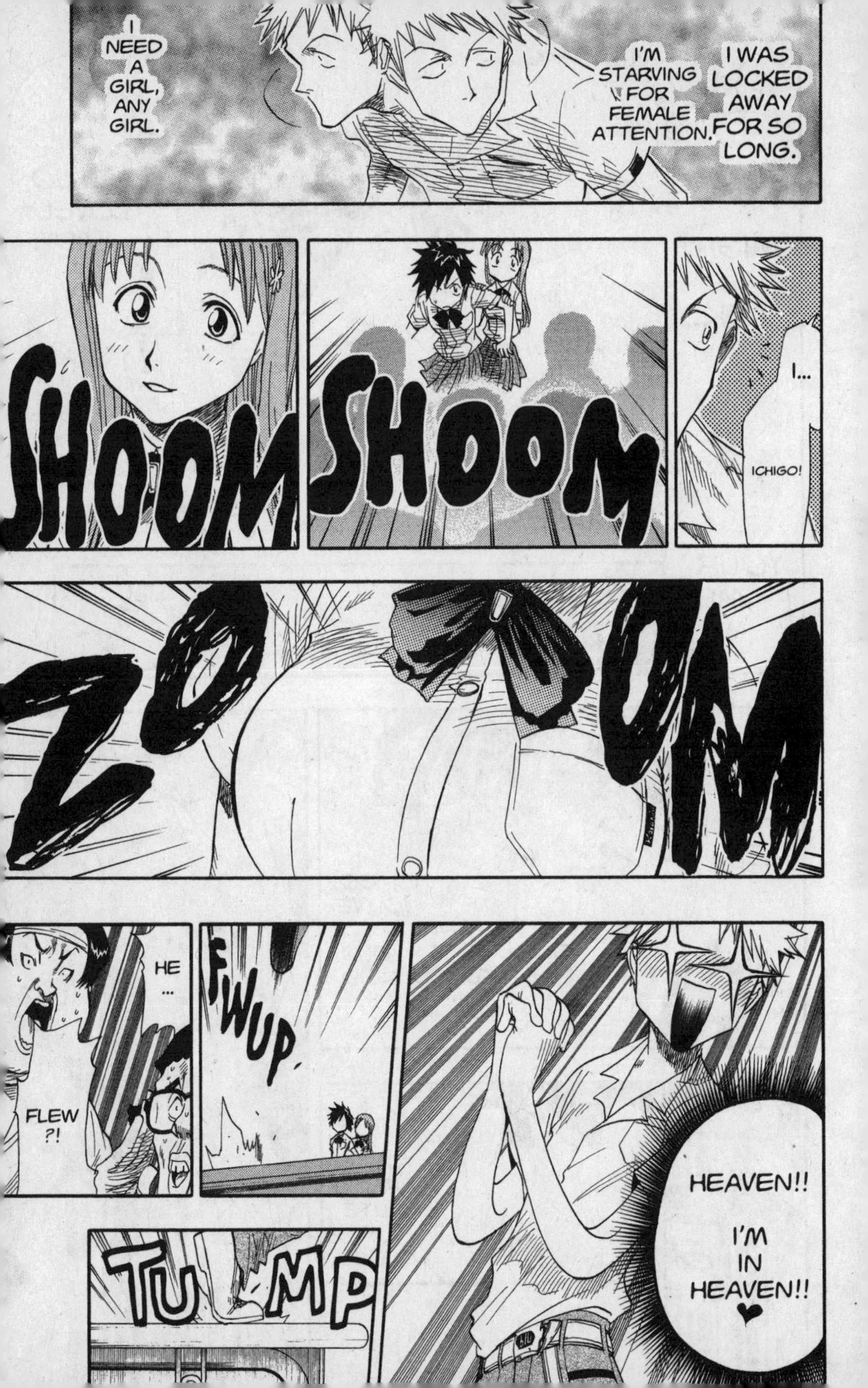
I WAS LOCKED AWAY FOR SO LONG.
I'M STARVING FOR FEMALE ATTENTION.
I NEED A GIRL, ANY GIRL.
I...
ICHIGO!
SHOOM
SHOOM
ZOOM
HEAVEN!!
I'M IN HEAVEN!! ♥
FWUP
HE...
FLEW?!
TUMP

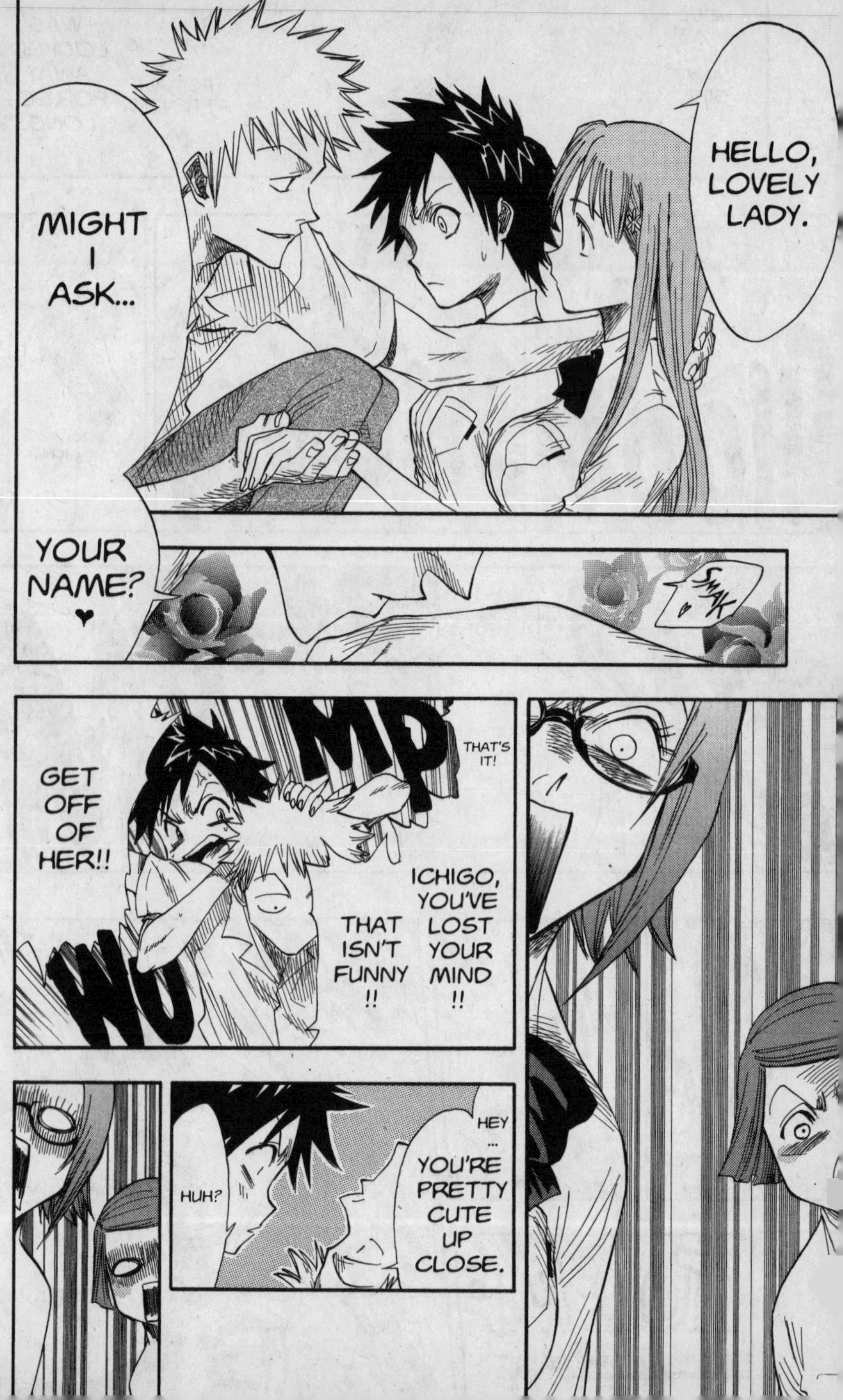
HELLO, LOVELY LADY.
MIGHT I ASK...
SMAK
YOUR NAME? ♥
THAT'S IT!
GET OFF OF HER!!
ICHIGO, YOU'VE LOST YOUR MIND!!
THAT ISN'T FUNNY!!
WHOMP
HEY... YOU'RE PRETTY CUTE UP CLOSE.
HUH?

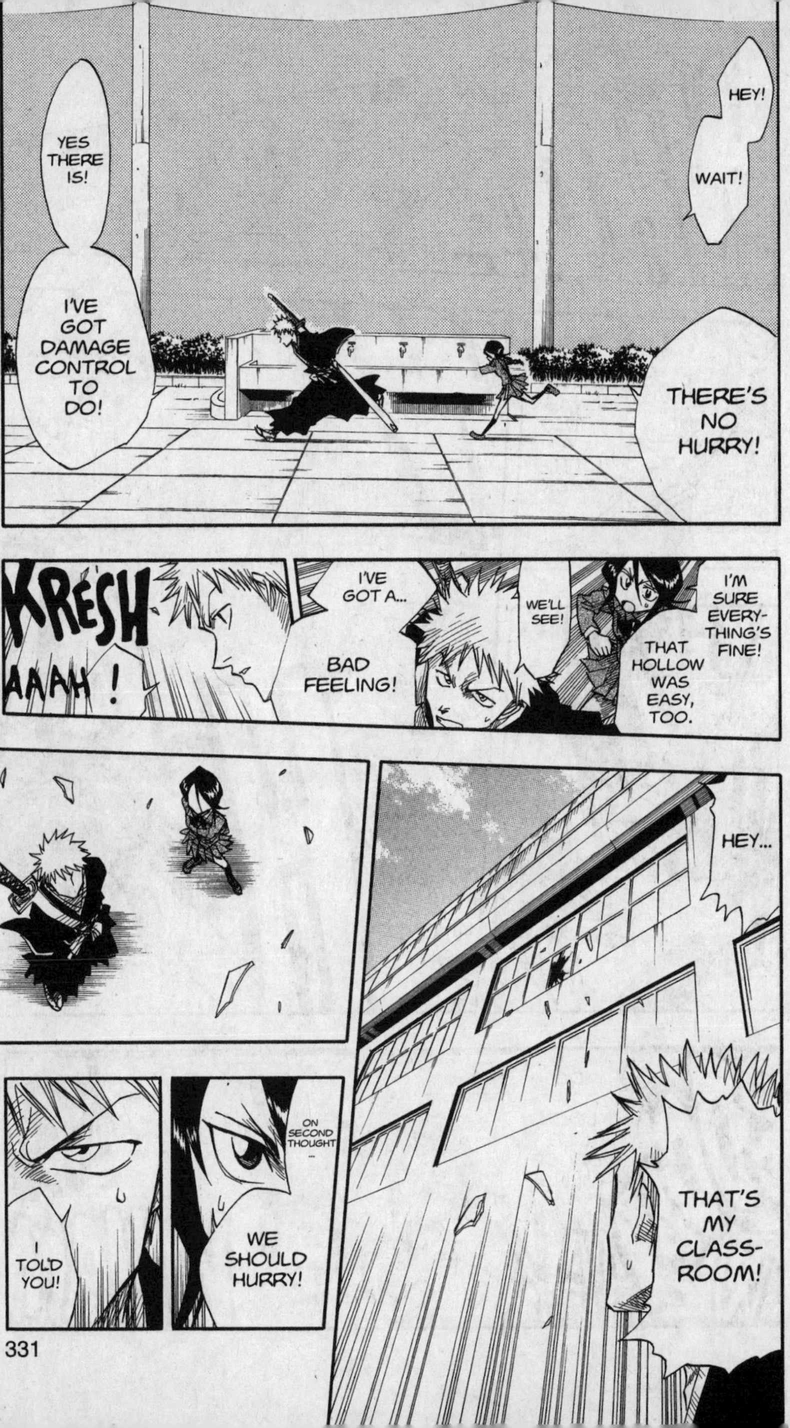
HEY!
WAIT!
THERE'S NO HURRY!
YES THERE IS!
I'VE GOT DAMAGE CONTROL TO DO!
I'M SURE EVERYTHING'S FINE!
THAT HOLLOW WAS EASY, TOO.
WE'LL SEE!
I'VE GOT A...
BAD FEELING!
KRESH
AAAH!
HEY...
THAT'S MY CLASSROOM!
ON SECOND THOUGHT...
WE SHOULD HURRY!
I TOLD YOU!

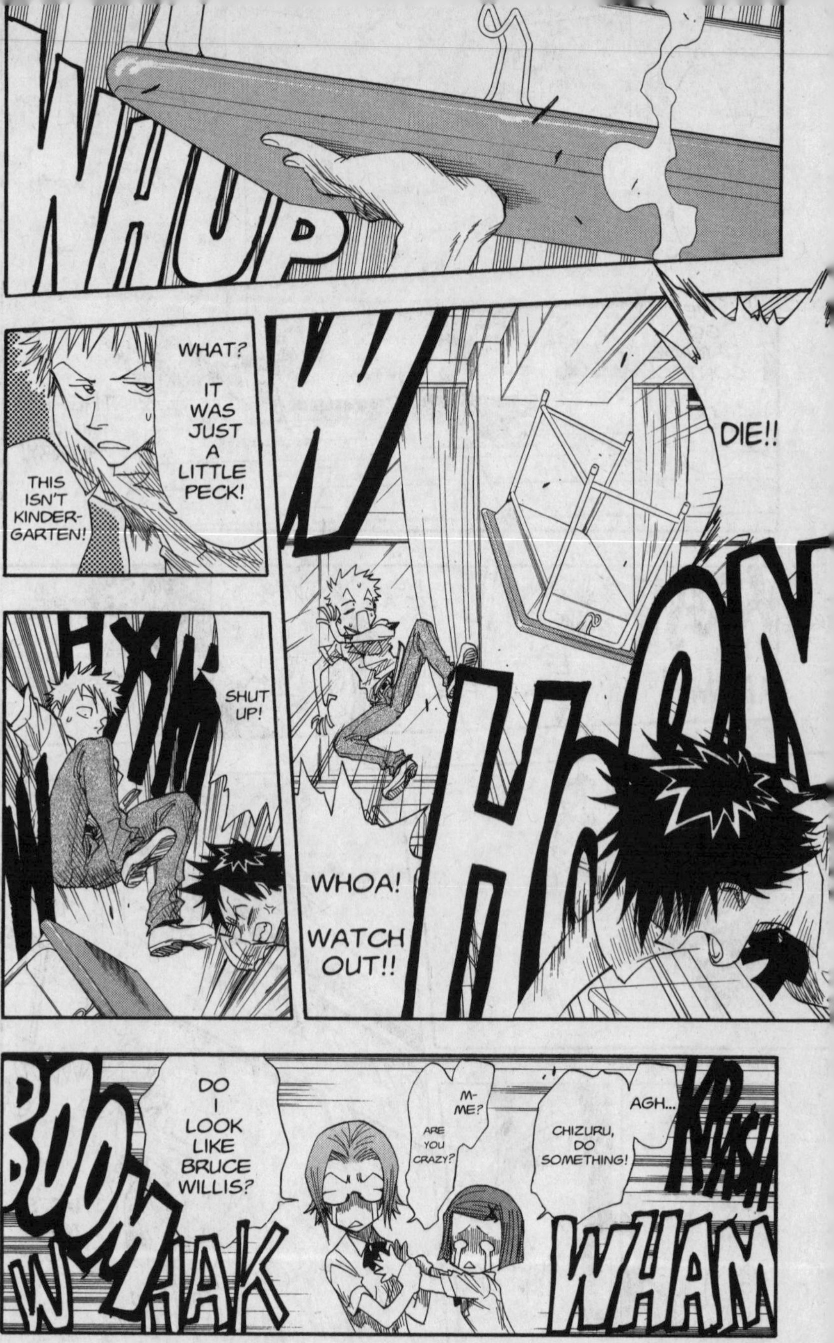
WHUP
DIE!!
WHOA!
WATCH OUT!!
WHAT?
IT WAS JUST A LITTLE PECK!
THIS ISN'T KINDER-GARTEN!
SHUT UP!
KRASH
WHAM
AGH...
CHIZURU, DO SOMETHING!
M-ME?
ARE YOU CRAZY?
DO I LOOK LIKE BRUCE WILLIS?
BOOM
WHAK

READ THIS WAY

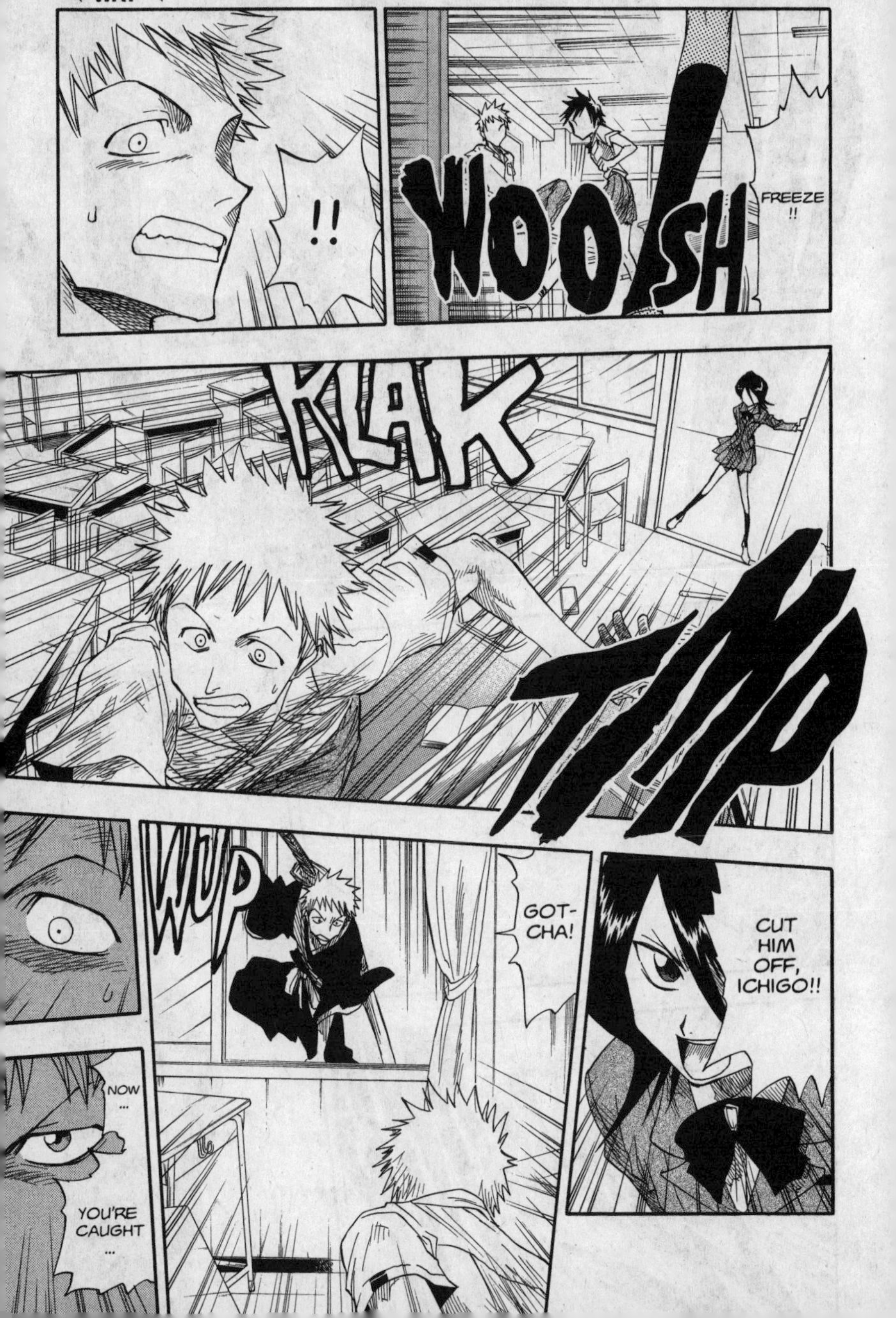
WOOSH
FREEZE !!
!!
KLAK
TAP
CUT HIM OFF, ICHIGO!!
GOT-CHA!
WUP
NOW ...
YOU'RE CAUGHT ...

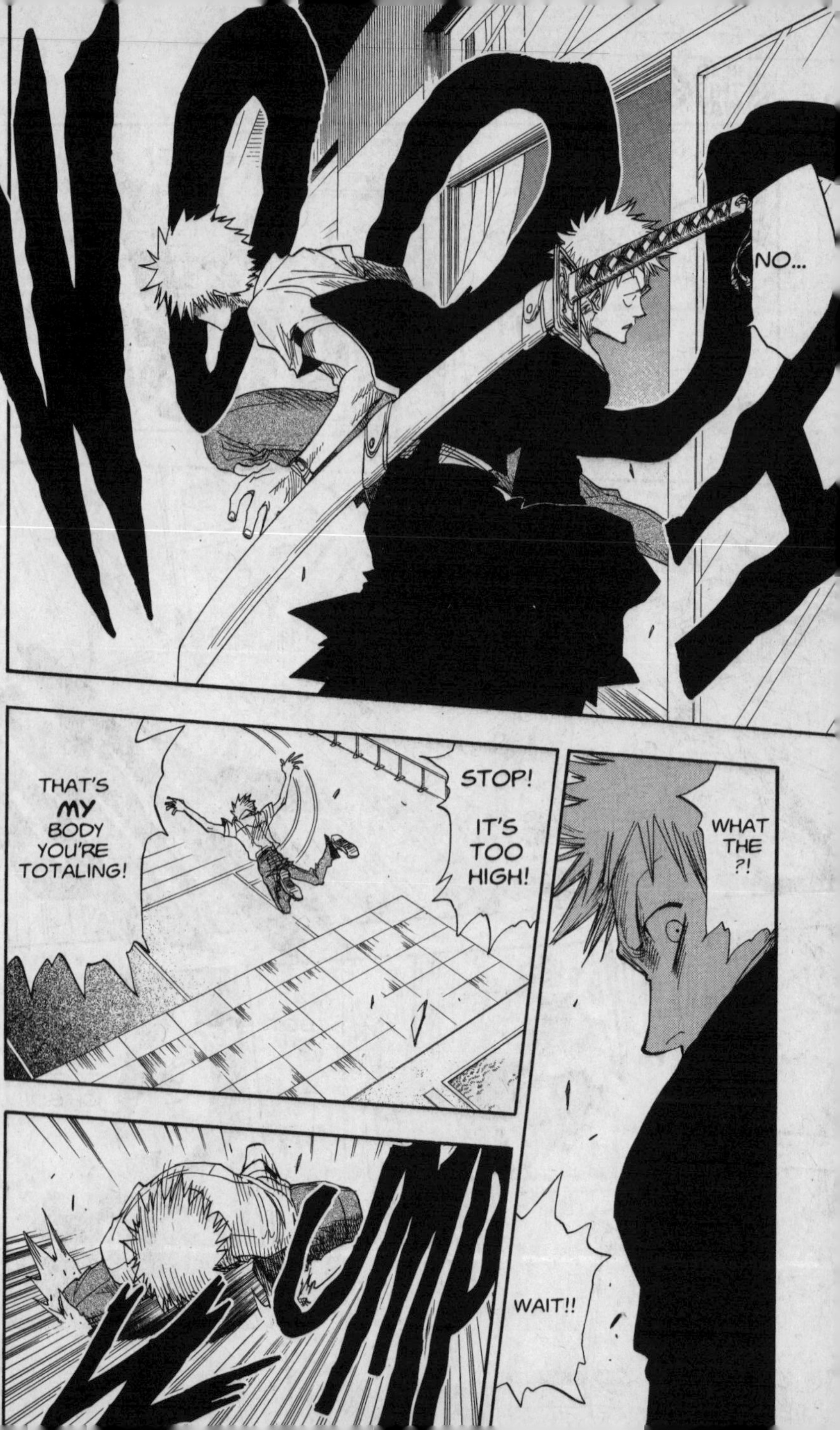
NO...
WHAT THE ?!
WAIT!!
STOP!
IT'S TOO HIGH!
THAT'S **MY** BODY YOU'RE TOTALING!

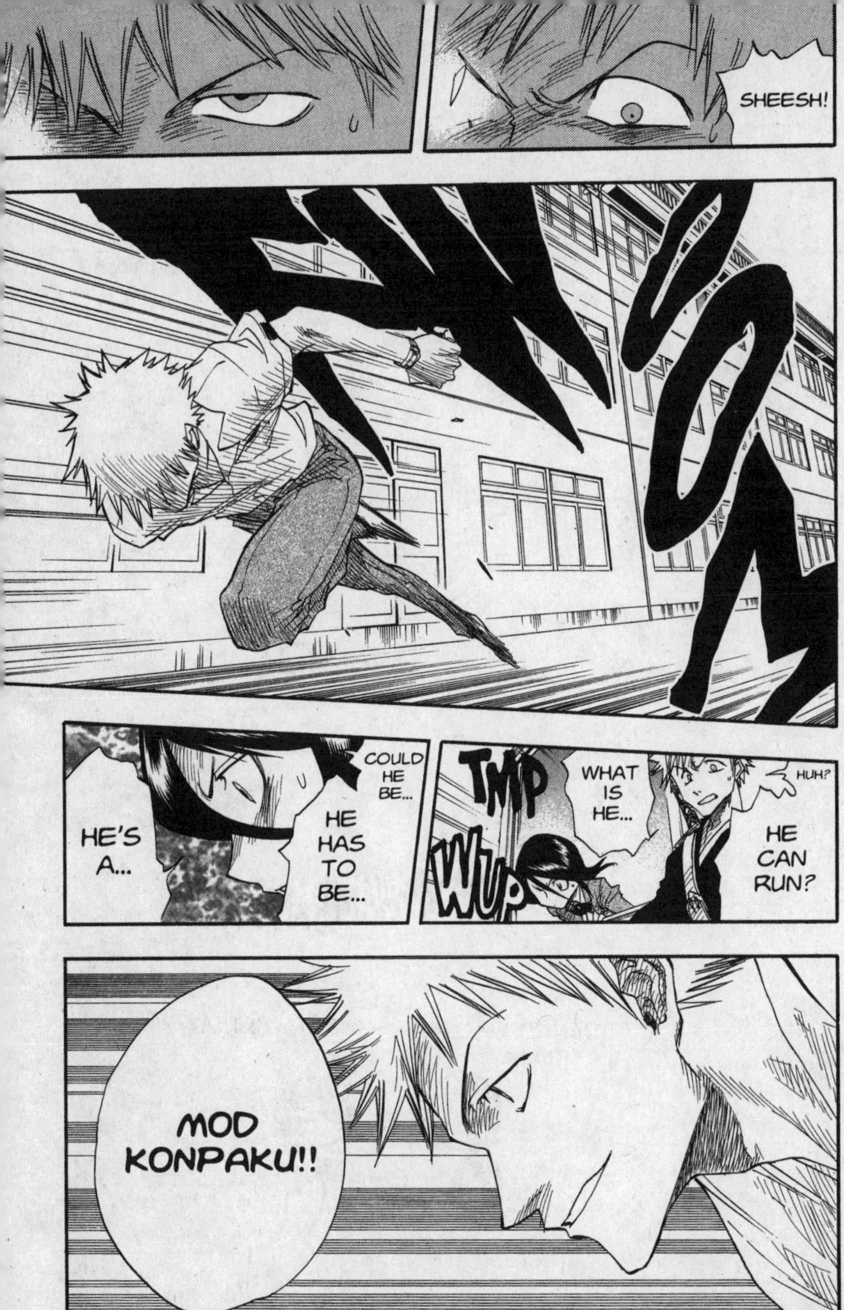
SHEESH!
HUH?
HE CAN RUN?
WHAT IS HE...
TMP
WUP
COULD HE BE...
HE HAS TO BE...
HE'S A...
MOD KONPAKU!!

KRASH WHAM BANG

I THINK IT WAS...
RUKIA?

WHAT WAS THAT?

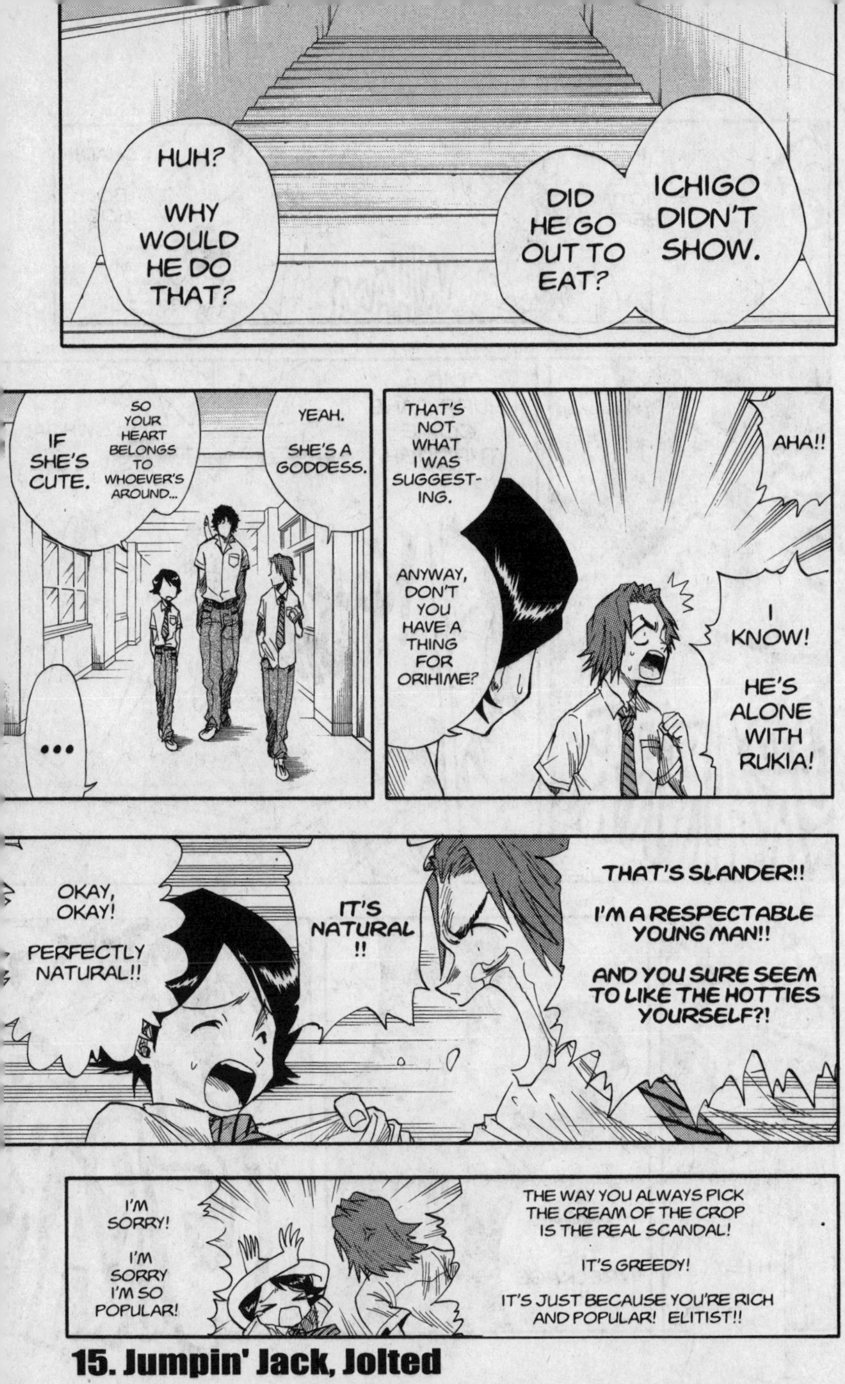
ICHIGO DIDN'T SHOW.
DID HE GO OUT TO EAT?
HUH? WHY WOULD HE DO THAT?
AHA!!
I KNOW! HE'S ALONE WITH RUKIA!
THAT'S NOT WHAT I WAS SUGGEST-ING.
ANYWAY, DON'T YOU HAVE A THING FOR ORIHIME?
YEAH. SHE'S A GODDESS.
SO YOUR HEART BELONGS TO WHOEVER'S AROUND...
IF SHE'S CUTE.
...
THAT'S SLANDER!! I'M A RESPECTABLE YOUNG MAN!! AND YOU SURE SEEM TO LIKE THE HOTTIES YOURSELF?!
IT'S NATURAL!!
OKAY, OKAY! PERFECTLY NATURAL!!
THE WAY YOU ALWAYS PICK THE CREAM OF THE CROP IS THE REAL SCANDAL! IT'S GREEDY! IT'S JUST BECAUSE YOU'RE RICH AND POPULAR! ELITIST!!
I'M SORRY! I'M SORRY I'M SO POPULAR!

15. Jumpin' Jack, Jolted

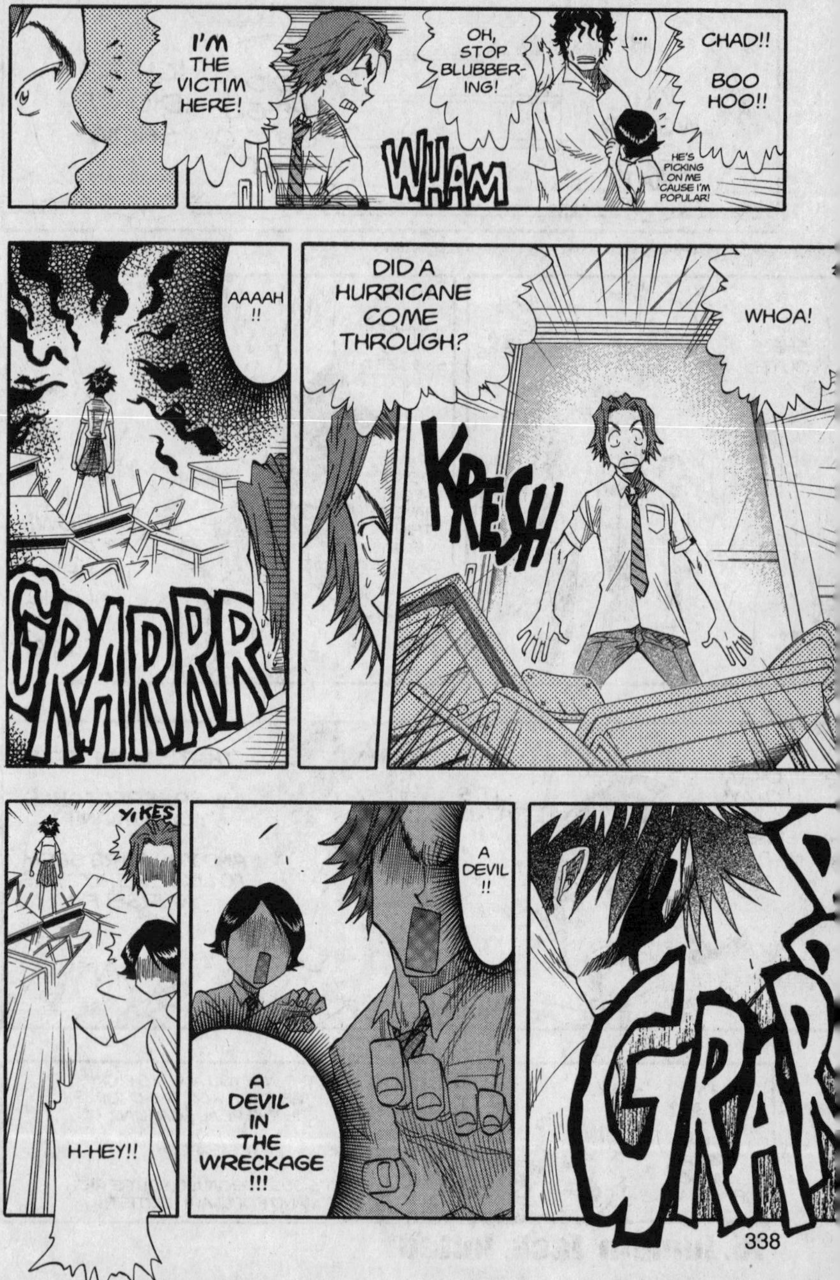
CHAD!! BOO HOO!!
HE'S PICKING ON ME 'CAUSE I'M POPULAR!
...
OH, STOP BLUBBER-ING!
WHAM
I'M THE VICTIM HERE!
WHOA!
DID A HURRICANE COME THROUGH?
KRESH
AAAAH !!
GRARRR
GRAR
A DEVIL !!
A DEVIL IN THE WRECKAGE !!!
YIKES
H-HEY!!

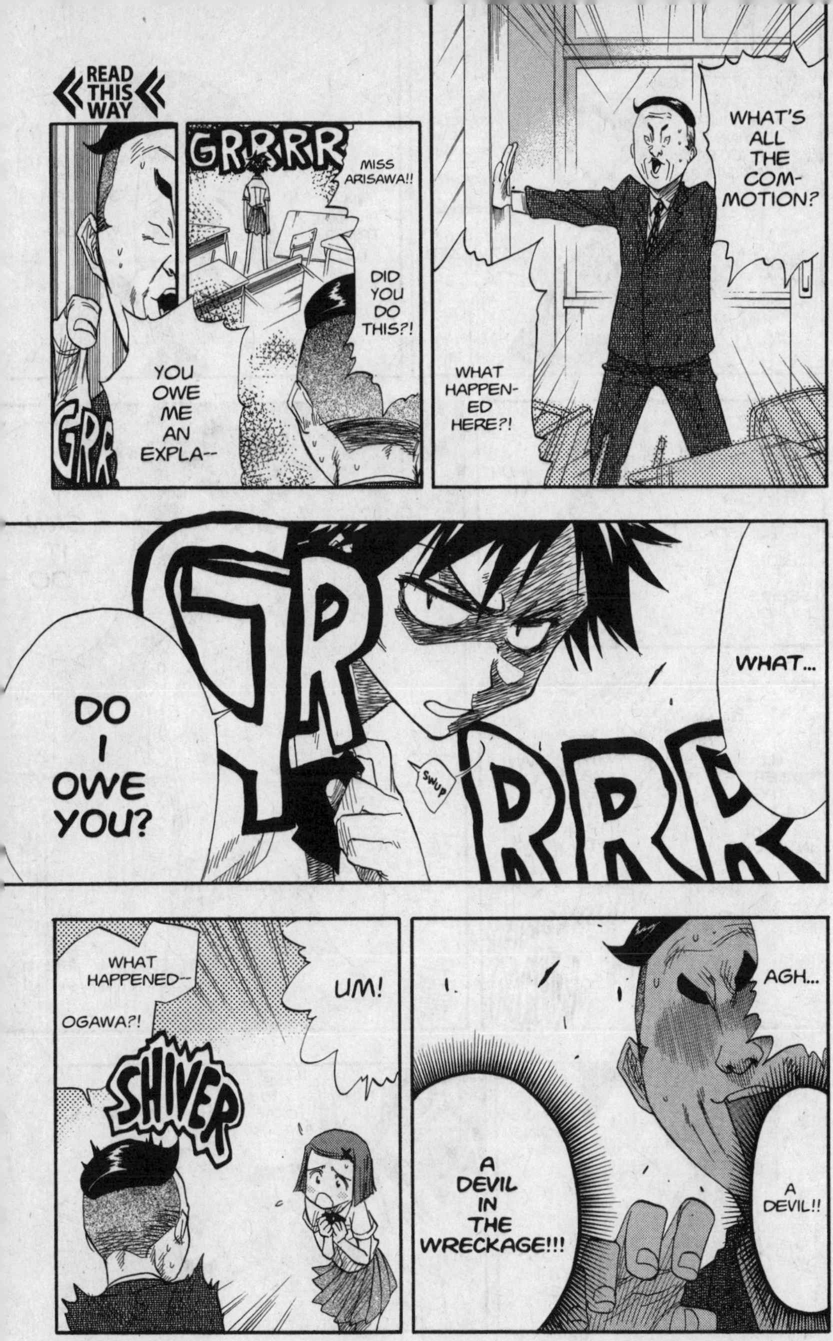
READ THIS WAY
WHAT'S ALL THE COMMOTION?
WHAT HAPPENED HERE?!
GRRRR
MISS ARISAWA!!
DID YOU DO THIS?!
YOU OWE ME AN EXPLA--
GRR
WHAT...
GRRRR
SWUP
DO I OWE YOU?
AGH...
A DEVIL!!
A DEVIL IN THE WRECKAGE!!!
UM!
WHAT HAPPENED--
OGAWA?!
SHIVER

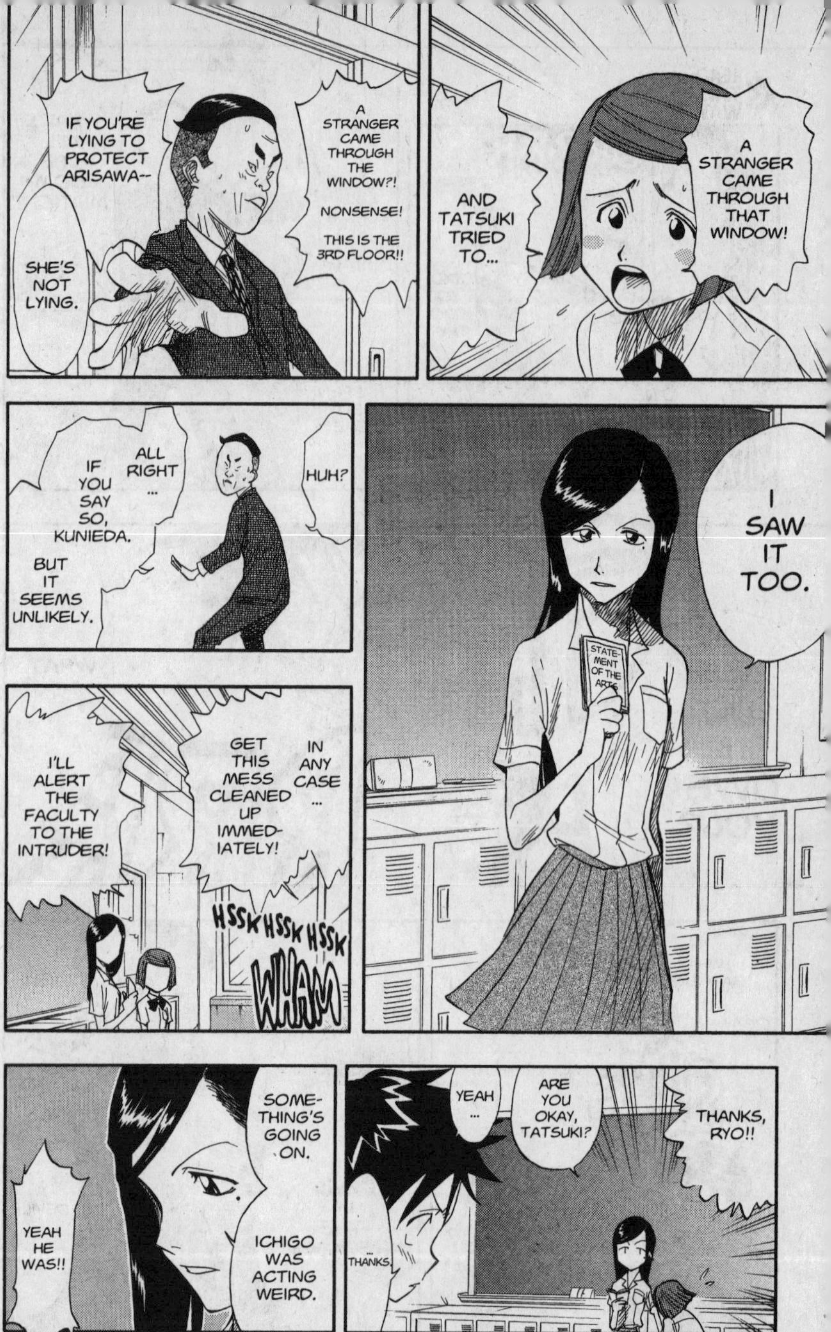
A STRANGER CAME THROUGH THAT WINDOW!
AND TATSUKI TRIED TO...
A STRANGER CAME THROUGH THE WINDOW?! NONSENSE! THIS IS THE 3RD FLOOR!!
IF YOU'RE LYING TO PROTECT ARISAWA--
SHE'S NOT LYING.
I SAW IT TOO.
STATEMENT OF THE ARTS
HUH?
ALL RIGHT ... IF YOU SAY SO, KUNIEDA.
BUT IT SEEMS UNLIKELY.
IN ANY CASE ...
GET THIS MESS CLEANED UP IMMEDIATELY!
I'LL ALERT THE FACULTY TO THE INTRUDER!
HSSK HSSK HSSK
WHAM
THANKS, RYO!!
ARE YOU OKAY, TATSUKI?
YEAH ...
... THANKS.
SOMETHING'S GOING ON.
ICHIGO WAS ACTING WEIRD.
YEAH HE WAS!!

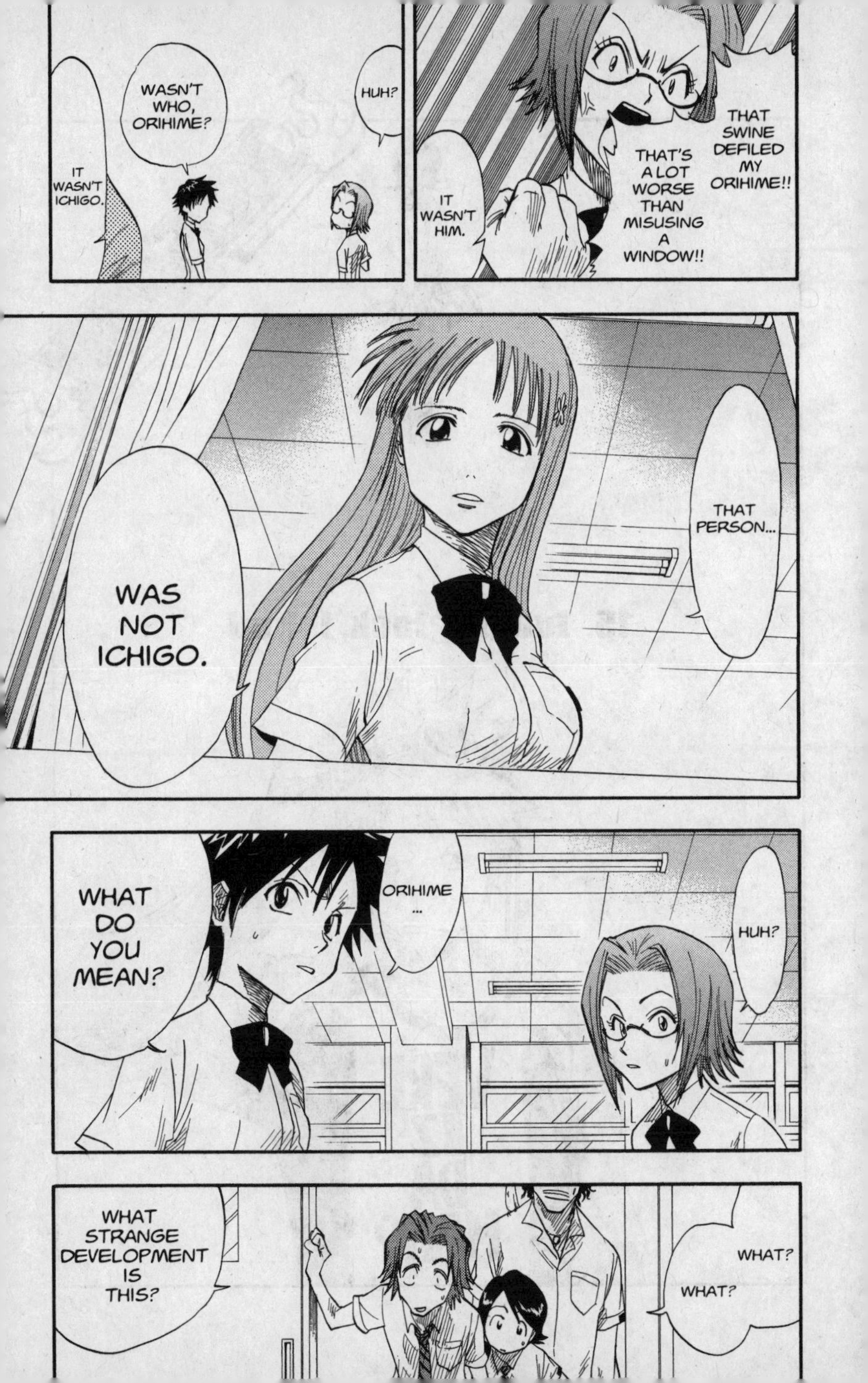
THAT SWINE DEFILED MY ORIHIME!!
THAT'S A LOT WORSE THAN MISUSING A WINDOW!!
IT WASN'T HIM.
HUH?
WASN'T WHO, ORIHIME?
IT WASN'T ICHIGO.
THAT PERSON...
WAS NOT ICHIGO.
HUH?
ORIHIME ...
WHAT DO YOU MEAN?
WHAT?
WHAT?
WHAT STRANGE DEVELOPMENT IS THIS?

15. Jumpin' Jack, Jolted

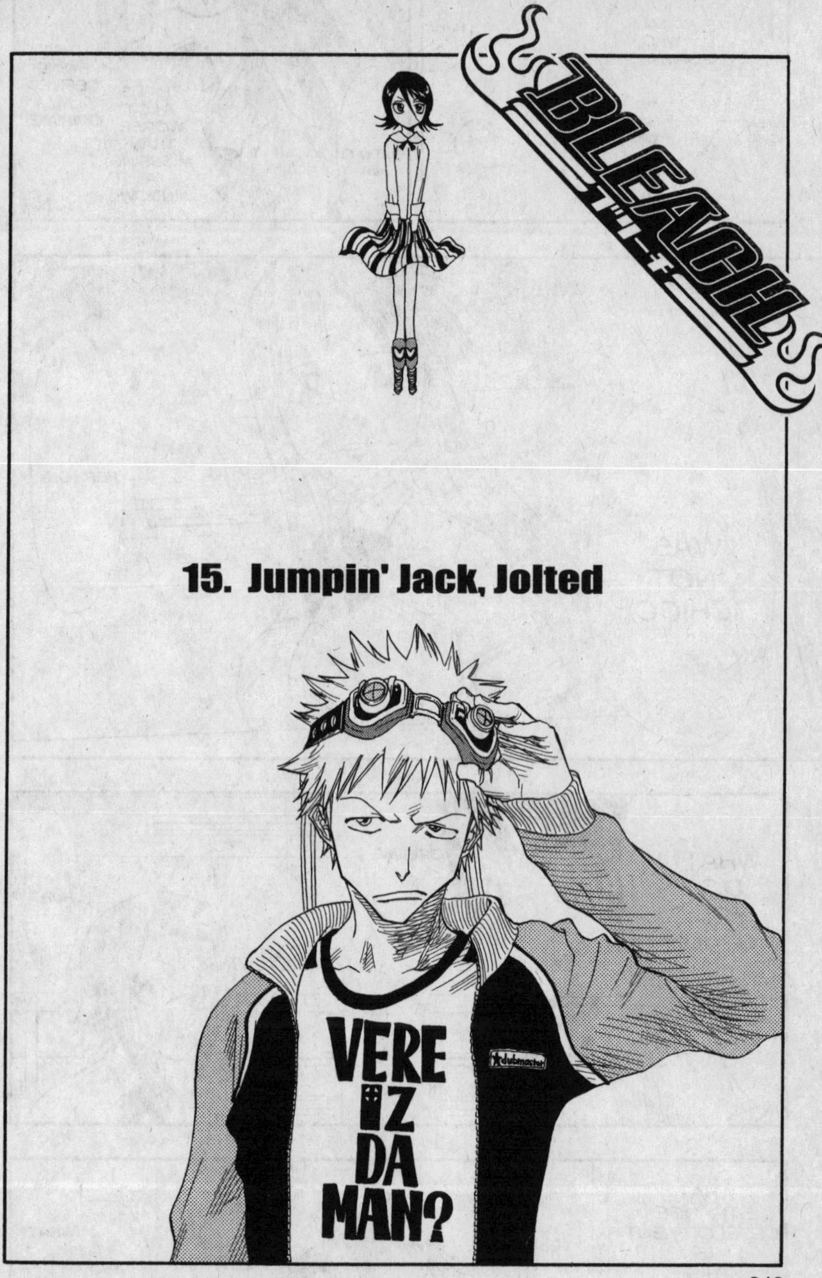
BLEACH
VERE IZ DA MAN?

READ THIS WAY

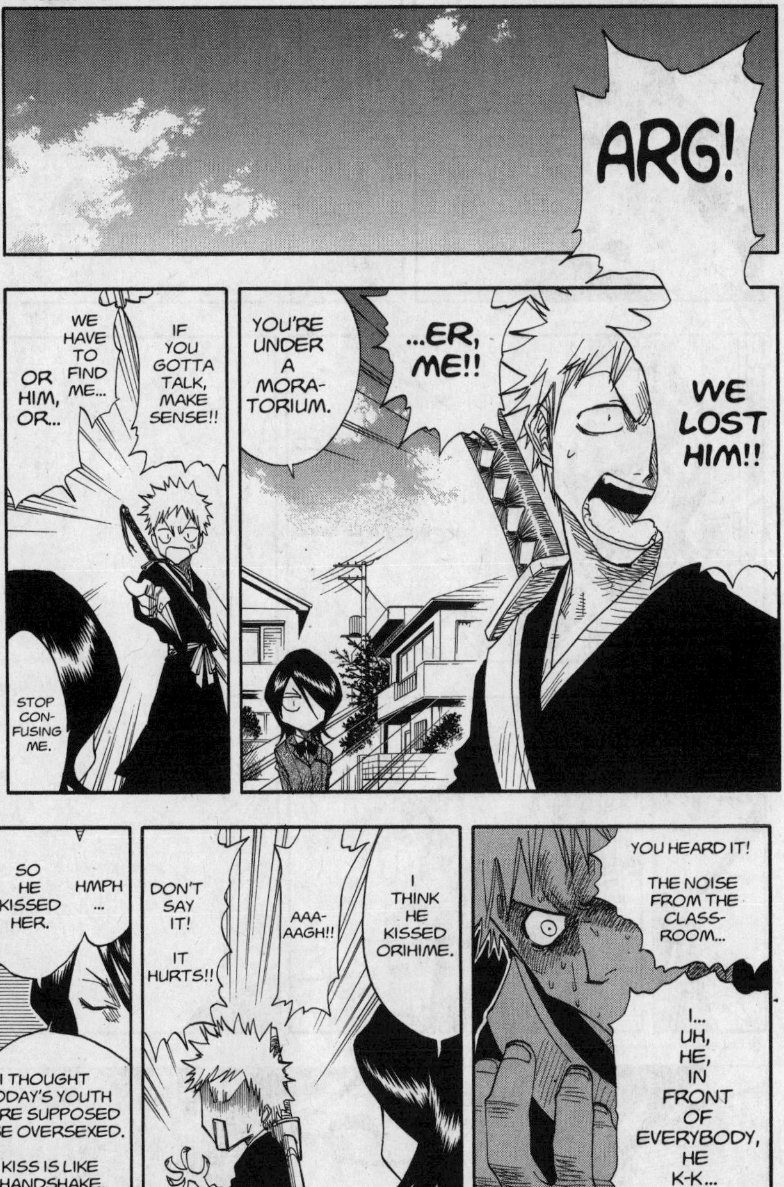
ARG!
WE LOST HIM!!
...ER, ME!!
YOU'RE UNDER A MORATORIUM.
IF YOU GOTTA TALK, MAKE SENSE!!
WE HAVE TO FIND ME...
OR HIM, OR...
STOP CONFUSING ME.
YOU HEARD IT!
THE NOISE FROM THE CLASSROOM...
I... UH, HE, IN FRONT OF EVERYBODY, HE K-K...
I THINK HE KISSED ORIHIME.
AAA-AAGH!!
DON'T SAY IT!
IT HURTS!!
HMPH...
SO HE KISSED HER.
I THOUGHT TODAY'S YOUTH WERE SUPPOSED TO BE OVERSEXED.
A KISS IS LIKE A HANDSHAKE.

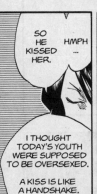

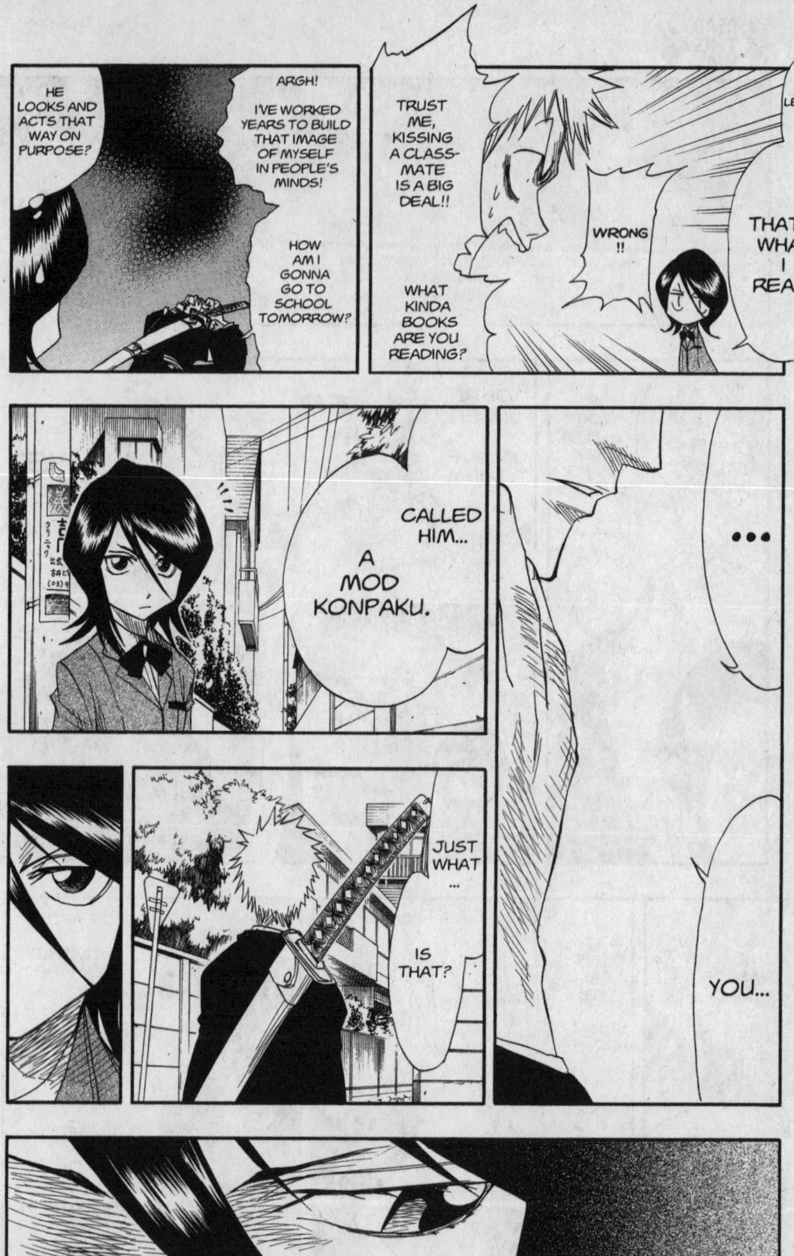
AT LEAST...
THAT'S WHAT I READ.
WRONG!!
TRUST ME, KISSING A CLASSMATE IS A BIG DEAL!!
WHAT KINDA BOOKS ARE YOU READING?
ARGH!
I'VE WORKED YEARS TO BUILD THAT IMAGE OF MYSELF IN PEOPLE'S MINDS!
HOW AM I GONNA GO TO SCHOOL TOMORROW?
HE LOOKS AND ACTS THAT WAY ON PURPOSE?
...
YOU...
CALLED HIM...
A MOD KONPAKU.
JUST WHAT...
IS THAT?

READ THIS WAY

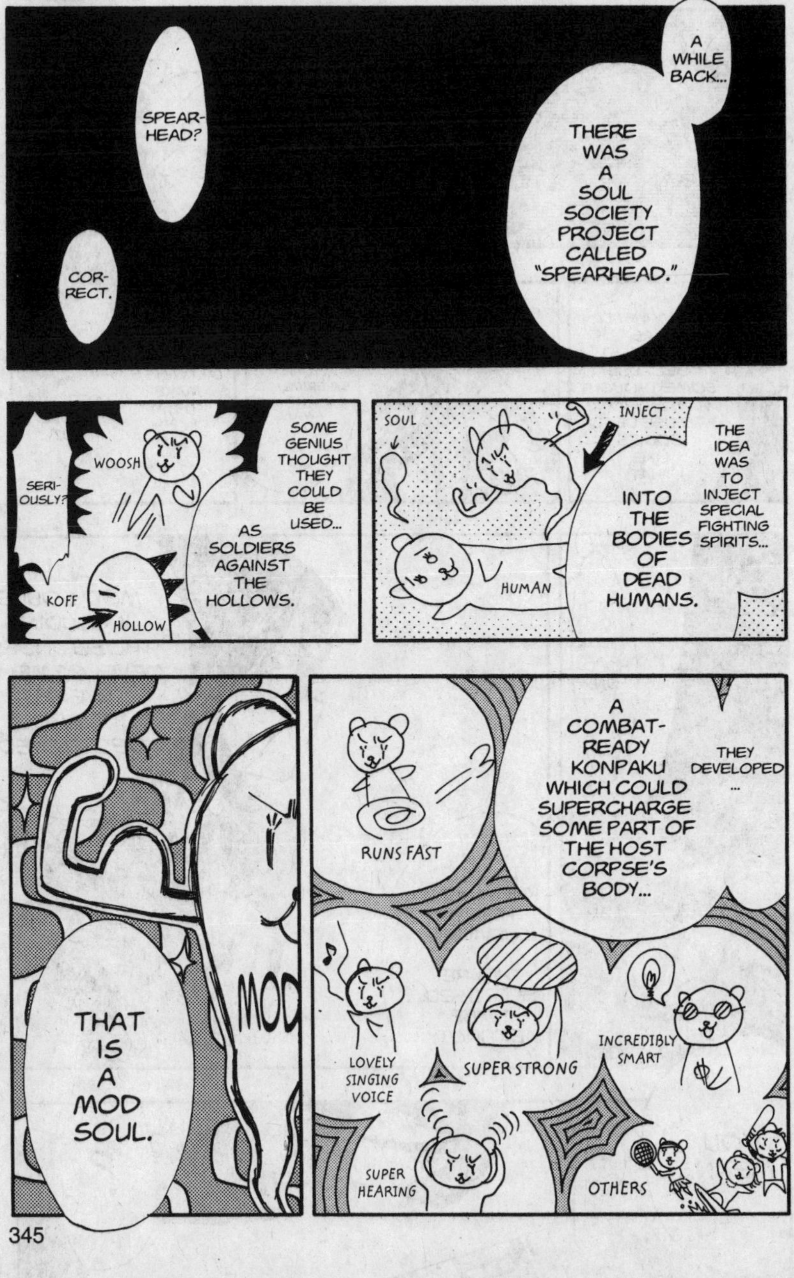
A WHILE BACK...
THERE WAS A SOUL SOCIETY PROJECT CALLED "SPEARHEAD."
SPEAR-HEAD?
COR-RECT.
THE IDEA WAS TO INJECT SPECIAL FIGHTING SPIRITS...
INTO THE BODIES OF DEAD HUMANS.
INJECT
SOUL
HUMAN
SOME GENIUS THOUGHT THEY COULD BE USED...
AS SOLDIERS AGAINST THE HOLLOWS.
WOOSH
SERI-OUSLY?
KOFF
HOLLOW
THEY DEVELOPED...
A COMBAT-READY KONPAKU WHICH COULD SUPERCHARGE SOME PART OF THE HOST CORPSE'S BODY...
RUNS FAST
INCREDIBLY SMART
SUPER STRONG
LOVELY SINGING VOICE
OTHERS
SUPER HEARING
MOD
THAT IS A MOD SOUL.

READ THIS WAY

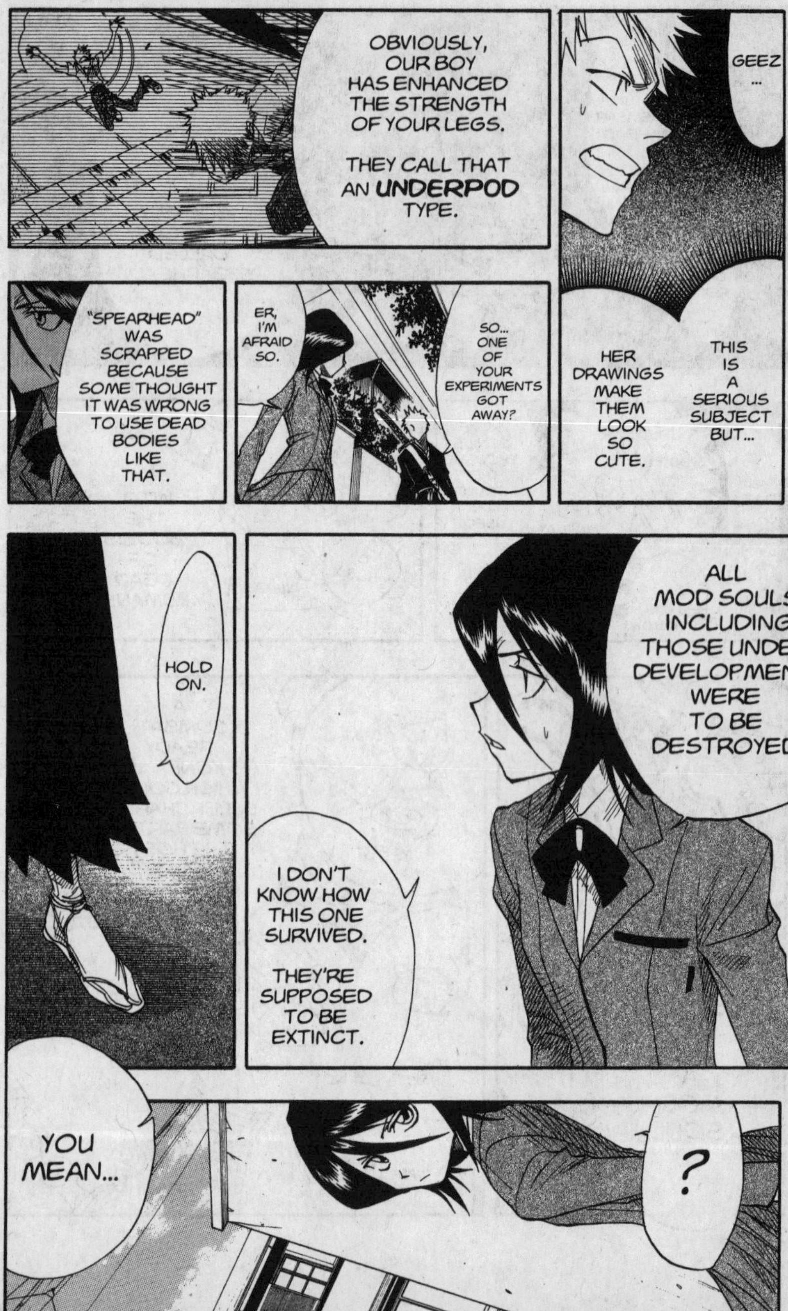
GEEZ...
OBVIOUSLY, OUR BOY HAS ENHANCED THE STRENGTH OF YOUR LEGS.
THEY CALL THAT AN **UNDERPOD** TYPE.
THIS IS A SERIOUS SUBJECT BUT...
HER DRAWINGS MAKE THEM LOOK SO CUTE.
SO... ONE OF YOUR EXPERIMENTS GOT AWAY?
ER, I'M AFRAID SO.
"SPEARHEAD" WAS SCRAPPED BECAUSE SOME THOUGHT IT WAS WRONG TO USE DEAD BODIES LIKE THAT.
ALL MOD SOULS, INCLUDING THOSE UNDER DEVELOPMENT, WERE TO BE DESTROYED.
I DON'T KNOW HOW THIS ONE SURVIVED.
THEY'RE SUPPOSED TO BE EXTINCT.
HOLD ON.
?
YOU MEAN...

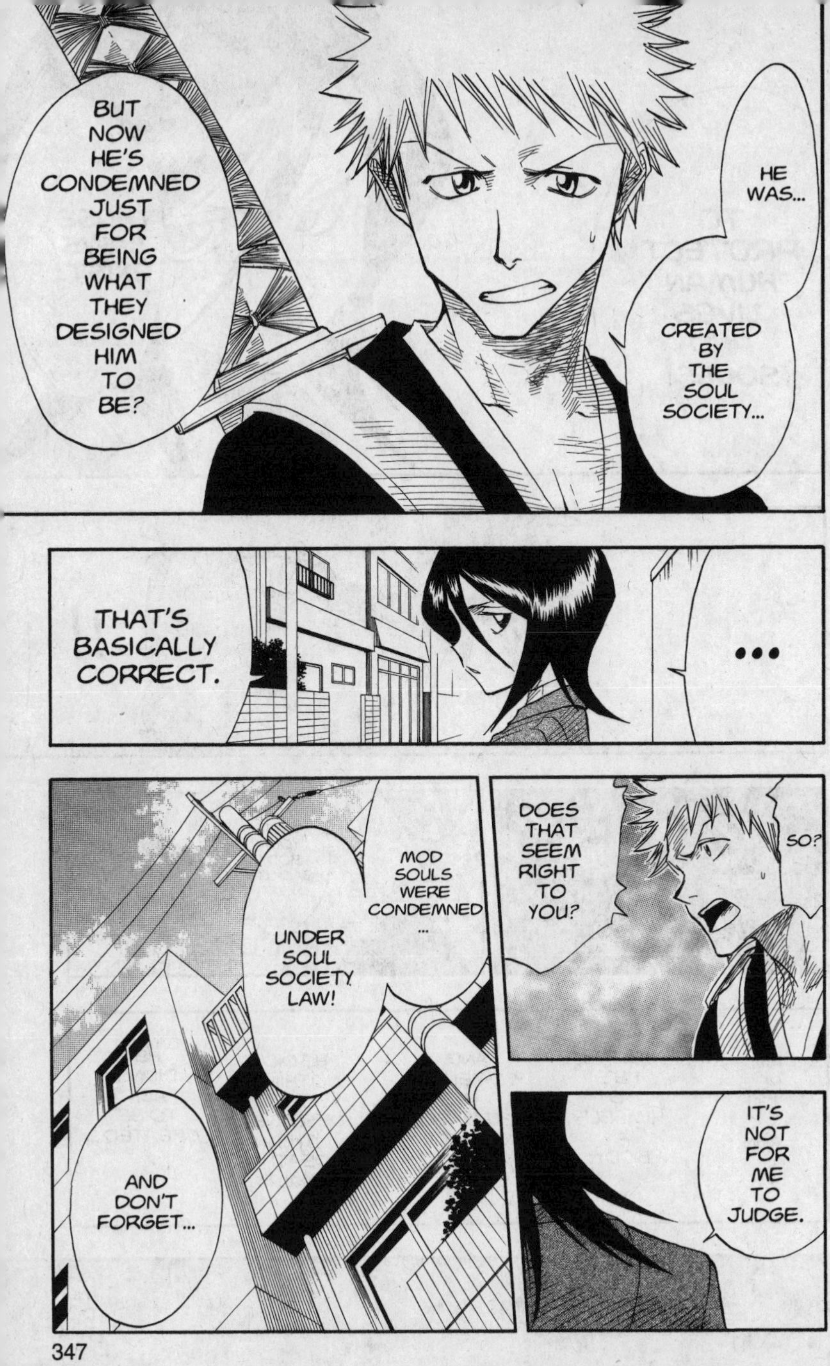
HE WAS...
CREATED BY THE SOUL SOCIETY...
BUT NOW HE'S CONDEMNED JUST FOR BEING WHAT THEY DESIGNED HIM TO BE?
...
THAT'S BASICALLY CORRECT.
SO?
DOES THAT SEEM RIGHT TO YOU?
IT'S NOT FOR ME TO JUDGE.
MOD SOULS WERE CONDEMNED...
UNDER SOUL SOCIETY LAW!
AND DON'T FORGET...

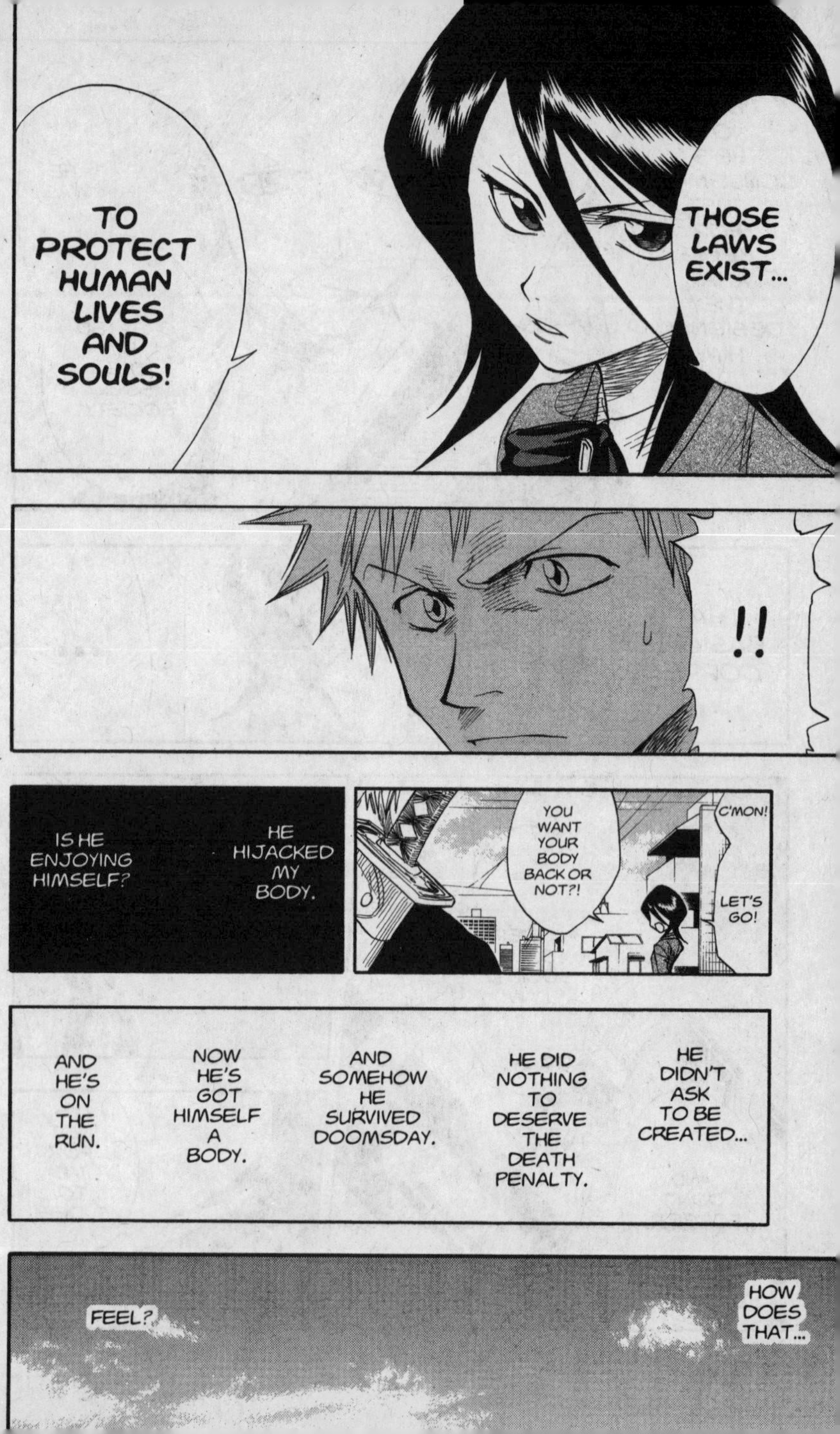
THOSE LAWS EXIST...
TO PROTECT HUMAN LIVES AND SOULS!
!!
C'MON!
YOU WANT YOUR BODY BACK OR NOT?!
LET'S GO!
HE HIJACKED MY BODY.
IS HE ENJOYING HIMSELF?
HE DIDN'T ASK TO BE CREATED...
HE DID NOTHING TO DESERVE THE DEATH PENALTY.
AND SOMEHOW HE SURVIVED DOOMSDAY.
NOW HE'S GOT HIMSELF A BODY.
AND HE'S ON THE RUN.
HOW DOES THAT...
FEEL?

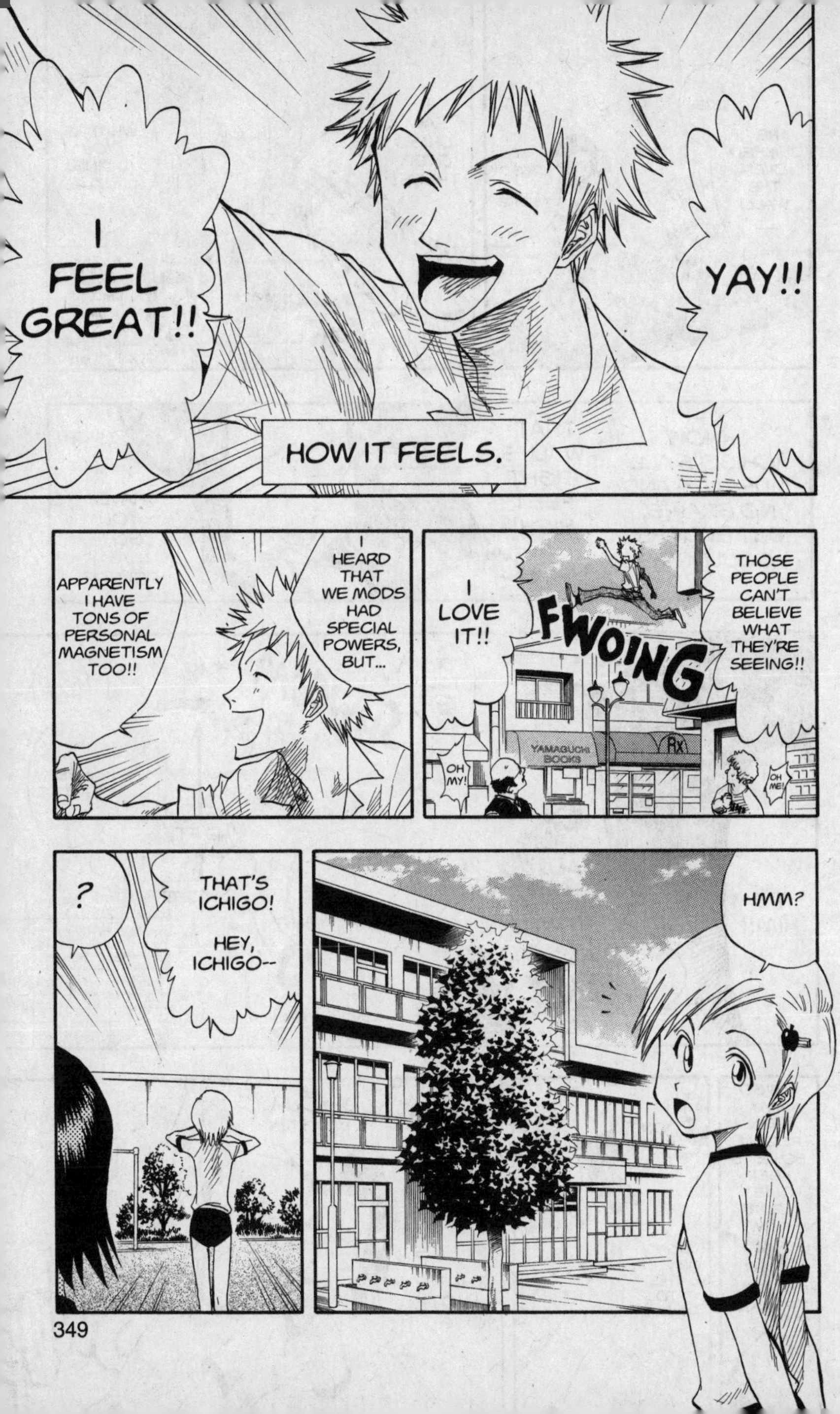
YAY!!
I FEEL GREAT!!
HOW IT FEELS.
THOSE PEOPLE CAN'T BELIEVE WHAT THEY'RE SEEING!!
FWOING
I LOVE IT!!
OH ME!
YAMAGUCHI BOOKS
RX
OH MY!
I HEARD THAT WE MODS HAD SPECIAL POWERS, BUT...
APPARENTLY I HAVE TONS OF PERSONAL MAGNETISM TOO!!
HMM?
THAT'S ICHIGO!
HEY, ICHIGO--
?

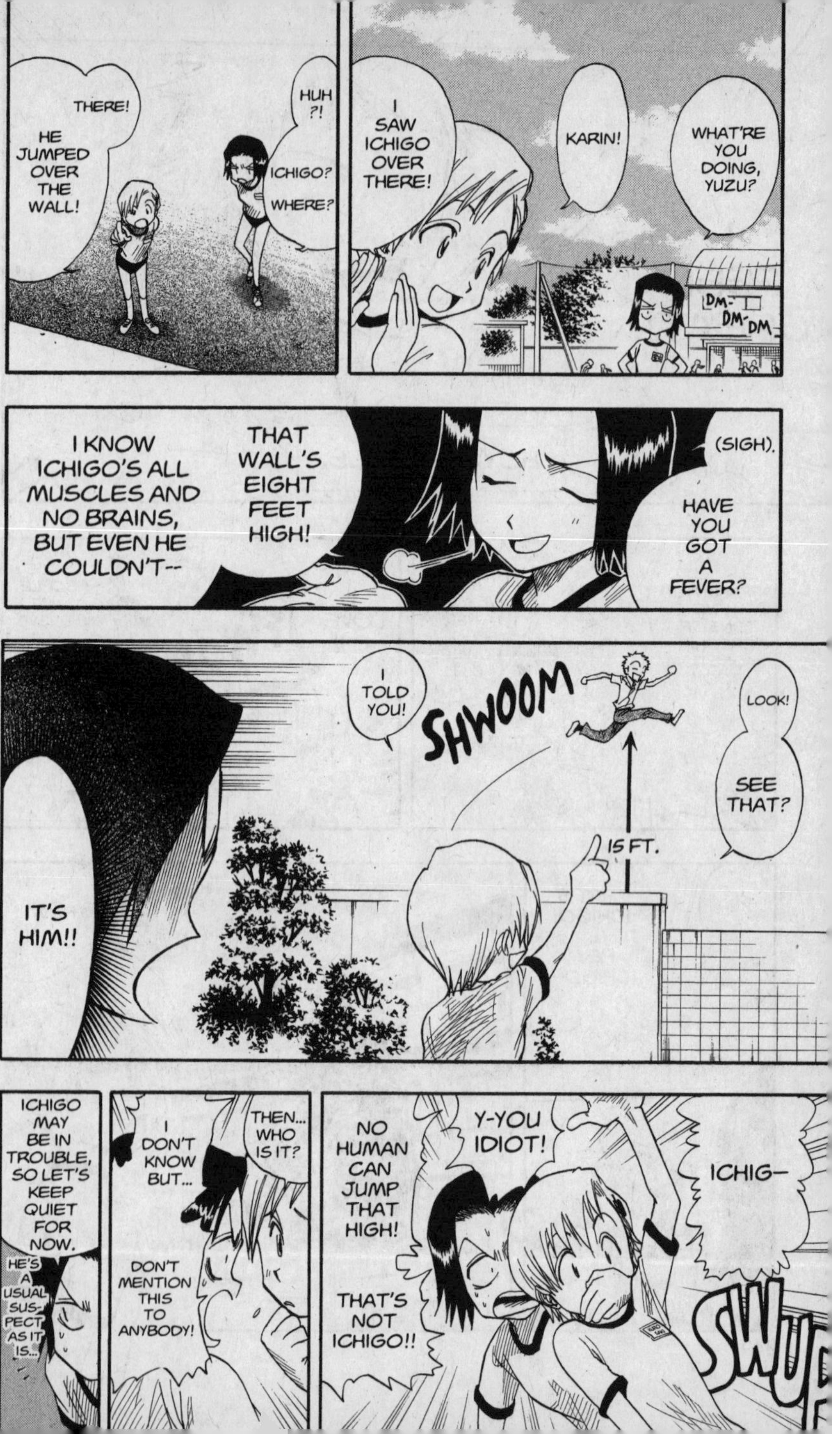
WHAT'RE YOU DOING, YUZU?
KARIN!
I SAW ICHIGO OVER THERE!
DM-DM-DM
HUH?!
ICHIGO? WHERE?
THERE!
HE JUMPED OVER THE WALL!
(SIGH).
HAVE YOU GOT A FEVER?
THAT WALL'S EIGHT FEET HIGH!
I KNOW ICHIGO'S ALL MUSCLES AND NO BRAINS, BUT EVEN HE COULDN'T--
LOOK!
SEE THAT?
I TOLD YOU!
SHWOOM
15 FT.
IT'S HIM!!
ICHIG—
SWUP
Y-YOU IDIOT!
NO HUMAN CAN JUMP THAT HIGH!
THAT'S NOT ICHIGO!!
THEN... WHO IS IT?
I DON'T KNOW BUT...
DON'T MENTION THIS TO ANYBODY!
ICHIGO MAY BE IN TROUBLE, SO LET'S KEEP QUIET FOR NOW.
HE'S A USUAL SUSPECT AS IT IS...

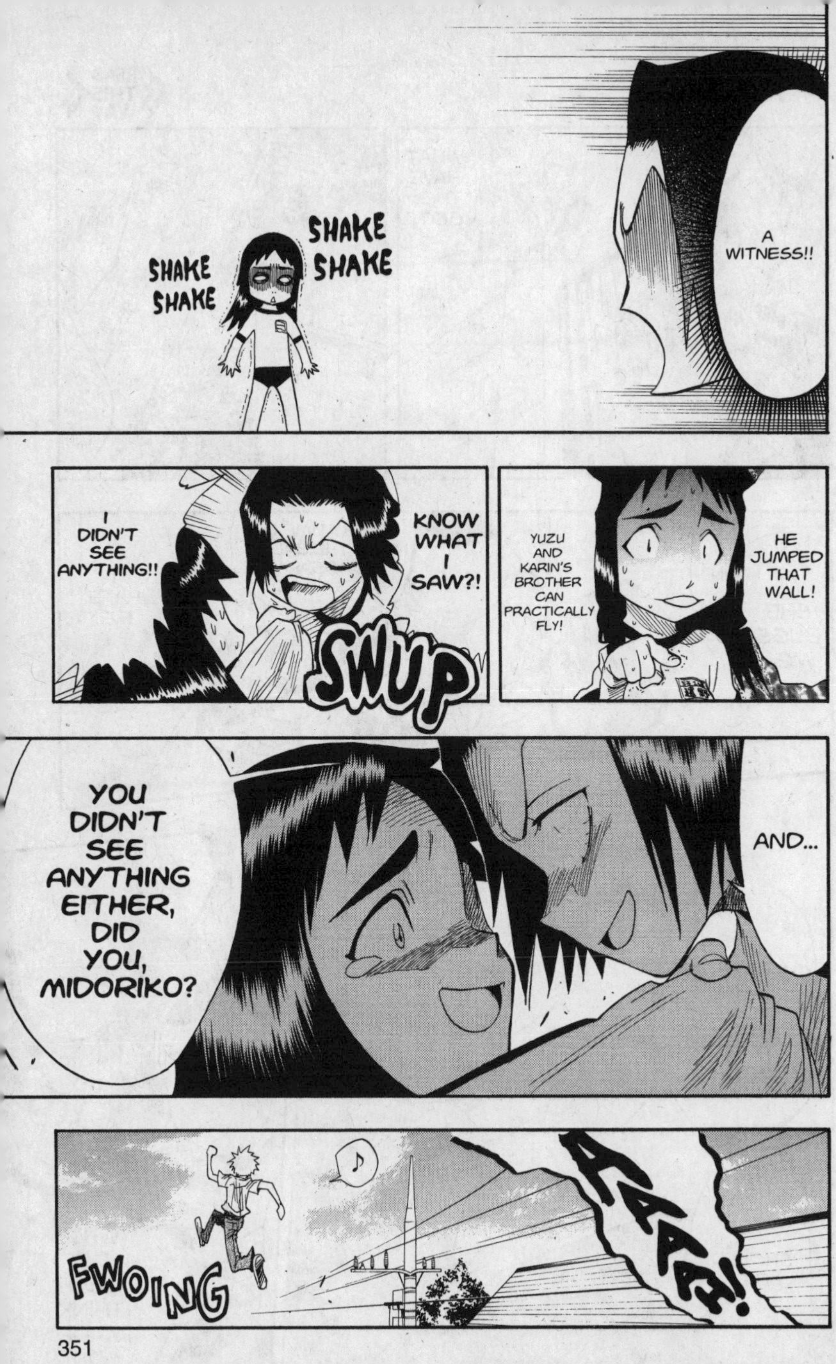
A WITNESS!!
SHAKE SHAKE
SHAKE SHAKE
HE JUMPED THAT WALL!
YUZU AND KARIN'S BROTHER CAN PRACTICALLY FLY!
KNOW WHAT I SAW?!
I DIDN'T SEE ANYTHING!!
SWUP
AND...
YOU DIDN'T SEE ANYTHING EITHER, DID YOU, MIDORIKO?
AAAAH!
♪
FWOING

READ THIS WAY

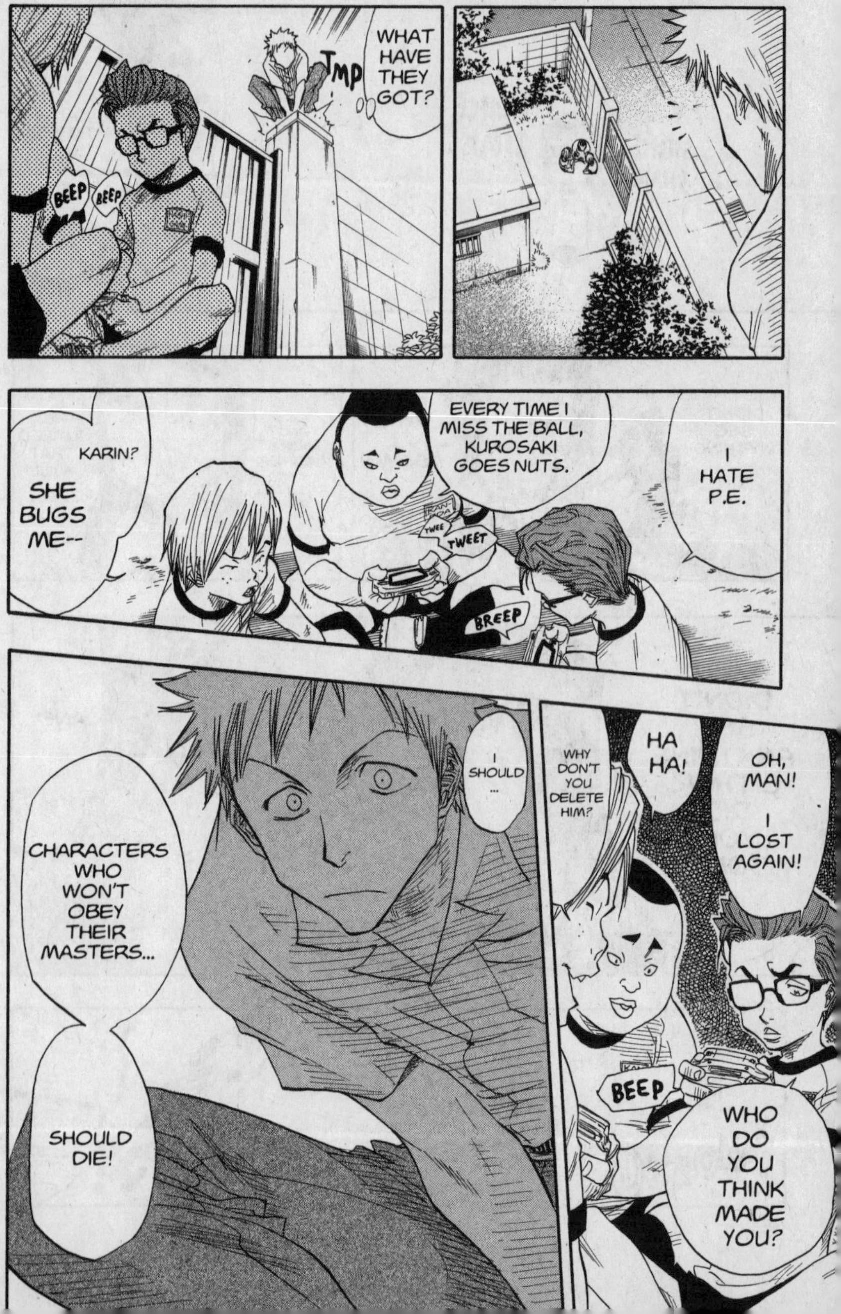
TMP
WHAT HAVE THEY GOT?
BEEP
BEEP
I HATE P.E.
BREEP
TWEET
TWEE
EVERY TIME I MISS THE BALL, KUROSAKI GOES NUTS.
KARIN?
SHE BUGS ME--
OH, MAN!
I LOST AGAIN!
HA HA!
WHY DON'T YOU DELETE HIM?
WHO DO YOU THINK MADE YOU?
BEEP
I SHOULD ...
CHARACTERS WHO WON'T OBEY THEIR MASTERS...
SHOULD DIE!

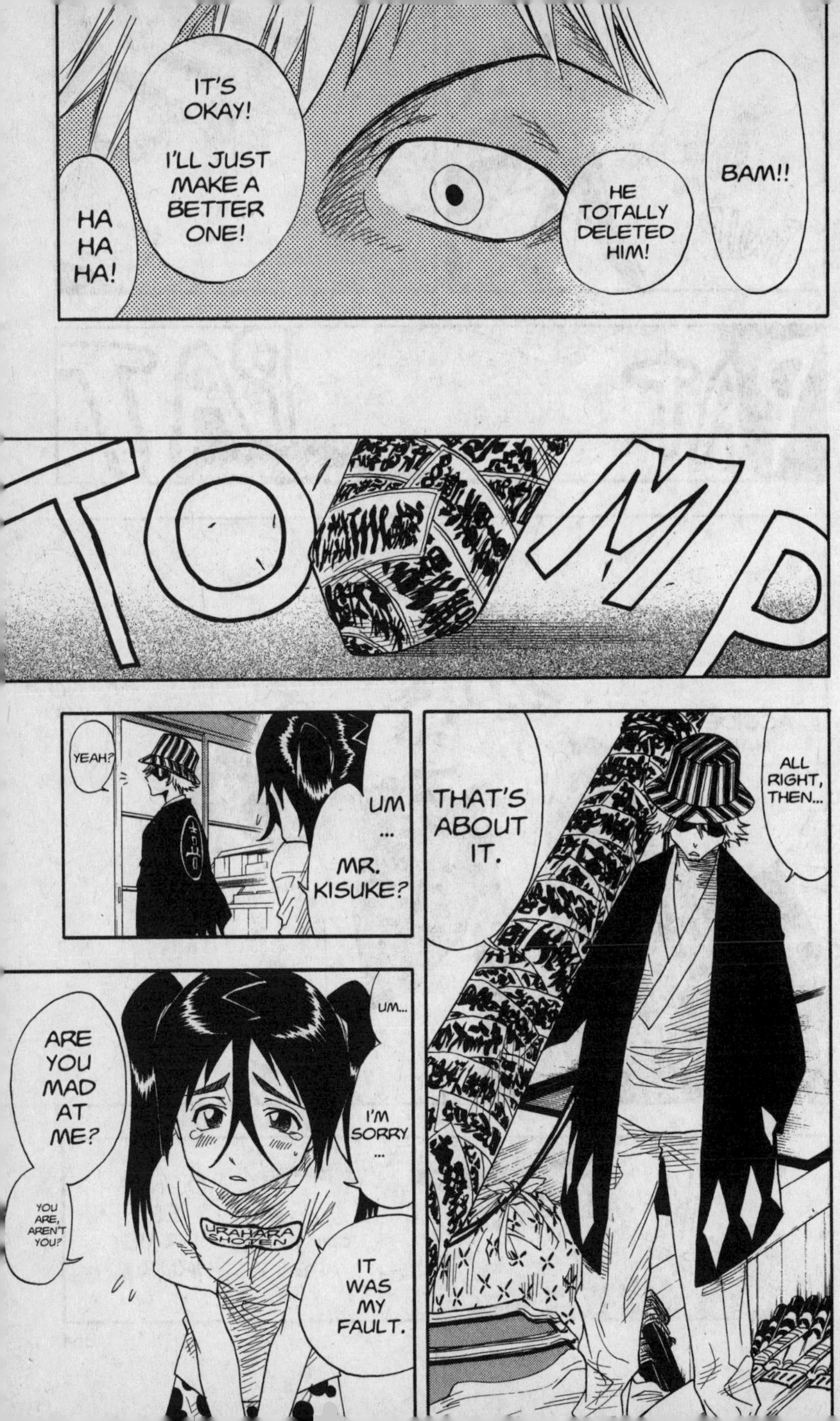
BAM!!
HE TOTALLY DELETED HIM!
IT'S OKAY! I'LL JUST MAKE A BETTER ONE!
HA HA HA!
TOMP
ALL RIGHT, THEN...
THAT'S ABOUT IT.
UM ... MR. KISUKE?
YEAH?
UM...
I'M SORRY ...
IT WAS MY FAULT.
ARE YOU MAD AT ME?
YOU ARE, AREN'T YOU?
URAHARA SHOTEN

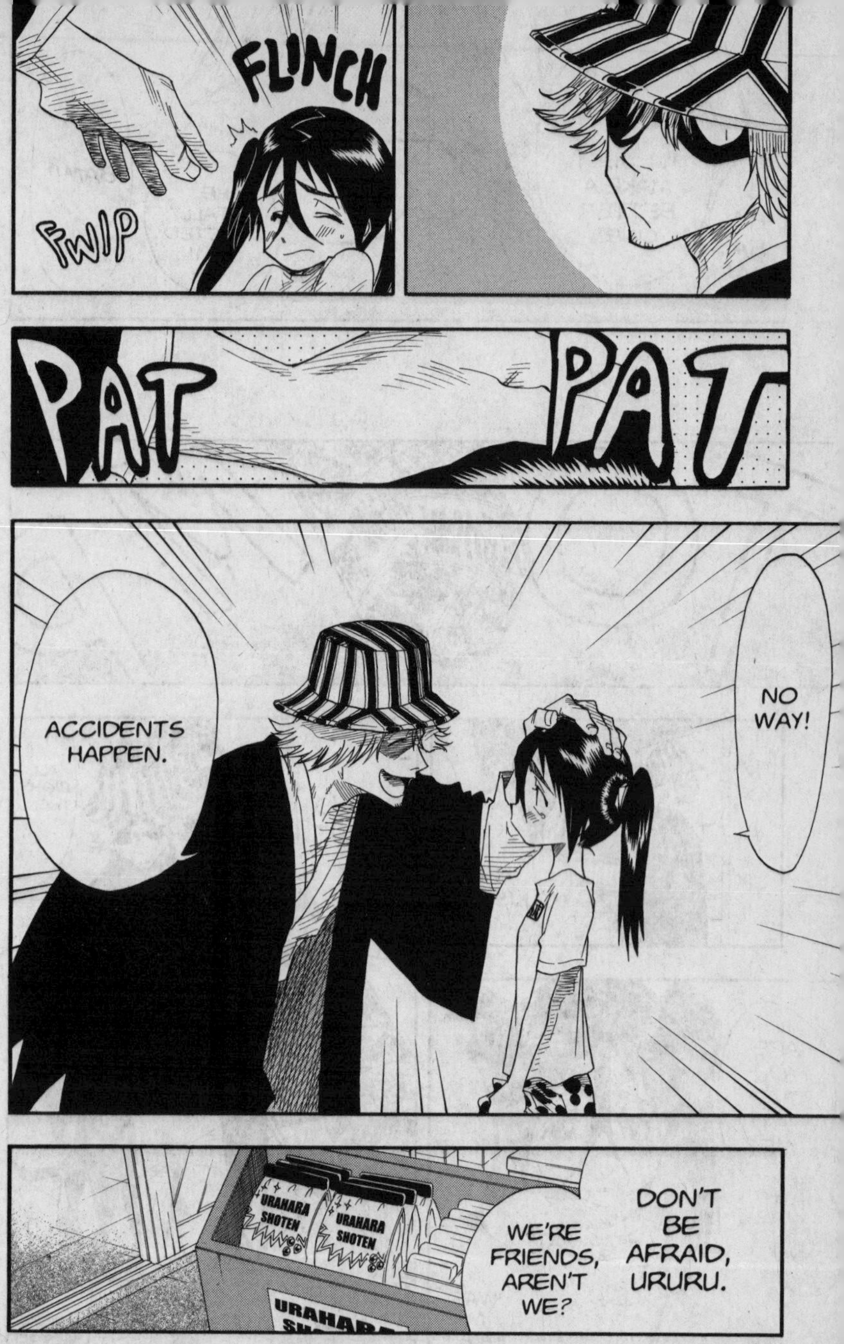
FLINCH
FWIP
PAT
PAT
NO WAY!
ACCIDENTS HAPPEN.
DON'T BE AFRAID, URURU.
WE'RE FRIENDS, AREN'T WE?
URAHARA SHOTEN
URAHARA SHOTEN

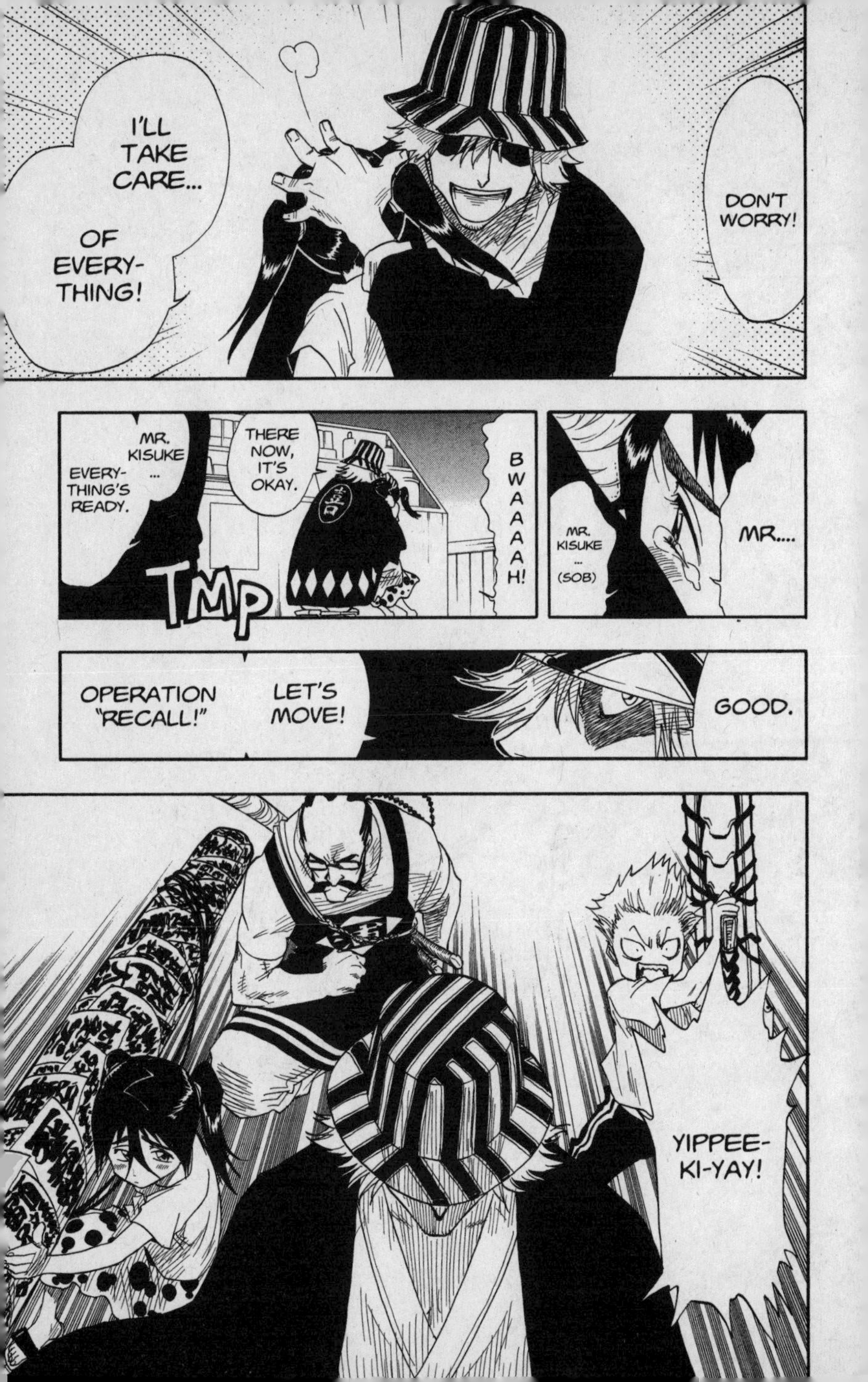
DON'T WORRY!
I'LL TAKE CARE... OF EVERY-THING!
MR....
MR. KISUKE... (SOB)
BWAAAAAH!
THERE NOW, IT'S OKAY.
MR. KISUKE... EVERY-THING'S READY.
TMP
GOOD.
LET'S MOVE!
OPERATION "RECALL!"
YIPPEE-KI-YAY!

THROWN BY TATSUKI.

HEY!!

MY DESK?!

16. Wasted but Wanted

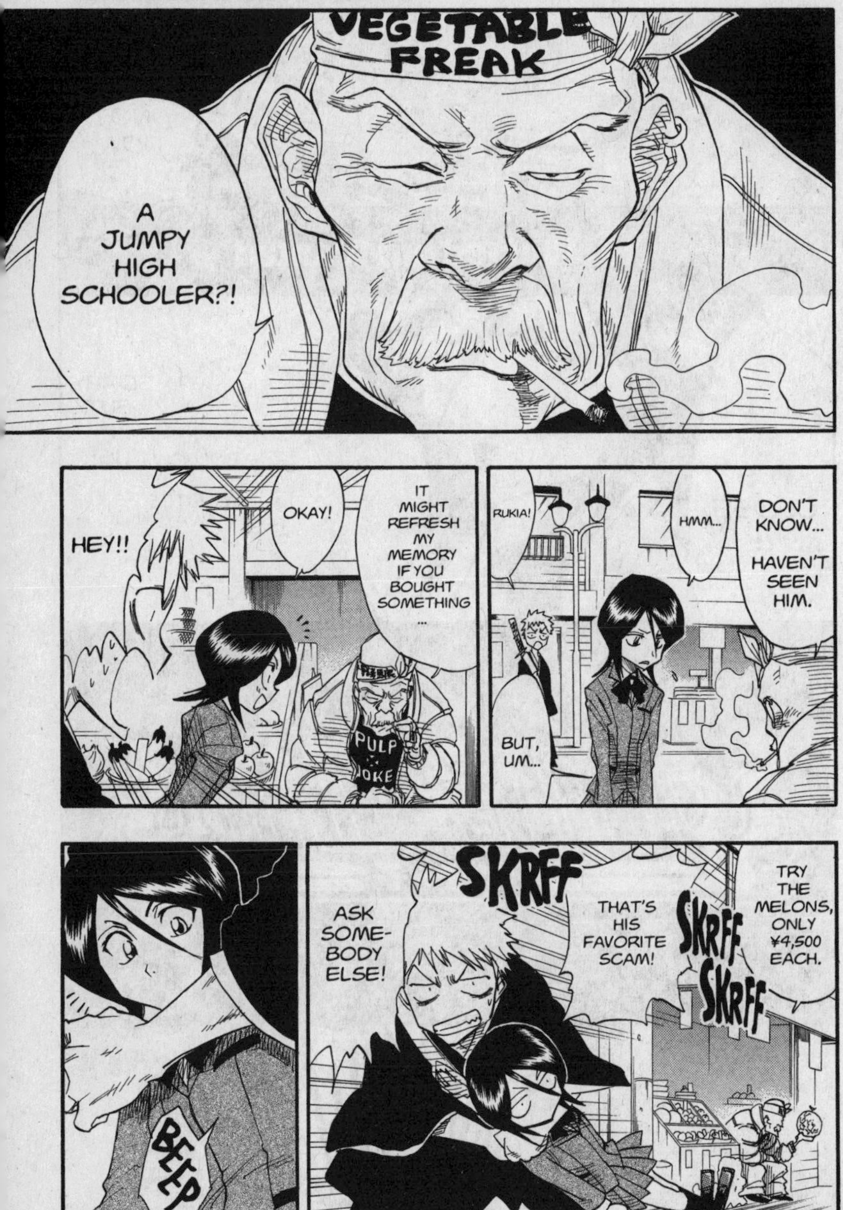
VEGETABLE FREAK
A JUMPY HIGH SCHOOLER?!
DON'T KNOW... HAVEN'T SEEN HIM.
HMM...
RUKIA!
BUT, UM...
IT MIGHT REFRESH MY MEMORY IF YOU BOUGHT SOMETHING ...
OKAY!
HEY!!
PULP
TRY THE MELONS, ONLY ¥4,500 EACH.
SKRFF SKRFF
THAT'S HIS FAVORITE SCAM!
SKRFF
ASK SOME-BODY ELSE!
BEEP

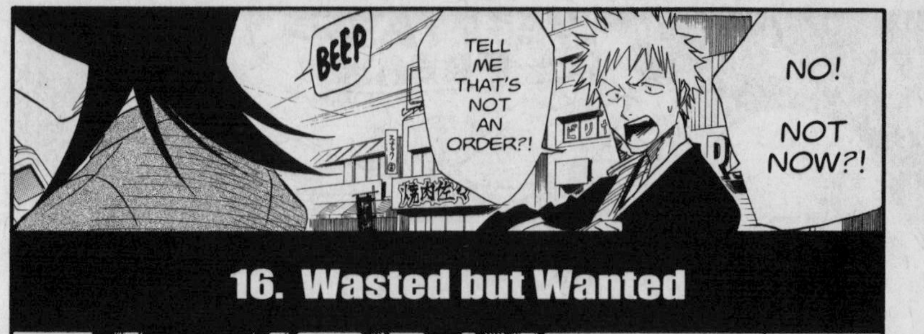
NO!
NOT NOW?!
TELL ME THAT'S NOT AN ORDER?!
BEEP

16. Wasted but Wanted

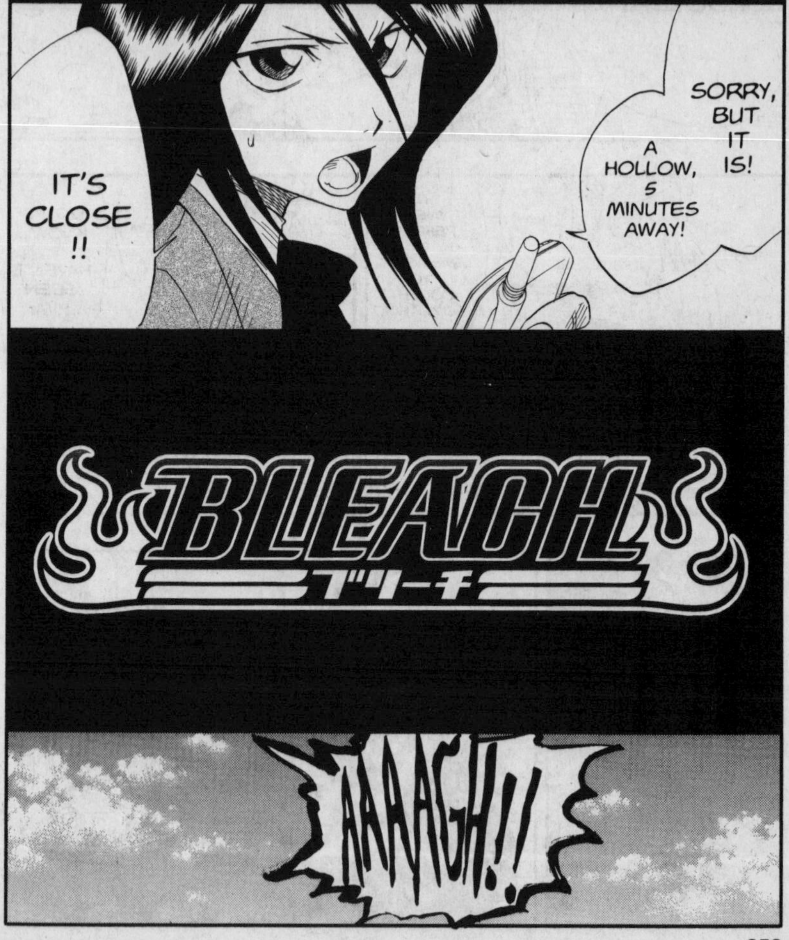
SORRY, BUT IT IS!
A HOLLOW, 5 MINUTES AWAY!
IT'S CLOSE !!
BLEACH
ブリーチ
AAAGH!!

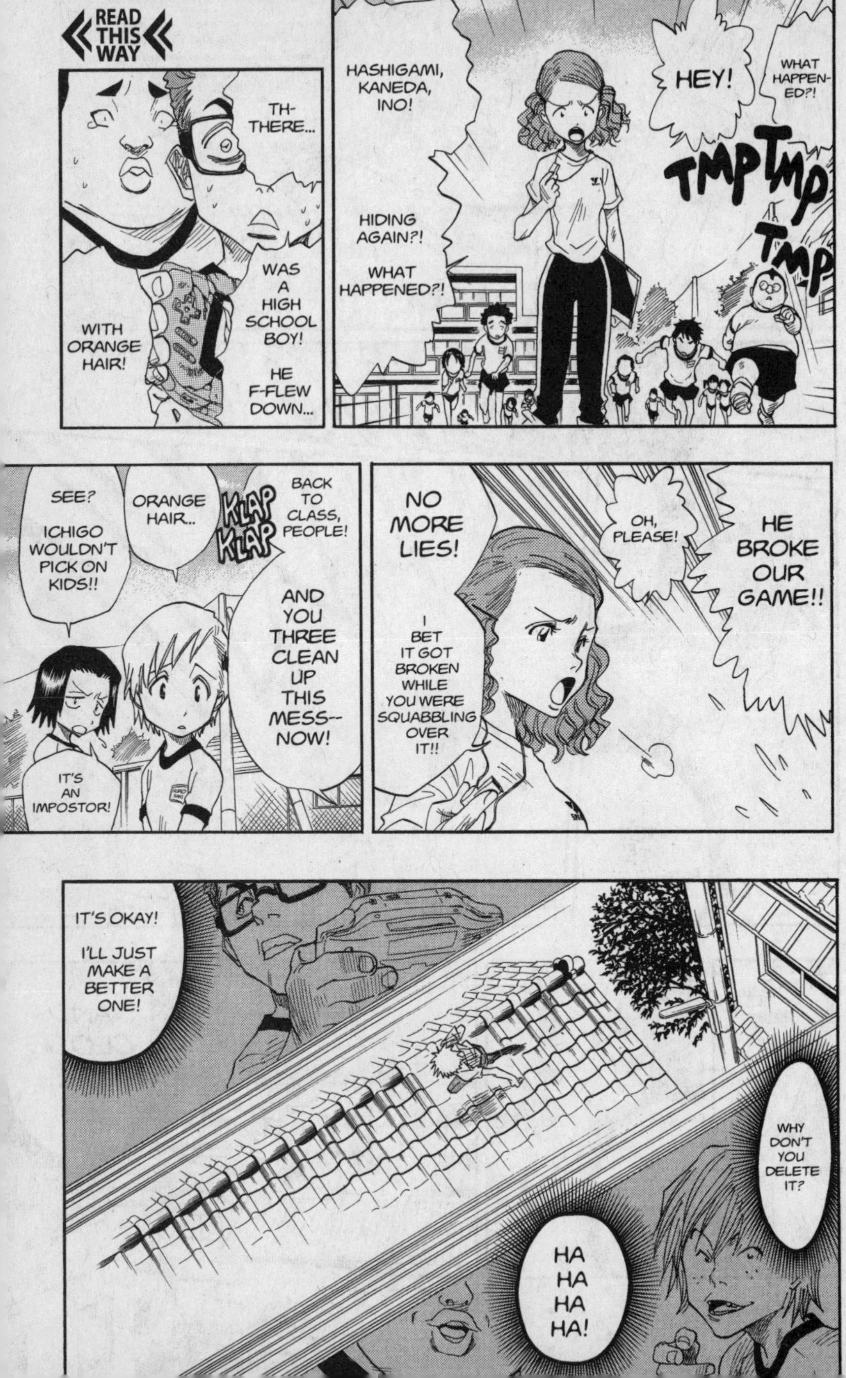
READ THIS WAY
HEY!
WHAT HAPPEN-ED?!
TMP TMP TMP
HASHIGAMI, KANEDA, INO!
HIDING AGAIN?!
WHAT HAPPENED?!
TH- THERE...
WAS A HIGH SCHOOL BOY!
HE F-FLEW DOWN...
WITH ORANGE HAIR!
HE BROKE OUR GAME!!
OH, PLEASE!
NO MORE LIES!
I BET IT GOT BROKEN WHILE YOU WERE SQUABBLING OVER IT!!
BACK TO CLASS, PEOPLE!
KLAP KLAP
AND YOU THREE CLEAN UP THIS MESS--NOW!
ORANGE HAIR...
SEE? ICHIGO WOULDN'T PICK ON KIDS!!
IT'S AN IMPOSTOR!
WHY DON'T YOU DELETE IT?
HA HA HA HA!
IT'S OKAY! I'LL JUST MAKE A BETTER ONE!

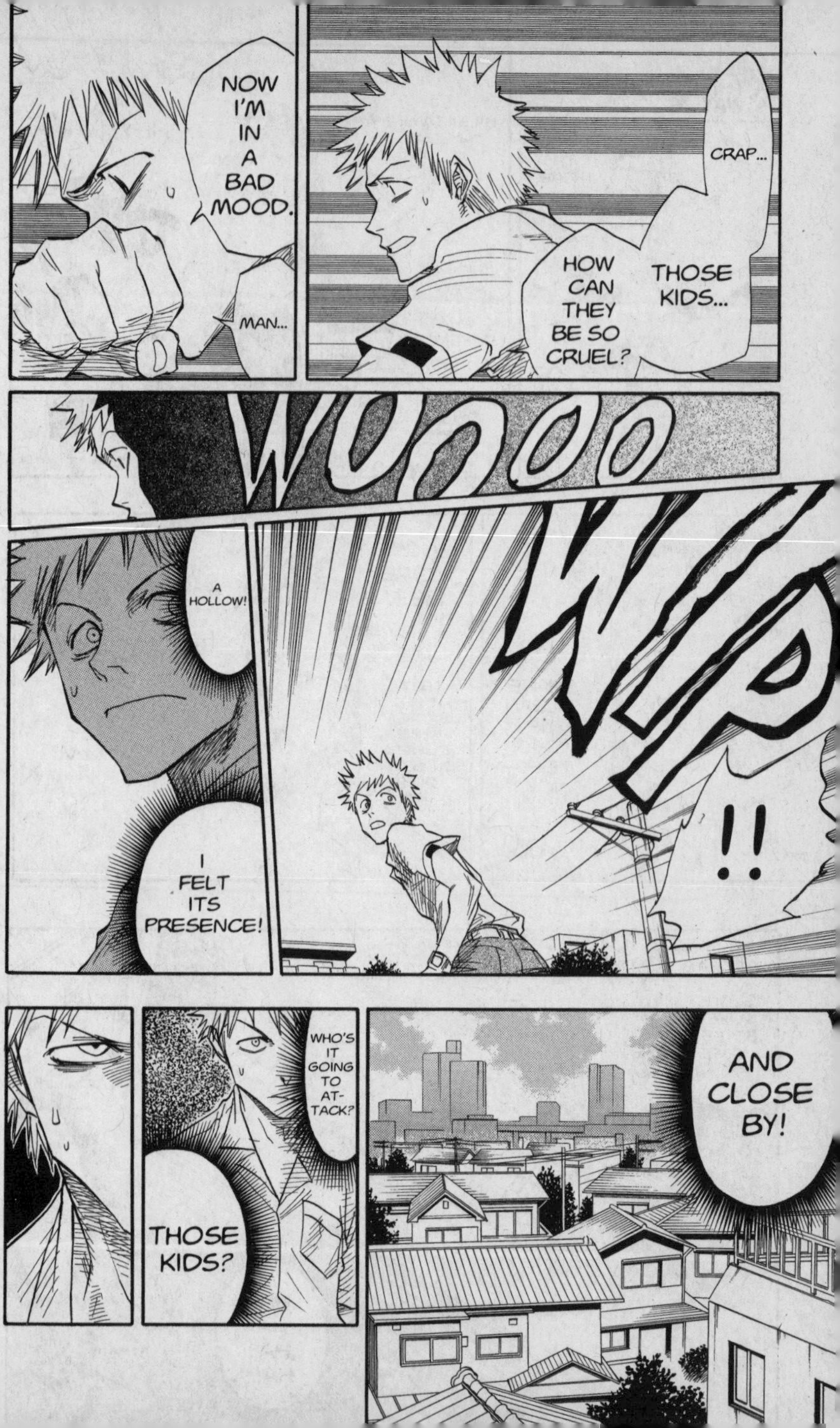
CRAP...
THOSE KIDS...
HOW CAN THEY BE SO CRUEL?
NOW I'M IN A BAD MOOD.
MAN...
WOOOO
WIP
!!
A HOLLOW!
I FELT ITS PRESENCE!
AND CLOSE BY!
WHO'S IT GOING TO AT-TACK?
THOSE KIDS?

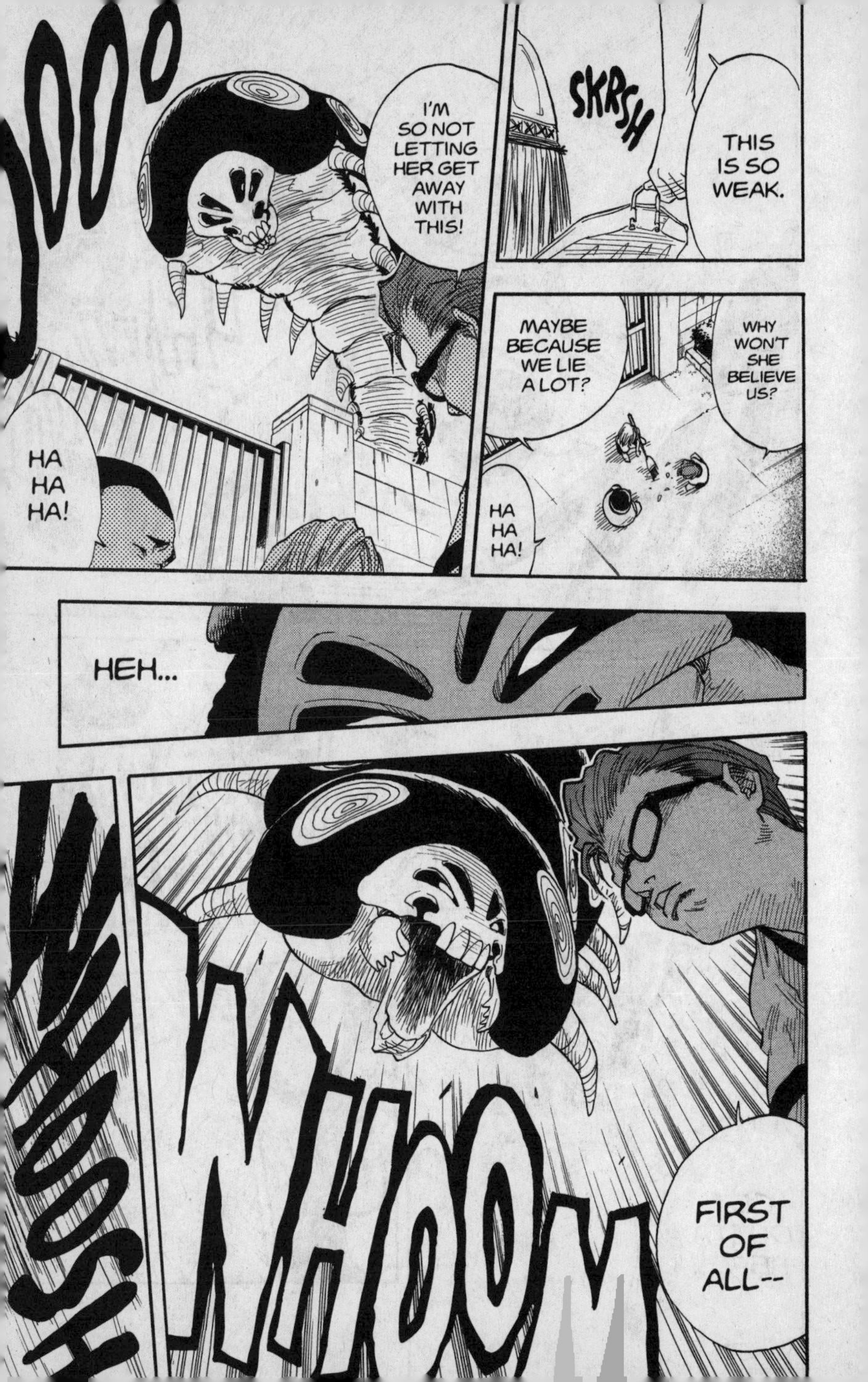
SKRSH
THIS IS SO WEAK.
WHY WON'T SHE BELIEVE US?
MAYBE BECAUSE WE LIE A LOT?
HA HA HA!
I'M SO NOT LETTING HER GET AWAY WITH THIS!
JOOOO
HA HA HA!
HEH...
FIRST OF ALL--
WHOOM
WHOOSH

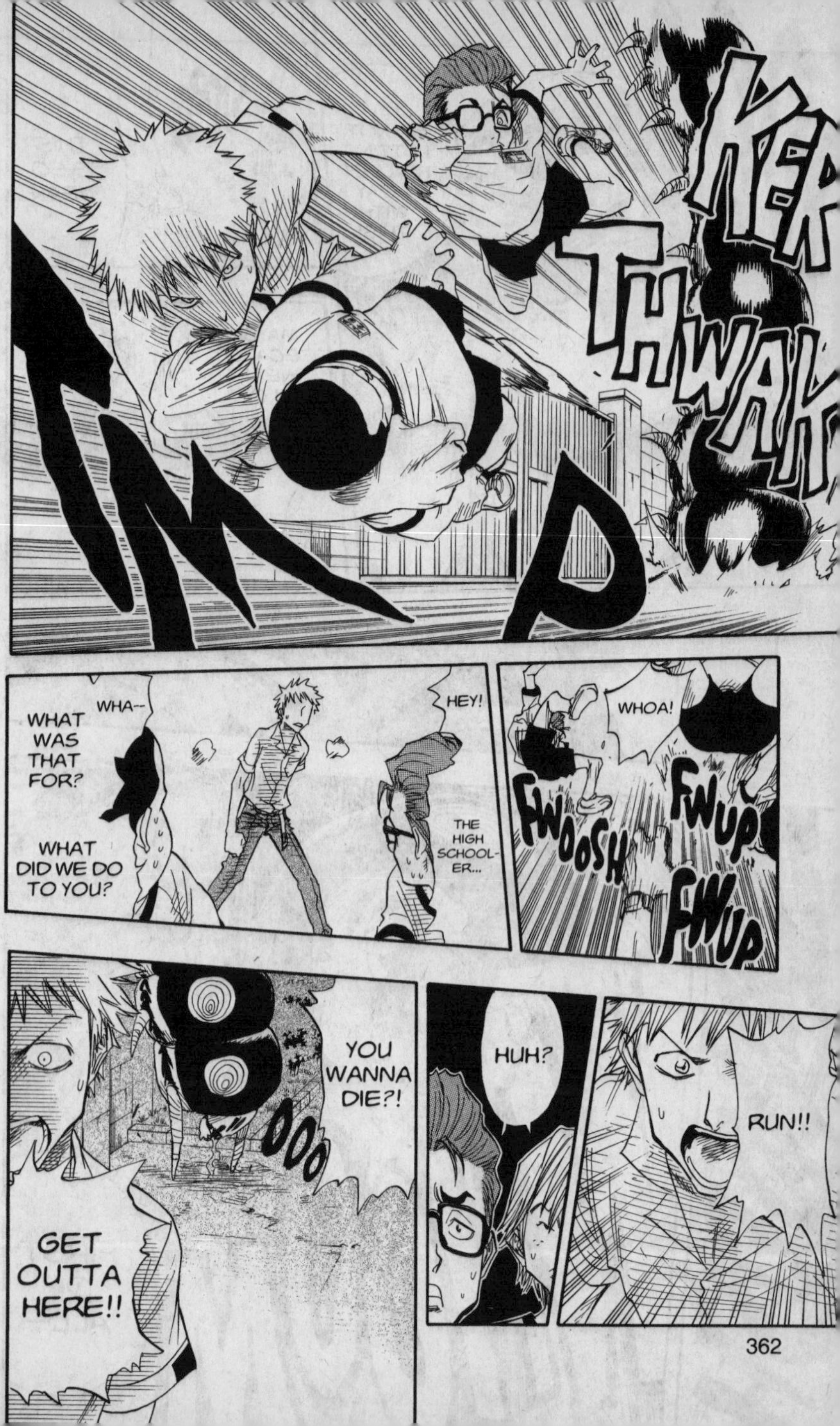
KER-THWAK
TMP
WHOA!
FWUP FWUP
FWOOSH
HEY!
THE HIGH SCHOOL-ER...
WHA--
WHAT WAS THAT FOR?
WHAT DID WE DO TO YOU?
RUN!!
HUH?
YOU WANNA DIE?!
OOO
GET OUTTA HERE!!

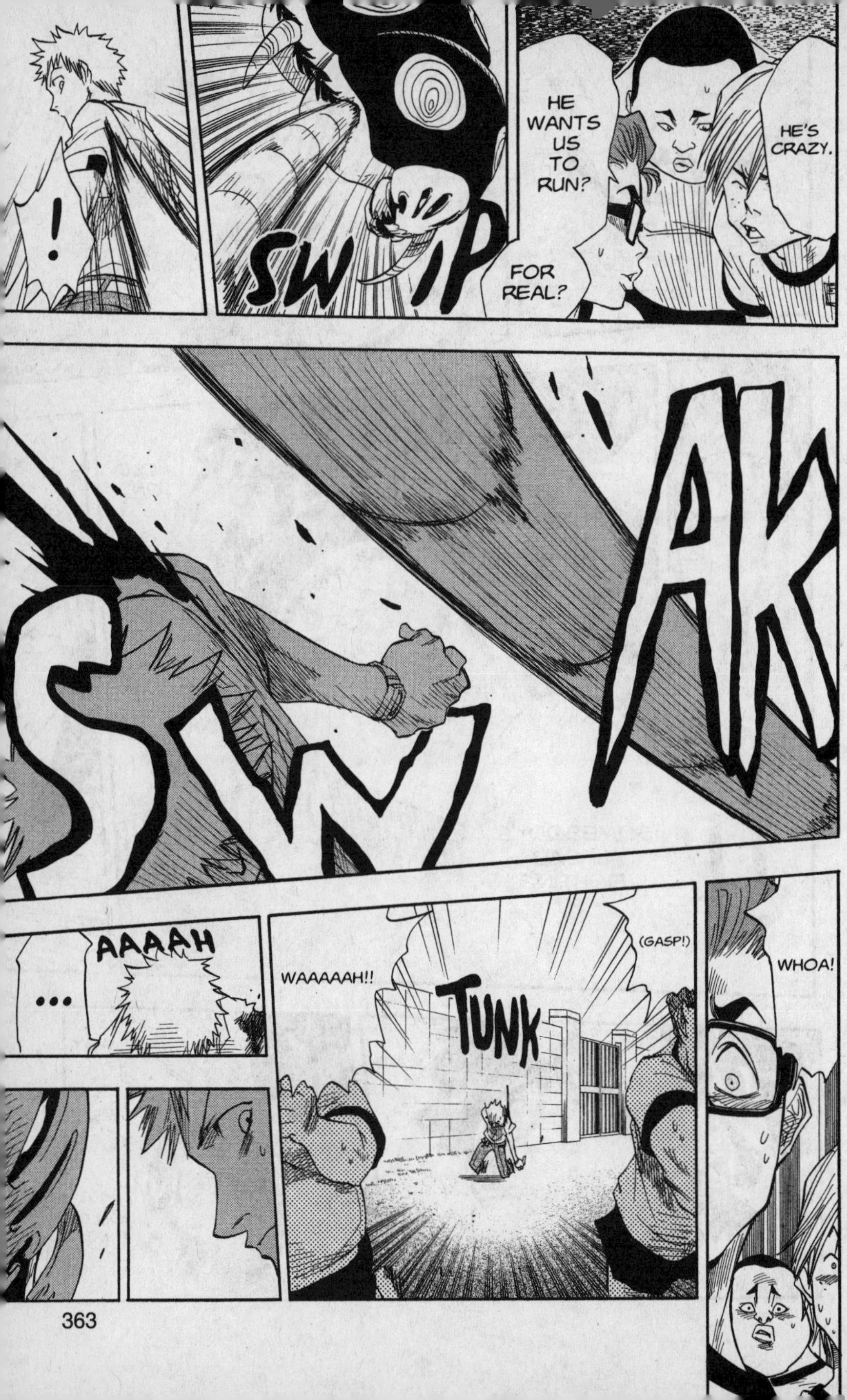
HE'S CRAZY.
HE WANTS US TO RUN?
FOR REAL?
SWIP
!
SWAK
WHOA!
(GASP!)
TUNK
WAAAAAH!!
AAAAH
...

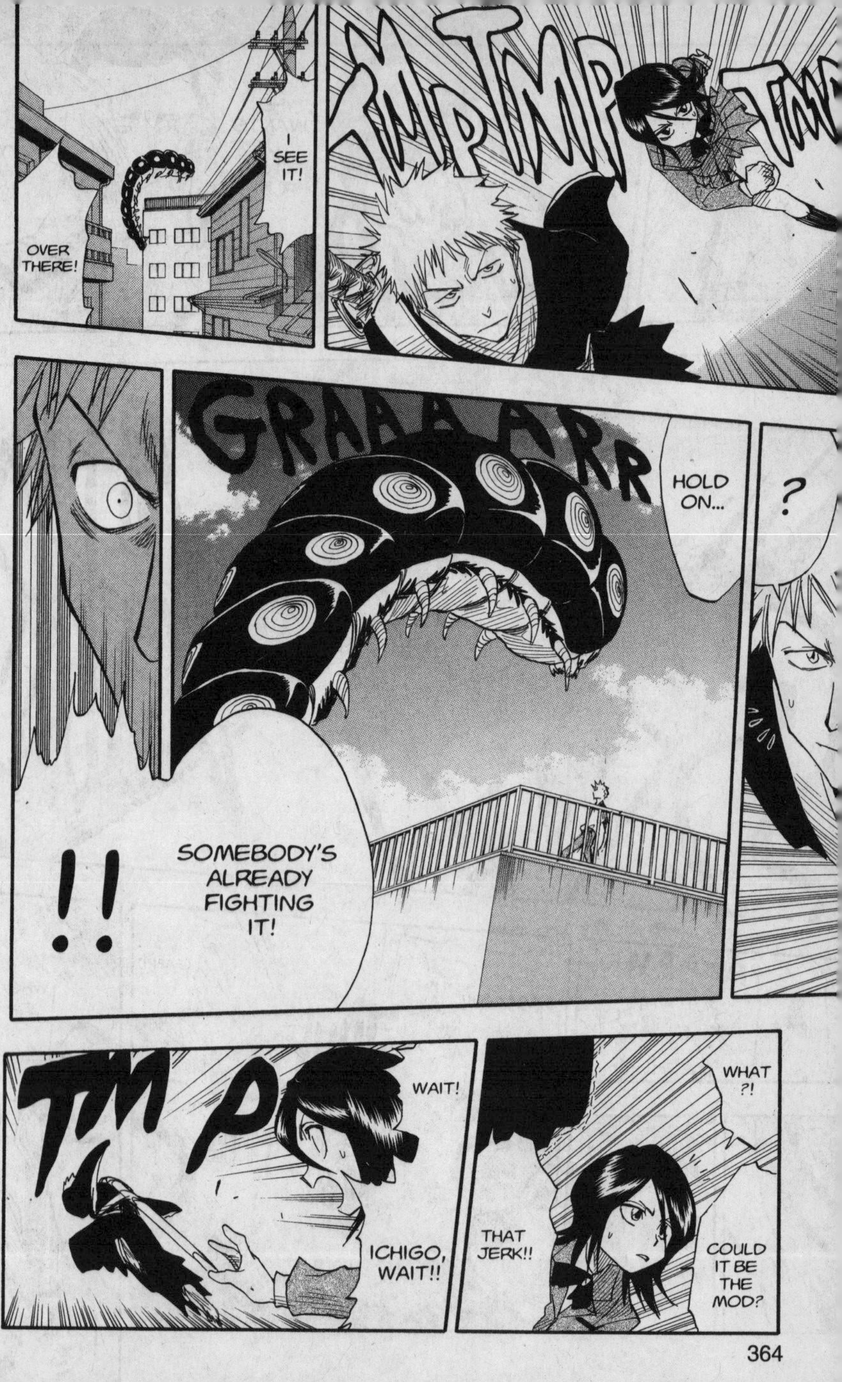
TMP TMP
I SEE IT!
OVER THERE!
HOLD ON...
?
GRAAAARR
SOMEBODY'S ALREADY FIGHTING IT!
!!
WHAT?!
COULD IT BE THE MOD?
THAT JERK!!
TMP
WAIT!
ICHIGO, WAIT!!

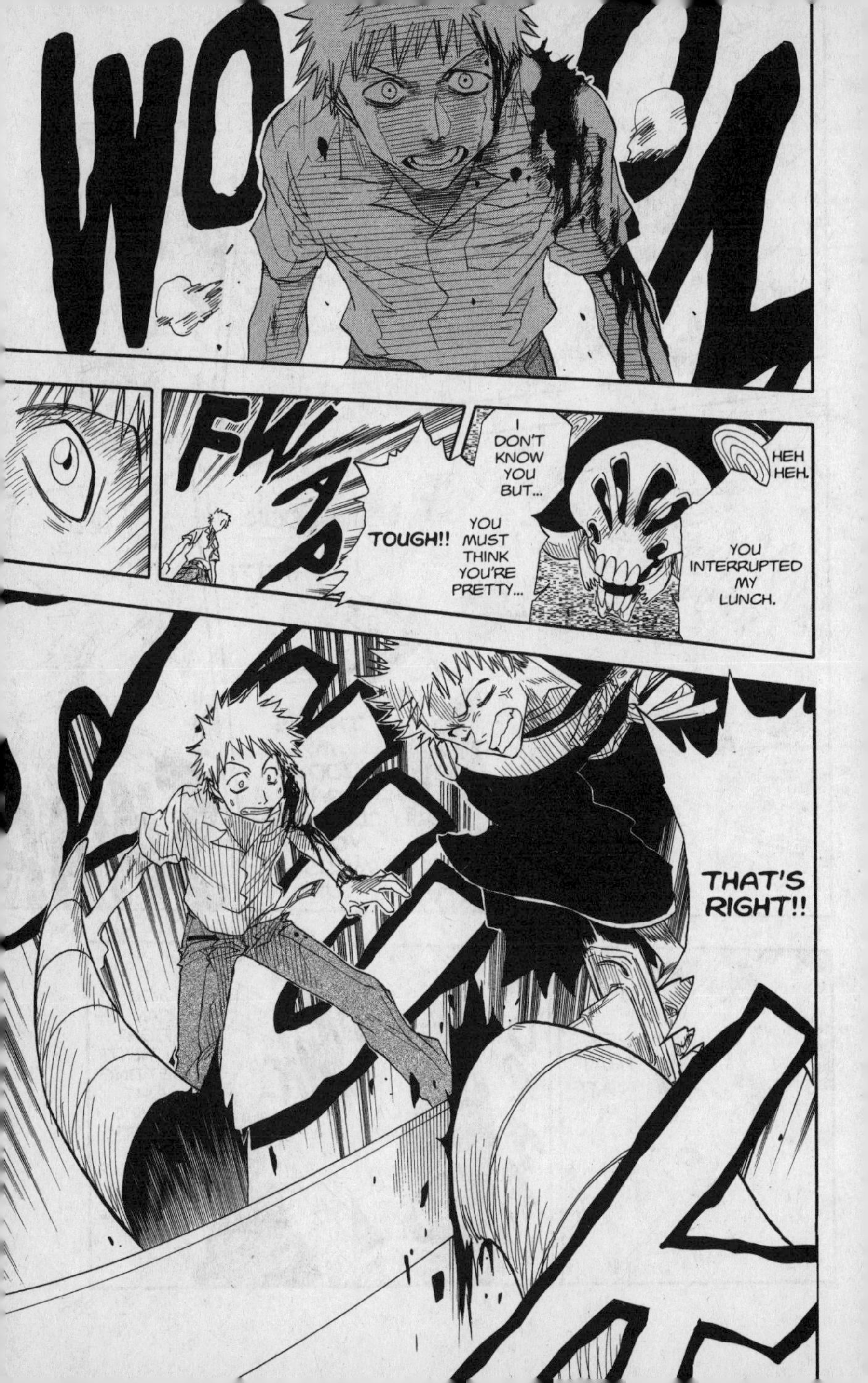
HEH HEH.
YOU INTERRUPTED MY LUNCH.
I DON'T KNOW YOU BUT...
YOU MUST THINK YOU'RE PRETTY...
TOUGH!!
FWAP
THAT'S RIGHT!!

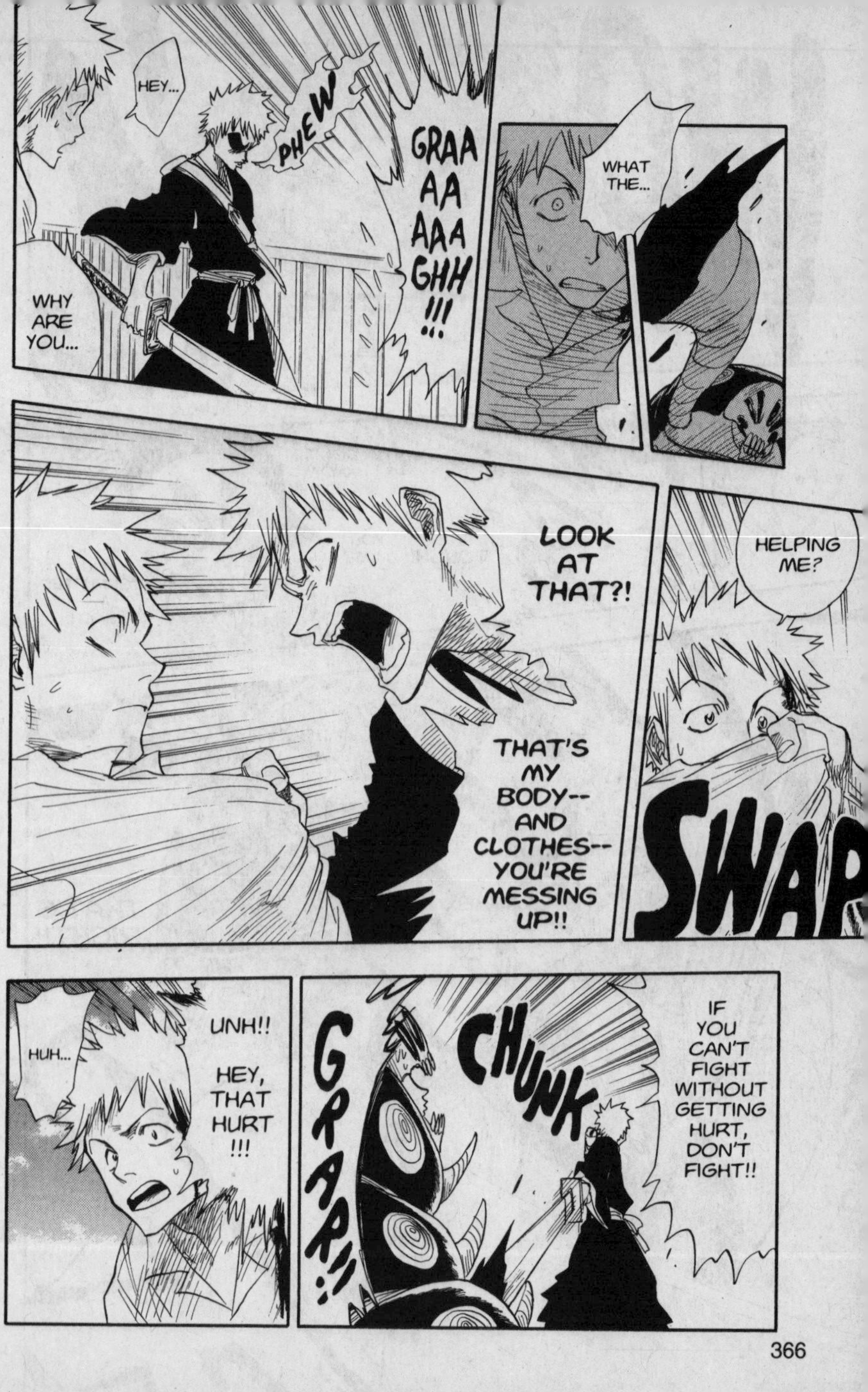
WHAT THE...
GRAA AA AAA GHH !!!
PHEW
HEY...
WHY ARE YOU...
HELPING ME?
SWAP
LOOK AT THAT?!
THAT'S MY BODY-- AND CLOTHES-- YOU'RE MESSING UP!!
IF YOU CAN'T FIGHT WITHOUT GETTING HURT, DON'T FIGHT!!
CHUNK
GRAR!!
UNH!!
HEY, THAT HURT !!!
HUH...

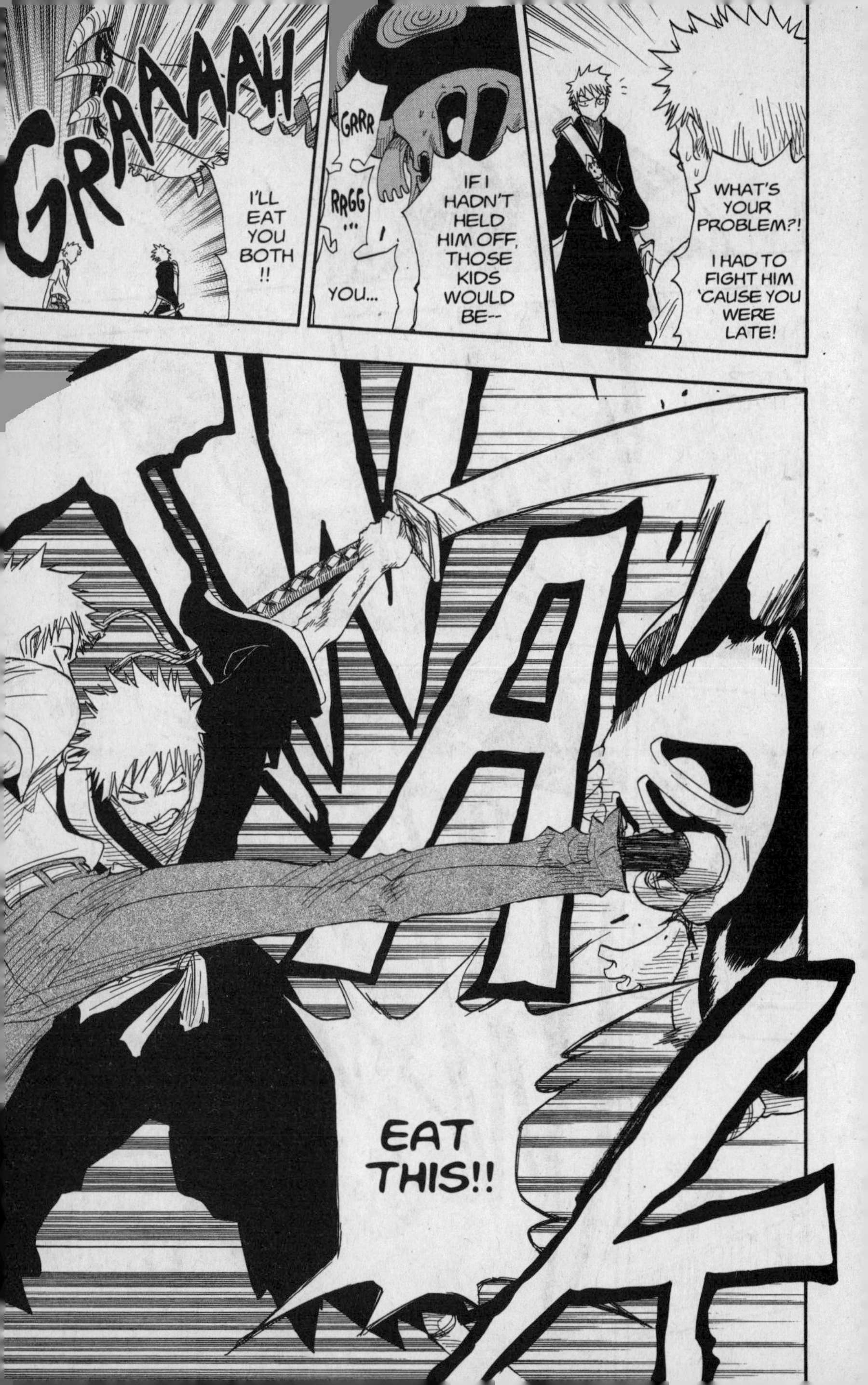
WHAT'S YOUR PROBLEM?!
I HAD TO FIGHT HIM 'CAUSE YOU WERE LATE!
IF I HADN'T HELD HIM OFF, THOSE KIDS WOULD BE--
GRRR
RRGG...
YOU...
GRAAAAH
I'LL EAT YOU BOTH!!
EAT THIS!!

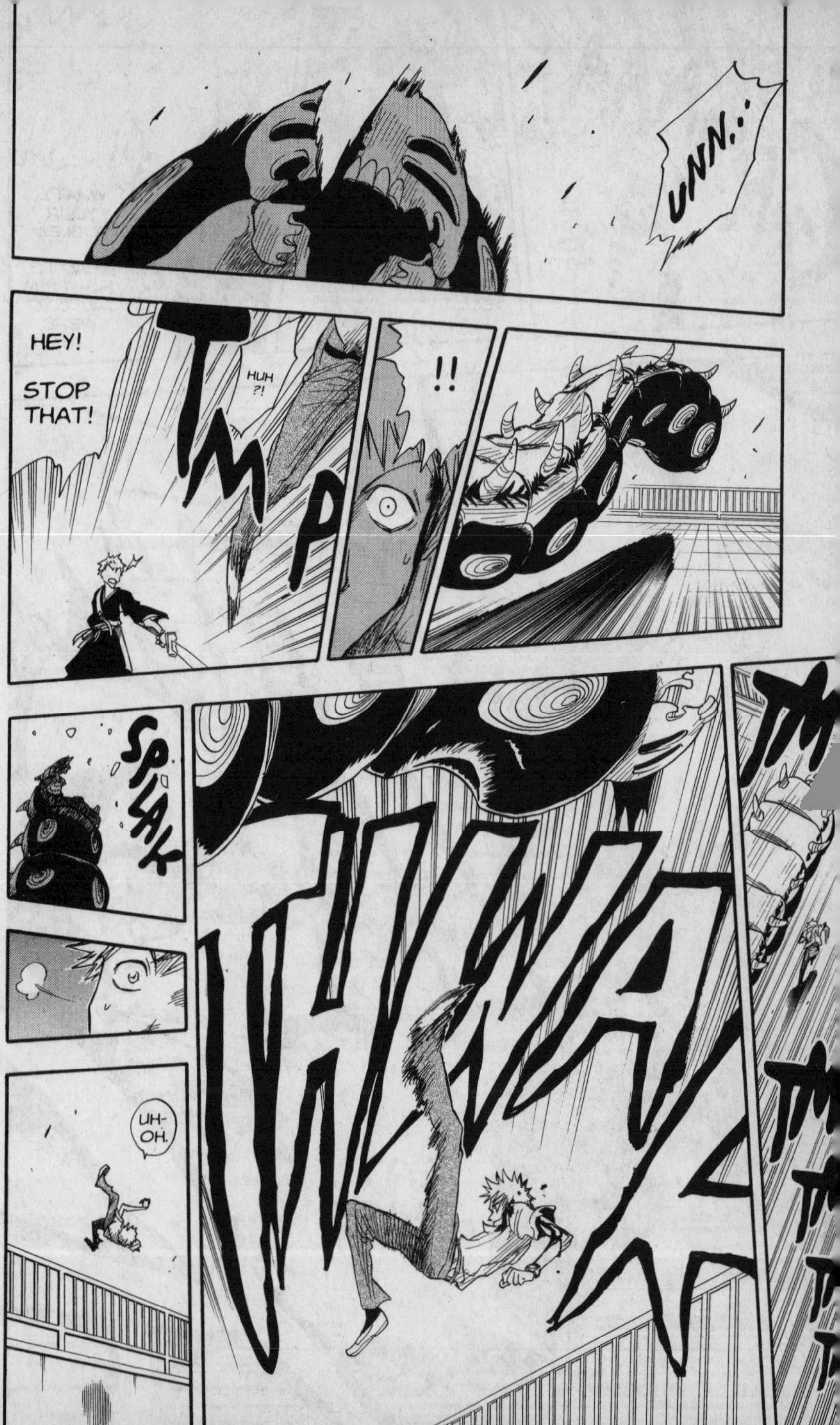
UNN...
!!
HUH ?!
TMP
HEY!
STOP THAT!
SPLAK
UH-OH.

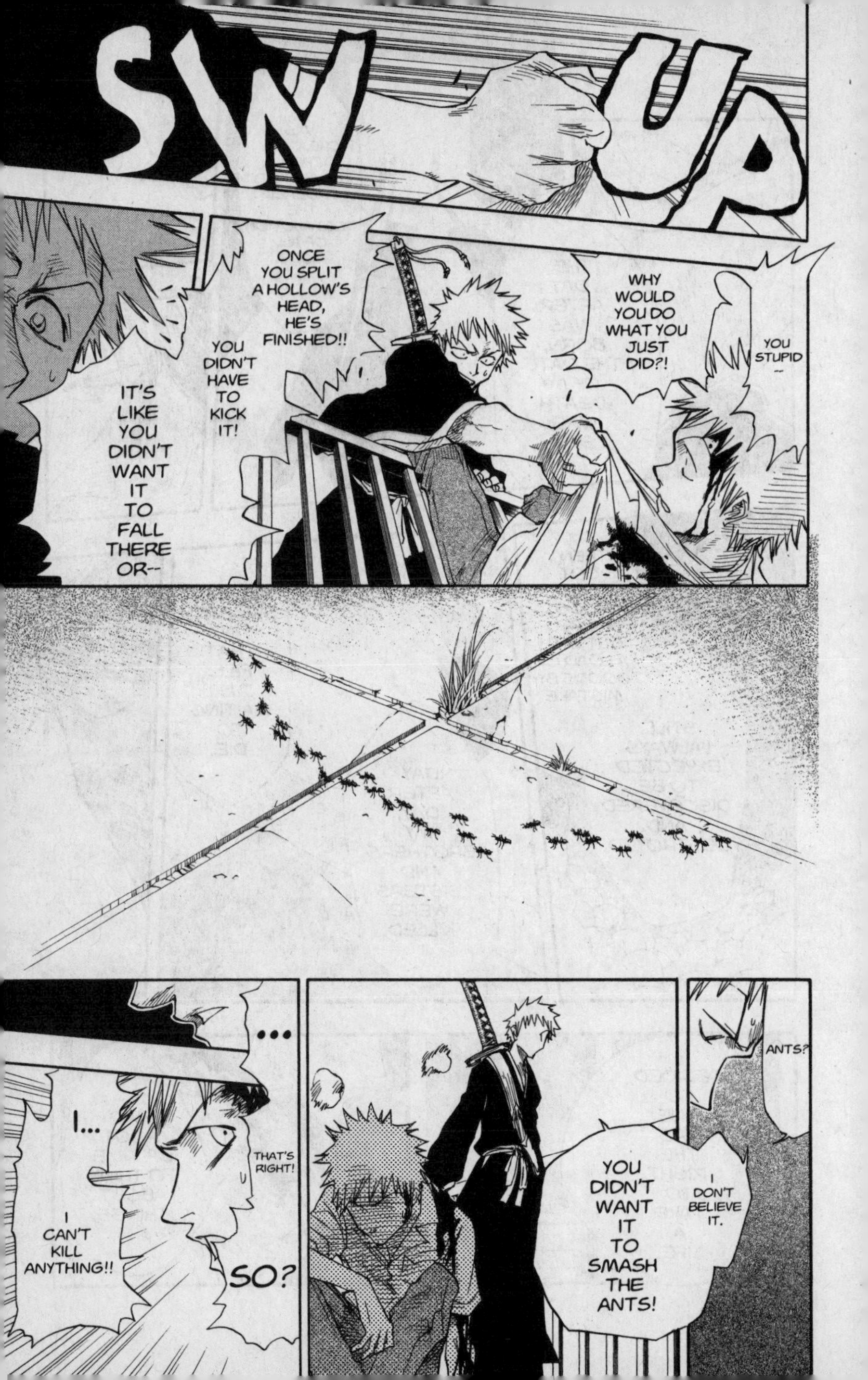
SWUP
YOU STUPID--
WHY WOULD YOU DO WHAT YOU JUST DID?!
ONCE YOU SPLIT A HOLLOW'S HEAD, HE'S FINISHED!!
YOU DIDN'T HAVE TO KICK IT!
IT'S LIKE YOU DIDN'T WANT IT TO FALL THERE OR--
ANTS?
I DON'T BELIEVE IT.
YOU DIDN'T WANT IT TO SMASH THE ANTS!
...
THAT'S RIGHT!
I...
I CAN'T KILL ANYTHING!!
SO?

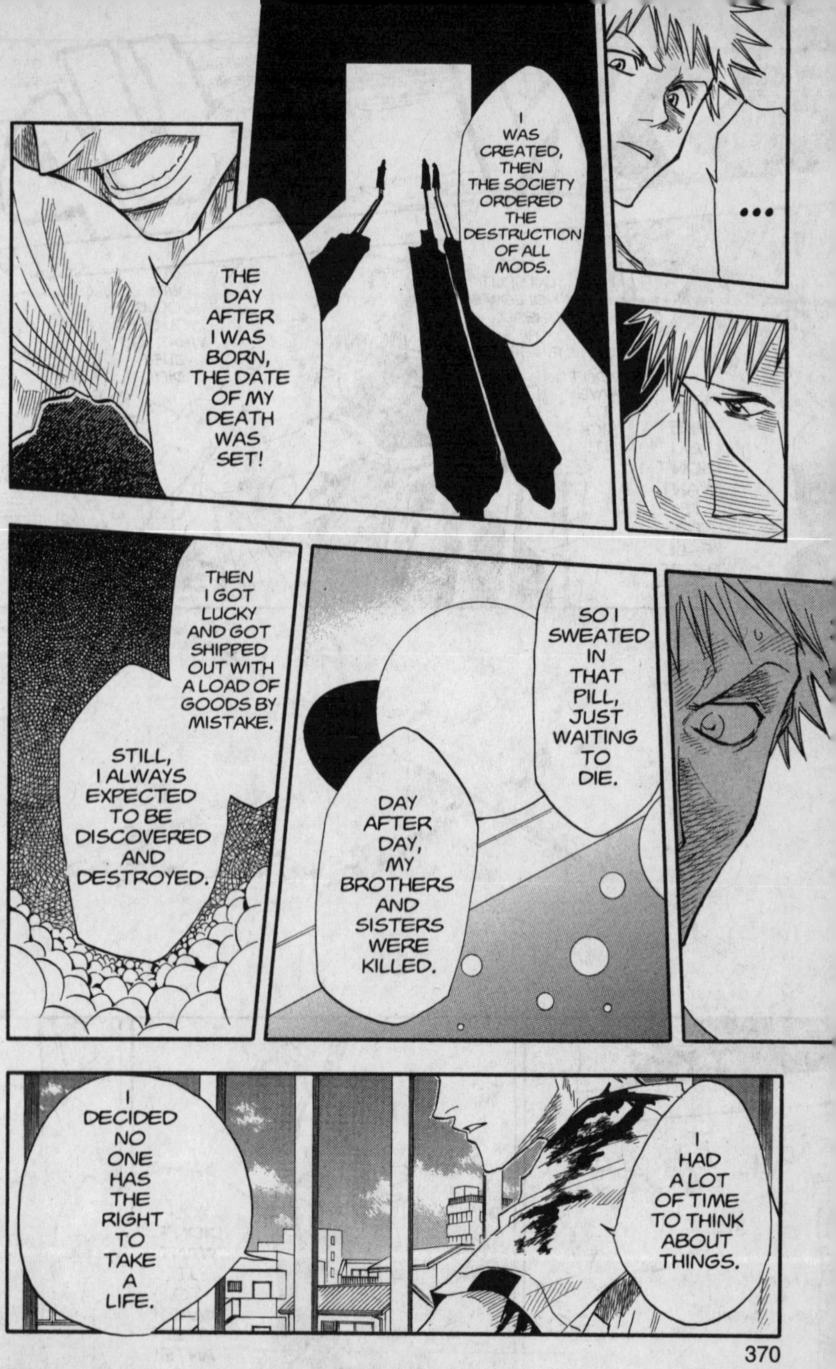
...
I WAS CREATED, THEN THE SOCIETY ORDERED THE DESTRUCTION OF ALL MODS.
THE DAY AFTER I WAS BORN, THE DATE OF MY DEATH WAS SET!
SO I SWEATED IN THAT PILL, JUST WAITING TO DIE.
DAY AFTER DAY, MY BROTHERS AND SISTERS WERE KILLED.
THEN I GOT LUCKY AND GOT SHIPPED OUT WITH A LOAD OF GOODS BY MISTAKE.
STILL, I ALWAYS EXPECTED TO BE DISCOVERED AND DESTROYED.
I HAD A LOT OF TIME TO THINK ABOUT THINGS.
I DECIDED NO ONE HAS THE RIGHT TO TAKE A LIFE.

I SHOULD HAVE THE RIGHT TO LIVE AND DIE FREELY!!

I EXIST!

I WON'T KILL...

NOT ANYTHING!

SO I REFUSE TO TAKE A LIFE.

LIKE HUMANS, OR EVEN BUGS.

EVEN A MOD...

SHOULD HAVE THAT RIGHT.

TOK

!!

WELL, LOOK HERE...

...

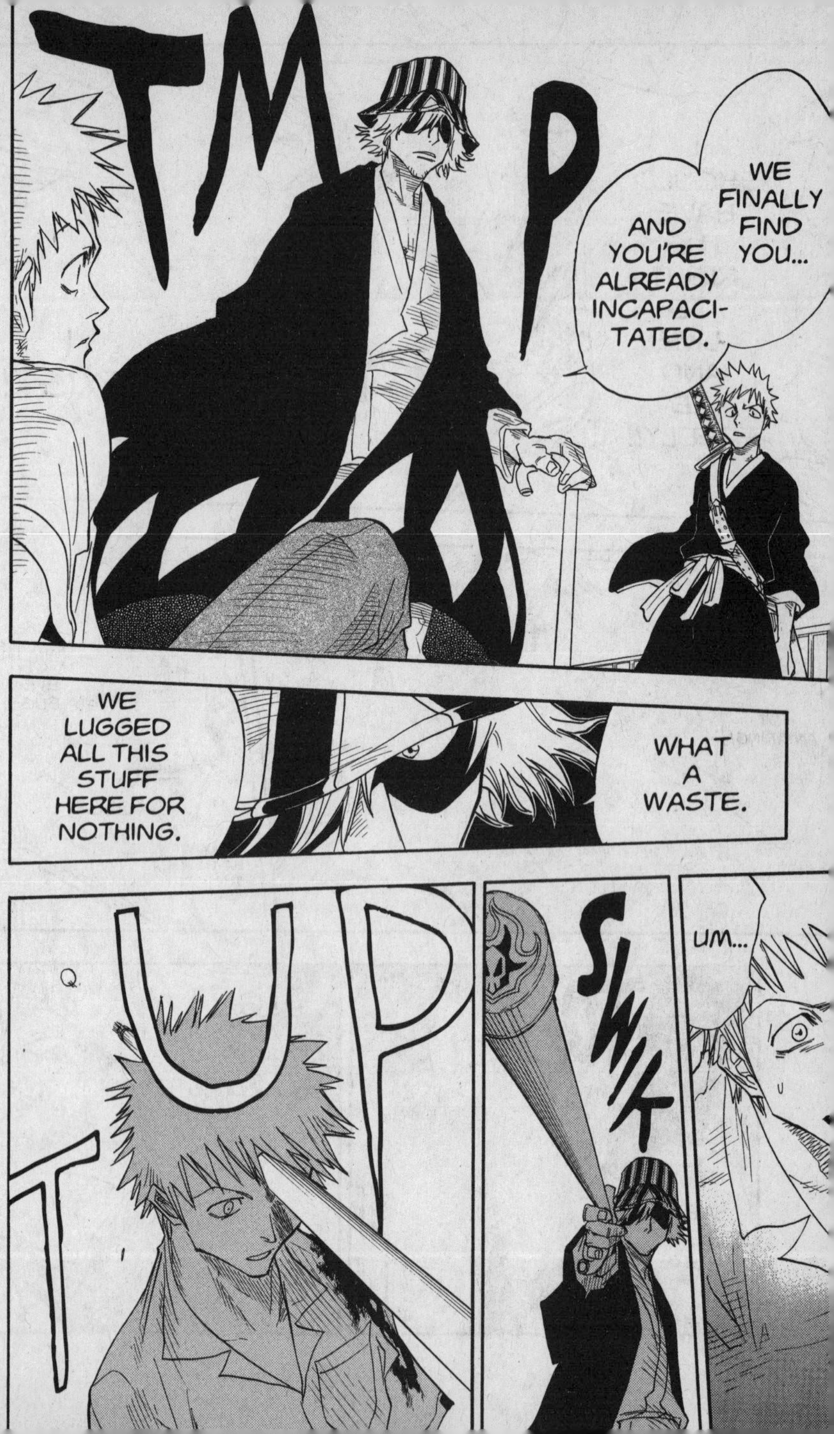
TMP
WE FINALLY FIND YOU...
AND YOU'RE ALREADY INCAPACITATED.
WHAT A WASTE.
WE LUGGED ALL THIS STUFF HERE FOR NOTHING.
UM...
SWIK
TUP

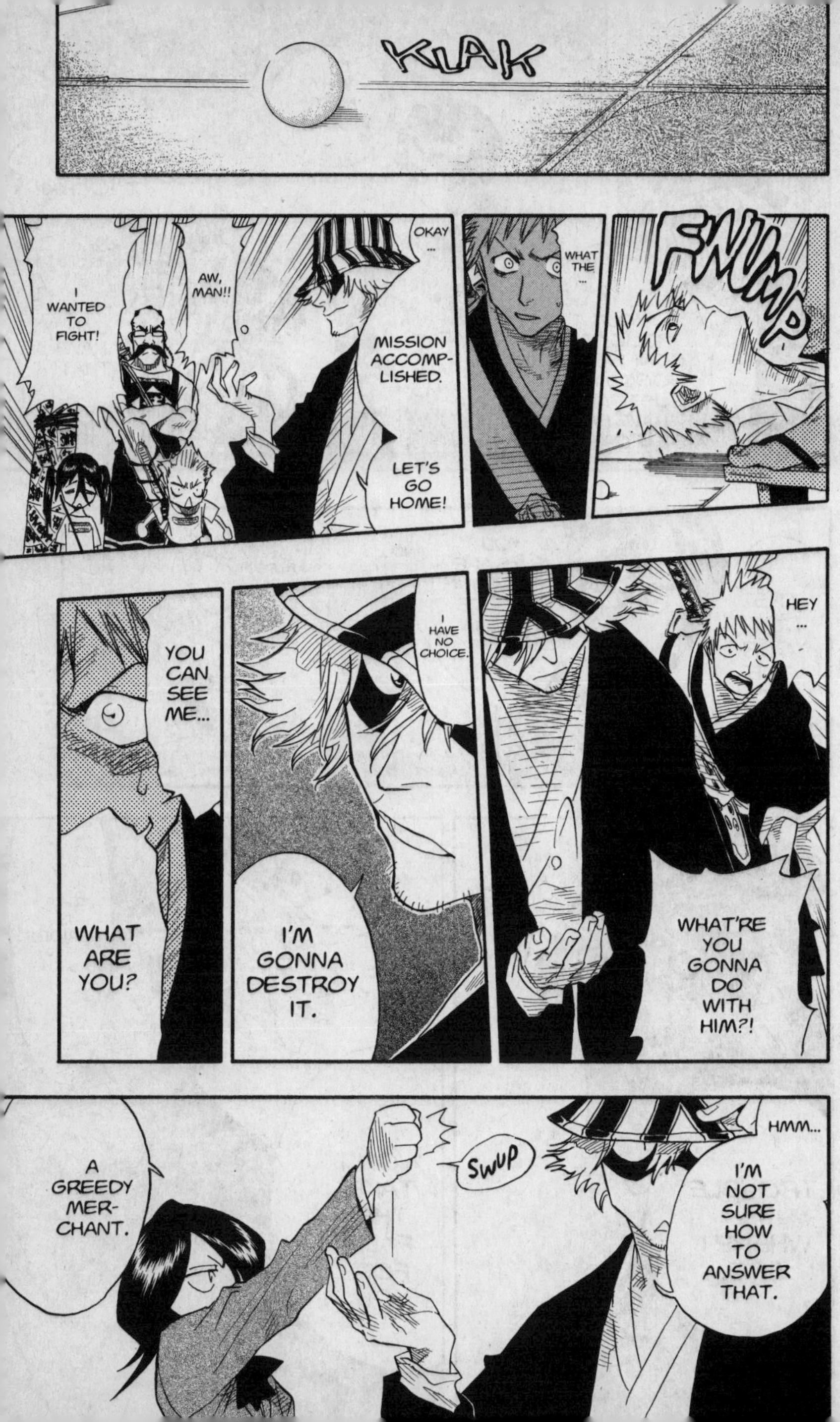
KLAK
FNUMP
WHAT THE ...
OKAY ...
MISSION ACCOMPLISHED.
LET'S GO HOME!
AW, MAN!!
I WANTED TO FIGHT!
HEY ...
WHAT'RE YOU GONNA DO WITH HIM?!
I HAVE NO CHOICE.
I'M GONNA DESTROY IT.
YOU CAN SEE ME...
WHAT ARE YOU?
HMM...
I'M NOT SURE HOW TO ANSWER THAT.
SWUP
A GREEDY MERCHANT.

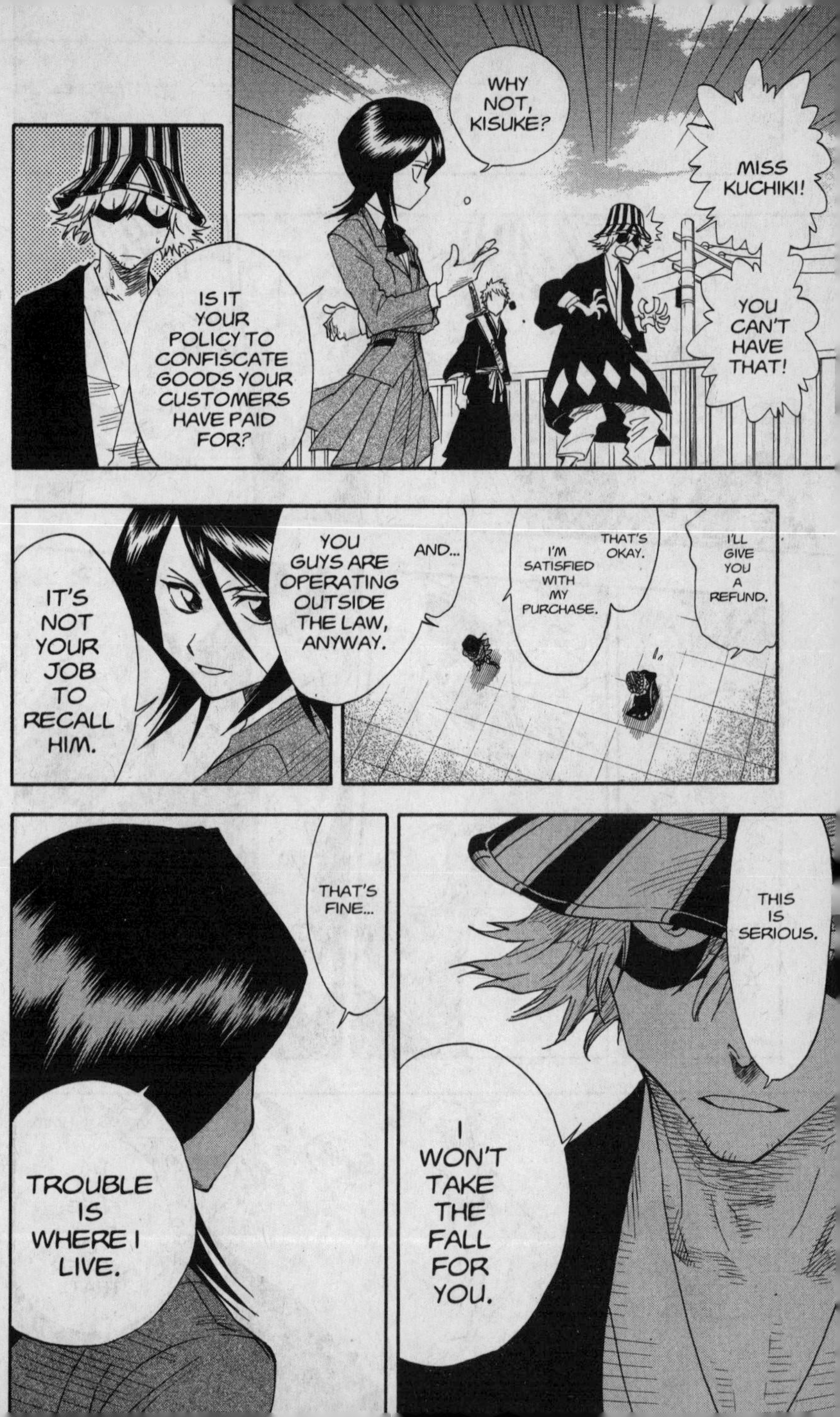
MISS KUCHIKI!
YOU CAN'T HAVE THAT!
WHY NOT, KISUKE?
IS IT YOUR POLICY TO CONFISCATE GOODS YOUR CUSTOMERS HAVE PAID FOR?
I'LL GIVE YOU A REFUND.
THAT'S OKAY.
I'M SATISFIED WITH MY PURCHASE.
AND...
YOU GUYS ARE OPERATING OUTSIDE THE LAW, ANYWAY.
IT'S NOT YOUR JOB TO RECALL HIM.
THIS IS SERIOUS.
I WON'T TAKE THE FALL FOR YOU.
THAT'S FINE...
TROUBLE IS WHERE I LIVE.

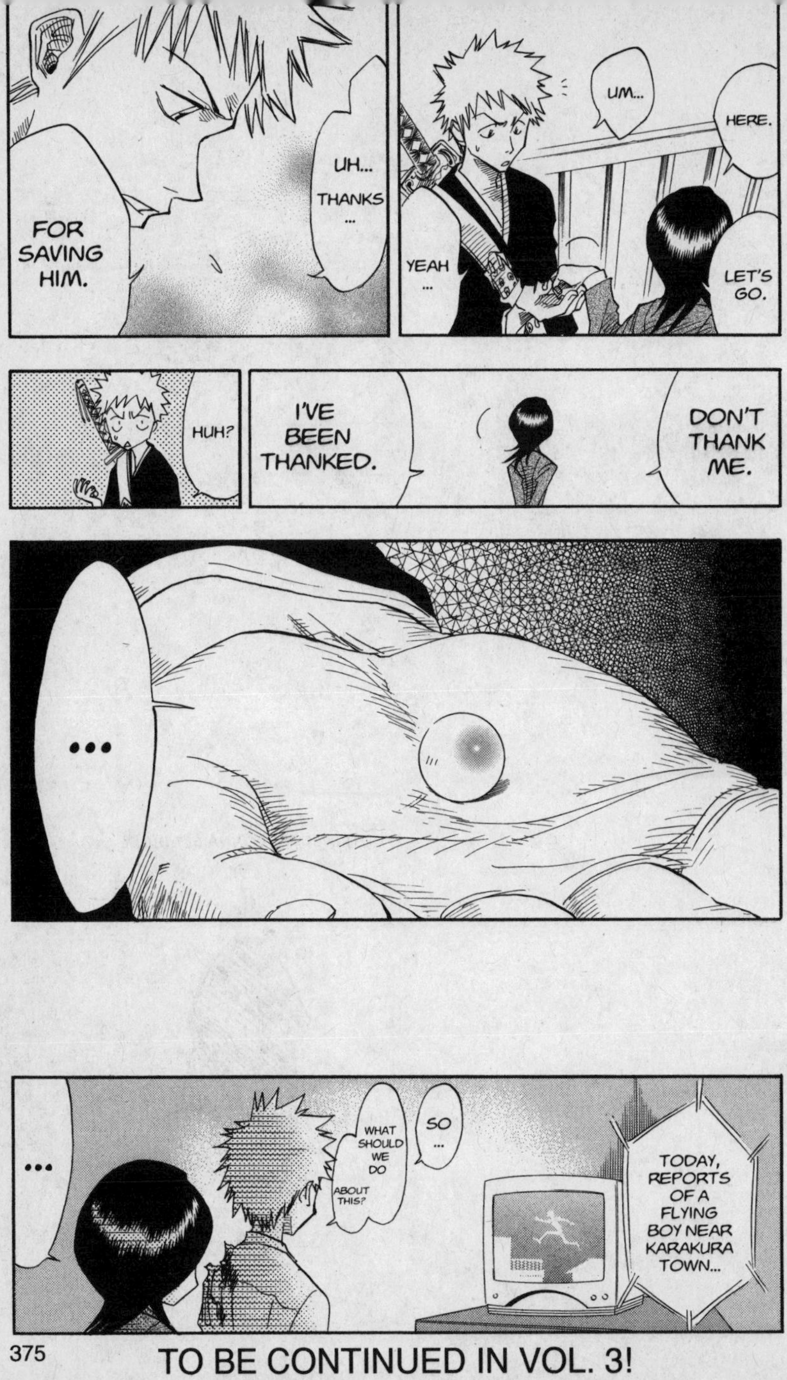
HERE.
UM...
LET'S GO.
YEAH ...
UH... THANKS ...
FOR SAVING HIM.
DON'T THANK ME.
I'VE BEEN THANKED.
HUH?
...
TODAY, REPORTS OF A FLYING BOY NEAR KARAKURA TOWN...
SO ...
WHAT SHOULD WE DO ABOUT THIS?
...

TO BE CONTINUED IN VOL. 3!

THINGS ARE GONNA GET DICEY.

EXTRA.

SOUL CANDY PACKAGE CATALOGUE

OTHER CHARACTERS

ALFRED

DIANA

CLAUDIA

GINOSUKE

GRINGO

BLUES

KANESHIRO

SCHTEINER

MOST POPULAR
"CHAPPY"

2ND MOST
POPULAR
"YUKI"

3RD MOST
POPULAR
"PUPPLES"

OVERALL ATTENDANCE 5	**ORIHIME**
FEMALE STUDENT 2	**INOUE**

ORIHIME INOUE

イノウエ・オリヒメ

157 CM
45 KG
BLOOD TYPE: BO
D.O.B. SEPTEMBER 3

○ LIKES ASIAN AND FLOWER PRINTS

○ LIKES COMEDY

○ DAYDREAMS A LOT

○ MOUTH OPEN WHEN DAYDREAMING

○ LIKES CHEESE AND BUTTER

○ PUTS BUTTER ON BAKED SWEET POTATOES

○ IS A STUDENT HEALTH ADVISOR

○ LOST BROTHER 3 YEARS AGO.
 STATUS OF PARENTS UNKNOWN.
 SUPPORTED BY RELATIVES

THEME SONG
ELSA
"T'EN VA PAS"
RECORDED IN
"L'ESSENTIAL ELSA"
1986-1993

OVERALL ATTENDANCE 16	YASUTORA "CHAD" SADO	サド・ヤストラ
MALE STUDENT 9		

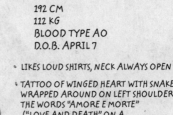

192 CM
112 KG
BLOOD TYPE AO
D.O.B. APRIL 7

° LIKES LOUD SHIRTS, NECK ALWAYS OPEN

° TATTOO OF WINGED HEART WITH SNAKE WRAPPED AROUND ON LEFT SHOULDER. THE WORDS "AMORE E MORTE" ("LOVE AND DEATH" ON A RIBBON ABOVE SNAKE)

° LIKES SMALL ANIMALS

° LIKES TOMATOES

° FAMILY STRUCTURE UNKNOWN

THEME SONG
THE HELLACOPTERS
"NO SONG UNHEARD"
RECORDED IN
"HIGH VISIBILITY"

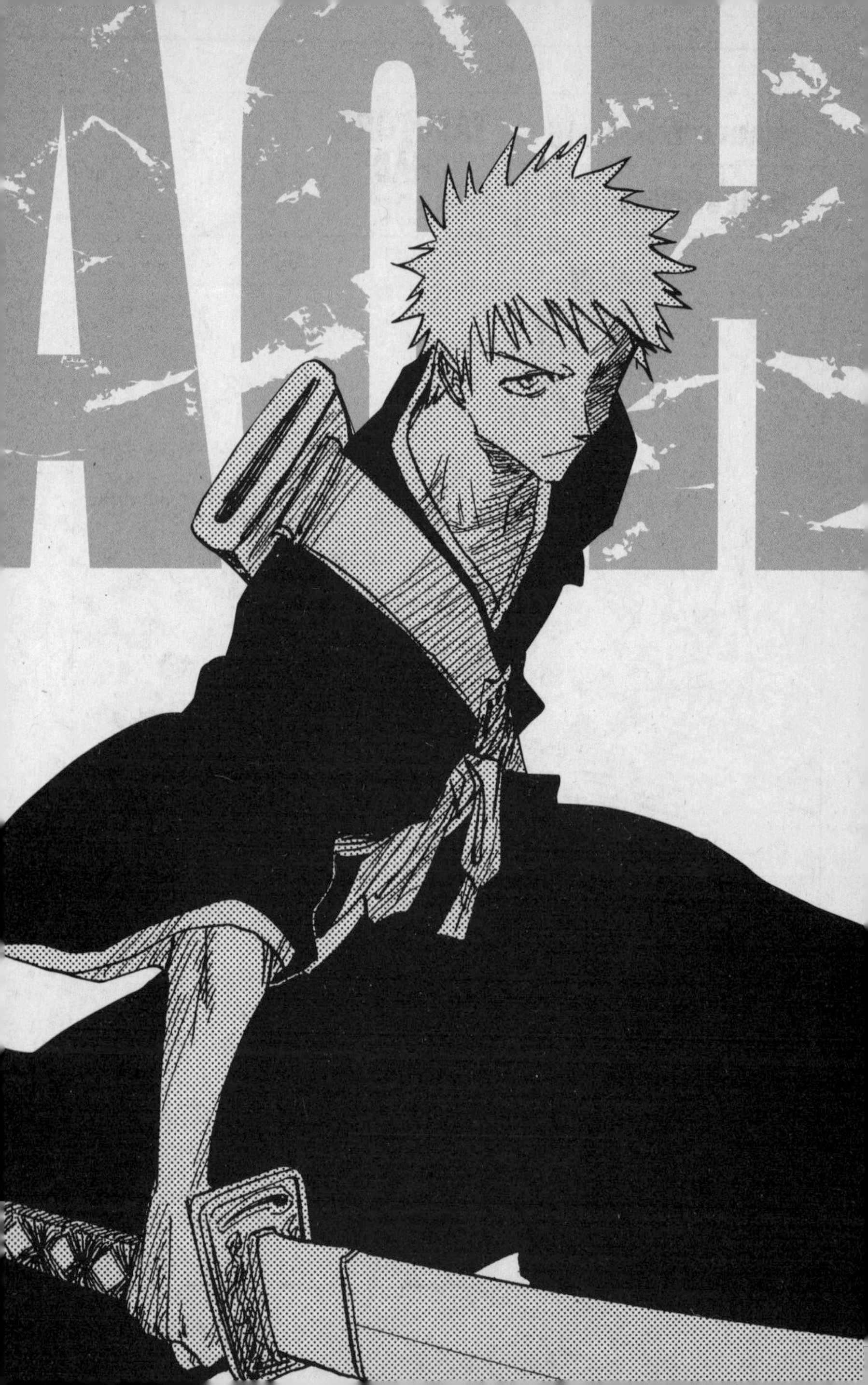

I tend to get worried about the seasons in
BLEACH as opposed to the actual seasons in
real life. The series started in the summer, but
at that time, it was May in the book. That
discrepancy has always bothered me. In this
volume, the introduction of Ichigo, the main
character, finally comes to an end. The
setting is June. Unexpectedly, this all
worked out quite well. If possible,
please read this on a rainy night.

-Tite Kubo

BLEACH

BLEACH
ブリーチ

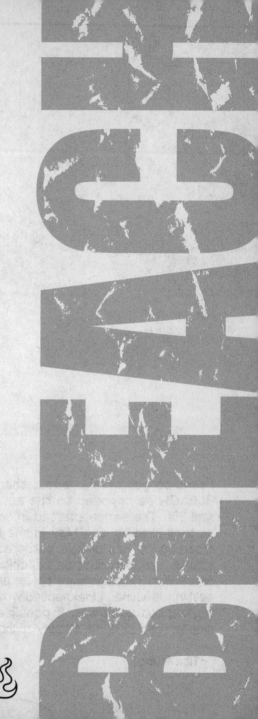

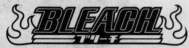

If I were rain,

That joins sky and earth that otherwise never touch,

Could I join two hearts as well?

BLEACH 3

memories in the rain

STARS AND

朽木ルキア

Rukia Kuchiki

Orihime Inoue

Ichigo Kurosaki

井上織姫

黒崎一護

plot

Ichigo Kurosaki, 15 years old. Except for being able to see ghosts, he is an ordinary (?) high school student. But when he meets the Soul Reaper Rukia Kuchiki, his life takes a dramatic turn for the bizarre, leading Ichigo to use his enormous spiritual energy to help Rukia do her job.

A Soul Reaper cleanses fallen souls called Hollows of their sins and guides them to the Soul Society. But as Ichigo fights an assortment of Hollows, he not only encounters souls who have lost their way in death, but one who had committed unforgivable crimes in life as well!

BLEACH ALL

黒崎真咲
Masaki Kurosaki

有沢竜貴
Tatsuki Arisawa

Isshin Kurosaki
黒崎一心

STORIES

BLEACH 3

memories in the rain

Contents

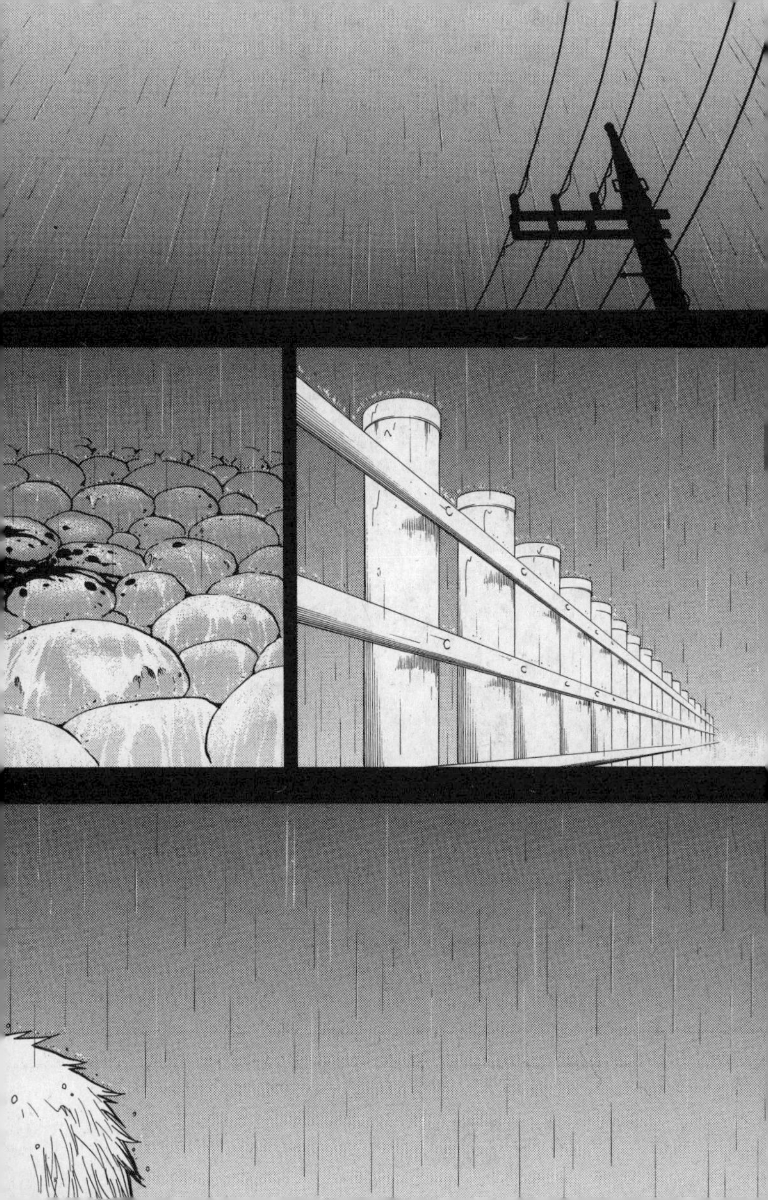

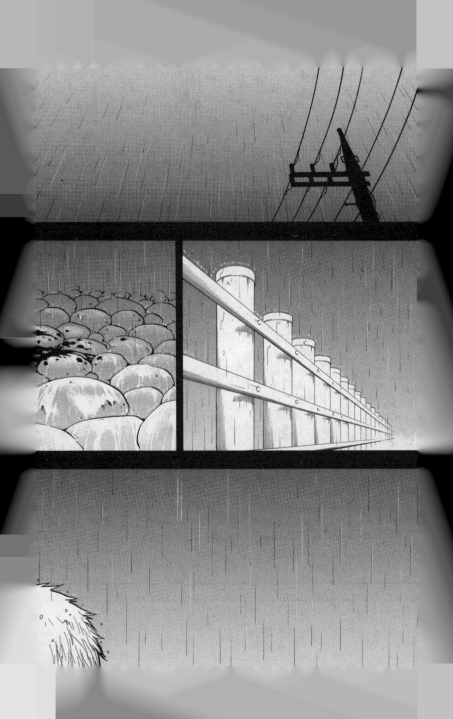

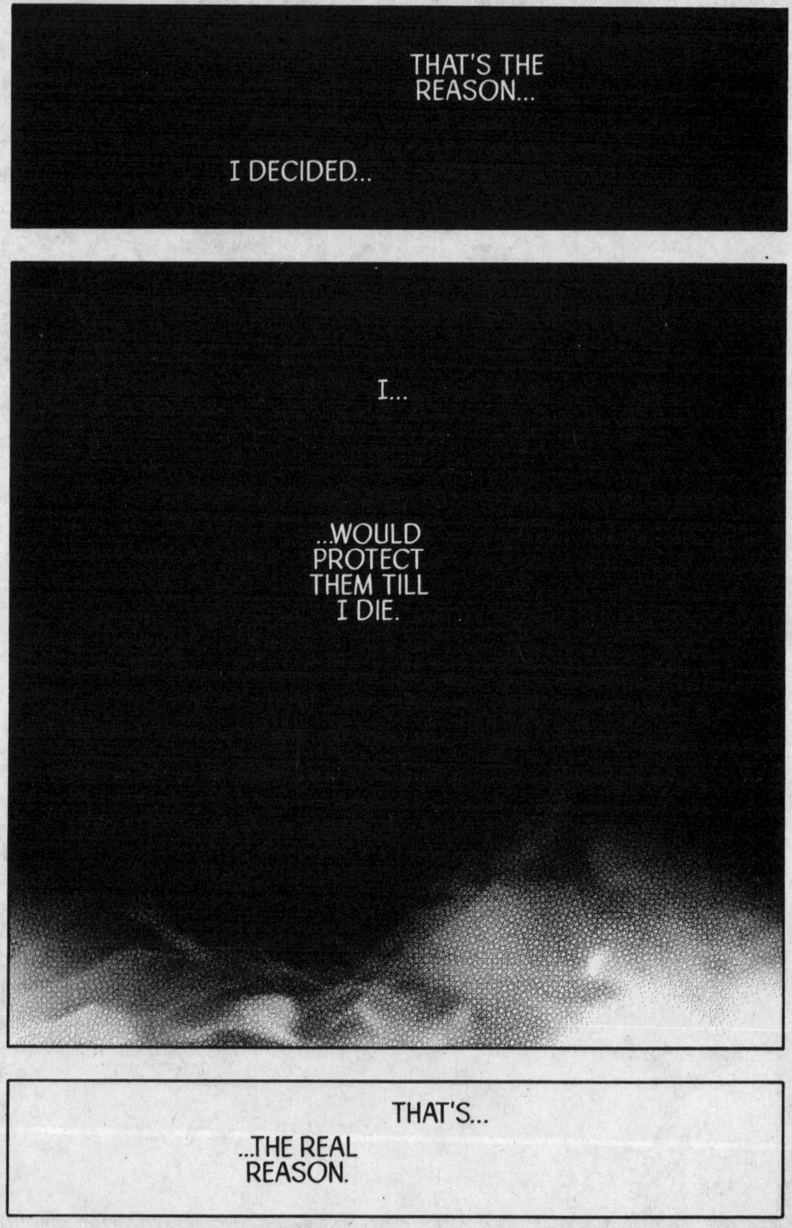
THAT'S THE REASON...
I DECIDED...
I...
...WOULD PROTECT THEM TILL I DIE.
THAT'S...
...THE REAL REASON.

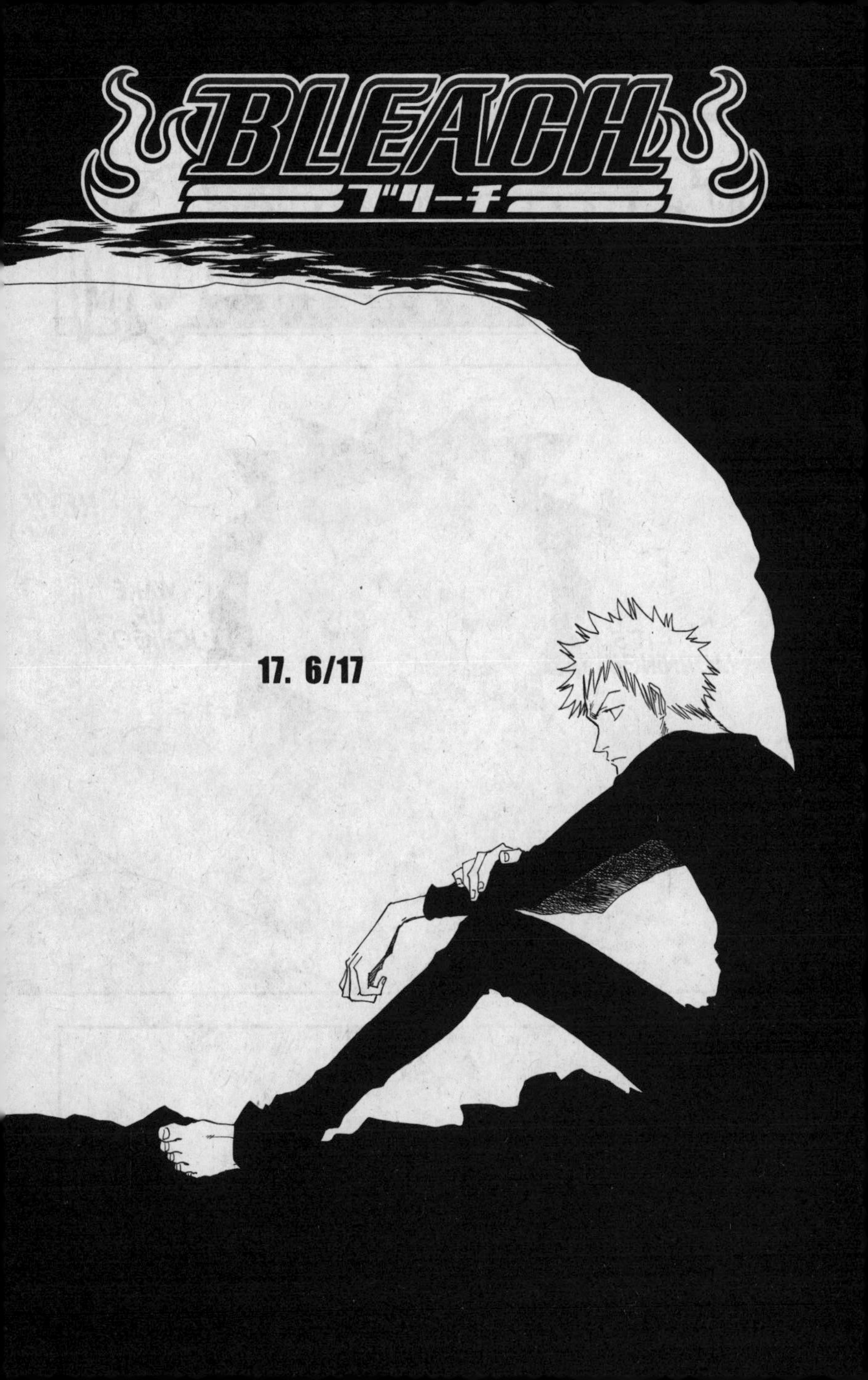
BLEACH
ブリーチ
17. 6/17

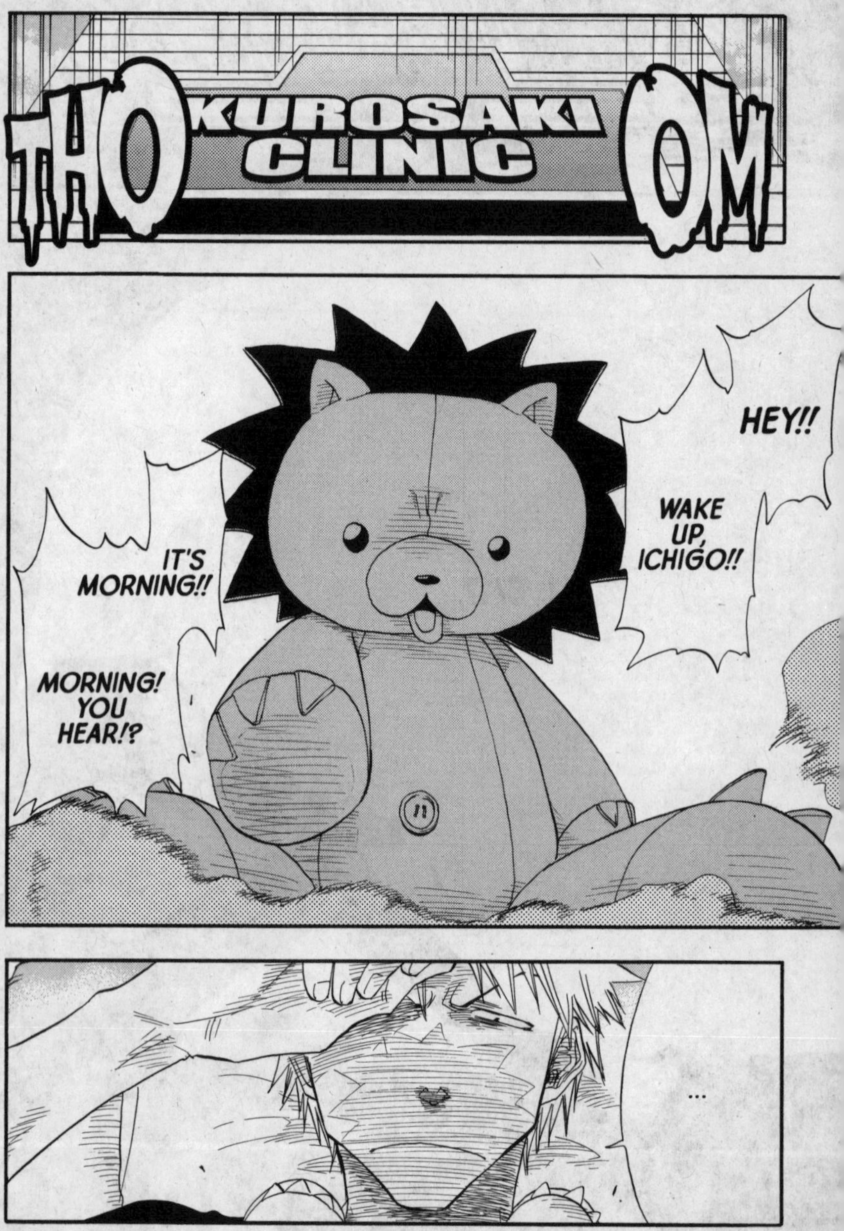
THOOM
KUROSAKI CLINIC
HEY!!
WAKE UP, ICHIGO!!
IT'S MORNING!!
MORNING! YOU HEAR!?
...

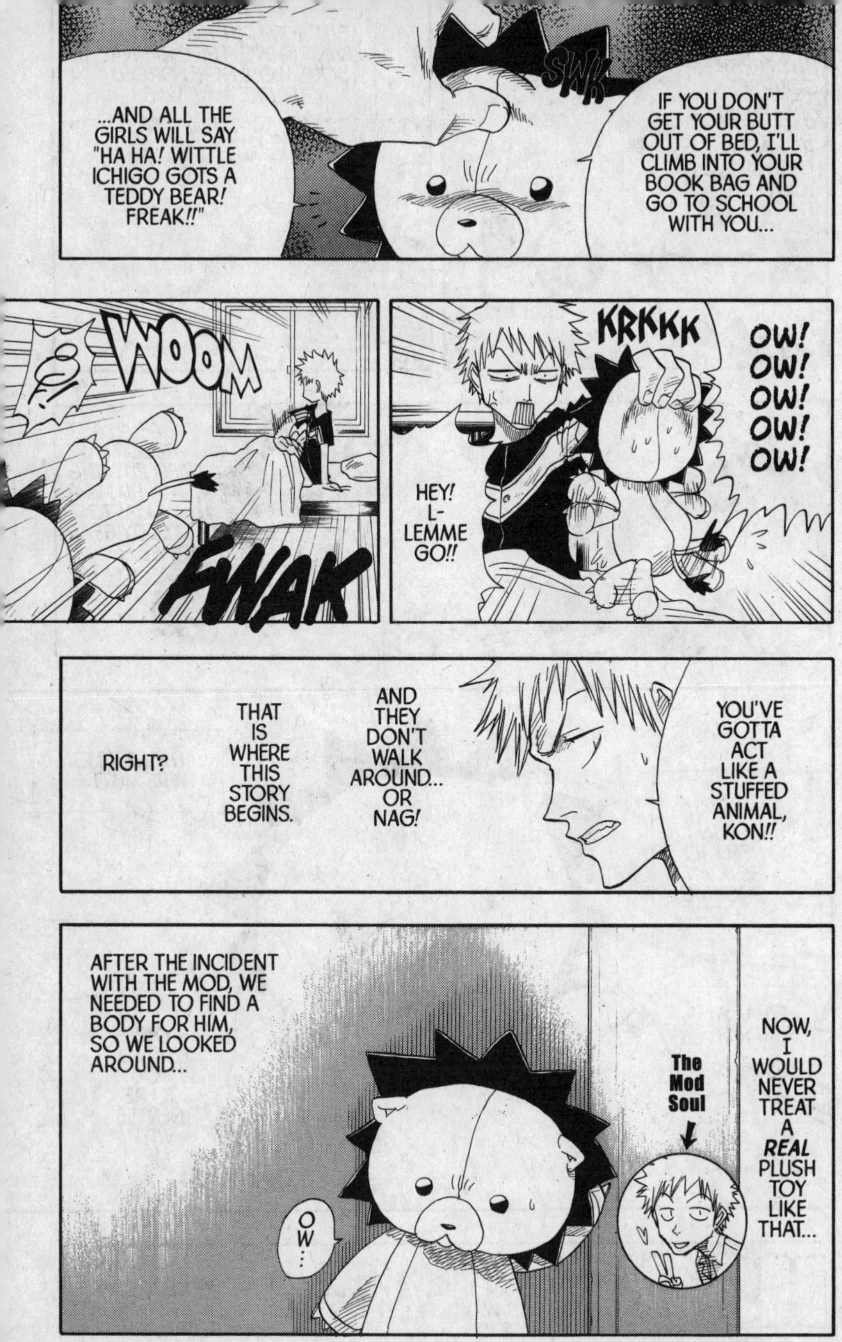
IF YOU DON'T GET YOUR BUTT OUT OF BED, I'LL CLIMB INTO YOUR BOOK BAG AND GO TO SCHOOL WITH YOU...
SWK
...AND ALL THE GIRLS WILL SAY "HA HA! WITTLE ICHIGO GOTS A TEDDY BEAR! FREAK!!"
KRKKK
OW! OW! OW! OW! OW!
HEY! L-LEMME GO!!
WOOM
FWAK
YOU'VE GOTTA ACT LIKE A STUFFED ANIMAL, KON!!
AND THEY DON'T WALK AROUND... OR NAG!
THAT IS WHERE THIS STORY BEGINS.
RIGHT?
NOW, I WOULD NEVER TREAT A *REAL* PLUSH TOY LIKE THAT...
The Mod Soul
OW...
AFTER THE INCIDENT WITH THE MOD, WE NEEDED TO FIND A BODY FOR HIM, SO WE LOOKED AROUND...

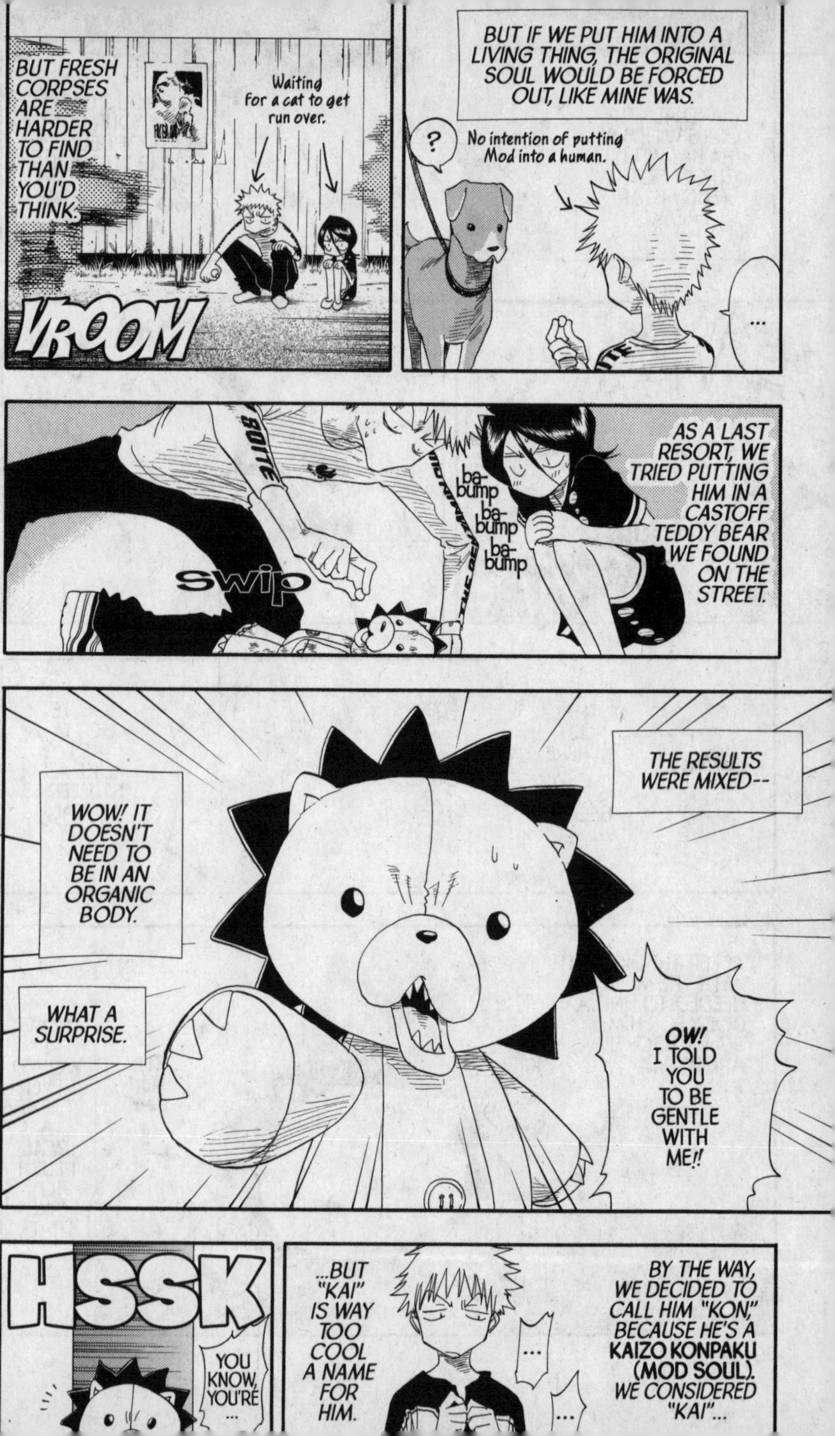
BUT IF WE PUT HIM INTO A LIVING THING, THE ORIGINAL SOUL WOULD BE FORCED OUT, LIKE MINE WAS.
?
No intention of putting Mod into a human.
...
BUT FRESH CORPSES ARE HARDER TO FIND THAN YOU'D THINK.
Waiting for a cat to get run over.
VROOM
AS A LAST RESORT, WE TRIED PUTTING HIM IN A CASTOFF TEDDY BEAR WE FOUND ON THE STREET.
ba-bump
ba-bump
ba-bump
swip
THE RESULTS WERE MIXED--
WOW! IT DOESN'T NEED TO BE IN AN ORGANIC BODY.
OW! I TOLD YOU TO BE GENTLE WITH ME!!
WHAT A SURPRISE.
BY THE WAY, WE DECIDED TO CALL HIM "KON," BECAUSE HE'S A **KAIZO KONPAKU** (MOD SOUL). WE CONSIDERED "KAI"...
...BUT "KAI" IS WAY TOO COOL A NAME FOR HIM.
...
...
HSSK
YOU KNOW, YOU'RE ...

READ THIS WAY

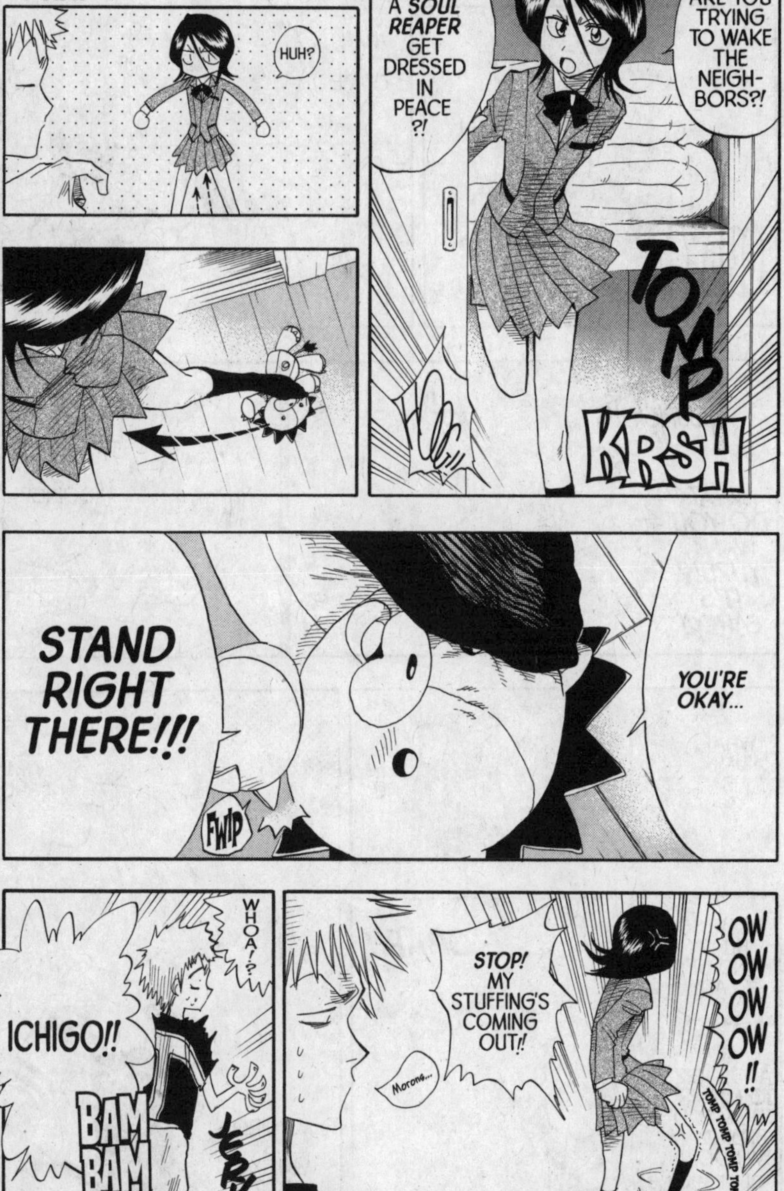
ARE YOU TRYING TO WAKE THE NEIGHBORS?!
CAN'T A *SOUL REAPER* GET DRESSED IN PEACE ?!
TOMP
KRSH
HUH?
YOU'RE OKAY...
STAND RIGHT THERE!!!
FWIP
OW OW OW OW!!
TOMP TOMP TOMP TOMP
STOP! MY STUFFING'S COMING OUT!!
Morons...
WHOA!?
ICHIGO!!
JERK
BAM BAM BAM

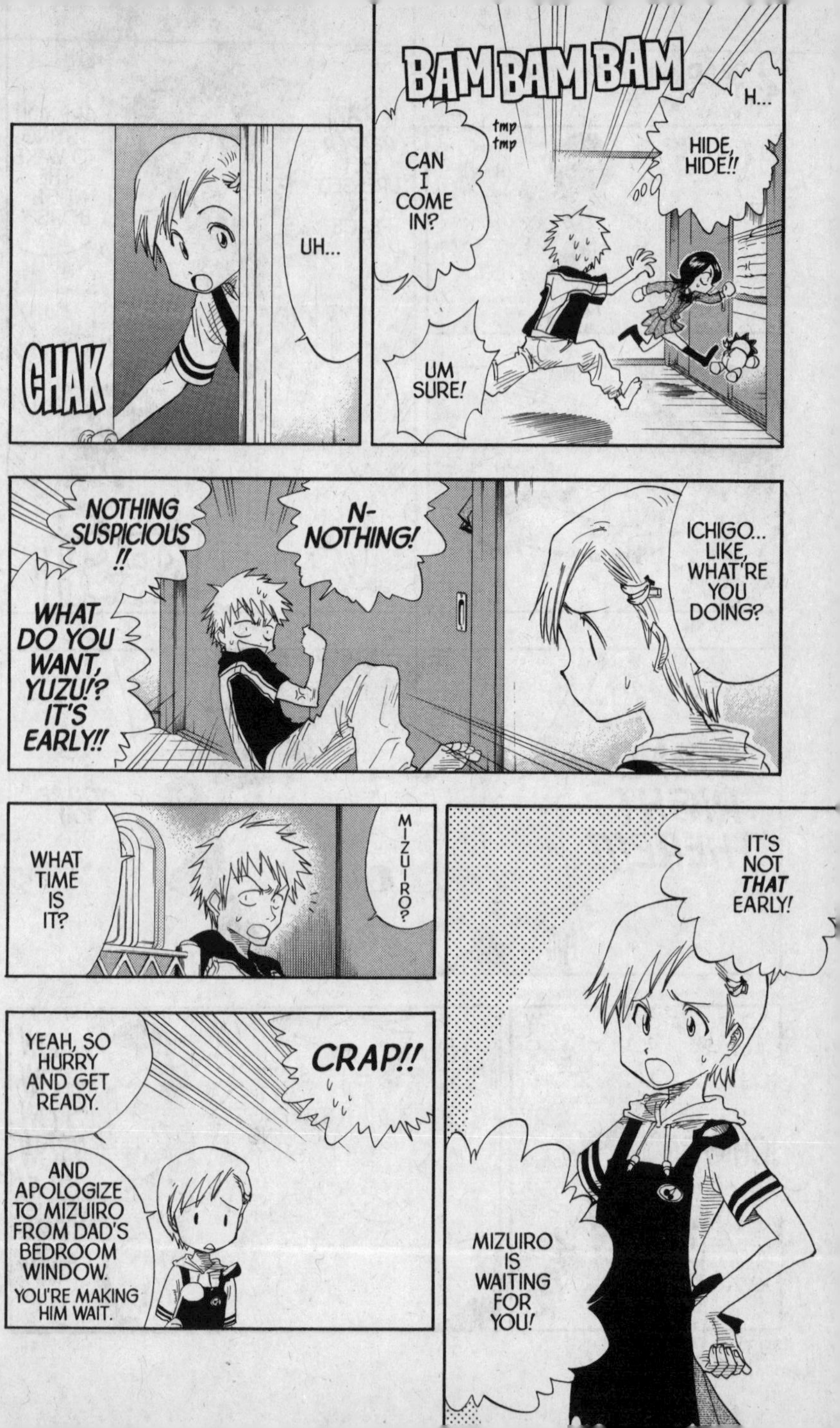
BAM BAM BAM
H...
HIDE, HIDE!!
CAN I COME IN?
tmp tmp
UM SURE!
UH...
CHAK
ICHIGO... LIKE, WHAT'RE YOU DOING?
N-NOTHING!
NOTHING SUSPICIOUS!!
WHAT DO YOU WANT, YUZU!? IT'S EARLY!!
IT'S NOT THAT EARLY!
MIZUIRO IS WAITING FOR YOU!
MIZUIRO?
WHAT TIME IS IT?
CRAP!!
YEAH, SO HURRY AND GET READY.
AND APOLOGIZE TO MIZUIRO FROM DAD'S BEDROOM WINDOW. YOU'RE MAKING HIM WAIT.

READ THIS WAY

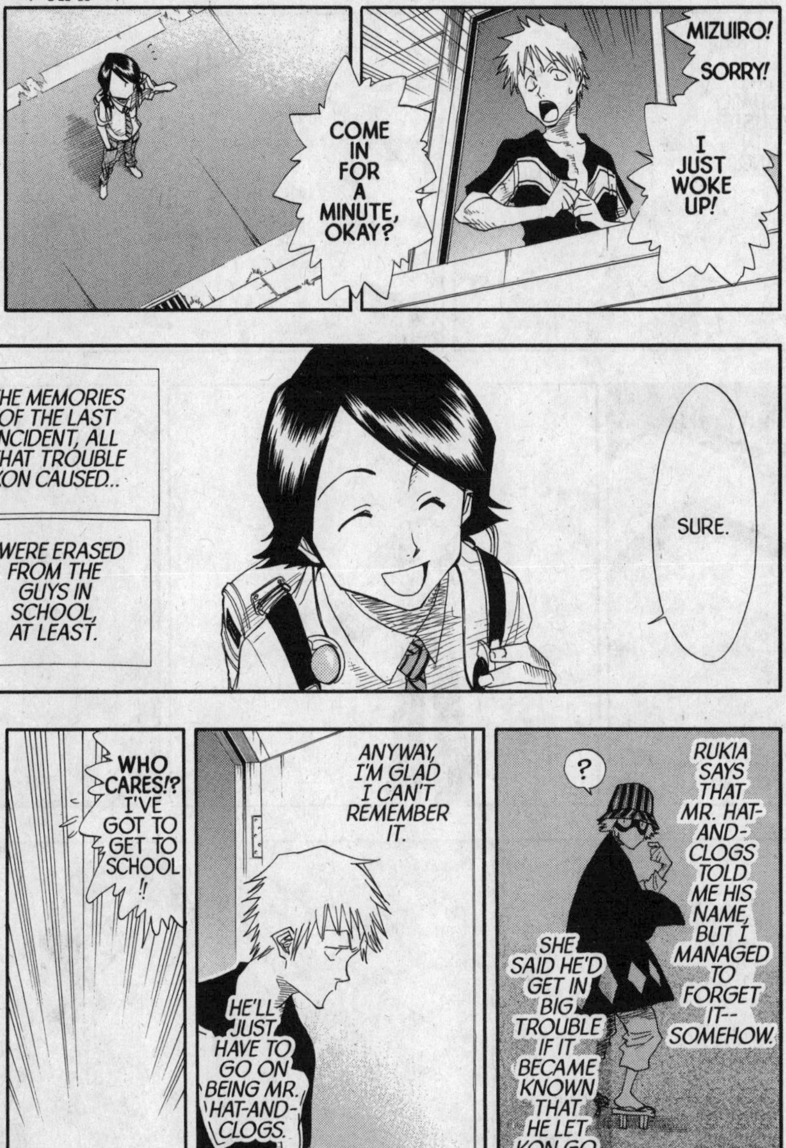
MIZUIRO!
SORRY!
I JUST WOKE UP!
COME IN FOR A MINUTE, OKAY?
SURE.
THE MEMORIES OF THE LAST INCIDENT, ALL THAT TROUBLE KON CAUSED...
...WERE ERASED FROM THE GUYS IN SCHOOL, AT LEAST.
RUKIA SAYS THAT MR. HAT-AND-CLOGS TOLD ME HIS NAME, BUT I MANAGED TO FORGET IT--SOMEHOW.
?
SHE SAID HE'D GET IN BIG TROUBLE IF IT BECAME KNOWN THAT HE LET KON GO.
ANYWAY, I'M GLAD I CAN'T REMEMBER IT.
HE'LL JUST HAVE TO GO ON BEING MR. HAT-AND-CLOGS.
WHO CARES!? I'VE GOT TO GET TO SCHOOL!!

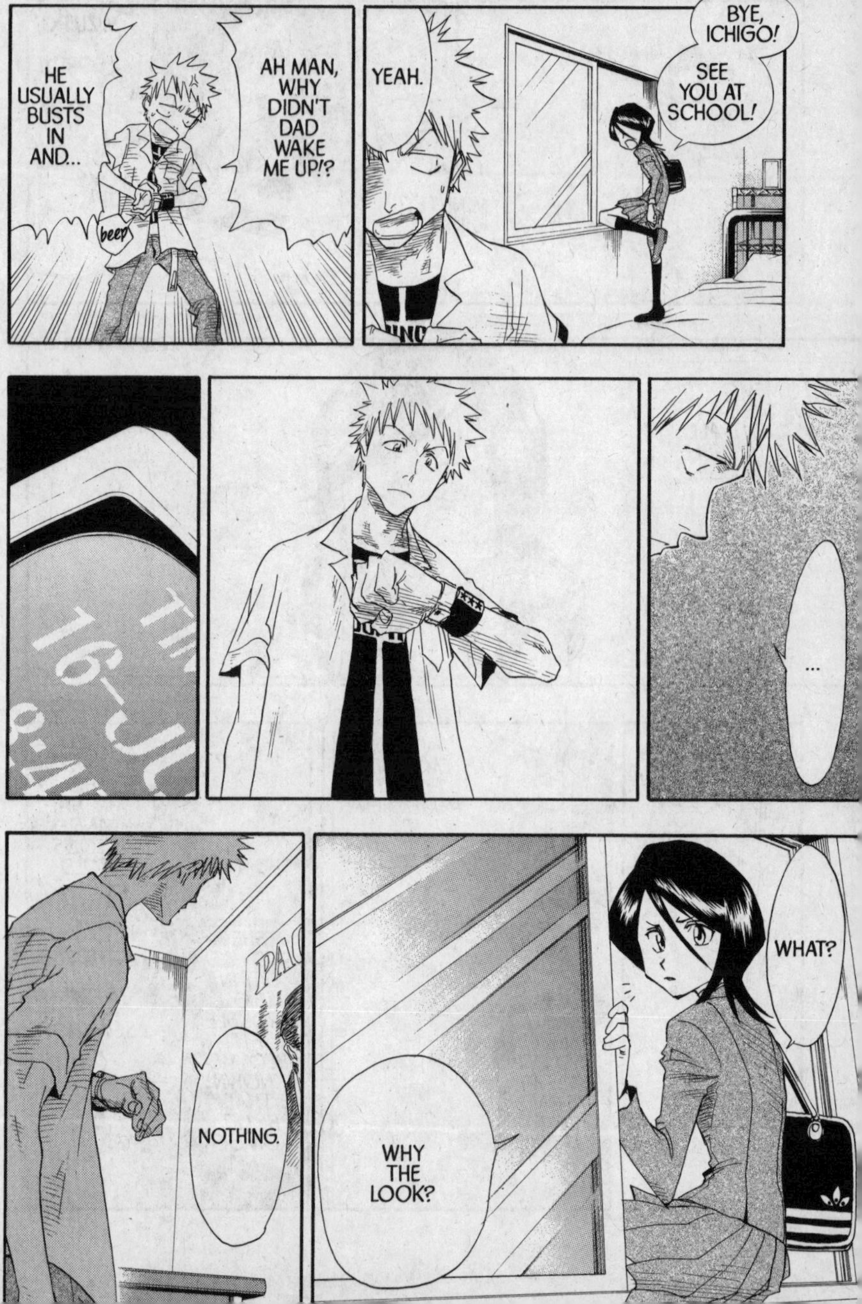
BYE, ICHIGO!
SEE YOU AT SCHOOL!
YEAH.
AH MAN, WHY DIDN'T DAD WAKE ME UP!?
HE USUALLY BUSTS IN AND...
beep
...
WHAT?
WHY THE LOOK?
NOTHING.

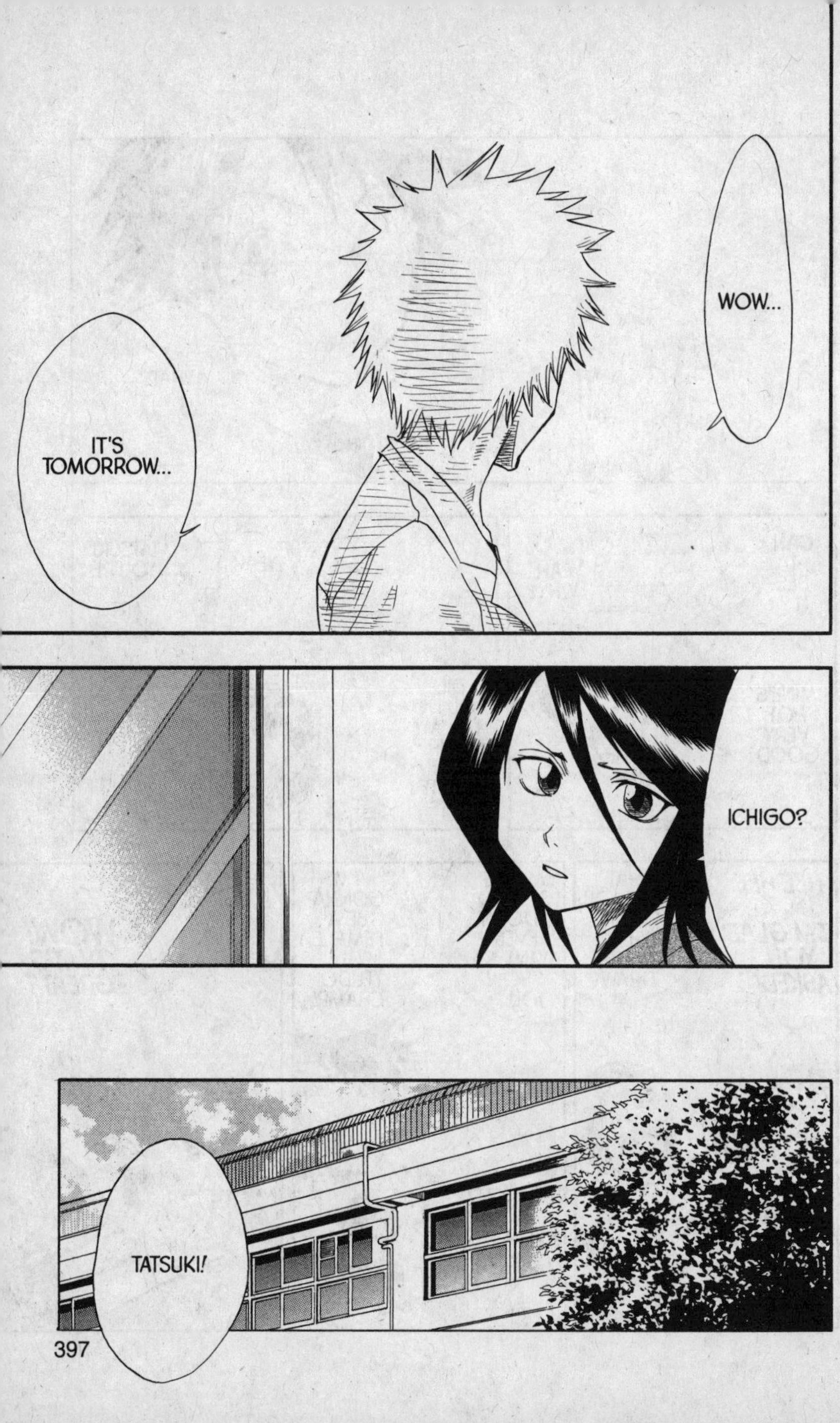
WOW...
IT'S TOMORROW...
ICHIGO?
TATSUKI!

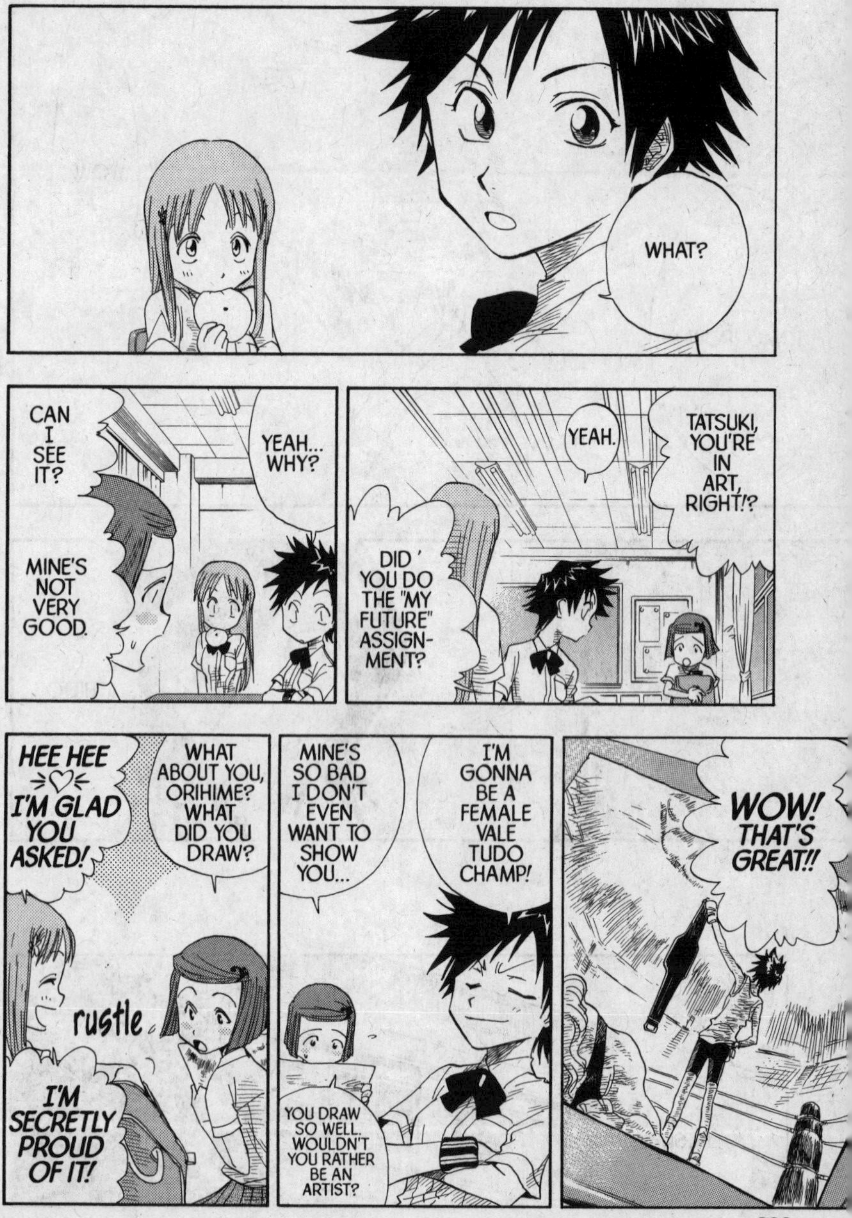
WHAT?
TATSUKI, YOU'RE IN ART, RIGHT!?
YEAH.
DID YOU DO THE "MY FUTURE" ASSIGNMENT?
YEAH... WHY?
CAN I SEE IT?
MINE'S NOT VERY GOOD.
WOW! THAT'S GREAT!!
I'M GONNA BE A FEMALE VALE TUDO CHAMP!
MINE'S SO BAD I DON'T EVEN WANT TO SHOW YOU...
YOU DRAW SO WELL. WOULDN'T YOU RATHER BE AN ARTIST?
WHAT ABOUT YOU, ORIHIME? WHAT DID YOU DRAW?
HEE HEE ♡ I'M GLAD YOU ASKED!
rustle
I'M SECRETLY PROUD OF IT!

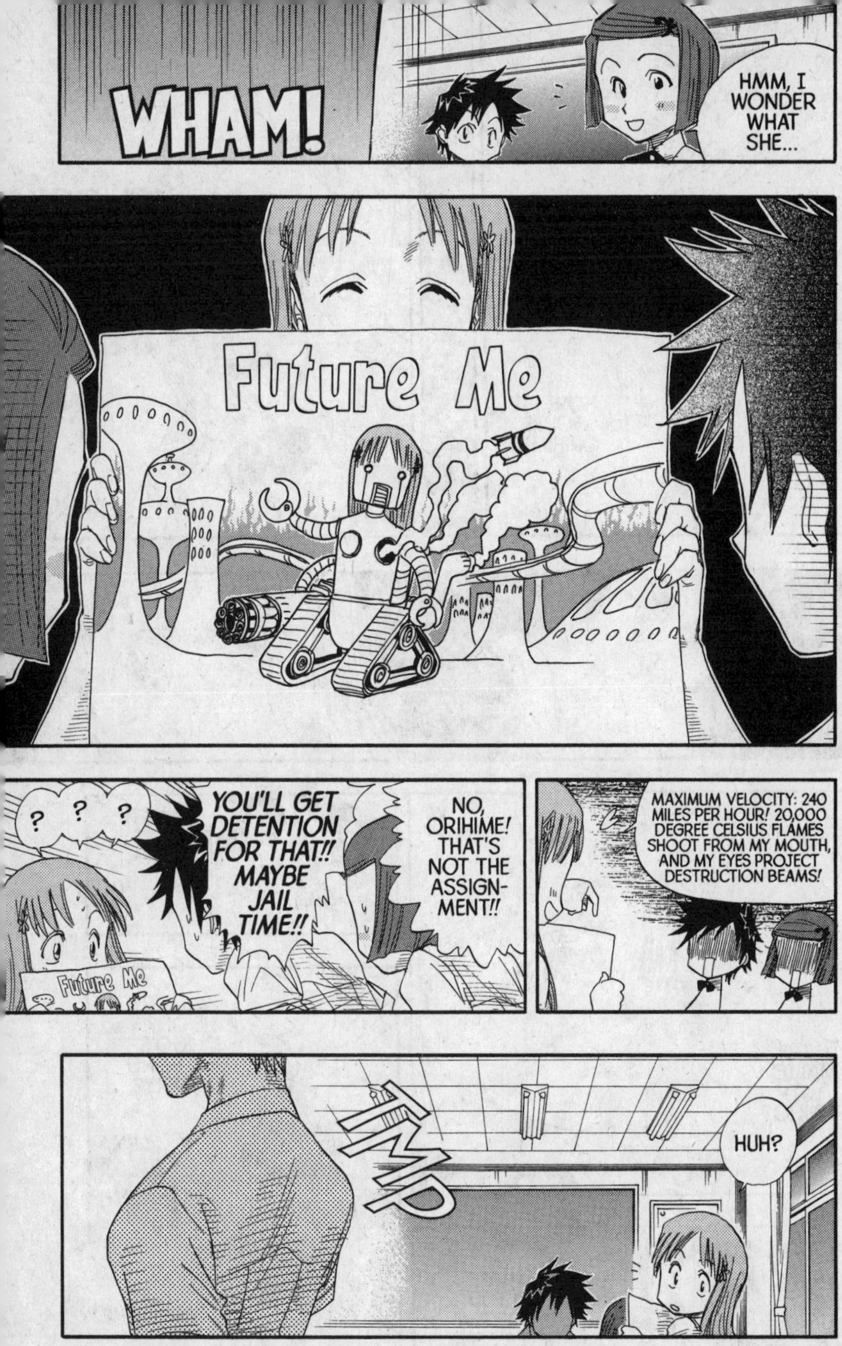
HMM, I WONDER WHAT SHE...
WHAM!
Future Me
MAXIMUM VELOCITY: 240 MILES PER HOUR! 20,000 DEGREE CELSIUS FLAMES SHOOT FROM MY MOUTH, AND MY EYES PROJECT DESTRUCTION BEAMS!
NO, ORIHIME! THAT'S NOT THE ASSIGN-MENT!!
YOU'LL GET DETENTION FOR THAT!! MAYBE JAIL TIME!!
? ? ?
Future Me
HUH?
TMP

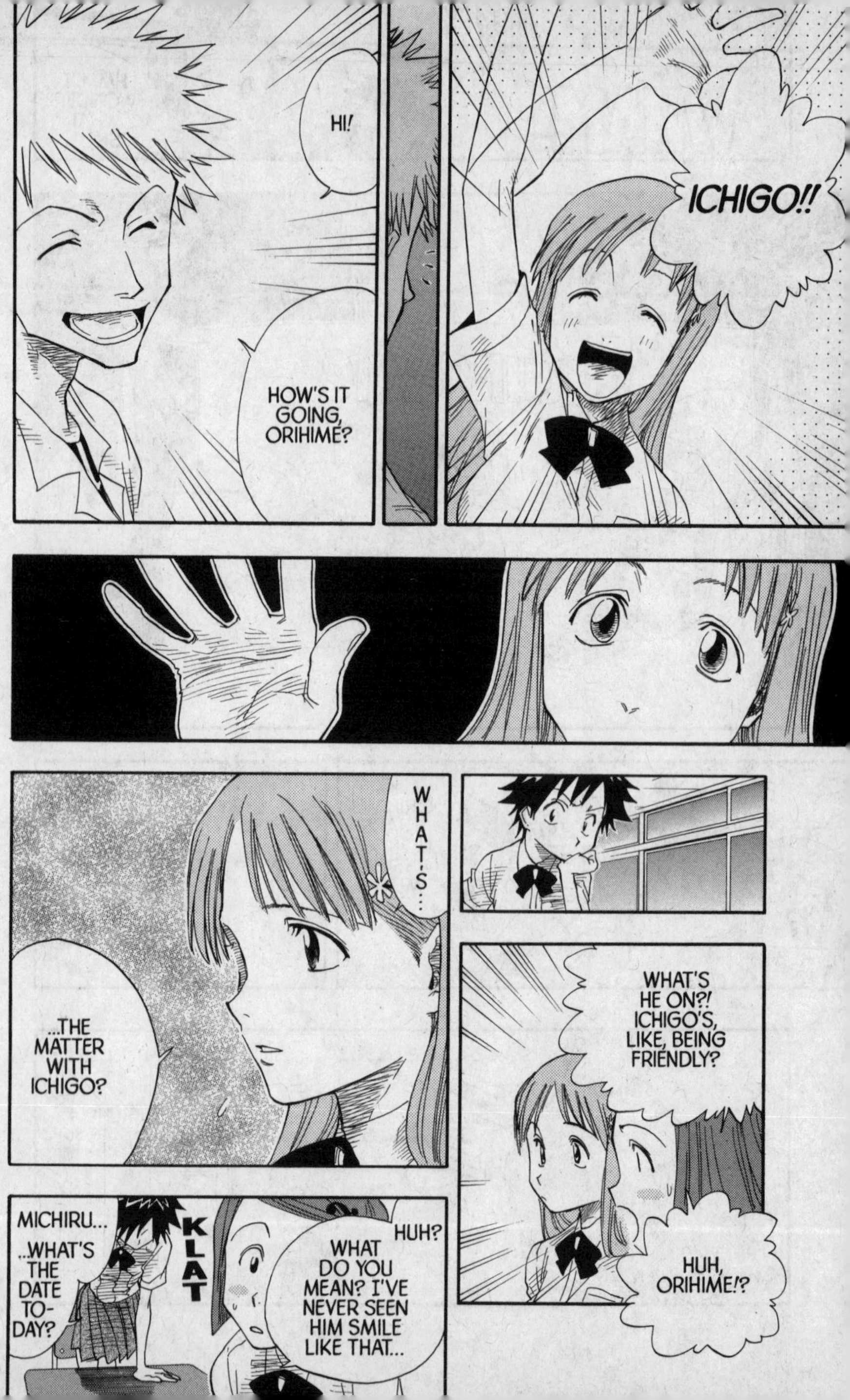
ICHIGO!!
HI!
HOW'S IT GOING, ORIHIME?
WHAT'S HE ON?! ICHIGO'S, LIKE, BEING FRIENDLY?
HUH, ORIHIME!?
WHAT'S...
...THE MATTER WITH ICHIGO?
HUH?
WHAT DO YOU MEAN? I'VE NEVER SEEN HIM SMILE LIKE THAT...
KLAT
MICHIRU...
...WHAT'S THE DATE TO-DAY?

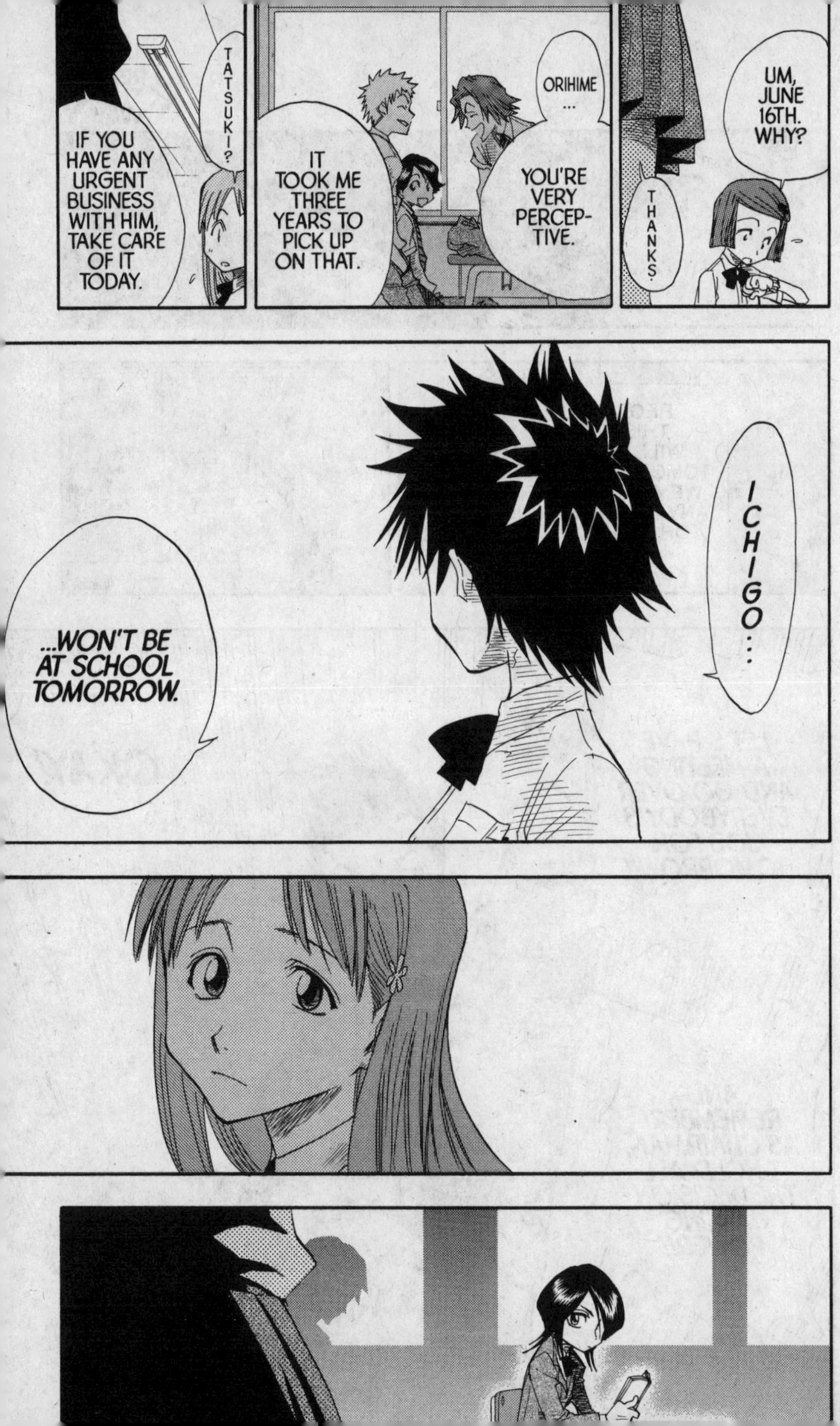
UM, JUNE 16TH. WHY?
THANKS.
ORIHIME...
YOU'RE VERY PERCEP-TIVE.
IT TOOK ME THREE YEARS TO PICK UP ON THAT.
TATSUKI?
IF YOU HAVE ANY URGENT BUSINESS WITH HIM, TAKE CARE OF IT TODAY.
ICHIGO...
...WON'T BE AT SCHOOL TOMORROW.

REGRETFULLY,
THIS FACILITY
WILL BE CLOSED
TOMORROW, JUNE 17.
WE APOLOGIZE FOR
ANY INCONVENIENCE
OR LOSS OF LIFE.
-- *MANAGEMENT
KUROSAKI CLINIC*

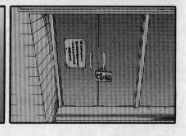

LET'S HAVE
A MEETING
AND GO OVER
EVERYBODY'S
JOB FOR
TOMORROW!!

OKAY!

AND
REMEMBER!
AS CHAIRMAN,
I HOLD ALL
THE DECISION-
MAKING
POWER!!

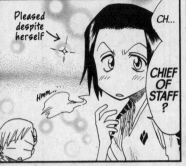

READ THIS WAY

AS IF! WHAT KIND OF MEETING IS THIS!?
HEY!
RAISE YOUR HAND IF YOU WISH TO SPEAK, CHIEF OF STAFF!!
wham
CH...
CHIEF OF STAFF?
Pleased despite herself
Hmm...
YUZU, YOU'LL BE IN CHARGE OF LUNCH, AS USUAL.
OKAY.
KARIN, YOU'LL LOAD THE PACKS.
HUH!?
AND THE LAST ITEM OF BUSINESS...I GOT A HAIR-CUT FOR THE OCCASION. HOW DO I LOOK?
EXACTLY THE SAME!!

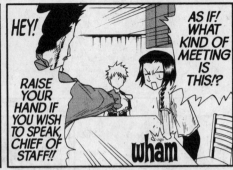

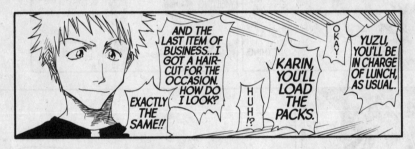

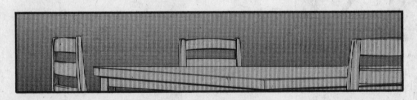

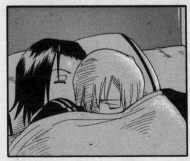

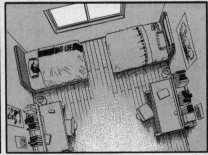

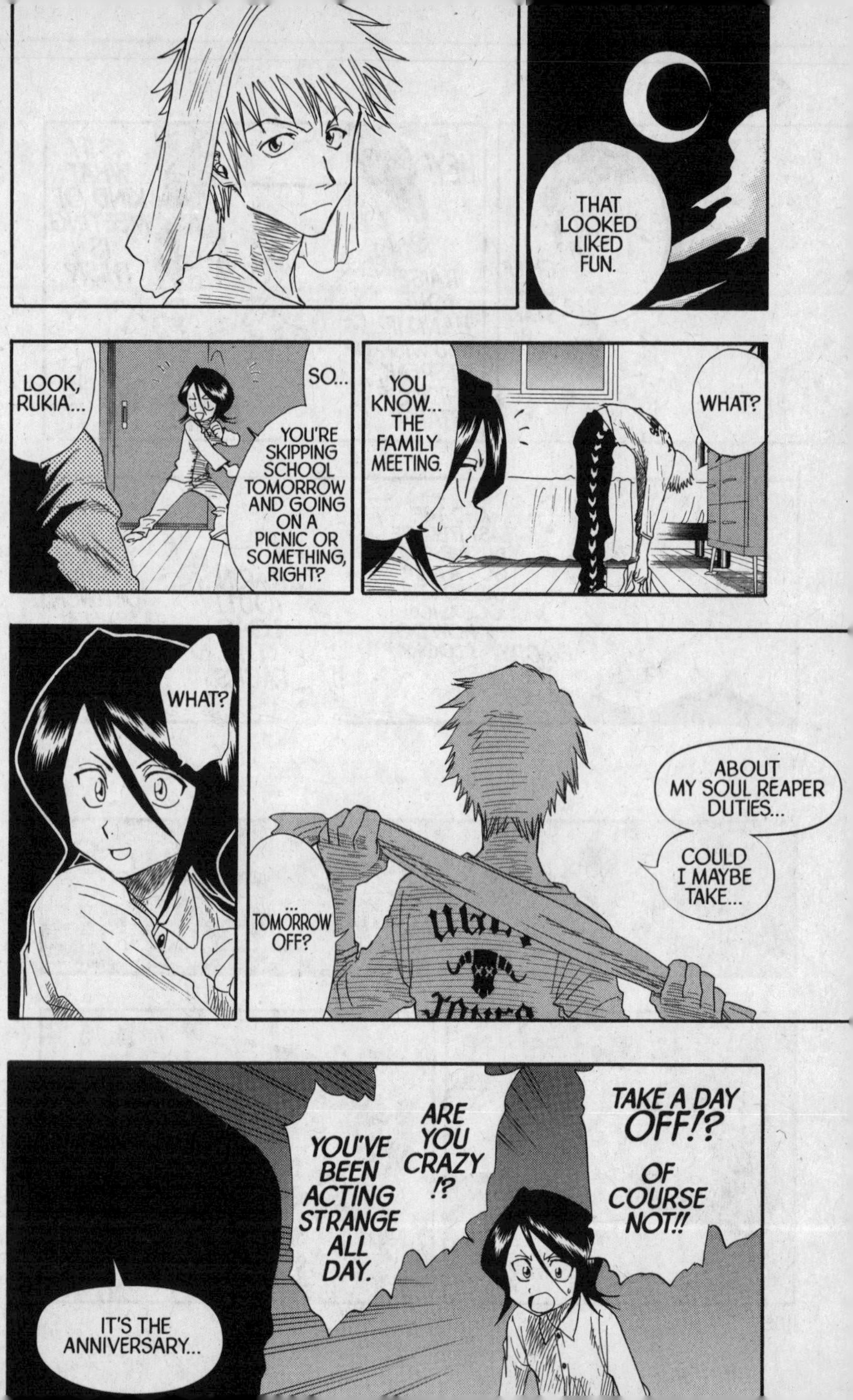
THAT LOOKED LIKED FUN.
WHAT?
YOU KNOW... THE FAMILY MEETING.
SO...
YOU'RE SKIPPING SCHOOL TOMORROW AND GOING ON A PICNIC OR SOMETHING, RIGHT?
LOOK, RUKIA...
ABOUT MY SOUL REAPER DUTIES...
COULD I MAYBE TAKE...
...TOMORROW OFF?
WHAT?
TAKE A DAY OFF!?
OF COURSE NOT!!
ARE YOU CRAZY!?
YOU'VE BEEN ACTING STRANGE ALL DAY.
IT'S THE ANNIVERSARY...

READ THIS WAY

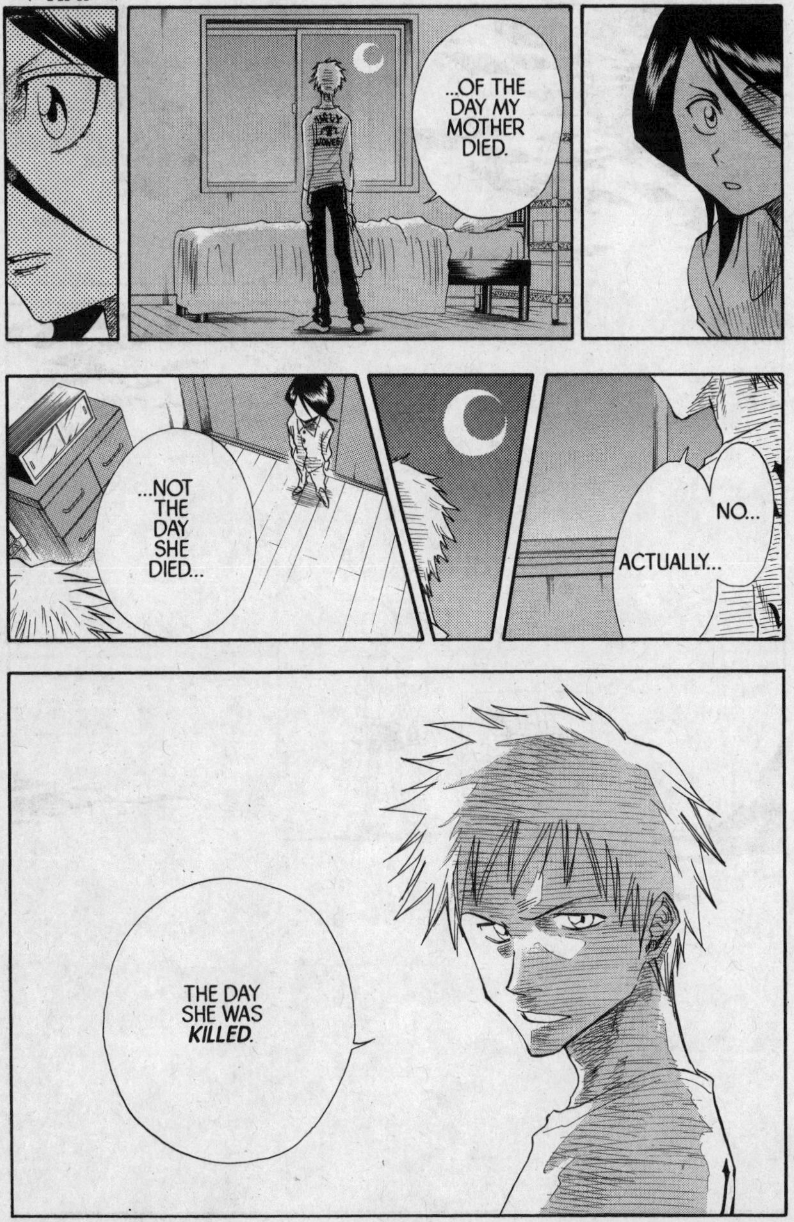

...OF THE DAY MY MOTHER DIED.
NO...
ACTUALLY...
...NOT THE DAY SHE DIED...
THE DAY SHE WAS *KILLED*.

18. 6/17 op. 2 Doesn't Smile Much Anymore

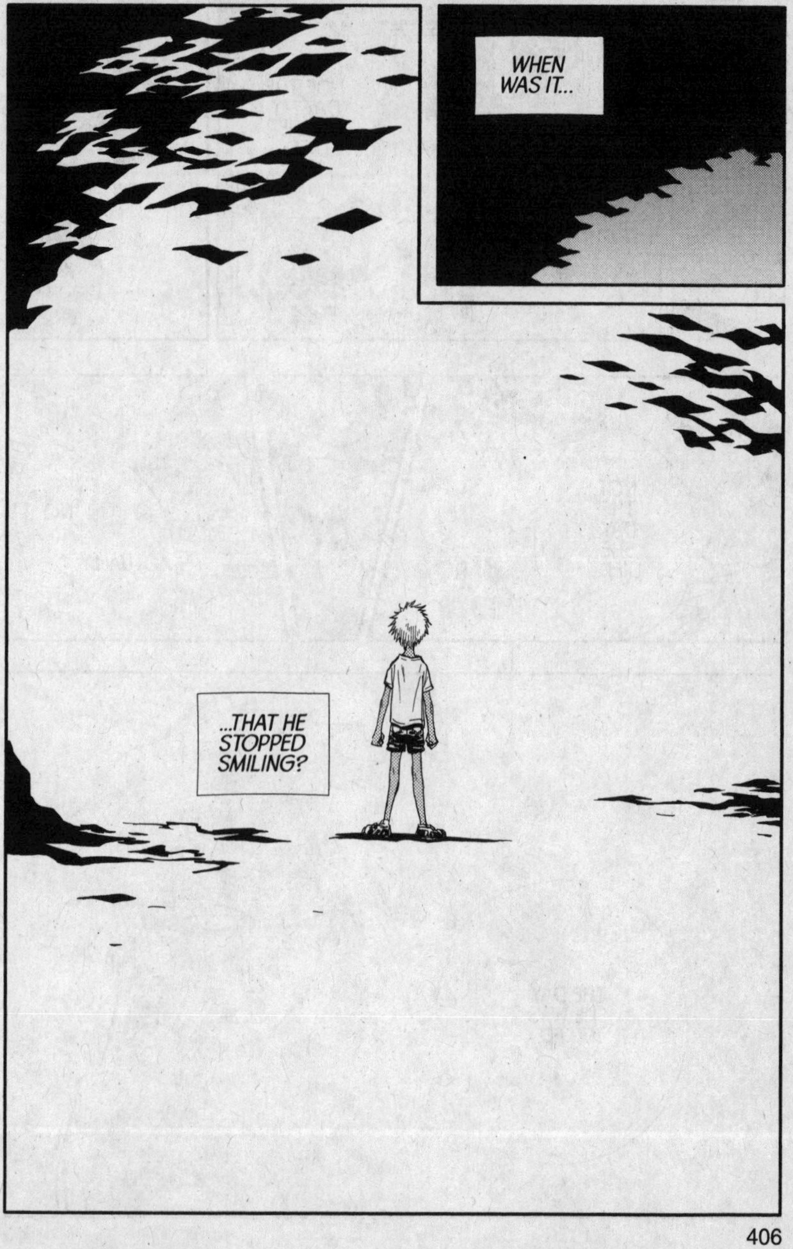
WHEN WAS IT...
...THAT HE STOPPED SMILING?

BLEACH
ブリーチ

18. 6/17 op. 2
Doesn't Smile Much Anymore

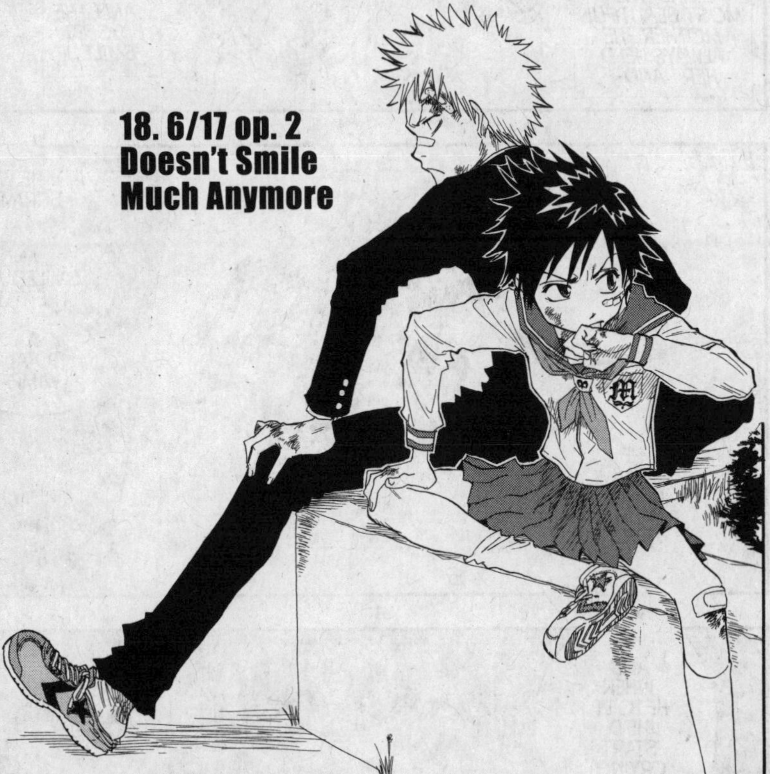

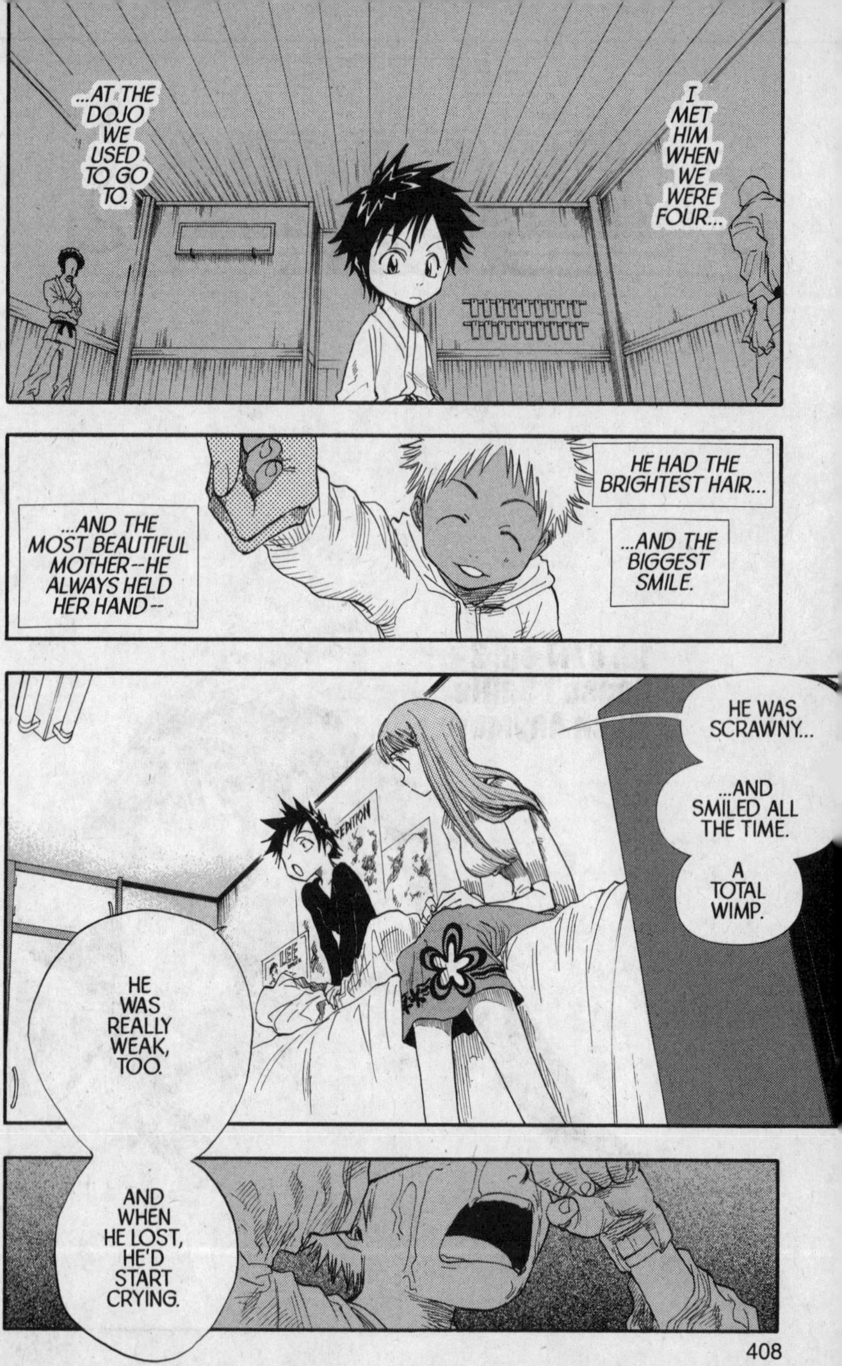
I MET HIM WHEN WE WERE FOUR...
...AT THE DOJO WE USED TO GO TO.
HE HAD THE BRIGHTEST HAIR...
...AND THE BIGGEST SMILE.
...AND THE MOST BEAUTIFUL MOTHER--HE ALWAYS HELD HER HAND--
HE WAS SCRAWNY...
...AND SMILED ALL THE TIME.
A TOTAL WIMP.
HE WAS REALLY WEAK, TOO.
AND WHEN HE LOST, HE'D START CRYING.

READ THIS WAY

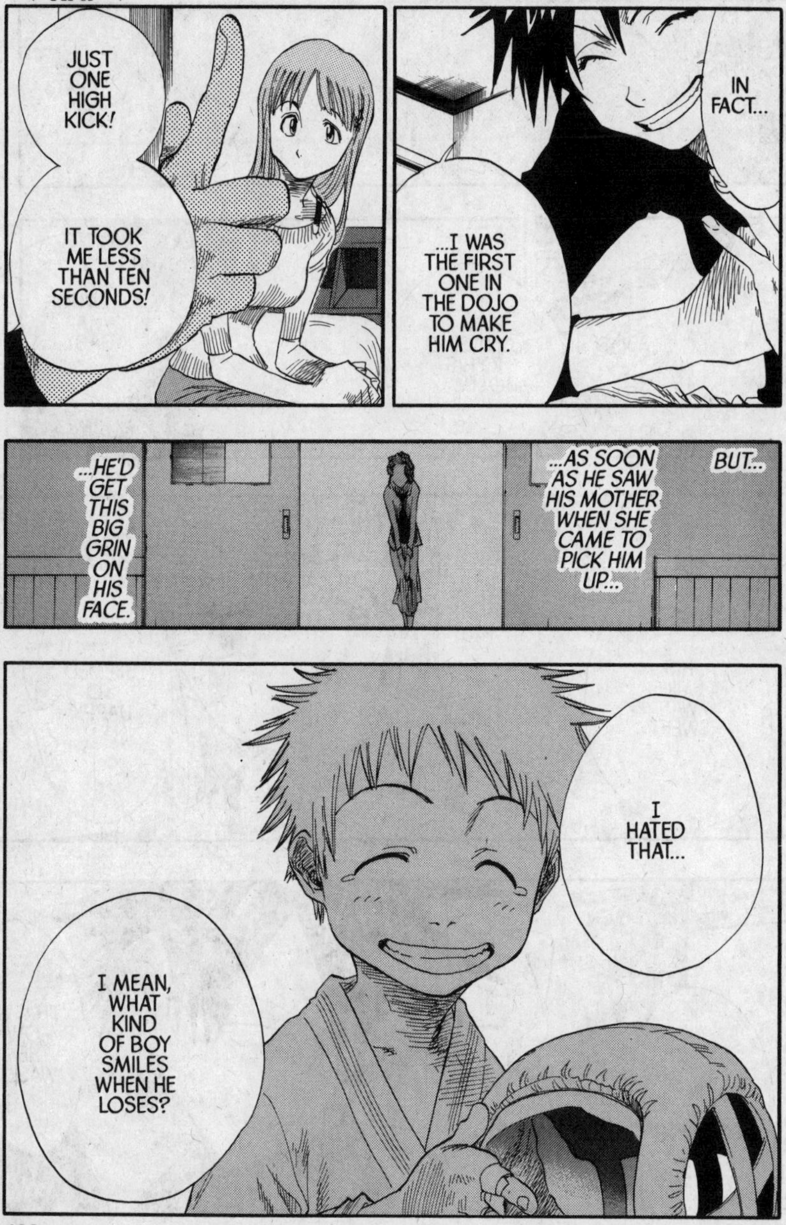
IN FACT...
...I WAS THE FIRST ONE IN THE DOJO TO MAKE HIM CRY.
JUST ONE HIGH KICK!
IT TOOK ME LESS THAN TEN SECONDS!
BUT...
...AS SOON AS HE SAW HIS MOTHER WHEN SHE CAME TO PICK HIM UP...
...HE'D GET THIS BIG GRIN ON HIS FACE.
I HATED THAT...
I MEAN, WHAT KIND OF BOY SMILES WHEN HE LOSES?

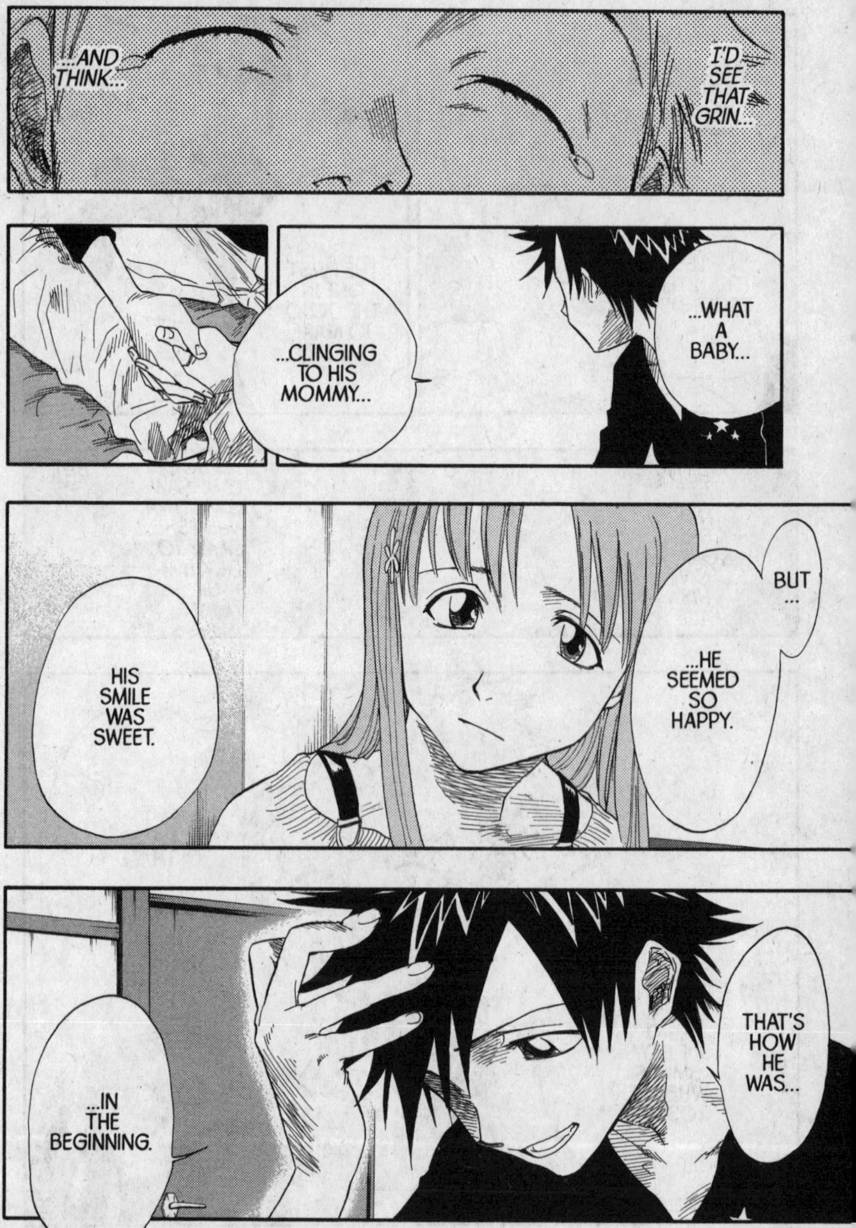
I'D SEE THAT GRIN...
...AND THINK...
...WHAT A BABY...
...CLINGING TO HIS MOMMY...
BUT...
...HE SEEMED SO HAPPY.
HIS SMILE WAS SWEET.
THAT'S HOW HE WAS...
...IN THE BEGINNING.

READ THIS WAY

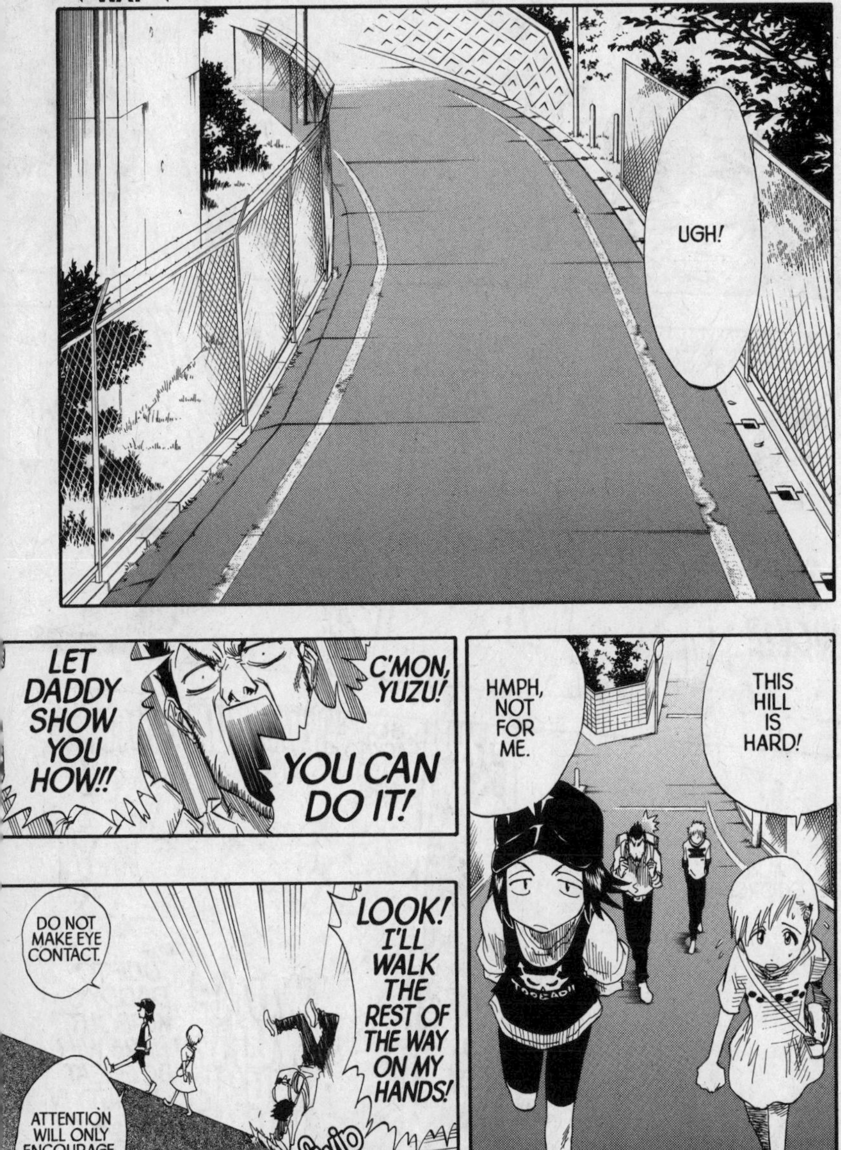

UGH!
THIS HILL IS HARD!
HMPH, NOT FOR ME.
C'MON, YUZU!
YOU CAN DO IT!
LET DADDY SHOW YOU HOW!!
LOOK! I'LL WALK THE REST OF THE WAY ON MY HANDS!
fwip
DO NOT MAKE EYE CONTACT.
ATTENTION WILL ONLY ENCOURAGE HIM.

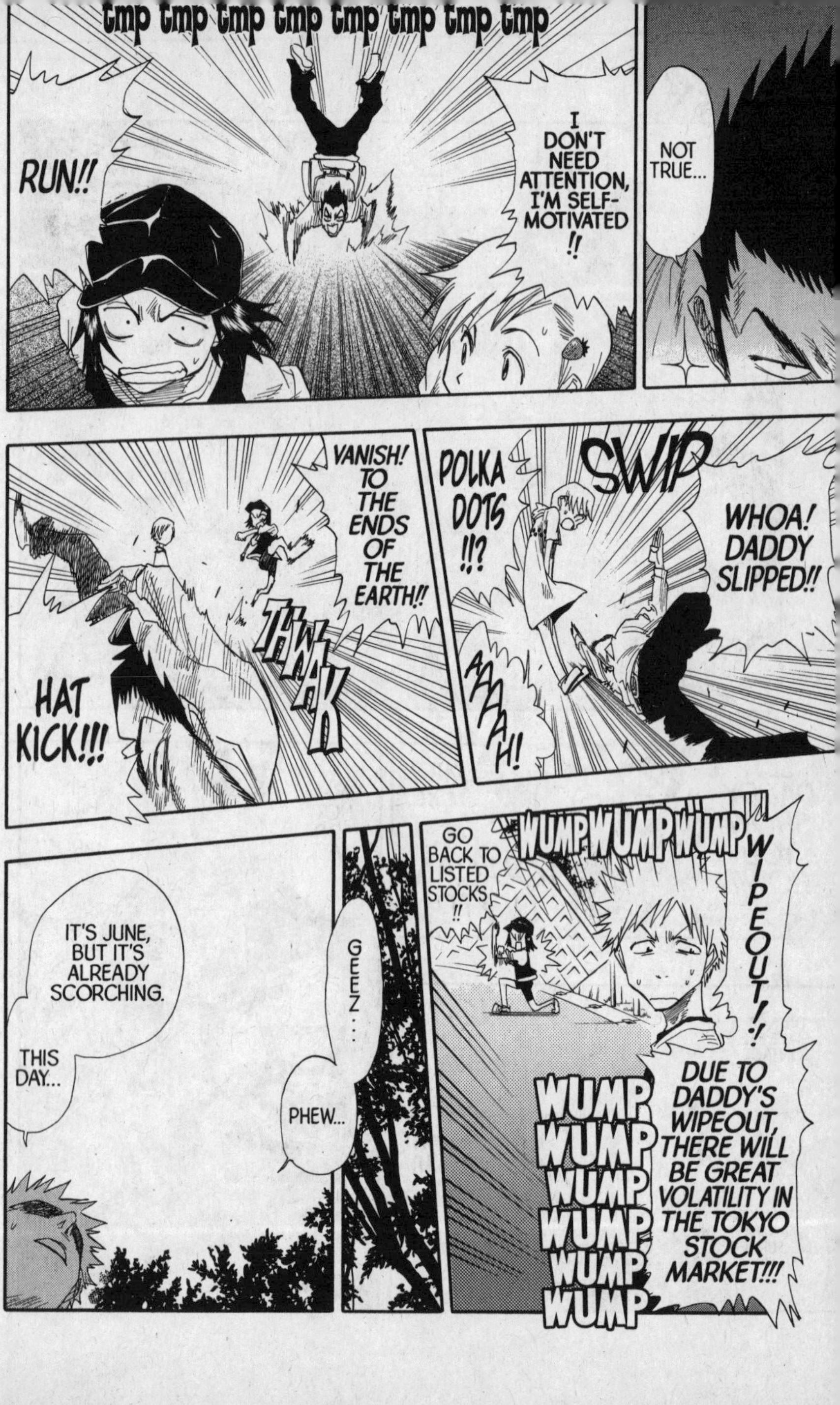
NOT TRUE...
tmp tmp tmp tmp tmp tmp tmp tmp
I DON'T NEED ATTENTION, I'M SELF-MOTIVATED!!
RUN!!
SWIP
WHOA! DADDY SLIPPED!!
POLKA DOTS!!?
AAAAH!
VANISH! TO THE ENDS OF THE EARTH!!
THWAK
HAT KICK!!!
WUMP WUMP WUMP
WIPEOUT!!
GO BACK TO LISTED STOCKS!!
DUE TO DADDY'S WIPEOUT, THERE WILL BE GREAT VOLATILITY IN THE TOKYO STOCK MARKET!!!
WUMP WUMP WUMP WUMP WUMP WUMP
GEEZ...
PHEW...
IT'S JUNE, BUT IT'S ALREADY SCORCHING.
THIS DAY...

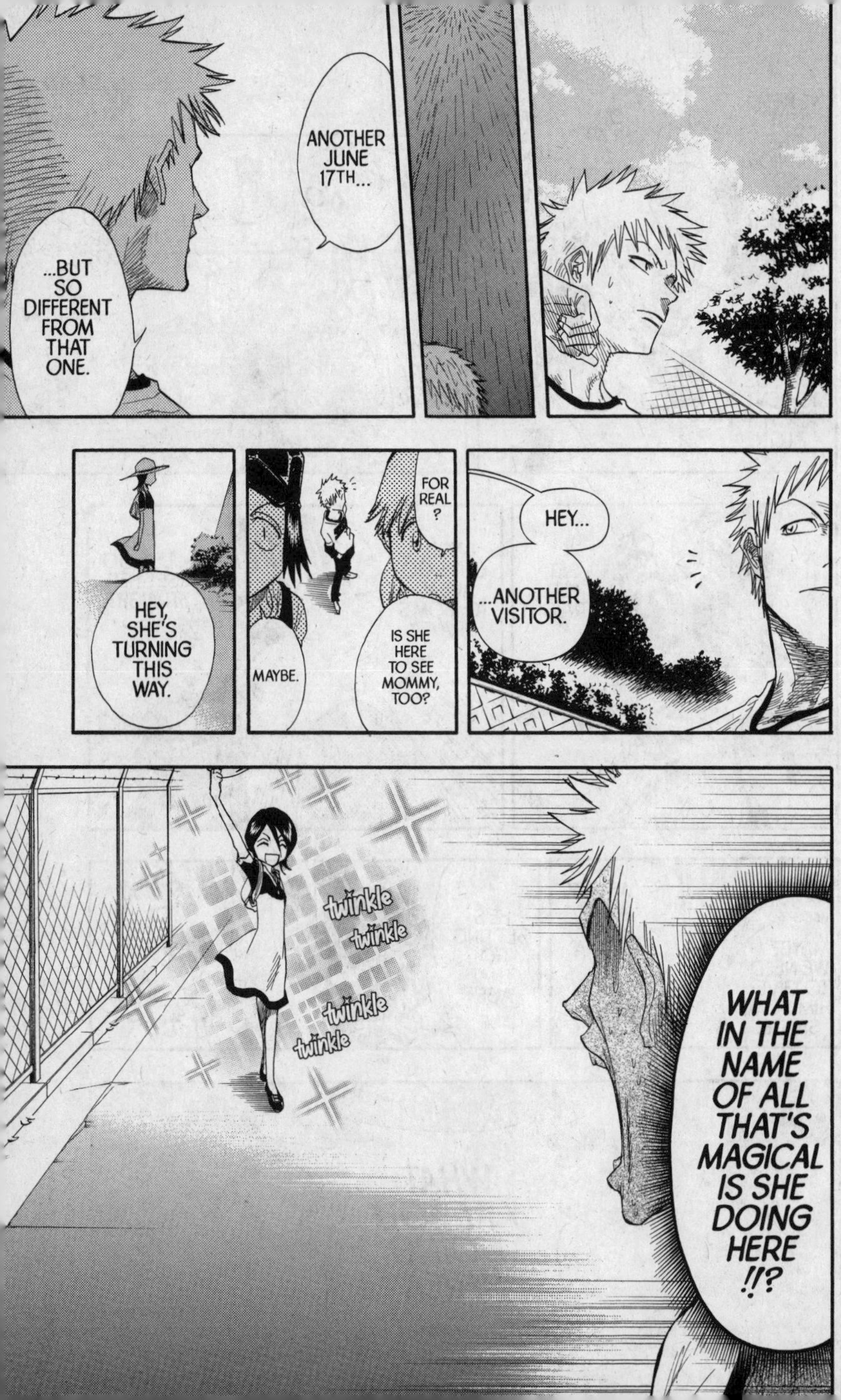
ANOTHER JUNE 17TH...
...BUT SO DIFFERENT FROM THAT ONE.
HEY...
...ANOTHER VISITOR.
FOR REAL?
IS SHE HERE TO SEE MOMMY, TOO?
MAYBE.
HEY, SHE'S TURNING THIS WAY.
WHAT IN THE NAME OF ALL THAT'S MAGICAL IS SHE DOING HERE!!?
twinkle
twinkle
twinkle
twinkle

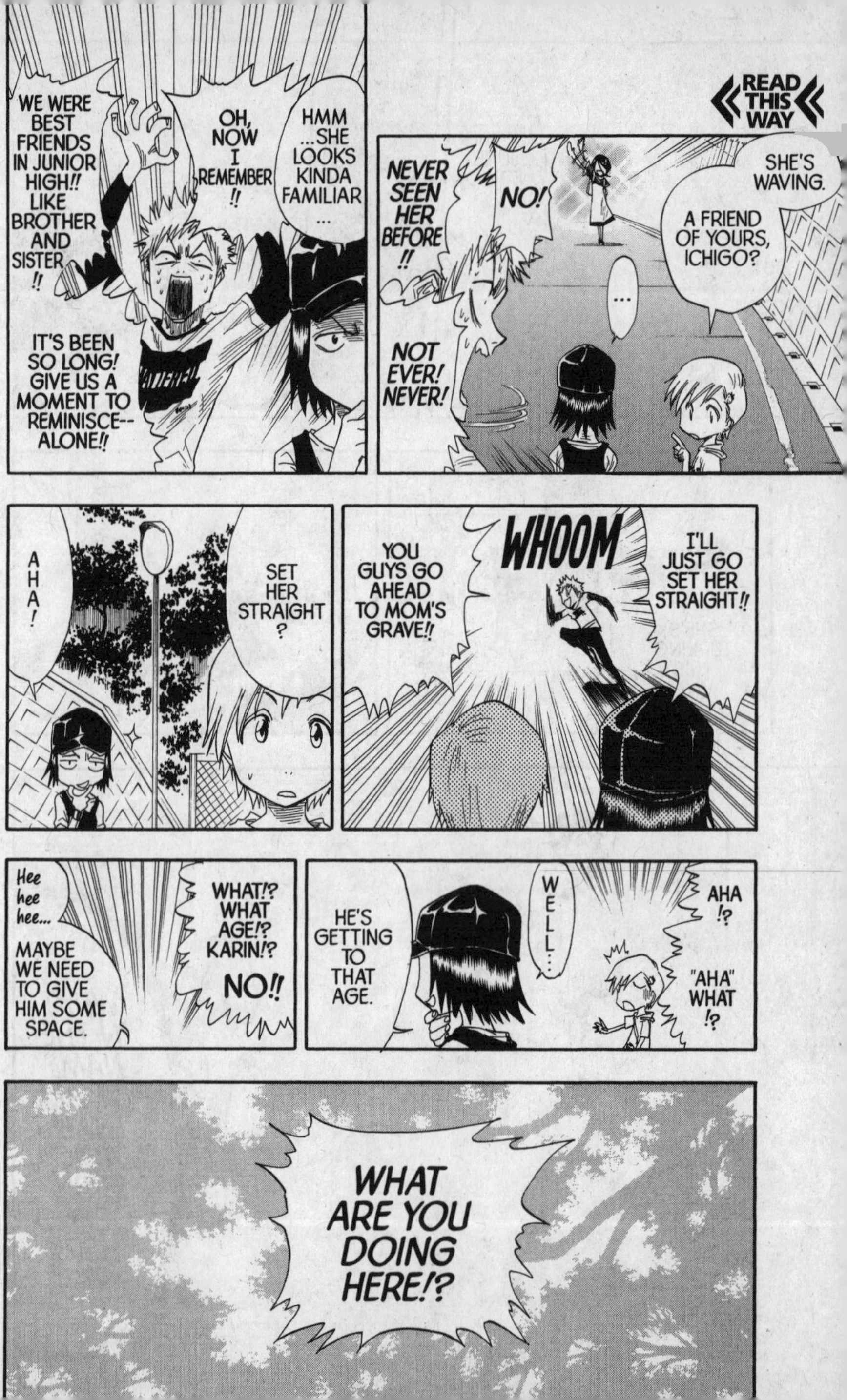
READ THIS WAY
SHE'S WAVING.
A FRIEND OF YOURS, ICHIGO?
...
NO!
NEVER SEEN HER BEFORE!!
NOT EVER! NEVER!
HMM ...SHE LOOKS KINDA FAMILIAR ...
OH, NOW I REMEMBER!!
WE WERE BEST FRIENDS IN JUNIOR HIGH!! LIKE BROTHER AND SISTER!!
IT'S BEEN SO LONG! GIVE US A MOMENT TO REMINISCE--ALONE!!
I'LL JUST GO SET HER STRAIGHT!!
WHOOM
YOU GUYS GO AHEAD TO MOM'S GRAVE!!
SET HER STRAIGHT?
AHA!
AHA!?
"AHA" WHAT!?
WELL...
HE'S GETTING TO THAT AGE.
WHAT!? WHAT AGE!? KARIN!?
NO!!
Hee hee hee...
MAYBE WE NEED TO GIVE HIM SOME SPACE.
WHAT ARE YOU DOING HERE!?

READ THIS WAY

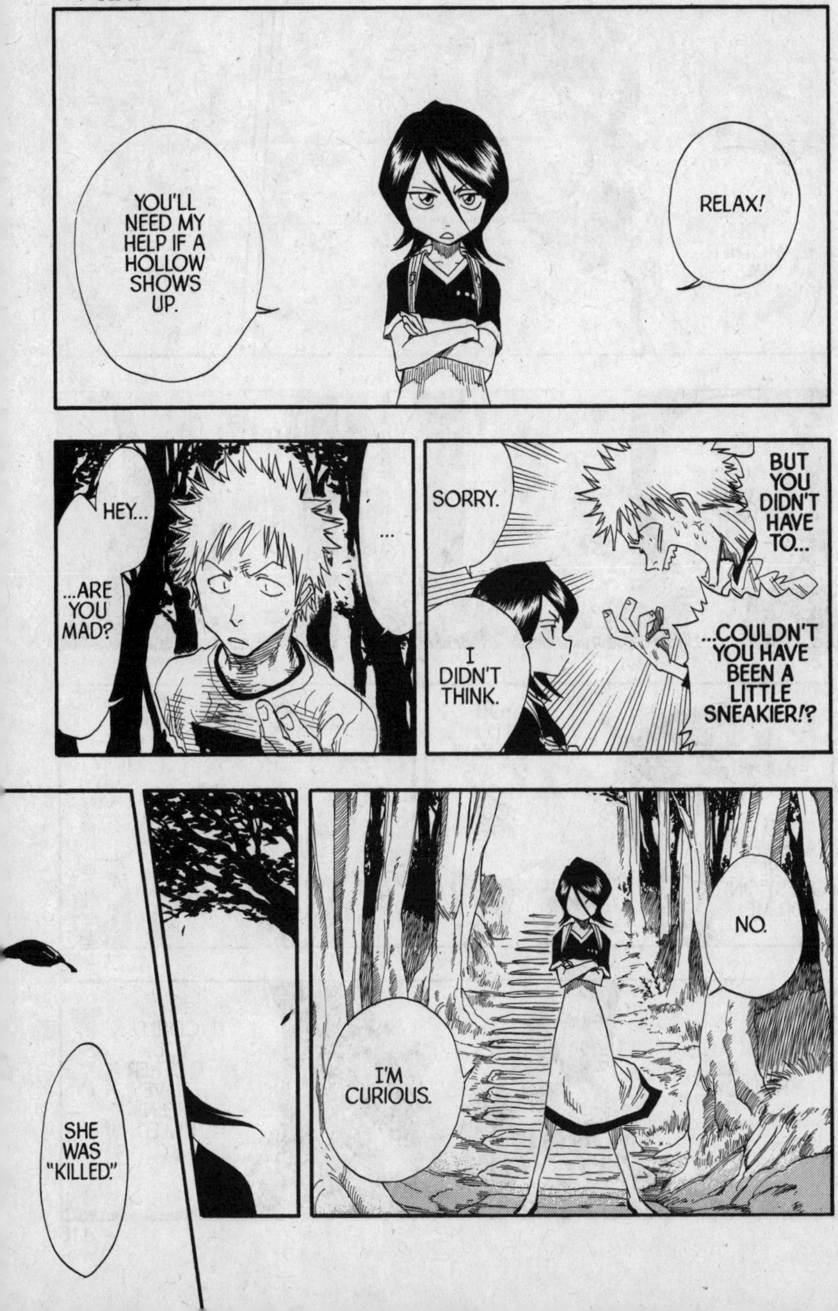

RELAX!
YOU'LL NEED MY HELP IF A HOLLOW SHOWS UP.
BUT YOU DIDN'T HAVE TO...
...COULDN'T YOU HAVE BEEN A LITTLE SNEAKIER!?
SORRY.
I DIDN'T THINK.
...
HEY...
...ARE YOU MAD?
NO.
I'M CURIOUS.
SHE WAS "KILLED."

READ THIS WAY

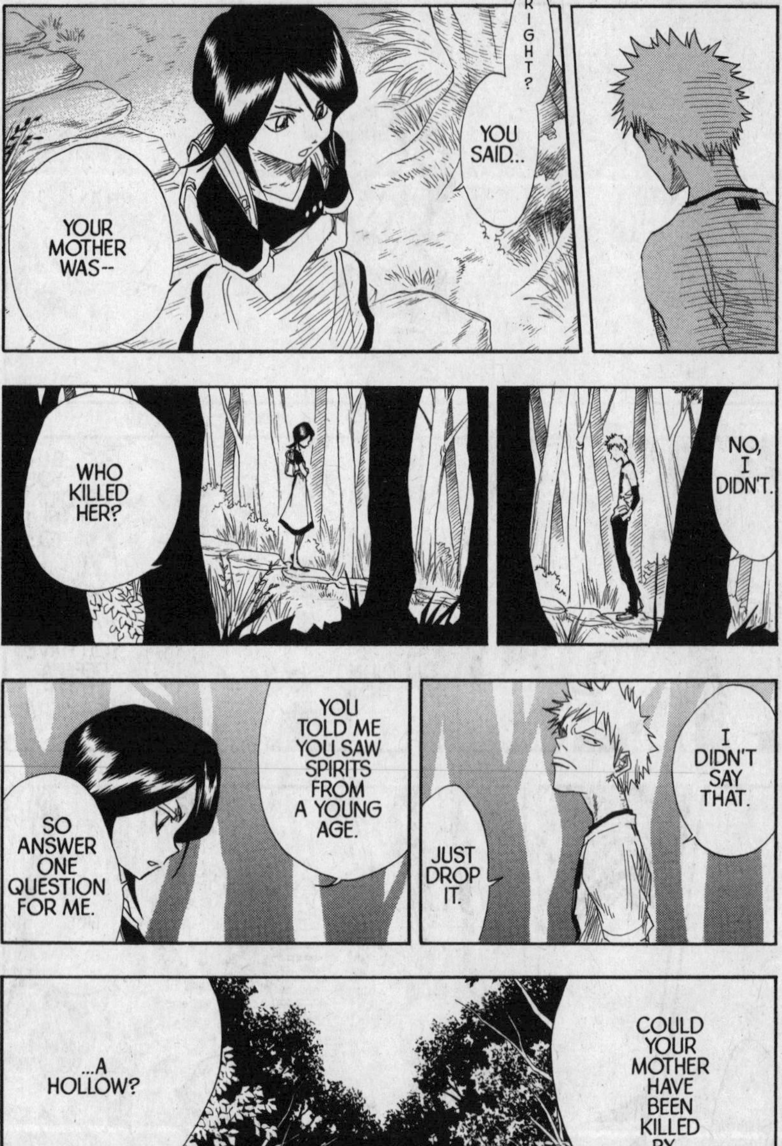
RIGHT?
YOU SAID...
YOUR MOTHER WAS--
NO, I DIDN'T.
WHO KILLED HER?
I DIDN'T SAY THAT.
JUST DROP IT.
YOU TOLD ME YOU SAW SPIRITS FROM A YOUNG AGE.
SO ANSWER ONE QUESTION FOR ME.
COULD YOUR MOTHER HAVE BEEN KILLED BY...
...A HOLLOW?

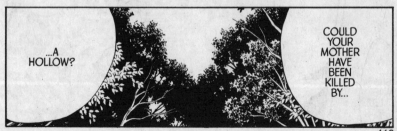

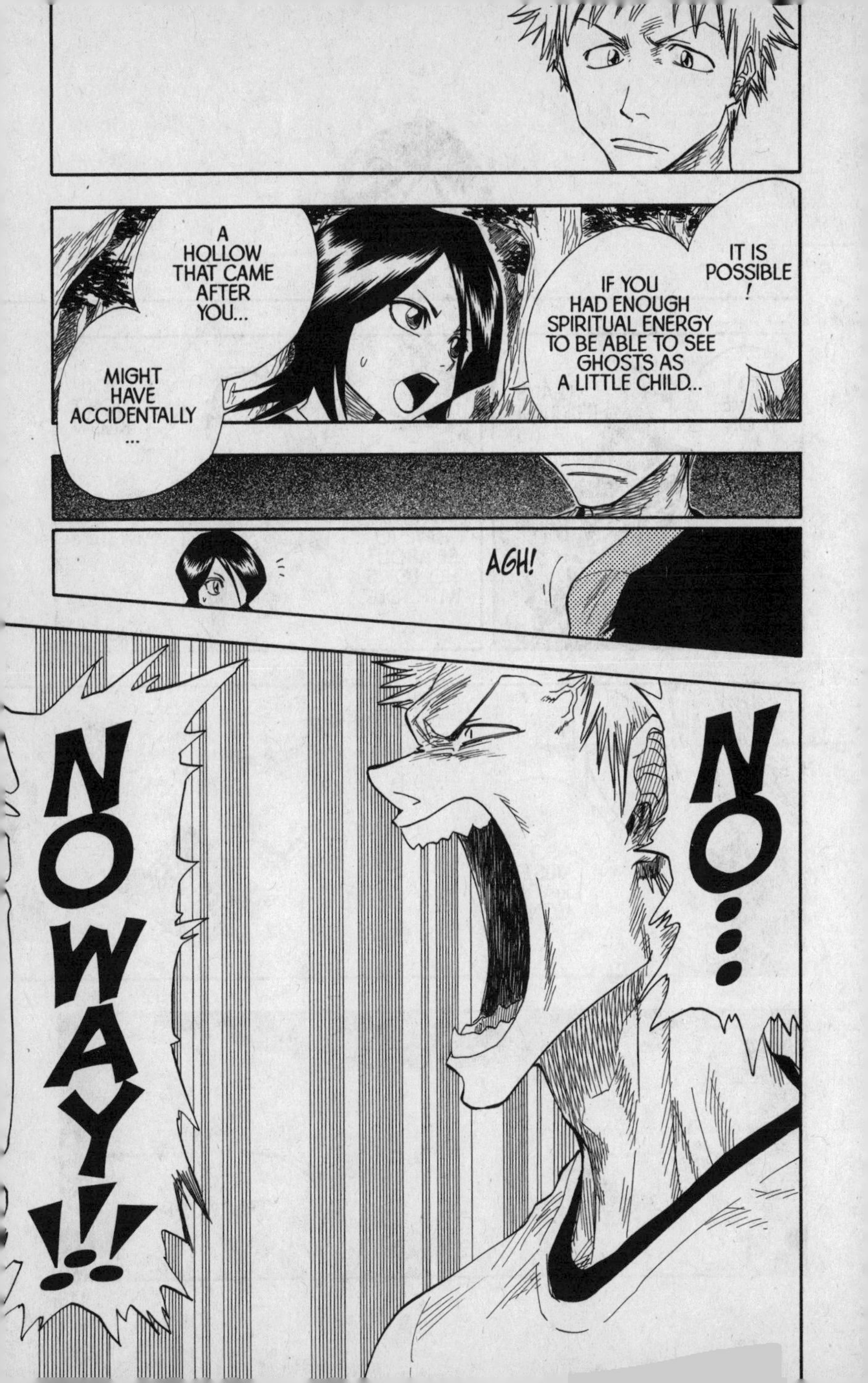
IT IS POSSIBLE!
IF YOU HAD ENOUGH SPIRITUAL ENERGY TO BE ABLE TO SEE GHOSTS AS A LITTLE CHILD...
A HOLLOW THAT CAME AFTER YOU...
MIGHT HAVE ACCIDENTALLY ...
AGH!
NO...
NO WAY!!!

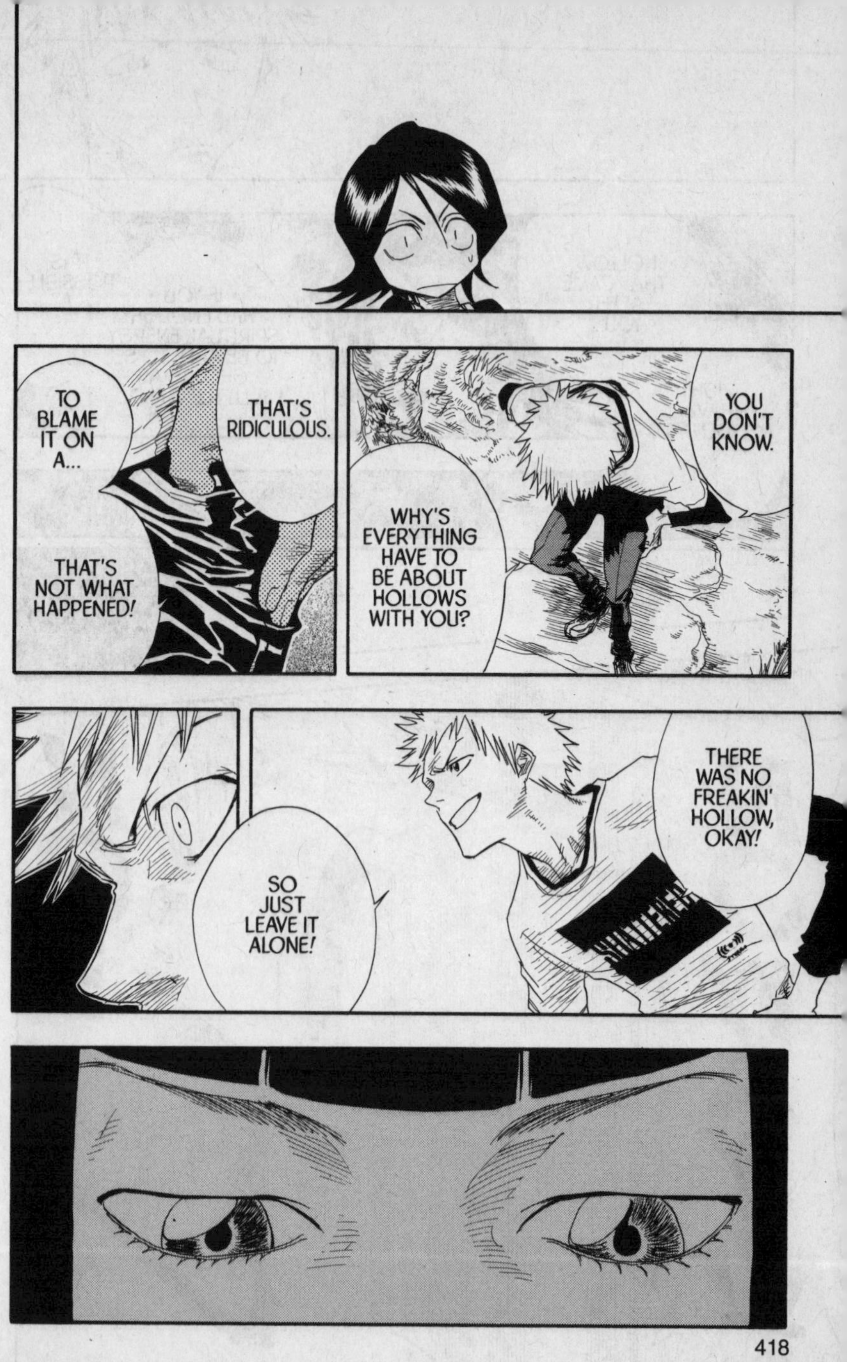
YOU DON'T KNOW.
WHY'S EVERYTHING HAVE TO BE ABOUT HOLLOWS WITH YOU?
THAT'S RIDICULOUS.
TO BLAME IT ON A...
THAT'S NOT WHAT HAPPENED!
THERE WAS NO FREAKIN' HOLLOW, OKAY!
SO JUST LEAVE IT ALONE!

READ THIS WAY

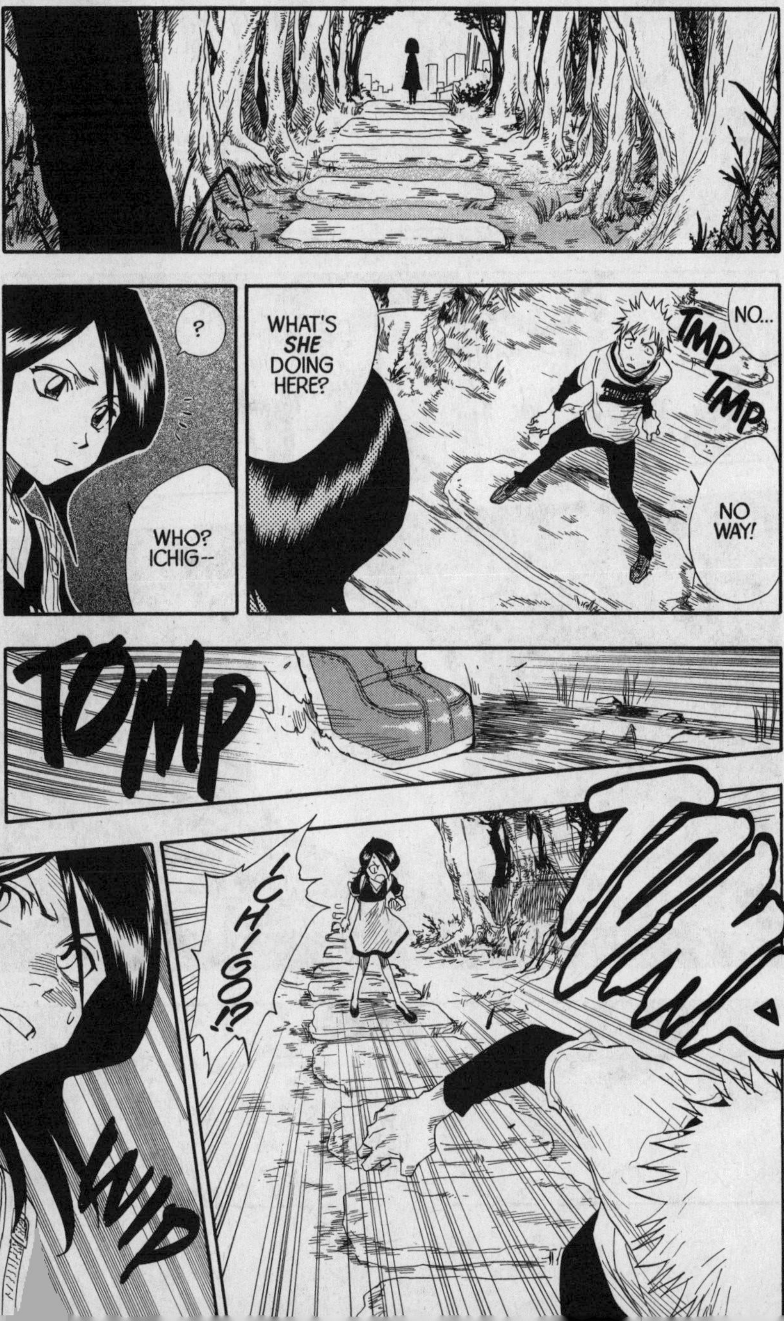
NO...
TMP TMP
WHAT'S SHE DOING HERE?
NO WAY!
?
WHO? ICHIG--
TOMP
TOMP
ICHIGO!?
TMP

READ THIS WAY

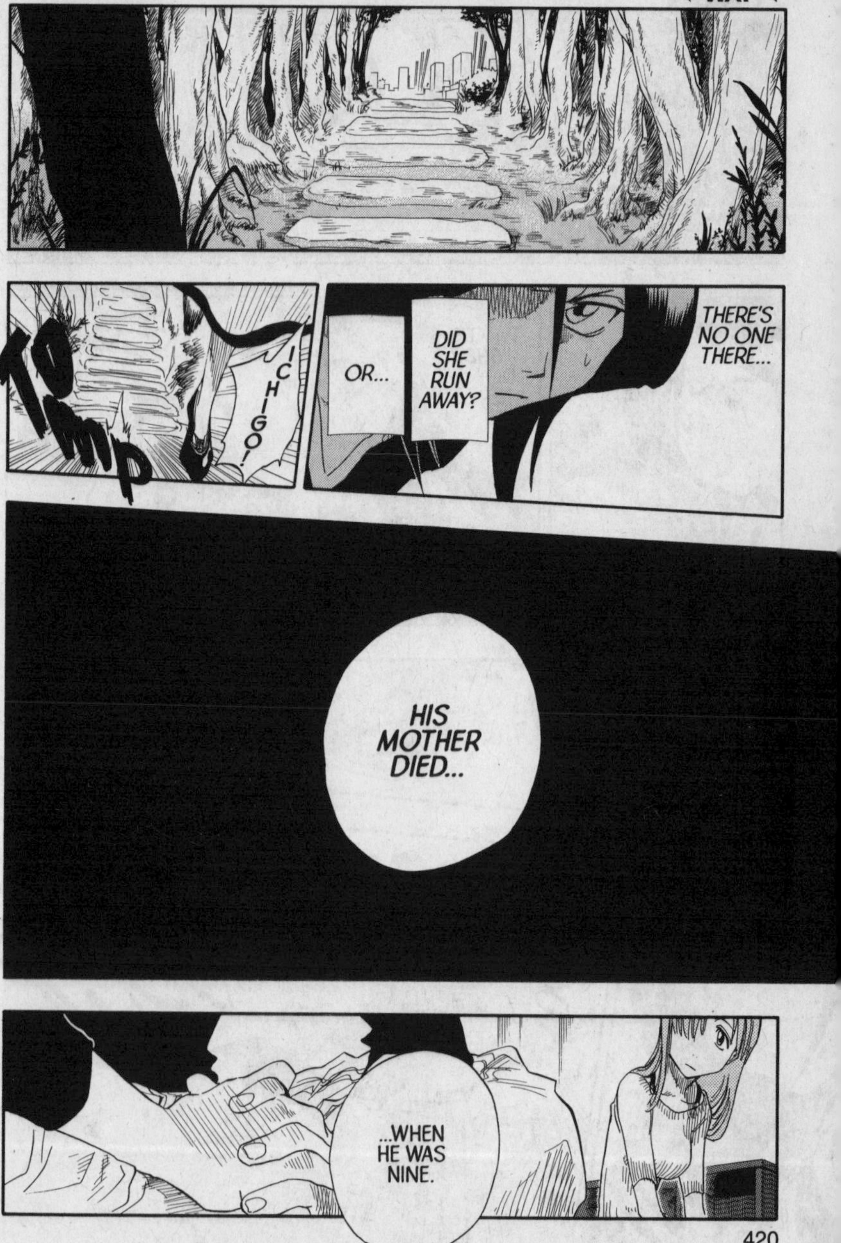
THERE'S NO ONE THERE...
DID SHE RUN AWAY?
OR...
ICHIGO!
TOMP
HIS MOTHER DIED...
...WHEN HE WAS NINE.

READ THIS WAY

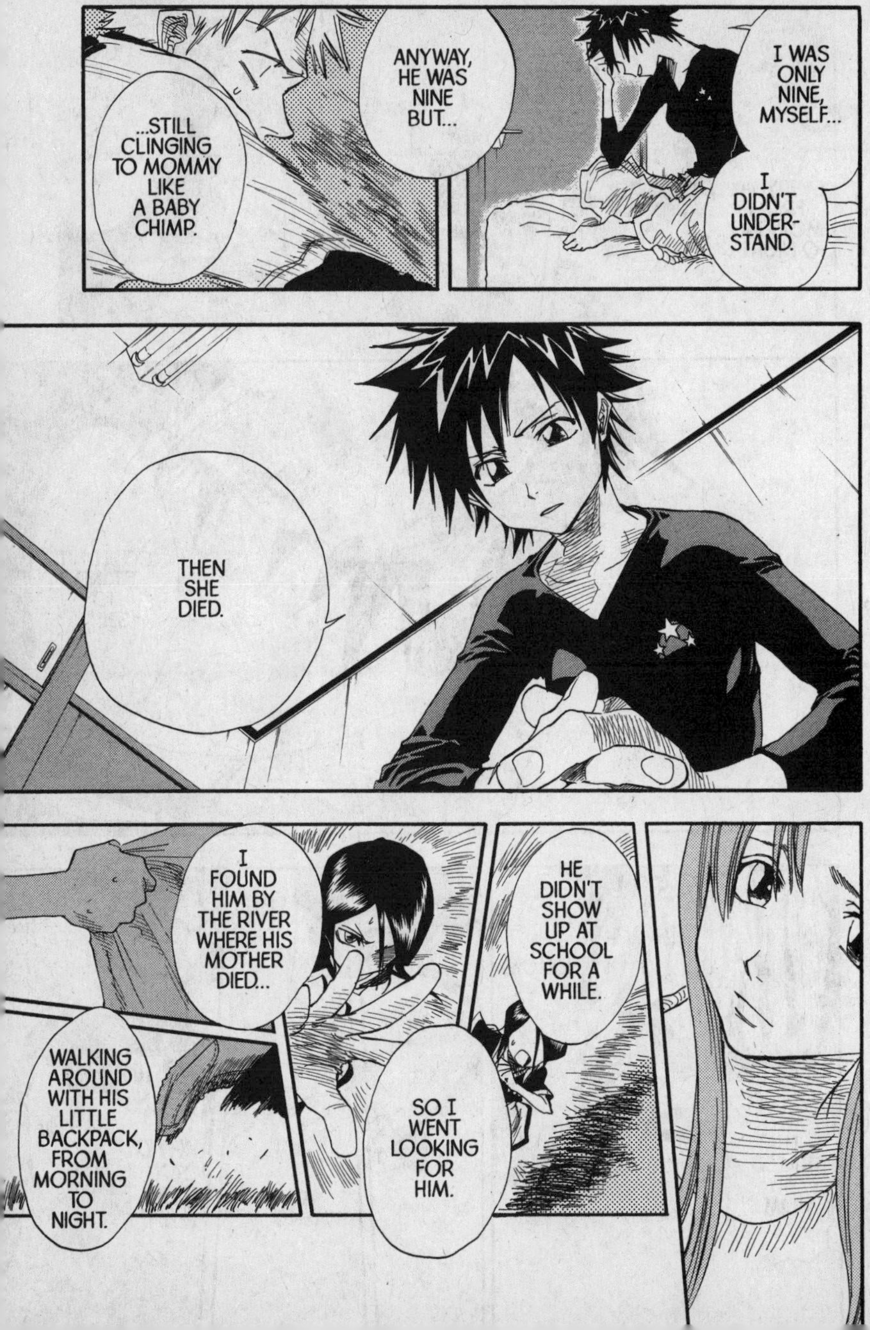
I WAS ONLY NINE, MYSELF...
I DIDN'T UNDER-STAND.
ANYWAY, HE WAS NINE BUT...
...STILL CLINGING TO MOMMY LIKE A BABY CHIMP.
THEN SHE DIED.
HE DIDN'T SHOW UP AT SCHOOL FOR A WHILE.
SO I WENT LOOKING FOR HIM.
I FOUND HIM BY THE RIVER WHERE HIS MOTHER DIED...
WALKING AROUND WITH HIS LITTLE BACKPACK, FROM MORNING TO NIGHT.

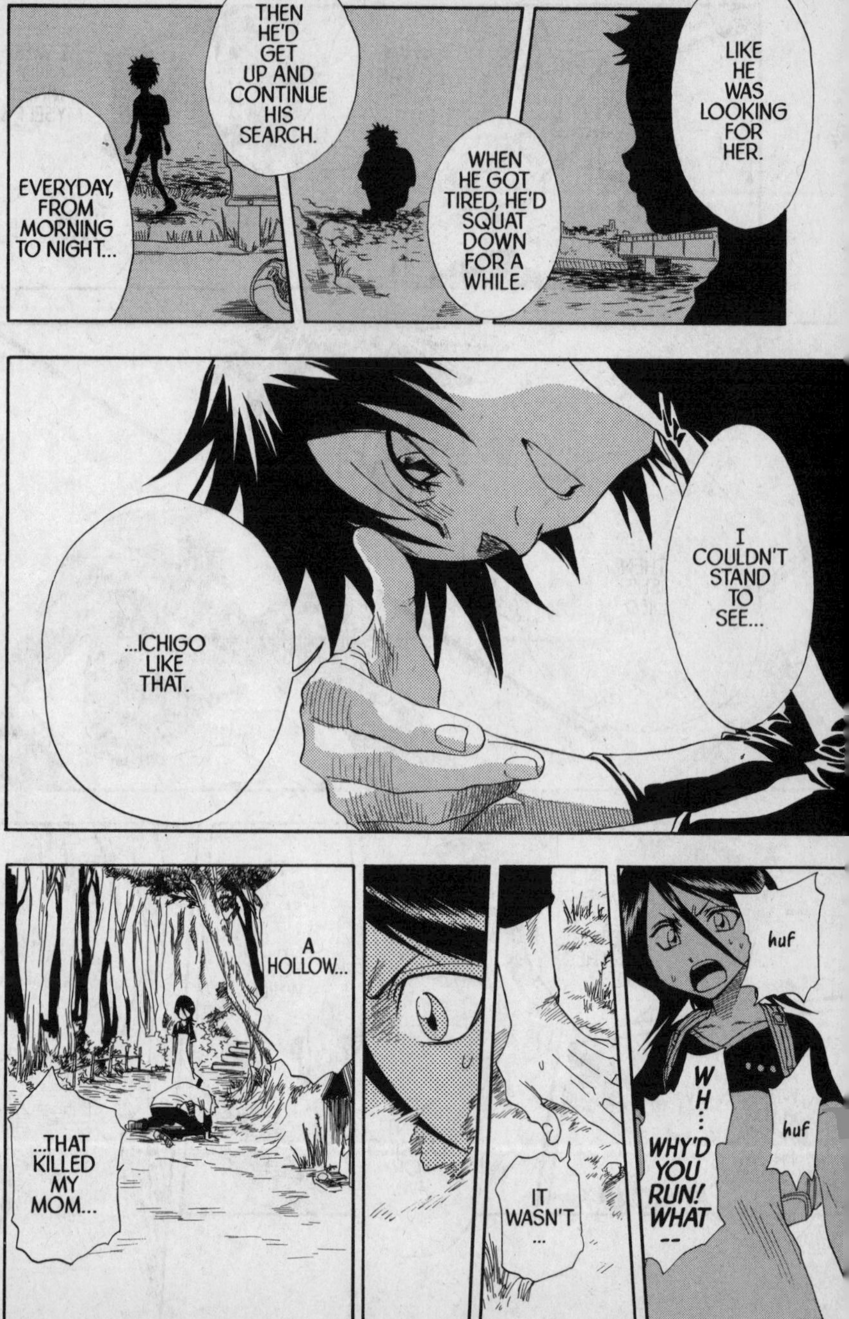
LIKE HE WAS LOOKING FOR HER.
WHEN HE GOT TIRED, HE'D SQUAT DOWN FOR A WHILE.
THEN HE'D GET UP AND CONTINUE HIS SEARCH.
EVERYDAY, FROM MORNING TO NIGHT...
I COULDN'T STAND TO SEE...
...ICHIGO LIKE THAT.
huf
WH... WHY'D YOU RUN! WHAT --
huf
IT WASN'T ...
A HOLLOW...
...THAT KILLED MY MOM...

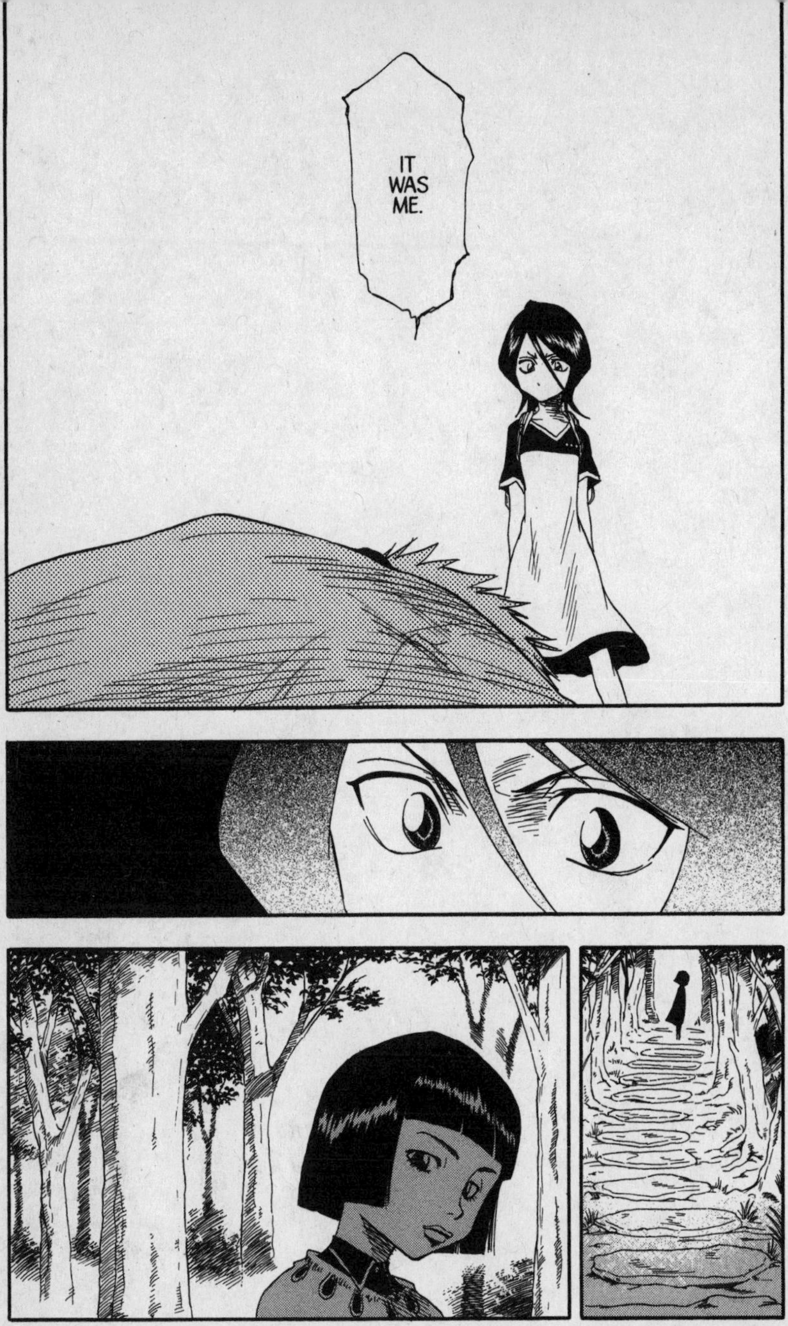
IT WAS ME.

Dressed unusually plain today.

Wonder why?

You'll find out in the last episode of this volume!!

19. 6/17 op. 3 memories in the rain

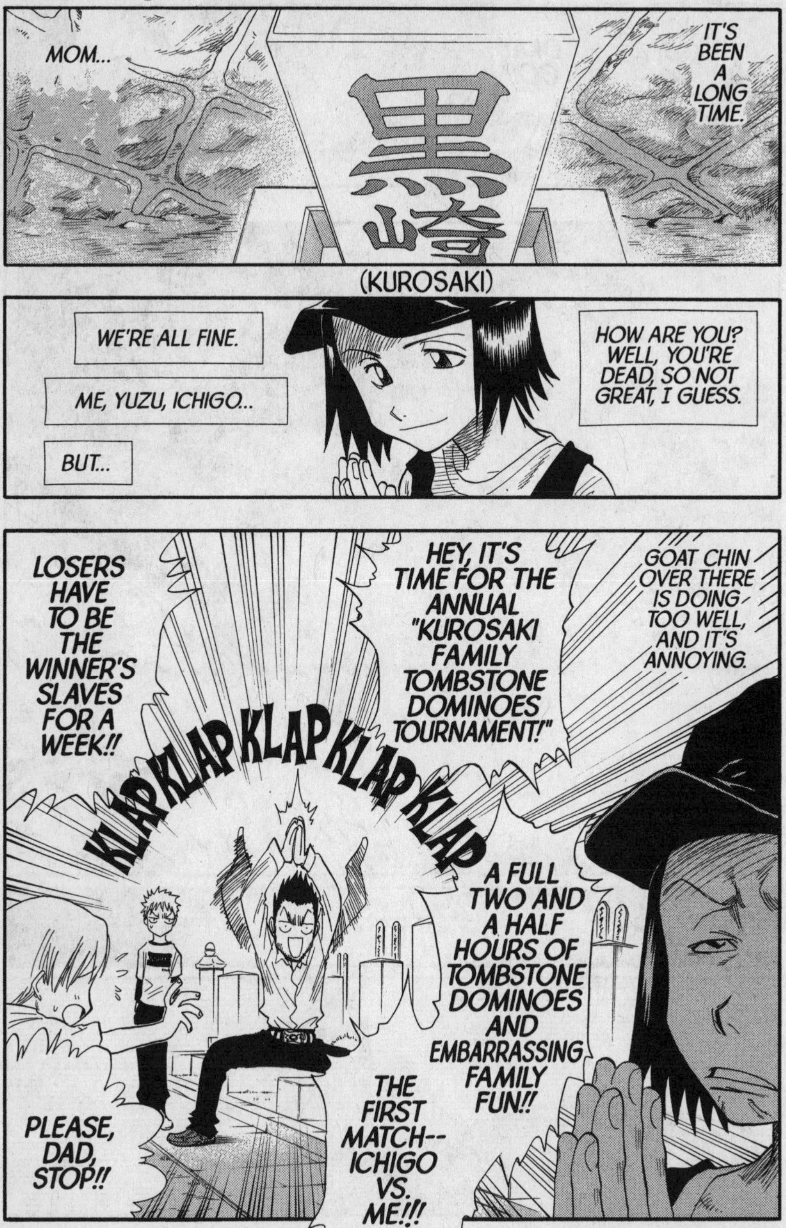
IT'S BEEN A LONG TIME.
MOM...
黒崎
(KUROSAKI)
HOW ARE YOU? WELL, YOU'RE DEAD, SO NOT GREAT, I GUESS.
WE'RE ALL FINE.
ME, YUZU, ICHIGO...
BUT...
GOAT CHIN OVER THERE IS DOING TOO WELL, AND IT'S ANNOYING.
HEY, IT'S TIME FOR THE ANNUAL "KUROSAKI FAMILY TOMBSTONE DOMINOES TOURNAMENT!"
LOSERS HAVE TO BE THE WINNER'S SLAVES FOR A WEEK!!
KLAP KLAP KLAP KLAP KLAP KLAP
A FULL TWO AND A HALF HOURS OF TOMBSTONE DOMINOES AND EMBARRASSING FAMILY FUN!!
THE FIRST MATCH-- ICHIGO VS. ME!!!
PLEASE, DAD, STOP!!

READ THIS WAY

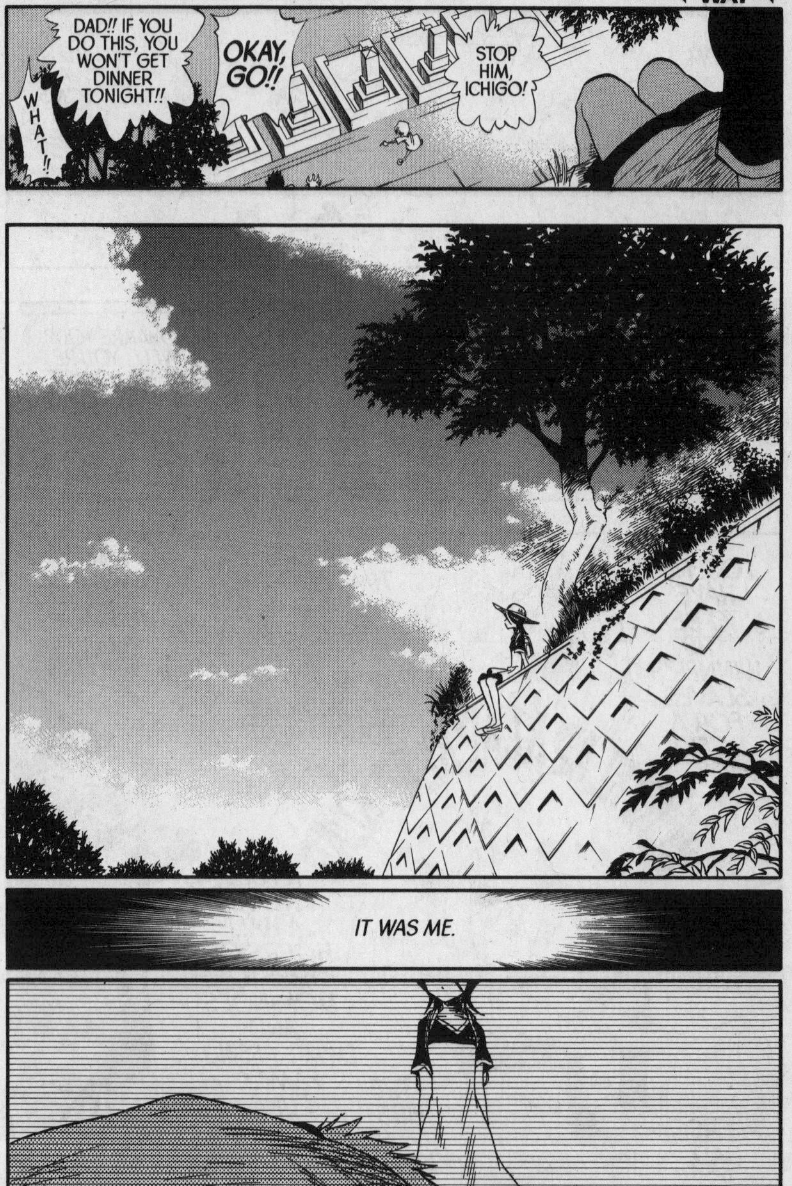

STOP HIM, ICHIGO!
OKAY, GO!!
DAD!! IF YOU DO THIS, YOU WON'T GET DINNER TONIGHT!!
WHAT!!
IT WAS ME.

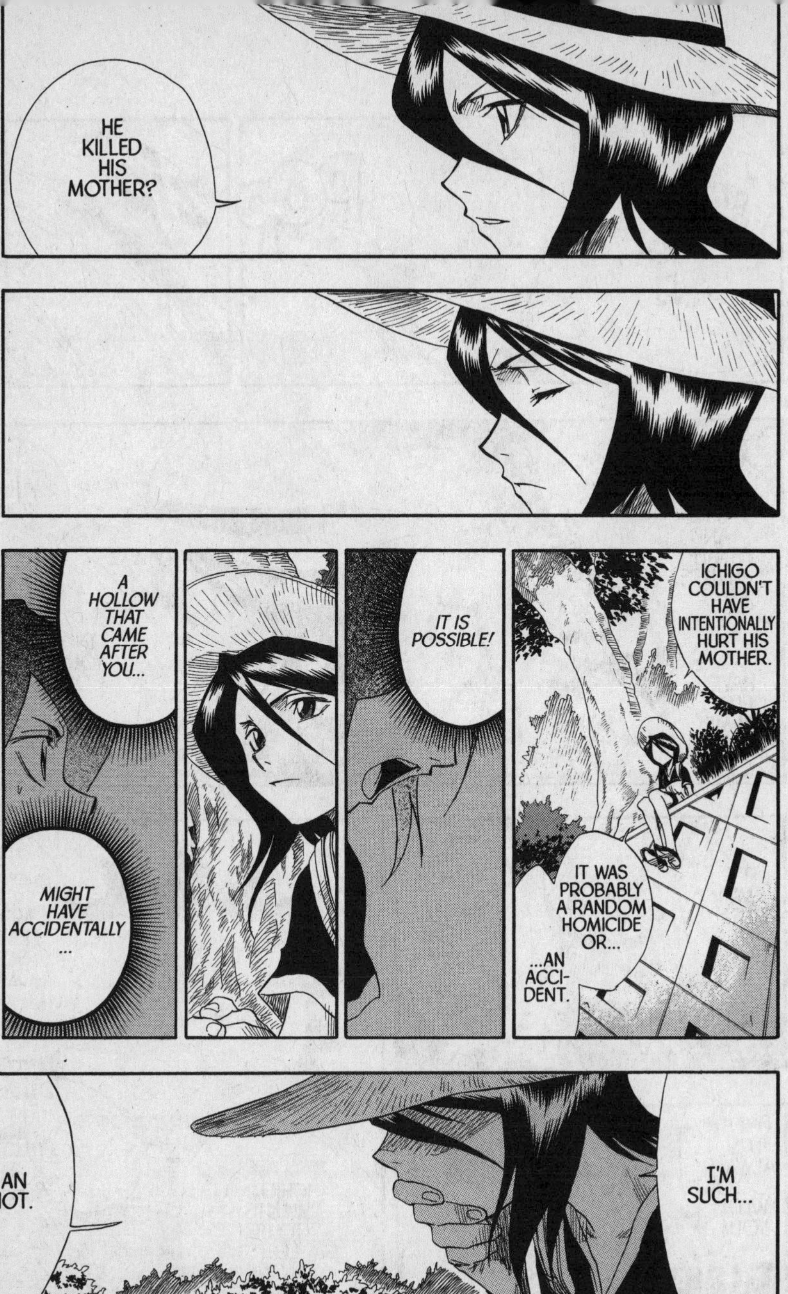
HE KILLED HIS MOTHER?
ICHIGO COULDN'T HAVE INTENTIONALLY HURT HIS MOTHER.
IT WAS PROBABLY A RANDOM HOMICIDE OR...
...AN ACCI-DENT.
IT IS POSSIBLE!
A HOLLOW THAT CAME AFTER YOU...
MIGHT HAVE ACCIDENTALLY ...
I'M SUCH...
...AN IDIOT.

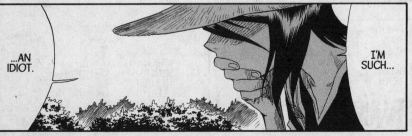

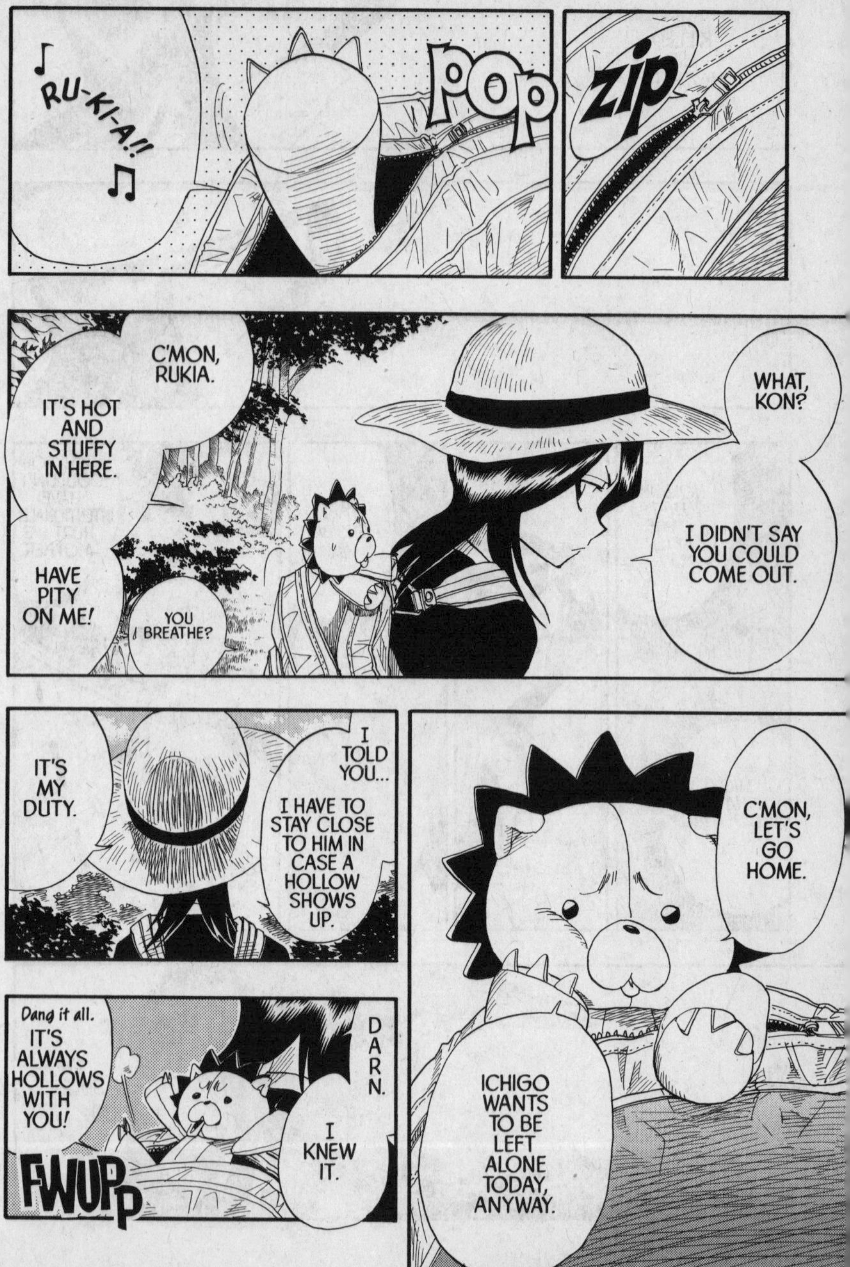
ZIP
RU-KI-A!!
POP
WHAT, KON?
I DIDN'T SAY YOU COULD COME OUT.
C'MON, RUKIA.
IT'S HOT AND STUFFY IN HERE.
HAVE PITY ON ME!
YOU BREATHE?
C'MON, LET'S GO HOME.
ICHIGO WANTS TO BE LEFT ALONE TODAY, ANYWAY.
I TOLD YOU...
I HAVE TO STAY CLOSE TO HIM IN CASE A HOLLOW SHOWS UP.
IT'S MY DUTY.
DARN.
I KNEW IT.
Dang it all.
IT'S ALWAYS HOLLOWS WITH YOU!
FWUPP

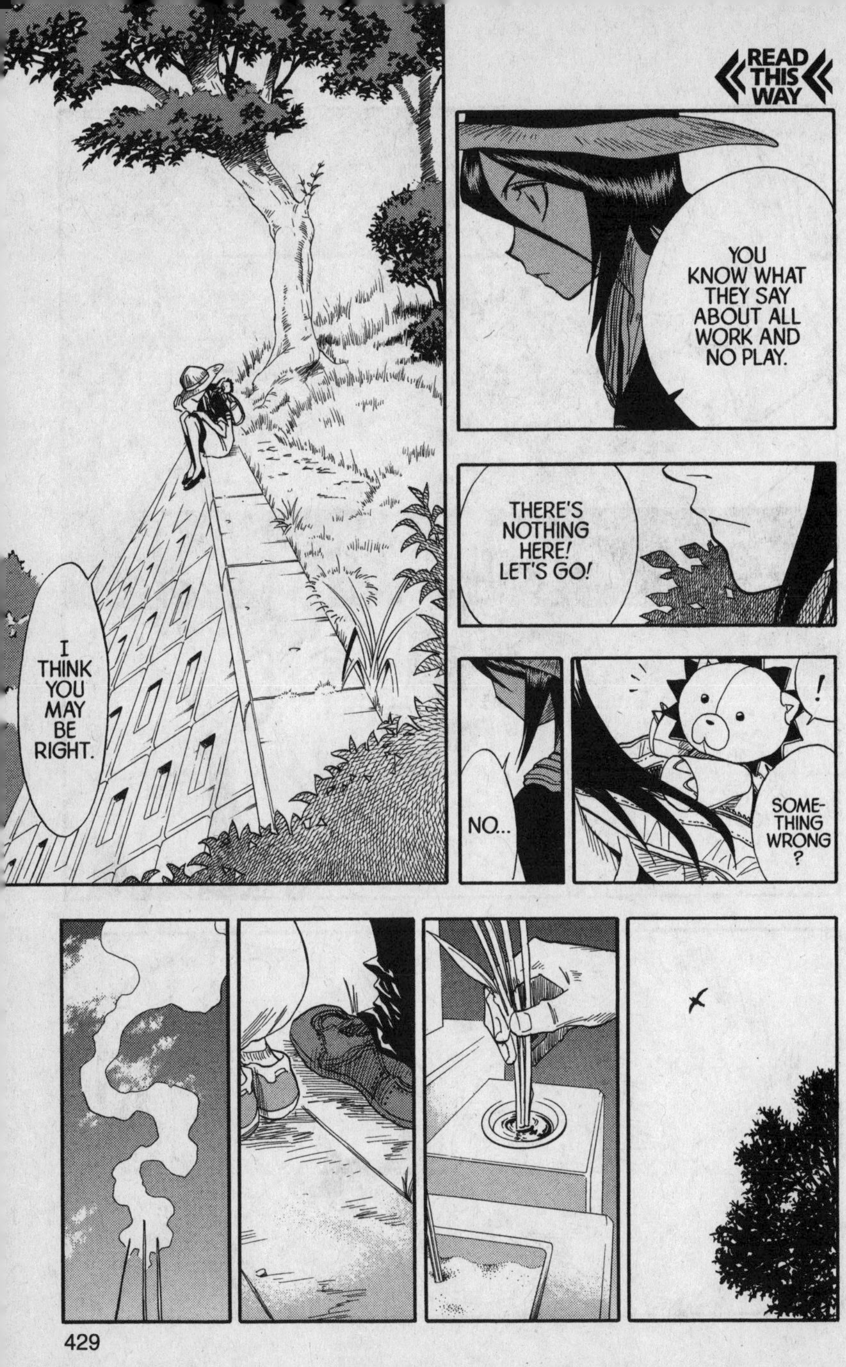
READ THIS WAY
YOU KNOW WHAT THEY SAY ABOUT ALL WORK AND NO PLAY.
THERE'S NOTHING HERE! LET'S GO!
!
SOME-THING WRONG?
NO...
I THINK YOU MAY BE RIGHT.

IS IT TRUE?
ICHIGO?
IS IT TRUE?
CAN YOU REALLY SEE GHOSTS?

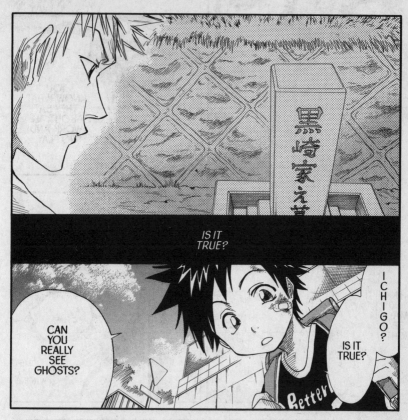

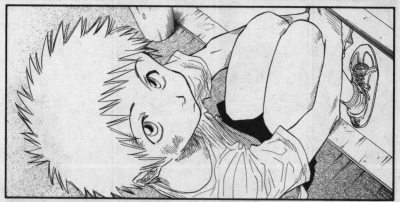

READ THIS WAY

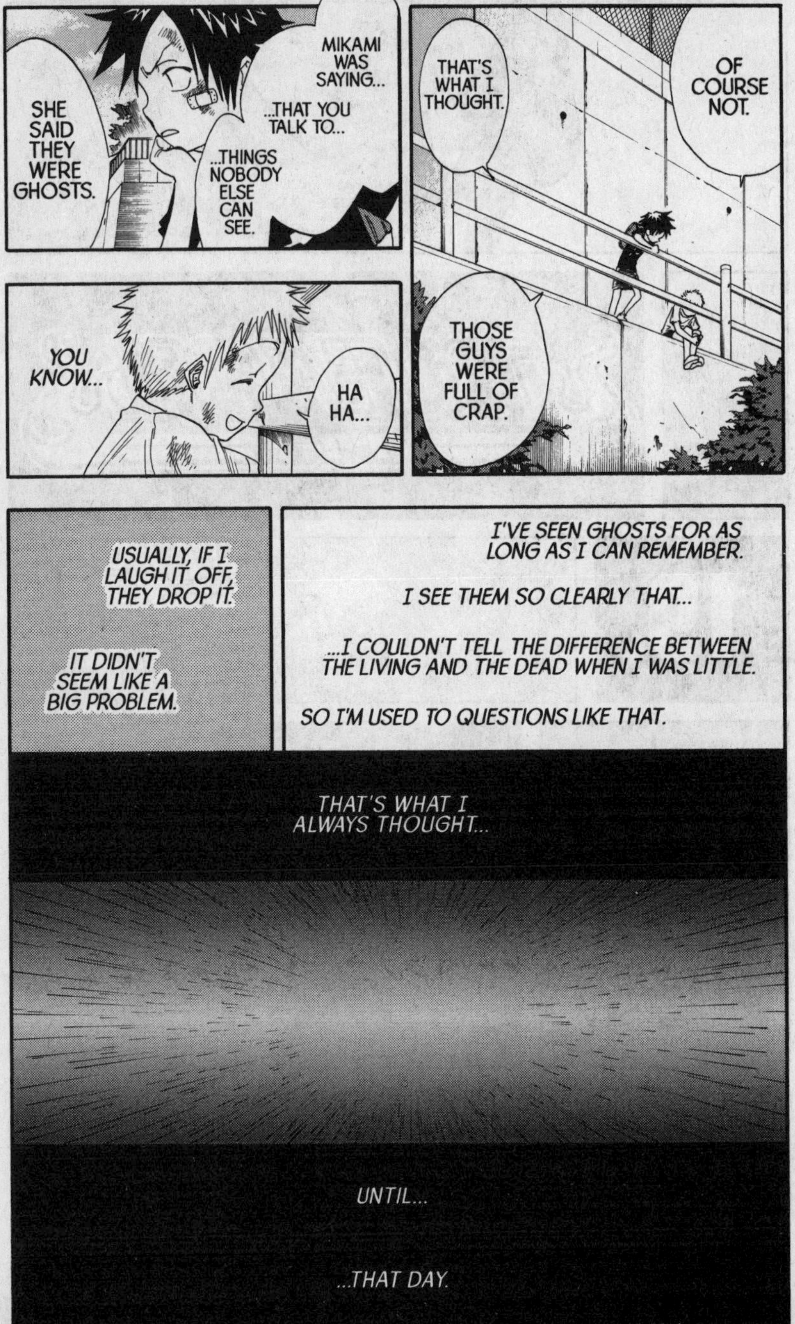

OF COURSE NOT.
THAT'S WHAT I THOUGHT.
THOSE GUYS WERE FULL OF CRAP.
MIKAMI WAS SAYING...
...THAT YOU TALK TO...
...THINGS NOBODY ELSE CAN SEE.
SHE SAID THEY WERE GHOSTS.
HA HA...
YOU KNOW...
I'VE SEEN GHOSTS FOR AS LONG AS I CAN REMEMBER.
I SEE THEM SO CLEARLY THAT...
...I COULDN'T TELL THE DIFFERENCE BETWEEN THE LIVING AND THE DEAD WHEN I WAS LITTLE.
SO I'M USED TO QUESTIONS LIKE THAT.
USUALLY, IF I LAUGH IT OFF, THEY DROP IT.
IT DIDN'T SEEM LIKE A BIG PROBLEM.
THAT'S WHAT I ALWAYS THOUGHT...
UNTIL...
...THAT DAY.

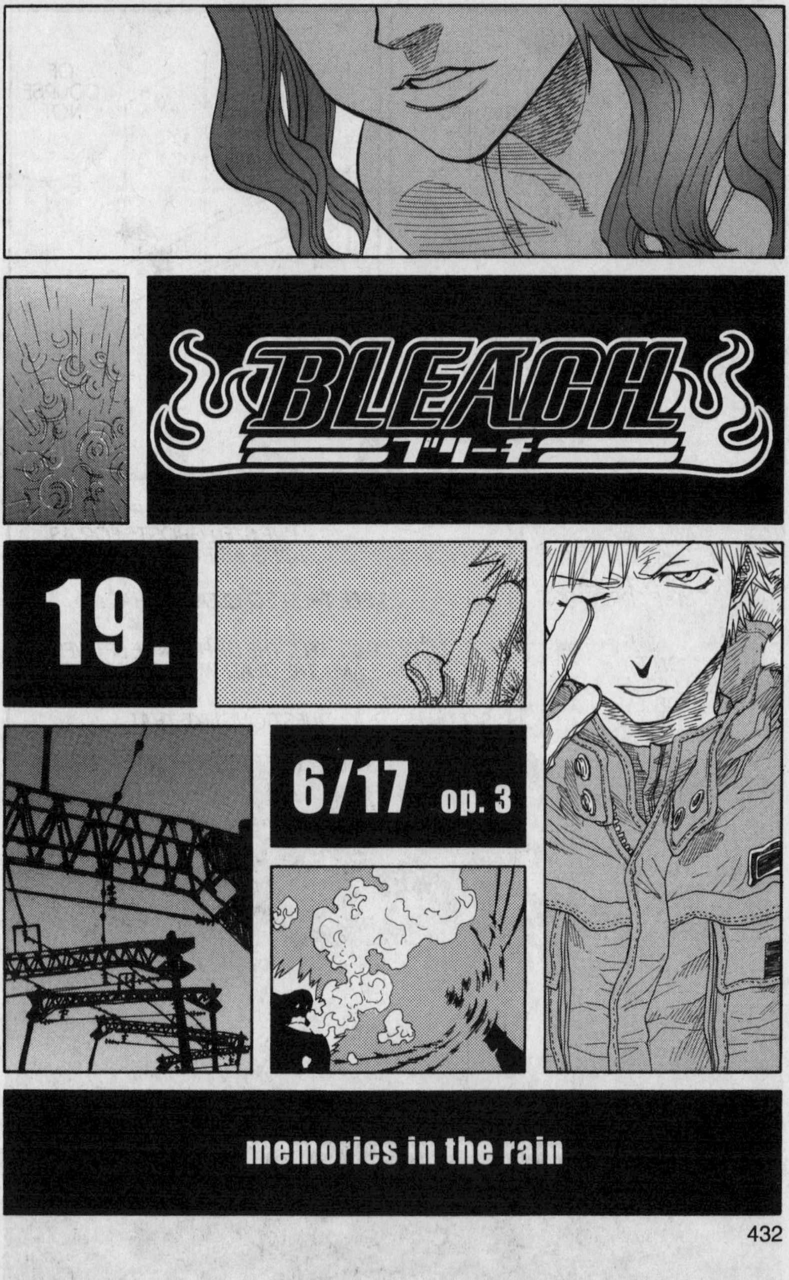
BLEACH
ブリーチ
19.
6/17 op. 3
memories in the rain

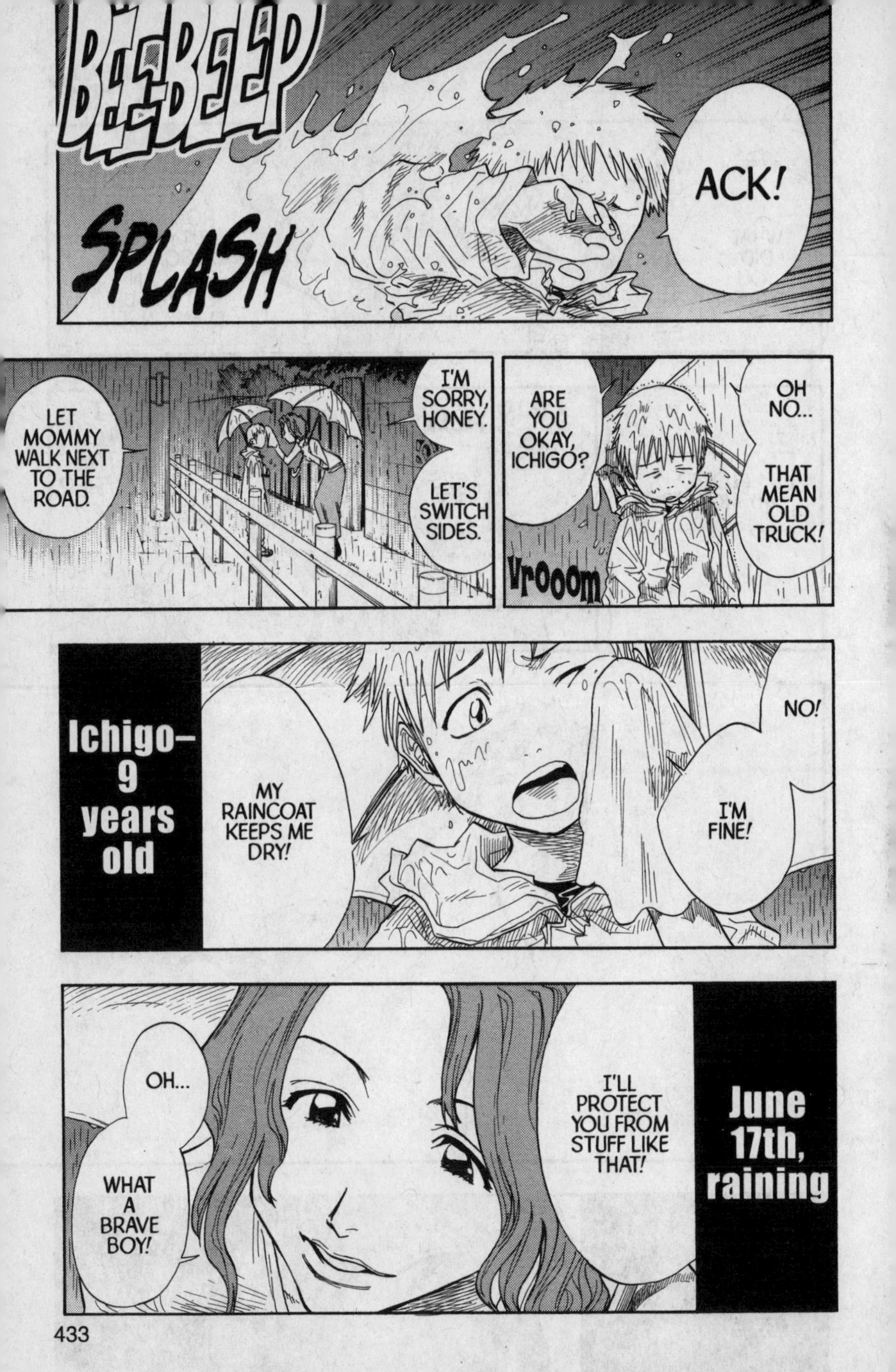

BEEBEEP
SPLASH
ACK!
OH NO... THAT MEAN OLD TRUCK!
ARE YOU OKAY, ICHIGO?
Vrooom
I'M SORRY, HONEY.
LET'S SWITCH SIDES.
LET MOMMY WALK NEXT TO THE ROAD.
NO!
I'M FINE!
MY RAINCOAT KEEPS ME DRY!
Ichigo– 9 years old
June 17th, raining
I'LL PROTECT YOU FROM STUFF LIKE THAT!
OH...
WHAT A BRAVE BOY!

READ THIS WAY

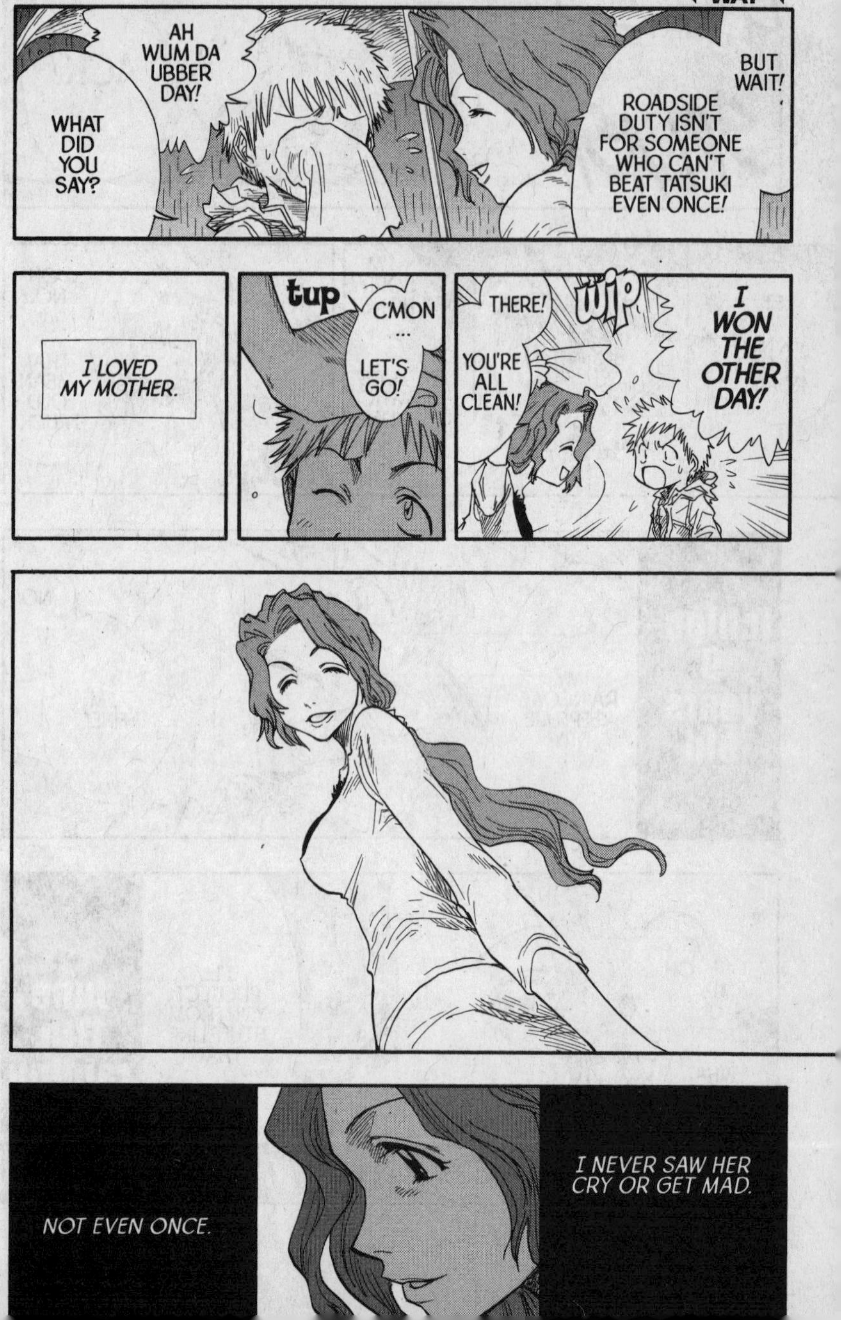
BUT WAIT!
ROADSIDE DUTY ISN'T FOR SOMEONE WHO CAN'T BEAT TATSUKI EVEN ONCE!
AH WUM DA UBBER DAY!
WHAT DID YOU SAY?
I WON THE OTHER DAY!
wip
THERE!
YOU'RE ALL CLEAN!
tup
C'MON ...
LET'S GO!
I LOVED MY MOTHER.
I NEVER SAW HER CRY OR GET MAD.
NOT EVEN ONCE.

READ THIS WAY

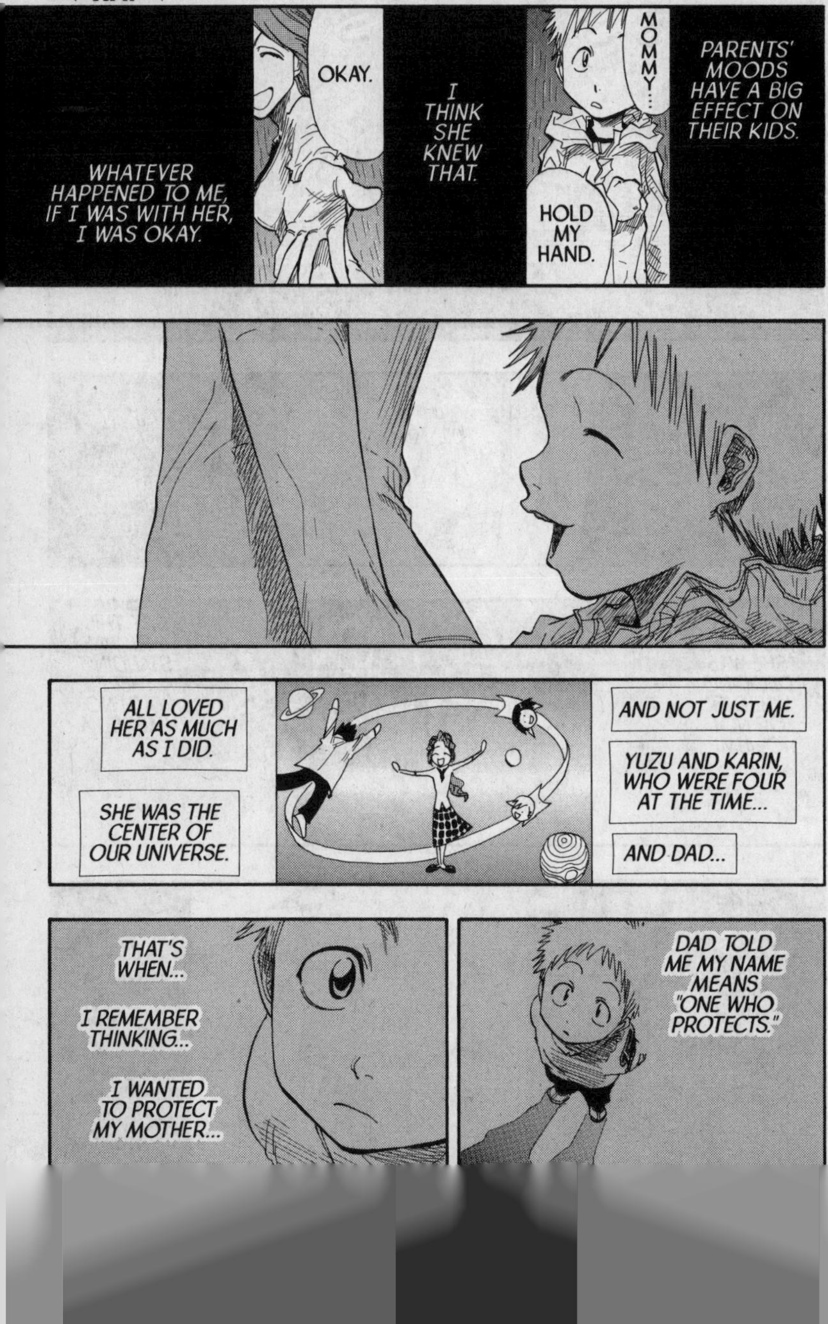
PARENTS' MOODS HAVE A BIG EFFECT ON THEIR KIDS.
MOMMY...
HOLD MY HAND.
I THINK SHE KNEW THAT.
OKAY.
WHATEVER HAPPENED TO ME, IF I WAS WITH HER, I WAS OKAY.
AND NOT JUST ME.
YUZU AND KARIN, WHO WERE FOUR AT THE TIME...
AND DAD...
ALL LOVED HER AS MUCH AS I DID.
SHE WAS THE CENTER OF OUR UNIVERSE.
DAD TOLD ME MY NAME MEANS "ONE WHO PROTECTS."
THAT'S WHEN...
I REMEMBER THINKING...
I WANTED TO PROTECT MY MOTHER...

READ THIS WAY

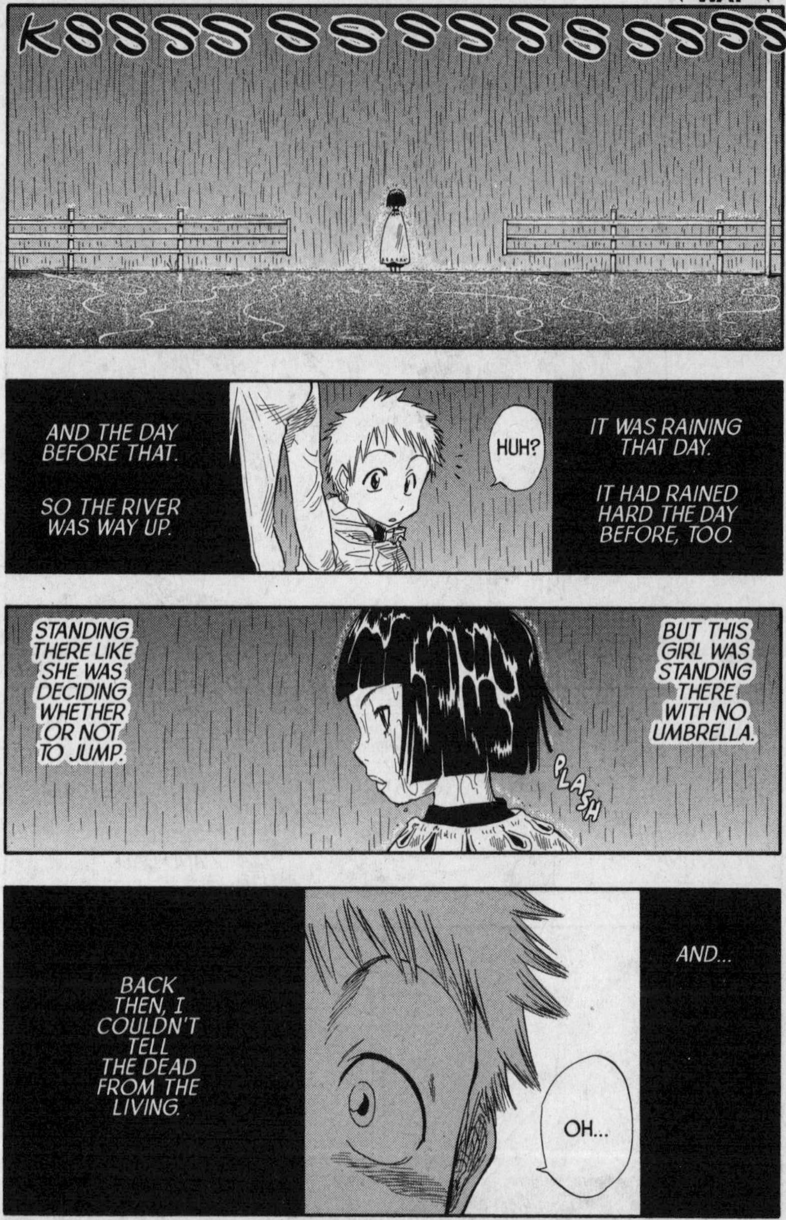
KSSSSSSSSSSSSSS
IT WAS RAINING THAT DAY.
IT HAD RAINED HARD THE DAY BEFORE, TOO.
HUH?
AND THE DAY BEFORE THAT.
SO THE RIVER WAS WAY UP.
BUT THIS GIRL WAS STANDING THERE WITH NO UMBRELLA.
PLASH
STANDING THERE LIKE SHE WAS DECIDING WHETHER OR NOT TO JUMP.
AND...
OH...
BACK THEN, I COULDN'T TELL THE DEAD FROM THE LIVING.

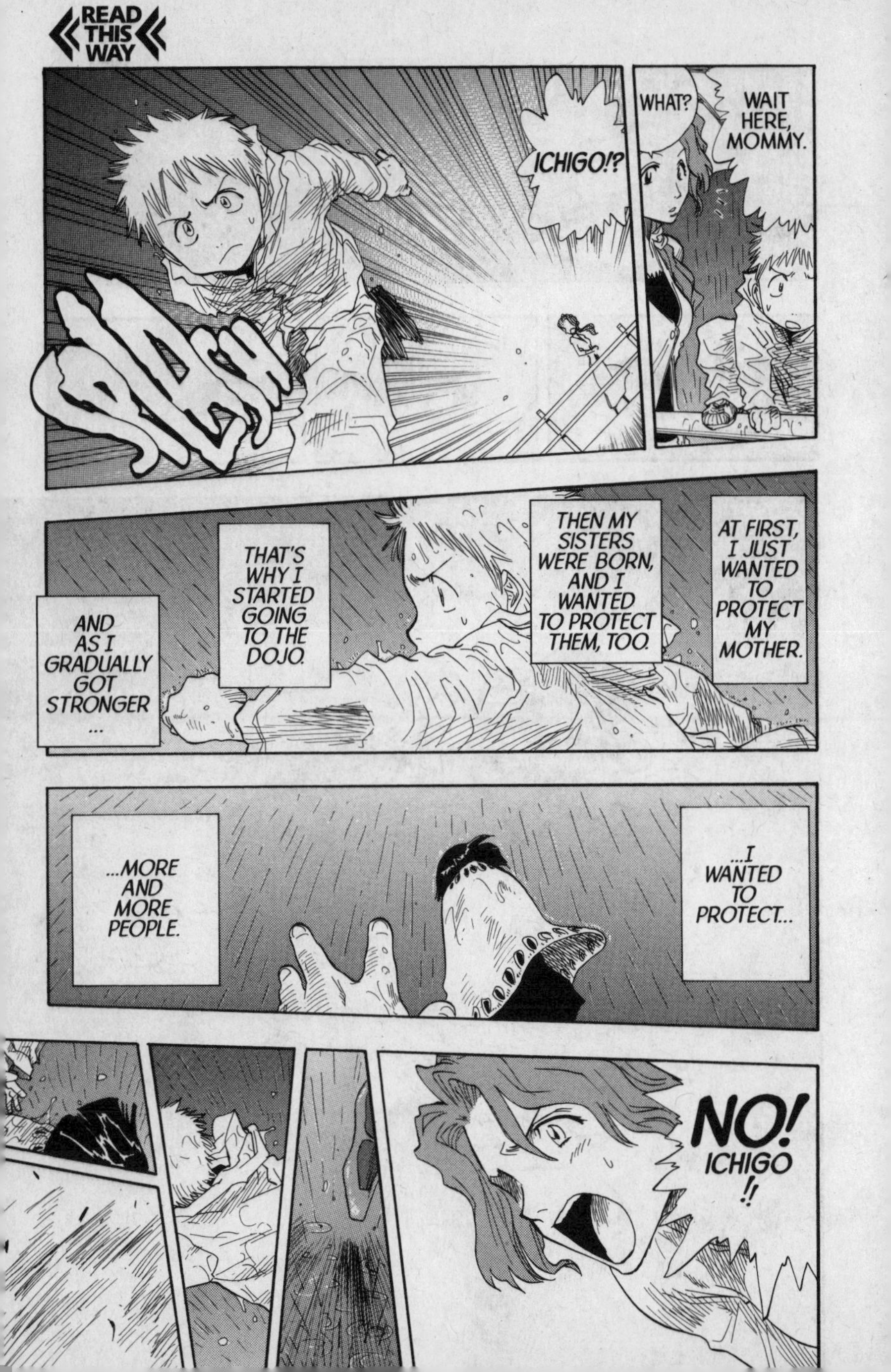
READ THIS WAY
WAIT HERE, MOMMY.
WHAT?
ICHIGO!?
AT FIRST, I JUST WANTED TO PROTECT MY MOTHER.
THEN MY SISTERS WERE BORN, AND I WANTED TO PROTECT THEM, TOO.
THAT'S WHY I STARTED GOING TO THE DOJO.
AND AS I GRADUALLY GOT STRONGER ...
...I WANTED TO PROTECT...
...MORE AND MORE PEOPLE.
NO! ICHIGO!!

READ THIS WAY

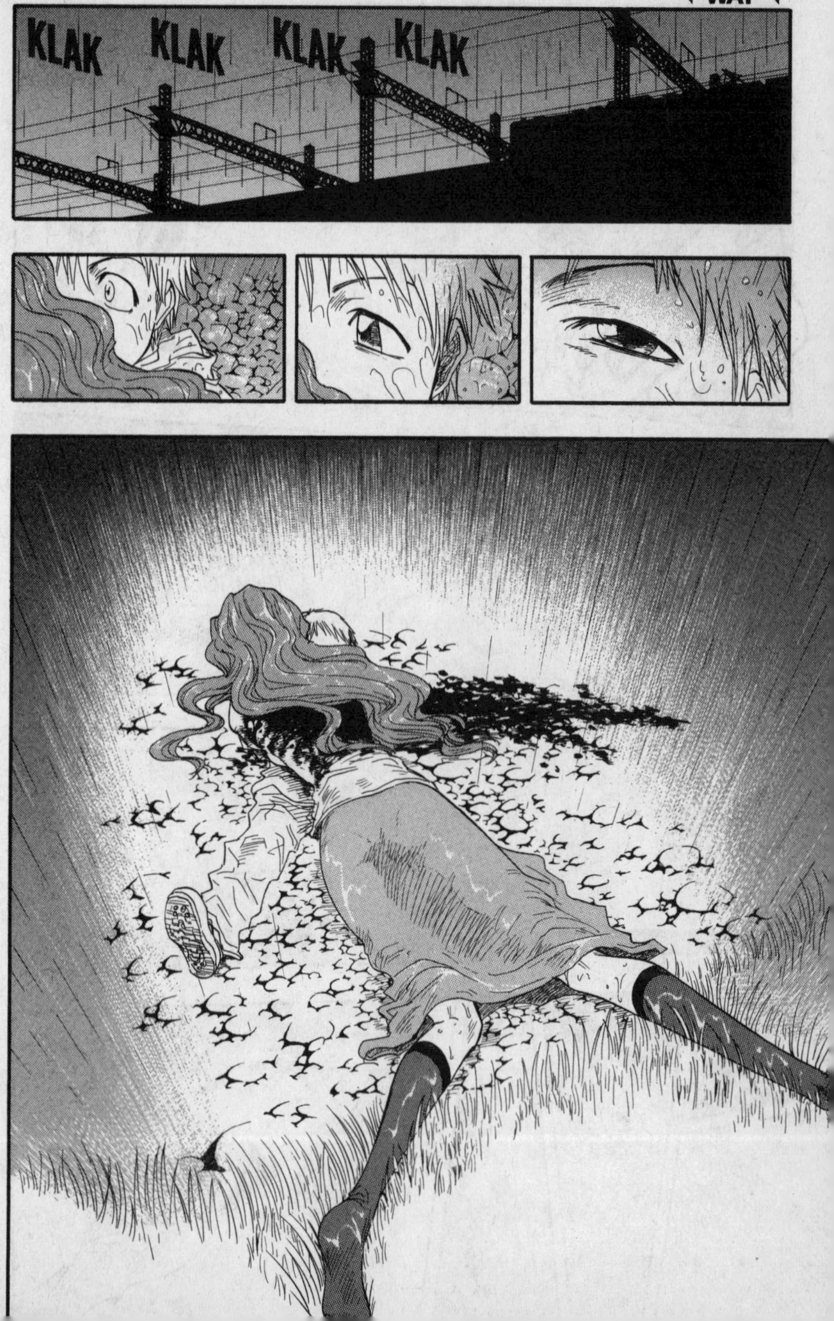
KLAK
KLAK
KLAK
KLAK

READ THIS WAY

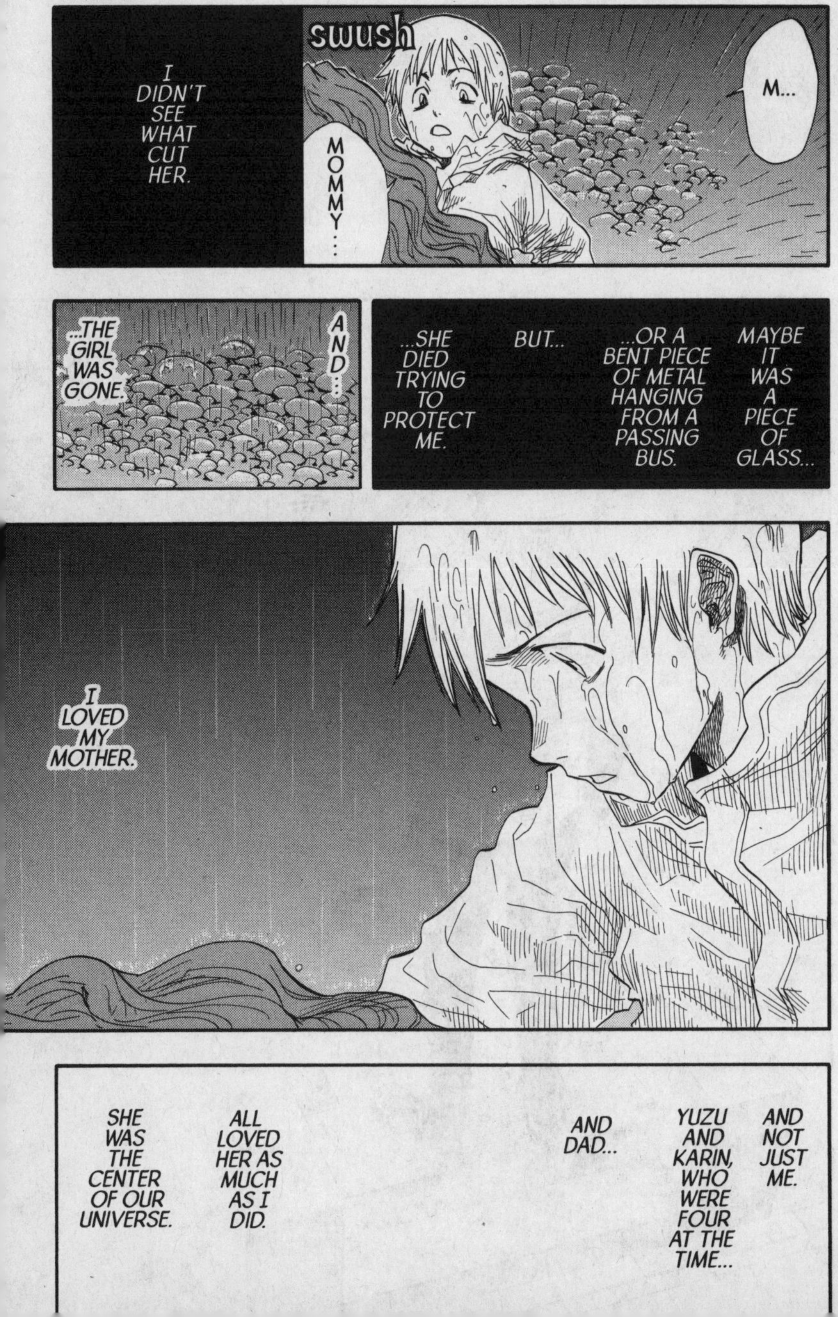
M...
swush
MOMMY...
I DIDN'T SEE WHAT CUT HER.
MAYBE IT WAS A PIECE OF GLASS...
...OR A BENT PIECE OF METAL HANGING FROM A PASSING BUS.
BUT...
...SHE DIED TRYING TO PROTECT ME.
AND...
...THE GIRL WAS GONE.
I LOVED MY MOTHER.
AND NOT JUST ME.
YUZU AND KARIN, WHO WERE FOUR AT THE TIME...
AND DAD...
ALL LOVED HER AS MUCH AS I DID.
SHE WAS THE CENTER OF OUR UNIVERSE.

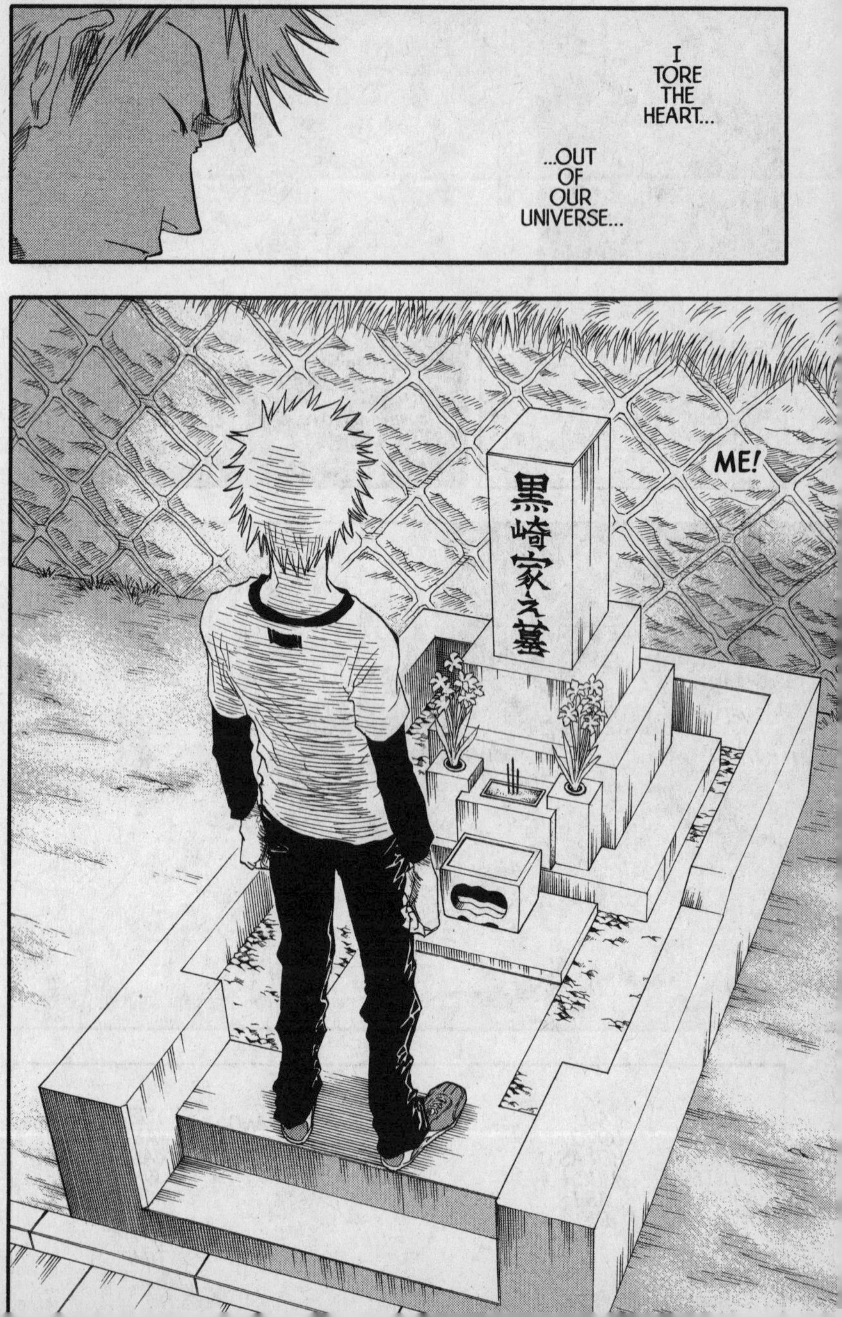
I TORE THE HEART...
...OUT OF OUR UNIVERSE...
ME!
黒崎家之墓

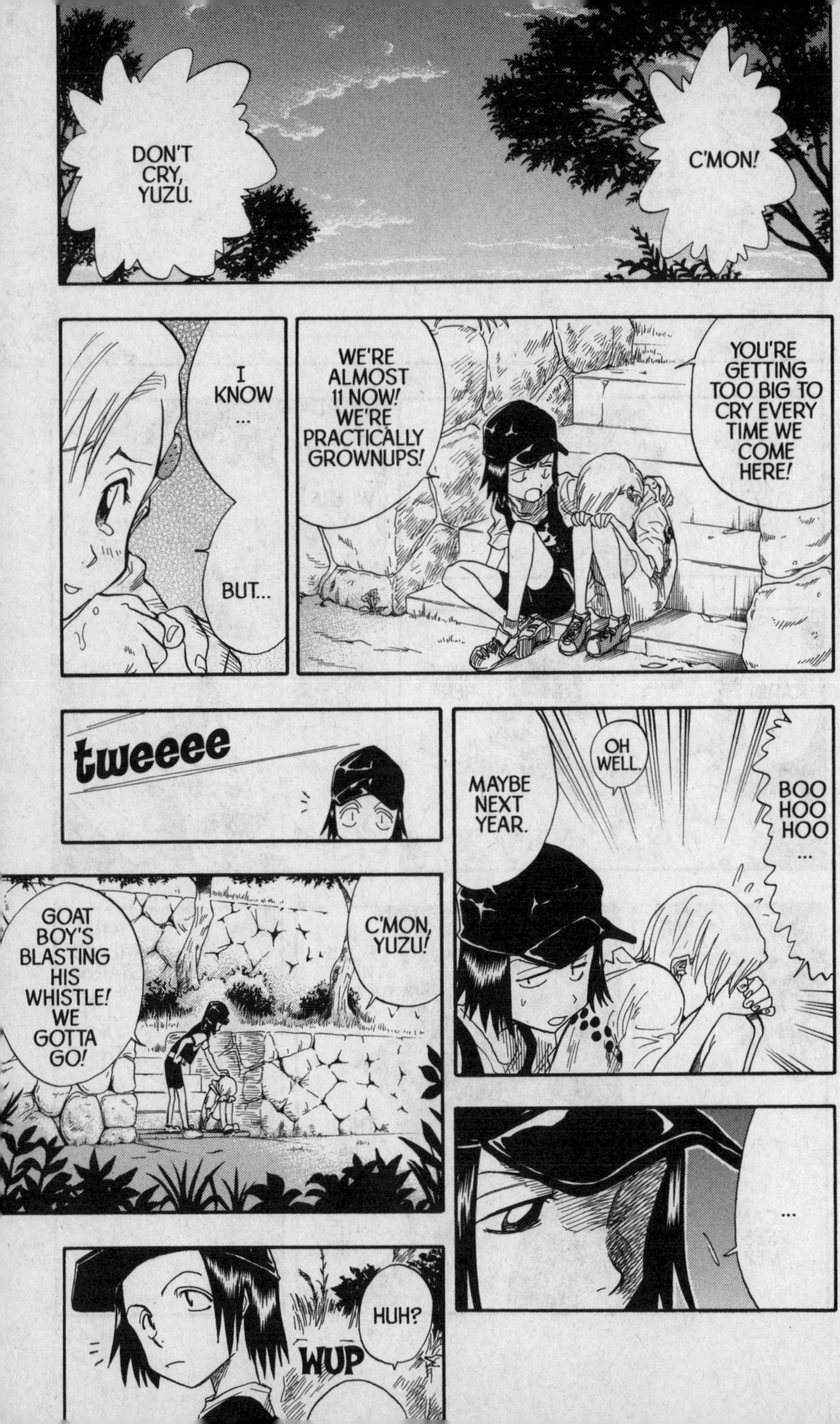
C'MON!
DON'T CRY, YUZU.
YOU'RE GETTING TOO BIG TO CRY EVERY TIME WE COME HERE!
WE'RE ALMOST 11 NOW! WE'RE PRACTICALLY GROWNUPS!
I KNOW ...
BUT...
BOO HOO HOO ...
OH WELL.
MAYBE NEXT YEAR.
tweeee
C'MON, YUZU!
GOAT BOY'S BLASTING HIS WHISTLE! WE GOTTA GO!
...
HUH?
WUP

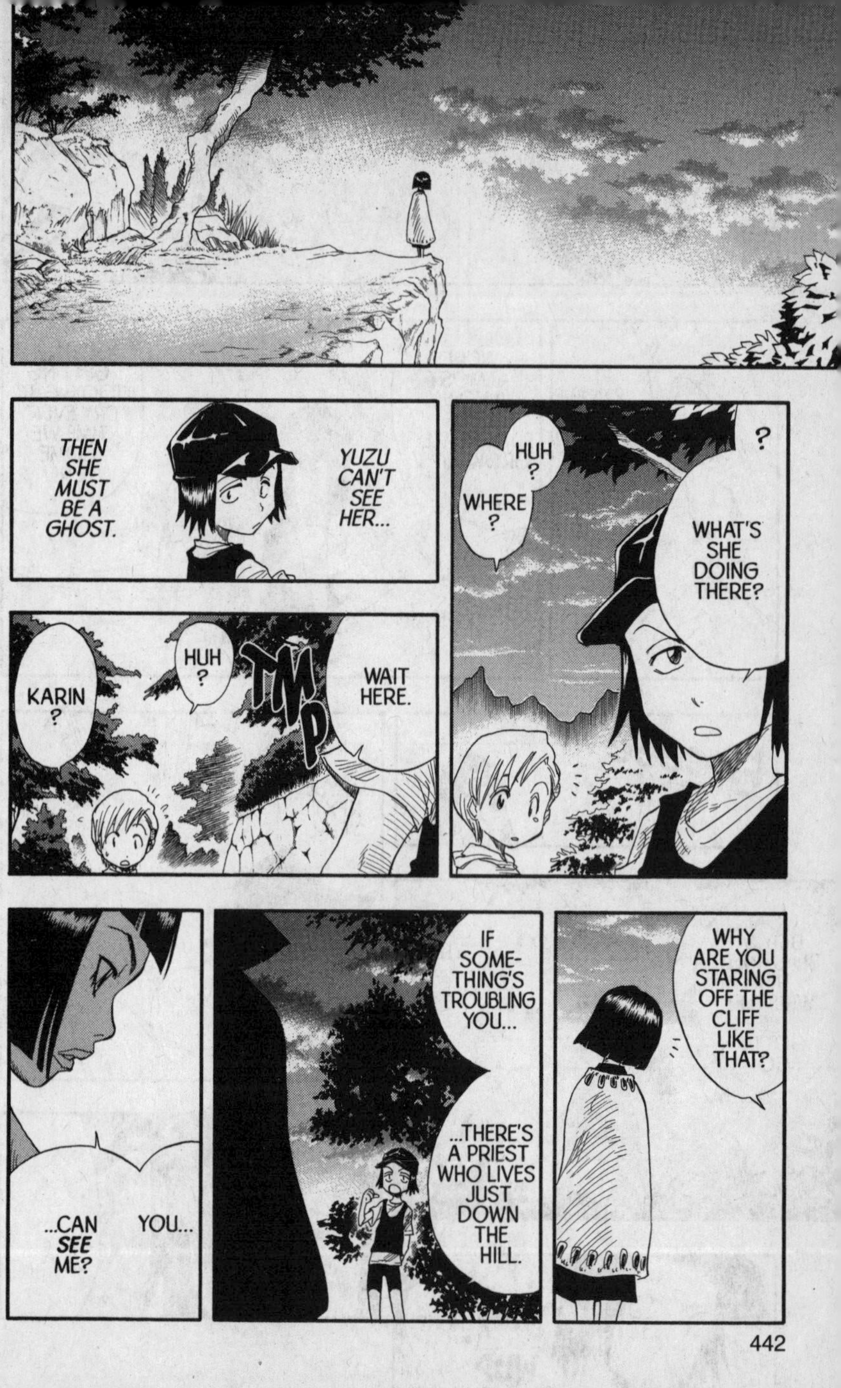
?
WHAT'S SHE DOING THERE?
HUH? WHERE?
YUZU CAN'T SEE HER...
THEN SHE MUST BE A GHOST.
WAIT HERE.
TMP
HUH?
KARIN?
WHY ARE YOU STARING OFF THE CLIFF LIKE THAT?
IF SOME-THING'S TROUBLING YOU...
...THERE'S A PRIEST WHO LIVES JUST DOWN THE HILL.
YOU...
...CAN *SEE* ME?

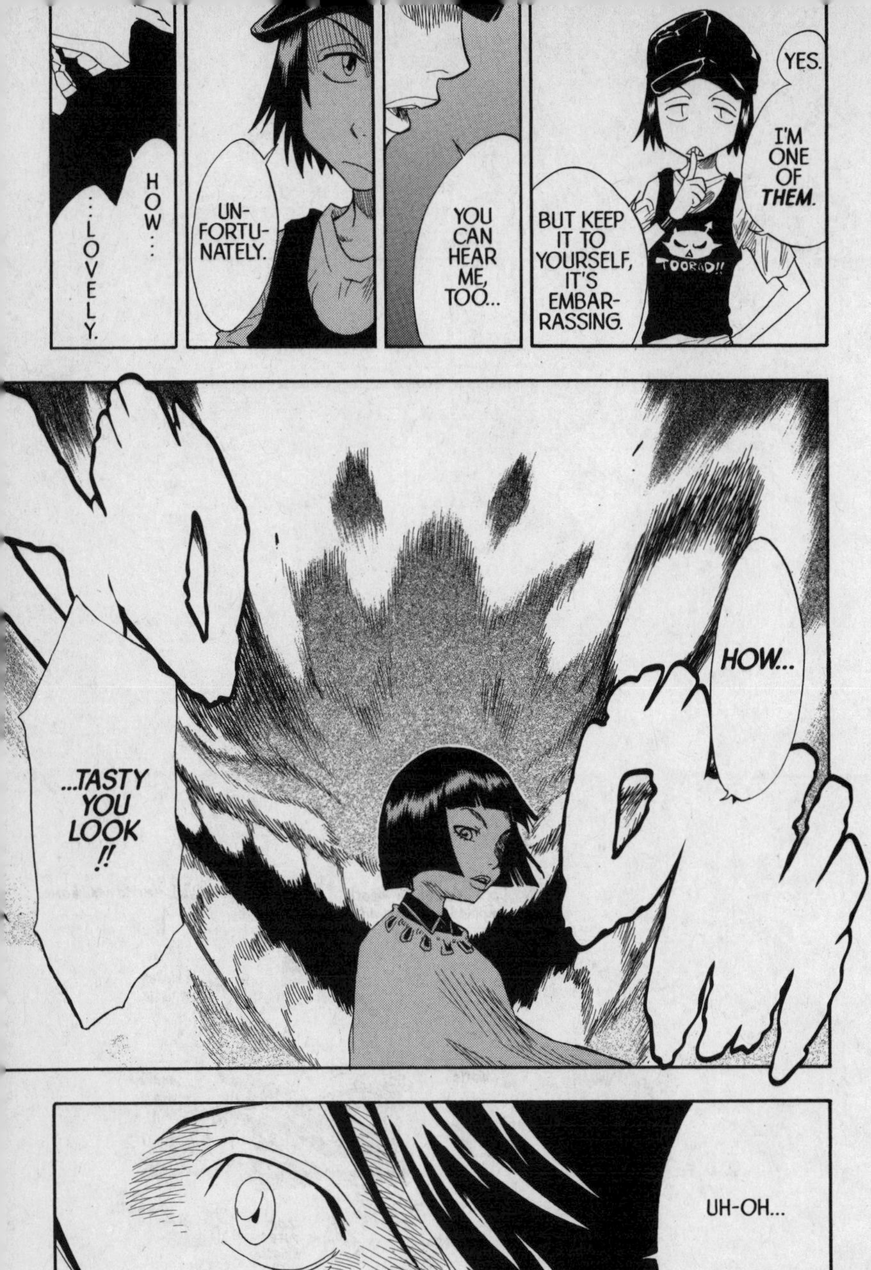
YES.
I'M ONE OF *THEM*.
BUT KEEP IT TO YOURSELF, IT'S EMBARRASSING.
YOU CAN HEAR ME, TOO...
UN-FORTUNATELY.
HOW...
...LOVELY.
HOW...
...TASTY YOU LOOK!!
UH-OH...

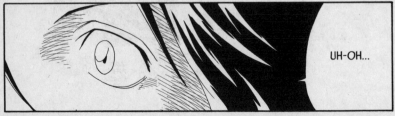

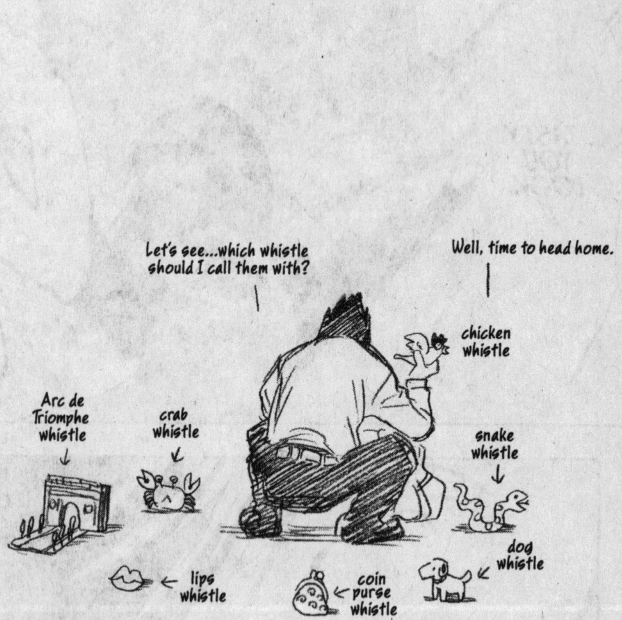
Well, time to head home.
Let's see...which whistle should I call them with?
chicken whistle
snake whistle
dog whistle
coin purse whistle
crab whistle
Arc de Triomphe whistle
lips whistle

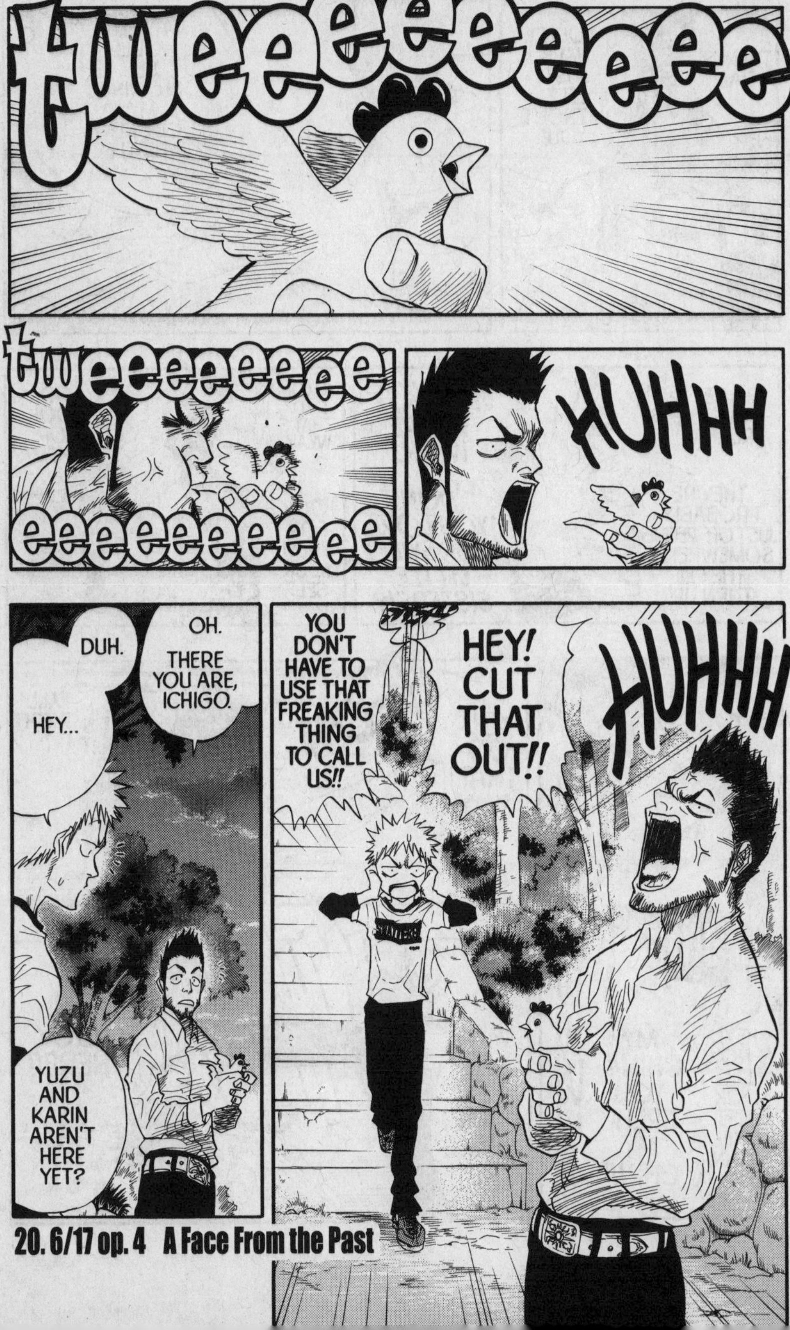
tweeeeeeeee
HUHHH
tweeeeeeeee
eeeeeeeeeee
HUHHH
HEY! CUT THAT OUT!!
YOU DON'T HAVE TO USE THAT FREAKING THING TO CALL US!!
OH.
THERE YOU ARE, ICHIGO.
DUH.
HEY...
YUZU AND KARIN AREN'T HERE YET?

20. 6/17 op. 4 A Face From the Past

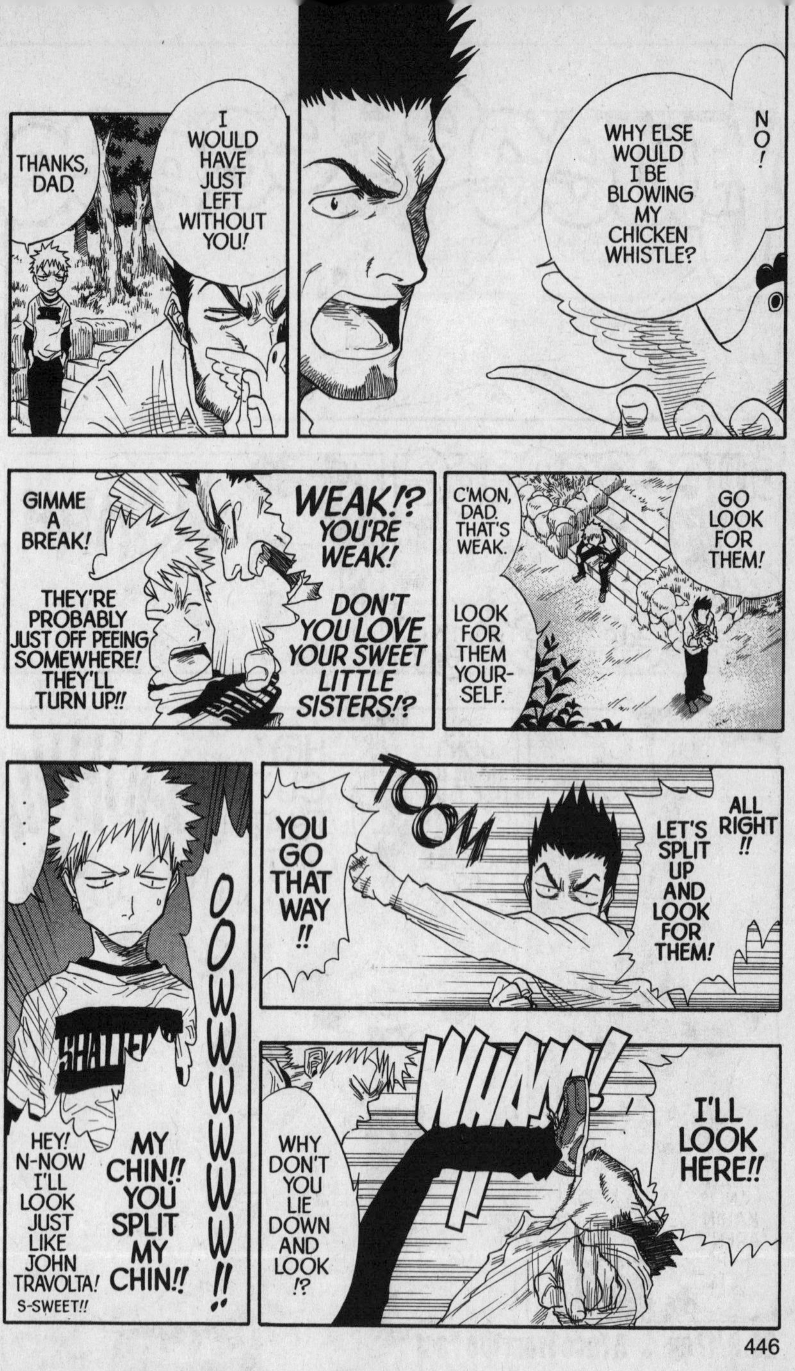
NO!
WHY ELSE WOULD I BE BLOWING MY CHICKEN WHISTLE?
I WOULD HAVE JUST LEFT WITHOUT YOU!
THANKS, DAD.
GO LOOK FOR THEM!
C'MON, DAD. THAT'S WEAK.
LOOK FOR THEM YOURSELF.
WEAK!? YOU'RE WEAK!
DON'T YOU LOVE YOUR SWEET LITTLE SISTERS!?
GIMME A BREAK!
THEY'RE PROBABLY JUST OFF PEEING SOMEWHERE! THEY'LL TURN UP!!
ALL RIGHT!!
LET'S SPLIT UP AND LOOK FOR THEM!
TOOM
YOU GO THAT WAY!!
I'LL LOOK HERE!!
WHAM!
WHY DON'T YOU LIE DOWN AND LOOK!?
...
OOWWWWWWWW!!
MY CHIN!! YOU SPLIT MY CHIN!!
HEY! N-NOW I'LL LOOK JUST LIKE JOHN TRAVOLTA!
S-SWEET!!

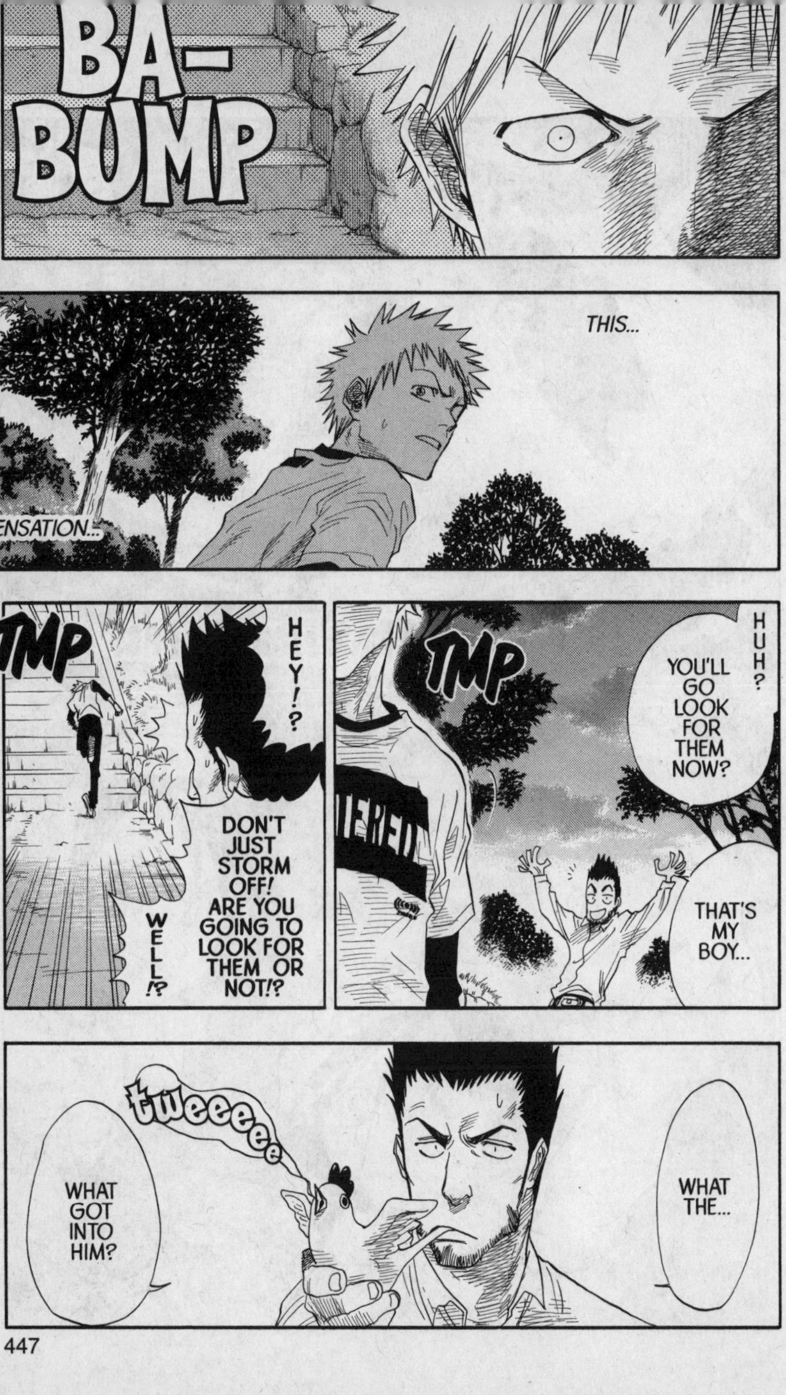
BA-BUMP
THIS...
...SENSATION...
HUH?
YOU'LL GO LOOK FOR THEM NOW?
TMP
THAT'S MY BOY...
HEY!?
DON'T JUST STORM OFF! ARE YOU GOING TO LOOK FOR THEM OR NOT!?
WELL!?
TMP
WHAT THE...
tweeeeee
WHAT GOT INTO HIM?

20. 6/17 op. 4 A Face From the Past

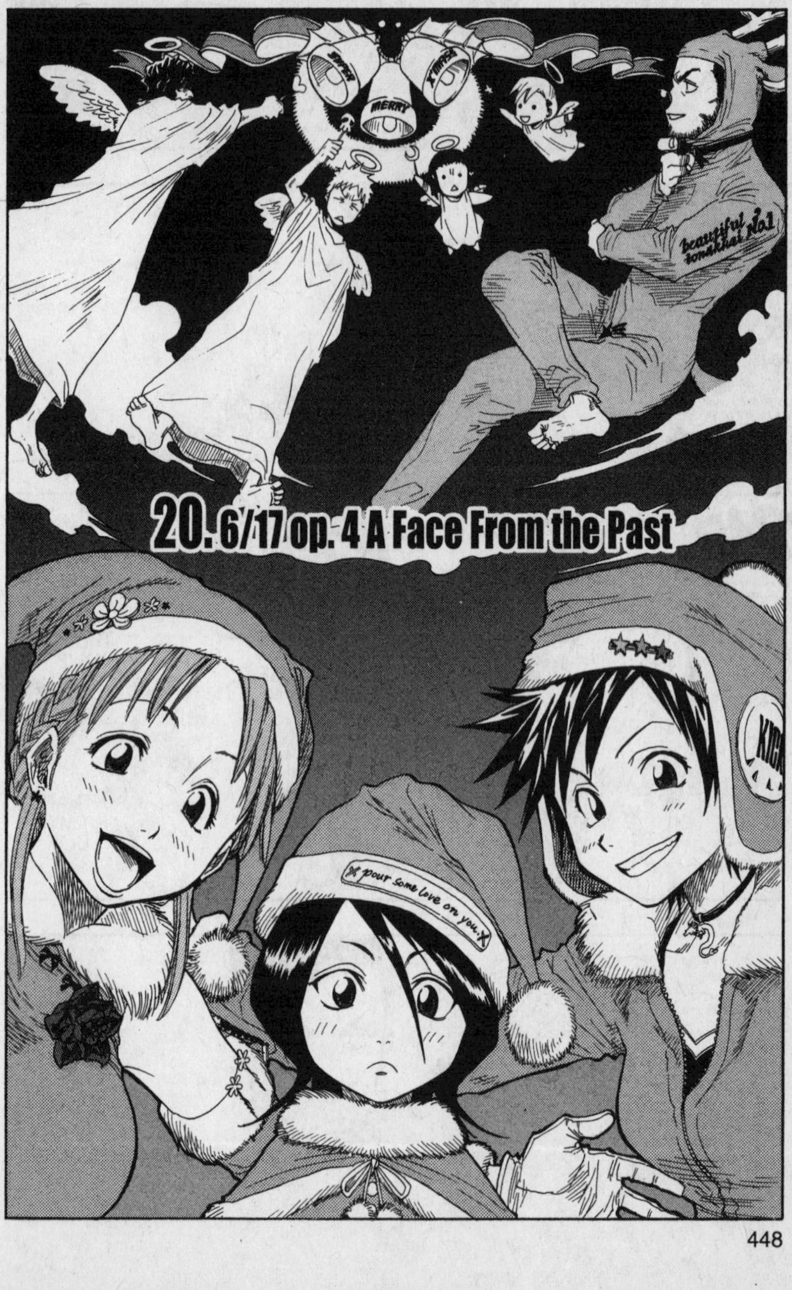
MERRY
pour some love on you.

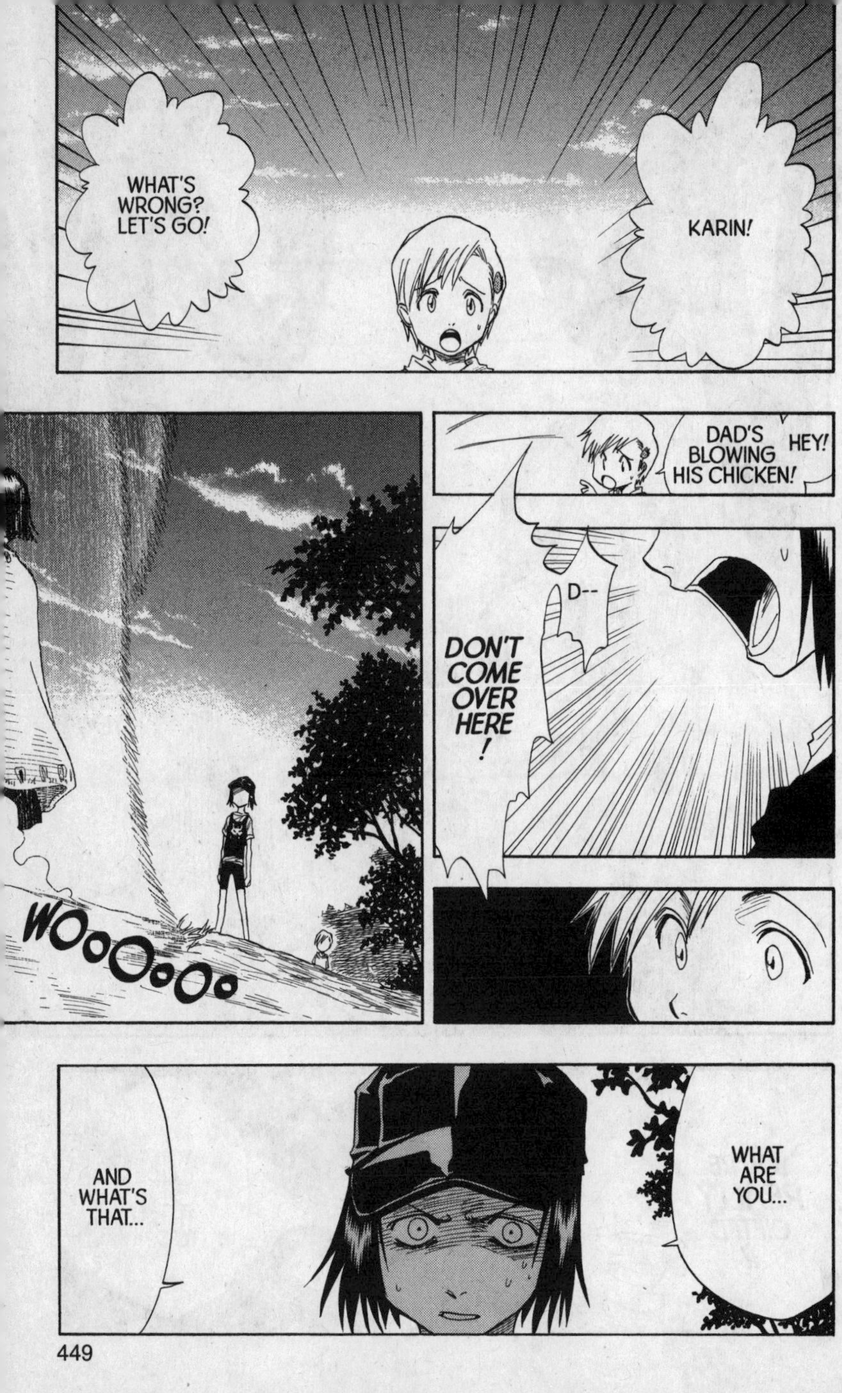
KARIN!
WHAT'S WRONG? LET'S GO!
HEY!
DAD'S BLOWING HIS CHICKEN!
D--
DON'T COME OVER HERE!
WOoOoOo
WHAT ARE YOU...
AND WHAT'S THAT...

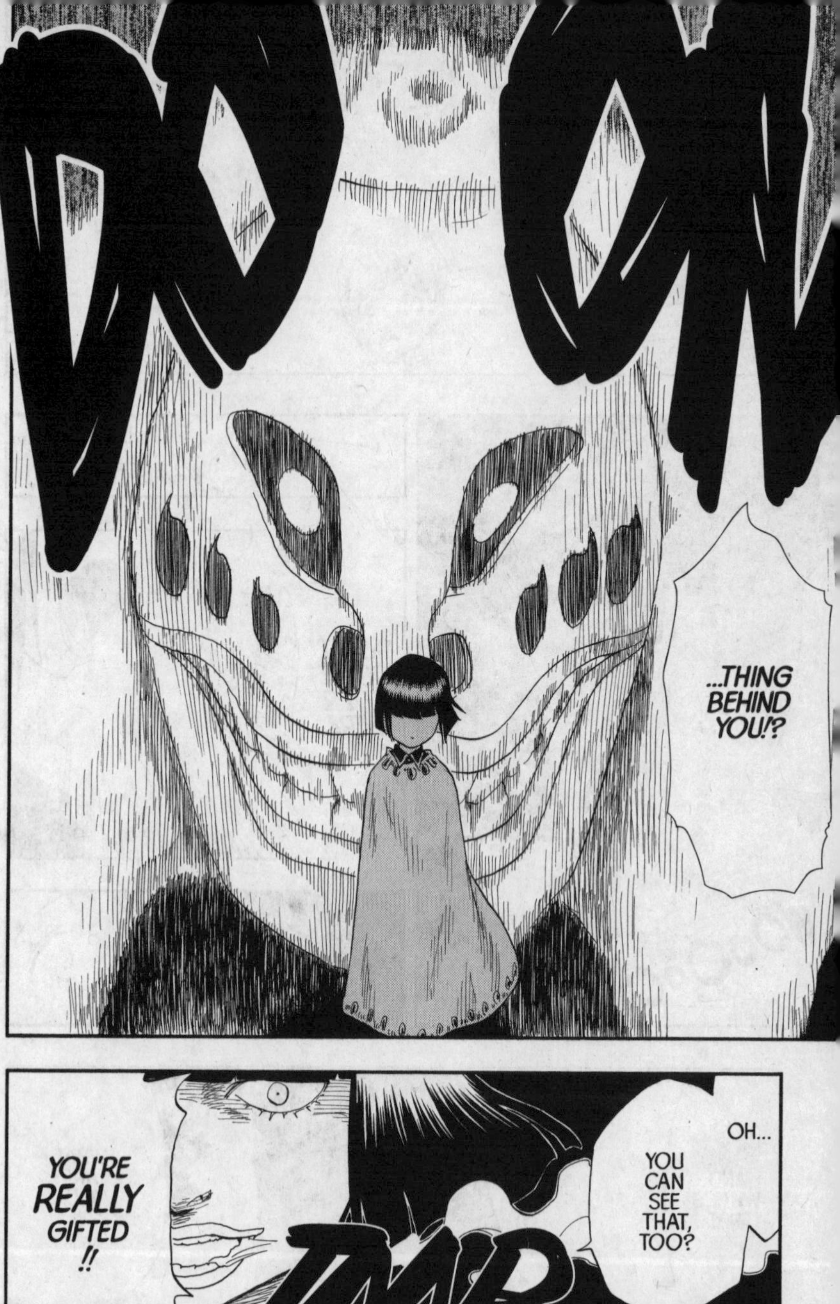
...THING BEHIND YOU!?
OH...
YOU CAN SEE THAT, TOO?
TMP
YOU'RE REALLY GIFTED!!

READ THIS WAY

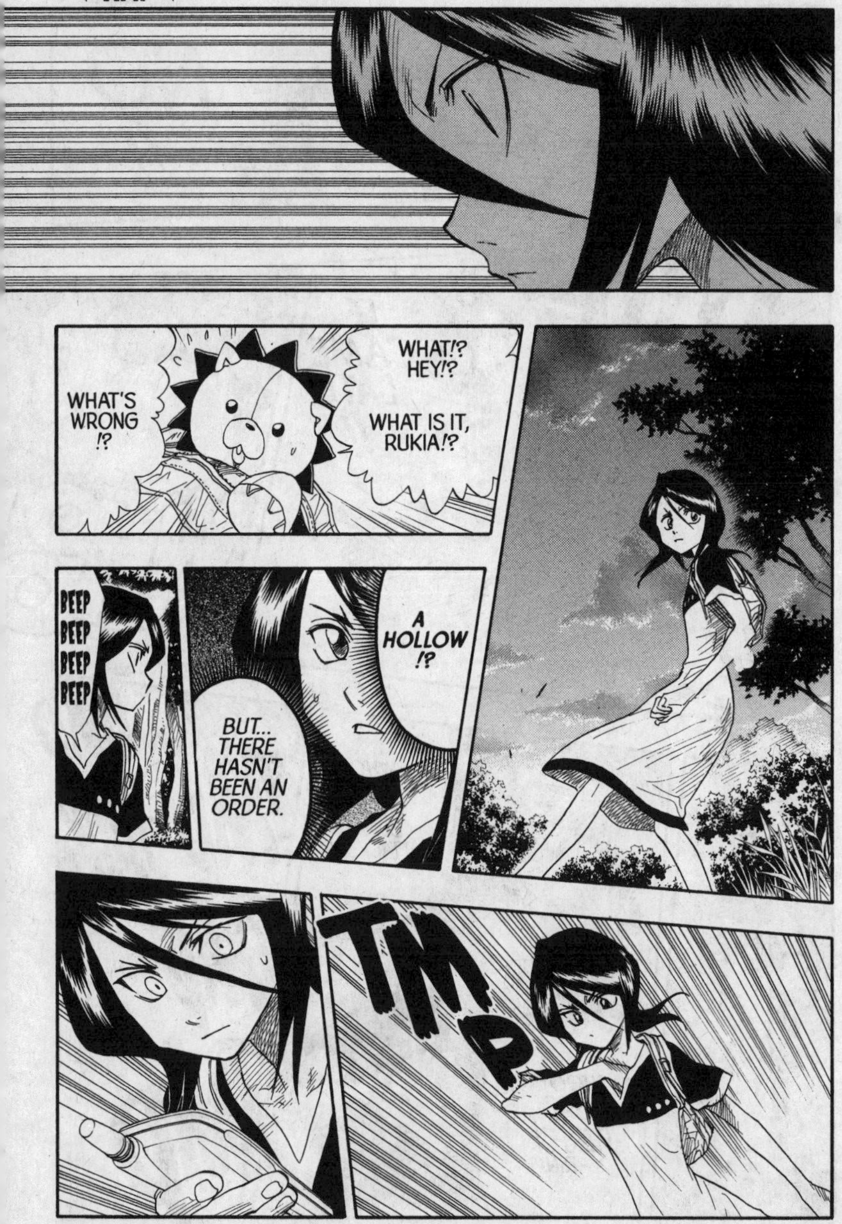
WHAT!? HEY!?
WHAT IS IT, RUKIA!?
WHAT'S WRONG !?
A HOLLOW !?
BUT... THERE HASN'T BEEN AN ORDER.
BEEP BEEP BEEP BEEP
TMP

READ THIS WAY

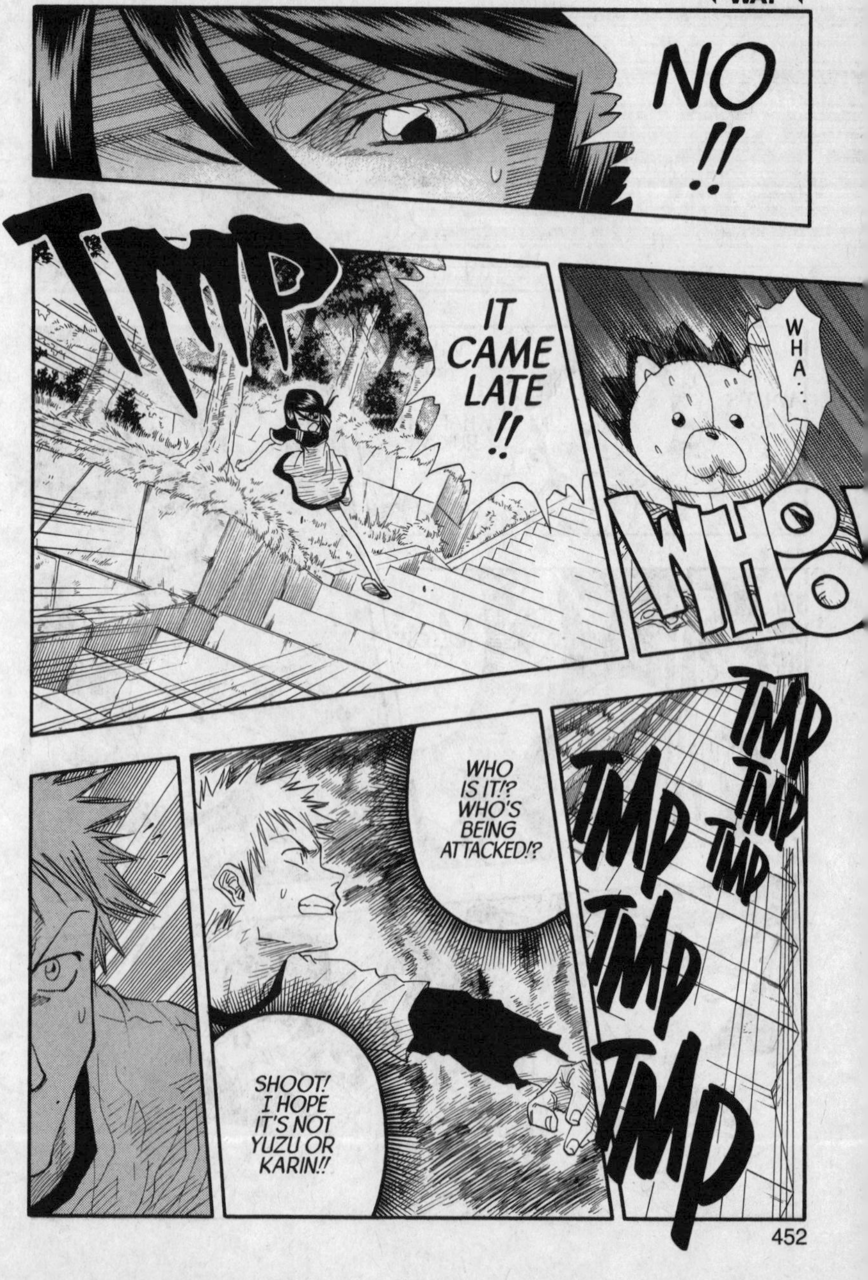

NO!!
WHA...
WHO
TMP
IT CAME LATE!!
TMP TMP TMP TMP TMP TMP
WHO IS IT!? WHO'S BEING ATTACKED!?
SHOOT! I HOPE IT'S NOT YUZU OR KARIN!!

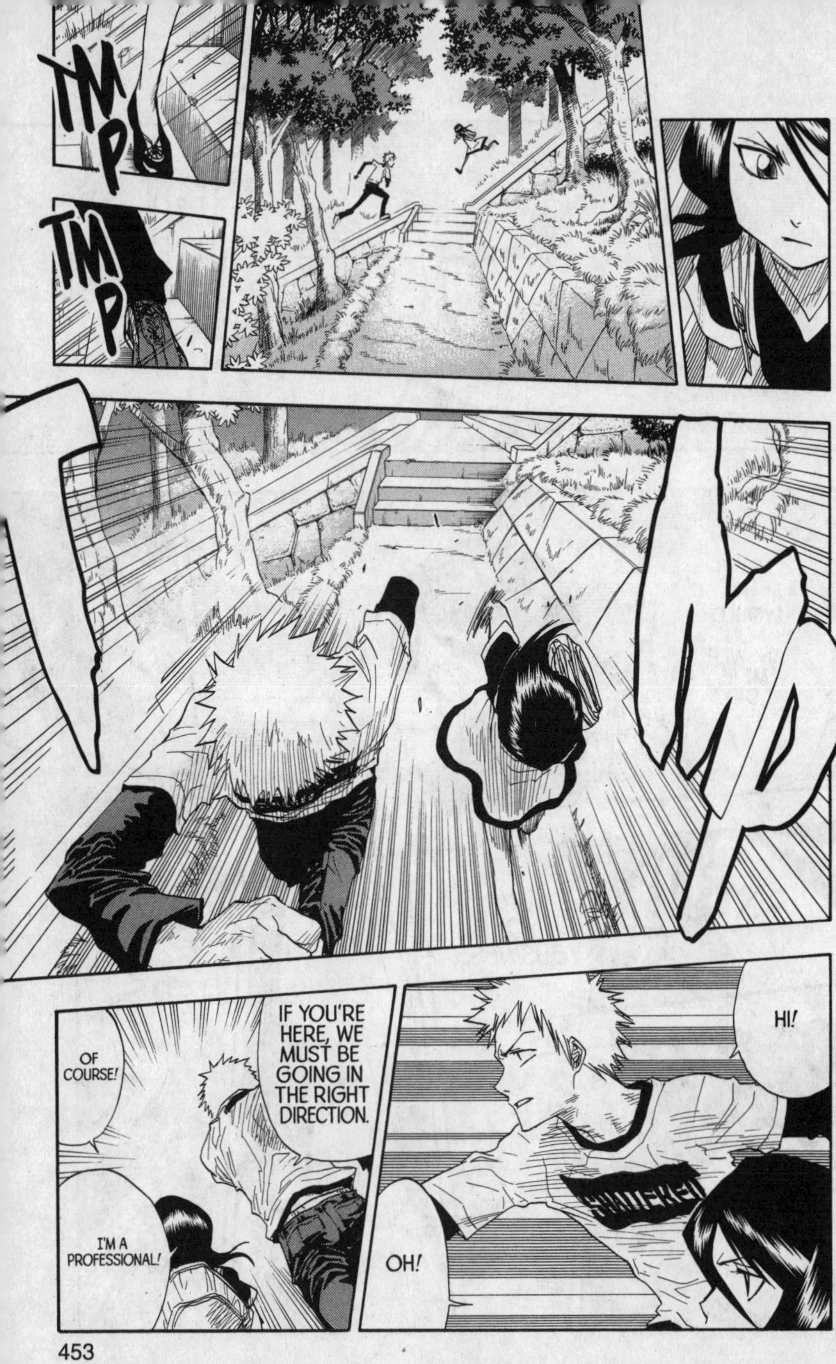
TMP
TMP
TMP
HI!
OH!
IF YOU'RE HERE, WE MUST BE GOING IN THE RIGHT DIRECTION.
OF COURSE!
I'M A PROFESSIONAL!

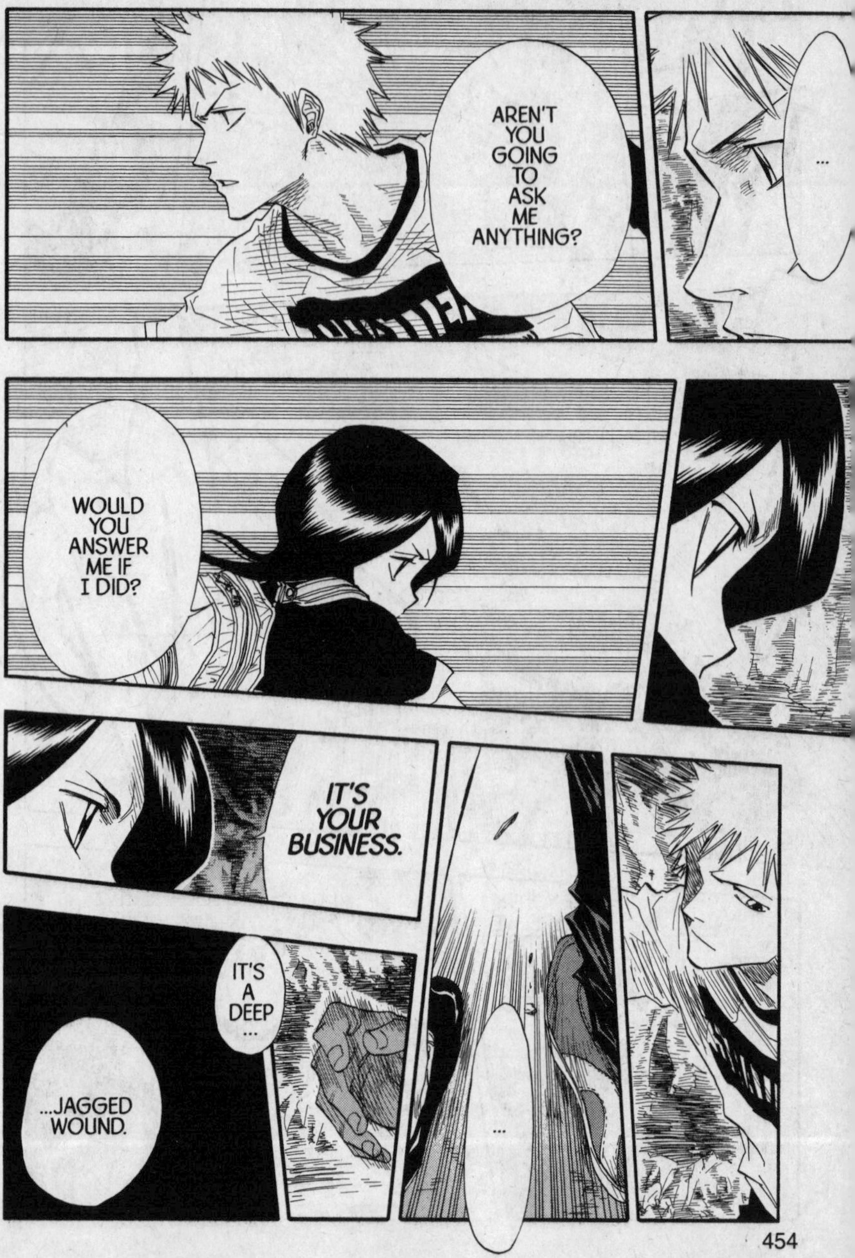
...
AREN'T YOU GOING TO ASK ME ANYTHING?
WOULD YOU ANSWER ME IF I DID?
...
IT'S YOUR BUSINESS.
IT'S A DEEP ...
...JAGGED WOUND.

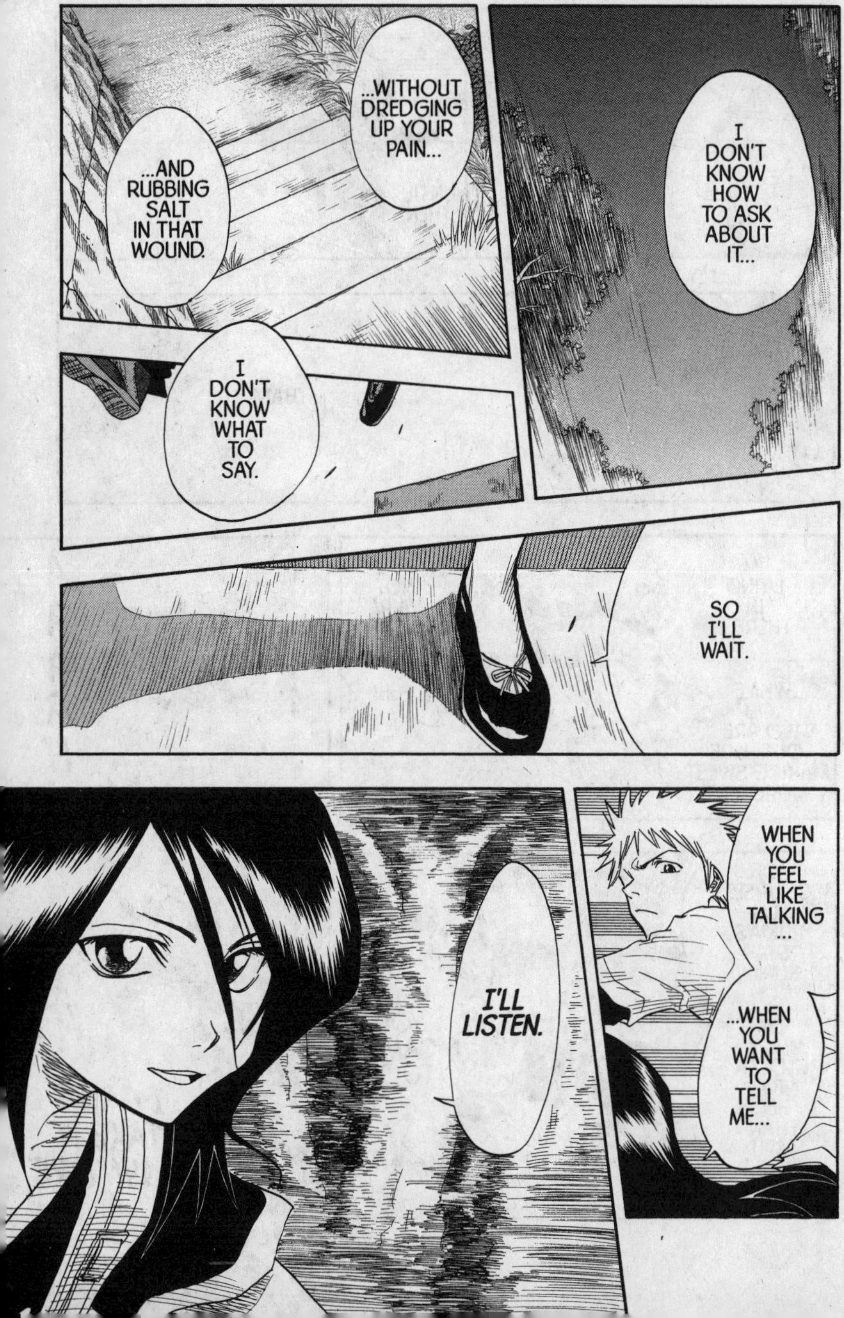
I DON'T KNOW HOW TO ASK ABOUT IT...
...WITHOUT DREDGING UP YOUR PAIN...
...AND RUBBING SALT IN THAT WOUND.
I DON'T KNOW WHAT TO SAY.
SO I'LL WAIT.
WHEN YOU FEEL LIKE TALKING...
...WHEN YOU WANT TO TELL ME...
I'LL LISTEN.

READ THIS WAY

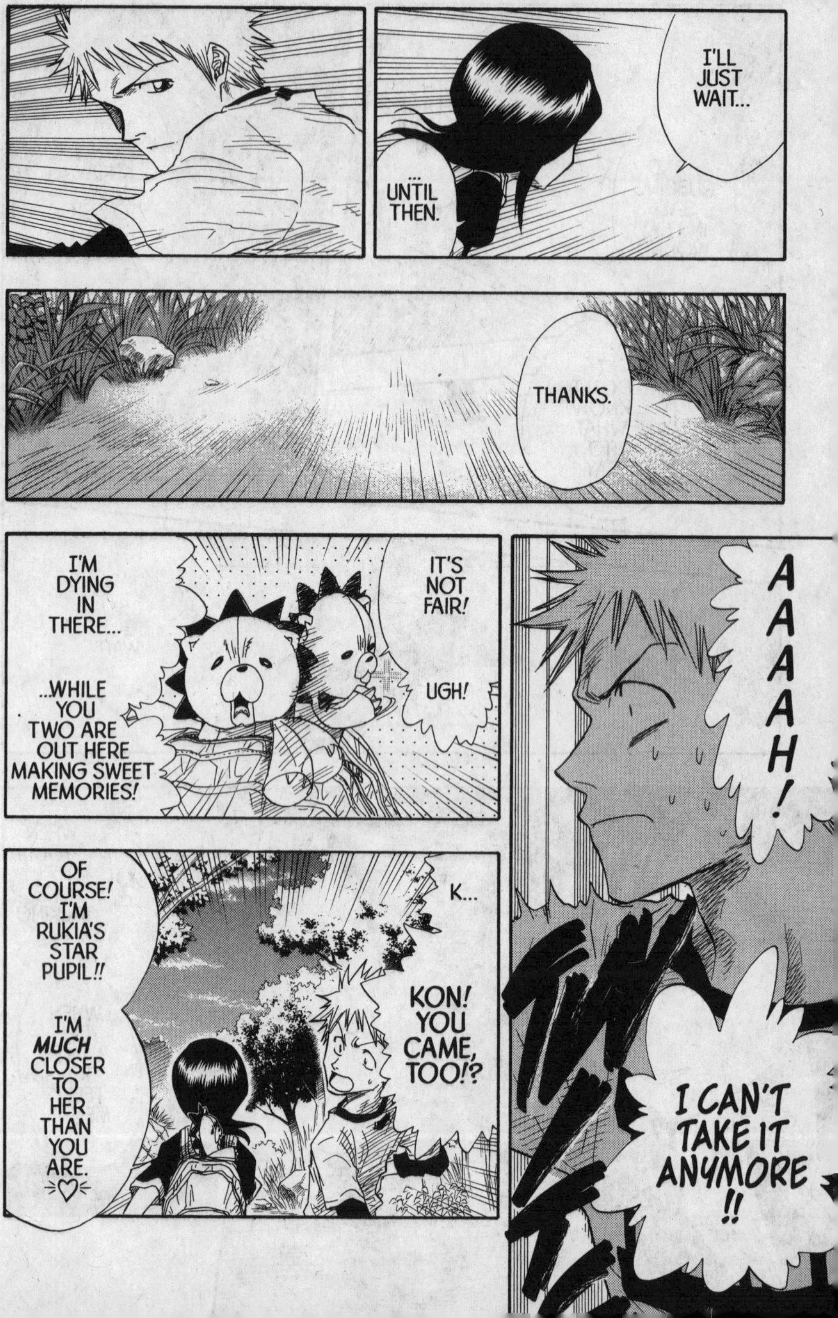
I'LL JUST WAIT...
...UNTIL THEN.
THANKS.
AAAAH!
I CAN'T TAKE IT ANYMORE!!
IT'S NOT FAIR!
UGH!
I'M DYING IN THERE...
...WHILE YOU TWO ARE OUT HERE MAKING SWEET MEMORIES!
K...
KON! YOU CAME, TOO!?
OF COURSE! I'M RUKIA'S STAR PUPIL!!
I'M MUCH CLOSER TO HER THAN YOU ARE. ♡

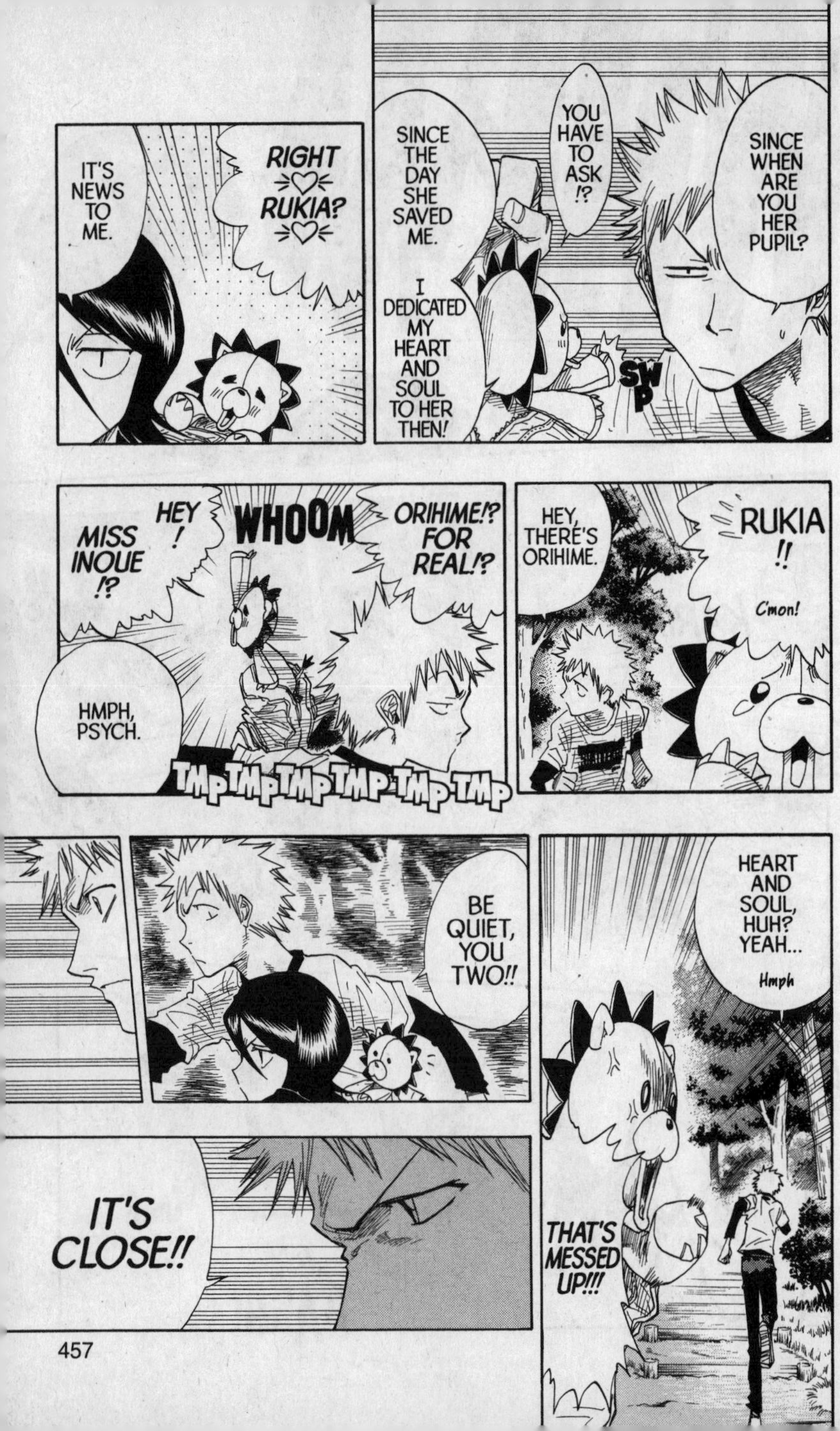
SINCE WHEN ARE YOU HER PUPIL?
YOU HAVE TO ASK!?
SINCE THE DAY SHE SAVED ME.
I DEDICATED MY HEART AND SOUL TO HER THEN!
SWP
RIGHT ♡ RUKIA? ♡
IT'S NEWS TO ME.
RUKIA!!
C'mon!
HEY, THERE'S ORIHIME.
ORIHIME!? FOR REAL!?
WHOOM
HEY!
MISS INOUE!?
HMPH, PSYCH.
TMP TMP TMP TMP TMP TMP
HEART AND SOUL, HUH? YEAH...
Hmph
THAT'S MESSED UP!!!
BE QUIET, YOU TWO!!
IT'S CLOSE!!

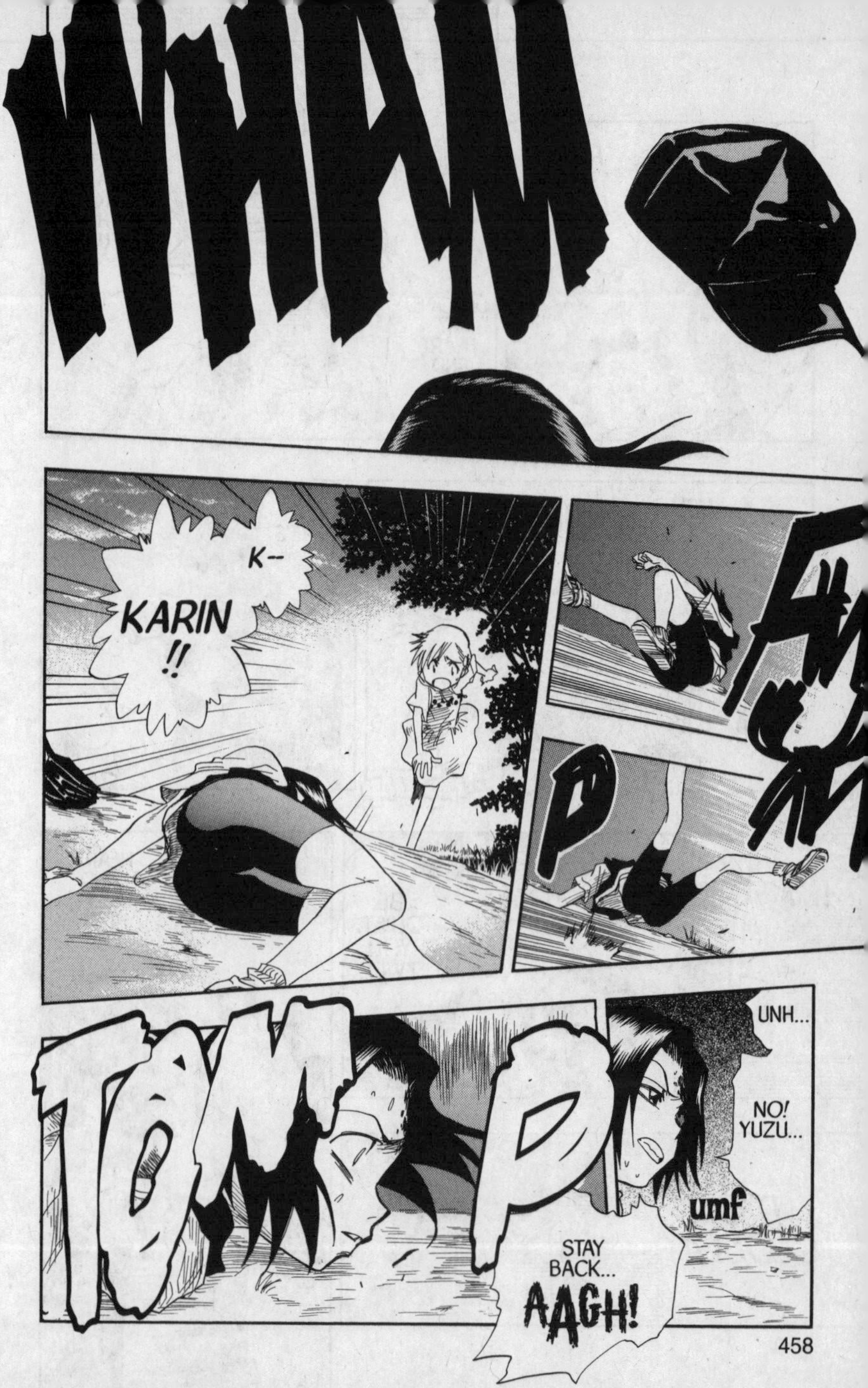
WHAM
K--
KARIN!!
UNH...
NO! YUZU...
umf
TOMP
STAY BACK... AAGH!

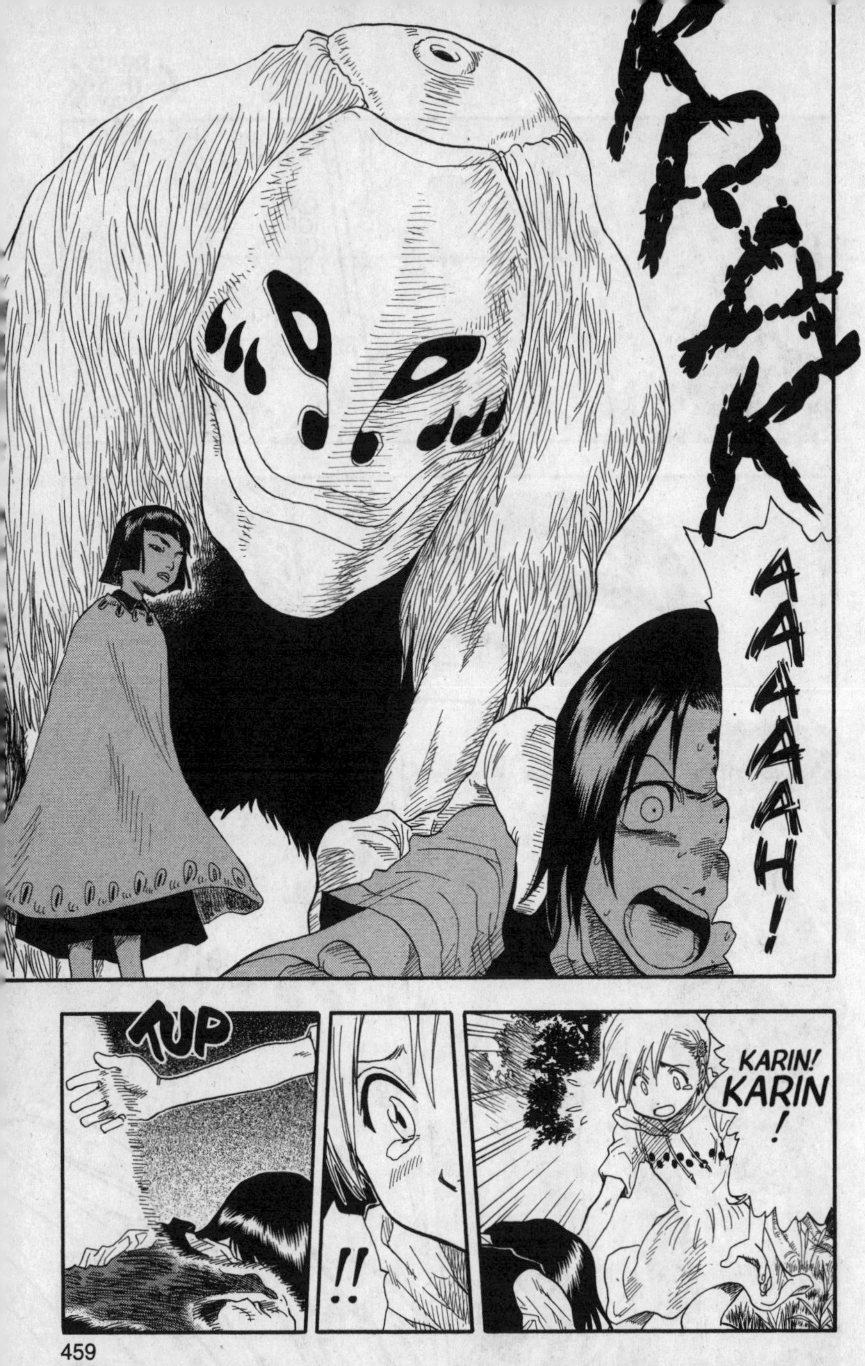

KRAK
AAAAAH!
KARIN! KARIN!
!!
TUP

READ THIS WAY

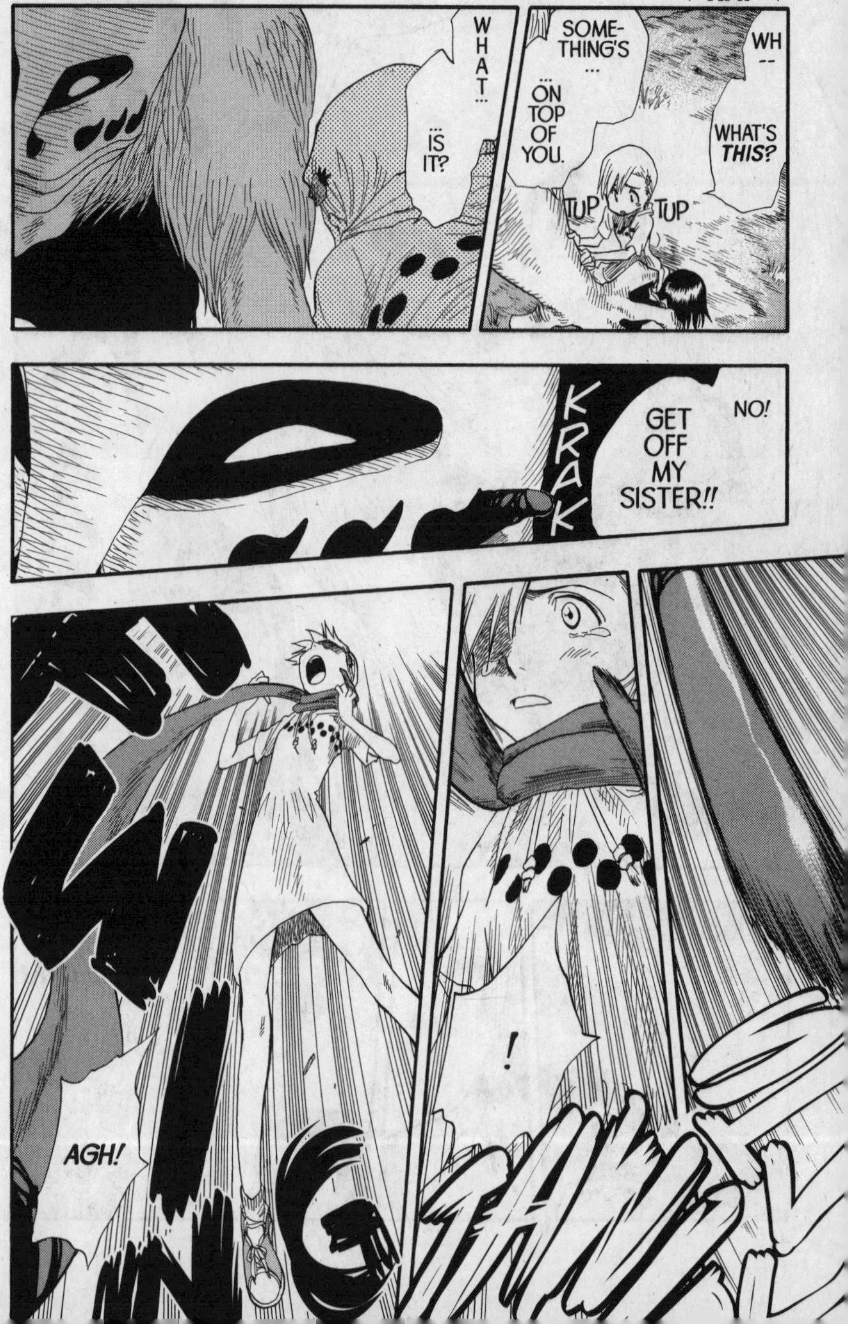
WH--
WHAT'S THIS?
SOME-THING'S... ...ON TOP OF YOU.
TUP TUP
WHAT... ...IS IT?
NO!
GET OFF MY SISTER!!
KRAK
!
THUD
SWING
AGH!

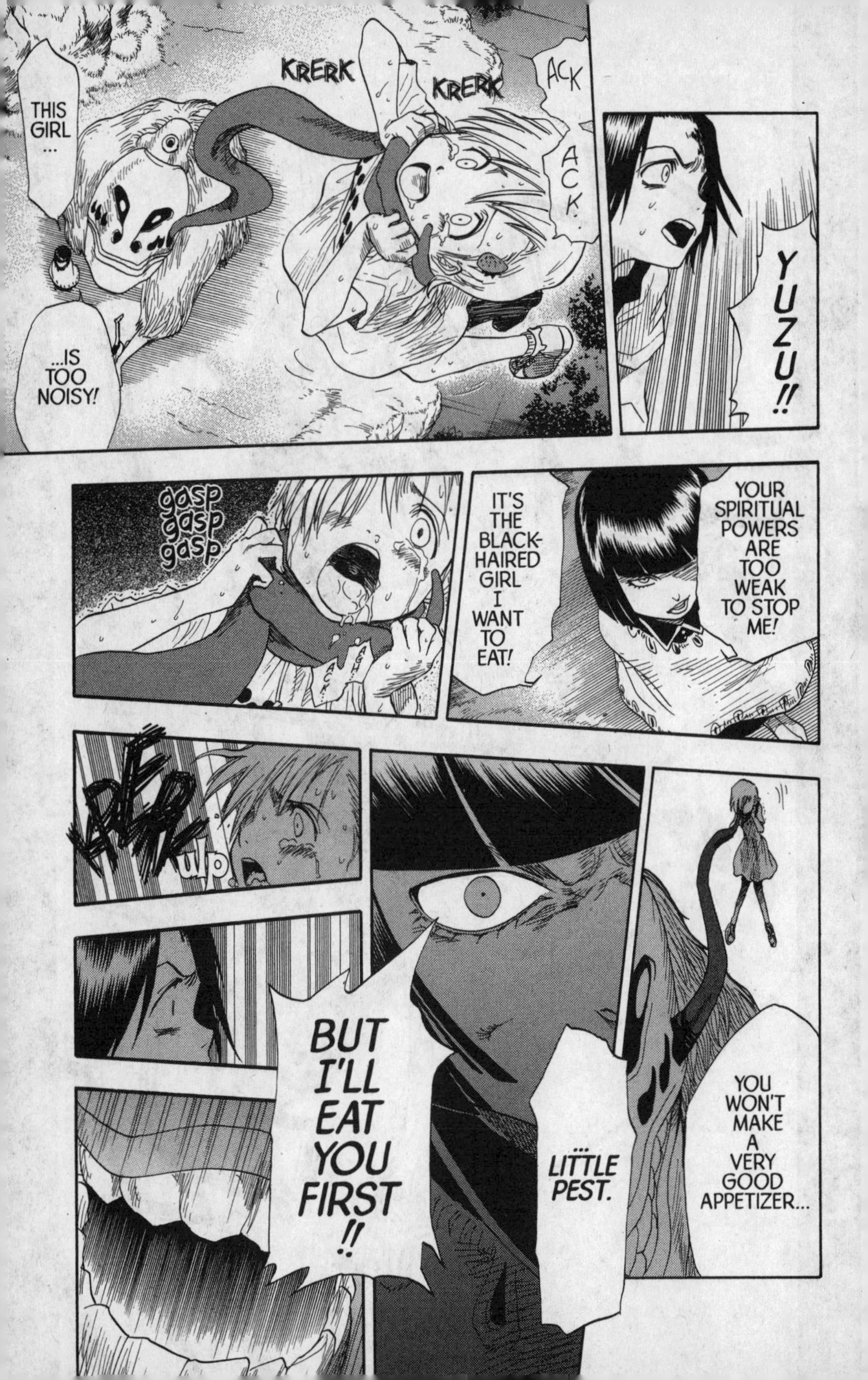
YUZU!!
ACK ACK.
KRERK
KRERK
THIS GIRL ...
...IS TOO NOISY!
YOUR SPIRITUAL POWERS ARE TOO WEAK TO STOP ME!
IT'S THE BLACK-HAIRED GIRL I WANT TO EAT!
gasp gasp gasp
AGH...
ACK...
YOU WON'T MAKE A VERY GOOD APPETIZER...
...LITTLE PEST.
BUT I'LL EAT YOU FIRST!!
gulp

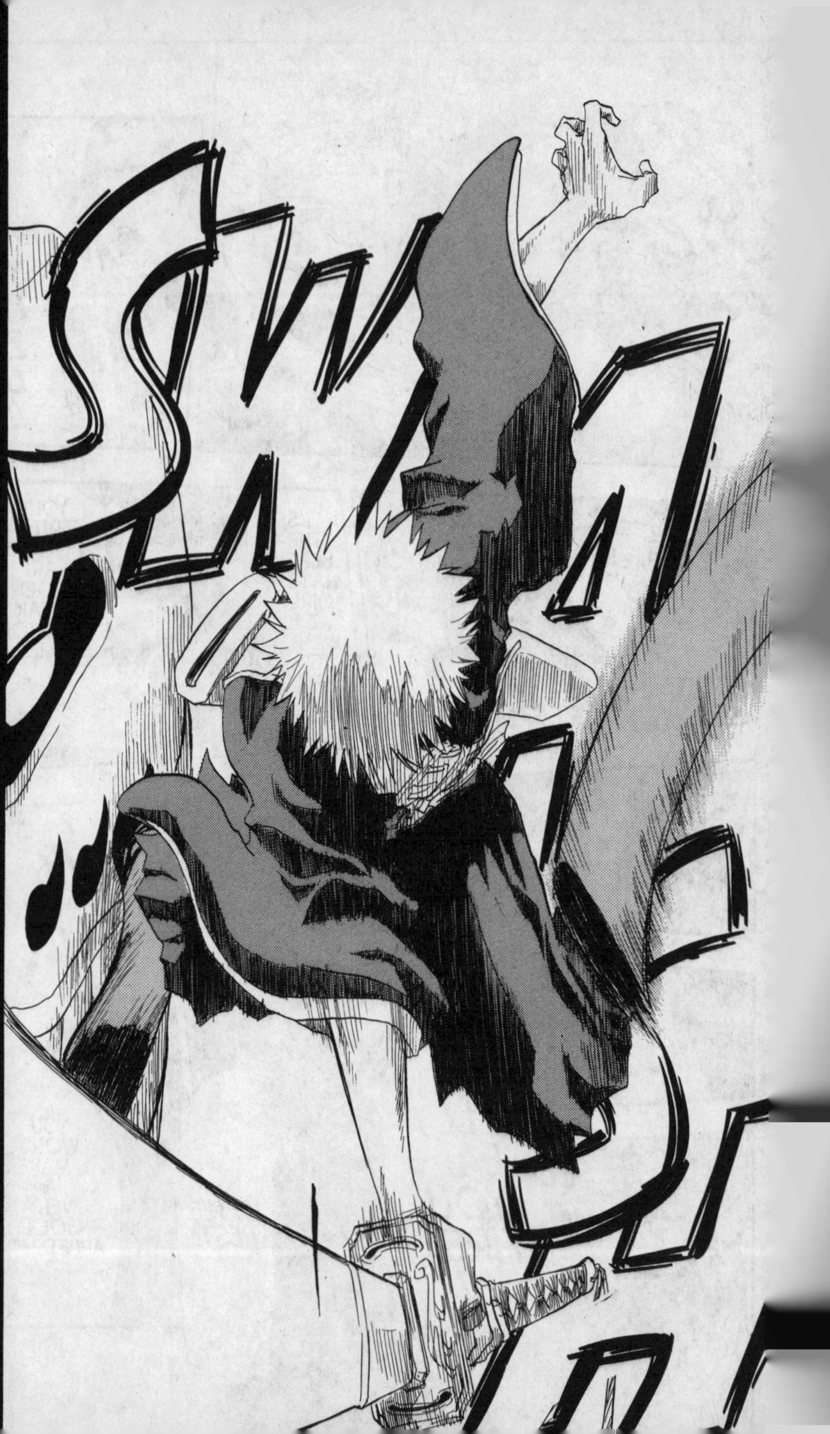

READ THIS WAY

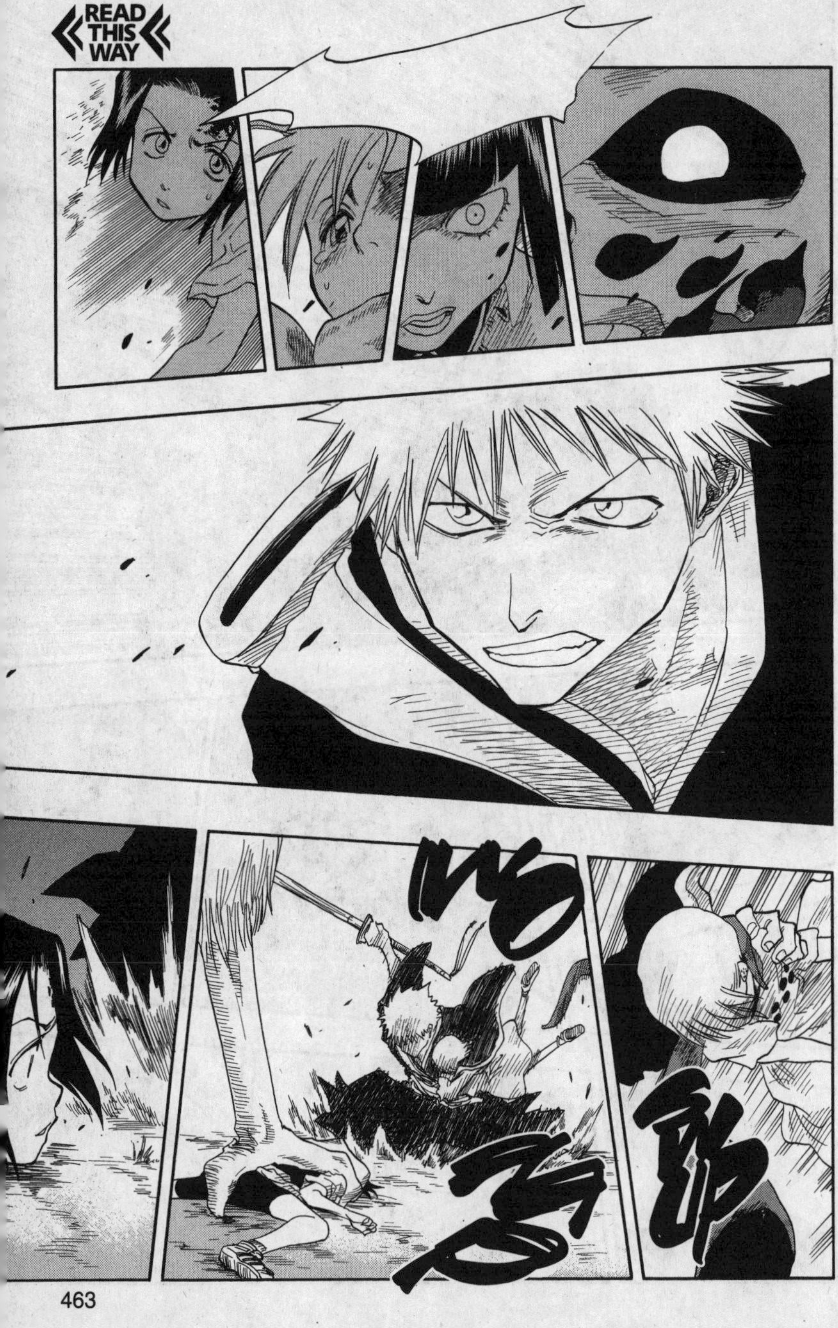

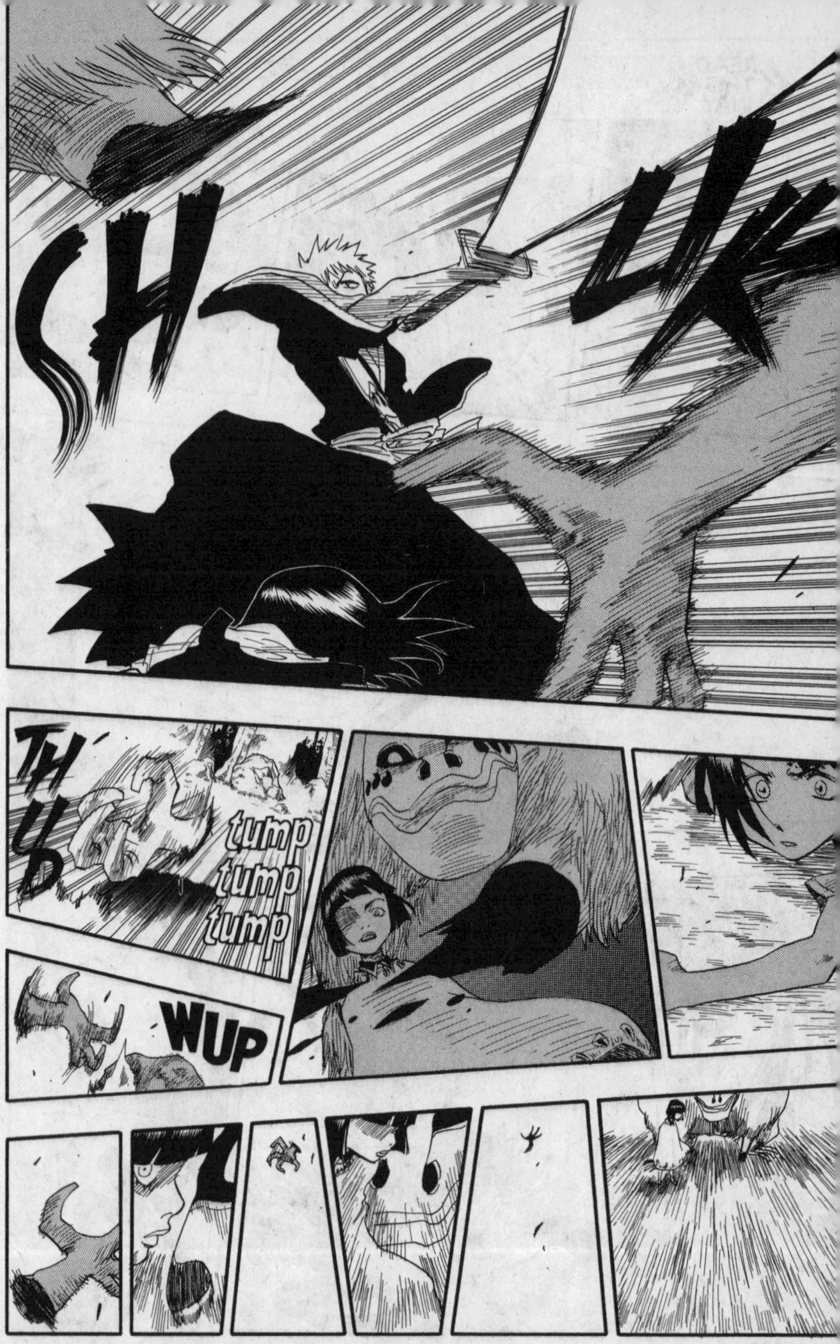
CHUK
THUD
tump
tump
tump
WUP

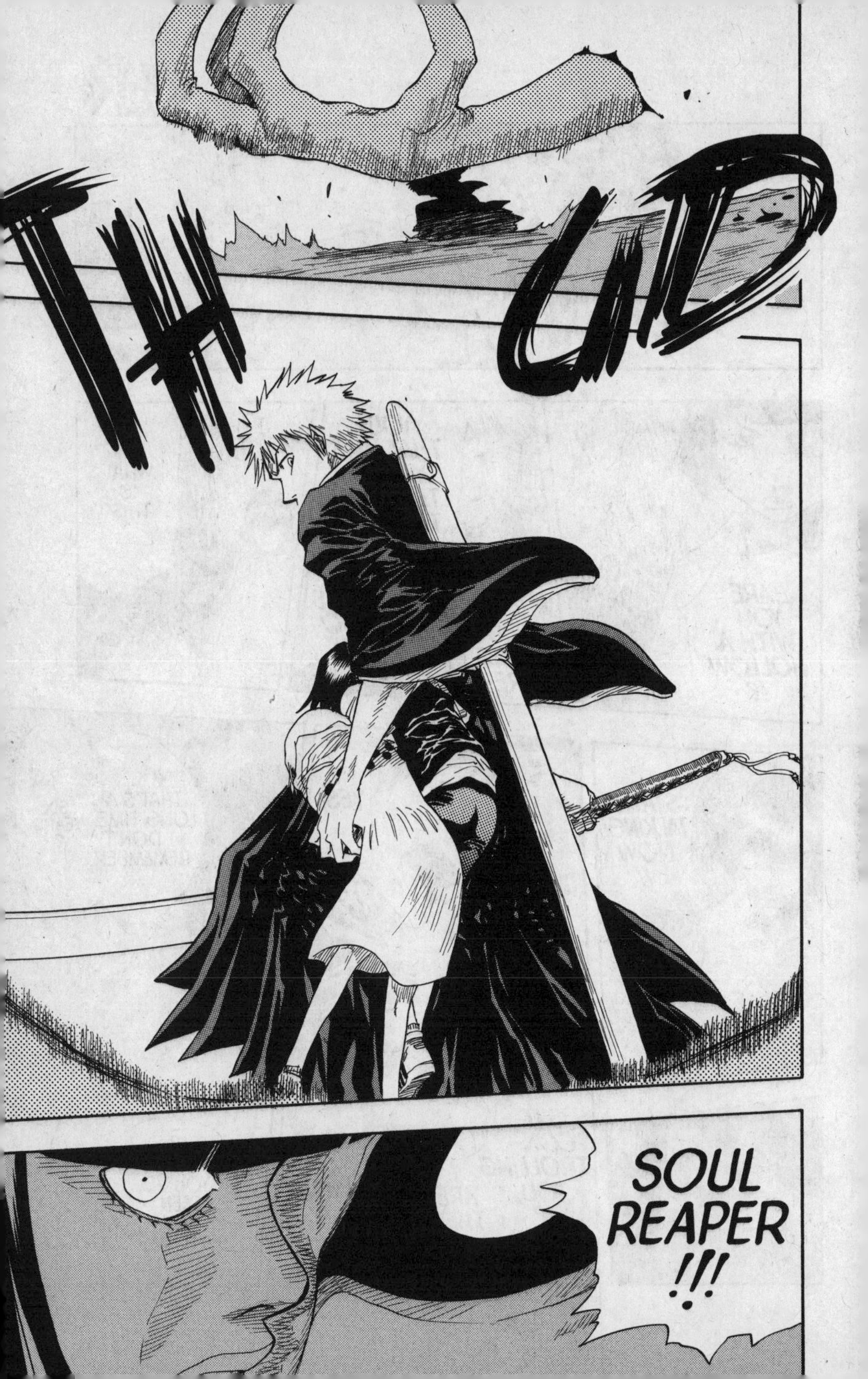
THUD
SOUL REAPER !!!

READ THIS WAY

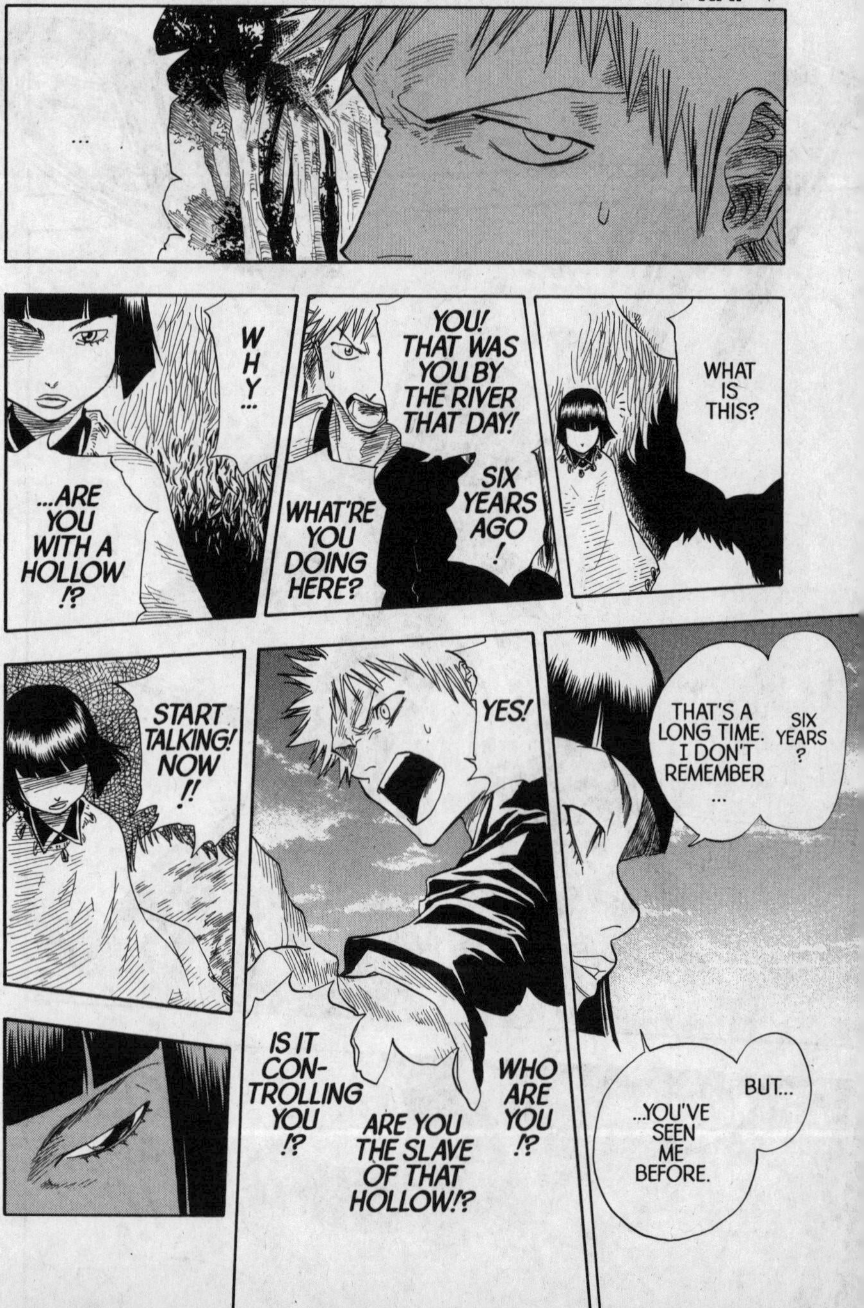
...
WHAT IS THIS?
YOU! THAT WAS YOU BY THE RIVER THAT DAY!
SIX YEARS AGO!
WHAT'RE YOU DOING HERE?
WHY...
...ARE YOU WITH A HOLLOW!?
SIX YEARS?
THAT'S A LONG TIME. I DON'T REMEMBER...
BUT...
...YOU'VE SEEN ME BEFORE.
YES!
WHO ARE YOU!?
ARE YOU THE SLAVE OF THAT HOLLOW!?
IS IT CONTROLLING YOU!?
START TALKING! NOW!!

READ THIS WAY

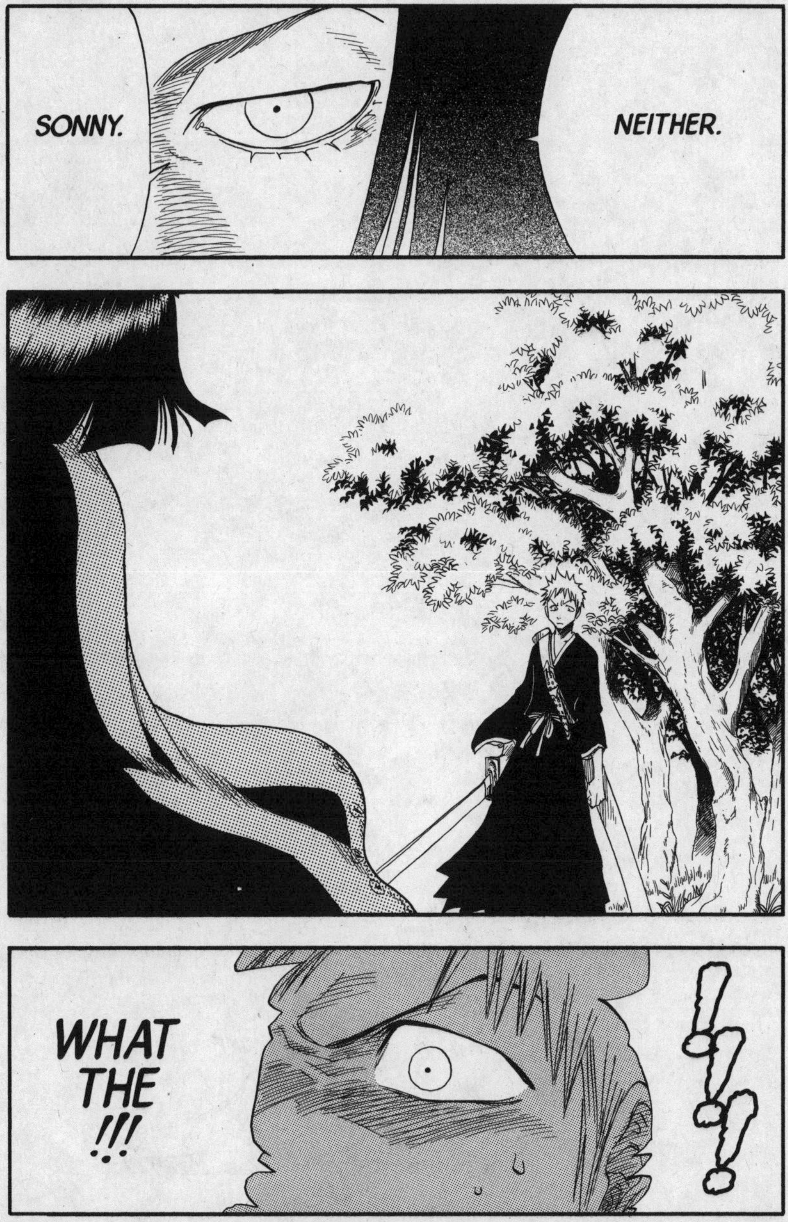
NEITHER.
SONNY.
!!!
WHAT THE !!!

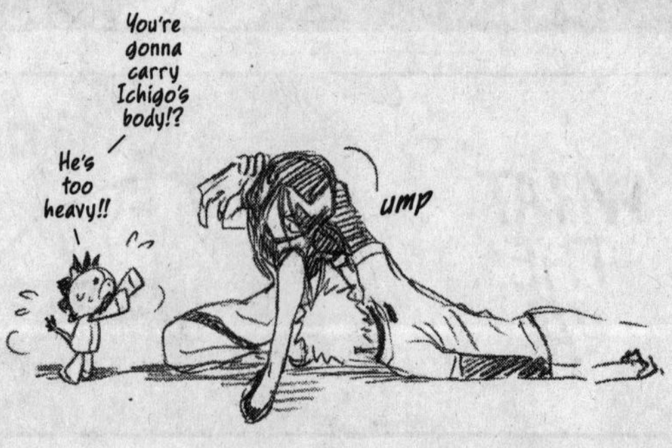
You're gonna carry Ichigo's body!?
ump
He's too heavy!!

21. 6/17 op. 5 A Fighting Boy

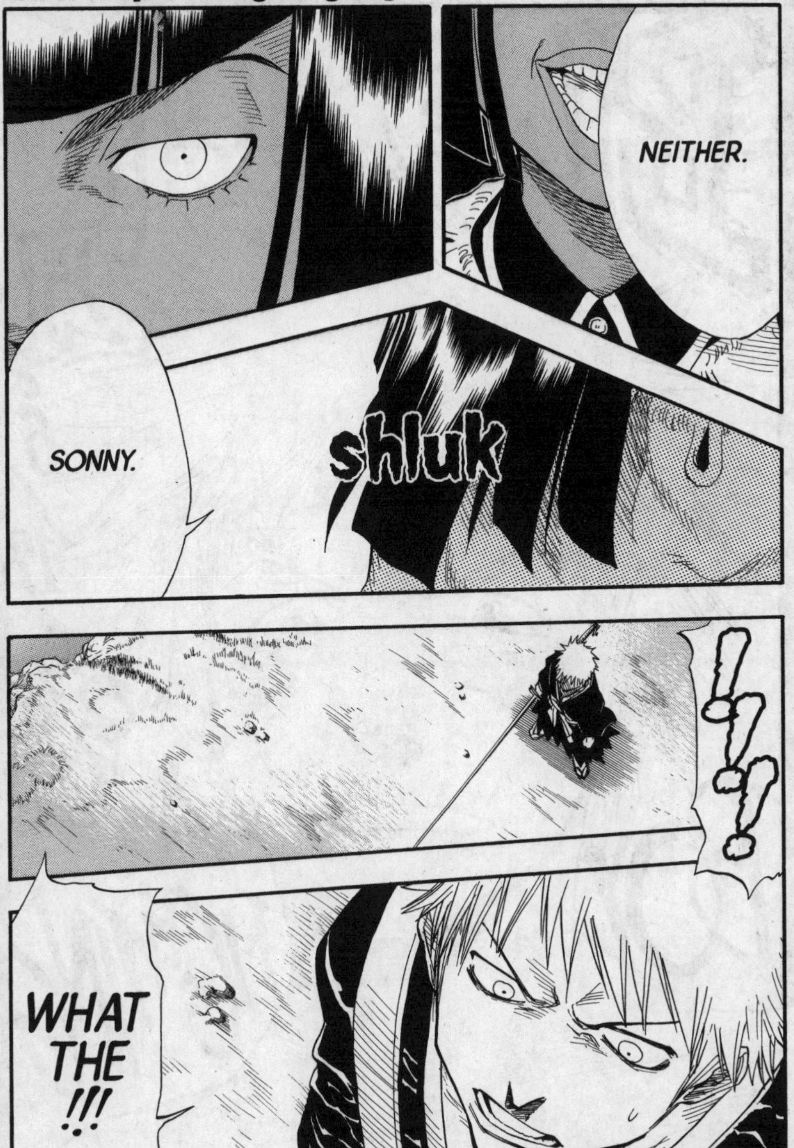
NEITHER.
SONNY.
shluk
!!?!
WHAT THE !!!

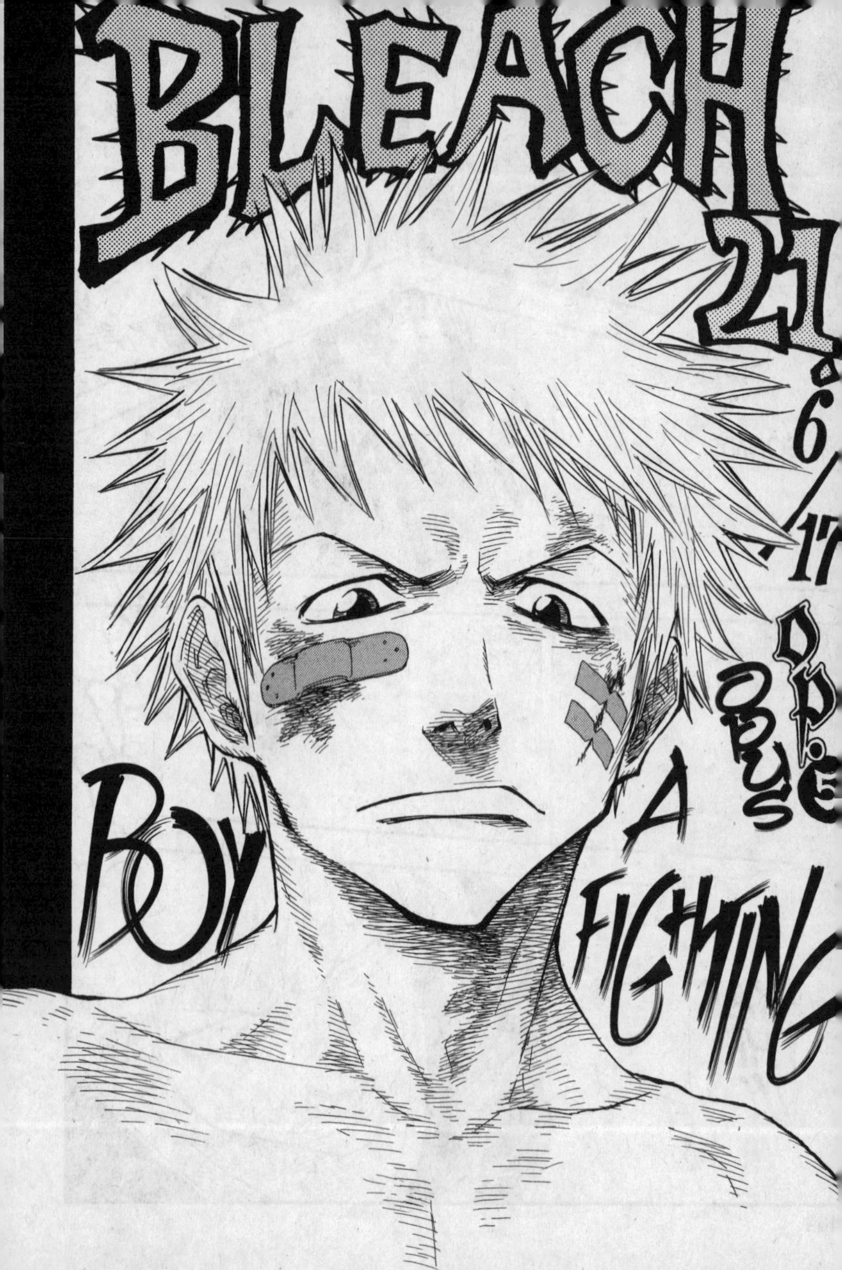
BLEACH
21
6/17
O.P.E
OBUS
A
FIGHTING
BOY

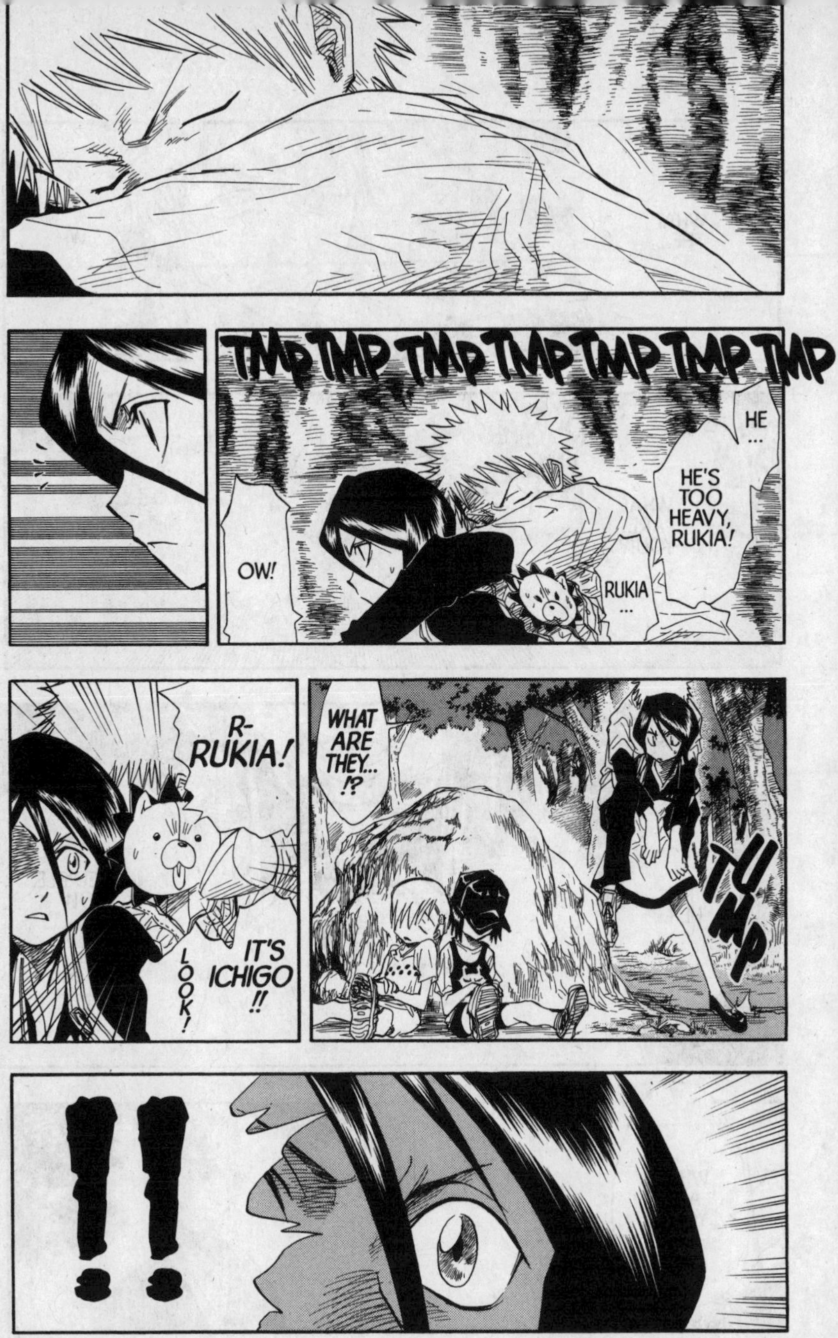
TMP TMP TMP TMP TMP TMP TMP
HE ...
HE'S TOO HEAVY, RUKIA!
RUKIA ...
OW!
WHAT ARE THEY... !?
TUMP
R-RUKIA!
IT'S ICHIGO !!
LOOK!
!!

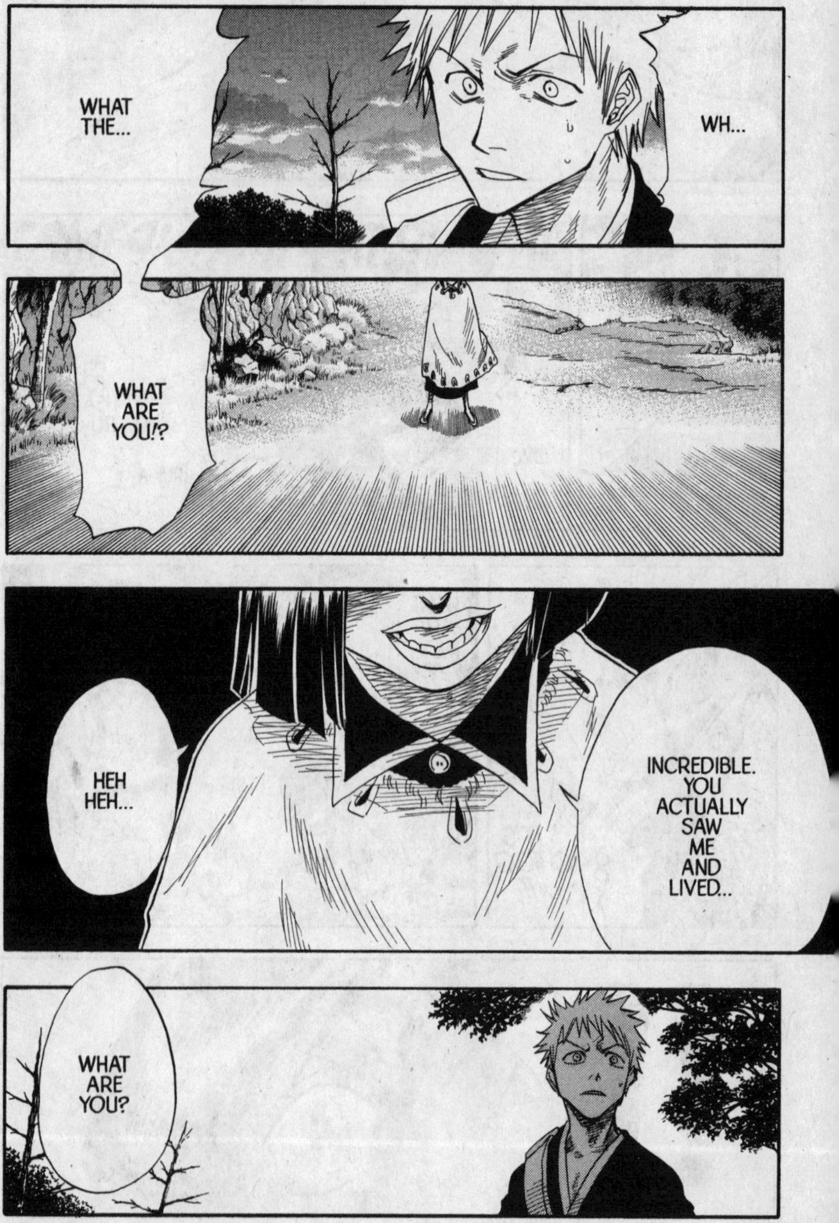
WH...
WHAT THE...
WHAT ARE YOU!?
INCREDIBLE. YOU ACTUALLY SAW ME AND LIVED...
HEH HEH...
WHAT ARE YOU?

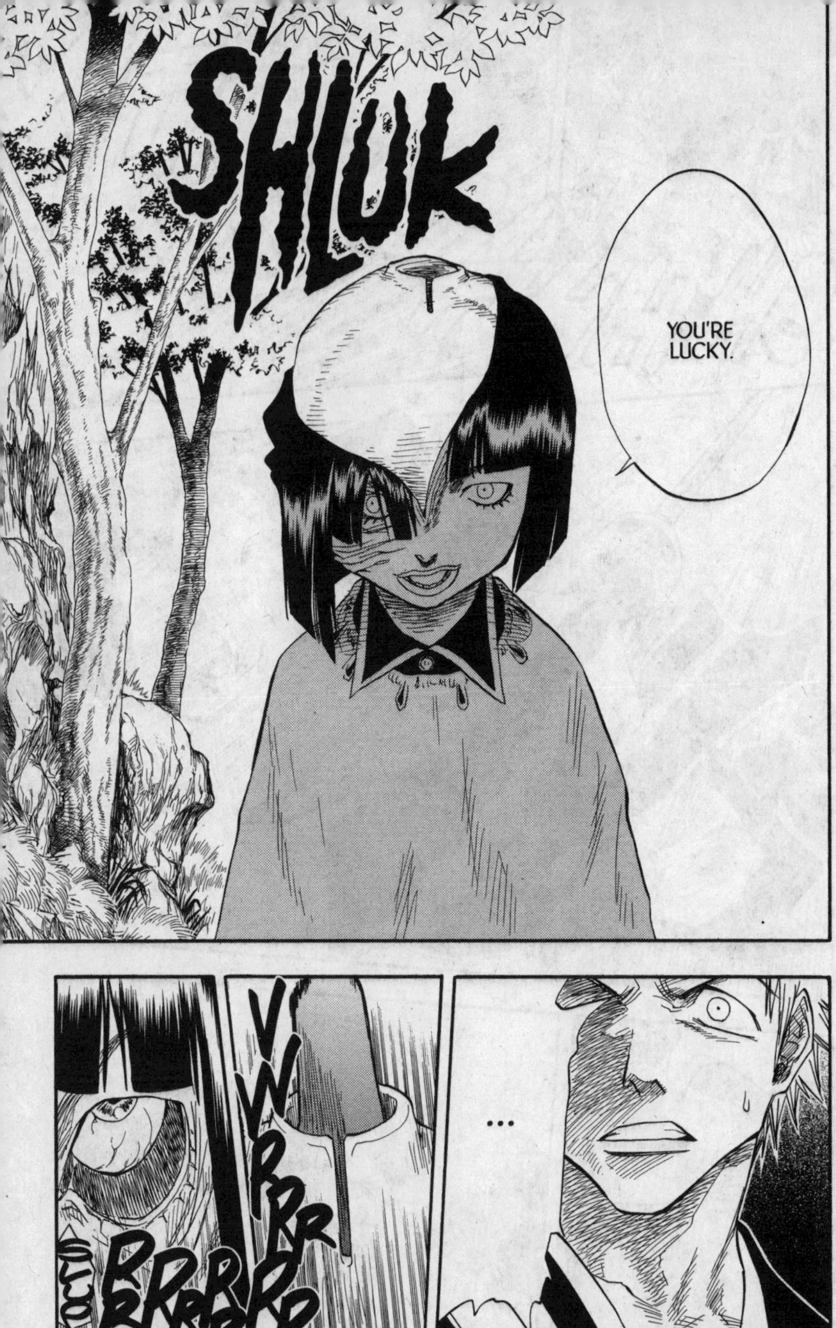
SHLUK
YOU'RE LUCKY.
...
VWRRRRRRRRRR

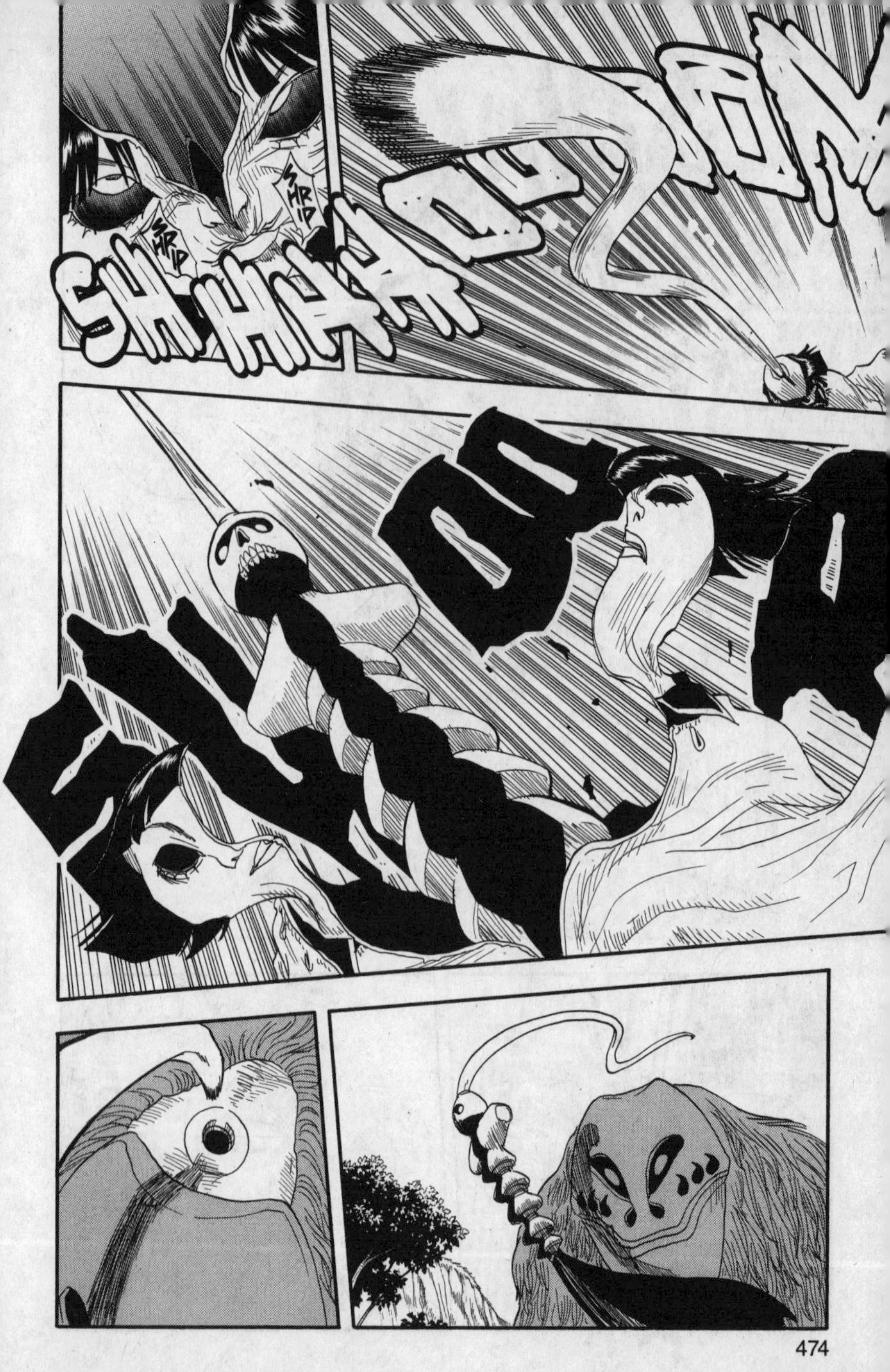
SHRIP
SHRIP

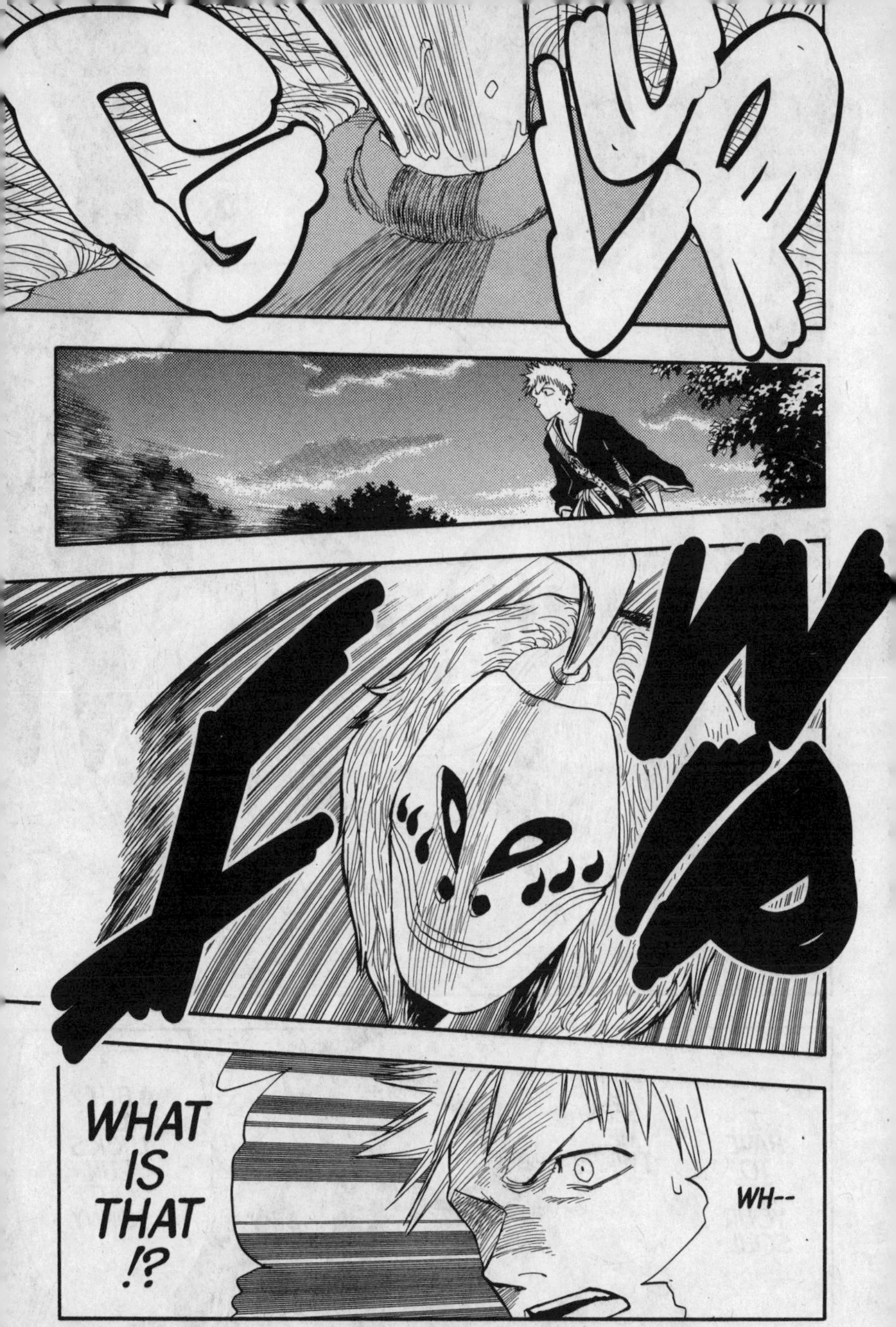
WH--
WHAT IS THAT !?

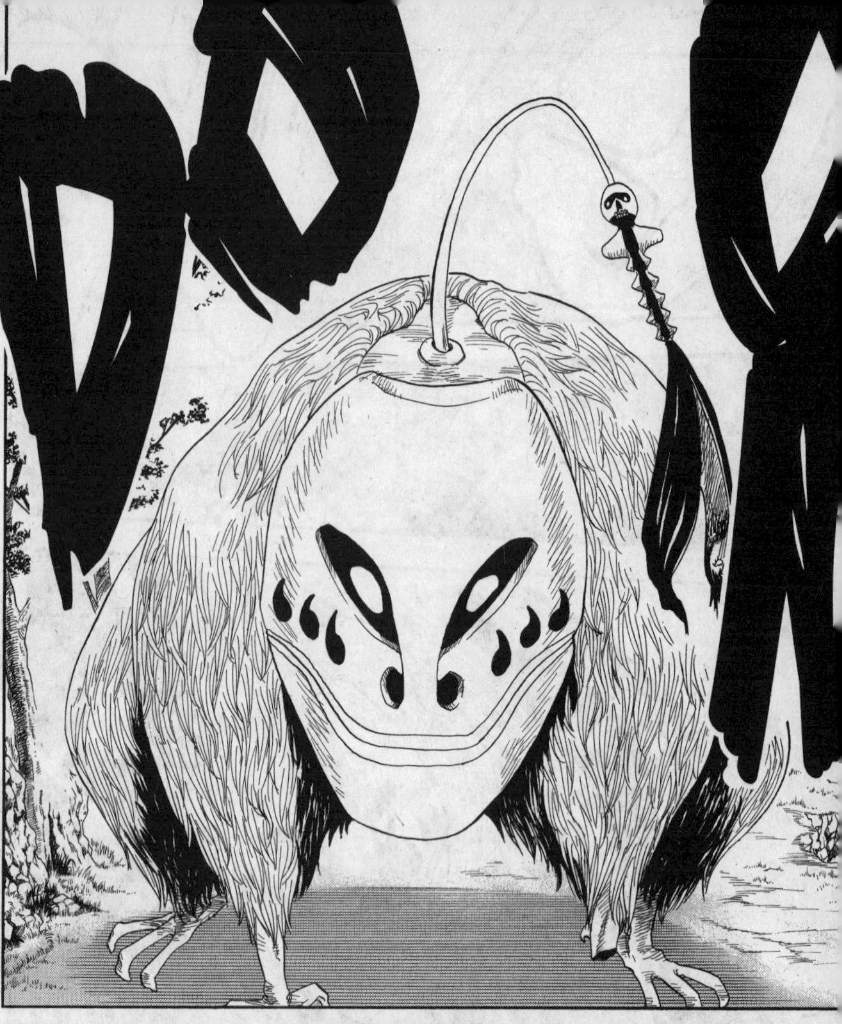
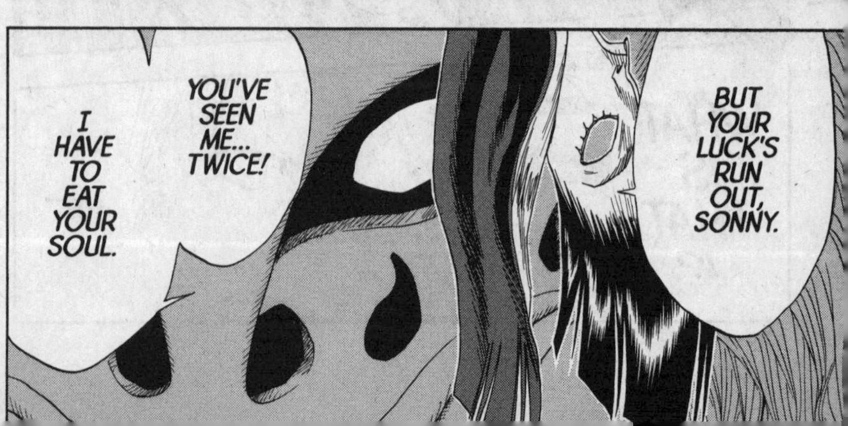
BUT YOUR LUCK'S RUN OUT, SONNY.
YOU'VE SEEN ME... TWICE!
I HAVE TO EAT YOUR SOUL.

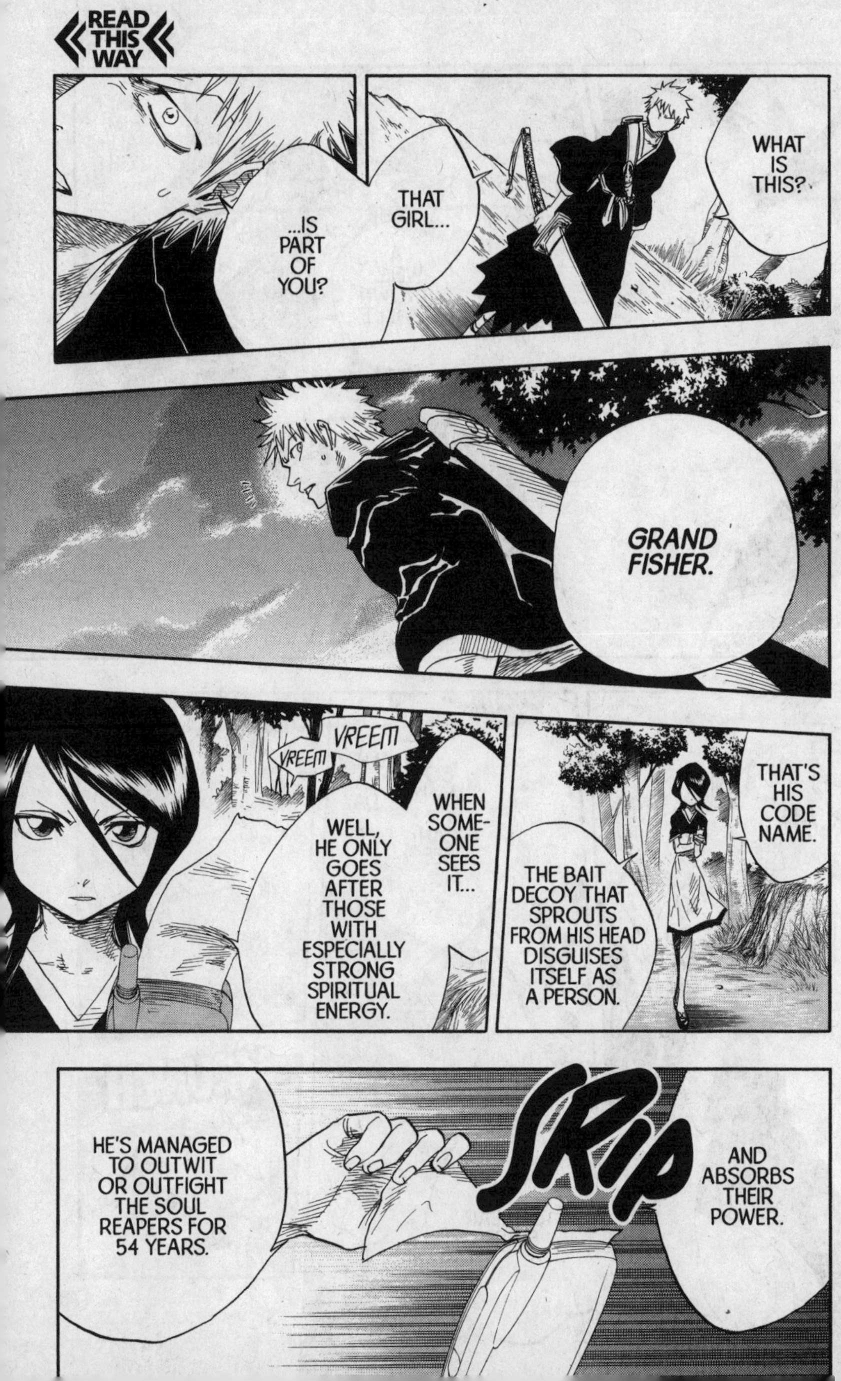
READ THIS WAY
WHAT IS THIS?
THAT GIRL...
...IS PART OF YOU?
GRAND FISHER.
THAT'S HIS CODE NAME.
THE BAIT DECOY THAT SPROUTS FROM HIS HEAD DISGUISES ITSELF AS A PERSON.
VREEM
VREEM
WHEN SOME-ONE SEES IT...
WELL, HE ONLY GOES AFTER THOSE WITH ESPECIALLY STRONG SPIRITUAL ENERGY.
AND ABSORBS THEIR POWER.
SKRIP
HE'S MANAGED TO OUTWIT OR OUTFIGHT THE SOUL REAPERS FOR 54 YEARS.

READ THIS WAY

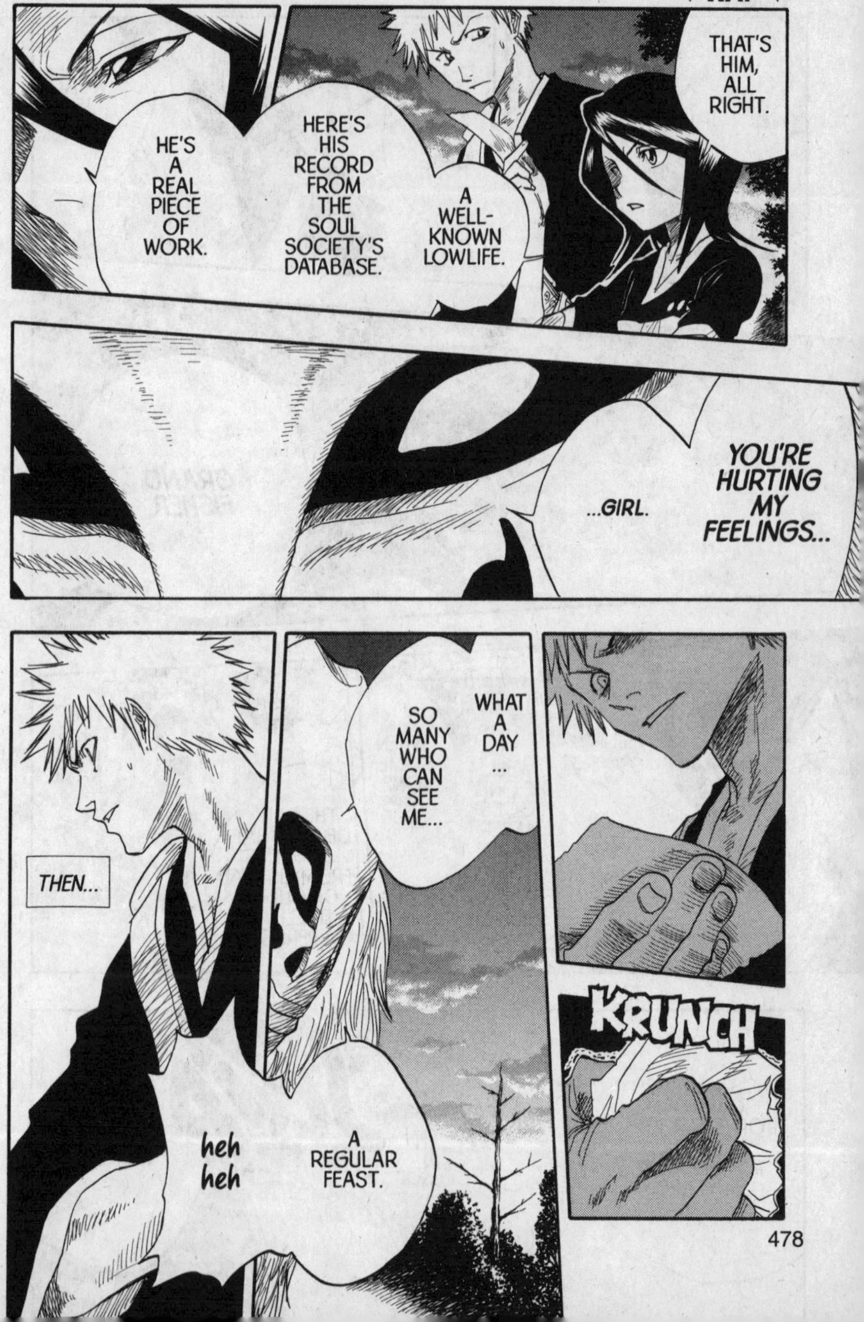

THAT'S HIM, ALL RIGHT.
A WELL-KNOWN LOWLIFE.
HERE'S HIS RECORD FROM THE SOUL SOCIETY'S DATABASE.
HE'S A REAL PIECE OF WORK.
YOU'RE HURTING MY FEELINGS...
...GIRL.
KRUNCH
WHAT A DAY...
SO MANY WHO CAN SEE ME...
A REGULAR FEAST.
heh heh
THEN...

READ THIS WAY

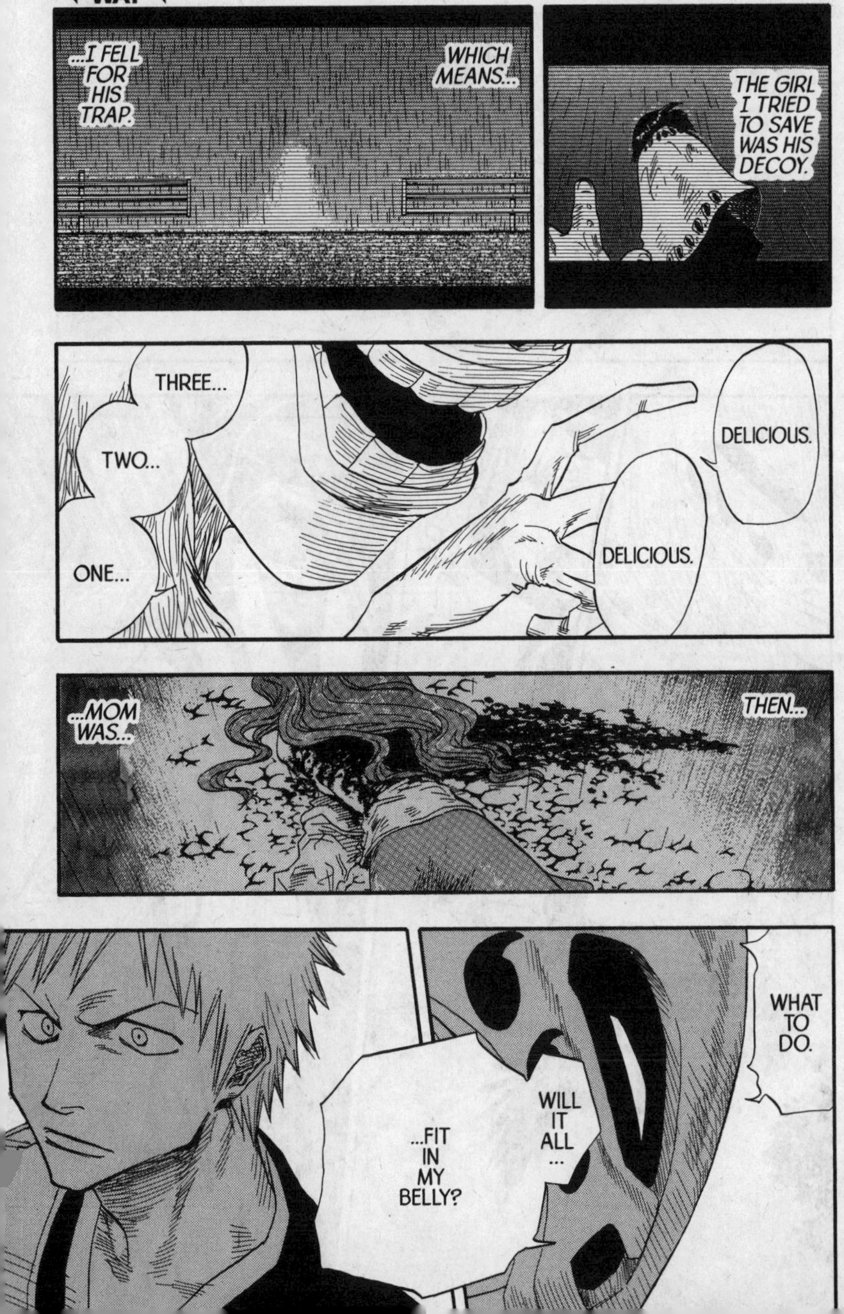
THE GIRL I TRIED TO SAVE WAS HIS DECOY.
WHICH MEANS...
...I FELL FOR HIS TRAP.
DELICIOUS.
DELICIOUS.
THREE...
TWO...
ONE...
THEN...
...MOM WAS...
WHAT TO DO.
WILL IT ALL ...
...FIT IN MY BELLY?

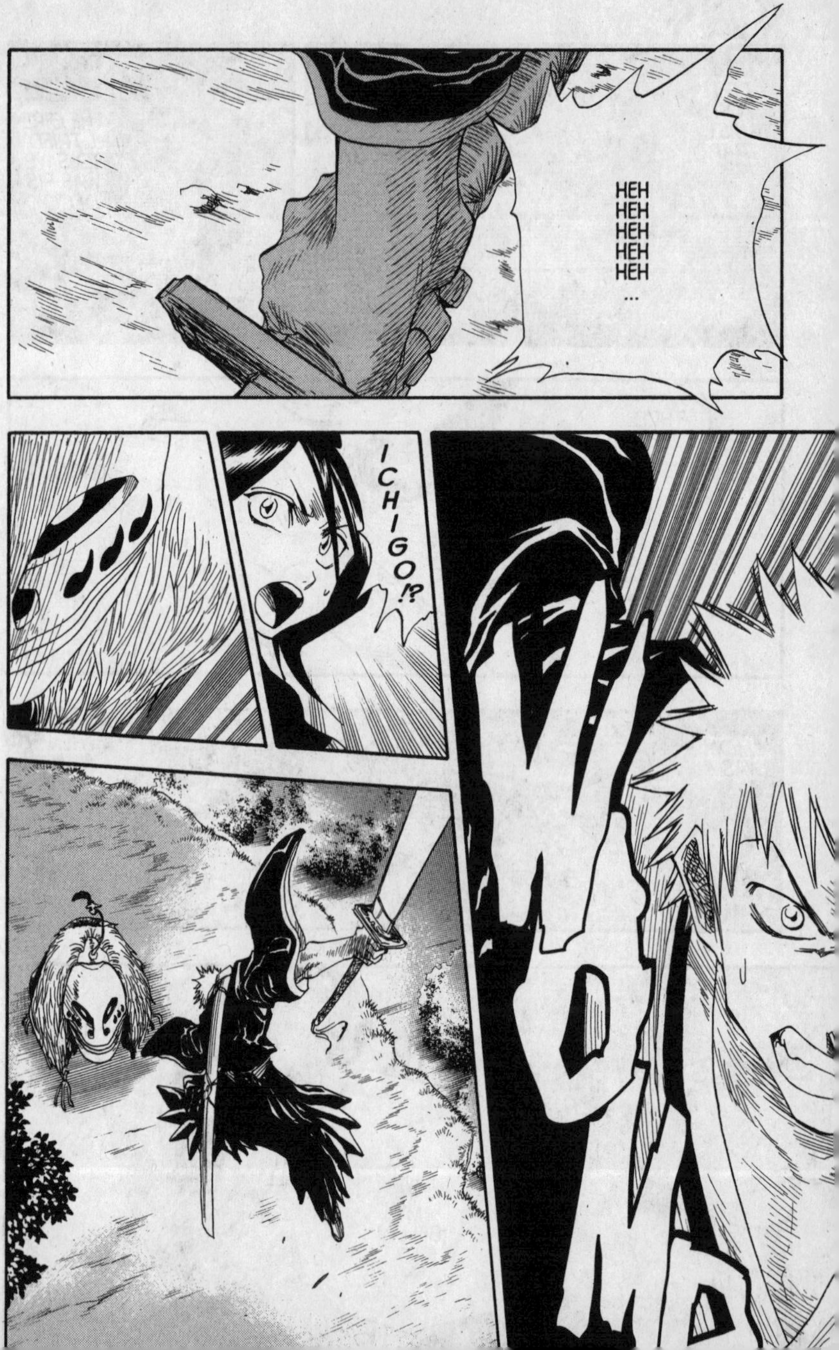
HEH
HEH
HEH
HEH
HEH
...
ICHIGO!?

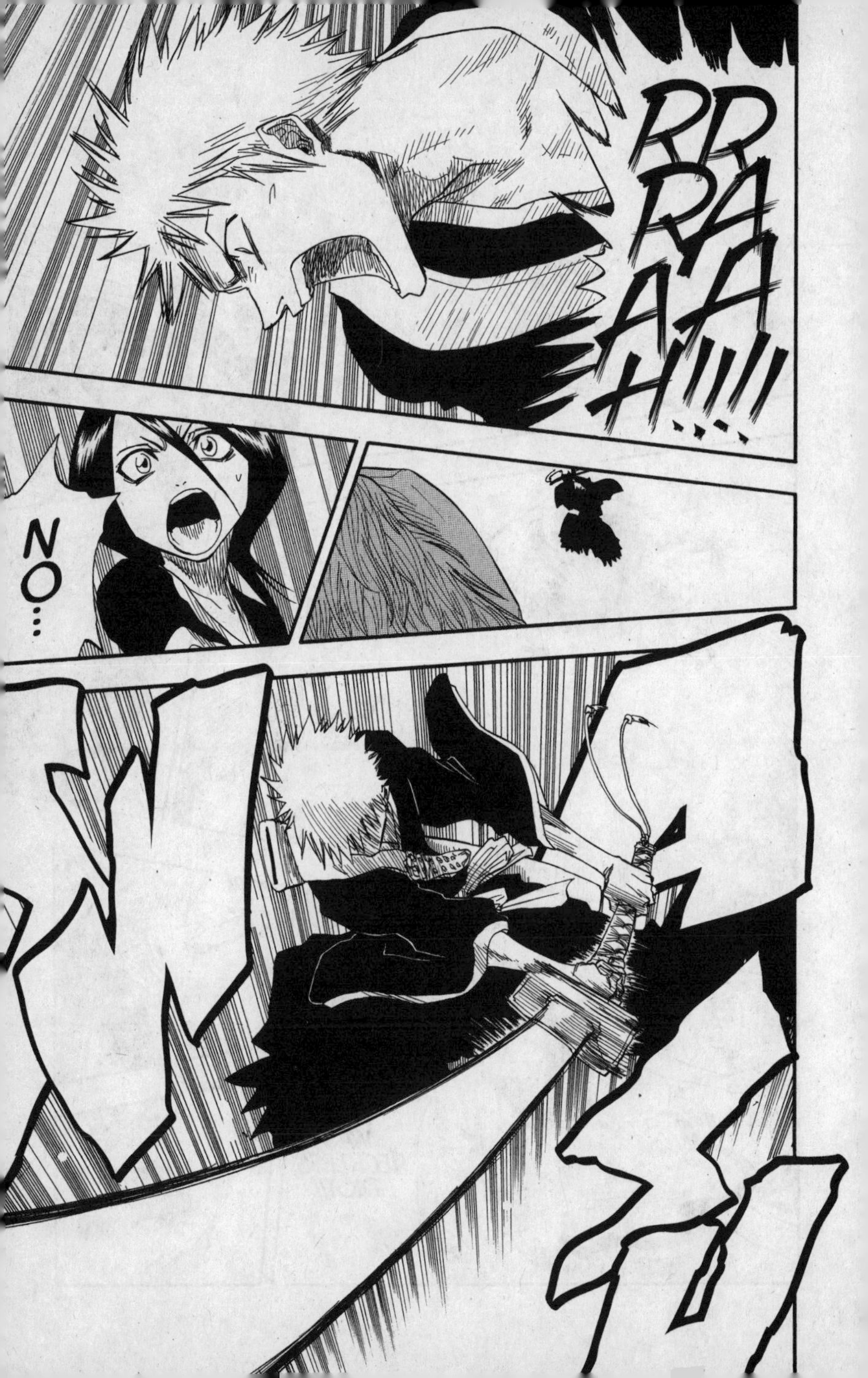
RRRAAH!!!!
....
NO...

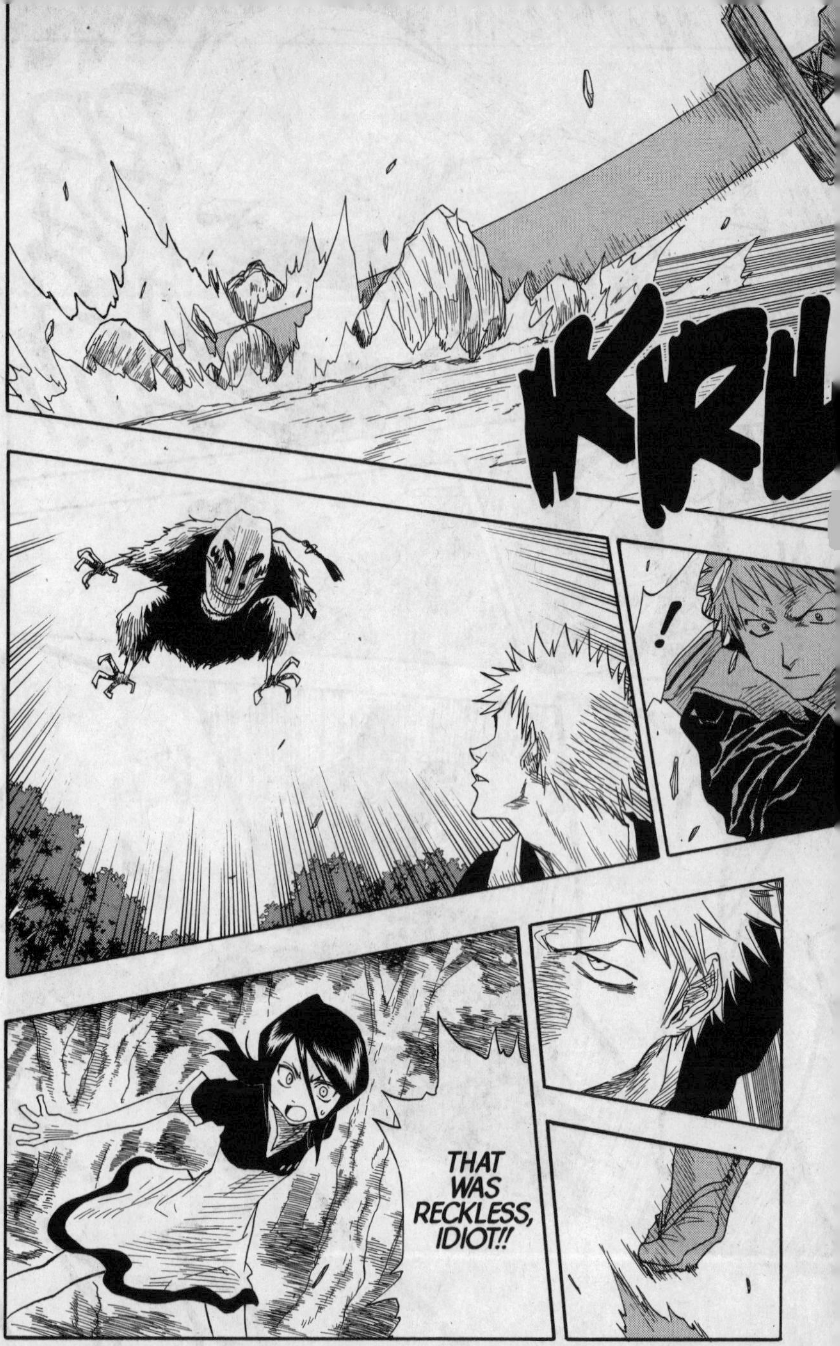
KRU
!
THAT WAS RECKLESS, IDIOT!!

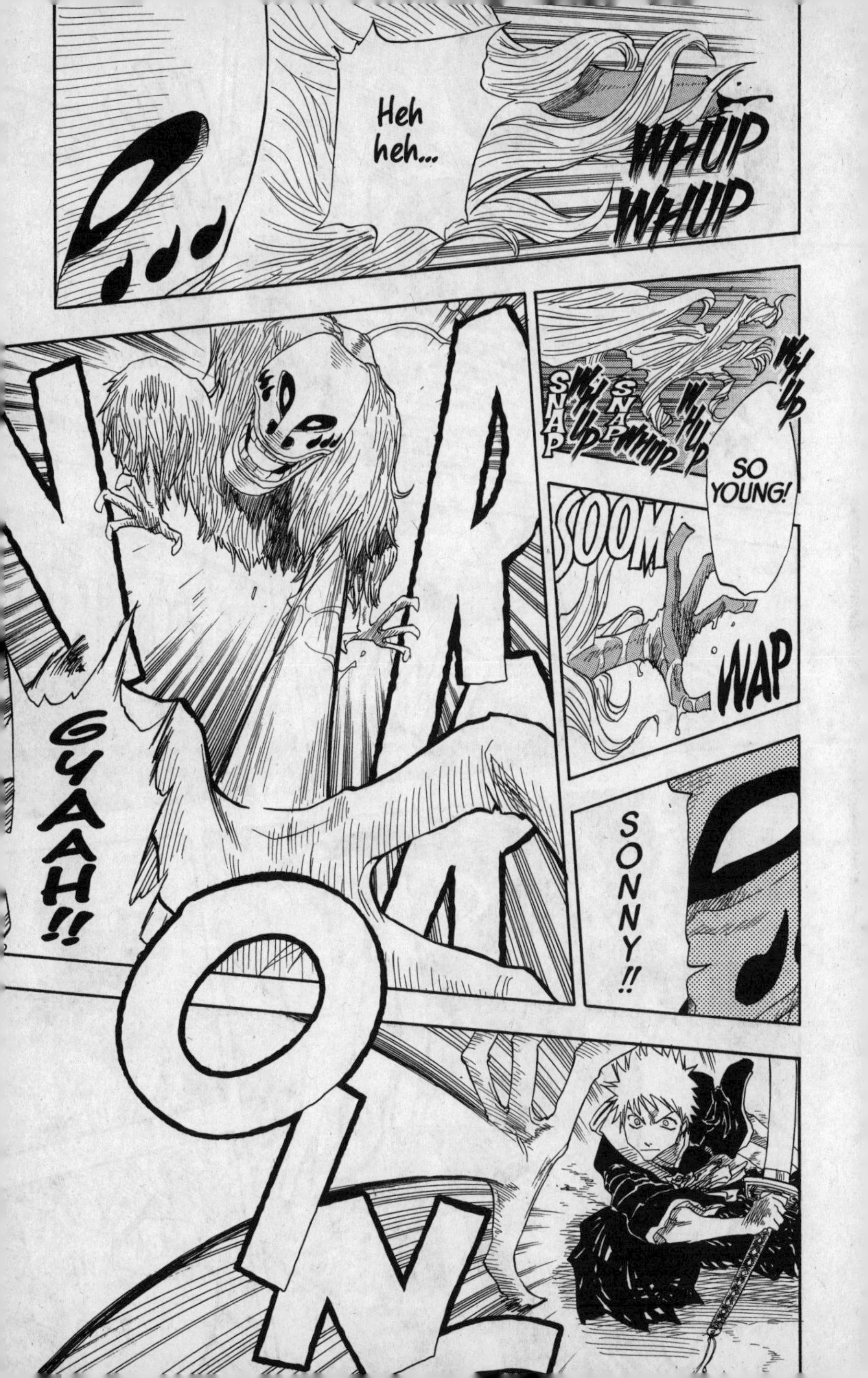
WHUP WHUP
Heh heh...
WHUP
WHUP
SNAP
WHUP
SNAP
WHUP
SO YOUNG!
SOOM
WAP
SONNY!!
WAP
GYAAH!!

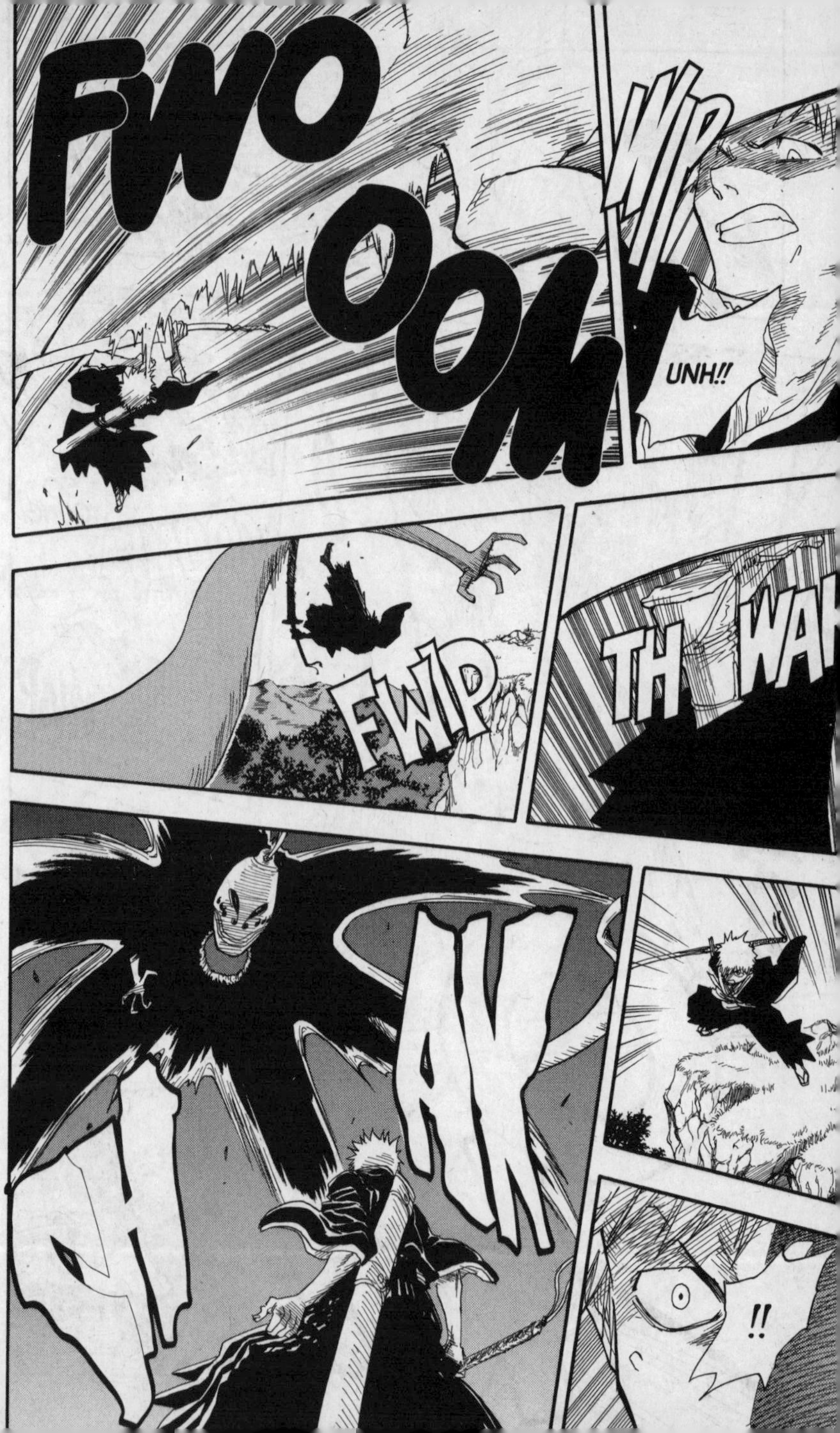
WIP
UNH!!
FWOOOM
THWAK
FWIP
!!

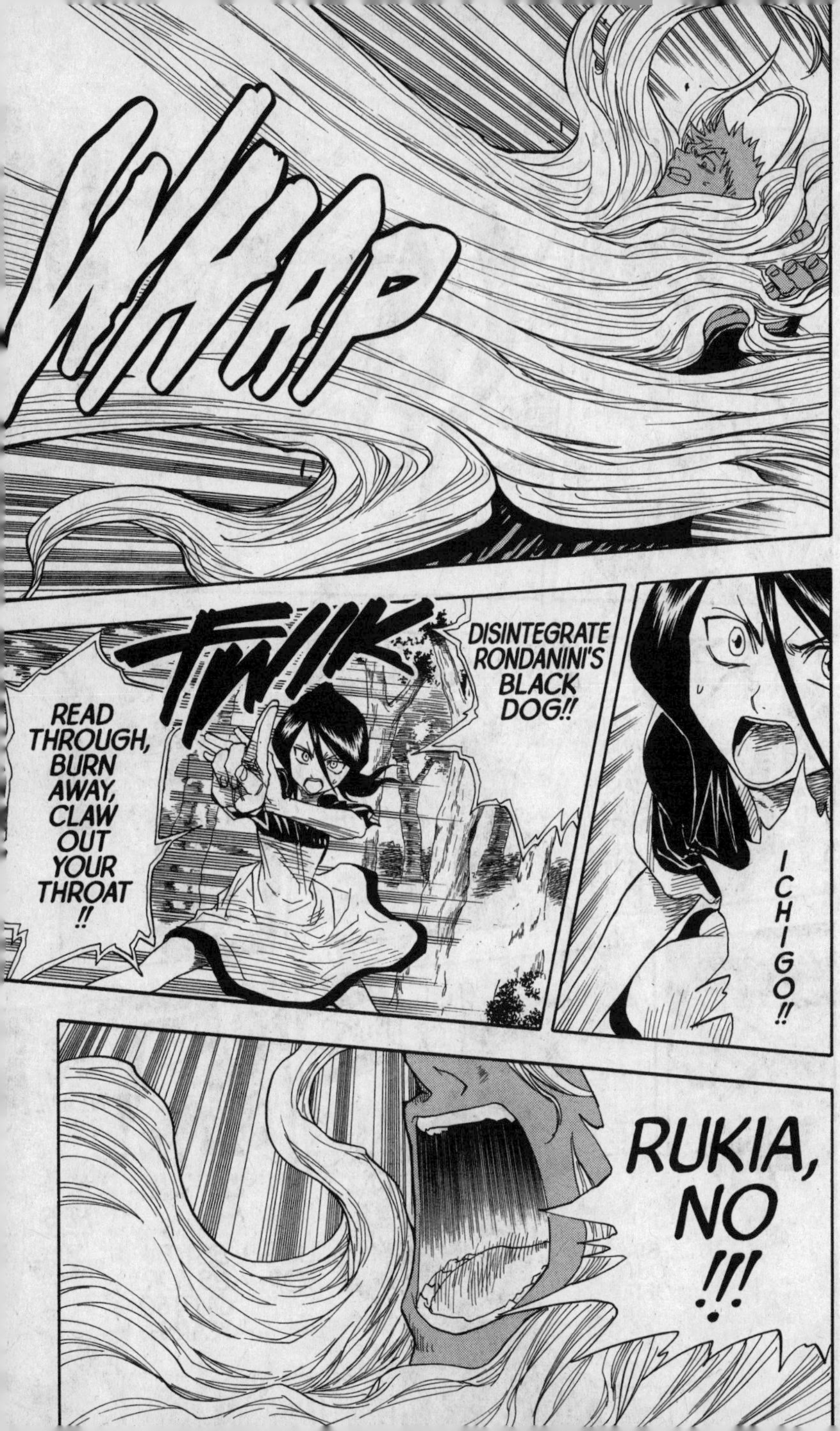
WHAP
ICHIGO!!
DISINTEGRATE RONDANINI'S BLACK DOG!!
TWIK
READ THROUGH, BURN AWAY, CLAW OUT YOUR THROAT!!
RUKIA, NO!!!

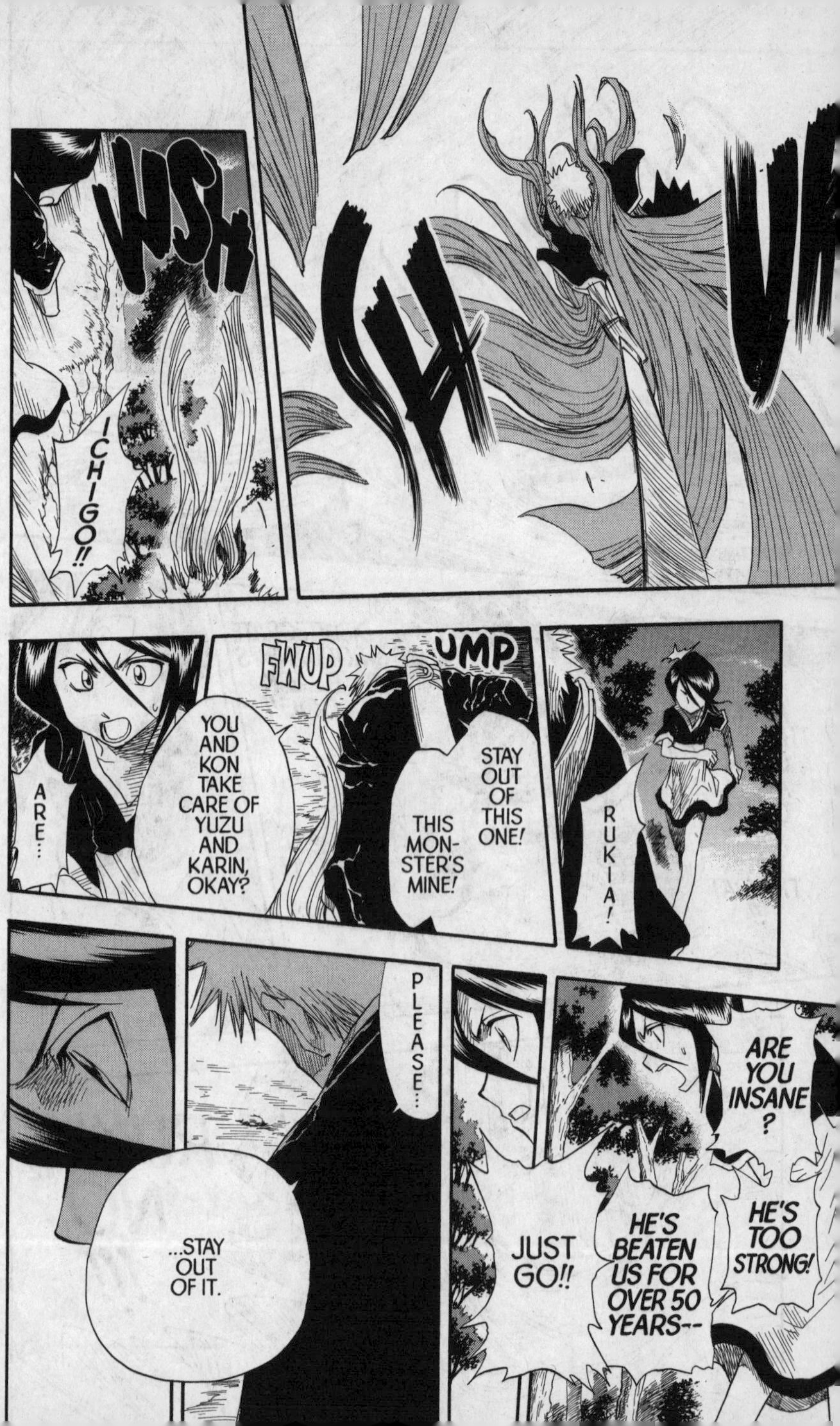
WSH
ICHIGO!!
RUKIA!
FWUP
UMP
STAY OUT OF THIS ONE!
THIS MONSTER'S MINE!
YOU AND KON TAKE CARE OF YUZU AND KARIN, OKAY?
ARE...
ARE YOU INSANE?
HE'S TOO STRONG!
HE'S BEATEN US FOR OVER 50 YEARS--
JUST GO!!
PLEASE...
...STAY OUT OF IT.

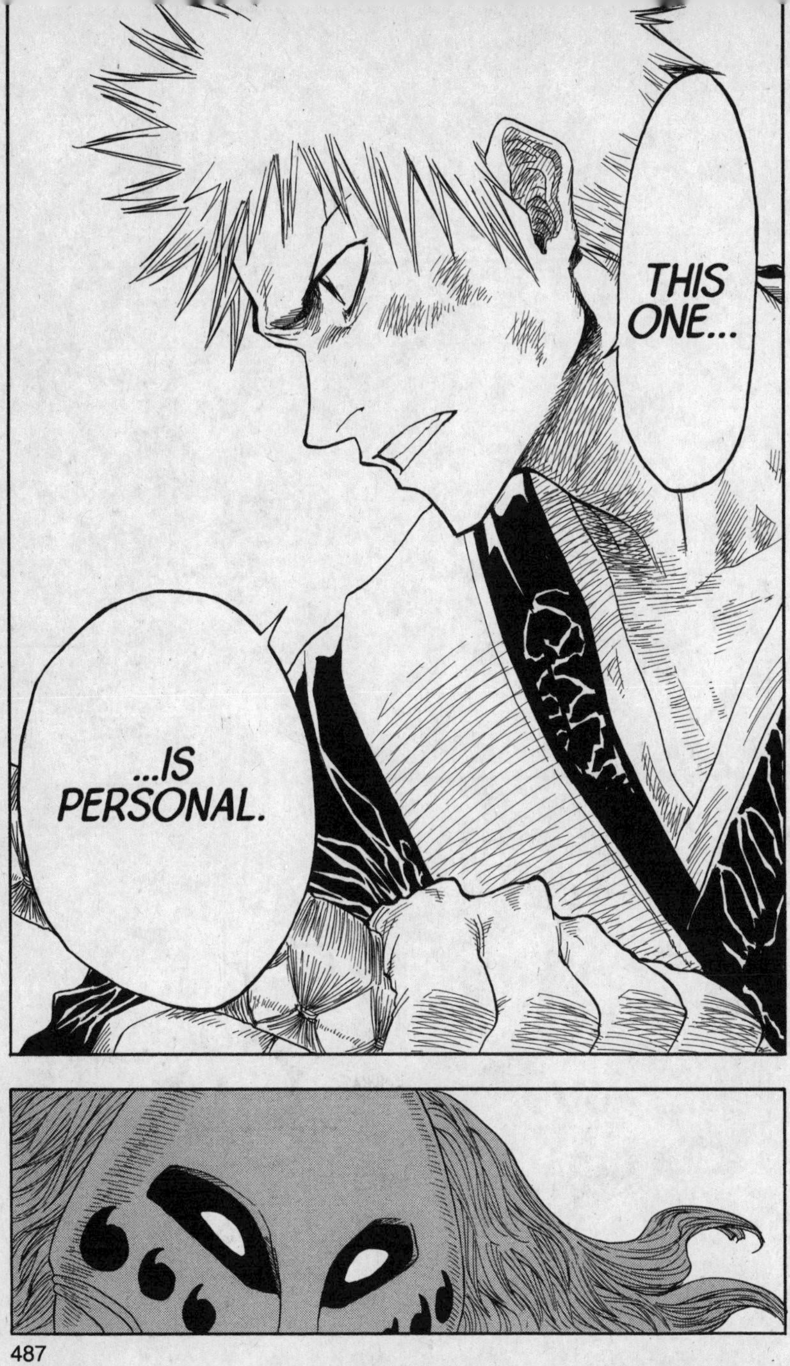
THIS ONE...
...IS PERSONAL.

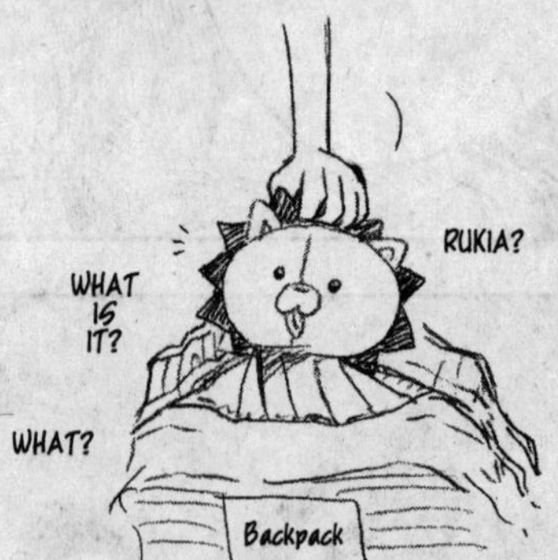
RUKIA?
WHAT IS IT?
WHAT?
Backpack

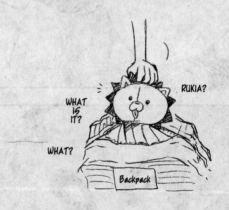

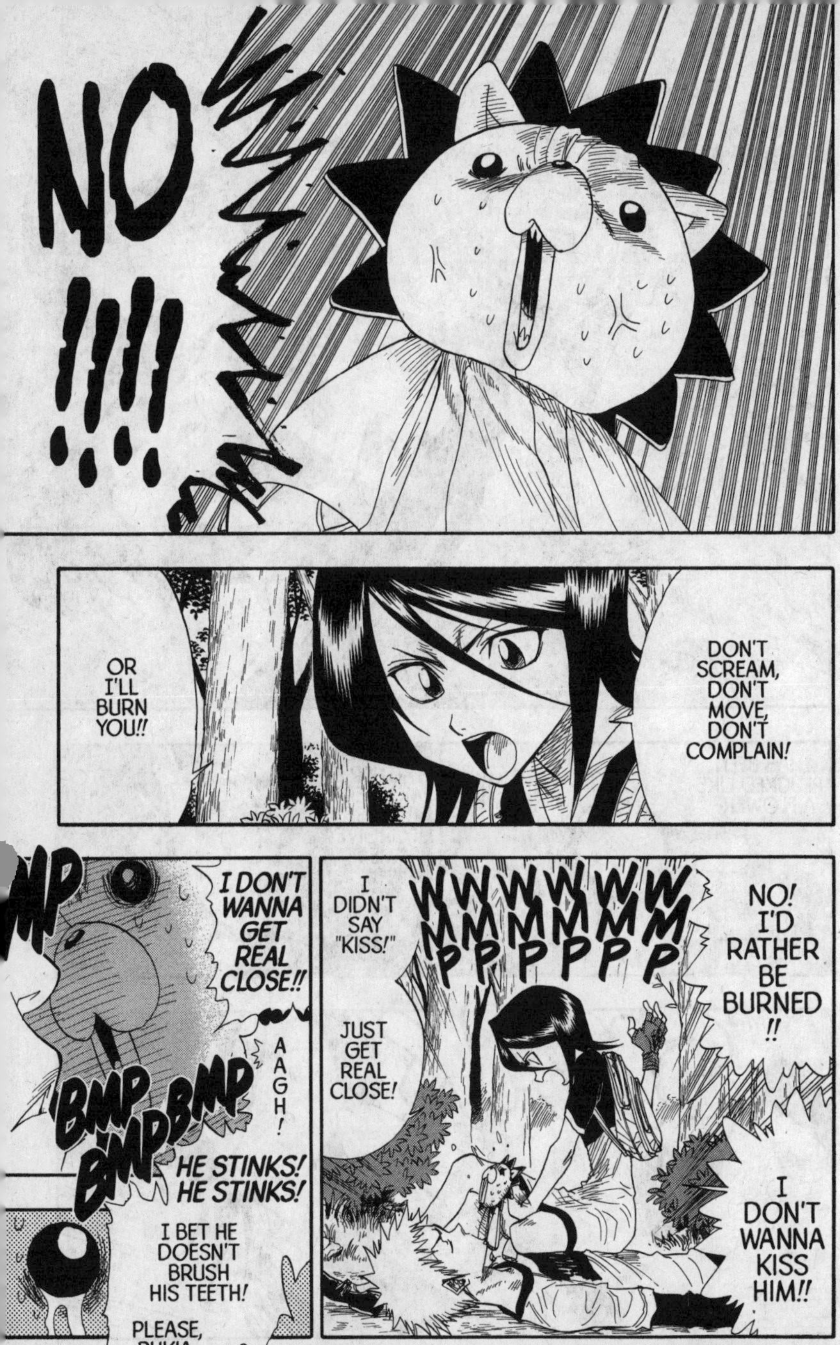
NO!!!!
DON'T SCREAM, DON'T MOVE, DON'T COMPLAIN!
OR I'LL BURN YOU!!
NO! I'D RATHER BE BURNED!!
WWWWWWW MMMMMMM PPPPPP
I DIDN'T SAY "KISS!"
JUST GET REAL CLOSE!
I DON'T WANNA KISS HIM!!
I DON'T WANNA GET REAL CLOSE!!
AAGH!
BMP BMP BMP BMP
HE STINKS! HE STINKS!
I BET HE DOESN'T BRUSH HIS TEETH!
PLEASE, RUKIA, NO!!
22. 6/17 op. 6 Battle in the Graveyard

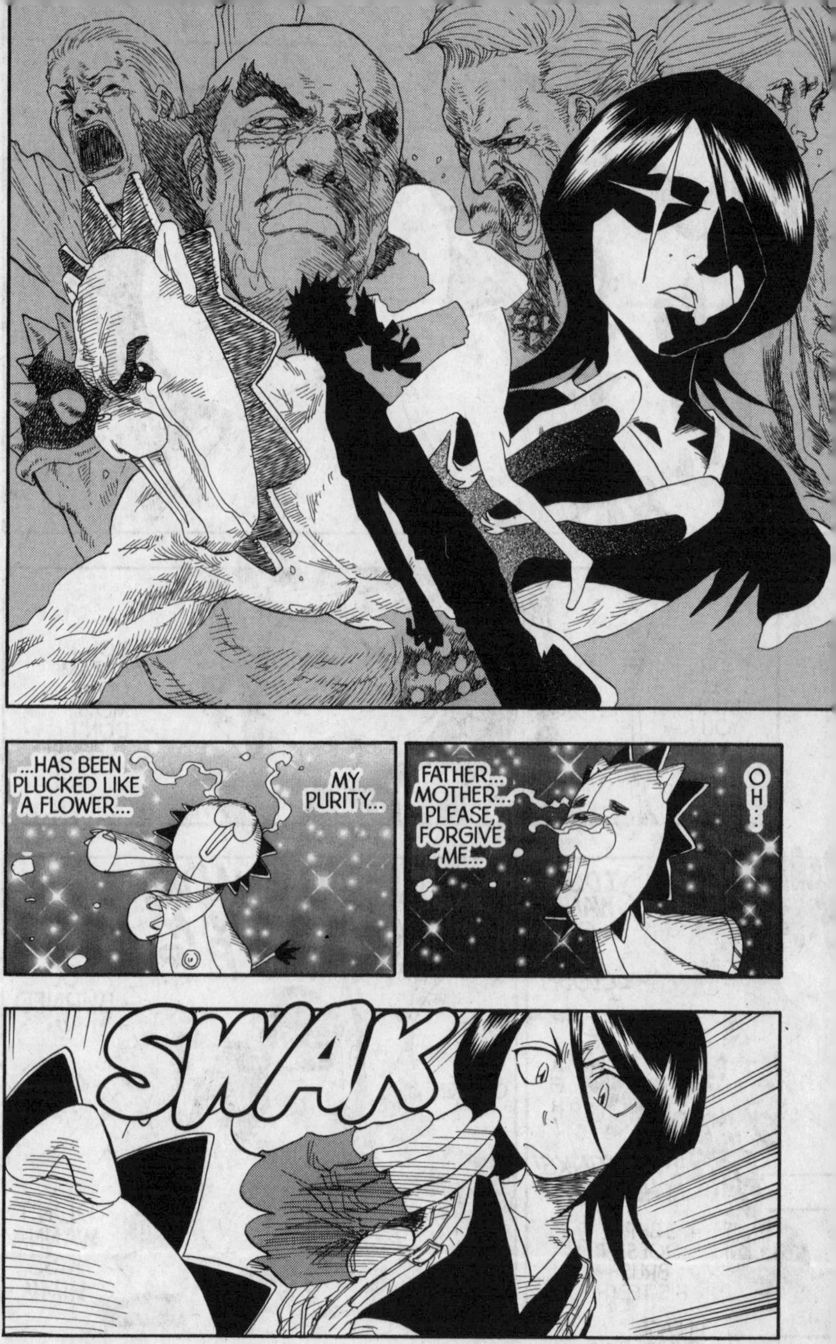
OH...
FATHER... MOTHER... PLEASE, FORGIVE ME...
MY PURITY...
...HAS BEEN PLUCKED LIKE A FLOWER...
SWAK

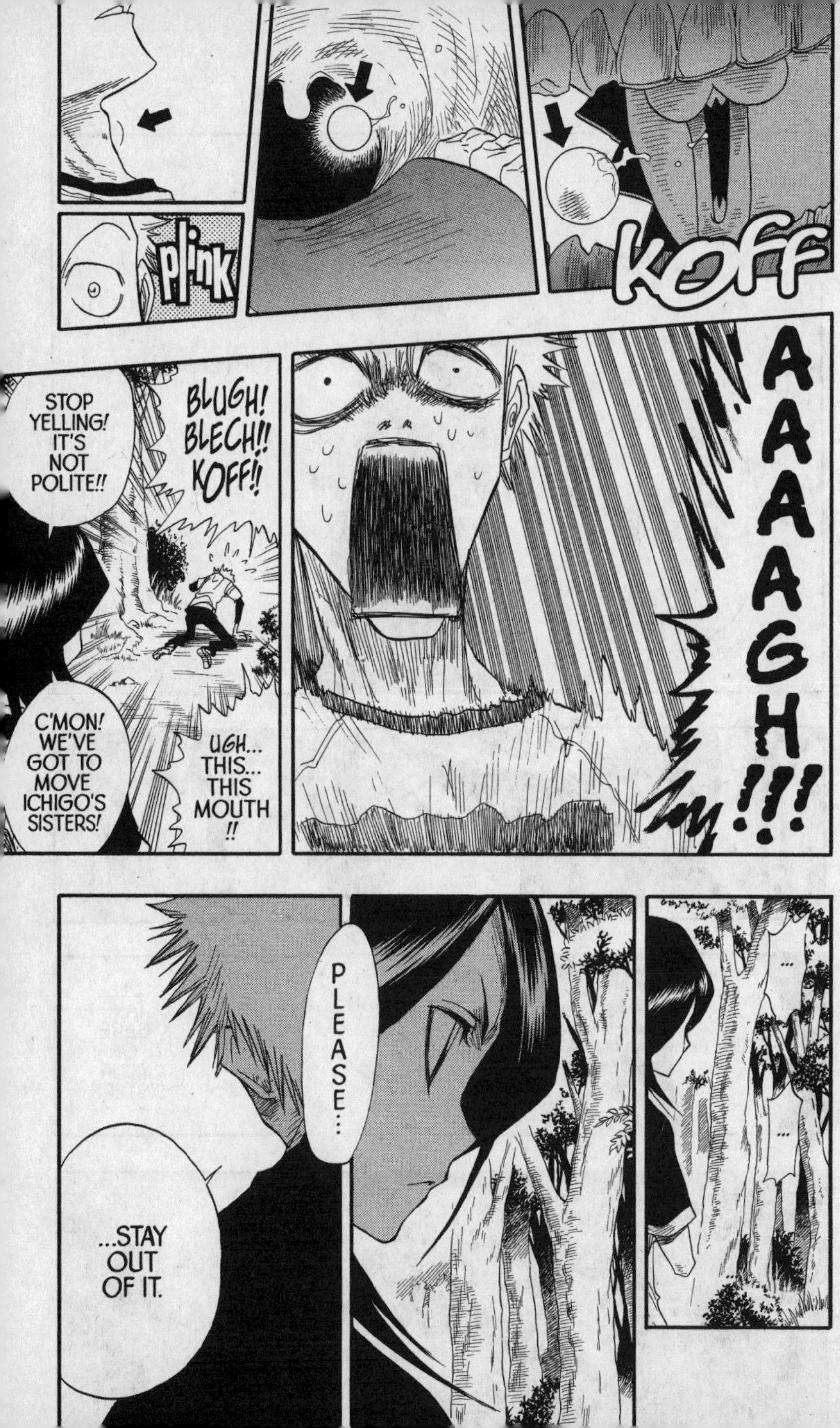
KOFF
plink
AAAAAGH!!!
BLUGH! BLECH!! KOFF!!
STOP YELLING! IT'S NOT POLITE!!
UGH... THIS... THIS MOUTH!!
C'MON! WE'VE GOT TO MOVE ICHIGO'S SISTERS!
...
...
PLEASE...
...STAY OUT OF IT.

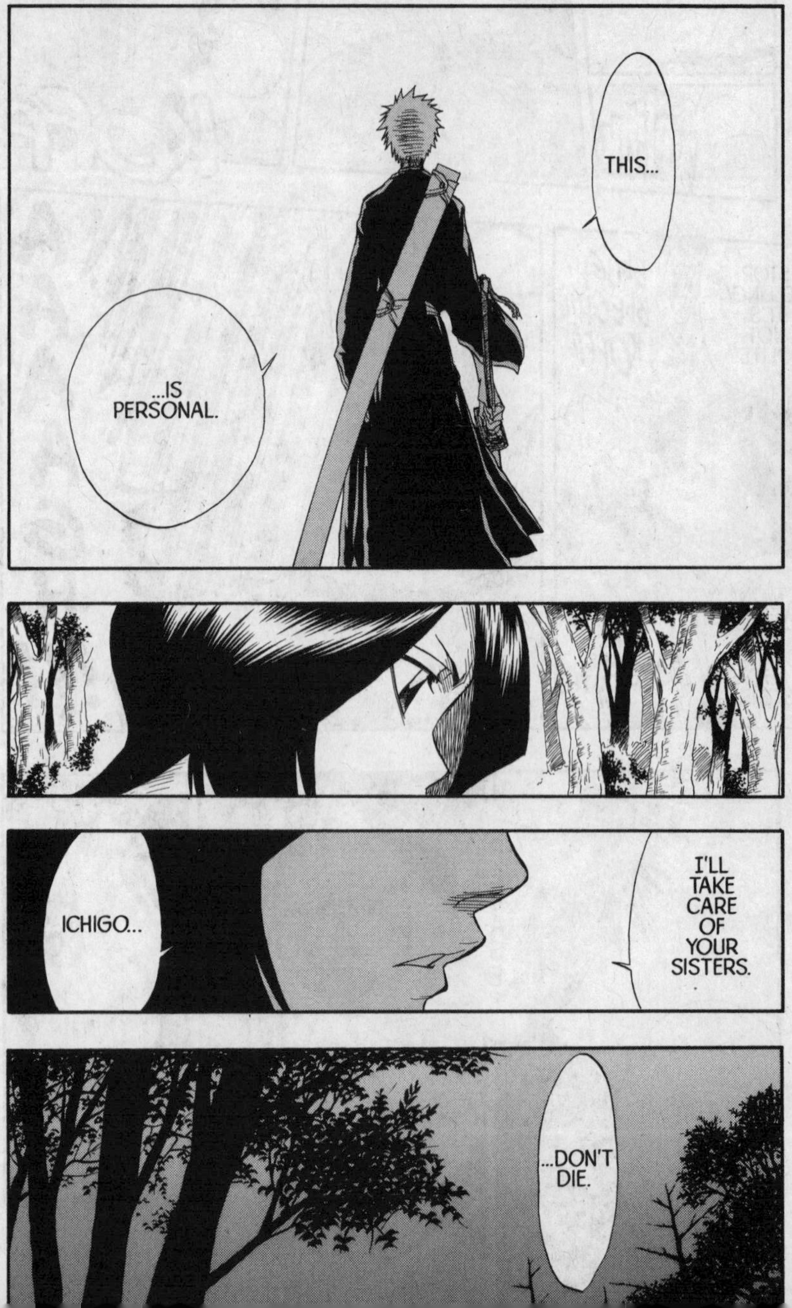
THIS...
...IS PERSONAL.
I'LL TAKE CARE OF YOUR SISTERS.
ICHIGO...
...DON'T DIE.

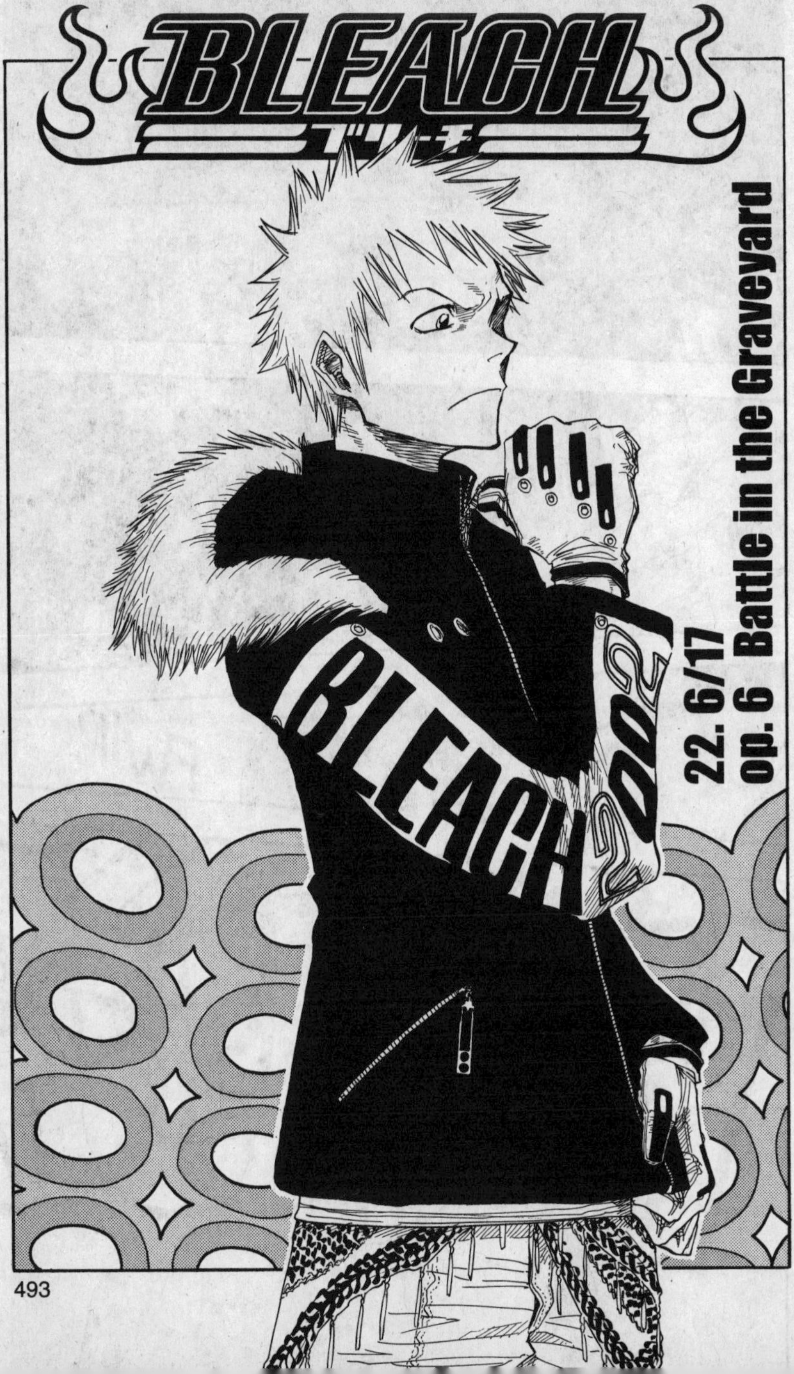
BLEACH
ブリーチ
22. 6/17
op. 6 Battle in the Graveyard
BLEACH 2002

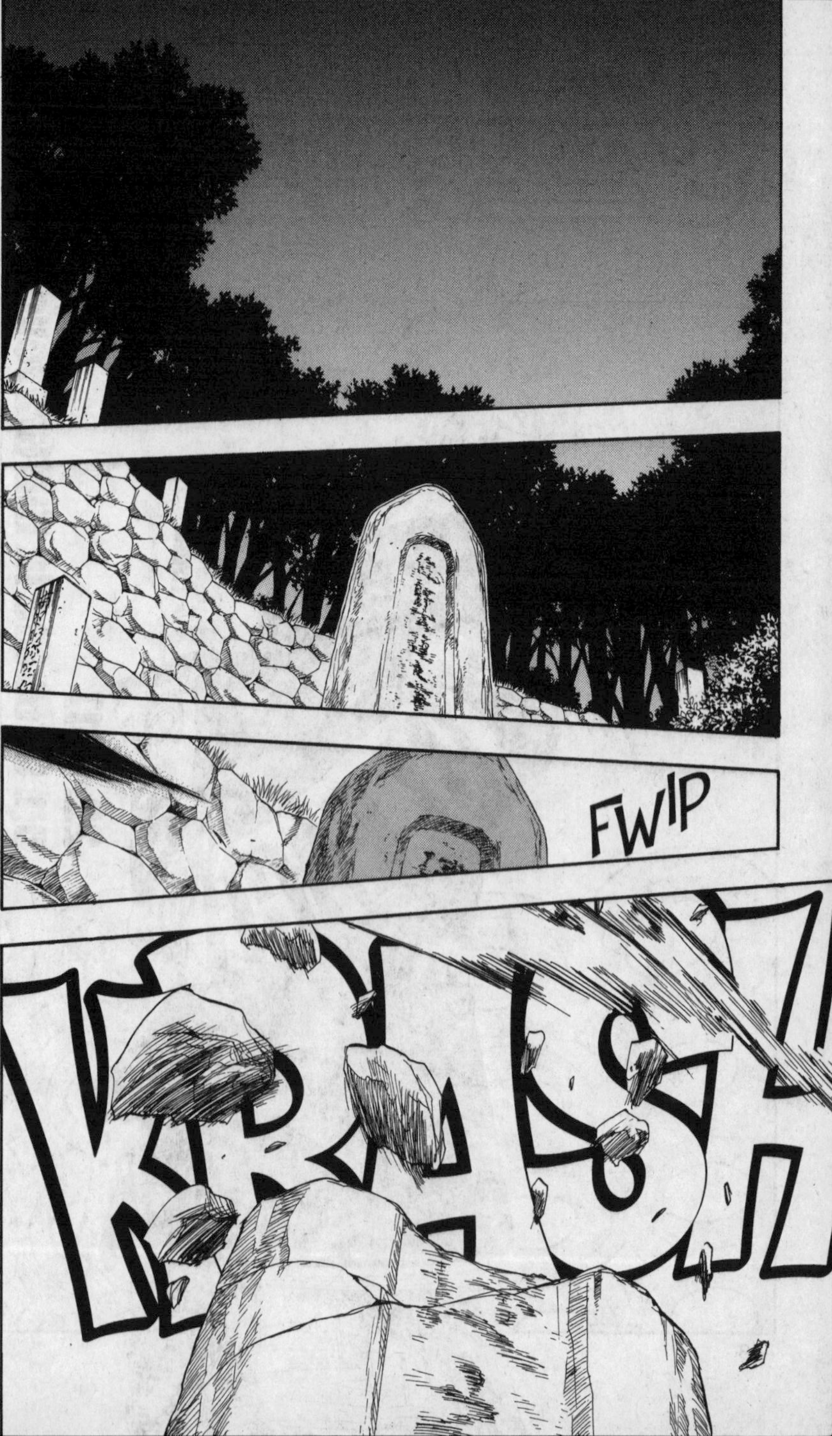
FWIP
KRASH

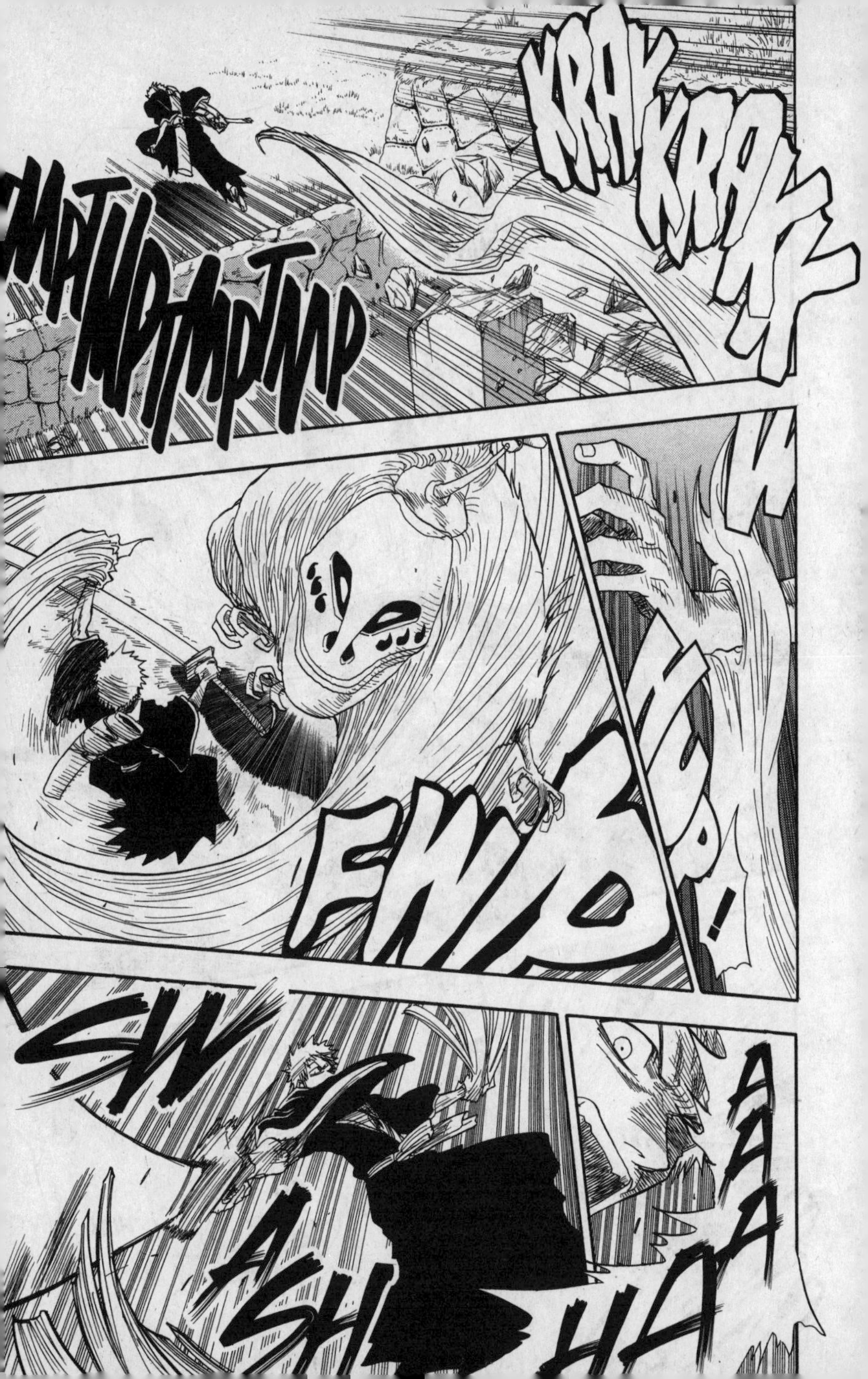
KRAK KRAK
SWASH

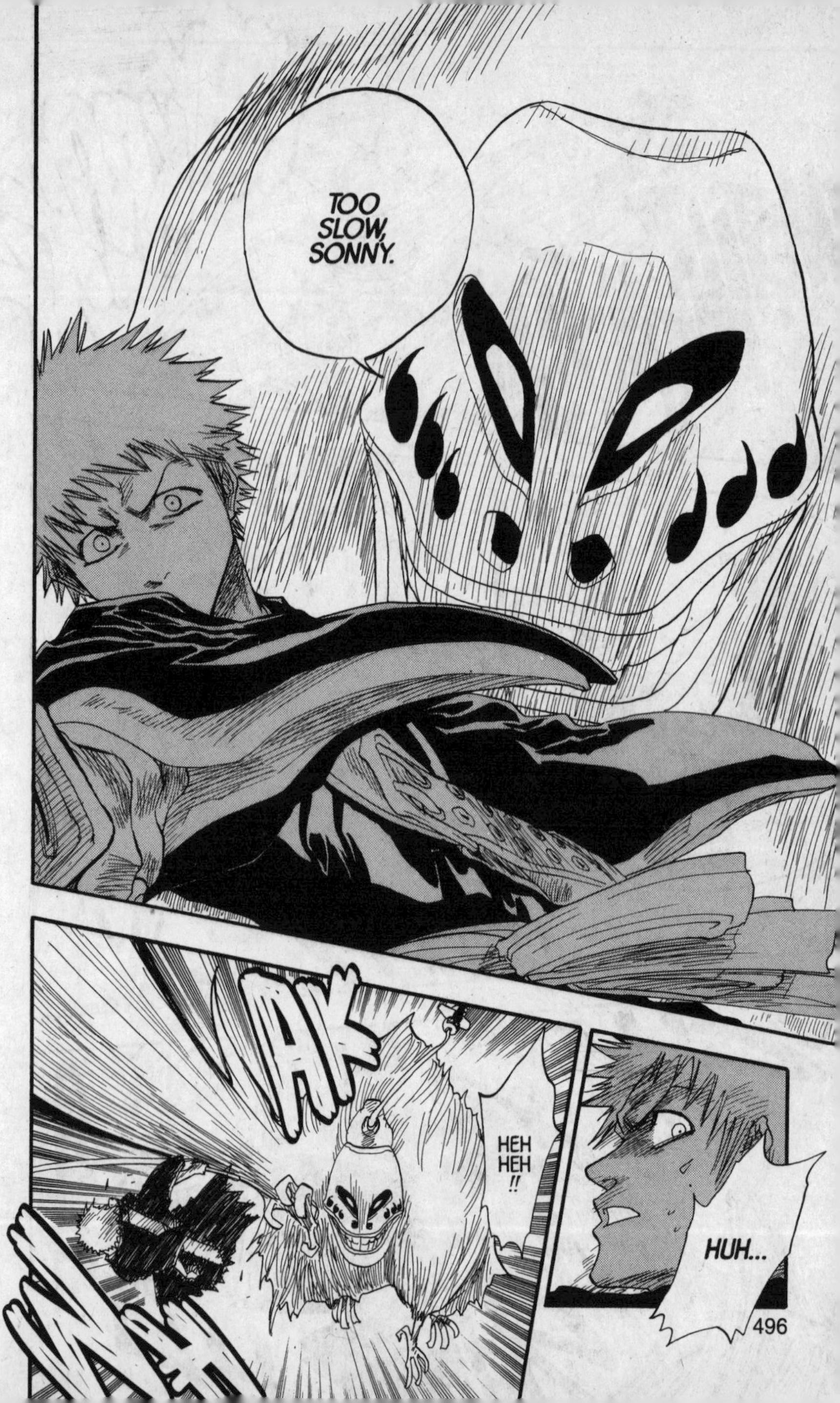
TOO SLOW, SONNY.
HUH...
HEH HEH!!

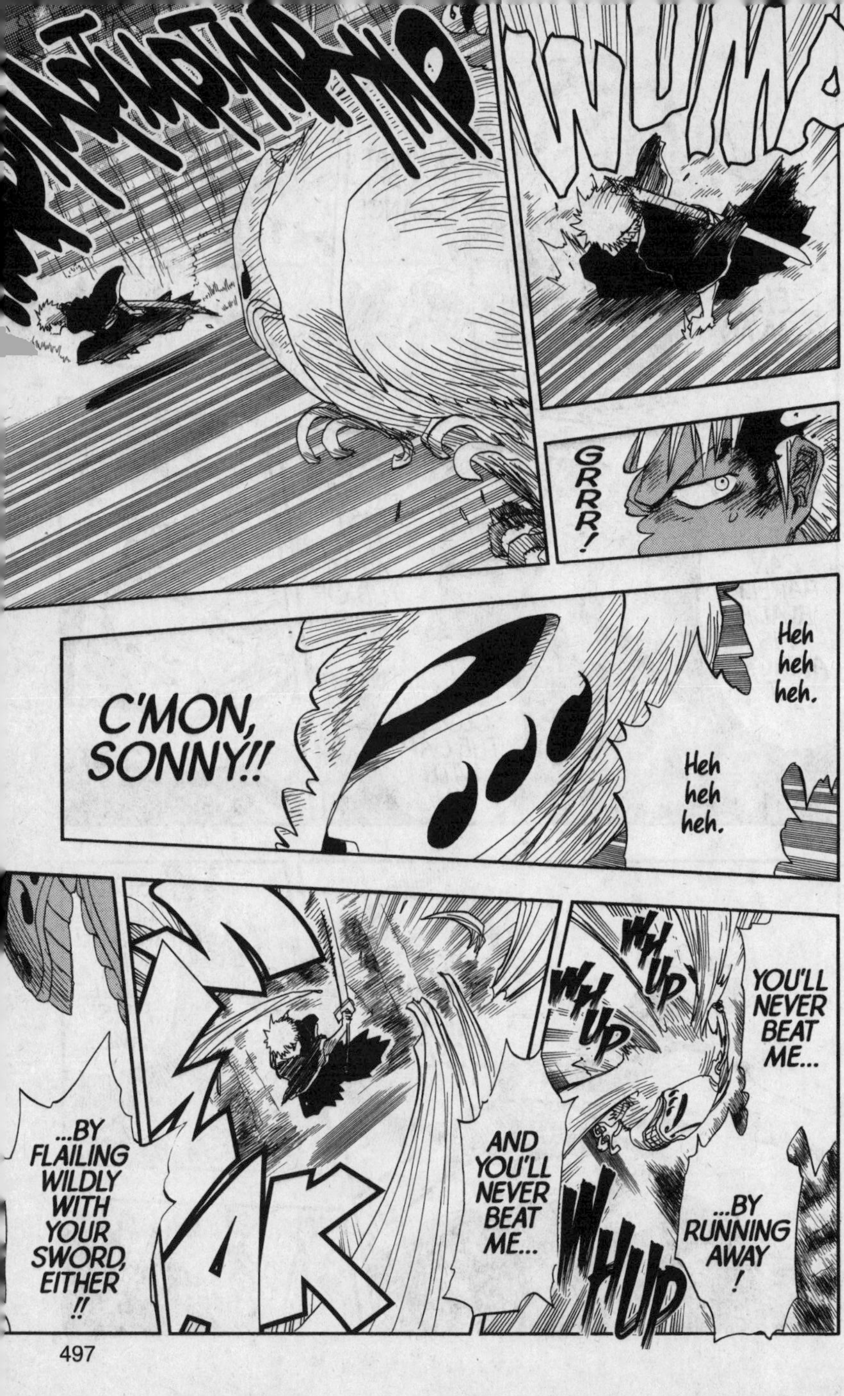

WUMP
WHAMPWHAMPWHAMP
GRRRR!
Heh heh heh.
Heh heh heh.
C'MON, SONNY!!
WHUP
WHUP
YOU'LL NEVER BEAT ME...
...BY RUNNING AWAY!
WHUP
AND YOU'LL NEVER BEAT ME...
...BY FLAILING WILDLY WITH YOUR SWORD, EITHER!!

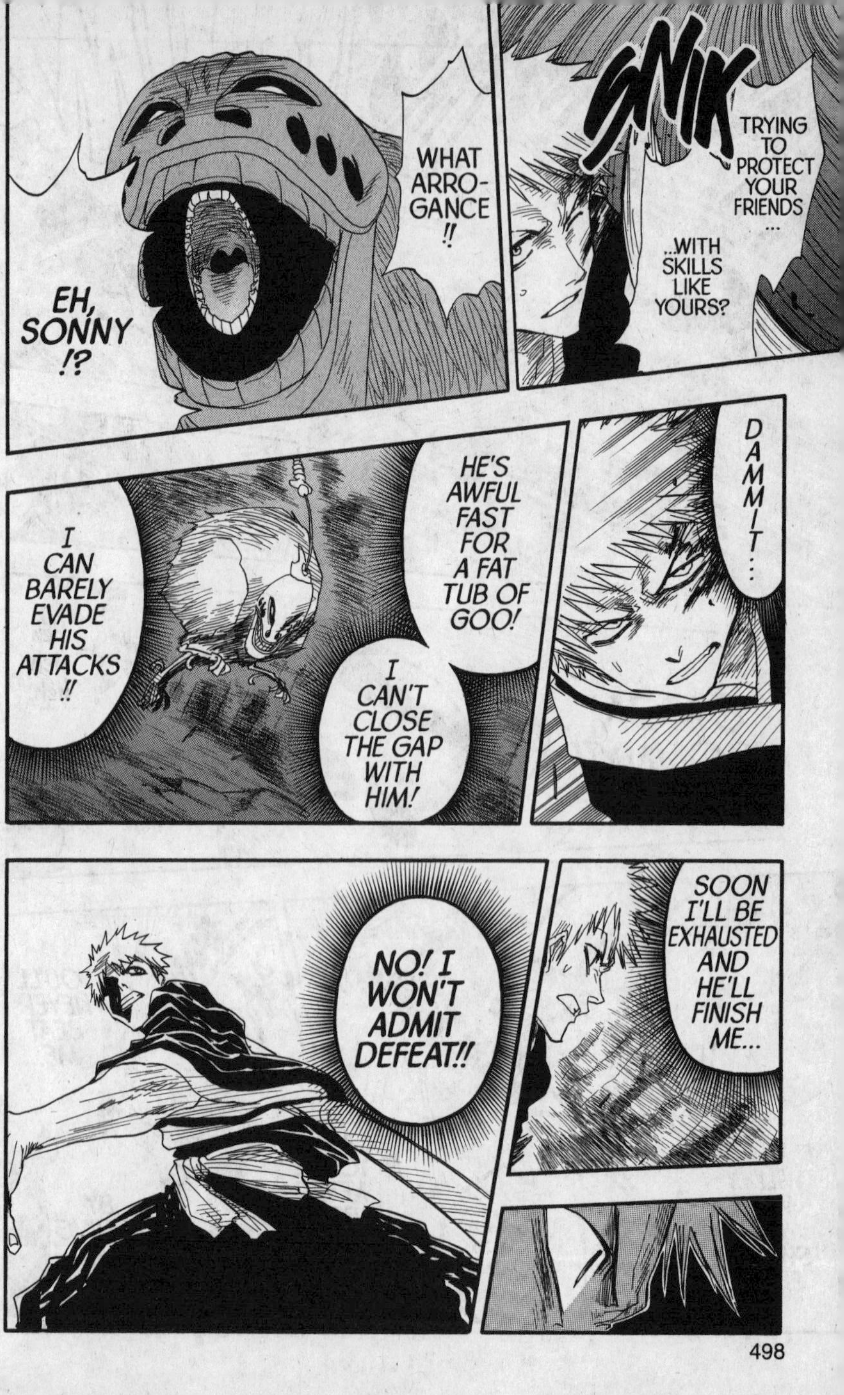
SNIK
TRYING TO PROTECT YOUR FRIENDS...
...WITH SKILLS LIKE YOURS?
WHAT ARRO-GANCE!!
EH, SONNY!?
DAMMIT...
HE'S AWFUL FAST FOR A FAT TUB OF GOO!
I CAN BARELY EVADE HIS ATTACKS!!
I CAN'T CLOSE THE GAP WITH HIM!
SOON I'LL BE EXHAUSTED AND HE'LL FINISH ME...
NO! I WON'T ADMIT DEFEAT!!

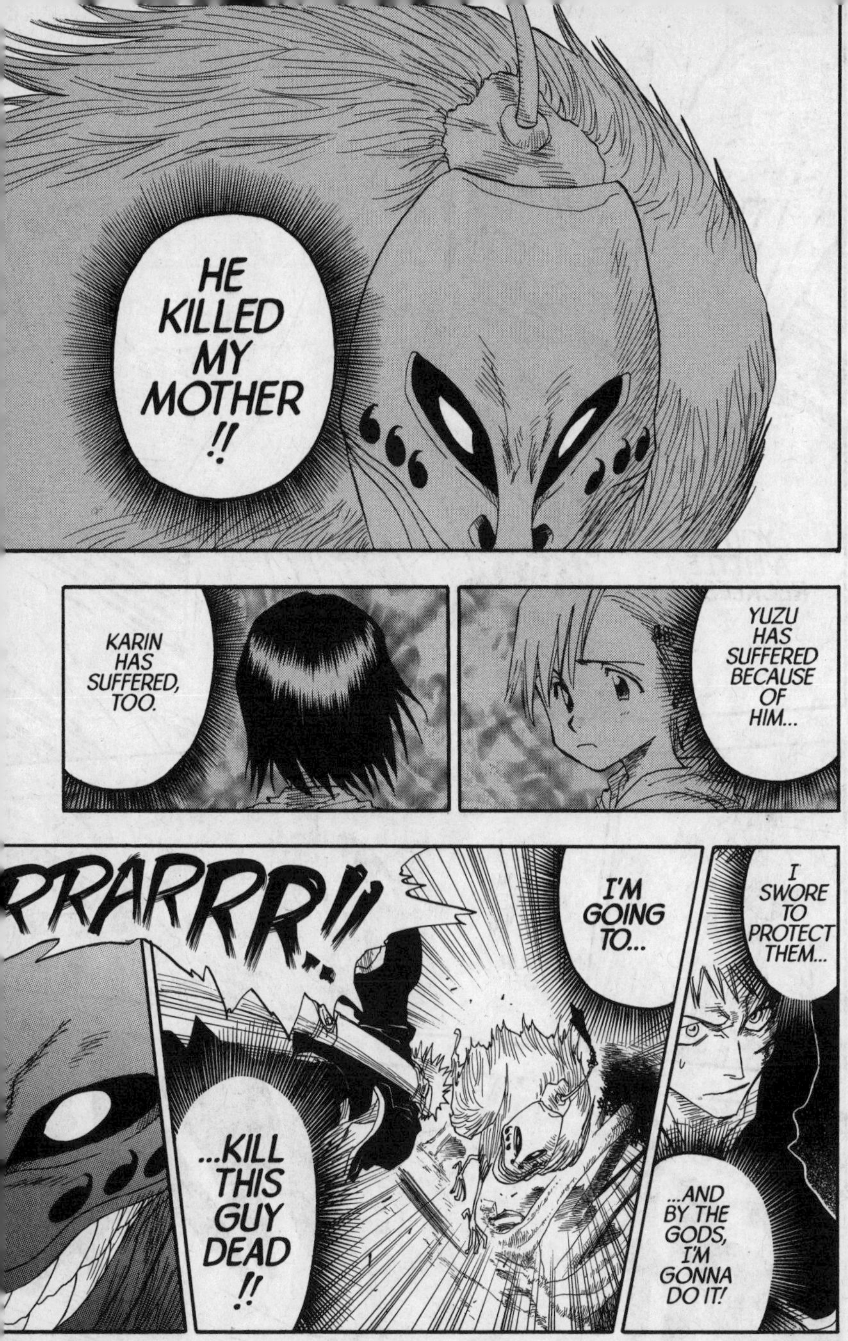
HE KILLED MY MOTHER !!
YUZU HAS SUFFERED BECAUSE OF HIM...
KARIN HAS SUFFERED, TOO.
I SWORE TO PROTECT THEM...
...AND BY THE GODS, I'M GONNA DO IT!
I'M GOING TO...
...KILL THIS GUY DEAD !!
RARRRR!!

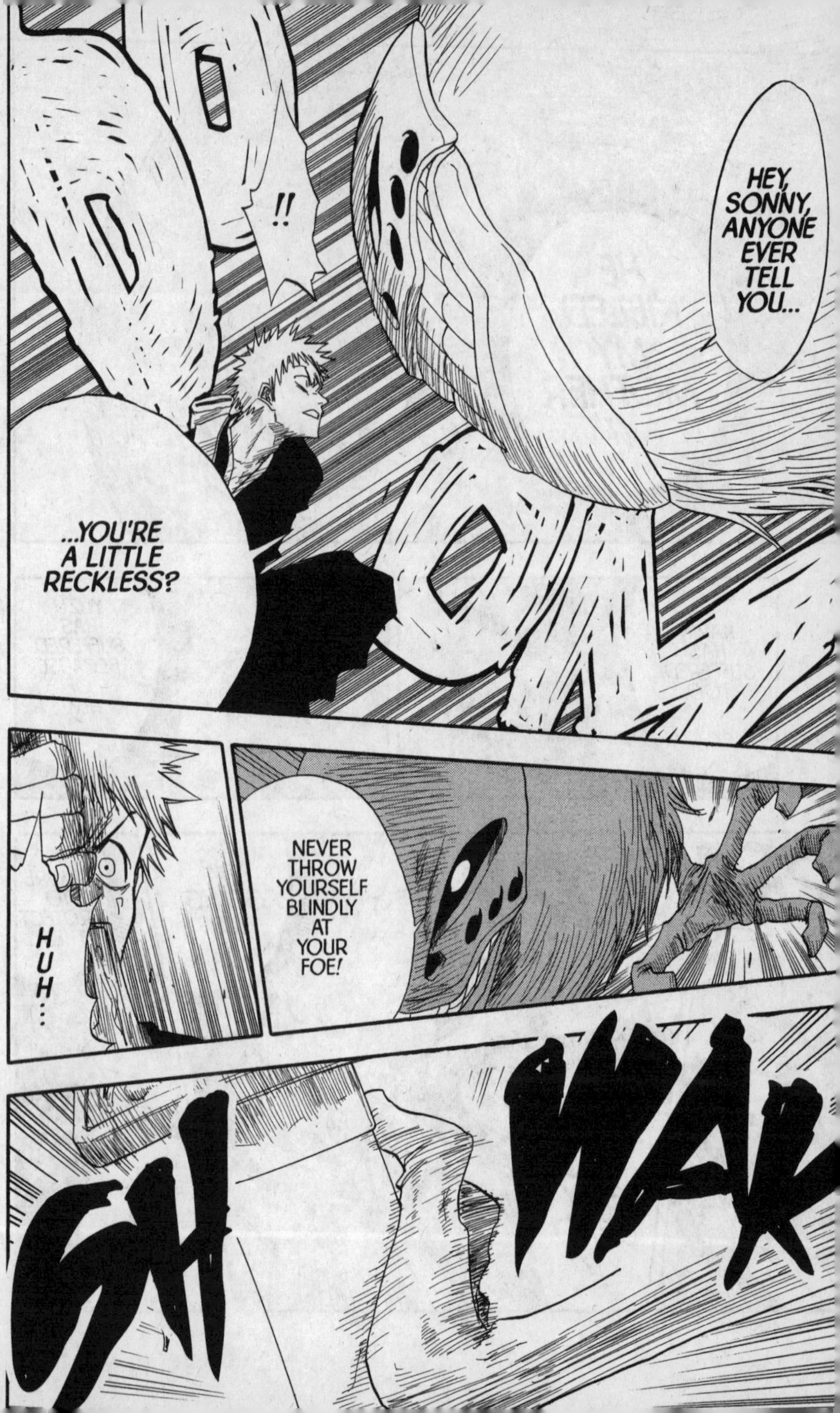
HEY, SONNY, ANYONE EVER TELL YOU...
!!
...YOU'RE A LITTLE RECKLESS?
NEVER THROW YOURSELF BLINDLY AT YOUR FOE!
HUH...
SHWAK

READ THIS WAY

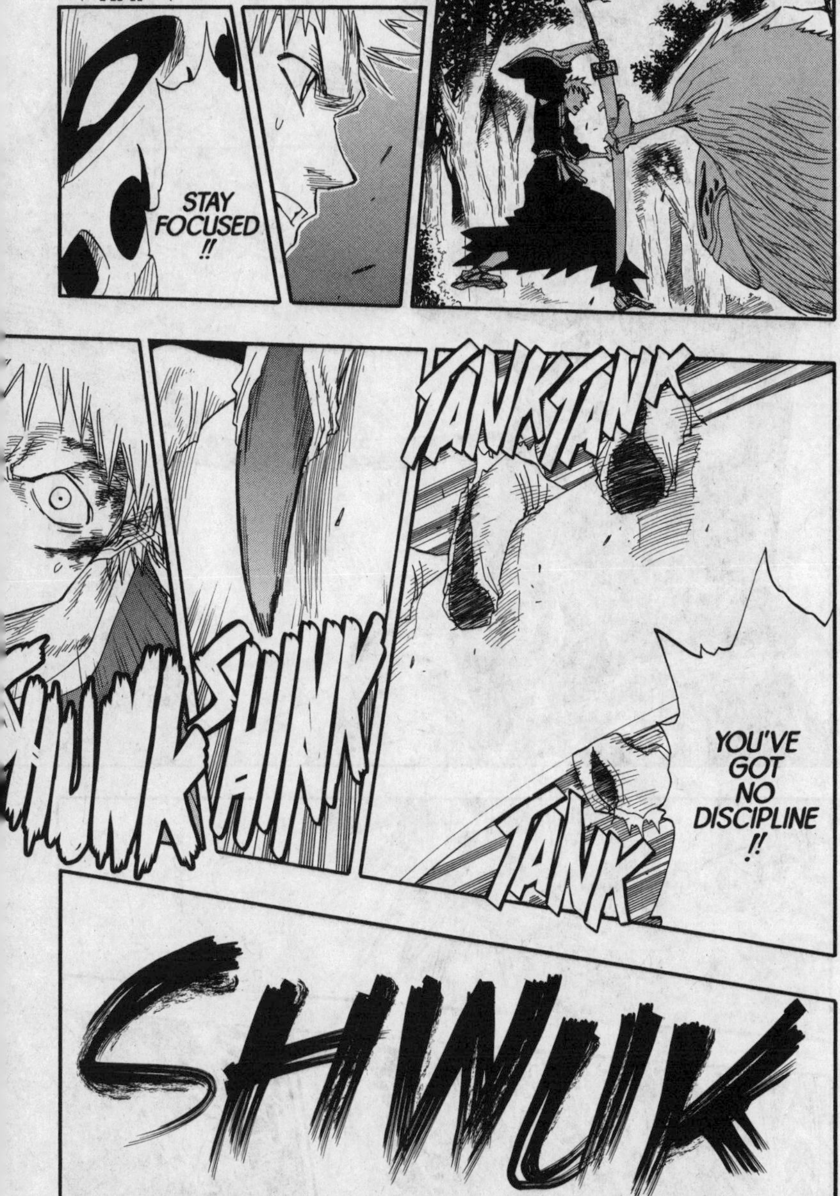
STAY FOCUSED !!
TANKTANK
YOU'VE GOT NO DISCIPLINE !!
TANK
SHINK
SHUNK
SHWUK

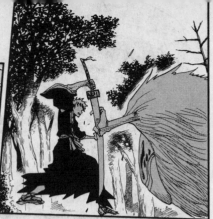

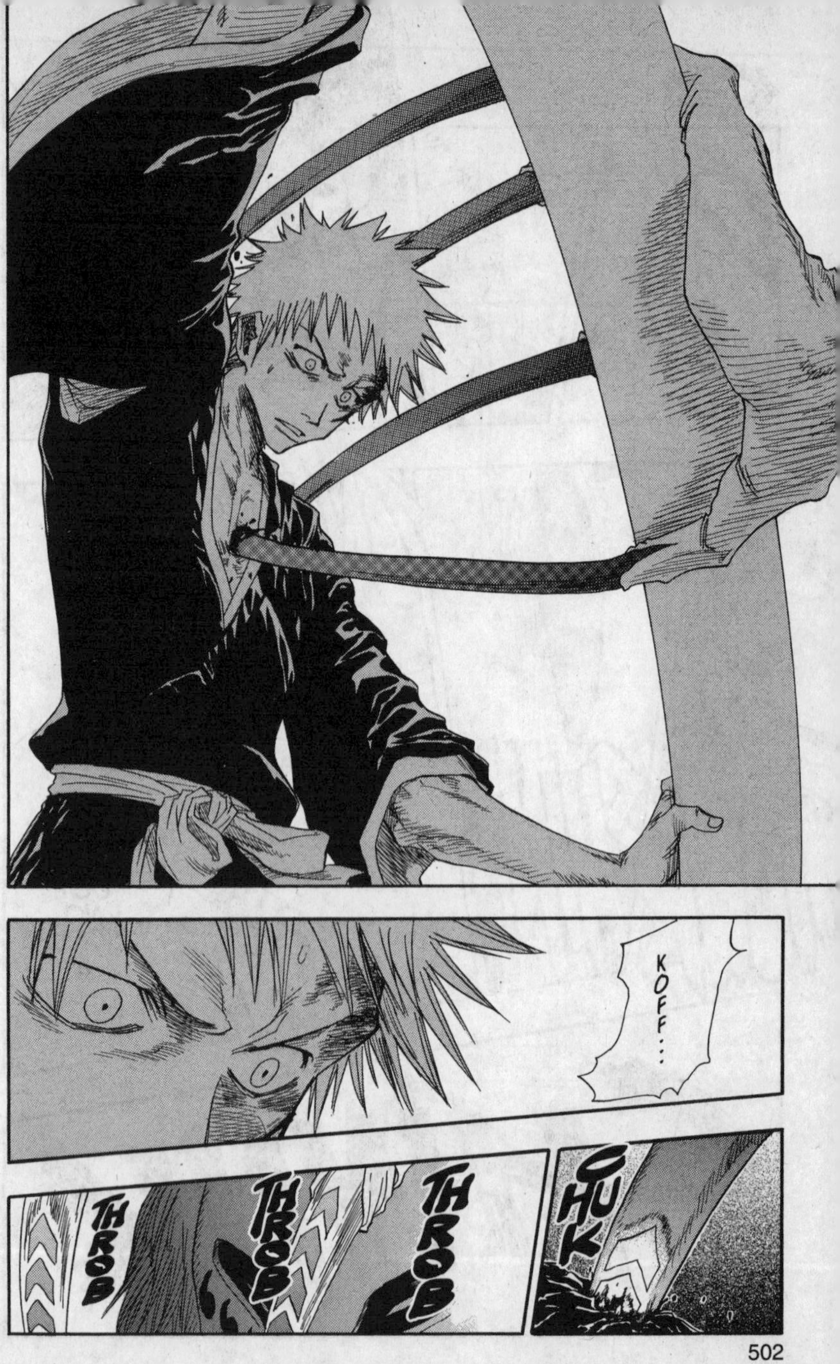
KOFF...
CHUK
THROB
THROB
THROB

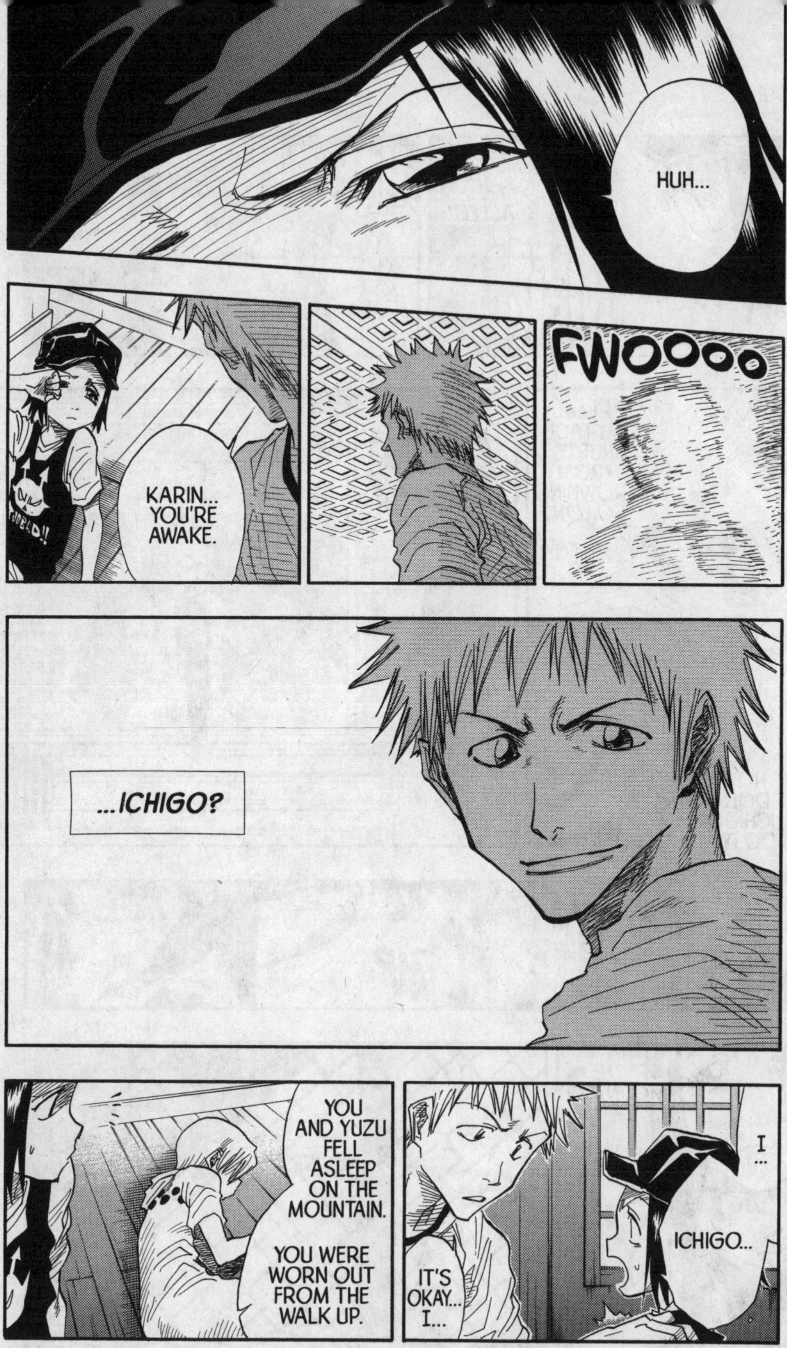
HUH...
FWOOOO
KARIN... YOU'RE AWAKE.
...ICHIGO?
I ...
ICHIGO...
IT'S OKAY... I...
YOU AND YUZU FELL ASLEEP ON THE MOUNTAIN.
YOU WERE WORN OUT FROM THE WALK UP.

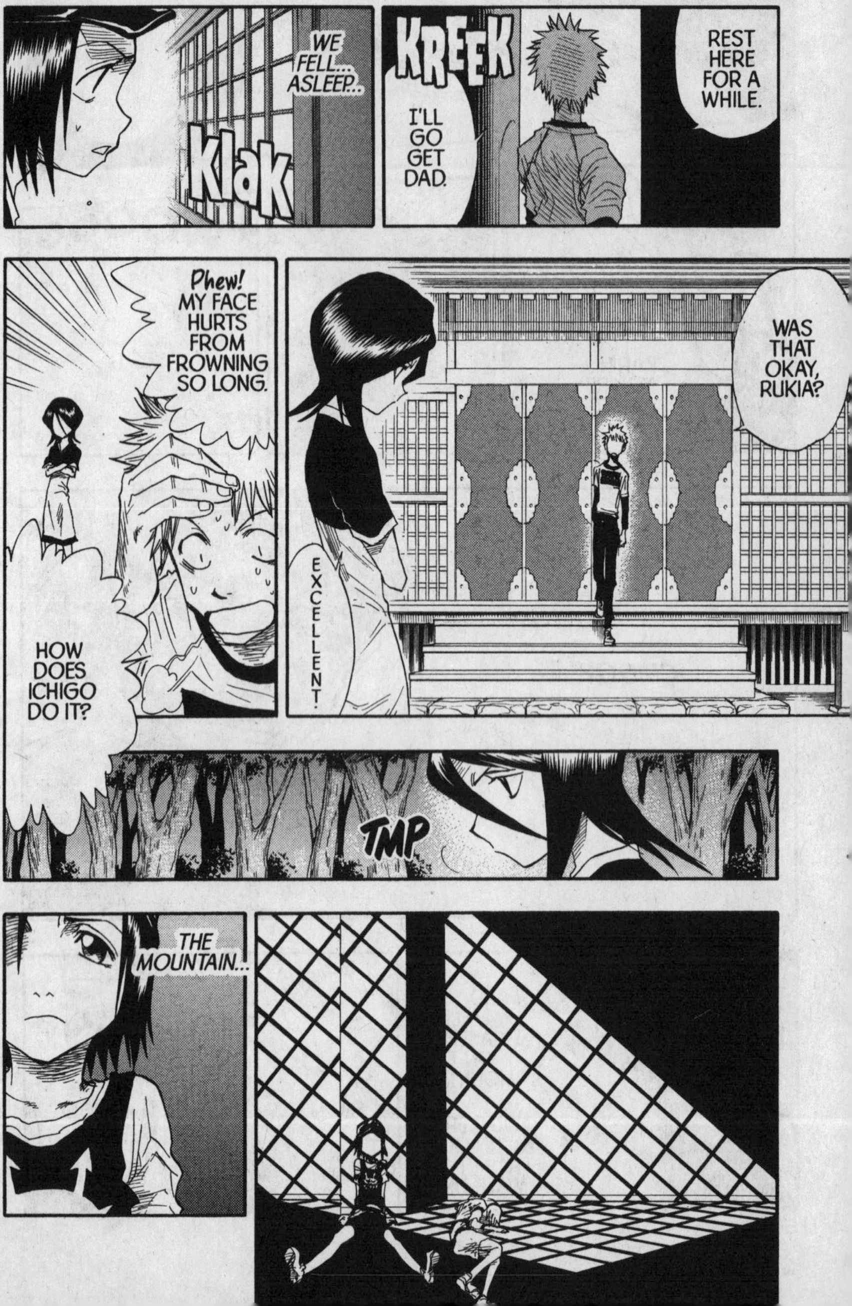
REST HERE FOR A WHILE.
KREEK
I'LL GO GET DAD.
WE FELL... ASLEEP...
Klak
WAS THAT OKAY, RUKIA?
EXCELLENT!
Phew! MY FACE HURTS FROM FROWNING SO LONG.
HOW DOES ICHIGO DO IT?
TMP
THE MOUNTAIN...

READ THIS WAY

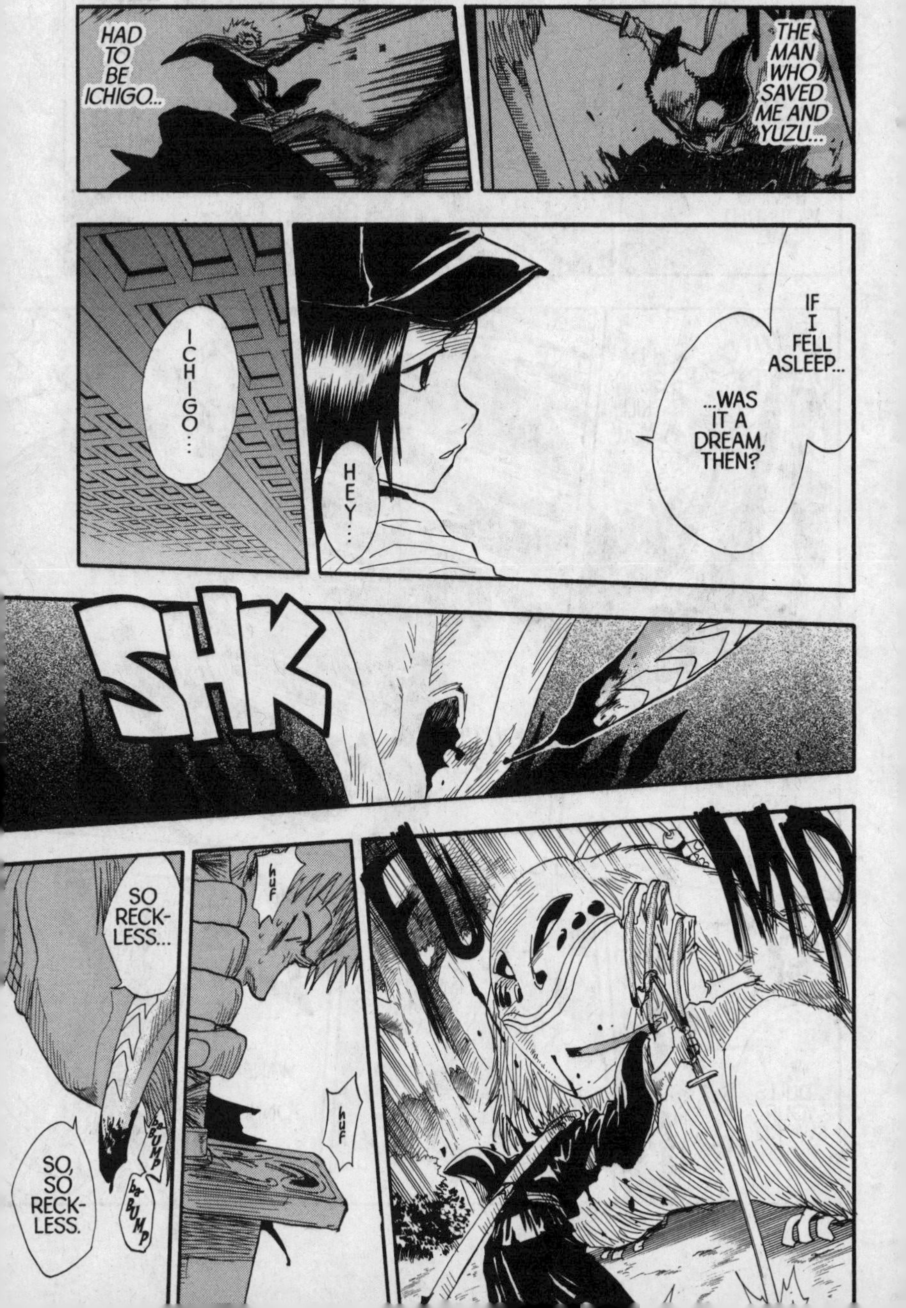
THE MAN WHO SAVED ME AND YUZU...
HAD TO BE ICHIGO...
IF I FELL ASLEEP...
...WAS IT A DREAM, THEN?
HEY...
ICHIGO...
SHK
FUMP
huf
huf
ba-BUMP
ba-BUMP
SO RECK-LESS...
SO, SO RECK-LESS.

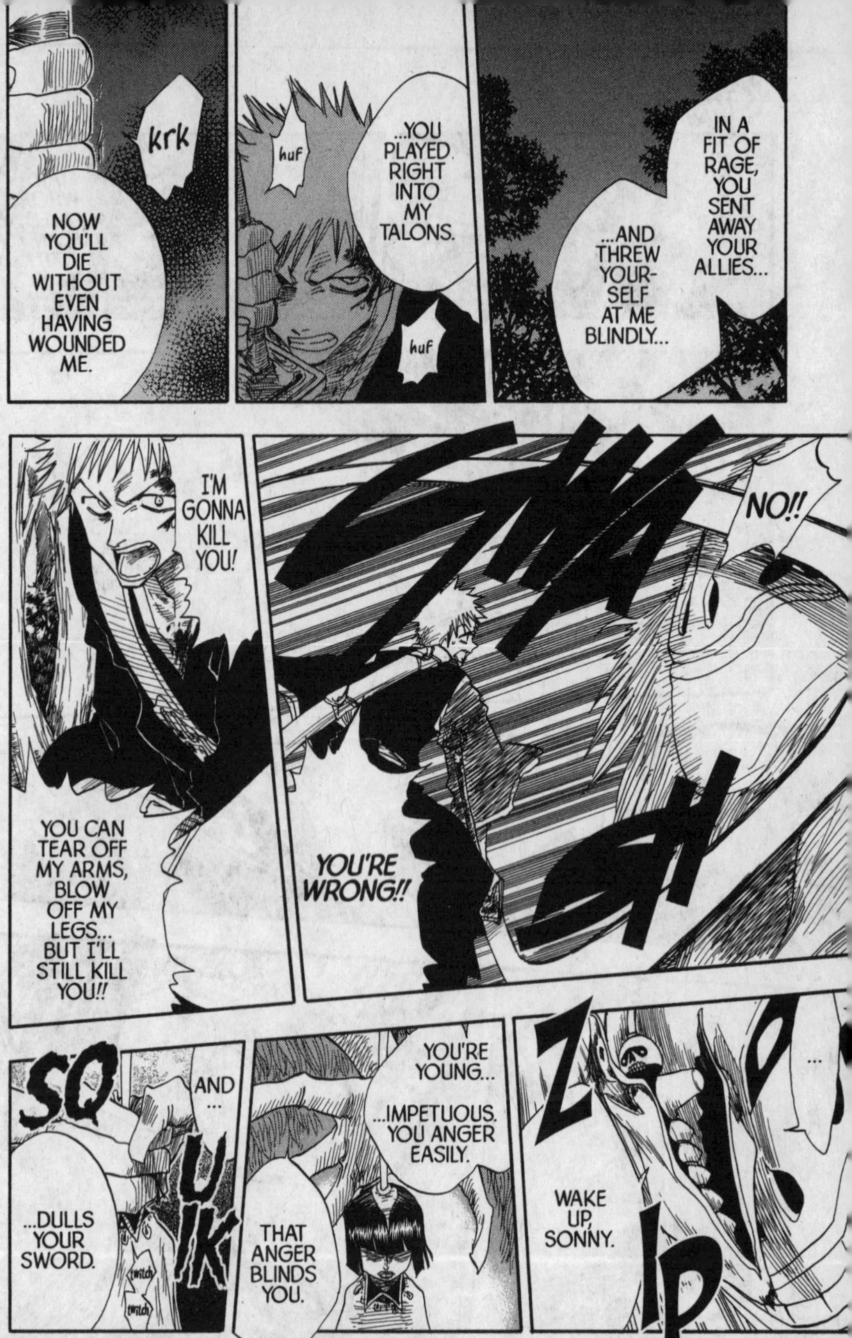
IN A FIT OF RAGE, YOU SENT AWAY YOUR ALLIES...
...AND THREW YOURSELF AT ME BLINDLY...
huf
...YOU PLAYED RIGHT INTO MY TALONS.
huf
krk
NOW YOU'LL DIE WITHOUT EVEN HAVING WOUNDED ME.
NO!!
YOU'RE WRONG!!
I'M GONNA KILL YOU!
YOU CAN TEAR OFF MY ARMS, BLOW OFF MY LEGS... BUT I'LL STILL KILL YOU!!
...
WAKE UP, SONNY.
YOU'RE YOUNG...
...IMPETUOUS. YOU ANGER EASILY.
THAT ANGER BLINDS YOU.
AND...
SQUK
...DULLS YOUR SWORD.
twitch
twitch

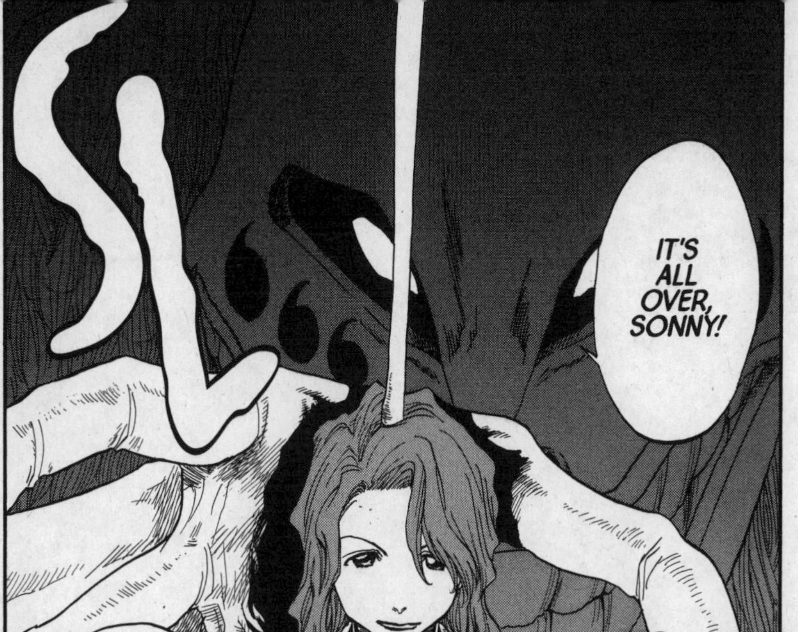
IT'S ALL OVER, SONNY!
YOU WERE MUCH TOO GREEN TO CHALLENGE ME!!
SUK

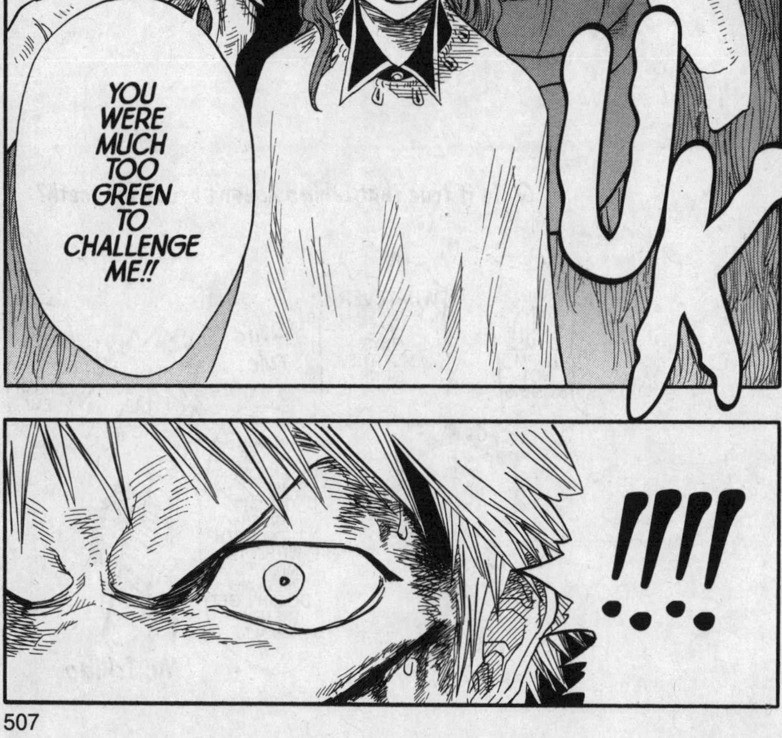
!!!!

Q: Is it true that Ichigo doesn't brush his teeth?

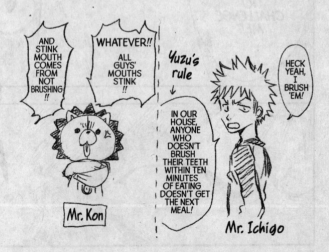

HECK YEAH, I BRUSH 'EM!
Mr. Ichigo
Yuzu's rule
IN OUR HOUSE, ANYONE WHO DOESN'T BRUSH THEIR TEETH WITHIN TEN MINUTES OF EATING DOESN'T GET THE NEXT MEAL!
WHATEVER!! ALL GUYS' MOUTHS STINK!!
AND STINK MOUTH COMES FROM NOT BRUSHING!!
Mr. Kon

23. 6/17 op. 7 Sharp Will, Dull Blade

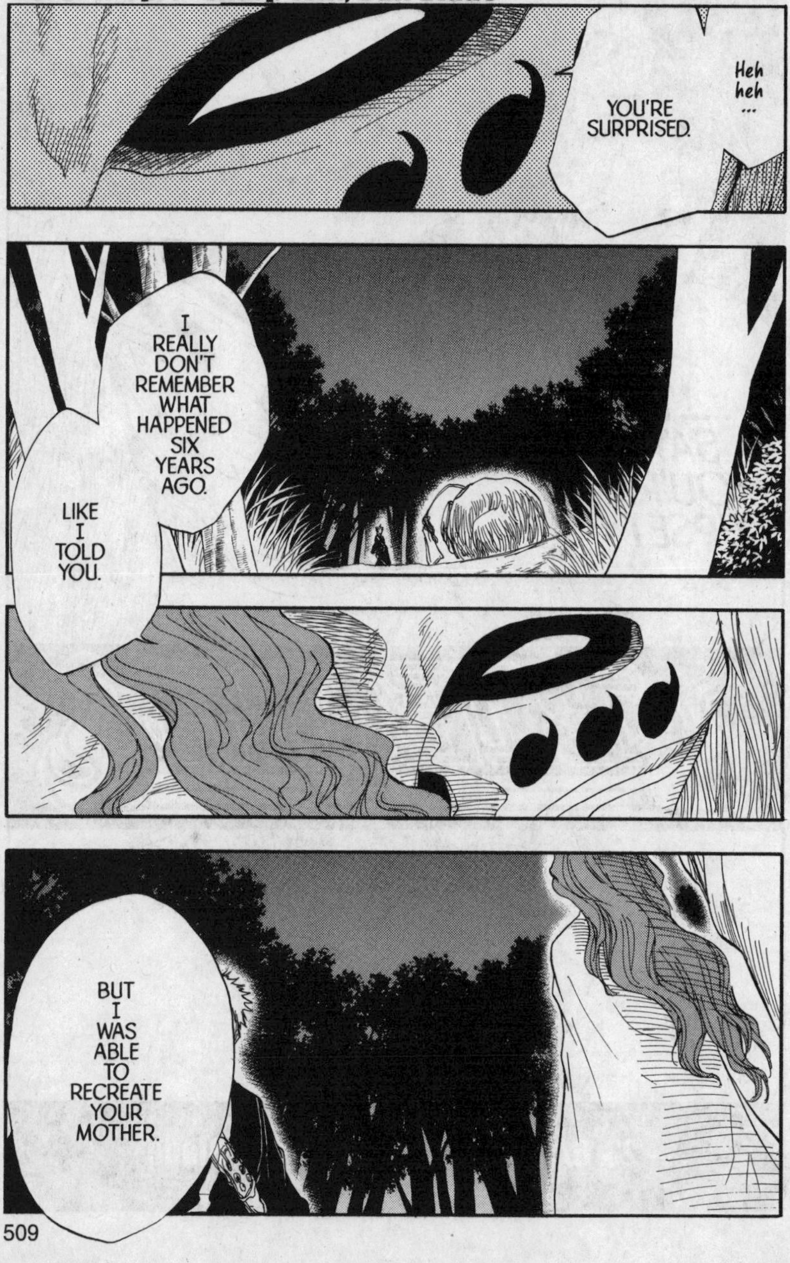
Heh heh ...
YOU'RE SURPRISED.
I REALLY DON'T REMEMBER WHAT HAPPENED SIX YEARS AGO.
LIKE I TOLD YOU.
BUT I WAS ABLE TO RECREATE YOUR MOTHER.

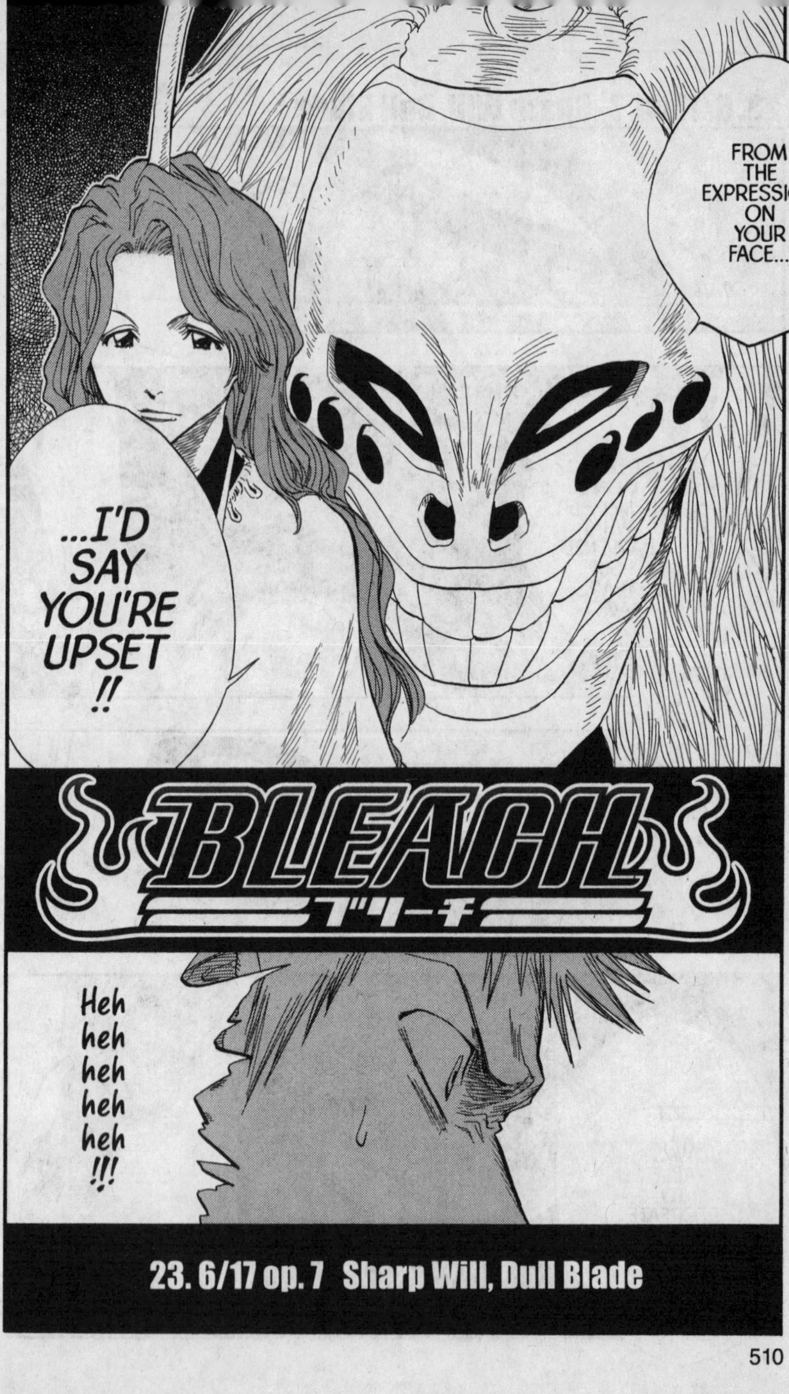
FROM THE EXPRESSION ON YOUR FACE...
...I'D SAY YOU'RE UPSET!!
BLEACH
ブリーチ
Heh heh heh heh heh!!!
23. 6/17 op. 7 Sharp Will, Dull Blade

READ THIS WAY

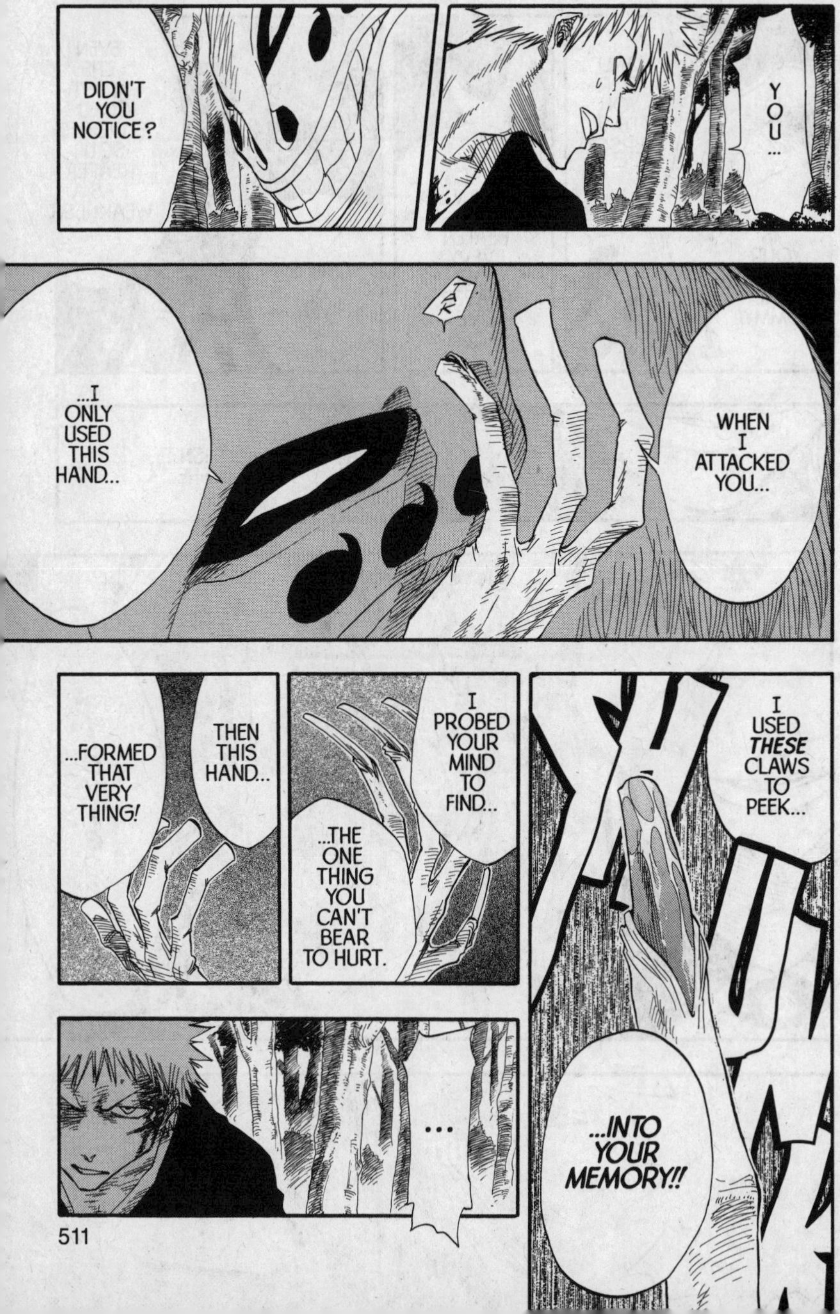
YOU...
DIDN'T YOU NOTICE?
WHEN I ATTACKED YOU...
TAK
...I ONLY USED THIS HAND...
I USED *THESE* CLAWS TO PEEK...
...INTO YOUR MEMORY!!
I PROBED YOUR MIND TO FIND...
...THE ONE THING YOU CAN'T BEAR TO HURT.
THEN THIS HAND...
...FORMED THAT VERY THING!
...

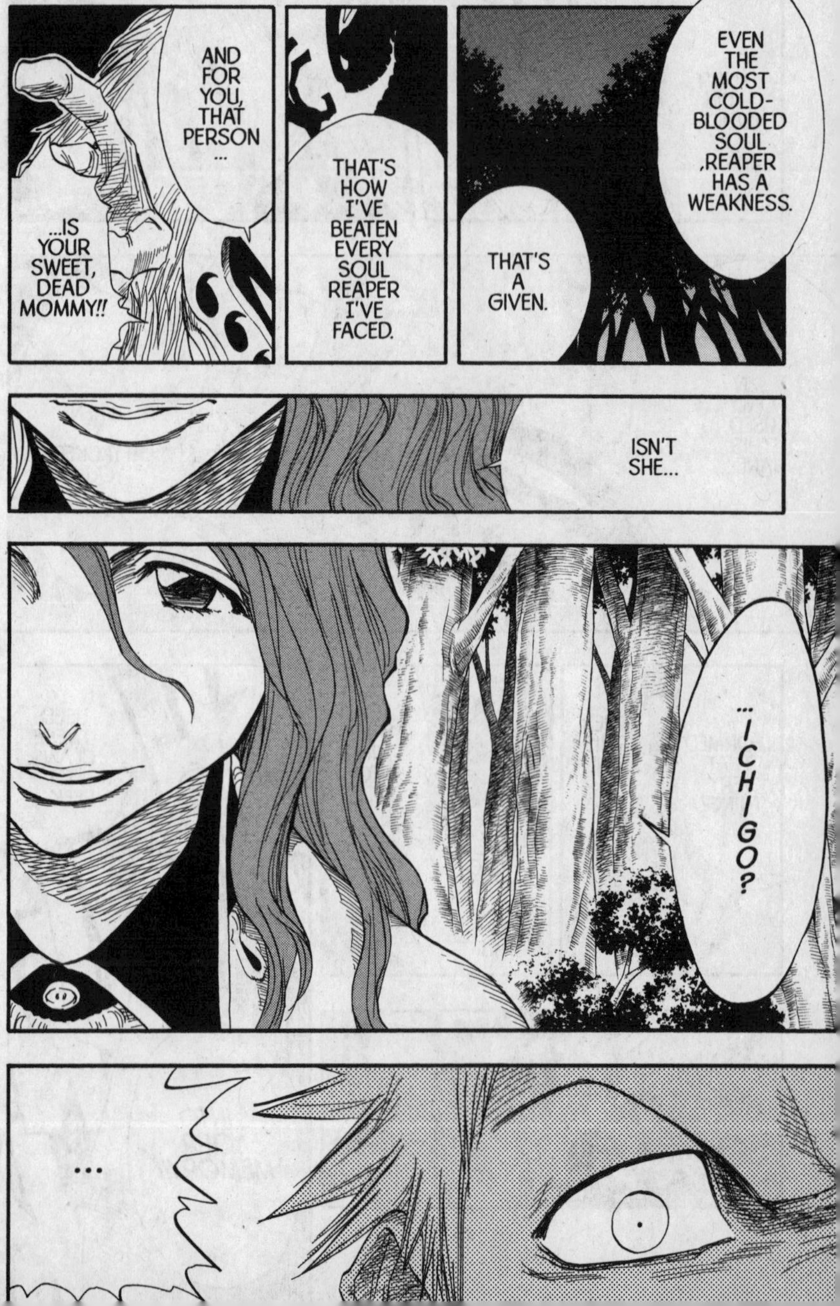
EVEN THE MOST COLD-BLOODED SOUL REAPER HAS A WEAKNESS.
THAT'S A GIVEN.
THAT'S HOW I'VE BEATEN EVERY SOUL REAPER I'VE FACED.
AND FOR YOU, THAT PERSON...
...IS YOUR SWEET, DEAD MOMMY!!
ISN'T SHE...
...ICHIGO?
...

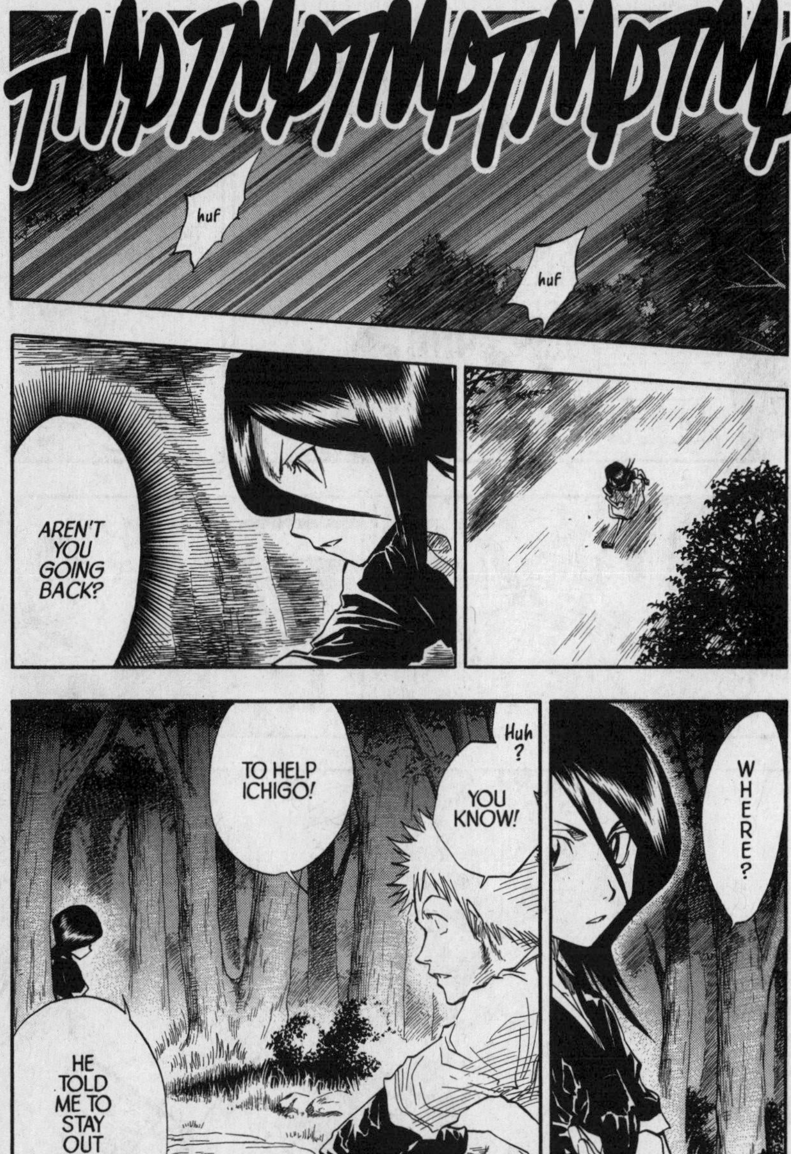
TMPTMPTMPTMPTMP
huf
huf
AREN'T YOU GOING BACK?
WHERE?
Huh?
YOU KNOW!
TO HELP ICHIGO!
HE TOLD ME TO STAY OUT OF IT.

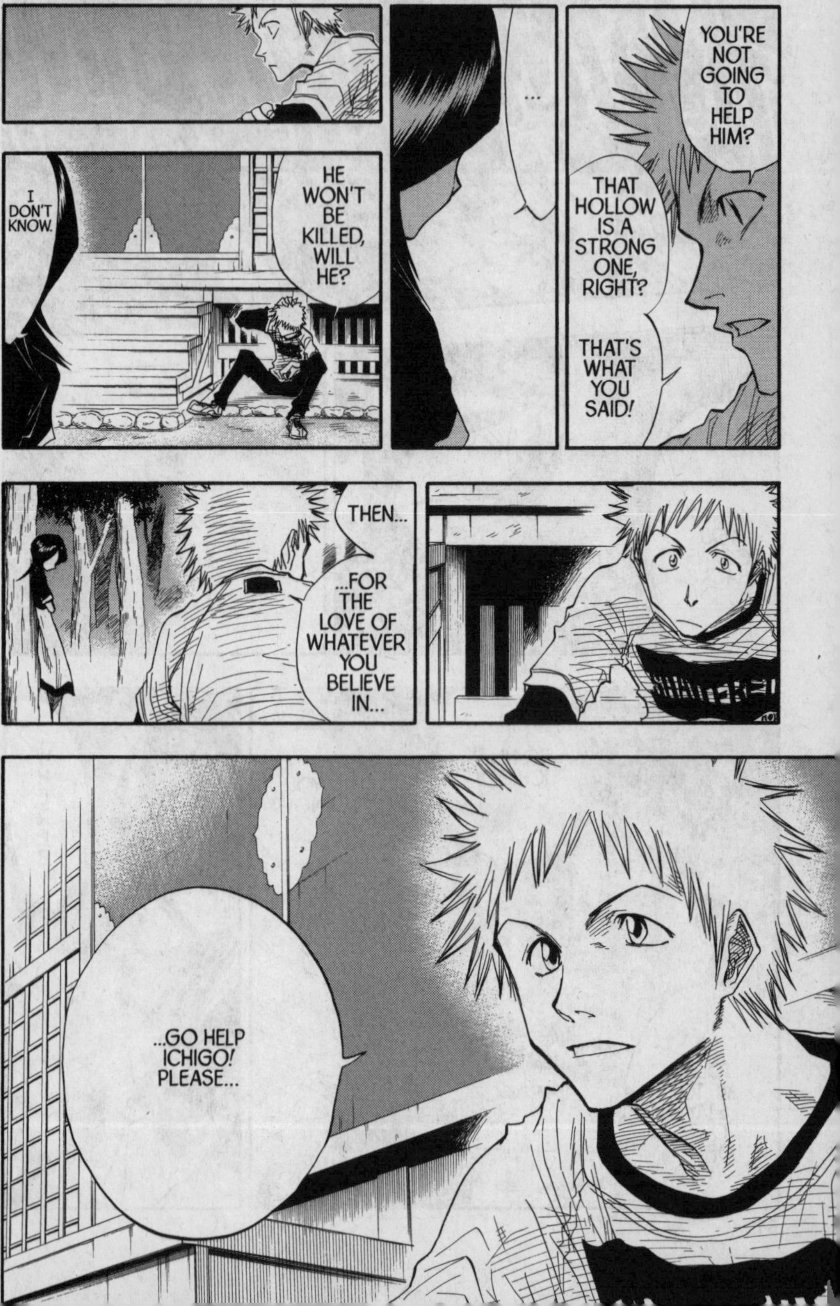
YOU'RE NOT GOING TO HELP HIM?
THAT HOLLOW IS A STRONG ONE, RIGHT?
THAT'S WHAT YOU SAID!
...
HE WON'T BE KILLED, WILL HE?
I DON'T KNOW.
THEN...
...FOR THE LOVE OF WHATEVER YOU BELIEVE IN...
...GO HELP ICHIGO! PLEASE...

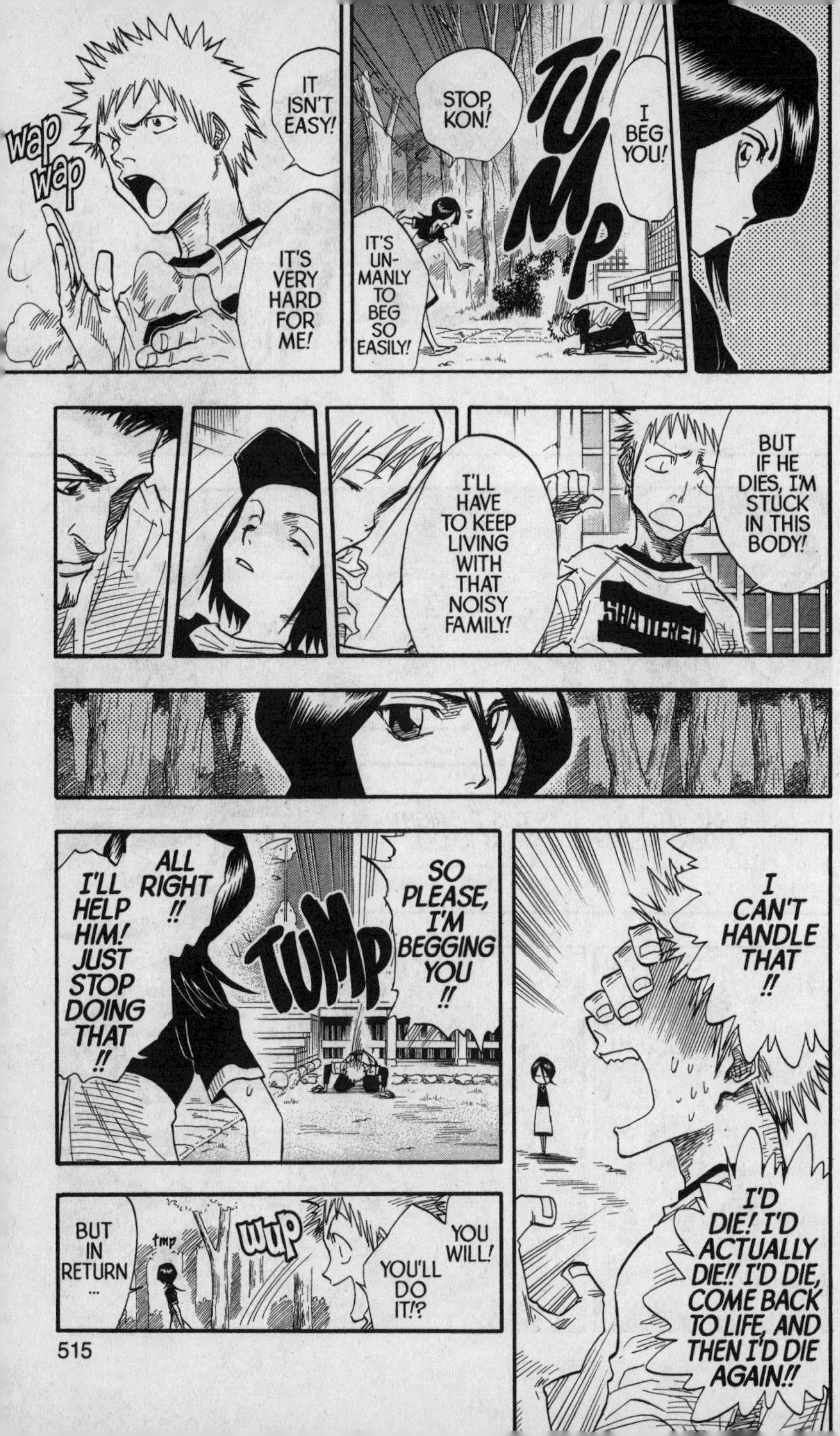

TUMP
I BEG YOU!
STOP, KON!
IT'S UNMANLY TO BEG SO EASILY!
IT ISN'T EASY!
wap wap
IT'S VERY HARD FOR ME!
BUT IF HE DIES, I'M STUCK IN THIS BODY!
SHATTERED
I'LL HAVE TO KEEP LIVING WITH THAT NOISY FAMILY!
I CAN'T HANDLE THAT!!
I'D DIE! I'D ACTUALLY DIE!! I'D DIE, COME BACK TO LIFE, AND THEN I'D DIE AGAIN!!
SO PLEASE, I'M BEGGING YOU!!
TUMP
ALL RIGHT!!
I'LL HELP HIM! JUST STOP DOING THAT!!
YOU WILL!
YOU'LL DO IT!?
wup
tmp
BUT IN RETURN ...

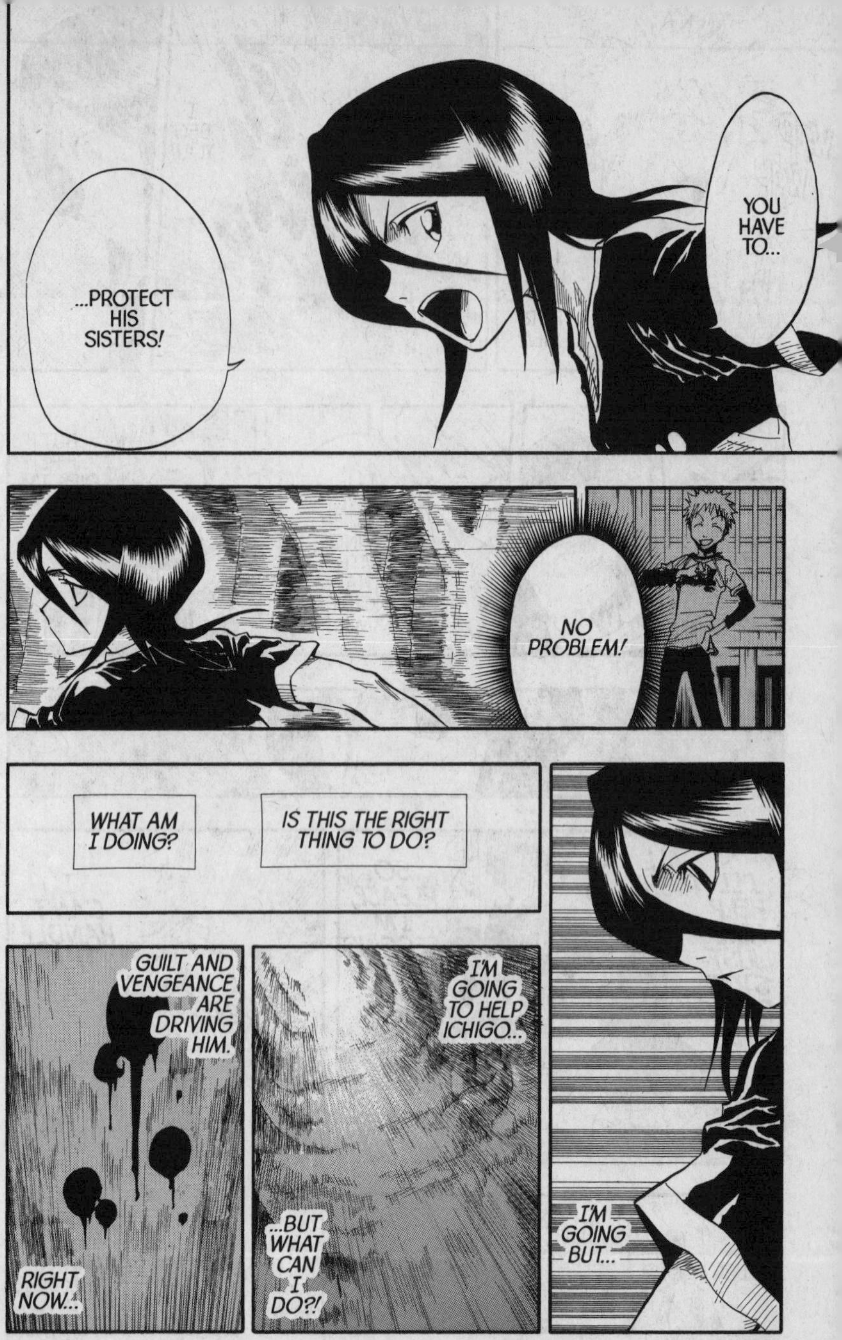
YOU HAVE TO...
...PROTECT HIS SISTERS!
NO PROBLEM!
I'M GOING BUT...
IS THIS THE RIGHT THING TO DO?
WHAT AM I DOING?
I'M GOING TO HELP ICHIGO...
...BUT WHAT CAN I DO?!
GUILT AND VENGEANCE ARE DRIVING HIM.
RIGHT NOW...

READ THIS WAY

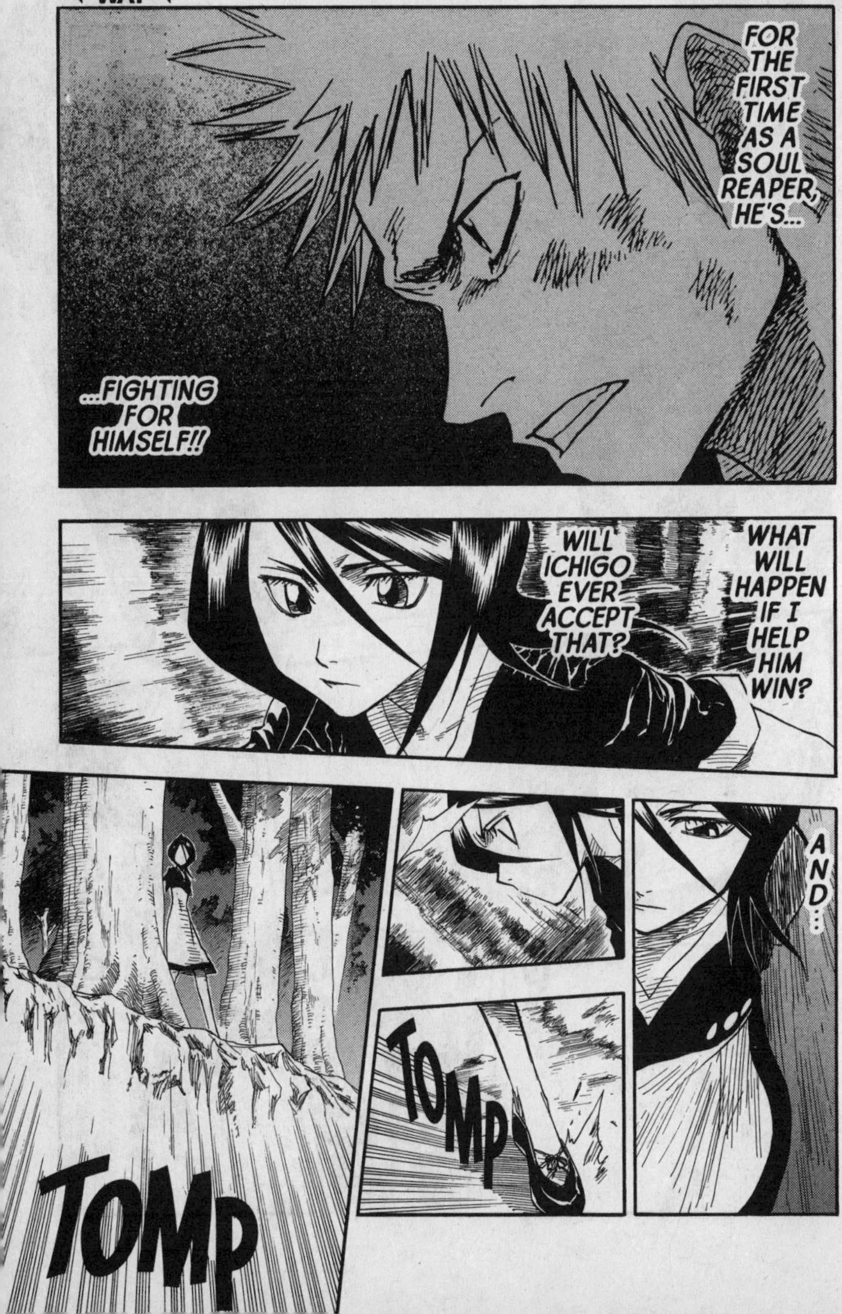

FOR THE FIRST TIME AS A SOUL REAPER, HE'S...
...FIGHTING FOR HIMSELF!!
WHAT WILL HAPPEN IF I HELP HIM WIN?
WILL ICHIGO EVER ACCEPT THAT?
AND...
TOMP
TOMP

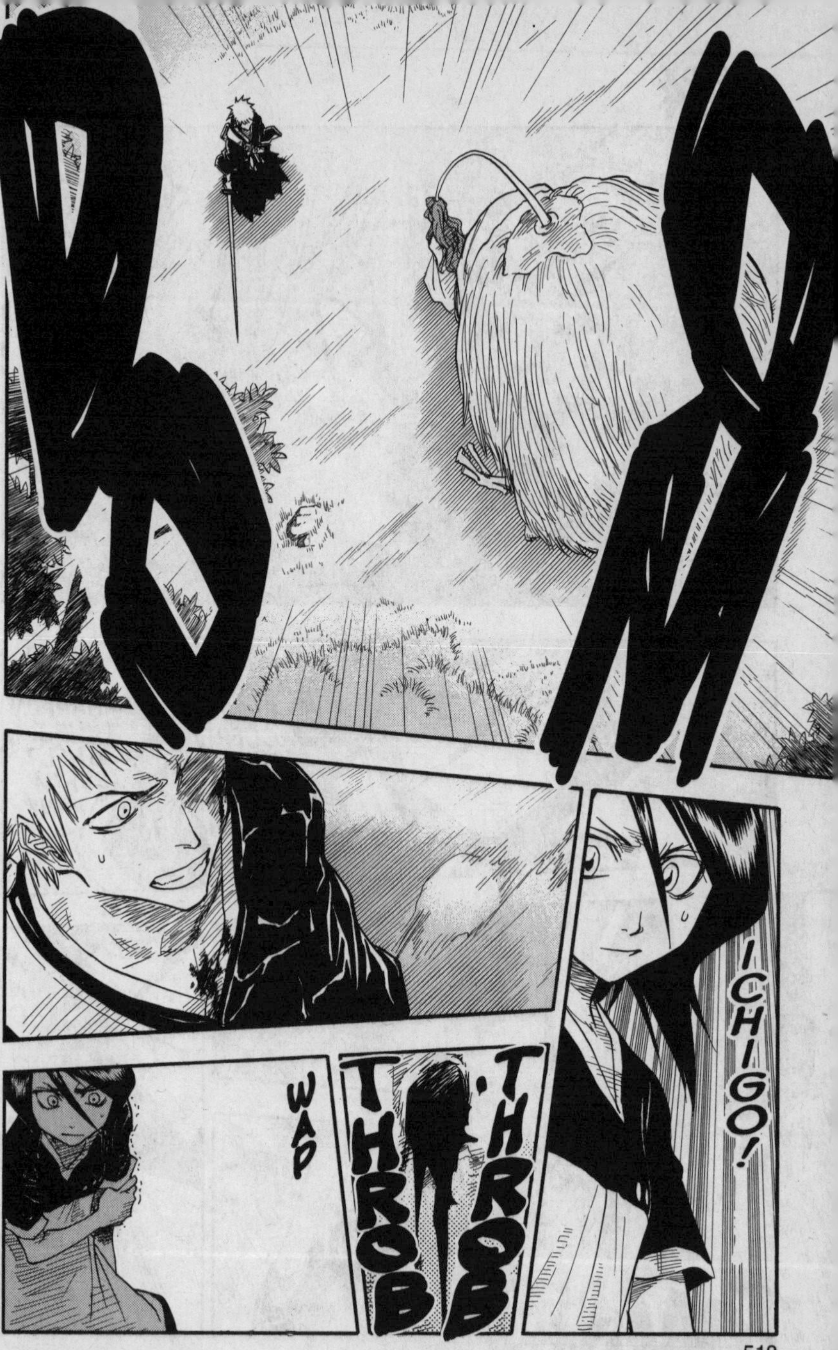
DOOM
ICHIGO!
THROB THROB
WAP

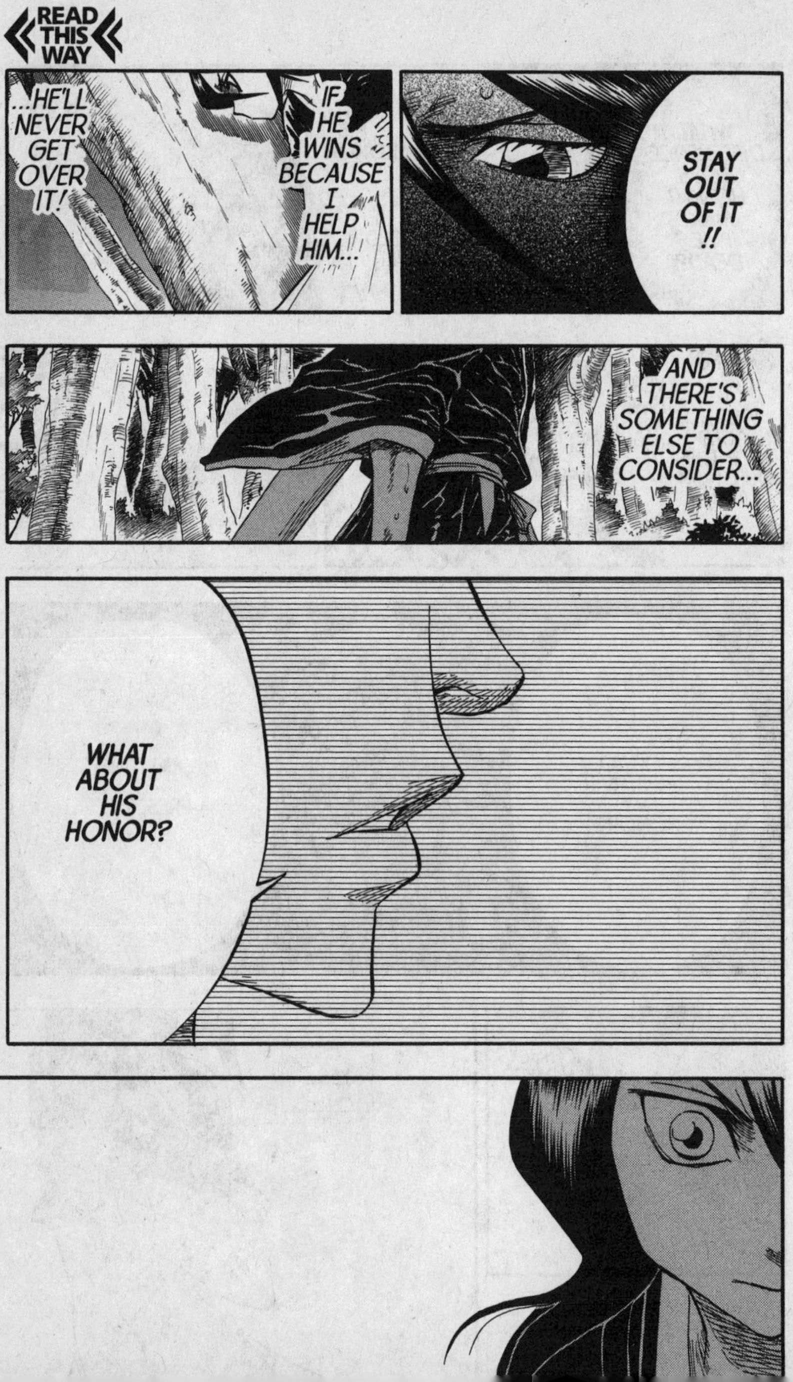
READ THIS WAY
STAY OUT OF IT !!
IF HE WINS BECAUSE I HELP HIM...
...HE'LL NEVER GET OVER IT!
AND THERE'S SOMETHING ELSE TO CONSIDER...
WHAT ABOUT HIS HONOR?

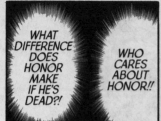

IF YOU HELP HIM NOW...
...HIS LIFE WILL BE SAVED...
BUT HIS HONOR...
...WILL BE DAMAGED FOREVER.
WHO CARES ABOUT HONOR!!
WHAT DIFFERENCE DOES HONOR MAKE IF HE'S DEAD?!
LISTEN...
...AND REMEMBER THIS WELL.
THERE ARE TWO KINDS OF BATTLE.
EVERY TIME WE FIGHT...
...WE'RE FACED WITH THIS QUESTION: AM I...
...FIGHTING TO PRESERVE LIFE...
...OR TO PRESERVE MY HONOR?
YES...
ICHIGO'S HONOR IS AT STAKE.

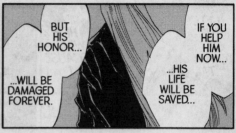

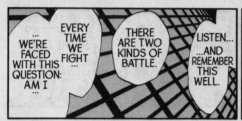

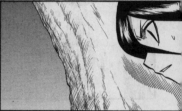

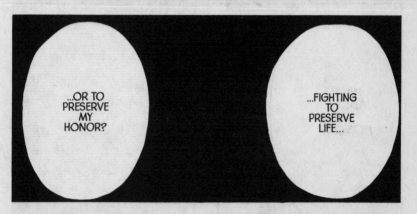

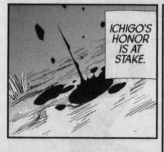

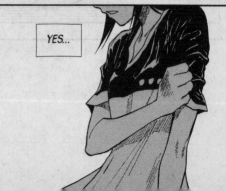

READ THIS WAY

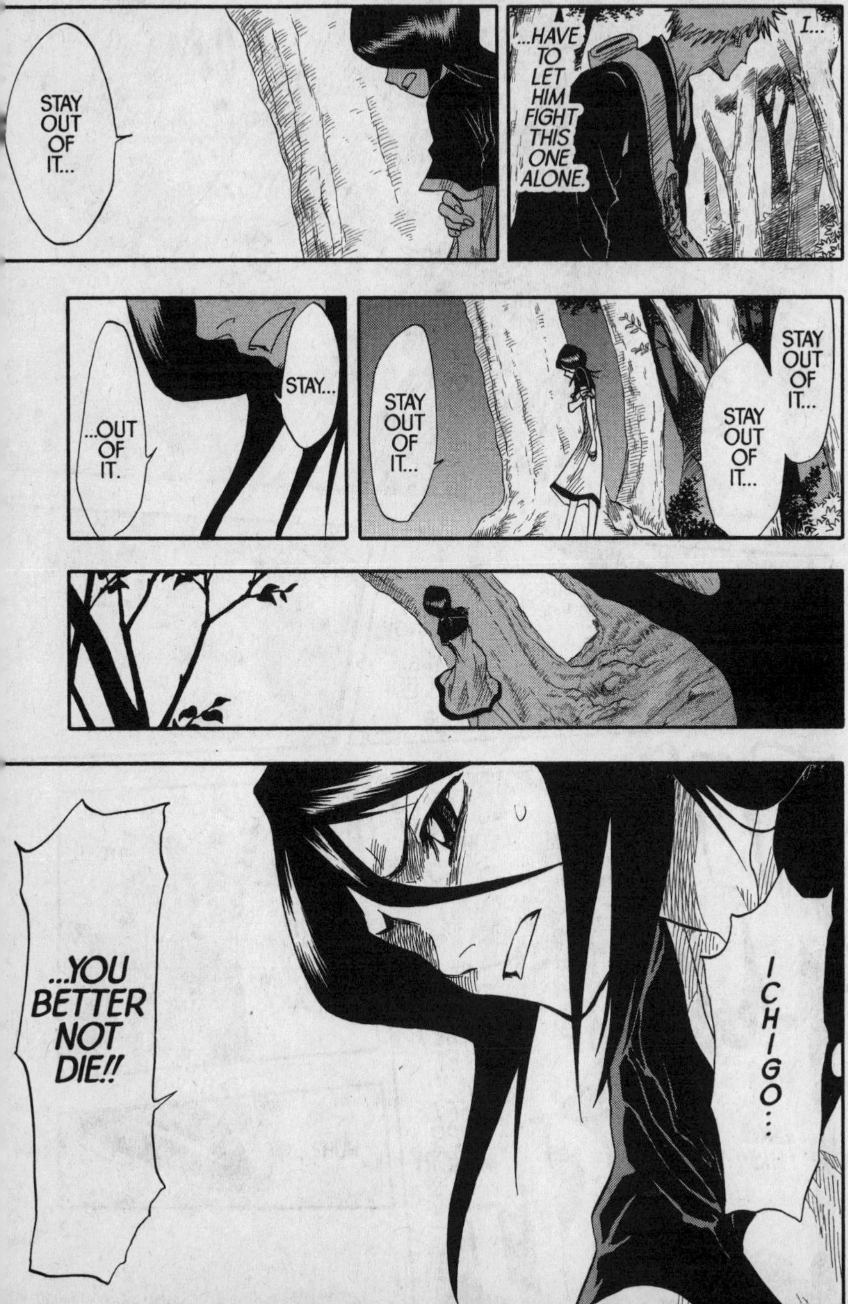
I...
...HAVE TO LET HIM FIGHT THIS ONE ALONE.
STAY OUT OF IT...
STAY OUT OF IT...
STAY OUT OF IT...
STAY OUT OF IT...
STAY...
...OUT OF IT.
ICHIGO...
...YOU BETTER NOT DIE!!

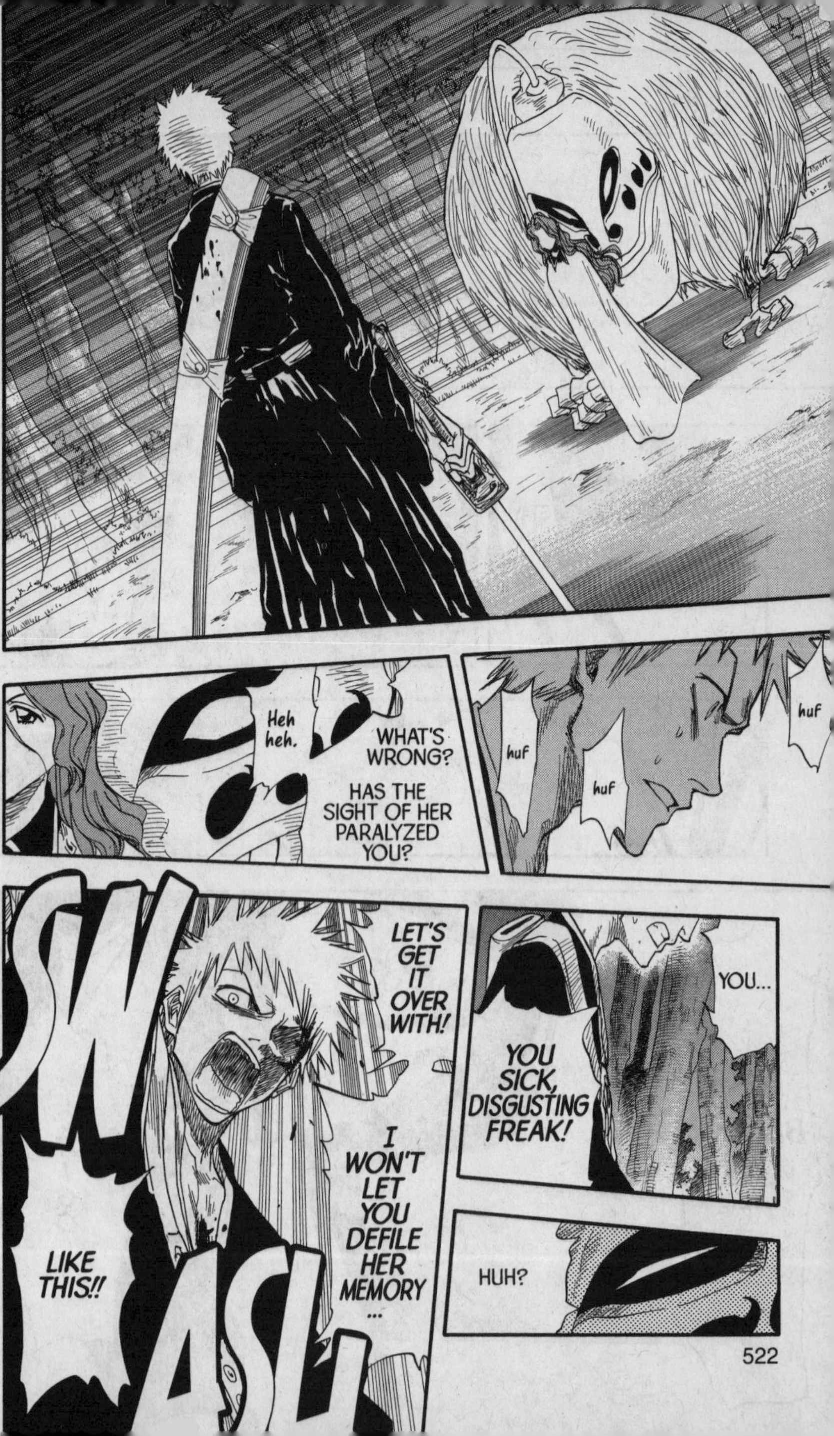
huf
huf
huf
Heh heh.
WHAT'S WRONG?
HAS THE SIGHT OF HER PARALYZED YOU?
YOU...
YOU SICK, DISGUSTING FREAK!
HUH?
LET'S GET IT OVER WITH!
I WON'T LET YOU DEFILE HER MEMORY ...
LIKE THIS!!
SWASH

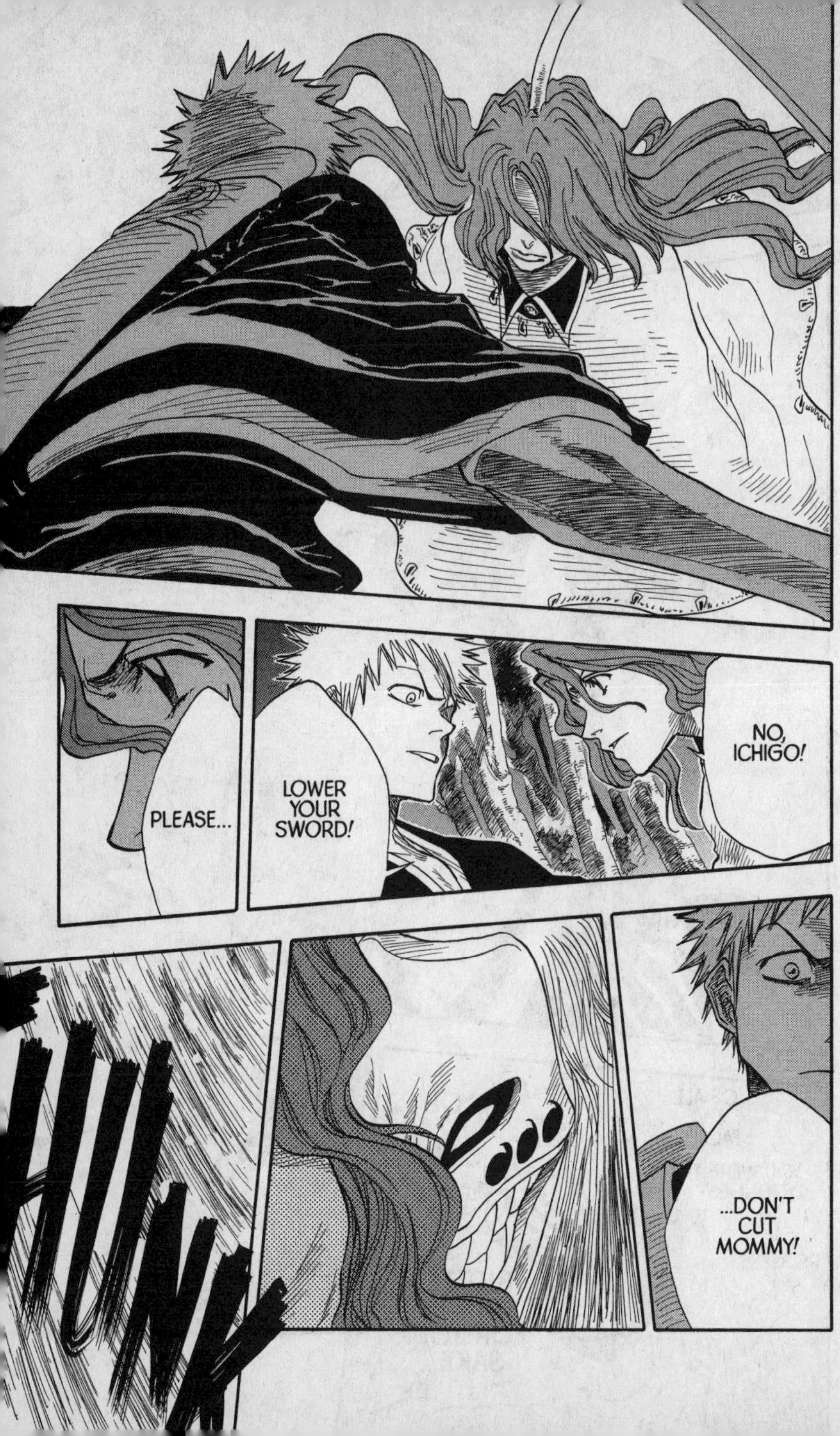
NO, ICHIGO!
LOWER YOUR SWORD!
PLEASE...
...DON'T CUT MOMMY!

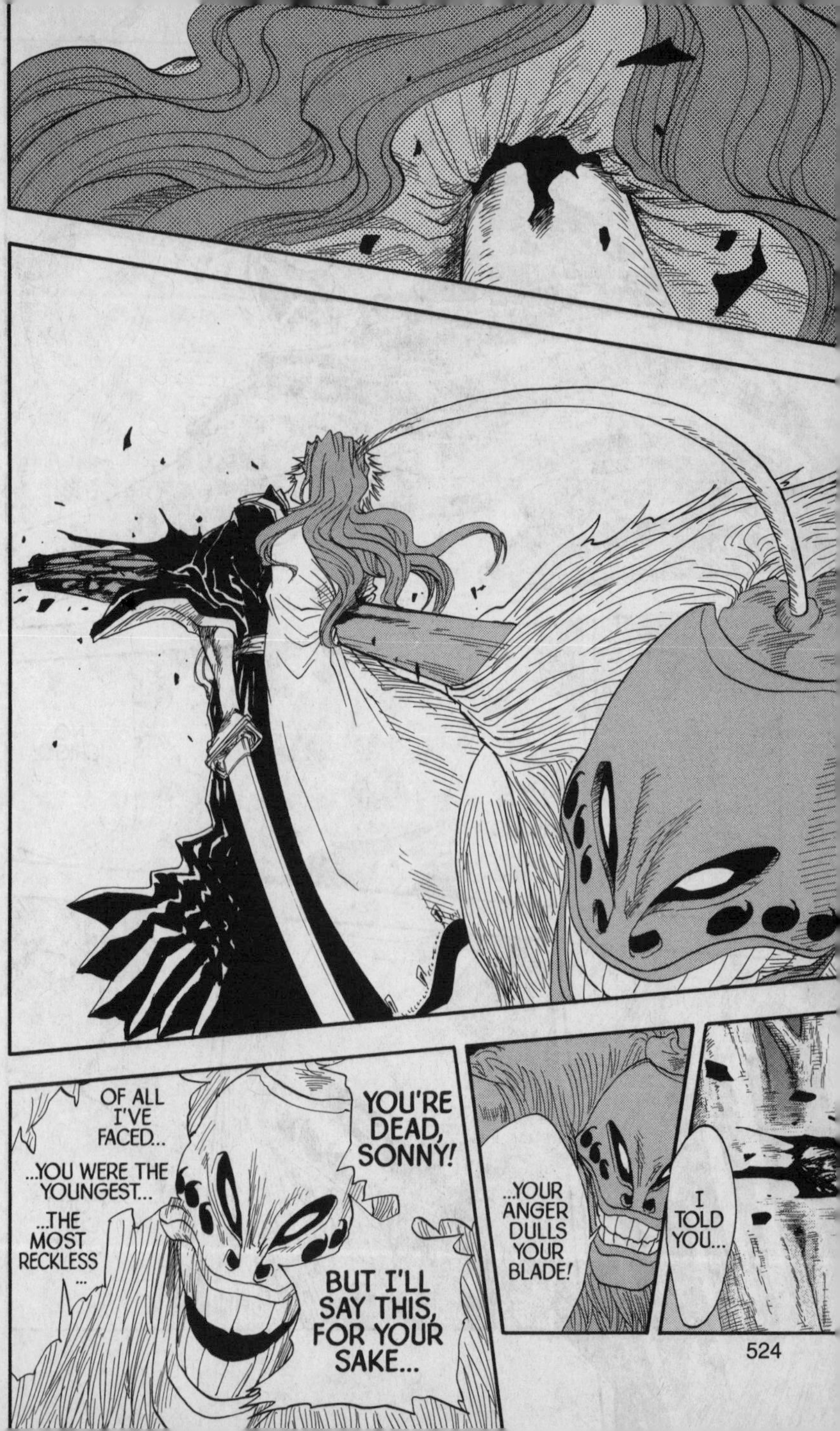
I TOLD YOU...
...YOUR ANGER DULLS YOUR BLADE!
YOU'RE DEAD, SONNY!
OF ALL I'VE FACED...
...YOU WERE THE YOUNGEST...
...THE MOST RECKLESS...
BUT I'LL SAY THIS, FOR YOUR SAKE...

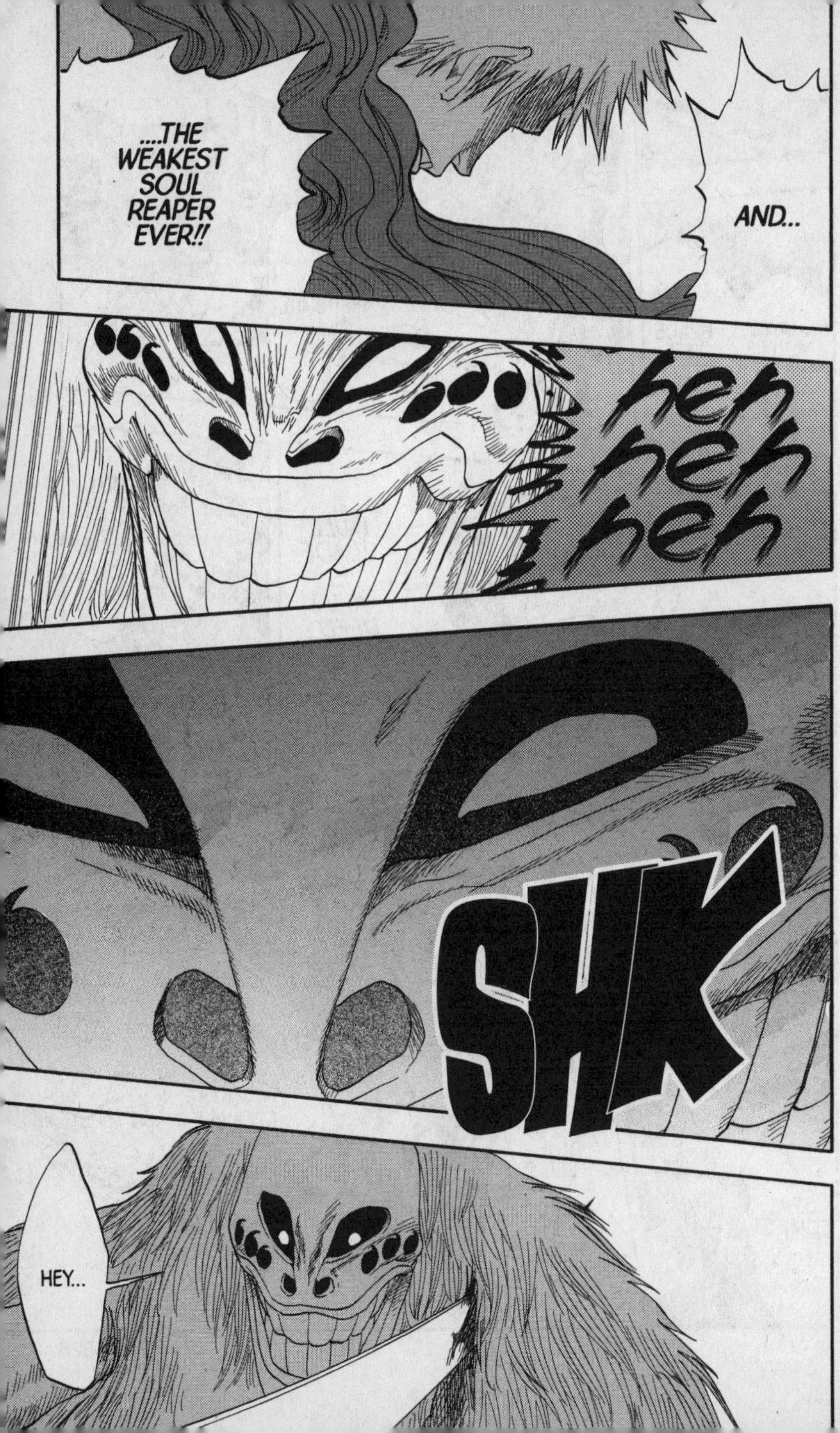
AND...
....THE WEAKEST SOUL REAPER EVER!!
heh heh heh
SHK
HEY...

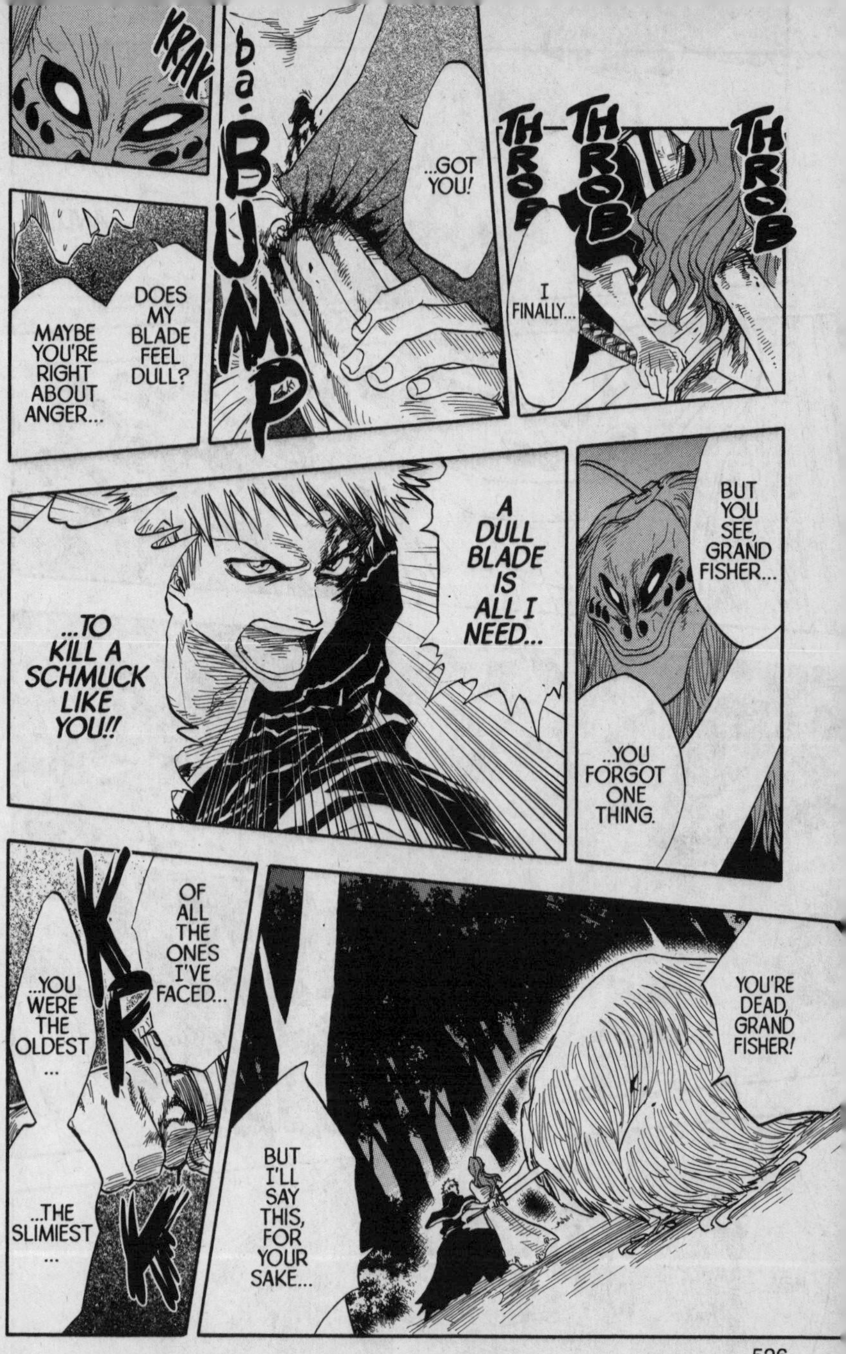
THROB THROB THROB
I FINALLY...
...GOT YOU!
ba-BUMP
KRAK
DOES MY BLADE FEEL DULL?
MAYBE YOU'RE RIGHT ABOUT ANGER...
BUT YOU SEE, GRAND FISHER...
...YOU FORGOT ONE THING.
A DULL BLADE IS ALL I NEED...
...TO KILL A SCHMUCK LIKE YOU!!
YOU'RE DEAD, GRAND FISHER!
BUT I'LL SAY THIS, FOR YOUR SAKE...
OF ALL THE ONES I'VE FACED...
...YOU WERE THE OLDEST...
...THE SLIMIEST...

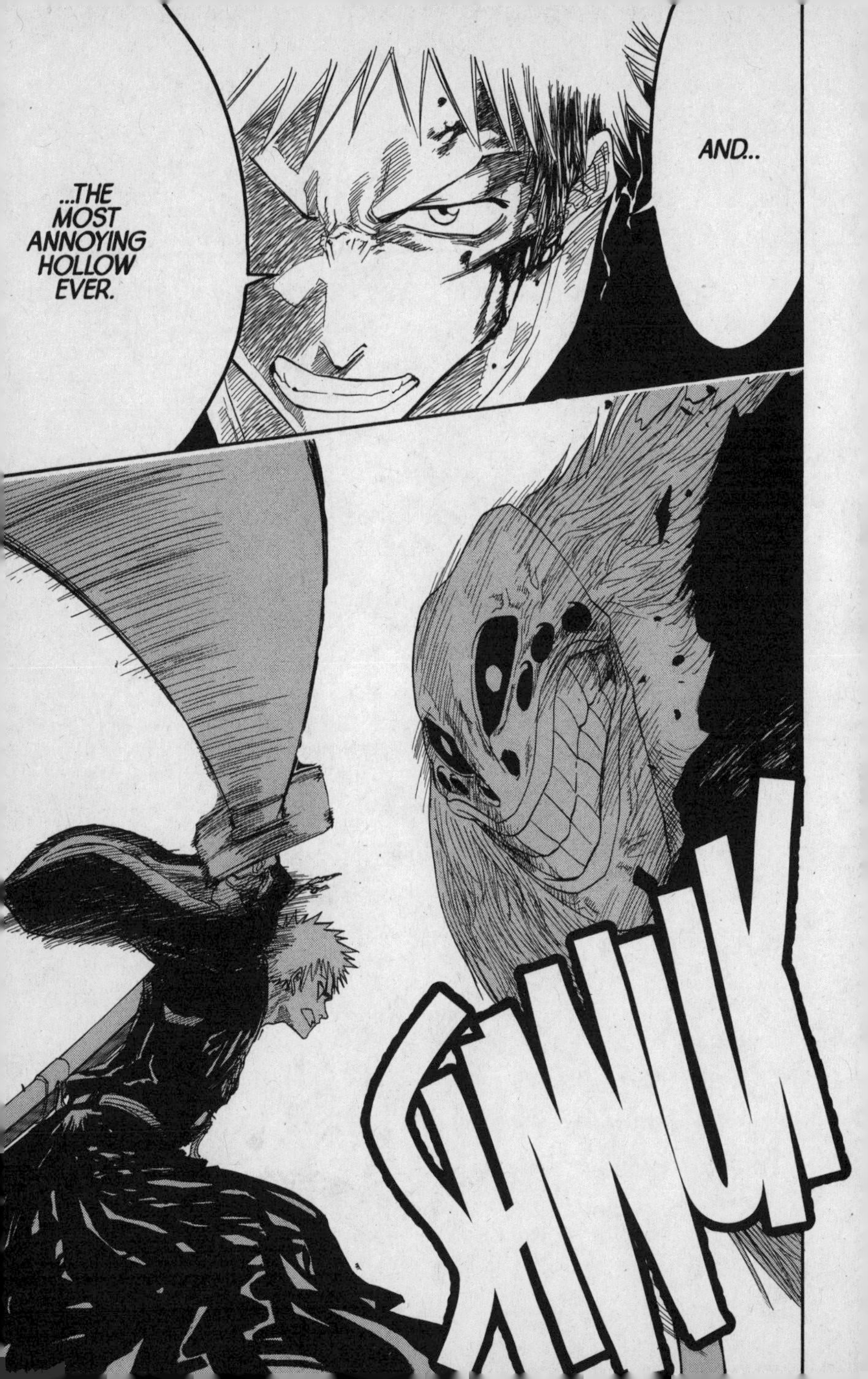
AND...
...THE MOST ANNOYING HOLLOW EVER.
SHWUK

PL◯UP

ksssssssssssssh

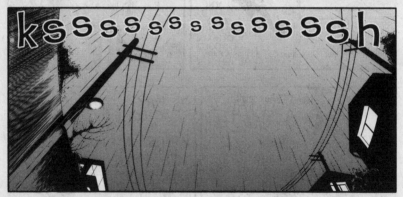

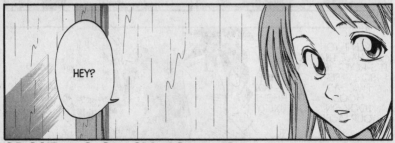

HEY?

24. 6/17 op. 8 One-Sided Sympathy

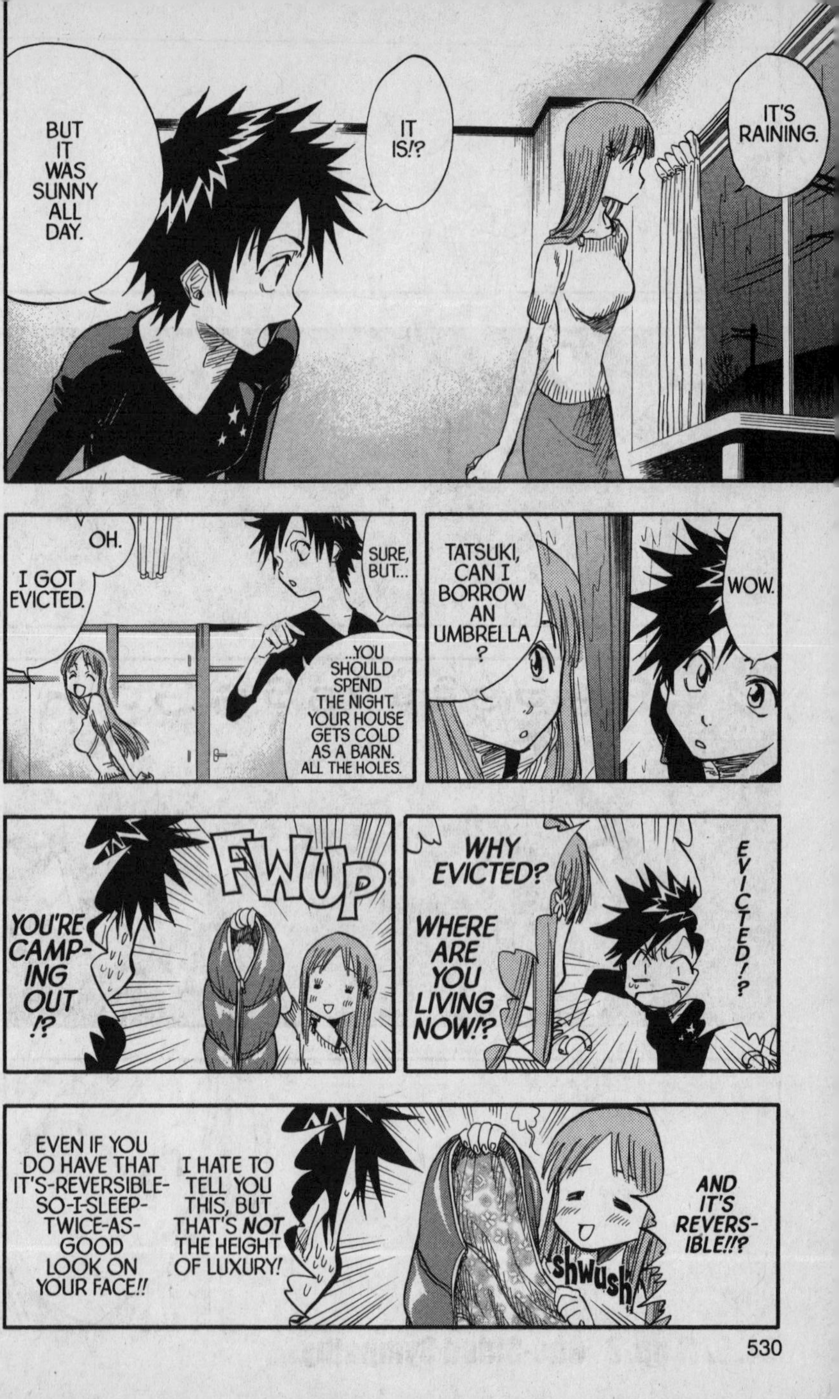

IT'S RAINING.
IT IS!?
BUT IT WAS SUNNY ALL DAY.
WOW.
TATSUKI, CAN I BORROW AN UMBRELLA?
SURE, BUT...
...YOU SHOULD SPEND THE NIGHT. YOUR HOUSE GETS COLD AS A BARN. ALL THE HOLES.
OH.
I GOT EVICTED.
EVICTED!?
WHY EVICTED?
WHERE ARE YOU LIVING NOW!?
FWUP
YOU'RE CAMPING OUT!?
AND IT'S REVERSIBLE!!?
shwush
I HATE TO TELL YOU THIS, BUT THAT'S ***NOT*** THE HEIGHT OF LUXURY!
EVEN IF YOU DO HAVE THAT IT'S-REVERSIBLE-SO-I-SLEEP-TWICE-AS-GOOD LOOK ON YOUR FACE!!

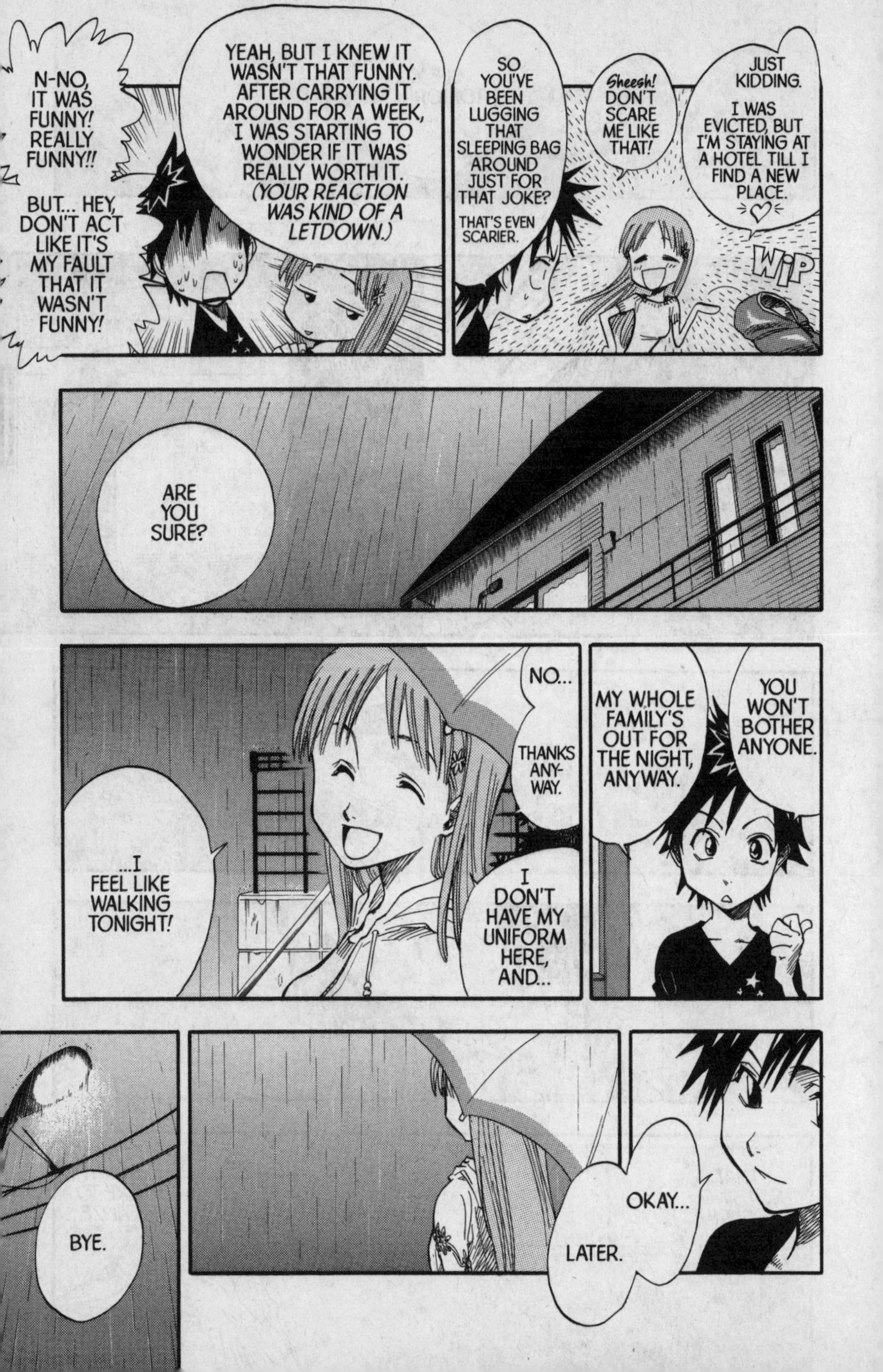
JUST KIDDING.
I WAS EVICTED, BUT I'M STAYING AT A HOTEL TILL I FIND A NEW PLACE. ♡
WIP
Sheesh! DON'T SCARE ME LIKE THAT!
SO YOU'VE BEEN LUGGING THAT SLEEPING BAG AROUND JUST FOR THAT JOKE?
THAT'S EVEN SCARIER.
YEAH, BUT I KNEW IT WASN'T THAT FUNNY. AFTER CARRYING IT AROUND FOR A WEEK, I WAS STARTING TO WONDER IF IT WAS REALLY WORTH IT. (YOUR REACTION WAS KIND OF A LETDOWN.)
N-NO, IT WAS FUNNY! REALLY FUNNY!!
BUT... HEY, DON'T ACT LIKE IT'S MY FAULT THAT IT WASN'T FUNNY!
ARE YOU SURE?
YOU WON'T BOTHER ANYONE.
MY WHOLE FAMILY'S OUT FOR THE NIGHT, ANYWAY.
NO...
THANKS ANY-WAY.
I DON'T HAVE MY UNIFORM HERE, AND...
...I FEEL LIKE WALKING TONIGHT!
OKAY...
LATER.
BYE.

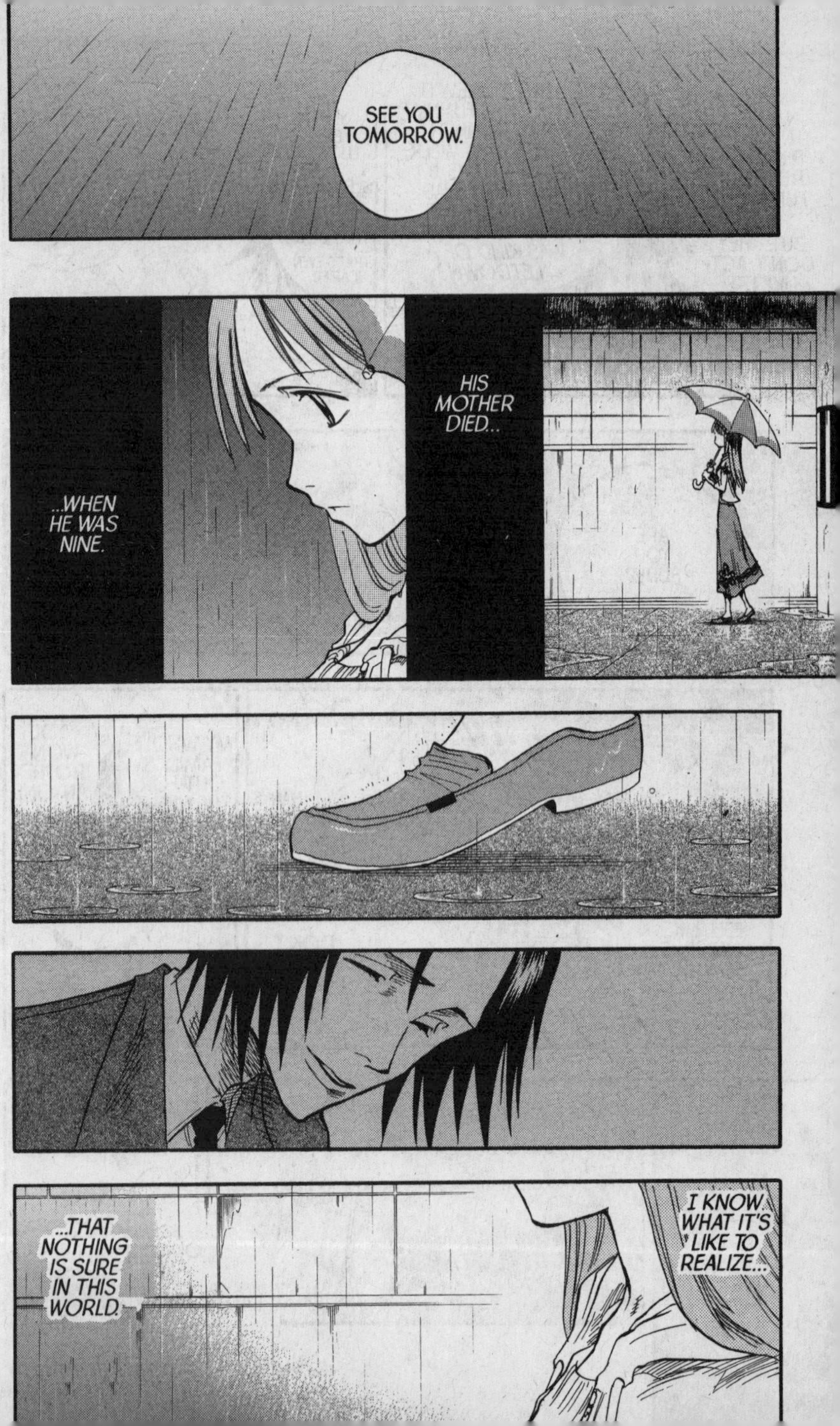
SEE YOU TOMORROW.
HIS MOTHER DIED...
...WHEN HE WAS NINE.
I KNOW WHAT IT'S LIKE TO REALIZE...
...THAT NOTHING IS SURE IN THIS WORLD.

READ THIS WAY

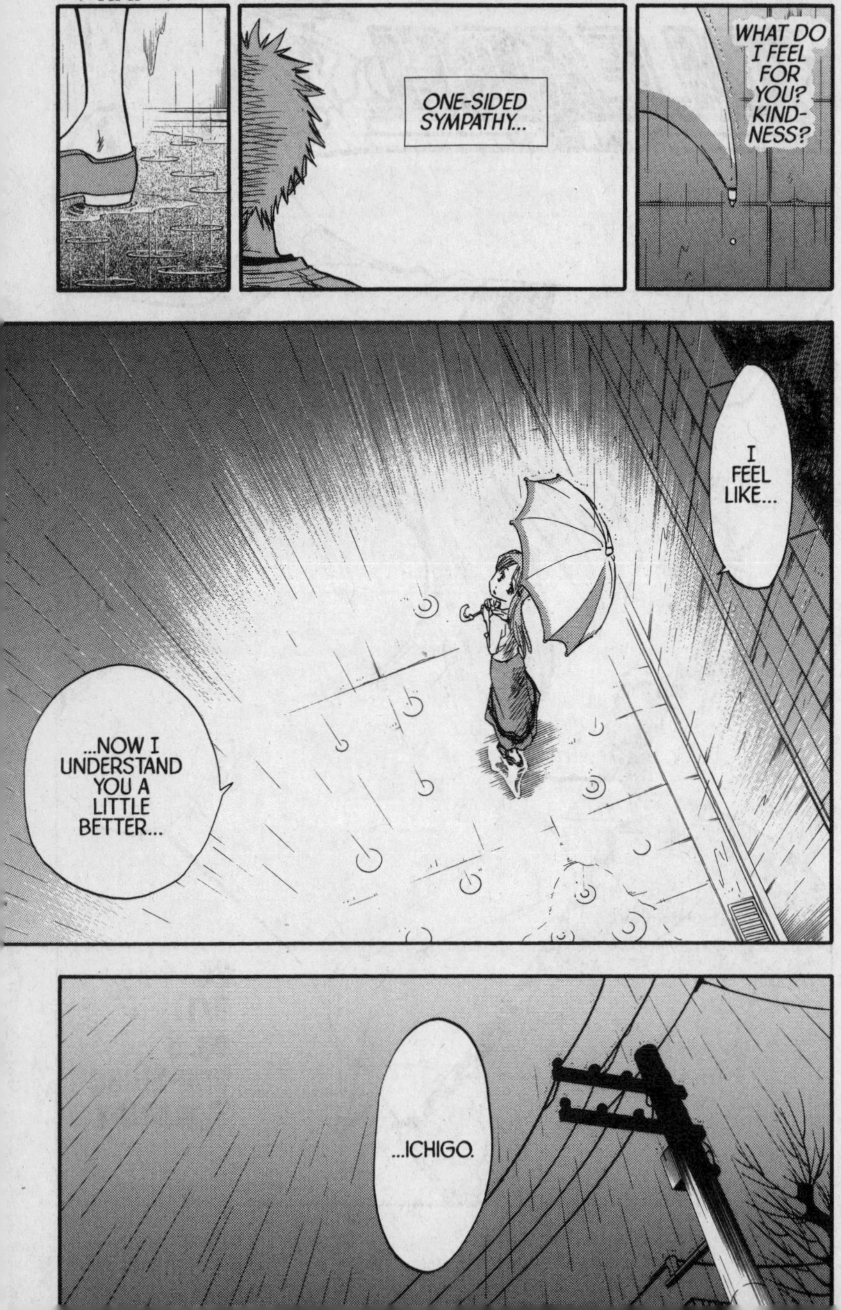
WHAT DO I FEEL FOR YOU? KINDNESS?
ONE-SIDED SYMPATHY...
I FEEL LIKE...
...NOW I UNDERSTAND YOU A LITTLE BETTER...
...ICHIGO.

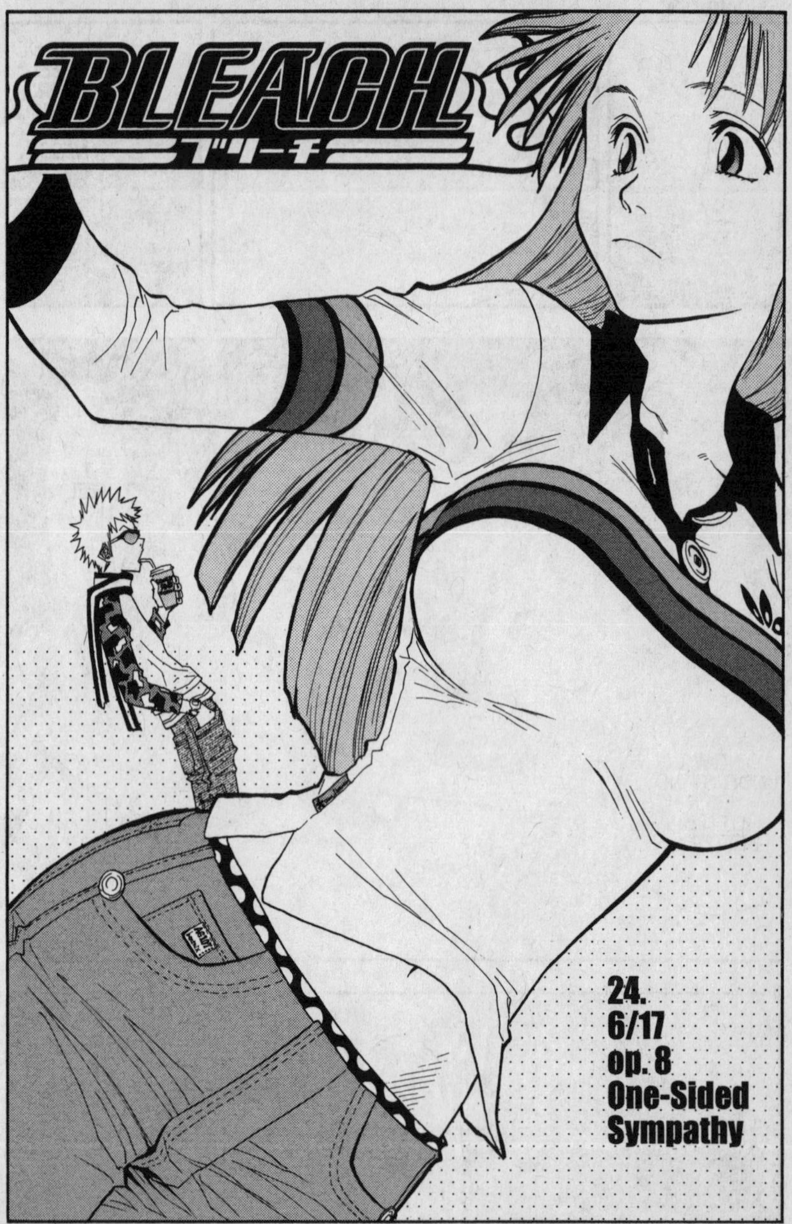
BLEACH
ブリーチ
24.
6/17
op. 8
One-Sided
Sympathy

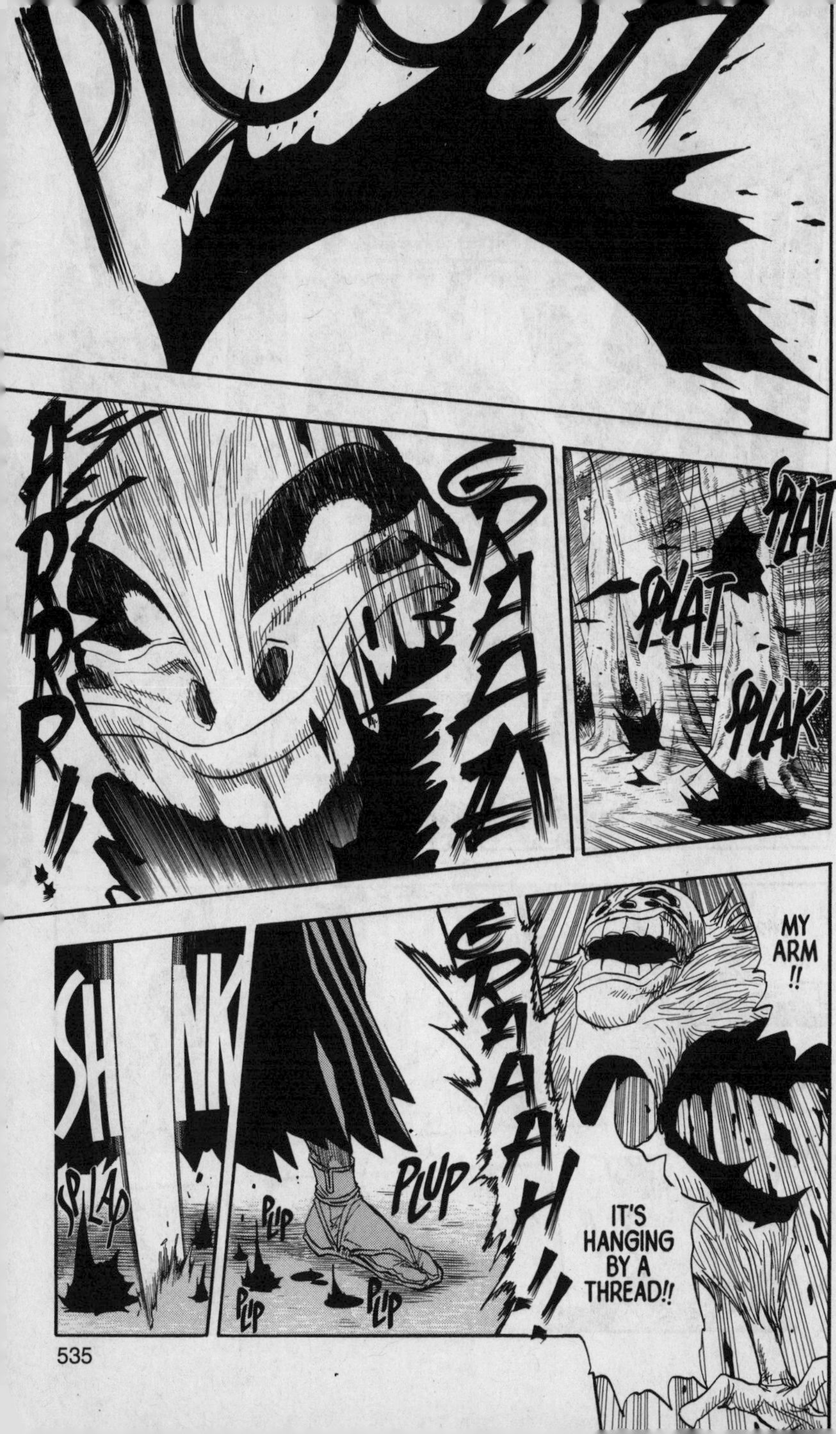
SPLAT
SPLAT
SPLAK
MY ARM!!
IT'S HANGING BY A THREAD!!
PLUP
PLIP
PLIP
PLIP
SPLAP

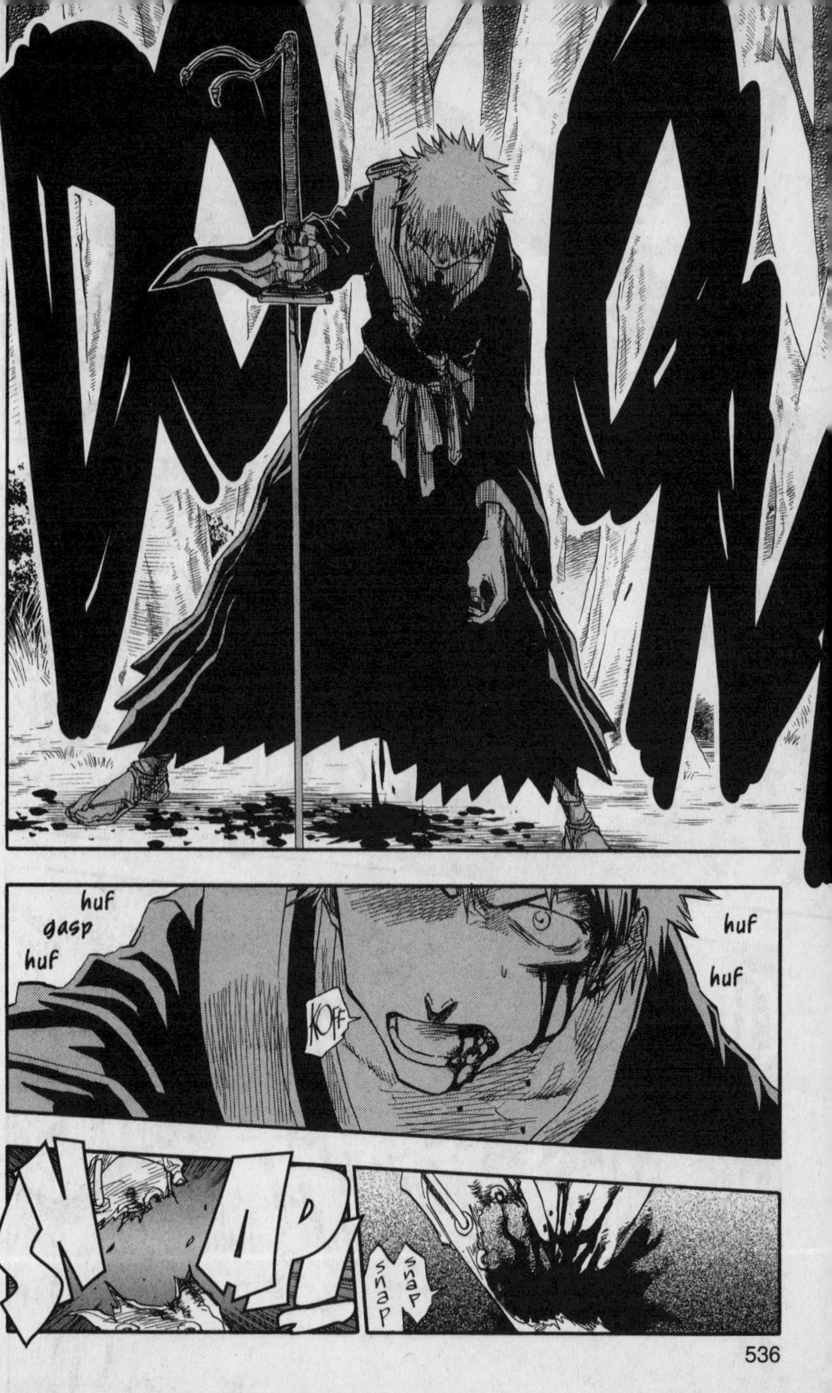
huf
huf
huf
gasp
huf
KOFF
snap
snap
SNAP!

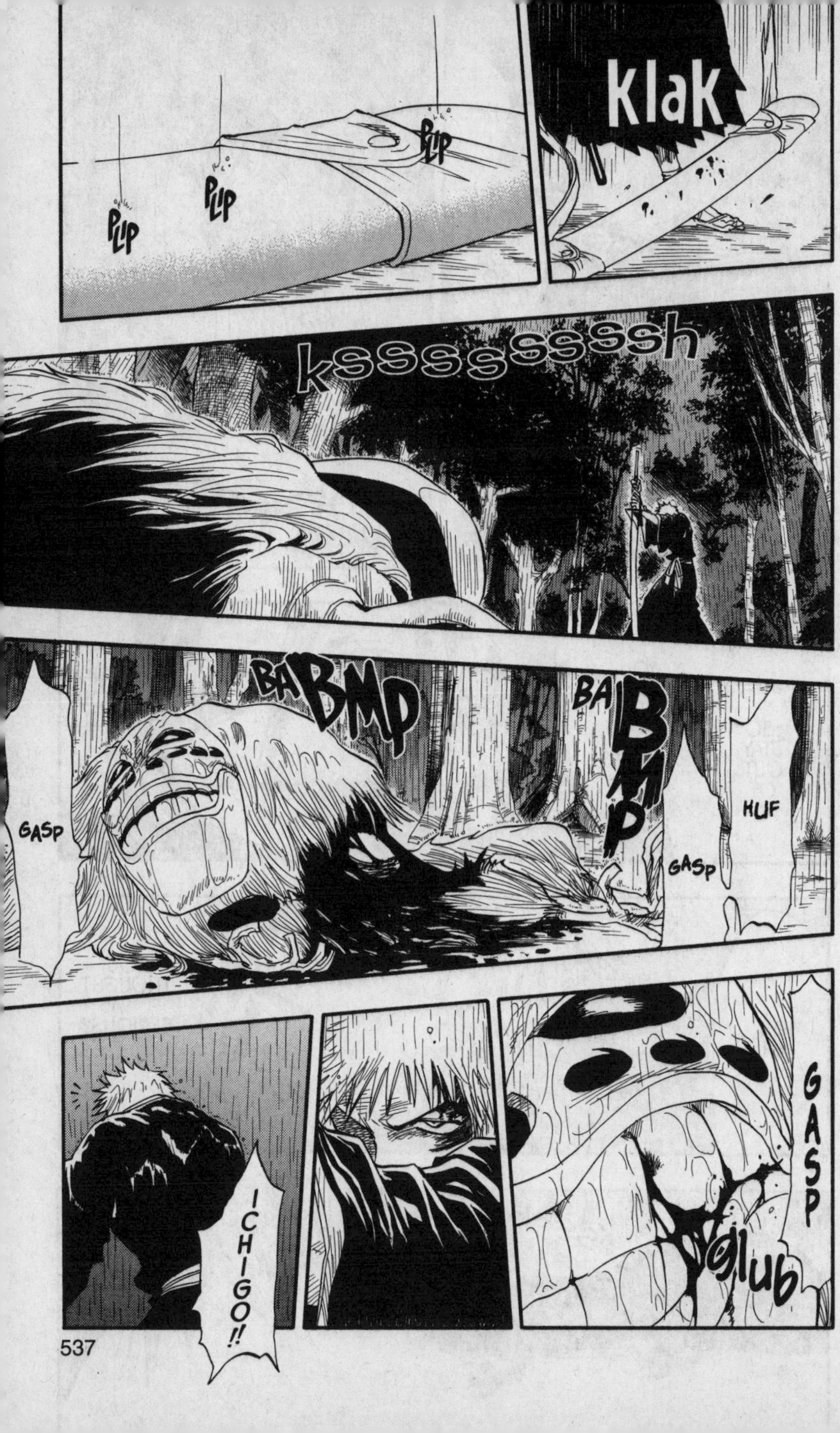

klak
PLIP
PLIP
PLIP
kssssssssh
HUF
GASP
BABMP
BABMP
GASP
GASP
glub
ICHIGO!!

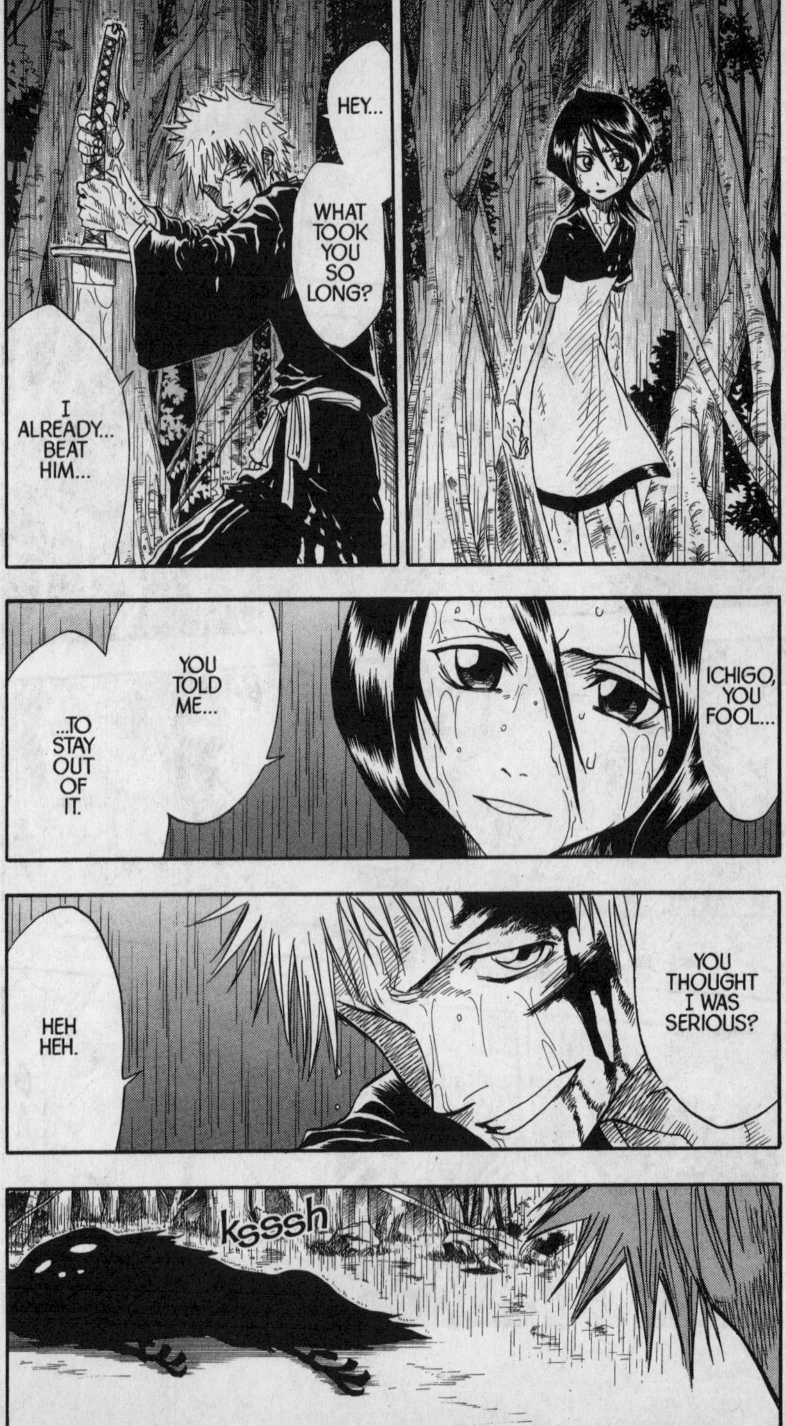
HEY...
WHAT TOOK YOU SO LONG?
I ALREADY... BEAT HIM...
ICHIGO, YOU FOOL...
YOU TOLD ME...
...TO STAY OUT OF IT.
YOU THOUGHT I WAS SERIOUS?
HEH HEH.
ksssh

READ THIS WAY

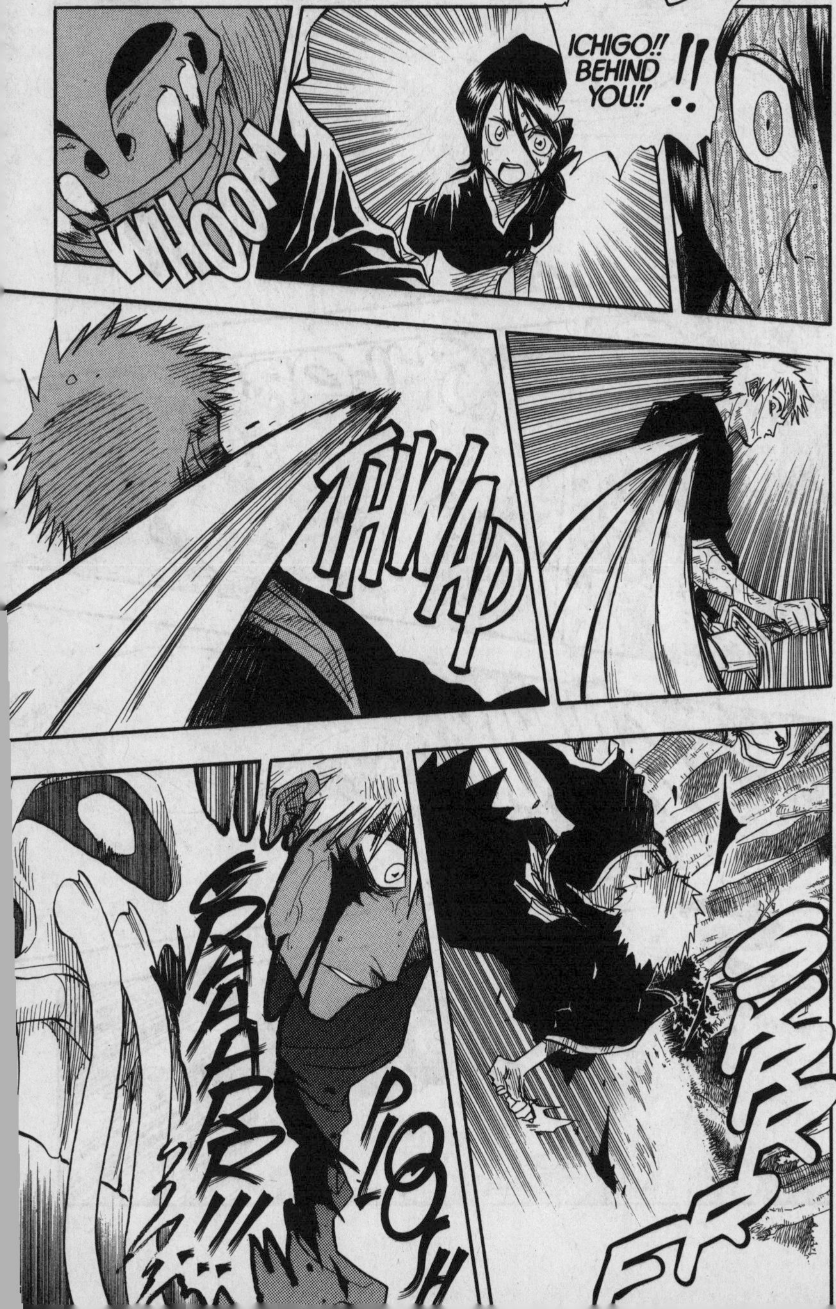
!!
ICHIGO!! BEHIND YOU!!
WHOOM
THWAP

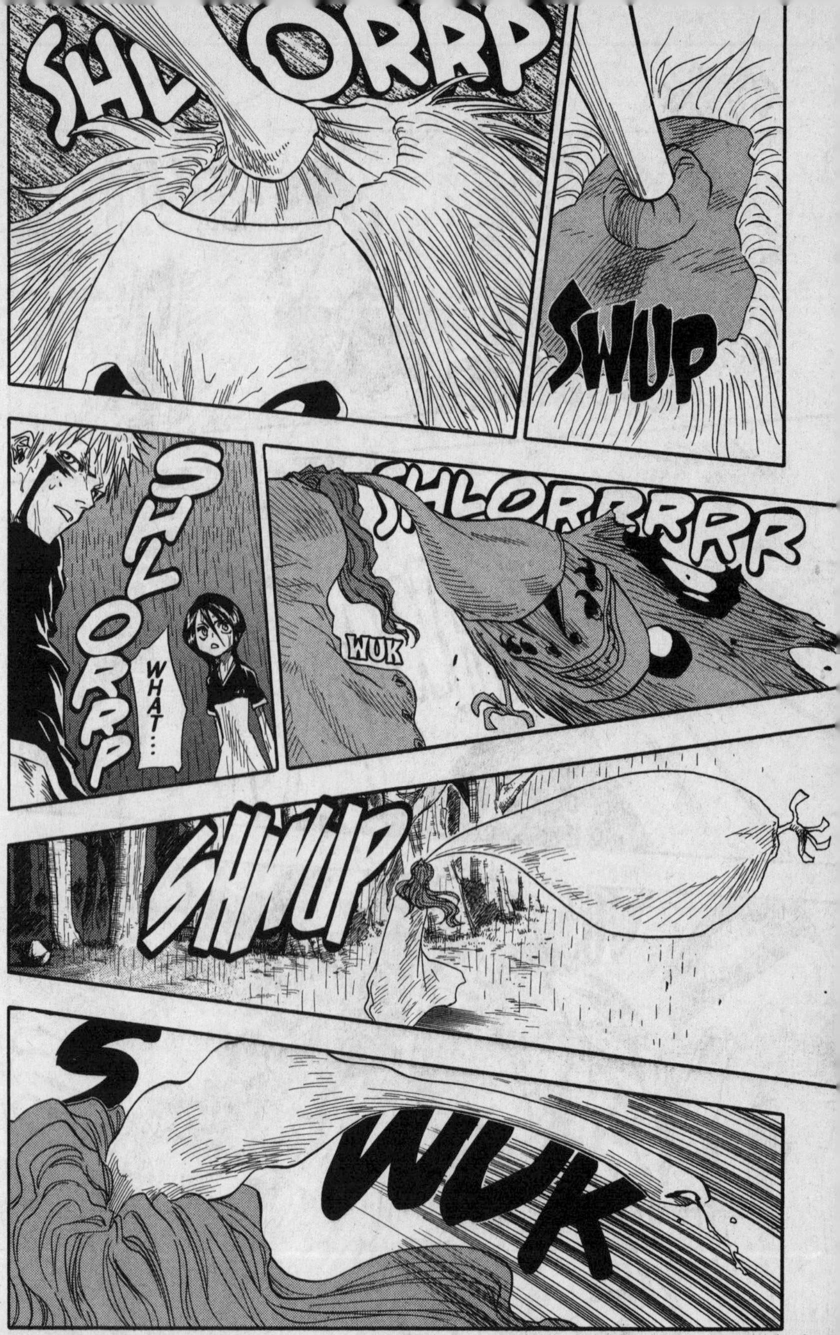
SWUP
SHLORRP
SHLORRRRR
WUK
SHLORRP
WHAT...
SHWUP
SWUK

READ THIS WAY

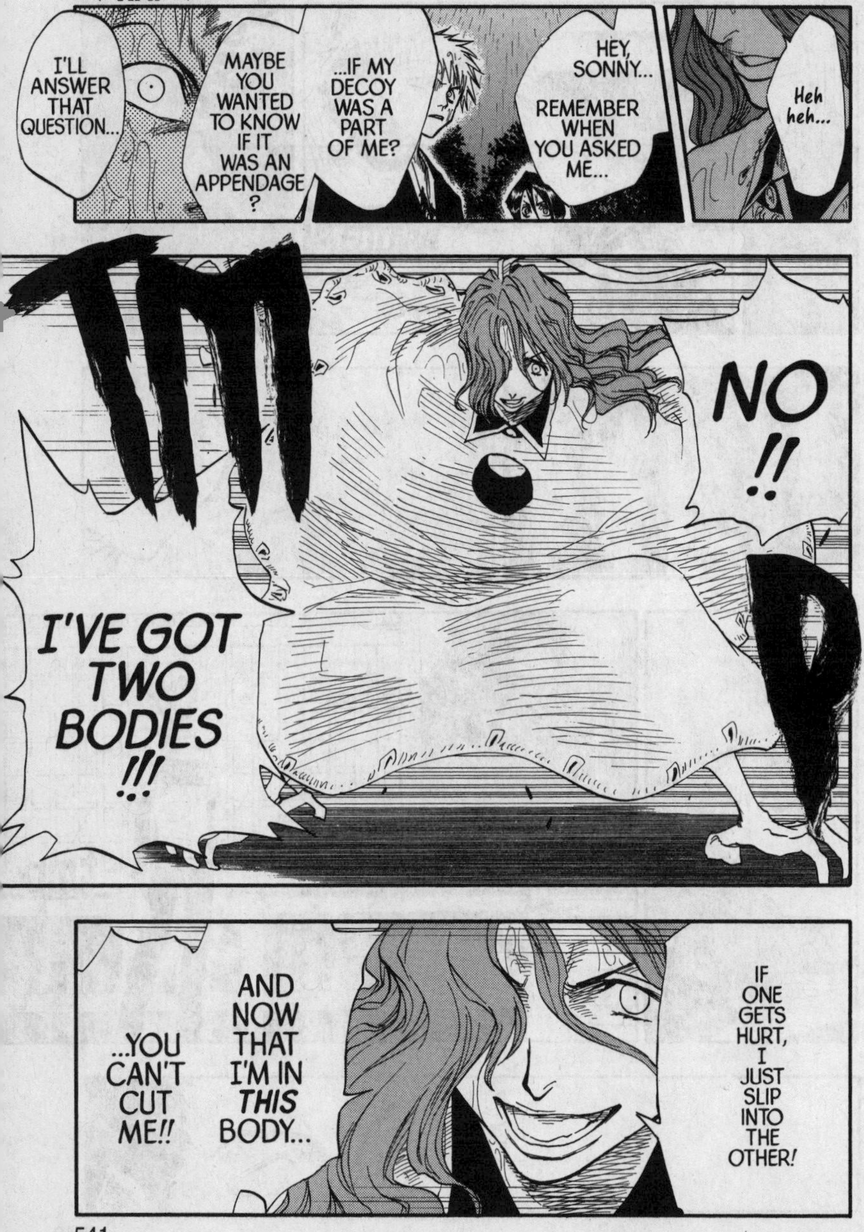
Heh heh...
HEY, SONNY... REMEMBER WHEN YOU ASKED ME...
...IF MY DECOY WAS A PART OF ME?
MAYBE YOU WANTED TO KNOW IF IT WAS AN APPENDAGE?
I'LL ANSWER THAT QUESTION...
NO!!
I'VE GOT TWO BODIES!!!
IF ONE GETS HURT, I JUST SLIP INTO THE OTHER!
AND NOW THAT I'M IN *THIS* BODY...
...YOU CAN'T CUT ME!!

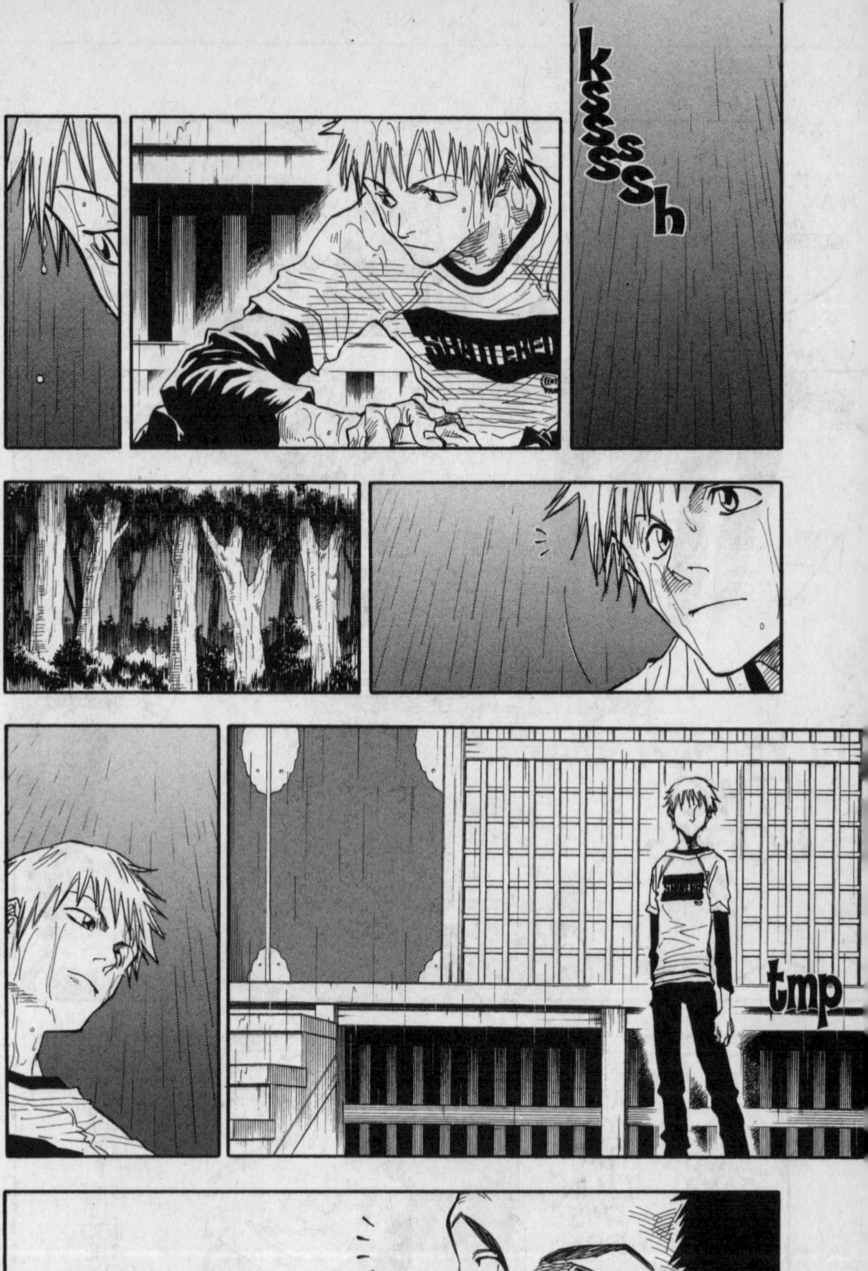
kssssh
tmp

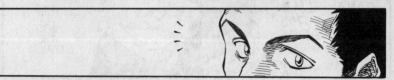

READ THIS WAY

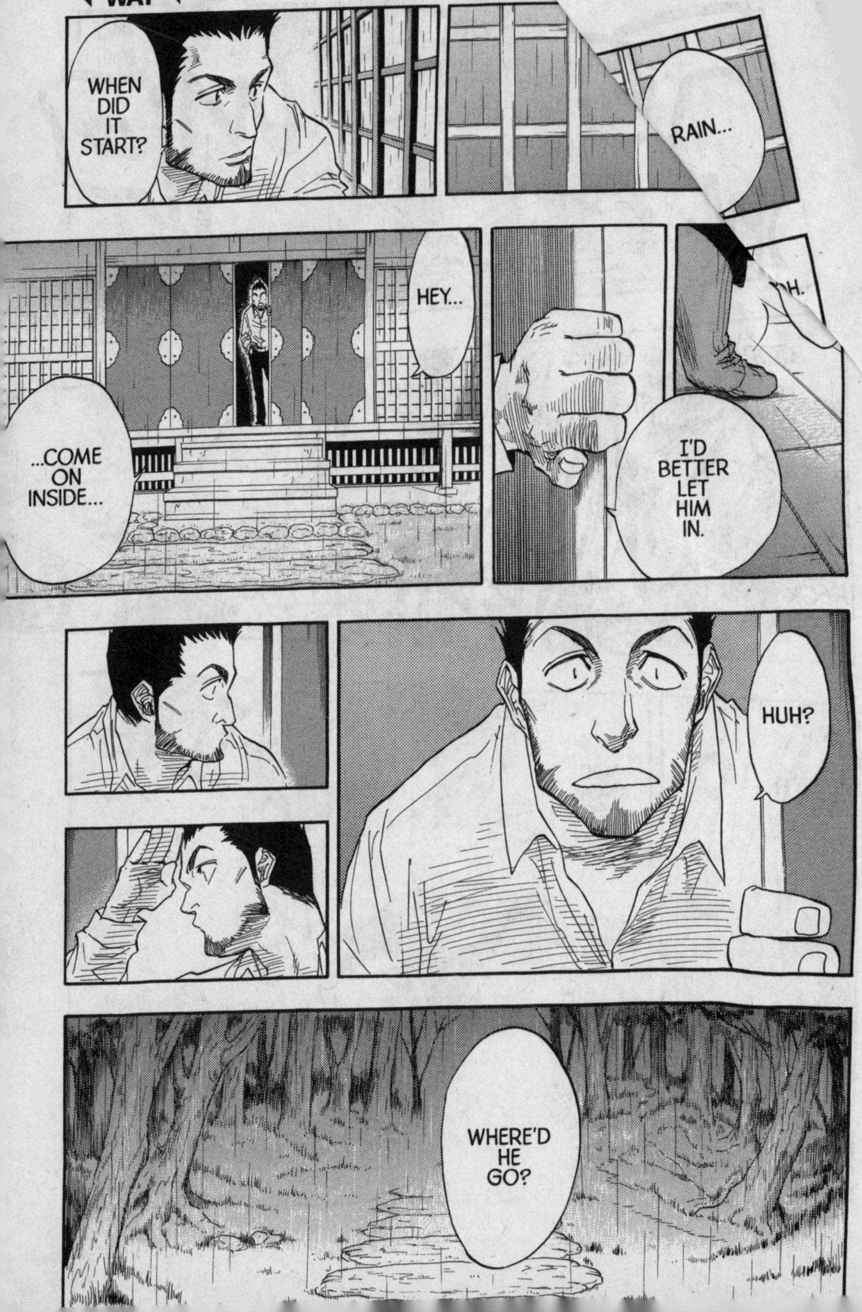
RAIN...
WHEN DID IT START?
I'D BETTER LET HIM IN.
HEY...
...COME ON INSIDE...
HUH?
WHERE'D HE GO?

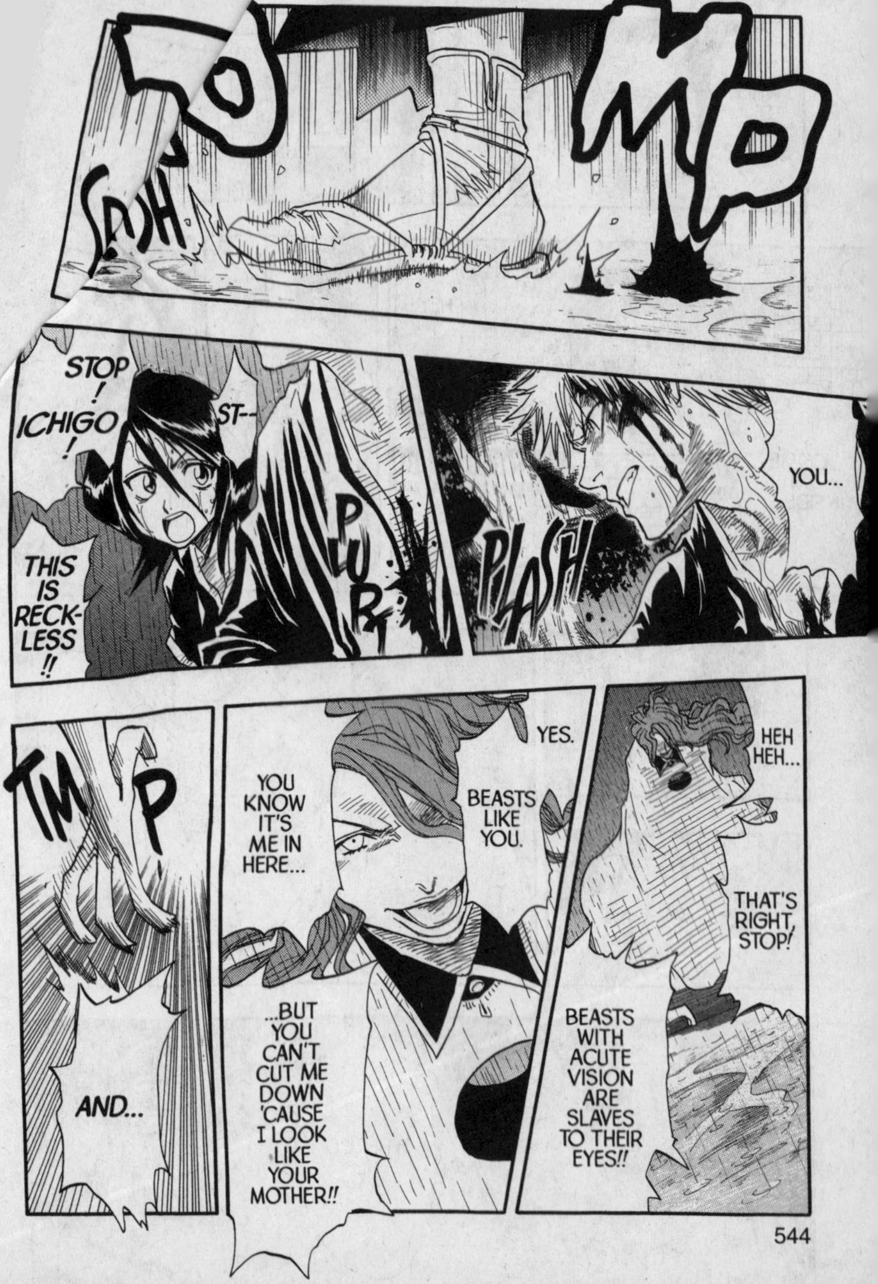
DO
MP
SPLSH
YOU...
PLASH
STOP! ICHIGO!
THIS IS RECKLESS!!
ST--
PLURT
HEH HEH...
THAT'S RIGHT, STOP!
BEASTS WITH ACUTE VISION ARE SLAVES TO THEIR EYES!!
YES.
BEASTS LIKE YOU.
YOU KNOW IT'S ME IN HERE...
...BUT YOU CAN'T CUT ME DOWN 'CAUSE I LOOK LIKE YOUR MOTHER!!
TMP
AND...

READ THIS WAY

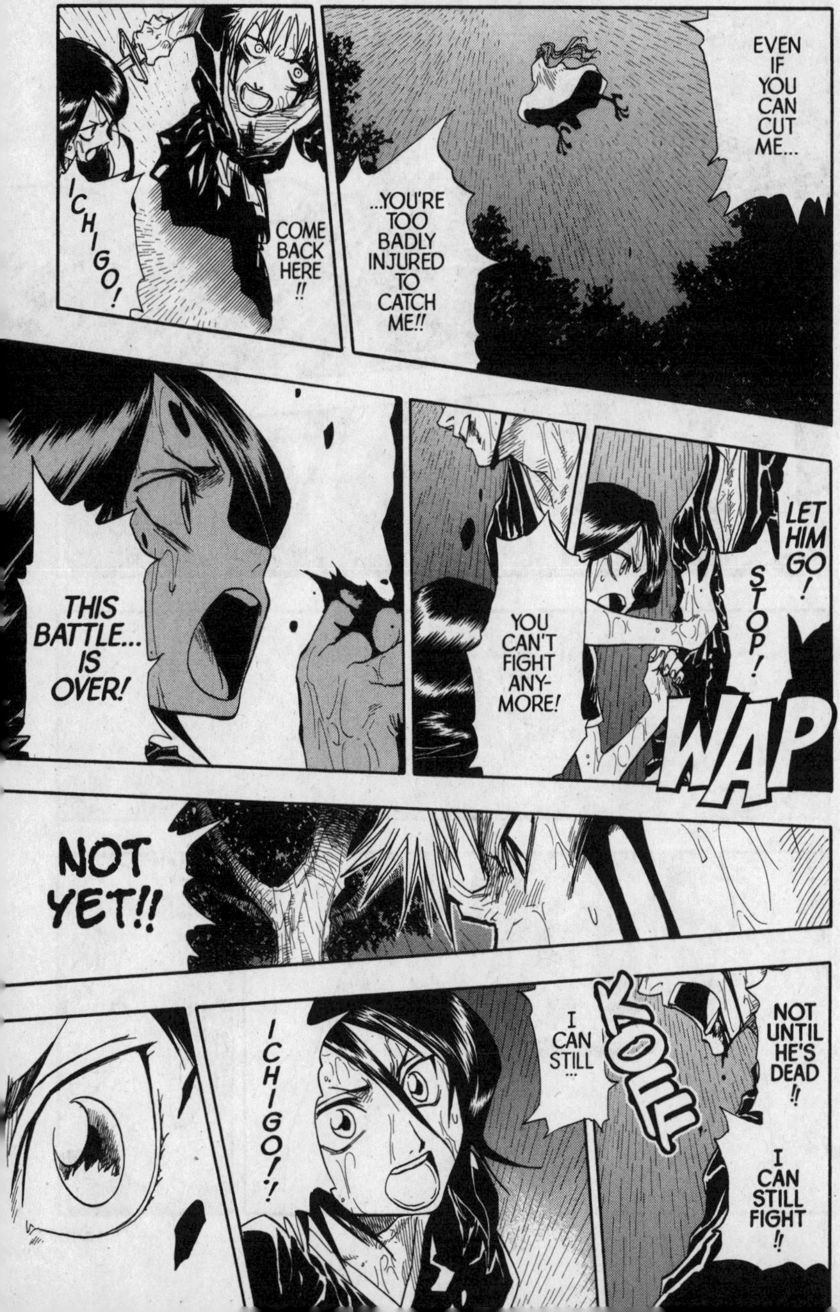

EVEN IF YOU CAN CUT ME...
...YOU'RE TOO BADLY INJURED TO CATCH ME!!
COME BACK HERE!!
ICHIGO!
LET HIM GO!
STOP!
YOU CAN'T FIGHT ANYMORE!
WAP
THIS BATTLE... IS OVER!
NOT YET!!
NOT UNTIL HE'S DEAD!!
I CAN STILL FIGHT!!
KOM
I CAN STILL...
ICHIGO!!

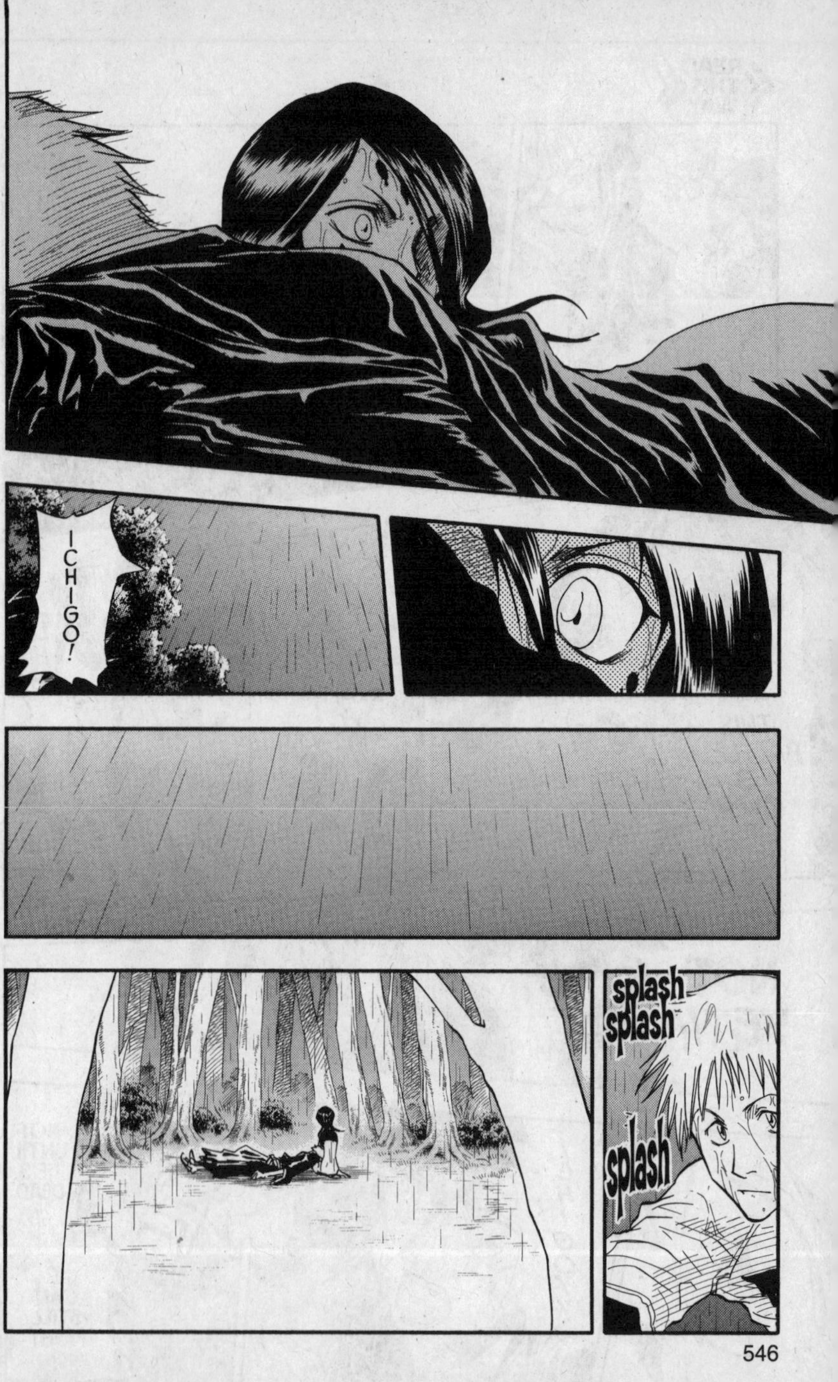
ICHIGO!
splash
splash
splash

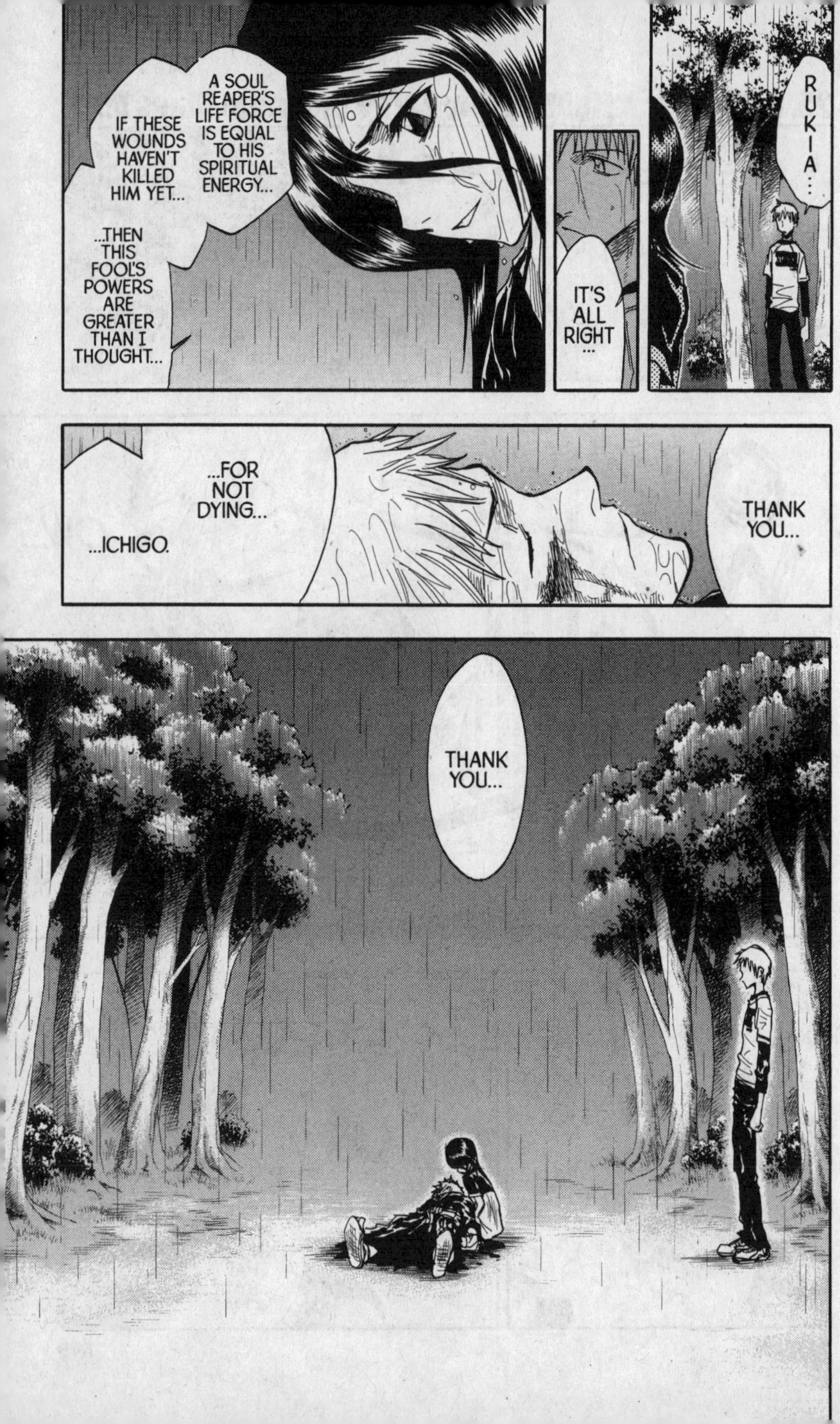
RUKIA...
IT'S ALL RIGHT...
A SOUL REAPER'S LIFE FORCE IS EQUAL TO HIS SPIRITUAL ENERGY...
IF THESE WOUNDS HAVEN'T KILLED HIM YET...
...THEN THIS FOOL'S POWERS ARE GREATER THAN I THOUGHT...
THANK YOU...
...FOR NOT DYING...
...ICHIGO.
THANK YOU...

25. 6/17 op. 9 A Fighting Boy 2 (The Cigarette Blues Mix)

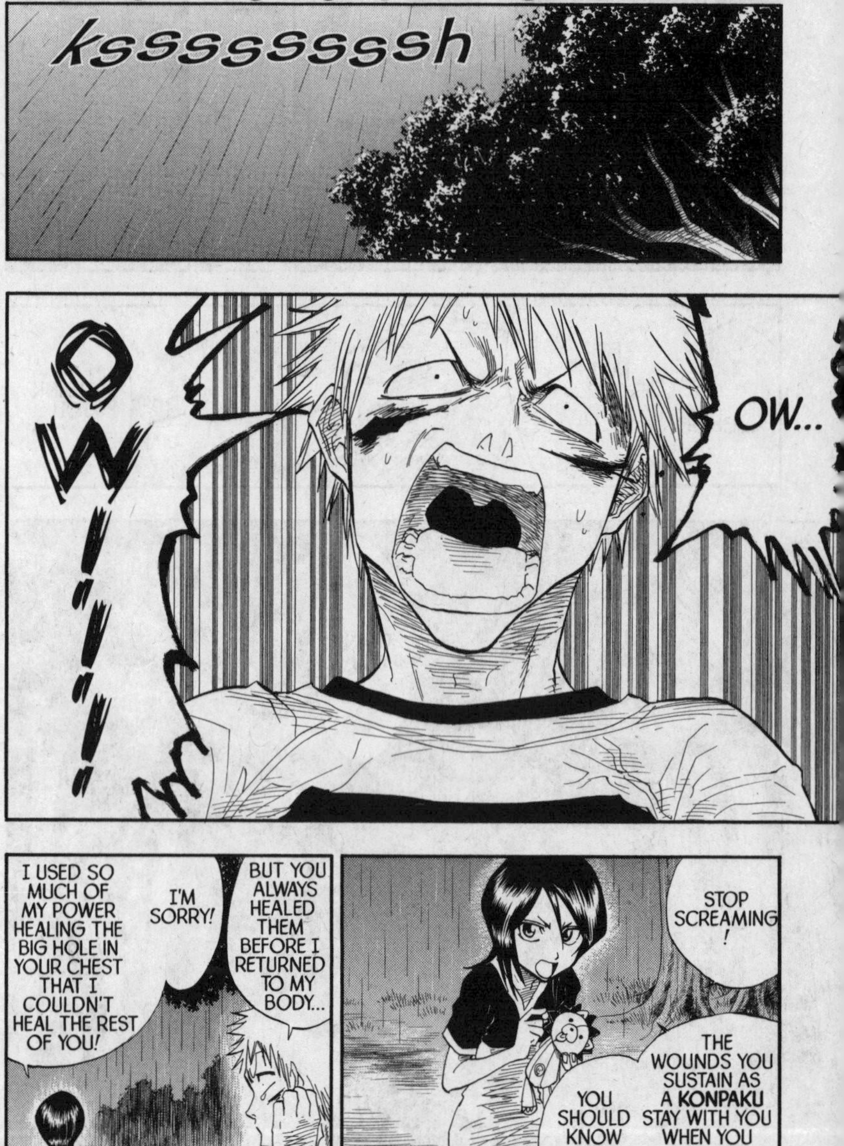
ksssssssh
OW...
OWW!!!!!!
STOP SCREAMING!
THE WOUNDS YOU SUSTAIN AS A **KONPAKU** STAY WITH YOU WHEN YOU RETURN TO YOUR MATERIAL BODY!
YOU SHOULD KNOW THAT BY NOW!
BUT YOU ALWAYS HEALED THEM BEFORE I RETURNED TO MY BODY...
I'M SORRY!
I USED SO MUCH OF MY POWER HEALING THE BIG HOLE IN YOUR CHEST THAT I COULDN'T HEAL THE REST OF YOU!

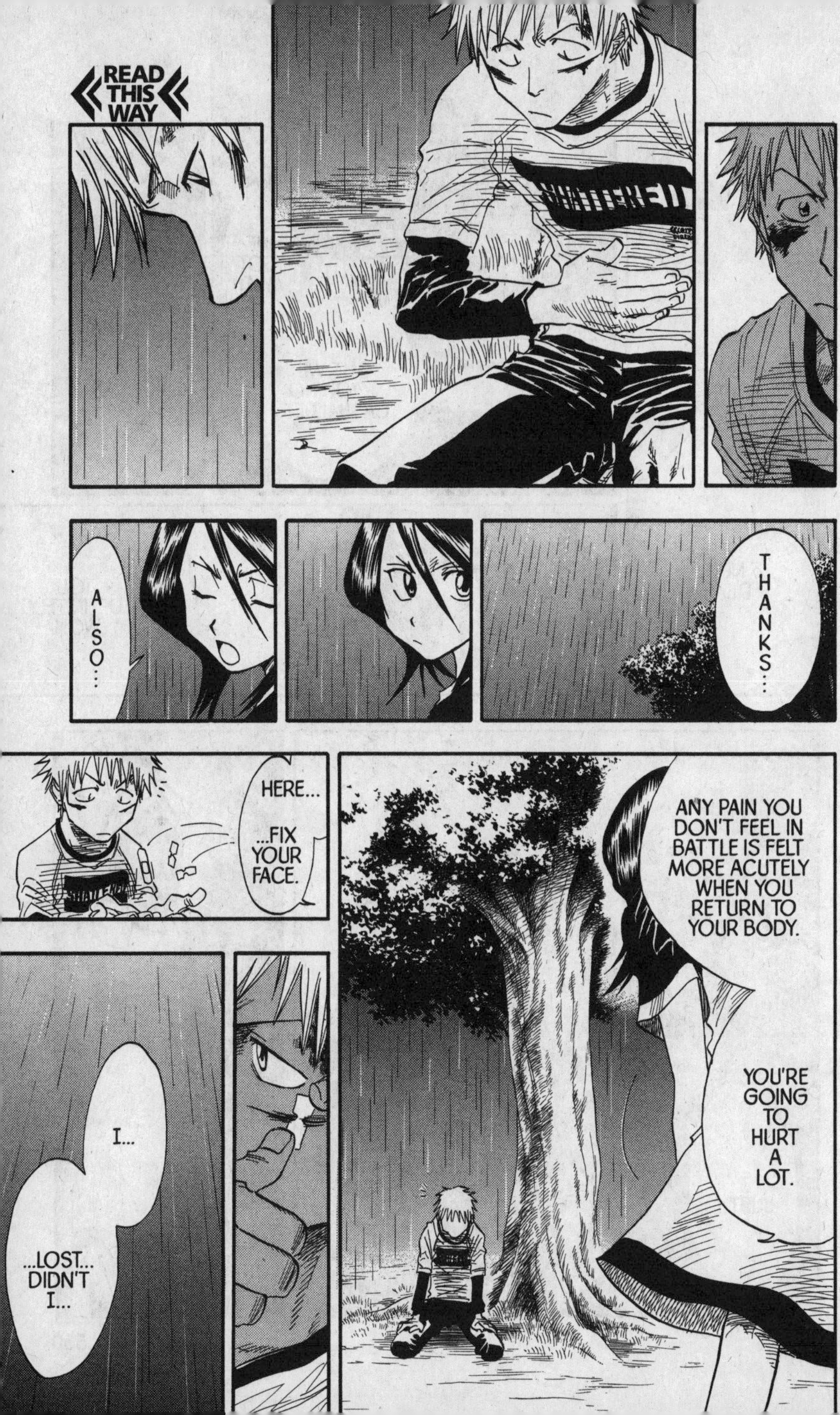
READ THIS WAY
THANKS...
ALSO...
ANY PAIN YOU DON'T FEEL IN BATTLE IS FELT MORE ACUTELY WHEN YOU RETURN TO YOUR BODY.
YOU'RE GOING TO HURT A LOT.
HERE... ...FIX YOUR FACE.
I...
...LOST... DIDN'T I...

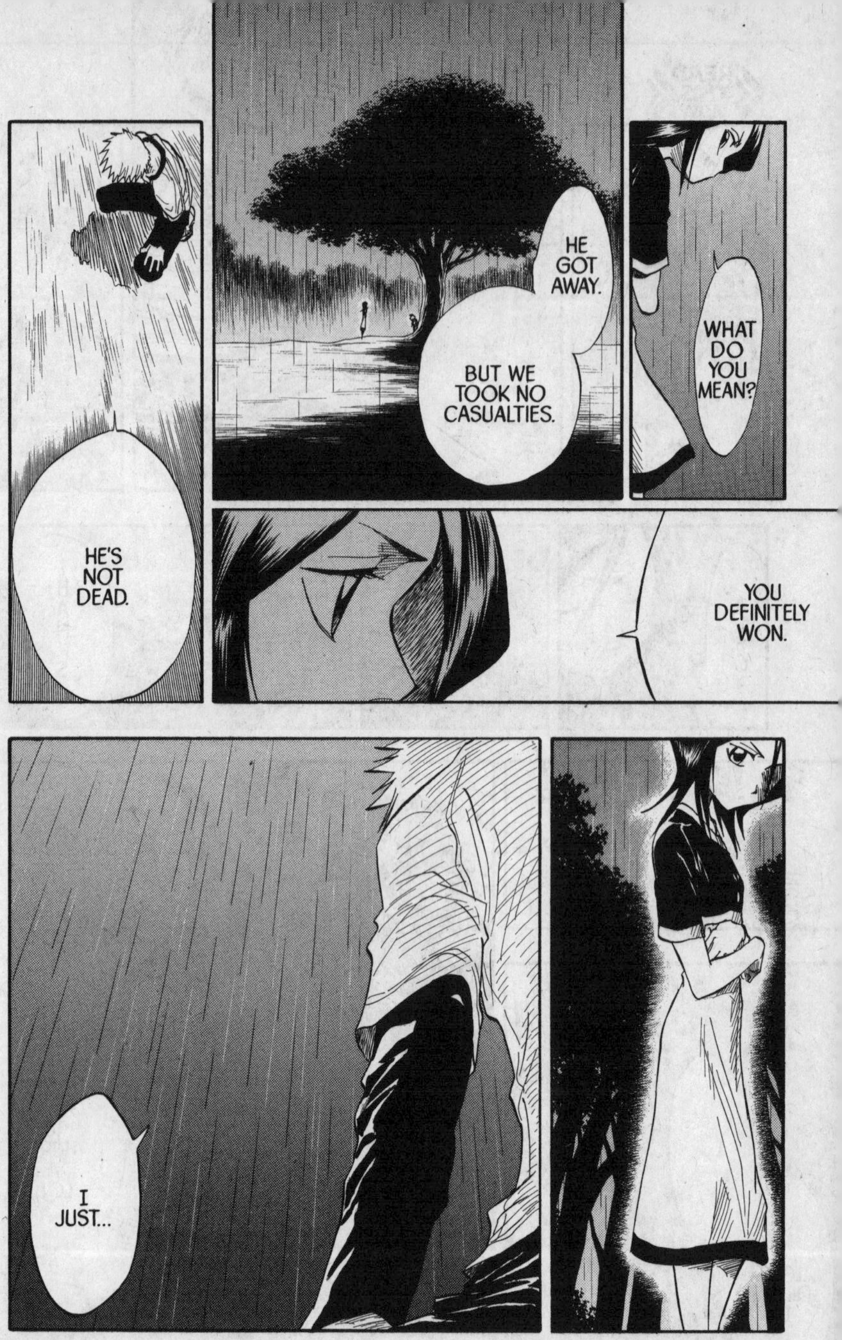
WHAT DO YOU MEAN?
HE GOT AWAY.
BUT WE TOOK NO CASUALTIES.
YOU DEFINITELY WON.
HE'S NOT DEAD.
I JUST...

READ THIS WAY

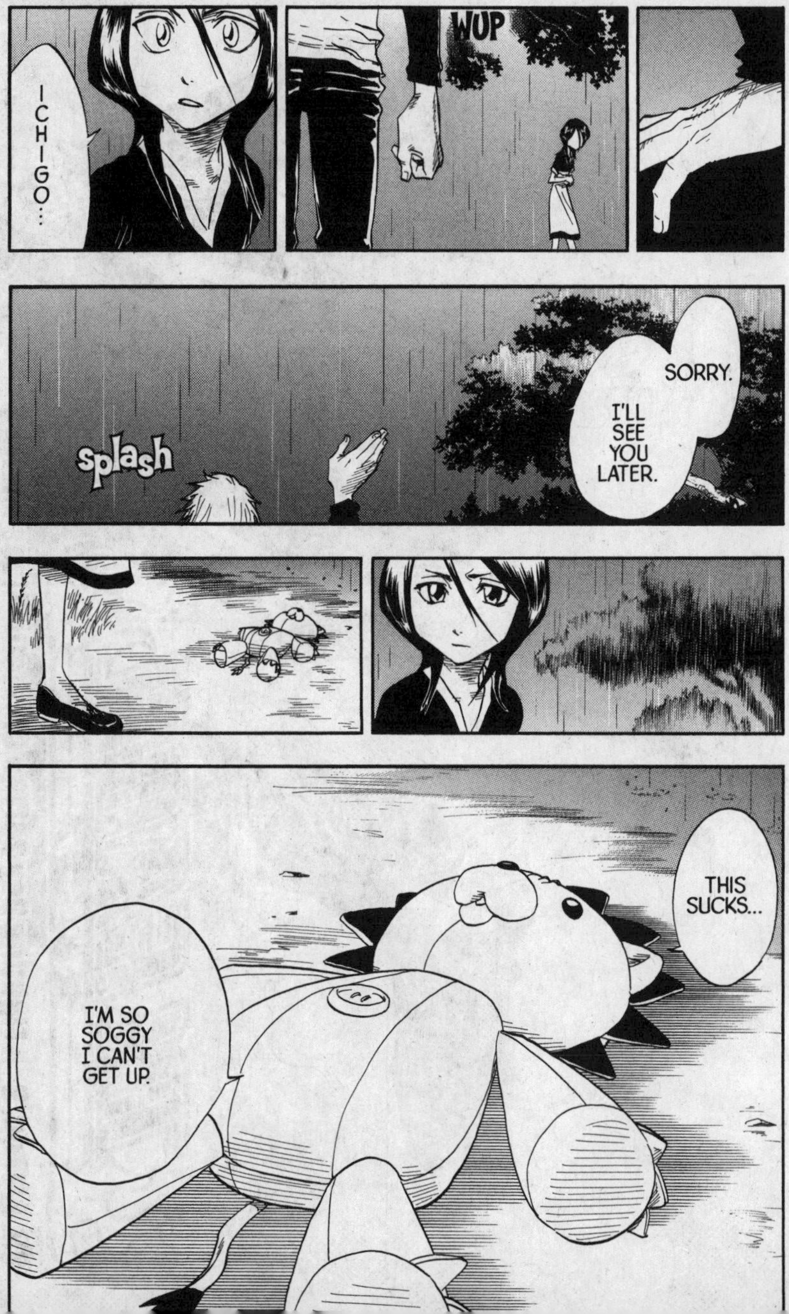
WUP
ICHIGO...
SORRY. I'LL SEE YOU LATER.
splash
THIS SUCKS...
I'M SO SOGGY I CAN'T GET UP.

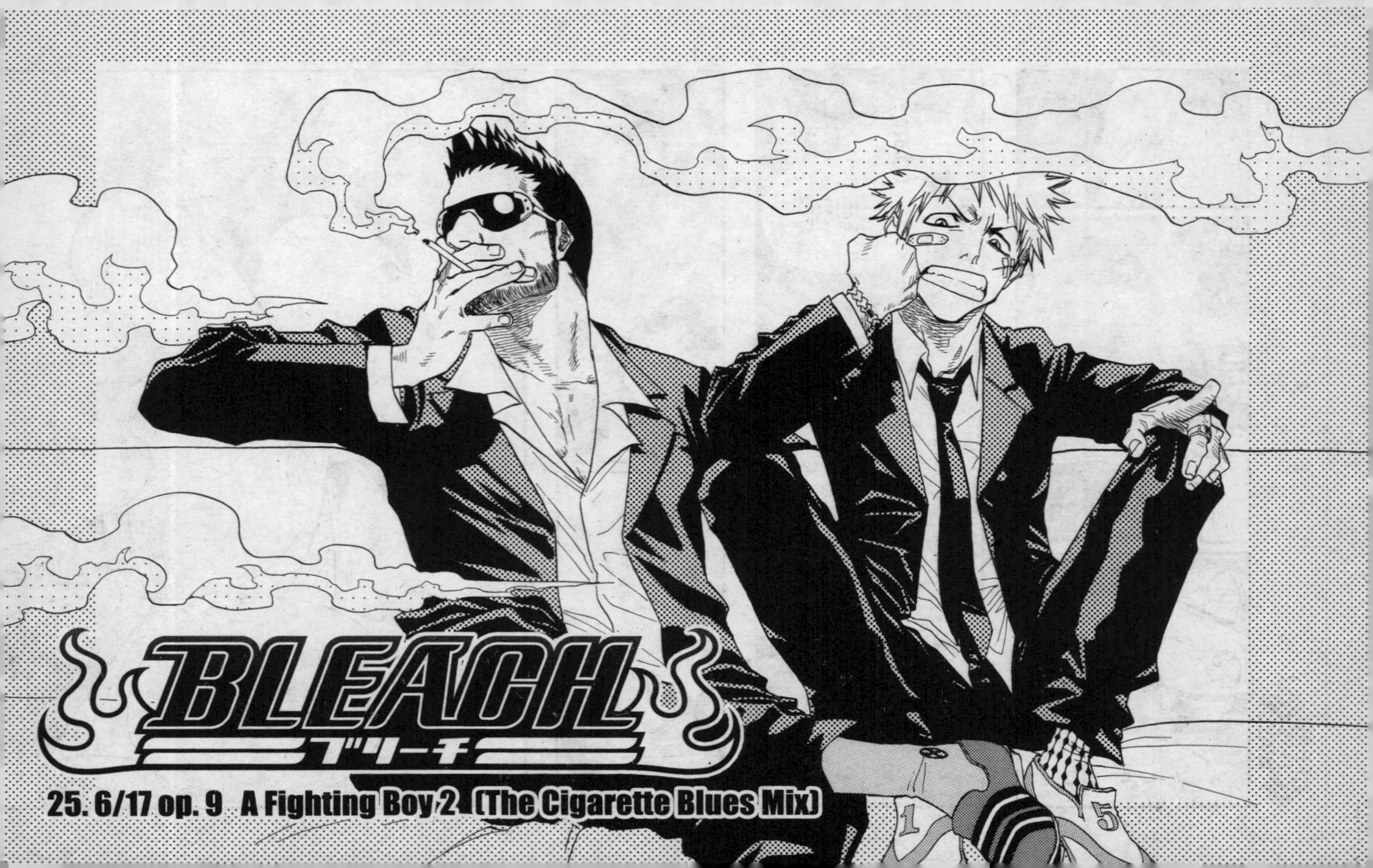
BLEACH
ブリーチ
25. 6/17 op. 9 A Fighting Boy 2 (The Cigarette Blues Mix)

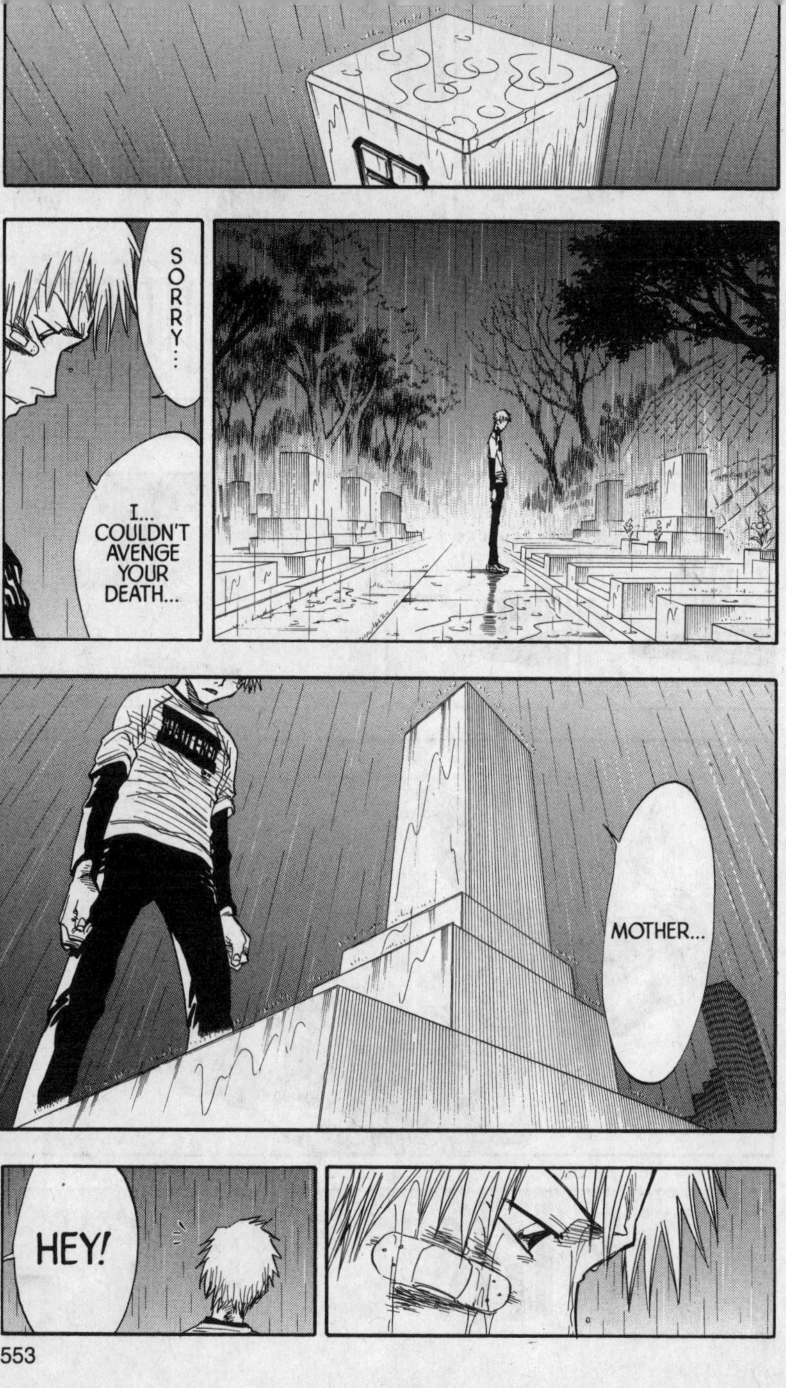
SORRY...
I... COULDN'T AVENGE YOUR DEATH...
MOTHER...
HEY!

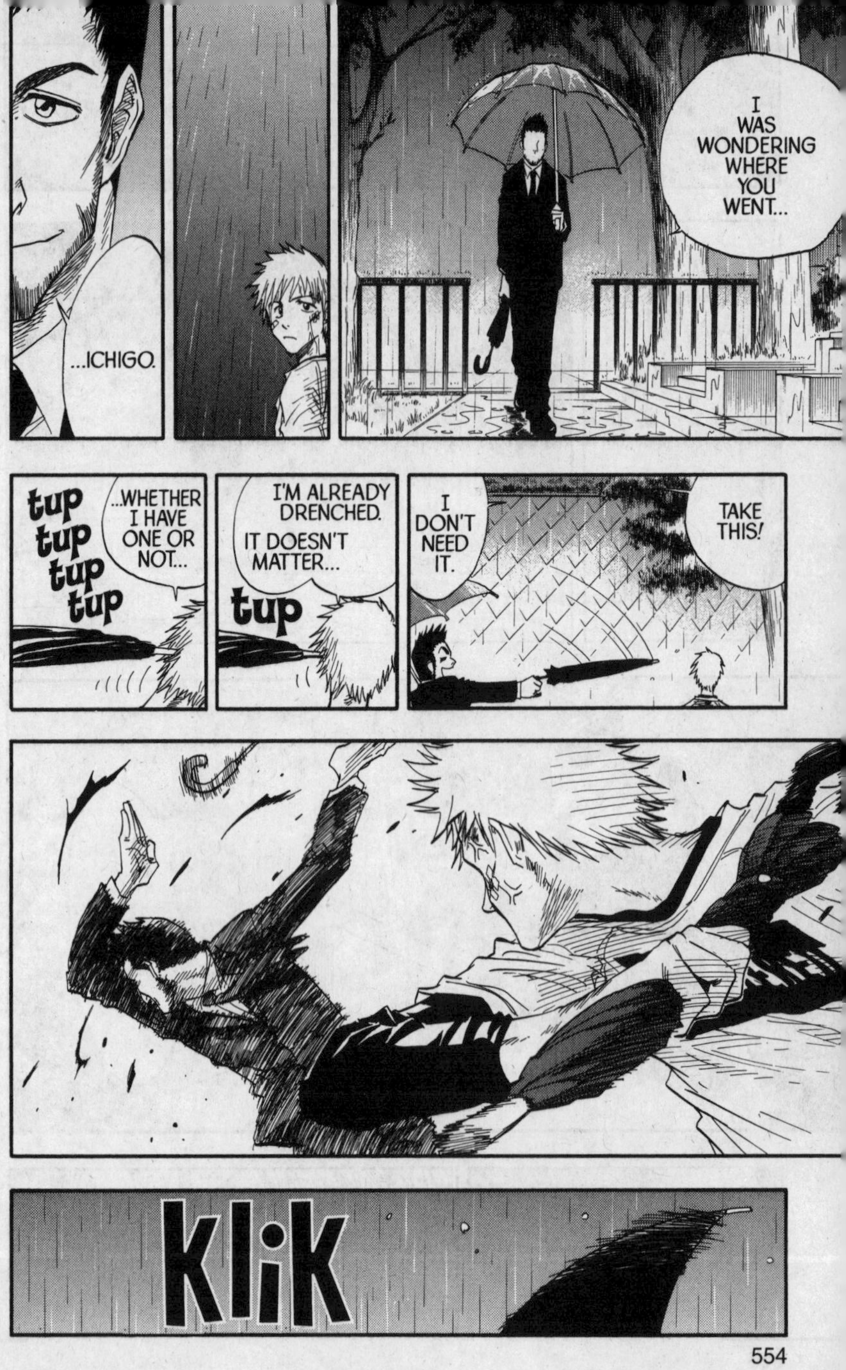
I WAS WONDERING WHERE YOU WENT...
...ICHIGO.
TAKE THIS!
I DON'T NEED IT.
I'M ALREADY DRENCHED.
IT DOESN'T MATTER...
tup
...WHETHER I HAVE ONE OR NOT...
tup tup tup tup
KliK

READ THIS WAY

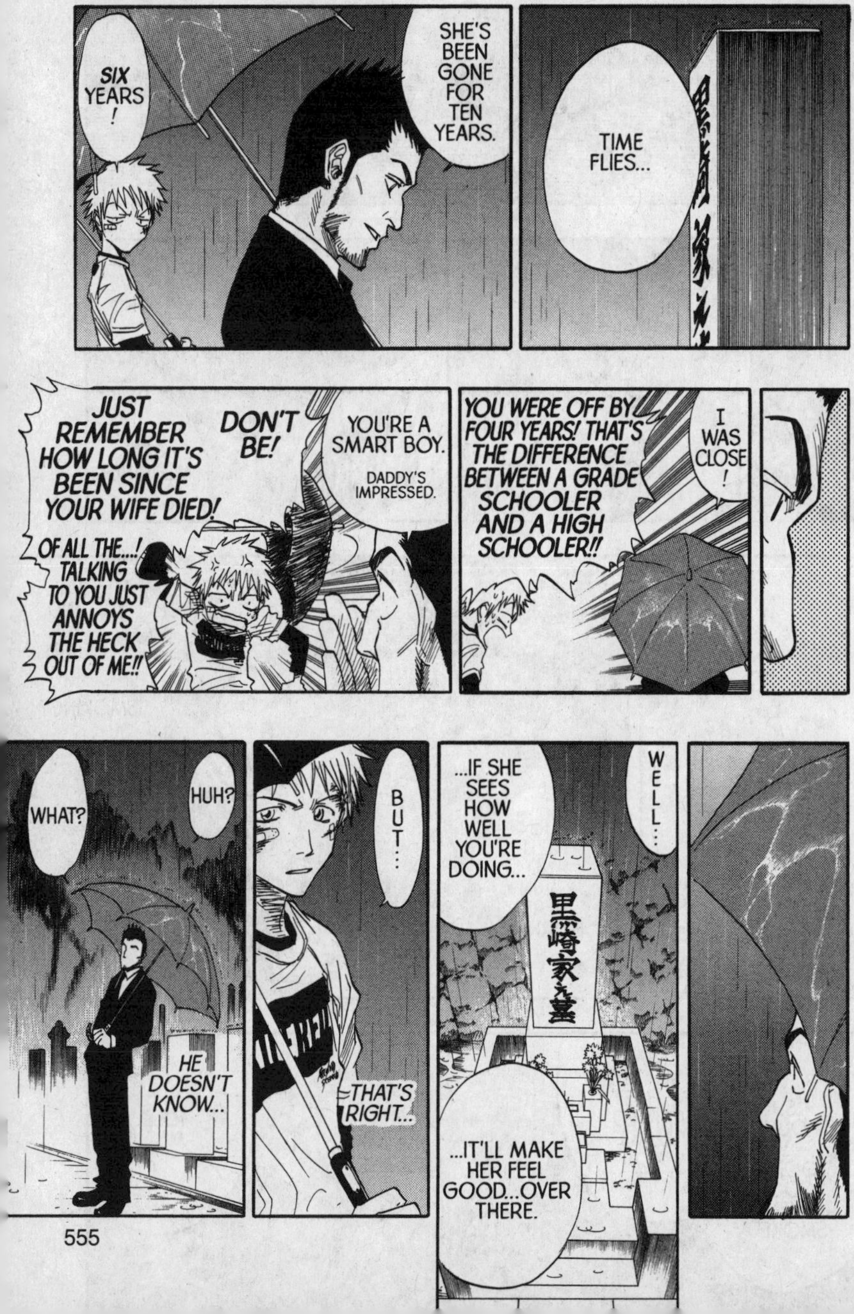
TIME FLIES...
SHE'S BEEN GONE FOR TEN YEARS.
SIX YEARS!
I WAS CLOSE!
YOU WERE OFF BY FOUR YEARS! THAT'S THE DIFFERENCE BETWEEN A GRADE SCHOOLER AND A HIGH SCHOOLER!!
YOU'RE A SMART BOY.
DADDY'S IMPRESSED.
DON'T BE!
JUST REMEMBER HOW LONG IT'S BEEN SINCE YOUR WIFE DIED!
OF ALL THE...! TALKING TO YOU JUST ANNOYS THE HECK OUT OF ME!!
WELL...
...IF SHE SEES HOW WELL YOU'RE DOING...
黒崎家之墓
...IT'LL MAKE HER FEEL GOOD...OVER THERE.
BUT...
THAT'S RIGHT...
HUH?
WHAT?
HE DOESN'T KNOW...

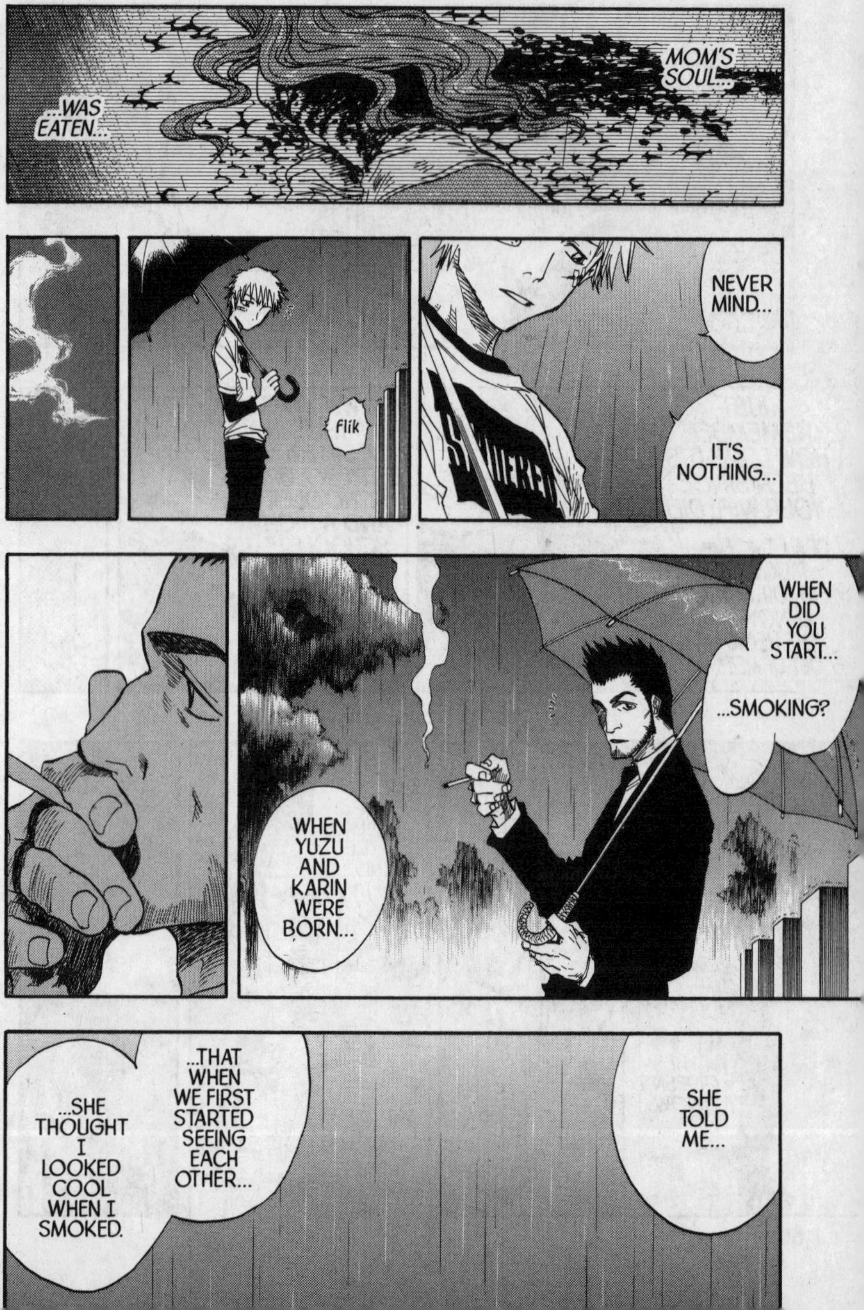
MOM'S SOUL...
...WAS EATEN...
NEVER MIND...
IT'S NOTHING...
Flik
WHEN DID YOU START...
...SMOKING?
WHEN YUZU AND KARIN WERE BORN...
SHE TOLD ME...
...THAT WHEN WE FIRST STARTED SEEING EACH OTHER...
...SHE THOUGHT I LOOKED COOL WHEN I SMOKED.

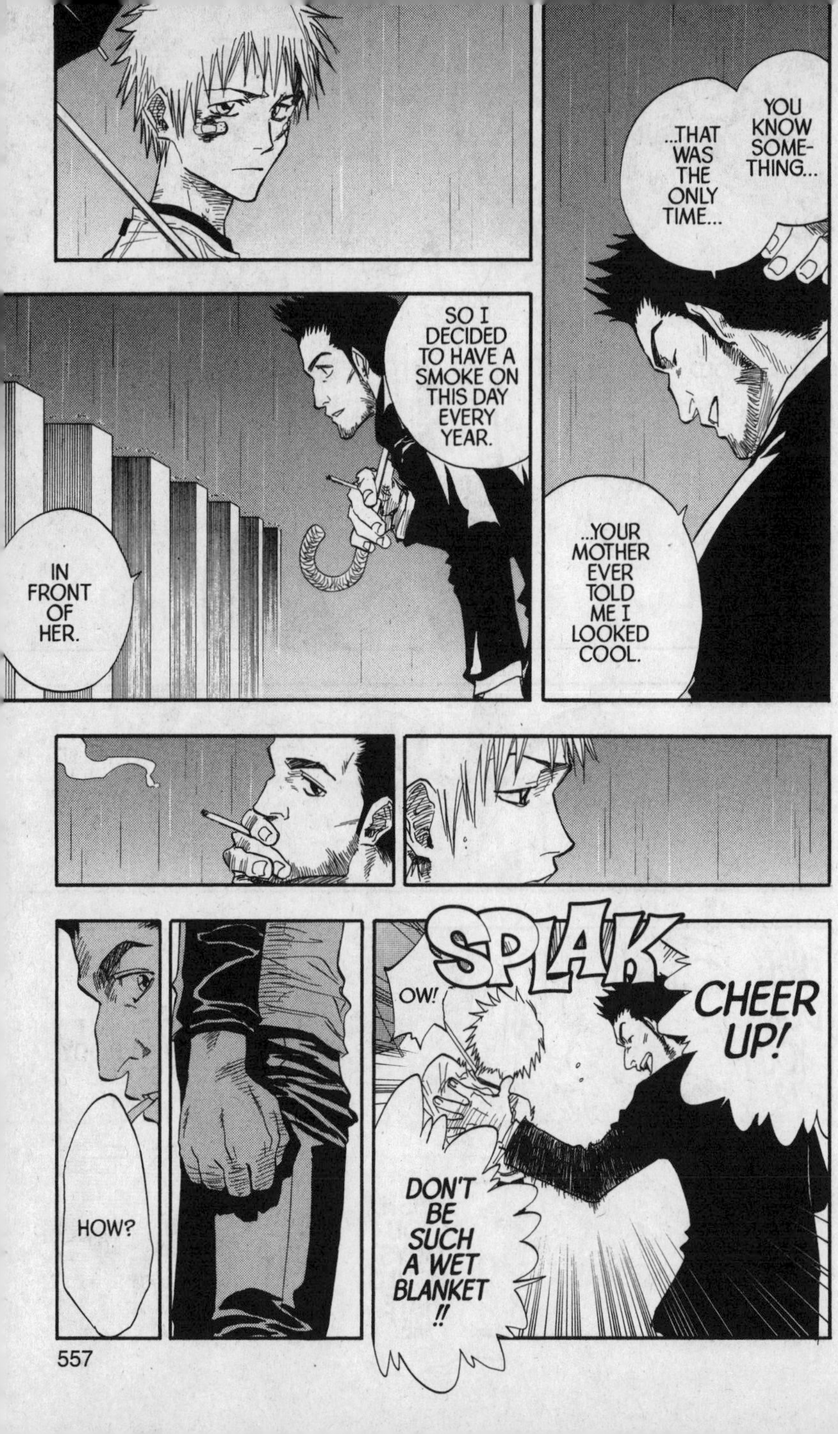
YOU KNOW SOMETHING...
...THAT WAS THE ONLY TIME...
...YOUR MOTHER EVER TOLD ME I LOOKED COOL.
SO I DECIDED TO HAVE A SMOKE ON THIS DAY EVERY YEAR.
IN FRONT OF HER.
SPLAK
CHEER UP!
OW!
DON'T BE SUCH A WET BLANKET!!
HOW?

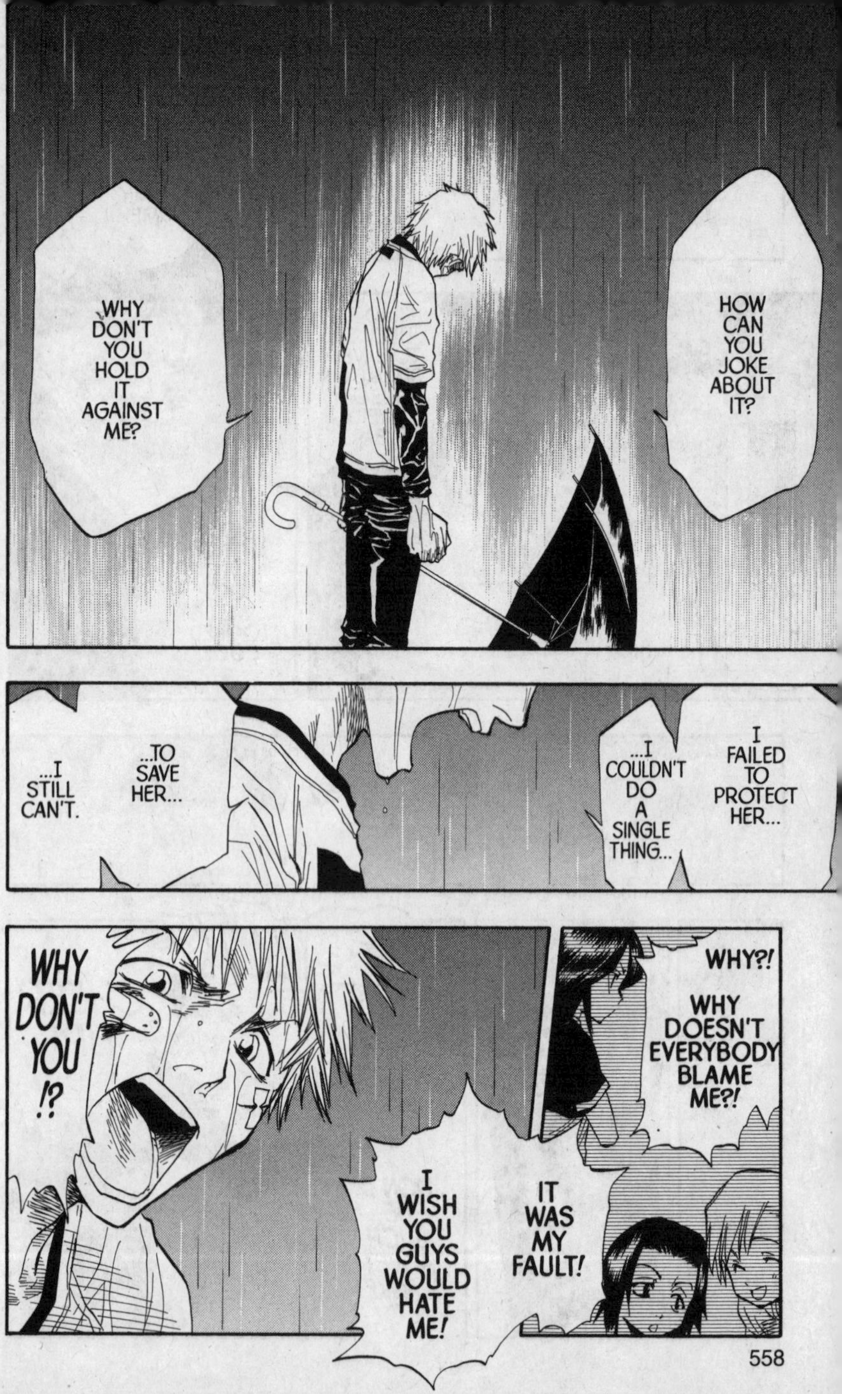
HOW CAN YOU JOKE ABOUT IT?
WHY DON'T YOU HOLD IT AGAINST ME?
I FAILED TO PROTECT HER...
...I COULDN'T DO A SINGLE THING...
...TO SAVE HER...
...I STILL CAN'T.
WHY?!
WHY DOESN'T EVERYBODY BLAME ME?!
IT WAS MY FAULT!
I WISH YOU GUYS WOULD HATE ME!
WHY DON'T YOU !?

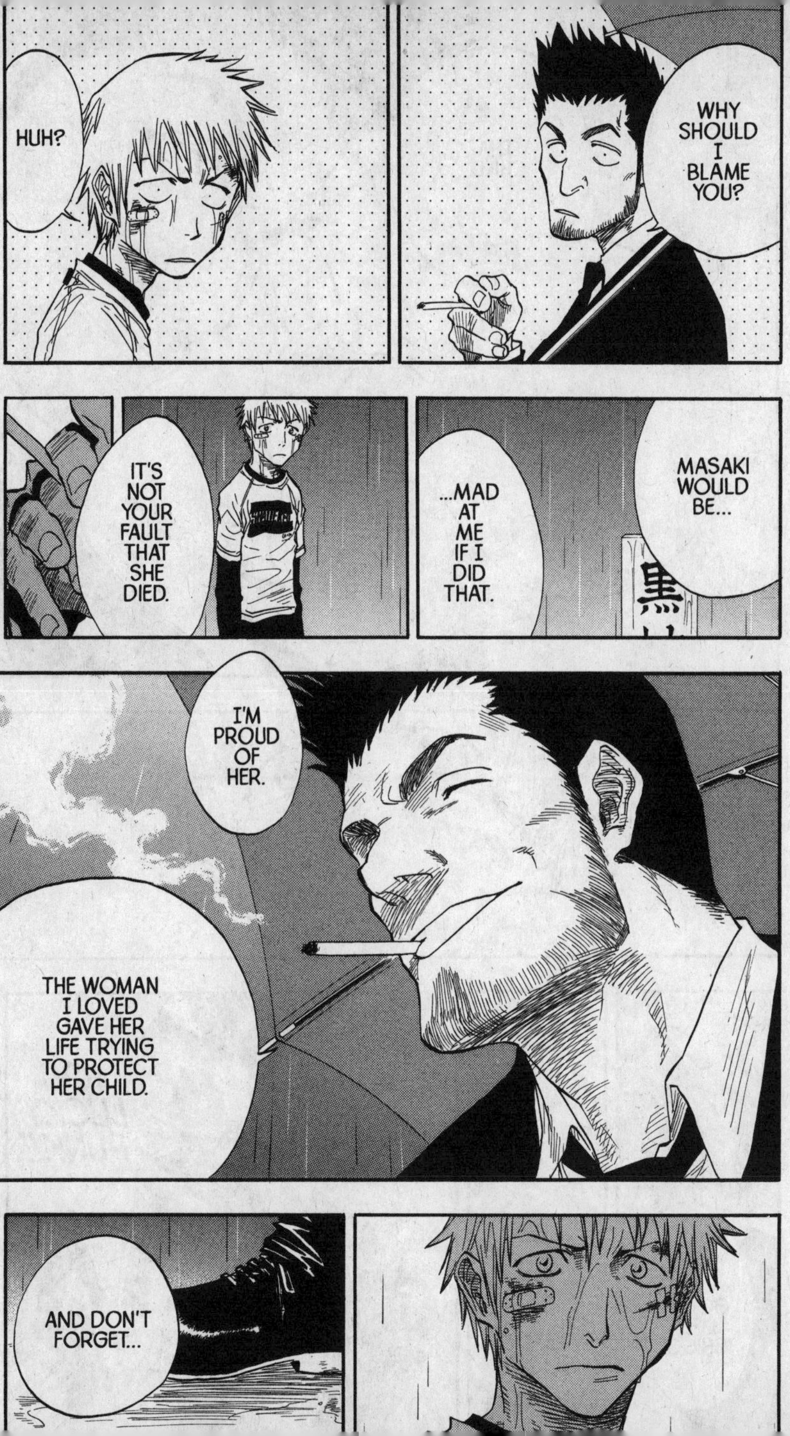
WHY SHOULD I BLAME YOU?
HUH?
MASAKI WOULD BE...
...MAD AT ME IF I DID THAT.
IT'S NOT YOUR FAULT THAT SHE DIED.
I'M PROUD OF HER.
THE WOMAN I LOVED GAVE HER LIFE TRYING TO PROTECT HER CHILD.
AND DON'T FORGET...

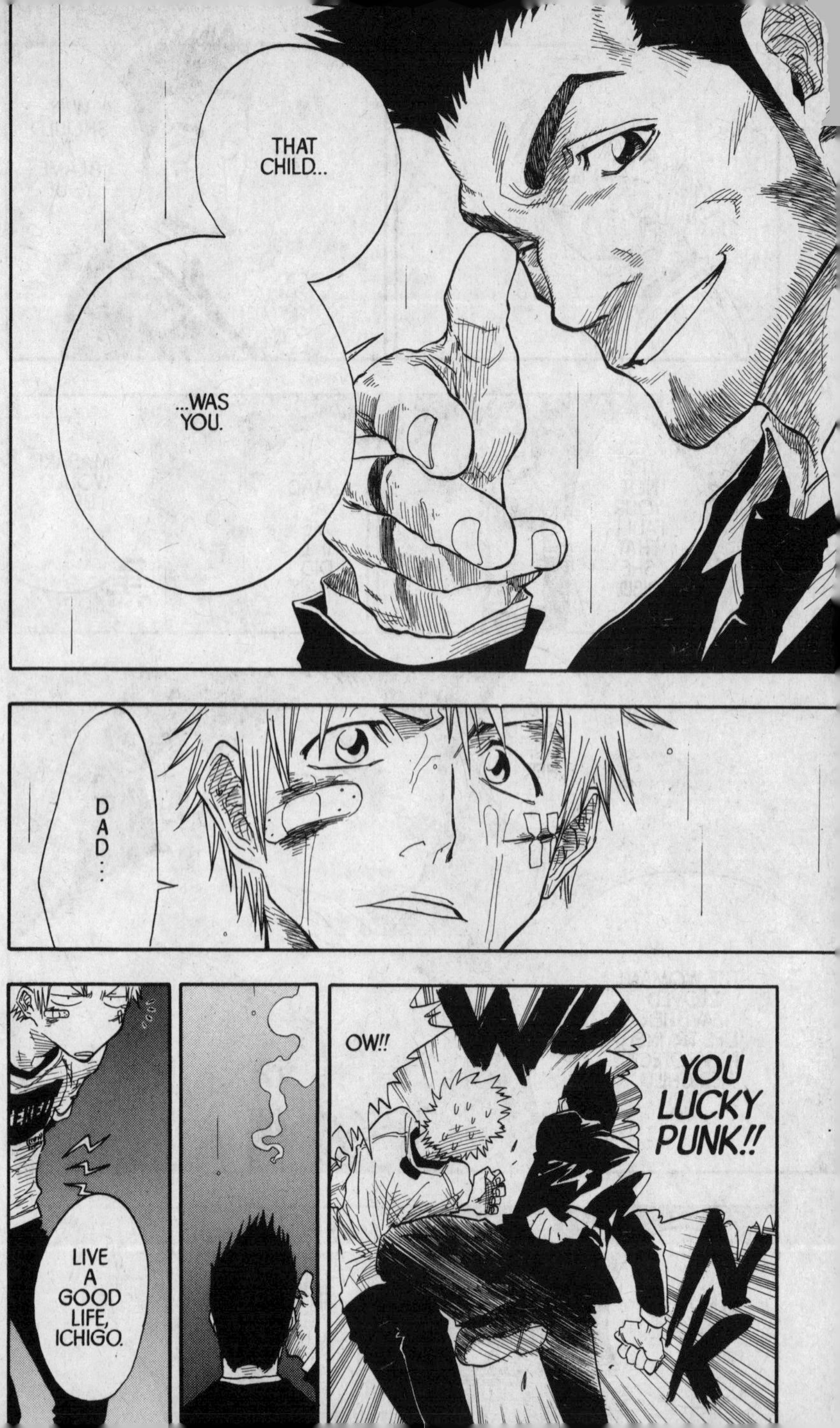
THAT CHILD...
...WAS YOU.
DAD...
YOU LUCKY PUNK!!
OW!!
LIVE A GOOD LIFE, ICHIGO.

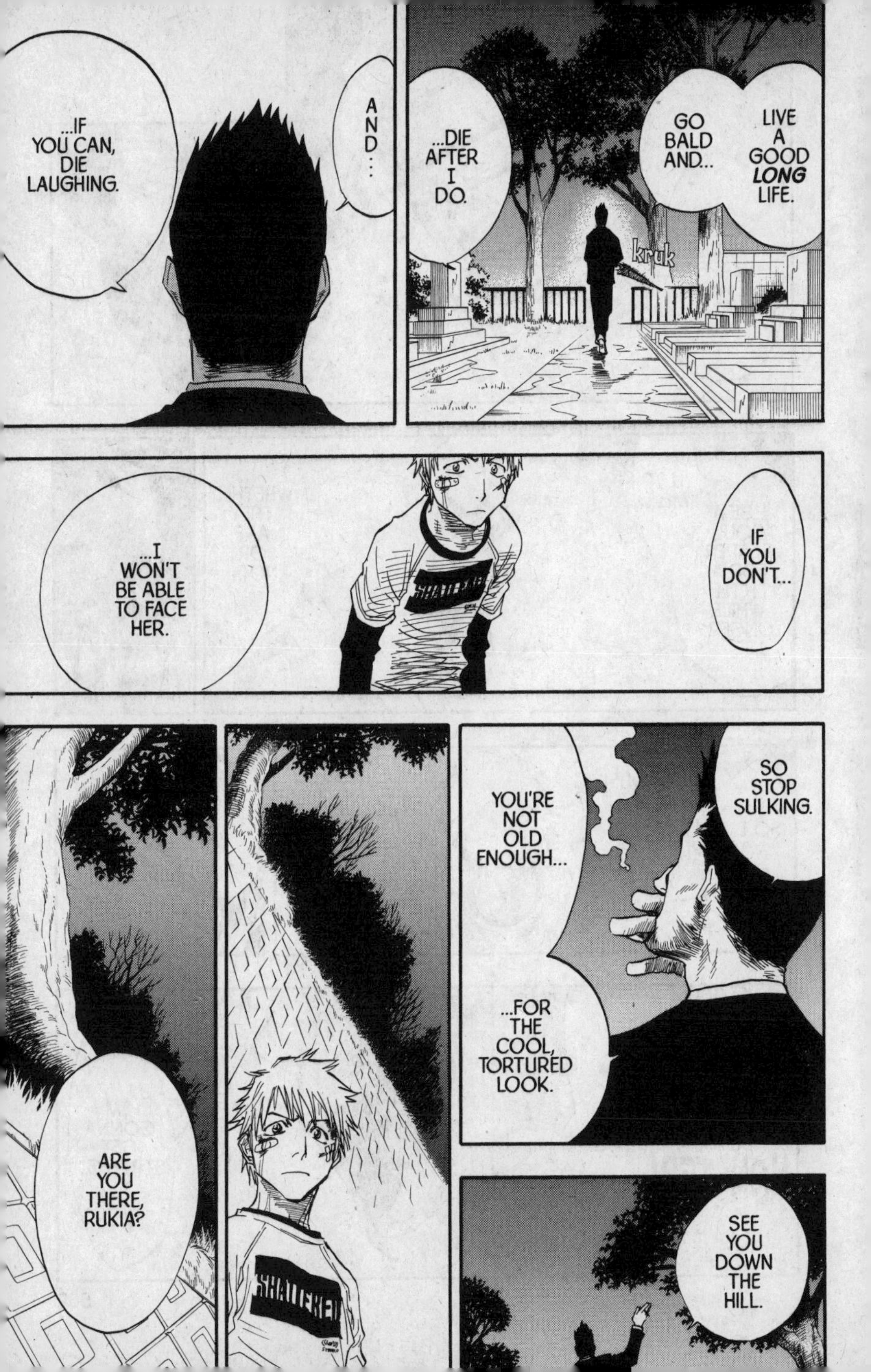
LIVE A GOOD LONG LIFE.
GO BALD AND...
...DIE AFTER I DO.
kruk
AND...
...IF YOU CAN, DIE LAUGHING.
IF YOU DON'T...
...I WON'T BE ABLE TO FACE HER.
SO STOP SULKING.
YOU'RE NOT OLD ENOUGH...
...FOR THE COOL, TORTURED LOOK.
SEE YOU DOWN THE HILL.
ARE YOU THERE, RUKIA?

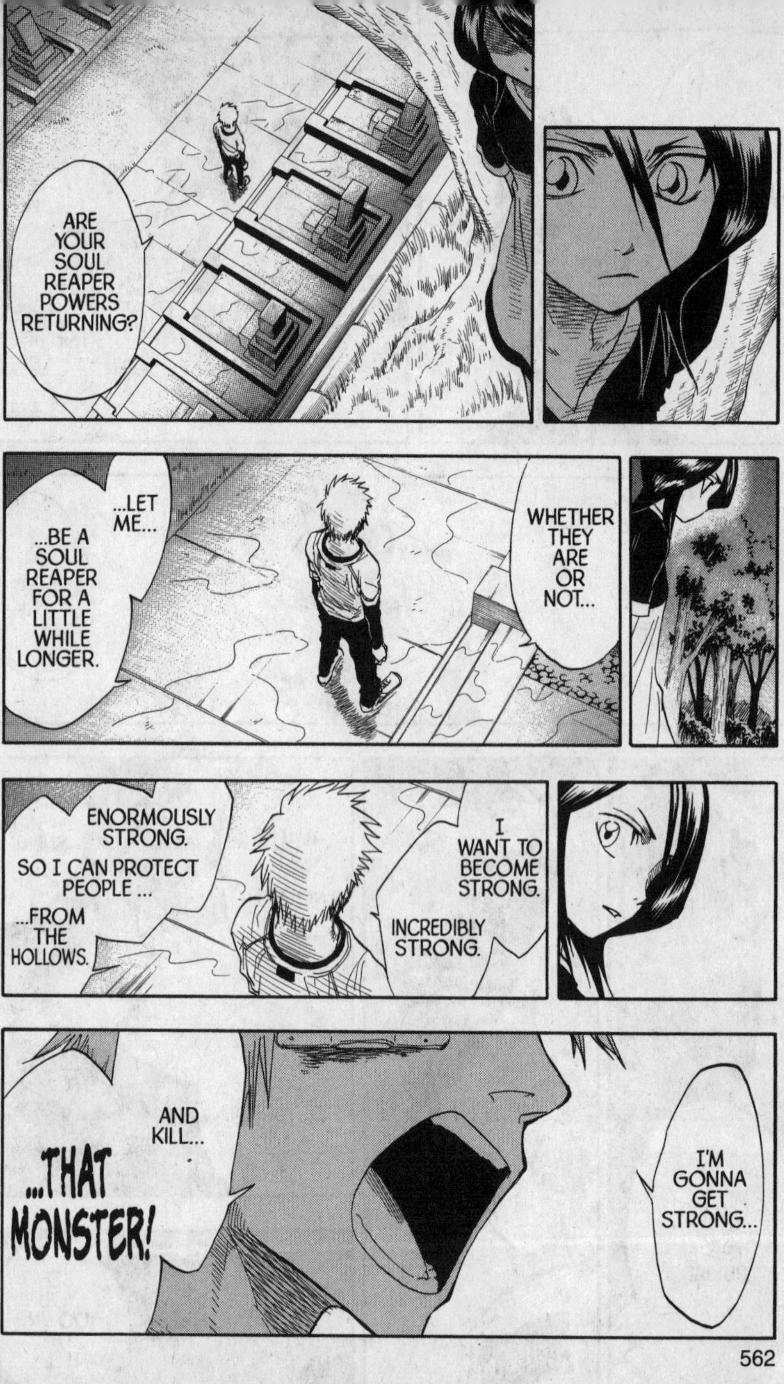
ARE YOUR SOUL REAPER POWERS RETURNING?
WHETHER THEY ARE OR NOT...
...LET ME...
...BE A SOUL REAPER FOR A LITTLE WHILE LONGER.
I WANT TO BECOME STRONG.
INCREDIBLY STRONG.
ENORMOUSLY STRONG.
SO I CAN PROTECT PEOPLE ...
...FROM THE HOLLOWS.
I'M GONNA GET STRONG...
AND KILL...
...THAT MONSTER!

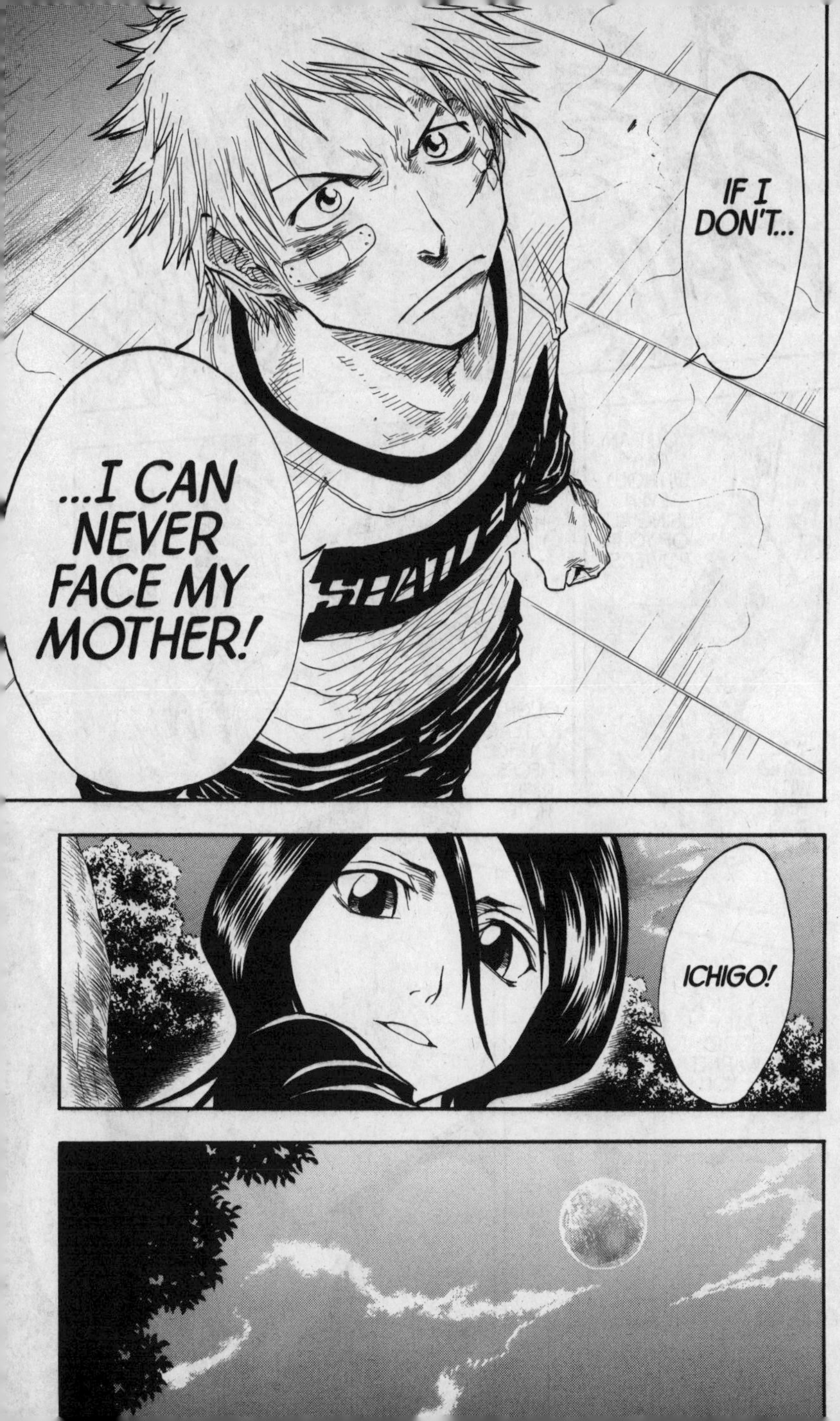
IF I DON'T...
...I CAN NEVER FACE MY MOTHER!
ICHIGO!

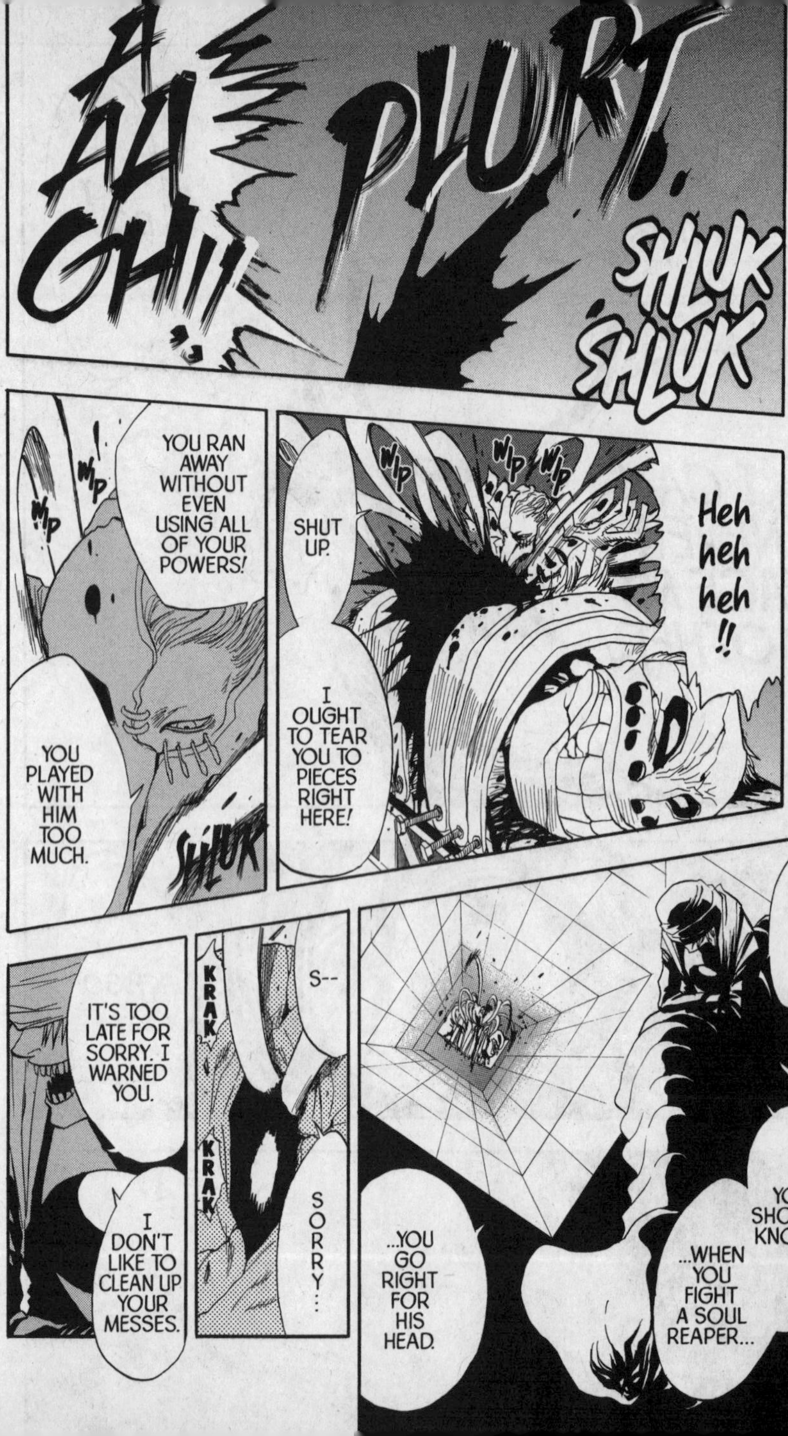
PLURT.
SHLUK
SHLUK
AAAGH!!
WIP WIP
WIP
Heh heh heh!!
SHUT UP.
I OUGHT TO TEAR YOU TO PIECES RIGHT HERE!
WIP
WIP
YOU RAN AWAY WITHOUT EVEN USING ALL OF YOUR POWERS!
YOU PLAYED WITH HIM TOO MUCH.
SHLUK
RIGHT.
YOU SHOULD KNOW...
...WHEN YOU FIGHT A SOUL REAPER...
...YOU GO RIGHT FOR HIS HEAD.
S--
KRAK
KRAK
SORRY...
IT'S TOO LATE FOR SORRY. I WARNED YOU.
I DON'T LIKE TO CLEAN UP YOUR MESSES.

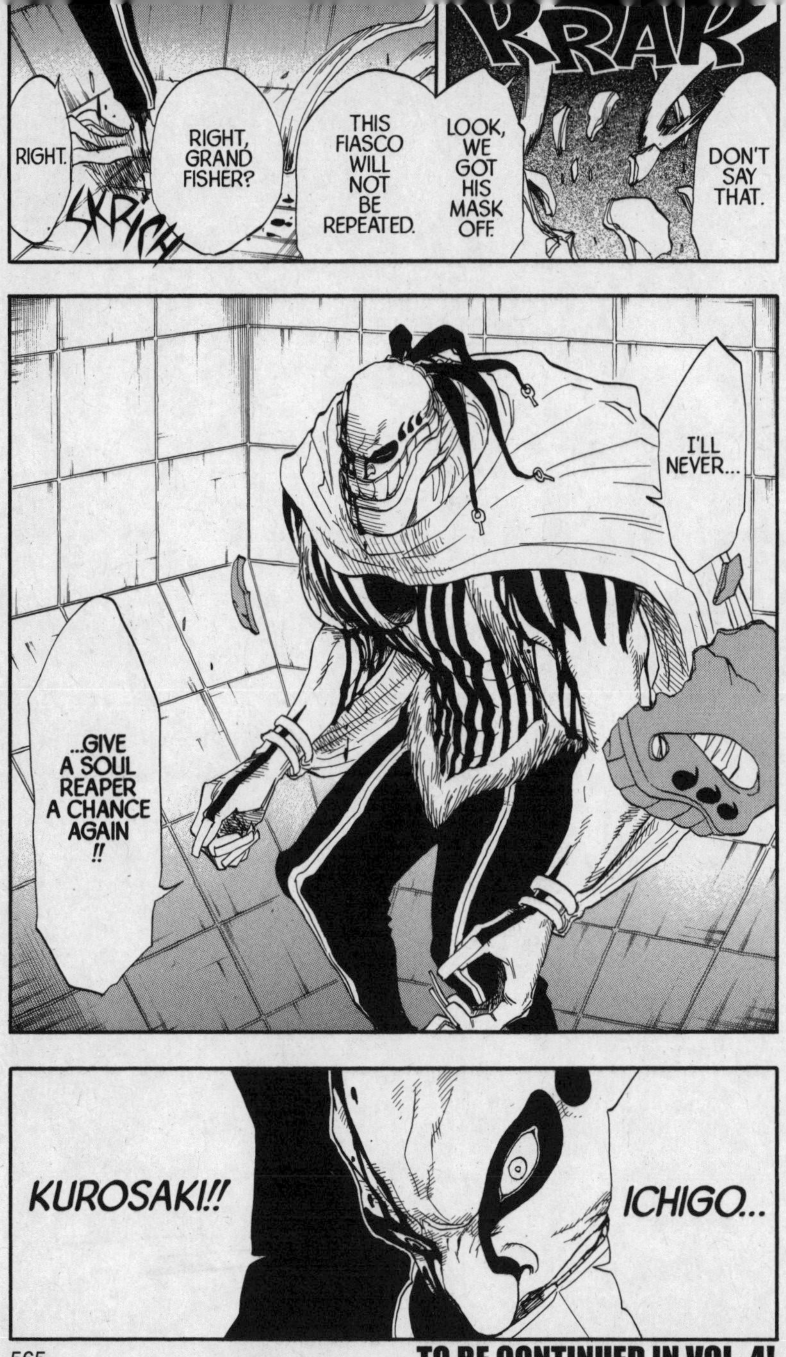
KRAK
DON'T SAY THAT.
LOOK, WE GOT HIS MASK OFF.
THIS FIASCO WILL NOT BE REPEATED.
RIGHT, GRAND FISHER?
SKRICH
RIGHT.
I'LL NEVER...
...GIVE A SOUL REAPER A CHANCE AGAIN!!
ICHIGO...
KUROSAKI!!

TO BE CONTINUED IN VOL. 4!

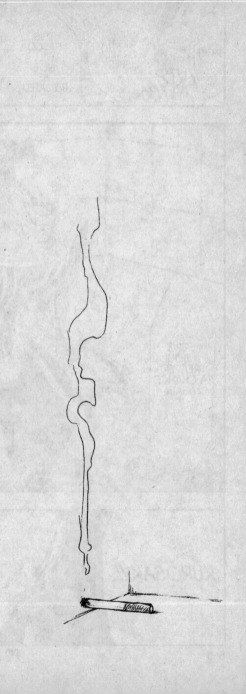

★★ here is the data of BLEACH!!

OVERALL ATTENDANCE NUMBER: 3	**TATSUKI ARISAWA**	アリサワ・タツキ
FEMALE STUDENT NUMBER: 1		

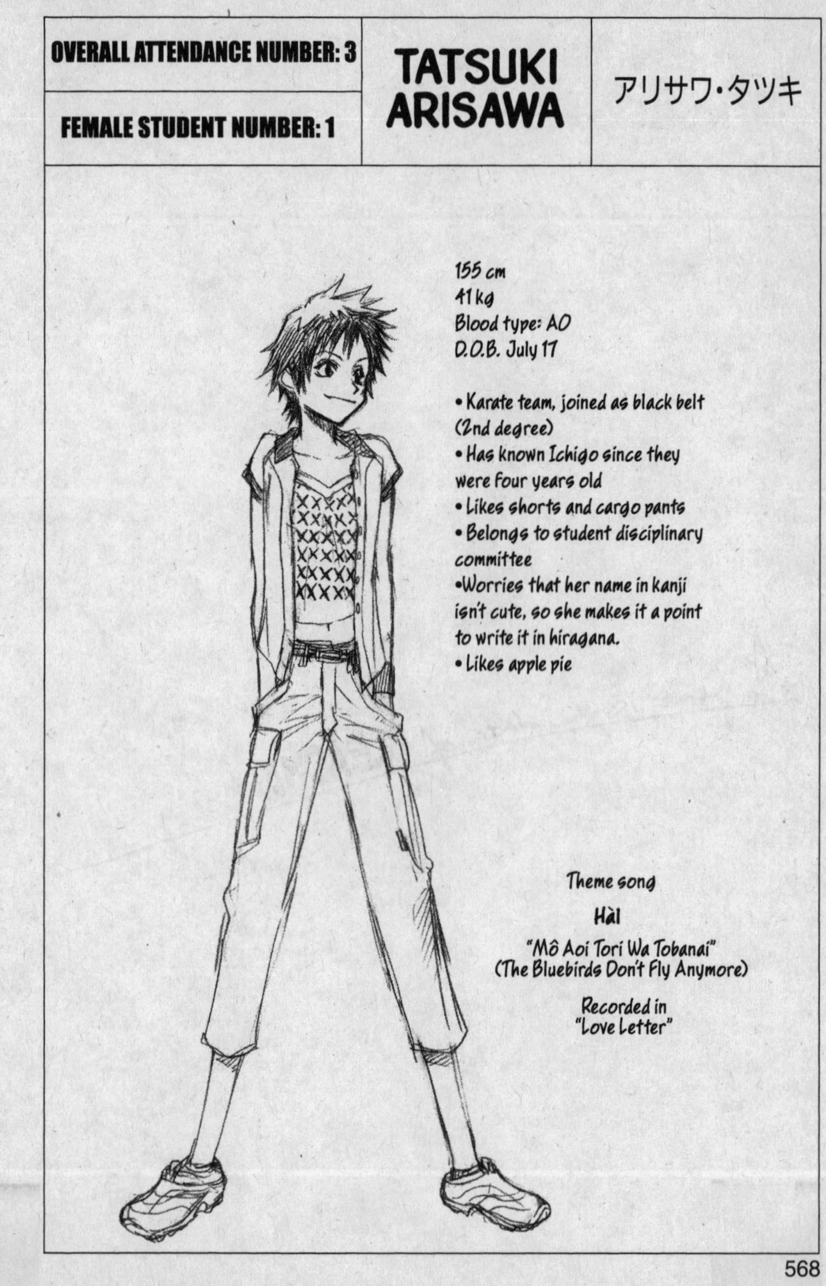

155 cm
41 kg
Blood type: AO
D.O.B. July 17

- Karate team, joined as black belt (2nd degree)
- Has known Ichigo since they were four years old
- Likes shorts and cargo pants
- Belongs to student disciplinary committee
- Worries that her name in kanji isn't cute, so she makes it a point to write it in hiragana.
- Likes apple pie

Theme song

Hàl

"Mô Aoi Tori Wa Tobanai"
(The Bluebirds Don't Fly Anymore)

Recorded in
"Love Letter"

ISSHIN KUROSAKI

クロサキ・イッシン

186 CM
80 KG
BLOOD TYPE: AB
D.O.B. DECEMBER 10

- HEAD OF KUROSAKI FAMILY
- LOCAL DOCTOR. CAN DO ANYTHING EXCEPT MAJOR SURGERY
- LIKES POTATO BEAN PASTE CAKES
- HE WAS ACTUALLY SUPPOSED TO BE A MORTICIAN INSTEAD OF A DOCTOR UNTIL THE VERY LAST MINUTE THIS MANGA WAS PUBLISHED, SO HE LOOKS BETTER IN A BLACK SUIT THAN A WHITE LAB COAT.

THEME SONG

SOCIAL DISTORTION

"DON'T DRAG ME DOWN"

RECORDED IN
"WHITE LIGHT,
WHITE HEAT,
WHITE TRASH"

Next Volume Preview

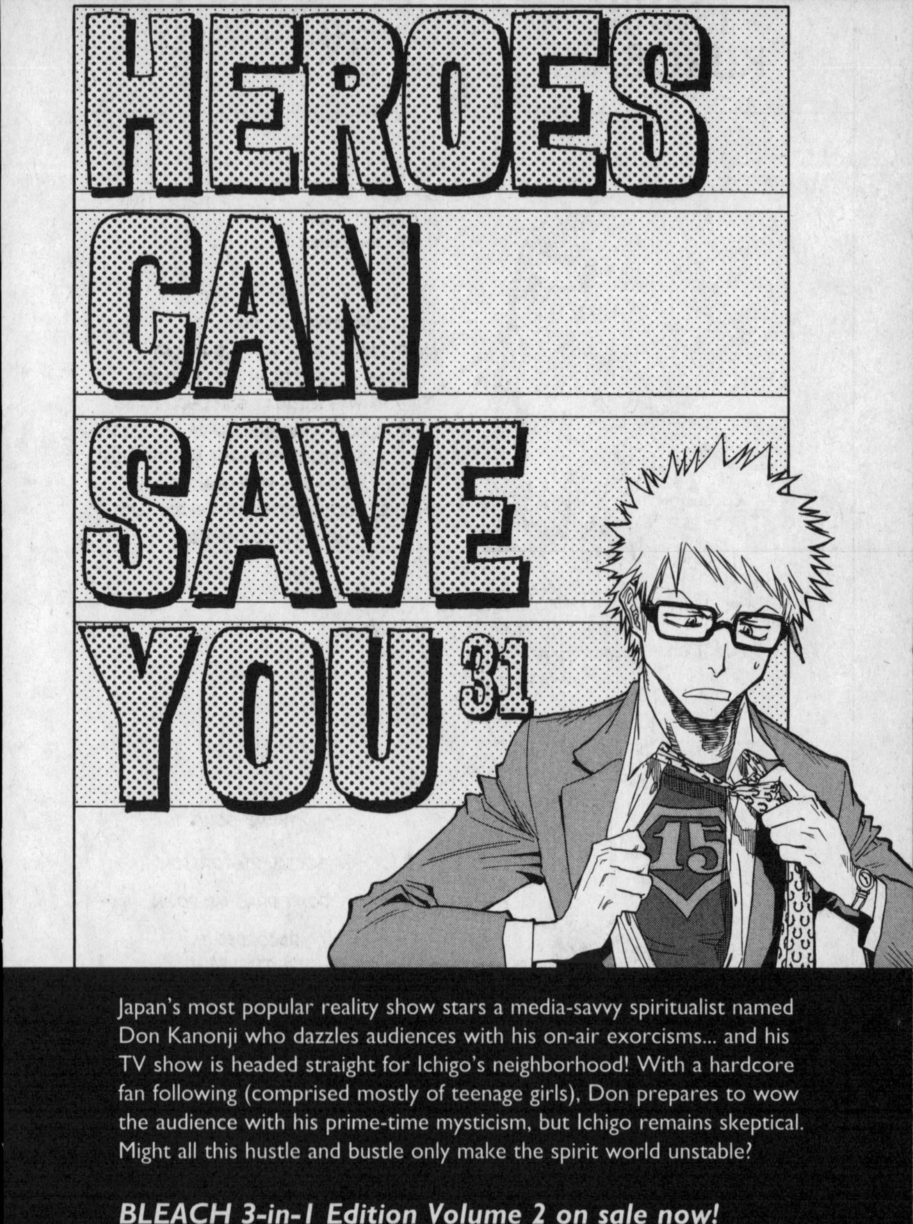
HEROES CAN SAVE YOU 31

Japan's most popular reality show stars a media-savvy spiritualist named Don Kanonji who dazzles audiences with his on-air exorcisms... and his TV show is headed straight for Ichigo's neighborhood! With a hardcore fan following (comprised mostly of teenage girls), Don prepares to wow the audience with his prime-time mysticism, but Ichigo remains skeptical. Might all this hustle and bustle only make the spirit world unstable?

BLEACH 3-in-1 Edition Volume 2 on sale now!

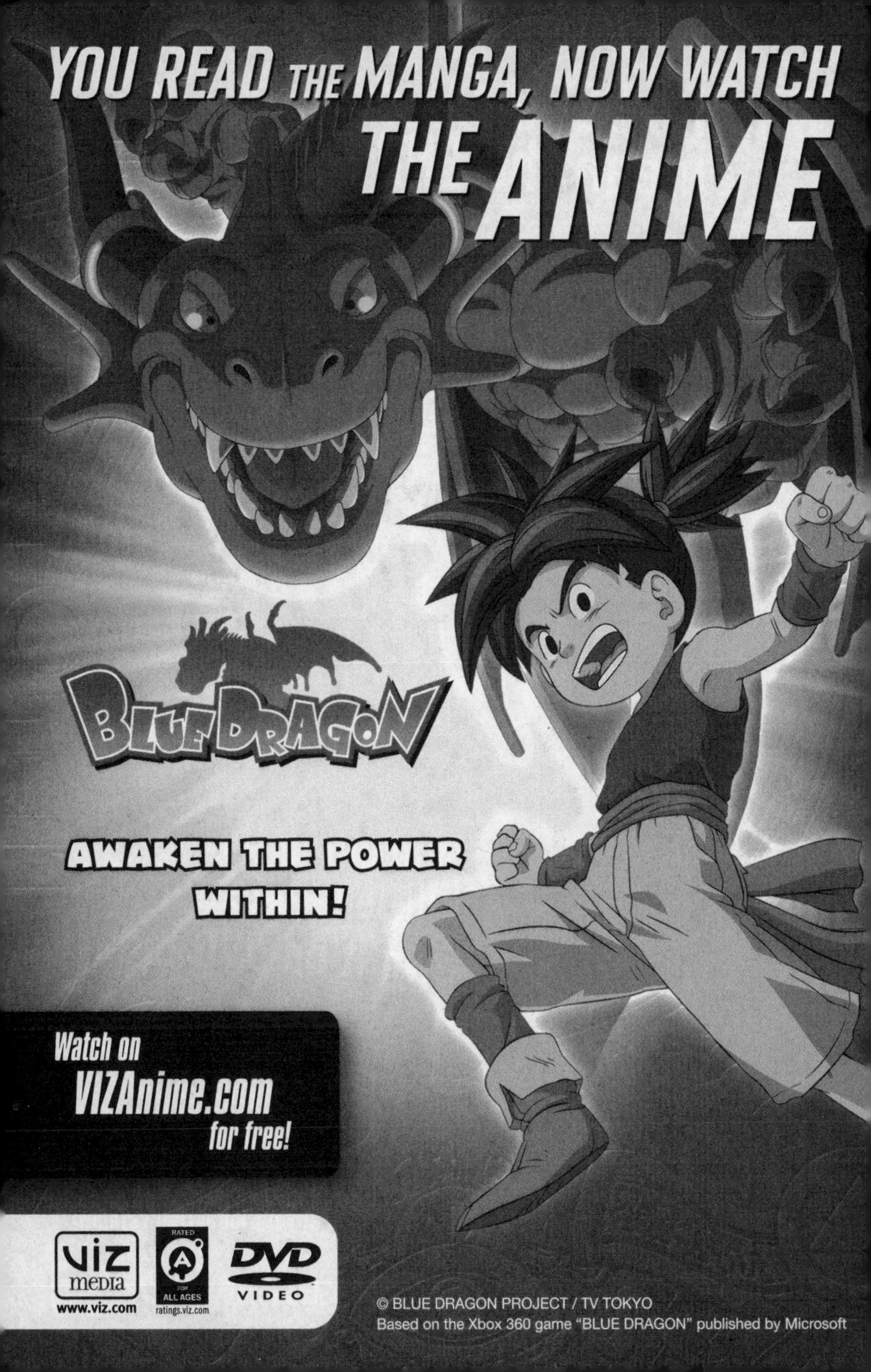

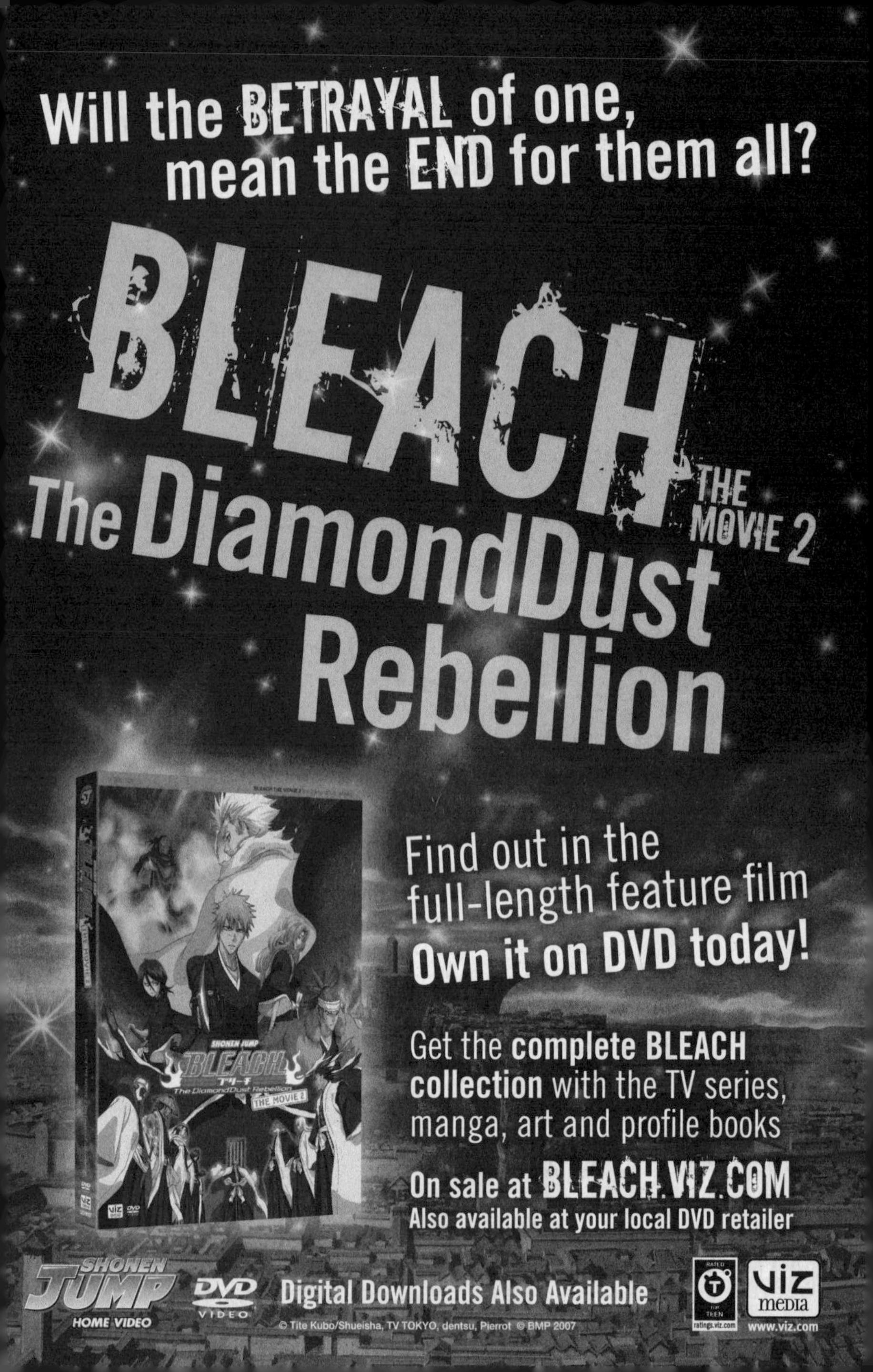

Will the BETRAYAL of one,
mean the END for them all?
BLEACH THE MOVIE 2
The DiamondDust Rebellion
Find out in the full-length feature film
Own it on DVD today!
Get the complete BLEACH collection with the TV series, manga, art and profile books
On sale at BLEACH.VIZ.COM
Also available at your local DVD retailer
SHONEN JUMP HOME VIDEO
DVD VIDEO
Digital Downloads Also Available
© Tite Kubo/Shueisha, TV TOKYO, dentsu, Pierrot © BMP 2007
RATED T FOR TEEN
ratings.viz.com
viz media
www.viz.com

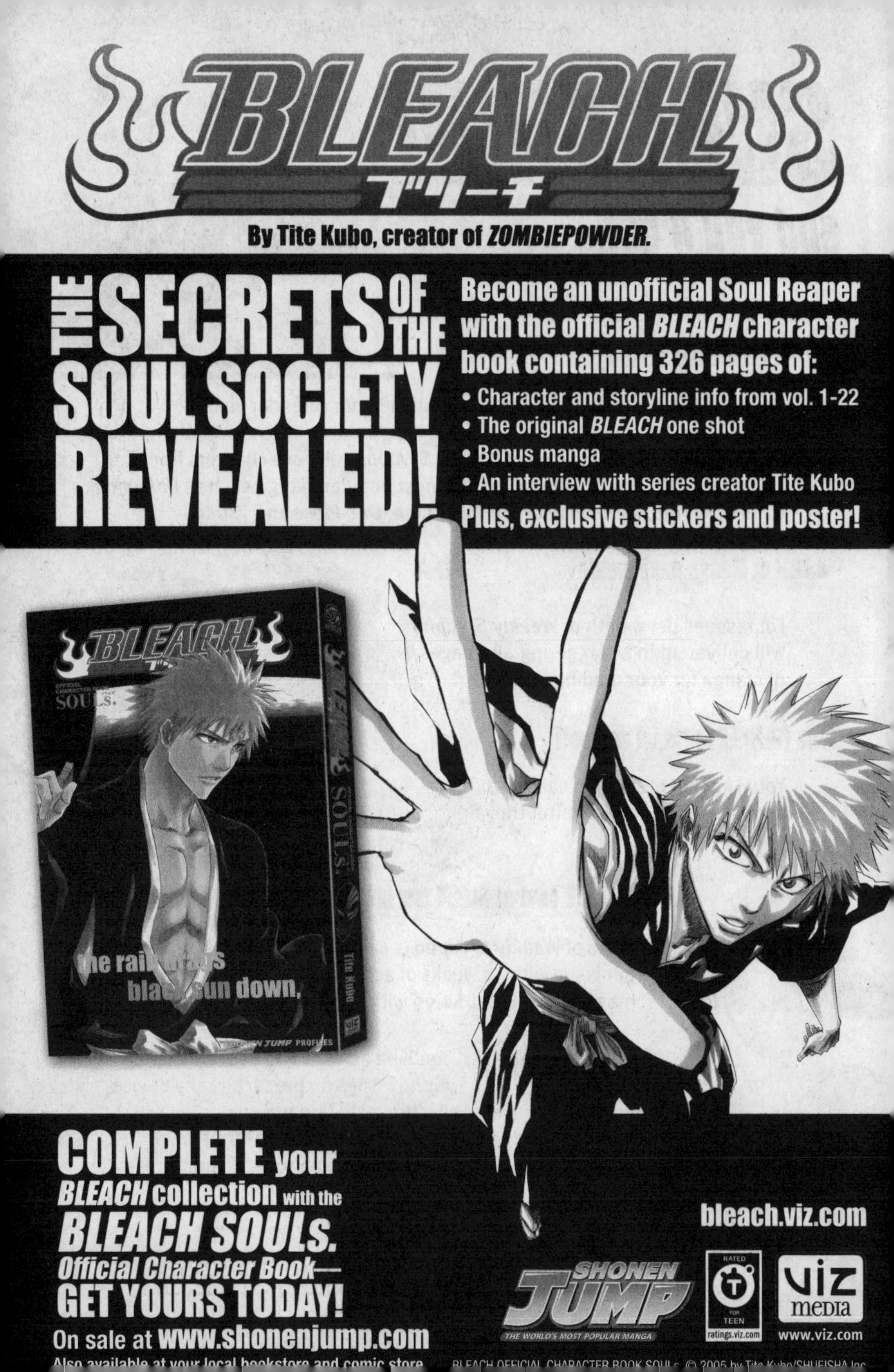
BLEACH
ブリーチ
By Tite Kubo, creator of ZOMBIEPOWDER.
THE SECRETS OF THE SOUL SOCIETY REVEALED!
Become an unofficial Soul Reaper with the official BLEACH character book containing 326 pages of:
• Character and storyline info from vol. 1-22
• The original BLEACH one shot
• Bonus manga
• An interview with series creator Tite Kubo
Plus, exclusive stickers and poster!
BLEACH
SOULs.
Tite Kubo
SHONEN JUMP PROFILES
COMPLETE your BLEACH collection with the BLEACH SOULs. Official Character Book—GET YOURS TODAY!
On sale at www.shonenjump.com
Also available at your local bookstore and comic store
bleach.viz.com
SHONEN JUMP
THE WORLD'S MOST POPULAR MANGA
RATED T FOR TEEN
ratings.viz.com
VIZ media
www.viz.com
BLEACH OFFICIAL CHARACTER BOOK SOULs. © 2005 by Tite Kubo/SHUEISHA Inc.